THE PHILOSO[PHICAL] QUEST

D0127507

A Cross-Cultural Reader

SECOND EDITION

Gail M. Presbey
University of Nairobi

Karsten J. Struhl
Adelphi University

Richard E. Olsen
Adelphi University

Boston   Burr Ridge, IL   Dubuque, IA   Madison, WI   New York   San Francisco   St. Louis
Bangkok   Bogotá   Caracas   Lisbon   London   Madrid   Mexico City   Milan
New Delhi   Seoul   Singapore   Sydney   Taipei   Toronto

McGraw-Hill Higher Education

A Division of The **McGraw-Hill** *Companies*

This book is printed on acid-free paper.

5 6 7 8 9 0 FGR/FGR   0 9 8 7 6 5 4 3

ISBN 0-07-289867-4

Editorial director: *Phillip A. Butcher*
Sponsoring editor: *Monica Eckman/Sarah Touborg Moyers*
Editorial coordinator: *Hannah Glover/Bennet Morrison*
Marketing manager: *Daniel Loch*
Project editor: *Susanne Riedell*
Production supervisor: *Rose Hepburn*
Freelance design coordinator: *Gino Cieslik*
Cover designer: *Stephanie Wicks*
Photo researcher: *Judy Kausal*
Supplement coordinator: *Craig S. Leonard*
Compositor: *Carlisle Communications, Ltd.*
Typeface: *10/12 Times Roman*
Printer: *Quebecor Printing Book Group/Fairfield*

Library of Congress Cataloging-in-Publication Data
The philosophical quest : a cross-cultural reader / [edited by] Gail
   M. Presbey, Karsten J. Struhl, Richard E. Olsen.—2nd ed.
       p. cm.
   Includes bibliographical references and index.
   ISBN 0-07-289867-4 (pbk.)
   1. Philosophy Introductions. I. Presbey, Gail M. II. Struhl,
Karsten J. III. Olsen, Richard E., 1941-   .
BD21.P466 2000
100—dc21   99-35392

http://www.mhhe.com

ABOUT THE AUTHORS

GAIL M. PRESBEY is presently J. William Fulbright Senior Scholar at the University of Nairobi, Kenya. She received her Ph.D. in philosophy from Fordham University. She has guest lectured and done research at many African universities in East, West, and Southern Africa. She has published articles on various issues in African philosophy, as well as political philosophy in journals such as *Research in African Literatures* and *New Political Science,* and in several edited book collections such as *Crossing Cultural Boundaries: Philosophy and Cultural Diversity,* and *Postcolonial African Philosophy: A Critical Reader.*

Professor Presbey studied Gandhian nonviolence and development at Gandhigram Rural University in Madurai, India, and has participated in community mediation programs and Nonviolent Conflict Resolution training in prisons. She cofounded and codirected Peace and Justice Studies programs at Albertus Magnus College and Fordham University. She has been the winner of several awards, including the Marist College Faculty Extraordinary Performance Award.

KARSTEN J. STRUHL teaches philosophy and political theory at Adelphi University, the New School for Social Research, John Jay College, and the College of New Rochelle. He has also taught at Long Island University, La Guardia Community College, the Queens House of Detention, Harlem Hospital, and several senior citizen centers. Professor Struhl's articles have appeared in philosophical, psychological, educational, and political journals and anthologies. He is the coeditor of *Philosophy Now: An Introductory Reader* (Random House) and *Ethics in Perspective* (McGraw-Hill), and he coauthored the entry on "Human Nature" for *The Encyclopedia of Bioethics* (Macmillan). He has spent considerable time traveling and conducting interviews in Russia and is currently at work on a philosophical-cultural-ideological comparison of that country and the United States. He is a member of the American Philosophical Association, the Radical Philosophy Association, the International Institute for Self-Management, and Educators for Social Responsibility.

RICHARD E. OLSEN is Professor of Philosophy at Adelphi University and chair of that university's philosophy department. He received his Ph.D. in philosophy from Brown University. He is the author of several journal articles and a book, *Karl Marx* (1979). He has also participated in National Endowment for the Humanities and Mellon Foundation grant projects. Professor Olsen has been a scholar of both Western and Asian philosophy for over twenty years and lived for a time as an ordained Buddhist monk in Thailand while pursuing his studies of Buddhism in that country. He is a member of the American Philosophical Association, the Phi Beta Kappa Society, and the Sigma Xi Honorary Science Fraternity.

CONTENTS

PREFACE

Education in the United States is presently confronting the challenge of multiculturalism. This term covers a variety of concerns: the inclusion in the curriculum of the history and points of view of different ethnic and racial groups; a greater emphasis on African-American, feminist, and gay and lesbian studies; and a greater sensitivity to the literature and history of non-Western cultures. All of the above senses of "multicultural" are included in our text, although the last may be properly termed "cross-cultural" and is emphasized in our text.

A number of disciplines have begun to respond to this challenge, most notably literature, history, sociology, and anthropology. For the most part, however, philosophy has been taught and continues to be taught as an essentially Western enterprise.

College students who studied philosophy in the 1950s and early 1960s were taught a historical canon that began with the Greeks, emphasizing Plato and Aristotle, passed quickly over the Middle Ages, and entered "modern philosophy" with Descartes in France, Locke and Berkeley in England, Hume in Scotland, and Kant, sometimes Hegel, and very occasionally Nietzsche in Germany. What was called contemporary philosophy might have taken a passing glance at phenomenology, existentialism, and American pragmatism but was for the most part positivism and the analytic school of Russell, Moore, Wittgenstein, Strawson, Austin, and so on. One could, in fact, go through a complete undergraduate and graduate curriculum in philosophy without ever encountering a non-Western philosopher. The introductory textbook anthologies of this era, reflecting this orientation, usually offered an almost exclusively Western "dialogue" within the traditional branches of philosophy—metaphysics, epistemology, ethics, social and political philosophy, and aesthetics.

In the late 1960s and early 1970s a new wave of introductory philosophy anthologies appeared, often labeled "relevance" textbooks (one of the editors of this anthology was a coeditor of such a textbook). These attempted both to expand the philosophical categories in a manner that made them more timely—human nature, philosophy of sexuality, the nature of consciousness, medical ethics, and so forth—and to include more specific ethical and political issues. The philosophical canon was broadened to include more continental (non-analytic European) philosophy and theoretical readings by authors in other disciplines. The late 1970s and the 1980s represented a return to a more traditional approach that yet retained some of the concerns of the 1960s—an integration of the old canon with what was rapidly becoming a new canon.

However, left out of these changing perspectives concerning the philosophical dialogue was any serious attempt to reflect upon non-Western philosophical traditions. At most a few Indian and Chinese authors might be thrown in as spice for an essentially Western philosophical brew.

This situation has now reached an almost embarrassing conjuncture. There are presently significantly more students from China, Japan, and other Asian countries, from the Middle East, from Latin America, and from Africa studying in Western universities. These students do not see themselves represented in either the traditional or the new canon, and they have begun to say so.

We know that many philosophers have wanted to respond to this deficiency but have been uncertain about how to begin. While there have been several recent conferences and workshops focusing on philosophy in a cross-cultural perspective, the standard complaint is that there is a general lack of adequate resources. This is especially true when it comes to introductory texts. It was our own frustration with the overall unavailability of a suitable cross-cultural introductory text as well as a recognition that others felt this same frustration that led us to collaborate on this anthology.

Our text is designed to be used in an introductory philosophy course, but it might also be used as part of a core humanities program and in a comparative philosophy course. An accompanying instructor's manual, available upon request from the publishers, includes additional syllabi for courses using this text. Courses include: Introduction to Asian Philosophy; Comparative Asian-Western Philosophy; Area Studies/Non-Western Philosophy; and Ethics with a Cross-Cultural Emphasis. Each of the text's nine chapters introduces the student to a fundamental question of philosophy through a wide variety of Western and non-Western philosophical readings. In fact, almost half of the selections in our text are by non-Western authors. The non-Western readings include classical and contemporary representatives of Asian, African, Middle Eastern, and Native American thought. Among the Western selections are classical and contemporary readings from diverse philosophical schools (analytic, positivist, pragmatist, phenomenological, and existential). We have also included selections from Russian, Iberian, and Latin American philosophy, which are on the periphery of the Western philosophical tradition and generally not included very much in standard introductory philosophical anthologies. These voices are also interesting because, while grounded in the Western tradition, they tend to speak in their own unique idioms. Finally, our text also includes African-American and both Western and non-Western feminist thinkers.

In this second edition of our text, we have felt a special need to include more African-American, Native American, Asian American, and Chicano authors (Patricia Hill Collins, Alain Locke, Laurence Thomas, M. L. King, Malcolm X, Vine Deloria, Black Elk, Paula Gunn Allen, Herbert John Benelly, Native Mesoamerican poets, Paula Moya, David Wong). We want philosophy to be able to speak to the lives of all Americans, and we want students to know that there are indeed philosophers from many different ethnic and racial backgrounds. For the same kinds of reasons, we have also endeavored to increase the number of women philosophers and feminist thinkers. We hope that such awareness might encourage more women and minorities to enter philosophy. As a recent American Philosophical report has shown, they are now clearly underrepresented in the field.[1]

Our purpose in constructing this cross-cultural reader is not merely to create a cultural smorgasbord. While authors rest side by side in this text, they are often engaged in a struggle not only over ideas but also over who is to be heard. In short, we recognize that in the real world there is not an equal exchange of ideas because there is an inequality of power between the participants. Some voices are more equal than others. The problems of unequal power and the struggle to be heard and understood are discussed by many of our authors (Vine Deloria, Leonardo and Clodovis Boff, Hassan Hanafi, Carol Christ, Fatima Mernissi, Elizabeth V. Spelman, Paula Gunn Allen, and Richard Mohr, among others, as well as those mentioned in the preceding paragraph).

Our text is organized thematically. Each chapter positions selections from Western and non-Western philosophical traditions in such a way as to highlight the parallels and differences between them and to present the writers from these different traditions in dialogue with each other. In addition, the Western readings in themselves often raise issues that reveal an awareness of non-Western philosophical traditions. An obvious example is an article by Derek Parfit, a contemporary analytic philosopher, who defends a Humean and Buddhist view of the self.

The juxtapositioning of non-Western philosophical readings beside Western ones within established philosophical categories has several other important functions. First, it serves to demonstrate the philosophical contributions of non-Western cultures. Second, it specifically emphasizes the way in which similar philosophical debates and concepts have occurred within these different philosophical traditions. Third, it shows the different ways in which these other traditions have interpreted and responded to these perennial questions. Finally, by presenting philosophical thinkers from different cultures in dialogue with one another, it expands the meaning of the traditional categories themselves.

Each chapter in our text has two or more sections. There is a general introduction to each chapter and a separate introduction to each of the sections within the chapter. There are questions for discussion at the end of each section within the chapter and some explanatory footnotes within the readings themselves. Each chapter introduction also refers the student to related readings that appear in other chapters. This cross-referencing will, we hope, enable the student to appreciate more clearly the interrelation of fundamental philosophical questions in a cross-cultural perspective.

As the second edition of this book reflects the work of many people who worked on the first editions, we would like to continue to thank Wayne Somers for his bibliographical expertise; Susan Weisser and Bernard Witlieb for reading and commenting on portions of the text; Liza Greenwald for help in selecting illustrations; Richard Schiffman for his suggestions concerning

---

[1] "Special Report of the Committee on the Status and Future of the Profession," *Proceedings and Addresses of the APA* 70, no. 2, pp. 131–53; see especially, pp. 134–35. As the APA statistics demonstrate in detail, "Three in five [undergraduate departments in philosophy] report no African-American, Hispanic-America, or Asian-American majors, with another one-quarter to one-third reporting only one or two majors in each ethnic category . . . A mere 12 percent report any Native American (First Nations) majors at all—and then usually only one or two." The same report states that "half of all departments reporting say that less than 30 percent of their majors are women, with another third indicating that women make up 30 to 40 percent of their majors . . . A quarter of the undergraduate departments report that women make up less than 15 percent of their undergraduate majors."

Asian sources; James Fenneley for consultation on Islamic sources; Alison Jaggar for suggestions concerning feminist sources; Barbara Kraeger for leads on Jewish sources; and Ofelia Schutte for suggestions about Latin American readings. We would also like to thank the following people for their contributions to the second edition: Susan Bendror, Olga Bukhina, Patricia Huntington, and Gina DiPietro.

The creation of a book requires considerable labor by those who often go unrecognized, those who do the editing, production, design, and so on. Our special thanks, therefore, go to those at McGraw-Hill who worked on the first edition: Cynthia Ward, Patricia Rodney, Judy Cornwell, and Tom Holton; and to those who worked on the second edition: Sarah Moyers, Rebecca Anderson, Ben Morrison, Monica Eckman, and Hannah Glover. We would like to make special mention of Susanne Riedell, the project manager for our text, and Rosalyn Sheff, our copy editor. These two individuals are the unsung heroes who have worked tirelessly and with loving attention to produce this book. Finally, we would like to thank Jo-Anne Naples for her persistent efforts to secure permissions for the readings that appear in our book in both editions.

Gail M. Presbey
Karsten J. Struhl
Richard E. Olsen

INTRODUCTION

*For this is essentially the pathos of a philosopher, to be astonished; there is
no other determining point of departure for philosophy than this.*
—PLATO

WONDER AND THE EXPERIENCE OF PHILOSOPHIZING

Wonder is probably as old as humanity; it is also the starting point of philosophy.

Perhaps we are most familiar with wonder as we ponder the remarkable accomplishments of humans throughout history and the astounding events of our times: the Egyptian pyramids, the Taj Mahal, the medieval cathedral in Chartres, the first astronaut's steps on the moon, and so on. Human history is filled with great accomplishments as well as great cruelties, both of which can stun the inquirer and send thought spinning. Likewise, nature's grandeur and terrors—oceans and mountain ranges, hurricanes and volcanoes—seize our attention and either mesmerize with their beauty or stupefy with their power. Witnessing a birth or a death can also bring to mind questions of human meaning with an urgency we do not often experience. At such times our everyday consciousness is arrested and we wonder why—we marvel at the fact of existence or we ponder the pain or joy that such sights evoke in us.

Karl Jaspers describes those moments that so often give rise to philosophical reflection. He speaks of them as times of either joy or despair that jar a person into a state of wonderment, where all former answers and beliefs are called into question. We all have probably had such experiences. We are all philosophers on at least some occasions.

Humans can certainly function practically in an immediate "survival" mode without wondering about these matters. But a lifetime of such shortsightedness may begin to feel unfulfilling. Of course, one could take a shortcut and bypass philosophical inquiry by embracing a prepackaged ideology that provides ready-made answers to our fundamental questions. The philosopher, however, strikes out on his or her own, searching for wisdom in a reflective fashion. It is this that we call the philosophical quest.

Here it might be helpful to contrast the informal sense of "having" a philosophy with the formal sense of "doing" philosophy, or philosophizing, where we scrutinize our experiences and beliefs in a search for insight and understanding. In the first sense, each of us already has a philosophy; indeed, we are creating our philosophy of life—more or less unconsciously—all the time. "Don't trust people," "pain can be a growth experience," "try new things," "don't be afraid," "there *is* life after death": such viewpoints, held unreflectively, influence our daily lives and guide our decisions. In contrast, when we engage directly in *doing* philosophy, it is a time to take inventory of our preconceptions and challenge them. With this more formal sense of philosophizing comes an emphasis on reason, analysis, and argumentation.

In fact, philosophy could be understood as the discipline that criticizes received opinions, in all subjects, from daily life to aesthetic and religious experience. In this sense we can say that philosophy is *radical* in the most literal meaning of the word; for whereas practitioners of a religion or citizens of a state may take for granted the validity of the assumptions of their belief systems, philosophers question those assumptions. Philosophers go to the "roots" of ideas by clarifying, questioning, and evaluating our most basic assumptions. Often this challenge to accepted norms and ideas can lead to views that are at odds with one's culture. Buddha challenged the Hindu views on caste and social position; Socrates challenged the Athenians on their notions of piety, justice, and wisdom; both the French existentialists and the logical positivists, in our own century, have questioned received religious opinion. In this way, philosophy never rests, never reaches the final answer; all past answers are subject to continuing scrutiny and revision by those who come after. Philosophy is, in short, a radical critical inquiry into the fundamental assumptions of any field of inquiry, including itself.

As we have seen, one doesn't have to be a professional "philosopher" to philosophize; wherever assumptions are being questioned and opinions are challenged, philosophizing is going on. Anyone willing to observe the overlooked, to reflect, to analyze, and to put forth an argument can be a philosopher. However, those who make philosophical reflection a lifetime habit perhaps most deserve the label "philosopher." For, with practice, comes skill. The more one philosophizes and studies the philosophies of the past, the more likely one is to gain real philosophic insight.

PHILOSOPHY IN WORLD PERSPECTIVE: THE EUROCENTRIC PROBLEM

People around the globe have been engaging in philosophical reflection for centuries. And yet the most often promulgated view of philosophy in so many Western introductory textbooks is that the Greeks began philosophy, the Romans continued it, and then the Germans, French, and British carried it to its present state. Some texts follow philosophy to the New World but only to observe its practice in the essentially Anglo-German cultures of English-speaking Canada and the United States. One gets the impression that other peoples in the world do not philosophize. What then were the Asian and African peoples, the Persians, Iberians, and Slavs doing and thinking over the centuries? What of the aboriginal societies in North, Central, and South America? The popular Western view is that others were content to wallow in superstition, unthinkingly perpetuating a system of belief that could never stand the scrutiny of Western reason. Whole continents have been seen as prereflective, never asking philosophical questions, never criticizing received opinions. It is the view of the editors, and of many now engaged in a careful study of the intellectual history of the world, that such a vision of philosophy goes against the facts and results from "Eurocentrism."

Often the contributions of other cultures to the foundations of Western philosophy are recognized at the time of the influence but then are downplayed in later historical accounts. Greece, considered the cradle of Western philosophy, was a seafaring nation that regularly interacted with many other cultures. But most modern Western readers will not realize that at the birth and heyday of Greek civilization, Greece was surrounded by advanced and powerful civilizations, such as Egypt, that had a detailed knowledge of medicine, science, and astronomy, and a practice of philosophical speculation and debate. That the Greeks built upon this background knowledge and came up with their own unique contributions to thought and method that radically clarified and furthered philosophy is not to be disputed; it is with real merit that the Greeks deserve an important place in the history of philosophy. But it is crucial to realize that the Greeks did not appear in a vacuum but rather in the context of an interactive dialogue with other civilizations.

Some contemporary thinkers, such as Enrique Dussel and W. E. B. DuBois, have developed theories to explain the seeming tunnel vision of many Western accounts of the history of philosophy. Since we are in the "West," we receive a view of our cultural heritage that emphasizes the accomplishments of those who are considered to be a part of this heritage; those who are historical enemies or rivals are always seen in the worst light. To take one example, the fledgling European nations were awed by the power of the Indian and Chinese empires and envied their riches. In the years of colonialism and imperialism, Britain conquered India militarily and came to dominate China during the Opium Wars. With the theory of the "white man's burden," Britain attempted to see itself as a civilizing influence bringing order where there had formerly been chaos, and instituting progress where there had formerly been backwardness. In such a context, it was difficult to admit the good points of cultures that were being forced to submit to British models of right and progress.

This same theory of military-political rivalry and/or domination affecting perceptions of cultural history can account, at least partially, for the meager attention paid to Islam, Africa, and Native America in Western philosophy texts. The Greco-Roman world and Western Europe were, throughout much of history, involved in military battles to check the spread of Islam westward. It is probably no accident, then, that the flourishing of Islamic philosophy between the tenth and fourteenth centuries is rarely mentioned in the more superficial Western accounts of philosophy, even though this Islamic philosophical renaissance directly influenced the West.

In a similar vein, it has been argued that the European and American engagement in the African slave trade encouraged thinkers to justify such an atrocity by interpreting African culture as primitive, asserting that Africans are not "rational animals." It is no wonder that G. W. F. Hegel, one of the greatest German philosophers of the nineteenth century, said in his *Philosophy of History* that Africans were not even a part of the unfolding human story of progress toward ultimate rationality. For, if Africans were humans with complex thought patterns and an insightful and sensitive relationship to the world and themselves, then how could their enslavement be justified? Earlier justifications of slavery based on the slave's "inferior nature" were first argued by Aristotle. Aristotle's arguments were resurrected by the Spanish conquistadores to defend their enslavement of Native Americans in Mexico and Central and South America.

Europe itself—and then later the United States—has had its own "peripheries," which have given rise to their own style of philosophy. Iberian, Latin American, and Russian philosophers often find themselves marginalized in most textbooks, if they find themselves included at all. Once again, coincidentally, the political marginalizations of these areas may account for their philosophical marginalization. Yet great thinkers such as Dostoevsky and Unamuno have pondered questions of life with marvelous insight and have earned themselves the spotlight of world renown. It has even been suggested that being on the periphery of a culture affords one a better perspective for asking the most basic questions, so necessary for philosophy.

The twentieth-century French philosopher Michel Foucault has observed that often so-called objective and impartial knowledge serves the powers-that-be. Fortunately for us, philosophy always entails the questioning of assumptions, so that later philosophical inquiry can expose the mistakes of former positions. In fact, all knowledge seems to be perspectival; no human being can have a God's-eye view of our world; each of us has been influenced by our culture to interpret our experience according to certain conceptual categories. Does this mean that objectivity is a goal never to be reached? This question is the focus of a centuries-long debate; all we editors wish to suggest is that objectivity can be encouraged by seeking out a multiplicity of perspectives on any given topic. Immanuel Kant referred to an "enlarged mentality" as the ability to represent the views of others in one's own mind, and he saw it as a crucial step in making a sound judgment. This text is structured with the idea that looking at multiple perspectives on any given issue will help the reader make a more informed judgment.

Our goal in this collection is not to pit civilizations against one another and rate their relative merits or demerits. Rather, our hope is to present each culture in its best light, with selections taken from its most interesting contributions to the philosophical dialogue. We also hope to dispel some misconceptions. For example, it is often suggested that all Hindu thought is alike, all Chinese thought is alike, and so on, and it is only in the Western tradition that we have truly interesting debate. The reality is, however, quite different. The Chinese philosophers debated a number of issues within the Taoist, Confucian, and Buddhist schools. Ancient China saw a lively debate concerning the question of whether human nature is good or evil. Debates concerning the compatibility of science and religion can be found within the Islamic tradition. Hinduism also saw debates between dualists, monists, and materialists. These and other such controversies are represented in this anthology. Also within this text the reader will find a number of parallel debates carried on within two or more cultures. Plato's world of the forms finds echoes in a Native American Lakota vision. Western skepticism concerning the problem of induction was preceded by Indian skepticism by several thousand years. Hume's critique of the self was preceded by the Buddha's and is revived by a contemporary British philosopher in the analytic tradition, Derek Parfit. Arguments for dualism, idealism, and materialism appear within the African, Indian, and Western traditions. Parallel debates concerning human nature occur within both China and the Western world.

The project of this book is embedded in a sociopolitical context; the contemporary educational setting demands such works. In our own American society, a web of interrelating immigrant cultures, we need to let all voices be heard. We have our own "peripheries," and those at the edge of power in our society, women, African-Americans, and other groups, have felt their voices stifled. Thus, we have included some of these voices as well.

THE PHILOSOPHICAL QUEST

A Cross-Cultural Reader

80°N

160°W   140°W   120°W   100°W   80°W   60°W   40°W   20°W

80°N

KALAALLIT NUNAAT
(DEN.)

60°N

ALASKA
(U.S.)

ICELAND

CANADA

UNITED
KINGDOM

IRELAND

40°N

UNITED STATES

ATLANTIC

FRAN

PORTUGAL

AZORES
(PORT.)

MADEIRA IS.
(PORT.)

CANARY IS.
(SP.)

WESTERN SAHARA
(MOR.)

MOR

MEXICO

BAHAMAS

Tropic of Cancer

20°N

HAWAII (U.S.)

CUBA

DOMINICAN
REPUBLIC

HAITI

27

MAURITANIA

BELIZE

JAMAICA

29

CAPE
VERDE

SENEGAL

HONDURAS

28

30

31

GUATEMALA

NICARAGUA

GRENADA

32

GAMBIA

EL SALVADOR

33

GUINEA BISSAU

GUINEA

COSTA RICA

34

SIERRA
LEONE

PANAMA

VENEZUELA

GUYANA

SURINAME

LIBERIA

FRENCH GUIANA (FR.)

CÔTE
D'IVOIRE

PACIFIC

COLOMBIA

EQUATOR

KIRIBATI

GALÁPAGOS IS.
(EC.)

ECUADOR

OCEAN

OCEAN

WESTERN
SAMOA

AMERICAN
SAMOA (U.S.)

FRENCH POLYNESIA
(FR.)

BRAZIL

PERU

TONGA

BOLIVIA

20°S

PARAGUAY

Tropic of Capricorn

CHILE

40°S

ARGENTINA

URUGUAY

FALKLAND IS. (U.K.)

60°S

80°S

0   1000   2000 Miles

0   1000   2000 Kilometers

1. NETHERLANDS
2. BELGIUM
3. LUXEMBOURG
4. ESTONIA
5. LATVIA
6. LITHUANIA
7. CZECH REPUBLIC
8. SLOVAKIA
9. SWITZERLAND
10. AUSTRIA
11. HUNGARY
12. SLOVENIA
13. CROATIA
14. BOSNIA AND HERCEGOVINA
15. YUGOSLAVIA
16. MACEDONIA
17. ALBANIA
18. MOLDOVA
19. GEORGIA
20. ARMENIA
21. AZERBAIJAN
22. LEBANON
23. ISRAEL
24. LAOS
25. THAILAND
26. CAMBODIA
27. PUERTO RICO (U.S.)
28. ST. KITTS AND NEVIS
29. ANTIGUA AND BARBUDA
30. DOMINICA
31. ST. LUCIA
32. ST. VINCENT AND THE GRENADINES
33. BARBADOS
34. TRINIDAD AND TOBAGO

THE PHILOSOPHICAL QUEST

A Cross-Cultural Reader

M. C. Escher, *Day and Night,* 1938, M. C. Escher Heirs, c/o Cordon Art, Baarn, Holland.

CHAPTER 1

APPEARANCE AND REALITY

The philosophical question concerning the distinction between appearance and reality—that is, the question that concerns itself with the relation between what things appear to be to the senses and what they really are—has been an especially prominent one in Western philosophy since the time of the scientific revolution. However, the puzzles of the appearance/reality distinction are neither specifically Western nor specifically modern. They seem to be both universal and universally deemed important, though the forms they take may vary from culture to culture and age to age.

The selections in Section One begin with Plato and include the famous parable of the cave, in which he likens the world of appearances to a world of shadows, a comparison that is echoed in the teachings of the Native American sage Black Elk. The "two-world" view advanced by these thinkers is not, however, shared by the final philosopher presented in the section; the modern philosopher Hannah Arendt argues that such theories of the world are both false and misleading. The second section presents a variety of views whose argument is that reality is created by the mind, the position that philosophers call "idealism," using this term in a technical sense that has little in common with its everyday meaning. It includes both Western and Asian thinkers as well as a glimpse at the pioneering work of Arthur Schopenhauer, who attempts to synthesize West and East. The section ends with a selection from Chinese Ch'an or Zen Buddhism, "The Sutra of Hui Neng." Zen, following the teachings of the ancient Indian Mahayana Buddhist philosophers, puts a special twist on the "idealist" theme, arguing that a true understanding of the nature of mind and its world pushes us beyond concepts and language. This is the view that is commonly called "mysticism." The reader will find it further explored in Chapters 3 and 5 of the book.

The last section presents those views of the world that see its appearances as grounded not in mind but in matter. "Materialists," those who hold that the world is entirely physical in its nature, have existed in most cultures that practice philosophical reflection, though their denial of an independent spiritual realm has often made them unpopular with their contemporaries. The selections presented here are taken from the seventeenth-century Chinese materialist Wang Fu-Chih and the famous German socialist Friedrich Engels, who is better known for his political than his philosophical efforts, being the coauthor with Karl Marx of the *Communist Manifesto* and several other revolutionary socialist works.

Readers interested in Section One, "The World of the Forms," may also want to refer to a further selection from Plato found in Chapter 5. Selections that deal with the topics of idealism and materialism are also to be found in that chapter.

THE WORLD OF THE FORMS

The ancient Greek philosopher Plato (427?–347? B.C.) sets the views of Socrates, his teacher, at odds with those of Socrates' companions in a selection from the famous dialogue *Symposium* with which this section begins. The occasion is a drinking party to celebrate the successful production of a friend's play. In order not to become too drunk, since some of the party are still suffering from hangovers from the previous night's festivities, the participants have decided to water their wine and test their poetic skills by making speeches in honor of the god of Love, the god that the Greeks called Eros. The selection begins with the speech of Socrates' playwright friend, Agathon, who waxes eloquent in his praises of the god, presenting a perfect foil for Socrates' speech, which follows. For Socrates maintains that Love is not a god at all but merely a messenger to the divine. Love is, however, he adds, not to be dismissed lightly on account of this, since, if he is used correctly, Love can lead you to the higher world of the perfect Forms where one will behold perfect everlasting Beauty and the supreme God that governs that realm. In making his case for this account of Love, Plato shows Socrates in bold contrast to Agathon and the speakers who came before him, not merely in the content of what he says but also in his method. Where Agathon and the others rely mainly upon references to mythology in presenting their accounts of Love, Socrates employs reasoned argument. We see his own teacher, the wisewoman Diotima, lead him through the series of questions and answers that were to become his staple and a staple in Greek philosophy, the Socratic dialogue or dialectic.

Plato returns to the subject of the perfect ideas or forms in the dialogue *Republic,* from which "The Parable of the Cave" is taken. This dialogue begins with a discussion between Socrates and some fellow Athenians concerning not appearance and reality but an ethical question—What is justice? Although it does, in its own way, continue always to hark back to that question, the dialogue takes us on several fascinating journeys in its attempt to dis-

cover the true meaning of what it is to be just. On one of these, Socrates speaks extensively of the forms, the underpinning of his philosophical world view—the metaphysics or first philosophy on which his ethical and other views are based. There is, he argues, as he did before, a higher world, the "world of mind," the realm of the forms, compared to which our tangible and visible world is an insubstantial copy, a world of "shadows," to use the metaphor he employs in the long analogy he draws between our own condition and that of prisoners confined in a dimly lit cave.

It is important to stress here that the "world of mind," or forms, as he speaks about it, is not something subjective and therefore *in* the mind, but an objective realm that is more deeply real, on his view, than is the realm of the senses. The ideas or "Forms" that the world of mind contains are not lodged in our consciousness any more than the things that our eyes see are lodged in our eyeballs. The mind, for Plato, is more like a sixth sense than a container. We apprehend the higher world through mind in much the same way that we apprehend this world with our eyes.

Though separated from Plato's Athens by an ocean and over 2,000 years in time, the metaphysics espoused by Socrates is also voiced by the Native American Sioux or Lakota shaman Black Elk in his account of the journey of his cousin, the famous holy man and war chief Crazy Horse, to a higher spirit world that seems indistinguishable from that which Socrates and Diotima sought. Being a horseback Indian of the Western American plains, he took his horse along on the journey; but aside from that, the nature of the quest appears to be nearly identical. It is also interesting to note the striking parallels between the account of Crazy Horse's character, which Black Elk presents, and those usually given of Socrates: They are both strange men, never wholly present, seemingly not subject to the needs of ordinary people, but loved by many for their unselfishness despite their strangeness, though feared by others because of it.

Black Elk presented this account of Crazy Horse in unfolding the story of his life to the poet and journalist John Niehardt in the early 1930s, when he was an old man in his 70s. In his lifetime, he had seen perhaps the most painful period in his people's history, beginning with a childhood of fear during the Sioux Indian Wars, when the Lakota were convinced that the whites meant to exterminate them. There were moments of glory, of course: He—like Crazy Horse—had visions, and he fought in the victory over the U.S. cavalry at Little Big Horn. But this was followed by defeat and demoralization and the vanishing of a way of life that the Sioux loved enough to fight fiercely to defend. It was only to preserve a little piece of this life, a fragment of its wisdom, that he agreed to tell John Niehardt things he had never told a white before.

Our final selection is taken from one of the later works of Hannah Arendt (1906–1975). Arendt was a German Jew born in Konigsberg, then the capital of East Prussia. She struggled to survive in Hitler's Germany and narrowly escaped with her life. Her early works, written after her arrival in the United States, focused on political philosophy, especially a critique of totalitarianism. Toward the end of her life she felt the need to turn her attention to thinking, willing, and judging, to provide a larger philosophical background for her political analyses.

Arendt here critiques Plato's "two-world theory." She objects to the dichotomy with its hierarchical ranking of a deeper underlying reality as compared to a shallower world of "appearance." Arendt thinks that the appearance is most important; entities, and people, exist in order to appear. Such notions are connected to her idea of the political realm as the space of appearance where people are seen and heard. If one read further in her work, one would see that her criticism of those who try to search behind appearances for reality is connected to her concerns regarding methods of terror, practiced in the French Revolution and later by Hitler and Stalin, which involve the attempt to unmask the hypocrite and search for the "enemy within." Arendt thinks that life in general, and politics in particular, would be less hostile if appearances were respected.

THE SYMPOSIUM

Plato

"Quite right, Phaidros," said Agathon, "I am ready to speak; Socrates will be there another time, and often, to talk to.

"First, then, I wish to describe how I ought to speak; then to speak. It seems to me that all who have spoken so far have not praised the god, but have congratulated mankind on the good things which the god has caused for them: what that god was himself who gave these gifts, no one has described. But the one right way for any laudation of anyone is to describe what he is, and then what he causes, whoever may be our subject. Thus, you see, with Love: we also should first praise him for what he is, and then praise his gifts.

"I say then that all gods are happy, but if it is lawful to say this without offence, I say that Love is happiest of them all, being most beautiful and best. And how he is most beautiful, I am about to describe. First of all, Phaidros, he is youngest of the gods. He himself supplies one great proof of what I say, for he flies in full flight away from Old Age, who is a quick one clearly, since he comes too soon to us all. Love hates him naturally and will not come anywhere near him. But he is always associated with the young, and with them he consorts, for the old saying is right, 'Like ever comes to like.' I am ready to admit many other things to Phaidros, but one I do not admit, that Love is older than Cronos and Iapetos[1]; no, I say he is youngest of the gods, and ever young; but that old business of the gods, which Hesiod and Parmenides tell about was done through Necessity and not through Love, if they told the truth; for if Love had been in them, there would have been no gelding or enchaining of each other and all those violent things, but friendship and peace, as there is now, and has been ever since Love has reigned over

---

[1]In Greek mythology these were two of the Titans who were children of Ouranos (Heaven) and Gaia (Earth). They existed even before Zeus.

the gods. So then he is young, and besides being young he is tender; but we need a poet like Homer to show the god's tenderness. For Homer says of Ate[2] that she was a god and tender—at least her feet were tender—when he says that

> Tender are her feet; she comes not near
> The ground, but walks upon the heads of men.

I think he gives good proof of her tenderness, that she walks not on the hard but on the soft. Then let us use the same proof for Love, that he is tender. For he walks not on the earth nor on top of heads, which are not so very soft, but both walks and abides in the softest things there are; for his abode is settled in the tempers and souls of gods and men, and again, not in all souls without exception; no, whenever he meets a soul with a hard temper, he departs, but where it is soft, he abides. So since he always touches with feet and all else the softest of the soft, he must needs be tender. You see, then, he is youngest and tenderest, but besides this his figure is supple, for if he were stiff, he could not fold himself in everywhere, or throughout every soul, and come in and go out unnoticed from the first. A great proof of his good proportion and supple shape is his gracefulness, which, as we all know, Love has in high degree; for there is always war between gracelessness and Love. Colours and beauty are testified by the god's nestling in flowers; for where there is no flower, or flower is past, in body and soul and everything else, Love sits not, but where the place is flowery and fragrant there he both sits and stays.

"Of the god's beauty much more might be said, but this is enough; the virtue of Love comes next. Chief is that Love wrongs not and is not wronged, wrongs no god and is wronged by none, wrongs no man and is wronged by none. Nothing that happens to him comes by violence, for violence touches not Love; nothing he does is violent, for everyone willingly serves Love in everything, and what a willing person grants to a willing, is just—so say 'the city's king, the laws.'[3] And besides justice, he is full of temperance. It is agreed that temperance is the mastery and control of pleasures and desires, and that no pleasure is stronger than Love. But if they are weaker, then Love would master and control them; and being master of pleasure and desires, Love would be especially temperate. Furthermore, in courage 'not even Ares[4] stands up against Love,' for it is not Ares that holds Love, but Love Ares—love of Aphrodite, as they say; stronger is he that holds than he that is held, and the master of the bravest of all would be himself bravest. Now the justice and temperance and courage of the god have been spoken of, and wisdom is left; so one must try to do the best one is able to do. And first, that I may honour our art as Eryximachos honoured his, Love is so wise a poet that he can make another the same; at least, everyone becomes a poet whom Love touches, even one who before that, had 'no music in his soul'.[5] This we may fittingly use as a proof that Love is a good poet[6] or active maker in practically all the creations of the fine arts; for what one has not or knows not, one can neither give to another nor teach another. Now take the making of all living things; who will dispute that they are the clever work of Love, by which all living things are made and begotten? And craftsmanship in the arts; don't we know that where this god is teacher, art turns out notable and illustrious, but where there is no touch of Love, it is all in the dark? Archery, again, and medicine and divination were invented by Apollo, led by desire and love, so that even he would be a pupil of Love; so also the Muses in music and Hephaistos in smithcraft and Athena in weaving and Zeus in 'pilotage of gods and men.' Hence you see also, all that business of the gods was arranged when Love came among them—love of beauty, that is plain, for there is no Love in ugliness. Before that, as I said at the beginning, many terrible things happened to the gods because of the reign of Necessity—so the story goes; but when this god Love was

---

[2]Ate, presumptuous Madness, something like Sin. Iliad xix. 92.
[3]Quoted from Alcidamas, a stylist.

[4]Ares, god of war. The quotation is from Sophocles' lost play *Thyestes,* fragment 235 N.
[5]Euripides. *Stheneboea,* fragment 663 N.
[6]The Greek word ποιητηδ, poet, means a maker, and he uses this here to indicate creative arts and crafts and even the "creation" of living things.

born, all became good both for gods and men from loving beautiful things.

"Thus it seems to me, Phaidros, that Love comes first, himself most beautiful and best, and thereafter he is cause of other such things in others. And I am moved to speak something of him in verse myself, that it is he who makes

> Peace among men, calm weather on the deep,
> Respite from winds, in trouble rest and sleep.[7]

He empties us of estrangement, and fills us with friendliness, ordaining all such meetings as this one, of people one with another, in feasts, in dances, in sacrifices becoming men's guide; he provides gentleness and banishes savagery; he loves to give good will, hates to give ill will; gracious, mild; illustrious to the wise, admirable to the gods; enviable to those who have none of him, treasured by those who have some of him; father of luxury, daintiness, delicacy, grace, longing, desire; careful of good things, careless of bad things; in hardship, in fear, in drinking,[8] in talk a pilot, a comrade, a stand-by[9] and the best of saviours; of all gods and men an ornament, a guide most beautiful and best, whom every man must follow, hymning him well, sharing in the song he sings as he charms the mind of gods and men.

"This, Phaidros, is my speech," he said; "may the god accept my dedication, partly play, partly modest seriousness, and the best that I am able to do."

When Agathon had spoken (Aristodemos told me), all applauded; the young man was thought to have spoken becomingly for himself and for the god. Then Socrates looked at Eryximachos, and said, "Now then, son of Acumenos, do you think there was no reason to fear in the fears I feared?[10] Was I not a prophet when I said, as I did just now, that Agathon would make a wonderful speech, and leave me with nothing to say?"

"Yes, to the first," said Eryximachos, "you were a prophet there, certainly, about the wonderful speech; but nothing to say? I don't think so!"

"Bless you," said Socrates, "and how have I anything to say, I or anyone else, when I have to speak after that beautiful speech, with everything in it? The first part was wonderful enough, but the end! The beauty of those words and phrases! It was quite overwhelming for any listener. The fact is, when I considered that I shall not be able to get anywhere near it, and I have nothing fine to say at all—I was so ashamed that I all but took to my heels and ran, but I had nowhere to go. The speech reminded me of Gorgias,[11] and I really felt quite as in Homer's story;[12] I was afraid that Agathon at the end of his speech might be going to produce the Gorgon's head of Gorgias—the terror in speech-making—directed against *my* speech, and turn me into stone with dumbness. And I understood then that I was a fool when I told you I would take my turn in singing the honours of Love, and admitted I was terribly clever in love affairs, whereas it seems I really had no idea how a eulogy ought to be made. For I was stupid enough to think that we ought to speak the truth about each person eulogised, and to make this the foundation, and from these truths to choose the most beautiful things and arrange them in the most elegant way; and I was quite proud to think how well I should speak, because I believed that I knew the truth. However, apparently this was not the right way to praise anything, but we should dedicate all that is greatest and most beautiful to the work, whether things are so or not; if they were false it did not matter. For it seems the task laid down was not for each of us to praise Love, but to seem to praise him. For this reason then, I think, you rake up every story, and dedicate it to Love, and say he is so-and-so and the cause of such-and-such, that he may seem to be most beautiful and best, of course to those who

---

[7]Compare *Odyssey* v. 391.

[8]This word "drinking" is doubtful in the Greek text.

[9]The three words used by Plato mean a ship's pilot, a fighter (not the driver) in a chariot or a marine on a ship, and a man who stands by another in battle.

[10]He puts in his own little drop of parody.

---

[11]Gorgias, the celebrated Sophist, adopted an artificial, affected style.

[12]*Odyssey* xi, 634. Odysseus, at the end of his visit to the Kingdom of the Dead, grew pale with fear that Persephone might out of Hades send upon him a Gorgon head, and turn him to stone.

don't know—not to those who do, I suppose—and the laudation is excellent and imposing. But indeed I did not know how an encomium was made, and it was without this knowledge that I agreed to take my part in praising. Therefore the tongue promised, but not the mind,[13] so good-bye to that. For I take it back now; I make no eulogy in this fashion: I could not do it. However, the truth, if you like: I have no objection to telling the truth, in my own fashion, not in rivalry with your speeches, or I should deserve to be laughed at. Then see whether you want a speech of that sort, Phaidros. Will you listen to the truth being told about Love, in any words and arrangement of phrases such as we may hit on as we go?"

Phaidros and the others (continued Aristodemos) told him to go on just as he thought best. "Then, Phaidros," he said, "let me ask Agathon a few little things, that I may get his agreement before I speak."

"Oh, I don't mind," said Phaidros, "ask away." After that Socrates began something like this:

"Indeed, my dear Agathon, I thought you were quite right in the beginning of your speech, when you said that you must first show what Love was like, and afterwards come to his works. That beginning I admire very much. Now then, about Love: you described what he is magnificently well, and so on; but tell me this too—is Love such as to be a love of something, or of nothing? I don't mean to ask if he is a love of mother or father; for that would be a ridiculous question, whether Love is love for mother or father; I mean it in the sense that one might apply to 'father' for instance; is the father a father of something or not? You would say, I suppose, if you wanted to answer right, that the father is father of son or daughter. Is that correct?"

"Certainly," said Agathon.

"And the same with the mother?"

This was agreed.

"Another, please," said Socrates, "answer me one or two more, that you may better understand what I want. What if I were to ask: 'A brother now, in himself, is he brother of something?' "

He said yes.

"Of a brother or sister?"

He agreed.

"Then tell me," he said, "about Love. Is Love love of nothing or of something?"

"Certainly he is love of something."

"Now then," said Socrates, "keep this in your memory, what the object of Love is;[14] and say whether Love desires the object of his love?"

"Certainly," said Agathon.

"Is it when he *has* what he desires and loves that he desires and loves it, or when he has not?"

"Most likely, when he has not," said he.

"Just consider," said Socrates, "put 'necessary' for 'likely'; isn't it necessary that the desiring desires what it lacks, or else does not desire if it does not lack? I think positively myself, Agathon, that it is absolutely necessary; what do you think?"

"I think the same," said he.

"Good. Then would one being big want to be big, or being strong want to be strong?"

"Impossible, according to what we have agreed."

"For I suppose he would not be lacking in whichever of these he is?"

"True."

"For if being strong he wanted to be strong," said Socrates, "and being swift he wanted to be swift, and being healthy he wanted to be healthy— you might go on forever like this, and you might think that those who were so-and-so and had such-and-such did also desire what they had; but to avoid our being deceived I say this—if you understand me, Agathon, it is obvious that these *must* have at this present time all they have, whether they wish to or not—and can anyone desire that? And when one says, 'I am healthy and want to be healthy,' 'I am rich and want to be rich,' 'I desire what I have,' we should answer, 'You, my good man, being possessed of riches and health and strength, wish to go on being possessed of them in the future, since at present you have them whether

---

[13]A modification of Euripides' Hippolytos 612.

[14]Agathon had just said it was beauty.

you want it or not; and when you say, "I desire what I have," consider—you mean only that you want to have in the future what you have now.' Wouldn't he agree?"

Agathon said yes.

Then Socrates went on, "Therefore this love for these blessings to be preserved for him into the future and to be always present for him—this is really loving that which is not yet available for him or possessed by him?"

"Certainly," he said.

"Then he, and every other who desires, desires what is not in his possession and not there, what he has not, and what he is not himself and what he lacks? Those are the sorts of things of which there is desire and love?"

"Certainly," he said.

"Come now," said Socrates, "let us run over again what has been agreed. Love is, first of all, of something; next, of those things which one lacks?"

"Yes," he said.

"This being granted, then, remember what things you said in your speech were the objects of Love. I will remind you, if you wish. I think you said something like this; the gods arranged their business through love of beautiful things, for there could not be a love for ugly things. Didn't you say something like that?"

"Yes, I did," said Agathon.

"And quite reasonably too, my friend," said Socrates; "and if this is so, would not Love be love of beauty, not of ugliness?"

He agreed.

"Well now, it has been agreed that he loves what he lacks and has not?"

"Yes," he said.

"Then Love lacks and has not beauty."

"That must be," said he.

"Very well: do you say that what lacks beauty and in no wise has beauty is beautiful?"

"Certainly not."

"Then if that is so, do you still agree that Love is beautiful?"

Agathon answered, "I fear, Socrates, I knew nothing of what I said!"

"Oh no," said he, "it was a fine speech, Agathon! But one little thing more: don't you think good things are also beautiful?"

"I do."

"Then if Love lacks beautiful things, and good things are beautiful, he should lack the good things too."

"Socrates," he said, "I really could not contradict you; let it be as you say."

"Contradict the truth, you should say, beloved Agathon," he replied; "you can't do that, but to contradict Socrates is easy enough.

"And now you shall have peace from me; but there is a speech about Love which I heard once from Diotima of Mantineia,[15] who was wise in this matter and in many others; by making the Athenians perform sacrifices before the plague she even managed to put off the disease for ten years. And she it was who taught me about love affairs. This speech, then, which she made I will try to narrate to you now, beginning with what is agreed between me and Agathon; I will tell it by myself, as well as I can. You will see that I must describe first, as you did, Agathon, who Love is and what like, and then his works. I think it easiest to do it as the lady did in examining me. I said to her very much what Agathon just now did to me, that Love was a great god, and was a love of beautiful things; and she convinced me by saying the same as I did to Agathon, that he is neither beautiful, according to my argument, nor good. Then I said, 'What do you mean, Diotima? Is Love then ugly and bad?' And she said, 'Hush, for shame! Do you think that what is not beautiful must necessarily be ugly?' 'Yes, I do.' 'And what is not wise, ignorant? Do you not perceive that there is something between wisdom and ignorance?' 'What is that?' 'To have right opinion without being able to give a reason,' she said, 'is neither to understand (for how could an unreasoned thing be understanding?) nor is it ignorance (for how can ignorance hit the truth?). Right

---

[15] A well-known Greek city in the Peloponnesus. The names perhaps suggest "the prophetess Fearthelord of Prophetville."

opinion is no doubt something between knowledge and ignorance.' 'Quite true,' I said. 'Then do not try to compel what is not beautiful to be ugly, or what is not good to be bad. So also with Love. He is not good and not beautiful, as you admit yourself, but do not imagine for that reason any the more that he must be ugly and bad, but something between these two,' said she. 'Well, anyway,' I said, 'he is admitted by all to be a great god.' 'All who don't know,' she said, 'or all who know too?' 'All without exception.' At this she said, with a laugh, 'And how could he be admitted to be a great god, Socrates, by those who say he is not a god at all?' 'Who are these?' said I. 'You for one,' said she, 'and I for another.' And I asked, 'How can that be?' She said, 'Easily. Tell me, don't you say that all the gods are happy and beautiful? Or would you dare to say that any one of them is not happy and beautiful?' 'Indeed I would not,' said I. 'Then don't you call happy those possessed of good and beautiful things?' 'Certainly.' 'Yet you admitted that Love, because of a lack of good and beautiful things, actually desired those things which he lacked.' 'Yes, I admitted that.' 'Then how could he be a god who has no share in beautiful and good things?' 'He could not be a god, as it seems.' 'Don't you see then,' said she, 'that you yourself deny Love to be a god?'

" 'Then what could Love be?' I asked. 'A mortal?' 'Not at all.' 'What then?' I asked. 'Just as before, between mortal and immortal.' 'What is he then, Diotima?' 'A great spirit, Socrates; for all the spiritual is between divine and mortal.' 'What power has it?' said I. 'To interpret and to ferry across to the gods things given by men, and to men things from the gods, from men petitions and sacrifices, from the gods commands and requitals in return; and being in the middle it completes them and binds all together into a whole. Through this intermediary moves all the art of divination, and the art of priests, and all concerned with sacrifice and mysteries and incantations, and all sorcery and witchcraft. For God mingles not with man, but through this comes all the communion and conversation of gods with men and men with gods, both awake and asleep; and he who is expert in this is a spiritual

man, but the expert in something other than this, such as common arts or crafts, is a vulgar man. These spirits are many and of all sorts and kinds, and one of them is Love.'

" 'Who was his father,' said I, 'and who was his mother?' She answered, 'That is rather a long story, but still I will tell you. When Aphrodite was born, the gods held a feast, among them Plenty,[16] the son of Neverataloss. When they had dined, Poverty came in begging, as might be expected with all that good cheer, and hung about the doors. Plenty then got drunk on the nectar—for there was no wine yet—and went into Zeus's park all heavy and fell asleep. So Poverty because of her penury made a plan to have a child from Plenty, and lay by his side and conceived Love. This is why Love has become follower and servant of Aphrodite, having been begotten at her birthday party, and at the same time he is by nature a lover busy with beauty because Aphrodite is beautiful. Then since Love is the son of Plenty and Poverty he gets his fortunes from them. First, he is always poor; and far from being tender and beautiful, as most people think, he is hard and rough and unshod and homeless, lying always on the ground without bedding, sleeping by the doors and in the streets in the open air, having his mother's nature, always dwelling with want. But from his father again he has designs upon beautiful and good things, being brave and go-ahead and high-strung, a mighty hunter, always weaving devices, and a successful coveter of wisdom, a philosopher all his days, a great wizard and sorcerer and sophist. He was born neither mortal nor immortal; but on the same day, sometimes he is blooming and alive, when he has plenty, sometimes he is dying; then again he gets new life through his father's nature; but what he procures in plenty always trickles away, so that Love is not in want nor in wealth, and again he is between wisdom and ignorance. The truth is this: no god seeks after wisdom or desires to become wise—for wise he is

---

[16]So Spenser calls him in the "Hymn to Love"; Lamb has "Resource, the son of Cunning," in his translation in the Loeb Classical Library.

already; nor does anyone else seek after wisdom, if he is wise already. And again, the ignorant do not seek after wisdom nor desire to become wise; for this is the worst of ignorance, that one who is neither beautiful and good[17] nor intelligent should think himself good enough, so he does not desire it, because he does not think he is lacking in what he does not think he needs.'

" 'Then who are the philosophers, Diotima,' said I, 'if those who seek after wisdom are neither the wise nor the ignorant?' 'That's clear enough even to a child,' she answered; 'they are those between these two, as Love is. You see, wisdom is one of the most beautiful things, and Love is a love for the beautiful, so Love must necessarily be a philosopher, and, being a philosopher, he must be between wise and ignorant. His birth is the cause of this, for he comes of a wise and resourceful father, but of a mother resourceless and not wise. Well then, dear Socrates, this is the nature of the spirit; but it was no wonder you thought Love what you did think. You thought, if I may infer it from what you say, that Love was the beloved, not the lover. That was why, I think, Love seemed to you wholly beautiful; for the thing loved is in fact beautiful and dainty and perfect and blessed, but the loving thing has a different shape, such as I have described.'

"Then I said, 'Very well, madam, what you say is right; but Love being such as you describe, of what use is he to mankind?' 'I will try to teach you that next, Socrates,' she said. 'Love then is like that, and born like that, and he is love of beautiful things, as you said he is. But suppose someone should ask us: "Socrates and Diotima, what is meant by love of beautiful things?"—I will put it more clearly: "He that loves beautiful things loves what?" ' Then I answered, 'To get them.' 'Still,' she said, 'that answer needs another question, like this: "What will he get who gets the beautiful things?" ' I said I could not manage at all to answer that question offhand. 'Well,' said she, 'suppose one should change "beau-

tiful" to "good" and ask that? See here, Socrates, I will say: "What does he love who loves good things?" ' 'To get them,' said I. 'And what will he get who gets the good things?' 'That's easier,' said I; 'I can answer that he will be happy.' 'Then,' said she, 'by getting good things the happy are happy, and there is no need to ask further, why he who wishes to be happy does wish that, but the answer seems to be finished.' 'Quite true,' said I. 'But do you think this wish and this love is common to all mankind,' Diotima said, 'and do you think that all men always wish to have the good things, or what do you say?' 'That's it,' said I, 'it's common to all.' 'Why then, Socrates,' said she, 'do we not say that all men are lovers, if they do in fact all love the same things and always, instead of saying that some are lovers and some are not?' 'That surprises me too,' I said. 'Don't let it surprise you,' she said. 'For we have taken one kind of love, and given it the name of the whole, love; and there are other cases in which we misapply other names.' 'For example?' said I. 'Here is one,' she said. 'You know that poetry is many kinds of making, for when anything passes from not-being to being, the cause is always making, or poetry, so that in all the arts the process is making, and all the craftsmen in these are makers, or poets.' 'Quite true,' I said. 'But yet,' said she, 'they are not all called poets; they have other names, and one bit of this making has been taken, that concerning music and verse, and this is called by the name of the whole. For this only is called poetry, and those who have this bit of making are called poets.' 'That is true,' I said. 'So with love, then; in its general sense it is all the desire for good things and for happiness—Love most mighty and all-ensnaring; but those who turn to him by any other road, whether by way of moneymaking, or of a taste for sports or philosophy, are not said to be in love and are not called lovers, but only those who go after one kind and are earnest about that have the name of the whole, love, and are said to love and to be lovers.' 'I think you are right there,' said I. 'And there is a story,' said she, 'that people in love are those who are seeking for their other half, but my story tells that love is not for a half, nor indeed the

---

[17]The Greeks meant by this what we might call a cultured gentleman.

whole, unless that happens to be something good, my friend; since men are willing to cut off their own hands and feet, if their own seem to them to be nasty. For really, I think, no one is pleased with his own thing, except one who calls the good thing his own and his property, and the bad thing another's; since there is nothing else men love but the good. Don't you think so?' 'Yes,' I said. 'Then,' said she, 'we may say simply that men love the good?' 'Yes,' I said. 'Shall we add,' she asked, 'that they love to have the good?' 'Yes, add that,' I said. 'Not only to have it, but always to have it?' 'Add that too.' 'Then to sum up,' she said, 'it is the love of having the good for oneself always.' 'Most true, indeed,' I said.

"She went on, 'Now if love is the love of having this always, what is the way men pursue it, and in what actions would their intense earnestness be expressed so as to be called love? What is this process? Can you tell me?' 'No,' said I, 'or else, Diotima, why should I, in admiration of your wisdom, have come to you as your pupil to find out these very matters?' 'Well then, I will tell you,' she said. 'It is a breeding in the beautiful, both of body and soul.' 'It needs divination,' I said, 'to tell what on earth you mean, and I don't understand.' 'Well,' she said, 'I will tell you clearer. All men are pregnant, Socrates, both in body and in soul; and when they are of the right age, our nature desires to beget. But it cannot beget in an ugly thing, only in a beautiful thing. And this business is divine, and this is something immortal in a mortal creature, breeding and birth. These cannot be in what is discordant. But the ugly is discordant with everything divine, and the beautiful is concordant. Beauty therefore is Portioner and Lady of Labour at birth. Therefore when the pregnant comes near to a beautiful thing it becomes gracious, and being delighted it is poured out and begets and procreates; when it comes near to an ugly thing, it becomes gloomy and grieved and rolls itself up and is repelled and shrinks back and does not procreate, but holds back the conception and is in a bad way. Hence in the pregnant thing swelling full already, there is great agitation about the beautiful thing because he that has it gains relief from great agony. Finally, Socrates, love is not for the

beautiful, as you think.' 'Why not?' 'It is for begetting and birth in the beautiful.' 'Oh, indeed?' said I. 'Yes indeed,' said she. 'Then why for begetting?' 'Because begetting is, for the mortal, something everlasting and immortal. But one must desire immortality along with the good, according to what has been agreed, if love is love of having the good for oneself always. It is necessary then from this argument that love is for immortality also.'

"All this she taught me at different times whenever she came to speak about love affairs; and once she asked, 'What do you think, Socrates, to be the cause of this love and desire? You perceive that all animals get into a dreadful state when they desire to procreate, indeed birds and beasts alike; all are sick and in a condition of love, about mating first, and then how to find food for their young, and they are ready to fight hard for them, the weakest against the strongest, and to die for them, and to suffer the agonies of starvation themselves in order to feed them, ready to do anything. One might perhaps think that man,' she said, 'would do all this from reasoning; but what about beasts? What is the cause of their enamoured state? Can you tell me?' And I said again that I did not know; and she said, 'Then how do you ever expect to become expert in love affairs, if you do not understand that?' 'Why, Diotima, this is just why I have come to you, as I said; I knew I needed a teacher. Pray tell me the cause of this, and all the other love lore.'

" 'Well then,' she said, 'if you believe love is by nature love of that which we often agreed on, don't be surprised. For on the same principle as before, here mortal nature seeks always as far as it can be to be immortal; and this is the only way it can, by birth, because it leaves something young in place of the old. Consider that for a while each single living creature is said to live and to be the same; for example, a man is said to be the same from boyhood to old age; he has, however, by no means the same things in himself, yet he is called the same: he continually becomes new, though he loses parts of himself, hair and flesh and bones and blood and all the body. Indeed, not only body, even in soul, manners, opinions, desires, pleasures, pains, fears, none of these remains the same, but some perish and others are born. And far stranger still, this happens to knowledge too; not only do some kinds of knowledge perish in us, not only are other kinds born, and not even in our knowledge are we ever the same, but the same happens even in each single kind of knowledge. For what is called study and practice means that knowledge is passing out; forgetting is knowledge leaving us, and study puts in new knowledge instead of that which is passing away, and preserves our knowledge so that it seems to be the same. In this way all the mortal is preserved, not by being wholly the same always, like the divine, but because what grows old and goes leaves behind something new like its past self. By this device, Socrates,' said she, 'mortality partakes of immortality, both in body and in all other respects; but it cannot otherwise. Then do not be surprised that everything naturally honours its own offspring; immortality is what all this earnestness and love pursues.'

"I heard this with admiration; and I said, 'Really, Diotima most wise! Is that really and truly so?' She answered as the complete Sophists do,[18] and said, 'You may be sure of that, Socrates. Just think, if you please, of men's ambition. You would be surprised at its unreasonableness if you didn't bear in mind what I have told you; observe what a terrible state they are in with love of becoming renowned, "and to lay up their fame for evermore"[19] and for this how ready they are to run all risks even more than for their children, and to spend money and endure hardship to any extent, and to die for it. Do you think Alcestis would have died for Admetos, or Achilles would have died over Patroclos, or your Codros[20] would have died for the royalty of his sons, if they had not thought that "immortal memory of Virtue" would be theirs, which we still keep! Far from it,' she said; 'for eternal virtue and glorious fame like that all men do everything, I think, and the better they

are, the more they do so; for the immortal is what they love. So those who are pregnant in body,' she said, 'turn rather to women and are enamoured in this way, and thus, by begetting children, secure for themselves, so they think, immortality and memory and happiness, "Providing all things for the time to come;"[21] but those who are pregnant in soul—for there are some,' she said, 'who conceive in soul still more than in body, what is proper for the soul to conceive and bear; and what is proper? wisdom and virtue in general—to this class belong all creative poets, and those artists and craftsmen who are said to be inventive. But much the greatest wisdom,' she said, 'and the most beautiful, is that which is concerned with the ordering of cities and homes, which we call temperance and justice. So again a man with divinity in him, whose soul from his youth is pregnant with these things, desires when he grows up to beget and procreate; and thereupon, I think, he seeks and goes about to find the beautiful thing in which he can beget; for in the ugly he never will. Being pregnant, then, he welcomes bodies which are beautiful rather than ugly, and if he finds a soul beautiful and generous and well-bred, he gladly welcomes the two body and soul together, and for a human being like that he has plenty of talks about virtue, and what the good man ought to be and to practise, and he tries to educate him. For by attaching himself to a person of beauty, I think, and keeping company with him, he begets and procreates what he has long been pregnant with; present and absent he remembers him, and with him fosters what is begotten, so that as a result these people maintain a much closer communion together and a firmer friendship than parents of children, because they have shared between them children more beautiful and more immortal. And everyone would be content to have such children born to him rather than human children; he would look to Homer and Hesiod and the other good poets, and wish to rival them,

---

[18]That is, she made a speech rather than answered questions.
[19]A line of poetry.
[20]A legendary King of Athens, who gave his life for this in the Dorian invasion.

---

[21]A line of poetry.

who leave such offspring behind them, which give their parents the same immortal fame and memory as they have themselves; or if you like,' she said, 'think what children Lycurgos[22] left in Lacedaimon, the saviours of Lacedaimon and, one may say, of all Hellas. Honour came to Solon also, in your country, by the begetting of his laws; and to many others in many countries and times, both Hellenes and barbarians, who performed many beautiful works and begat all kinds of virtue; in their names many sanctuaries have been made because they had such children, but never a one has been so honoured because of human children.

" 'These are some of the mysteries of Love, Socrates, in which perhaps even you may become an initiate; but as for the higher revelations, which initiation leads to if one approaches in the right way, I do not know if you could ever become an adept. At least I will instruct you,' she said, 'and no pains will be lacking; you try to follow if you can. It is necessary,' she said, 'that one who approaches in the right way should begin this business young, and approach beautiful bodies. First, if his leader leads aright, he should love one body and there beget beautiful speech; then he should take notice that the beauty in one body is akin to the beauty in another body, and if we must pursue beauty in essence, it is great folly not to believe that the beauty in all such bodies is one and the same. When he has learnt this, he must become the lover of all beautiful bodies, and relax the intense passion for one, thinking lightly of it and believing it to be a small thing. Next he must believe beauty in souls to be more precious than beauty in the body; so that if anyone is decent in soul, even if it has little bloom, it should be enough for him to love and care for, and to beget and seek such talks as will make young people better; that he may moreover be compelled to contemplate the beauty in our pursuits and customs, and to see that all beauty is of one and the same kin, and that so

he may believe that bodily beauty is a small thing. Next, he must be led from practice to knowledge, that he may see again the beauty in different kinds of knowledge, and, directing his gaze from now on towards beauty as a whole, he may no longer dwell upon one, like a servant, content with the beauty of one boy or one human being or one pursuit, and so be slavish and petty; but he should turn to the great ocean of beauty, and in contemplation of it give birth to many beautiful and magnificent speeches and thoughts in the abundance of philosophy, until being strengthened and grown therein he may catch sight of some one knowledge, the one science of this beauty now to be described. Try to attend,' she said, 'as carefully as you can.

" 'Whoever shall be guided so far towards the mysteries of love, by contemplating beautiful things rightly in due order, is approaching the last grade. Suddenly he will behold a beauty marvellous in its nature, that very Beauty, Socrates, for the sake of which all the earlier hardships had been borne: in the first place, everlasting, and never being born nor perishing, neither increasing nor diminishing; secondly, not beautiful here and ugly there, not beautiful now and ugly then, not beautiful in one direction and ugly in another direction, not beautiful in one place and ugly in another place. Again, this beauty will not show itself to him like a face or hands or any bodily thing at all, nor as a discourse or a science, nor indeed as residing in anything, as in a living creature or in earth or heaven or anything else, but being by itself with itself always in simplicity; while all the beautiful things elsewhere partake of this beauty in such manner, that when *they* are born and perish *it* becomes neither less nor more and nothing at all happens to it; so that when anyone by right boy-loving goes up from these beautiful things to that beauty, and begins to catch sight of it, he would almost touch the perfect secret. For let me tell you, the right way to approach the things of love, or to be led there by another, is this: beginning from these beautiful things, to mount for that beauty's sake ever upwards, as by

---

[22]The Spartan lawgiver.

a flight of steps, from one to two, and from two to all beautiful bodies, and from beautiful bodies to beautiful pursuits and practices, and from practices to beautiful learnings, so that from learnings he may come at last to that perfect learning which is the learning solely of that beauty itself, and may know at last that which is the perfection of beauty. There in life and there alone, my dear Socrates,' said the inspired woman, 'is life worth living for man, while he contemplates Beauty itself. If ever you see this, it will seem to you to be far above gold and raiment and beautiful boys and men, whose beauty you are now entranced to see and you and many others are ready, so long as they see their darlings and remain ever with them, if it could be possible, not to eat nor drink but only to gaze at them and to be with them. What indeed,' she said, 'should we think, if it were given to one of us to see beauty undefiled, pure, unmixed, not adulterated with human flesh and colours and much other mortal rubbish, and if he could behold beauty in perfect simplicity? Do you think it a mean life for a man,' she said, 'to be looking thither and contemplating that and abiding with it? Do you not reflect,' said she, 'that there only it will be possible for him, when he sees the beautiful with the mind, which alone can see it, to give birth not to likenesses of virtue, since he touches no likeness, but to realities, since he touches reality; and when he has given birth to real virtue and brought it up, will it not be granted him to be the friend of God, and immortal if any man ever is?'

"This then, Phaidros and gentlemen, is what Diotima said, and I am quite convinced, and, being convinced, I try to persuade other people also to believe that to attain this possession one could not easily find a better helper for human nature than Love. And so I say that every man ought to honour Love, and I honour love matters myself, and I practise them particularly and encourage others; and now and always I sing the praises of Love's power and courage, as much as I am able. Then let this be my speech of eulogy to Love, if you please, Phaidros, or call it anything else you like."

THE PARABLE OF THE CAVE

Plato

"Next, then," I said, "take the following parable of education and ignorance as a picture of the condition of our nature. Imagine mankind as dwelling in an underground cave with a long entrance open to the light across the whole width of the cave; in this they have been from childhood, with necks and legs fettered, so they have to stay where they are. They cannot move their heads round because of the fetters, and they can only look forward, but light comes to them from fire burning behind them higher up at a distance. Between the fire and the prisoners is a road above their level, and along it imagine a low wall has been built, as puppet showmen have screens in front of their people over which they work their puppets."

"I see," he said.

"See, then, bearers carrying along this wall all sorts of articles which they hold projecting above the wall, statues of men and other living things,[1] made of stone or wood and all kinds of stuff, some of the bearers speaking and some silent, as you might expect."

"What a remarkable image," he said, "and what remarkable prisoners!"

"Just like ourselves," I said. "For, first of all, tell me this: What do you think such people would have seen of themselves and each other except their shadows, which the fire cast on the opposite wall of the cave?"

"I don't see how they could see anything else," said he, "if they were compelled to keep their heads unmoving all their lives!"

"Very well, what of the things being carried along? Would not this be the same?"

"Of course it would."

"Suppose the prisoners were able to talk together, don't you think that when they named the shadows which they saw passing they would believe they were naming things?"[2]

---

[1]Including models of trees, etc.
[2]Which they had never seen. They would say "tree" when it was only a shadow of the model of a tree.

"Necessarily."

"Then if their prison had an echo from the opposite wall, whenever one of the passing bearers uttered a sound, would they not suppose that the passing shadow must be making the sound? Don't you think so?"

"Indeed I do," he said.

"If so," said I, "such persons would certainly believe that there were no realities except those shadows of handmade things."[3]

"So it must be," said he.

"Now consider," said I, "what their release would be like, and their cure from these fetters and their folly; let us imagine whether it might naturally be something like this. One might be released, and compelled suddenly to stand up and turn his neck round, and to walk and look towards the firelight; all this would hurt him, and he would be too much dazzled to see distinctly those things whose shadows he had seen before. What do you think he would say, if someone told him that what he saw before was foolery, but now he saw more rightly, being a bit nearer reality and turned towards what was a little more real? What if he were shown each of the passing things, and compelled by questions to answer what each one was? Don't you think he would be puzzled, and believe what he saw before was more true than what was shown to him now?"

"Far more," he said.

"Then suppose he were compelled to look towards the real light, it would hurt his eyes, and he would escape by turning them away to the things which he was able to look at, and these he would believe to be clearer than what was being shown to him."

"Just so," said he.

"Suppose, now," said I, "that someone should drag him thence by force, up the rough ascent, the steep way up, and never stop until he could drag him out into the light of the sun, would he not be distressed and furious at being dragged; and when he came into the light, the brilliance would fill his eyes and he would not be able to see even one of the things now called real?"[4]

"That he would not," said he, "all of a sudden."

"He would have to get used to it, surely, I think, if he is to see the things above. First he would most easily look at shadows, after that images of mankind and the rest in water, lastly the things themselves. After this he would find it easier to survey by night the heavens themselves and all that is in them, gazing at the light of the stars and moon, rather than by day the sun and the sun's light."

"Of course."

"Last of all, I suppose, the sun; he could look on the sun itself by itself in its own place, and see what it is like, not reflections of it in water or as it appears in some alien setting."

"Necessarily," said he.

"And only after all this he might reason about it, how this is he who provides seasons and years, and is set over all there is in the visible region, and he is in a manner the cause of all things which they saw."

"Yes, it is clear," said he, "that after all that, he would come to this last."

"Very good. Let him be reminded of his first habitation, and what was wisdom in that place, and of his fellow-prisoners there; don't you think he would bless himself for the change, and pity them?"

"Yes, indeed."

"And if there were honours and praises among them and prizes for the one who saw the passing things most sharply and remembered best which of them used to come before and which after and which together, and from these was best able to prophesy accordingly what was going to come— do you believe he would set his desire on that, and envy those who were honoured men or potentates among them? Would he not feel as Homer says,[5] and heartily desire rather to be serf of some landless man on earth and to endure anything in the world, rather than to opine as they did and to live in that way?"

---

[3]Shadows of artificial things, not even the shadow of a growing tree: another stage from reality.

[4]To the next stage of knowledge: the real thing, not the artificial puppet.
[5]*Odyssey* xi, 489.

"Yes, indeed," said he, "he would rather accept anything than live like that."

"Then again," I said, "just consider; if such a one should go down again and sit on his old seat, would he not get his eyes full of darkness coming in suddenly out of the sun?"

"Very much so," said he.

"And if he should have to compete with those who had been always prisoners, by laying down the law about those shadows while he was blinking before his eyes were settled down—and it would take a good long time to get used to things—wouldn't they all laugh at him and say he had spoiled his eyesight by going up there, and it was not worthwhile so much as to try to go up? And would they not kill anyone who tried to release them and take them up, if they could somehow lay hands on him and kill him?"[6]

"That they would!" said he.

"Then we must apply this image, my dear Glaucon," said I, "to all we have been saying. The world of our sight is like the habitation in prison, the firelight there to the sunlight here, the ascent and the view of the upper world is the rising of the soul into the world of mind; put it so and you will not be far from my own surmise, since that is what you want to hear; but God knows if it is really true. At least, what appears to me is, that in the world of the known, last of all,[7] is the idea of the good, and with what toil to be seen! And seen, this must be inferred to be the cause of all right and beautiful things for all, which gives birth to light and the king of light in the world of sight, and, in the world of mind, herself the queen produces truth and reason; and she must be seen by one who is to act with reason publicly or privately."

"I believe as you do," he said, "in so far as I am able."

"Then believe also, as I do," said I, "and do not be surprised, that those who come thither are not willing to have part in the affairs of men, but their souls ever strive to remain above; for that surely may be expected if our parable fits the case."

---

[6]Plato probably alludes to the death of Socrates.
[7]The end of our search.

"Quite so," he said.

"Well then," said I, "do you think it surprising if one leaving divine contemplations and passing to the evils of men is awkward and appears to be a great fool, while he is still blinking—not yet accustomed to the darkness around him, but compelled to struggle in law courts or elsewhere about shadows of justice, or the images which make the shadows, and to quarrel about notions of justice in those who have never seen justice itself?"

"Not surprising at all," said he.

"But any man of sense," I said, "would remember that the eyes are doubly confused from two different causes, both in passing from light to darkness and from darkness to light; and believing that the same things happen with regard to the soul also, whenever he sees a soul confused and unable to discern anything he would not just laugh carelessly; he would examine whether it had come out of a more brilliant life, and if it were darkened by the strangeness; or whether it had come out of greater ignorance into a more brilliant light, and if it were dazzled with the brighter illumination. Then only would he congratulate the one soul upon its happy experience and way of life, and pity the other; but if he must laugh, his laugh would be a less downright laugh than his laughter at the soul which came out of the light above."

"That is fairly put," said he.

"Then if this is true," I said, "our belief about these matters must be this, that the nature of education is not really such as some of its professors say it is; as you know, they say that there is not understanding in the soul, but they put it in, as if they were putting sight into blind eyes."

"They do say so," said he.

"But our reasoning indicates," I said, "that this power is already in the soul of each, and is the instrument by which each learns; thus if the eye could not see without being turned with the whole body from the dark towards the light, so this instrument must be turned round with the whole soul away from the world of becoming until it is able to endure the sight of being and the most brilliant light of being: and this we say is the good, don't we?"

"Yes."

CRAZY HORSE'S VISION

Black Elk

Crazy Horse's father was my father's cousin, and there were no chiefs in our family before Crazy Horse; but there were holy men; and he became a chief because of the power he got in a vision when he was a boy. When I was a man, my father told me something about that vision. Of course he did not know all of it; but he said that Crazy Horse dreamed and went into the world where there is nothing but the spirits of all things. That is the real world that is behind this one, and everything we see here is something like a shadow from that world. He was on his horse in that world, and the horse and himself on it and the trees and the grass and the stones and everything were made of spirit, and nothing was hard, and everything seemed to float. His horse was standing still there, and yet it danced around like a horse made only of shadow, and that is how he got his name, which does not mean that his horse was crazy or wild, but that in his vision it danced around in that queer way.

It was this vision that gave him his great power, for when he went into a fight, he had only to think of that world to be in it again, so that he could go through anything and not be hurt. Until he was murdered by the Wasichus[1] at the Soldiers' Town on White River, he was wounded only twice, once by accident and both times by someone of his own people when he was not expecting trouble and was not thinking; never by an enemy. He was fifteen years old when he was wounded by accident; and the other time was when he was a young man and another man was jealous of him because the man's wife liked Crazy Horse.

They used to say too that he carried a sacred stone with him, like one he had seen in some vision, and that when he was in danger, the stone al-ways got very heavy and protected him somehow. That, they used to say, was the reason no horse he ever rode lasted very long. I do not know about this; maybe people only thought it; but it is a fact that he never kept one horse long. They wore out. I think it was only the power of his great vision that made him great.

Now and then he would notice me and speak to me before this; and sometimes he would have the crier call me into his tepee to eat with him. Then he would say things to tease me, but I would not say anything back, because I think I was a little afraid of him. I was not afraid that he would hurt me; I was just afraid. Everybody felt that way about him, for he was a queer man and would go about the village without noticing people or saying anything. In his own tepee he would joke, and when he was on the warpath with a small party, he would joke to make his warriors feel good. But around the village he hardly ever noticed anybody, except little children. All the Lakotas[2] like to dance and sing; but he never joined a dance, and they say nobody ever heard him sing. But everybody liked him, and they would do anything he wanted or go anywhere he said. He was a small man among the Lakotas and he was slender and had a thin face and his eyes looked through things and he always seemed to be thinking hard about something. He never wanted to have many things for himself, and did not have many ponies like a chief. They say that when game was scarce and the people were hungry, he would not eat at all. He was a queer man. Maybe he was always partway into that world of his vision. He was a very great man, and I think if the Wasichus had not murdered him down there, maybe we should still have the Black Hills and be happy. They could not have killed him in battle. They had to lie to him and murder him. And he was only about thirty years old when he died.

---

[1]"Wasichus" is the name Black Elk uses for the whites (Eds.).

[2]Lakota or Dakota is the name the Sioux call themselves (Eds.).

THE VALUE OF THE SURFACE

Hannah Arendt

1 THE WORLD'S PHENOMENAL NATURE

The world men are born into contains many things, natural and artificial, living and dead, transient and sempiternal, all of which have in common that they *appear* and hence are meant to be seen, heard, touched, tasted, and smelled, to be perceived by sentient creatures endowed with the appropriate sense organs. Nothing could appear, the word "appearance" would make no sense, if recipients of appearances did not exist—living creatures able to acknowledge, recognize, and react to—in flight or desire, approval or disapproval, blame or praise— what is not merely there but appears to them and is meant for their perception. In this world which we enter, appearing from a nowhere, and from which we disappear into a nowhere, *Being and Appearing coincide.* Dead matter, natural and artificial, changing and unchanging, depends in its being, that is, in its appearingness, on the presence of living creatures. Nothing and nobody exists in this world whose very being does not presuppose a *spectator.* In other words, nothing that is, insofar as it appears, exists in the singular; everything that is is meant to be perceived by somebody. Not Man but men inhabit this planet. Plurality is the law of the earth.

Since sentient beings—men and animals, to whom things appear and who as recipients guarantee their reality—are themselves also appearances, meant and able both to see and be seen, hear and be heard, touch and be touched, they are never mere subjects and can never be understood as such; they are no less "objective" than stone and bridge. The worldliness of living things means that there is no subject that is not also an object and appears as such to somebody else, who guarantees its "objective" reality. What we usually call "consciousness," the fact that I am aware of myself and therefore in a sense can appear to myself, would never suffice to guarantee reality.

• • •

Seen from the perspective of the world, every creature born into it arrives well equipped to deal with a world in which Being and Appearing coincide; they are fit for worldly existence. Living beings, men and animals, are not just in the world, they are *of the world,* and this precisely because they are subjects and objects—perceiving and being perceived—at the same time.

Nothing perhaps is more surprising in this world of ours than the almost infinite diversity of its appearances, the sheer entertainment value of its views, sounds, and smells, something that is hardly ever mentioned by the thinkers and philosophers.

• • •

This diversity is matched by an equally astounding diverseness of sense organs among the animal species, so that what actually appears to living creatures assumes the greatest variety of form and shape: every animal species lives in a world of its own. Still, all sense-endowed creatures have appearance as such in common, first, an appearing world and second, and perhaps even more important, the fact that they themselves are appearing and disappearing creatures, that there always was a world before their arrival and there always will be a world after their departure.

To be alive means to live in a world that preceded one's own arrival and will survive one's own departure. On this level of sheer being alive, appearance and disappearance, as they follow upon each other, are the primordial events, which as such mark out time, the time span between birth and death. The finite life span allotted to each living creature determines not merely its life expectancy but also its time experience; it provides the secret prototype for all time measurements no matter how far these then may transcend the allotted life span into past and future. Thus, the lived experience of the length of a year changes radically throughout our life. A year that to a five-year-old constitutes a full fifth of his existence must seem much longer than when it will constitute a mere twentieth or thirtieth of his time on earth. We all know how the years revolve quicker and quicker as we get older, until, with the approach of old age, they slow down again because we begin to measure them against the psychologically and somatically anticipated date of our departure. Against this clock, inherent in living beings who are born and die, stands "objective" time, according to which the length of a year never changes. This is the time of the world, and its underlying assumption—regardless of any religious or scientific beliefs—is that the world has neither beginning nor end, an assumption that seems only natural for beings who always come into a world that preceded them and will survive them.

In contrast to the inorganic thereness of lifeless matter, living beings are not mere appearances. To be alive means to be possessed by an urge toward self-display which answers the fact of one's own appearingness. Living things *make their appearance* like actors on a stage set for them. The stage is common to all who are alive, but it *seems* different to each species, different also to each individual specimen. Seeming—the it-seems-to-me, *dokei moi*—is the mode, perhaps the only possible one, in which an appearing world is acknowledged and perceived. To appear always means to seem to others, and this seeming varies according to the standpoint and the perspective of the spectators. In other words, every appearing thing acquires, by virtue of its appearingness, a kind of disguise that may indeed—but does not have to—hide or disfigure it. Seeming corresponds to the fact that every appearance, its identity notwithstanding, is perceived by a plurality of spectators.

The urge toward self-display—to respond by showing to the overwhelming effect of being shown—seems to be common to men and animals. And just as the actor depends upon stage, fellow-actors, and spectators, to make his entrance, every living thing depends upon a world that solidly appears as the location for its own appearance, on fellow-creatures to play with, and on spectators to acknowledge and recognize its existence. Seen from the viewpoint of the spectators to whom it appears and from whose view it finally

disappears, each individual life, its growth and decline, is a developmental process in which an entity unfolds itself in an upward movement until all its properties are fully exposed; this phase is followed by a period of standstill—its bloom or epiphany, as it were—which in turn is succeeded by the downward movement of disintegration that is terminated by complete disappearance. There are many perspectives in which this process can be seen, examined, and understood, but our criterion for what a living thing essentially is remains the same: in everyday life as well as in scientific study, it is determined by the relatively short time span of its full appearance, its epiphany. The choice, guided by the sole criteria of completeness and perfection in appearance, would be entirely arbitrary if reality were not first of all of a phenomenal nature.

The primacy of appearance for all living creatures to whom the world appears in the mode of an it-seems-to-me is of great relevance to . . . those mental activities by which we distinguish ourselves from other animal species. For although there are great differences among these activities, they all have in common a *withdrawal* from the world as it appears and a bending back toward the self. This would cause no great problem if we were mere spectators, godlike creatures thrown into the world to look after it or enjoy it and be entertained by it, but still in possession of some other region as our natural habitat. However, *we are of the world and not merely in it;* we, too, are appearances by virtue of arriving and departing, of appearing and disappearing; and while we come from a nowhere, we arrive well equipped to deal with whatever appears to us and to take part in the play of the world. These properties do not vanish when we happen to be engaged in mental activities and close the eyes of our body, to use the Platonic metaphor, in order to be able to open the eyes of the mind. The two-world theory belongs among the metaphysical fallacies but it would never have been able to survive for so many centuries if it had not so plausibly corresponded to some basic experiences. As Merleau-Ponty once put it, "I can flee being only into being,"[1] and since Being and Appearing coincide for men, this means that I can flee appearance only into appearance. And that does not solve the problem, for the problem concerns the fitness of thought to appear at all, and the question is whether thinking and other invisible and soundless mental activities are meant to appear or whether in fact they can never find an adequate home in the world.

2 (TRUE) BEING AND (MERE) APPEARANCE: THE TWO-WORLD THEORY

We may find a first consoling hint regarding this subject if we turn to the old metaphysical dichotomy of (true) Being and (mere) Appearance, because it, too, actually relies on the primacy, or at least on the priority, of appearance. In order to find out what truly *is,* the philosopher must *leave* the world of appearances among which he is naturally and originally at home—as Parmenides did when he was carried upward, beyond the gates of night and day, to the divine way that lay "far from the beaten path of men,"[2] and as Plato did, too, in the Cave parable.[3] The world of appearances is *prior* to whatever region the philosopher may *choose* as his "true" home but into which he was not born. It has always been the very appearingness of this world that suggested to the philosopher, that is, to the human mind, the notion that something must exist that is not appearance: *"Nehmen wir die Welt als Erscheinung so beweiset sie gerade zu das Dasein von Etwas das nicht Erscheinung ist"* ("If we look upon the world as appearance, it demonstrates the existence of something that is not appearance"), in the words of Kant.[4] In other words, when the philosopher takes leave of the world given to our senses and does a turnabout (Plato's *periagōgē*) to the life

of the mind, he takes his clue from the former, looking for something to be revealed to him that would explain its underlying truth. This truth—*a-lētheia,* that which is disclosed (Heidegger)—can be conceived only as another "appearance," another phenomenon originally hidden but of a supposedly higher order, thus signifying the lasting predominance of appearance. Our mental apparatus, though it can withdraw from *present* appearances, remains geared to Appearance. The mind, no less than the senses, in its search . . . expects that something will appear to it.

Something quite similar seems to be true for science, and especially for modern science, which—according to an early remark of Marx's—relies on Being and Appearance having parted company, so that the philosopher's special and individual effort is no longer needed to arrive at some "truth" behind the appearances. The scientist, too, depends on appearances, whether, in order to find out what lies beneath the surface, he cuts open the visible body to look at its interior or catches hidden objects by means of all sorts of sophisticated equipment that deprives them of the exterior properties through which they show themselves to our natural senses. The guiding notion of these philosophical and scientific efforts is always the same: Appearances, as Kant said, "must themselves have grounds which are not appearances."[5] This, in fact, is an obvious generalization of the way natural things grow and "appear" into the light of day out of a ground of darkness, except that it was now assumed that this ground possessed a higher rank of reality than what merely appeared and after a while disappeared again. And just as the philosophers' "conceptual efforts" to find something beyond appearances have always ended with rather violent invectives against "mere appearances," the eminently practical achievements of the scientists in laying bare what appearances themselves never show without being interfered with have been made at their expense.

---

[1] Thomas Langan, *Merleau-Ponty's Critique of Reason,* New Haven, London, 1966, p. 93.
[2] Frag. 1.
[3] *Republic,* VII, 514a–521b.
[4] Kant, *Opus Postumum,* ed. Erich Adickes, Berlin, 1920, p. 44. Probable date of this remark is 1788.

---

[5] *Critique of Pure Reason,* B565.

The primacy of appearance is a fact of everyday life which neither the scientist nor the philosopher can ever escape, to which they must always return from their laboratories and studies, and which shows its strength by never being in the least changed or deflected by whatever they may have discovered when they withdrew from it. "Thus the 'strange' notions of the new physics . . . [surprise] common sense . . . without changing anything of its categories."[6] Against this unshakable common-sense conviction stands the age-old theoretical supremacy of Being and Truth over mere appearance, that is, the supremacy of the *ground* that does not appear over the surface that does. This ground supposedly answers the oldest question of philosophy as well as of science: How does it happen that something or somebody, including myself, appears at all and what makes it appear in this form and shape rather than in any other? The question itself asks for a *cause* rather than a base or ground, but the point of the matter is that our tradition of philosophy has transformed the base from which something rises into the cause that produces it and has then assigned to this producing agent a higher rank of reality than is given to what merely meets the eye. The belief that a cause should be of higher rank than the effect (so that an effect can easily be disparaged by being retraced to its cause) may belong to the oldest and most stubborn metaphysical fallacies. Yet here again we are not dealing with a sheer arbitrary error; the truth is, not only do appearances never reveal what lies beneath them of their own accord but also, generally speaking, they never just reveal; they also conceal—"No thing, no side of a thing, shows itself except by actively hiding the others."[7] They expose, and they also protect from exposure, and, as far as what lies beneath is concerned, this protection may even be their most important function. At any rate, this is true for living

things, whose surface hides and protects the inner organs that are their source of life.

The elementary logical fallacy of all theories that rely on the dichotomy of Being and Appearance is obvious and was early discovered and summed up by the sophist Gorgias in a fragment from his lost treatise *On Non-Being or On Nature*—supposedly a refutation of Eleatic philosophy: "Being is not manifest since it does not appear [to men: *dokein*]; appearing [to men] is weak since it does not succeed in being."[8]

Modern science's relentless search for the base underneath mere appearances has given new force to the old argument. It has indeed forced the ground of appearances into the open so that man, a creature fitted for and dependent on appearances, can catch hold of it. But the results have been rather perplexing. No man, it has turned out, can live among "causes" or give full account in normal human language of a Being whose truth can be scientifically demonstrated in the laboratory and tested practically in the real world through technology. It does look as though Being, once made manifest, overruled appearances—except that nobody so far has succeeded in *living* in a world that does not manifest itself of its own accord.

3 THE REVERSAL OF THE METAPHYSICAL HIERARCHY: THE VALUE OF THE SURFACE

The everyday common-sense world, which neither the scientist nor the philosopher ever eludes, knows error as well as illusion. Yet no elimination of errors or dispelling of illusions can arrive at a region beyond appearance. "For when an illusion dissipates, when an appearance suddenly breaks up, it is always for the profit of a new appearance which takes up again for its own account the ontological function of the first . . . The dis-illusion is the loss of one evidence only because it is the acquisition of *an-*

---

[6]Maurice Merleau-Ponty, *The Visible and the Invisible,* Evanston, 1968, p. 17.
[7]Maurice Merleau-Ponty, *Signs,* Evanston, 1964, Introduction, p. 20.

[8]Hermann Diels and Walter Kranz, *Die Fragmente der Vorsokratiker,* Berlin, 1959, Vol. II, B26.

other evidence . . . there is no *Schein* without an *Erscheinung,* every *Schein* is the counterpart of an *Erscheinung.*"[9] That modern science, in its relentless search for *the* truth behind *mere* appearances, will ever be able to resolve this predicament is, to say the least, highly doubtful, if only because the scientist himself belongs to the world of appearances although his perspective on this world may differ from the common-sense perspective.

Historically speaking, it seems that an irremovable doubt has been inherent in the whole enterprise ever since its beginnings with the rise of science in the modern age. The first entirely new notion brought in by the new age—the seventeenth-century idea of an unlimited *progress,* which after a few centuries became the most cherished dogma of *all* men living in a scientifically oriented world—seems intended to take care of the predicament: though one expects to progress further and further, no one seems ever to have believed in reaching a final absolute goal of truth.

It is obvious that consciousness of the predicament should be most acute in the sciences that deal directly with men, and the answer—reduced to its lowest common denominator—of the various branches of biology, sociology, and psychology is to interpret all appearances as functions of the life process. The great advantage of functionalism is that it presents us again with a unitary world view, and the old metaphysical dichotomy of (true) Being and (mere) Appearance, together with the old prejudice of Being's supremacy over appearance, is still kept intact, albeit in a different manner. The argument has shifted; appearances are no longer depreciated as "secondary qualities" but understood as necessary conditions for essential processes that go on inside the living organism.

This hierarchy has recently been challenged in a way that seems to me highly significant. Could it not be that appearances are not there for the sake of the life process but, on the contrary, that the life process is there for the sake of appearances? Since we live in an *appearing* world, is it not much more plausible that the relevant and the meaningful in this world of ours should be located precisely on the surface?

In a number of publications on the various shapes and forms in animal life, the Swiss zoologist and biologist Adolf Portmann has shown that the facts themselves speak a very different language from the simplistic functional hypothesis that holds that appearances in living beings serve merely the twofold purpose of self-preservation and preservation of the species. From a different, and, as it were, more innocent viewpoint, it rather looks as though, on the contrary, the inner, nonappearing organs exist only in order to bring forth and maintain the appearances. "Prior to all functions for the purpose of preservation of the individual and the species . . . we find the simple fact of appearing as self-display *that makes these functions meaningful*" (italics added).[10]

Moreover, Portmann demonstrates with a great wealth of fascinating example, what should be obvious to the naked eye—that the enormous variety of animal and plant life, the very richness of display in its sheer functional *superfluity,* cannot be accounted for by the common theories that understand life in terms of functionality. Thus, the plumage of birds, "which, at first, we consider to be of value as a warm, protective covering, is thus in addition so formed that its visible parts—and these only—build up a coloured garment, the intrinsic worth of which lies solely in its visible appearance."[11] Generally speaking, "the functional form pure and simple, so much extolled by some as befitting Nature [adequate to nature's purpose], is a rare and special case."[12] Hence, it is wrong to take into account only the functional process that goes on inside the living organism and to regard everything that is outside and "offers itself to the senses as the more or less subordinate consequence of the much more essential, 'central,' and

---

[9] *The Visible and the Invisible,* pp. 40–41.

[10] *Das Tier als Soziales Wesen,* Zürich, 1953, p. 252.
[11] *Animal Forms and Patterns,* trans. Hella Czech, New York, 1967, p. 19.
[12] *Ibid.,* p. 34.

'real' processes."[13] According to that prevailing mis-interpretation, "the external shape of the animal serves to conserve the essential, the inside apparatus, through movement and intake of food, avoidance of enemies, and finding sexual partners."[14] Against this approach Portmann proposes his "morphology," a new science that would reverse the priorities: "*Not what something is, but how it 'appears' is the research problem*" (italics added).[15]

This means that the very shape of an animal "must be appraised as a special organ of reference in relationship to a beholding eye. . . . The eye and what is to be looked at form a functional unit which is fitted together according to rules as strict as those obtaining between food and digestive organs."[16] And in accordance with this reversal, Portmann distinguishes between "authentic appearances," which come to light of their own accord, and "inauthentic" ones, such as the roots of a plant or the inner organs of an animal, which become visible only through interference with and violation of the "authentic" appearance.

Two facts of equal importance give this reversal its main plausibility. First, the impressive phenomenal difference between "authentic" and "inauthentic" appearances, between outside shapes and the inside apparatus. The outside shapes are infinitely varied and highly differentiated; among the higher animals we can usually tell one individual from another. Outside features of living things, moreover, are arranged according to the law of symmetry so that they appear in a definite and pleasing order. Inside organs, on the contrary, are never pleasing to the eye; once forced into view, they look as though they had been thrown together piecemeal and, unless deformed by disease or some peculiar abnormality, they appear alike; not even the various animal species, let alone the individuals, are easy to tell from each other by the mere inspection of their intestines. When Portmann defines life as "the appearance of an inside in an outside,"[17] he seems to fall victim to the very views he criticizes; for the point of his own findings is that what appears outside is so hopelessly *different* from the inside that one can hardly say that the inside ever appears at all. The inside, the functional apparatus of the life process, is covered up by an outside which, as far as the life process is concerned, has only one function, namely, to hide and protect it, to prevent its exposure to the light of an appearing world. If this inside were to appear, we would all look alike.

There is, second, the equally impressive evidence for the existence of an innate impulse—no less compelling than the merely functional instinct of preservation—which Portmann calls "the urge to self-display" (*Selbstdarstellung*). This instinct is entirely gratuitous in terms of life-preservation; it far transcends what may be deemed necessary for sexual attraction. These findings suggest that the predominance of outside appearance implies, in addition to the sheer receptivity of our senses, a spontaneous activity: *whatever can see wants to be seen, whatever can hear calls out to be heard, whatever can touch presents itself to be touched*. It is indeed as though everything that is alive—in addition to the fact that its surface is made for appearance, fit to be seen and meant to appear to others—has an *urge to appear*, to fit itself into the world of appearances by displaying and showing, not its "inner self" but itself as an individual. (The word "self-display," like the German *Selbstdarstellung*, is equivocal: it can mean that I actively make my presence felt, seen, and heard, or that I display my *self*, something inside me that otherwise would not appear at all—that is, in Portmann's terminology, an "inauthentic" appearance. In the following we shall use the word in the first meaning.) It is precisely this self-display, quite prominent already in the higher forms of animal life, that reaches its climax in the human species.

---

[13]*Das Tier als Soziales Wesen*, p. 232.
[14]*Ibid.*
[15]*Ibid.*, p. 127.
[16]*Animal Forms and Patterns*, pp. 112–113.

---

[17]*Das Tier als Soziales Wesen*, p. 64.

Portmann's morphological reversal of the usual priorities has far-reaching consequences, which he himself, however—perhaps for very good reasons—does not elaborate. They point to what he calls "the value of the surface," that is, to the fact that "the appearance shows a maximum power of expression compared with the internal, whose functions are of a more primitive order."[18] The use of the word "expression" shows clearly the terminological difficulties an elaboration of these consequences is bound to encounter. For an "expression" cannot but express something, and to the inevitable question, What does the expression express? (that is, press out), the answer will always be: something inside—an idea, a thought, an emotion. The expressiveness of an appearance, however, is of a different order; it "expresses" nothing but itself, that is, it exhibits or displays. It follows from Portmann's findings that our habitual standards of judgment, so firmly rooted in metaphysical assumptions and prejudices—according to which the essential lies beneath the surface, and the surface is "superficial"—are wrong, that our common conviction that what is inside ourselves, our "inner life," is more relevant to what we "are" than what appears on the outside is an illusion; but when it comes to correcting these fallacies, it turns out that our language, or at least our terminological discourse, fails us.

QUESTIONS FOR DISCUSSION

1. Why does Socrates believe that Love is not a god, even though Love was traditionally accepted as a god by the Greek people? Do you think that Socrates' argument concerning Love's true nature is a sound one? Why or why not?

2. If there were a time machine that could carry Black Elk to Socrates' Athens or Socrates to the American plains, Black Elk and Socrates surely would have had much in common to talk about, despite their great differences in culture. What might they say to each other? What might seem familiar? What would seem strange? Invent an imaginary conversation between the two where they explore their similarities and differences.

3. Why does Arendt feel that the "appearance/reality" distinction is false and misleading? Do you agree with her criticism of "two-world theories" that rely on the distinction? Why or why not?

---

[18]*Biologie und Geist,* Zürich, 1956, p. 24.

IDEALISM: WESTERN AND ASIAN

Concerned about the loss of spirituality he observed in a Europe increasingly turning to science for its answers, the Anglo-Irish philosopher-bishop George Berkeley (1685–1753) argued that the world of appearance *is* reality and reality is totally dependent on mind; the things around us are, that is to say, ideas in our minds, though ultimately they do have their origins in ideas that are contained in the mind of God. This view of reality is called in philosophy "idealism," not in the sense that its proponents are necessarily high-minded idealists but in the more basic sense that they view the world as mental or a mere idea. This is not to say that such philosophers deny totally the world's objectivity. It is just rather that, for them, the objective world, which people commonly call *material,* is, in fact, not material but the product of mind.

Beginning about 800 B.C.—more than 2,500 years before the time of Bishop Berkeley—in the great river valleys of North India, small groups of men turned their backs on established society in order to undertake a journey deep within themselves to find their own true nature and the true nature of God. Out of these spiritual journeys came the philosophical reflections known to the world as Vedanta or the *Upanishads,* a word which, roughly translated, means teachings received sitting at a sage's feet. Over time, these teachings were accepted as scriptural by the priests of the emerging Hindu religion. These scriptures in turn were interpreted in a variety of ways by the philosophers and theologians of Hinduism.

Our first selection begins with what is, perhaps, the most famous *Upanishad* of all, the dialogue in which a father instructs his son Svetaketu about his true nature, "Thou art that," from the *Chandogya Upanishad.* It is followed by a second passage in which "Brahman" or God is equated with the true nature of the self. In the second selection, the modern Indian sage Sri Ramana Maharshi (1880–1950) presents a philosophical interpretation of these and related passages that is known as Advaita Vedanta. "Advaita" in the Sanskrit language means "non-

dual" or "Absolute," to use a technical term for nonduality taken from the Western tradition. The *Upanishads,* on Ramana's view, teach that God or Brahman is in reality identical to the true Self or Atman in that they form together a nondual unity. The world and the false self that we usually mistakenly take ourselves to be are, on the other hand, mere appearances of God and not the underlying reality. The material world is thus, from God's point of view, a purely mind-created entity, a product of God's consciousness with no substance of its own. This form of idealism is often termed "objective idealism" in order to contrast it with Berkeley's "subjective" variety, which begins with human subjective experience and not an apprehension of a spiritual existence beyond the human form.

The transcendence of individual consciousness in objective idealism and the nondualism it implies cannot be given too much emphasis, as they are central to its teachings. It is because of this that Sri Ramana remarks that the scriptures' characterization of the Self as tiny and "subtler than the subtlest" and similar assertions are mere metaphors with "no foundation in fact" and that being the Self and realizing it are equivalent. There is, in the apprehension of the nondual Absolute (the Self), no distinction between the knower and the known. The Absolute is not a One in contrast to a Many. It is the inexpressible unity that precedes the idea of the One and the Many. This is, on Ramana's interpretation, what the seers of the *Upanishads* uncovered in their forest retreats.

The task is not so much to find something as to discard one's false beliefs. And the method that Sri Ramana employs is the traditional method of the *Upanishads* themselves, the method of *jnana* or "knowledge" that Svetaketu's father employed nearly 3,000 years ago. It is a method that uses philosophy more as a tool than as an end in itself, negative in its approach but positive in its goals. Thus, the selection is arranged in dialogue form, as Sri Ramana attempts to help the questioner throw off his beliefs in the plurality of existence—an attempt that looks upon the problem from many angles in the hope that somewhere a breakthrough can be made.

Absolute idealism is not, however, a purely Indian invention. In Germany in the early nineteenth century, following suggestions in the work of the great philosopher Immanuel Kant, several philosophers began exploring this avenue of understanding. When translations of classical Indian philosophy began to appear at around this same time in Germany, they were greeted with amazed enthusiasm. This, in turn, was reinforced by the discovery of the common ancestry of most European and North Indian languages. It was as if, in India, a long lost if distant cousin had been found. Of all the German idealists, the most knowledgeable on the subject of Indian idealism and the one working most closely in spirit to the Indians was Arthur Schopenhauer (1788–1860). Indeed, he often referred to himself as a Buddhist. In the selection from *The World as Will and Idea* presented here, he relates his own work to the famous "Thou art that" passage from the *Chandogya Upanishad* with which the Indian selections began.

To appreciate fully the claims Schopenhauer makes in the selection requires some background concerning his thought. To obtain this and see how Schopenhauer accomplishes his synthesis of East and West, it is necessary, first of all, to look at his point of departure in the philosophy of Kant. Like Berkeley before him, Kant had seen the world of human experience as having its existence in the mind. Unlike the bishop, however, Kant refused to draw the conclusion that reality itself was a product of the mind, positing instead a realm of the "thing-in-itself," which formed the ground of our mind-conditioned human experience. Since these mysterious "entities" existed, by definition, beyond and outside of human experience, it was natural for those philosophers who followed Kant to question their existence and collapse the system into a full-blown idealism.

Once this is accomplished, however, the idealism that results looks more like that of the *Upanishads* than that of Bishop Berkeley. For Kant had begun his account of the world with an argument that space and time are themselves forms of human "intuition" and not properties of the realm of things-in-themselves.

For Schopenhauer, this means that consciousness is not yet multiple and individual until the *principium individuationis,* the principle of individuation, a "potential for plurality" that space and time create, is brought into play by the mind. For space and time are what divides the world into a plurality. The very notion of plurality only exists in experience; that is, it only exists when the forms of space and time separate experience into the things and creatures of this world. Prior to that, consciousness is a nondual Absolute, which Schopenhauer identifies explicitly with the Brahman of the *Upanishads*.

This Absolute, moreover, reveals itself as having two aspects. It is first of all manifest as idea or the world as idea, the content of consciousness that constitutes the world's ideal nature in much the same way that Bishop Berkeley's mind-dependent universe did. Its second aspect is "will" or, more specifically, the "one will to live." This is the real "thing-in-itself" behind experience, not some unknowable "object in itself" into which "Kant's thing-in-itself unfortunately degenerated in the course of his work." For, just as we know our own bodies both as idea in perception when we look at and feel ourselves, and as will when we engage in deliberate action, so every object in the world is an expression of the will, an "objectification of will in the world." Otherwise, Schopenhauer argues, we must assume that our body is an object, "different from all others; that it alone of all objects is at once both will and idea, while the rest are only ideas, i.e., only phantoms."

In identifying the motive power of existence with the will to live conceived as the Absolute, Schopenhauer's characterization of the world resembles not only the Hindu but also the Buddhist view, which, like his, sees will as bringing into being the illusory conventional world we mistakenly believe ourselves to inhabit. Unlike Orthodox Buddhism, however, he interprets "karma" and reincarnation in our selection as a mere "myth" rather than a literal expression of the will. But like the Buddhism of Hui Neng in the next selection, Schopenhauer's view of subject and object characterizes them as "both mere abstractions . . . parts of one whole which comprises both," each existing only relative to the other. The Absolute—being both and neither subject and object—is ultimately beyond thought and words. Hui Neng (638–713), the sixth patriarch of the Ch'an or Zen school, following the Mahayana tradition in Buddhism, expresses this fact by referring to it as *sunya,* that is to say, "void" or "emptiness." In the Zen teaching, since it is beyond words, knowledge of the Absolute must be transmitted outside any scripture from the heart of the teacher directly to the student's heart.

Legend says that Buddha each day would retire with his monks at day's end and lecture them on his teachings. On one occasion, however, instead of speaking, he merely held up before them a bouquet of flowers, which a lay follower had given him earlier in the day. All the monks but one were puzzled. Only Kasyapa smiled and understood. Buddha therefore handed him the flowers, saying, "There is a teaching which is beyond words. I have given this teaching to Maha Kasyapa." This, says the legend, was the birth of Zen Buddhism.

Many centuries later, says another legend, the Indian monk Bodhidharma carried the teachings over the mountains to China. At this time they were called "Dhyana," though the Zen school seems to put no special emphasis on the Dhyana or trance states induced by intense meditative concentration. Like Buddha with Kasyapa, Bodhidharma—if we are to believe the legend—brought the Chinese not trance but a teaching beyond words, a teaching that was "a direct pointing into the heart that we might see our true nature." The Chinese took up Bodhidharma's teachings, calling them "Ch'an" because they couldn't pronounce "Dhyana." They mixed the teaching also with styles derived from their indigenous Taoist mysticism. When Ch'an was brought to Japan in its Chinese form by Chinese monks, the Japanese in turn mispronounced Ch'an as Zen. It was in their Japanese form that the teachings first became popular in the West. They are, however, a very pure form of mysticism, the doctrine that reality cannot be expressed in language; their ultimate origin is actually Indian, as the legends suggest, and a version of the school can be found in several Buddhist countries.

SUBJECTIVE IDEALISM

George Berkeley

THE FIRST DIALOGUE

Philonous: Good morrow, Hylas: I did not expect to find you abroad so early.

Hylas: It is indeed something unusual: but my thoughts were so taken up with a subject I was discoursing of last night, that finding I could not sleep, I resolved to rise and take a turn in the garden.

Phil: It happened well, to let you see what innocent and agreeable pleasures you lose every morning. Can there be a pleasanter time of the day, or a more delightful season of the year?

• • •

But I am afraid I interrupt your thoughts; for you seemed very intent on something.

Hyl: It is true, I was, and shall be obliged to you if you will permit me to go on in the same vein; not that I would by any means deprive myself of your company, for my thoughts always flow more easily in conversation with a friend, than when I am alone: but my request is, that you would suffer me to impart my reflections to you.

Phil: With all my heart, it is what I should have requested myself, if you had not prevented me.

Hyl: I was considering the odd fate of those men who have in all ages, through an affectation of being distinguished from the vulgar, or some unaccountable turn of thought, pretended either to believe nothing at all, or to believe the most extravagant things in the world. This however might be borne, if their paradoxes and scepticism did not draw after them some consequences of general disadvantage to mankind. But the mischief lieth here; that when men of less leisure see them who are supposed to have spent their whole time in the pursuits of knowledge, professing an entire ignorance of all things, or advancing such notions as are repugnant to plain and commonly received principles, they will be tempted to entertain suspicions concerning the most important truths, which they had hitherto held sacred and unquestionable.

Phil: I entirely agree with you, as to the ill tendency of the affected doubts of some philosophers, and fantastical conceits of others. I am even so far gone of late in this way of thinking, that I have quitted several of the sublime notions I had got in their schools for vulgar opinions. And I give it you on my word, since this revolt from metaphysical notions to the plain dictates of nature and common sense, I find my understanding strangely enlightened, so that I can now easily comprehend a great many things which before were all mystery and riddle.

Hyl: I am glad to find there was nothing in the accounts I heard of you.

Phil: Pray, what were those?

Hyl: You were represented in last night's conversation, as one who maintained the most extravagant opinion that ever entered into the mind of man, to wit, that there is no such thing as *material substance* in the world.

Phil: That there is no such thing as what philosophers call *material substance,* I am seriously persuaded: but if I were made to see any thing absurd or sceptical in this, I should then have the same reason to renounce this, that I imagine I have now to reject the contrary opinion.

Hyl: What! can any thing be more fantastical, more repugnant to common sense, or a more manifest piece of scepticism, than to believe there is no such thing as *matter?*

Phil: Softly, good Hylas. What if it should prove, that you who hold there is, are by virtue of that opinion a greater sceptic, and maintain more paradoxes and repugnancies to common sense, than I who believe no such thing?

Hyl: You may as soon persuade me, the part is greater than the whole, as that, in order to avoid absurdity and scepticism, I should ever be obliged to give up my opinion in this point.

Phil: Well then, are you content to admit that opinion for true, which upon examination shall appear most agreeable to common sense, and remote from scepticism?

Hyl: With all my heart. Since you are for raising disputes about the plainest things in nature, I am content for once to hear what you have to say.

Phil: Pray, Hylas, what do you mean by a *sceptic?*

Hyl: I mean what all men mean, one that doubts of every thing.

Phil: He then who entertains no doubt concerning some particular point, with regard to that point cannot be thought a *sceptic.*

Hyl: I agree with you.

Phil: Whether doth doubting consist in embracing the affirmative or negative side of a question?

Hyl: In neither; for whoever understands English, cannot but know that *doubting* signifies a suspense between both.

Phil: He then that denieth any point, can no more be said to doubt of it than he who affirmeth it with the same degree of assurance.

Hyl: True.

Phil: And consequently, for such his denial is no more to be esteemed a *sceptic* than the other.

Hyl: I acknowledge it.

Phil: How cometh it to pass then, Hylas, that you pronounce me a *sceptic,* because I deny what you affirm, to wit, the existence of matter? Since, for ought you can tell, I am as peremptory in my denial, as you in your affirmation.

Hyl: Hold, Philonous, I have been a little out in my definition; but every false step a man makes in discourse is not to be insisted on. I said, indeed, that a *sceptic* was one who doubted of every thing; but I should have added, or who denies the reality and truth of things.

Phil: What things? Do you mean the principles and theorems of sciences? but these you know are universal intellectual notions, and consequently independent of matter; the denial therefore of this doth not imply the denying them.

Hyl: I grant it. But are there no other things? What think you of distrusting the senses, of denying the real existence of sensible things, or pretending to know nothing of them? Is not this sufficient to denominate a man a *sceptic?*

Phil: Shall we therefore examine which of us it is that denies the reality of sensible things, or professes the greatest ignorance of them; since, if I take you rightly, he is to be esteemed the greatest *sceptic?*

Hyl: That is what I desire.

Phil: What mean you by sensible things?

Hyl: Those things which are perceived by the senses. Can you imagine that I mean any thing else?

Phil: Pardon me, Hylas, if I am desirous clearly to apprehend your notions, since this may much shorten our inquiry. Suffer me then to ask you this further question. Are those things only perceived by the senses which are perceived immediately? or may those things properly be said to be *sensible,* which are perceived mediately, or not without the intervention of others?

Hyl: I do not sufficiently understand you.

Phil: In reading a book, what I immediately perceive are the letters, but mediately, or by means of these, are suggested to my mind the notions of God, virtue, truth, &c. Now that the letters are truly sensible things, or perceived by sense, there is no doubt: but I would know whether you take the things suggested by them to be so too.

Hyl: No, certainly, it were absurd to think *God* or *virtue* sensible things, though they may be signified and suggested to the mind by sensible marks, with which they have an arbitrary connexion.

Phil: It seems then, that by *sensible things* you mean those only which can be perceived immediately by sense.

Hyl: Right.

Phil: Doth it not follow from this, that though I see one part of the sky red, and another blue, and that my reason doth thence evidently conclude there must be some cause of that diversity of colours, yet that cause cannot be said to be a sensible thing, or perceived by the sense of seeing?

Hyl: It doth.

Phil: In like manner, though I hear variety of sounds, yet I cannot be said to hear the causes of those sounds.

Hyl: You cannot.

Phil: And when by my touch I perceive a thing to be hot and heavy, I cannot say with any truth or propriety, that I feel the cause of its heat or weight.

Hyl: To prevent any more questions of this kind, I tell you once for all, that by *sensible things* I mean those only which are perceived by sense, and that in truth the senses perceive nothing which they do not perceive immediately: for they make no inferences. The deducing therefore of causes or occasions from effects and appearances, which alone are perceived by sense, entirely relates to reason.

Phil: This point then is agreed between us, that *sensible things are those only which are immediately perceived by sense.* You will further inform me, whether we immediately perceive by sight any thing beside light, and colours, and figures: or by hearing any thing but sounds: by the palate, any thing besides tastes: by the smell, besides odours: or by the touch, more than tangible qualities.

Hyl: We do not.

Phil: It seems therefore, that if you take away all sensible qualities, there remains nothing sensible.

Hyl: I grant it.

Phil: Sensible things therefore are nothing else but so many sensible qualities, or combinations of sensible qualities.

Hyl: Nothing else.

Phil: Heat then is a sensible thing.

Hyl: Certainly.

Phil: Doth the reality of sensible things consist in being perceived? or, is it something distinct from their being perceived, and that bears no relation to the mind?

Hyl: To *exist* is one thing, and to be *perceived* is another.

Phil: I speak with regard to sensible things only; and of these I ask, whether by their real existence you mean a subsistence exterior to the mind, and distinct from their being perceived?

Hyl: I mean a real absolute being, distinct from, and without any relation to their being perceived.

Phil: Heat, therefore, if it be allowed a real being, must exist without the mind.

Hyl: It must.

Phil: Tell me, Hylas, is this real existence equally compatible to all degrees of heat, which we perceive: or is there any reason why we should attribute it to some, and deny it others? and if there be, pray let me know that reason.

Hyl: Whatever degree of heat we perceive by sense, we may be sure the same exists in the object that occasions it.

Phil: What, the greatest as well as the least?

Hyl: I tell you, the reason is plainly the same in respect of both: they are both perceived by sense; nay, the greater degree of heat is more sensibly perceived; and consequently, if there is any difference, we are more certain of its real existence than we can be of the reality of a lesser degree.

Phil: But is not the most vehement and intense degree of heat a very great pain?

Hyl: No one can deny it.

Phil: And is any unperceiving thing capable of pain or pleasure?

Hyl: No, certainly.

Phil: Is your material substance a senseless being, or a being endowed with sense and perception?

Hyl: It is senseless without doubt.

Phil: It cannot therefore be the subject of pain.

Hyl: By no means.

Phil: Nor consequently of the greatest heat perceived by sense, since you acknowledge this to be no small pain.

Hyl: I grant it.

Phil: What shall we say then of your external object; is it a material substance, or no?

Hyl: It is a material substance with the sensible qualities inhering in it.

Phil: How then can a great heat exist in it, since you own it cannot in a material substance? I desire you would clear this point.

Hyl: Hold, Philonous; I fear I was out in yielding intense heat to be a pain. It should seem rather, that pain is something distinct from heat, and the consequence or effect of it.

Phil: Upon putting your hand near the fire, do you perceive one simple uniform sensation, or two distinct sensations?

Hyl: But one simple sensation.

Phil: Is not the heat immediately perceived?

Hyl: It is.

Phil: And the pain?

Hyl: True.

Phil: Seeing therefore they are both immediately perceived at the same time, and the fire affects you only with one simple, or uncompounded idea, it follows that this same simple idea is both the intense heat immediately perceived, and the pain; and consequently, that the intense heat immediately perceived, is nothing distinct from a particular sort of pain.

Hyl: It seems so.

Phil: Again, try in your thoughts, Hylas, if you can conceive a vehement sensation to be without pain, or pleasure.

Hyl: I cannot.

Phil: Or can you frame to yourself an idea of sensible pain or pleasure in general, abstracted from every particular idea of heat, cold, tastes, smells, &c.?

Hyl: I do not find that I can.

Phil: Doth it not therefore follow, that sensible pain is nothing distinct from those sensations or ideas, in an intense degree?

Hyl: It is undeniable; and to speak the truth, I begin to suspect a very great heat cannot exist but in a mind perceiving it.

Phil: What! are you then in that *sceptical* state of suspense, between affirming and denying?

Hyl: I think I may be positive in the point. A very violent and painful heat cannot exist without the mind.

Phil: It hath not therefore, according to you, any real being.

Hyl: I own it.

Phil: Is it therefore certain, that there is no body in nature really hot?

Hyl: I have not denied there is any real heat in bodies. I only say, there is no such thing as an intense real heat.

Phil: But did you not say before, that all degrees of heat were equally real: or if there was any difference, that the greater were more undoubtedly real than the lesser?

Hyl: True: but it was, because I did not then consider the ground there is for distinguishing between them, which I now plainly see. And it is this: because intense heat is nothing else but a particular kind of painful sensation; and pain cannot exist but in a perceiving being; it follows that no intense heat can really exist in an unperceiving corporeal substance. But this is no reason why we should deny heat in an inferior degree to exist in such a substance.

Phil: But how shall we be able to discern those degrees of heat which exist only in the mind, from those which exist without it?

Hyl: That is no difficult matter. You know, the least pain cannot exist unperceived; whatever therefore degree of heat is a pain, exists only in the mind. But as for all other degrees of heat, nothing obliges us to think the same of them.

Phil: I think you granted before, that no unperceiving being was capable of pleasure, any more than of pain.

Hyl: I did.

Phil: And is not warmth, or a more gentle degree of heat than what causes uneasiness, a pleasure?

Hyl: What then?

Phil: Consequently it cannot exist without the mind in any unperceiving substance, or body.

Hyl: So it seems.

Phil: Since therefore, as well those degrees of heat that are not painful, as those that are, can exist only in a thinking substance; may we not conclude that external bodies are absolutely incapable of any degree of heat whatsoever?

Hyl: On second thoughts, I do not think it so evident that warmth is a pleasure, as that a great degree of heat is a pain.

Phil: I do not pretend that warmth is as great a pleasure as heat is a pain. But if you grant it to be even a small pleasure, it serves to make good my conclusion.

Hyl: I could rather call it an *indolence*. It seems to be nothing more than a privation of both pain and pleasure. And that such a quality or state as this may agree to an unthinking substance, I hope you will not deny.

Phil: If you are resolved to maintain that warmth, or a gentle degree of heat, is no pleasure, I know not how to convince you otherwise, than by appealing to your own sense. But what think you of cold?

Hyl: The same that I do of heat. An intense degree of cold is a pain; for to feel a very great cold, is to perceive a great uneasiness: it cannot therefore exist without the mind; but a lesser degree of cold may, as well as a lesser degree of heat.

Phil: Those bodies therefore, upon whose application to our own we perceive a moderate degree of heat, must be concluded to have a moderate degree of heat or warmth in them; and those, upon whose application we feel a like degree of cold, must be thought to have cold in them.

Hyl: They must.

Phil: Can any doctrine be true that necessarily leads a man into an absurdity?

Hyl: Without doubt it cannot.

Phil: Is it not an absurdity to think that the same thing should be at the same time both cold and warm?

Hyl: It is.

Phil: Suppose now one of your hands hot, and the other cold, and that they are both at once put into the same vessel of water, in an intermediate state; will not the water seem cold to one hand, and warm to the other?

Hyl: It will.

Phil: Ought we not therefore by your principles to conclude, it is really both cold and warm at the same time, that is, according to your own concession, to believe an absurdity?

Hyl: I confess it seems so.

Phil: Consequently, the principles themselves are false, since you have granted that no true principle leads to an absurdity.

Hyl: But after all, can any thing be more absurd than to say, *there is no heat in the fire?*

Phil: To make the point still clearer; tell me, whether in two cases exactly alike, we ought not to make the same judgment?

Hyl: We ought.

Phil: When a pin pricks your finger, doth it not rend and divide the fibres of your flesh?

Hyl: It doth.

Phil: And when a coal burns your finger, doth it any more?

Hyl: It doth not.

Phil: Since therefore you neither judge the sensation itself occasioned by the pin, nor any thing like it to be in the pin; you should not, conformably to what you have now granted, judge the sensation occasioned by the fire, or any thing like it, to be in the fire.

Hyl: Well, since it must be so, I am content to yield this point, and acknowledge, that heat and cold are only sensations existing in our minds: but there still remain qualities enough to secure the reality of external things.

Phil: But what will you say, Hylas, if it shall appear that the case is the same with regard to all other sensible qualities, and that they can no more be supposed to exist without the mind, than heat and cold?

Hyl: Then indeed you will have done something to the purpose; but that is what I despair of seeing proved.

Phil: Let us examine them in order. What think you of tastes, do they exist without the mind, or no?

Hyl: Can any man in his senses doubt whether sugar is sweet, or wormwood bitter?

Phil: Inform me, Hylas. Is a sweet taste a particular kind of pleasure or pleasant sensation, or is it not?

Hyl: It is.

Phil: And is not bitterness some kind of uneasiness or pain?

Hyl: I grant it.

Phil: If therefore sugar and wormwood are unthinking corporeal substances existing without the mind, how can sweetness and bitterness, that is, pleasure and pain, agree to them?

Hyl: Hold, Philonous; I now see what it was deluded me all this time. You asked whether heat and cold, sweetness and bitterness, were not particular sorts of pleasure and pain; to which I answered simply, that they were. Whereas I should have thus distinguished: those qualities, as perceived by us, are pleasures or pains, but not as existing in the external objects. We must not therefore conclude absolutely, that there is no heat in the fire, or sweetness in the sugar, but only that heat or sweetness, as perceived by us, are not in the fire or sugar. What say you to this?

Phil: I say it is nothing to the purpose. Our discourse proceeded altogether concerning sensible things, which you defined to be the things we *immediately perceive by our senses.* Whatever other qualities therefore you speak of, as distinct from these, I know nothing of them, neither do they at all belong to the point in dispute. You may indeed pretend to have discovered certain qualities which you do not perceive, and assert those insensible qualities exist in fire and sugar. But what use can be made of this to your present purpose, I am at a loss to conceive. Tell me then once more, do you acknowledge that heat and cold, sweetness and bitterness (meaning those qualities which are perceived by the senses), do not exist without the mind?

Hyl: I see it is to no purpose to hold out, so I give up the cause as to those mentioned qualities. Though I profess it sounds oddly, to say that sugar is not sweet.

Phil: But for your further satisfaction, take this along with you: that which at other times seems sweet, shall to a distempered palate appear bitter. And nothing can be plainer, than that divers persons perceive different tastes in the same food, since that which one man delights in, another abhors. And how could this be, if the taste was something really inherent in the food?

Hyl: I acknowledge I know not how.

Phil: In the next place, odours are to be considered. And with regard to these, I would fain know, whether what hath been said of tastes doth not exactly agree to them? Are they not so many pleasing or displeasing sensations?

Hyl: They are.

Phil: Can you then conceive it possible that they should exist in an unperceiving thing?

Hyl: I cannot.

Phil: Or can you imagine, that filth and ordure affect those brute animals that feed on them out of choice, with the same smells which we perceive in them?

Hyl: By no means.

Phil: May we not therefore conclude of smells, as of the other forementioned qualities, that they cannot exist in any but a perceiving substance or mind?

Hyl: I think so.

Phil: Then as to sounds, what must we think of them: are they accidents really inherent in external bodies, or not?

Hyl: That they inhere not in the sonorous bodies, is plain from hence; because a bell struck in the exhausted receiver of an air-pump, sends forth no sound. The air therefore must be thought the subject of sound.

Phil: What reason is there for that, Hylas?

Hyl: Because when any motion is raised in the air, we perceive a sound greater or lesser, in proportion to the air's motion; but without some motion in the air, we never hear any sound at all.

Phil: And granting that we never hear a sound but when some motion is produced in the air, yet I do not see how you can infer from thence, that the sound itself is in the air.

Hyl: It is this very motion in the external air, that produces in the mind the sensation of *sound.* For striking on the drum of the ear, it causeth a vibration, which by the auditory nerves being communicated to the brain, the soul is thereupon affected with the sensation called *sound.*

Phil: What! is sound then a sensation?

Hyl: I tell you, as perceived by us, it is a particular sensation in the mind.

Phil: And can any sensation exist without the mind?

Hyl: No, certainly.

Phil: How then can sound, being a sensation, exist in the air, if by the *air* you mean a senseless substance existing without the mind.

Hyl: You must distinguish, Philonous, between sound, as it is perceived by us, and as it is in itself; or, (which is the same thing) between the sound we immediately perceive, and that which exists without us. The former indeed is a particular kind of sensation, but the latter is merely a vibrative or undulatory motion in the air.

Phil: I thought I had already obviated that distinction by the answer I gave when you were applying it in a like case before. But to say no more of that: are you sure then that sound is really nothing but motion?

Hyl: I am.

Phil: Whatever therefore agrees to real sound, may with truth be attributed to motion.

Hyl: It may.

Phil: It is then good sense to speak of *motion,* as of a thing that is *loud, sweet, acute,* or *grave.*

Hyl: I see you are resolved not to understand me. Is it not evident, those accidents or modes belong only to sensible sound, or *sound* in the common acceptation of the word, but not to *sound* in the real and philosophic sense, which, as I just now told you, is nothing but a certain motion of the air?

Phil: It seems then there are two sorts of sound, the one vulgar, or that which is heard, the other philosophical and real.

Hyl: Even so.

Phil: And the latter consists in motion.

Hyl: I told you so before.

Phil: Tell me, Hylas, to which of the senses, think you, the idea of motion belongs: to the hearing?

Hyl: No, certainly, but to the sight and touch.

Phil: It should follow then, that according to you, real sounds may possibly be *seen* or *felt,* but never *heard.*

Hyl: Look you, Philonous, you may if you please make a jest of my opinion, but that will not alter the truth of things. I own, indeed, the inferences you draw me into sound something oddly: but common language, you know, is framed by, and for the use of the vulgar: we must not therefore wonder, if expressions adapted to exact philosophic notions, seem uncouth and out of the way.

Phil: Is it come to that? I assure you, I imagine myself to have gained no small point, since you make so light of departing from common phrases and opinions; it being a main part of our inquiry, to examine whose notions are widest of the common road, and most repugnant to the general sense of the world. But can you think it no more than a philosophical paradox, to say that *real sounds are never heard,* and that the idea of them is obtained by some other sense. And is there nothing in this contrary to nature and the truth of things?

Hyl: To deal ingenuously, I do not like it. And after the concessions already made, I had as well grant that sounds too have no real being without the mind.

Phil: And I hope you will make no difficulty to acknowledge the same of colours.

Hyl: Pardon me; the case of colours is very different. Can any thing be plainer, than that we see them on the objects?

Phil: The objects you speak of are, I suppose, corporeal substances existing without the mind.

Hyl: They are.

Phil: And have true and real colours inhering in them?

Hyl: Each visible object hath that colour which we see in it.

Phil: How! is there any thing visible but what we perceive by sight.

Hyl: There is not.

Phil: And do we perceive any thing by sense, which we do not perceive immediately?

Hyl: How often must I be obliged to repeat the same thing? I tell you, we do not.

Phil: Have patience, good Hylas; and tell me once more whether there is any thing immediately perceived by the senses, except sensible qualities. I know you asserted there was not: but I would now be informed, whether you still persist in the same opinion.

Hyl: I do.

Phil: Pray, is your corporeal substance either a sensible quality or made up of sensible qualities?

Hyl: What a question that is! who ever thought it was?

Phil: My reason for asking was, because in saying, *each visible object hath that colour which we see in it,* you make visible objects to be corporeal substances; which implies either that corporeal substances are sensible qualities, or else that there is something beside sensible qualities perceived by sight: but as this point was formerly agreed between us, and is still maintained by you, it is a clear consequence, that your corporeal substance is nothing distinct from sensible qualities.

Hyl: You may draw as many absurd consequences as you please, and endeavour to perplex the plainest things; but you shall never persuade me out

of my senses. I clearly understand my own meaning.

Phil: I wish you would make me understand it too. But since you are unwilling to have your notion of corporeal substance examined, I shall urge that point no further. Only be pleased to let me know, whether the same colours which we see, exist in external bodies, or some other.

Hyl: The very same.

Phil: What! are then the beautiful red and purple we see on yonder clouds, really in them? Or do you imagine they have in themselves any other form than that of a dark mist or vapour?

Hyl: I must own, Philonous, those colours are not really in the clouds as they seem to be at this distance. They are only apparent colours.

Phil: Apparent call you them? how shall we distinguish these apparent colours from real?

Hyl: Very easily. Those are to be thought apparent, which, appearing only at a distance, vanish upon a nearer approach.

Phil: And those I suppose are to be thought real, which are discovered by the most near and exact survey.

Hyl: Right.

Phil: Is the nearest and exactest survey made by the help of a microscope, or by the naked eye?

Hyl: By a microscope, doubtless.

Phil: But a microscope often discovers colours in an object different from those perceived by the unassisted sight. And in case we had microscopes magnifying to any assigned degree; it is certain, that no object whatsoever viewed through them, would appear in the same colour which it exhibits to the naked eye.

Hyl: And what will you conclude from all this? You cannot argue that there are really and naturally no colours on objects; because by artificial managements they may be altered, or made to vanish.

Phil: I think it may evidently be concluded from your own concessions, that all the colours we see with our naked eyes, are only apparent as those on the clouds, since they vanish upon a more close and accurate inspection, which is afforded us by a microscope. Then as to what you say by way of prevention;

I ask you, whether the real and natural state of an object is better discovered by a very sharp and piercing sight, or by one which is less sharp.

Hyl: By the former without doubt.

Phil: Is it not plain from *dioptrics,* that microscopes make the sight more penetrating, and represent objects as they would appear to the eye, in case it were naturally endowed with a most exquisite sharpness?

Hyl: It is.

Phil: Consequently the microscopical representation is to be thought that which best sets forth the real nature of the thing, or what it is in itself. The colours therefore by it perceived, are more genuine and real, than those perceived otherwise.

Hyl: I confess there is something in what you say.

Phil: Besides, it is not only possible but manifest, that there actually are animals, whose eyes are by nature framed to perceive those things, which by reason of their minuteness escape our sight. What think you of those inconceivably small animals perceived by glasses? must we suppose they are all stark blind? Or, in case they see, can it be imagined their sight hath not the same use in preserving their bodies from injuries, which appears in that of all other animals? And if it hath, is it not evident, they must see particles less than their own bodies, which will present them with a far different view in each object, from that which strikes our senses? Even our own eyes do not always represent objects to us after the same manner. In the *jaundice,* every one knows that all things seem yellow. Is it not therefore highly probable, those animals in whose eyes we discern a very different texture from that of ours, and whose bodies abound with different humours, do not see the same colours in every object that we do? From all of which, should it not seem to follow that all colours are equally apparent, and that none of those which we perceive are really inherent in any outward object?

Hyl: It should.

Phil: The point will be past all doubt, if you consider, that in case colours were real properties or affections inherent in external bodies, they could admit of no alteration, without some change wrought in the very bodies themselves; but is it not evident from what hath been said, that upon the use of microscopes, upon a change happening in the humours of the eye, or a variation of distance, without any manner of real alteration in the thing itself, the colours of any object are either changed, or totally disappear? Nay, all other circumstances remaining the same, change but the situation of some objects, and they shall present different colours to the eye. The same thing happens upon viewing an object in various degrees of light. And what is more known, than that the same bodies appear differently coloured by candle-light from what they do in the open day? Add to these the experiment of a prism, which, separating the heterogeneous rays of light, alters the colour of any object; and will cause the whitest to appear of a deep blue or red to the naked eye. And now tell me, whether you are still of opinion, that every body hath its true, real colour inhering in it; and if you think it hath, I would fain know further from you, what certain distance and position of the object, what peculiar texture and formation of the eye, what degree or kind of light is necessary for ascertaining that true colour, and distinguishing it from apparent ones.

Hyl: I own myself entirely satisfied, that they are all equally apparent; and that there is no such thing as colour really inhering in external bodies, but that it is altogether in the light. And what confirms me in this opinion, is, that in proportion to the light, colours are still more or less vivid; and if there be no light, then are there no colours perceived. Besides, allowing there are colours on external objects, yet how is it possible for us to perceive them? For no external body affects the mind, unless it act first on our organs of sense. But the only action of bodies is motion; and motion cannot be communicated otherwise than by impulse. A distant object therefore cannot act on the eye, nor consequently make itself or its properties perceivable to the soul. Whence it plainly follows, that it is immediately some contiguous substance, which operating on the eye occasions a perception of colours: and such is light.

Phil: How! is light then a substance?

Hyl: I tell you, Philonous, external light is nothing but a thin fluid substance, whose minute particles being agitated with a brisk motion, and in various manners reflected from the different surfaces of outward objects to the eyes, communicate different motions to the optic nerves; which being propagated to the brain, cause therein various impressions: and these are attended with the sensations of red, blue, yellow, &c.

Phil: It seems, then, the light doth no more than shake the optic nerves.

Hyl: Nothing else.

Phil: And consequent to each particular motion of the nerves the mind is affected with a sensation, which is some particular colour.

Hyl: Right.

Phil: And these sensations have no existence without the mind.

Hyl: They have not.

Phil: How then do you affirm that colours are in the light, since by *light* you understand a corporeal substance external to the mind?

Hyl: Light and colours, as immediately perceived by us, I grant cannot exist without the mind. But in themselves they are only the motions and configurations of certain insensible particles of matter.

Phil: Colours then, in the vulgar sense, or taken for the immediate objects of sight, cannot agree to any but a perceiving substance.

Hyl: That is what I say.

Phil: Well then, since you give up the point as to those sensible qualities, which are alone thought colours by all mankind beside, you may hold what you please with regard to those invisible ones of the philosophers. It is not my business to dispute about them; only I would advise you to bethink yourself, whether, considering the inquiry we are upon, it be prudent for you to affirm *the red and blue which we see are not real colours, but certain unknown motions and figures which no man ever did or can see, are truly so.* Are not these shocking notions, and are not they subject to as many ridiculous inferences, as those you were obliged to renounce before in the case of sounds?

Hyl: I frankly own, Philonous, that it is in vain to stand out any longer. Colours, sounds, tastes, in a word, all those termed *secondary qualities,* have certainly no existence without the mind. But by this acknowledgment I must not be supposed to derogate any thing from the reality of matter or external objects, seeing it is no more than several philosophers maintain, who nevertheless are the furthest imaginable from denying matter. For the clearer understanding of this, you must know sensible qualities are by philosophers divided into *primary* and *secondary.* The former are extension, figure, solidity, gravity, motion, and rest. And these they hold exist really in bodies. The latter are those above enumerated; or briefly, all sensible qualities beside the primary, which they assert are only so many sensations or ideas existing no where but in the mind. But all this, I doubt not, you are already apprised of. For my part, I have been a long time sensible there was such an opinion current among philosophers, but was never thoroughly convinced of its truth till now.

Phil: You are still then of opinion, that extension and figures are inherent in external unthinking substances.

Hyl: I am.

Phil: But what if the same arguments which are brought against secondary qualities, will hold proof against these also?

Hyl: Why then I shall be obliged to think, they too exist only in the mind.

Phil: Is it your opinion, the very figure and extension which you perceive by sense, exist in the outward object or material substance?

Hyl: It is.

Phil: Have all other animals as good grounds to think the same of the figure and extension which they see and feel?

Hyl: Without doubt, if they have any thought at all.

Phil: Answer me, Hylas. Think you the senses were bestowed upon all animals for their preservation and well-being in life? or were they given to men alone for this end?

Hyl: I make no question but they have the same use in all other animals.

Phil: If so, is it not necessary they should be enabled by them to perceive their own limbs, and those bodies which are capable of harming them?

Hyl: Certainly.

Phil: A mite therefore must be supposed to see his own foot, and things equal or even less than it, as bodies of some considerable dimension; though at the same time they appear to you scarce discernible, or at best as so many visible points.

Hyl: I cannot deny it.

Phil: And to creatures less than the mite they will seem yet larger.

Hyl: They will.

Phil: Insomuch that what you can hardly discern, will to another extremely minute animal appear as some huge mountain.

Hyl: All this I grant.

Phil: Can one and the same thing be at the same time in itself of different dimensions?

Hyl: That were absurd to imagine.

Phil: But from what you have laid down it follows, that both the extension by you perceived, and that perceived by the mite itself, as likewise all those perceived by lesser animals, are each of them the true extension of the mite's foot, that is to say, by your own principles you are led into an absurdity.

Hyl: There seems to be some difficulty in the point.

Phil: Again, have you not acknowledged that no real inherent property of any object can be changed, without some change in the thing itself?

Hyl: I have.

Phil: But as we approach to or recede from an object, the visible extension varies, being at one distance ten or a hundred times greater than at another. Doth it not therefore follow from hence likewise, that it is not really inherent in the object?

Hyl: I own I am at a loss what to think.

Phil: Your judgment will soon be determined, if you will venture to think as freely concerning this quality, as you have done concerning the rest. Was it not admitted as a good argument, that neither heat nor cold was in the water, because it seemed warm to one hand, and cold to the other?

Hyl: It was.

Phil: Is it not the very same reasoning to conclude, there is no extension or figure in an object, because to one eye it shall seem little, smooth, and round, when at the same time it appears to the other, great, uneven, and angular?

Hyl: The very same. But doth this latter fact ever happen?

Phil: You may at any time make the experiment, by looking with one eye bare, and with the other through a microscope.

Hyl: I know not how to maintain it, and yet I am loath to give up *extension,* I see so many odd consequences following upon such a concession.

Phil: Odd, say you? After the concessions already made, I hope you will stick at nothing for its oddness. But on the other hand should it not seem very odd, if the general reasoning which includes all other sensible qualities did not also include extension? If it be allowed that no idea nor any thing like an idea can exist in an unperceiving substance, then surely it follows, that no figure or mode of extension, which we can either perceive or imagine, or have any idea of, can be really inherent in matter; not to mention the peculiar difficulty there must be, in conceiving a material substance, prior to and distinct from extension, to be the *substratum* of extension. Be the sensible quality what it will, figure, or sound, or colour; it seems alike impossible it should subsist in that which doth not perceive it.

Hyl: I give up the point for the present, reserving still a right to retract my opinion, in case I shall hereafter discover any false step in my progress to it.

Phil: That is a right you cannot be denied. Figures and extension being despatched, we proceed next to *motion.* Can a real motion in any external body be at the same time both very swift and very slow?

Hyl: It cannot.

Phil: Is not the motion of a body swift in a reciprocal proportion to the time it takes up in describing any given space? Thus a body that describes a mile in an hour, moves three times faster than it would in case it described only a mile in three hours.

Hyl: I agree with you.

Phil: And is not time measured by the succession of ideas in our minds?

Hyl: It is.

Phil: And is it not possible ideas should succeed one another twice as fast in your mind, as they do in mine, or in that of some spirit of another kind.

Hyl: I own it.

Phil: Consequently the same body may to another seem to perform its motion over any space in half the time that it doth to you. And the same reasoning will hold as to any other proportion: that is to say, according to your principles (since the motions perceived are both really in the object) it is possible one and the same body shall be really moved the same way at once, both very swift and very slow. How is this consistent either with common sense, or with what you just now granted?

Hyl: I have nothing to say to it.

Phil: Then as for *solidity:* either you do not mean any sensible quality by that word, and so it is beside our inquiry: or if you do, it must be either hardness or resistance. But both the one and the other are plainly relative to our senses: it being evident, that what seems hard to one animal, may appear soft to another, who hath greater force and firmness of limbs. Nor is it less plain, that the resistance I feel is not in the body.

Hyl: I own the very sensation of resistance, which is all you immediately perceive, is not in the *body,* but the cause of that sensation is.

Phil: But the causes of our sensations are not things immediately perceived, and therefore not sensible. This point I thought had been already determined.

Hyl: I own it was; but you will pardon me if I seem a little embarrassed: I know not how to quit my old notions.

Phil: To help you out, do but consider, that if extension be once acknowledged to have no existence without the mind, the same must necessarily be granted of motion, solidity, and gravity, since they all evidently suppose extension. It is therefore su-perfluous to inquire particularly concerning each of them. In denying extension, you have denied them all to have any real existence.

• • •

THE SECOND DIALOGUE

Hylas: I beg your pardon, Philonous, for not meeting you sooner. All this morning my head was so filled with our late conversation, that I had not leisure to think of the time of the day, or indeed of any thing else.

Philonous: I am glad you were so intent upon it, in hopes if there were any mistakes in your concessions, or fallacies in my reasonings from them, you will now discover them to me.

Hyl: I assure you, I have done nothing ever since I saw you, but search after mistakes and fallacies, and with that view have minutely examined the whole series of yesterday's discourse: but all in vain, for the notions it led me into, upon review appear still more clear and evident; and the more I consider them, the more irresistibly do they force my assent.

Phil: And is not this, think you, a sign that they are genuine, that they proceed from nature, and are conformable to right reason? Truth and beauty are in this alike, that the strictest survey sets them both off to advantage. While the false lustre of error and disguise cannot endure being reviewed, or too nearly inspected.

Hyl: I own there is a great deal in what you say. Nor can any one be more entirely satisfied of the truth of those odd consequences, so long as I have in view the reasonings that lead to them. But when these are out of my thoughts, there seems on the other hand something so satisfactory, so natural and intelligible in the modern way of explaining things, that I profess I know not how to reject it.

Phil: I know not what way you mean.

Hyl: I mean the way of accounting for our sensations or ideas.

Phil: How is that?

Hyl: It is supposed the soul makes her residence in some part of the brain, from which the nerves take their rise, and are thence extended to all parts of the body: and that outward objects, by the different impressions they make on the organs of sense, communicate certain vibrative motions to the nerves; and these being filled with spirits, propagate them to the brain or seat of the soul, which according to the various impressions or traces thereby made in the brain, is variously affected with ideas.

Phil: And call you this an explication of the manner whereby we are affected with ideas?

Hyl: Why not, Philonous? have you any thing to object against it?

Phil: I would first know whether I rightly understand your hypothesis. You make certain traces in the brain to be the causes or occasions of our ideas. Pray tell me, whether by the *brain* you mean any sensible thing?

Hyl: What else think you I could mean?

Phil: Sensible things are all immediately perceivable; and those things which are immediately perceivable, are ideas; and these exist only in the mind. Thus much you have, if I mistake not, long since agreed to.

Hyl: I do not deny it.

Phil: The brain therefore you speak of, being a sensible thing, exists only in the mind. Now, I would fain know whether you think it reasonable to suppose, that one idea or thing existing in the mind, occasions all other ideas. And if you think so, pray how do you account for the origin of that primary idea or brain itself?

Hyl: I do not explain the origin of our ideas by that brain which is perceivable to sense, this being itself only a combination of sensible ideas, but by another which I imagine.

Phil: But are not things imagined as truly in the mind as things perceived?

Hyl: I must confess they are.

Phil: It comes therefore to the same thing; and you have been all this while accounting for ideas, by certain motions or impressions in the brain, that is, by some alterations in an idea, whether sensible or imaginable, it matters not.

Hyl: I begin to suspect my hypothesis.

Phil: Beside spirits, all that we know or conceive are our own ideas. When therefore you say, all ideas are occasioned by impressions in the brain, do you conceive this brain or no? If you do, then you talk of ideas imprinted in an idea, causing that same idea, which is absurd. If you do not conceive it, you talk unintelligibly, instead of forming a reasonable hypothesis.

Hyl: I now clearly see it was a mere dream. There is nothing in it.

Phil: You need not be much concerned at it; for after all, this way of explaining things, as you called it, could never have satisfied any reasonable man. What connexion is there between a motion in the nerves, and the sensations of sound or colour in the mind? Or how is it possible these should be the effect of that?

Hyl: But I could never think it had so little in it, as now it seems to have.

Phil: Well then, are you at length satisfied that no sensible things have a real existence; and that you are in truth an arrant *sceptic?*

Hyl: It is too plain to be denied.

Phil: Look! are not the fields covered with a delightful verdure?

• • •

The motion and situation of the planets, are they not admirable for use and order. Were those . . . globes ever known to stray, in their repeated journeys through the pathless void? Do they not measure areas round the sun ever proportioned to the times? So fixed, so immutable are the laws by which the unseen Author of nature actuates the universe.

• • •

Is not the whole system immense, beautiful, glorious beyond expression and beyond thought? What treatment then do those philosophers deserve, who would deprive these noble and delightful scenes of all reality? How should those principles be entertained, that lead us to think all the visible beauty of the creation a false imaginary glare? To be plain, can you expect this scepticism of yours will not be thought extravagantly absurd by all men of sense?

Hyl: Other men may think as they please: but for your part you have nothing to reproach me with. My comfort is, you are as much a *sceptic* as I am.

Phil: There, Hylas, I must beg leave to differ from you.

Hyl: What! have you all along agreed to the premises, and do you now deny the conclusion, and leave me to maintain those paradoxes by myself which you led me into? This surely is not fair.

Phil: I deny that I agreed with you in those notions that led to scepticism. You indeed said, the reality of sensible things consisted in an *absolute existence* out of the minds of spirits, or distinct from their being perceived. And pursuant to this notion of reality, you are obliged to deny sensible things any real existence: that is, according to your own definition, you profess yourself a *sceptic.* But I neither said nor thought the reality of sensible things was to be defined after that manner. To me it is evident, for the reasons you allow of, that sensible things cannot exist otherwise than in a mind or spirit. Whence I conclude, not that they have no real existence, but that seeing they depend not on my thought, and have an existence distinct from being perceived by me, *there must be some other mind wherein they exist.* As sure therefore as the sensible world really exists, so sure is there an infinite, omnipresent Spirit who contains and supports it.

Hyl: What! this is no more than I and all Christians hold; nay, and all others too who believe there is a God, and that he knows and comprehends all things.

Phil: Ay, but here lies the difference. Men commonly believe that all things are known or perceived by God, because they believe the being of a God, whereas I, on the other side, immediately and necessarily conclude the being of a God, because all sensible things must be perceived by him.

THOU ART THAT

The Upanishads

"As the bees, my son, make honey by collecting the juices of distant trees, and reduce the juice into one form,

"And as these juices have no discrimination, so that they might say, I am the juice of this tree or that, in the same manner, my son, all these creatures, when they have become merged in the True (either in deep sleep or in death), know not that they are merged in the True.

"Whatever these creatures are here, whether a lion, or a wolf, or a boar, or a worm, or a midge, or a gnat, or a musquito, that they become again and again.

"Now that which is that subtle essence, in it all that exists has its self. It is the True. It is the Self, and thou, O *S*vetaketu, art it."

"Please, Sir, inform me still more," said the son.

"Be it so, my child," the father replied.

"These rivers, my son, run, the eastern (like the Gangâ) toward the east, the western (like the Sindhu) toward the west. They go from sea to sea (i.e., the clouds lift up the water from the sea to the sky, and send it back as rain to the sea). They become indeed sea. And as those rivers, when they are in the sea, do not know, I am this or that river,

"In the same manner, my son, all these creatures, when they have come back from the True, know not that they have come back from the True. Whatever these creatures are here, whether a lion, or a wolf, or a boar, or a worm, or a midge, or a gnat, or a musquito, that they become again and again.

"That which is that subtle essence, in it all that exists has its self. It is the True. It is the Self, and thou, O *S*vetaketu, art it."

"Please, Sir, inform me still more," said the son.

"Be it so, my child," the father replied.

"If some one were to strike at the root of this large tree here, it would bleed, but live. If he were to strike at its stem, it would bleed, but live. If he were to strike at its top, it would bleed, but live. Pervaded by the living Self that tree stands firm, drinking in its nourishment and rejoicing;

"But if the life (the living Self) leaves one of its branches, that branch withers; if it leaves a second, that branch withers; if it leaves a third, that branch withers. If it leaves the whole tree, the whole tree withers. In exactly the same manner, my son, know this." Thus he spoke:

"This (body) indeed withers and dies when the living Self has left it; the living Self dies not.

"That which is that subtle essence, in it all that exists has its self. It is the True. It is the Self, and thou, *S*vetaketu, art it."

"Please, Sir, inform me still more," said the son.

"Be it so, my child," the father replied.

"Fetch me from thence a fruit of the Nyagrodha tree."

"Here is one, Sir."

"Break it."

"It is broken, Sir."

"What do you see there?"

"These seeds, almost infinitesimal."

"Break one of them."

"It is broken, Sir."

"What do you see there?"

"Not anything, Sir."

The father said: "My son, that subtle essence which you do not perceive there, of that very essence this great Nyagrodha tree exists.

"Believe it, my son. That which is the subtle essence, in it all that exists has its self. It is the True. It is the Self, and thou, O *S*vetaketu, art it."

"Please, Sir, inform me still more," said the son.

"Be it so, my child," the father replied.

"Place this salt in water, and then wait on me in the morning."

The son did as he was commanded.

The father said to him: "Bring me the salt, which you placed in the water last night."

The son having looked for it, found it not, for, of course, it was melted.

The father said: "Taste it from the surface of the water. How is it?"

The son replied: "It is salt."

"Taste it from the middle. How is it?"

The son replied: "It is salt."

"Taste it from the bottom. How is it?"

The son replied: "It is salt."

The father said: "Throw it away and then wait on me."

He did so: but salt exists for ever.

Then the father said: "Here also, in this body, forsooth, you do not perceive the True (Sat[1]), my son; but there indeed it is.

"That which is the subtle essence, in it all that exists has its self. It is the True. It is the Self, and thou, O *S*vetaketu, art it."

• • •

All this is Brahman. Let a man meditate on that (visible world) as beginning, ending, and breathing in it (the Brahman).

Now man is a creature of will. According to what his will is in this world, so will he be when he has departed this life. Let him therefore have this will and belief:

The intelligent, whose body is spirit, whose form is light, whose thoughts are true, whose nature is like ether (omnipresent and invisible), from whom all works, all desires, all sweet odours and tastes proceed; he who embraces all this, who never speaks, and is never surprised,

He is my self within the heart, smaller than a corn of rice, smaller than a corn of barley, smaller than a mustard seed, smaller than a canary seed or the kernel of a canary seed. He also is my self within the heart, greater than the earth, greater than the sky, greater than heaven, greater than all these worlds.

He from whom all works, all desires, all sweet odours and tastes proceed, who embraces all this, who never speaks and who is never surprised, he, my self within the heart, is that Brahman. When I shall have departed from hence, I shall obtain him (that Self). He who has this faith has no doubt; thus said *Sând*ilya, yea, thus he said.

A COMMENTARY ON THE UPANISHADS

Sri Ramana Maharshi

Q: What is reality?

A: Reality must be always real. It is not with forms and names. That which underlies these is the

---

[1]The Sanskrit word *Sat* refers to truth, usually in the sense of deep or ultimate or spiritual truth (Eds.).

reality. It underlies limitations, being itself limit-less. It is not bound. It underlies unrealities, itself being real. Reality is that which is. It is as it is. It transcends speech. It is beyond the expressions "ex-istence, non-existence," etc.

The reality which is the mere consciousness that remains when ignorance is destroyed along with knowledge of objects, alone is the Self [*atma*]. In that *Brahma-swarupa* [real form of *Brahman*], which is abundant Self-awareness, there is not the least ignorance.

The reality which shines fully, without misery and without a body, not only when the world is known but also when the world is not known, is your real form [*nija-swarupa*].

The radiance of consciousness-bliss, in the form of one awareness shining equally within and without, is the supreme and blissful primal reality. Its form is silence and it is declared by *jnanis* to be the final and unobstructable state of true knowledge [*jnana*].

Know that *jnana* alone is non-attachment; *jnana* alone is purity; *jnana* is the attainment of God; *jnana* which is devoid of forgetfulness of Self alone is immortality; *jnana* alone is everything.

Q: What is this awareness and how can one ob-tain and cultivate it?

A: You are awareness. Awareness is another name for you. Since you are awareness there is no need to attain or cultivate it. All that you have to do is to give up being aware of other things, that is of the not-Self. If one gives up being aware of them then pure awareness alone remains, and that is the Self.

Q: If the Self is itself aware, why am I not aware of it even now?

A: There is no duality. Your present knowledge is due to the ego and is only relative. Relative knowledge requires a subject and an object, whereas the aware-ness of the Self is absolute and requires no object.

Remembrance also is similarly relative, requir-ing an object to be remembered and a subject to re-member. When there is no duality, who is to remember whom?

The Self is ever-present. Each one wants to know the Self. What kind of help does one require to know oneself? People want to see the Self as

something new. But it is eternal and remains the same all along. They desire to see it as a blazing light etc. How can it be so? It is not light, not dark-ness. It is only as it is. It cannot be defined. The best definition is "I am that I am." The *srutis* [scriptures] speak of the Self as being the size of one's thumb, the tip of the hair, an electric spark, vast, subtler than the subtlest, etc. They have no foundation in fact. It is only being, but different from the real and the unreal; it is knowledge, but different from knowledge and ignorance. How can it be defined at all? It is simply being.

Q: When a man realises the Self, what will he see?

A: There is no seeing. Seeing is only being. The state of Self-realisation, as we call it, is not attain-ing something new or reaching some goal which is far away, but simply being that which you always are and which you always have been. All that is needed is that you give up your realisation of the not-true as true. All of us are regarding as real that which is not real. We have only to give up this prac-tice on our part. Then we shall realise the Self as the Self; in other words, "Be the Self." At one stage you will laugh at yourself for trying to discover the Self which is so self-evident. So, what can we say to this question?

That stage transcends the seer and the seen. There is no seer there to see anything. The seer who is seeing all this now ceases to exist and the Self alone remains.

Q: How to know this by direct experience?

A: If We talk of knowing the Self, there must be two selves, one a knowing self, another the self which is known, and the process of knowing. The state we call realisation is simply being oneself, not knowing anything or becoming anything. If one has realised, one is that which alone is and which alone has always been. One cannot describe that state. One can only be that. Of course, we loosely talk of Self-realisation, for want of a better term. How to "real-ise" or make real that which alone is real?

• • •

Q: God is described as manifest and unmanifest. As the former he is said to include the world as a part of his being. If that is so, we as part of that world should have easily known him in the manifested form.

A: Know yourself before you seek to decide about the nature of God and the world.

Q: Does knowing myself imply knowing God?

A: Yes, God is within you.

Q: Then, what stands in the way of my knowing myself or God?

A: Your wandering mind and perverted ways.

Q: Is God personal?

A: Yes, he is always the first person, the I, ever standing before you. Because you give precedence to worldly things, God appears to have receded to the background. If you give up all else and seek him alone, he alone will remain as the "I," the Self.

Q: Is God apart from the Self?

A: The Self is God. "I am" is God. This question arises because you are holding on to the ego self. It will not arise if you hold onto the true Self. For the real Self will not and cannot ask anything. If God be apart from the Self he must be a Self-less God, which is absurd. God, who seems to be nonexistent, alone truly exists, whereas the individual, who seems to be existing, is ever non-existent. Sages say that the state in which one thus knows one's own non-existence [*sunya*] alone is the glorious supreme knowledge.

You now think that you are an individual, that there is the universe and that God is beyond the cosmos. So there is the idea of separateness. This idea must go. For God is not separate from you or the cosmos.

• • •

Q: Is God the same as Self?

A: The Self is known to everyone, but not clearly. You always exist. The be-ing is the Self. "I am" is the name of God. Of all the definitions of God, none is indeed so well put as the Biblical statement "I am that I am" in Exodus 3. There are other statements, such as *Brahmaivaham* [*Brahman* am I], *aham Brahmasmi* [I am *Brahman*] and *soham* [I am he]. But none is so direct as the name Jehovah which means "I am." The absolute being is what is. It is the Self. It is God.

Knowing the Self, God is known. In fact God is none other than the Self.

Q: God seems to be known by many different names. Are any of them justified?

A: Among the many thousands of names of God, no name suits God, who abides in the Heart, devoid of thought, so truly, aptly, and beautifully as the name "I" or "I am." Of all the known names of God, the name of God "I"—"I" alone will resound triumphantly when the ego is destroyed, rising as the silent supreme word [*mouna-para-vak*] in the Heart-space of those whose attention is Selfward-facing. Even if one unceasingly meditates upon that name "I-I" with one's attention on the feeling "I," it will take one and plunge one into the source from which thought rises, destroying the ego, the embryo, which is joined to the body.

Q: What is the relationship between God and the world? Is he the creator or sustainer of it?

A: Sentient and insentient beings of all kinds are performing actions only by the mere presence of the sun, which rises in the sky without any volition. Similarly all actions are done by the Lord without any volition or desire on his part. In the mere presence of the sun, the magnifying lens emits fire, the lotus-bud blossoms, the water-lily closes and all the countless creatures perform actions and rest.

The order of the great multitude of worlds is maintained by the mere presence of God in the same manner as the needle moves in front of a magnet, and as the moonstone emits water, the water-lily blossoms and the lotus closes in front of the moon.

In the mere presence of God, who does not have even the least volition, the living beings, who are engaged in innumerable activities, after embarking upon many paths to which they are drawn according to the course determined by their own *karmas,* finally realise the futility of action, turn back to Self and attain liberation.

The actions of living beings certainly do not go and affect God, who transcends the mind, in the same manner as the activities of the world do not affect that sun and as the qualities of the conspicuous four elements [earth, water, fire and air] do not affect the limitless space.

Q: Why is samsara—*creation and manifestation as finitised—so full of sorrow and evil?*

A: God's will!

Q: Why does God will it so?

A: It is inscrutable. No motive can be attributed to that power—no desire, no end to achieve can be asserted of that one infinite, all-wise and all-powerful being. God is untouched by activities, which take place in his presence. Compare the sun and the world activities. There is no meaning in attributing responsibility and motive to the one before it becomes many.

Q: Does everything happen by the will of God?

A: It is not possible for anyone to do anything opposed to the ordinance of God, who has the ability to do everything. Therefore to remain silent at the feet of God, having given up all the anxieties of the wicked, defective and delusive mind, is best.

Q: Is there a separate being Iswara *[personal God] who is the rewarder of virtue and punisher of sins? Is there a God?*

A: Yes.

Q: What is he like?

A: Iswara has individuality in mind and body, which are perishable, but at the same time he has also the transcendental consciousness and liberation inwardly.

Iswara, the personal God, the supreme creator of the universe really does exist. But this is true only from the relative standpoint of those who have not realised the truth, those people who believe in the reality of individual souls. From the absolute standpoint the sage cannot accept any other existence than the impersonal Self, one and formless.

Iswara has a physical body, a form and a name, but it is not so gross as this material body. It can be seen in visions in the form created by the devotee. The forms and names of God are many and various and differ with each religion. His essence is the same as ours, the real Self being only one and without form. Hence forms he assumes are only creations or appearances.

Iswara is immanent in every person and every object throughout the universe. The totality of all things and beings constitutes God. There is a power

out of which a small fraction has become all this universe, and the remainder is in reserve. Both this reserve power plus the manifested power as material world together constitute *Iswara.*

Q: So ultimately Iswara *is not real?*

A: Existence of *Iswara* follows from our conception of *Iswara.* Let us first know whose concept he is. The concept will be only according to the one who conceives. Find out who you are and the other problems will solve themselves.

Iswara, God, the creator, the personal God, is the last of the unreal forms to go. Only the absolute being is real. Hence, not only the world, not only the ego, but also the personal God are of unreality. We must find the absolute—nothing less.

THE WORLD AS WILL AND IDEA

Arthur Schopenhauer

THE WORLD AS IDEA

"The world is my idea:"—this is a truth which holds good for everything that lives and knows, though man alone can bring it into reflective and abstract consciousness. If he really does this, he has attained to philosophical wisdom. It then becomes clear and certain to him that what he knows is not a sun and an earth, but only an eye that sees a sun, a hand that feels an earth; that the world which surrounds him is there only as idea, *i.e.,* only in relation to something else, the consciousness, which is himself. If any truth can be asserted *a priori,* it is this: for it is the expression of the most general form of all possible and thinkable experience: a form which is more general than time, or space, or causality, for they all presuppose it; and each of these, which we have seen to be just so many modes of the principle of sufficient reason, is valid only for a particular class of ideas;

whereas the antithesis of object and subject is the common form of all these classes, is that form under which alone any idea of whatever kind it may be, abstract or intuitive, pure or empirical, is possible and thinkable. No truth therefore is more certain, more independent of all others, and less in need of proof than this, that all that exists for knowledge, and therefore this whole world, is only object in relation to subject, perception of a perceiver, in a word, idea. This is obviously true of the past and the future, as well as of the present, of what is farthest off, as of what is near; for it is true of time and space themselves, in which alone these distinctions arise. All that in any way belongs or can belong to the world is inevitably thus conditioned through the subject, and exists only for the subject. The world is idea.

This truth is by no means new. It was implicitly involved in the sceptical reflections from which Descartes started. Berkeley, however, was the first who distinctly enunciated it, and by this he has rendered a permanent service to philosophy, even though the rest of his teaching should not endure. Kant's primary mistake was the neglect of this principle . . . How early again this truth was recognised by the wise men of India, appearing indeed as the fundamental tenet of the Vedânta philosophy ascribed to Vyasa, is pointed out by Sir William Jones in the last of his essays: "On the philosophy of the Asiatics," where he says, "The fundamental tenet of the Vedanta school consisted not in denying the existence of matter, that is, of solidity, impenetrability, and extended figure (to deny which would be lunacy), but in correcting the popular notion of it, and in contending that it has no essence independent of mental perception; that existence and perceptibility are convertible terms." These words adequately express the compatibility of empirical reality and transcendental ideality.

In this first book,[1] then, we consider the world only from this side, only so far as it is idea. The in-

ward reluctance with which any one accepts the world as merely his idea, warns him that this view of it, however true it may be, is nevertheless one-sided, adopted in consequence of some arbitrary abstraction. And yet it is a conception from which he can never free himself. The defectiveness of this view will be corrected in the next book by means of a truth which is not so immediately certain as that from which we start here; a truth at which we can arrive only by deeper research and more severe abstraction, by the separation of what is different and the union of what is identical. This truth, which must be very serious and impressive if not awful to every one, is that a man can also say and must say, "the world is my will."

In this book, however, we must consider separately that aspect of the world from which we start, its aspect as knowable, and therefore, in the meantime, we must, without reserve, regard all presented objects, even our own bodies (as we shall presently show more fully), merely as ideas, and call them merely ideas. By so doing we always abstract from will (as we hope to make clear to every one further on), which by itself constitutes the other aspect of the world. For as the world is in one aspect entirely *idea,* so in another it is entirely *will.* A reality which is neither of these two, but an object in itself (into which the thing in itself has unfortunately dwindled in the hands of Kant), is the phantom of a dream, and its acceptance is an *ignis fatuus* in philosophy.

That which knows all things and is known by none is the subject. Thus it is the supporter of the world, that condition of all phenomena, of all objects which is always pre-supposed throughout experience; for all that exists, exists only for the subject. Every one finds himself to be subject, yet only in so far as he knows, not in so far as he is an object of knowledge. But his body is object, and therefore from this point of view we call it idea. For the body is an object among objects, and is conditioned by the laws of objects, although it is an immediate object. Like all objects of perception, it lies within the universal forms of knowledge, time and space, which are the conditions of multiplicity. The subject, on the contrary, which is always the

---

[1]The first book, with which the selection begins, concerns the world as only idea or appearances. In the second book below, Schopenhauer deals with the world in its other aspect as will, the thing which gives the world of idea its objectivity (Eds.).

knower, never the known, does not come under these forms, but is presupposed by them; it has therefore neither multiplicity nor its opposite unity. We never know it, but it is always the knower wherever there is knowledge.

So then the world as idea, the only aspect in which we consider it at present, has two fundamental, necessary, and inseparable halves. The one half is the object, the forms of which are space and time, and through these multiplicity. The other half is the subject, which is not in space and time, for it is present, entire and undivided, in every percipient being. So that any one percipient being, with the object, constitutes the whole world as idea just as fully as the existing millions could do; but if this one were to disappear, then the whole world as idea would cease to be. These halves are therefore inseparable even for thought, for each of the two has meaning and existence only through and for the other, each appears with the other and vanishes with it. They limit each other immediately; where the object begins the subject ends.

• • •

THE WORLD AS WILL

In the first book we were reluctantly driven to explain the human body as merely idea of the subject which knows it, like all the other objects of this world of perception. But it has now become clear that what enables us consciously to distinguish our own body from all other objects which in other respects are precisely the same, is that our body appears in consciousness in quite another way *toto genere* different from idea, and this we denote by the word *will;* and that it is just this double knowledge which we have of our own body that affords us information about it, about its action and movement following on motives, and also about what it experiences by means of external impressions; in a word, about what it is, not as idea, but as more than idea; that is to say, what it is *in itself.* None of this information have we got directly with regard to the nature, action, and experience of other real objects.

It is just because of this special relation to one body that the knowing subject is an individual. For regarded apart from this relation, his body is for him only an idea like all other ideas. But the relation through which the knowing subject is an *individual,* is just on that account a relation which subsists only between him and one particular idea of all those which he has. Therefore he is conscious of this one idea, not merely as an idea, but in quite a different way as a will. If, however, he abstracts from that special relation, from that twofold and completely heterogeneous knowledge of what is one and the same, then that *one,* the body, is an idea like all other ideas. Therefore, in order to understand the matter, the individual who knows must either assume that what distinguishes that one idea from others is merely the fact that his knowledge stands in this double relation to it alone; that insight in two ways at the same time is open to him only in the case of this one object of perception, and that this is to be explained not by the difference of this object from all others, but only by the difference between the relation of his knowledge to this one object, and its relation to all other objects. Or else he must assume that this object is essentially different from all others; that it alone of all objects is at once both will and idea, while the rest are only ideas, *i.e.,* only phantoms.

• • •

We have recognised *temporal justice,* which has its seat in the state, as requiting and punishing, and have seen that this only becomes justice through a reference to the *future.* For without this reference all punishing and requiting would be an outrage without justification, and indeed merely the addition of another evil to that which has already occurred, without meaning or significance. But it is quite otherwise with *eternal justice,* which was referred to before, and which rules not the state but the world, is not dependent upon human institutions, is not subject to chance and deception, is not uncertain, wavering, and erring, but infallible, fixed, and sure. The conception of requital implies that of time; therefore *eternal justice* cannot be requital. Thus it cannot, like temporal justice, admit of respite and delay, and require time in order to triumph, equalising the evil deed by the evil consequences only by means of time. The punishment must here be so bound up with the offence that both are one.

• • •

Now that such an eternal justice really lies in the nature of the world will soon become completely evident to whoever has grasped the whole of the thought which we have hitherto been developing.

The world, in all the multiplicity of its parts and forms, is the manifestation, the objectivity, of the one will to live. Existence itself, and the kind of existence, both as a collective whole and in every part, proceeds from the will alone. The will is free, the will is almighty. The will appears in everything, just as it determines itself in itself and outside time. The world is only the mirror of this willing; and all finitude, all suffering, all miseries, which it contains, belong to the expression of that which the will wills, are as they are because the will so wills. Accordingly with perfect right every being supports existence in general, and also the existence of its species and its peculiar individuality, entirely as it is and in circumstances as they are, in a world such as it is, swayed by chance and error, transient, ephemeral, and constantly suffering; and in all that it experiences, or indeed can experience, it always gets its due. For the will belongs to it; and as the will is, so is the world. Only this world itself can bear the responsibility of its own existence and nature—no other; for by what means could another have assumed it? Do we desire to know what men, morally considered, are worth as a whole and in general, we have only to consider their fate as a whole and in general. This is want, wretchedness, affliction, misery, and death. Eternal justice reigns; if they were not, as a whole, worthless, their fate, as a whole, would not be so sad. In this sense we may say, the world itself is the judgment of the world. If we could lay all the misery of the world in one scale of the balance, and all the guilt of the world in the other, the needle would certainly point to the centre.

Certainly, however, the world does not exhibit itself to the knowledge of the individual as such, de-

veloped for the service of the will, as it finally reveals itself to the inquirer as the objectivity of the one and only will to live, which he himself is. But the sight of the uncultured individual is clouded, as the Hindus say, by the veil of Mâyâ.[1] He sees not the thing-in-itself but the phenomenon in time and space, the *principium individuationis,* and in the other forms of the principle of sufficient reason. And in this form of his limited knowledge he sees not the inner nature of things, which is one, but its phenomena as separated, disunited, innumerable, very different, and indeed opposed. For to him pleasure appears as one thing and pain as quite another thing: one man as a tormentor and a murderer, another as a martyr and a victim; wickedness as one thing and evil as another. He sees one man live in joy, abundance, and pleasure, and even at his door another die miserably of want and cold. Then he asks, Where is the retribution? And he himself, in the vehement pressure of will which is his origin and his nature, seizes upon the pleasures and enjoyments of life, firmly embraces them, and knows not that by this very act of his will he seizes and hugs all those pains and sorrows at the sight of which he shudders. He sees the ills and he sees the wickedness in the world, but far from knowing that both of these are but different sides of the manifestation of the one will to live, he regards them as very different, and indeed quite opposed, and often seeks to escape by wickedness, *i.e.,* by causing the suffering of another, from ills, from the suffering of his own individuality, for he is involved in the *principium individuationis,* deluded by the veil of Mâyâ. Just as a sailor sits in a boat trusting to his frail barque in a stormy sea, unbounded in every direction, rising and falling with the howling mountainous waves; so in the midst of a world of sorrows the individual man sits quietly, supported by and trusting to the *principium individuationis,* or the way in which the individual knows things as phenomena. The bound-

---

[1]"Maya" literally is a veil, but Western writers still persist in using the phrase "the veil of Maya" as if "Maya" had a veil. The metaphor of a veil that hides reality and produces illusion is a common one in Indian thought, especially in the *Upanishads* (Eds.).

less world, everywhere full of suffering in the infinite past, in the infinite future, is strange to him, indeed is to him but a fable; his ephemeral person, his extensionless present, his momentary satisfaction, this alone has reality for him; and he does all to maintain this, so long as his eyes are not opened by a better knowledge. Till then, there lives only in the inmost depths of his consciousness a very obscure presentiment that all that is after all not really so strange to him, but has a connection with him, from which the *principium individuationis* cannot protect him. From this presentiment arises that ineradicable *awe* common to all men (and indeed perhaps even to the most sensible of the brutes) which suddenly seizes them if by any chance they become puzzled about the *principium individuationis,* because the principle of sufficient reason in some one of its forms seems to admit of an exception. For example, if it seems as if some change took place without a cause, or some one who is dead appears again, or if in any other way the past or the future becomes present or the distant becomes near. The fearful terror at anything of the kind is founded on the fact that they suddenly become puzzled about the forms of knowledge of the phenomenon, which alone separate their own individuality from the rest of the world. But even this separation lies only in the phenomenon, and not in the thing-in-itself; and on this rests eternal justice. In fact, all temporal happiness stands, and all prudence proceeds, upon ground that is undermined. They defend the person from accidents and supply its pleasures; but the person is merely phenomenon, and its difference from other individuals, and exemption from the sufferings which they endure, rests merely in the form of the phenomenon, the *principium individuationis.* According to the true nature of things, every one has all the suffering of the world as his own, and indeed has to regard all merely possible suffering as for him actual, so long as he is the fixed will to live, *i.e.,* asserts life with all his power. For the knowledge that sees through the *principium individuationis,* a happy life in time, the gift of chance or won by prudence, amid the sorrows of innumerable others, is only the dream of a beggar in which he is a

king, but from which he must awake and learn from experience that only a fleeting illusion had separated him from the suffering of his life.

Eternal justice withdraws itself from the vision that is involved in the knowledge which follows the principle of sufficient reason in the *principium individuationis;* such vision misses it altogether unless it vindicates it in some way by fictions. It sees the bad, after misdeeds and cruelties of every kind, live in happiness and leave the world unpunished. It sees the oppressed drag out a life full of suffering to the end without an avenger, a requiter appearing. But that man only will grasp and comprehend eternal justice who raises himself above the knowledge that proceeds under the guidance of the principle of sufficient reason, bound to the particular thing, and recognises the Ideas, sees through the *principium individuationis,* and becomes conscious that the forms of the phenomenon do not apply to the thing-in-itself. Moreover, he alone, by virtue of the same knowledge, can understand the true nature of virtue, as it will soon disclose itself to us in connection with the present inquiry, although for the practice of virtue this knowledge in the abstract is by no means demanded. Thus it becomes clear to whoever has attained to the knowledge referred to, that because the will is the in-itself of all phenomena, the misery which is awarded to others and that which he experiences himself, the bad and the evil, always concerns only that one inner being which is everywhere the same, although the phenomena in which the one and the other exhibits itself exist as quite different individuals, and are widely separated by time and space. He sees that the difference between him who inflicts the suffering and him who must bear it is only the phenomenon, and does not concern the thing-in-itself, for this is the will living in both, which here, deceived by the knowledge which is bound to its service, does not recognise itself, and seeking an increased happiness in *one* of its phenomena, produces great suffering in *another,* and thus, in the pressure of excitement, buries its teeth in its own flesh, not knowing that it always injures only itself, revealing in this form, through the medium of individuality, the conflict with itself which it bears in its inner nature. The inflicter of suffering and the sufferer are one. The former errs in that he believes he is not a partaker in the suffering; the latter, in that he believes he is not a partaker in the guilt. If the eyes of both were opened, the inflicter of suffering would see that he lives in all that suffers pain in the wide world, and which, if endowed with reason, in vain asks why it was called into existence for such great suffering, its desert of which it does not understand. And the sufferer would see that all the wickedness which is or ever was committed in the world proceeds from that will which constitutes *his* own nature also, appears also in *him,* and that through this phenomenon and its assertion he has taken upon himself all the sufferings which proceed from such a will and bears them as his due, so long as he is this will. From this knowledge speaks the profound poet Calderon in "Life a Dream"—

> For the greatest crime of man
> Is that he ever was born.

Why should it not be a crime, since, according to an eternal law, death follows upon it? Calderon has merely expressed in these lines the Christian dogma of original sin.

The living knowledge of eternal justice, of the balance that inseparably binds together the *malum culpæ* with the *malum pœnæ,* demands the complete transcending of individuality and the principle of its possibility. Therefore it will always remain unattainable to the majority of men, as will also be the case with the pure and distinct knowledge of the nature of all virtue, which is akin to it, and which we are about to explain. Accordingly the wise ancestors of the Hindu people have directly expressed it in the Vedas, which are only allowed to the three regenerate castes, or in their esoteric teaching, so far at any rate as conception and language comprehend it, and their method of exposition, which always remains pictorial and even rhapsodical, admits; but in the religion of the people, or exoteric teaching, they only communicate it by means of myths. The direct exposition we find in the Vedas, the fruit of the highest human

knowledge and wisdom, the kernel of which has at last reached us in the Upanishads as the greatest gift of this century. It is expressed in various ways, but especially by making all the beings in the world, living and lifeless, pass successively before the view of the student, and pronouncing over every one of them that word which has become a formula, and as such has been called the Mahavakya: Tatoumes,—more correctly, Tat twam asi,—which means, "This thou art." But for the people, that great truth, so far as in their limited condition they could comprehend it, was translated into the form of knowledge which follows the principle of sufficient reason. This form of knowledge is indeed, from its nature, quite incapable of apprehending that truth pure and in itself, and even stands in contradiction to it, yet in the form of a myth it received a substitute for it which was sufficient as a guide for conduct. For the myth enables the method of knowledge, in accordance with the principle of sufficient reason, to comprehend by figurative representation the ethical significance of conduct, which itself is ever foreign to it. This is the aim of all systems of religion, for as a whole they are the mythical clothing of the truth which is unattainable to the uncultured human intellect. In this sense this myth might, in Kant's language, be called a postulate of the practical reason; but regarded as such, it has the great advantage that it contains absolutely no elements but such as lie before our eyes in the course of actual experience and can therefore support all its conceptions with perceptions. What is here referred to is the myth of the transmigration of souls. It teaches that all sufferings which in life one inflicts upon other beings must be expiated in a subsequent life in this world, through precisely the same sufferings; and this extends so far, that he who only kills a brute must, some time in endless time, be born as the same kind of brute and suffer the same death. It teaches that wicked conduct involves a future life in this world in suffering and despised creatures, and, accordingly, that one will then be born again in lower castes, or as a woman, or as a brute, as Pariah or Tschandala, as a leper, or as a crocodile, and so forth. All the pains which the myth threatens it supports with perceptions from actual life, through suffering creatures which do not know how they have merited their misery, and it does not require to call in the assistance of any other hell. As a reward, on the other hand, it promises re-birth in better, nobler forms, as Brahmans, wise men, or saints. The highest reward, which awaits the noblest deeds and the completest resignation, which is also given to the woman who in seven successive lives has voluntarily died on the funeral pile of her husband, and not less to the man whose pure mouth has never uttered a single lie,—this reward the myth can only express negatively in the language of this world by the promise, which is so often repeated, that they shall never be born again, *Non adsumes iterum existentiam apparentem;* or, as the Buddhists, who recognise neither Vedas nor castes, express it, "Thou shalt attain to Nirvâna," *i.e.,* to a state in which four things no longer exist—birth, age, sickness, and death.

Never has a myth entered, and never will one enter, more closely into the philosophical truth which is attainable to so few than this primitive doctrine of the noblest and most ancient nation. Broken up as this nation now is into many parts, this myth yet reigns as the universal belief of the people, and has the most decided influence upon life to-day, as four thousand years ago. Therefore Pythagoras and Plato have seized with admiration on that *ne plus ultra* of mythical representation, received it from India or Egypt, honoured it, made use of it, and, we know not how far, even believed it. We, on the contrary, now send the Brahmans English clergymen and evangelical linen-weavers to set them right out of sympathy, and to show them that they are created out of nothing, and ought thankfully to rejoice in the fact. But it is just the same as if we fired a bullet against a cliff. In India our religions will never take root. The ancient wisdom of the human race will not be displaced by what happened in Galilee. On the contrary, Indian philosophy streams back to Europe, and will produce a fundamental change in our knowledge and thought.

THE SUTRA OF HUI NENG*

Hui Neng

Once, when the Patriarch had arrived at Pao Lin Monastery, Prefect Wei of Shao Chou and other officials went there to ask him to deliver public lectures on Buddhism in the hall of Ta Fan Temple in the City (of Canton).

In due course, there were assembled (in the lecture hall) Prefect Wei, government officials and Confucian scholars about thirty each, and bhikkhus, bhikkhunis,[1] Taoists and laymen to the number of about one thousand. After the Patriarch had taken his seat, the congregation in a body paid him homage and asked him to preach on the fundamental laws of Buddhism. Whereupon, His Holiness delivered the following address:

Learned Audience, our Essence of Mind (literally, self-nature) which is the seed or kernel of enlightenment (Bodhi) is pure by nature, and by making use of this mind alone we can reach Buddhahood directly. Now let me tell you something about my own life and how I came into possession of the esoteric teaching of the Dhyana (or the Zen) School.

My father, a native of Fan Yang, was dismissed from his official post and banished to be a commoner in Hsin Chou in Kwangtung. I was unlucky in that my father died when I was very young, leaving my mother poor and miserable. We moved to Kwang Chou (Canton) and were then in very bad circumstances.

I was selling firewood in the market one day, when one of my customers ordered some to be brought to his shop. Upon delivery being made and payment received, I left the shop, outside of which I found a man reciting a sutra. As soon as I heard the text of this sutra

---

*A "sutra" is a short discourse usually delivered by the Buddha himself or a Bodhisattva or Buddhist saint. This sutra is, in fact, the sole exception to this general rule as Hui Neng, though enlightened, is usually identified as neither (Eds.).

[1]"Bhikkhus and Bhikkhunis" are Buddhist monks and nuns (Eds.).

my mind at once became enlightened. Thereupon I asked the man the name of the book he was reciting and was told that it was the Diamond Sutra (Vajracchedika or Diamond Cutter). I further enquired whence he came and why he recited this particular sutra. He replied that he came from Tung Ch'an Monastery in the Huang Mei District of Ch'i Chou; that the Abbot in charge of this temple was Hung Yen, the Fifth Patriarch; that there were about one thousand disciples under him; and that when he went there to pay homage to the Patriarch, he attended lectures on this sutra. He further told me that His Holiness used to encourage the laity as well as the monks to recite this scripture, as by doing so they might realise their own Essence of Mind, and thereby reach Buddhahood directly.

It must be due to my good karma in past lives that I heard about this, and that I was given ten taels for the maintenance of my mother by a man who advised me to go to Huang Mei to interview the Fifth Patriarch. After arrangements had been made for her, I left for Huang Mei, which took me less than thirty days to reach.

I then went to pay homage to the Patriarch, and was asked where I came from and what I expected to get from him. I replied, "I am a commoner from Hsin Chou of Kwangtung. I have travelled far to pay you respect and I ask for nothing but Buddhahood." "You are a native of Kwangtung, a barbarian? How can you expect to be a Buddha?" asked the Patriarch. I replied, "Although there are northern men and southern men, north and south make no difference to their Buddha-nature. A barbarian is different from Your Holiness physically, but there is no difference in our Buddha-nature." He was going to speak further to me, but the presence of other disciples made him stop short. He then ordered me to join the crowd to work.

"May I tell Your Holiness," said I, "that Prajna (transcendental Wisdom) often rises in my mind. When one does not go astray from one's own Essence of Mind, one may be called the 'field of merits.'[2] I do not know what work Your Holiness would ask me to do."

"This barbarian is too bright," he remarked. "Go to the stable and speak no more." I then withdrew myself to the backyard and was told by a lay brother to split firewood and to pound rice.

More than eight months after, the Patriarch saw me one day and said, "I know your knowledge of Buddhism is very sound, but I have to refrain from speaking to you lest evil doers should do you harm. Do you understand?" "Yes, Sir, I do," I replied. "To avoid people taking notice of me, I dare not go near your hall."

The Patriarch one day assembled all his disciples and said to them, "The question of incessant rebirth is a momentous one. Day after day, instead of trying to free yourselves from this bitter sea of life and death, you seem to go after tainted merits only (*i.e.,* merits which will cause rebirth). Yet merits will be of no help, if your Essence of Mind is obscured. Go and seek for Prajna (wisdom) in your own mind and then write me a stanza (*gatha*) about it. He who understands what the Essence of Mind is will be given the robe (the insignia of the Patriarchate) and the Dharma (*i.e.,* the esoteric teaching of the Dhyana School), and I shall make him the Sixth Patriarch. Go away quickly. Delay not in writing the stanza, as deliberation is quite unnecessary and of no use. The man who has realised the Essence of Mind can speak of it at once, as soon as he is spoken to about it; and he cannot lose sight of it, even when engaged in battle."

Having received this instruction, the disciples withdrew and said to one another, "It is of no use for us to concentrate our mind to write the stanza and submit it to His Holiness, since the Patriarchate is bound to be won by Shen Hsiu, our instructor. And if we write perfunctorily, it will only be a waste of energy." Upon hearing this, all of them made up their minds not to write and said, "Why should we take the trouble? Hereafter, we will simply follow our instructor, Shen Hsiu, wherever he goes, and look to him for guidance."

Meanwhile, Shen Hsiu reasoned thus with himself. "Considering that I am their teacher, none of them will take part in the competition. I wonder whether I should write a stanza and submit it to His Holiness. If I do not, how can the Patriarch know

[2]A title of honour given to monks, as they afford the best opportunities to others to sow the 'seed' of merits.

how deep or superficial my knowledge is? If my object is to get the Dharma, my motive is a pure one. If I were after the Patriarchate, then it would be bad. In that case, my mind would be that of a worldling and my action would amount to robbing the Patriarch's holy seat. But if I do not submit the stanza, I shall never have a chance of getting the Dharma. A very difficult point to decide, indeed!"

In front of the Patriarch's hall there were three corridors, the walls of which were to be painted by a court artist, named Lu Chen, with pictures from the Lankavatara (Sutra) depicting the transfiguration of the assembly, and with scenes showing the genealogy of the five Patriarchs for the information and veneration of the public.

When Shen Hsiu had composed his stanza he made several attempts to submit it to the Patriarch, but as soon as he went near the hall his mind was so perturbed that he sweated all over. He could not screw up courage to submit it, although in the course of four days he made altogether thirteen attempts to do so.

Then he suggested to himself, "It would be better for me to write it on the wall of the corridor and let the Patriarch see it for himself. If he approves it, I shall come out to pay homage, and tell him that it is done by me; but if he disapproves it, then I shall have wasted several years in this mountain in receiving homage from others which I by no means deserve! In that case, what progress have I made in learning Buddhism?"

At 12 o'clock that night he went secretly with a lamp to write the stanza on the wall of the south corridor, so that the Patriarch might know what spiritual insight he had attained. The stanza read:

> Our body is the Bodhi-tree,
> And our mind a mirror bright.
> Carefully we wipe them hour by hour,
> And let no dust alight.

As soon as he had written it he left at once for his room; so nobody knew what he had done. In his room he again pondered: "When the Patriarch sees my stanza tomorrow and is pleased with it, I shall be ready for the Dharma; but if he says that it is

badly done, it will mean that I am unfit for the Dharma, owing to the misdeeds in previous lives which thickly becloud my mind. It is difficult to know what the Patriarch will say about it!" In this vein he kept on thinking until dawn, as he could neither sleep nor sit at ease.

But the Patriarch knew already that Shen Hsiu had not entered the door of enlightenment, and that he had not known the Essence of Mind.

In the morning, he sent for Mr. Lu, the court artist, and went with him to the south corridor to have the walls there painted with pictures. By chance, he saw the stanza. "I am sorry to have troubled you to come so far," he said to the artist. "The walls need not be painted now, as the Sutra says, 'All forms or phenomena are transient and illusive.' It will be better to leave the stanza here, so that people may study it and recite it. If they put its teaching into actual practice, they will be saved from the misery of being born in these evil realms of existence (*gatis*). The merit gained by one who practises it will be great indeed!"

He then ordered incense to be burnt, and all his disciples to pay homage to it and to recite it, so that they might realise the Essence of Mind. After they had recited it, all of them exclaimed, "Well done!"

At midnight, the Patriarch sent for Shen Hsiu to come to the hall, and asked him whether the stanza was written by him or not. "It was, Sir," replied Shen Hsiu. "I dare not be so vain as to expect to get the Patriarchate, but I wish Your Holiness would kindly tell me whether my stanza shows the least grain of wisdom."

"Your stanza," replied the Patriarch, "shows that you have not yet realised the Essence of Mind. So far you have reached the 'door of enlightenment,' but you have not yet entered it. To seek for supreme enlightenment with such an understanding as yours can hardly be successful.

"To attain supreme enlightenment, one must be able to know spontaneously one's own nature or Essence of Mind, which is neither created nor can it be annihilated. From ksana to ksana (thought-moment to thought-moment), one should be able to realise the Essence of Mind all the time. All things will then be free from restraint (*i.e.*, emancipated). Once the Tathata (Suchness, another name for the Essence of Mind) is known, one will be free from delusion for ever; and in all circumstances one's mind will be in a state of 'Thusness.' Such a state of mind is absolute Truth. If you can see things in such a frame of mind you will have known the Essence of Mind, which is supreme enlightenment.

"You had better go back to think it over again for a couple of days, and then submit me another stanza. If your stanza shows that you have entered the 'door of enlightenment,' I will transmit you the robe and the Dharma."

Shen Hsiu made obeisance to the Patriarch and left. For several days, he tried in vain to write another stanza. This upset his mind so much that he was as ill at ease as if he were in a nightmare, and he could find comfort neither in sitting nor in walking.

Two days after, it happened that a young boy who was passing by the room where I was pounding rice recited loudly the stanza written by Shen Hsiu. As soon as I heard it, I knew at once that the composer of it had not yet realised the Essence of Mind. For although I had not been taught about it at that time, I already had a general idea of it.

"What stanza is this?" I asked the boy. "You barbarian," he replied, "don't you know about it? The Patriarch told his disciples that the question of incessant rebirth was a momentous one, that those who wished to inherit his robe and Dharma should write him a stanza, and that the one who had an understanding of the Essence of Mind would get them and be made the Sixth Patriarch. Elder Shen Hsiu wrote this 'Formless' Stanza on the wall of the south corridor and the Patriarch told us to recite it. He also said that those who put its teaching into actual practice would attain great merit, and be saved from the misery of being born in the evil realms of existence."

I told the boy that I wished to recite the stanza too, so that I might have an affinity with its teaching in future life. I also told him that although I had been pounding rice there for eight months I had never been to the hall, and that he would have to show me where the stanza was to enable me to make obeisance to it.

The boy took me there and I asked him to read it to me, as I am illiterate. A petty officer of the Chiang Chou District named Chang Tih-Yung, who happened to be there, read it out to me. When he had finished reading I told him that I also had composed a stanza, and asked him to write it for me. "Extraordinary indeed," he exclaimed, "that you also can compose a stanza!"

"Don't despise a beginner," said I, "if you are a seeker of supreme enlightenment. You should know that the lowest class may have the sharpest wit, while the highest may be in want of intelligence. If you slight others, you commit a very great sin."

"Dictate your stanza," said he. "I will take it down for you. But do not forget to deliver me, should you succeed in getting the Dharma!"
My stanza read:

> There is no Bodhi-tree,
> Nor stand of a mirror bright.
> Since all is void,
> Where can the dust alight?

When he had written this, all disciples and others who were present were greatly surprised. Filled with admiration, they said to one another, "How wonderful! No doubt we should not judge people by appearance. How can it be that for so long we have made a Bodhisattva incarnate work for us?"

Seeing that the crowd was overwhelmed with amazement, the Patriarch rubbed off the stanza with his shoe, lest jealous ones should do me injury. He expressed the opinion, which they took for granted, that the author of this stanza had also not yet realised the Essence of Mind.

Next day the Patriarch came secretly to the room where the rice was pounded. Seeing that I was working there with a stone pestle, he said to me, "A seeker of the Path risks his life for the Dharma. Should he not do so?" Then he asked, "Is the rice ready?" "Ready long ago," I replied, "only waiting for the sieve." He knocked the mortar thrice with his stick and left.

Knowing what his message meant, in the third watch of the night I went to his room. Using the robe as a screen so that none could see us, he expounded the Diamond Sutra to me. When he came to the sentence, "One should use one's mind in such a way that it will be free from any attachment,"[3] I at once became thoroughly enlightened, and realised that all things in the universe are the Essence of Mind itself.

"Who would have thought," I said to the Patriarch, "that the Essence of Mind is intrinsically pure! Who would have thought that the Essence of Mind is intrinsically free from becoming or annihilation! Who would have thought that the Essence of Mind is intrinsically self-sufficient! Who would have thought that the Essence of Mind is intrinsically free from change! Who would have thought that all things are the manifestation of the Essence of Mind!"

Knowing that I had realised the Essence of Mind, the Patriarch said, "For him who does not know his own mind there is no use learning Buddhism. On the other hand, if he knows his own mind and sees intuitively his own nature, he is a Hero, a 'Teacher of gods and men,' 'Buddha'."

Thus, to the knowledge of no one, the Dharma was transmitted to me at midnight, and consequently I became the inheritor of the teaching of the 'Sudden' School as well as of the robe and the begging bowl.

"You are now the Sixth Patriarch," said he. "Take good care of yourself, and deliver as many sentient beings as possible. Spread and preserve the teaching, and don't let it come to an end. Take note of my stanza:

---

[3]Note by Dhyana Master Hui An:

" 'To be free from any attachment' means not to abide in form or matter, not to abide in sound, not to abide in delusion, not to abide in enlightenment, not to abide in the quintessence, not to abide in the attribute. 'To use the mind' means to let the 'One Mind' (i.e., the Universal mind) manifest itself everywhere. When we let our mind dwell on piety or on evil, piety or evil manifests itself, but our Essence of Mind (or Primordial mind) is thereby obscured. But when our mind dwells on nothing, we realise that all the worlds of the ten quarters are nothing but the manifestation of 'One Mind.'

"The above commentary is most accurate and to the point. Scholastic Buddhist scholars can never give an explanation as satisfactory as this. For this reason Dhyana Masters (National Teacher Hui An being one of them) are superior to the so-called Scriptural Expounders."

Sentient beings who sow the seeds of enlightenment
In the field of causation will reap the fruit of
    Buddhahood.
Inanimate objects void of Buddha-nature
Sow not and reap not.

He further said, "When the Patriarch Bodhidharma first came to China, most Chinese had no confidence in him, and so this robe was handed down as a testimony from one Patriarch to another. As to the Dharma, this is transmitted from heart to heart, and the recipient must realise it by his own efforts. From time immemorial it has been the practice for one Buddha to pass to his successor the quintessence of the Dharma, and for one Patriarch to transmit to another the esoteric teaching from heart to heart. As the robe may give cause for dispute, you are the last one to inherit it. Should you hand it down to your successor, your life would be in imminent danger. Now leave this place as quickly as you can, lest some one should do you harm."

"Whither should I go?" I asked. "At Huai you stop and at Hui you seclude yourself," he replied.

Upon receiving the robe and the begging bowl in the middle of the night, I told the Patriarch that, being a Southerner, I did not know the mountain tracks, and that it was impossible for me to get to the mouth of the river (to catch a boat). "You need not worry," said he. "I will go with you."

He then accompanied me to Kiukiang, and there ordered me into a boat. As he did the rowing himself, I asked him to sit down and let me handle the oar. "It is only right for me to carry you across," he said (an allusion to the sea of birth and death which one has to go across before the shore of Nirvana can be reached). To this I replied, "While I am under illusion, it is for you to get me across; but after enlightenment, I should cross it by myself. (Although the term 'to go across' is the same, it is used differently in each case.) As I happen to be born on the frontier, even my speaking is incorrect in pronunciation, (but in spite of this) I have had the honour to inherit the Dharma from you. Since I am now enlightened, it is only right for me to cross the sea of birth and death myself by realising my own Essence of Mind."

"Quite so, quite so," he agreed. "Beginning from you the Dhyana School will become very popular. Three years after your departure from me I shall leave this world. You may start on your journey now. Go as fast as you can towards the South. Do not preach too soon, as Buddhism is not so easily spread."

After saying good-bye, I left him and walked towards the South. In about two months' time, I reached the Ta Yü Mountain. There I noticed that several hundred men were in pursuit of me with the intention of robbing me of my robe and begging bowl.

Among them there was a monk named Hui Ming, whose lay surname was Ch'en. He was a general of the fourth rank in lay life. His manner was rough and his temper hot. Of all the pursuers, he was the most vigilant in search of me. When he was about to overtake me, I threw the robe and the begging bowl on a rock, saying, "This robe is nothing but a symbol. What is the use of taking it away by force?" (I then hid myself.) When he got to the rock, he tried to pick them up, but found he could not. Then he shouted out, "Lay Brother, Lay Brother, (for the Patriarch had not yet formally joined the Order) I come for the Dharma, not for the robe."

Whereupon I came out from my hiding place and squatted on the rock. He made obeisance and said, "Lay Brother, preach to me, please."

"Since the object of your coming is the Dharma," said I, "refrain from thinking of anything and keep your mind blank. I will then teach you." When he had done this for a considerable time, I said, "When you are thinking of neither good nor evil, what is at that particular moment, Venerable Sir, your real nature (literally, original face)?"

As soon as he heard this he at once became enlightened. But he further asked, "Apart from those esoteric sayings and esoteric ideas handed down by the Patriarch from generation to generation, are there any other esoteric teachings?" "What I can tell you is not esoteric," I replied. "If you turn your light inwardly,[4] you will find what is esoteric within you."

"In spite of my staying in Huang Mei," said he, "I did not realise my self-nature. Now thanks to your guidance, I know it as a water-drinker knows how hot or how cold the water is. Lay Brother, you are now my teacher."

I replied, "If that is so, then you and I are fellow disciples of the Fifth Patriarch. Take good care of yourself."

In answering his question whither he should go thereafter, I told him to stop at Yuan and to take up his abode in Meng. He paid homage and departed.

Sometime after I reached Ts'ao Ch'i. There the evildoers again persecuted me and I had to take refuge in Szu Hui, where I stayed with a party of hunters for a period as long as fifteen years.

Occasionally I preached to them in a way that befitted their understanding. They used to put me to watch their nets, but whenever I found living creatures therein I set them free. At meal times I put vegetables in the pan in which they cooked their meat. Some of them questioned me, and I explained to them that I would eat the vegetables only, after they had been cooked with the meat.

One day I bethought myself that I ought not to pass a secluded life all the time, and that it was high time for me to propagate the Law. Accordingly I left there and went to the Fa Hsin Temple in Canton.

---

[4] The most important point in the teaching of the Dhyana School lies in 'Introspection,' which means the turning of one's own 'light' to reflect inwardly. To illustrate, let us take the analogy of a lamp. We know that the light of a lamp, when surrounded by a shade, will reflect inwardly with its radiance centering on itself, whereas the rays of a naked flame will diffuse and shine outwardly. Now when we are engrossed with criticising others, as is our wont, we hardly turn our thoughts on ourselves, and hence scarcely know anything about ourselves. Contrary to this, the followers of the Dhyana School turn their attention completely within and reflect exclusively on their own 'real nature,' known in Chinese as one's 'original face.'

Lest our readers should overlook this important passage, let it be noted that in China alone thousands of Buddhists have attained enlightenment by acting on this wise saying of the Sixth Patriarch.—DIH PING TSZE.

At that time Bhikkhu Yin Tsung, Master of the Dharma, was lecturing on the Maha Parinirvana Sutra in the Temple. It happened that one day, when a pennant was blown about by the wind, two Bhikkhus entered into a dispute as to what it was that was in motion, the wind or the pennant. As they could not settle their difference I submitted to them that it was neither, and that what actually moved was their own mind. The whole assembly was startled by what I said, and Bhikkhu Yin Tsung invited me to take a seat of honour and questioned me about various knotty points in the Sutras.

Seeing that my answers were precise and accurate, and that they showed something more than book-knowledge, he said to me, "Lay Brother, you must be an extraordinary man. I was told long ago that the inheritor of the Fifth Patriarch's robe and Dharma had come to the South. Very likely you are the man."

To this I politely assented. He immediately made obeisance and asked me to show the assembly the robe and the begging bowl which I had inherited.

He further asked what instructions I had when the Fifth Patriarch transmitted me the Dharma. "Apart from a discussion on the realisation of the Essence of Mind," I replied, "he gave me no other instruction, nor did he refer to Dhyana and Emancipation." "Why not?" he asked. "Because that would mean two ways," I replied. "And there cannot be two ways in Buddhism. There is one way only."

He asked what was the only way. I replied, "The Maha Parinirvana Sutra which you expound explains that Buddha-nature is the only way. For example, in that Sutra King Kao Kuei-Teh, a Bodhisattva, asked Buddha whether or not those who commit the four acts of gross misconduct,[5] or the five deadly sins,[6] and those who are *icchantika* (heretics) etc., would eradicate their 'element of goodness' and their Buddha-nature. Buddha

replied, 'There are two kinds of 'element of goodness,' the eternal and the non-eternal. Since Buddha-nature is neither eternal nor non-eternal, therefore their 'element of goodness' is not eradicated. Now Buddhism is known as having no two ways. There are good ways and evil ways, but since Buddha-nature is neither, therefore Buddhism is known as having no two ways. From the point of view of ordinary folks, the component parts of a personality (*skandhas*) and factors of consciousness (*dhatus*) are two separate things: but enlightened men understand that they are not dual in nature. Buddha-nature is non-duality."

Bhikkhu Yin Tsung was highly pleased with my answer. Putting his two palms together as a sign of respect, he said, "My interpretation of the Sutra is as worthless as a heap of debris, while your discourse is as valuable as genuine gold." Subsequently he conducted the ceremony of hair-cutting for me (*i.e.,* the ceremony of Initiation into the Order) and asked me to accept him as my pupil.

Thenceforth, under the Bodhi-tree I preached the teaching of the Tung Shan School (the School of the Fourth and the Fifth Patriarchs, who lived in Tung Shan).

Since the time when the Dharma was transmitted to me in Tung Shan, I have gone through many hardships and my life often seemed to be hanging by a thread. Today, I have had the honour of meeting you in this assembly, and I must ascribe this to our good connection in previous *kalpas* (cyclic periods), as well as to our common accumulated merits in making offerings to various Buddhas in our past reincarnations; otherwise, we should have had no chance of hearing the above teaching of the 'Sudden' School, and thereby laying the foundation of our future success in understanding the Dharma.

This teaching was handed down from the past Patriarchs, and it is not a system of my own invention. Those who wish to hear the teaching should first purify their own mind, and after hearing it they should each clear up their own doubts in the same way as the Sages did in the past."

At the end of the address, the assembly felt rejoiced, made obeisance and departed.

---

[5]Killing, stealing, carnality and lying.
[6]Patricide, matricide, setting the Buddhist Order in discord, killing an Arhat, and causing blood to flow from the body of a Buddha.

QUESTIONS FOR DISCUSSION

1. Berkeley claims that his philosophy is compatible with the views of the ordinary person (the "vulgar" to use his own term, although that word has since taken on negative connotations it didn't have in his day). Why does he claim that he speaks for the ordinary human? Do you think he is correct in making this claim? Why or why not?
2. Why does Ramana Maharshi claim "the personal God is the last of the unreal forms to go"?

Do you agree with his characterization of God? If so, why? If not, why not?
3. Evaluate Schopenhauer's claim that, if the misery of the world were weighed against its guilt, the needle would balance at the center.
4. Why does Hui Neng challenge Shen Hsiu's interpretation of the Zen teachings? How does the concept of the Absolute (the "void") inform Hui Neng's own interpretation of the "essence of mind"?

MATERIALISM

Just as philosophical idealism in no way implies an idealistic attitude in the popular sense of this term, so also philosophical materialism implies no preoccupation with the acquisition of material goods. Rather, as "idealism" in philosophy refers to a doctrine that teaches that the world is the product of mind, "materialism" refers to the opposite position; the world, in its view, consists only of independent physical things, the mind being not the creator of the material world but its product. Where idealists like Bishop Berkeley claim that the brain is paradoxically lodged in the mind, the materialist sees the brain as the source of the mind, as something which is either actually identical with the mind or a necessary prerequisite for mind to exist in the world. This, of course, challenges most religious beliefs and puts materialism in direct conflict with spiritual interpretations of the world.

The first selection presented comes from the work of the seventeenth-century Neo-Confucian philosopher Wang Fu-Chi (1619–1692), who argues that both *Tao,* the "way," and *Li* or "principle," are not prior to Chi or "material force" but inseparable from it. In this he challenges all other Neo-Confucians who generally hold the view that *Li* is prior to *Chi,* that is to say, that a conscious intelligence is necessary for the operation of the laws of physical nature, that a Supreme Principle or a Supreme Being governs the world. As a materialist, Wang has come in for much praise in recent years in China, where the officially materialist Communist regime views him as a traditional ally and forerunner of its official world view.

Friedrich Engels (1820–1895), the cofounder of Marxism and Karl Marx's lifelong collaborator, provides the second selection. The selection begins with his account of the origin and development of the world in exclusively scientific terms—a world of matter and energy governed wholly by natural law. Very quickly, however, he moves on to the question of humanity's place in this world of unthinking matter, ending with a faith that, though intelligent life is eventually likely to perish here on this planet, it will emerge elsewhere in the universe in matter's "eternal cycle."

NEO-CONFUCIAN MATERIALISM

Wang Fu-Chih

THE WORLD OF CONCRETE THINGS

The world consists only of concrete things. The Way (*Tao*) is the Way of concrete things, but concrete things may not be called concrete things of the Way. People generally are capable of saying that without its Way there cannot be the concrete thing. However, if there is the concrete thing, there need be no worry about there not being its Way. A sage knows what a superior man does not know, but an ordinary man or woman can do what a sage cannot do. A person may be ignorant of the Way of a thing, and the concrete thing therefore cannot be completed. But not being completed does not mean that there is no concrete thing. Few people are capable of saying that without a concrete thing there cannot be its Way, but it is certainly true.

In the period of wilderness and chaos, there was no Way to bow and yield a throne. At the time of Yao and Shun,[1] there was no Way to pity the suffering people and punish the sinful rulers. During the Han (206 B.C.–A.D. 220) and T'ang (618–907) dynasties there were no Ways as we have today, and there will be many in future years which we do not have now. Before bows and arrows existed, there was no Way of archery. Before chariots and horses existed, there was no Way to drive them. Before sacrificing oxen and wine, presents of jade and silk,

---

[1]Legendary emperors (3rd millennium B.C.).

or bells, chimes, flutes, and strings existed, there were no Ways of ceremonies and music. Thus there is no Way of the father before there is a son, there is no Way of the elder brother before there is a younger brother, and there are many potential Ways which are not existent. Therefore without a concrete thing, there cannot be its Way. This is indeed a true statement. Only people have not understood it.

Sages of antiquity could manage concrete things but could not manage the Way. What is meant by the Way is the management of concrete things. When the Way is fulfilled, we call it virtue. When the concrete thing is completed, we call it operation. When concrete things function extensively, we call it transformation and penetration. When its effect becomes prominent, we call it achievement. . .

By "what exists before physical form" [and is therefore without it][2] does not mean there is no physical form. There is already physical form. As there is physical form, there is that which exists before it. Even if we span past and present, go through all the myriad transformations, and investigate Heaven, Earth, man, and things to the utmost, we will not find any thing existing before physical form [and is without it]. Therefore it is said, "It is only the sage who can put his physical form into full use."[3] He puts into full use what is within a physical form, not what is above it. Quickness of apprehension and intelligence are matters of the ear and the eye, insight and wisdom those of the mind and thought, humanity that of men, righteousness that of events, equilibrium and harmony those of ceremonies and music, great impartiality and perfect correctness those of reward and punishment, advantage and utility those of water, fire, metal, and wood, welfare that of grains, fruits, silk, and hemp, and correct virtue that of the relationship between ruler and minister and between father and son. If one discarded these and sought for that which existed before concrete things, even if he spanned past and present, went through all the myr-

iad transformations, and investigated Heaven, Earth, man, and things to the utmost, he would not be able to give it a name. How much less could he find its reality! Lao Tzu was blind to this and said that the Way existed in vacuity. But vacuity is the vacuity of concrete things. The Buddha was blind to this and said that the Way existed in silence. But silence is the silence of concrete things. One may keep on uttering such extravagant words to no end, but one can never escape from concrete things. Thus if one plays up some name that is separated from concrete things as though he were a divine being, whom could he deceive?

SUBSTANCE AND FUNCTION

All functions in the world are those of existing things. From their functions I know they possess substance. Why should we entertain any doubt? Function exists to become effect, and substance exists to become nature and feelings. Both substance and function exist, and each depends on the other to be concrete. Therefore all that fills the universe demonstrates the principle of mutual dependence. Therefore it is said, "Sincerity (realness) is the beginning and end of things. Without sincerity there will be nothing."[4]

What is the test for this? We believe in what exists but doubt what does not exist. I live from the time I was born to the time I die. As there were ancestors before, so there will be descendants later. From observing the transformations throughout heaven and earth, we see the productive process. Is any of these facts doubtful? . . . Hold on to the concrete things and its Way will be preserved. Cast aside the concrete things and its Way will be destroyed . . . Therefore those who are expert in speaking of the Way arrive at substance from function but those who are not expert in speaking of the Way erroneously set up substance and dismiss function in order to conform to it.

• • •

[2]*Changes,* "Appended Remarks," pt. 1, ch. 12, Cf. Legge, trans., *Yi King,* 377.
[3]*Mencius,* 7A:38.
[4]*The Mean*, ch. 25.

PRINCIPLE AND MATERIAL FORCE

Principle depends on material force. When material force is strong, principle prevails. When Heaven accumulates strong and powerful material force, there will be order, and transformations will be refined and totally renewed. This is why on the day of religious fasting an emperor presents an ox [to Heaven] so that the material force will fill the universe and sincerity will penetrate everything. All products in the world are results of refined and beautiful material force. Man takes the best of it to nourish his life, but it is all from Heaven. Material force naturally becomes strong. Sincerity naturally becomes solidified. And principle naturally becomes self-sufficient. If we investigate into the source of these phenomena, we shall find that it is the refined and beautiful transformation of Heaven and Earth.

At bottom principle is not a finished product that can be grasped. It is invisible. The details and order of material force is principle that is visible. Therefore the first time there is any principle is when it is seen in material force.

MATERIALISM AND THE SCIENTIFIC WORLD VIEW*

Friedrich Engels

The new conception of nature was complete in its main features; all rigidity was dissolved, all fixity dissipated, all particularity that had been regarded as eternal became transient, the whole of nature shown as moving in eternal flux and cyclical course.

Thus we have once again returned to the point of view of the great founders of Greek philosophy, the view that the whole of nature, from the smallest element to the greatest, from grains of sand to suns,

from protista[1] to men, has its existence in eternal coming into being and passing away, in ceaseless flux, in unresting motion and change, only with the essential difference that what for the Greeks was a brilliant intuition, is in our case the result of strictly scientific research in accordance with experience, and hence also it emerges in a much more definite and clear form. It is true that the empirical proof of this motion is not wholly free from gaps, but these are insignificant in comparison with what has already been firmly established, and with each year they become more and more filled up. And how could the proof in detail be otherwise than defective when one bears in mind that the most essential branches of science—trans-planetary astronomy, chemistry, geology—have a scientific existence of barely a hundred years, and the comparative method in physiology one of barely fifty years, and that the basic form of almost all organic development, the cell, is a discovery not yet forty years old?

The innumerable suns and solar systems of our island universe,[2] bounded by the outermost stellar rings of the Milky Way, developed from swirling, glowing masses of vapour, the laws of motion of which will perhaps be disclosed after the observations of some centuries have given us an insight into the proper motion of the stars. Obviously, this development did not proceed everywhere at the same rate. Recognition of the existence of dark bodies, not merely planetary in nature, hence extinct suns in our stellar system, more and more forces itself on astronomy (Mädler); on the other hand (according to Secchi) a part of the vaporous nebular patches belong to our stellar system as suns not yet fully formed, whereby it is not excluded that other nebulæ, as Mädler maintains, are distant independent

*The notes in the text which explain and, at times, correct and update Engels' science are those of the 20th century scientist, J.B.S. Haldane, who edited the translation used here (Eds.).

[1]*Protista.* Single-celled animals and plants such as Paramœcium, Amœba, Bacillus.
[2]This refers to the system of stars of which the sun is one, and the Milky Way represents the densest portions. Mädler was right in maintaining that many of the other bodies then described as nebulæ were similar masses of stars. His view that there are extinct suns is more doubtful. Nor is it clear that the gaseous nebulæ are likely to condense into suns.

island universes, the relative stage of development of which must be determined by the spectroscope.

How a solar system develops from an individual nebular mass has been shown in detail by Laplace in a manner still unsurpassed; subsequent science has more and more confirmed him.[3]

On the separate bodies so formed—suns as well as planets and satellites—the form of motion of matter at first prevailing is that which we call heat. There can be no question of chemical compounds of the elements even at a temperature like that still possessed by the sun; the extent to which heat is transformed into electricity or magnetism[4] under such conditions, continued solar observations will show; it is already as good as proved that the mechanical motion taking place in the sun arises solely from the conflict of heat with gravity.

The smaller the individual bodies, the quicker they cool down, the satellites, asteroids, and meteors first of all, just as our moon has long been extinct. The planets cool more slowly, the central body slowest of all.

With progressive cooling the interplay of the physical forms of motion which become transformed into one another comes more and more to the forefront until finally a point is reached from when on chemical affinity begins to make itself felt, the previously chemically indifferent elements become differentiated chemically one after another, obtain chemical properties, and enter into combination with one another. These compounds change continually with the decreasing temperature, which affects differently not only each element but also each separate compound of the elements, changing also with the consequent passage of part of the gaseous matter first to the liquid and then the solid state, and with the new conditions thus created.

The period when the planet has a firm shell and accumulations of water on its surface coincides with that when its intrinsic heat diminishes more and more in comparison to the heat emitted to it from the central body. Its atmosphere becomes the arena of meteorological phenomena in the sense in which we now understand the word; its surface becomes the arena of geological changes in which the deposits resulting from atmospheric precipitation become of ever greater importance in comparison to the slowly decreasing external effects of the hot fluid interior.

If, finally, the temperature becomes so far equalised that over a considerable portion of the surface at least it does not exceed the limits within which protein is capable of life, then, if other chemical conditions are favourable, living protoplasm is formed. What these conditions are, we do not yet know, which is not to be wondered at since so far not even the chemical formula of protein has been established—we do not even know how many chemically different protein bodies there are—and since it is only about ten years ago that the fact became known that completely structureless protein[5] exercises all the essential functions of life, digestion, excretion, movement, contraction, reaction to stimuli, and reproduction.

Thousands of years may have passed before the conditions arose in which the next advance could take place and this formless protein produce the first cell by formation of nucleus and cell membrane. But this first cell also provided the foundation for the morphological development of the whole organic world; the first to develop, as it is permissible to assume from the whole analogy of the palæontological record, were innumerable species of non-cellular and cellular protista, of

---

[3]Laplace's theory is fairly certainly incorrect.

[4]Huge magnetic fields have been discovered in the sunspots, and it is also known that the matter shot out in solar prominences is electrically charged. Both these facts were unsuspected by most, if not all, astronomers when Engels wrote.

---

[5]*Structureless protein: Bathybius Haeckeli,* which was supposed to be an organism composed of a mere mass of structureless protein, proved to be an artifact, that is to say not a natural object, but one produced by the chemicals intended to preserve it. However Engels was fundamentally right. Some of the "viruses," that is to say the smallest agents of disease, are simply large protein molecules, as first shown by Stanley in 1936. They do not appear to exercise all the functions of life, but only some of them.

which *Eozoon canadense*[6] alone has come down to us, and of which some were gradually differentiated into the first plants and others into the first animals. And from the first animals were developed, essentially by further differentiation, the numerous classes, orders, families, genera, and species of animals; and finally mammals, the form in which the nervous system attains its fullest development; and among these again finally that mammal in which nature attains consciousness of itself—man.

Man too arises by differentiation. Not only individually, by differentiation from a single egg cell to the most complicated organism that nature produces—no, also historically. When after thousands of years[7] of struggle the differentiation of hand from foot, and erect gait, were finally established, man became distinct from the monkey and the basis was laid for the development of articulate speech and the mighty development of the brain that has since made the gulf between man and monkey an unbridgeable one. The specialisation of the hand—this implies the *tool,* and the tool implies specific human activity, the transforming reaction of man on nature, production. Animals in the narrower sense also have tools, but only as limbs of their bodies: the ant, the bee, the beaver; animals also produce, but their productive effect on surrounding nature in relation to the latter amounts to nothing at all. Man alone has succeeded in impressing his stamp on nature, not only by shifting the plant and animal world from one place to another, but also by so altering the aspect and climate of his dwelling place, and even the plants and animals themselves, that the consequences of his activity can disappear only with the general extinction of the terrestrial globe. And he has accomplished this primarily and essentially by means of *the hand.* Even the steam engine, so far his most powerful tool for the transformation of nature, depends, because it

is a tool, in the last resort on the hand. But step by step with the development of the hand went that of the brain; first of all consciousness of the conditions for separate practically useful actions, and later, among the more favoured peoples and arising from the preceding, insight into the natural laws governing them. And with the rapidly growing knowledge of the laws of nature the means for reacting on nature also grew; the hand alone would never have achieved the steam engine if the brain of man had not attained a correlative development with it, and parallel to it, and partly owing to it.

With men we enter *history.* Animals also have a history, that of their derivation and gradual evolution to their present position. This history, however, is made for them, and in so far as they themselves take part in it, this occurs without their knowledge or desire. On the other hand, the more that human beings become removed from animals in the narrower sense of the word, the more they make their own history consciously, the less becomes the influence of unforeseen effects and uncontrolled forces on this history, and the more accurately does the historical result correspond to the aim laid down in advance. If, however, we apply this measure to human history, to that of even the most developed peoples of the present day, we find that there still exists here a colossal disproportion between the proposed aims and the results arrived at, that unforeseen effects predominate, and that the uncontrolled forces are far more powerful than those set into motion according to plan. And this cannot be otherwise as long as the most essential historical activity of men, the one which has raised them from bestiality to humanity and which forms the material foundation of all their other activities, namely the production of their requirements of life, that is to-day social production, is above all subject to the interplay of unintended effects from uncontrolled forces and achieves its desired end only by way of exception and, much more frequently, the exact opposite. In the most advanced industrial countries we have subdued the forces of nature and pressed them into the service of mankind; we have thereby infinitely multiplied production, so that a child now produces more than a hundred adults pre-

---

[6]*Eozoon canadense* is almost certainly not an organic product. Nevertheless there is every reason to believe in the essential truth of this paragraph.

[7]The geological time-scale is longer than was believed fifty years ago. "Millions of years" would be more correct.

viously did. And what is the result? Increasing over-work and increasing misery of the masses, and every ten years a great collapse. Darwin did not know what a bitter satire he wrote on mankind, and especially on his countrymen, when he showed that free competition, the struggle for existence, which the economists celebrate as the highest historical achievement, is the normal state of the *animal kingdom.* Only conscious organisation of social production, in which production and distribution are carried on in a planned way, can lift mankind above the rest of the animal world as regards the social aspect, in the same way that production in general has done this for men in their aspect as species. Historical evolution makes such an organisation daily more indispensable, but also with every day more possible. From it will date a new epoch of history, in which mankind itself, and with mankind all branches of its activity, and especially natural science, will experience an advance that will put everything preceding it in the deepest shade.

Nevertheless, "all that comes into being deserves to perish." Millions of years may elapse, hundreds of thousands of generations be born and die, but inexorably the time will come when the declining warmth of the sun[8] will no longer suffice to melt the ice thrusting itself forward from the poles; when the human race, crowding more and more about the equator, will finally no longer find even there enough heat for life; when gradually even the last trace of organic life will vanish; and the earth, an extinct frozen globe like the moon, will circle in deepest darkness and in an ever narrower orbit about the equally extinct sun, and at last fall into it. Other planets will have preceded it, others will follow it; instead of the bright, warm solar system with

its harmonious arrangement of members, only a cold, dead sphere will still pursue its lonely path through universal space. And what will happen to our solar system will happen sooner or later to all the other systems of our island universe; it will happen to all the other innumerable island universes, even to those the light of which will never reach the earth while there is a living human eye to receive it.

And when such a solar system has completed its life history and succumbs to the fate of all that is finite, death, what then? Will the sun's corpse roll on for all eternity through infinite space, and all the once infinitely diverse, differentiated natural forces pass for ever into one single form of motion, attraction? "Or"—as Secchi asks—"do forces exist in nature which can re-convert the dead system into its original state of an incandescent nebula and re-awake it to new life? We do not know."

At all events we do not know in the sense that we know that $2 \times 2 = 4$, or that the attraction of matter increases and decreases according to the square of the distance. In theoretical natural science, however, which as far as possible builds up its view of nature into a harmonious whole, and without which nowadays even the most thoughtless empiricist cannot get anywhere, we have very often to reckon with incompletely known magnitudes; and logical consistency of thought must at all times help to get over defective knowledge. Modern natural science has had to take over from philosophy the principle of the indestructibility of motion; it cannot any longer exist without this principle. But the motion of matter is not merely crude mechanical motion, mere change of place, it is heat and light, electric and magnetic stress, chemical combination and dissociation, life and, finally, consciousness. To say that matter during the whole unlimited time of its existence has only once, and for what is an infinitesimally short period in comparison to its eternity, found itself able to differentiate its motion and thereby to unfold the whole wealth of this motion, and that before and after this remains restricted for eternity to mere change of place—this is equivalent to maintaining that matter is mortal and motion transitory. The indestructibility of motion cannot be

---

[8]Until quite recently these rather gloomy conclusions appeared inevitable, even if the time-scale proved to be vastly longer than was supposed. But in 1936–1938 Milne and Dirao independently arrived at the conclusion that the laws of nature themselves evolve, and in particular (according to Milne) that chemical changes are speeded up (at the rate of about one two-thousand-millionth part per year) in relation to physical changes. If so it is at least conceivable that this process may be rapid enough to compensate for the cooling of the stars, and that life may never become impossible.

merely quantitative, it must also be conceived qualitatively; matter whose purely mechanical change of place includes indeed the possibility under favourable conditions of being transformed into heat, electricity, chemical action, or life, but which is not capable of producing these conditions from out of itself, such matter has *forfeited motion;* motion which has lost the capacity of being transformed into the various forms appropriate to it may indeed still have *dynamis* but no longer *energeia,*[9] and so has become partially destroyed. Both, however, are unthinkable.

This much is certain: there was a time when the matter of our island universe had *transformed* a quantity of motion—of what kind we do not yet know—into heat, such that there could be developed from it the solar systems appertaining to (according to Mädler) at least twenty million stars, the gradual extinction of which is likewise certain. How did this transformation take place? We know just as little as Father Secchi knows whether the future *caput mortuum* of our solar system will once again be converted into the raw material of a new solar system. But here either we must have recourse to a creator, or we are forced to the conclusion that the incandescent raw material for the solar system of our universe was produced in a natural way by transformations of motion which are *by nature inherent* in moving matter, and the conditions of which therefore also must be reproduced by matter, even if only after millions and millions of years and more or less by chance but with the necessity that is also inherent in chance.

The possibility of such a transformation is more and more being conceded. The view is being arrived at that the heavenly bodies are ultimately destined to fall into one another, and one even calculates the amount of heat which must be developed on such collisions. The sudden flaring up of new stars, and the equally sudden increase in brightness of familiar ones, of which we are informed by astronomy, is most easily explained[10] by such collisions. Not only does our group of planets move about the sun, and our sun within our island universe, but our whole island universe also moves in space in temporary, relative equilibrium with the other island universes, for even the relative equilibrium of freely moving bodies can only exist where the motion is reciprocally determined; and it is assumed by many that the temperature in space is not everywhere the same. Finally, we know that, with the exception of an infinitesimal portion, the heat of the innumerable suns of our island universe vanishes into space and fails to raise the temperature of space even by a millionth of a degree centigrade.[11] What becomes of all this enormous quantity of heat? Is it for ever dissipated in the attempt to heat universal space, has it ceased to exist practically, and does it only continue to exist theoretically, in the fact that universal space has become warmer by a decimal fraction of a degree beginning with ten or more noughts? The indestructibility of motion forbids such an assumption, but it allows the possibility that by the successive falling into one another of the bodies of the universe all existing mechanical motion will be converted into heat and the latter radiated into space, so that in spite of all "indestructibility of force" all motion in general would have ceased. (Incidentally it is seen here how inaccurate is the term "indestructibility of force"[12] instead of "indestructibility of motion.") Hence we arrive at the conclusion that in some way, which it will later be the task of scientific research to demonstrate, the heat radiated into space must be able to become transformed into another form of motion, in which it can once more be stored up and rendered active. Thereby the chief difficulty in the way of the reconversion of extinct suns into incandescent vapour disappears.

---

[9]"Dynamis" and "energeia" are Greek words used by Aristotle. They can roughly be translated as "power" and "activity."

[10]The flaring up of new stars is now generally explained not by collision, but by an internal crisis in the star, in fact in a more dialectical manner.

[11]Actually the temperature of dust particles in the space between the galaxies is probably several degrees above absolute zero.

[12]Engels rightly protests against the use of the same word "Kraft" for "force" and "energy."

For the rest, the eternally repeated succession of worlds in infinite time is only the logical complement to the co-existence of innumerable worlds in infinite space—a principle the necessity of which has forced itself even on the anti-theoretical Yankee brain of Draper.[13]

It is an eternal cycle[14] in which matter moves, a cycle that certainly only completes its orbit in periods of time for which our terrestrial year is no adequate measure, a cycle in which the time of highest development, the time of organic life and still more that of the life of beings conscious of nature and of themselves, is just as narrowly restricted as the space in which life and self-consciousness come into operation; a cycle in which every finite mode of existence of matter, whether it be sun or nebular vapour, single animal or genus of animals, chemical combination or dissociation, is equally transient, and wherein nothing is eternal but eternally changing, eternally moving matter and the laws according to which it moves and changes. But however often, and however relentlessly, this cycle is completed in time and space, however many millions of suns and earths may arise and pass away, however long it may last before the conditions for organic life develop, however innumerable the organic beings that have to arise and to pass away before animals with a brain capable of thought are developed from their midst, and for a short span of time find conditions suitable for life, only to be exterminated later without mercy, we have the certainty that matter remains eternally the same in all its transformations, that none of its attributes can ever be lost, and therefore, also, that with the same iron necessity that it will exterminate on the earth its highest creation, the thinking mind, it must somewhere else and at another time again produce it.

---

[13]"The multiplicity of worlds in infinite space leads to the conception of a succession of worlds in infinite time." J. W. Draper, *History of the Intellectual Development of Europe,* 1864. Vol. 2, p. 325. [*Note by F. Engels.*]

[14]At present physicists are divided on this question. A few take Engels' view that the universe goes through cyclical changes, entropy being somehow diminished by processes at present unknown (*e.g.* formation of matter from radiation in interstellar space). Others think as Clausius did, that it will run down. But there is a third possibility. As pointed out above, the work of Milne suggests that the universe as a whole has a history, though probably an infinite one both in the past and the future. It is almost certain that Engels would have welcomed this idea, although he here admits the eternity of the laws according to which matter moves and changes.

QUESTIONS FOR DISCUSSION

1. Where Engels speaks of scientifically derived natural laws, Wang Fu-Chi speaks of "principle." Do you think these two notions can be equated? That is, is Wang Fu-Chi's materialism at bottom the same as that of Engels or significantly different from it?

2. Engels presents a picture of the universe without a God or any other sort of Supreme Being. Do you agree with this materialist picture of the world? Why or why not?

The Problem of Method

Charles Sanders Peirce, *The Fixation of Belief*
Paul Feyerabend, *Against Method*
Sandra Harding, *Is Science Multicultural?*
Patricia Hill Collins, *An Afrocentric Feminist
  Epistemology*
Ayatollah Murtaza Mutahhari, *The Limits of Science*

The Limits of Reason and the Limits of Knowledge

Chuang Tzu, *Knowledge and Relativity*
Jorge Luis Borges, *Averroës' Search*
Daisetz T. Suzuki, *Zen Knowledge*

Jacob Lawrence, *The Library,* 1960, National Museum of American Art, Washington, D.C./Art Resource, NY

CHAPTER 2

KNOWLEDGE AND SCIENCE

The theory of knowledge, which is also known as *epistemology,* has been seen as central to philosophy by most Western philosophers in the period since the scientific revolution. As the prestige of science has grown, the philosophy of science has in turn been increasingly seen as central to most epistemological investigations. In this chapter, knowledge is examined both generally and in its specifically "scientific" form. The chapter begins with the question of method in knowledge gathering: What is the scientific method? Does such a method really, in practice, exist? Is it sufficient for a full understanding of the world? Is there, in addition to scientific knowledge, spiritual or religious knowledge of the world? What of the knowledge that we seem to obtain through the arts and our cul-

tural traditions? Are there cultural limitations on the acquisition of knowledge? Can all understanding be contained within the bounds of reason? These questions are debated by thinkers from a variety of times and cultures, with special emphasis being given to contemporary thought. For the problems of knowledge have become more acute than ever before in the world's history, as Marshall McLuhan's "global village" and the post–Cold War global market begin to take shape.

Those readers interested in the Chuang Tzu selection may want to look also at the selections from Chuang Tzu and other Taoist authors in Chapter 8. The subject of Zen is also addressed in "The Sutra of Hui Neng" in Chapter 1 and in Section Three of Chapter 5.

THE PROBLEM OF METHOD

The question of method—that is, What method or methods prove best in ensuring reliable knowledge? —is a question that has both great practical and great theoretical importance. It therefore is one of the most central questions in epistemology. In the West and other industrialized parts of the world today, the methods of science are held in high esteem. In the first selection presented in this section, the American philosopher Charles Sanders Peirce (pronounced "Purse") (1839–1914) attempts in a cheerfully open-minded manner to demonstrate why science is, for many purposes at least, superior to other methods of knowledge gathering or—to put the matter in his own terms—for the "fixing of belief." In doing this, he very briefly sketches out some main features of the "method of scientific investigation." The question of whether the view of scientific investigation presented here really *is* the method employed by working scientists is left, however, unexamined by him.

If we are to believe the next author, the answer is far less clear-cut than is usually assumed. Contemporary philosopher Paul Feyerabend, in a selection taken from his critique of science "Against Method," claims that the scientists' decisions concerning the role that experience will play in their work is far more arbitrary than it is ordinarily taken to be. There is no scientific method, argues Feyerabend; the claim that there is a single foolproof method in science is merely a piece of propaganda that scientists use to undercut their opponents. The truth is that science enjoys no special monopoly on knowledge. "Science" is more a fraternity of specialists with vested interests than a method for knowledge acquisition.

In bolstering his case, Paul Feyerabend relies heavily on the history of science. So also does another contemporary philosopher, Sandra Harding of the University of Delaware, when she explores the cultural nature of science in "Is Science Multicultural?" In the article, she breaks this issue down into three related but essentially independent questions: Does

modern science have non-Western origins? Have there been or could there be other comparable non-Western sciences? And, in what ways, in fact, is modern science specifically Western or "European-American"? Like Feyerabend, she is skeptical of many of the claims made in defense of modern science to the effect that it constitutes a unique and uniquely superior method of knowledge acquisition, though her critique of science is far more tempered than his.

Less temperate are the claims of contemporary sociologist Patricia Hill Collins (1947–) in the next selection. She questions the superiority of what she terms the "positivist approaches" of scientific investigation—which is to say, those very approaches that Peirce had said recommended science over other methods of fixing belief. Instead, she suggests that the alternative methods forged in the experiences of black American women, as well as, by implication, the methods arrived at by numerous other social groupings, deserve a fair hearing, which they have never received in the courts of official epistemology.

The view that official science has its limits was also championed by the Iranian cleric and scholar Murtaza Mutahhari, who looks at the scientific enterprise in the light of the Islamic world view, an approach to life with a long history that, as we have seen in Sandra Harding's article, has often been intermingled with the history of science itself.

Islamic civilization was at one time the most powerful in the world, not merely politically and militarily but also in terms of its widespread intellectual influence. Islamic thinkers not only acted as a conduit for classical philosophy and science in both Europe and Africa, they also added to it, making significant contributions to astronomy, philosophy, architecture, medicine, and mathematics. Today, however, Islam finds itself frustrated, treated as if it were a barbarous backwater, valued more for its oil reserves than its knowledge and wisdom.

In this situation, a movement has arisen that is usually referred to as "Islamic fundamentalism." This movement has made great inroads both politically and intellectually in most major Islamic countries. In Iran, the movement has actually seized the reins of power. The Ayatollah Murtaza Muttahhari was an important figure in the Iranian revolution. Popular with traditionalists and author of several works on Islamic theology, he was a student of the Ayatollah Khomeini and held political office under him. Mutahhari's political and religious career was, however, cut short when he was assassinated by a car bomb relatively early in the history of the Khomeini regime.

THE FIXATION OF BELIEF

Charles Sanders Peirce

DOUBT AND BELIEF

We generally know when we wish to ask a question and when we wish to pronounce a judgment, for there is a dissimilarity between the sensation of doubting and that of believing.

But this is not all which distinguishes doubt from belief. There is a practical difference. Our beliefs guide our desires and shape our actions. The Assassins, or followers of the Old Man of the Mountain, used to rush into death at his least command, because they believed that obedience to him would insure everlasting felicity. Had they doubted this, they would not have acted as they did. So it is with every belief, according to its degree. The feeling of believing is a more or less sure indication of there being established in our nature some habit which will determine our actions.[1] Doubt never has such an effect.

[1]Doubt, however, is not usually hesitancy about what is to be done then and there. It is anticipated hesitancy about what I shall do hereafter, or a feigned hesitancy about a fictitious state of things. It is the power of making believe we hesitate, together with the pregnant fact that the decision upon the merely make-believe dilemma goes toward forming a bona fide habit that will be operative in a real emergency. It is these two things in conjunction that constitute us intellectual beings.

Nor must we overlook a third point of difference. Doubt is an uneasy and dissatisfied state from which we struggle to free ourselves and pass into the state of belief; while the latter is a calm and satisfactory state which we do not wish to avoid, or to change to a belief in anything else.

On the contrary, we cling tenaciously, not merely to believing, but to believing just what we do believe.

Thus, both doubt and belief have positive effects upon us, though very different ones. Belief does not make us act at once, but puts us into such a condition that we shall behave in some certain way, when the occasion arises. Doubt has not the least such active effect, but stimulates us to inquiry until it is destroyed. This reminds us of the irritation of a nerve and the reflex action produced thereby; while for the analogue of belief, in the nervous system, we must look to what are called nervous associations—for example, to that habit of the nerves in consequence of which the smell of a peach will make the mouth water.

THE END OF INQUIRY

The irritation of doubt causes a struggle to attain a state of belief. I shall term this struggle *Inquiry,* though it must be admitted that this is sometimes not a very apt designation.

The irritation of doubt is the only immediate motive for the struggle to attain belief. It is certainly best for us that our beliefs should be such as may truly guide our actions so as to satisfy our desires; and this reflection will make us reject every belief which does not seem to have been so formed as to insure this result. But it will only do so by creating a doubt in the place of that belief. With the doubt, therefore, the struggle begins, and with the cessation of doubt it ends. Hence, the sole object of inquiry is the settlement of opinion. We may fancy that this is not enough for us, and that we seek, not merely an opinion, but a true opinion. But put this fancy to the test, and it proves groundless; for as soon as a firm belief is reached we are entirely satisfied, whether the belief be true or false. And it is clear that nothing out of the sphere of our knowledge can be our object, for nothing which does not affect the mind can be the motive for mental effort. The most that can be maintained is, that we seek for a belief that we shall *think* to be true. But we think each one of our beliefs to be true, and, indeed, it is mere tautology to say so.[2]

That the settlement of opinion is the sole end of inquiry is a very important proposition. It sweeps away, at once, various vague and erroneous conceptions of proof. A few of these may be noticed here.

1. Some philosophers have imagined that to start an inquiry it was only necessary to utter a question whether orally or by setting it down upon paper, and have even recommended us to begin our studies with questioning everything! But the mere putting of a proposition into the interrogative form does not stimulate the mind to any struggle after belief. There must be a real and living doubt, and without this all discussion is idle.

2. It is a very common idea that a demonstration must rest on some ultimate and absolutely indubitable propositions. These, according to one school, are first principles of a general nature; according to another, are first sensations. But, in point of fact, an inquiry, to have that completely satisfactory result called demonstration, has only to start with propositions perfectly free from all actual doubt. If the premises are not in fact doubted at all, they cannot be more satisfactory than they are.[3]

3. Some people seem to love to argue a point after all the world is fully convinced of it. But no further advance can be made. When doubt ceases, mental action on the subject comes to an end; and, if it did go on, it would be without a purpose.

METHODS OF FIXING BELIEF

If the settlement of opinion is the sole object of inquiry, and if belief is of the nature of a habit, why should we not attain the desired end, by taking as answer to a question any we may fancy, and constantly reiterating it to ourselves, dwelling on all which may conduce to that belief, and learning to turn with contempt and hatred from anything that might disturb it? This simple and direct method is really pursued by many men. I remember once being entreated not to read a certain newspaper lest it might change my opinion upon free-trade. "Lest I might be entrapped by its fallacies and misstatements," was the form of expression. "You are not," my friend said, "a special student of political economy. You might, therefore, easily be deceived by fallacious arguments upon the subject. You might, then, if you read this paper, be led to believe in protection. But you admit that free-trade is the true doctrine; and you do not wish to believe what is not true." I have often known this system to be deliberately adopted. Still oftener, the instinctive dislike of an undecided state of mind, exaggerated into a vague dread of doubt, makes men cling spasmodically to the views they already take. The man feels that, if he only holds to his belief without wavering, it will be entirely satisfactory. Nor can it be denied that a steady and immovable faith yields great peace of mind. It may, indeed, give rise to inconveniences, as if a man should resolutely continue to believe that fire would not burn him, or that he would be eternally damned if he received his *ingesta* otherwise than through a stomach-pump. But then the man who adopts this method will not allow that its inconveniences are greater than its advantages. He will say, "I hold steadfastly to the truth, and the truth is always wholesome." And in many cases it may very well be that the pleasure he derives from his calm faith overbalances any inconveniences resulting from its deceptive character. Thus, if it be true

---

[2]For truth is neither more nor less than that character of a proposition which consists in this, that belief in the proposition would, with sufficient experience and reflection, lead us to such conduct as would tend to satisfy the desires we should then have. To say that truth means more than this is to say that it has no meaning at all.—1903.

[3]We have to acknowledge that doubts about them may spring up later; but we can find no propositions which are not subject to this contingency. We ought to construct our theories so as to provide for such discoveries; first, by making them rest on as great a variety of different considerations as possible, and second, by leaving room for the modifications which cannot be foreseen but which are pretty sure to prove needful.

that death is annihilation, then the man who believes that he will certainly go straight to heaven when he dies, provided he have fulfilled certain simple observances in this life, has a cheap pleasure which will not be followed by the least disappointment. A similar consideration seems to have weight with many persons in religious topics, for we frequently hear it said, "Oh, I could not believe so-and-so, because I should be wretched if I did." When an ostrich buries its head in the sand as danger approaches, it very likely takes the happiest course. It hides the danger, and then calmly says there is no danger; and, if it feels perfectly sure there is none, why should it raise its head to see? A man may go through life, systematically keeping out of view all that might cause a change in his opinions, and if he only succeeds—basing his method, as he does, on two fundamental psychological laws—I do not see what can be said against his doing so. It would be an egotistical impertinence to object that his procedure is irrational, for that only amounts to saying that his method of settling belief is not ours. He does not propose to himself to be rational, and, indeed, will often talk with scorn of man's weak and illusive reason. So let him think as he pleases.

But this method of fixing belief, which may be called the method of tenacity, will be unable to hold its ground in practice. The social impulse is against it. The man who adopts it will find that other men think differently from him, and it will be apt to occur to him, in some saner moment, that their opinions are quite as good as his own, and this will shake his confidence in his belief. This conception, that another man's thought or sentiment may be equivalent to one's own, is a distinctly new step, and a highly important one. It arises from an impulse too strong in man to be suppressed, without danger of destroying the human species. Unless we make ourselves hermits, we shall necessarily influence each other's opinions; so that the problem becomes how to fix belief, not in the individual merely, but in the community.

Let the will of the state act, then, instead of that of the individual. Let an institution be created which shall have for its object to keep correct doctrines before the attention of the people, to reiterate them perpetually, and to teach them to the young; having at the same time power to prevent contrary doctrines from being taught, advocated, or expressed. Let all possible causes of a change of mind be removed from men's apprehensions. Let them be kept ignorant, lest they should learn of some reason to think otherwise than they do. Let their passions be enlisted, so that they may regard private and unusual opinions with hatred and horror. Then, let all men who reject the established belief be terrified into silence. Let the people turn out and tar-and-feather such men, or let inquisitions be made into the manner of thinking of suspected persons, and when they are found guilty of forbidden beliefs, let them be subjected to some signal punishment. When complete agreement could not otherwise be reached, a general massacre of all who have not thought in a certain way has proved a very effective means of settling opinion in a country. If the power to do this be wanting, let a list of opinions be drawn up, to which no man of the least independence of thought can assent, and let the faithful be required to accept all these propositions, in order to segregate them as radically as possible from the influence of the rest of the world.

This method has, from the earliest times, been one of the chief means of upholding correct theological and political doctrines, and of preserving their universal or catholic character. In Rome, especially, it has been practised from the days of Numa Pompilius to those of Pius Nonus. This is the most perfect example in history; but wherever there is a priesthood—and no religion has been without one—this method has been more or less made use of. Wherever there is an aristocracy, or a guild, or any association of a class of men whose interests depend, or are supposed to depend, on certain propositions, there will be inevitably found some traces of this natural product of social feeling. Cruelties always accompany this system; and when it is consistently carried out, they become atrocities of the most horrible kind in the eyes of any rational man. Nor should this occasion surprise, for the officer of a society does not feel justified in surrendering the interests of that society for the sake of mercy, as he might his own private interests. It is natural, therefore, that sympathy and fellowship should thus produce a most ruthless power.

In judging this method of fixing belief, which may be called the method of authority, we must, in the first place, allow its immeasurable mental and moral superiority to the method of tenacity. Its success is proportionately greater; and, in fact, it has over and over again worked the most majestic results. The mere structures of stone which it has caused to be put together—in Siam, for example, in Egypt, and in Europe—have many of them a sublimity hardly more than rivaled by the greatest works of Nature. And, except the geological epochs, there are no periods of time so vast as those which are measured by some of these organized faiths. If we scrutinize the matter closely, we shall find that there has not been one of their creeds which has remained always the same; yet the change is so slow as to be imperceptible during one person's life, so that individual belief remains sensibly fixed. For the mass of mankind, then, there is perhaps no better method than this. If it is their highest impulse to be intellectual slaves, then slaves they ought to remain.

But no institution can undertake to regulate opinions upon every subject. Only the most important ones can be attended to, and on the rest men's minds must be left to the action of natural causes. This imperfection will be no source of weakness so long as men are in such a state of culture that one opinion does not influence another—that is, so long as they cannot put two and two together. But in the most priest-ridden states some individuals will be found who are raised above that condition. These men possess a wider sort of social feeling; they see that men in other countries and in other ages have held to very different doctrines from those which they themselves have been brought up to believe; and they cannot help seeing that it is the mere accident of their having been taught as they have, and of their having been surrounded with the manners and associations they have, that has caused them to believe as they do and not far differently. Nor can their candour resist the reflection that there is no reason

to rate their own views at a higher value than those of other nations and other centuries; thus giving rise to doubts in their minds.

They will further perceive that such doubts as these must exist in their minds with reference to every belief which seems to be determined by the caprice either of themselves or of those who originated the popular opinions. The willful adherence to a belief, and the arbitrary forcing of it upon others, must, therefore, both be given up. A different new method of settling opinions must be adopted, that shall not only produce an impulse to believe, but shall also decide what proposition it is which is to be believed. Let the action of natural preferences be unimpeded, then, and under their influence let men, conversing together and regarding matters in different lights, gradually develop beliefs in harmony with natural causes. This method resembles that by which conceptions of art have been brought to maturity. The most perfect example of it is to be found in the history of metaphysical philosophy. Systems of this sort have not usually rested upon any observed facts, at least not in any great degree. They have been chiefly adopted because their fundamental propositions seemed "agreeable to reason." This is an apt expression; it does not mean that which agrees with experience, but that which we find ourselves inclined to believe. Plato, for example, finds it agreeable to reason that the distances of the celestial spheres from one another should be proportional to the different lengths of strings which produce harmonious chords. Many philosophers have been led to their main conclusions by considerations like this;[4] but this is the lowest and least developed form which the method takes, for it is clear that another

---

[4]Let us see in what manner a few of the greatest philosophers have undertaken to settle opinion, and what their success has been. Descartes, who would have a man begin by doubting everything, remarks that there is one thing he will find himself unable to doubt, and that is, that he does doubt; and when he reflects that he doubts, he can no longer doubt that he exists. Then, because he is all the while doubting whether there are any such things as shape and motion, Descartes thinks he must be persuaded that shape and motion do not belong to his nature, or anything else but consciousness. This is taking it for granted that nothing in his nature lies hidden beneath the surface.

man might find Kepler's theory, that the celestial spheres are proportional to the inscribed and circumscribed spheres of the different regular solids, more agreeable to *his* reason. But the shock of opinions will soon lead men to rest on preferences of a far more universal nature. Take, for example, the doctrine that man only acts selfishly—that is, from the consideration that acting in one way will afford him more pleasure than acting in another. This rests on no fact in the world, but it has had a wide acceptance as being the only reasonable theory.

This method is far more intellectual and respectable from the point of view of reason than either of the others which we have noticed. Indeed, as long as no better method can be applied, it ought to be followed, since it is then the expression of instinct which must be the ultimate cause of belief in all cases. But its failure has been the most manifest. It makes of inquiry something similar to the development of taste; but taste, unfortunately, is always more or less a matter of fashion, and accordingly metaphysicians have never come to any fixed agreement, but the pendulum has swung backward and forward between a more material and a more spiritual philosophy, from the earliest times to the latest. And so from this, which has been called the *a priori* method, we are driven, in Lord Bacon's phrase, to a true induction. We have examined into this *a priori* method as something which promised to deliver our opinions from their accidental and capricious element. But development, while it is a process which eliminates the effect of some casual circumstances, only magnifies that of others. This method, therefore, does not differ in a very essential way from that of authority. The government may not have lifted its finger to influence my convictions; I may have been left outwardly quite free to choose, we will say, between monogamy and polygamy, and, appealing to my conscience only, I may have concluded that the latter practice is in itself licentious. But when I come to see that the chief obstacle to the spread of Christianity among a people of as high culture as the Hindoos has been a conviction of the immorality of our way of treating women, I cannot help seeing that, though govern-

ments do not interfere, sentiments in their development will be very greatly determined by accidental causes. Now, there are some people, among whom I must suppose that my reader is to be found, who, when they see that any belief of theirs is determined by any circumstance extraneous to the facts, will from that moment not merely admit in words that that belief is doubtful, but will experience a real doubt of it, so that it ceases in some degree at least to be a belief.

To satisfy our doubts, therefore, it is necessary that a method should be found by which our beliefs may be determined by nothing human, but by some external permanency—by something upon which our thinking has no effect. Some mystics imagine that they have such a method in a private inspiration from on high. But that is only a form of the method of tenacity, in which the conception of truth as something public is not yet developed. Our external permanency would not be external, in our sense, if it was restricted in its influence to one individual. It must be something which affects, or might affect, every man. And, though these affections are necessarily as various as are individual conditions, yet the method must be such that the ultimate conclusion of every man shall be the same. Such is the method of science. Its fundamental hypothesis, restated in more familiar language, is this: There are Real things, whose characters are entirely independent of our opinions about them; those Reals affect our senses according to regular laws, and, though our sensations are as different as are our relations to the objects, yet, by taking advantage of the laws of perception, we can ascertain by reasoning how things really and truly are; and any man, if he have sufficient experience and he reason enough about it, will be led to the one True conclusion. The new conception here involved is that of Reality. It may be asked how I know that there are any Reals. If this hypothesis is the sole support of my method of inquiry, my method of inquiry must not be used to support my hypothesis. The reply is this: (1) If investigation cannot be regarded as proving that there are Real things, it at least does not lead to a contrary conclusion; but the method and the conception on which it is based remain ever in harmony. No doubts of the method, therefore, necessarily arise from its practice, as is the case with all the others. (2) The feeling which gives rise to any method of fixing belief is a dissatisfaction at two repugnant propositions. But here already is a vague concession that there is some *one* thing which a proposition should represent. Nobody, therefore, can really doubt that there are Reals, for, if he did, doubt would not be a source of dissatisfaction. The hypothesis, therefore, is one which every mind admits. So that the social impulse does not cause men to doubt it. (3) Everybody uses the scientific method about a great many things, and only ceases to use it when he does not know how to apply it. (4) Experience of the method has not led us to doubt it, but, on the contrary, scientific investigation has had the most wonderful triumphs in the way of settling opinion. These afford the explanation of my not doubting the method or the hypothesis which it supposes; and not having any doubt, nor believing that anybody else whom I could influence has, it would be the merest babble for me to say more about it. If there be anybody with a living doubt upon the subject, let him consider it.

To describe the method of scientific investigation is the object of this series of papers. At present I have only room to notice some points of contrast between it and other methods of fixing belief.

This is the only one of the four methods which presents any distinction of a right and a wrong way. If I adopt the method of tenacity, and shut myself out from all influences, whatever I think necessary to doing this, is necessary according to that method. So with the method of authority: the state may try to put down heresy by means which, from a scientific point of view, seem very ill-calculated to accomplish its purposes; but the only test *on that method* is what the state thinks; so that it cannot pursue the method wrongly. So with the *a priori* method. The very essence of it is to think as one is inclined to think. All metaphysicians will be sure to do that, however they may be inclined to judge each other to be perversely wrong. The Hegelian system recognizes every natural tendency of thought as logi-

cal, although it be certain to be abolished by counter-tendencies. Hegel thinks there is a regular system in the succession of these tendencies, in consequence of which, after drifting one way and the other for a long time, opinion will at last go right. And it is true that metaphysicians do get the right ideas at last; Hegel's system of Nature represents tolerably the science of his day; and one may be sure that whatever scientific investigation shall have put out of doubt will presently receive *a priori* demonstration on the part of the metaphysicians. But with the scientific method the case is different. I may start with known and observed facts to proceed to the unknown; and yet the rules which I follow in doing so may not be such as investigation would approve. The test of whether I am truly following the method is not an immediate appeal to my feelings and purposes, but, on the contrary, itself involves the application of the method. Hence it is that bad reasoning as well as good reasoning is possible; and this fact is the foundation of the practical side of logic.

It is not to be supposed that the first three methods of settling opinion present no advantage whatever over the scientific method. On the contrary, each has some peculiar convenience of its own. The *a priori* method is distinguished for its comfortable conclusions. It is the nature of the process to adopt whatever belief we are inclined to, and there are certain flatteries to the vanity of man which we all believe by nature, until we are awakened from our pleasing dream by rough facts. The method of authority will always govern the mass of mankind; and those who wield the various forms of organized force in the state will never be convinced that dangerous reasoning ought not to be suppressed in some way. If liberty of speech is to be untrammeled from the grosser forms of constraint, then uniformity of opinion will be secured by a moral terrorism to which the respectability of society will give its thorough approval. Following the method of authority is the path of peace. Certain non-conformities are permitted; certain others (considered unsafe) are forbidden. These are different in different countries and in different ages; but, wherever you are, let it be known that you seriously hold a tabooed belief, and you may be perfectly sure of being treated with a cruelty less brutal but more refined than hunting you like a wolf. Thus, the greatest intellectual benefactors of mankind have never dared, and dare not now, to utter the whole of their thought; and thus a shade of *prima facie* doubt is cast upon every proposition which is considered essential to the security of society. Singularly enough, the persecution does not all come from without; but a man torments himself and is oftentimes most distressed at finding himself believing propositions which he has been brought up to regard with aversion. The peaceful and sympathetic man will, therefore, find it hard to resist the temptation to submit his opinions to authority. But most of all I admire the method of tenacity for its strength, simplicity, and directness. Men who pursue it are distinguished for their decision of character, which becomes very easy with such a mental rule. They do not waste time in trying to make up their minds what they want, but, fastening like lightning upon whatever alternative comes first, they hold to it to the end, whatever happens, without an instant's irresolution. This is one of the splendid qualities which generally accompany brilliant, unlasting success. It is impossible not to envy the man who can dismiss reason, although we know how it must turn out at last.

· · ·

Yes, the other methods do have their merits: a clear logical conscience does cost something—just as any virtue, just as all that we cherish, costs us dear. But we should not desire it to be otherwise. The genius of a man's logical method should be loved and reverenced as his bride, whom he has chosen from all the world. He need not condemn the others; on the contrary, he may honor them deeply, and in doing so he only honors her the more. But she is the one that he has chosen, and he knows that he was right in making that choice. And having made it, he will work and fight for her, and will not complain that there are blows to take, hoping that there may be as many and as hard to give, and will

strive to be the worthy knight and champion of her from the blaze of whose splendors he draws his inspiration and his courage.

AGAINST METHOD

Paul Feyerabend

The following essay has been written in the conviction that *anarchism,* while perhaps not the most attractive *political* philosophy, is certainly an excellent foundation for *epistemology,* and for the *philosophy of science.*

The reason is not difficult to find.

"History generally, and the history of revolutions in particular, is always richer in content, more varied, more manysided, more lively and 'subtle' than even" the best historian and the best methodologist can imagine.[1] "Accidents and conjunctures, and curious juxtapositions of events"[2] are the very substance of history, and the "complexity of human change and the unpredictable character of the ultimate consequences of any given act or decision of men"[3] its most conspicuous feature. Are we really to believe that a bunch of rather naive and simpleminded rules will be capable of explaining such a "maze of interactions"?[4] And is it not clear that a person who *participates* in a complex process of this kind will succeed only if he is a ruthless *opportunist,* and capable of quickly changing from one method to another?

This is indeed the lesson that has been drawn by intelligent and thoughtful observers. "From this

[1] V. I. Lenin, *'Left Wing' Communism, an Infantile Disorder* (Peking: Foreign Language Press, 1965), p. 100. Lenin speaks of parties and the revolutionary vanguard rather than of scientists and methodologists. The lesson is, however, the same.
[2] H. Butterfield, *The Whig Interpretation of History* (New York: Norton, 1965), p. 66.
[3] *Ibid.,* p. 21.
[4] *Ibid.,* p. 25.

[character of the historical process]," writes Lenin, continuing the passage just quoted, "follow two very important practical conclusions: first, that in order to fulfill its task, the revolutionary class [i.e., the class of those who want to change either a part of society, such as science, or society as a whole] must be able to master *all* forms and sides of social activity [it must be able to understand, and to apply not only one particular methodology, but any methodology, and any variation thereof it can imagine], without exception; second, [it] must be ready to pass from one to another in the quickest and most unexpected manner."[5] "The external conditions," writes Einstein, "which are set for [the scientist] by the facts of experience do not permit him to let himself be too much restricted in the construction of his conceptual world by the adherence to an epistemological system. He therefore must appear to the systematic epistemologist as a type of unscrupulous opportunist . . ."[6]

The difference between epistemological (political, theological) *theory* and scientific (political, religious) *practice* that emerges from these quotations is usually formulated as a difference between "certain and infallible" (or, at any rate, clear, systematic, and objective) *rules,* or *standards,* and "our fallible and uncertain faculties [which] depart from them and fall into error."[7] Science as it should be, third-world science,[8] agrees with the proscribed rules. Science as we actually find it in history is a combination of such rules and of *error.* It follows that the scientist who works in a particular historical situation must learn how to recognize er-

ror and how to live with it, always keeping in mind that he himself is liable to add fresh error at any stage of the investigation. He needs a *theory of error* in addition to the "certain and infallible" rules which define the "approach to the truth."

Now error, being an expression of the idiosyncrasies of an individual thinker, observer, even of an individual measuring instrument, *depends* on circumstances, on the particular phenomena or theories one wants to analyze, and it *develops* in highly unexpected ways. *Error is itself a historical phenomenon.* A theory of error will therefore contain rules of thumb, useful hints, heuristic suggestions rather than general laws, and it will relate these hints and these suggestions to historical episodes so that one sees in detail how some of them have led some people to success in some situations. It will develop the imagination of the student without ever providing him with cut-and-dried prescriptions and procedures. It will be more a collection of stories than a theory in the proper sense and it will contain a sizable amount of aimless gossip from which everyone may choose what fits in with his intentions. Good books on the art of recognizing and avoiding error will have much in common with good books on the art of singing, or boxing, or making love. Such books consider the great variety of character, of vocal (muscular, glandular, emotional) equipment, of personal idiosyncrasies, and they pay attention to the fact that each element of this variety may develop in most unexpected directions (a woman's voice may bloom forth after her first abortion). They contain numerous rules of thumb, useful hints, and they leave it to the reader to choose what fits his case. Clearly the reader will not be able to make the correct choice unless he has already *some* knowledge of vocal (muscular, emotional) matters and this knowledge he can acquire only by throwing himself into the process of learning and hoping for the best. In the case of singing he must start using his organs, his throat, his brain, his diaphragm, his buttocks before he really knows how to use them, and he must learn from their reactions the way of learning most appropriate to him. And this is true of all learning: choosing a certain way the student, or the "mature scientist," creates a situation as

---

[5]Lenin, *'Left Wing' Communism,* p. 100. It is interesting to see how a few substitutions can turn a political lesson into a lesson for methodology which, after all, is part of the process by means of which we move from one historical stage to another.
[6]P. A. Schilpp; ed., *Albert Einstein, Philosopher-Scientist* (Evanston, Ill.: Tudor, 1948), p. 683.
[7]D. Hume, *A Treatise of Human Nature* (Oxford: Oxford University Press, 1888), p. 180.
[8]Popper and his followers distinguish between the sociopsychological process of science where errors abound and rules are constantly broken and a "third world" where knowledge is changed in a rational manner, and without interference from "mob psychology."

yet unknown to him from which he must learn how best to approach situations of this kind. This is not as paradoxical as it sounds as long as we keep our options open and as long as we refuse to settle for a particular method, including a particular set of rules, without having examined alternatives. "Let people emancipate themselves," says Bakunin, "and they will instruct themselves of their own accord."[9] In the case of *science* the necessary tact can be developed only by *direct participation* (where "participation" means something different for different individuals) or, if such direct participation cannot be had, or seems undesirable, from a study of past episodes in the *history* of the subject. *Considering their great and difficult complexity these episodes must be approached with a novelist's love for character and for detail*, or with a gossip columnist's love for scandal and for surprising turns; they must be approached with insight into the positive function of strength as well as of weakness, of intelligence as well as of stupidity, of love for truth as well as of the will to deceive, of modesty as well as of conceit, rather than with the crude and laughably inadequate instruments of the logician. For nobody can say in abstract terms, without paying attention to idiosyncrasies of person and circumstance, what precisely it was that led to progress in the past, and nobody can say what moves will succeed in the future.

Now it is of course possible to simplify the historical medium in which a scientist works by simplifying its main actors. The history of science, after all, consists not only of facts and conclusions drawn therefrom. It consists also of ideas, interpretations of facts, problems created by a clash of interpretations, actions of scientists, and so on. On closer analysis we even find that there are no "bare facts" at all but that the facts that enter our knowledge are already viewed in a certain way and are therefore essentially ideational. This being the case the history of science will be as complex, as chaotic, as full of error, and as entertaining as the ideas it contains and these ideas in turn will be as complex, as chaotic, as full of error, and as entertaining as are the minds of those who invented them. Conversely, a little brainwashing will go a long way in making the history of science more simple, more uniform, more dull, more "objective," and more accessible to treatment by "certain and infallible" rules: a theory of errors is superfluous when we are dealing with well-trained scientists who are kept in place by an internal slave master called "professional conscience" and who have been convinced that it is good and rewarding to attain, and then to forever keep, one's "professional integrity."[10]

Scientific education as we know it today has precisely this purpose. It has the purpose of carrying out a rationalistic simplification of the process "science" by simplifying its participants. One proceeds as follows. First, a domain of research is defined. Next, the domain is separated from the remainder of history (physics, for example, is separated from metaphysics and from theology) and receives a "logic" of its own.[11] A thorough training in such a logic then conditions those working in the domain so that they may not unwittingly disturb the purity (read: the sterility) that has already been achieved. An essential part of the training is the inhibition of intuitions that might lead to a blurring of boundaries. A person's religion, for example, or his metaphysics, or his sense of humor must not have the slightest connection with his scientific activity. His imagination is restrained[12] and even his language will cease to be his own.[13]

---

[9] E. H. Carr, *Michael Bakunin* (London: Macmillan, 1937), pp. 8–9.

[10] Thus external pressure is replaced by bad conscience, and freedom remains restricted as before.

[11] "This unique prevalence of the *inner* logic of a subject over and above the outer influences is not . . . to be found at the beginning of modern science." H. Blumenberg, *Die Kopernikanische Wende* (Frankfurt: Suhrkamp, 1965), p. 8.

[12] "Nothing is more dangerous to reason than the flights of the imagination . . ." Hume, *A Treatise of Human Nature*, p. 267.

[13] An *expert* is a man or a woman who has decided to achieve excellence in a narrow field at the expense of a balanced development. He has decided to subject himself to standards which restrict him in many ways, his style of writing and the patterns of his speech included, and he is prepared to conduct most of his waking life in accordance with these standards (this being the case, it is likely that his dreams will be governed by these standards, too).

It is obvious that such an education, such a cutting up of domains and of consciousness, cannot be easily reconciled with a humanitarian attitude. It is in conflict "with the cultivation of individuality which [alone] produces, or can produce well developed human beings";[14] it "maim[s] by compression, like a Chinese lady's foot, every part of human nature which stands out prominently, and tends to make a person markedly dissimilar in outline"[15] from the ideal of rationality that happens to be fashionable with the methodologists.

Now it is precisely such an ideal that finds expression either in "certain and infallible rules" or else in *standards* which separate what is correct, or rational, or reasonable, or "objective" from what is incorrect, or irrational, or unreasonable, or "subjective." Abandoning the ideal as being unworthy of a free man means abandoning standards and relying on theories of error entirely. Only these theories, these hints, these rules of thumb must now be renamed. Without universally enforced standards of truth and rationality we can no longer speak of universal error. We can only speak of what does, or does not, seem appropriate when viewed from a particular and restricted point of view, different views, temperaments, attitudes giving rise to different judgments and different methods of approach. Such an *anarchistic epistemology*—for this is what our theories of error now turn out to be—is not only a better means for improving knowledge, or of understanding history. It is also more appropriate for a free man to use than are its rigorous and "scientific" alternatives.

We need not fear that the diminished concern for law and order in science and society that is entailed by the use of anarchistic philosophies will lead to chaos. The human nervous system is too well organized for that.[16] Of course, there may arrive an epoch when it becomes necessary to give reason a temporary advantage and when it is wise to defend *its* rules to the exclusion of everything else. I do not think we are living in such an epoch today.

> When we see that we have arrived at the utmost extent of human [understanding] we sit down contented. HUME[17]
>
> The more solid, well defined, and splendid the edifice erected by the understanding, the more restless the urge of life . . . to escape from it into freedom. [Appearing as] reason it is negative and dialectical, for it dissolves into nothing the detailed determinations of the understanding. HEGEL[18]
>
> Although science taken as whole is a nuisance, one can still learn from it. BENN[19]

• • •

The idea of a method that contains firm, unchanging, and absolutely binding principles for conducting the business of science gets into considerable difficulty when confronted with the results of historical research. We find, then, that there is not a single rule, however plausible, and however firmly grounded in epistemology, that is not violated at some time or other. It becomes evident that such violations are not accidental events, they are not the results of insufficient knowledge or of inattention which might have been avoided. On the contrary, we see that they are necessary for progress. Indeed, one of the most striking features of recent discussions in the history and philosophy of science is the realization that developments such as the Copernican Revolution, or the rise of atomism in antiquity and recently (kinetic theory; dispersion theory;

---

[14]John Stuart Mill, *On Liberty,* quoted from *The Philosophy of John Stuart Mill,* ed. Marshall Cohen (New York: Modern Library, 1961), p. 258.

[15]*Ibid.,* p. 265.

[16]Even in undetermined and ambiguous situations uniformity of action is soon achieved, and adhered to tenaciously. Cf. M. Sherif, *The Psychology of Social Norms* (New York: Harper Torchbooks, 1964).

[17]*A Treatise of Human Nature,* p. xxii. The word "reason" has been replaced by "understanding" in order to establish coherence with the terminology of the German idealists.

[18]The first part of the quotation, up to "appearing as," is taken from *Differenz des Fichte'schen und Schelling'schen Systems der Philosophie,* ed. G. Lasson (Hamburg: Felix Meiner, 1962), p. 13. The second part is from the *Wissenschaft der Logik,* vol. I (Hamburg: Felix Meiner, 1965), p. 6.

[19]Letter to Gert Micha Simon of October 11, 1949. Quoted from *Gottfried Benn, Lyrik und Prosa, Briefe und Dokuments* (Wiesbaden: Limes Verlag, 1962), p. 235.

stereochemistry; quantum theory), or the gradual emergence of the wave theory of light occurred either because some thinkers *decided* not to be bound by certain "obvious" methodological rules or because they *unwittingly broke* them.[20]

This liberal practice, I repeat, is not just a *fact* of the history of science. It is not merely a manifestation of human inconstancy and ignorance. It is reasonable *and absolutely necessary* for the growth of knowledge. More specifically, the following can be shown: considering any rule, however "fundamental," there are always circumstances when it is advisable not only to ignore the rule, but to adopt its opposite. For example, there are circumstances when it is advisable to introduce, elaborate, and defend ad hoc hypotheses, or hypotheses which contradict well-established and generally accepted experimental results, or hypotheses whose content is smaller than the content of the existing and empirically adequate alternatives, or self-inconsistent hypotheses, and so on.[21]

There are even circumstances—and they occur rather frequently—when argument loses its forward-looking aspect and becomes a hindrance to progress. Nobody wants to assert that the teaching of *small children* is exclusively a matter of argument (though argument may enter into it and should enter into it to a larger extent than is customary), and almost everyone now agrees that what looks like a result of reason—the mastery of a language, the existence of a richly articulated perceptual world, logical ability—is due partly to indoctrination, partly to a process of growth that proceeds with the force of natural law. And where arguments do seem to have an effect this must often be ascribed to their *physical repetition* rather than to their *semantic content*.[22] This much having been admitted, we must also concede the possibility of non-argumentative growth in the *adult* as well as in (the theoretical parts of) *institutions* such as science, religion, and prostitution. We certainly cannot take it for granted that what is possible for a small child—to acquire new modes of behavior on the slightest provocation, to slide into them without any noticeable effort—is beyond the reach of his elders. One should expect that catastrophic changes of the physical environment, wars, the breakdown of encompassing systems of morality, political revolutions, will transform adult reaction patterns, too, including important patterns of argumentation. This may again be an entirely natural process and rational argument may but increase the mental tension that precedes and causes the behavioral outburst.

Now, if there are events, not necessarily arguments, which cause us to adopt new standards, including new and more complex forms of argumentation, will it then not be up to the defenders of the status quo to provide, not just arguments, but also contrary causes? (Virtue without terror is ineffective, says Robespierre.) And if the old forms of argumentation turn out to be too weak a cause, must not these defenders either give up or resort to stronger and more "irrational" means? (It is very difficult, and perhaps entirely impossible, to combat

[20]For details and further literature see "Problems of Empiricism, Part II," in *The Nature and Function of Scientific Theory*, ed. R. G. Colodny (Pittsburgh: University of Pittsburgh Press, 1970).

[21]One of the few physicists to see and to understand this feature of the development of scientific knowledge was Niels Bohr: ". . . he would never try to outline any finished picture, but would patiently go through all the phases of the development of a problem, starting from some apparent paradox, and gradually leading to its elucidation. In fact, he never regarded achieved results in any other light than as starting points for further exploration. In speculating about the prospects of some line of investigation, he would dismiss the usual considerations of simplicity, elegance or even consistency with the remark that such qualities can only be properly judged *after* [my italics] the event . . ." L. Rosenfeld in S. Rozental, ed., *Niels Bohr, His Life and Work as Seen by His Friends and Colleagues* (New York: Interscience, 1967), p. 117.

[22]Commenting on his early education by his father, and especially on the explanations he received on matters of logic, J. S. Mill made the following observations: "The explanations did not make the matter at all clear to me at the time; but they were not therefore useless; they remained as a nucleus for my observations and reflections to crystallize upon; the import of his general remarks being interpreted to me, by the particular instances which came under my notice afterwards." *Autobiography* (London: Oxford University Press, 1963), p. 16. In "Problems of Empiricism, Part II" I have argued that the development of science exhibits phase differences of precisely this kind.

the effects of brainwashing by argument.) Even the most puritanical rationalist will then be forced to stop reasoning and to use, say, *propaganda* and *coercion,* not because some of his *reasons* have ceased to be valid, but because the *psychological conditions* which make them effective, and capable of influencing others, have disappeared. And what is the use of an argument that leaves people unmoved?

Of course, the problem never arises quite in this form. The teaching of standards never consists in merely putting them before the mind of the student and making them as *clear* as possible. The standards are supposed to have maximal *causal efficacy* as well. This makes it very difficult to distinguish between the *logical force* and the *material effect* of an argument. Just as a well-trained pet will obey his master no matter how great the confusion he finds himself in and no matter how urgent the need to adopt new patterns of behavior, in the very same way a well-trained rationalist will obey the mental image of *his* master, he will conform to the standards of argumentation he has learned, he will adhere to these standards no matter how great the difficulty he finds himself in, and he will be quite unable to discover that what he regards as the "voice of reason" is but a *causal aftereffect* of the training he has received. We see here very clearly how the appeal to "reason" works. At first sight this appeal seems to be to some *ideas* which *convince* a man instead of *pushing* him. But conviction cannot remain an ethereal state; it is supposed to lead to *action*. It is supposed to lead to the *appropriate* action, and it is supposed to *sustain* this action as long as necessary. What is the force that upholds such a development? It is the causal efficacy of the standards to which appeal was made and this causal efficacy in turn is but an effect of training, as we have seen. It follows that appeal to argument either has no content at all, and can be made to agree with any procedure, or else will often have a conservative function: it will set limits to what is about to become a natural way of behavior. In the latter case, however, the appeal is nothing but a concealed *political maneuver.* This becomes very clear when a rationalist wants to restore an earlier point of view. Basing his argument on natural habits of reasoning which either have become extinct or have no point of attack in the new situation, such a champion of "rationality" must first restore the earlier material and psychological conditions. This, however, involves him in "a struggle of interests and forces, not of argument."[23]

That interests, forces, propaganda, brainwashing techniques play a much greater role in the growth of our knowledge and, a fortiori, of science than is commonly believed can also be seen from an analysis of the *relation between idea and action.* One often takes it for granted that a clear and distinct understanding of new ideas precedes and should precede any formulation and any institutional expression of them. (An investigation starts with a problem, says Popper.) *First,* we have an idea, or a problem; *then* we act, i.e., either speak, or build, or destroy. This is certainly not the way in which small children develop. They use words, they combine them, they play with them until they grasp a meaning that so far has been beyond their reach. And the initial playful activity is an essential presupposition of the final act of understanding. There is no reason why this mechanism should cease to function in the adult. On the contrary, we must expect, for example, that the *idea* of liberty could be made clear only by means of the very same actions which were supposed to *create* liberty. Creation of a *thing,* and creation plus full understanding of a *correct idea* of the thing, *very often are parts of one and the same indivisible process* and they cannot be separated without bringing the process to a standstill. The process itself is not guided by a well-defined program; it cannot be guided by such a program for it contains the conditions of the realization of programs. It is rather guided by a vague urge, by a "passion" (Kierkegaard). The passion gives rise to specific be-

---

[23]Leon Trotsky, *The Revolution Betrayed,* trans. M. Eastman (Garden City, N.Y.: Doubleday, 1937), pp. 86–87.

havior which in turn creates the circumstances and the ideas necessary for analyzing and explaining the whole development, for making it "rational."

The development of the Copernican point of view from Galileo up to the twentieth century is a perfect example of the situation we want to describe. We start with a strong belief that runs counter to contemporary reason. The belief spreads and finds support from other beliefs which are equally unreasonable, if not more so (law of inertia; telescope). Research now gets deflected in new directions, new kinds of instruments are built, "evidence" is related to theories in new ways until there arises a new ideology that is rich enough to provide independent arguments for any particular part of it and mobile enough to find such arguments whenever they seem to be required. *Today* we can say that Galileo was on the right track, for his persistent pursuit of what once seemed to be a silly cosmology created the material needed for the defense of this cosmology against those of us who accept a view only if it is told in a certain way and who trust it only if it contains certain magical phrases, called "observational reports."[24] And this is not an exception—it is the normal case: theories become clear and "reasonable" only *after* incoherent parts of them have been used for a long time. Such unreasonable, nonsensical, unmethodical foreplay thus turns out to be an unavoidable precondition of clarity and of empirical success.[25]

Trying to describe developments of this kind in a general way, we are of course obliged to appeal to the existing forms of speech which do not take them into account and which must be distorted, misused, and beaten into new patterns in order to fit unforeseen situations (without a constant misuse of language there cannot be any discovery and any progress). "Moreover, since the traditional categories are the gospel of everyday thinking (including ordinary scientific thinking) and of everyday practice, [such an attempt at understanding] in effect presents rules and forms of false thinking and action—false, that is, from the standpoint of [scientific] commonsense."[26] This is how *dialectical thinking* arises as a form of thought that "dissolves into nothing the detailed determinations of the understanding."[27]

It is clear, then, that the idea of a fixed method, or of a fixed (theory of) rationality, arises from too naive a view of man and of his social surroundings. To those who look at the rich material provided by history, and who are not intent on impoverishing it in order to please their lower instincts, their craving for intellectual security as it is provided, for example, by clarity and precision, to such people it will seem that there is only one principle that can be defended under all circumstances, and in *all* stages of human developments. It is the principle: *anything goes.*[28]

---

[24]The phrase "magical" is quite appropriate, for the inclusion of well-formed observational reports was demanded in books on magic, down to Agrippa's *De occulta philosophia.*

[25]Our understanding of ideas and concepts, says Hegel (*Gymnasialreden*; quoted from K. Loewith and J. Riedel, eds., *Hegel, Studienausgabe*, vol. I, Frankfurt: Fischer Bücherei, 1968, p. 54), starts with "an uncomprehended knowledge of them . . ."

It is also interesting to note to what extent Kierkegaard's ideas about the role of faith, passion, subjectivity apply to our scientific life (provided, of course, we are interested in fundamental discoveries, and not just in the preservation of the status quo, in methodology, and elsewhere). Cf. *Concluding Unscientific Postscript*, trans. David F. Swensen and Walter Lowrie (Princeton, N.J.: Princeton University Press, 1941), especially chapter II: "Truth as Subjectivity."

[26]H. Marcuse, *Reason and Revolution* (London: Oxford University Press, 1941), p. 130. The quotation is about Hegel's logic.

[27]Cf. note 18.

[28]"It would be absurd to formulate a recipe or general rule . . . to serve all cases. One must use one's own brains and be able to find one's bearings in each separate case." Lenin, *'Left Wing' Communism*, p. 64.

The reader should remember that despite all my praise for Marxism and its various proponents I am defending its *anarchistic* elements only and that I am defending those elements only insofar as they can be used for a criticism of epistemological and moral rules.

IS SCIENCE MULTICULTURAL?

Sandra Harding

I. CHALLENGES AND RESOURCES

Are the natural sciences multicultural? Could they and should they be? Such questions initially may seem ignorant or, at least odd, since it is exactly the lack of cultural fingerprints that conventionally is held responsible for the great successes of the sciences. The sciences " work"—they are universally valid, it is said, because they transcend culture. They can tell us how nature really functions instead of only how the British, Native Americans, or Chinese fear or want it to work.

There are good reasons to wonder if one should regard this universal science claim as ending the matter, however. Multicultural perspectives are providing more comprehensive and less distorted understandings of history, literature, arts, and social sciences. They are beginning to reshape public consciousness as they are disseminated through television specials, new elementary and high school history and literature textbooks and, indeed, daily news reports of perspectives on the West (or should one say the "North"?) that conflict with the conventional beliefs that many Westerners now understand to be Eurocentric. Do the challenges raised by multicultural perspectives in other fields have no consequences for the natural sciences?

We can identify three central questions for anyone who wishes to explore this issue. First, to what extent does modern science have origins in non-European cultures? Second, have there been and could there be other sciences, culturally distinctive ones, that also "work" and thus are universal in this sense? Third, in what ways is modern science culturally European or European-American? Fortunately, pursuit of these questions has been made easier by the appearance in English recently of a small but rich set of writings on such topics. These "postcolonial science studies," as I shall refer to them, are authored by scientists and engineers, a few anthropologists, and historians of science. These authors are of European and Third-World descent; the latter live in the Third and First Worlds.

• • •

Now is none too soon to note that the terms of this discussion are and must be controversial, for who gets to name natural and social realities gets to control how they will be organized. Moreover, it is not just language at issue but also a "discourse"—a conceptual framework with its logic linking my words in ways already familiar to readers—that is adequate to the project of this essay. For example, for conventional science theorists, it is controversial to use the term "science" to refer to sciences' social institutions, technologies and applications, metaphors, language, and social meanings. They insist on restricting the term's reference to sciences' abstract cognitive core—the laws of nature—and/or the legendary scientific method, thereby excluding the other parts of sciences' practices and culture which many contemporary science theorists insist also are fundamental constituents of sciences.

Moreover, the terms of multicultural discourse are and must be controversial. Do my references to "Western" replicate dualistic, orientalist thinking that has been so widely criticized? Isn't it precisely from the borderlands between "Western" and "non-Western" that this paper and the thought of its cited authors arises?[1] How "Western" is Western science anyway (a topic to be pursued below)? Moreover, which of the diverse peoples currently living in Europe and North America get to count as Western? And is Japan "non-Western" and "Third World"? Additionally, Third-World cultures are immensely diverse, and they are internally heterogeneous by class, gender, ethnicity, religion, politics, and other features. Doesn't ignoring or marginalizing these differences disseminate characteristic Eurocentric tendencies to homogenize and refuse to think care-

---

[1]The term "borderlands" is from Gloria Anzaldúa's *Borderlands/La Frontera: The New Mestiza* (San Francisco: Spinsters/Aunt Lute Book Company: 1987). The notion appears in the writing of many other "borderlands" thinkers.

fully about peoples that Westerners have constructed as their Others? Furthermore, doesn't "neocolonial" designate better than "postcolonial" the present relations between the West and its former colonies? And are African-Americans and indigenous Americans appropriately thought of as "colonized"? What are the politics of continuing to refer to the First and Third Worlds when this contrast is the product of the Eurocentric Cold War? Finally, should the knowledge traditions of non-Western cultures be referred to as "sciences" rather than only as "ethnosciences" (a topic I take up below)?

We cannot settle such questions easily. In some cases, it is the familiar languages that are at issue in the questions raised in this essay. In other cases, less controversial terms have not yet been found or have not yet reached general circulation. Moreover, changing language sometimes advances the growth of knowledge but, in other cases, it simply substitutes an acceptable veneer under which ignorance and exploitative politics can continue to flourish. Discourses, conceptual schemes, paradigms, and epistemes are at issue, not just words. I hope readers can hear beyond these inadequate languages to the issues that can help us develop less problematic thinking, speech, and actions. I shall primarily use the terms the postcolonial authors use, though their own usages are diverse and sometimes conflicting.

One term worth clarifying, however, is "Eurocentrism." Here I refer to a cluster of assumptions, central among which are that peoples of European descent, their institutions, practices and conceptual schemes, express the unique heights of human development, and that Europeans and their civilization are fundamentally self-generated, owing little or nothing to the institutions, practices, conceptual schemes, or peoples of other parts of the world.[2] If Western sciences and science studies turn out to be Eurocentric, we are likely to discover possibilities of multiculturalism in the natural sciences that have been hidden from view.

One last issue: who is the "we" of this paper? In relation to its topics, I am positioned as a woman of European descent, and economically privileged. But the "we" I invoke is meant to include all people, regardless of their ethnicity, "race," nationality, class, gender, or other significant features of their location in local and global social relations, who are concerned to rethink critically those social relations past and present, the role of sciences in them, and who wish to bring about more effective links between scientific projects and those of advancing democratic social relations.

The universal science view—that modern sciences are uniquely successful exactly because they have eliminated cultural fingerprints from their results of research—contains some important insights, but it also incorporates some assumptions that are probably false but, at any rate, have not been supported by evidence. For example, it assumes that no other sciences could generate the laws of gravity or antibiotics; that modern science also does not "work" for producing human and natural disasters; that what has worked best to advance the West will and should work best to advance other societies; that modern sciences are the best ones to discover all of the laws of nature; and that the kinds of projects for which modern sciences have worked best in the past are the ones at which any possible sciences, past, present, and future, should want to succeed.[3] In spite of these problematic assumptions, the conventional view contains important insights. Such insights are more reasonably explained, however, in ways that give up these problematic assumptions and locate

---

[2]See, e.g., Samir Amin, *Eurocentrism* (New York: Monthly Review Press, 1989).

[3]Scientists usually claim that all they mean by the statement that "science works" is that it makes accurate predictions. However, in the next breath they usually defend the extraordinarily high US investment in scientific establishments on what I take to be the only grounds anyone could find reasonable in a society professing a commitment to democratic social relations; namely, that the results of science improve social life. Thus "science works" in this enlarged sense which is conflated with the more technical sense of the phrase. As we shall see below, the success of science's empirical predictions depends in part on social relations; there are good historical reasons for the conflation.

modern sciences on the more accurate historical and geographical maps produced by the postcolonial accounts.[4]

Let us turn to the three questions that will help to determine the degree to which science, or the sciences, may be multicultural.

II. DOES MODERN SCIENCE HAVE NON-WESTERN ORIGINS?

Least controversial is to acknowledge that modern sciences have borrowed from other cultures. Most people are aware of at least a couple of such examples. However, the borrowings have been far more extensive and important for the development of modern sciences than the conventional histories reveal. Modern sciences have been enriched by contributions not only from the so-called "complex" cultures of China, India, and others in east-Asian and Islamic societies, but also from the so-called "simpler" ones of Africa, pre-Columbian Americas, and others that interacted with the expansion of European cultures.

To list just a few examples, Egyptian mystical philosophies and premodern European alchemical traditions were far more useful to the development of sciences in Europe than is suggested by the conventional view that these are only irrational and marginally valuable elements of immature Western sciences.[5] The Greek legacy of scientific and mathematical thought was not only fortuitously preserved but also developed in Islamic culture, to be claimed by the sciences of the European Renaissance.[6] Furthermore, the identification of Greek culture as European is questionable on several counts. For one thing, the idea of Europe and the social relations such an idea made possible came into existence centuries later. Some would date the emergence of "Europe" to Charlemagne's achievements, others to fifteenth-century events. Another point here is that through the spread of Islam, diverse cultures of Africa and Asia can also claim Greek culture as their legacy.[7]

Some knowledge traditions that were appropriated and fully integrated into modern sciences are not acknowledged at all. Thus the principles of pre-Columbian agriculture, that provided potatoes for almost every European ecological niche and thereby had a powerful effect on the nutrition and subsequent history of Europe, was subsumed into European science.[8] Mathematical achievements from India and Arabic cultures provide other examples. The magnetic needle, rudder, gunpowder, and many other technologies useful to Europeans and the advancement of their sciences (were these not part of scientific instrumentation?) were borrowed from China. Knowledge of local geographies, geologies, animals, plants, classification schemes, medicines, pharmacologies, agriculture, navigational techniques, and local cultures that formed significant parts of European sciences' picture of

---

[4]I am tempted to keep inserting "Western" into "modern science"—modern *Western* science—to avoid the standard Eurocentric assumption that non-Western traditions, including their scientific practices and cultures, are static; that only Western sciences are dynamic and thus have developed since the fifteenth century. However, that locution has other problems; it emphasizes the dualistic "West versus the rest" framework, and ignores the non-Western components of modern science.

[5]Frances Yates, *Giordano Bruno and the Hermetic Tradition* (New York: Vintage, 1969).

[6]Donald F. Lach, *Asia in the Making of Europe,* Vol. 2 (Chicago: University of Chicago Press, 1977); Seyyed Hossein Nasr, "Islamic Science, Western Science: Common Heritage, Diverse Destinies," in *The Revenge of Athena,* ed. Z. Sardar, pp. 239–48.

[7]See Martin Bernal, *Black Athena: The Afroasiatic Roots of Classical Civilization,* Vol. I (New Brunswick: Rutgers University Press, 1987); Cheikh Anta Diop, *The African Origin of Civilization: Myth or Reality?* tr. M. Cook (Westport, CT: L. Hill, 1974); Lacinay Keita, "African Philosophical Systems: A Rational Reconstruction," *Philosophical Forum,* 9, 2–3 (1977–78), pp. 169–89; Lach, *Asia in the Making of Europe;* I. A. Sabra, "The Scientific Enterprise," in *The World of Islam,* ed. B. Lewis (London: Thames and Hudson, 1976); E. Frances White, "Civilization Denied: Questions on *Black Athena*," *Radical America,* 21, 5 (1987), pp. 38–40.

[8]Jack Weatherford, *Indian Givers: What the Native Americans Gave to the World* (New York: Crown, 1988).

nature were provided in part by the knowledge traditions of non-Europeans. ("We took on board a native of the region, and dropped him off six weeks further up the coast," report the voyagers' accounts.) Summarizing the consequences for modern sciences of British imperialism in India, one recent account points out that in effect "India was added as a laboratory to the edifice of modern science."[9] We could say the same for all of the lands to which the "voyages of discovery" and later colonization projects took the Europeans.[10]

Thus modern science already is multicultural, at least in the sense that elements of the knowledge traditions of many different non-European cultures have been incorporated into it. There is nothing unusual about such scientific borrowing. It is evident in the ordinary, everyday borrowing that occurs when scientists revive models, metaphors, procedures, technologies, or other ideas from older European scientific traditions, when they borrow such elements from the culture outside their laboratories and field stations, or from other contemporary sciences.[11] After all, a major point of professional conferences and international exchange programs, not to mention "keeping up with the literature," is to permit everyone to borrow everyone else's achievements. As we shall see shortly, without such possibilities, sciences wither and lose their creativity. What is at issue here is only the Eurocentric failure to acknowledge the origins and importance to "real science" of these borrowings from non-European cultures, and also, thereby, to trivialize the achievements of their scientific traditions.

To give up this piece of Eurocentrism does not challenge the obvious accomplishments of modern sciences. Every thinking person should be able to accept the claim that modern science is multicultural in this sense. Of course it is one thing to accept a claim that conflicts with one's own, and quite another to use it to transform one's own thinking. To do the latter would require that historians of science and the rest of us locate our accounts on a global civilizational map rather than only on the Eurocentric map of Europe that we all learned.

There are implications here also for philosophies and social studies of science. For example, the standard contrasts between the objectivity, rationality, and progressiveness of modern scientific thought versus the only locally valid, irrational, and backwards or primitive thought of other cultures begins to seem less explanatorily useful and, indeed, accurate after the postcolonial accounts. Whether overtly stated or only discretely assumed, these contrasts damage our ability not only to appreciate the strengths of other scientific traditions but also to grasp the real strengths and limitations of modern sciences.

These accounts of multicultural origins do not directly challenge conventional beliefs that modern sciences uniquely deserve to be designated sciences, however, or that they are universally valid because their cognitive/technical core transcends culture. Other arguments in the postcolonial accounts do.

III. HAVE THERE BEEN OR COULD THERE BE OTHER, DISTINCTIVE SCIENCES THAT "WORK"?

Do any other knowledge traditions deserve to be called sciences? The conventional view is that only modern sciences are entitled to this designation. In such accounts, science is treated as a cultural emergent in early modern Europe. While a shift in social conditions may have made it possible in the first place, what emerged was a form of knowledge-seeking that is fundamentally self-generating; its "internal logic" is responsible for its great successes. This "logic of scientific research" has been characterized in various

---

[9] R. K. Kochhar, "Science in British India," Parts I and II, *Current Science* (India), 63, 11, p. 694. Cf. also 64, 1 (1992–93), pp. 55–62.

[10] And, as V. Y. Mudimbe pointed out to me, of Europe itself, for European sciences also constituted European lands, cities, and peoples as their laboratories. Consider, for example, the way women, the poor, children, the sick, the mad, rural and urban populations, and workers have been continuously studied by natural and social sciences.

[11] Susantha Goonatilake makes this point in "The Voyages of Discovery and the Loss and Re-Discovery of 'Other's' Knowledge," *Impact of Science on Society,* 167 (1993), pp. 241–64.

ways—as inductivism, crucial experiments, the hypothetico-deductive method, a cycle of normal science–revolution–normal science. Whatever the logic attributed to scientific research, it is conceptualized as "inside" science and not "outside" it "in society." Though Chinese or African astronomers may have made discoveries before Europeans, this is not sufficient to indicate that the former were really doing what is reasonably regarded as "science."[12] Thus while science is said to need a supportive social climate to flourish, the particular form of that climate is claimed to leave no distinctive cultural fingerprints on science's results of research.

Is this a reasonable position? Is the content of the successes of modern sciences due entirely to the sciences' "internal" features? For one, not all of the successes attributed to Western sciences are unique to it. In many cases,

> what has been ascribed to the European tradition has been shown on closer examination to have been done elsewhere by others earlier. (Thus Harvey was not the first to discover the circulation of blood, but an Arabic scientist was; Paracelsus did not introduce the fourth element "salt" and start the march towards modern chemistry, but a twelfth-century alchemist from Kerala did so teaching in Saudi Arabia.)[13]

Many other cultures made sophisticated astronomical observations which were repeated centuries later in Europe. For example, many of the observations that Galileo's telescope made possible were known to the Dogon peoples of West Africa more

than 1,500 years earlier. Either they had invented some sort of telescope, or they had extraordinary eyesight.[14] Many mathematical achievements of Indians and other Asian peoples were adopted or invented in Europe much later. Indeed, it is as revealing to examine the ideas European sciences *did not* borrow from the knowledge traditions they encountered as it is to examine what they did borrow. Among the notions "unborrowed" are the ability to deal with very large numbers (such as 10^{-53}), the zero as a separate number with its own arithmetical logic, and irrational and negative numbers.[15] Needham points out that "between the first century B.C. and fifteenth century A.D. Chinese civilization was much more efficient than the occidental in applying human natural knowledge to practical human needs . . . in many ways this was much more congruent with modern science than was the world outlook of Christendom."[16] Thus other knowledge traditions "worked" at projects Western sciences could not accomplish until much later. If the achievements of modern science should be attributed to its "internal logic," then evidently this logic is not unique to it.

This brings us to a second point. Nobody has discovered an eleventh commandment handed down from the heavens specifying what may and may not be counted as a science. Obviously the project of drawing a line between science and nonscience is undertaken because it emphasizes a contrast thought to be important. Belief in the reality of this demarcation, as in the reality of the science versus pseudoscience duality, is necessary to preserve the mystique of the uniqueness and purity of the West's knowledge-seeking. Thus the sciences, as well as the philosophies that are focused on describing and explaining that kind of rationality so highly valued in the modern West, have been partners with an-

---

[12]For one thing, Westerners note that Chinese or African astronomy is done within culturally local projects of a sort devalued by scientific rationality, such as (in some cases) astrology, or culturally local meanings of the heavens or other natural phenomena. So, whatever their accuracy, such astronomical discoveries could not be admitted as "real science" without permitting the possibility of assigning such a status also to astrology or Confucian religious beliefs. Alternatively, one could say that any but only those discoveries of other cultures that are duplicated by Western sciences count as scientific; this has the paradoxical consequence that as Western sciences develop, other cultures also (retroactively!) get more scientific. Nancy Brickhouse's questions helped me to clarify this point.

[13]Goonatilake, "A Project for Our Time," in *The Revenge of Athens,* ed. Z. Sardar, p. 226.

[14]See the section on astronomy in Ivan Van Sertima, *Blacks in Science* (New Brunswick: Transaction Press, 1986).

[15]Goonatilake, "The Voyages of Discovery," p. 256.

[16]Joseph Needham, *The Grand Titration: Science and Society in East and West* (Toronto: University of Toronto Press, 1969), p. 55–6.

thropology in maintaining a whole series of Eurocentric contrasts, whether or not individual scientists, philosophers, or anthropologists so intended. The self-image of the West depends on contrasts not only between the rational and irrational, but also between civilization and the savage or primitive, the advanced or progressive and the backwards, dynamic and static societies, developed and undeveloped, the historical and the natural, the rational and the irrational, and other contrasts through which the European Self has constructed its Other, and thereby justified its exploitative treatment of various peoples.[17] My point here is that even though there clearly are obvious and large differences between modern sciences and the traditions of seeking systematic knowledge of the natural world to be found in other cultures, it is useful to think of them all as sciences to gain a more objective understanding of the causes of Western successes, the achievements of other sciences, and possible directions for future local and global sciences.[18]

One cannot avoid noticing, moreover, that European scholars disagree on the exact distinctive features responsible for the success of European sciences. It is instructive to look at four accounts of Western scientific uniqueness made by distinguished and otherwise progressive Western analysts—ones whose work has in important ways challenged conventional Eurocentric assumptions. Anthropologist Robin Horton, who has shown how African traditional thought is surprisingly similar to Western scientific thought, attributes the residual crucial differences to the fact that modern scientific thought takes a critical stance toward tradition and is aided in this project by its rejection of magical

relations between language and the world; it holds that we can manipulate language without changing the world.[19] However, as philosopher J. E. Wiredu points out, Horton undervalues the extent of noncritical and dogmatic assumptions in modern Western scientific thought. After all, "classical" British empiricism is "traditional thought" for Western scientific communities and those who value scientific rationality; the once-radical claims of Locke and Hume have become uncontroversial assumptions for us. An anthropologist from another culture might refer to them as our "folk beliefs." So how accurate is it to claim that a critical approach to tradition is responsible for the successes of modern sciences? Moreover, if science is modern in its rejection of magical relations between language and the world, scientists surely aren't, Wiredu continues, since many also hold religious beliefs that invest in just such magical relations.[20] Many commentators have noted that sacred—dare one say "magical"—faith in the accuracy and progressiveness of modern science characteristic of many scientists and the "educated classes" more generally.

Historian Thomas Kuhn would agree with Wiredu's assessment that Western sciences are in significant respects uncritical of conventional assumptions; indeed, he argues that they are dogmatic in rejecting a thoroughgoing critical attitude. However, he has explained that this scientific dogmatism is not an obstacle to scientific progress but, instead, a crucial element in its success. A field becomes a science only when it no longer questions a founding set of assumptions within which it can then get on with the business of designing research projects to resolve the puzzles that such assumptions have brought into focus. He attributes the unique successes of modern

---

[17]See, e.g., Susan Bordo, *The Flight to Objectivity* (Albany: State University of New York Press, 1987); Genevieve Lloyd, *The Man of Reason* (Minneapolis: University of Minnesota Press, 1984); Tzvetan Todorov, *The Conquest of America: The Question of the Other,* tr. Richard Howard (New York: Harper and Row, 1984).

[18]See Needham's discussion of seven conceptual errors in standard Western thought about "universal science" that lead to erroneous devaluations of the scientific achievements of non-European sciences in *The Grand Titration.*

[19]Robin Horton, "African Traditional Thought and Western Science," parts 1 and 2, *Africa,* 37 (1967), pp. 50–71, 155–87.

[20]J. E. Wiredu, "How Not to Compare African Thought with Western Thought," in *African Philosophy,* ed. Richard Wright, 3rd ed. (Lanham, MD; University Press of America, 1984), pp. 149–62.

sciences to the distinctive (progressive?) organization of Western scientific communities:

> only the civilizations that descended from Hellenic
> Greece have possessed more than the most rudimen-
> tary science. The bulk of scientific knowledge is a
> product of Europe in the last four centuries. No other
> place and time has supported the very special com-
> munities from which scientific productivity comes.[21]

Though one might think that a social community is
not "internal" to the logic of science, Kuhn insists
that in an important sense it is; the very special scientific communities are ones trained to follow modern science's success-producing internal logic of
paradigm creation, puzzle-solving with anomaly
tolerance, paradigm breakdown, and then, eventually, another paradigm shift. Kuhn directed attention to the importance of the distinctive social
organization of modern scientific communities.
However, one can also see that Kuhn's problematic
here—his concern to identify a different, distinctive
cause of modern science's successes—is inseparable in his thought from the widespread Eurocentric
assumptions he articulates about the origins and
virtues of European civilization.

Historian Joseph Needham refers to Chinese
knowledge traditions as sciences when comparing
them to those of the modern West. He would contest Kuhn's characterization of non-European sciences as primitive and the West's as uniquely
descended from the Greek, and proposes yet another kind of cause of the success of modern European sciences.

> When we say that modern science developed only in
> Western Europe at the time of Galileo in the late Re-
> naissance, we mean surely that there and then alone
> there developed the fundamental bases of the structure
> of the natural sciences as we have them today, namely
> the application of mathematical hypotheses to Nature,
> the full understanding and use of the experimental
> method, the distinction between primary and second-
> ary qualities, the geometrization of space, and the ac-

ceptance of the mechanical model of reality. Hypotheses of primitive or medieval type distinguish
themselves quite clearly from those of modern type.[22]

For Needham, it is not the attitudes on which Horton focuses, or the organization of scientific communities that appears so important to Kuhn, but a
specific set of assumptions about the nature of reality and appropriate methods of research.

Finally, sociologist Edgar Zilsel, asking why
modern science emerged only in Renaissance Europe rather than in China or some other "high culture," claims that the emergence of a new social
class that, in contrast to the classes of aristocratic or
slave societies, was permitted to combine a trained
intellect with willingness to do manual labor, allowed the invention of experimental method. Only
in early modern Europe where there was an absence
of slavery and challenges to aristocracy was there a
progressive culture, he implies, that gave individuals reasons to want to obtain intellectual and manual training.[23]

No doubt one could find additional features of
the cultures and practices of modern sciences to
which other historians would attribute their successes. These different purported causes are probably not entirely independent of each other, and
some readers will find one more plausible than another of such proposals. However, my point is that
there is no general agreement even among the most
distinguished and progressive Western science theorists about the distinctive causes of modern science, and that the search for such an explanation
and the kinds of accounts on which such scholars
settle usually remain tied to Eurocentric dualisms.

A third source of skepticism about conventional
claims for the unique efficacy of Western sciences
arises from an oft-repeated argument in the postcolonial accounts. European sciences advanced because they focused on describing and explaining
those aspects of nature's regularities that permitted

---

[21]Thomas S. Kuhn, *The Structure of Scientific Revolutions,* 2nd
ed. (Chicago: University of Chicago Press, 1970), p. 167.

[22]Needham, *The Grand Titration,* p. 14–15.
[23]Edgar Zilsel, "The Sociological Roots of Science," *American
Journal of Sociology,* 47 (1942), pp. 544–62.

the upper classes of Europeans to multiply and thrive, especially through the prospering of their military, imperial, and otherwise expansionist projects. Interestingly, evidence for this claim now can be gathered easily from many of the museum exhibits and scholarly publications associated with the 1992 quincennial of the Columbian encounter. They drew attention, intentionally or not, to the numerous ways European expansion in the Americas advanced European sciences. A detailed account of how British colonialism in India advanced European sciences is provided by Kochhar. The British needed better navigation, so they built observatories, funded astronomers, and kept systematic records of their voyages. The first European sciences to be established in India were, not surprisingly, geography and botany.[24] Nor is the intimate relation between scientific advance in the West and expansionist efforts only a matter of the distant past (or only of expansion into foreign lands, as noted earlier). By the end of World War II, the development of US physics had been almost entirely handed over to the direction of US militarism and nationalism, as historian Paul Forman has shown in detail.[25]

Thus European expansionism has changed the "topography" of global scientific knowledge, causing the advance of European sciences and the decline or underdevelopment of scientific traditions of other cultures:

> The topography of the world of knowledge before the last few centuries could be delineated as several hills of knowledge roughly corresponding to the regional

civilizations of, say, West Asia, South Asia, East Asia and Europe. The last few centuries have seen the levelling of the other hills and from their debris the erection of a single one with its base in Europe.[26]

These arguments begin to challenge the idea that the causes of modern sciences' achievements are to be located entirely in their purported inherently transcultural character. It turns out that what makes them "work," and to appear uniquely to do so, is at least partly a consequence of their focus on the kinds of projects that European expansion could advance and benefit from while simultaneously clearing the field of potentially rival scientific traditions. To make such claims is not to deny that Western sciences can claim many great and, so far, unique scientific achievements. Instead, it is to argue, contrary to conventional views, that scientific "truths," no less than false beliefs, are caused by social relations as well as by nature's regularities and the operations of reason.[27]

But could there be other, culturally distinctive sciences that also "work"? The postcolonial accounts have shown the rich and sophisticated scientific traditions of Asia, Islam, and "simpler" societies of the past. But what about the future? We return to this issue shortly.

IV. IS MODERN SCIENCE CULTURALLY "WESTERN"?

The very accounts describing the histories of other scientific traditions also show the distinctive cultural features of modern sciences. These features are precisely, for better and worse, the features that are responsible for their successes, as the discussions above began to reveal. That is, the distinctive social/political history of the development of modern sciences is not external to their content; it appears in the image of nature's regularities and underlying

---

[24]Kochhar, "Science in British India"; Alfred Crosby, *Ecological Imperialism: The Biological Expansion of Europe* (Cambridge: Cambridge University Press, 1987); V. V. Krishna, "The Colonial 'Model' and the Emergence of National Science in India: 1876–1920," in *Science and Empires,* Petitjean et al., pp. 57–72; Deepak Kumar, "Problems in Science Administration: A Study of the Scientific Surveys in British India 1757–1900," in *Science and Empires,* Petitjean et al., pp. 69–80.

[25]Paul Forman, "Behind Quantum Electronics: National Security as Bases for Physical Research in the US, 1940–1960," *Historical Studies in Physical and Biological Sciences,* 18 (1987) pp. 149–229.

[26]Susantha Goonatilake, "A Project for Our Times," p. 235–6. (Should not African and indigenous American civilizations also count as regional ones containing scientific traditions?)

[27]The "Strong Programme" in the sociology of knowledge has developed this analysis. See, e.g., David Bloor, *Knowledge and Social Imagery* (London: Routledge and Kegan Paul, 1977).

causal tendencies they produce, including the "laws of nature" that form their cognitive/technical core. Here, I can identify only five of the distinctively "Western" features persistently noted in the postcolonial literature.

First, as indicated above, which aspects of nature modern sciences describe and explain, and how they are described and explained, have been selected, in part, by the conscious purposes and unconscious interests of European expansion. Of course, these are not the only purposes and interests shaping these sciences—androcentric, religious, local bourgeois, and others also have had powerful effects as many recent accounts have shown—but they are significant. The "problems" that count as scientific are those for which expansionist Europe needed solutions; conversely those aspects of nature about which the beneficiaries of expansionism have not needed or wanted to know have remained uncharted. Thus, the culturally distinctive patterns of systematic knowledge and systematic ignorance in modern sciences' picture of nature's regularities and their underlying causal tendencies can be detected from the perspective of cultures with different preoccupations. For example, modern sciences answered questions about how to: improve European land and sea travel: mine ores; identify the economically useful minerals, plants, and animals of other parts of the world; manufacture and farm for the benefit of Europeans living in Europe, the Americas, Africa, and India; improve their health and occasionally that of the workers who produced profit for them; protect settlers in the colonies from settlers of other nationalities; gain access to the labor of the indigenous residents; and do all this to benefit only local European citizens—the Spanish versus the Portuguese, French, or British. These sciences have not been concerned to explain how the consequences of interventions in nature for the benefit of Europeans of the advantaged gender, classes, and ethnicities would change the natural resources available to the majority of the world's peoples, or what the economic, social, political, and ecological costs to less-advantaged groups in and outside Europe would be of the interventions in nature and so-

cial relations that sciences' experimental methods "foresaw" and to which it directed policymakers. Sciences with other purposes—explaining how to shift from unrenewable to renewable natural resources, to maintain a healthy but less environmentally destructive standard of living in the overdeveloped societies, to clean up toxic wastes, to benefit women in every culture, etc.—could generate other, perhaps sometimes conflicting, descriptions and explanations of nature's regularities and underlying causal tendencies.

Second, early modern sciences' conception of nature was distinctively Western or, at least, alien to many other cultures. For the resident of medieval Europe, nature was enchanted; the "disenchantment of nature" was a crucial element in the shift from the medieval to the modern mentality, from feudalism to capitalism, from Ptolemaic to Galilean astronomy, and from Aristotelian to Newtonian physics.[28] Modern science related to a worldly power in nature, not to power that lay outside the material universe. To gain power over nature for modern man would violate no moral or religious principles.

Moreover, the Western conception of laws of nature drew on Judeo–Christian religious beliefs and the increasing familiarity in early modern Europe with centralized royal authority, with royal absolutism. Needham points out that this Western idea that the universe was a "great empire, ruled by a divine Logos"[29] was never comprehensible at any time in the long history of Chinese science since a common thread in the diverse Chinese traditions was that nature was self-governed, a web of relationships without a weaver, with which humans interfered at their own peril.

> Universal harmony comes about not by the celestial fist of some King of Kings, but by the spontaneous co-operation of all beings in the universe brought about

---

[28]See, e.g., Morris Berman, *The Reenchantment of the World* (Ithaca: Cornell University Press, 1981); Bordo, *The Flight to Objectivity;* Carolyn Merchant, *The Death of Nature: Women, Ecology and the Scientific Revolution* (New York: Harper and Row, 1980); Nasr, "Islamic Science, Western Science."
[29]Needham, *The Grand Titration,* p. 302.

by their following the internal necessities of their own natures. . . . [A]ll entities at all levels behave in accordance with their position in the greater patterns (organisms) of which they are parts.[30]

Compared to Renaissance science, the Chinese conception of nature was problematic, blocking their interest in discovering "precisely formulated abstract laws ordained from the beginning by a celestial lawgiver for nonhuman nature."

> There was no confidence that the code of Nature's laws could be unveiled and read, because there was no assurance that a divine being, even more rational than ourselves, had ever formulated such a code capable of being read.[31]

Of course, such notions of "command and duty in the 'Laws' of Nature" have disappeared from modern science and have been replaced by the notion of statistical regularities that describe rather than prescribe nature's order—in a sense, a return, Needham comments, to the Taoist perspective. And yet other residues of the earlier conception remain. Evelyn Fox Keller has pointed to the positive political implications of conceptualizing nature simply as ordered rather than as law-governed.[32] My point here is that Western conceptions of nature have been intimately linked to historically shifting Western religious and political ideals.

Third, the European-Christian conception of the laws of nature was just one kind of regional resource used to develop European sciences. Elements of medieval scientific and classical Greek thought, and other religious, national, class, and gender metaphors, models, and assumptions also were available for use in developing European sciences. The adoption of these cultural resources are familiar from the writings of conventional historians of Western sciences. In the context of the postcolonial literatures, these now appear as distinctively European cultural elements, ones that make modern sciences foreign to peoples in many other cultures.

Another kind of regional resource available only in Europe was created through the intermingling and integration of non-European elements with each other and with resources already available in Europe to make more useful elements for modern science. That is, those non-European elements indicated above were not only borrowed, but also were frequently transformed through processes possible only for a culture at the center of global exchanges. Thus the map and route of European expansion could be traced in the expansion of the content of European sciences. Prior to European expansion African, Asian, and indigenous American cultures had long traded scientific and technological ideas among themselves as they exchanged other products, but this possibility was reduced or eliminated for them and transferred to Europe during the "voyages of discovery."[33]

Fourth, the way peoples of European descent distribute and account for the consequences of modern sciences appears distinctively Western. The benefits are distributed disproportionately to already overadvantaged groups in Europe and elsewhere, and the costs disproportionately to everyone else. Whether one looks at sciences intended to improve the military, agriculture, manufacturing, health, or even the environment, the expanded opportunities they make possible have been distributed predominantly to small minorities of already privileged people primarily but not entirely of European descent, and the costs to the already poorest,

---

[30]Ibid., p. 323.

[31]Ibid., p. 327.

[32]"[L]aws of nature, like laws of the state, are historically imposed from above and obeyed from below." In contrast, "the concept of order, wider than law and free from its coercive, hierarchical, and centralizing implications has the potential to expand our conception of science. Order is a category comprising patterns of organization that can be spontaneous, self-generated, or externally imposed." Evelyn Fox Keller, *Reflections on Gender and Science* (New Haven: Yale University Press, 1984), p. 131–2. See also the interesting discussion of Needham's argument in Jatinder K. Bajaj, "Francis Bacon, the First Philosopher of Modern Science: A Non-Western View," in *Science, Hegemony and Violence: A Requiem for Modernity,* ed. Ashis Nandy (Delhi: Oxford, 1990).

[33]See Bruno Latour's discussion of the importance to science of "centres of calculation," in Chapter 6 of his *Science in Action* (Cambridge: Harvard University Press).

racial and ethnic minorities and women located at the periphery of local and global economic and political networks.[34]

The causes of this distribution are not mysterious or unforeseen. For one thing, it is not "man" whom sciences enable to make better use of nature's resources, but only those already positioned in social hierarchies. As Khor Kok Peng puts the point, the latter already own and control nature in the form of land with its forests, water, plants, animals, and minerals as well as having the tools to extract and process such resources. These people are in a position to decide "what to produce, how to produce it, what resources to use up to produce, and what technology to use."

> We thus have this spectacle, on the one hand, of the powerful development of technological capacity, so that the basic and human needs of every human being could be met if there were an appropriate arrangement of social and production systems; and, on the other hand, of more than half the world's population (and something like two-thirds of the Third-World's people) living in conditions where their basic and human needs are not met.[35]

Not only are the benefits and costs of modern sciences distributed in ways that disproportionately benefit elites in the West and elsewhere, but sciences' accounting practices are distorted to make this distribution invisible to those who gain the benefits. All consequences of sciences and technologies that are not planned or intended are externalized as "not science."[36] The critics argue that such an "internalization of profits and externalization of costs is the normal consequence when na-

ture is treated as if its individual components were isolated and unrelated.[37]

Finally, even if modern sciences bore none of the above cultural fingerprints, their value-neutrality would itself mark them as culturally distinctive. Of course, this is a contradiction ("If it's value-free, then it's not value-free."), or at least highly paradoxical. The point is that maximizing cultural neutrality, not to mention claiming it, is itself a culturally specific value; the reality and the claim are at issue here. Most cultures do not value neutrality, so one that does is easily identifiable. Moreover, the claim to neutrality is itself characteristic of the administrators of modern Western cultures organized by principles of scientific rationality.[38] Surprisingly, it turns out that abstractness and formality express distinctive cultural features, not the absence of any culture at all. Thus when modern science is introduced into many other societies, it is experienced as a rude and brutal cultural intrusion precisely because of the feature. Modern sciences' "neutrality" devalues not only local scientific traditions, but also the culturally defining values and interests that make a tradition Confucian rather than Protestant or Islamic. Claims for modern sciences' universality and objectivity are "a politics of disvaluing local concerns and knowledge and legitimating 'outside experts'."[39]

Interesting issues emerge from the discovery of the cultural specificity of modern sciences. For example, the conventional understanding of the universality of modern science is contested in two ways in these accounts. First, these accounts argue that universality is established as an empirical consequence of European expansion, not as an episte-

---

[34]The complexity of these sentences arises from the fact that elites in Third-World cultures also enjoy luxurious access to the benefits of modern sciences, and the majority of citizens in most First-World cultures—that is, the poor and other disadvantaged groups—do not.

[35]Khor, Kok Peng, "Science and Development: Underdeveloping the Third World," in *The Revenge of Athena,* ed. Z. Sardar, pp. 207–8.

[36]Claude Alvares, "Science, Colonialism and Violence: A Luddite View," in *Science, Hegemony and Violence: A Requiem for Modernity,* ed. Ashis Nandy, p. 108.

[37]J. Bandyopadhyay and V. Shiva, "Science and Control: Natural Resources and their Exploitation," in *The Revenge of Athena,* ed. Z. Sardar, p. 63.

[38]Dorothy Smith is especially eloquent on this point. See *The Conceptual Practices of Power* (Boston: Northeastern University Press, 1990) and *The Everyday World as Problematic: A Feminist Sociology* (Boston: Northeastern University Press, 1987). However, abstractness is not unique to such cultures. As Paola Bachetta pointed out (by letter), certain forms of ancient Hinduism are based on philosophical abstractions.

[39]Bandyopadhyay and Shiva, "Science and Control," p. 60.

mological cause of valid claims, to be located "inside science"—for example, in its method. As pointed out by one author:

> The epistemological claim of the "universality of science" . . . covers what is an empirical fact, the material and intellectual construction of this "universal science" and its "international character." The "universality of science" does not appear to be the cause but the effect of a process that we cannot explain or understand merely by concentrating our attention on epistemological claims.[40]

Second, a wedge has been driven between the universality of a science and its cultural neutrality. The laws of nature "discovered" by modern sciences that explain, for instance, how gravity and antibiotics work, will have their effects on us regardless of our cultural location, but they are not the only possible such universal laws of nature; there could be many universally valid but culturally distinctive sciences.

> [I]f we were to picture physical reality as a large blackboard, and the branches and shoots of the knowledge tree as markings in white chalk on this blackboard, it becomes clear that the yet unmarked and unexplored parts occupy a considerably greater space than that covered by the chalk tracks. The socially structured knowledge tree has thus explored only certain partial aspects of physical reality, explorations that correspond to the particular historical unfoldings of the civilization within which the knowledge tree emerged.
>
> Thus entirely different knowledge systems corresponding to different historical unfoldings in different civilizational settings become possible. This raises the possibility that in different historical situations and contexts sciences very different from the European tradition could emerge. Thus an entirely new set of "universal" but socially determined natural science laws are possible.[41]

These accounts thus provide additional evidence for the claim that fully modern sciences could be constructed within other cultures—the argument I left incomplete in the last section. Significant cultural features of modern sciences have not blocked their development as fully modern, according to the postcolonial accounts; indeed, they are responsible for these successes.[42] Moreover, one can now ask: which of the original cultural purposes of modern sciences that continue today to shape their conceptual framework are still desirable? Should we want to continue to develop sciences that, intentionally or not, succeed by extinguishing or obscuring all other scientific traditions, directing limitless consumption of scarce and unrenewable resources, distributing their benefits internally and their costs externally, and so forth? These questions show that if culture shapes sciences, then changes in local and global cultures can shape different sciences "here" as well as "there."

AN AFROCENTRIC FEMINIST EPISTEMOLOGY*

Patricia Hill Collins

Black feminist thought, like all specialized thought, reflects the interests and standpoint of its creators. Tracing the origin and diffusion of any body of specialized thought reveals its affinity to the power of

[40]Xavier Polanco, "World-Science: How Is the History of World-Science to Be Written?" in *Science and Empires,* Petitjean et al., p. 225.
[41]Susantha Goonatilake, *Aborted Discovery: Science and Creativity in the Third World* (London: Zed Press, 1984), pp. 229–30.

[42]This kind of critique enables one to see that sleeping in the feminist science analyses lies a direct challenge to conventional assumptions about the necessity of value-neutrality to the universality of science. A form of this challenge has been to the necessity of value-neutrality to the maximal objectivity of science. Cf. my "After the Neutrality Ideal: Science, Politics and 'Strong Objectivity'," *Social Research,* 59, 3 (Fall 1992), pp. 568–87; reprinted in *The Politics of Western Science, 1640–1990,* ed. Margaret Jacob (Atlantic Highlands: Humanities Press, 1994).
*This selection is taken from a longer work of Patricia Collins, *Black Feminist Thought: Knowledge, Consciousness and the Politics of Empowerment* (New York: Routledge, 1991).

the group that created it. Because elite white men and their representatives control structures of knowledge validation, white male interests pervade the thematic content of traditional scholarship. As a result, Black women's experiences with work, family, motherhood, political activism, and sexual politics have been routinely distorted in or excluded from traditional academic discourse.

Black feminist thought as specialized thought reflects the thematic content of African-American women's experiences. But because Black women have had to struggle against white male interpretations of the world in order to express a self-defined standpoint, Black feminist thought can best be viewed as subjugated knowledge. The suppression of Black women's efforts for self-definition in traditional sites of knowledge production has led African-American women to use alternative sites such as music, literature, daily conversations, and everyday behavior as important locations for articulating the core themes of a Black feminist consciousness.

Investigating the subjugated knowledge of subordinate groups—in this case a Black women's standpoint and Black feminist thought—requires more ingenuity than that needed to examine the standpoints and thought of dominant groups. I found my training as a social scientist inadequate to the task of studying the subjugated knowledge of a Black women's standpoint. This is because subordinate groups have long had to use alternative ways to create independent self-definitions and self-valuations and to rearticulate them through our own specialist. Like other subordinate groups, African-American women have not only developed a distinctive Black women's standpoint, but have done so by using alternative ways of producing and validating knowledge.

Epistemology is the study of the philosophical problems in concepts of knowledge and truth. The techniques I use in this volume to rearticulate a Black women's standpoint and to further Black feminist thought may appear to violate some of the basic epistemological assumptions of my training as a social scientist. In choosing the core themes in Black feminist thought that merited investigation, I consulted established bodies of academic research. But I also searched my own experiences and those of African-American women I know for themes we thought were important. My use of language signals a different relationship to my material than that which currently prevails in social sciences literature. For example, I often use the pronoun "our" instead of "their" when referring to African-American women, a choice that embeds me in the group I am studying instead of distancing me from it. In addition, I occasionally place my own concrete experiences in the text. To support my analysis, I cite few statistics and instead rely on the voices of Black women from all walks of life. These conscious epistemological choices signal my attempts not only to explore the thematic content of Black feminist thought but to do so in a way that does not violate its basic epistemological framework.

One key epistemological concern facing Black women intellectuals is the question of what constitutes adequate justifications that a given knowledge claim, such as a fact or theory, is true. In producing the specialized knowledge of Black feminist thought, Black women intellectuals often encounter two distinct epistemologies: one representing elite white male interests and the other expressing Afrocentric feminist concerns. Epistemological choices about who to trust, what to believe, and why something is true are not benign academic issues. Instead, these concerns tap the fundamental question of which versions of truth will prevail and shape thought and action.

THE EUROCENTRIC, MASCULINIST KNOWLEDGE VALIDATION PROCESS

Institutions, paradigms, and other elements of the knowledge validation procedure controlled by elite white men constitutes the Eurocentric masculinist knowledge validation process. The purpose of this process is to represent a white male standpoint. Although it reflects powerful white males interest, various dimensions of the process are not necessarily managed by white men themselves. Scholars, publishers, and other experts represent specific interests and credentialing processes, and their knowledge claims must satisfy the political and epistemological criteria of the contexts in which they reside.

Two political criteria influence the knowledge validation process. First, knowledge claims are evaluated by a community of experts whose members represent the standpoints of the groups from which they originate. Within the Eurocentric masculinist process this means that a scholar making a knowledge claim must convince a scholarly community controlled by white men that a given claim is justified. Second, each community of experts must maintain its credibility as defined by the larger group in which it is situated and from which it draws its basic, taken-for-granted knowledge. This means that scholarly communities that challenge basic beliefs held in the culture at large will be deemed less credible than those which support popular perspectives.

When white men control the knowledge validation process, both political criteria can work to suppress Black feminist thought. Given that the general culture shaping the taken-for-granted knowledge of the community of experts is permeated by widespread notions of Black and female inferiority, new knowledge claims that seem to violate these fundamental assumptions are likely to be viewed as anomalies.[1] Moreover, specialized thought challenging notions of Black and female inferiority is unlikely to be generated from within a white-male-controlled academic community because both the kinds of questions that could be asked and the explanations that would be found satisfying would necessarily reflect a basic lack of familiarity with Black women's reality.

The experiences of African-American women scholars illustrate how individuals who wish to rearticulate a Black women's standpoint through Black feminist thought can be suppressed by a white-male-controlled knowledge validation process. Exclusion from basic literacy, quality educational experiences, and faculty and administrative positions has limited Black women's access to influential academic positions. While Black women can produce knowledge claims that contest those advanced by the white male community, this community does not grant that Black women scholars have competing knowledge claims based in another knowledge validation process. As a consequence, any credentials controlled by white male academicians can be denied to Black women producing Black feminist thought on the grounds that it is not credible research.

Black women with academic credentials who seek to exert the authority that our status grants us to propose new knowledge claims about African-American women face pressures to use our authority to help legitimate a system that devalues and excludes the majority of Black women. When an outsider group—in this case, African-American women—recognizes that the insider group—namely, white men—requires special privileges from the larger society, a special problem arises of keeping the outsiders out and at the same time having them acknowledge the legitimacy of this procedure. Accepting a few "safe" outsiders addresses this legitimation problem.[2] One way of excluding the majority of Black women from the knowledge validation process is to permit a few Black women to acquire positions of authority in institutions that legitimate knowledge, and to encourage us to work within the taken-for-granted assumptions of Black female inferiority shared by the scholarly community and by the culture at large. Those Black women who accept these assumptions are likely to be rewarded by their institutions, often at significant personal cost. Those challenging the assumptions run the risk of being ostracized.

African-American women academicians who persist in trying to rearticulate a Black women's standpoint also face potential rejection of our knowledge claims on epistemological grounds. Just as the material realities of the powerful and the dominated produce separate standpoints, each group may also have distinctive epistemologies or theories of knowledge.

[1]See Thomas Kuhn, *The Structure of Scientific Revolutions* (Chicago: University of Chicago Press, 1962).

[2]See Peter L. Berger, and Thomas Luckmann, *The Social Construction of Reality* (New York: Doubleday, 1966).

Black women scholars may know that something is true but be unwilling or unable to legitimate our claims using Eurocentric, masculinist criteria for consistency with substantiated knowledge and criteria for methodological adequacy. For any body of knowledge, new knowledge claims must be consistent with an existing body of knowledge that the group controlling the interpretive context accepts as true. The methods used to validate knowledge claims must also be acceptable to the group controlling the knowledge validation process.

The criteria for the methodological adequacy of positivism illustrate the epistemological standards that Black women scholars would have to satisfy in legitimating Black feminist thought using a Eurocentric masculinist epistemology. While I describe Eurocentric masculinist approaches as a single process, many schools of thought or paradigms are subsumed under this one process. Moreover, my focus on positivism should be interpreted neither to mean that all dimensions of positivism are inherently problematic for Black women nor that nonpositivist frameworks are better. For example, most traditional frameworks that women of color internationally regard as oppressive to women are not positivist, and Eurocentric feminist critiques of positivism may have less political importance for women of color, especially those in traditional societies, than they have for white feminists.

Positivist approaches aim to create scientific descriptions of reality by producing objective generalizations. Because researchers have widely differing values, experiences, and emotions, genuine science is thought to be unattainable unless all human characteristics except rationality are eliminated from the research process. By following strict methodological rules, scientists aim to distance themselves from the values, vested interests, and emotions generated by their class, race, sex, or unique situation. By decontextualizing themselves, they allegedly become detached observers and manipulators of nature. Moreover, this researcher decontextualization is paralleled by comparable efforts to remove the objects of study from their contexts. The result of this entire process is often the separation of information from meaning.

Several requirements typify positivist methodological approaches. First, research methods generally require a distancing of the researcher from her or his "object" of study by defining the researcher as a "subject" with full human subjectivity and by objectifying the "object" of study. A second requirement is the absence of emotions from the research process. Third, ethics and values are deemed inappropriate in the research process, either as the reason for scientific inquiry or as a part of the research process itself. Finally, adversarial debates, whether written or oral, become the preferred method of ascertaining truth: the arguments that can withstand the greatest assault and survive intact become the strongest truths.

Such criteria ask African-American women to objectify ourselves, devalue our emotional life, displace our motivations for furthering knowledge about Black women, and confront in an adversarial relationship those with more social, economic and professional power. It therefore seems unlikely that Black women would use a positivist epistemological stance in rearticulating a Black women's standpoint. Black women are more likely to choose an alternative epistemology for assessing knowledge claims, one using different standards that are consistent with Black women's criteria for substantiated knowledge and with our criteria for methodological adequacy. If such an epistemology exists, what are its contours? Moreover, what is its role in the production of Black feminist thought?

THE CONTOURS OF AN AFROCENTRIC FEMINIST EPISTEMOLOGY

Africanist analyses of the Black experience generally agree on the fundamental elements of an Afrocentric standpoint. Despite varying histories, Black societies reflect elements of a core African value system that existed prior to and independently of racial oppression. Moreover, as a result of colonialism, imperialism, slavery, apartheid, and other systems of racial domination, Black people share a common experience of oppression. These two factors foster shared Afrocentric values that permeate the family structure, religious institutions, culture, and community life of Blacks in varying parts of

Africa, the Caribbean, South America, and North America. This Afrocentric consciousness permeates the shared history of people of African descent through the framework of a distinctive Afrocentric epistemology.[3]

Feminist scholars advance a similar argument by asserting that women share a history of gender oppression, primarily through sex/gender hierarchies. These experiences transcend divisions among women created by race, social class, religion, sexual orientation, and ethnicity and form the basis of a women's standpoint with a corresponding feminist consciousness and epistemology.

Because Black women have access to both the Afrocentric and the feminist standpoints, an alternative epistemology used to rearticulate a Black women's standpoint should reflect elements of both traditions. The search for the distinguishing features of an alternative epistemology used by African-American women reveals that values and ideas Africanist scholars identify as characteristically "Black" often bear remarkable resemblance to similar ideas claimed by feminist scholars as characteristically "female."[4] This similarity suggests that the material conditions of race, class, and gender oppression can vary dramatically and yet generate some uniformity in the epistemologies of subordinate groups. Thus the significance of an Afrocentric feminist epistemology may lie in how such an epistemology enriches our understanding of how subordinate groups create knowledge that fosters resistance.

The parallels between the two conceptual schemes raise a question: Is the worldview of women of African descent more intensely infused with the overlapping feminine/Afrocentric standpoints than is the case for either African-American men or white women? While an Afrocentric feminist epistemol-ogy reflects elements of epistemologies used by African-Americans and women as groups, it also paradoxically demonstrates features that may be unique to Black women. On certain dimensions Black women may more closely resemble Black men; on others, white women; and on still others Black women may stand apart from both groups. Black women's both/and conceptual orientation, the act of being simultaneously a member of a group and yet standing apart from it, forms an integral part of Black women's consciousness. Black women negotiate these contradictions, a situation Bonnie Thornton Dill labels the "dialectics of Black womanhood," by using this both/and conceptual orientation.[5]

Rather than emphasizing how a Black women's standpoint and its accompanying epistemology are different from those in Afrocentric and feminist analyses, I use Black women's experiences to examine points of contact between the two. Viewing an Afrocentric feminist epistemology in this way challenges additive analyses of oppression claiming that Black women have a more accurate view of oppression than do other groups. Such approaches suggest that oppression can be quantified and compared and that adding layers of oppression produces a potentially clearer standpoint. One implication of standpoint approaches is that the more subordinated the group, the purer the vision of the oppressed group. This is an outcome of the origins of standpoint approaches in Marxist social theory, itself an analysis of social structure rooted in Western either/or dichotomous thinking. Ironically, by quantifying and ranking human oppressions, standpoint theorists invoke criteria for methodological adequacy characteristic of positivism. Although it is tempting to claim that Black women are more oppressed than everyone else and therefore have the best standpoint from which to understand the mechanisms, processes, and effects of oppression, this simply may not be the case.

Like a Black women's standpoint, an Afrocentric feminist epistemology is rooted in the everyday experiences of African-American women. In spite of

---

[3]See James Turner, *The Next Decade: Theoretical and Research Issues in Africana Studies* (Ithaca: Cornell University, 1984).

[4]In critiques of the Eurocentric, masculinist knowledge validation process, what Africanist scholars label "white" and "Eurocentric" feminist scholars describe as "male-dominated" and "masculinist." Although he does not emphasize its patriarchal and racist features, Morris Berman's *The Reenchantment of the World* (1981) provides an important discussion of Western thought.

[5]Bonnie Thornton Dill, "The Dialectics of Black Womanhood," *Signs* 4, no. 3, pp. 543–55.

diversity that exists among women, what are the dimensions of an Afrocentric feminist epistemology?

CONCRETE EXPERIENCE AS A CRITERION OF MEANING

"My aunt used to say, 'A heap see, but a few know,'" remembers Carolyn Chase, a 31-year-old inner-city Black woman. This saying depicts two types of knowing—knowledge and wisdom—and taps the first dimension of an Afrocentric feminist epistemology. Living life as Black women requires wisdom because knowledge about the dynamics of race, gender, and class oppression has been essential to Black women's survival. African-American women give such wisdom high credence in assessing knowledge.

Allusions to these two types of knowing pervade the words of a range of African-American women. Zilpha Elaw, a preacher of the mid-1800s, explains the tenacity of racism: "The pride of a white skin is a bauble of great value with many in some parts of the United States, who readily sacrifice their intelligence to their prejudices, and possess more knowledge than wisdom." In describing differences separating African-American and white women, Nancy White invokes a similar rule: "When you come right down to it, white women just think they are free. Black women *know* they ain't free."[6] Geneva Smitherman, a college professor specializing in African-American linguistics, suggests that "from a black perspective, written documents are limited in what they can teach about life and survival in the world. Blacks are quick to ridicule 'educated fools,' . . . they have 'book learning' but no 'mother wit,' knowledge, but not wisdom."[7] Mabel Lincoln eloquently summarizes the distinction between knowledge and wisdom: "To black people like me, a fool is funny—you know, people who

love to break bad, people you can't tell anything to, folks that would take a shotgun to a roach."

African-American women need wisdom to know how to deal with the "educated fools" who would "take a shotgun to a roach." As members of a subordinate group, Black women cannot afford to be fools of any type, for our objectification as the Other denies us the protections that white skin, maleness, and wealth confer. This distinction between knowledge and wisdom, and the use of experience as the cutting edge dividing them, has been key to Black women's survival. In the context of race, gender, and class oppression, the distinction is essential. Knowledge without wisdom is adequate for the powerful, but wisdom is essential to the survival of the subordinate.

For most African-American women those individuals who have lived through the experiences about which they claim to be experts are more believable and credible than those who have merely read or thought about such experiences. Thus concrete experience as a criterion for credibility frequently is invoked by Black women when making knowledge claims. For instance, Hannah Nelson describes the importance personal experience has for her: "Our speech is most directly personal, and every black person assumes that every other black person has a right to a personal opinion. In speaking of grave matters, your personal experience is considered very good evidence. With us, distant statistics are certainly not as important as the actual experience of a sober person."[8] Similarly, Ruth Shays uses her concrete experiences to challenge the idea that formal education is the only route to knowledge: "I am the kind of person who doesn't have a lot of education, but both my mother and my father had good common sense. Now, I think that's all you need. I might not know how to use thirty-four words where three would do, but that does not mean that I don't know what I'm talking about . . . . I know what I'm talking about because I'm talking about myself. I'm talking about what I have lived."

[6]Quoted in John Langston Gwaltney, *Drylongso: A Self-Portrait of Black America* (New York: Vintage, 1980), p. 147.
[7]Geneva Smitherman, *Talkin' and Testifyin': The Language of Black America* (Boston: Houghton Mifflin, 1977), p. 76.
[8]Gwaltney, *op. cit.,* p. 7.

Implicit in Ms. Shay's self-assessment is a critique of the type of knowledge that obscures the truth, the "thirty-four words" that cover up a truth that can be expressed in three.

Even after substantial mastery of white masculinist epistemologies, many Black women scholars invoke our own concrete experiences and those of other African-American women in selecting topics for investigation and methodologies used. For example, Elsa Barkley Brown subtitles her essay on Black women's history, "how my mother taught me to be an historian in spite of my academic training." Similarly, Joyce Ladner maintains that growing up as a Black woman in the South gave her special insights in conducting her study of Black adolescent women. Lorraine Hansberry alludes to the potential epistemological significance of valuing the concrete: "In certain peculiar ways, we have been conditioned to think not small—but tiny. And the thing, I think, which has strangled us most is the tendency to turn away from the world in search of the universe. That is chaos in science—can it be anything else in art?"[9]

Experience as a criterion of meaning with practical images as its symbolic vehicles is a fundamental epistemological tenet in African-American thought systems. "Look at my arm!" Sojourner Truth proclaimed: "I have ploughed, and planted, and gathered into barns, and no man could head me! And ain't I a woman?" By invoking concrete practical images from her own life to symbolize new meanings, Truth deconstructed the prevailing notions of woman. Stories, narratives, and Bible principles are selected for their applicability to the lived experiences of African-Americans and become symbolic representations of a whole wealth of experience. Bible tales are often told for the wisdom they express about everyday life, so their interpretation involves no need for scientific historical verification. The narrative method requires that the story be told,

not torn apart in analysis, and trusted as core belief, not "admired as science."[10]

June Jordan's essay about her mother's suicide illustrates the multiple levels of meaning that can occur when concrete experiences are used as a criterion of meaning. Jordan describes her mother, a woman who literally died trying to stand up, and the effect her mother's death had on her own work:[11]

> I think all of this is really about women and work. Certainly this is all about me as a woman and my life work. I mean I am not sure my mother's suicide was something extraordinary. Perhaps most women must deal with a similar inheritance, the legacy of a woman whose death you cannot possibly pinpoint because she died so many, many times and because, even before she became your mother, the life of that woman was taken. . . . I came too late to help my mother to her feet. By way of everlasting thanks to all of the women who have helped me to stay alive I am working never to be late again.

While Jordan has knowledge about the concrete act of her mother's death, she also strives for wisdom concerning the meaning of that death.

Some feminist scholars offer a similar claim that women as a group are more likely than men to use concrete knowledge in assessing knowledge claims. For example, a substantial number of the 135 women in a study of women's cognitive development were "connected knowers" and were drawn to the sort of knowledge that emerges from firsthand observation. Such women felt that because knowledge comes from experience, the best way of understanding another person's ideas was to develop empathy and share the experiences that led the person to form those ideas.

In valuing the concrete, African-American women invoke not only an Afrocentric tradition but a women's tradition as well. Some feminist theories suggest that women are socialized in complex relational nexuses where contextual rules versus abstract

[9]Lorraine Hansberry, *To Be Young, Gifted and Black* (New York: Signet, 1969), p. 134.

[10]Henry H. Mitchell, and Nicholas Cooper Lewter, *Soul Theology: The Heart of American Black Culture* (San Francisco: Harper & Row, 1986), p. 8.

[11]June Jordan, *On Call* (Boston: South End Press, 1985), p. 20.

principles govern behavior. This socialization process is thought to stimulate characteristic ways of knowing. These theorists suggest that women are more likely to experience two modes of knowing: one located in the body and the space it occupies and the other passing beyond it. Through their child-rearing and nurturing activities, women mediate these two modes and use the concrete experiences of their daily lives to assess more abstract knowledge claims.

Although valuing the concrete may be more representative of women than men, social class differences among women may generate differential expression of this women's value. One study of working-class women's ways of knowing found that both white and African-American women rely on common sense and intuition. These forms of knowledge allow for subjectivity between the knower and the known, rest in the women themselves (not in higher authorities), and are experienced directly in the world (not through abstractions).

Amanda King, a young African-American mother, describes how she used the concrete to assess the abstract and points out how difficult mediating these two modes of knowing can be:

> The leaders of the ROC [a labor union] lost their jobs too, but it just seemed like they were used to losing their jobs . . . This was like a lifelong thing for them, to get out there and protest. They were like, what do you call them—intellectuals . . . You got the ones that go to the university that are supposed to make all the speeches, they're the ones that are supposed to lead, you know, put this little revolution together, and then you got the little ones . . . that go to the factory everyday, they be the ones that have to fight. I had a child and I thought I don't have the time to be running around with these people. . . . I mean I understand some of that stuff they were talking about, like the bourgeoisie, the rich and the poor and all that, but I had surviving on my mind for me and my kid.[12]

For Ms. King abstract ideals of class solidarity were mediated by the concrete experience of motherhood and the connectedness it involved.

In traditional African-American communities Black women find considerable institutional support for valuing concrete experience. Black women's centrality in families, churches, and other community organizations allows us to share our concrete knowledge of what it takes to be self-defined Black women with younger, less experienced sisters. "Sisterhood is not new to Black women," asserts Bonnie Thornton Dill, but "while Black women have fostered and encouraged sisterhood, we have not used it as the anvil to forge our political identities."[13] Though not expressed in explicitly political terms, this relationship of sisterhood among Black women can be seen as a model for a whole series of relationships African-American women have with one another.

Given that Black churches and families are both woman-centered, Afrocentric institutions, African-American women traditionally have found considerable institutional support for this dimension of an Afrocentric feminist epistemology. While white women may value the concrete, it is questionable whether white families—particularly middle-class nuclear ones—and white community institutions provide comparable types of support. Similarly, while Black men are supported by Afrocentric institutions, they cannot participate in Black women's sisterhood. In terms of Black women's relationships with one another, African-American women may find it easier than others to recognize connectedness as a primary way of knowing, simply because we are encouraged to do so by a Black women's tradition of sisterhood.

THE USE OF DIALOGUE IN ASSESSING KNOWLEDGE CLAIMS

"Dialogue implies talk between two subjects, not the speech of subject and object. It is a humanizing speech, one that challenges and resists domination," asserts Bell Hooks.[14] For Black women new knowledge claims are rarely worked out in isolation

---

[12]Victoria Byerly, *Hard Times Cotton Mills Girls* (Ithaca: Cornell University, 1986), p. 198.

[13]Bonnie Thornton Dill, "Race, Class and Gender," *Feminist Studies* 9, 1, 1983, p. 134.
[14]Bell Hooks, *Talking Back: Thinking Feminist, Thinking Black* (Boston: South End Press, 1987), p. 131.

from other individuals and are usually developed through dialogues with other members of a community. A primary epistemological assumption underlying the use of dialogue in assessing knowledge claims is that connectedness rather than separation is an essential component of the knowledge validation process.

This belief in connectedness and the use of dialogue as one of its criteria for methodological adequacy has Afrocentric roots. In contrast to Western, either/or dichotomous thought, the traditional African worldview is holistic and seeks harmony. "One must understand that to become human, to realize the promise of becoming human, is the only important task of the person," posits Molefi Asante.[15] People become more human and empowered only in the context of a community, and only when they "become seekers of the type of connections, interactions, and meetings that lead to harmony." The power of the word generally, and dialogues specifically, allows this to happen.

Not to be confused with adversarial debate, the use of dialogue has deep roots in an African-based oral tradition and in African-American culture. Ruth Shays describes the importance of dialogue in the knowledge validation process of enslaved African-Americans:

> They would find a lie if it took them a year. . . . The foreparents found the truth because they listened and they made people tell their part many times. Most often you can hear a lie. . . . Those old people was everywhere and knew the truth of many disputes. They believed that a liar should suffer the pain of his lies, and they had all kinds of ways of bringing liars to judgement.[16]

The widespread use of the call-and-respond discourse mode among African-Americans illustrates the importance placed on dialogue. Composed of spontaneous verbal and nonverbal interaction between speaker and listener in which all of the speaker's statements, or "calls," are punctuated by expressions, or "responses," from the listener, this Black discourse mode pervades African-American culture. The fundamental requirement of this interactive network is active participation of all individuals. For ideas to be tested and validated, everyone in the group must participate. To refuse to join in, especially if one really disagrees with what has been said, is seen as "cheating."

June Jordan's analysis of Black English points to the significance of this dimension of an alternative epistemology:

> Our language is a system constructed by people constantly needing to insist that we exist. . . . Our language devolves from a culture that abhors all abstraction, or anything tending to obscure or delete the fact of the human being who is here and now/the truth of the person who is speaking or listening. Consequently, *there is no passive voice construction possible in Black English.* For example, you cannot say, "Black English is being eliminated." You must say, instead, "White people eliminating Black English." The assumption of the presence of life governs all of Black English . . . every sentence assumes the living and active participation of at least two human beings, the speaker and the listener.[17]

Many Black women intellectuals invoke the relationships and connectedness provided by use of dialogue. When asked why she chose the themes she did, novelist Gayl Jones replied: "I was . . . interested . . . in oral traditions of storytelling—Afro-American and others, in which there is always the consciousness and importance of the hearer."[18] In describing the difference in the way male and female writers select significant events and relationships, Jones points out that "with many women writers, relationships within family, community, between men and women, and among women—from slave narratives by black women writers on—are treated as complex and significant relationships, whereas with many men the significant relationships are those that

---

[15]Molefi Asante, *The Afrocentric Idea* (Philadelphia: Temple University, 1987), p. 185.
[16]Gwaltney, *op. cit.,* p. 32.

[17]June Jordan, *op. cit.,* p. 129.
[18]Claudia Tate, *Black Women Writers at Work* (New York: Continuum, 1983), p. 91.

involve confrontations—relationships outside the family and community." Alice Walker's reaction to Zora Neale Hurston's book, *Mules and Men*, is another example of the use of dialogue in accessing knowledge claims. In *Mules and Men* Hurston chose not to become a detached observer of the stories and folktales she collected but instead, through extensive dialogues with the people in the communities she studied, placed herself in the center of her analysis. Using a similar process, Walker tests the truth of Hurston's knowledge claims:

> When I read *Mules and Men* I was delighted. Here was this perfect book! The "perfection" of which I immediately tested on my relatives, who are such typical Black Americans they are useful for every sort of political, cultural, or economic survey. Very regular people from the South, rapidly forgetting their Southern cultural inheritance in the suburbs and ghettos of Boston and New York, they sat around reading the book themselves, listening to me read the book, listening to each other read the book, and a kind of paradise was regained.[19]

Black women's centrality in families and community organizations provides African-American women with a high degree of support for invoking dialogue as a dimension of an Afrocentric feminist epistemology. However, when African-American women use dialogues in assessing knowledge claims, we might be invoking a particularly female way of knowing as well. Feminist scholars contend that men and women are socialized to seek different types of autonomy—the former based on separation, the latter seeking connectedness—and that this variation in types of autonomy parallels the characteristic differences between male and female ways of knowing. For instance, in contrast to the visual metaphors (such as equating knowledge with illumination, knowing with seeing, and truth with light) that scientists and philosophers typically use, women tend to ground their epistemological premises in metaphors suggesting finding a voice, speak-

ing, and listening. The words of the Black woman who struggled for her education at Medgar Evers College resonate with the importance placed on voice: "I was basically a shy and reserved person prior to the struggle at Medgar, but I found my voice—and I used it! Now, I will never lose my voice again!"

While significant differences exist between Black women's family experiences and those of middle-class white women, African-American women clearly are affected by general cultural norms prescribing certain familial roles for women. Thus in terms of the role of dialogue in an Afrocentric feminist epistemology, Black women may again experience a convergence of the values of the African-American community and women's experiences.

THE LIMITS OF SCIENCE

Ayatollah Murtaza Mutahhari

THREE WORLD VIEWS

World views or schemes of world knowledge (the ways man defines or explains the world) generally fall into three classes: scientific, philosophic, and religious.

Scientific World View

Science is based on two things: hypothesis and experiment. In the scientist's mind, to discover and explain a phenomenon, one first forms a hypothesis, and then one subjects it to concrete experiment, in the laboratory. If the experiment supports the hypothesis, it becomes an accepted scientific principle. As long as no more comprehensive hypothesis, better supported by experimentation, appears, that scientific principle retains its standing. The more comprehensive hypothesis with its advent clears the field for itself. Science thus engages in discovering

---
[19]Alice Walker, "Zora Neale Hurston" in the forward to Robert Hemenway's *Zora Neale Hurston* (Urbana: University of Illinois, 1977).

causes and effects: Through concrete experiments, it discovers a thing's cause or effect; then it pursues the cause of that cause or the effect of that effect. It continues this course of discovery as far as possible.

The work of science, in being based on concrete experiments, has advantages and shortcomings. The greatest advantage of scientific research is that it is exact, precise, and discriminating. Science is able to give man thousands of data about some slight being; it can fill a book with knowledge about a leaf. Because it acquaints man with the special laws of every being, it enables man to control and dominate that being. Thus, it brings about industry and technology.

But precisely because of these qualities, the compass of science is also limited to experiment. It advances as far as can be subjected to experiment. But can one bring all of being in all its aspects within the confines of experiment? Science in practice pursues causes and effects to a certain limit and then reaches a point where it must say "I don't know." Science is like a powerful searchlight in the long winter night, illuminating a certain area without disclosing anything beyond its border. Can one determine by experiment whether the universe has a beginning and an end or is limitless in time? Or does the scientist, on reaching this point, consciously or unconsciously mount the pinions of philosophy in order to express an opinion?

From the standpoint of science, the universe is like an old book the first and last pages of which have been lost. Neither the beginning nor the end is known. Thus, the world view of science is a knowledge of the part, not of the whole. Our science acquaints us with the situation of some parts of the universe, not with the shape, mien, and character of the whole universe. The scientist's world view is like the knowledge about the elephant gained by those who touched it in the dark. The one who felt the elephant's ear supposed the animal to be shaped like a fan; the one who felt its leg supposed it to be shaped like a column; and the one who felt its back supposed it to be shaped like a throne.

Another shortcoming of the scientific world view as a basis for an ideology is that science is un-

stable and unenduring from a theoretical standpoint, that is, from the standpoint of presenting reality as it is or of attracting faith to the nature of the reality of being. From the viewpoint of science, the face of the world changes from day to day because science is based on hypothesis and experiment, not on rational and self-evident first principles. Hypothesis and experiment have a provisional value; so the scientific world view is shaky and inconsistent and cannot serve as a foundation for faith. Faith demands a firmer, an unshakable foundation, a foundation characterized by eternity.

The scientific world view, in accordance with the limitations that the tools of science (hypothesis and experiment) have inevitably brought about for science, falls short of answering a series of basic cosmological questions that an ideology is obliged to answer decisively, such as: Where did the universe come from? Where is it going? How are we situated within the totality of being? Does the universe have a beginning and an end in time or in space? Is being in its totality right or a mistake, true or vain, beautiful or ugly? Do inevitable and immutable norms preside over the universe, or does no immutable norm exist? Is being in its totality a single living, conscious entity, or is it dead and unconscious, man's existence being an aberration, an accident? Can that which exists cease to exist? Can that which does not exist come into existence? Is the return of that which has lapsed from existence possible or impossible? Are the universe and history exactly repeatable, even after billions of years (the cyclical theory)? Does unity truly preside, or does multiplicity? Is the universe divisible into the material and the nonmaterial, and is the material universe a small part of the universe as a whole? Is the universe under guidance and seeing, or is it blind? Is the universe transacting with man? Does the universe respond in kind to man's good and evil? Does an enduring life exist after this transient one?

Science arrives at "I don't know" in trying to answer all these questions because it cannot subject them to experiment. Science answers limited, partial questions but is incapable of representing the totality of the universe. An analogy will clarify this point. It is possible for an individual to be well acquainted with a neighborhood or a quarter of Tehran. For instance, he may know South Tehran or some part of it in detail, such that he can sketch the streets, alleys, and even the houses of that area from memory. Someone else may know another neighborhood, a third person, a third area, and so on. If we bring together everything they know, we shall know enough of Tehran, part by part. But if we learn about Tehran in this way, shall we have learned about Tehran from every standpoint? Can we gain a complete picture of Tehran? Is it circular? Is it square? Is it shaped like the leaf of a tree? Of what tree? What relationships do the neighborhoods have with one another? Which bus lines connect how many neighborhoods? Is Tehran as a whole beautiful or ugly? If we want to inform ourselves on subjects such as these, if, for instance, we want to learn what the shape of Tehran is, or whether it is beautiful or ugly, we must board a plane and take in the whole city from above. In this sense, science is incapable of answering the most basic questions, as a world view must; that is, it can form no general conceptions of the universe as a whole and of its form.

The importance of the scientific world view lies in its practical, technical value, not in its theoretical value. What can serve as the support for an ideology is a theoretical value, not a practical one. The theoretical value of science lies in the reality of the universe being just as it is represented in the mirror of science. The practical and technical value of science lies in science's empowering man in his work and being fruitful, whether or not it represents reality. Today's industry and technology display the practical and technical value of science.

One of the remarkable things about science in today's world is that, to the extent that its practical and technical value increases, its theoretical value diminishes. Those on the sidelines suppose that the progress of science as an illumination of the human conscience and as a source of faith and certitude relative to reality (which is how science represents itself) is in direct proportion to the extent of irrefutable concrete progress, whereas the truth is just the opposite.

An ideology requires a world view that, first, answers the basic cosmological questions of relevance to the universe as a whole, not just to some certain part; second, provides a well-grounded, reliable, and eternally valid comprehension, not a provisional, transient one; and third, provides something of theoretical, not purely practical and technical value, something revealing reality. The scientific world view, for all its advantages from other standpoints, fails to fulfill these three conditions.

Philosophical World View

Although the philosophical world view lacks the exactitude and definition of the scientific world view, it enjoys an assurance and has none of the instability of the scientific world view. The reason for this is that it rests on a series of principles that are in the first place self-evident and undeniable to the mind, carried forward by demonstration and deduction, and in the second place general and comprehensive (in the language of philosophy, they relate to that by virtue of which the being is being). The world view of philosophy answers those same questions on which ideologies rest. Philosophical thought discerns the mien of the universe as a whole.

The scientific world view and the philosophical world view both conduce to action, but in two different ways. The scientific world view conduces to action by giving man the power and capacity to "change" and to "control" nature; it allows him to render nature subservient to his own desires. But the philosophical world view conduces to action and influences action by distinguishing the reasons for action and the criteria for human choice in life. The philosophical world view is influential in the way man encounters and responds to the universe. It fixes the attitude of man to the universe and shapes his outlook toward being and the universe. It gives man ideas or takes them away. It imparts meaning to his life or draws him into futility and emptiness. Thus, science is incapable but philosophy is capable of giving man a world view as the foundation of an ideology.

Religious World View

If we regard every general viewpoint expressed toward being and the universe as philosophical, regardless of the source of that world view (that is, syllogism, demonstration, and deduction or revelation received from the unseen world), we must regard the religious world view as philosophical. The religious world view and the philosophic world view cover the same domain, by contrast with the scientific world view. But if we take into account the source of knowledge, we must certainly admit that the religious and the philosophical cosmologies are different in kind. In some religions, such as Islam, the religious cosmology within the religion has taken on a philosophical quality, that is, a rational quality. It relies on reason and deduction and adduces demonstrations in answering the questions that are raised. From this standpoint, the Islamic world view is likewise a rational and philosophical world view.

Among the advantages of the religious world view (in addition to the two advantages it shares with the philosophical world view—stability and eternality, and generality and comprehensiveness) is its sanctification of the bases of the world view.

An ideology demands faith. For a school of thought to attract faith calls not only for a belief in that eternity and immutability of its principles, which the scientific world view in particular lacks, but for a respect approaching reverence. Thus, a world view becomes the basis of ideology and the foundation of belief when it takes on a religious character. A world view can become the basis of an ideology when it has attained the firmness and breadth of philosophical thought as well as the holiness and sanctity of religious principles.

CRITERIA FOR A WORLD VIEW

The good, sublime world view has the following characteristics:

1. It can be deduced and proven (is supported by reason and logic).

2. It gives meaning to life; it banishes from minds the ideas that life is vain and futile, that all roads lead to vanity and nothingness.
3. It gives rise to ideals, enthusiasm, and aspiration.
4. It has the power to sanctify human aims and social goals.
5. It promotes commitment and responsibility.

That a world view is logical paves the way to rational acceptance of it and renders it admissible to thought. It eliminates the ambiguities and obscurities that are great barriers to action.

That the world view of a school of thought gives rise to ideals lends it a magnetism as well as a fervor and force.

That a world view sanctifies the aims of a school of thought leads to individuals' easily making sacrifices and taking risks for the sake of these aims. So long as a school is unable to sanctify its aims, to induce feelings in individuals of worshipfulness, sacrifice, and idealism in relation to the aims of the school, that school of thought has no assurance that its aims will be carried out.

That a world view promotes commitment and responsibility commits the individual, to the depths of his heart and conscience, and makes him responsible for himself and society.

THE ALL-ENCOMPASSING WORLD VIEW OF TAUHID

All the features and properties that are organic to a good world view are summed up in the world view of *tauhid,* which is the only world view that can have all these features. The world view of *tauhid* means perceiving that the universe has appeared through a sagacious will and that the order of being is founded on goodness, generosity, and mercy, to convey existents to attainments worthy of them. The world view of *tauhid* means the universe is unipolar and uniaxial. The world view of *tauhid* means the universe has for its essence "from Him-ness" (*inna lillah*) and "to Him-ness" (*inna ilayhi raji'un*) [Qur'an 2:156].

The beings of the universe evolve in a harmonious system in one direction, toward one center. No being is created in vain, aimlessly. The universe is regulated through a series of definitive rules named the divine norms (*sunan ilahiya*). Man enjoys a special nobility and greatness among beings and has a special role and mission. He is responsible for his own evolution and upbringing and for the improvement of his society. The universe is the school for man, and God rewards every human being according to his right intention and right effort.

The world view of *tauhid* is backed by the force of logic, science, and reason. In every particle of the universe, there are indications of the existence of a wise, omniscient God; every tree leaf is a compendium of knowledge of the solicitous Lord.

The world view of *tauhid* gives meaning, spirit, and aim to life because it sets man on the course of perfection that stops at no determinate limit but leads ever onward.

The world view of *tauhid* has a magnetic attraction; it imparts joy and confidence to man; it presents sublime and sacred aims; and it leads individuals to be self-sacrificing.

The world view of *tauhid* is the only world view in which individuals' mutual commitment and responsibility find meaning, just as it is the only world view that saves man from falling into the terrible valley of belief in futility and worship of nothingness.

The Islamic world view is the world view of *tauhid. Tauhid* is presented in Islam in the purest form and manner. According to Islam, God has no peer—"There is nothing like Him" (42:11). God resembles nothing and no thing can be compared to God. God is the Absolute without needs; all need Him; He needs none—"You are the ones needing God, and God is the One Free of Need, the Praiseworthy" (35:15). "He is aware of all things" (42:12) and "He is capable of all things" (22:6). He is everywhere, and nowhere is devoid of Him; the highest heaven and the depths of the earth bear the same relationship to Him. Wherever we turn we face Him—"Wherever you turn, there is the presence of God" (2:115). He is aware of all the secrets of the heart, all the thoughts passing through the mind, all the intentions and designs, of everyone—"We created man, and We know what his soul whispers to him, and We are nearer to him than his jugular vein" (50:16). He is the summation of all perfections and is above and devoid of all defect—"The most beautiful names belong to God" (7:180). He is not a body; He is not to be seen with the eye—"No visions can grasp Him, but He comprehends all vision" (6:103).

According to the Islamic world view, the world view of *tauhid,* the universe is a created thing preserved through the divine providence and will. If for an instant this divine providence were withdrawn from the world, it would cease to be.

The universe has not been created in vain, in jest. Wise aims are at work in the creation of the universe and of man. Nothing inappropriate, devoid of wisdom and value, has been created. The existing order is the best and most perfect of possible orders. The universe rests on justice and truth. The order of the universe is based on causes and effects, and one must seek for every result in its unique cause and antecedents. One must expect a unique cause for every result and a unique result for every cause. Divine decree and foreordination bring about the existence of every being only through its own unique cause. A thing's divinely decreed fate is identical with the fate decreed for it by the sequence of causes leading to it.

The intent of the divine will operates in the world in the form of a norm (*sunna*), that is, in the form of a universal law and principle. The divine norms do not change.

QUESTIONS FOR DISCUSSION

1. Compare Feyerabend's view of science with that of Peirce. With which of the two do you find yourself in the most agreement? Why?
2. Evaluate Feyerabend's claim that the only epistemological principle that can be adequately defended for all times and places is "Anything goes."
3. Do you agree with Patricia Hill Collins' contention that "white male interests pervade the thematic content of traditional scholarship"? If so, why do you find yourself in agreement with her? If not, why do you disagree?

4. Ayatollah Mutahhari criticizes science, in large part, on the basis of its failure to attain certainty in knowledge. Evaluate his critique of science. Evaluate his more positive attitude toward religion as a source of knowledge.

5. Compare Sandra Harding's attitude toward scientific investigation with that of Feyerabend.

Compare her views with those of Patricia Hill Collins.

6. All of the authors in this section except for Peirce seem critical of the scientific enterprise. What common themes, if any, do you find in their critiques of science? What differences can you find in their views?

THE LIMITS OF REASON AND THE LIMITS OF KNOWLEDGE

This cross-cultural reader is predicated on the assumption that significant communication between cultures is possible. Yet, in true philosophical spirit, it must nevertheless be asked what the limits of such communication might be. Chuang Tzu, the well-known Taoist mystic of fourth-century B.C. China, asks this question at an even deeper level, testing the limits of understanding between species. In a famous paradox, he observes that he once dreamt that he was a butterfly, a dream so vivid that, when he awoke, he did not know whether the dream was his or the butterfly's. Another paradoxicalist, the modern Argentine writer Jorge Luis Borges (1899–1986), poignantly dramatizes our limitations in an imaginary account of the very real Islamic philosopher Averroës and his futile search to understand Aristotle's theory of drama while living in a culture that has no theater! In a final irony, Borges notes the absurdity of his own position, a twentieth-century Argentine trying to understand a medieval Arab intellectual.

The question of the limits of our knowledge is coupled in this section with the question of the limits of reason in knowledge, a question that the twentieth-century scholar of Japanese Buddhism D. T. Suzuki (1870–1966) addresses in an analysis of the mystical knowledge of Zen Buddhism, a subject that we examined previously from a slightly different angle in "The Sutra of Hui Neng" in Chapter 1. Suzuki experienced satori, or "sudden enlightenment," as a disciple of the Zen Master Soen. After his enlightenment, he dedicated himself to making Zen better known in the West.

KNOWLEDGE AND RELATIVITY

Chuang Tzu

How can Tao be so obscured that there should be a distinction of true and false? How can speech be so obscured that there should be a distinction of right and wrong? Where can you go and find Tao not to exist? Where can you go and find speech impossible? Tao is obscured by petty biases and speech is obscured by flowery expressions. Therefore there have arisen the controversies between the Confucianists and the Moists, each school regarding as right what the other considers as wrong, and regarding as wrong what the other considers as right. But to show that what each regards as right is wrong or to show that what each regards as wrong is right, there is no better way than to use the light (of Nature).

There is nothing that is not the "that" and there is nothing that is not the "this." Things do not know that they are the "that" of other things; they only know what they themselves know. Therefore I say that the "that" is produced by the "this" and the "this" is also caused by the "that." This is the theory of mutual production.[1] Nevertheless, when there is life there is death,[2] and when there is death there is life. When there is possibility, there is impossibility, and when there is impossibility, there is possibility. Because of the right, there is the wrong, and because of the wrong, there is the right. Therefore the sage does not proceed along these lines (of right and wrong, and so forth) but illuminates the matter with Nature. This is the reason.

The "this" is also the "that." The "that" is also the "this." The "this" has one standard of right and wrong, and the "that" also has a standard of right and wrong. Is there really a distinction between "that" and "this"? Or is there really no distinction between "that" and "this"? When "this" and "that" have no opposites,[3] there is the very axis of Tao.

---

[1]According to Ch'ien Mu, *Chuang Tzu tsuan-chien* (Collected Commentaries on the *Chuang Tzu*), 1951, *fang-sheng* means simultaneously coming into being. It means simultaneous production or causation. The idea is that one implies or involves the other, or coexistence. The emphasis here, however, is the causal relation rather than coexistence.

[2]The same saying appears in Hui Shih's (380–305 B.C.) paradoxes.

[3]Interpretation following Kuo Hsiang, whose commentary on *Chuang Tzu* is the most important of all. However, Kuo's commentary is more a system of his own philosophy than explanation of the text.

Only when the axis occupies the center of a circle can things in their infinite complexities be responded to. The right is an infinity. The wrong is also an infinity. Therefore I say that there is nothing better than to use the light (of Nature).

To take a mark (*chih*) to show that a mark is not a mark is not as good as to take a non-mark to show that a mark is not a mark. To take a horse to show that a [white] horse is not a horse (as such) is not as good as to take a non-horse to show that a horse is not a horse.[4] The universe is but one mark, and all things are but a horse. When [people say], "All right," then [things are] all right. When people say, "Not all right," then [things are] not all right. A road becomes so when people walk on it,[5] and things become so-and-so [to people] because people call them so-and-so. How have they become so? They have become so because [people say they are] so. How have they become not so? They have become not so because [people say they are] not so. In their own way things are so-and-so. In their own way things are all right. There is nothing that is not so-and-so. There is nothing that is not all right. Let us take, for instance, a large beam and a small beam, or an ugly woman and Hsi-shih (famous beauty of ancient China), or generosity, strangeness, deceit, and abnormality. The Tao identifies them all as one. What is division [to some] is production [to others], and what is production [to others] is destruction [to some]. Whether things are produced or destroyed, [Tao] again identifies them all as one.

Only the intelligent knows how to identify all things as one. Therefore he does not use [his own judgment] but abides in the common [principle]. The common means the useful and the useful means identification. Identification means being at ease with oneself. When one is at ease with himself, one is near Tao. This is to let it (Nature) take its own course.[6] He has arrived at this situation,[7] and does not know it. This is Tao.

Those who wear out their intelligence to try to make things one without knowing that they are really the same may be called "three in the morning." What is meant by "three in the morning"? A monkey keeper once was giving out nuts and said, "Three in the morning and four in the evening." All the monkeys became angry. He said, "If that is the case, there will be four in the morning and three in the evening." All the monkeys were glad. Neither the name nor the actuality has been reduced but the monkeys reacted in joy and anger [differently]. The keeper also let things take their own course. Therefore the sage harmonizes the right and wrong and rests in natural equalization. This is called following two courses at the same time.

The knowledge of the ancients was perfect. In what way was it perfect? There were those who believed that nothing existed. Such knowledge is indeed perfect and infinite and cannot be improved. The next were those who believed there were things but there was no distinction between them. Still the next were those who believed there was distinction but there was neither right nor wrong. When the distinction between right and wrong became prominent, Tao was thereby reduced. Because Tao was reduced, individual bias was formed. But are there really production and reduction? Is there really no production or reduction? That there are production and reduction is like Chao Wen[8] playing the lute [with petty opinions produced in his mind]. That there is no production or reduction is like Chao Wen not playing the lute,[9] [thus leaving things alone]. Chao Wen played the lute. Master K'uang[10] wielded the stick to keep time. And Hui Tzu[11] leaned against a drayanda tree [to argue]. The knowledge of these three gentlemen was almost perfect, and therefore they practiced their art to the end of their lives. Because they liked it, they became different from others, and they wished to enlighten others with what they liked. They were not to be

---

[4]This is clearly a criticism of Kung-sun Lung (b. 380 B.C.?).
[5]According to Wang Hsien-ch'ien, *tao* here does not mean Tao but a road.
[6]Other interpretations: (1) This is because he relies on this (that is, Tao); (2) he stops with this.
[7]Another interpretation: He has stopped.

---

[8]Identity unknown.
[9]Kuo Hsiang said in his commentary, "Not all sounds can be produced."
[10]Ancient musician famous for his sharpness in listening.
[11]Hui Shih.

enlightened and yet they insisted on enlightening them. Therefore Hui Tzu lived throughout his life discussing the obscure doctrines of hardness and whiteness.[12] And Chao Wen's son devoted his whole life to his heritage but ended with no success. Can these be called success? If so, even I am a success. Can these not be called success? If so, then neither I nor anything else can be called a success. Therefore the sage aims at removing the confusions and doubts that dazzle people. Because of this he does not use [his own judgment] but abides in the common principle. This is what is meant by using the light (of Nature).

Suppose we make a statement. We don't know whether it belongs to one category or another. Whether one or the other, if we put them in one, then one is not different from the other. However, let me explain. There was a beginning. There was a time before that beginning. And there was a time before the time which was before that beginning. There was being. There was non-being. There was a time before that non-being. And there was a time before the time that was before that non-being. Suddenly there is being and there is non-being, but I don't know which of being and non-being is really being or really non-being. I have just said something, but I don't know if what I have said really says something or says nothing.

There is nothing in the world greater than the tip of a hair that grows in the autumn, while Mount T'ai is small. No one lives a longer life than a child who dies in infancy, but P'eng-tsu (who lived many hundred years) died prematurely. The universe and I exist together, and all things and I are one. Since all things are one, what room is there for speech? But since I have already said that all things are one, how can speech not exist? Speech and the one then make two. These two (separately) and the one (the two together) make three. Going from this, even the best mathematician cannot reach [the final number]. How much less can ordinary people! If we proceed from nothing to something and arrive at three, how much more shall we reach if we proceed

from something to something! Let us not proceed. Let us let things take their own course.[13]

In reality Tao has no limitation, and speech has no finality. Because of this there are clear demarcations. Let me talk about clear demarcations. There are the left and the right. There are discussions and theories. There are analyses and arguments. And there are competitions and quarrels. These are called the eight characteristics. What is beyond the world, the sage leaves it as it exists and does not discuss it. What is within the world, the sage discusses but does not pass judgment. About the chronicles of historical events and the records of ancient kings, the sage passes judgments but does not argue. Therefore there are things which analysis cannot analyze, and there are things which argument cannot argue. Why? The sage keeps it in his mind while men in general argue in order to brag before each other. Therefore it is said that argument arises from failure to see [the greatness of Tao].

Great Tao has no appellation. Great speech does not say anything. Great humanity (*jen*) is not humane (through any special effort).[14] Great modesty is not yielding. Great courage does not injure. Tao that is displayed is not Tao. Speech that argues is futile. Humanity that is specially permanent or specially attached to someone or something will not be comprehensive.[15] Modesty that is too apparent is not real. Courage that injures the nature of things will not succeed. These five are all-comprehensive and all-embracing but tend to develop sharp edges. Therefore he who knows to stop at what he does not know is perfect. Who knows the argument that requires no speech or the Tao that cannot be named? If anyone can know, he is called the store of Nature (which embraces all). This store is not full when more things are added and not empty when things

---

[12]In ch. 5 of the *Chuang Tzu,* NHCC, 2:44a, Giles, pp. 69–70, Chuang Tzu refers to Hui Tzu's discussion and doctrines.

[13]Another interpretation is: Let us stop.

[14]It means that a man of humanity is not humane in a deliberate or artificial way, and that he is not partial. The word *jen* is often rendered as love, kindness, human-heartedness, true mankind, etc. In its broad sense, it denotes the general virtue.

[15]This is Kuo Hsiang's interpretation.

are taken out. We don't know where it comes from. This is called dimmed light.[16]

Of old Emperor Yao said to Shun,[17] "I want to attack the states of Tsung, Kuei, and Hsü'ao. Since I have been on the throne, my mind has not been free from them. Why?"

"The rulers of these states are as lowly as weeds," replied Shun. "Why is your mind not free from them? Once there were ten suns shining simultaneously and all things were illuminated. How much more can virtue illuminate than the suns?"

Nieh Ch'üeh asked Wang I,[18] "Do you know in what respect all things are right?"

"How can I know?" replied Wang I.

"Do you know that you do not know?"

Wang I said, "How can I know?"

"Then have all things no knowledge?"

"How can I know?" answered Wang I. "Nevertheless, I will try to tell you. How can it be known that what I call knowing is not really not knowing and that what I call not knowing is not really knowing? Now let me ask you this: If a man sleeps in a damp place, he will have a pain in his loins and will dry up and die. Is that true of eels? If a man lives up in a tree, he will be frightened and tremble. Is that true of monkeys? Which of the three knows the right place to live? Men eat vegetables and flesh, and deer eat tender grass. Centipedes enjoy snakes, and owls and crows like mice. Which of the four knows the right taste? Monkey mates with the dog-headed female ape and the buck mates with the doe, and eels mate with fishes. Mao Ch'iang[19] and Li Chi[20] were considered by men to be beauties, but at the sight of them fish plunged deep down in the water, birds soared high up in the air, and deer dashed away. Which of the four knows the right kind of beauty? From my point of view, the principle of humanity and righteousness and the doctrines of right and wrong are mixed and confused. How do I know the difference among them?"

"If you do not know what is beneficial and what is harmful," said Nieh Ch'üeh, "does it mean that the perfect man does not know them also?"

"The perfect man is a spiritual being," said Wang I. "Even if great oceans burned up, he would not feel hot. Even if the great rivers are frozen, he would not feel cold. And even if terrific thunder were to break up mountains and the wind were to upset the sea, he would not be afraid. Being such, he mounts upon the clouds and forces of heaven, rides on the sun and the moon, and roams beyond the four seas. Neither life nor death affects him. How much less can such matters as benefit and harm?"

Ch'ü-ch'iao Tzu asked Ch'ang-wu Tzu,[21] "I have heard from my grand master (Confucius) that the sage does not devote himself to worldly affairs. He does not go after gain nor avoid injury. He does not like to seek anything and does not purposely adhere to Tao. He speaks without speaking, and he does not speak when he speaks. Thus he roams beyond this dusty world. My grand master regarded this as a rough description of the sage, but I regard this to be the way the wonderful Tao operates. What do you think, sir?"

"What you have said would have perplexed even the Yellow Emperor," replied Ch'ang-wu Tzu. "How could Confucius be competent enough to know?" Moreover, you have drawn a conclusion too early. You see an egg and you immediately want a cock to crow, and you see a sling and you immediately want to roast a dove. Suppose I say a few words to you for what they are worth and you listen to them for what they are worth. How about it?

---

[16]This phrase is obscure. Each commentator has his own interpretation, which is mostly subjective.
[17]Legendary sage-emperors (3rd millennium B.C.).
[18]A virtuous man at the time of Yao, and teacher of Nieh Ch'üeh.
[19]Concubine of a king of Yüeh, which state ended in 334 B.C.
[20]Favorite of Duke Hsien (r. 676–651 B.C.) of Chin.

[21]The identities of these men have not been established. Most probably they are fictitious, products of Chuang Tzu's creative imagination. Yü Yüeh (1821–1906), in his *Chu-tzu p'ing-i* (Textual Critiques of the Various Philosophers), ch. 17, 1899 ed., 17:6b, argues that since the term "grand master" which is the honorific for Confucius, is used, the questioner must have been a pupil of Confucius. This is not necessarily the case, for Chuang Tzu freely put words into the mouths of people, historic or imaginary.

"The sage has the sun and moon by his side. He grasps the universe under the arm. He blends everything into a harmonious whole, casts aside whatever is confused or obscured, and regards the humble as honorable. While the multitude toil, he seems to be stupid and nondiscriminative. He blends the disparities of ten thousand years into one complete purity. All things blended like this and mutually involve each other.

"How do I know that the love of life is not a delusion? And how do I know that the hate of death is not like a man who lost his home when young and does not know where his home is to return to? Li Chi was the daughter of the border warden of Ai. When the Duke of Chin first got her, she wept until the bosom of her dress was drenched with tears. But when she came to the royal residence, shared with the duke his luxurious couch and ate delicate food, she regretted that she had wept. How do I know that the dead will not repent having previously craved for life?

"Those who dream of the banquet may weep the next morning, and those who dream of weeping may go out to hunt after dawn. When we dream we do not know that we are dreaming. In our dreams we may even interpret our dreams. Only after we are awake do we know we have dreamed. Finally there comes a great awakening, and then we know life is a great dream. But the stupid think they are awake all the time, and believe they know it distinctly. Are we (honorable) rulers? Are we (humble) shepherds? How vulgar! Both Confucius and you were dreaming. When I say you were dreaming, I am also dreaming. This way of talking may be called perfectly strange. If after ten thousand generations we could meet one great sage who can explain this, it would be like meeting him in as short a time as in a single morning or evening.

"Suppose you and I argue. If you beat me instead of my beating you, are you really right and am I really wrong? If I beat you instead of your beating me, am I really right and are you really wrong? Or are we both partly right and partly wrong? Or are we both wholly right and wholly wrong? Since between us neither you nor I know which is right, others are naturally in the dark. Whom shall we ask to arbitrate? If we ask someone who agrees with you, since he has already agreed with you, how can he arbitrate? If we ask someone who agrees with me, since he has already agreed with me, how can he arbitrate? If we ask someone who disagrees with both you and me to arbitrate, since he has already disagreed with you and me, how can he arbitrate? If we ask someone who agrees with both you and me to arbitrate, since he has already agreed with you and me, how can he arbitrate? Thus among you, me, and others, none knows which is right. Shall we wait for still others? The great variety of sounds are relative to each other just as much as they are not relative to each other. To harmonize them in the functioning of Nature[22] and leave them in the process of infinite evolution is the way to complete our lifetime."[23]

"What is meant by harmonizing them with the functioning of Nature.?"

"We say this is right or wrong, and is so or is not so. If the right is really right, then the fact that it is different from the wrong leaves no room for argument. If what is so is really so, then the fact that it is different from what is not so leaves no room for argument. Forget the passage of time (life and death) and forget the distinction of right and wrong. Relax in the realm of the infinite and thus abide in the realm of the infinite."

The Shade asks the Shadow, "A little while ago you moved, and now you stop. A little while ago you sat down and now you stand up. Why this instability of purpose?"

"Do I depend on something else to be this way?" answered the Shadow. "Does that something on which I depend also depend on something else? Do I depend on anything any more than a snake depends on its discarded scale or a cicada on its new wings? How can I tell why I am so or why I am not so?"

Once I, Chuang Chou,[24] dreamed that I was a butterfly and was happy as a butterfly. I was con-

---

[22]This interpretation follows Kuo Hsiang. Ma Hsü-lun in his *Chuang Tzu i-cheng* (Textual Studies of the Meaning of the *Chuang Tzu*), 1930, 2:23b, says that it means the revolving process of Nature.

[23]In the text these two sentences follow the next four. Following some editions, I have shifted them here. It seems a most logical thing to do.

[24]Chuang Tzu here refers to himself as Chuang Chou (Eds.).

scious that I was quite pleased with myself, but I did not know that I was Chou. Suddenly I awoke, and there I was, visibly Chou. I do not know whether it was Chou dreaming that he was a butterfly or the butterfly dreaming that it was Chou. Between Chou and the butterfly there must be some distinction. [But one may be the other.] This is called the transformation of things.

• • •

THE JOY OF FISHES

Chuang Tzu and Hui Tzu
Were crossing Hao river
By the dam.

Chuang said:
"See how free
The fishes leap and dart:
That is their happiness."

Hui replied:
"Since you are not a fish
How do you know
What makes fishes happy?"

Chuang said:
"Since you are not I
How can you possibly know
That I do not know
What makes fishes happy?"

Hui argued:
"If I, not being you,
Cannot know what you know
It follows that you
Not being a fish
Cannot know what they know."

Chuang said:
"Wait a minute!
Let us get back
To the original question.
What you asked me was
'How do you know
What makes fishes happy?'
From the terms of your question

You evidently know I know
What makes fishes happy.

"I know the joy of fishes
In the river
Through my own joy, as I go walking
Along the same river."

AVERROËS' SEARCH

Jorge Luis Borges

*S'imaginant que la tragédie
n'est autre que l'art de louer . . .*
—ERNEST RENAN, *AVERROËS,* 48 (1861).

Abu-al-Walid Muhammad ibn-Ahmad ibn-Rushd (a century would be needed for this lengthy name to become simply Averroës, after first becoming Benraist and then Avenryz and even Aben-Rassad and Filius Rosadis) was busy redacting the eleventh chapter of the *Tahāfut al Tahāfut* ("The Incoherence of Incoherence"), in which he maintains against the opinion of the Persian ascetic al-Ghazzāli,[1] author of the *Tahāfut al Falasifa* ("The Incoherence of Philosophers"), that the Divinity knows only the general laws of the universe, those concerning the species, not those relating to the individual. He wrote with slow assurance, from right to left; the task of composing syllogisms and of linking up vast paragraphs did not prevent him from feeling, as if it were a sense of well-being, the cool deep house around him. In the depths of the siesta hour, amorous doves cooed huskily; from some invisible patio arose the murmur of a fountain; something in the blood of Averroës, whose ancestors came from Arabian deserts, was grateful for the constancy of water. Down below lay the gardens, the orchard;

---

[1]A selection from the work of Al-Ghazzāli is found in Chapter 4 of this volume (Eds.).

down below, the bustling Guadalquivir, and beyond, the beloved city of Córdoba, no less illustrious than Baghdad or Cairo, like a complex and delicate instrument; and all around (Averroës heard and felt it, too), the land of Spain stretched out to the border, the land of Spain, where there are few things, but where each one seems to exist in a substantive and eternal way.

His pen raced across the page, his proofs, irrefutable, interwove themselves; but a slight preoccupation dimmed Averroës' felicity. It was not the fault of the *Tahāfut,* a fortuitous piece of work, but was caused by a problem of a philological nature, relating to the monumental work which would justify him in the eyes of mankind: his commentary on Aristotle. Fountainhead of all wisdom, the Greek had been given to the world to teach men all they might know. Averroës' lofty purpose was to interpret his books in the way that the ulema interpret the Koran. History records few acts more beautiful and more pathetic than this Arabic physician's consecration to the thoughts of a man from whom he was separated by fourteen centuries. To the intrinsic difficulties we should add the fact that Averroës, who had no knowledge of Syriac or Greek, was working on the translation of a translation. On the previous evening he had been nonplussed by two equivocal words at the beginning of the *Poetics:* the words *tragedy* and *comedy.* He had encountered them years before in the third book of the *Rhetoric.* No one within the compass of Islam intuited what they meant. Averroës had exhausted the pages of Alexander of Aphrodisia in vain; vainly he had collated the versions of the Nestorian philosopher Hunain ibn-Ishaq and of abu-Bashar Mata. The two arcane words pollulated in the text of the *Poetics;* it was impossible to elude them.

Averroës put down his pen. He told himself (without too much conviction) that whatever we seek is never very far away. He put aside the manuscript of the *Tahāfut* and went over to the book shelf where the many volumes of the *Mohkam,* composed by blind Abensida and copied by Persian calligraphers, stood in a row. It was ludicrous to think that he might not have consulted them already, but he

was tempted anew by the idle pleasure of turning their pages again: From this deliberate distraction he was in turn distracted by a kind of melody. He looked down over the railed balcony; below, in the narrow earthen patio, some half-clad boys were playing. One of them, standing on the shoulders of another, was obviously acting the part of the muezzin; with his eyes closed tight he chanted *There is no god but God.* The boy who sustained him, unmoving, was the minaret. A third, abjectly on his knees in the dust, was the congregation of the Faithful. The game did not last long: each one wanted to be the muezzin, no one cared to be the congregation or the tower. Averroës heard them arguing in *gross* dialect: that is, in the incipient Spanish of the Peninsula's Moslem plebs. He opened the *Quitah Ul-Ain* of Jalal and thought proudly of how in all Córdoba (perhaps even in all Al-Andalus) there was not another copy of that perfect work, only this one which the emir Yacub Almansur had sent him from Tangier. The name of this seaport reminded him that the traveler Abulcasim Al-Ashari, who had just come back from Morocco, would be dining with him that evening at the home of the Koranic scholar Farach. Abulcasim claimed to have voyaged as far as the dominions of the Empire of Shin (China). His detractors, equipped with the peculiar logic supplied by hatred, swore that he had never set foot in China and that he had blasphemed against Allah in that country's temples. The gathering would, inevitably, last several hours. Hurriedly, Averroës resumed writing his *Tahāfut.* He worked until nightfall.

At Farach's house, the conversation went from a discussion of the incomparable virtues of the Governor to those of his brother the emir; later, in the garden, they spoke of roses. Abulcasim, who had not looked at them, swore that there were no roses like those which decorate the country houses of Andalusia. Farach did not let himself be flattered; he observed that the learned ibn-Qutaiba describes an excellent variety of perpetual rose which grows in the gardens of Hindustan and whose petals—blood red—have characters written on them saying: *There is no other god like God. Mohammed is the Apostle of God.* He added that Abulcasim surely knew of these roses. Abulcasim looked at him with alarm. If he answered that he did, everyone would judge him, justifiably, the readiest and most gratuitous of imposters; if he replied that he did not, they would consider him an infidel. He chose to mumble that the keys to occult matters are kept by the Lord, and that in all the earth there is nothing, either green or faded, that is not noted in His Book. These words are part of one of the first sutras of the Koran, and they were received with a murmur of reverence. Stimulated by this dialectical victory, Abulcasim was about to announce that the Lord is perfect in His works, and inscrutable. Whereupon Averroës, prefiguring the remote arguments of an as yet problematical Hume, declared:

"It is easier for me to admit of an error in the learned ibn-Qutaiba, or in the copyists, than admit that the earth yields roses embodying a profession of Faith."

"Just so. Great words and true," said Abulcasim.

"One traveler speaks of a tree whose fruit are green birds," recalled the poet Abdalmalik. "It would take a less painful effort for me to believe in that tree than in roses which bore words."

"The color of the birds," said Averroës, "would seem to favor the first mentioned prodigy. Besides, fruits and birds belong to the natural world, but writing is an art. To go from leaves to birds is easier than to go from roses to letters."

Another guest indignantly denied that writing was an art, inasmuch as the original of the Koran— *the mother of the Book*—is older than the Creation and is kept in Heaven. Another man cited Chahiz of Basra, who had said that the Koran is an essence which can take the form of a man or of an animal, an opinion apparently in concord with the theory that it has two faces. Farach then lengthily expounded the orthodox doctrine. The Koran, he said, is one of the attributes of God, like His mercy; it is copied in a book, it is pronounced with the tongue, it is remembered in one's heart, and the language and the signs and the writing are all works of man, while the Koran is eternal and irrevocable. Averroës, who had written a commentary on the *Republic,* could have mentioned that the mother of the

Book is something on the order of its Platonic model, but he had already noticed that theology was a subject altogether inaccessible to Abulcasim.

Others, who had also noticed the same thing, urged Abulcasim to tell them the tale of some marvel. Then as now the world was an atrocious place; the audacious could move about in it, and so could the poor in spirit, the wretches who adjusted to anything. Abulcasim's memory was a mirror of intimate acts of cowardice. What tale could he tell? Besides, they demanded marvels of him, and marvels are probably not communicable; the moon in Bengal is not the same as the moon in the Yemen, though it be described by the same words. Abulcasim hesitated; then he spoke:

"Whoever travels through climes and cities," he unctuously announced, "will see many things worthy of credit. For instance, the following, which I have related only once before, to the King of the Turks. It took place at Sin Kalan (Canton), where the river of the Water of Life spills into the sea."

Farach asked if the city was to be found many leagues away from the Wall which had been built by Iskandar Zul Qarnain (Alexander Bicornis of Macedonia) to halt Gog and Magog.

"Deserts separate them," said Abulcasim, with involuntary arrogance. "It would take a *kafila* (a caravan) forty days to get within sight of its towers, and another forty days, they say, to reach it. I don't know of a single man in Sin Kalan who has ever seen the Wall, or who has ever seen anyone who did."

Terror of the crassly infinite, of mere space, of mere matter, laid a hand on Averroës for an instant. He gazed on the symmetrical garden; he knew himself grown old, useless, unreal. Abulcasim was saying:

"One afternoon, the Moslem merchants in Sin Kalan led me to a painted wood house inhabited by a large number of people. It is impossible to describe that house, which was more like a single room, with rows of chambers or of balconies, one on top of the other. People were eating and drinking in these cavities; the same activity was taking place on the floor and on a terrace. The people on the terrace played on drums and lutes, except for some score or so (who wore crimson masks) who were praying, singing, and conversing. They suffered imprisonment, but no one could see the prison: they rode on horseback, but no one saw the horse; they fought in combat, but their swords were reeds; they died and then stood up again."

"The activity of madmen," said Farach, "goes beyond the previsions of the sane."

"They were not mad," Abulcasim was forced to explain. "They were representing a story, a merchant told me."

No one understood, no one seemed to want to understand. In confusion, Abulcasim turned from the narrative which they had heard to cumbersome explanations. With the help of his hands, he said:

"Let us imagine that someone shows a story instead of telling it. Suppose this story is the one about the Seven Sleepers of Ephesus. We see them retire to the cave, we see them pray and sleep, sleep with their eyes open, we see them growing while they sleep, we see them awake at the end of three hundred and nine years, we see them awake in Paradise, we see them awake with the dog. Something of the sort was shown us that afternoon by the persons on the terrace."

"Did these people speak?" asked Farach.

"Of course they spoke," said Abulcasim, now become the apologist for a performance he scarcely remembered and which had only vexed him at the time. "They spoke and sang and perorated!"

"In that case," said Farach, "there was no need for *twenty* people. A single speaker can relate anything, however complex it may be."

Everyone approved this dictum. The virtues of Arabic were next extolled, for it is the language used by God to direct the angels; and Arabic poetry was praised. Abdalmalik, after properly considering the subject, held that the poets of Damascus or Córdoba who insisted on pastoral images and a Bedouin vocabulary were old-fashioned. He said it was absurd that a man before whose eyes the Guadalquivir ran wide should celebrate the still waters of a well. He urged the convenience of renovating the ancient metaphors; he stated that at the time Zuhair compared Destiny with a blind camel, this figure of speech could

move people to astonishment, but that five centuries of wonder had exhausted the surprise. This dictum, too, was approved by all: they had heard it often, from many men. Averroës was silent. But at last he spoke, less for the sake of the others than for himself.

"With less eloquence," said Averroës, "but with arguments of the same order, I have defended the proposition now sustained by Abdalmalik. In Alexandria, they say that the only man incapable of a crime is the man who has already committed it and already repented; to be free of error, let us add, it is well to have professed it. In his *mohalaca,* Zuhair stated that in the course of eighty years of pain and glory he has often seen Destiny suddenly trample men, like a blind camel. Abdalmalik finds that this figure of speech can no longer cause wonder. Many rejoinders could be made to this objection. The first, that if the end purpose of the poem was surprise, its life would be measured not by centuries but by days and hours and even perhaps by minutes. The second, that a renowned poet is less an inventor than he is a discoverer. In praise of ibn-Sharaf of Berja it has been said and repeated that only he could imagine that the stars at dawn fall slowly, like leaves falling from a tree; if such an attribution were true, it would be evidence that the image is worthless. An image one man alone can compose is an image that touches no man. There are an infinite number of things on earth; any one of them can be equated to any other. To equate stars to leaves is no less arbitrary than to equate them with fishes or birds. On the other hand, there is no one who has not felt at some time that Destiny is hard and awkward, that it is innocent and also inhuman. It was with this conviction in mind, a conviction which may be ephemeral or may be continuous but which no one may elude, that Zuhair's verse was written. What was said in that verse will not ever be said better. Besides (and perhaps here lies the essence of my reflections), time, which despoils fortresses, enriches verses. When Zuhair composed his verse in Araby, it served to bring two images face to face: the image of the old camel and the image of Destiny. Repeated now, it serves to evoke the memory of Zuhair and to fuse our regrets with those of the dead Arabian. The figure had two terms then, and now it has four. Time dilates the compass of verse, and I know of some which, like music, are all things to all men. Thus, when years ago in Marrakesh I was tormented by memories of Córdoba, I took pleasure in repeating the apostrophe Abdurrahman addressed to an African palm in the gardens of Ruzafa:

> You, too, O palm!
> are a stranger to this shore . . .

And this is the singular merit of poetry: that words written by a King who longed for the East served me, an exile in Africa, in my nostalgia for Spain."

Averroës then spoke of the first poets, of those who in the Time of Ignorance, before Islam, already said everything there was to say and said it in the infinite language of the desert. Alarmed—not without reason—by ibn-Sharaf's ostentation, he pointed out that all poetry was summarized in the ancients and in the Koran, and he condemned the ambition to innovate as both illiterate and vainglorious. The other guest heard him with pleasure, for he vindicated tradition.

The muezzins were calling the Faithful to early morning prayer when Averroës entered his library again. (In the harem, the raven-haired slave girls had been torturing a red-haired slave girl, but Averroës wouldn't know about this until that afternoon.) The sense of the two equivocal words had somehow been revealed to him. With a firm and careful calligraphy he added the following lines to the manuscript.

Aristu (Aristotle) *calls panegyrics by the name of tragedy, and satires and anathemas he calls comedies. The Koran abounds in remarkable tragedies and comedies, and so do the* mohalacas *of the sanctuary.*

He felt sleepy, he felt a bit cold. He unwound his turban and looked at himself in a metal mirror. I do not know what his eyes saw, for no historian has ever described the forms of his face. I do know that he suddenly disappeared, as if fulminated by a bolt of flameless fire, and that with him disappeared the house and the invisible fountain and the books and the manuscripts and the doves and the many raven-haired slave girls and the quivering red-haired slave girl and Farach and Abulcasim and the rose trees and perhaps even the Guadalquivir.

In the foregoing story I have striven to narrate the process involved in a defeat. I thought, first, of the Bishop of Canterbury who proposed to demonstrate the existence of God; then, of the alchemists who sought the philosopher's stone; next, of the vain trisectors of the angle and squarers of the circle. Later I reflected that even more poetic is the case of the man who sets himself a goal not inaccessible to other men, but inaccessible to him. I remembered Averroës, who, circumscribed by the compass of Islam, could never know the significance of the words *tragedy* and *comedy*. I told the tale; as I progressed, I felt what the god mentioned by Buffon must have felt, the god who set out to create a bull and instead created a buffalo. I sensed that the work was making mock of me. I sensed that Averroës, striving to imagine a drama without ever having suspected what a theater was, was no more absurd than I, who strove to imagine Averroës with no material other than some fragments from Renan, Lane, and Asín Palacios. I sensed, on the last page, that my narrative was a symbol of the man I was while I wrote it, and that to write that story I had to be that man, and that to be that man I had to write that story, and so to infinity. (The instant I stop believing in him, "Averroës" disappears.)

ZEN KNOWLEDGE

Daisetz T. Suzuki

Satori is a Japanese term, *wu* in Chinese. The Sanskrit *bodhi* and *buddha* come from the same root, *bud,* "to be aware of," "to wake." *Buddha* is thus "the awakened one," "the enlightened one," while *bodhi* is "enlightenment." "Buddhism" means the teaching of the enlightened one, that is to say, Buddhism is the doctrine of enlightenment. What Buddha teaches, therefore, is the realisation of bodhi, which is satori. Satori is the centre of all Buddhist teachings. Some may think satori is characteristic of Mahayana Buddhism, but it is not so. Earlier Buddhists also talk about this, the realization of *bodhi;* and as long as they talk about *bodhi* at all they must be said to base their doctrine on the experience of satori.

We have to distinguish between *prajna* and *vijnana.* We can divide knowledge into two categories: intuitive knowledge which is *prajna* whereas discursive knowledge is *vijnana.* To distinguish further: *prajna* grasps reality in its oneness, in its totality; *vijnana* analyses it into subject and object. Here is a flower; we can take this flower as representing the universe itself. We talk about the petals, pollen, stamen and stalk; that is physical analysis. Or we can analyse it chemically into so much hydrogen, oxygen, etc. Chemists analyse a flower, enumerate all its elements and say that the aggregate of all those elements makes up the flower. But they have not exhausted the flower; they have simply analyzed it. That is the *vijnana* way of understanding a flower. The *prajna* way is to understand it just as it is without analysis or chopping in into pieces. It is to grasp it in its oneness, in its totality, in its suchness (*sono mame*) in Japanese.

We are generally attracted to analytical knowledge or discriminative understanding, and we divide reality into several pieces. We dissect it and by dissecting it we kill reality. When we have finished our analysis we have murdered reality, and this dead reality we think is our understanding of it. When we see reality dead, after analysing it, we say that we understand it, but what we understand is not reality itself but its corpse after it has been mutilated by our intellect and senses. We fail to see that this result of dissection is not reality itself, and when we take this analysis as a basis of our understanding it is inevitable that we go astray, far away from the truth. Because in this way we shall never reach the final solution of the problem of reality.

Prajna grasps this reality in its oneness, in its totality, in its suchness. *Prajna* does not divide reality into any form of dichotomy; it does not dissect it ei-

ther metaphysically or physically or chemically. The dividing of reality is the function of *vijnana* which is very useful in a practical way; but *prajna* is different.

Vijnana can never reach infinity. When we write the numbers 1, 2, 3, etc, we never come to an end, for the series goes on to infinity. By adding together all those individual numbers we try to reach the total of the numbers, but as numbers are endless this totality can never be reached. *Prajna,* on the other hand, intuits the whole totality instead of moving through 1, 2, 3 to infinity; it grasps things as a whole. It does not appeal to discrimination; it grasps reality from inside, as it were. Discursive *vijnana* tries to grasp reality objectively, that is, by addition objectively one after another. But this objective method can never reach its end because things are infinite, and we can never exhaust them objectively. Subjectively, however, we turn that position upside down and get to the inside. By looking at this flower objectively we can never reach its essence or life, but when we turn that position inside out, enter into the flower, and become the flower itself, we live through the process of growth: I am the shoot, I am the stem, I am the bud, and finally I am the flower and the flower is me. That is the *prajna* way of comprehending the flower.

In Japan there is a seventeen syllable poem called *haiku,* and one composed by a modern woman-poet reads in literal translation:

> Oh, Morning Glory!
> Bucket taken captive,
> I beg for water.

The following was the incident that led her to compose it. One early morning the poet came outdoors to draw water from the well, and saw the morning glory winding round the bamboo pole attached to the bucket. The morning glory in full bloom looks its best in the early morning after a dewy night. It is bright, refreshing, vivifying; it reflects heavenly glory not yet tarnished by things earthly. She was so struck with its untainted beauty that she remained silent for a little while; she was so absorbed in the flower that she lost the power of speech. It took a few seconds at least before she could exclaim: "Oh, Morning Glory!" Physically, the interval was a space of a second or two or perhaps more; but metaphysically, it was eternity as beauty itself is. Psychologically, the poet was the unconscious itself in which there was no dichotomization of any kind.

The poet was the morning glory and the morning glory was the poet. There was self-identity of flower and poet. It was only when she became conscious of herself seeing the flower that she cried: "Oh, Morning Glory!" When she said that, consciousness revived in her. But she did not like to disturb the flower, because although it is not difficult to unwind the flower from the bamboo pole she feared that to touch the flower with human hands would be the desecration of the beauty. So she went to a neighbour and asked for water.

When you analyse that poem you can picture to yourself how she stood before the flower, losing herself. There was then no flower, no human poet; just a "something" which was neither flower nor poet. But when she recovered her consciousness, there was the flower, there was herself. There was an object which was designated as morning glory and there was one who spoke—a bifurcation of subject-object. Before the bifurcation there was nothing to which she could give expression, she herself was non-existent. When she uttered, "Oh, Morning Glory!" the flower was created and along with it herself, but before that bifurcation, that dualisation of subject and object, there was nothing. And yet there was a "something" which could divide itself into subject-object, and this "something" which had not yet divided itself, not become subject to bifurcation, to discriminative understanding (i.e. before *vijnana* asserted itself)—this is *prajna*. For *Prajna* is subject and at the same time object; it divides itself into subject-object and also stands by itself, but that standing by itself is not to be understood on the level of duality. Standing by itself, being absolute in its complete totality or oneness—that is the moment which the poet realised, and that is satori. Satori consists in not staying in that oneness, not remaining with itself, but in awak-

ening from it and being just about to divide itself into subject and object. Satori is the staying in oneness and yet rising from it and dividing itself into subject-object. First, there is "something" which has not divided itself into subject-object, this is oneness as it is. Then this "something," becoming conscious of itself, divides itself into flower and poet. The becoming conscious is the dividing. Poet now sees flower and flower sees poet, there is mutual seeing. When this seeing each other, not just from one side alone but from the other side as well when this kind of seeing actually takes place, there is a state of satori.

When I talk like this it takes time. There is something which has not divided itself but which then becomes conscious of itself, and this leads to an utterance, and so on. But in actual satori there is no time interval, hence no consciousness of the bifurcation. The oneness dividing itself into subject-object and yet retaining its oneness at the very moment that there is the awakening of a consciousness—this is satori.

From the human point of view we talk of *prajna* and *vijnana* as the integral understanding and the discriminative understanding of reality respectively. We speak of these things in order to satisfy our human understanding. Animals and plants do not divide themselves; they just live and act, but humans have awakened this consciousness. By the awakening of consciousness we become conscious of this and that, and this universe of infinite diversity arises. Because of this awakening we discriminate, and because of discrimination we talk of *prajna* and *vijnana* and make these distinctions, which is characteristic of human beings. To satisfy this demand we talk about having satori, or the awakening of this self-identity consciousness.

When the poet saw the flower, that very moment before she spoke even a word there was an intuitive apprehension of something which eludes our ordinary intuition. This *sui generis* intuition is what I would call *prajna*-intuition. The moment grasped by *prajna*-intuition is satori. That is what made Buddha the Enlightened one. Thus, to attain satori, *prajna*-intuition is to be awakened.

That is more or less a metaphysical explanation of satori, but psychologically satori may be said to take place this way. Our consciousness contains all things; but there must be at least two things whereby consciousness is possible. Consciousness takes place when two things stand opposing one another. In our ordinary life, consciousness is kept too busy with all things going on in it and has not time to reflect within itself. Consciousness has thus no opportunity to become conscious of itself. It is so deeply involved in action, it is in fact action itself. Satori never takes place as long as consciousness is kept turning outwardly, as it were. Satori is born of self-consciousness. Consciousness must be made to look within itself before it is awakened to satori.

To get satori, all things which crowd into our daily-life consciousness must be wiped off clean. This is the function of *samadhi,* which Indian philosophers emphasize so much. "Entering into *samadhi*" is to attain uniformity of consciousness, i.e. to wipe consciousness clean, though practically speaking, this wiping clean is something almost impossible. But we must try to do it in order to attain this state of uniformity, which, according to early Buddhist thinkers, is a perfect state of mental equilibrium, for here there are no passions, no intellectual functions, but only a perfectly balanced state of indifference. When this takes place it is known as *samadhi,* or entering into the fourth stage of *dhyana* or *jhana,* as described in most early Buddhist sutras. This is not, however, a state of satori. *Samadhi* is not enough, which is no more than the unification of consciousness. There must be an awakening from this state of unification or uniformity. The awakening is becoming aware of consciousness in its own activities. When consciousness starts to move, begins to divide itself into subject-object and says: I am sorry, or glad, or I hear, and so on—this very moment as it moves on is caught up in satori. But as soon as you say "I have caught it" it is no more there. Therefore, satori is not something you can take hold of and show to others, saying, "See, it is here!"

Consciousness is something which never ceases to be active though we may be quite unconscious of it, and what we call perfect uniformity is not a state of sheer quietness, that is, of death. As conscious-

ness thus goes on unceasingly, no one can stop it for inspection. Satori must take place while consciousness is going through stages or instant points of becoming. Satori is realised along with the becoming, which knows no stoppage. Satori is no particular experience like other experiences of our daily life. Particular experiences are experiences of particular events while the satori experience is the one that runs through all experiences. It is for this reason that satori cannot be singled out of other experiences and pronounced, "See, here is my satori!" It is always elusive and alluring. It can never be separated from our everyday life, it is forever there, inevitably there. Becoming, not only in its each particularisable moment but through its never-terminating totality, is the body of satori.

The nature of human understanding and reasoning is to divide reality into the dichotomy of this and that, of "A" and "not-A" and then to take reality so divided as really reality. We do not seem to understand reality in any other way. This being so, as long as we are depending on "the understanding," there will be no grasping of reality, no intuitive taking hold of reality, and satori is no other than this intuitive taking hold of reality. There is no reality beside becoming, becoming is reality and reality is becoming. Therefore, the satori intuition of reality consists in identifying oneself with becoming, to take becoming as it goes on becoming. We are not to cut becoming into pieces, and, picking up each separate piece which drops from "becoming," to say to people, "Here is reality." While making this announcement we will find that becoming is no more there; reality is flown away into the realm of the irrevocable past.

This is illustrated by a Zen story. A woodman went to the mountains and saw a strange animal on the other side of the tree which he was cutting. He thought: "I might kill that animal." The animal then spoke to the woodman and said: "Are you going to kill me?" Having his mind read, the woodman got angry and wondered what to do. The animal said: "Now you are thinking what to do with me." Whatever thought the woodman had, the animal intuited, and told him so. Finally, the woodman said: "I will stop thinking about the animal and go on cutting wood." While he was so engaged the top of the axe flew off and killed the animal.

This illustrates that when you are thinking of it there is satori. When you try to realise satori, the more you struggle the farther it is away. You cannot help pursuing satori, but so long as you make that special effort satori will never be gained. But you cannot forget about it altogether. If you expect satori to come to you of its own accord, you will not get it.

To realise satori is very difficult, as the Buddha found. When he wished to be liberated from the bondage of birth and death he began to study philosophy, but this did not avail him, so he turned to asceticism. This made him so weak that he could not move, so he took milk and decided to go on with his search for liberation. Reasoning did not do any good and pursuing moral perfection did not help him either. Yet the urge to solve this problem was still there. He could go no farther, yet he could not retreat, so he had to stay where he was, but even that would not do. This state of spiritual crisis means that you cannot go on, nor retreat, nor stay where you are. When this dilemma is genuine, there pre-vails a state of consciousness ready for satori. When we really come to this stage (but we frequently think that what is not real is real), when we find ourselves at this critical moment, something is sure to rise from the depths of reality, from the depths of our own being. When this comes up there is satori. Then you understand all things and are at peace with the world as well as with yourself.

QUESTIONS FOR DISCUSSION

1. Chuang Tzu says he knows the joy of fishes through his own joy, while walking by the river in which they swim. Do you think this empathy is a reliable indicator? Or are we being too literal in thus trying to understand Chuang Tzu?

2. Compare Borges's views on knowledge with those of Chuang Tzu.

3. Suzuki says that, so long as we depend on "the understanding," there will be no grasping of re-ality. Do you agree with this mystical conclu-sion? Why or why not?

Theistic Arguments and Atheist Challenges
  A. C. Ewing, *Proofs of God's Existence*
  Antony Flew, *Theology and Falsification*
  Sigmund Freud, *A Philosophy of Life*

The Religious Experience
  Sarvepalli Radhakrishnan, *Personal Experience of God*
  Buddhadasa, *No Religion*
  Vine Deloria, *Transforming Reality*

Religions, Society, and Politics
  Karl Marx and Friedrich Engels, *Critique of Religion*
  Leonardo and Clodovis Boff, *Liberation Theology*
  Sulak Sivaraksa, *Engaged Buddhism*
  Hassan Hanafi, *Islam and Revolution*
  Carol P. Christ, *Why Women Need the Goddess*

William H. Johnson, *I Baptize Thee,* c. 1940, National Museum of American Art, Washington, D.C./Art Resource, NY.

CHAPTER 3

PHILOSOPHY OF RELIGION

The contemporary German-born psychoanalyst and social thinker Erich Fromm claims that all cultures and, indeed, all human beings are religious in that they develop a general frame of orientation to understand the fundamental problems of human existence. Such a framework attempts to locate one's own life within a larger scheme of things. Whether or not we want to conceptualize religion so broadly, it is clear that from the dawn of human civilization every culture has been concerned with what it identified as a religious dimension of life and embodied this concern in a specific set of religious institutions and ritual practices. In this more specific sense, religion points to an ultimate spiritual foundation of physical reality and human existence, a spiritual dimension that can provide us with an answer to questions of life and death, that attempts to explain the relation of the individual to the universe, and that can offer a guide to human self-development and ethical conduct. Such a spiritual source has been most often, although not always, identified with the idea of God. It is for this reason that in the first section of this chapter we consider the philosophical question: Does God exist?

Philosophy of religion in the Western tradition has been to a large extent the attempt to answer this question by providing, analyzing, and criticizing rational demonstrations, or proofs of God's existence. In the first section the contemporary British philosopher A. C. Ewing presents three of these proofs and gives qualified support to two of them. The second two selections in this section—by the contemporary British philosopher Antony Flew and the renowned founder of psychoanalysis Sigmund Freud—answer the question in the negative.

Philosophical proofs of the existence of God have been a much more important philosophical enterprise within the West than they have been for other religious traditions. In part this is because these other traditions tend to be more concerned with religious experience as such, or what is sometimes called "the mystical experience." In the second section of this chapter, the twentieth-century Indian philosopher Sarvepalli Radhakrishnan attempts to characterize this experience and to evaluate its cross-cultural significance. While those who have had such experiences often talk about them as experiences of God, they do not always do so. In fact, while religious or mystical experiences as such seem to be cross-cultural, they tend to be interpreted through the cultural and philosophical categories of each religious tradition. This leads to the proposition expressed by the contemporary Thai Buddhist Buddhadassa that the essence of religion transcends all religions. In contrast, the last reading in the second section claims that tribal religious experience is fundamentally different from the religious experiences of the major world's religions.

In the final section of this chapter we examine the relation of religion to social and political change. While the nineteenth-century revolutionary German philosopher Karl Marx characterized religion as the "opium of the people," religion has also been used to challenge the ruling powers. In Latin America, for example, a powerful revolutionary current has emerged in the last several decades known as "liberation theology." The selection by two Brazilian theologians and priests who are also brothers, Leonardo and Clodovis Boff, attempts to explain the political, theological, and philosophical significance of this movement. But the emphasis on action against the status quo is not limited to the Christian tradition in Latin America. We can find forms of liberation theology in every major religious tradition and in every corner of the world. The selections by Sulak Sivaraksa on engaged Buddhism and by Hassan Hanafi on the revolutionary implications of Islam illustrate this point. Finally, the last selection by the feminist writer Carol Christ challenges the patriarchal categories of traditional religious thought and suggests that women might do well to disavow God the Father and embrace the Goddess.

Readers of Section Two and Section Three who want to know more about Hinduism should see another reading by Radhakrishnan in Section One of Chapter 6, the selections from the Upanishads in Section Two of Chapter 1 and Section Two of Chapter 5 and the commentary on the Upanishads by Sri Ramana Maharshi in Section Two of Chapter 1, the selections from the Bhadavad-Gita in Section Two of Chapter 5 and Section One of Chapter 7, and the reading by Satyavrata Siddhantalankar in Section Two of Chapter 9. Those who want to know more about the Buddhist approach should consult first H. Saddhatissa's discussion of the Four Noble Truths reprinted in Section One of Chapter 8 and Gunapala Dharmasiri's discussion of Buddhist ethics in Section Two of Chapter 7. There are three selections concerning the Buddhist view of self in Section Two of Chapter 5, the classic "Questions of King Melinda" and the selections by T. R. V. Murti and Toshiko Izutsu. The last writer is a Zen Buddhist. For other selections by Zen Buddhists see Daisetz T. Suzuki in Section Two of Chapter 2 and Kitaro Nishida in Section Three of Chapter 6. Those interested in Tibetan Buddhism should read the Tibetan Book of the Dead in Section Five of Chapter 5 and the selection by the Dalai Lama in Section Three of Chapter 8. Those interested in learning more about Islam should see the selections by Ayatollah Murtaza Mutahhari in Section One of Chapter Two, by Al-Ghazali and Fatima Mernissi in Section Two of Chapter 4, and by Tabatabai in Section One of Chapter 8.

THEISTIC ARGUMENTS AND ATHEIST CHALLENGES

The Bible does not attempt to prove the existence of God but rather assumes it. For those who lived in the community for whom it was originally meaningful, God's existence was beyond question. It is only when a system of beliefs begins to break down that people feel the need to question it. This happens when one culture meets another or when the development of a new mode of thinking emerges. Modern science is such a new mode of thinking.

The scientific ethos puts belief in God in question in two ways. First, it insists that ideas about the world must be, in some way, verified in experience. Secondly, specific theories of science pose challenges to, at least, some traditional Western religious beliefs. Before Galileo looked through his telescope and found evidence that Copernicus was right, it was generally assumed that God created the earth at the center of the universe so that His human creation would also be so situated. Darwin's theory of evolution challenged the idea of Adam and Eve as a separate creation. And Sigmund Freud's psychoanalytic theories imply that belief in God might have less than spiritual motives.

While the main arguments for the existence of God were originally formulated in the Middle Ages or earlier, they take on a special urgency in the modern scientific era. In the first selection of this section A. C. Ewing, a twentieth-century British philosopher, presents a version of three classical arguments. The first, the ontological argument which attempts to deduce the existence of God from the very concept of God, Ewing finds unsatisfying. But he gives qualified support to the cosmological argument, which assumes that we need an ultimate reason or First Cause to account for the existence of the world, and the argument from design (sometimes called the teleological argument), which argues from the appearance of orderliness and design in the universe to the existence of a Grand Designer. These arguments, Ewing asserts, do not provide a definitive proof of God's existence but give the world view of the *theist* (one who believes in the ex-

istence of God) a higher probability value than the world view of the *atheist* (one who denies God's existence). In the last analysis, Ewing claims that "it does remain incredible that the physical universe should just have happened."

Antony Flew, the contemporary British philosopher and proponent of logical positivism, is the second author in this section. Logical positivism is a philosophical method that assumes that a statement about the world is meaningful only if we can say what kinds of conditions and observations would lead us to accept it as true or false. Emphasizing the later consideration, Flew insists that for a statement to be meaningful it must in principle be capable of falsification. This is known as the falsifiability criteria. Using a parable of an invisible gardener, Flew attempts to show that the falsifiability criteria cannot be satisfied with regard to statements about God and, therefore, such assertions as "God exists" or "God loves us" are neither true nor false but simply meaningless.

It is important to note that when Flew claims that statements about God are not meaningful, he is denying their cognitive status, not talking about whether they have emotional significance for our lives. It is hardly to be doubted that for many people in the world belief in the existence of God is of great psychological importance. Indeed, some might argue that this fact alone establishes the existence of God. How is it possible for so many people to believe in God, if the belief itself is false or meaningless? Sigmund Freud, in the last article in this section, speaks directly to this question. Freud uses his psychoanalytic method to trace the origin of belief in God to the child's helplessness in relation to his or her parents. For Freud, "God the Father" functions precisely as the infant once viewed his or her real father—as a creator of his or her existence, as an omnipotent protector, and one who imposes prohibitions and threatens punishment. Religion, then, is a fantasy that attempts to relive this aspect of our childhood experiences. In this sense, it speaks to some real human desires and fears, but it remains an illusion that cannot provide an adequate account of the real world. For that we need the scientific world view. In another of his works, *The Future of an Illusion,* Freud describes religion as a universal cultural neurosis that must be transcended if civilization as a whole is to move from its childhood to maturity.

PROOFS OF GOD'S EXISTENCE

A. C. Ewing

By "God" I shall understand a supreme mind regarded as either omnipotent or at least more powerful than anything else and supremely good and wise. It is not within the scope of a purely philosophical work to discuss the claims of revelation on which belief in God and his attributes has so often been based, but philosophers have also formulated a great number of *arguments* for the existence of God.

THE ONTOLOGICAL ARGUMENT

To start with the most dubious and least valuable of these, the *ontological* argument claims to prove the existence of God by a mere consideration of our idea of him. God is defined as the most perfect being or as a being containing all positive attributes.[1] It is then argued that existence is a "perfection" or a positive attribute, and that therefore, if we are to avoid contradicting ourselves, we must grant the existence of God. The most important of the objections to the argument is to the effect that existence is not a "perfection" or an attribute. To say that

something exists is to assert a proposition of a very different kind from what we assert when we ascribe any ordinary attribute to a thing. It is not to increase the concept of the thing by adding a new characteristic, but merely to affirm that the concept is realized in fact. This is one of the cases where we are apt to be misled by language. Because "cats exist" and "cats sleep," or "cats are existent" and "cats are carnivorous," are sentences of the same grammatical form, people are liable to suppose that they also express the same form of proposition, but this is not the case. To say that cats are carnivorous is to ascribe an additional quality to beings already presupposed as existing; to say that cats are existent is to say that propositions ascribing to something the properties which constitute the definition of a cat are sometimes true. The distinction is still more obvious in the negative case. If "dragons are not existent animals" were a proposition of the same form as "lions are not herbivorous animals," to say that dragons are not existent would already be to presuppose their existence. A lion has to exist in order to have the negative property of not being herbivorous, but in order to be nonexistent a dragon need not first exist.[2] "Dragons are non-existent" means that nothing has the properties commonly implied by the word "dragon."

It has sometimes been said that "the ontological proof" is just an imperfect formulation of a principle which no one can help admitting and which is a necessary presupposition of all knowledge. This is the principle that what we really must think must be true of reality. ("Must" here is the logical, not the psychological must.) If we did not assume this principle, we should never be entitled to accept something as a fact because it satisfies our best intellectual criteria, and therefore we should have no ground for asserting anything at all. Even experience would not help us, since any proposition contradicting experience might well be true if the law

---

[1]"Positive" (1) enables us to exclude evil attributes on the ground that they are negative, (2) implies the infinity of God, for there would be an element of negativity in him if he possessed any attribute in any limited degree, i.e. superior degrees would be denied of him.

[2]We can of course say that dragons are not herbivorous if we are merely making a statement about the content of fictitious stories of dragons.

of contradiction were not assumed to be objectively valid. This, however, is so very different from what the ontological proof as formulated by its older exponents says that it should not be called by the same name. And in any case the principle that what we must think must be true of reality could only be used to establish the existence of God if we already had reached the conclusion that we must think this, i.e. had already justified the view that God exists (or seen it to be self-evident).

THE FIRST CAUSE ARGUMENT

The *cosmological* or first cause argument is of greater importance. The greatest thinker of the Middle Ages, St. Thomas Aquinas (*circ.* 1225–74), while rejecting the ontological argument, made the cosmological the main intellectual basis of his own theism, and in this respect he has been followed by Roman Catholic orthodoxy. To this day it is often regarded in such circles as proving with mathematical certainty the existence of God. It has, however, also played a very large part in Protestant thought; and an argument accepted in different forms by such varied philosophers of the highest eminence as Aristotle, St. Thomas, Descartes, Locke, Leibniz, and many modern thinkers certainly ought not to be despised. The argument is briefly to the effect that we require a reason to account for the world and this ultimate reason must be of such a kind as itself not to require a further reason to account for it. It is then argued that God is the only kind of being who could be conceived as self-sufficient and so as not requiring a cause beyond himself but being his own reason. The argument has an appeal because we are inclined to demand a reason for things, and the notion of a first cause is the only alternative to the notion of an infinite regress, which is very difficult and seems even self-contradictory. Further, if any being is to be conceived as necessarily existing and so not needing a cause outside itself, it is most plausible to conceive God as occupying this position. But the argument certainly makes assumptions which may be questioned. It assumes the principle of causation in a form in which the cause is held to

give a reason for the effect, a doctrine with which I have sympathy but which would probably be rejected by the majority of modern philosophers outside the Roman Catholic Church. Further, it may be doubted whether we can apply to the world as a whole the causal principle which is valid within the world; and if we say that the causal principle thus applied is only analogous to the latter the argument is weakened. Finally, and this I think the most serious point, it is exceedingly difficult to see how anything could be its own reason. To be this it would seem that it must exist necessarily *a priori*.[3] Now we can well see how it can be necessary *a priori* that something, p, should be true if something else, q, is, or again how it can be necessary *a priori* that something self-contradictory should not exist, but it is quite another matter to see how it could be *a priori* necessary in the logical sense that something should positively exist. What contradiction could there be in its not existing?[4] In the mere blank of nonexistence there can be nothing to contradict. I do not say that it can be seen to be absolutely impossible that a being could be its own logical reason, but I at least have not the faintest notion how this could be. The advocates of the cosmological proof might, however, contend that God was necessary in some non-logical sense, which is somewhat less unplausible though still quite incomprehensible to us.

Can the cosmological argument, clearly invalid as a complete proof, be stated in a form which retains some probability value? It may still be argued that the world will at least be more rational if it is as the theist pictures it than if it is not, and that it is more reasonable to suppose that the world is rational than to suppose that it is irrational. Even the latter point would be contradicted by many modern thinkers, but though we cannot prove the view they reject to be true, we should at least note that it is the view which is presupposed by

---

[3] *a priori* is a Latin phrase meaning, literally, "from what comes before." In philosophy, it refers to something that precedes or is independent of sensory experience. Thus, what is *a priori* is true, valid, or exists by necessity (Eds.).

[4] It is one of the objections to the ontological proof that it claims to find a contradiction in God not existing.

science, often unconsciously, in its own sphere. For, as we have seen, practically no scientific propositions can be established by strict demonstration and/or observation alone. Science could not advance at all if it did not assume some criterion beyond experience and the laws of logic and mathematics. What is this criterion? It seems to be coherence in a rational system. We have rejected the view that this is the only criterion, but it is certainly one criterion of truth. For of two hypotheses equally in accord with the empirical facts, scientists will always prefer the one which makes the universe more of a rational system to the one which does not. Science does this even though neither hypothesis is capable of rationalizing the universe completely or even of giving a complete ultimate explanation of the phenomena in question. It is sufficient that the hypothesis adopted brings us a step nearer to the ideal of a fully coherent, rationally explicable world. Now theism cannot indeed completely rationalize the universe till it can show how God can be his own cause, or how it is that he does not need a cause, and till it can also overcome the problem of evil completely, but it does come nearer to rationalizing it than does any other view. The usual modern philosophical views opposed to theism do not try to give any rational explanation of the world at all, but just take it as a brute fact not to be explained, and it must certainly be admitted that we come at least nearer to a rational explanation if we regard the course of the world as determined by purpose and value than if we do not. So it may be argued that according to the scientific principle that we should accept the hypothesis which brings the universe nearest to a coherent rational system theism should be accepted by us. The strong point of the cosmological argument is that after all it does remain incredible that the physical universe should just have happened, even if it be reduced to the juxtaposition of some trillions of electrons. It calls out for some further explanation of some kind.

THE ARGUMENT FROM DESIGN

The *teleological argument* or the *argument from design* is the argument from the adaptation of the living bodies of organisms to their ends and the ends of their species. This is certainly very wonderful:

there are thousands of millions of cells in our brain knit together in a system which works; twenty or thirty different muscles are involved even in such a simple act as a sneeze; directly a wound is inflicted or germs enter an animal's body all sorts of protective mechanisms are set up, different cells are so cunningly arranged that, if we cut off the tail of one of the lower animals, a new one is grown, and the very same cells can develop according to what is needed into a tail or into a leg. Such intricate arrangements seem to require an intelligent purposing mind to explain them. It may be objected that, even if such an argument shows wisdom in God, it does not show goodness and is therefore of little value. The reply may be made that it is incredible that a mind who is so much superior to us in intelligence as to have designed the whole universe should not be at least as good as the best men and should not, to put it at its lowest, care for his offspring at least as well as a decent human father and much more wisely because of his superior knowledge and intellect. Still it must be admitted that the argument could not at its best establish all that the theist would ordinarily wish to establish. It might show that the designer was very powerful, but it could not show him to be omnipotent or even to have created the world as opposed to manufacturing it out of given material; it might make it probable that he was good, but it could not possibly prove him perfect. And of course the more unpleasant features of the struggle for existence in nature are far from supporting the hypothesis of a good God.

But does the argument justify any conclusion at all? It has been objected that it does not on the following ground. It is an argument from analogy, it is said, to this effect: animal bodies are like machines, a machine has a designer, therefore animal bodies have a designer. But the strength of an argument from analogy depends on the likeness between what is compared. Now animal bodies are really not very like machines, and God is certainly not very like a man. Therefore the argument from analogy based on our experience of men designing machines has not enough strength to give much probability to its conclusion. This criticism, I think, would be valid if the argument from design were really in the main an argument from analogy,[5] but I do not think it is. The force of the argument lies not in the analogy, but in the extraordinary intricacy with which the details of a living body are adapted to serve its own interests, an intricacy far too great to be regarded as merely a coincidence. Suppose we saw pebbles on the shore arranged in such a way as to make an elaborate machine. It is theoretically possible that they might have come to occupy such positions by mere chance, but it is fantastically unlikely, and we should feel no hesitation in jumping to the conclusion that they had been thus deposited not by the tide but by some intelligent agent. Yet the body of the simplest living creature is a more complex machine than the most complex ever devised by a human engineer.

Before the theory of evolution was accepted the only reply to this argument was to say that in an infinite time there is room for an infinite number of possible combinations, and therefore it is not, even apart from a designing mind, improbable that there should be worlds or stages in the development of worlds which display great apparent purposiveness. If a monkey played with a typewriter at random, it is most unlikely that it would produce an intelligible book; but granted a sufficient number of billions of years to live and keep playing, the creature would probably eventually produce quite by accident a great number. For the number of possible combinations of twenty-six letters in successions of words is finite, though enormously large, and therefore given a sufficiently long time it is actually probable that any particular one would be reached. This may easily be applied to the occurrence of adaptations in nature. Out of all the possible combinations of things very few would display marked adaptation; but if the number of ingredients of the universe is finite the number of their combinations is also finite, and therefore it is only probable that, given an infinite time, some worlds or some stages in a world process should appear highly purposeful, though they are only the result of a chance combination of atoms. The plausibility of this reply is diminished when we reflect what our attitude would be to somebody who, when playing bridge, had thirteen spades in his hand several times running—according to the laws of probability an enormously less improbable coincidence than would be an unpurposed universe with so much design unaccounted for—and then used such an argument to meet the charge of cheating. Our attitude to his reply would surely hardly be changed even if we believed that people had been playing bridge for an infinite time. If only we were satisfied that matter had existed and gone on changing for ever, would we conclude that the existence of leaves or pebbles on the ground in such positions as to make an intelligible book no longer provided evidence making it probable that somebody had deliberately arranged them? Surely not. And, if not, why should the supposition that matter had gone on changing for ever really upset the argument from design? Of course the appearance of design *may be* fortuitous; the argument from design never claims to give certainty but only probability. But, granted the universe as we have it, is it not a much less improbable hypothesis that it should really have been designed than that it should constitute one of the fantastically rare stages which showed design in an infinite series of chance universes? Further, that matter has been changing for an infinite time is a gratuitous assumption and one not favoured by modern science.[6]

But now the theory of evolution[7] claims to give an alternative explanation of the adaptation of organisms

---

[5]Hume's criticisms of it in the famous *Dialogues concerning Natural Religion* depend mainly on the assumption that it is such an argument.

---

[6]Strictly speaking, what is required by those who put forward the objection in question to the argument from design is not necessarily that matter should have been changing for an infinite time but only for a sufficiently long, though finite, time. But the length of time allowed by modern science for the development of the earth and indeed for that of the whole universe does not in the faintest degree approach what would be needed to make the appearance of organized beings as a result of mere random combinations of atoms anything less than monstrously improbable.

[7]The *theory of evolution* is a theory developed by Charles Darwin (1809–1882) that proposes a scientific explanation of the development of different species. In brief, the theory argues that all known living organisms have evolved from the simplest living organism through a process known as "natural selection," through the capacities of certain accidental new characteristics to adapt to the environment. Evolutionary theory is generally accepted by the scientific community and is the foundation for much of modern biology (Eds.).

that removes the improbability of which we have complained. Once granted the existence of some organisms their offspring would not all be exactly similar. Some would necessarily be somewhat better equipped than others for surviving and producing offspring in their turn, and their characteristics would therefore tend to be more widely transmitted. When we take vast numbers into account, this will mean that a larger and larger proportion of the species will have had relatively favourable variations transmitted to them by their parents, while unfavourable variations will tend to die out. Thus from small beginnings accumulated all the extraordinarily elaborate mechanism which now serves the purpose of living creatures.

There can be no question for a properly informed person of denying the evolution theory, but only of considering whether it is adequate by itself to explain the striking appearance of design. If it is not, it may perfectly well be combined with the metaphysical hypothesis that a mind has designed and controls the universe. Evolution will then be just the way in which God's design works out. Now in reply to the purely evolutionary explanation it has been said that for evolution to get started at all some organisms must have already appeared. Otherwise the production of offspring and their survival or death in the struggle for existence would not have come into question at all. But even the simplest living organism is a machine very much more complex than a motor car. Therefore, if it would be absurd to suppose inorganic matter coming together fortuitously of itself to form a motor car, it would be even more absurd to suppose it thus coming together to form an organism, so without design the evolutionary process would never get started at all. Nor, even granting that this miracle had occurred, could the evolutionists claim that they had been altogether successful in removing the antecedent improbability of such an extensive adaptation as is in fact shown by experience. It has been urged that, since we may go wrong in a vast number of ways for one in which we may go right, the probability of favourable variations is very much less than that of unfavourable; that in order to produce the effect on

survival required a variation would have to be large, but if it were large it would usually lessen rather than increase the chance of survival, unless balanced by other variations the occurrence of which simultaneously with the first would be much more improbable still; and that the odds are very great against either a large number of animals in a species having the variations together by chance or their spreading from a single animal through the species by natural selection. The arguments suggest that, so to speak, to weight the chances we require a purpose, which we should not need, however, to think of as intervening at odd moments but as controlling the whole process. The establishment of the evolution theory no doubt lessens the great improbability of the adaptations having occurred without this, but the original improbability is so vast as to be able to survive a great deal of lessening, and it does not remove it.

Some thinkers would regard it as adequate to postulate an unconscious purpose to explain design, but it is extraordinarily difficult to see what such a thing as an unconscious purpose could be. In one sense indeed I can understand such a phrase. "Unconscious" might mean "unintrospected" or "unintrospectible," and then the purpose would be one which occurred in a mind that did think on the matter but did not self-consciously notice its thinking. But this sense will not do here, for it already presupposes a mind. To talk of a purpose which is not present in any mind at all seems to me as unintelligible as it would be to talk of rectangles which had no extension. The argument from design has therefore to my mind considerable, though not, by itself at least, conclusive force. It is also strange that there should be so much beauty in the world, that there should have resulted from an unconscious unintelligent world beings who could form the theory that the world was due to chance or frame moral ideals in the light of which they could condemn it. It might be suggested that a mind designed the organic without designing the inorganic, but the connection between organic and inorganic and the unity of the world in general are too close to make this a plausible view.

The counter argument from evil is of course formidable, but I shall defer discussion of it to a later stage in the chapter, as it is rather an argument against theism in general than a specific objection to the argument from design. I must, however, make two remarks here. First, it is almost a commonplace that the very large amount of apparent waste in nature is a strong prima facie argument against the world having been designed by a good and wise being. But is there really much "wasted"? A herring may produce hundreds of thousands or millions of eggs for one fish that arrives at maturity, but most of the eggs which come to grief serve as food for other animals. We do not look on the eggs we eat at breakfast, when we can get them, as "wasted," though the hen might well do so. It is certainly very strange that a good God should have designed a world in which the living beings can only maintain their life by devouring each other, but this is part of the general problem of evil and not a specific problem of waste in nature. Secondly, the occurrence of elaborate adaptations to ends is a very much stronger argument for the presence of an intelligence than its apparent absence in a good many instances is against it. A dog would see no purpose whatever in my present activity, but he would not therefore have adequate grounds for concluding that I had no intelligence. If there is a God, it is only to be expected *a priori* that in regard to a great deal of his work we should be in the same position as the dog is in regard to ours, and therefore the fact that we are in this position is no argument that there is no God. The occurrence of events requiring intelligence to explain them is positive evidence for the presence of intelligence, but the absence of results we think worth while in particular cases is very slight evidence indeed on the other side where we are debating the existence of a being whose intelligence, if he exists, we must in any case assume to be as much above ours as that of the maker of the whole world would have to be. The existence of positive evil of course presents a greater difficulty to the theist.

THEOLOGY AND FALSIFICATION

Antony Flew

Let us begin with a parable. It is a parable developed from a tale told by John Wisdom in his haunting and revelatory article "Gods."[1] Once upon a time two explorers came upon a clearing in the jungle. In the clearing were growing many flowers and many weeds. One explorer says, "Some gardener must tend this plot." The other disagrees, "There is no gardener." So they pitch their tents and set a watch. No gardener is ever seen. "But perhaps he is an invisible gardener." So they set up a barbed-wire fence. They electrify it. They patrol with bloodhounds. (For they remember how H. G. Wells's *The Invisible Man* could be both smelt and touched though he could not be seen.) But no shrieks ever suggest that some intruder has received a shock. No movements of the wire ever betray an invisible climber. The bloodhounds never give cry. Yet still the Believer is not convinced. "But there is a gardener, invisible, intangible, insensible to electric shocks, a gardener who has no scent and makes no sound, a gardener who comes secretly to look after the garden which he loves." At last the Sceptic despairs, "But what remains of your original assertion? Just how does what you call an invisible, intangible, eternally elusive gardener differ from an imaginary gardener or even from no gardener at all?"

In this parable we can see how what starts as an assertion, that something exists or that there is some analogy between certain complexes of phenomena, may be reduced step by step to an altogether different status, to an expression perhaps of a "picture preference."[2] The Sceptic says there is no gardener.

---

[1]*P.A.S.,* 1944–5, reprinted as Ch. X of *Logic and Language,* Vol I (Blackwell, 1951), and in his *Philosophy and Psychoanalysis* (Blackwell, 1953).
[2]Cf. J. Wisdom, "Other Minds," *Mind,* 1940; reprinted in his *Other Minds* (Blackwell, 1952).

The Believer says there is a gardener (but invisible, etc.). One man talks about sexual behaviour. Another man prefers to talk of Aphrodite[3] (but knows that there is not really a superhuman person additional to, and somehow responsible for, all sexual phenomena). The process of qualification may be checked at any point before the original assertion is completely withdrawn and something of that first assertion will remain (Tautology). Mr. Wells's invisible man could not, admittedly, be seen, but in all other respects he was a man like the rest of us. But though the process of qualification may be, and of course usually is, checked in time, it is not always judiciously so halted. Someone may dissipate his assertion completely without noticing that he has done so. A fine brash hypothesis may thus be killed by inches, the death by a thousand qualifications.

And in this, it seems to me, lies the peculiar danger, the endemic evil, of theological utterance. Take such utterances as "God has a plan," "God created the world," "God loves us as a father loves his children." They look at first sight very much like assertions, vast cosmological assertions. Of course, this is no sure sign that they either are, or are intended to be, assertions. But let us confine ourselves to the cases where those who utter such sentences intend them to express assertions. (Merely remarking parenthetically that those who intend or interpret such utterances as crypto-commands, expressions of wishes, disguised ejaculations, concealed ethics, or as anything else but assertions, are unlikely to succeed in making them either properly orthodox or practically effective).

Now to assert that such and such is the case is necessarily equivalent to denying that such and such is not the case.[4] Suppose then that we are in doubt as to what someone who gives vent to an utterance is asserting, or suppose that, more radically, we are sceptical as to whether he is really asserting anything at all, one way of trying to understand (or perhaps it will be to expose) his utterance is to attempt to find what he would regard as counting against, or as being incompatible with, its truth. For if the utterance is indeed an assertion, it will necessarily be equivalent to a denial of the negation of that assertion. And anything which would count against the assertion, or which would induce the speaker to withdraw it and to admit that it had been mistaken, must be part of (or the whole of) the meaning of the negation of that assertion. And to know the meaning of the negation of an assertion, is as near as makes no matter, to know the meaning of that assertion.[5] And if there is nothing which a putative assertion denies then there is nothing which it asserts either: and so it is not really an assertion. When the Sceptic in the parable asked the Believer, "Just how does what you call an invisible, intangible, eternally elusive gardener differ from an imaginary gardener or even from no gardener at all?" he was suggesting that the Believer's earlier statement had been so eroded by qualification that it was no longer an assertion at all.

Now it often seems to people who are not religious as if there was no conceivable event or series of events the occurrence of which would be admitted by sophisticated religious people to be a sufficient reason for conceding "There wasn't a God after all" or "God does not really love us then." Someone tells us that God loves us as a father loves his children. We are reassured. But then we see a child dying of inoperable cancer of the throat. His earthly father is driven frantic in his efforts to help, but his Heavenly Father reveals no obvious sign of concern. Some qualification is made—God's love is "not a merely human love" or it is "an inscrutable love," perhaps—and we realize that such sufferings are quite compatible with the truth of the assertion that "God loves us as a father (but, of course, . . .)." We are reassured again. But then perhaps we ask: what is this assurance of God's (appropriately qualified) love worth, what is this apparent guarantee really a guarantee against? Just what would have to happen not merely (morally and wrongly) to tempt

---

[3]Aphrodite, in ancient Greek mythology, is the Goddess of love, sex, and beauty. In Roman mythology, she was called "Venus" (Eds.).

[4]For those who prefer symbolism: $p \equiv \sim\sim p$.

[5]For by simply negating $\sim p$ we get $p: \sim\sim p \equiv p$.

but also (logically and rightly) to entitle us to say "God does not love us" or even "God does not exist"? I therefore put to the succeeding symposiasts the simple central questions, "What would have to occur or to have occurred to constitute for you a disproof of the love of, or of the existence of, God?"

A PHILOSOPHY OF LIFE

Sigmund Freud

If we are to give an account of the grandiose nature of religion, we must bear in mind what it undertakes to do for human beings. It gives them information about the origin and coming into existence of the universe, it assures them of its protection and of ultimate happiness in the ups and downs of life and it directs their thoughts and actions by precepts which it lays down with its whole authority. Thus it fulfills three functions. With the first of them it satisfies the human thirst for knowledge; it does the same thing that science attempts to do with *its* means, and at that point enters into rivalry with it. It is to its second function that it no doubt owes the greatest part of its influence. Science can be no match for it when it soothes the fear that men feel of the dangers and vicissitudes of life, when it assures them of a happy ending and offers them comfort in unhappiness. It is true that science can teach us how to avoid certain dangers and that there are some sufferings which it can successfully combat; it would be most unjust to deny that it is a powerful helper to men; but there are many situations in which it must leave a man to his suffering and can only advise him to submit to it. In its third function, in which it issues precepts and lays down prohibitions and restrictions, religion is furthest away from science. For science is content to investigate and to establish facts, though it is true that from its applications rules and advice are derived on the conduct of life. In some circumstances these are the same as those

offered by religion, but, when this is so, the reasons for them are different.

The convergence between these three aspects of religion is not entirely clear. What has an explanation of the origin of the universe to do with the inculcation of certain particular ethical precepts? The assurances of protection and happiness are more intimately linked with the ethical requirements. They are the reward for fulfilling these commands; only those who obey them may count upon these benefits, punishment awaits the disobedient. Incidentally, something similar is true of science. Those who disregard its lessons, so it tells us, expose themselves to injury.

The remarkable combination in religion of instruction, consolation and requirements can only be understood if it is subjected to a genetic analysis. This may be approached from the most striking point of the aggregate, from its instruction on the origin of the universe; for why, we may ask, should a cosmogony be a regular component of religious systems? The doctrine is, then, that the universe was created by a being resembling a man, but magnified in every respect, in power, wisdom, and the strength of his passions—an idealized super-man. Animals as creators of the universe point to the influence of totemism, upon which we shall have a few words at least to say presently. It is an interesting fact that this creator is always only a single being, even when there are believed to be many gods. It is interesting, too, that the creator is usually a man, though there is far from being a lack of indications of female deities; and some mythologies actually make the creation begin with a male god getting rid of a female deity, who is degraded into being a monster. Here the most interesting problems of detail open out; but we must hurry on. Our further path is made easy to recognize, for this god-creator is undisguisedly called "father." Psychoanalysis infers that he really is the father, with all the magnificence in which he once appeared to the small child. A religious man pictures the creation of the universe just as he pictures his own origin.

This being so, it is easy to explain how it is that consoling assurances and strict ethical demands are combined with a cosmogony. For the same person to whom the child owed his existence, the father (or more correctly, no doubt, the parental agency compounded of the father and mother), also protected and watched over him in his feeble and helpless state, exposed as he was to all the dangers lying in wait in the external world; under his father's protection he felt safe. When a human being has himself grown up, he knows, to be sure, that he is in possession of greater strength, but his insight into the perils of life has also grown greater, and he rightly concludes that fundamentally he still remains just as helpless and unprotected as he was in his childhood, that faced by the world he is still a child. Even now, therefore, he cannot do without the protection which he enjoyed as a child. But he has long since recognized, too, that his father is a being of narrowly restricted power, and not equipped with every excellence. He therefore harks back to the mnemic image of the father whom in his childhood he so greatly overvalued. He exalts the image into a deity and makes it into something contemporary and real. The effective strength of this mnemic image and the persistence of his need for protection jointly sustain his belief in God.

The third main item in the religious programme, the ethical demand, also fits into this childhood situation with ease. I may remind you of Kant's famous pronouncement in which he names, in a single breath, the starry heavens and the moral law within us. However strange this juxtaposition may sound—for what have the heavenly bodies to do with the question of whether one human creature loves another or kills him?—it nevertheless touches on a great psychological truth. The same father (or parental agency) which gave the child life and guarded him against its perils, taught him as well what he might do and what he must leave undone, instructed him that he must adapt himself to certain restrictions on his instinctual wishes, and made him understand what regard he was expected to have for his parents and brothers and sisters, if he wanted to become a tolerated and welcome member of the family circle and later on of larger associations. The child is brought up to a knowledge of his social du-

ties by a system of loving rewards and punishments, he is taught that his security in life depends on his parents (and afterwards other people) loving him and on their being able to believe that he loves them. All these relations are afterwards introduced by men unaltered into their religion. Their parents' prohibitions and demands persist within them as a moral conscience. With the help of this same system of rewards and punishments, God rules the world of men. The amount of protection and happy satisfaction assigned to an individual depends on his fulfilment of the ethical demands; his love of God and his consciousness of being loved by God are the foundations of the security with which he is armed against the dangers of the external world and of his human environment. Finally, in prayer he has assured himself a direct influence on the divine will and with it a share in the divine omnipotence.

• • •

The scientific spirit, strengthened by the observation of natural processes, has begun, in the course of time, to treat religion as a human affair and to submit it to a critical examination. Religion was not able to stand up to this. What first gave rise to suspicion and scepticism were its tales of miracles, for they contradicted everything that had been taught by sober observation and betrayed too clearly the influence of the activity of the human imagination. After this its doctrines explaining the origin of the universe met with rejection, for they gave evidence of an ignorance which bore the stamp of ancient times and to which, thanks to their increased familiarity with the laws of nature, people knew they were superior. The idea that the universe came into existence through acts of copulation or creation analogous to the origin of individual people had ceased to be the most obvious and self-evident hypothesis since the distinction between animate creatures with a mind and an inanimate Nature had impressed itself on human thought—a distinction which made it impossible to retain belief in the original animism. Nor must we overlook the influence of the comparative study of different religious systems and the impression of their mutual exclusiveness and intolerance.

Strengthened by these preliminary exercises, the scientific spirit gained enough courage at last to venture on an examination of the most important and emotionally valuable elements of the religious *Weltanschauung.*[1] People may always have seen, though it was long before they dared to say so openly, that the pronouncements of religion promising men protection and happiness if they would only fulfill certain ethical requirements had also shown themselves unworthy of belief. It seems not to be the case that there is a Power in the universe which watches over the well-being of individuals with parental care and brings all their affairs to a happy ending. On the contrary, the destinies of mankind can be brought into harmony neither with the hypothesis of a Universal Benevolence nor with the partly contradictory one of a Universal Justice. Earthquakes, tidal waves, conflagrations, make no distinction between the virtuous and pious and the scoundrel or unbeliever. Even where what is in question is not inanimate Nature but where an individual's fate depends on his relations to other people, it is by no means the rule that virtue is rewarded and that evil finds its punishment. Often enough the violent, cunning or ruthless man seizes the envied good things of the world and the pious man goes away empty. Obscure, unfeeling and unloving powers determine men's fate; the system of rewards and punishments which religion ascribes to the government of the universe seems not to exist.

• • •

The last contribution to the criticism of the religious *Weltanschauung* was effected by psychoanalysis, by showing how religion originated from the helplessness of children and by tracing its contents to the survival into maturity of the wishes and needs of childhood. This did not precisely mean a contradiction of religion, but it was nevertheless a

necessary rounding-off of our knowledge about it, and in one respect at least it was a contradiction, for religion itself lays claim to a divine origin. And, to be sure, it is not wrong in this, provided that our interpretation of God is accepted.

In summary, therefore, the judgement of science on the religious *Weltanschauung* is this. While the different religions wrangle with one another as to which of them is in possession of the truth, our view is that the question of the truth of religious beliefs may be left altogether on one side. Religion is an attempt to master the sensory world in which we are situated by means of the wishful world which we have developed within us as a result of biological and psychological necessities. But religion cannot achieve this. Its doctrines bear the imprint of the times in which they arose, the ignorant times of the childhood of humanity. Its consolations deserve no trust. Experience teaches us that the world is no nursery. The ethical demands on which religion seeks to lay stress need, rather, to be given another basis; for they are indispensable to human society and it is dangerous to link obedience to them with religious faith. If we attempt to assign the place of religion in the evolution of mankind, it appears not as a permanent acquisition but as a counterpart to the neurosis which individual civilized men have to go through in their passage from childhood to maturity.

• • •

The struggle of the scientific spirit against the religious *Weltanschauung* is, as you know, not at an end: it is still going on to-day under our eyes. Though as a rule psycho-analysis makes little use of the weapon of controversy, I will not hold back from looking into this dispute. In doing so I may perhaps throw some further light on our attitude to *Weltanschauung.* You will see how easily some of the arguments brought forward by the supporters of religion can be answered, though it is true that others may evade refutation.

The first objection we meet with is to the effect that it is an impertinence on the part of science to make religion a subject for its investigations, for religion is something sublime, superior to any operation

---

[1]*Weltanschauung,* from the German, literally means "world view." The term refers to one's general framework or system of beliefs about the universe and life. In this essay, Freud is contrasting the religious world view with the general assumptions of science (Eds.).

of the human intellect, something which may not be approached with hair-splitting criticisms. In other words, science is not qualified to judge religion: it is quite serviceable and estimable otherwise, so long as it keeps to its own sphere. But religion is not its sphere, and it has no business there. If we do not let ourselves be put off by this brusque repulse and en-quire further what is the basis of this claim to a posi-tion exceptional among all human concerns, the reply we receive (if we are thought worthy of any reply) is that religion cannot be measured by human measure-ments, for it is of divine origin and was given us as a revelation by a Spirit which the human spirit cannot comprehend. One would have thought that there was nothing easier than the refutation of this argument: it is a clear case of *petitio principii,* of "begging the question"—I know of no good German equivalent expression. The actual question raised is whether there *is* a divine spirit and a revelation by it; and the matter is certainly not decided by saying that this question cannot be asked, since the deity may not be put in question. The position here is what it occasion-ally is during the work of analysis. If a usually sensi-ble patient rejects some particular suggestion on specially foolish grounds, this logical weakness is ev-idence of the existence of a specially strong motive for the denial—a motive which can only be of an af-fective nature, an emotional tie.

We may also be given another answer, in which a motive of this kind is openly admitted: religion may not be critically examined because it is the highest, most precious, and most sublime thing that the human spirit has produced, because it gives ex-pression to the deepest feelings and alone makes the world tolerable and life worthy of men. We need not reply by disputing this estimate of religion but by drawing attention to another matter. What we do is to emphasize the fact that what is in question is not in the least an invasion of the field of religion by the scientific spirit, but on the contrary an invasion by religion of the sphere of scientific thought. What-ever may be the value and importance of religion, it has no right in any way to restrict thought—no right, therefore, to exclude itself from having thought applied to it.

Scientific thinking does not differ in its nature from the normal activity of thought, which all of us, believers and unbelievers, employ in looking after our affairs in ordinary life. It has only developed certain features: it takes an interest in things even if they have no immediate, tangible use; it is con-cerned carefully to avoid individual factors and af-fective influences; it examines more strictly the trustworthiness of the sense-perceptions on which it bases its conclusions; it provides itself with new perceptions which cannot be obtained by everyday means and it isolates the determinants of these new experiences in experiments which are deliberately varied. Its endeavour is to arrive at correspondence with reality—that is to say, with what exists outside us and independently of us and, as experience has taught us, is decisive for the fullfilment or disap-pointment of our wishes. This correspondence with the real external world we call "truth." It remains the aim of scientific work even if we leave the prac-tical value of that work out of account. When, there-fore, religion asserts that it can take the place of science, that, because it is beneficent and elevating, it must also be true, that is in fact an invasion which must be repulsed in the most general interest. It is asking a great deal of a person who has learnt to conduct his ordinary affairs in accordance with the rules of experience and with a regard to reality, to suggest that he shall hand over the care of what are precisely his most intimate interests to an agency which claims as its privilege freedom from the pre-cepts of rational thinking. And as regards the pro-tection which religion promises its believers, I think none of us would be so much as prepared to enter a motor-car if its driver announced that he drove, un-perturbed by traffic regulations, in accordance with the impulses of his soaring imagination.

The prohibition against thought issued by reli-gion to assist in its self-preservation is also far from being free from danger either for the individual or for human society. Analytic experience has taught us that a prohibition like this, even if it is originally limited to a particular field, tends to widen out and thereafter to become the cause of severe inhibitions in the subject's conduct of life. This result may be observed, too, in the female sex, following from their being forbidden to have anything to do with their sexuality even in thought. Biography is able to point to the damage done by the religious inhibition of thought in the life stories of nearly all eminent individuals in the past. On the other hand intellect—or let us call it by the name that is familiar to us, reason—is among the powers which we may most expect to exercise a unifying influence on men—on men who are held together with such difficulty and whom it is therefore scarcely possible to rule. It may be imagined how impossible human society would be, merely if everyone had his own multiplication table and his own private units of length and weight. Our best hope for the future is that intellect—the scientific spirit, reason—may in process of time establish a dictatorship in the mental life of man. The nature of reason is a guarantee that afterwards it will not fail to give man's emotional impulses and what is determined by them the position they deserve. But the common compulsion exercised by such a dominance of reason will prove to be the strongest uniting bond among men and lead the way to further unions. Whatever, like religion's prohibition against thought, opposes such a development, is a danger for the future of mankind.

• • •

And what, finally, is the aim of these passionate disparagements of science? In spite of its present incompleteness and of the difficulties attaching to it, it remains indispensable to us and nothing can take its place. It is capable of undreamt-of improvements, whereas the religious *Weltanschauung* is not. This is complete in all essential respects; if it was a mistake, it must remain one for ever. No belittlement of science can in any way alter the fact that it is attempting to take account of our dependence on the real external world, while religion is an illusion and it derives its strength from its readiness to fit in with our instinctual wishful impulses.

QUESTIONS FOR DISCUSSION

1. In what respects, if at all, do you think the statement "God exists" is a meaningful one? In what respects, if any, is it a meaningless assertion? In your answer refer to Flew's article and to at least one other reading in this section.

2. Ewing claims that the religious world view is a more adequate explanation for the universe than that of the atheist. Freud argues for atheism on the basis of the scientific world view. Who is right? Or do you believe that science and religion are ultimately compatible?

3. Freud claims that religion is an illusion, a fantasy derived from early childhood memories and wishes. Explain his interpretation of religion. Is he correct? Why or why not?

THE RELIGIOUS EXPERIENCE

The readings in the previous section focused primarily on the Western theistic tradition in which God is understood as a transcendent being whose proof requires rational demonstration through philosophical argument. As we have seen, such arguments are problematic and lend themselves easily to the atheist's challenge which, in the scientific spirit, insists upon the experiential verification. However, there is also an undercurrent within the Western tradition that talks about an immediate experiential encounter with God—Moses and the burning bush, the Jewish mystics of the Kaballah, and such Christian mystics as Meister Eckhart and Saint Teresa of Avila. But what is only an undercurrent in Western religions is given emphasis in the Asian traditions—Hinduism, Buddhism, and Taoism. "Experience," writes Sarvepalli Radhakrishnan, "is the soul of religion." The readings in this section explore the nature of the religious experience.

Sarvepalli Radhakrishnan (1888–1975) is an Indian philosopher well known for his ability to make Hindu philosophy accessible to Western philosophers. After a long academic career he entered politics and became vice president of India in 1952 and president of India ten years later. In the first selection of this section, he analyzes the essential characteristics of religious, or mystical, experiences. These experiences are described as being beyond our ordinary sensory and intellectual consciousness. The boundaries dividing the individual from the universe have been broken, and the self merges with an undifferentiated unity that is experienced as a higher realm. How do we know that this is not simply an hallucination? The mystic's answer is that the experience presents itself with a sense of its own validity. Beyond that not much more can be said, and, in fact, the experience is often described as ineffable.

How should we evaluate this experience? The religious or mystical experience itself, as characterized above, seems to be cross-cultural, occurring within every major religious tradition. The descriptions of Jewish, Christian, Islamic, Hindu, and Buddhist mystics sound remarkably similar. However, according to Radhakrishnan, we must distinguish between the experience itself and the interpretation of that experience. Within the Western religious traditions, the tendency has been to identify the mystical experience as an experience of God and, within each religious tradition, to interpret it through the theological preconceptions of that religion. Thus, a Christian might say that he had an encounter with the Holy Ghost and a Buddhist, having the same experience, might speak of having achieved Nirvana. Radhakrishnan concludes that such interpretations are, therefore, cultural constructions that must be distinguished from the experience itself.

The next selection in this section is by the twentieth-century Thai Buddhist monk and meditation master Buddhadasa, who considers further implications of the religious experience and comes to a surprising conclusion. Buddhadasa argues that the religious experience opens up a deeper level of understanding in which all religions, however they may conventionally appear to be different from one another (and however they tend to divide people), are ultimately the same. This recognition of the universality of all religions is not, for him, the final truth, for at the deepest level of understanding the mystical experience points to a dimension of existence that is beyond religion itself. From this vantage point, various religions are simply different vehicles to realize the ultimate reality, and when the Ultimate is finally grasped, the vehicles are no longer necessary. In other words, at the deepest level of understanding, there is no religion.

The last selection in this section is by Vine Deloria, a Sioux Indian who is widely known as a social activist as well as a legal theorist and academic (he was a member of the department of political science at the University of Arizona). In the 1960s he was executive director of the National Congress of American Indians and achieved considerable recognition for his work *Custer Died for Your Sins: An Indian Manifesto*. With the work from which this selection is drawn, *The Metaphysics of Modern Existence,* written in 1979, Deloria turns his attention to philosophical, religious, and spiritual themes.

Deloria claims that tribal religious experience is fundamentally different from what is articulated in the traditional world's religions, especially from what is described within Western religions. Whereas Western religion tends to divide reality into the world of ordinary experience and the ultimate reality that exists over and above the ordinary world, tribal religions recognize the unity of the spiritual, the psychological, and the natural world. Whereas the world's main religions denigrate nature in favor of the social and of the idea of a higher reality, tribal societies see nature as one big society in which all life forms are interconnected and have equal status. Tribal individuals develop their spirituality not in opposition to nature but in communion with it. The natural universe is, for them, a space–time unity that is energized by an all-pervasive power (mana) that can concentrate itself in certain spaces, giving them a sacral character. Deloria observes that this tribal religious vision of reality has echoes in modern science and, we may note, in the ecology movement today.

PERSONAL EXPERIENCE OF GOD

Sarvepalli Radhakrishnan

PERSONAL EXPERIENCE OF GOD

All the religions owe their inspiration to the personal insights of their prophet founders. The Hindu religion, for example, is characterized by its adherence to fact. In its pure form, at any rate, it never leaned as heavily as other religions do on authority. It is not a "founded" religion; nor does it centre round any historical events. Its distinctive characteristic has been its insistence on the inward life of

spirit. To know, possess and be the spirit in this physical frame, to convert an obscure plodding mentality into clear spiritual illumination, to build peace and self-existent freedom in the stress of emotional satisfactions and sufferings, to discover and realize the life divine in a body subject to sickness and death has been the constant aim of the Hindu religious endeavour. The Hindus look back to the Vedic period[1] as the epoch of their founders. The Veda, the wisdom, is the accepted name for the highest spiritual truth of which the human mind is capable. It is the work of the *ṛṣis* or the seers. The truths of the *ṛṣis* are not evolved as the result of logical reasoning or systematic philosophy but they are the products of spiritual intuition, *dṛṣṭi* or vision. The *ṛṣis* are not so much the authors of the truths recorded in the Vedas as the seers who were able to discern the eternal truths by raising their life-spirit to the plane of the universal spirit. They are the pioneer researchers in the realm of spirit who saw more in the world than their fellows. Their utterances are based not on transitory vision but on a continuous experience of resident life and power. When the Vedas are regarded as the highest authority, all that is meant is that the most exacting of all authorities is the authority of facts.

If experience is the soul of religion, expression is the body through which it fulfils its destiny. We have the spiritual facts and their interpretations by which they are communicated to others, *śruti* or what is heard, and *smṛti* or what is remembered. Śaṁkara equates them with *pratyakṣa* or intuition and *anumāna* or inference. It is the distinction between immediacy and thought. Intuitions abide, while interpretations change. *Śruti* and *smṛti* differ as the authority of fact and the authority of interpretation. Theory, speculation, dogma, change from time to time as the facts become better understood. Their value is acquired from their adequacy to

---

[1]The Vedic period, as Radhakrishnan here uses this term, refers especially to the later Veda or Vedanta, which consists of the *Upanishads* and *Bhagavad Gita.* Selections from these can be found in Chapters 1, 5, and 7. The reader might want to look at these in conjunction with this selection (Eds.).

experience. When forms dissolve and the interpretations are doubted, it is a call to get back to the experience itself and reformulate its content in more suitable terms. While the experiential character of religion is emphasized in the Hindu faith, every religion at its best falls back on it.

The whole scheme of Buddhism centres on Buddha's enlightenment. Moses saw God in the burning bush, and Elijah heard the still small voice. In *Jeremiah* we read: "This is the covenant which I will make with the house of Israel after those days, saith the Lord. I will put my hand in their inward parts, and in their heart will I write it."[2] Jesus's experience of God is the basic fact for Christianity: "As he came up out of the river he saw the heavens parted above him and the spirit descending like a dove towards him: and he heard a voice sounding out of the heavens and saying 'Thou art my beloved son. I have chosen thee.'" According to St Mark, the baptism in the Jordan by John was to Jesus the occasion of a vivid and intense religious experience, so much so that he felt that he had to go for a time into absolute solitude to think it over.[3] He obviously spoke of the ineffable happening, the sudden revelation, the new peace and joy in words that have come down to us. He emphasized the newness of the reborn soul as something which marks him off from all those who are religious only at second hand. "Verily I say unto you, among men born of women there hath not arisen a greater than John the Baptist; but the least in the Kingdom of God is greater than he."[4] The vision that came to Saul on the Damascus road and turned the persecutor into an apostle[5] is another illustration. Faith means in St James acceptance of dogma; in St Paul it is the surrender of heart and mind to Christ; but in the Epistle to the Hebrews, faith is defined as that outreaching of the mind by which we become aware of the invisible world.[6] The life of Mohammad is full of mystic ex-

periences. Witnesses to the personal sense of the divine are not confined to the East. Socrates and Plato, Plotinus and Porphyry, Augustine and Dante, Bunyan and Wesley, and numberless others, testify to the felt reality of God. It is as old as humanity and is not confined to any one people. The evidence is too massive to run away from.

CHARACTER OF RELIGIOUS EXPERIENCE

To study the nature of this experience is rather a difficult matter. All that one can hope to do is to set down a few general impressions. It is a type of experience which is not clearly differentiated into a subject-object state, an integral, undivided consciousness in which not merely this or that side of man's nature but his whole being seems to find itself. It is a condition of consciousness in which feelings are fused, ideas melt into one another, boundaries broken and ordinary distinctions transcended. Past and present fade away in a sense of timeless being. Consciousness and being are not there different from each other. All being is consciousness and all consciousness being. Thought and reality coalesce and a creative merging of subject and object results. Life grows conscious of its incredible depths. In this fulness of felt life and freedom, the distinction of the knower and the known disappears. The privacy of the individual self is broken into and invaded by a universal self which the individual feels as his own.

The experience itself is felt to be sufficient and complete. It does not come in a fragmentary or truncated form demanding completion by something else. It does not look beyond itself for meaning or validity. It does not appeal to external standards of logic or metaphysics. It is its own cause and explanation. It is sovereign in its own rights and carries its own credentials. It is self-established (*svatassiddha*) self-evidencing (*svasaṁvedya*) self-luminous (*svayam-prakāśa*). It does not argue or explain but it knows and is. It is beyond the bounds of proof and so touches completeness. It comes with a constraint that brooks no denial. It is pure comprehension, en-

[2]xxxi. 37.
[3]Mark I. 10.
[4]See also Matt. xi. II.
[5]Acts ix. 1-9.
[6]See also I Cor. xiii. 12; Romans viii. 18-25; Rev. xxi. 22.

tire significance, complete validity. Patañjali, the author of the *Yoga Sūtra,* tells us that the insight is truth-filled, or truth-bearing.[7]

The tension of normal life disappears, giving rise to inward peace, power and joy. The Greeks called it ataraxy, but the word sounds more negative than the Hindu term '*Śānti*' or peace, which is a positive feeling of calm and confidence, joy and strength in the midst of outward pain and defeat, loss and frustration. The experience is felt as profoundly satisfying, where darkness is turned into light, sadness into joy, despair into assurance. The continuance of such an experience constitutes dwelling in heaven, which is not a place where God lives, but a mode of being which is fully and completely real.

However much we may quarrel about the implications of this kind of experience, we cannot question the actuality of the experience itself. While the profound intuitions do not normally occur, milder forms are in the experience of all who feel an answering presence in deep devotion or share the spell which great works of art cast on us. When we experience the illumination of new knowledge, the ecstasy of poetry or the subordination of self to something greater, family or nation, the self-abandonment of falling in love, we have faint glimpses of mystic moods. Human love perhaps takes us nearest to them. It can become an experience deep and profound, a portal through which we enter the realm of the sublime. "My life, My all, My more," said Sappho to Philaenis. To have one's heart and mind absorbed in love seems to unveil the mystery of the universe. We forget the sense of the outward world in our communion with the grandeur beyond. Religious mysticism often falls into the language of passionate love. It has been so from the Upaniṣads and the Song of Songs.

Since the intuitive experiences are not always given but occur only at rare intervals, they possess the character of revelation. We cannot command or continue them at our will. We do not know how or why they occur. They sometimes occur even against our will. Their mode of comprehension is beyond the understanding of the normal, and the supernormal is traced to the supernatural. Those who are gifted with the insight tend to regard themselves as the chosen ones, the privileged few. Conscious of a light which other men had not, they feel inclined to believe that the light has been directed on them and that they are not only the seekers but the sought. "Only he who is chosen by the Supreme is able to realize it."

If all our experience were possessed of intrinsic validity (*svataḥprāmāṇya*) there would be no question of truth and falsehood. There would be nothing with which our experience will have to cohere or to correspond. There would not arise any need or desire to test its value. All our experience will be self-valid, i.e. all reality will be present in its own immediate validity. But even the noblest human minds have only glimpses of self-valid experiences. The moments of vision are transitory and intermittent. We therefore do not attain an insight, permanent and uninterrupted, where reality is present in its own immediate witness. But we are convinced that such an ideal is not an impossible one.

So long as the experience lasts, the individual remains rapt in contemplation, but no man can rest in that state for all time. Life is a restless surge. Scarcely is the seer assured of the unique character of the experience than he is caught in the whirl of desire and temptation, discord and struggle. During the vision, its influence was so potent and overwhelming that he had neither the power nor the desire to analyse it. Now that the vision is no more, he strives to recapture it and retain in memory what cannot be realized in fact. The process of reflection starts. He cannot forget the blessed moments which have a weight for the rest of his life and give to his beliefs a power and a vividness that nothing can shake. The individual adopts an attitude of faith which is urged by its own needs to posit the transcendental reality. He affirms that the soul has dealings, direct, intimate and luminous, with a plane of being different from that with which the senses deal, a world

---

[7]Rtambharā tatra prajñā (*Yoga Sūtra,* I. 48).

more resplendent but not less real than the conventional one. The experience is felt as of the nature of a discovery or a revelation, not a mere conjecture or a creation. The real was there actually confronting us, it was not conjured out of the resources of our mind.[8] He claims for his knowledge of reality an immediate and intuitive certainty, transcending any which mere reason can reach. No further experience or rational criticism can disturb his sense of certainty. Doubt and disbelief are no more possible. He speaks without hesitation and with the calm accents of finality. Such strange simplicity and authoritativeness do we find in the utterances of the seers of the Upaniṣads, of Buddha, of Plato, of Christ, of Dante, of Eckhart, of Spinoza, of Blake. They speak of the real, not as the scribes, but as those who were in the immediate presence of "that which was, is and ever shall be." St Theresa says: "If you ask how it is possible that the soul can see and understand that she has been in God, since during the union she has neither sight nor understanding, I reply that she does not see it then, but that she sees it clearly later, after she has returned to herself, not by any vision, but by a certitude which abides with her and which God alone can give her."[9]

In addition to the feeling of certitude is found the sense of the ineffability of the experience. It transcends expression even while it provokes it. It is just what it is and not like anything else. There is no experience by which we can limit it, no conception by which we can define it. The *Kena Upaniṣad* says that "it is other than the known and above the unknown."[10] As Lao Tze expresses it at the beginning of his *Tao Teh King:*[11] "The Tao which can be expressed is not the unchanging Tao; the Name which can be named is not the unchanging Name."

The unquestionable content of the experience is that about which nothing more can be said.[12] Indian scriptures give cases of teachers who dispelled the doubts of their pupils by assuming an attitude of silence on this question.[13] When we hear enthusiastic descriptions about the ultimate reality, let us remember the dictum of Lao Tze that he who knows the Tao may be recognized by the fact that he is reluctant to speak of it.

Conceptual substitutes for ineffable experiences are not adequate. They are products of rational thinking. All forms, according to Śaṁkara, contain an element of untruth and the real is beyond all forms. Any attempt to describe the experience falsifies it to an extent. In the experience itself the self is wholly integrated and is therefore both the knower and the known, but it is not so in any intellectual description of the experience. The profoundest being of man cannot be brought out by mental pictures or logical counters. God is too great for words to explain. He is like light, making things luminous but himself invisible.

And yet we cannot afford to be absolutely silent. Though the tools of sense and understanding cannot describe adequately, creative imagination with its symbols and suggestions may be of assistance. The profoundest wisdom of the past is transmitted to us in the form of myths and metaphors which do not have any fixed meaning and therefore can be interpreted as life requires. The seers who were at least as wise and as subtle as ourselves, by letting their imagination work on experience, devised symbolic conceptions such as crossing the ocean of *saṁsāra,* ascending into heaven, meeting God face to face. Plato expressed his deepest convictions, which were incapable of proof, in the language of poetry, saying,

---

[8]Śaṁkara on *Brahma Sūtra,* i. I. I.
[9]James: *Varieties of Religious Experience* (1906), p. 409.
[10]i. 3.
[11]Lao Tze and *Tao Teh King* are alternative English spellings of Lao Tzu and the *Tao Te Ching.* A selection from Lao Tzu appears in this book in Section Two of Chapter 8 (Eds.).

---

[12]There is an endless world, O my brother, and there is the Nameless Being, of whom nought can be said.
Only he knows it who has reached that region: it is other than all that is heard and said.
No form, no body, no length, no breadth is seen there: how can I tell you that which it is?
(*Kabir:* Rabindranath Tagore's E.T., 76)
[13]Cp. Lao Tze: "To teach without words and to be useful without action, few among men are capable of this."

"Not this perhaps, but something like this must be true." If we insist on interpreting these symbols literally, difficulties arise. But if we go behind the words to the moods they symbolize, agreement is possible.

The symbols and suggestions employed are derived from the local and historical traditions. An Orphic describes to us Charon and the spring on either side of the road and the tall cypress tree. The Vaiṣṇava speaks to us of the cowherd, the Brindāvan and the river Yamunā. The myths require to be changed as they lose their meaning with the lapse of time, but they are in no case to be accepted as literal truths. They require to be interpreted "according to their meaning and not their lisping expression," as Aristotle suggests in speaking of Empedocles. Much of the rationalistic criticism of the sacred scriptures is due to a confusion between symbolic statements and literal truths. It is easy to prove that the world was not made in seven days or that Eve was not made out of Adam's rib. What they say is not scientifically true; what they mean is a different matter.

5. EXPERIENCE AND THE VARIETY OF EXPRESSIONS

If all our experiences were adequately intuited at once, such immediate intuitions could not be doubted under any circumstances; but, as it is, we are compelled to relate our intuitive experiences with others and here we are obliged to employ formulas. The pedestrian function of consolidation and revaluation seems to be indispensable. The only way to impart our experiences to others and elucidate their implications for the rest of our life and defend their validity against hostile criticism is by means of logic. When we test the claim of the experience to truth, we are really discussing the claims of the forms or propositions in which the nature of the experience is unfolded. In the utterances of the seers, we have to distinguish the given and the interpreted elements. What is regarded as immediately given may be the product of inference. Immediacy does not mean absence of psychological mediation, but only non-mediation by conscious thought. Ideas which seem to come to us with compelling force, without any mediate intellectual process of which we are aware, are generally the results of previous training in traditions imparted to us in our early years. Our past experience supplies the materials to which the new insight adds fresh meanings. When we are told that the souls have felt in their lives the redeeming power of Kṛṣṇa or Buddha, Jesus or Mohammad, we must distinguish the immediate experience or intuition which might conceivably be infallible and the interpretation which is mixed up with it. St. Theresa tells us that after her experience she learned to understand the Trinity. Surely she would not have recognized the revelation as that of the Trinity if she had not already known something of the Trinity.[14] Similarly, if Paul had not learned something about Jesus, he would not have identified the voice that came to him on the Damascus road as Jesus's. We must distinguish the simple facts of religion from the accounts which reach us through the depth of theological preconceptions. That the soul is in contact with a mighty spiritual power other than its normal self and yet within and that its contact means the beginning of the creation of a new self is the fact, while the identification of this power with the historic figures of Buddha or Christ, the confusion of the simple realization of the universal self in us with a catastrophic revelation from without, is an interpretation, a personal confession and not necessarily an objective truth. Something is directly experienced but it is unconsciously interpreted in the terms of the tradition in which the individual is trained. The frame of reference which each individual adopts is determined by heredity and culture.

Again, there is no such thing as pure experience, raw and undigested. It is always mixed up with layers of interpretation. The alleged immediate datum is psychologically mediated. The scriptural statements give us knowledge, or interpreted experience, a that-what. The "that" is merely the affirmation of a fact, of a self-existent spiritual experience in which all distinctions are blurred and the individual seems

---

[14]Evelyn Underhill: *Mysticism,* p. 132, 5th Ed.

to overflow into the whole and belong to it. The experience is real though inarticulate.

Among the religious teachers of the world, Buddha is marked out as the one who admitted the reality of the spiritual experience and yet refused to interpret it as a revelation of anything beyond itself. For him the view that the experience gives us direct contact with God is an interpretation and not an immediate datum. Buddha gives us a report of the experience rather than an interpretation of it, though strictly speaking there are no experiences which we do not interpret. It is only a question of degree. But Buddha keeps closest to the given and is content with affirming that a deeper world of spirit penetrates the visible and the tangible world. Such a world certified as valid by the witness of perfect intuition exists beyond or rather within the world of multiplicity and change which the senses and understanding present to us. The primary reality is an unconditional existence beyond all potentiality of adequate expression by thought or description by symbol, in which the word "existence" itself loses its meaning and the symbol of *nirvāna* alone seems to be justified. The only liberty in which Buddha indulges when obliged to give a positive content to it is to identify it with Eternal righteousness (*dharma*), which is the principle of the universe[15] and the foundation of all conduct. It is on account of it that we have the implicit belief in the worth of life.

The Hindu thinkers admit the ineffability of the experience but permit themselves a graduated scale of interpretations from the most "impersonal" to the most "personal." The freedom of interpretation is responsible for what may be called the hospitality of the Hindu mind. The Hindu tradition by its very breadth seems to be capable of accommodating varied religious conceptions.

Hinduism admits that the unquestionable content of the experience is a *that* about which nothing more can be said. The deeper and more intimate a spiritual experience, the more readily does it dispense with signs and symbols. Deep intuition is utterly silent. Through silence we "confess without confession"

that the glory of spiritual life is inexplicable and beyond the reach of speech and mind. It is the great unfathomable mystery and words are treacherous.

The empirical understanding is quite competent within its own region, but it cannot be allowed to criticize its foundation, that which it, along with other powers of man, takes for granted. The Supreme is not an object presented to knowledge but is the condition of knowledge. While for Buddha, who was ethically disposed, the eternal spirit is righteousness or *dharma,* in the strength of which we live and struggle, for many Hindu thinkers it is the very condition of knowledge. It is the eternal light which is not one of the things seen but the condition of seeing. The ultimate condition of being where all dualities disappear, where life and death do not matter since they spring from it, where spirit seems to enjoy spirit and reason does not stir, can be expressed only in negative terms. The Upanisads and Śamkara[16] try to express the nature of the ultimate being in negative terms. "The eye goes not thither nor speech nor mind."[17]

There is a danger in these negative descriptions. By denying all attributes and relations we expose ourselves to the charge of reducing the ultimate being to bare existence which is absolute vacuity. The negative account is intended to express the soul's sense of the transcendence of God, the "wholly other," of whom naught may be predicted save in negations, and not to deprive God of his positive being. It is the inexhaustible positivity of God that bursts through all conceptual forms. When we call it nothing we mean that

---

[15]See Appendix to the writer's work on *Indian Philosophy,* vol. I, 2nd Ed. (1929).

---

[16]The *Upanishads,* a Sanskrit word that means teachings received sitting at the feet of the sage, are the last and most philosophical part of the *Vedas* (see footnote 1). There are 108 authenticated *Upanishads,* thirteen of which are taken to be major texts. They are perhaps the best known of Hindu scriptural literature and are taken as the basis of Hindu philosophy. *Samkara* is an alternative English spelling of *Shankara,* a ninth-century Indian philosopher who is the most famous interpreter of the *Upanishads.* Selections from the *Upanishads* appear in Section Two of Chapter 1 and Section Two of Chapter 5 (Eds.).
[17]*Bṛhadāraṇyaka Upaniṣad,* iii. 8. 8. For Śaṁkara it is *nirguna* (without qualities), *nirākāra* (without form), *nirviśeṣa* (without particularity), *nirupādhika* (without limitations). It is what it is. Isaiah's words are true, "Verily, thou art a God that hidest thyself." For Dionysius the Areopagite, God is the nameless supraessential one elevated above goodness itself. St. Augustine speaks of the Absolute, selfsame One, that which is.

it is nothing which created beings can conceive or name and not that it is nothing absolutely. The scriptures do not demonstrate or describe him but only bear witness to him. The three noteworthy features of spiritual experience are reality, awareness and freedom. If some parts of our experience come to us with these characteristics, it implies the possibility that all experience is capable of being received in the same manner. The consciousness to which all experience is present in its own immediacy, revealedness and freedom from anything which is not itself is the divine consciousness, that which is our ideal. We picture it as a glowing fire, a lucid flame of consciousness ever shining and revealing itself. In the divine status reality is its own immediate witness, its own self-awareness, its own freedom of complete being. There is nothing which is not gathered up in its being, nothing which is not revealed in it, and there is utter absence of all discord. It is perfect being, perfect consciousness and perfect freedom, *sat, cit* and *ānanda*. Being, truth and freedom are distinguished in the divine but not divided. The true and ultimate condition of the human being is the divine status. The essence of life is the movement of the universal being; the essence of emotion is the play of the self-existent delight in being; the essence of thought is the inspiration of the all-pervading truth; the essence of activity is the progressive realization of a universal and self-effecting good. Thought and its formations, will and its achievements, love and its harmonies are all based on the Divine Spirit. Only the human counterparts involve duality, tension, strain, and so are inadequate to the fulness of the divine. The supreme is real, not true, perfect, not good. Its freedom is its life, its essential spontaneity.

NO RELIGION

Buddhadasa

When I come to speak here, it is not to give any form of sermon or lecture, but to have an informal talk. I hope that you all agree to this, because then we can speak and listen to each other without formality and so our talk here can be somewhat different and unusual. Another thing; I intend to speak only about the most essential matters, important topics which are thought to be profound; therefore, if you don't listen carefully you will find it difficult to follow and probably will misunderstand, especially those of you who have not heard the previous talks which relate to this one. As a matter of fact, it is also difficult for me, for with each new talk I must maintain a connection with the previous ones. Last time we dealt with "voidness." This time I intend to talk about "No Religion." If you find it strange or incomprehensible, or if do not agree, please think it over for a while. It is not necessary to believe or subscribe to it right away.

Meeting together with you this time, I feel there is something which prevents us from understanding each other, and that is none other than the problem of language itself. Language as it is conventionally spoken we will call "People language," the language of common man. This is one kind of language. Then there is the language which is spoken by those who know reality (Dhamma),[1] especially those who know and understand reality in the ultimate sense. This is another kind of language. Sometimes only a few words, or even just a few syllables, are uttered, one who listens finds it paradoxical, completely opposite to the language of ordinary people. So please take note that there are two languages in use all the time. "People language" is used by ordinary people who do not understand Dhamma and worldlings so dense that they are blind to every thing other than material things. And then, there is also the language of those who really know the highest truth (Dhamma); that is a different language. We will call it "Dhamma language," the "Inner language"[2] pointing to the inner truths.

---

[1]*Dhamma* is a Pali term (*Dharma* in Sanskrit) that has been translated variously as ultimate truth, ultimate reality, the teachings of the Buddha, the underlying laws of the universe, and so on (Eds.).

[2]"A special kind of religious language embodying the "inner world," the culture of mind, of the heart." ". . . speaking from the view-point of absolute truth by keeping in mind the truth hidden in between the letters or behind the sound of speech." (*Christianity and Buddhism* by the Ven. Bhikkhu Buddhadasa Indapañño).

Therefore, you must take care to discriminate as to which language is being spoken.

People who are blind to the true reality (Dhamma) speak only "People language," the conventional language of ordinary people. On the other hand, the person who has genuinely realized the ultimate Truth (truly real Dhamma) can speak either one. He can handle People language quite well and is also comfortable using Inner (Dhamma) language, especially when speaking with someone else who knows reality or who has already realized the Truth (Dhamma). At that time it is only the inner reality (Dhamma) that is discussed and Inner language is used exclusively, that language of Dhamma which is unintelligible to ordinary people. Inner language is understood only by those who are in the know. What is more, in Inner language it is not even necessary to make a sound: For example, a finger is pointed or an eyebrow raised and the ultimate meaning of reality is understood. Therefore, I ask you to please keep in mind that there are two languages, People language and Inner language.

Now let us take up the following example: The ordinary, ignorant worldling is under the impression that there is this religion and that religion and that they are all different, different to the extent of being hostilely opposed. For instance, he considers "Christianity," "Islam," "Buddhism," and calls them "different," "incompatible," and even "bitter enemies." Speech like this is that of common man speaking, speaking in accordance with the impressions held by common people. And so, because of speech like this, there do exist different religions hostilely opposed to each other.

If one has penetrated to the essential nature (Dhamma) of religion, he will regard all religions as being the same. Although he may say there is Buddhism, Christianity, Islam, etc., he will also say that essentially they are all the same. However, if he should go on to a deeper and deeper understanding of Dhamma until finally he knows the Absolute Truth (Highest Dhamma), he would discover that there is no such thing called religion:—that there is no Buddhism; there is no Christianity; there is no Islam. Therefore, how can they be the same or conflicting?—it just isn't possible: Thus the words "No

religion!" is actually Dhamma language at its highest level. Whether it will be understood or not is something else, for this depends upon the listener and has nothing to do with the truth or with religion.

I will now give an example in People language, the language of materialism. Let us consider water. A person who does not know very much about even the simplest things thinks that there are many different kinds of water. He will view these various kinds of water as if they have nothing in common. He sees rain-water, well-water, underground-water, water in canals, water in swamps, water in ditches, water in gutters, water in sewers, water in toilets, urine-water, feces-water, water, water, water. This average common man will insist these waters are completely different. This is because his judgment depends on external criteria. A person with some knowledge however, knows that no matter what kind of water it is, in it pure water can be found or be distilled. If you take rain-water and distil it you can get pure water. If you take river-water and distil it you can get pure water. If you take canal-water, sewer-water or water out of a toilet and distil it, you can still get pure water.

A person who thinks in this way knows that all those different kinds of waters are the same as far as water is concerned. As for those elements which make it impure and look different, they are not water. They may combine with water, and alter water, but they still are not water. If you look through the polluting elements you can see water that is in every case identical, for in every case the essential nature of water is the same.

To sum up, however many kinds of water, they are all the same as far as the essential nature of water is concerned. If you look at things from this viewpoint, you can see that all religions are the same. If they appear different it is because you are making judgments on the basis of external forms.

If you are even smarter than this, you will take that pure water and examine it further. Then you will have to conclude that there is no water:—only two parts of hydrogen to one part of oxygen. Hydrogen and oxygen: that is not water. That substance which we have been calling water has disappeared, been voided—it is void, it is voidness.

Thus it becomes even more apparent that all those forms of "water" are the same. Two parts of hydrogen and one part of oxygen are the same everywhere—in the sky, in the ground, or wherever they may happen to be found; the substance water has ceased to exist, since we no longer use the term "water." And so, for one who has penetrated to the truth at this level, there is no such thing as water. In the same way one who has attained to the ultimate truth sees that there is no such thing as religion! There is only a kind of nature which you can call whatever you like—you can call it "dhamma," you can call it "truth," but you should not particularize that "Dhamma" or that "Truth" as Buddhism, Christianity or Islam, for whatever it is, it is, you cannot confine it by labelling.[3] The reason this division of Buddhism, Christianity and Islam exists is because the truth has not yet been realized; only outer forms are being taken into account, just as with canal-water and muddy water and the rest.

TRANSFORMING REALITY

Vine Deloria

A DIVIDED VISION

More than we would like to admit, our understanding of reality depends upon what we want to believe is true. The most sophisticated insights of physical science and the most intense religious experiences count for nothing in the popular mind if they do not conform to a general belief in what the reality of the world is. Thus our understanding of Western culture and civilization depends upon the manner in which we examine the general conceptions of reality held by Western peoples rather than upon a precise knowledge of what the most advanced thinkers have intuited. In approaching the Western conception of reality, therefore, we must fall back upon the religious and philosophical beliefs traditionally held in Western civilization.

One of the chief distinguishing characteristics of Western peoples in these fields has been the belief that ultimate reality exists over and above the transitory experiences of daily life. Arthur O. Lovejoy (1873–1962), American philosopher and historian of ideas, in his classic *The Great Chain of Being,* traces this belief to the Platonic dilemma of ensuring the validity of human knowledge and Plato's subsequent division of the world into otherworldly and this-worldly realms. Lovejoy says that the otherworldly attitude that originated most concretely with Platonic thinking is characterized by "the belief that both the genuinely 'real' and the truly good are radically antithetic in their essential characteristics to anything to be found in man's natural life, in the ordinary course of human experience, however normal, however intelligent, and however fortunate."[1] Divinity, reality, and eternity existed above and beyond the passing parade of life which we experience, and thus knowledge of the world was not an ultimate understanding but merely hinted at a more permanent structure to the moral and physical universe. The task of Greek philosophy, before and after Plato, was to divine from the welter of phenomena the ultimate constituent of the universe.

When this dualism was merged with Christian theology in the controversies over the status of Jesus, the meaning of historical revelation, and the fear of the last judgment, Greek thought was considered capable of articulating the philosophical aspects of the Christian religion and was welcomed. God existed in the Heavenly City where the faithful would be rewarded by eternal life, and all values of importance became those of the other world. Anthropologist Gregory Bateson describes

---

[3]In the light of this, there is no further need to translate the word "dhamma" or "Dhamma," but remember, "In the dictionary of nature there are no nouns, only verbs."

[1]Lovejoy, *The Great Chain of Being,* p. 25.

the attitudes toward the world that form when this picture of reality dominates:

> If you put God outside and set him vis-à-vis his cre-
> ation and if you have the idea that you are created in
> his image, you will logically and naturally see your-
> self as outside and against the things around you. And
> you will arrogate all mind to yourself, you will see the
> world around you as mindless and therefore not enti-
> tled to moral or ethical consideration. The environ-
> ment will seem to be yours to exploit. Your survival
> unit will be you and your folks or conspecifics against
> the environment of other social units, other races and
> the brutes and vegetables.[2]

It is this precise attitude toward the world that has characterized Western peoples and that today is crumbling before the realities of the present situa-tion in which we cannot continue to exploit the brutes and vegetables and in which the non-Western peoples reject Western exclusivity.

But the phenomena of *this-world* still had to make sense to Western peoples because these expe-riences and events affected them and determined their lives. One could not exist within human soci-ety believing it had no ultimate value and that life had no value. Two beliefs arose to fill this vacuum: a strong nationalism and a reliance on history as a repository of human values. History became not simply a record of past events but a record of *our* past events, a justification of the present by refer-ence to its chronological antecedents with the evi-dence amassed indicating that contemporary men and women had transcended their ancestors in many important ways.

History became such a dominant form of inter-preting the human experience that Western peoples ascribed a reality to it in itself, particularly when it was expressed in Christian theological concepts. All human existence had meaning because a divine plan was coordinating each and every event preparatory to a grand climactic judgment. Thus rather than negate daily existence, Western peoples became frantically concerned that every human act

had cosmic significance that would be revealed at the Last Judgment. Rigid rules and regulations arose to guide the individual through his or her pe-riod of testing in order to escape eternal damnation.

• • •

TRIBAL RELIGIOUS REALITIES

Primitive people do not differentiate their world of experience into two realms that oppose or comple-ment each other. They seem to maintain a consistent understanding of the unity of all experience. "Among the primitives," according to Joachim Wach, "there is no clear distinction between the no-tions of spiritual and material, psychical and physi-cal."[3] Rather than seeking underlying causes or substances, primitives report the nature and inten-sity of their experience. Carl Jung clarified this ap-proach to experience somewhat when he wrote that "thanks to our one-sided emphasis on so-called nat-ural causes, we have learned to differentiate what is subjective and psychic from what is objective and "natural." For primitive man, on the contrary, the psychic and the objective coalesce in the external world. In the face of something extraordinary it is not he who is astonished, but rather the thing that is astonishing."[4]

The traditional picture that Western thinkers have painted of primitive peoples is one of fear, supersti-tion, and ignorance, the intense desire to come to grips with natural forces, and a tendency to attribute powers and intentions to the unusual acts of nature. Jung's suggestion that the astonishment occurs in the objective world rather than in the observer would seem to indicate that primitives have a rather keen sense of observation and are intensely aware of the nature of the physical world in which they live, constantly encountering the unique in everything they meet. Such an attitude is indeterminate, not ab-solute, and would seem to transcend fear and super-

[2]Bateson, *Steps to an Ecology of Mind,* p. 462.

[3]Wach, *The Comparative Study of Religions,* p. 93.
[4]Jung, "Archaic Man," in *Civilization in Transition,* Collected Works, Volume 10, p. 63.

stition. At the very minimum, the fact that the astonishment occurs in the objective world means that the
identity of the primitive in a personal sense is preserved from destructive psychic disruptions.

But we must not consider the life of the primitive
one series of astonishing events after another. Primitive peoples rapidly become accustomed to the apparent periodic movements of nature, and it is the
unusual that attracts them. Carl Jung cautioned that
"primitive man's belief in an arbitrary power does
not arise out of thin air, as was always supposed, but
is grounded in experience. The grouping of chance
occurrences justifies what we call his superstition,
for there is a real measure of probability that unusual events will coincide in time and place. We
must not forget that our experience is apt to leave us
in the lurch here. Our observation is inadequate because our point of view leads us to overlook these
matters."[5] The first step in understanding the alternative world view of primitive peoples, therefore, is
to recognize that they do not derive their beliefs out
of "thin air" but that all beliefs and institutions derive from experience.

Although Jung warned that we tend to overlook
unusual coincidences and relationships that primitive peoples discern, we must recognize that
primitive peoples exist on the same planet as we
do and therefore have the same basic types of daily
experiences as we do. Their insights into the nature of reality, therefore, while occasionally more
specific or emotional, or even more intuitive, than
ours, refer to the same external reality. Their failure or refusal to differentiate subjective from objective, spiritual from material, seems to form the
basic difference that separates them from us. Thus
when we examine their system of beliefs, their
myths, or their social and political organizations,
we must remember that some things that have utmost importance for primitive peoples can be
found within the Western scheme of knowledge
but perhaps in a differentiated form that makes it
difficult to identify properly.

Thus it is with the most common feature of primitive awareness of the world—the feeling or belief
that the universe is energized by a pervading power.
Scholars have traditionally called the presence of this
power *mana,* following Polynesian beliefs, but we
find it among tribal peoples, particularly American
Indian tribes, as *wakan, orenda,* or *manitou.* Regardless of the technical term used, there is general agreement that a substantial number of primitive peoples
recognize the existence of a power in the universe
that affects and influences them. "The mana theory
maintains that there is something like a widely distributed power in the external world that produces all
those extraordinary effects," Carl Jung explained.
And he suggested that "everything that exists acts,
otherwise it would not *be.* It can *be* only by virtue of
its inherent energy. Being is a field of force. The
primitive idea of mana, as you can see, has in it the
beginnings of a crude theory of energy."[6]

It would be comforting, of course, to claim that
primitive peoples derived the principles of modern-
energy theory from their religious experiences
thousands of years before Western scientists formulated their complicated explanations, but it is not
necessary to be extravagant. It is sufficient to note
that the observations and experiences of primitive
peoples were so acute that they were able to recognize a basic phenomenon of the natural world religiously rather than scientifically. They felt power
but did not measure it. Today we measure power but
are unable to feel it except on extremely rare occasions. We conclude that energy forms the basic constituent of the universe through experimentation,
and the existence of energy is truly a conclusion of
scientific experimentation. For primitive peoples,
on the other hand, the presence of energy and power
is the starting point of their analyses and understanding of the natural world. It is their cornerstone
for further exploration.

Western thinkers continually misinterpret the
recognition of power by primitive peoples as if it
were a conclusion they had reached rather than a

---

[5]Ibid., p. 60.

[6]Ibid., p. 69.

beginning they were making. Thus Paul Tillich wrote that "the conception of nature that we find earliest in history, so far as we have knowledge of it, is the magical-sacramental conception. According to it, everything is filled with a sort of material energy which gives to things and to parts of things, even to the body and the parts of the body, a sacral power. The word 'sacral' in this context, however, does not signify something in opposition to the profane. Indeed, at this phase of cultural development the distinction between the sacred and the profane is not a fundamental one."[7] Such an explanation is incorrect because it is phrased in the traditional language of Western thinkers, which separates spiritual and material into two distinct aspects of reality. Primitive peoples refuse to make such distinctions. We are not dealing, therefore, with a conception of nature in the same way that Western thinkers conceive of things, but with a simple recognition of the force-field that seems to constitute the natural world.

The implications of understanding the proper sense in which primitive peoples experienced the natural world is important because it bears directly on the manner in which they understand themselves. Ernst Cassirer, writing of the attitudes of primitive peoples, maintained that for them "nature becomes one great society, the *society of life*. Man is not endowed with outstanding rank in this society. He is a part of it but he is in no respect higher than any other member."[8] All species, all forms of life, have equal status before the presence of the universal power to which all are subject. The religious requirement for all life-forms is thus harmony, and this requirement holds for every species, ours included. The natural world has a great bond that brings together all living entities, each species gaining an identity and meaning as it forms a part of the complex whole. If ever there were a truly evolutionary theological position, primitive peoples would represent it.

Primitive peoples somehow maintain this attitude toward the world and toward other life-forms. As long as the bond of life is respected, all species have value and meaning, emotions and intuitions remain a constant factor of experience, and harmony is maintained. The elimination of emotional intensity and intuitive insights into the world, which is accomplished by the great "world" religions, twists this basic apprehension of reality. "No religion could ever think of cutting or even loosening the bond between nature and man," Ernst Cassirer wrote. "But in the great ethical religions this bond is tied and fastened in a new sense. . . . Nature is not, as in polytheistic religions, the great and benign mother, the divine lap from which all life originates. It is conceived as the sphere of law and lawfulness."[9]

The great innovation of the world religions is to reduce natural events to a sequence containing some form of predictability, to introduce the conception of law and regularity into the natural world. Such an innovation is wholly artificial and may be understood by primitive peoples as the original sin. Certainly the acquisition of knowledge is understood in Genesis as the original sin, and it is ironic that in attempting to refine religious experiences into a more precise understanding that the great world religions commit the sin that alienates our species from the rest of the natural world. Paul Tillich noted that the primitive understanding of reality changes "when the system of powers is replaced by the correlation of self and world, of subjectivity and objectivity. Man becomes an epistemological, legal, and moral center, and things become objects of his knowledge, his work, and his use."[10] This point of departure separates primitive people from the rest of the human species; it distinguishes civilized from primitive, and unleashes the energies of our species on a path of conquest of the rest of nature, which has now been reduced to the status of an object.

---

[7]Tillich, *The Protestant Era,* pp. 99–100.
[8]Cassirer, *An Essay on Man,* p. 83.

[9]Ibid., p. 100.
[10]Tillich, *The Protestant Era,* p. 120.

It is curious that Tillich would support the tendency of the great world religions to reduce the natural world to an objective status, thereby artificially elevating our species above other life forms. Granted that we seek knowledge continually; knowledge is more than the ability to deal with theories. The curiosity arises because Tillich suggested that the "man who transforms the world into a universal machine serving his purposes has to adapt himself to the laws of the machine. The mechanized world of things draws man into itself and makes him a cog, driven by the mechanical necessities of the whole. *The personality that deprives nature of its power in order to elevate itself above it becomes a powerless part of its own creation.*"[11] It would appear, therefore, that organizing and systematizing religious experiences into reliable and predictable knowledge is a major theological transgression and a movement away from intimate understanding of our place in the world in an epistemological sense.

Arnold Toynbee described the severance of the bond of nature and our species in different terms than did Cassirer, and Toynbee's analysis gives us insight into the problems created by the expansion and sophistication of the great world religions. "The worship of Nature tends to unite the members of different communities because it is not self-centered," Toynbee maintained, "it is the worship of a power in whose presence all human beings have the identical experience of being made aware of their own human weakness." In contrast to the unifying effect which nature has on human communities, Toynbee suggested that "the worship of parochial communities tends to set their respective members at variance because this religion is an expression of self-centredness; because self-centredness is the source of all strife; and because the collective ego is a more dangerous object of worship than the individual ego is."[12]

The characteristic that purports to save members of world religions, while conceived on an idealistic and precise basis, is the very thing that destroys the members thereof—concentrating on the self to the exclusion of the world. Perhaps the best illustration we can find is the comparative status that primitive peoples and adherents of world religions enjoy vis-à-vis each other. Joachim Wach wrote that "in most primitive religions a strong tie binds the members of a tribal cult together, and on the level of great religions, spiritual brotherhood surpasses physical ties between brothers. A 'father or mother in God,' a 'brother or sister in God,' may be closer to us than our physical parents and relatives."[13] This claim may have a certain validity for specific individuals, but on the larger scale it does not appear to be operative. Wach himself noted that "whatever the prevailing mood, the religious association takes precedence over all other forms of fellowship. Religious loyalty, in theory at least, outranks any other loyalty everywhere except in the modern Western world."[14] The result of the teachings of the world religions, which center on the care and salvation of the individual, is, of course, the creation of the solitary individual, apart from any community of concern.

Most adherents of world religions would dispute the accusation that their tradition isolates individuals; yet their teachings appear designed to break the traditional ties that have bound communities together. "In order to create a new and profound spiritual brotherhood based on the principles enunciated by the new faith," Wach explained, "old bonds have to be broken. This break of sociological ties becomes one of the marks of the willingness to begin a new life. To become a disciple of the Buddha means to leave parents and relatives, wife and child, home and property and all else, as flamingos leave their lakes."[15] Theoretically, at least, the new community, which is formed according to the principles of the new faith, is superior to the sociological, family, and

---

[11]Ibid., p. 123. Italics mine.
[12]Toynbee, *An Historian's Approach to Religion,* p. 34.

[13]Wach, *The Comparative Study of Religions,* p. 125.
[14]Ibid., p. 139.
[15]Ibid., p. 128.

community ties, which are severed in the primitive community. The product, again, is not what the world religions claim it to be. "Modern Western man is all too prone to think of the solitary individual first and last," Wach wrote, "yet the study of primitive religions shows that, individual experiences notwithstanding, religion is generally a group affair."[16]

The attraction of the world religions appears to be their knowledge and idealism, their precise manner of articulating answers to perennial human questions about life, death, and meaning, and their ability to preach and teach methods of living that will enable people to survive in a world that often seems hostile. But clarity in articulating beliefs is not necessarily a benefit. Carl Jung suggested that "it is not ethical principles, however lofty, or creeds, however orthodox, that lay the foundations for the freedom and autonomy of the individual, but simply and solely the empirical awareness, the incontrovertible experience of an intensely personal, reciprocal relationship between man and an extramundane authority which acts as the counterpoise to the 'world' and its reason.' "[17] The great bond of experience with nature, no matter how vaguely defined, incorporates the emotional and intuitive dimension of our lives much better than do the precise creeds, doctrines, and dogmas of the great world religions and as such provides us with continuing meaning as long as we treat our apprehension of the great mystery with respect.

The first and great difference between primitive religious thought and the world religions, therefore, is that primitive peoples maintain a sense of mystery through their bond with nature; the world religions sever the relationship and attempt to establish a new, more comprehensible one. Foremost among the religious leaders who fought the great natural bond between our species and the other life-forms and processes of nature were the Hebrew prophets, with their constant warfare against the Baals. "The

significance of prophetic criticism," Paul Tillich wrote, "lies in the fact that it dissolves the primitive unity between the holy and the real. To the prophets the holy is primarily a demand. . . . Nature as such is deprived of its sacred character and becomes profane. Immediate intercourse with nature no longer possesses religious significance."[18] In this criticism, therefore, we have a reductionism that severs the holy from its origin and makes it an intellectual ethical requirement. A demand can only originate in a system of duties and responsibilities, a legalism and can only produce another legal system and more duties and responsibilities. The collective ego of the new community, which becomes the object of worship, be it the Christian church or whatever, must itself be given structure and a means of operation, and religion becomes a group of humans examining their own beliefs rather than continuing to fulfill a role in the great process of nature.

Primitive relationships with nature have been subjected to criticism from many points of view. They are regarded as remnants of former days when our species had no scientific understanding of the natural world. Tillich defined primitive relationships with nature as "objectification" and suggested that "the objectification of the divine in time and space and in anthropomorphic conceptions, which takes place in myth, is disrupted by prophetic religion, regarded as inadequate by mysticism and dismissed as unworthy and absurd by philosophical religion."[19] Tillich's statement poses important questions for understanding primitive perceptions of religions and, ultimately, natural reality. Our first task is to examine the suggestion that primitive peoples in fact do objectify the divine in time and space.

We have suggested earlier that the major difference between Christianity and Buddhism is that one absolutizes time and human affairs and the other absolutizes natural processes, and ultimately space. By contrast, primitive peoples maintain the unity of space-time and refuse to use either concept as their

---

[16]Ibid., pp. 121–22.
[17]Jung, "Religion as the Counterbalance to Mass-Mindedness," in *Civilization in Transition,* Collected Works, Volume 10, p. 258.

[18]Tillich, *The Protestant Era,* p. 108.
[19]Paul Tillich, "Myth and Religion," in Pelikan, ed., *Twentieth Century Theology in the Making,* Volume 2, p. 346.

analytical tool for understanding the world. Ernst Cassirer, writing about the society of natural life that characterizes primitive perceptions of nature, said that "we find the same principle—that of the solidarity and unbroken unity of life—if we pass from space to time. It holds not only in the order of simultaneity but also in the order of succession."[20] Like the modern physicist, the primitive holds the unity of experience in a continuum that transcends traditional Western divisions of space and time.

But there is an additional parallel between primitive peoples' perception of experiences and the theories of modern physics: space may conceivably have priority over time in that time occurs within space and must give way, at least conceptually, to spatial recognitions. "A native thinker makes the penetrating comment," Claude Levi-Strauss notes, "that 'all sacred things must have their place . . .' It could even be said that being in their place is what makes them sacred for if they were taken out of their place, even in thought, the entire order of the universe would be destroyed. Sacred objects therefore contribute to the maintenance of order in the universe by occupying the places allocated to them."[21] Far from objectifying the sacred in time and space here is a recognition that religious perceptions in fact occur in the natural world and go a substantial distance in giving it structure. We have not only the recognition that a divine energy pervades the natural world but that it is able to reveal itself in particular objects and places. To deny this possibility would be to deny the possibility of an ultimate sense of reality itself. But it is important to note that primitives are dealing with recognitions, not beliefs that have an intellectual content; and recognitions, like perceptions, involve the totality of personality.

Tillich himself admitted that "the holy appears only in special places, in special contexts." But instead of recognizing that the preservation of memories concerning the appearance of the holy is the first stage in structuring the world view of the primitive, that is, the holy mountain, the sacred river or lake, the point of emergence from the underworld, Tillich argued that "the concentration of the sacramental in special places, in special rites, is the expression of man's ambiguous situation."[22] It is difficult to understand why recognizing sacred places and rites creates ambiguity. Primitive peoples are certainly not confused about the places and rites they consider sacred, for these form the basis of their community and provide an identity that incorporates rather than transcends the space-time dimensions. Ambiguity would only seem to appear if one wished to universalize the sacred nature of experience, thereby, in effect, lifting the sacred from its context of the natural world and holding it in one's mind as a set of concepts. Ambiguity only appears when one attempts to control the appearance of divinity and establish regular guidelines for any relationship that might ensue with divinity.

Whenever we begin to discuss the role of time and space for primitive peoples, we become embroiled in controversy because Western thinkers have traditionally separated space and time, unconsciously we might suggest, always considering them homogenous entities in their own right. Thus it is important to clarify the primitive perceptions of space and time so that we can be sure we understand the manner in which primitive peoples perceive experiences. "Primitive thought is not only incapable of thinking of a system of space," Ernst Cassirer wrote, "it cannot even conceive a scheme of space." And, he continued, "Its concrete space cannot be brought into a *schematic* shape. Ethnology shows us that primitive tribes usually are gifted with an extraordinarily sharp perception of space. A native of these tribes has an eye for all the nicest details of his environment."[23] The primitive easily comprehends the places of his or her experience, but he or she does not abstract from them a scheme of space in a Euclidian or Newtonian sense. The primitive person is thus in direct immediate

[20]Cassirer, *An Essay on Man*, p. 83.
[21]Levi-Strauss, *The Savage Mind*, p. 10.

[22]Tillich, *The Protestant Era*, p. 111.
[23]Cassirer, *An Essay on Man*, p. 45.

relationship with his or her environment but fails to extend abstract principles continuously to conceive of "endless" dimensional existence. In view of our discussion of the conceptions of space-time in modern physics, it would appear that primitive peoples, in their religious perceptions of the natural world, coincide with the contemporary conceptual understanding of the world.

This view of primitive peoples provides them with an understanding of the natural world that immediately incorporates all aspects of experience. Thus primitive descriptions of events contain all elements of knowledge that Western scientists have traditionally extracted and organized into distinct academic disciplines. Whenever scholars have attempted to return to the primitive perception and illustrate the wholistic understanding contained in primitive mythologies, they have had to bring in the primitive perception of space as a means of demonstrating their thesis. Thus Claude Levi-Strauss suggests that there is a symmetry between anthropology and history in primitive thought-forms, making the two disciplines parallel, interwoven developments. Levi-Strauss encounters difficulty with his academic colleagues in advocating this position, and he complains that "this symmetry between history and anthropology seems to be rejected by philosophers who implicitly or explicitly deny that distribution in space and succession in time afford equivalent perspectives. In their eyes some special prestige seems to attach to the temporal dimension, as if a diachrony were to establish a kind of intelligibility not merely superior to that provided by a synchrony, but above all more specifically human."[24]

When we admit the equivalency of temporal and spatial dimensions as perspectives for understanding, we can answer the accusations of the prophets, the mystics, and the expositors of philosophical religion. Perceptions of experience articulated in predominantly spatial terms incorporate the immediacy of the situation without including prior causations and future projections as part of the original experience.

Thus the immediate event is passed forward as it occurred, without editorial reordering, and primitive peoples preserve "chunks" of experience, not interpretive patterns of activity. Rather than being a demeaning manner of understanding, which fails to comprehend cause and effect and temporality, the primitive form of apprehension may be more sophisticated. Marshall McLuhan comments on this possibility in *Understanding Media*, suggesting that although "our ideas of cause and effect in the literate West have long been in the form of things in sequence and succession," such a way of understanding the world is "an idea that strikes any tribal or auditory culture as quite ridiculous, and *one that has lost its prime place in our own new physics and biology.*"[25]

We conclude that primitive peoples' perceptions of reality, particularly their religious experiences and awareness of divinity, occupy a far different place in their lives than do the conceptions of the world religions, their experiences, and theologies, philosophies, doctrines, dogmas, and creeds. Primitive peoples preserve their experiences fairly intact, understand them as a manifestation of the unity of the natural world, and are content to recognize these experiences as the baseline of reality. World religions take the raw data of religious experience and systematize elements of it, using either the temporal or the spatial dimensions as a framework, and attempt to project meaning into the unexamined remainder of human experience. Ethics becomes an abstract set of propositions attempting to relate individuals to one another in the world religions, while kinship duties, customs, and responsibilities, often patterned after relationships in the natural world, parallel the ethical considerations of religion in the primitive peoples. Primitive peoples always have a concrete reference—the natural world—and the adherents of the world religions continually deal with abstract and ideal situations on an intellectual plane. "Who is my neighbor?" becomes a question of great debate in the tradition of the world reli-

---

[24]Levi-Strauss, *The Savage Mind,* p. 256.

[25]McLuhan, *Understanding Media; The Extensions of Man,* p. 86. Italics mine.

gions, and the face of the neighbor changes continually as new data about people becomes available. Such a question is not even within the world view of primitives. They know precisely who their relatives are and what their responsibilities toward them entail.

QUESTIONS FOR DISCUSSION

1. For Radhakrishnan mystical or religious experiences have certain universal characteristics. Discuss several of these characteristics. In your discussions consider at least two of the following: (a) whether or not there is any value to these experiences; (b) the epistemological status of the experience; and (c) whether they are experiences of God.

2. Evaluate Buddhadassa's claim that while from the perspective of ordinary language religions are different, on a deeper level they are all the same. Then, evaluate his further claim that on a still deeper level there are no religions. In your answer to the last question consider his comparison of religion at the deepest level and water as ultimately two parts hydrogen and one part oxygen.

3. We generally feel justified in calling something real if it is capable of being publicly verified. But mystical experiences are, by their very nature, private. How then, if at all, can we distinguish between a mystical experience and a hallucination?

4. Discuss Deloria's characterization of tribal religious experience. To what extent is the tribal religious understanding of reality different from the way in which the major world's religions view reality? Is tribal religious experience fundamentally different from the experience described by mystics within the world's major religions? Or is tribal religious experience a form of the mystical experience? To what extent do you think that the tribal religious vision of reality is useful for confronting the world today?

RELIGION, SOCIETY, AND POLITICS

Religion has always had an ambivalent relation to those in power. "Render unto Caesar," said Jesus Christ, "what is due to Caesar," but left unclear what fits into this category. Although often supporting the status quo, religion has been also used by revolutionaries against the status quo. How, then, should we evaluate its social and political significance?

The first reading in this section is composed of excerpts from the works of the nineteenth-century social theorists and revolutionaries Karl Marx and Friedrich Engels. For these thinkers, religion is an expression of an oppressive and alienated society. Since human beings experience intense suffering in such a world, they create an illusory happiness in a world beyond (the reader might want to compare this analysis of religion as an illusion with Freud's psychological analysis in Section one of this chapter). It is in this sense that religion is "the opium of the people." Just as the using of actual opiate derivatives or other similar drugs tends to reinforce the status quo by pacifying people and diverting their attention from the problems that make them need drugs in the first place, so religion pacifies and diverts people's attention from the social roots of their suffering. In addition, both Marx and Engels believed that the class that wields economic and political power, the ruling class, uses religion directly as an instrument to legitimate its interest and its rule. Marx notes that Christianity in particular has historically justified slavery, serfdom, and capitalist exploitation, and that it has attempted to justify these forms of oppression as "either the just punishment of original sin and other sins or trials that the Lord in his infinite wisdom imposes on those redeemed." Religion, Marx claims, will not vanish through the force of rational argument but only when the oppressive social conditions that generate the need for it have been overthrown. "The demand to give up the illusions about its condition is the demand to give up a condition which needs illusions. The criticism of religion is therefore in embryo the criticism of the vale of woe, the halo of which is religion."

Nevertheless, even Marx knows that there is another side to religion. In the same text that he discusses religion as "the opium of the people" he also calls religion "the protest against real distress" and the "heart of a heartless world." And Engels writes that Christianity "was originally a movement of oppressed people" and that it, like socialism, preaches a liberation from oppression. The problem, however, is that "Christianity places this salvation in a life beyond, after death, in heaven," while "socialism places it in this world in a transformation of society."

In 1968, in Medellín, Colombia, 130 Catholic Bishops met and called for a radical social transformation with an emphasis on the "option for the poor." This call spoke to a movement that was already emerging known as "liberation theology," and this movement was to become a dynamic movement for and by the poor in every country in Latin America. It was often led by priests who helped their parishioners establish "Christian base communities" that were often engaged in revolutionary struggle.

In this section, the Brazilian theologians and priests Leonardo Boff and Clodovis Boff (they are brothers) discuss some of the key theological and philosophical foundations of liberation theology. Liberation from oppression, according to liberation theology, does not await a life beyond, after death, as Engels would have it, because God's Kingdom exists not only in eternity but also within history.

While liberation theology is revolutionary, it is also still theology. The poor are not merely Marx's proletariat but all the oppressed who are represented by the "disfigured Son of God." The revolutionary stance of liberation theology is rooted in what Boff and Boff call a "hermeneutics of liberation," a rereading of the Bible from the standpoint of the poor. This also entails reinterpreting the fundamental stories and symbols from the Old and New Testament as revolutionary indicators. The Exodus is the story of a God who stands with the oppressed against their oppressors. The Prophets present a revolutionary challenge to all forms of social injustice. Christ is the symbol of liberation itself. The Holy Spirit struggles with the people against their oppressors. Mary is the liberating woman of the people.

Liberation theology is a current within Christianity, specifically within Catholicism, but there are currents that parallel it in every major world religion. In 1972, a number of well-known thinkers from different religious traditions were asked to respond to liberation theology. They were explicitly asked to read two significant works, one of which was *Introducing Liberation Theology,* written by Leonardo and Clodovis Boff (their reading in this section is from that book). One of the respondents was Sulak Sivaraksa, who was director of the Santi Prak Institute in Bangkok and a leading expositor of Hindu and Buddhist thought. Sivaraksa's response, which also appears in this section, offers a favorable assessment of a growing tendency within the Buddhist tradition, often called by its advocates (including the Dalai Lama, among others) "engaged Buddhism." This contemporary current challenges the idea of Buddhism as quietistic and escapist and insists that Buddhism's commitment to personal liberation cannot be separated from a commitment to social change. Engaged Buddhism takes the position that Buddhist practitioners should seek to create the social conditions necessary for the development of Buddhist values on a global scale and that such an agenda presents a radical challenge to the status quo.

Sivaraksa recognizes that Buddhism has often been used to maintain the status quo (just as has every religion) but argues that this is antithetical to the true spirit of Buddha's message. The Buddha, he recounts, emphasized the problem of human suffering and the means necessary to overcome that suffering. Buddha recognized the role played by greed, hatred, and ignorance in causing that suffering. In today's world, greed is fostered by consumerism, which is, in turn, promoted by multinational corporations. Hatred and ignorance are fostered by oppression and militarism. Therefore, Buddhism must become engaged in the struggle against consumerism, oppression, and militarism and against the economic and political institutions that sustain them.

However, engaged Buddhism does insist that the struggle against these evils must not be motivated by hatred, that one should struggle against oppression but not hate the oppressors, who are themselves suffering as result of their greed and ignorance. Here, engaged Buddhism distinguishes itself from liberation theology's preferential option for the poor, being ultimately concerned with all those who suffer from the effects of an oppressive system—the oppressors as well as the oppressed. While Buddhist social activists need to ally themselves with the oppressed, they also need to enlighten those who work in exploitative industries and unjust governmental bureaucracies.

Engaged Buddhism also distinguishes itself from secular social activism in that it seeks not only to create conditions that can satisfy basic desires but also to liberate individuals from self-seeking desires. It seeks not only social goals but spirituality in social action. It employs the Buddhist practice of mindfulness (a form of meditation) that can enable the social activist to struggle with a calm and peaceful mind.

Finally, engaged Buddhism challenges the attachment to ideology. Sivaraksa quotes the Vietnamese Buddhist Zen master Thich Nhat Hanh: "Do not be idolatrous or bound to any ideology, even Buddhist ones. . . . Peace can only be achieved when we are not attached to a view, when we are free from fanaticism."

In the United States and much of the Western world, Islam is often associated with fanaticism, terrorism, and the support of dictatorial regimes. This association conflates Islam with only one of its forms—fundamentalism. Hassan Hanafi, a professor of philosophy at the University of Cairo and president of the Egyptian Philosophical Association, presents a different understanding of Islam. Hanafi is very much a cosmopolitan, public intellectual (he received his doctorate at the Sorbonne and has been a visiting professor in the United States, Belgium, and Kuwait) who is willing to dialogue with the fundamentalists. In the selection in this section, reprinted from his book *Islam in the Modern World,* Hanafi argues for the revolutionary significance of Islam. Basing his analysis on the primary sources of the Qur'an and the Hadith, he claims that the etymological meaning of Islam as submission, or surrender, has been misunderstood and manipulated to justify submission to political rulers and to the status quo. In Islam, he asserts, there is only one kind of legitimate surrender, submission to God, who he refers to more neutrally (nonanthropomorphically) as the Transcendence. From this it follows that adherents to Islam must refuse to give their ultimate allegiance to any temporal political power. No worldly political power can ever claim absolute authority, as only the Transcendence can have such authority. In short, no ruler can legitimately claim to be God's representative, and a despotic ruler deserves to be overthrown. All the prophets, Hanafi points out, struggle against the status quo; and all revolutions, he claims, are functions of the Transcendence.

Hanafi also argues that Islam is committed to a vision of an egalitarian society in which there is complete freedom of expression, in which there is no gap between rich and poor, and in which there are no class divisions. This vision, however, should not be confused with its secular political counterparts, as Hanafi also argues that one form of oppression is "the rule of Muslims by a secular minority in the name of secular political ideologies: Liberalism, Socialism, Nationalism, Marxism, etc." Hanafi also attempts to explain Islamic fundamentalism as an understandable reaction to Westernization and its threat to Islamic cultural identity and, while subscribing to a universal code of ethics, advocates a return to the unity of the Muslim world. The symbols of Islam are not, for Hanafi, mere packaging for a universal revolutionary message.

Symbols in general and religious symbols in particular have profound psychological and political significance. Carol Christ, a feminist writer—she is the author of *Laughter of Aphrodite*—involved in the movement of women's spirituality, observes that symbols shape our cultural ethos and resonate at a deep unconscious level. But, with perhaps the exception of Mary, the symbols of Western religion—and we might add, of all the major reli-

gions—are overwhelmingly male. Of special significance is the symbol of God the Father, which Carol Christ claims devalues and delegitimizes the power of women. Thus, in the last selection in this section and in this chapter, Christ argues in favor of asserting the symbol of the Goddess as an affirmation of female power.

CRITIQUE OF RELIGION

Karl Marx and Friedrich Engels

The basis of irreligious criticism is: *Man makes religion,* religion does not make man. In other words, religion is the self-consciousness and self-feeling of man who has either not yet found himself or has already lost himself again. But *man* is no abstract being squatting outside the world. Man is *the world of man,* the state, society. This state, this society, produce religion, *a reversed world-consciousness,* because they are *a reversed world.* Religion is the general theory of that world, its encyclopaedic compendium, its logic in a popular form, its spiritualistic *point d'honneur,* its enthusiasm, its moral sanction, its solemn completion, its universal ground for consolation and justification. It is *the fantastic realization* of the human essence because the *human essence* has no true reality. The struggle against religion is therefore mediately the fight against *the other world,* of which religion is the spiritual *aroma.*

Religious distress is at the same time the *expression* of real distress and the *protest* against real distress. Religion is the sigh of the oppressed creature, the heart of a heartless world, just as it is the spirit of a spiritless situation. It is the *opium* of the people.

The abolition of religion as the *illusory* happiness of the people is required for their *real* happiness. The demand to give up the illusions about its condition is the *demand to give up a condition which needs illusions.* The criticism of religion is therefore *in embryo the criticism of the vale of woe,* the *halo* of which is religion.

Criticism has plucked the imaginary flowers from the chain not so that man will wear the chain without any fantasy or consolation but so that he will shake off the chain and cull the living flower. The criticism of religion disillusions man to make him think and act and shape his reality like a man who has been disillusioned and has come to reason, so that he will revolve round himself and therefore round his true sun. Religion is only the illusory sun which revolves round man as long as he does not revolve round himself.

The task of history, therefore, once the *world beyond the truth* has disappeared, is to establish the *truth of this world.* The immediate *task of philosophy,* which is at the service of history, once the *saintly form* of human self-alienation has been unmasked, is to unmask self-alienation in its *unholy forms.* Thus the criticism of heaven turns into the criticism of the earth, the *criticism of religion* into the *criticism of right* and the *criticism of theology* into the *criticism of politics.*[1]

• • •

The religious world is but the reflex of the real world. And for a society based upon the production of commodities,[2] in which the producers in general enter into social relations with one another by treating their products as commodities and values, whereby they reduce their individual private labour to the standard of homogeneous human labour—for such a society, Christianity with its *cultus* of abstract man, more especially in its bourgeois developments, Protestantism, Deism, &c., is the most fitting form of religion. In the ancient Asiatic and other ancient modes of production,[3] we find that the conversion of products into commodities, and therefore the conversion of men into producers of commodities, holds a subordinate place, which, however, increases in importance as the primitive communities approach nearer and nearer to their dissolution. Trading nations, properly so called, exist in the ancient world only in its interstices, like the gods of Epicurus in the Intermundia,[4] or like Jews in the pores of Polish society. Those ancient social organisms of production are, as compared with bourgeois society, extremely simple and transparent. But they are founded either on the immature development of man individually, who has not yet severed the umbilical cord that unites him with his fellowmen in a primitive tribal community, or upon direct relations of subjection. They can arise and exist only when the development of the productive power of labour has not risen beyond a low stage, and when, therefore, the social relations within the sphere of material life, between man and man, and between man and nature, are correspondingly narrow. This narrowness is reflected in the ancient worship of nature, and in the other elements of the popular religions. The religious reflex of the real world can, in any case, only then finally vanish, when the practical relations of every-day life offer to man none but perfectly intelligible and reasonable relations with regard to his fellowmen and to nature.

The life-process of society, which is based on the process of material production, does not strip off its mystical veil until it is treated as production by freely associated men, and is consciously regulated by them in accordance with a settled plan.[5] This, however, demands for society a certain material

---

[1]Marx is referring here to the German philosopher Ludwig Feuerbach's (1804–1872) critique of religion as an alienated projection of human nature. Marx is arguing that it is not enough to expose religion as self-alienation but that we must further expose the alienating social and political conditions that provide the ground for religious self-alienation (Eds.).

[2]Commodities are not just objects for use but objects to be bought and sold. A society based upon the production of commodities is a capitalist society (Eds.).

[3]A mode of production is the economic structure of a society in both its physical and social dimensions. According to Marx there have been several different modes of production throughout history: ancient (Asiatic and slave), feudal, and capitalist (Eds.).

[4]Epicurus (341–270 B.C.E. [Before the common era]) was an Ancient Greek philosopher who speculated that the gods were material, pleasure-seeking beings who exist in a realm separate from the human world—Intermundia—and who pursue their own affairs without concern for human beings (Eds.).

[5]This was Marx's concept of a communist society (Eds.).

groundwork or set of conditions of existence which in their turn are the spontaneous product of a long and painful process of development.

• • •

All religion, however, is nothing but the fantastic reflection in men's minds of those external forces which control their daily life, a reflection in which the terrestrial forces assume the form of supernatural forces. In the beginnings of history it was the forces of nature which were first so reflected and which in the course of further evolution underwent the most manifold and varied personifications among the various peoples. This early process has been traced back by comparative mythology, at least in the case of the Indo-European peoples, to its origin in the Indian Vedas, and in its further evolution it has been demonstrated in detail among the Indians, Persians, Greeks, Romans, Germans and, so far as material is available, also among the Celts, Lithuanians and Slavs. But it is not long before, side by side with the forces of nature, social forces begin to be active—forces which confront man as equally alien and at first equally inexplicable, dominating him with the same apparent natural necessity as the forces of nature themselves. The fantastic figures, which at first only reflected the mysterious forces of nature, at this point acquire social attributes, become representatives of the forces of history. At a still further stage of evolution, all the natural and social attributes of the numerous gods are transferred to *one* almighty god, who is but a reflection of the abstract man. Such was the origin of monotheism, which was historically the last product of the vulgarized philosophy of the later Greeks and found its incarnation in the exclusively national god of the Jews, Jehovah. In this convenient, handy and universally adaptable form, religion can continue to exist as the immediate, that is, the sentimental form of men's relation to the alien natural and social forces which dominate them, so long as men remain under the control of these forces. However, we have seen repeatedly that in existing bourgeois society men are dominated by the economic conditions created by themselves, by the means of

production which they themselves have produced, as if by an alien force. The actual basis of the reflective activity that gives rise to religion therefore continues to exist, and with it the religious reflection itself. And although bourgeois political economy has given a certain insight into the causal connection of this alien domination, this makes no essential difference. Bourgeois economics can neither prevent crises in general, nor protect the individual capitalists from losses, bad debts and bankruptcy, nor secure the individual workers against unemployment and destitution. It is still true that man proposes and God (that is, the alien domination of the capitalist mode of production) disposes. Mere knowledge, even if it went much further and deeper than that of bourgeois economic science, is not enough to bring social forces under the domination of society. What is above all necessary for this, is a social *act*. And when this act has been accomplished, when society, by taking possession of all means of production and using them on a planned basis, has freed itself and all its members from the bondage in which they are now held by these means of production which they themselves have produced but which confront them as an irresistible alien force; when therefore man no longer merely proposes, but also disposes—only then will the last alien force which is still reflected in religion vanish; and with it will also vanish the religious reflection itself, for the simple reason that then there will be nothing left to reflect.

• • •

The history of early Christianity has notable points of resemblance with the modern working-class movement. Like the latter, Christianity was originally a movement of oppressed people: it first appeared as the religion of slaves and emancipated slaves, of poor people deprived of all rights, of peoples subjugated or dispersed by Rome. Both Christianity and the workers' socialism preach forthcoming salvation from bondage and misery; Christianity places this salvation in a life beyond, after death, in heaven; socialism places it in this world, in a transformation of society. Both are persecuted and baited, their adherents are despised and made the objects of exclusive laws, the former as enemies of the human race, the latter as enemies of the state, enemies of religion, the family, social order. And in spite of all persecution, nay, even spurred on by it, they forge victoriously, irresistibly ahead. Three hundred years after its appearance Christianity was the recognized state religion in the Roman World Empire, and in barely sixty years socialism has won itself a position which makes its victory absolutely certain.

If, therefore, Prof. Anton Menger wonders in his *Right to the Full Product of Labour* why, with the enormous concentration of landownership under the Roman emperors and the boundless sufferings of the working class of the time, which was composed almost exclusively of slaves, "socialism did not follow the overthrow of the Roman Empire in the West," it is because he cannot see that this "socialism" did in fact, as far as it was possible at the time, exist and even became dominant—in Christianity. Only this Christianity, as was bound to be the case in the historic conditions, did not want to accomplish the social transformation in this world, but beyond it, in heaven, in eternal life after death, in the impending "millennium."

•   •   •

Besides income tax, the Consistorial Councillor has another means of introducing communism as he conceives it:

"What is the alpha and omega of Christian faith? The dogma of original sin and the redemption. And therein lies the solidary link between men at its highest potential; one for all and all for one."

Happy people! The *cardinal question* is solved for ever. Under the double wings of the Prussian eagle and the Holy Ghost the proletariat will find two inexhaustible sources of life: first the surplus of income tax over and above the ordinary and extraordinary needs of the state, a surplus which is equal to nought; second, the revenues from the heavenly domains of original sin and the redemption which are also equal to nought. These two noughts provide a splendid ground for one-third of the nation who

have no ground for their subsistence and a wonderful support for another third which is on the decline. In any case, the imaginary surpluses, original sin and the redemption, will appease the hunger of the people in quite a different way than the long speeches of the liberal deputies!

Further we read:

"In the 'Our Father' we say: lead us not into temptation. And we must practise towards our neighbour what we ask for ourselves. But our social conditions tempt man and excessive need incites to crime."

And we, the honourable bureaucrats, judges and consistorial councillors of the Prussian state, take this into consideration by having people racked on the wheel, beheaded, imprisoned, and flogged and thereby "lead" the proletarians "into temptation" to have us later similarly racked on the wheel, beheaded, imprisoned and flogged. And that will not fail to happen.

"Such conditions," the Consistorial Councillor declares, "a Christian state *cannot* tolerate, it must find a remedy for them."

Yes, with absurd prattle on society's duties of solidarity, with imaginary surpluses and unprovided bills drawn on God the Father, Son and Co.

"We can also be spared the already boring talk about communism," our observant Consistorial Councillor asserts. "If only those whose calling it is to develop the social principles of Christianity do so, the Communists will soon be put to silence."

The social principles of Christianity have now had eighteen hundred years to develop and need no further development by Prussian consistorial councillors.

The social principles of Christianity justified the slavery of Antiquity, glorified the serfdom of the Middle Ages and equally know, when necessary, how to defend the oppression of the proletariat, although they make a pitiful face over it.

The social principles of Christianity preach the necessity of a ruling and an oppressed class, and all they have for the latter is the pious wish the former will be charitable.

The social principles of Christianity transfer the consistorial councillors' adjustment of all infamies to heaven and thus justify the further existence of those infamies on earth.

The social principles of Christianity declare all vile acts of the oppressors against the oppressed to be either the just punishment of original sin and other sins or trials that the Lord in his infinite wisdom imposes on those redeemed.

The social principles of Christianity preach cowardice, self-contempt, abasement, submission, dejection, in a word all the qualities of the *canaille;* and the proletariat, not wishing to be treated as *canaille,* needs its courage, its self-feeling, its pride and its sense of independence more than its bread.

The social principles of Christianity are sneakish and the proletariat is revolutionary.

So much for the social principles of Christianity.

LIBERATION THEOLOGY

Leonardo and Clodovis Boff

What lies behind liberation theology? Its starting point is the perception of scandals . . . which exist not only in Latin America but throughout the Third World. According to "conservative" estimates, there are in those countries held in underdevelopment:

- five-hundred million persons starving;
- one billion, six-hundred million persons whose life expectancy is less than sixty years (when a person in one of the developed countries reaches the age of forty-five, he or she is reaching middle age; in most of Africa or Latin America, a person has little hope of living to that age);
- one billion persons living in absolute poverty;
- one billion, five-hundred million persons with no access to the most basic medical care;
- five-hundred million with no work or only occasional work and a per capita income of less than $150 a year;
- eight-hundred-fourteen million who are illiterate;
- two billion with no regular, dependable water supply.

Who cannot be filled with righteous anger at such a human and social hell? Liberation theology presupposes an energetic protest at such a situation, for that situation means:

- on the social level: collective oppression, exclusion, and marginalization;
- on the individual level: injustice and denial of human rights;
- on the religious level: social sinfulness, "contrary to the plan of the Creator and to the honor that is due to him" (Puebla, §28).[1]

Without a minimum of "suffering with" this suffering that affects the great majority of the human race, liberation theology can neither exist nor be understood. Underlying liberation theology is a prophetic and comradely commitment to the life, cause, and struggle of these millions of debased and marginalized human beings, a commitment to ending this historical-social iniquity. The Vatican Instruction, "Some Aspects of Liberation Theology" (August 6, 1984), put it well: "It is not possible for a single instant to forget the situations of dramatic poverty from which the challenge set to theologians springs—the challenge to work out a genuine theology of liberation."

MEETING THE POOR CHRIST
IN THE POOR

Every true theology springs from a spirituality— that is, from a true meeting with God in history. Liberation theology was born when faith con-

---

[1]The Latin American bishops' conference, CELAM, has held three General Conferences since the Second Vatican Council. The second, held at Medellín, Colombia, in 1968, can be considered the "official launching" of the theme of liberation. The third, held at Puebla, Mexico, in 1979, with Pope John Paul II in attendance, developed in some ways, but also watered down, the conclusions reached at Medellín. Puebla produced its own "Final Document," published in England as *Puebla: Evangelization at Present and in the Future: Conclusions of the Third General Conference of the Latin American Bishops.* Catholic Institute for International Relations (Slough, Berkshire: St. Paul Publications, 1979) and in the U.S.A. as *Puebla and Beyond: Documentation and Commentary.* Ed. John Eagleson and Philip Scharper (Maryknoll, N.Y.: Orbis, 1979).—TRANS.

fronted the injustice done to the poor. By "poor" we do not really mean the poor individual who knocks on the door asking for alms. We mean a collective poor, the "popular classes," which is a much wider category than the "proletariat" singled out by Karl Marx (it is a mistake to identify the poor of liberation theology with the proletariat, though many of its critics do): the poor are also the workers exploited by the capitalist system; the underemployed, those pushed aside by the production process—a reserve army always at hand to take the place of the employed; they are the laborers of the countryside, and migrant workers with only seasonal work.

All this mass of the socially and historically oppressed makes up the poor as a social phenomenon. In the light of faith, Christians see in them the challenging face of the Suffering Servant, Jesus Christ. At first there is silence, silent and sorrowful contemplation, as if in the presence of a mystery that calls for introspection and prayer. Then this presence speaks. The Crucified in these crucified persons weeps and cries out: "I was hungry . . . in prison . . . naked" (Matt. 25:31–46).

Here what is needed is not so much contemplation as effective action for liberation. The Crucified needs to be raised to life. We are on the side of the poor only when we struggle alongside them against the poverty that has been unjustly created and forced on them. Service in solidarity with the oppressed also implies an act of love for the suffering Christ, a liturgy pleasing to God.

THE FIRST STEP: LIBERATING ACTION, LIBER-A(C)TION[2]

What is the action that will effectively enable the oppressed to move out of their inhuman situation? Many years of reflection and practice suggest that it

___

[2]The Portuguese word for "liberation" is *liberação,* which is composed of the root *liber,* "free," and, by chance, the Portuguese word for "action," *ação.* This coupling cannot be reproduced in English.—TRANS.

has to go beyond two approaches that have already been tried: aid and reformism.

"Aid" is help offered by individuals moved by the spectacle of widespread destitution. They form agencies and organize projects: the "Band-Aid" or "corn-plaster" approach to social ills. But however perceptive they become and however well-intentioned—and successful—aid remains a strategy for helping the poor, but treating them as (collective) objects of charity, not as subjects of their own liberation. The poor are seen simply as those who have nothing. There is a failure to see that the poor are oppressed and made poor *by others;* and what they do possess—strength to resist, capacity to understand their rights, to organize themselves and transform a subhuman situation— tends to be left out of account. Aid increases the dependence of the poor, tying them to help from others, to decisions made by others: again, not enabling them to become their own liberators.

"Reformism" seeks to improve the situation of the poor, but always within existing social relationships and the basic structuring of society, which rules out greater participation by all and diminution in the privileges enjoyed by the ruling classes. Reformism can lead to great feats of development in the poorer nations, but this development is nearly always at the expense of the oppressed poor and very rarely in their favor. For example, in 1964 the Brazilian economy ranked 46th in the world; in 1984 it ranked 8th. The last twenty years have seen undeniable technological and industrial progress, but at the same time there has been a considerable worsening of social conditions for the poor, with exploitation, destitution, and hunger on a scale previously unknown in Brazilian history. This has been the price paid by the poor for this type of elitist, exploitative, and exclusivist development in which, in the words of Pope John Paul II, the rich become ever richer at the expense of the poor who become ever poorer.

The poor can break out of their situation of oppression only by working out a strategy better able to change social conditions: the strategy of liberation. In liberation, the oppressed come together, come to understand their situation through the process of conscientization,[3] discover the causes of their oppression, organize themselves into movements, and act in a coordinated fashion. First, they claim everything that the existing system can give: better wages, working conditions, health care, education, housing, and so forth; then they work toward the transformation of present society in the direction of a new society characterized by widespread participation, a better and more just balance among social classes and more worthy ways of life.

In Latin America, where liberation theology originated, there have always been movements of liberation since the early days of the Spanish and Portuguese conquest. Amerindians, slaves, and the oppressed in general fought against the violence of the colonizers, created redoubts of freedom, such as the *quilombos* and *reducciones,*[4] led movements of revolt and independence. And among the colonizers were bishops such as Bartolomé de Las Casas, Antonio Valdivieso, and Toribio de Mogrovejo, and other missionaries and priests who defended the rights of the colonized peoples and made evangelization a process that included advancement of their rights.

Despite the massive and gospel-denying domination of the colonial centuries, dreams of freedom were never entirely extinguished. But it is only in the past few decades that a new consciousness of liberation has become widespread over the whole of Latin America. The poor, organized and conscientized, are beating at their masters' doors, demanding life, bread, liberty, and dignity. Courses of action are being taken with a view to release the liberty that is

now held captive. Liberation is emerging as the strategy of the poor themselves, confident in themselves and in their instruments of struggle: free trade unions, peasant organizations, local associations, action groups and study groups, popular political parties, base Christian communities.[5] They are being joined by groups and individuals from other social classes who have opted to change society and join the poor in their struggle to bring about change.

The growth of regimes of "national security" (for which read "capital security"), of military dictatorships, with their repression of popular movements in many countries of Latin America, is a reaction against the transforming and liberating power of the organized poor.

THE SECOND STEP: FAITH REFLECTS ON LIBERATING PRACTICE

Christians have always been and still are at the heart of these wider movements for liberation. The great majority of Latin Americans are not only poor but also Christian. So the great question at the beginning and still valid today was—and is—what role Christianity has to play. How are we to be Christians in a world of destitution and injustice? There can be only one answer: we can be followers of Jesus and true Christians only by making common cause with the poor and working out the gospel of liberation. Trade union struggles, battles for land and for the territories belonging to Amerindians, the fight for human rights and all other forms of commitment always pose the same question: What part is Christianity playing in motivating and carrying on the process of liberating the oppressed?

Inspired by their faith—which must include commitment to one's neighbor, particularly to the poor, if

---

[3]"Conscientization" was a term brought into general use by the Brazilian educator Paulo Freire. In his work with illiterate Brazilians, the basic learning unit was always linked with the social and political context of the learner, as distinguished from purely objective learning or indoctrination.—TRANS.
[4]*Quilombos* were villages formed and inhabited by runaway slaves. *Reducciones* were enclaves of relative freedom from colonial powers for baptized Latin Americans, especially Amerindians, supervised by religious orders, especially the Jesuits, in Paraguay and elsewhere in the seventeenth and eighteenth centuries.—TRANS.

[5]The Portuguese term *comunidade* (in Spanish, *comunidad*) *eclesial de base* is variously translated "base church community," "basic Christian community," "grass-roots community," etc. They are small groups that come together for Bible study, liturgy, and social action, usually without a priest but with trained leaders. Smaller than parishes, they represent the "base" of society. They are the operational base of liberation theology in practice.—TRANS.

it is to be true (Matt. 25:31–46)—and motivated by the proclamation of the kingdom of God—which begins in this world and culminates only in eternity— and by the life, deeds, and death of Christ, who made a historic option for the poor, and by the supremely liberating significance of his resurrection, many Christians—bishops, priests, religious, nuns, lay men and women—are throwing themselves into action alongside the poor, or joining the struggles already taking place. The Christian base communities, Bible societies, groups for popular evangelization, movements for the promotion and defense of human rights, particularly those of the poor, agencies involved in questions of land tenure, indigenous peoples, slums, marginalized groups, and the like, have all shown themselves to have more than a purely religious and ecclesial significance, and to be powerful factors for mobilization and dynamos of liberating action, particularly when they have joined forces with other popular movements.

Christianity can no longer be dismissed as the opium of the people, nor can it be seen as merely fostering an attitude of critique: it has now become an active commitment to liberation. Faith challenges human reason and the historical progress of the powerful, but in the Third World it tackles the problem of poverty, now seen as the result of oppression. Only from this starting point can the flag of liberation be raised.

The gospel is not aimed chiefly at "modern" men and women with their critical spirit, but first and foremost at "nonpersons," those whose basic dignity and rights are denied them. This leads to reflection in a spirit of prophecy and solidarity aimed at making nonpersons full human beings, and then new men and women, according to the design of the "new Adam," Jesus Christ.

Reflecting on the basis of practice, within the ambit of the vast efforts made by the poor and their allies, seeking inspiration in faith and the gospel for the commitment to fight against poverty and for the integral liberation of all persons and the whole person— that is what liberation theology means.

Christians who have been inspired by its principles and who live out its practices have chosen the harder way, exposing themselves to defamation, persecution, and even martyrdom. Many have been led by its insights and the practice of solidarity at its origins to a process of true conversion. Archbishop Oscar Romero of San Salvador, who had been conservative in his views, became a great advocate and defender of the poor when he stood over the dead body of Fr. Rutilio Grande, assassinated for his liberating commitment to the poor. The spilt blood of the martyr acted like a salve on his eyes, opening them to the urgency of the task of liberation. And he himself was to follow to a martyr's death in the same cause.

Commitment to the liberation of the millions of the oppressed of our world restores to the gospel the credibility it had at the beginning and at the great periods of holiness and prophetic witness in history. The God who pitied the downtrodden and the Christ who came to set prisoners free proclaim themselves with a new face and in a new image today. The eternal salvation they offer is mediated by the historical liberations that dignify the children of God and render credible the coming utopia of the kingdom of freedom, justice, love, and peace, the kingdom of God in the midst of humankind.

From all this, it follows that if we are to understand the theology of liberation, we must first understand and take an active part in the real and historical process of liberating the oppressed. In this field, more than in others, it is vital to move beyond a merely intellectual approach that is content with comprehending a theology through its purely theoretical aspects, by reading articles, attending conferences, and skimming through books. We have to work our way into a more biblical framework of reference, where "knowing" implies loving, letting oneself become involved body and soul, communing wholly—being committed, in a word—as the prophet Jeremiah says: "He used to examine the cases of poor and needy, then all went well. Is not that what it means to know me?—it is Yahweh who speaks" (Jer. 22:16). So the criticisms made of liberation theology by those who judge it on a purely conceptual level, devoid of any real commitment to the oppressed, must be seen as radically irrelevant. Liberation theology responds to such criticism with just one question: What part have *you* played in the effective and integral liberation of the oppressed?

• • •

ENLARGING ON THE CONCEPT OF "THE POOR"

The Poor as Blacks, Indigenous Peoples, Women

Liberation theology is about liberation of the oppressed—in their totality as persons, body and soul—and in their totality as a class: the poor, the subjected, the discriminated against. We cannot confine ourselves to the purely socioeconomic aspect of oppression, the "poverty" aspect, however basic and "determinant" this may be. We have to look also to other levels of social oppression, such as:

• racist oppression: discrimination against blacks;
• ethnic oppression: discrimination against indigenous peoples or other minority groups;
• sexual oppression: discrimination against women.

Each of these various oppressions—or discriminations—and more (oppression of children, juveniles, the elderly) has its specific nature and therefore needs to be treated (in both theory and practice) specifically. So we have to go beyond an exclusively "classist" concept of the oppressed, which would restrict the oppressed to the socio-economically poor. The ranks of the oppressed are filled with others besides the poor.

Nevertheless, we have to observe here that the socio-economically oppressed (the poor) do not simply exist *alongside* other oppressed groups, such as blacks, indigenous peoples, women—to take the three major categories in the Third World. No, the "class-oppressed"—the socio-economically poor— are the infrastructural expression of the process of oppression. The other groups represent "superstructural" expressions of oppression and because of this are deeply conditioned by the infrastructural. It is one thing to be a black taxi-driver, quite another to be a black football idol; it is one thing to be a woman working as a domestic servant, quite another to be the first lady of the land; it is one thing to be an

Amerindian thrown off your land, quite another to be an Amerindian owning your own farm.

This shows why, in a class-divided society, class struggles—which are a fact and an ethical demonstration of the presence of the injustice condemned by God and the church—are the main sort of struggle. They bring antagonistic groups, whose basic interests are irreconcilable, face to face. On the other hand, the struggles of blacks, indigenes, and women bring groups that are not naturally antagonistic into play, whose basic interests can in principle be reconciled. Although exploiting bosses and exploited workers can never finally be reconciled (so long as the former remain exploiters and the latter exploited), blacks can be reconciled with whites, indigenes with nonindigenes, and women with men. We are dealing here with nonantagonistic contradictions mixed in with the basic, antagonist class conflict in our societies. But it must also be noted that noneconomic types of oppression aggravate preexisting socio-economic oppression. The poor are additionally oppressed when, besides being poor, they are also black, indigenous, women, or old.

The Poor as "Degraded and Deprived"

The socio-analytical approach is undoubtedly important for a critical understanding of the situation of the poor and all classes of oppressed. Nevertheless, its insight into oppression is limited to what an academic sort of approach can achieve. Such an approach has its limitations, which are those of analytical scholarship. It can only (but this is already a great deal) grasp the basic and overall structure of oppression; it leaves out of account all the shadings that only direct experience and day-by-day living can appreciate. Attending just to the rational, scientific understanding of oppression falls into rationalism and leaves more than half the reality of the oppressed poor out of account.

The oppressed are more than what social analysts—economists, sociologists, anthropologists—can tell us about them. We need to listen to the oppressed themselves. The poor, in their popular wisdom, in fact "know" much more about poverty than does any economist. Or rather, they know in another way, in much greater depth.

For example, what is "work" for popular wisdom and what is it for an economist? For the latter it is usually a simple category or a statistical calculation, whereas for the people, "work" means drama, anguish, dignity, security, exploitation, exhaustion, life—a whole series of complex and even contradictory perceptions. Again, what does "land" mean to an agricultural worker and what does it mean to a sociologist? For the former, it is much more than an economic and social entity; it is human greatness, with a deeply affective and even mystical significance. And if it is your ancestral land, then it means even more.

Finally, "poor" for the people means dependence, debt, exposure, anonymity, contempt, and humiliation. The poor do not usually refer to themselves as "poor," which would offend their sense of honor and dignity. It is the non-poor who call them poor. So a poor woman from Tacaimbó in the interior of Pernambuco, hearing someone call her poor, retorted: "Poor, no! Poor is the end. We are the dispossessed, but fighting!"

From which we conclude that liberation theologians in contact with the people cannot be content with social analyses but also have to grasp the whole rich interpretation made by the poor of their world, linking the socio-analytical approach with the indispensable understanding provided by folk wisdom.

The Poor as the Disfigured Son of God

Finally, the Christian view of the poor is that they are all this and more. Faith shows us the poor and all the oppressed in the light that liberation theology seeks to project (and here we anticipate the hermeneutical mediation):

- the disfigured image of God;
- the Son of God made the suffering servant and rejected;
- the memorial of the poor and persecuted Nazarene;
- the sacrament of the Lord and Judge of history.

Without losing any of its specific substance, the conception of the poor is thus infinitely enlarged through being opened up to the Infinite. In this way, seen from the standpoint of faith and the mission of the church, the poor are not merely human beings with needs; they are not just persons who are socially oppressed and at the same time agents of history. They are all these and more: they are also bearers of an "evangelizing potential" (Puebla, §1147) and beings called to eternal life.

HERMENEUTICAL MEDIATION[6]

Once they have understood the real situation of the oppressed, theologians have to ask: What has the word of God to say about this? This is the second stage in the theological construct—a specific stage, in which discourse is *formally* theological.

It is therefore a question, at this point, of seeing the "oppression/liberation" process "in the light of faith." What does this mean? The expression does not denote something vague or general; it is something that has a positive meaning in scripture, where we find that "in the light of faith" and "in the light of the word of God" have the same meaning.

The liberation theologian goes to the scriptures bearing the whole weight of the problems, sorrows, and hopes of the poor, seeking light and inspiration from the divine word. This is a new way of reading the Bible: the hermeneutics of liberation.

• • •

The Marks of a Theological-Liberative Hermeneutics

The rereading of the Bible done from the basis of the poor and their liberation project has certain characteristic marks.

---

[6]Hermeneutics is the process of interpreting the deeper meaning of a text. In this context it is the attempt to interpret scriptures through the categories of liberation and oppression. The scriptures are, thus, mediated by those categories (Eds.).

It is a hermeneutics that favors *application* rather than explanation. In this the theology of liberation takes up the kind of probing that has been the perennial pursuit of all true biblical reading, as can be seen, for example, in the church fathers—a pursuit that was neglected for a long time in favor of a rationalistic exegesis concerned with dragging out the meaning-in-itself.

Liberative hermeneutics reads the Bible as a book of life, not as a book of strange stories. The textual meaning is indeed sought, but only as a function of the *practical* meaning: the important thing is not so much interpreting the text of the scriptures as interpreting life "according to the scriptures." Ultimately, this old/new reading aims to find contemporary actualization (practicality) for the textual meaning.

Liberative hermeneutics seeks to discover and activate the *transforming energy* of biblical texts. In the end, this is a question of finding an interpretation that will lead to individual change (conversion) and change in history (revolution). This is not a reading from ideological preconceptions: biblical religion is an open and dynamic religion thanks to its messianic and eschatological character. Ernst Bloch once declared: "It would be difficult to make a revolution without the Bible."

Finally, without being reductionist, this theological-political rereading of the Bible stresses the *social context* of the message. It places each text in its historical context in order to construct an appropriate—not literal—translation into our own historical context. For example, liberative hermeneutics will stress (but not to the exclusion of other aspects) the social context of oppression in which Jesus lived and the markedly political context of his death on the cross. Obviously, when it is approached in this way, the biblical text takes on particular relevance in the context of the oppression now being experienced in the Third World, where liberating evangelization has immediate and serious political implications—as the growing list of martyrs in Latin America proves.

Biblical Books Favored by Liberation Theology

Theology must, of course, take all the books of the Bible into account. Nevertheless, hermeneutical preferences are inevitable and even necessary, as the liturgy and the practice of homiletics demonstrate. The books most appreciated by liberation theology, on its three levels—professional, pastoral, and especially popular—are:

- *Exodus,* because it recounts the epic of the politico-religious liberation of a mass of slaves who, through the power of the covenant with God, became the people of God;
- the *Prophets,* for their uncompromising defense of the liberator God, their vigorous denunciation of injustices, their revindication of the rights of the poor, and their proclamation of the messianic world;
- the *Gospels,* obviously, for the centrality of the divine person of Jesus, with his announcement of the kingdom, his liberating actions, and his death and resurrection—the final meaning of history;
- the *Acts of the Apostles,* because they portray the ideal of a free and liberating Christian community;
- *Revelation,* because in collective and symbolic terms it describes the immense struggles of the people of God against all the monsters of history.

SOME KEY THEMES OF LIBERATION THEOLOGY

1. Living and true faith includes the practice of liberation. Faith is the original standpoint of all theology, including liberation theology. Through the act of faith we place our life, our pilgrimage through this world, and our death in God's hands. By the light of faith we see that divine reality penetrates every level of history and the world. As a way of life, faith enables us to discern the presence or negation of God in various human endeavors. It is living faith that provides a contemplative view of the world.

But faith also has to be true, the faith necessary for salvation. In the biblical tradition it is not enough for faith to be true in the terms in which it is expressed (orthodoxy); it is verified, made true, when it is informed by love, solidarity, hunger and thirst for justice. St. James teaches that "faith without good deeds is useless" and that believing in the one God is not enough, for "the demons have the same belief" (2:21, 20). Therefore, ortho-doxy has to be accompanied by ortho-praxis.[7] Living and true faith enables us to hear the voice of the eschatological Judge in the cry of the oppressed: "I was hungry . . ." (Matt. 25:35). This same faith bids us give heed to that voice, resounding through an act of liberation: "and you gave me to eat." Without this liberating practice that appeases hunger, faith barely plants a seed, let alone produces fruit: not only would we be failing to love our sisters and brothers but we would be failing to love God too: "If a man who was rich enough in this world's goods saw that one of his brothers was in need, but closed his heart to him, how could the love of God be living in him?" (1 John 3:17). Only the faith that leads on to love of God and love of others is the faith that saves, and therefore promotes integral liberation: "Our love is not to be just words and mere talk, but something real and active" (1 John 3:18).

It is the task of liberation theology to recover the practical dimension inherent in biblical faith: in the world of the oppressed this practice can only be liberating.

2. The living God sides with the oppressed against the pharaohs of this world. In a world in which death from hunger and repression have become commonplace, it is important to bring out those characteristics of the Christian God that directly address the practice of liberation. God will always

be God and as such will constitute the basic mystery of our faith. We cannot struggle with God; we can only cover our faces and, like Moses, adore God (Exod. 3:6). God, who "dwells in inaccessible light" (1 Tim. 6:16), is beyond the scope of our understanding, however enlightened. But beyond the divine transcendence, God is not a terrifying mystery, but full of tenderness. God is especially close to those who are oppressed; God hears their cry and resolves to set them free (Exod. 3:7–8). God is father of all, but most particularly father and defender of those who are oppressed and treated unjustly. Out of love for them, God takes sides, takes *their* side against the repressive measures of all the pharaohs.

This partiality on God's part shows that life and justice should be a universal guarantee to all, starting with those who are at present denied them; no one has the right to offend another human being, the image and likeness of God. God is glorified in the life-sustaining activities of men and women; God is worshiped in the doing of justice. God does not stand by impassively watching the drama of human history, in which, generally speaking, the strong impose their laws and their will on the weak. The biblical authors often present Yahweh as *Go'el,* which means: he who does justice to the weak, father of orphans and comforter of widows (see Ps. 146:9; Isa. 1:17; Jer. 7:6, 22:3; Job 29:13, 31:16).

In the experience of slavery in Egypt, which bound the Israelites together as a people, they realized their longing for liberation and witnessed to the intervention of Yahweh as liberator. The liberation from slavery in Egypt was a political event, but one that became the basis for the religious experience of full liberation—that is, liberation also from sin and death. As the bishops of Latin America said at Medellín in 1968:

> Just as formerly the first people, Israel, experienced the saving presence of God when he set them free from slavery in Egypt, so we too, the new people of God, cannot fail to feel his saving deliverance when there is real development—that is, deliverance for each and every one from less human to more human conditions of life [Introduction to Conclusions, no. 6].

---

[7]*Praxis* literally means "practice" in German but refers philosophically to the unity of thought and action, theory and practice. *Ortho-praxis* is, then, the unity of faith and social activism. According to liberation theology, that "ortho-doxy has to be accompanied by ortho-praxis" means that true faith must be accompanied by political struggle for liberation (Eds.).

Finally, the Christian God is a trinity of persons, Father, Son, and Holy Spirit. Each distinct from the other, they coexist eternally in a relationship of absolute equality and reciprocity. In the beginning there was not merely the oneness of a divine nature, but the full and perfect communion of three divine persons. This mystery provides the prototype for what society should be according to the plan of the triune God: by affirming and respecting personal individuality, it should enable persons to live in such communion and collaboration with each other as to constitute a unified society of equals and fellow citizens. The society we commonly find today, full of divisions, antagonisms, and discriminations, does not offer an environment in which we can experience the mystery of the Holy Trinity. It has to be transformed if it is to become the image and likeness of the communion of the divine persons.

3. The kingdom of God's project in history and eternity. Jesus Christ, second person of the Blessed Trinity, incarnated in our misery, revealed the divine plan that is to be realized through the course of history and to constitute the definitive future in eternity; the kingdom of God. The kingdom is not just in the future, for it is "in our midst" (Luke 17:21); it is not a kingdom "of this world" (John 18:36), but it nevertheless begins to come about in this world. The kingdom or reign of God means the full and total liberation of all creation, in the end, purified of all that oppresses it, transfigured by the full presence of God.

No other theological or biblical concept is as close to the ideal of integral liberation as this concept of the kingdom of God. This was well expressed by the bishops at Puebla, in the hearing of John Paul II:

> There are two complementary and inseparable elements. The first is liberation from all the forms of bondage, from personal and social sin, and from everything that tears apart the human individual and society; all this finds its source in egotism, in the mystery of iniquity. The second element is liberation for progressive growth in being through communion with God and other human beings; this reaches its culmination in the perfect communion of heaven, where God is all in all and weeping forever ceases [§482; cf. *Evangelii nuntiandi,* no. 9].

Because the kingdom is the absolute, it embraces all things: sacred and profane history, the church and the world, human beings and the cosmos. Under different sacred and profane signs, the kingdom is always present where persons bring about justice, seek comradeship, forgive each other, and promote life. However, the kingdom finds a particular expression in the church, which is its perceptible sign, its privileged instrument, its "initial budding forth" and principle (see Puebla, §§227–28) insofar as it lives the gospel and builds itself up from day to day as the Body of Christ.

Seeing the kingdom as God's universal project helps us to understand the link joining creation and redemption, time and eternity. The kingdom of God is something more than historical liberations, which are always limited and open to further perfectioning, but it is anticipated and incarnated in them in time, in preparation for its full realization with the coming of the new heaven and the new earth.

4. Jesus, the Son of God, took on oppression in order to set us free. Jesus is God in our human misery, the Son of God became an individual Jew, at a certain time in history and in a particular social setting. The incarnation of the Word of God implies the assumption of human life as marked by the contradictions left by sin, not in order to consecrate them, but in order to redeem them. In these conditions, Jesus became a "servant" and made himself "obedient even to death on a cross" (Phil. 2:6–11; Mark 10:45). His first public word was to proclaim that the kingdom of God was "at hand" and already present as "good news" (Mark 1:14). When he publicly set out his program in the synagogue in Nazareth (Luke 4:16–21), he took on the hopes of the oppressed and announced that they were now— "this day"—being fulfilled. So the Messiah is the one who brings about the liberation of all classes of unfortunates. The kingdom is also liberation from sin (Luke 24:27; Acts 2:38; 5:31; 13:38), but this must not be interpreted in a reductionist sense to the point where the infrastructural dimension in Jesus' preaching stressed by the evangelists is lost sight of.

The kingdom is not presented simply as something to be hoped for in the future; it is already being made concrete in Jesus' actions. His miracles and healings, besides demonstrating his divinity, are designed to show that his liberating proclamation is already being made history among the oppressed, the special recipients of his teaching and first beneficiaries of his actions. The kingdom is a gift of God offered gratuitously to all. But the way into it is through the process of conversion. The conversion demanded by Jesus does not mean just a change of convictions (theory) but above all a change of attitude (practice) toward all one's previous personal, social, and religious relationships.

The liberation wrought by Jesus outside the law and customs of the time, and his radical requirements for a change of behavior along the lines of the Beatitudes, led him into serious conflict with all the authorities of his age. He knew defamation and demoralization, persecution and the threat of death. His capture, torture, judicial condemnation, and crucifixion can be understood only as a consequence of his activity and his life. In a world that refused to listen to his message and to take up the way of conversion, the only alternative open to Jesus as a way of staying faithful to the Father and to his own preaching was to accept martyrdom. The cross is the expression of the human rejection of Jesus, on the one hand, and of his sacrificial acceptance by the Father, on the other.

The resurrection uncovers the absolute meaning of the message of the kingdom, and of Jesus' life and death. It is the definitive triumph of life and of hope for a reconciled kingdom in which universal peace is the fruit of divine justice and the integration of all things in God. The resurrection has to be seen as full liberation from all the obstacles standing in the way of the lordship of God and the full realization of all the dynamic forces for life and glory placed by God within human beings and the whole of creation.

The resurrection also, and especially, reveals the meaning of the death of the innocent, of those who are rejected for having proclaimed a greater justice—God's justice—and of all those who, like Jesus, support a good cause and are anonymously liquidated. It was not a Caesar at the height of his power who was raised from the dead, but someone destroyed by crucifixion on Calvary. Those who have been unjustly put to death in a good cause share in his resurrection.

Following Jesus means taking up his cause, being ready to bear the persecution it brings and brave enough to share his fate in the hope of inheriting the full liberation that the resurrection offers us.

5. *The Holy Spirit, "Father of the poor," is present in the struggles of the oppressed.* Like the Son, the Holy Spirit was sent into the world to further and complete the work of integral redemption and liberation. The special field of action for the Spirit is history. Like the wind (the biblical meaning of "spirit"), the Spirit is present in everything that implies movement, transformation, growth. No one and nothing is beyond the reach of the Spirit, inside and outside the Christian sphere. The Spirit takes hold of persons, fills them with enthusiasm, endows them with special charisms and abilities to change religion and society, break open rigid institutions and make things new. The Spirit presides over the religious experience of peoples, not allowing them to forget the dimension of eternity or succumb to the appeals of the flesh.

The Holy Spirit becomes a participant in the struggles and resistance of the poor in a quite special way. Not without reason is the Spirit called "Father of the poor" in the liturgy: giving them strength, day after day, to face up to the arduous struggle for their own survival and that of their families, finding the strength to put up with a socio-economic system that oppresses them, one that they have no hope of changing from one day to the next; helping keep alive their hope that some things will get better and that, united, they will eventually set themselves free. Their piety, their sense of God; their solidarity, hospitality, and fortitude; their native wisdom, fed on suffering and experience; their love for their own children and those of others; their capacity for celebration and joy in the midst of the most painful conflicts; the serenity with which they face the harshness of their struggle for life; their perception of what is possible and viable; their moderation in the use of force and their virtually limitless powers of resistance to the persistent, daily aggression of the socio-economic system with its consequent social marginalization—all these qualities are gifts of the Holy Spirit, forms of the ineffable presence and activity of the Spirit among the oppressed.

But this activity is seen even more clearly when they rise up, decide to take history into their own hands, and organize themselves to bring about the transformation of society in the direction of the dream in which there will be a place for all with dignity and peace. The history of the struggles of the oppressed for their liberation is the history of the call of the Holy Spirit to the heart of a divided world. It is because of the Spirit that the ideals of equality and fellowship, the utopia of a world in which it will be easier to love and recognize in the face of the other the maternal and paternal features of God, will never be allowed to die or be forgotten under the pressure of resignation.

It is also in the light of the action of the Spirit that the emergence of base Christian communities should be understood. More a happening than an institution, they bring into the present the movement Jesus started and commit themselves to the justice of the kingdom of God. This is where the church can be seen to be the sacrament of the Holy Spirit, endowed with many charisms, ministries and services for the good of all and the building of the kingdom in history.

6. Mary is the prophetic and liberating woman of the people. The people's devotion to Mary has deep dogmatic roots: she is the Mother of God, the Immaculate Conception, the Virgin of Nazareth, and the one human being taken up into heavenly glory in all her human reality. From the standpoint of liberation, certain characteristics of hers stand out as dear to Christians of the base communities committed in the light of their faith to the transformation of society.

In the first place, all the theological greatness of Mary is based on the lowliness of her historical condition. She is Mary from Nazareth, a woman of the people, who observed the popular religious customs of the time (the presentation of Jesus in the temple and the pilgrimage to Jerusalem [Luke 2:21ff. and 41ff.]),

who visited her relatives (Luke 1:39ff.), who would not miss a wedding (John 2), who worried about her son (Luke 2:48–51; Mark 3:31–32), and who followed him to the foot of the cross, as any devoted mother would have done (John 19:25). Because of this ordinariness, and not in spite of it, Mary was everything that faith proclaims her to be, for God did "great things" for her (Luke 1:49).

In the second place, Mary is the perfect example of faith and availability for God's purpose (Luke 1:45, 38). She certainly did not understand the full extent of the mystery being brought about through her—the coming of the Holy Spirit upon her and the virginal conception of the eternal Son of the Father in her womb (Luke 1:35; Matt. 1:18), but even so she trusted in God's purpose. She thinks not of herself but of others, of her cousin Elizabeth (Luke 1:39ff.), of her son lost on the pilgrimage (Luke 2:43), of those who have no wine at the marriage feast at Cana (John 2:3). Persons can be liberators only if they free themselves from their own preoccupations and place their lives at the service of others, as did Mary, Jesus, and Joseph.

In the third place, Mary is the prophetess of the Magnificat. Anticipating the liberating proclamation of her son, she shows herself attentive and sensitive to the fate of the humiliated and debased; in a context of praising God, she raises her voice in denunciation and invokes divine revolution in the relationship between oppressors and oppressed. Paul VI gave excellent expression to this whole liberating dimension of Mary in his apostolic exhortation *Marialis Cultus* of 1974:

> Mary of Nazareth, despite her total submission to the will of God, was far from being a passively submissive woman or one given to an alienating religiosity; she was a woman who had no hesitation in affirming that God is the avenger of the humble and oppressed, who pulls down the mighty of this world from their thrones (Luke 1:51–53). We can recognize in Mary, "who stands out among the poor and humble of the Lord" (LG 55), a strong woman, who knew poverty, suffering, flight, and exile (Matt. 2:13–23)—situations that cannot escape the attention of those who with an

evangelical spirit seek to channel the liberating energies of man and society [no. 37].

Finally, Mary is as she appears in the popular religion of Latin America. There is no part of Latin America in which the name of Mary is not given to persons, cities, mountains, and innumerable shrines. Mary loves the poor of Latin America. She took on the dark face of the slaves and the persecuted Amerindians. She is the *Morenita* ("little dark girl") in Guadalupe, Mexico; she is Nossa Senhora da Aparecida, bound like the slaves in Brazil; she is the dark-complexioned Virgin of Charity in Cuba; the list is endless.

The masses of the poor bring their troubles to the centers of Marian pilgrimage; they dry their tears there and are filled with renewed strength and hope to carry on struggling and surviving. In these places Mary becomes "the sacramental presence of the maternal features of God" (Puebla, §291), the "ever-renewed star of evangelization" (*Evangelii nuntiandi,* no. 81), and together with Christ her son, in union with the oppressed, the "protagonist of history" (Puebla, §293).

ENGAGED BUDDHISM

Sulak Sivaraksa

At present, there is no such thing as a solid global-scale Buddhist liberative vision. Unlike disciples of other great world religions, Buddhists have no recognized international religious leaders like the Pope to prescribe specific dogmas on social justice for the faithful. Nor do Buddhists have an international organization like the World Council of Churches or the World Muslim League whose resolutions often have an impact on various local communities. Although the present Dalai Lama is greatly revered, he is the spiritual head of the Tibetan tradition only. As a result, perhaps, Buddhists have not been at the forefront in planning desirable societies, nor, it

should be added, can any Buddhist community be considered as an ideal example.

It appears, too, that, as is the case with all religions, there are some Buddhists who can claim spiritual happiness despite the fact that in many so-called Buddhist countries, the majority of people face enormous suffering.

Thus, it may be easy for those who have not made a profound study of Buddhism to fall into the belief that Buddhism is merely a way of personal salvation for escapists in search of spiritual enlightenment.

This, however, is an erroneous assumption. Buddhism strongly asserts that social imperfections can be reduced by the reduction of greed, hatred, and ignorance, and by compassionate action guided by wisdom. In the *Anguttara Nikaya* (Gradual Sayings), the Buddha is quoted as saying:

> He who has understanding and great wisdom does not think of harming himself or another, nor of harming both alike. He rather thinks of his own welfare, and that of others, and that of both, and of the welfare of the whole world. In that way one shows understanding and great wisdom.

Examination of the Buddha's messages on compassion show that he was certainly not indifferent to human suffering. Buddhists are taught to believe that social misery can be remedied, at least partly. The Buddha's discourses in the *Digha Nikaya* demonstrate that early Buddhists were very much concerned with the creation of social conditions favorable to the cultivation of Buddhist values.

Buddhist teachings, such as the insistence on the interrelatedness of all life, and the ideals of compassion for all beings and nonviolence, have been leading some contemporary Buddhists to broader and deeper interpretations of the relationship between social, environmental, racial, and sexual justice and peace, and have inspired them to become engaged in today's society by attempting to come to grips with, and work towards solving, some of the problems which exist.

Ken Jones, a well-known Buddhist activist from the United Kingdom, writes the following:

> The task of Buddhists in both East and West in the 21st century is to interpret Buddhism in terms of the needs

of industrial-age man and woman in the social conditions of their time, and to demonstrate its acute and urgent relevance to the ills of that society.[1]

In this respect, people need to know how to apply the four Noble Truths and the Noble Eightfold Path today in the context of their surroundings, and how these methods can inspire people to work towards the creation of a desirable society in the future.

Liberation theology and engaged Buddhism have many more similarities than differences, and it is my hope that increased understanding through greater communication and mutual respect will open the door further to a constructive coordination of efforts against the forces of oppression in an interreligious context.

• • •

CURRENT GLOBAL PROBLEMS

Obviously, it is impossible in this one chapter to analyze all of the problems existing in the world today. To simplify the examination of the present human predicament, it might be helpful to look at problems and the social institutions and values that perpetuate them, in the context of the Buddhist concept of the three root causes of suffering—greed, delusion, and hatred.

Greed

Consumer culture and technology are being used to replace spiritual virtues with new values. Greed is now encouraged. Ill-begotten wealth and power are to be admired. So-called "development models" often serve to propagate the message of "the richer the better, the bigger the better, the quicker the better." They degrade human beings and leave no room for spiritual development or respect for indigenous local cultures. Advertising, for the consumer culture, is the new gospel for "progress" in economic development.

This modernization has forced peasants to depend on the market for clothing, electricity, water, fuel, construction materials, fertilizers, pesticides, livestock, and agricultural tools, rather than allowing them to live in the self-sufficient cooperative manner in which they once did.

Greed has brought about the large-scale depletion of natural resources, the majority of which have gone to benefit the "advanced" societies in Japan and the West and the privileged elite in third-world areas, and not for consumption by the peasantry. The poor are gradually losing their land through debt, and millions flock to urban centers each year. In Thailand, young women work as servants or unskilled factory workers, or are forced into prostitution. Indeed, the country has more prostitutes than monks. As people pour into the cities, industry cannot absorb them, and many are forced to resort to crime.

Zen writer David Brandon has this to say of the present situation:

> Cravings have become cemented into all forms of social structures and institutions. People who are relatively successful at accumulating goods and social position wish to ensure that they remain successful. Both in intended and unintended ways they erect barriers of education, finance and law to protect their property and other interests. These structures and their protective institutions continue to exacerbate and amplify the basic human inequalities in housing, health care, education and income. They reward greed, selfishness and exploitation rather than love, sharing and compassion. Certain people's lifestyles, characterized by greed and overconsumption, become dependent on the deprivation of the many. The oppressors and the oppressed fall into the same trap.[2]

Buddhadasa Bhikkhu, who preaches and writes for the liberation of all human beings, has vehemently criticized materialism, especially the worship of money and technology. While denouncing blind technological progress, the consumer culture, militarism, and multinational corporations, he has also condemned mainstream education and mass

[1]Ken Jones, *Buddhism and Social Action* (Kandy, Sri Lanka: Buddhist Publication Society, 1981).

[2]David Brandon, *Zen and the Art of Helping* (London: Routledge and Kegan Paul, 1976).

media for promoting greed. Proper education, he feels, should go beyond the intellect to link the heart and the mind to reduce self-centeredness and encourage selflessness. He urges us to live in such a way that we consume appropriately rather than excessively, and to return to the true essence of our spiritual teachings.

Many Christian groups have done studies on multinational corporations and international banking. Buddhists should learn from them and use these findings to form a Buddhist position.

It should be noted here that greed for money or power is not ingrained solely in the capitalist system. It pervades all walks of life, and its effects can be seen today in suffering throughout the world.

Delusion

In order to lead a meaningful life, one must be conditioned by righteousness (*dhamma*). If we are not mindful, our lives become conditioned by fear or the search for fame or hedonism, neither of which can be satisfied. This is a path of pure heedlessness, rooted in ignorance and delusion, and many in our society have fallen victim to it. For example, the majority of politicians work only for their own political ends. Some even misuse certain passages of the Scriptures to support their position. In many parts of the world, political power is used to oppress various social groups such as women, political opponents, racial and religious communities, and the poor.

When the essence of spiritual teachings is misunderstood or deliberately misinterpreted, considerable harm can be done in the name of religion. Buddhism, often linked with politics, has been used to maintain the status quo. Those who are suffering are told to be complacent about their situation, as it is the inevitable result of bad karma in previous lives. The Buddhist monkhood has even been used to legitimize the military who act as the main forces of oppression in some areas.

Thus, engaged Buddhists feel that religion must offer spiritual guidance applicable to today's crises. Religion's meaning must not be lost in ritual or politics if we are to achieve true progress as a species.

Hatred

Buddhism teaches us that even if we are struggling against oppression, we must not hate the oppressor. Evil can never be countered constructively with evil. The *Dhammapada* says, "Never by hatred is hatred appeased, but it is appeased by kindness." "One should conquer anger through kindness, wickedness through goodness, selfishness through charity and falsehood through truthfulness." This does not imply that one must lie down and accept oppression. It merely points out that violence is not a viable answer, even as a last resort.

Hatred in its most violent form leads to war. This hatred is often fanned by those in power who have their own masked stakes in a war. Costs of violent conflicts in terms of money, manpower, and lives have been outrageous, all in the name of defending ourselves from each other. Human rights are often forgotten when we are consumed with hatred. We are no longer able to see the interrelatedness of all life that Buddhism preaches.

It seems, then, that the three root causes of suffering—greed, delusion, and hatred—and the social institutions and norms that support them must be dealt with alongside their effects or symptoms, such as poverty, human rights violations, and discrimination.

In order for Buddhists effectively to tackle the problems existing in the world today, we must first determine where we want to go. Each religious tradition must understand its own ideals before its adherents can effectively put them into practice. The next section, therefore, is concerned with the ideal society from a Buddhist perspective.

THE IDEAL SOCIETY

It may be helpful to use the traditional *sila,* or basic rules for Buddhist morality, as a framework for building desirable societies. They are:

1. to abstain from killing;
2. to abstain from stealing;
3. to abstain from sexual misconduct;

4. to abstain from false speech;

5. to abstain from intoxicants that cause heedlessness.

These are not commandments. Rather, they are guiding principles that can be voluntarily undertaken to help one lead a more socially just life. To practice them is to be endowed with five ennobling virtues, namely:

1. loving kindness and compassion;

2. right means of livelihood and generosity;

3. sexual restraint;

4. truthfulness and sincerity;

5. mindfulness and heedfulness.

Living in such a way would allow one to achieve true human development.

There is no doubt that peace, happiness, and freedom are the supreme goals of Buddhism. All three are synonyms for Nibbana or Nirvana. Thai Buddhist scholar and writer Phra Devavedi (Prayudh Payutto) has much to say regarding liberation and has set out four levels of freedom that lead to the realization of Nibbana.[3] Progression from one level to the next depends on the attainment of the preceding level. The four levels are:

1. Physical freedom. The basic needs of life must be met (i.e. food, shelter, clothing and health care). And one must be safe from life-threatening calamities and unfavorable natural conditions which implies a positive environment and the wise use of natural resources, life and technology so as to enhance the quality of life for all while not allowing man to become a slave to these quests.

2. Social freedom. This category includes freedom from oppression, persecution, exploitation, injustice, discrimination, violence and conflict. This means that one must have good relationships with others as well as full human rights, equality, tolerance and a cooperative outlook.

3. Emotional freedom. This level refers to a state of freedom from all mental defilements and suffering which leaves one purified, secure and profoundly happy and peaceful. For example, to attain this level of freedom, one would have to be endowed with love, compassion, confidence, mindfulness, conscience, generosity, forbearance and tranquility.

4. Intellectual freedom. This is freedom through knowledge and wisdom without any distortion, bias or ulterior motives; the cultivation of the insight into the true nature of things.

The third and fourth levels can be combined under the heading "spiritual freedom." Ideally, all people should have the right to conditions which might allow them to realize Nibbana. Many liberation theologians have expressed similar views. Buddhists can support the kind of grassroots theology in the Christian liberation tradition and take inspiration from it—particularly the flow of cooperation, communication, and inspiration between the "popular, pastoral and professional" levels. However, Buddhists have not adopted a "preferential option for the poor" and are encouraged to work towards the reduction of suffering for all those who are oppressed.

It has been said that ideal conditions can be realized through righteous ruling. In any society, leaders or coordinators must emerge. Buddhism regards politics as a necessary evil in which the rulers and the ruled must not exploit each other or their environment. Political institutions should act as a framework where justice, peace, mercy, equality, decency, friendliness, and basic human rights can prevail. Politics, on the one hand, gives powers and legitimation to the rulers to use a set of laws to run the country in the name of, and for the benefit of, the people who are being ruled. On the other hand, if people refuse that authority or question that legitimacy, the rulers no longer have the right to rule. This last statement is a basic Buddhist concept regarding national politics. It was quoted by Mongkut, the first "modern" Siamese king to open his country to the West in the 1850s. Many believe that this open-door policy allowed us to remain independent while our neighbors were colonized by the great Western powers.

---

[3]Prayudh Payutto, *Freedom: Individual and Social* (Bangkok, 1987).

In Buddhism, there are ten *dhamma* of kingship. They are:

dana (generosity)	*tapo* (self-restraint)
sila (morality)	*akkodha* (non-anger)
pariccaga (liberality)	*avihimsa* (non-hurtfulness)
ajjava (uprightness)	*khanti* (forbearance)
maddava (gentleness)	*avirodhana* (non-opposition)

This is the ideal, and not what has happened historically in Buddhist lands. There has been only one leader who ruled righteously in the true Buddhist sense—Emperor Ashoka of India. Buddhist scholar Walpola Rahula has this to say about Ashoka's reign (274–236 B.C.E.):

> Buddhism arose in India as a spiritual force against social injustices, against degrading superstitious rites, ceremonies and sacrifices; it denounced the tyranny of the caste system and advocated the equality of all men; it emancipated women and gave her complete spiritual wisdom.[4]

Political power, then, should be used to fashion and sustain a society whose citizens are free to live in dignity, harmony, and mutual respect, free from the degradation of poverty and war.

Right leadership will also include right economic policy. E. F. Schumacher, in his book *Small Is Beautiful,* explains the essence of Buddhist economics as follows:

> While the materialist is mainly interested in goods, the Buddhist is mainly interested in liberation. . . . The keynote of Buddhist economics is simplicity and nonviolence. . . . It is a question of finding the right path of development, the Middle Way, between materialist heedlessness and traditional immobility, in short, of finding "Right Livelihood."[5]

Buddhist economics, according to Schumacher, would involve a sufficient range of material goods (and no more), production based on appropriate technology, and harmony with the environment.

Prominent Thai economist Puey Ungphakorn, one of the first in Thailand to praise E. F. Schumacher's book, set forth a program for the correct development path of a nation. To start with, an efficient society, liberty for the people, and justice are required, and the people must care for one another. Then what he terms four "virtues" necessary for right development are peace within and without (which implies good administration), worthy development goals, well-planned developmental procedures, and power both carefully used and properly checked. Finally, he sees the goals of development to be increased income and improved health standards, economic stability, and equitable distribution of the fruits of production.

In an ideal Buddhist society, under righteous and effective administration, there would be no poverty. Everyone would enjoy economic self-reliance and self-sufficiency, except for the community of monks and nuns who would be deliberately sustained by the lay society's surplus of material resources, in order that lay people could be guided by the clergy's lifestyles and spiritual progress over life and death. In addition to a religious tradition of social ethics, a spirit of nonalignment, a respect for local culture and customs, and a commitment to decentralization would contribute to an Asian model of a just society—with less affluence, perhaps, but with more self-respect and freedom.

Buddhist social action must be directed towards realizing Buddhist ideals. These Buddhist ideals have much in common with the ideals of other religious communities. Meaningful communication and cooperation leading to an interreligious solidarity in striving towards common values would certainly be beneficial to all involved. Thus, exchange and learning between Buddhists and non-Buddhists should be encouraged.

One of the main driving forces behind engaged Buddhism is compassion. The question is how to use compassion and other Buddhist principles to deal with global problems and work towards a more ideal society where all citizens have the

---

[4]Walpola Rahula, *Zen and the Taming of the Bull: Essays* (Gordon Fraser, 1978).

[5]E. F. Schumacher, *Small Is Beautiful: Economics as if Human Beings Mattered* (Blond and Briggs, 1973).

right to realize Nibbana. The next section examines possible paths leading from the present conditions in society towards the realization of a better future.

THE PATH—A SOCIALLY ENGAGED SPIRITUALITY

Objectives

The secular humanist activist and the engaged Buddhist contemplate social action in a fundamentally different way. Buddhadasa Bhikkhu explains it in the following way:

> From the worldly standpoint, development can proceed when desires are increased or satisfied. From the religious standpoint, the more desires can be reduced, the further development can proceed.[6]

Thus, Buddhism seeks to liberate us from our own grasping desires as well as from external oppression.

In the past, development has ignored faith and culture—both vital sources of human values. Activists, even those of agnostic tendency, should try to remain open to the liberative dimensions of these institutions. Even the self-help ideology of grassroots development needs to be reoriented to the local context. Peasants, fishermen, industrial workers, women, and all oppressed factions in any country should be encouraged to explore their religion and the roots of their culture in order to draw inspiration and sustenance from them.

At the same time, we should strengthen and extend the liberation potential within the Buddhist tradition to make it relevant to today's world, and to allow each local community to gain a global perspective, making each aware of global problems, especially the suffering of the poor. If more people were conscious of the problem, it could be solved more efficiently. Further, people suffering under similar oppression should be encouraged to come together to share their experience and insights and to coordinate actions.

We need a better understanding of society and its systems on all levels. For example, much of the trend towards consumerism is fostered or controlled by multinational corporations. If people cannot understand the cause of suffering, they cannot put an end to it.

In this day and age, we do not need to expend more energy gaining converts for our religions. What we need, beyond a return to our own spiritual and cultural core, is conscientization and solidarity, to join with friends of various religious and cultural backgrounds, to work towards social justice. In this aspect, we can learn from liberation theology with its theory of grassroots conscientization, organization, and coordination. However, we need to enlighten not only the oppressed, but also those who are working in multinational corporations, exploitative industries, international banking, unjust governments, and bureaucracies, so that they come to understand that unjust economic systems and indiscriminate use of high technologies are as harmful to those who propagate them as to those subjected to them. Poisonous food, dangerous medicines, or chemical production and the arms race may bring their creators wealth, but eventually they will also become victims. In addition, concerned first-worlders must link themselves meaningfully with those of the Third World to create a more effective movement towards global awareness.

While trying to educate the rich and powerful, we must always communicate with the poor and oppressed. Indeed, if we must choose sides, we should be with the poor, share their suffering, remain humble, and learn from them, especially regarding their culture and lifestyle. The simpler our livelihood is, the less our natural resources will be exploited. The less we imitate the rich, the more we will be free from the harmful effects of consumer culture and high technology. If, through conscientization, we could learn along with the poor not to join the rich people's club or any system of oppression, then it would be the first step away from *economic* development towards full *human* development. This would not really involve a new lifestyle, but a return to our spiritual traditions.

---

[6]Buddhadasa Bhikku, *Dhammic Socialism.*

Once our awareness is raised, we must not be afraid to speak out against oppression or war, and participate in the solution.

As Buddhists, we should promote the study and discussion of major social issues (for example, those pertaining to war, the environment, human rights, economics and right livelihood, technology, discrimination, medicine, mass media, education, crime, and intoxicants) in order to formulate appropriate Buddhist responses, and then act together with friends who are seeking similar changes from inside and outside our heritage.

The Role of the Sangha

Unlike the lay community, the Sangha reverses the process of degeneration of the human race described in the Buddhist creation myths: coercion is replaced by cooperation, private property by propertylessness, family and home by the community of wanderers of both sexes, hierarchy by egalitarian democracy. The Sangha symbolizes the unification of means and ends in Buddhist philosophy. That is, the movement working for the resolution of conflict must embody a sane and peaceful process itself. The discipline of the early monastic Sangha was designed to channel expected conflicts of interest among the monks and nuns into processes of peaceful democratic resolution. In order to spread peace and stability in their societies, the monastic Sangha sought to establish moral hegemony over the state, to guide their societies with a code of nonviolent ethics in the interest of social welfare.

However, since the passing away of the Buddha some 2,530 years ago, the historical Sangha has been divided vertically and horizontally by cultural, economic, and political alliances. Sectors of the Sangha in many different countries became dependent on state patronage for their growing communities. With the growth of monastic wealth and land-holding came the integration of the Sangha into society as a priest-class of teachers, ritual performers, and chanters of magic formulas—a sector of the landowning elite with its own selfish interests and tremendous cultural power.

With centralization and hierarchization of the Sangha came increasing elite and state control, so that instead of applying the ethics of nonviolence to the state, a part of the Sangha was increasingly called upon to rationalize violence and injustice.

On the other hand, at the base of society, frequently impoverished and poorly educated, there have always been propertyless and familyless radical clergy who maintain the critical perspective of the Buddha. To this day, scattered communities of Buddhists continue in a radical disregard, and sometimes fiery condemnation, of the official "State Buddhism" with its elite hierarchical structures and its legacies of secular accommodation and corruption.

In looking to the future of humankind, it is, therefore, necessary to look back and place the state and its elites, with their natural tendency towards acquisitive conflict, under the hegemony of the popular institutions that embody the process of nonviolent, democratic, conflict resolution. In traditional Buddhist terms, the king should always be under the influence of the Sangha, and not vice versa.

It is imperative that we support the radical clergy in maintaining this critical perspective of the Buddha. We should wholeheartedly support the Sangha in its efforts to lead the local communities towards self-reliance and away from domination by the elites or their consumerism, and stand together with them to denounce unjust systems.

Indeed, many of the local and agrarian societies still have nonviolent means of livelihood, and respect for each individual as well as for animals, trees, rivers, and mountains.

Although the government and multinational corporations have introduced various technological "advances" and chemical fertilizers and have advertised to make villagers turn away from their traditional ways of life and opt for jeans, Coca Cola and fast food as well as worship of the state and its warlike apparatus, their efforts have been successfully countered by those of the critical Sangha. Some of them have even reintroduced meditation practices for farmers and established rice banks and buffalo banks which are owned by the communities and are for their benefit. Monks are also currently involved in traditional medicine projects among the people, and have even gained recognition from the Public Health Ministry in Thailand. This movement promises to evolve into an alternative road to development—a grassroots Buddhist development model.

Hopeful Signs

Along with the efforts of some members of the Sangha in Thailand to become involved in social and development work, there are many other positive signs in Buddhism today. Although it would be impossible to mention all of them, here are a few examples:

The Vietnamese monk, Thich Nhat Hanh, is a very well-known engaged Buddhist. His Order of Interbeing is designed to explicitly address social justice and peace issues, sensitizing people to test their behavior in relation to the needs of the larger community, while freeing them from limiting patterns. In directing the individual to focus on his or her interconnection with other beings, Thich Nhat Hanh is asking us to experience the continuity between the inner and outer world, and to act in collaboration and in mutuality with others in the dynamic unfolding of the truth that nurtures justice and creates peace.

Buddhadasa Bhikkhu and his Garden of Liberation in southern Thailand has urged a return to authentic Buddha-dhamma, replacing merit-making with a serious quest for Nibbana, the memorization of Abhidhamma philosophy with an understanding of the Suttas, the performance of magical rituals with the practice of meditation, and an emphasis on the monk with concern for the entire community, lay and monastic.

The Buddhist Peace Fellowships in many Western countries seem to have put Buddhist practice into proper perspective by attempting to improve individually members as well as society and their surroundings, collectively. Rather than sitting on the fence, they have taken a firm Buddhist stand for justice through loving kindness and nonviolence.

Positive action has also been taken by some Japanese Buddhist monks in their movement against armaments and nuclear war. They have worked in Sri Lanka towards reconciliation and have become involved in a number of human rights issues within their country and internationally. Also, the Rishokosakai organization in Japan has established the Niwano Press Prize and the Niwano Foundation to encourage studies toward a peaceful world.

Many promising projects have recently been initiated in the field of alternative education. An example here in Thailand is Dr. Prawase Wasi's village school in Kanchanaburi, about 125 miles west of Bangkok. The school is recognized by the Thai government. Yet, it stresses love and freedom rather than academic competition and applies Buddhist principles of critical self-awareness. Rather than focusing exclusively on the scholarly attainment of higher education, this school promotes self-reliance, good neighborliness, righteous livelihood, contentment, the ability to adapt to the natural environment, and the appreciation of folk arts and indigenous culture.

● ● ●

Spirituality in Activism

All religions contain an inherent tradition of social concern; thus, one is encouraged to become involved in society and not simply seek personal liberation. The message of the importance of social action in spirituality is fairly obvious.

It might be helpful to talk briefly about the other side of that argument—the importance of spirituality in social action. Certainly engaged Buddhists would agree with liberation theologians that the two should not be separated from each other.

For Buddhists, meditation is particularly important for maintaining awareness, both outwardly and inwardly. On this subject, Thich Nhat Hanh preaches, "Do not lose yourself in dispersion and in your surroundings. Learn to practice breathing in order to regain composure of the body and mind, to practice mindfulness, and to develop true concentration and understanding."[7] This may be something that Bud-

---

[7]Thich Nhat Hahn, *Being Peace* (Berkeley, CA: Parallax Press).

dhists can share and participate in with people from other religious backgrounds.

Indeed, internal and external development must take place at the same time if we are to be effective and constructive in our work. Each person must strive to find and keep their balance. Once one becomes aware of one's own ego and discovers the fallacy of it, one becomes less emotionally invested and more able to do what compassion requires. When we try to change our external world without training our mind to be calm and selfless, it becomes difficult to see things the way they really are, and thus it is impossible to carry out our tasks objectively. On working without developing mindfulness, Ken Jones has written:

> Dedication to a great cause can give meaning to life and a heartwarming sense of righteousness and group solidarity, even though these gratifications may filter out a lot of reality. Similarly, doing good to other people can make me feel good at the expense of undermining their dignity and autonomy.[8]

Yet, Buddhists are discouraged from paying uncritical respect to the Buddha's words. Cultivating blind attachment to any ideology on a collective level can be extremely dangerous. Thich Nhat Hanh says, "Do not be idolatrous or bound to any doctrine, theory or ideology, even Buddhist ones. All systems of thought are guiding means; they are not absolute truth. . . . If you have a gun, you can shoot one, two, three, five people, but if you have an ideology and stick to it, thinking it is the absolute truth, you can kill millions. . . . Peace can only be achieved when we are not attached to a view, when we are free from fanaticism."[9]

It is in this context that spirituality is important in social action—"as a guiding means." With critical self-awareness, we can genuinely understand and respect others of various religions and beliefs.

Our common enemies are consumerism, oppression, and militarism. Buddhists and Christians should join hands in working for peace and social justice, and in liberating themselves from our geocentricity, selfishness, and intolerance, so that we can act as normal people without fear, insecurity, or feelings of superiority or inferiority. It is important to realize that many of the divergences existing among religions are often complementary visions, which should not be seen as conflictual, but rather as differences which lead to deeper, more universal positions through a process of dialogue. It is crucial, then, that this process is guaranteed to take place by the religions, their institutions, and by society and the state.

• • •

[I]t is my view that people of different religious backgrounds not only can, but must, work together. It is not enough to look back to the essential teachings of our own heritage; we must find good friends beyond our religious affiliations if we are to achieve true liberation, justice, and peace.

In closing, perhaps a quote from the Dalai Lama seems most appropriate:

> Today we have become so interdependent and so closely connected with each other that without a sense of universal responsibility, irrespective of different ideologies and faiths, our very existence or survival would be difficult.

ISLAM AND REVOLUTION*

Hassan Hanafi

1—INTRODUCTION

1–1 Contrary to the general and common idea that Islam etymologically means submission, surrendering, servitude or even slavery, this paper tries to

---

[8]Ken Jones, *Buddhism and Social Action.*
[9]Thich Nhat Hahn, *Being Peace.*

---

*A Contribution in United Nations University project "Perceptions of Desirable societies in different religions, and ethical systems, Vol. I, Islamic Perspective," Tokyo, Japan, 1987. Also published in Theory and Practice of Liberation at the end of XXth Century, Bruylant, Bruxelles, 1988.

prove just the opposite, that Islam is a protest, an opposition and a revolution. The term *Aslama,* in fact, is ambiguous. It means to surrender to God, not to yield to any other power. It implies a double act: First, a rejection of all non-Transcendental yokes; Second an acceptance of the Transcendental Power. Islam, by this function is a double act of negation and affirmation. This double act is expressed in the utterance "I witness that there are no gods except the God."

1–2 This ambiguity of the verb *Aslama* and the noun Islam has been intentionally misused to lean Islam on one of its sides, namely, that of submission. Afterwards, the submission to the ruler is substituted to the submission to God, once the individual consciousness is psychologically structured on submission. The intention of this study is to show the other aspect of Islam, intentionally hidden, namely the rejection, the opposition and the revolt, taking into consideration the actual needs of the Muslim Masses. Since any religion, including Islam, is anchored in society, it takes on the societal shape, social structure and political power of the society in question. The ambiguity of the word Islam is consequently a reflection of the dual socio-political structure of society: Islam as both submission to the political power and the upper classes, and as revolt by the ruled majority and the poor classes.

1–3 Therefore, by concentrating the double-meaning of Islam on one of the two meanings submission or revolt, one is not really engaging in disinterested research for the sake of formulating a theory, but is rather involved in the choice of a practical option, whether to defend the status quo of political regimes through the interpretation of Islam as submission, or to initiate a socio-political change against the status quo by interpreting Islam as revolt. The conflict of interpretations is not a theoretical, scientific and purely academic conflict, but rather a power struggle between the ruling elite and the upper class interested in the continuation of the status quo on the one hand, and the ruled majority and the poor class interested in social change on the other hand. This study on the

revolution of the Transcendence is not only a theory but also a practice. It is a part of the research which is taking into consideration the actual state of the art in Islamic Studies.

1–4 The term "Transcendence" is used instead of the term "God." The term "God" has been so often used in respect to different meanings, concepts and usages that it has become unoperational whether it be in everyday expression or in scholarly communication. It is fully loaded with conceptions and misconceptions through the repetition of its common usages of the term, supported mostly by Dictionaries and history of religions textbooks. On the contrary, the term "Transcendence" is less loaded with misconceptions and can be used more easily in expressing and communicating any new idea such as the other meaning of the word Islam, namely, revolt, rejection, opposition and revolution. The term "Transcendence" is nonanthropomorphic, impersonal, rational, universal, nontheological, nonsectraian, etc. It can be understood by all rational human beings. It is a common experience in all religions. It expresses a human experience, common to everyone, going always beyond the limits of given situations.

1–5 The revolt of the Transcendence can be understood by everybody irrespective of his religion, his sect or his ideology. Although the case of Islam is specific, it can be generalized and extended to all other cases through asking the famous question: Is religion the "opium of the people" or the "sigh of the oppressed"? Is the "Perception of Desirable Society" a wishful thought, an alienation from the real world, or is it an alternative ideology for the status quo, an active plan for the future? The Transcendence can then be a dialogue, a theme not only in regard to religion, but also between religions and philosophies. It offers a common ground for interreligious as well as intercultural dialogue.

1–6 Only primary sources have been used to substantiate the theoretical underpinnings of this study. The Qur´an is the first source of Islam. The Hadith is a secondary source. Islamic disciplines including theology, philosophy, jurisprudence, mysticism, comprise material for a third. Because traditional studies on Islamic political thought have been based primarily on theology, the doctrine of the Imamate or jurisprudence, the qualities, the nomination and the destitution of the Imam, may have tended to concentrate on speculative argument and legal reasoning at the expense of the Qur'an. The "Revolution of Transcendence," therefore, restitutes the Qur'an as its primary source. Content analysis of scriptural arguments is relevant to the phenomenological description of the meanings as essences in the living experiences. Exhaustive references make scholarship an end in itself. A simple, clear and evident description is sometimes more persuasive than more accumulation of marginal notes.

2—THE AUTONOMY OF REASON

2–1 The Transcendence is a reality which can be conceived of by Human Reason. Any affirmation beyond human reason is impossible since an affirmation needs to be understood by reason and expressed in words. The Transcendence is not an arbitrary decision of the Will expressing a personal faith or a group choice. The Transcendence has no particularities or preferences contrary to its Universalism. The Transcendence as an act of the soul or of pure feeling is not enough as an act of cognition. A feeling is a common human experience generating in situations while the meaning is the universal essence of these experiences understood by human reason. That is why communication between individuals, mutual consultations and converging views, are possible.[1] The reflection on revelation, nature and human destiny would lead to the Transcendence as an overall reality transpiring everywhere. The Transcendence is not an external and visible object to be reflected upon by a subject, but the whole Reality including the object and the subject together.

• • •

4—THE CENTRALITY OF MAN

4–1 The revolution of the Transcendence appears in man as the centre of the Universe. Everything is human. He is not a particular man belonging to a specific geographical area or to an ethnic group but is man as such, the Universal Man. He is the perfect man, the knowledgeable man. The greatness of man is in his perfection and knowledge.[2]

• • •

4–3 Man is created out of nothing and the whole world has been created for him.[3] Although man is created from earth, from clay, from congealed blood, from sperm and from water, he can transcend his material creation to the Transcendental world.[4] Man is the king of the Universe. Nature has been created for him. Nature is subservient to him. He can discover its laws and reflects upon them for his benefit. Sun, Moon, Earth, Sea, Day and Night are all subservient to Man.[5]

---

[1]The Qur'an uses the *motto* "Don't you reason?" 19 times, "in order that you may reason" 8 times and "if you reason" twice.

[2]The word Man (*Insan*) is mentioned in the Qur'an 65 times as definite singular *Al-Insan*. "We have indeed created man in the best of moulds" (95:4); "Thought man that which he know not" (95:5). "He has created man. He has taught him speech and intelligence" (55:2–3).

[3]"But does not man call to mind that we created him before out of nothing" (19:67); "Has there not been over man a long period of time, when he was nothing (not even) mentioned?" (76:1).

[4]"Man We did create from a quintessence (of clay)" (23:12); "He who has made everything which He has created most good. He began the creation of man with (nothing more than) clay" (32:7); "We created man from sounding clay, from mud moulded into shape" (15:26); "He created man from sounding clay like unto pottery" (55:14); "Doth not man see that it is We Who created him from sperm . . ." (36:77); "Verily, we created man from a drop of mingled sperm . . ." (76:2); "He has created man from a sperm-drop . . ." (16:4); "created man out of a (mere) clot of congealed blood" (96:2); "Now, let man think from what he is created. He is created from a drop emitted, proceeding from between the backbone and the ribs" (86:5–7).

[5]The word *Sakhara,* which means to be subservient to, is mentioned in the Qur'an 22 times. All are used in the same meaning. See, H. Hanafi: Human Subservience of Nature, Stockholm, Sweden, 1980.

4–4 Man has a double existence, fragile and solid. He is at the same time weak and strong, miserable and great. The weakness of man is not only physical but essentially psychological. Man thinks of God only in time of danger. After danger is eliminated, God is forgotten. The Transcendence has a permanent presence, not only in times of distress but also in comfort. When the danger is overcome man attributes this success to himself and forgets his previous invocations. Is man so ungrateful? Man is happy when he receives something good but he becomes unfaithful and ungrateful when something bad occurs to him! Certainly, man is ungrateful and unjust.[6] Man is also avaricious, scared, arrogant, tyrannical, hasty, dialectical, suspicious, impatient, etc.[7] He is limited by his emotions and desires.

4–5 However, Man is also great. His greatness appears in his free will, efforts, work and perseverance. Man is productive. He strives, struggles and even suffers pain. Life is a test, a trial. Man is capable of passing it successfully given his reason, his intelligence, his work and his assiduity. Through work and effort man can be saved.[8] Therefore, the Transcendence is not only a theory but it is also a practice. The Transcendence is not only an Idea, a Principle or a Universal Rule but also a real structure for the individual and for society. Life is a challenge and man has accepted it freely given his powers of reason and his free will.[9]

• • •

5—THE EGALITARIAN SOCIETY

5–1 The revolution of the Transcendence appears in society for the implementation of social justice and the foundation of an egalitarian society. Transcendence means universal equality between all individuals in the same society. The Universality of the Transcendence is the prerequisite for the equality of individuals. The Unity of the Transcendence is the foundation of the affiliation of all individuals to One Principle. The Unity of the community is the reflection of the Unity of God.[10]

[6]"For Man was created weak (in flesh)" (4:28); "when trouble toucheth a man, He crieth unto Us (in all postures) lying down on his side or sitting, or standing. But when We have solved his trouble, he passeth on his way as if he had never cried to Us for a trouble that touched him" (10:12); "When distress seizes you at sea, those that ye call upon-besides Himself leave you in the lurch! But when He brings you back safe to and, ye turn away (from Him) most ungrateful is man" (17:67); "Now, when trouble touches Man, He cries to Us. But when we bestow a favour upon him as from Ourselves, he says: This has been given to me because of a certain knowledge (I have)" (39:49); "Man does not weary of asking for good (things), but if ill touches him, he gives up all hope (and) is lost in despair. When we give him a taste, of some mercy from Ourselves after some adversity has touched him, he is sure to say: This is due to my (merit) . . ." (41:50); "When We bestow favours on man, he turns away, and gets himself remote on his side (instead of coming to Us); And when evil seizes him, (he comes) full of prolonged prayers" (51:51); "And truly when we give man a taste of a mercy from Ourselves, he doth exalt thereat, but when some ill happens to him, on account of the deed which his hands have sent forth, truly then is man ungrateful!" (42:48); we give man a taste of mercy from Ourselves, and then withdraw it from him. Behold! He is in despair and (falls into) blasphemy" (11:9); "Verily, man is given up to injustice and ingratitude" (14:34); Truly, man is a most ungrateful creature!" (27:66); "Truly man is a blasphemous ingrate avowed" (43:15).
[7]"For man is given to hastiness" (17:11); "Man is created from haste" (21:37); "For man is (ever) niggardly" (17:100); "But man is in most things contentious" (18:54); "It was We who created man and we know what dark suggestions his soul makes to him" (50:16); "Truly, man is created very impatient" (70:19); "Nay, but man doth transgress all bounds" (96:7).

[8]"Every man's fate we have fastened on his own neck" (17:13); "That man can have nothing but what he strives for" (53:39); "O thou man Verily thou art ever toiling on towards thy Lord, painfully toiling, but thou shalt meet Him" (86:6); Verily "We have created man into toil and struggle" (90:4); "Verily man is in loss, except such as have faith and do righteous deeds and (join together) in the mutual teaching of truth and of patience and constancy" (103:2–3); "That day will man say: Where is the refuge" (75:10); "That day will man be told (all) that he put forward and all that he put back" (75:13); "Nay man will be evidence against himself" (75:14).
[9]The challenge is metaphorized in the Qur'an as the Devil. "For Satan is to man as avowed enemy" (12:5; 17:53); "Like the evil one, when he says to man: Deny god; But when man denies God, the evil one says: I am free of thee. I do fear God, the Lord of the World" (49:16); "We did indeed offer the Trust to Heavens and Earth and the Mountains; but they refused to undertake it, being afraid thereof. But Man undertook it."
[10]"And verily this brotherhood of yours is a single brotherhood and I am your Lord and Cherisher" (23:52; 21:92).

5–2 Since ownership is one of the main reasons of inequality, the affiliation of Man to the Transcendence would protect him from holding something as private property. The World cannot be owned. It belongs to the Eminent Ownership of the Transcendence. The World, including Man, is in the realm of Being, not of Having. Ownership is only a social function. Man is only entrusted with what he has. What he has is only a trust or a deposit.[11] Man in relation to things has the right to use not to misuse, to invest not to capitalize, to develop not to monopolize. If he does not, the legal authority in the community representing the common interests has the right to confiscate, to depossess and to nationalize.

5–3 Modes of production related to common welfare cannot be individually owned. They belong to the public sector and include such things as agriculture, industry, mining.[12] All that comes from Earth, beneath or above such as raw materials, cannot be privately owned.

5–4 National Wealth cannot be left in the hands of a few persons. Wealth must circulate between all individuals belonging to the same community.[13] The Social Order will collapse in any society where there is a palace towering over a neglected well.[14] The poor have a right to the wealth of the rich, not as simple charity left to individual assessment and piety, but as a legal right in the name of the Transcendence. The inequality between rich and poor is contrary to the unity and the universality of the Transcendence.

5–5 The egalitarian society is a society without classes. A society based upon an upper and a lower class is against the Transcendence. It is a society without rich and poor, satiety and hunger.[15] Hunger is something substantial in life, not merely an accident.[16] The revolt of the Transcendence is against fear.[17] Hunger is a punishment while satiety is a reward. Hunger and satiety are symbolized by Hell and Paradise.[18] Hunger is also coupled with nudity as an image of extreme poverty and misery. Hunger, fear, lack of funds, lack of agriculture and fully realized development are all components of underdeveloped societies. All are signs of damnation and Hell.

5–6 Work is the only source of value. Work means effort, energy and sweat. No surplus value is admitted. That is why usury is absolutely prohibited since usury is earning without effort. Money does not generate money. Capital increases only through human effort. Interest *Riba* is also prohibited for the same reason.[19] Commerce is not interest, since commerce implies effort and energy. Charity is simply the opposite of usury, giving is the opposite of taking.[20]

---

[11]"And spend out of the (substance) whereof He has made you heirs" (57:7).

[12]This is the famous prophetic tradition "People share three things: Water, Grass and Fire."

[13]"What God has bestowed on His Apostle (and taken away) from the people of the townships—belongs to God, to this Apostle and to kindred and orphans, the needy and the wayfarer. In order that it may not (merely) make a circuit between the wealthy among you." (59:7).

[14]"How many populations have we destroyed, which were given to wrongdoing? They tumbled down on their roofs. And how many wells are lying idle and neglected and castles lofty and well-built?" (22:45).

[15]"Be sure We shall test you with something of fear and hunger, some loss in goods or lives or the fruits (of your toil) . . ." (2:155): "God set forth a parable: A city enjoying security and guilt, abundantly supplied with sustenance from every place. Yet, was it ungrateful for the favours of God. So God made it taste of hunger and terror . . ." (16:112).

[16]Hunger is mentioned in the Qur'an 5 times, 4 times as a noun and one time as a verb, which means that hunger is substantive, not merely accidental.

[17]"Let them adore the Lord of this House. Who provides them with food against hunger and with security against fear" (106:2–4).

[18]"Then, We said: O Adam! Verily, this is an enemy to thee and thy wife: So let him not get you both out of Garden so that thou art landed in misery. There is therein (enough provision) for thee not to go naked" (70:117–118); "No food will there be for them but a bitter *dhari*, which will neither nourish nor satisfy hunger" (88:7).

[19]The word *Riba* is mentioned in the Qur'an 8 times. The prohibition 5 times such as "O ye who believe! Fear God, and give up what remains of your demand of usury, if ye are indeed believers" (2:278); "O ye who believe, devour not usury, doubled and multiplied. But fear God; that ye may (really) prosper" (3:130); "That they took usury, though they were forbidden. And they devoured men's substance wrongfully" (4:161).

[20]"Those who devour usury will not stand except as stands one whom the Evil One by his touch hath driven to madness. That is because they say: Trade is like usury. But God has permitted trade and forbidden usury" (2:275); "God will deprive usury of all blessing, but will give increase for the deed of charity" (2:276).

6—THE RULE OF THE LAW

6–1 The Transcendence appears in society as an application of the Law *Sharia* to give the individual and the society a formal structure through the State and its Institutions. The revolution of the Transcendence occurs every time human power becomes an absolute authority and a source of legislation. God is the Ruler, the Sovereign and the Judge.[21]

6–2 Since Law is not man-made, but Divinely given, it is impartial, universal and objective. It can be applied in any time and in any place and for any community.[22] It is something similar to the universal declaration of human rights combined with another universal declaration, that of People's rights. The Universal Intentions of the Law, according to classical Jurisprudence, are four: First, the affirmation of common interests and Welfare of all individuals and societies including the rights of food, clothing, shelter, work, security and peace. In case of an apparent opposition between the textual law and the concrete common interest, the textual law yields. The law is not an end in itself but only a means for the realization of individuals' and people's welfare. Second, the common understanding of the Law by all men is a condition for its implementation. The understanding of the law, its purpose and intent, its different modes of application and its capability of realizing human welfare, make its application a free choice and a responsible and accountable act. Third, the assimilation of the Law makes it a part of human activities. The objectivity of the Law becomes a part of human subjectivity. Fourth, the application of the Law is an individual and societal commitment. It is the belief-system put into practice.[23]

6–3 The Law is not a formal Law but a positive one based on the analysis of the human condition and the structure of human behaviour. Human action is a contextual. It is based on reasons, causes and motivations. It is realized easily and normally or else suspended because of difficulties and hindrances. It can be radical and absolute in an ideal form. It can be also adaptive and relative in a practical form.[24] Since all human actions are motivated, only intentions can validate actions and cut short all possibilities of casuistics. Therefore, the penal code is not formal regardless of the situation. Punishment *per se* is not intentional but is only an application of the Law of Merit, and this in two ways: reward for good deeds and punishment for bad deeds. Rights are given before duties are requested. Individual sacrifices may preserve the common welfare. Capital punishment generates life for the whole community.[25]

6–4 Since the State and its Institutions are the manifestation of the Transcendence in society, no human power, namely political power, can present itself as an absolute power. The Transcendence is the origin of authority. Sovereignty comes from the Law which is a manifestation of the Transcendence. The Ruler is not God's representative. He is only chosen by the community to implement the Law. Whoever is knowledgeable, capable, just and honest can be the Ruler. He is neither a king to legate

---

[21]"If any do fail to judge by what God hath revealed, they are unbelievers . . . The wrong doers . . . those who rebel . . ." (5:44–45, 47);"Truly God has judged between his servants" (40:48); "The Command rests with none but God. He declares the truth and he is the best of judges" (6:57); "Is not His the Command?" (6:62); "The Command is for none but God" (12:40; 12.67).

[22]"We have sent down to thee the book of truth that thou mightest judge between men as guided by God." (4:105): "Let the people of the Gospel judge by what God hath revealed therein." (5:50): "And this judge thou between them by what God hath revealed, and follow not their vain desires . . ." (5:52).

[23]These four intentions of the revelation called the intentions of the Legislator are greatly expounded by al-Shatibi in Al-Muu'afaqat.

[24]In many verses necessities are recognized. "But if one is forced by necessity without wilful disobedience, nor transgressing due limits, then is he guiltless." (2:173; 6:145; 16:115); "But if one is forced by hunger with no inclination to transgression, God is indeed off-giving, most merciful" (5:4); "Why should ye not eat on which God's name hath been pronounced, when he hath explained to you in detail what is forbidden to you except under a compulsion of necessity?" (6:119).

[25]"In the law of equality there is (saving of) life, to you O ye men of understanding" (2:179).

his kingdom to his posterity nor an usurper coming to power after a coup d'etat.[26]

6–5 In case the Ruler becomes a despot, the revolution of the Transcendence protects individuals and people's freedom. Since the Ruler has been chosen to implement the Law, any intentional failure to assume his duties will elicit a response from those who are knowledgeable in the Law, the intellectual vanguard of the society, through the regular sermons of the Friday prayer speeches and through open and vocal condemnation. If the Ruler continues his obstinacy, he is officially reminded by the practice of the legal device of Ordering the Good to be done and preventing evil from being done through direct confrontation between the Scholars and the Ruler. If he still continues his negligence or disobedience, he is then declared as unfit to rule by the judiciary, the high judge. If he is still in contempt of the Law, a mass revolt led by the scholars, the guardians of people's rights, is launched aiming at his complete removal from office.[27]

6–6 Therefore, the scholars of the Law are the real guardians of the city. They are the educators of the people and the conscience of the rulers. They can denounce the tyrants and mobilize the masses. Their words are substantiated by their deeds. Their ideas correspond to their feelings. The revolution of

Transcendence is a revolution of Thought, of knowledge and of Science.[28]

7—PROGRESS IN HISTORY

7–1 The revolt of the Transcendence is continuous in history. Since man first existed on Earth the Transcendence was equal to his individual consciousness and to the social order. All the prophets revolted against the status quo in the name of the Transcendence. All future revolutions will also be launched, directly or indirectly, in the name of the Transcendence. Prophets did not only preach the revolutions but they also led them. They enter into the political struggle and take the side of the poor, the oppressed and the wretched of the earth.[29]

7–2 The function of revelation was to liberate human consciousness from the yokes of the natural and socio-political orders. The Power of the Transcendence is greater than the power of Nature and that of the Tyrants. Individual consciousness will be elevated, deepened and strengthened by the Transcendence. Affiliation to the Transcendence is unique and exclusive. The first act of faith in Islam is an utterance, a recognition that there are no other gods than the only true God.[30] The prophet is this individual consciousness freed from the collective consciousness which has become autonomous and free. Those who believe with him in

---

[26]In the Qur'an, there is a radical rejection of kingdoms and Tyrannies. "She said: kings when they enter a county, despoil it, and made the noblest of its people its meanest, thus do they behave" (27:34); The word *tyrant* is mentioned in the Qur'an 10 times such as: "Thy intention is none other than to become a powerful violent man in the land" (28:19); "And when ye exert your strong hand do ye do it like men of absolute power" (26:130); "And following the command of every powerful, obstinate transgressor" (11:59).

[27]The word *advice* is mentioned in the Qur'an 13 times such as: "I gave you good counsel but ye love not good counsellors" (7:79); "I have you good counsel" (7:93); This is also substanciated by the Hadith "Religion is the good advice." Ordering to do good and preventing to do evil is a legal office in Islamic institutions based on well-known Qur'anic verses such as: "Let there arise out of you a band of people inviting to all that is good enjoining what is right and forbidding what is wrong" (3:104); "Ye are the best of peoples, evolved for mankind, enjoining what is right, forbidding what is wrong." (3:110; 3:114; 7:157; 9:71; 9:112; 22:41; 31:17).

[28]"Is it not a sign to them that the learned of the children of Israel knew it?" (26:197); "Those truly fear God among his servants, who have knowledge" (35:28).

[29]"How many of the prophets fought and with them large hands of godly men? But they never lost heart if they met with disaster in God's way, nor did they weaken nor give in" (3:146); "Whenever we sent a prophet to a town we took up its people in suffering and adversity, in order that they might learn humility" (7:94); "Apostle, rouse the believers to the fight . . ." (8:65); "O prophet, strive hard against the unbelievers and the hypocrites and be firm against them" (9:73; 66:9).

[30]"It is not (possible) that a man, to whom is given the Books and wisdom and the Prophetic Office should say to the people: Be ye my worshippers rather than God's. On the contrary (He would say): Be ye worshippers of Him who is truly the cherisher of all. For ye have taught the Book and ye have studied it earnestly. Nor would he instruct you to take angels and prophets for Lords and Patrons . . ." (3:79–80).

God are likewise individual "consciousnesses" aligning themselves with the group.[31]

7–3 All prophets struggled for the change of the status quo for a better and more ethical socio-political order. Lot fought homosexuality, Abraham struggled against idolotry, Moses strived for the liberation of his community from political oppression. Jesus sought to liberate the Jews from the formalism of the Law, and Muhammad attempted to establish a society of equality and justice.[32]

• • •

7–6 The Transcendence appears wherever socio-political struggle may be. The Transcendence is at the same time a theoretical structure of the world and a dialectic in history. The Transcendence is not a simple faith. Without works, an internal illumination for spiritual beauty and mystical beautification, but rather a social struggle and a historical dialectic. The Transcendence is a permanent struggle between Reason and Passion, Good and Mischief, Unity and Disparity, Peace and Discord, Construction and Destruction, Life and Death, etc.[33]

7–7 Therefore, Islam is not submission or servitude, but rather the revolution of the Transcendence, a dynamic structure for the individual consciousness, for the social order and for progress in history. The common and wrong idea combined with another common and wrong practice serve as a basis for the perpetuation of the stereotyped images in a time where images, through the powerful mass media, became substitutes to realities. If the conflict of interpretations is indeed a power struggle on the level of society, the conflict of images is also another power struggle on the level of history.

7–8 The revolt of the Transcendence is not a utopian thought. It happened in history, in the Islamic World and Culture, during the classical era. Once the Transcendence eclipsed in the hearts and minds of the Muslims, it eclipsed also in their societies and in their history. All efforts to change the state of the mind, the social order or even the course of history of the Muslims in the name of secular ideologies of modernization apart from the revolution of the Transcendence will have always partial successes and several setbacks, one step forward and two steps backward, as modern history of Muslim societies would tell.

Only through the revolution of the Transcendence that Muslims can return back to their individual souls, to their Law in society and to their vocation in history.

7–9 All revolutions occurred in history as the function of the Transcendence. Islam only gave the prototype. Since Spartacus and the revolt of the slaves in ancient Rome till the Islamic revolution in Iran, people's power in the Philippines and mass demonstrations in South Korea, all revolutions were against political and social tyrannies. The great French, Russian, and American revolutions are different manifestations of the revolution of the Transcendence, especially as motivations in the beginning. All movements for the unity of peoples such as the German, the Italian and the American unities are also indirectly made in the name of the Transcendence. The heroic era of decolonization in the Third World was also one of the late manifestations of the revolution of the Transcendence.

---

[31]"Did ye wonder that there hath come to you a message from your Lord, through a man of your own people to warn you so that ye may fear God and happily receive his mercy" (7:63; 7:69); "Is it a matter of wonderment to men that we have sent our inspiration to a man from among themselves that he should warn mankind and give the good news to the believers that they have before their Lord the lofty rank of truth" (10:2); "Is there not among you a single right-minded man?" (11:78). "Then there came running from the farthest part of the city. A man saying: O people, obey the apostle" (36:20); "A believer, a man from among the people of Pharoah who had concealed his faith and said: Will ye slay a man because he says: My Lord is God . . ." (40:28).

[32]"But we destroyed those who transgressed beyond bounds" (21:9); "How many were the populations we utterly destroyed because of their iniquities, setting up in their places other peoples" (20:11); "Thus we have placed leaders in every town, its wicked men, to plot therein" (6:123); "When we decide to destroy a population we send a definite order to those among them who are given the good things of this life and yet transgress. So that the word is proved true against them. Then, we destroy them truly." (17:16).

[33]"And did not God check one set of people by means of another, the earth would indeed be full of mischief" (2:251); "Mischief has appeared on the land and sea because of that the hands of men have earned, that (God) may give them a taste of some of their deeds" (30:41). (The translation used is that of Abdullah Yusuf Ali, *The Holy Qur'an,* Text, Translation and Commentary, Dar Al-Arabia, Beirut, Lebanon, 1968).

The argument of practicality is often misused. Instrumentalism was always a justification of war. Peace is an endeavour, an effort to spend, a struggle to endure. But, it is before all a conviction, then a striving. If humanity yields to interests, small or big, it will sink down into continuous wars. If humanity identifies itself with the Universal Code of Ethics, it will lift-up itself to Eternal Peace. It is up to humanity to choose between failure of nerves and moral courage, between eternal damnation and eternal salvation.

8—REALITIES OF THE MUSLIM WORLD TODAY

8–1 It may be argued that the realities of the Muslim World nowadays: violence, civil wars, kidnapping, hijacking, tortures, assassinations . . . etc. are far away from this ideal described just now: Islam as a religion of peace and a Universal Code of Ethics. If this ideal is not practiced by the Muslims themselves, how far can it be applied to non-Muslims in the rest of the world? Indeed, such an argument could be valid if the Muslims had tried to apply the ideal and failed. On the contrary, the realities of the Muslim World are as such because of the absence of this Ideal. Muslim Societies are not yet prepared for life in peace. Peace is not reigning neither in the external nor in the internal world, neither on Earth nor in the Soul. Muslim Societies are suffering from the most horrible forms of social, economic and political injustices. As far as these forms continue, Muslim Societies will not be prepared for life in peace. Once these forms are lifted-up, peace would reign. The intention of the gradual Revelation in history was to prepare peoples, societies and nations for life in peace and security. Once the purpose of Revelation is fulfilled, the distance between the Ideal and the Real would disappear.

8–2 In the Muslim World nowadays, there are seven forms of injustices which are behind all kinds of violence and disturbance in the public Order on the international as well as on the national scenes. They are at heart everywhere, motivating individuals and dissident groups for action and inviting peoples for revolt. First, the occupation of the land as a leftover of the colonial era. In spite of the huge process of decolonization, parts of the Muslim World are still occupied: Palestine, Afghanistan, Kashmir . . . etc. Occupation can be also indirect such as the presence of foreign military bases in many parts of the Muslim World (Saudi Arabia, Turkey . . . etc.). In Islam, the Kingdom of God is in Heavens and on Earth, not only a Kingdom in Heavens (Christianism) or a Kingdom on Earth (Judaism). Decolonization is a just war. *Jihad* is legitimate for those expelled out of their homes and become expatriated.[34] The *Jihad* as explained is a defensive war to reestablish justice and order. Occupation occurs by aggressive wars and ends by liberating wars.

8–3 Second, internal oppression and dictatorial regimes are behind a lot of internal violence in the Muslim World. The rule of Muslim majority by secular minority in the name of secular political ideologies: Liberalism, Socialism, Nationalism, Marxism . . . etc. is an usurpation of power. The source of authority in Islam is neither heredity (Kingdoms), nor coups d'Etat by Free Officers (People's republics) nor referendums (Parliamentary systems) but Islamic Law. The political power is only an executive power neither a legislative nor a judiciary power. In Islamic Rule freedom of expression is the duty of every Muslim man and Muslim woman knowing the Law. He has to order the good to be done and prevent the evil from being done.[35] He has to begin by the peaceful advice, then by appealing to the judiciary and finally by a revolt against the despot who does not apply the rule of the Law. Although the high Judge is nominated by the head of the State, he cannot be dismissed by him. On the contrary, the head of State can be dismissed by the high

---

[34]"To those against whom war is made, permission is given (to fight) because they are wronged; and verily, God is most powerful for their aid. (They are), those who have been expelled from their homes in defiance of right (for no cause) except that they say: Our Lord is God . . ." (22:39).

[35]"Let there arise out of you a band of people inviting to all that is good, enjoying what is right, and forbidding what is wrong" (3:104); "Ye are the best of Peoples, evolved for mankind enjoying what is right, forbidding what is wrong . . ." (3:110).

Judge if the former does not hear and obey the advice of the knowledgeable people and before a revolt against him occurs. As far as political regimes in the Muslim World continue to rule in the name of secular ideologies practicing the most horrible forms of oppression and dictatorship, violence would always continue to destabilize these regimes supported by foreign Powers. Muslim societies can be prepared for life in peace once freedom of expression stipulated upon in Islam is implemented in practice.

8–4 Third, the polarity between rich and poor inside Muslim societies reached a stage where a few people own almost all the wealth and the majority is starving. The maldistribution of wealth between those who have and those who have not, between oil-rich countries and poor countries, between royal families and populace, between multimillionaires and the majority living under the poverty line is a major cause of social unrest. The national capital flew to the international capital and national sovereignty yielded to multinational corporations. In Islam, wealth cannot be in the hands of the minority ruling the majority. It has to be divided and given to all social classes in the whole nation.[36] Wealth and the whole world belong to God. Man is only a depositary. He has the right to use, to invest and to spend according to his needs. But he has no right to misuse, to monopolize or to exploit. If he does, the State representing mass interests intervenes. The State has the right to nationalize, to confiscate and to own. General interests cannot be owned individually such as grass (agriculture), fire (industry) and salt (big Trade). God in Islam is defined in terms of human needs: food against hunger as well as security against fear.[37] A society would collapse and the State be destroyed if it has a high Palace looking

over a closed well, that means the domination by the wealthy minority of the poor majority.[38] As long as few are dying from satiety and over-filled stomachs and millions are dying from drought, hunger and poverty Muslim societies are not yet prepared for life in peace.

8–5 Fourth, the dismantlement of the Muslim World, the breaking of its undestructable tie, the dismemberment of one organic body continue to be one major cause of violence, borders clashes and internal civil wars. Before the era of colonization, the Muslim World was one united world. Every Muslim could travel from one corner to the other looking for knowledge without barriers, or frontiers. After decolonization, new National States were created [against] the will of the people and contrary to their long Traditions. With ignorance, backwardness and foreign conspiracies to strengthen ethnic and religious differences, wars began on the borders between two countries or inside the same country.[39] The old Roman dictum *Diuide ut imperas* was successfully implemented by big Powers to divide the Muslim World and to swallow it piecemeal. As long as the dismantlement of the Muslim World continues, border clashes from the outside and civil wars from the inside will also continue. Once the Muslim World returns back to its unity, at the image of God's Unity, there will be no more violence and bloodshed.[40] The desire of unity is so deep in the present as well as in the past. The Muslim World is inspiring to its unity antagonized by big Powers in all its forms, even the partial ones between any two neighbouring States, in the name of Arab or African Unity or in the name of Afro-Asian Solidarity or the Non-Alignment movements.

---

[36]"What God has bestowed on His Apostle (and taken away) from the people of the townships, belongs to God, to his Apostle and to Kindred and Orphans, the needy and the wayfarer in order that it may not (merely) make a circuit between the wealthy among you" (59:7).

[37]"Let them adore the Lord of this House, who provide them with food against hunger and with security against fear (of danger)" (56:3-4).

---

[38]"How many populations have We destroyed, which were given to wrongdoing? They tumbled down on their roofs. And how many wells are lying idle and neglected and castles lofty and well-built?" (22:45).

[39]Wars between two countries such as Iran and Iraq, Egypt and Libya. . . etc. Wars inside the same country such as in Sudan (North-South), Morocco (Polizario), Lebanon (civil war). The Philippines (Muslims in Mindanao) . . . etc.

[40]"Verily, this Brotherhood of yours is a single Brotherhood and I am your Lord and cherisher" (21:29; 23:52).

8–6 Fifth, the backwardness of the Muslim World called in modern terms underdeveloped or developing countries is another cause of disturbance. The lack of infrastructure on all levels especially public services makes the whole society living in distress and constantly depressed. All phenomena of underdevelopment such as: dependency in food and nutrition, foreign aid, increase of import and decrease of export, lack of heavy industry, widespread consumerism, deficit in balance of payment, foreign debts, open-door policies, tax evasions, the rise of new middle classes, corruption, foreign banks flowing money from inside to outside, black markets, brain-drain, lack of planning . . . etc. create a psychosis of frustration in those who cannot compete in the new life-style. Therefore, crime increases, and security decreases. As long as Muslim societies continue in that kind of social disorder, neither peace nor security will reign. It is quite easy through Islam, to prepare Muslim Societies for life in peace by asserting the sense of Vocation of a Muslim in particular and a human being in general as a Vice-Gerant of God on Earth fulfilling his message and realizing his Word.[41] The struggle against underdevelopment is a struggle for peace.

8–7 Sixth, Westernization of Muslim Societies and the threats to cultural identity are behind the upsurge of Islamic Fundamentalism and the practice of violence against the symbols of Western imitation and pro-Western policies. As long as the process of Westernization continues, a counterreaction will be always generated in defense of indigenous Tradition. The polarity between the Self and the Other will reach a point of no return. Development does not mean necessarily the adoption of the Western model: growth, modernization, consumerism . . . etc. Endogenous development rather than the exogenous one would protect Cultural Identity. As long as the relation between the Center and Periphery continues as it is now: Trainer and the trainee, Master and disciple, Teacher and pupil, knowledgable and ignorant, a one way relation from those who have to those who have not and a dissemination of Knowledge from the centre to the periphery, the complex of superiority created in the Other and the complex of inferiority created in the Self would continue as one of the major sources of violence and causes of revolt. Once all nations become equal partners, having an equal share in the making of humanity, once the process of Knowledge and learning is a double-way process, once the whole history of all mankind is not reduced to one of its phases, that of European Modern Times, Muslim Societies at that time will be better prepared for life in peace.[42]

8–8 Seventh, the lack of mass-mobilization in the Muslim World for a huge project of a global Renaissance leaves the masses an easy target for all kinds of underground movements to expand. Violence, bloodshed and wars are not inherent in human nature. It is an exception to the Rule. Violence is usually committed by secret organizations (for instance *Jihad* group and *Hizballah* in Lebanon) or by big Powers (the American invasion of Grenada and bombing of Libya and the Russian invasion of Afghanistan). The global commons are peaceful. The abolition of all political parties, the permission of one usually in power or the acceptance of a multiparty system without any equal balance of power and with an election result of 99.99% for the ruling party make the presence of an illicit, secret and militant Islamic party an attraction to Muslim youth. It is very astonishing that in the whole Muslim World,

---

[41]"Behold, Thy Lord said to the angels: I will create a Vicegerant on Earth . . ." (2:30); "O David! We did indeed make thee a Vice-gerant on Earth . . ." (38:26); "It is He who hath made you (His) agents, inheritors of the Earth . . ." (6:165; 10:73; 35:39; 7:69; 7:74; 27:62).

[42]"To each among you have We prescribed a Law and an Open Way. If God had so willed, He would have made you a single people but (His plan is) to test you in what He hath given you: so strive as in a race in all virtues . . ." (5:51); "If the Lord has so willed, He could have made mankind one people, but they will not cease to differ . . ." (9:118; 16:93).

there is no one legal and popular Islamic party which would fill the gap in the political life, in spite of the complaint expressed by all political leaders about the political vacuum in their respective societies. The idea of a militant Islamic party is at heart in every Muslim Society.[43] Once that party is allowed, Muslim Masses will have a legal channel of expression. All underground Islamic Movements will have an open forum to express its grievances against the status quo and its hopes for their ideal societies.

8–9 As long as these actual dramas of the Muslim World are not resolved, Muslim Societies will be unprepared for life in Peace and be the victim of the most horrible forms of violence and war. Nuclear arms, star-wars and problems of disarmaments are more linked to Western Societies. If it is easy to find solutions for nuclear threats through bilateral agreements between nuclear powers and through East-West Summits, it is very difficult to solve the seven dramas of the Muslim World. The Threats to the Western World are recent, only since the second World War and made by Western Powers themselves. The dramas of the Muslim World are the heritage of a long history since its decadence and caused mostly by the other. The preparation of Western Societies for life in peace requires political treaties on the nonproliferation of nuclear weapons. The preparation of Muslim Societies for life in peace requires a change in the course of history.

WHY WOMEN NEED THE GODDESS

Carol P. Christ*

At the close of Ntozake Shange's stupendously successful Broadway play "For Colored Girls Who Have Considered Suicide When the Rainbow Is Enuf," a tall beautiful black woman rises from despair to cry out, "I found God in myself and I loved her fiercely."[1] Her discovery is echoed by women around the country who meet spontaneously in small groups on full moons, solstices, and equinoxes to celebrate the Goddess as symbol of life and death powers and waxing and waning energies in the universe and in themselves.[2]

> It is the night of the full moon. Nine women stand in a circle, on a rocky hill above the city. The western sky is rosy with the setting sun; in the east the moon's face begins to peer above the horizon. . . . The woman pours out a cup of wine onto the earth, refills it and raises it high. "Hail, Tana, Mother of mothers!" she cries. "Awaken from your long sleep, and return to your children again!"[3]

What are the political and psychological effects of this fierce new love of the divine in themselves for women whose spiritual experience has been focused by the male God of Judaism and Christianity? Is the spiritual dimension of feminism a passing diversion, an escape from difficult but necessary political work? Or does the emergence of the symbol

---

[43]In the *Qur'an,* there is a duality between the party of the Devil applied to the actual secular party of God which is usually a secret militant Islamic group. The party of the devil such as "The Evil One has got the better of them. So he has made them lose the remembrance of God. They are the party of the Evil One. Truly, It is the party of the Evil One that will perish" (58:19); "But people have cut off their affair (of unity) between them into sects; Each party rejoices in that which is with itself" (23:63; 30:32); The party of God such as: "As to those who turn (for friendship) to God, His Apostle and the (Fellowship of) believers. It is the fellowship of God that must certainly triumph" (5:56); "they are the party of God. Truly it is the party of God that will achieve felicity" (58:22).

---

*The author has requested the following: "This essay is published in a slightly shortened form. Ellipsis dots indicate places where Christ's discussion of feminist art and ritual illustrating her points was cut. Carol P. Christ is an internationally known feminist thealogian. Her book *Laughter of Aphrodite: Reflections on a Journey to the Goddess* (Harper and Row) discusses issues raised in this essay in greater detail."
[1]From the original cast album, Buddah Records, 1976.
[2]See Susan Rennie and Kristen Grimstad, "Spiritual Explorations Cross-Country," *Quest,* 1975, *I* (4), 49–51; and *WomanSpirit* magazine.
[3]See Starhawk, "Witchcraft and Women's Culture."

of Goddess among women have significant political and psychological ramifications for the feminist movement?

To answer this question, we must first understand the importance of religious symbols and rituals in human life and consider the effect of male symbolism of God on women. According to anthropologist Clifford Geertz, religious symbols shape a cultural ethos, defining the deepest values of a society and the persons in it. "Religion," Geertz writes "is a system of symbols which act to produce powerful, pervasive, and long-lasting moods and motivations"[4] in the people of a given culture. A "mood" for Geertz is a psychological attitude such as awe, trust, and respect, while a "motivation" is the *social* and *political* trajectory created by a mood that transforms mythos into ethos, symbol system into social and political reality. Symbols have both psychological and political effects, because they create the inner conditions (deep-seated attitudes and feelings) that lead people to feel comfortable with or to accept social and political arrangements that correspond to the symbol system.

Because religion has such a compelling hold on the deep psyches of so many people, feminists cannot afford to leave it in the hands of the fathers. Even people who no longer "believe in God" or participate in the institutional structure of patriarchal religion still may not be free of the power of the symbolism of God the Father. A symbol's effect does not depend on rational assent, for a symbol also functions on levels of the psyche other than the rational. Religion fulfills deep psychic needs by providing symbols and rituals that enable people to cope with limit situations[5] in human life (death, evil, suffering) and to pass through life's important transitions (birth, sexuality, death). Even people who consider themselves completely secularized will often find themselves sitting in a church or syn-

agogue when a friend or relative gets married, or when a parent or friend has died. The symbols associated with these important rituals cannot fail to affect the deep or unconscious structures of the mind of even a person who has rejected these symbolisms on a conscious level—especially if the person is under stress. The reason for the continuing effect of religious symbols is that the mind abhors a vacuum. Symbol systems cannot simply be rejected, they must be replaced. Where there is not any replacement, the mind will revert to familiar structures at times of crisis, bafflement, or defeat.

Religions centered on the worship of a male God create "moods" and "motivations" that keep women in a state of psychological dependence on men and male authority, while at the same legitimating the *political* and *social* authority of fathers and sons in the institutions of society.

Religious symbol systems focused around exclusively male images of divinity create the impression that female power can never be fully legitimate or wholly beneficent. This message need never be explicitly stated (as, for example, it is in the story of Eve) for its effect to be felt. A woman completely ignorant of the myths of female evil in biblical religion nonetheless acknowledges the anomaly of female power when she prays exclusively to a male God. She may see herself as like God (created in the image of God) only by denying her own sexual identity and affirming God's transcendence of sexual identity. But she can never have the experience that is freely available to every man and boy in her culture, of having her full sexual identity affirmed as being in the image and likeness of God. In Geertz' terms, her "mood" is one of trust in male power as salvific and distrust of female power in herself and other women as inferior or dangerous. Such a powerful, pervasive, and long-lasting "mood" cannot fail to become a "motivation" that translates into social and political reality.

In *Beyond God the Father*, feminist theologian Mary Daly detailed the psychological and political ramifications of father religion for women. "If God in 'his' heaven is a father ruling his people," she

---

[4]"Religion as a Cultural System," in William L. Lessa and Evon V. Vogt, eds., *Reader in Comparative Religion,* 2nd ed. (New York: Harper & Row, 1972), p. 206.
[5]Geertz, p. 210.

wrote, "then it is the 'nature' of things and according to divine plan and the order of the universe that society be male dominated. Within this context, a *mystification of roles* takes place: The husband dominating his wife represents God 'himself.' The images and values of a given society have been projected into the realm of dogmas and 'Articles of Faith,' and these in turn justify the social structures which have given rise to them and which sustain their plausibility."[6]

Philosopher Simone de Beauvoir was well aware of the function of patriarchal religion as legitimater of male power. As she wrote, "Man enjoys the great advantage of having a god endorse the code he writes; and since man exercises a sovereign authority over women it is especially fortunate that this authority has been vested in him by the Supreme Being. For the Jew, Mohammedans, and Christians, among others, man is Master by divine right; the fear of God will therefore repress any impulse to revolt in the downtrodden female."[7]

This brief discussion of the psychological and political effects of God religion puts us in an excellent position to begin to understand the significance of the symbol of Goddess for women. In discussing the meaning of the Goddess, my method will first be phenomenological. I will isolate a meaning of the symbol of the Goddess as it has emerged in the lives of contemporary women. I will then discuss its psychological and political significance by contrasting the "moods" and "motivations" engendered by Goddess symbols with those engendered by Christian symbolism. I will also correlate Goddess symbolism with themes that have emerged in the women's movement, in order to show how Goddess symbolism undergirds and legitimates the concerns of the women's movement, much as God symbolism in Christianity undergirded the interests of men in patriarchy. I will discuss four aspects of Goddess symbolism here: the Goddess as affirmation of female power, the female body, the female will, and

women's bonds and heritage. There are, of course, many other meanings of the Goddess that I will not discuss here.

The sources for the symbol of the Goddess in contemporary spirituality are traditions of Goddess worship and modern women's experience. The ancient Mediterranean, pre-Christian European, native American, Mesoamerican, Hindu, African, and other traditions are rich sources for Goddess symbolism. But these traditions are filtered through modern women's experiences. Traditions of Goddesses, subordination to Gods, for example, are ignored. Ancient traditions are tapped selectively and eclectically, but they are not considered authoritative for modern consciousness. The Goddess symbol has emerged spontaneously in the dreams, fantasies, and thoughts of many women around the country in the past several years. Kirsten Grimstad and Susan Rennie reported that they were surprised to discover widespread interest in spirituality, including the Goddess, among feminists around the country in the summer of 1974.[8] *WomanSpirit* magazine, which published its first issue in 1974 and has contributors from across the United States, has expressed the grass roots nature of the women's spirituality movement. In 1976, a journal, *Lady Unique,* devoted to the Goddess emerged. In 1975, the first women's spirituality conference was held in Boston and attended by 1,800 women. In 1978, a University of Santa Cruz course on the Goddess drew over 500 people. Sources for this essay are these manifestations of the Goddess in modern women's experiences as reported in *WomanSpirit, Lady Unique,* and elsewhere, and as expressed in conversations I have had with women who have been thinking about the Goddess and women's spirituality.

The simplest and most basic meaning of the symbol of Goddess is the acknowledgement of the legitimacy of female power as a beneficient and independent power. A woman who echoes Ntosake Shange's dramatic statement, "I found God in myself and loved her fiercely," is saying "Female

---

[6]Boston: Beacon Press, 1974, p. 13, italics added.
[7]*The Second Sex,* trans. H. M. Parshleys (New York: Alfred A. Knopf, 1953).

[8]See Grimstad and Rennie.

power is strong and creative." She is saying that the divine principle, the saving and sustaining power, is in herself, that she will no longer look to men or male figures as saviors. The strength and independence of female power can be intuited by contemplating ancient and modern images of the Goddess.

• • •

The affirmation of female power contained in the Goddess symbol has both psychological and political consequences. Psychologically, it means the defeat of the view engendered by patriarchy that women's power is inferior and dangerous. This new "mood" of affirmation of female power also leads to new "motivations"; it supports and undergirds women's trust in their own power and the power of other women in family and society.

If the simplest meaning of the Goddess symbol is an affirmation of the legitimacy and beneficence of female power, then a question immediately arises, "Is the Goddess simply female power writ large, and if so, why bother with the symbol of Goddess at all? Or does the symbol refer to a Goddess 'out there' who is not reducible to a human potential?" The many women who have rediscovered the power of Goddess would give three answers to this question: (1) The Goddess is divine female, a personification who can be invoked in prayer and ritual; (2) the Goddess is symbol of the life, death, and rebirth energy in nature and culture, in personal and communal life and (3) the Goddess is symbol of the affirmation of the legitimacy and beauty of female power (made possible by the new becoming of women in the women's liberation movement). If one were to ask these women which answer is the "correct" one, different responses would be given. Some would assert that the Goddess definitely is *not* "out there," that the symbol of a divinity "out there" is part of the legacy of patriarchal oppression, which brings with it the authoritarianism, hierarchicalism, and dogmatic rigidity associated with biblical monotheistic religions. They might assert that the Goddess symbol reflects the sacred power within women and nature, suggesting the connectedness between women's cycles of men-

struation, birth, and menopause, and the life and death cycles of the universe. Others seem quite comfortable with the notion of Goddess as a divine female protector and creator and would find their experience of Goddess limited by the assertion that she is not *also* out there as well as within themselves and in all natural processes. When asked what the symbol of Goddess means, feminist priestess Starhawk replied, "It all depends on how I feel. When I feel weak, she is someone who can help and protect me. When I feel strong, she is the symbol of my own power. At other times I feel her as the natural energy in my body and the world."[9] How are we to evaluate such a statement? Theologians might call these the words of a sloppy thinker. But my deepest intuition tells me they contain a wisdom that Western theological thought has lost.

To theologians, these differing views of the "meaning" of the symbol of Goddess might seem to threaten a replay of the trinitarian controversies. Is there, perhaps, a way of doing theology, which would not lead immediately into dogmatic controversy, which would not require theologians to say definitively that one understanding is true and the others are false? Could people's relation to a common symbol be made primary and varying interpretations be acknowledged? The diversity of explications of the meaning of the Goddess symbol suggests that symbols have a richer significance than any explications of their meaning can express, a point literary critics have long insisted on. This phenomenological fact suggests that theologians may need to give more than lip service to a theory of symbol in which the symbol is viewed as the primary fact and the meanings are viewed as secondary. It also suggests that a *thealogy*[10] of the Goddess would be very different from the *theology* we have known in the West. But to spell out this notion of the primacy of *symbol* in thealogy in contrast to the primacy of the *explanation* in theology would be the topic of another paper. Let me

---

[9] Personal communication.
[10] A term coined by Naomi Goldenberg to refer to reflection on the meaning of the symbol of Goddess.

simply state that women, who have been deprived of a female religious symbol system for centuries, are therefore in an excellent position to recognize the power and primacy of symbols. I believe women must develop a theory of symbol and thealogy congruent with their experience at the same time as they "remember and invent" new symbol systems.

A second important implication of the Goddess symbol for women is the affirmation of the female body and the life cycle expressed in it. Because of women's unique position as menstruants, birth-givers, and those who have traditionally cared for the young and the dying, women's connection to the body, nature, and this world has been obvious. Women were denigrated because they seemed more carnal, fleshy, and earthy than the culture-creating males.[11] The misogynist anti*body* tradition in Western thought is symbolized in the myth of Eve who is traditionally viewed as a sexual temptress, the epitome of women's carnal nature. This tradition reaches its nadir in the *Malleus Maleficarum (The Hammer of Evil-Doing Women),* which states, "All witchcraft stems from carnal lust, which in women is insatiable."[12] The Virgin Mary, the positive female image in Christianity does not contradict Christian denigration of the female body and its powers. The Virgin Mary is revered because she, in her perpetual virginity, transcends the carnal sexuality attributed to most women.

The denigration of the female body is expressed in cultural and religious taboos surrounding menstruation, childbirth, and menopause in women. While menstruation taboos may have originated in a perception of the awesome powers of the female body,[13] they degenerated into a simple perception that there is something "wrong"

with female bodily functions. Menstruating women were forbidden to enter the sanctuary in ancient Hebrew and premodern Christian communities. Although only Orthodox Jews still enforce religious taboos against menstruant women, few women in our culture grow up affirming their menstruation as a connection to sacred power. Most women learn that menstruation is a curse and grow up believing that the bloody facts of menstruation are best hidden away. Feminists challenge this attitude to the female body. Judy Chicago's art piece "Menstruation Bathroom" broke these menstrual taboos. In a sterile white bathroom, she exhibited boxes of Tampax and Kotex on an open shelf, and the wastepaper basket was overflowing with bloody tampons and sanitary napkins.[14] Many women who viewed the piece felt relieved to have their "dirty secret" out in the open.

The denigration of the female body and its powers is further expressed in Western culture's attitudes toward childbirth.[15] Religious iconography does not celebrate the birthgiver, and there is no theology or ritual that enables a woman to celebrate the process of birth as a spiritual experience. Indeed, Jewish and Christian traditions also had blood taboos concerning the woman who had recently given birth. While these religious taboos are rarely enforced today (again, only by Orthodox Jews), they have secular equivalents. Giving birth is treated as a disease requiring hospitalization, and the woman is viewed as a passive object, anesthetized to ensure her acquiescence to the will of the doctor. The women's liberation movement has challenged these cultural attitudes, and many feminists have joined with advocates of natural childbirth and home birth in emphasizing the need for women to control and take pride in their bodies, including the birth process.

Western culture also gives little dignity to the postmenopausal or aging woman. It is no secret that

---

[11]This theory of the origins of the Western dualism is stated by Rosemary Ruether in *New Woman: New Earth* (New York: Seabury Press, 1975), and elsewhere.

[12]Heinrich Kramer and Jacob Sprenger (New York: Dover, 1971), p. 47.

[13]See Rita M. Gross, "Menstruation and Childbirth as Ritual and Religious Experience in the Religion of the Australian Aborigines," in *The Journal of the American Academy of Religion,* 1977, 45 (4). Supplement 1147–1181.

[14]*Through the Flower* (New York: Doubleday & Company, 1975), plate 4, pp. 106–107.

[15]See Adrienne Rich, *Of Woman Born* (New York: Bantam Books, 1977), chaps. 6 and 7.

our culture is based on a denial of aging and death, and that women suffer more severely from this denial than men. Women are placed on a pedestal and considered powerful when they are young and beautiful, but they are said to lose this power as they age. As feminists have pointed out, the "power" of the young woman is illusory, since beauty standards are defined by men, and since few women are considered (or consider themselves) beautiful for more than a few years of their lives. Some men are viewed as wise and authoritative in age, but old women are pitied and shunned. Religious iconography supports this cultural attitude towards aging women. The purity and virginity of Mary and the female saints is often expressed in the iconographic convention of perpetual youth. Moreover, religious mythology associates aging women with evil in the symbol of the wicked old witch. Feminists have challenged cultural myths of aging women and have urged women to reject patriarchal beauty standards and to celebrate the distinctive beauty of women of all ages.

The symbol of Goddess aids the process of naming and reclaiming the female body and its cycles and processes. In the ancient world and among modern women, the Goddess symbol represents the birth, death, and rebirth processes of the natural and human worlds. The female body is viewed as the direct incarnation of waxing and waning, life and death, cycles in the universe. This is sometimes expressed through the symbolic connection between the twenty-eight-day cycles of menstruation and the twenty-eight-day cycles of the moon. Moreover, the Goddess is celebrated in the triple aspect of youth, maturity, and age, or maiden, mother, and crone. The potentiality of the young girl is celebrated in the nymph or maiden aspect of the Goddess. The Goddess as mother is sometimes depicted giving birth, and giving birth is viewed as a symbol of all the creative, life-giving powers of the universe.[16] The life-giving

powers of the Goddess in her creative aspect are not limited to physical birth, for the Goddess is also seen as the creator of all the arts of civilization, including healing, writing, and the giving of just law. Women in the middle of life who are not physical mothers may give birth to poems, songs, and books, or nurture other women, men, and children. They too are incarnations of the Goddess in her creative, life-giving aspect. At the end of life, women incarnate the crone aspect of the Goddess. The wise old woman, the woman who knows from experience what life is about, the woman whose closeness to her own death gives her a distance and perspective on the problems of life, is celebrated as the third aspect of the Goddess. Thus, women learn to value youth, creativity, and wisdom in themselves and other women.

• • •

A third important implication of the Goddess symbol for women is the positive valuation of will in a Goddess-centered ritual, especially in Goddess-centered ritual magic and spellcasting in womanspirit and feminist witchcraft circles. The basic notion behind ritual magic and spellcasting is energy as power. Here the Goddess is a center or focus of power and energy; she is the personification of the energy that flows between beings in the natural and human worlds. In Goddess circles, energy is raised by chanting or dancing. According to Starhawk, "Witches conceive of psychic energy as having form and substance that can be perceived and directed by those with a trained awareness. The power generated within the circle is built into a cone form, and at its peak is released—to the Goddess, to reenergize the members of the coven, or to do a specific work such as healing." In ritual magic, the energy raised is directed by willpower. Women who celebrate in Goddess circles believe they can achieve their wills in the world.

The emphasis on the will is important for women, because women traditionally have been taught to devalue their wills, to believe that they cannot achieve their will through their own power, and even to suspect that the assertion of will is evil.

[16]See James Mellaart, *Earliest Civilizations of the Near East* (New York: McGraw-Hill, 1965), p. 92.

• • •

Patriarchal religion has enforced the view that female initiative and will are evil through the juxtaposition of Eve and Mary. Eve caused the fall by asserting her will against the command of God, while Mary began the new age with her response to God's initiative, "Let it be done to me according to thy word" (Luke 1:38). Even for men, patriarchal religion values the passive will subordinate to divine initiative. The classical doctrines of sin and grace view sin as the prideful assertion of will and grace as the obedient subordination of the human will to the divine initiative or order. While this view of will might be questioned from a human perspective, Valerie Saiving has argued that it has particularly deleterious consequences for women in Western culture. According to Saiving, Western culture encourages males in the assertion of will, and thus it may make some sense to view the male form of sin as an excess of will. But since culture discourages females in the assertion of will, the traditional doctrines of sin and grace encourage women to remain in their form of sin, which is self-negation or insufficient assertion of will.[17] One possible reason the will is denigrated in a patriarchal religious framework is that both human and divine will are often pictured as arbitrary, self-initiated, and exercised without regard for other wills.

In a Goddess-centered context, in contrast, the will is valued. *A woman is encouraged to know her will, to believe that her will is valid, and to believe that her will can be achieved in the world,* three powers traditionally denied to her in patriarchy. In a Goddess-centered framework, a woman's will is not subordinated to the Lord God as king and ruler, nor to men as his representatives. Thus a woman is not reduced to waiting and acquiescing in the wills of others as she is in patriarchy. But neither does she adopt the egocentric form of will that pursues self-interest without regard for the interests of others.

The Goddess-centered context provides a different understanding of the will than that available in the traditional patriarchal religious framework. In the Goddess framework, will can be achieved only when it is exercised in harmony with the energies and wills of other beings. Wise women, for example, raise a cone of healing energy at the full moon or solstice when the lunar or solar energies are at their high points with respect to the earth. This discipline encourages them to recognize that not all times are propitious for the achieving of every will. Similarly, they know that spring is a time for new beginnings in work and love, summer a time for producing external manifestations of inner potentialities, and fall or winter times for stripping down to the inner core and extending roots. Such awareness of waxing and waning processes in the universe discourages arbitrary ego-centered assertion of will, while at the same time encouraging the assertion of individual will in cooperation with natural energies and the energies created by the wills of others. Wise women also have a tradition that whatever is sent out will be returned and this reminds them to assert their wills in cooperative and healing rather than egocentric and destructive ways. This view of will allows women to begin to recognize, claim, and assert their wills without adopting the worst characteristics of the patriarchal understanding and use of will. In the Goddess-centered framework, the "mood" is one of positive affirmation of personal will in the context of the energies of other wills or beings. The "motivation" is for women to know and assert their wills in cooperation with other wills and energies. This of course does not mean that women always assert their wills in positive and life-affirming ways. Women's capacity for evil is, of course, as great as men's. My purpose is simply to contrast the differing attitudes toward the exercise of will *per se,* and the female will in particular, in Goddess-centered religion and in the Christian God-centered religion.

The fourth and final aspect of Goddess symbolism that I will discuss here is the significance of the Goddess for a revaluation of woman's bonds and heritage. As Virginia Woolf has said, "Chloe liked Olivia," a statement about a woman's relation to another woman, is a sentence that rarely occurs in fic-

[17]"The Human Situation: A Feminine View," in *Journal of Religion,* 1960, *40,* 100–112.

tion. Men have written the stories, and they have written about women almost exclusively in their relations to men.[18] The celebrations of women's bonds to each other, as mothers and daughters, as colleagues and coworkers, as sisters, friends, and lovers, is beginning to occur in the new literature and culture created by women in the women's movement. While I believe that the revaluing of each of these bonds is important, I will focus on the mother-daughter bond, in part because I believe it may be the key to the others.

Adrienne Rich has pointed out that the mother-daughter bond, perhaps the most important of women's bonds, "resonant with charges . . . the flow of energy between two biologically alike bodies, one of which has lain in amniotic bliss inside the other, one of which has labored to give birth to the other,"[19] is rarely celebrated in patriarchal religion and culture. Christianity celebrates the father's relation to the son and the mother's relation to the son, but the story of mother and daughter is missing. So, too, in patriarchal literature and psychology the mothers and the daughters rarely exist. Volumes have been written about the oedipal complex, but little has been written about the girl's relation to her mother. Moreover, as de Beauvoir has noted, the mother-daughter relation is distorted in patriarchy because the mother must give her daughter over to men in a male-defined culture in which women are viewed as inferior. The mother must socialize her daughter to become subordinate to men, and if her daughter challenges patriarchal norms, the mother is likely to defend the patriarchal structures against her own daughter.[20]

These patterns are changing in the new culture created by women in which the bonds of women to women are beginning to be celebrated. Holly Near has written several songs that celebrate women's bonds and women's heritage. In one of her finest songs she writes of an "old-time woman" who is "waiting to die." A young woman feels for the life that has passed the old woman by and begins to cry, but the old woman looks her in the eye and says, "If I had not suffered, you wouldn't be wearing those jeans/Being an old-time woman ain't as bad as it seems."[21] This song, which Near has said was inspired by her grandmother, expresses and celebrates a bond and a heritage passed down from one woman to another. In another of Near's songs, she sings of a "a hiking-boot mother who's seeing the world/For the first time with her own little girl." In this song, the mother tells the drifter who has been traveling with her to pack up and travel alone if he thinks "traveling three is a drag" because "I've got a little one who loves me as much as you need me/And darling, that's loving enough."[22] This song is significant because the mother places her relationship to her daughter above her relationship to a man, something women rarely do in patriarchy.[23]

Almost the only story of mothers and daughters that has been transmitted in Western culture is the myth of Demeter and Persephone that was the basis of religious rites celebrated by women only, the Thesmophoria, and later formed the basis of the Eleusian mysteries, which were open to all who spoke Greek. In this story, the daughter, Persephone, is raped away from her mother, Demeter, by the God of the underworld. Unwilling to accept this state of affairs, Demeter rages and withholds fertility from the earth until her daughter is returned to her. What is important for women in this story is that a mother fights for her daughter and for her relation to her daughter. This is completely different from the mother's relation to her daughter in patriarchy. The "mood" created by the story of Demeter and Persephone is one of celebration of the mother-daughter bond, and the "motivation" is for mothers and daughters to affirm the heritage passed on from mother to daughter and to reject the patriarchal

[18]*A Room of One's Own* (New York Harcourt Brace Jovanovich, 1928), p. 86.
[19]Rich, p. 226.
[20]De Beauvior, pp. 448–449.
[21]"Old Time Woman," lyrics by Jeffrey Langley and Holly Near, from *Holly Near: A Live Album,* Redwood Records, 1974.
[22]"Started Out Fine," by Holly Near from *Holly Near: A Live Album.*
[23]Rich, p. 223.

pattern where the primary loyalties of mother and daughter must be to men.

The symbol of Goddess has much to offer women who are struggling to be rid of the "powerful, pervasive, and long-lasting moods and motivations" of devaluation of female power, denigration of the female body, distrust of female will, and denial of the women's bonds and heritage that have been engendered by patriarchal religion. As women struggle to create a new culture in which women's power, bodies, will, and bonds are celebrated, it seems natural that the Goddess would reemerge as symbol of the newfound beauty, strength, and power of women.

QUESTIONS FOR DISCUSSION

1. Discuss Marx's claim that religion is "the opium of the people." What does he mean by this? Is he right?
2. Is liberation theology simply Marxism with a Christian face, or is it a genuine theology in its own right? Be specific.
3. Both Marx and Freud believe that religion is an illusion, but their respective analysis of the origin and function of this illusion is quite different. Compare their respective positions. Who is right? Or are their different analyses compatible and perhaps even complementary?
4. The goal of Buddhist practice is Enlightenment, and, according to Buddha, one can only achieve Enlightenment through one's own efforts (see H. Saddhatissa's discussion of Buddha's Four Noble Truths in Section One of Chapter 8). For this reason, Buddhism has often been considered quietistic and characterized as an attempt to escape from the world. In light of these considerations, evaluate the perspective of engaged Buddhism and its commitment to social change. What, if anything, does engaged Buddhism add to the commitment of the secular social activist?
5. In the Western world, Islam has often been characterized as a conservative and even fanatical religion. In light of this characterization, evaluate Hanafi's claim that Islam is a revolutionary religion that refuses to submit to any secular power (even those that bear the banner of Islam) and that is committed to egalitarianism and complete freedom of expression.
6. Is worshipping the Goddess more or less problematic than worshipping God? Are both equally problematic? For those who worship the Goddess, is the Goddess real or simply a useful fiction?

Universal Human Nature

Is Human Nature Good or Evil? A Chinese Debate
Mencius, *Human Nature Is Good*
Hsün Tsu, *Human Nature Is Evil*
Thomas Hobbes, *Human Nature as Competitive*
Petr Kropotkin, *Mutual Aid*
Ashley Montagu, *War and Aggression*
Jean-Paul Sartre, *There Is No Human Nature*
Francisco Miró Quesada, *Man without Theory*

Gender Nature

Women's Nature: Two Islamic Views
Al-Ghazali, *The Proper Role for Women*
Fatima Mernissi, *Beyond the Veil*
Simone de Beauvoir, *The Second Sex*

José Ortega y Gasset, *Woman as Body*
Elizabeth V. Spelman, *Gender and Race*
Paula Gunn Allen, *The Sacred Hoop*

Sexual Nature

Richard D. Mohr, *Is Homosexuality Unnatural?*
Ruth Hubbard, *The Social Construction of Sexuality*

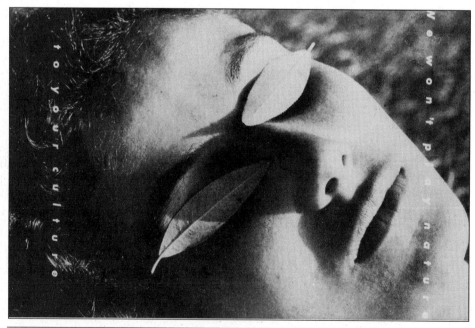

Barbara Kruger, *Untitled (We Won't Play Nature to Your Culture)*, 1983, Collection Ydessa Hendeles, Toronto. Courtesy Ydessa Hendeles Art Foundation. Photo: Robert Keziere.

CHAPTER 4

HUMAN NATURE

What does it mean to be human? Behind this seemingly straightforward question is a set of inter-related issues. What distinguishes human beings from nonhuman animals? That human beings are featherless bipeds is true but not very enlightening. Some other definitions are more interesting. Human beings are rational animals (Aristotle), symbolic animals (language users), tool makers; the human being is the only animal who can laugh, who can be bored, who can fear its own death. But these answers still do not go far enough. We do not merely want a taxonomy. We want to know whether there are certain modes of feeling, thinking, and behaving that are *natural* and that, because they are natural, have profound implications for our individual and collective lives. In other words, are there certain innate psychological characteristics that are socially significant and that can be ascribed to all human beings throughout history? Such characteristics would determine the limits of personal or social change, or would suggest possibilities for a more human existence. This may be called the universal and transhistorical concept of human nature.

The readings in Section One of this chapter examine the idea of a universal human nature and its implication for personal and social change. It begins with a Chinese debate in the Confucian tradition concerning whether human nature is good or evil. This question recurs in more modern forms: The seventeenth-century British philosopher Thomas Hobbes argues that human nature is aggressive, competitive, selfish, and, if left to its own devices, destructive. The nineteenth-century Russian naturalist and political anarchist Petr Kropotkin argues that human beings are naturally cooperative and altruistic. The contemporary British-American anthropologist Ashley Montagu challenges the claim that human warfare is the result of an innate aggressive or territorial drive. The French existentialist philosopher Jean-Paul Sartre claims that there is no human nature. Finally, in the last selection in this section on universal human nature, the contemporary Peruvian philosopher Francisco Miró Quesada argues that the whole theoretical enterprise is a mistake, because any attempt to develop a general theory about human nature will be both philosophically inadequate and morally pernicious.

Not all theories of human nature are universal. Some theories make a point of noting the social differences between human beings and claim that these differences derive from certain innate characteristics. Such theories tend to justify the dominance of one group over the other; specifically, they tend to legitimate racial, class, or sexual domination. The readings in the second section of this chapter will focus on the problem of gender nature. Is there a woman's nature distinct from a man's nature? If so, do their differences justify each sex occupying different social positions with different advantages and responsibilities? Or is gender itself a social construction, a set of social meanings ascribed to sexual embodiment? The readings in this section begin with two perspectives concerning the role of women within Islam, one by Abuhami Muhammad Al-Ghazali, an eleventh-century Islamic philosopher, who argues that women must be taught to be obedient to men. The second perspective is by the Moroccan sociologist and feminist Fatima Mernissi who argues that implicit in Islam is the idea of women as too powerful and, therefore, in need of being controlled by men. The underlying premise is that humanity is essentially male.

This idea has its modern counterpart in the idea that the criteria for being human is the male and that woman is by nature the subordinate sex whose essence is her physicality. The second set of readings, by two

twentieth-century existentialist philosophers—the French feminist theorist Simone de Beauvoir and the Spanish cultural critic Ortega y Gasset—address this issue from diametrically opposed standpoints. The last two selections—by Elizabeth V. Spelman and Paula Gunn Allen—expand the question of gender by analyzing, respectively, its relation to racial oppression and the ways in which women were regarded in American Indian societies before the conquest.

If men and women were truly equal, what would happen to sex itself? Would heterosexuality still be the norm? Is there anything unnatural or immoral about homosexuality? Or bisexuality? Or is sexual orientation itself socially constructed? The readings in the last section of this chapter—by the contemporary philosopher and gay theorist Richard D. Mohr and the biologist and feminist theorist Ruth Hubbard—attempt to answer these and related questions.

Those reading Section Two of this chapter might also want to read the selections by Sandra Harding and Patricia Hill Collins in Section One of Chapter 2, by Carol Christ in the third section of Chapter 3, by Nancy Holmstrom in the third section of Chapter 6, by Virginia Held in the first section of Chapter 7, and by Peggy McIntosh, Laurence Thomas, and Paula M. L. Moya in the first section of Chapter 9.

UNIVERSAL HUMAN NATURE

"**M**an's Nature is naturally good," writes Mencius, "just as water naturally flows downward." Mencius (372–289 B.C.E.) was one of the most illustrious followers of Confucius and was himself a pupil of Confucius' grandson. In making the above claim, he thought he was only making explicit what he took to be already implicit in Confucian thought. However, as the Chinese debate in this section demonstrates, not all followers of Confucius agreed. In order to appreciate the nuances of this Chinese debate, which spans a period from ancient to medieval times, it is important to reflect upon the Confucian tradition within which it took place. For Confucius, the individual was immediately a social being. Individual and society were inseparable. The goal of social organization and government was to bring about the happiness of the individual within it, and it was the task of these individuals to take their place within the social order by following *Li,* often translated "ritual," "rules of propriety," "etiquette," and "principles." In effect, *Li* was a set of social conventions that held society together and through which, according to Confucius, an individual became a social and ethical being. It is important to add that Confucius did not believe in following all social conventions, but only those that were morally correct. *Li* originally meant "sacrifice," and indeed the following of *Li* required the sacrifice of self-discipline, as it imposed upon each individual a set of obligations that had to be willingly assumed. This self-discipline, Confucius believed, required extensive education that was at once moral and intellectual. From this followed the special esteem that Confucius accorded the role of the teacher.

To return to Mencius, human nature is good because human beings have within them a sense of right and wrong, a natural sympathy for those who suffer, and a sense of propriety; in effect, the desire to conform to *Li* is already within our original nature. Therefore, Mencius argues that "if you let people follow their feelings (original nature), they will be able to do good." If this is so, how do we account

for the differences in human moral behavior? Mencius' answer is to compare it to the way in which the same kind of seed fares differently in different soils. In other words, our original goodness needs cultivation and nourishment, or it will be corrupted and decay. For Mencius, like Confucius, education was extremely important in order to cultivate our innate moral sense.

Hsün Tzu (298–238 B.C.E.), a contemporary of Mencius and a significant figure within the Confucian tradition, also extolled education but saw its function as extremely different. For Hsün Tzu, human nature was fundamentally evil. What was innate within us was greed, envy, and hatred. Realizing this, the sage kings—the wise rulers of even more ancient times—created certain "ritual principles" —*Li*—in order to control our natural (evil) emotions. It was only by being educated to follow these principles that the unruly impulses of human beings could be controlled. Morality, then, did not derive from our original nature but was opposed to it and had to be painfully inculcated in each individual. If we did away with these principles and, Hsün adds, the authority of the ruler, "chaos and destruction" would surely follow. In Hsün Tzu's words, we are originally a "warped piece of wood" that must be "laid against the straightening board."

The debate concerning whether human nature is good or evil can be found in a variety of cultures from ancient times to the modern era. Echoing Hsün Tzu, the seventeenth-century British philosopher Thomas Hobbes (1588–1679) argues that human beings are naturally competitive, greedy, antisocial, and bellicose, and that left to themselves they would be in continuous war with one another—a war of each against each. The result would be that life would be "nasty, brutish, and short" (remember that Hsün Tzu had declared that without moral education there would be chaos and destruction). Hobbes' *Leviathan,* from which this reading was excerpted, appeared in 1654, shortly after the British Revolution of 1648. This Revolution had convinced Hobbes, who sympathized with the monarchy against the parliament, that it was folly for there to be a division of authority and that peace and order required a Leviathanlike state—the Leviathan was a crocodile in the Old Testament who ruled the animal kingdom and who, because of his tough scales, could not be overthrown—that had absolute authority over its subjects. Thus, just as Hsün Tzu emphasizes the need for moral principles to control our evil impulses, Hobbes argues for the necessity of an absolute sovereign to accomplish the same purpose.

Although Hobbes was long dead by the time Charles Darwin wrote his *Origins of the Species,* his analysis of human nature is often taken to be a precursor of Darwin's "survival of the fittest." Darwin had used this phrase to indicate the mechanism through which evolutionary development, or "natural selection," occurred. Certain new traits, or mutations, that appeared accidentally would survive if they were adaptive to the environmental conditions within which the organism lived. If so, a new species developed that was "fit" to survive. Those who did not survive were "unfit."

In the hands of the British philosopher and sociologist Herbert Spencer[1] (1820–1903), the idea of the survival of the fittest came to imply that social progress was like biological evolution in that it was the result of a competition between individuals—and, he asserted, also races—in which the superior, whom he identified with the economically prosperous, overcomes the inferior, whom he identified with the poor. The latter then tended to die off, leaving the human species with a greater stock of superior characteristics. This, he argued, gave scientific credence to laissez-faire economics, as it implied that social welfare measures would retard social progress.

Spencer's theory, which became known as Social Darwinism, was popularized in the United States by William Graham Sumner, a major economist and sociologist, who specifically equated the

"fittest" with the rich and wrote an entire work justifying the concentration of wealth. Sumner's ideas were adopted by the Episcopalian minister Henry Ward Beecher, who had such luminaries in his congregation as J. P. Morgan and John D. Rockefeller. They, needless to say, found Social Darwinism a very agreeable doctrine. Rockefeller is quoted as having said: "The growth of a large business is merely the survival of the fittest . . . It is merely the working-out of a law of nature and a law of God."

What Social Darwinists failed to note was that Darwin himself was at least ambivalent about the ethical implications of his ideas. He had argued that the "social instinct," which he considered the biological basis for morality, was an adaptive trait; specifically, that human tribal groups whose members were altruistic and who engaged in mutual support had an evolutionary advantage over those tribes whose members lacked these traits. From this it is not very difficult to draw the conclusion that cooperation and mutual support rather than rapacious competition is what helped the human species to survive.

It was precisely this interpretation of Darwinism that was advanced by Prince Petr Kropotkin (1842–1921), a Russian aristocrat who eventually renounced his social standing. Kropotkin was a renowned naturalist and political anarchist known for his work in geography and zoology—he studied animal life in Siberia for several years—as well as his work in sociology, politics, and history. His goal in writing *Mutual Aid,* from which the reading in this chapter is taken, was to put his anarcho-communist ideas on a scientific foundation. In this work he argues that Darwin's "fittest" should not be equated with the strong who dominate the weak but rather with the species whose members learn to cooperate and support one another for their mutual advantage. Competition within a species, then, is ultimately disadvantageous. With numerous examples of animal life and early human societies he attempts to demonstrate that mutual aid is a general rule and that it, rather than mutual struggle, is the major force of evolution. In the reading reprinted in this chapter he specifically attacks Hobbes' notion of the state of nature, pointing out that rather than being character-

[1]Spencer was, in fact, the first to use the phrase "survival of the fittest" to describe Darwin's idea. Darwin himself subsequently borrowed the term from Spencer in the fifth edition of his *Origin of the Species.*

ized by a war of each against each, early human so-cieties, and most higher mammals, lived in tribes or bands based on mutual aid.

Who is right? Is human nature essentially good or is it evil? Is it essentially competitive and selfish or cooperative and altruistic? Closely connected to these questions is the question of whether human beings have an innate aggressive drive or instinct. In recent times, evolutionary theory has been used to argue that such a drive is an adaptive trait. One popularizer of this idea is the German ethologist Konrad Lorenz, who in his book *On Aggression* ar-gued that the aggressive instinct evolved through natural selection in various animal species because it served certain life-preserving functions. For ex-ample, territorial aggression helps disperse mem-bers of the same species over a larger area, thus preventing overcrowding and enabling more of them to secure food. Other survival functions in-clude selection of the strongest for reproduction, defense of the young, and the establishment of a hi-erarchy that aids the group in coordinating its func-tions. In a species armed with sharp teeth or claws, the aggressive instinct, said Lorenz, was usually ac-companied by an inhibitory mechanism that gener-ally prevented animals from fighting to the death. Thus, inasmuch as human beings were not naturally armed, there was no need for such an inhibitory mechanism and so it did not develop. With the de-velopment of weapons, however, the absence of such a mechanism was often lethal, and with the ad-vent of modern warfare the aggressive instinct has become a threat to the survival of the species.

Is aggression an innate drive? Is modern war an outgrowth of it? Are we by nature condemned to for-ever be fighting wars? In the next selection in this sec-tion, Ashley Montagu, a world-famous contemporary anthropologist, argues that human beings "have evolved as the most malleable, flexible, and educable of all creatures" and that the brain is itself an organ of inhibition, an organ "which permits voluntary rather than biologically predetermined inhibition." In short, there was no evolutionary need for human beings to develop an aggressive instinct and an inhibitory mech-anism against killing. Addressing himself specifically

to the problem of war, Montagu points out that our closest evolutionary relatives, gorillas and chim-panzees, are nonterritorial and that hunter-gatherer so-cieties were generally unwarlike. He further suggests that modern warfare is exceptionally artificial, ab-stract, and impersonal and, therefore, "represents one of the least aggressive forms of man's behavior."

Can human beings choose not to engage in war or aggressive behavior? Can they choose to be good or evil, competitive or cooperative? The importance of choice receives special emphasis in the work of the contemporary French philosopher Jean-Paul Sartre (1905–1980). Sartre is perhaps the best-known pro-ponent of existentialism, whose main thesis he char-acterizes as "existence precedes essence." This means that there is no objective human essence, that human-ity does not have within itself any necessary function or goal. From this it follows that there is nothing that a person necessarily is or has to be. What we are indi-vidually is the result of our past choices and actions, and each of us will be what we choose to be. Thus, each person must accept total responsibility for what he or she has become and will become. We cannot blame human nature, because there is no universal, unchangeable nature shared by everyone. In the course of our lives we create our specific natures and, in so doing, we give this choice the import of univer-sal values; in other words, by choosing we simultane-ously define what it is to be human and create our own values. Of course, others may choose differently, giv-ing their choice equally universal import. There is, then, a plurality of human "natures," each based upon individual human choice. But what can guide this choice? Sartre's answer is that there are no external standards, no God, and no human nature that can make us choose or tell us how to choose. And yet, we must choose, for deciding not to choose is still a choice. We are, therefore, "condemned to freedom."

The last piece in this section is written by the con-temporary Peruvian philosopher Francisco Miró Quesada, who holds doctorates in mathematics and philosophy as well as a law degree. His writing ranges widely, from phenomenology to mathematical logic, from epistemology to political philosophy. In the se-lection in this section, from his book *El hombre sin teoría,* Miró Quesada argues that no theory of human nature will ever be adequate to the nature of human beings. He argues this on the basis of two claims: first, that human reality is too complex to be encompassed by theory; and, second, that human beings are free and, therefore, that their actions are inherently unpredictable. This, however, creates a dilemma, as human beings seem unable to live without theory and that, in any case, all theories about the world and language itself seem to imply a theory about human beings. Miró Quesada argues that we can escape the horns of the dilemma—that a theory of human nature is necessary and that it is impossible—by distinguishing between two kind of theories: between a theory that is implicit and spontaneous and one that is philosophical and consciously elaborated. It is the second of these that we can avoid with respect to human beings. Miró Quesada also suggests another reason that we should stop developing philosophical theories about human beings: Human beings tend to create bizarre and often inflexible consequences from such theorizing. Theories about human nature have been all too often used to support absolute ideologies that leave no room for real human beings. They have been used to support killing and torture and any number of other immoral actions. In the last analysis, says Miró Quesada, what we need is not a "theory of man" but a decision to struggle against exploitation and suffering and for the betterment of humankind.

IS HUMAN NATURE GOOD OR EVIL?
A CHINESE DEBATE

HUMAN NATURE IS GOOD

Mencius

Kao Tzu said, "Human nature is like the willow tree, and righteousness is like a cup or a bowl. To turn human nature into humanity and righteousness is like turning the willow into cups and bowls." Mencius said, "Sir, can you follow the nature of the willow tree and make the cups and bowls, or must you violate the nature of the willow tree before you can make the cups and bowls? If you are going to violate the nature of the willow tree in order to make cups and bowls, then must you also violate human nature in order to make it into humanity and righteousness? Your words, alas! would lead all people in the world to consider humanity and righteousness as calamity [because they required the violation of human nature]!"

Kao Tzu said, "Man's nature is like whirling water. If a breach in the pool is made to the east it will flow to the east. If a breach is made to the west it will flow to the west. Man's nature is indifferent to good and evil, just as water is indifferent to east and west." Mencius said, "Water, indeed, is indifferent to the east and west, but is it indifferent to high and low? Man's nature is naturally good just as water naturally flows downward. There is no man without this good nature; neither is there water that does not flow downward. Now you can strike water and cause it to splash upward over your forehead, and by damming and leading it, you can force it uphill. Is this the nature of water? It is the forced circumstance that makes it do so. Man can be made to do evil, for his nature can be treated in the same way."

Kao Tzu said, "What is inborn is called nature." Mencius said, "When you say that what is inborn is called nature, is that like saying that white is white?" "Yes." "Then is the whiteness of the white feather the same as the whiteness of snow? Or, again, is the whiteness of snow the same as the whiteness of white jade?" "Yes." "Then is the nature of a dog the same as the nature of an ox, and is the nature of an ox the same as the nature of a man?"

Kao Tzu said, "By nature we desire food and sex. Humanity is internal and not external, whereas righteousness is external and not internal." Mencius said, "Why do you say that humanity is internal and righteousness external?" "When I see an old man and respect him for his age, it is not that the oldness is within me, just as, when something is white and I call it white, I am merely observing its external appearance. I therefore say that righteousness is external." Mencius said, "There is no difference between our considering a white horse to be white and a white man to be white. But is there no difference between acknowledging the age of an old horse and the age of an old man? And what is it that we call righteousness, the fact that a man is old or the fact that we honor his old age?" Kao Tzu said, "I love my own younger brother but do not love the younger brother of, say, a man from the state of Ch'in. This is because I am the one to determine that pleasant feeling. I therefore say that humanity comes from within. On the other hand, I respect the old men of the state of Ch'u as well as my own elders. What determines my pleasant feeling is age itself. Therefore I say that righteousness is external." Mencius said, "We love the roast meat of Ch'in as much as we love our own. This is even so with respect to material things. Then are you going to say that our love of roast meat is also external?"

• • •

Kung-tu Tzu said, "Kao Tzu said that man's nature is neither good nor evil. Some say that man's nature may be made good or evil, therefore when King Wen and King Wu[1] were in power the people loved virtue, and when Kings Yu and Li[2] were in power people loved violence. Some say that some men's nature is good and some men's nature is evil. Therefore even under (sage-emperor) Yao there was Hsiang [who daily plotted to kill his brother], and even with a bad father Ku-sou, there was [a most filial] Shun (Hsiang's brother who succeeded Yao), and even with (wicked king) Chou as uncle and ruler, there were Viscount Ch'i of Wei and Prince Pi-kan. Now you say that human nature is good. Then are those people wrong?"

Mencius said, "If you let people follow their feelings (original nature), they will be able to do good. This is what is meant by saying that human nature is good. If man does evil, it is not the fault of his natural endowment. The feeling of commiseration is found in all men; the feeling of shame and dislike is found in all

men; the feeling of respect and reverence is found in all men; and the feeling of right and wrong is found in all men. The feeling of commiseration is what we call humanity; the feeling of shame and dislike is what we called righteousness; the feeling of respect and reverence is what we called propriety (*li*); and the feeling of right and wrong is what we called wisdom. Humanity, righteousness, propriety, and wisdom are not drilled into us from outside. We originally have them with us. Only we do not think [to find them]. Therefore it is said, 'Seek and you will find it, neglect and you will lose it.' [Men differ in the development of their endowments], some twice as much as others, some five times, and some to an incalculable degree, because no one can develop his original endowment to the fullest extent. The *Book of Odes* says, 'Heaven produces the teeming multitude. As there are things there are their specific principles. When the people keep their normal nature they will love excellent virtue.' Confucius said, 'The writer of this poem indeed knew the Way (Tao). Therefore as there are things, there must be their specific principles, and since people keep to their normal nature, therefore they love excellent virtue.' "

• • •

Mencius said, "In good years most of the young people behave well. In bad years most of them abandon themselves to evil. This is not due to any difference in the natural capacity endowed by Heaven. The abandonment is due to the fact that the mind is allowed to fall into evil. Take for instance the growing of wheat. You sow the seeds and cover them with soil. The land is the same and the time of sowing is also the same. In time they all grow up luxuriantly. When the time of harvest comes, they are all ripe. Although there may be a difference between the different stalks of wheat, it is due to differences in the soil, as rich or poor, to the unequal nourishment obtained from the rain and the dew, and to differences in human effort. Therefore all things of the same kind are similar to one another. Why should there be any doubt about men? The sage and I are the same in kind. Therefore Lung Tzu said, 'If a man makes shoes without knowing the size of people's feet, I know that he will at least not make them to be like baskets.' Shoes are alike because people's feet are

[1]Sage-kings who founded the Chou dynasty (r. 1171–1122 B.C. and 1121–1116 B.C., respectively).
[2]Wicked kings (r. 781–771 B.C. and 878–842 B.C., respectively).

alike. There is a common taste for flavor in our mouths. I-ya was the first to know our common taste for food. Suppose one man's taste for flavor is different from that of others, as dogs and horses differ from us in belonging to different species, then why should the world follow I-ya in regard to flavor? Since in the matter of flavor the whole world regards I-ya as the standard, it shows that our tastes for flavor are alike. The same is true of our ears. Since in the matter of sounds the whole world regards Shih-k'uang as the standard, it shows that our ears are alike. The same is true of our eyes. With regard to Tzu-tu, none in the world did not know that he was handsome. Any one who did not recognize his handsomeness must have no eyes. Therefore I say there is a common taste for flavor in our mouths, a common sense for sound in our ears, and a common sense for beauty in our eyes. Can it be that in our minds alone we are not alike? What is it that we have in common in our minds? It is the sense of principle and righteousness (*i-li,* moral principles). The sage is the first to possess what is common in our minds. Therefore moral principles please our minds as beef and mutton and pork please our mouths."

• • •

Mencius said, "The trees of the Niu Mountain were once beautiful. But can the mountain be regarded any longer as beautiful since, being in the borders of a big state, the trees have been hewed down with axes and hatchets? Still with the rest given them by the days and nights and the nourishment provided them by the rains and the dew, they were not without buds and sprouts springing forth. But then the cattle and the sheep pastured upon them once and again. That is why the mountain looks so bald. When people see that it is so bald, they think that there was never any timber on the mountain. Is this the true nature of the mountain? Is there not [also] a heart of humanity and righteousness originally existing in man? The way in which he loses his originally good mind is like the way in which the trees are hewed down with axes and hatchets. As trees are cut down day after day, can a mountain retain its beauty? To be sure, the days and nights do the heal-

ing, and there is the nourishing air of the calm morning which keeps him normal in his likes and dislikes. But the effect is slight, and is disturbed and destroyed by what he does during the day. When there is repeated disturbance, the restorative influence of the night will not be sufficient to preserve (the proper goodness of the mind). When the influence of the night is not sufficient to preserve it, man becomes not much different from the beast. People see that he acts like an animal, and think that he never had the original endowment (for goodness). But is that his true character? Therefore with proper nourishment and care, everything grows, whereas without proper nourishment and care, everything decays. Confucius said, 'Hold it fast and you preserve it. Let it go and you lose it. It comes in and goes out at no definite time and without anyone's knowing its direction.' He was talking about the human mind."

• • •

Kung-tu Tzu asked, "We are all human beings. Why is it that some men become great and others become small?" Mencius said, "Those who follow the greater qualities in their nature become great men and those who follow the smaller qualities in their nature become small men." "But we are all human beings. Why is it that some follow their greater qualities and others follow their smaller qualities?" Mencius replied, "When our senses of sight and hearing are used without thought and are thereby obscured by material things, the material things act on the material senses and lead them astray. That is all. The function of the mind is to think. If we think, we will get them (the principles of things). If we do not think, we will not get them. This is what Heaven has given to us. If we first build up the nobler part of our nature, then the inferior part cannot overcome it. It is simply this that makes a man great."

• • •

Kung-sun Ch'ou asked, "May I venture to ask, sir, how you maintain an unperturbed mind and how Kao Tzu maintains an unperturbed mind. May I be told?" Mencius answered, "Kao Tzu said, 'What is not attained in words is not to be sought in the mind, and what is not attained in the mind is not to be sought in the vital force.' It is all right to say that what is not attained in the mind is not to be sought in the vital force, but it is not all right to say that what is not attained in words is not to be sought in the mind. The will is the leader of the vital force, and the vital force pervades and animates the body. The will is the highest; the vital force comes next. Therefore I say, 'Hold the will firm and never do violence to the vital force.' "

Ch'ou said, "You said that the will is the highest and that the vital force comes next. But you also say to hold the will firm and never to do violence to the vital force. Why?"

Mencius said, "If the will is concentrated, the vital force [will follow it] and become active. If the vital force is concentrated, the will [will follow it] and become active. For instance, here is a case of a man falling or running. It is his vital force that is active, and yet it causes his mind to be active too."

Ch'ou asked, "May I venture to ask, sir, in what you are strong?"

Mencius replied, "I understand words. And I am skillful in nourishing my strong, moving power."

"May I ask what is meant by the strong, moving power?"

"It is difficult to describe. As power, it is exceedingly great and exceedingly strong. If nourished by uprightness and not injured, it will fill up all between heaven and earth. As power, it is accompanied by righteousness and the Way. Without them, it will be devoid of nourishment. It is produced by the accumulation of righteous deeds but is not obtained by incidental acts of righteousness. When one's conduct is not satisfactory to his own mind, then one will be devoid of nourishment. I therefore said that Kao Tzu never understood righteousness because he made it something external."

• • •

"Always be doing something without expectation. Let the mind not forget its objective, but let there be no artificial effort to help it grow. Do not be like the man of Sung. There was a man of Sung who was sorry that his corn was not growing, and so he pulled it up. Having been tired out he went home and said to his people, 'I am all tired. I have helped the corn to grow.' When his son ran to look at it, the corn had already withered."

• • •

Mencius said, "All men have the mind which cannot bear [to see the suffering of][3] others. The ancient kings had this mind and therefore they had a government that could not bear to see the suffering of the people. When a government that cannot bear to see the suffering of the people is conducted from a mind that cannot bear to see the suffering of others, the government of the empire will be as easy as making something go round in the palm."

"When I say that all men have the mind which cannot bear to see the suffering of others, my meaning may be illustrated thus: Now, when men suddenly see a child about to fall into a well, they all have a feeling of alarm and distress, not to gain friendship with the child's parents, nor to seek the praise of their neighbors and friends, nor because they dislike the reputation [of lack of humanity if they did not rescue the child]. From such a case, we see that a man without the feeling of commiseration is not a man; a man without the feeling of shame and dislike is not a man; a man without the feeling of deference and compliance is not a man; and a man without the feeling of right and wrong is not a man. The feeling of commiseration is the beginning of humanity; the feeling of shame and dislike is the beginning of righteousness; the feeling of deference and compliance is the beginning of propriety; and the feeling of right and wrong is the beginning of wisdom. Men have these Four Beginnings just as they have their four limbs. Having these Four Beginnings, but saying that they cannot develop them is to destroy themselves. When they say that their ruler cannot develop them, they are destroying their ruler. If anyone with these Four Beginnings in him knows how to give them the fullest extension and development, the result will be like fire beginning

---

[3]According to Chao Ch'i, "cannot bear to do evil to others."

to burn or a spring beginning to shoot forth. When they are fully developed, they will be sufficient to protect all people within the four seas (the world). If they are not developed, they will not be sufficient even to serve one's parents."

. . .

Kung-sun Ch'ou said, "Why is it that the superior man does not teach his son himself?" Mencius said, "The circumstance is such that it cannot be done. To teach is necessarily to inculcate correct principles. When these correct principles are not practiced, anger will follow. As anger follows, feelings will be hurt. [The son would say], 'My master teaches me the correct principles but he himself does not proceed according to correct principles.' This means that the father and son hurt each other's feelings. When father and son hurt each other's feelings, it is bad. The ancients exchanged their sons, one teaching the son of another. Between father and son there should be no reproving admonition to what is good. Such reproofs lead to alienation, and nothing is more inauspicious than alienation."

HUMAN NATURE IS EVIL

Hsün Tzu

Man's nature is evil; goodness is the result of conscious activity. The nature of man is such that he is born with a fondness for profit. If he indulges this fondness, it will lead him into wrangling and strife, and all sense of courtesy and humility will disappear. He is born with feelings of envy and hate, and if he indulges these, they will lead him into violence and crime, and all sense of loyalty and good faith will disappear. Man is born with the desires of the eyes and ears, with a fondness for beautiful sights and sounds. If he indulges these, they will lead him into license and wantonness, and all ritual principles and correct forms will be lost. Hence, any man who follows his

nature and indulges his emotions will inevitably become involved in wrangling and strife, will violate the forms and rules of society, and will end as a criminal. Therefore, man must first be transformed by the instructions of a teacher and guided by ritual principles, and only then will he be able to observe the dictates of courtesy and humility, obey the forms and rules of society, and achieve order. It is obvious from this, then, that man's nature is evil, and that his goodness is the result of conscious activity.

A warped piece of wood must wait until it has been laid against the straightening board, steamed, and forced into shape before it can become straight; a piece of blunt metal must wait until it has been whetted on a grindstone before it can become sharp. Similarly, since man's nature is evil, it must wait for the instructions of a teacher before it can become upright, and for the guidance of ritual principles before it can become orderly. If men have no teachers to instruct them, they will be inclined towards evil and not upright; and if they have no ritual principles to guide them, they will be perverse and violent and lack order. In ancient times the sage kings realized that man's nature is evil, and that therefore he inclines toward evil and violence and is not upright or orderly. Accordingly they created ritual principles and laid down certain regulations in order to reform man's emotional nature and make it upright, in order to train and transform it and guide it in the proper channels. In this way they caused all men to become orderly and to conform to the Way. Hence, today any man who takes to heart the instructions of his teacher, applies himself to his studies, and abides by ritual principles may become a gentleman, but anyone who gives free rein to his emotional nature, is content to indulge his passions, and disregards ritual principles becomes a petty man. It is obvious from this, therefore, that man's nature is evil, and that his goodness is the result of conscious activity.

Mencius states that man is capable of learning because his nature is good, but I say that this is wrong. It indicates that he has not really understood man's nature nor distinguished properly between the basic nature and conscious activity. The nature is that which is given by Heaven; you cannot learn it, you cannot acquire it by effort. Ritual principles, on the other hand, are created by sages; you can learn to apply them, you can work to bring them to completion. That part of man which cannot be learned or acquired by effort is called the nature; that part of him which can be acquired by learning and brought to completion by effort is called conscious activity. This is the difference between nature and conscious activity.

It is a part of man's nature that his eyes can see and his ears can hear. But the faculty of clear sight can never exist separately from the eye, nor can the faculty of keen hearing exist separately from the ear. It is obvious, then, that you cannot acquire clear sight and keen hearing by study. Mencius states that man's nature is good, and that all evil arises because he loses his original nature. Such a view, I believe, is erroneous. It is the way with man's nature that as soon as he is born he begins to depart from his original naïveté and simplicity, and therefore he must inevitably lose what Mencius regards as his original nature. It is obvious from this, then, that the nature of man is evil.

Those who maintain that the nature is good praise and approve whatever has not departed from the original simplicity and naïveté of the child. That is, they consider that beauty belongs to the original simplicity and naïveté and goodness to the original mind in the same way that clear sight is inseparable from the eye and keen hearing from the ear. Hence, they maintain that [the nature possesses goodness] in the same way that the eye possesses clear vision or the ear keenness of hearing. Now it is the nature of man that when he is hungry he will desire satisfaction, when he is cold he will desire warmth, and when he is weary he will desire rest. This is his emotional nature. And yet a man, although he is hungry, will not dare to be the first to eat if he is in the presence of his elders, because he knows that he should yield to them, and although he is weary, he will not dare to demand rest because he knows that he should relieve others of the burden of labor. For a son to yield to his father or a younger brother to yield to his elder brother, for a son to relieve his father of work or a younger brother to relieve his elder brother—acts such as these are all contrary to man's nature and run counter to his emotions. And yet they represent the way of filial piety and the proper forms enjoined by ritual principles. Hence, if men follow their emotional nature, there will be no courtesy or humility; courtesy and humility in fact run counter to man's emotional nature. From this it is obvious, then, that man's nature is evil, and that his goodness is the result of conscious activity.

Someone may ask: if man's nature is evil, then where do ritual principles come from? I would reply: all ritual principles are produced by the conscious activity of the sages; essentially they are not products of man's nature. A potter molds clay and makes a vessel, but the vessel is the product of the conscious activity of the potter, not essentially a product of his human nature. A carpenter carves a piece of wood and makes a utensil, but the utensil is the product of the conscious activity of the carpenter, not essentially a product of his human nature. The sage gathers together his thoughts and ideas, experiments with various forms of conscious activity, and so produces ritual principles and sets forth laws and regulations. Hence, these ritual principles and laws are the products of the conscious activity of the sage, not essentially products of his human nature.

Phenomena such as the eye's fondness for beautiful forms, the ear's fondness for beautiful sounds, the mouth's fondness for delicious flavors, the mind's fondness for profit, or the body's fondness for pleasure and ease—these are all products of the emotional nature of man. They are instinctive and spontaneous; man does not have to do anything to produce them. But that which does not come into being instinctively but must wait for some activity to bring it into being is called the product of conscious activity. These are the products of the nature and of conscious activity respectively, and the proof that they are not the same. Therefore, the sage transforms his nature and initiates conscious activity; from this conscious activity he produces ritual principles, and when they have been produced he sets up rules and regulations. Hence, ritual principles and rules are produced by the sage. In respect to human nature the sage is the same as all other men and does not surpass them; it is only in his conscious activity that he differs from and surpasses other men.

It is man's emotional nature to love profit and desire gain. Suppose now that a man has some wealth to be divided. If he indulges his emotional nature, loving profit and desiring gain, then he will quarrel and wrangle even with his own brothers over the division. But if he has been transformed by the proper forms of ritual principle, then he will be capable of yielding even to a complete stranger. Hence, to indulge the emotional nature leads to the quarreling of brothers, but to be transformed by ritual principles makes a man capable of yielding to strangers.

Every man who desires to do good does so precisely because his nature is evil. A man whose accomplishments are meager longs for greatness; an ugly man longs for beauty; a man in cramped quarters longs for spaciousness; a poor man longs for wealth; a humble man longs for eminence. Whatever a man lacks in himself he will seek outside. But if a man is already rich, he will not long for wealth, and if he is already eminent, he will not long for greater power. What a man already possesses in himself he will not bother to look for outside. From this we can see that men desire to do good precisely because their nature is evil. Ritual principles are certainly not a part of man's original nature. Therefore, he forces himself to study and to seek to possess them. An understanding of ritual principles is not a part of man's original nature, and therefore he ponders and plans and thereby seeks to understand them. Hence, man in the state in which he is born neither possesses nor understands ritual principles. If he does not possess ritual principles, his behavior will be chaotic, and if he does not understand them, he will be wild and irresponsible. In fact, therefore, man in the state in which he is born possesses this tendency towards chaos and irresponsibility. From this it is obvious, then, that man's nature is evil, and that his goodness is the result of conscious activity.

Mencius states that man's nature is good, but I say that this view is wrong. All men in the world, past and present, agree in defining goodness as that which is upright, reasonable, and orderly, and evil as that which is prejudiced, irresponsible, and chaotic. This is the distinction between good and evil. Now suppose that man's nature was in fact intrinsically

upright, reasonable, and orderly—then what need would there be for sage kings and ritual principles? The existence of sage kings and ritual principles could certainly add nothing to the situation. But because man's nature is in fact evil, this is not so. Therefore, in ancient times the sages, realizing that man's nature is evil, that it is prejudiced and not upright, irresponsible and lacking in order, for this reason established the authority of the ruler to control it, elucidated ritual principles to transform it, set up laws and standards to correct it, and meted out strict punishments to restrain it. As a result, all the world achieved order and conformed to goodness. Such is the orderly government of the sage kings and the transforming power of ritual principles. Now let someone try doing away with the authority of the ruler, ignoring the transforming power of ritual principles, rejecting the order that comes from laws and standards, and dispensing with the restrictive power of punishments, and then watch and see how the people of the world treat each other. He will find that the powerful impose upon the weak and rob them, the many terrorize the few and extort from them, and in no time the whole world will be given up to chaos and mutual destruction. It is obvious from this, then, that man's nature is evil, and that his goodness is the result of conscious activity.

Those who are good at discussing antiquity must demonstrate the validity of what they say in terms of modern times; those who are good at discussing Heaven must show proofs from the human world. In discussions of all kinds, men value what is in accord with the facts and what can be proved to be valid. Hence if a man sits on his mat propounding some theory, he should be able to stand right up and put it into practice, and show that it can be extended over a wide area with equal validity. Now Mencius states that man's nature is good, but this is neither in accord with the facts, nor can it be proved to be valid. One may sit down and propound such a theory, but he cannot stand up and put it into practice, nor can he extend it over a wide area with any success at all. How, then, could it be anything but erroneous?

If the nature of man were good, we could dispense with sage kings and forget about ritual principles. But if it is evil, then we must go along with the sage kings and honor ritual principles. The straightening board is made because of the warped wood; the plumb line is employed because things are crooked; rulers are set up and ritual principles elucidated because the nature of man is evil. From this it is obvious, then, that man's nature is evil, and that his goodness is the result of conscious activity. A straight piece of wood does not have to wait for the straightening board to become straight; it is straight by nature. But a warped piece of wood must wait until it has been laid against the straightening board, steamed, and forced into shape before it can become straight, because by nature it is warped. Similarly, since man's nature is evil, he must wait for the ordering power of the sage kings and the transforming power of ritual principles; only then can he achieve order and conform to goodness. From this it is obvious, then, that man's nature is evil, and that his goodness is the result of conscious activity.

Someone may ask whether ritual principles and concerted conscious activity are not themselves a part of man's nature, so that for that reason the sage is capable of producing them. But I would answer that this is not so. A potter may mold clay and produce an earthen pot, but surely molding pots out of clay is not a part of the potter's human nature. A carpenter may carve wood and produce a utensil, but surely carving utensils out of wood is not a part of the carpenter's human nature. The sage stands in the same relation to ritual principles as the potter to the things he molds and produces. How, then, could ritual principles and concerted conscious activity be a part of man's basic human nature?

As far as human nature goes, the sages Yao and Shun possessed the same nature as the tyrant Chieh or Robber Chih, and the gentleman possesses the same nature as the petty man. Would you still maintain, then, that ritual principles and concerted conscious activity are a part of man's nature? If you do so, then what reason is there to pay any particular honor to Yao, Shun, or the gentleman? The reason people honor Yao, Shun, and the gentleman is that they are able to transform their nature, apply themselves to conscious activity, and produce ritual prin-

ciples. The sage, then, must stand in the same relation to ritual principles as the potter to the things he molds and produces. Looking at it this way, how could ritual principles and concerted conscious activity be a part of man's nature? The reason people despise Chieh, Robber Chih, or the petty man is that they give free rein to their nature, follow their emotions, and are content to indulge their passions, so that their conduct is marked by greed and contentiousness. Therefore, it is clear that man's nature is evil, and that his goodness is the result of conscious activity.

HUMAN NATURE AS COMPETITIVE

Thomas Hobbes

Nature hath made men so equal, in the faculties of the body, and mind; as that though there be found one man sometimes manifestly stronger in body, or of quicker mind than another; yet when all is reckoned together, the difference between man, and man, is not so considerable, as that one man can thereupon claim to himself any benefit, to which another may not pretend, as well as he. For as to the strength of body, the weakest has strength enough to kill the strongest, either by secret machination, or by confederacy with others, that are in the same danger with himself.

And as to the faculties of the mind, setting aside the arts grounded upon words, and especially that skill of proceeding upon general, and infallible rules, called science; which very few have, and but in few things; as being not a native faculty, born with us; nor attained, as prudence, while we look after somewhat else, I find yet a greater equality amongst men, than that of strength. For prudence, is but experience; which equal time, equally bestows on all men, in those things they equally apply themselves unto. That which may perhaps make such equality incredible, is but a vain conceit of one's own wisdom, which almost all men think they have in a greater degree, than the vulgar; that is, than all men but themselves, and a few others, whom by fame, or for concurring with themselves, they approve. For such is the nature of men, that howsoever they may acknowledge many others to be more witty, or more eloquent, or more learned; yet they will hardly believe there be many so wise as themselves; for they see their own wit at hand, and other men's at a distance. But this proveth rather that men are in that point equal, than unequal. For there is not ordinarily a greater sign of the equal distribution of any thing, than that every man is contented with his share.

From equality proceeds diffidence. From this equality of ability, ariseth equality of hope in the attaining of our ends. And therefore if any two men desire the same thing, which nevertheless they cannot both enjoy, they become enemies; and in the way to their end, which is principally their own conservation, and sometimes their delectation only, endeavour to destroy, or subdue one another. And from hence it comes to pass, that where an invader hath no more to fear, than another man's single power; if one plant, sow, build, or possess a convenient seat, others may probably be expected to come prepared with forces united, to dispossess, and deprive him, not only of the fruit of his labour, but also of his life, or liberty. And the invader again is in the like danger of another.

And from this diffidence of one another, there is no way for any man to secure himself, so reasonable, as anticipation; that is, by force, or wiles, to master the persons of all men he can, so long, till he see no other power great enough to endanger him: and this is no more than his own conservation requireth, and is generally allowed. Also because there be some, that taking pleasure in contemplating their own power in the acts of conquest, which they pursue farther than their security requires; if others, that otherwise would be glad to be at ease within modest bounds, should not by invasion increase their power, they would not be able, long time, by standing only on their defence, to subsist. And by consequence, such augmentation of dominion over men being necessary to a man's conservation, it ought to be allowed him.

Again, men have no pleasure, but on the contrary a great deal of grief, in keeping company, where there is no power able to over-awe them all. For every man looketh that his companion should value him, at the same rate he sets upon himself: and upon all signs of contempt, or undervaluing, naturally endeavours, as far as he dares, (which amongst them that have no common power to keep them in quiet, is far enough to make them destroy each other), to extort a greater value from his contemners, by damage; and from others, by the example.

So that in the nature of man, we find three principal causes of quarrel. First, competition; secondly, diffidence; thirdly, glory.

The first, maketh men invade for gain; the second, for safety; and the third, for reputation. The first use violence, to make themselves masters of other men's persons, wives, children, and cattle; the second, to defend them; the third, for trifles, as a word, a smile, a different opinion, and any other sign of undervalue, either direct in their persons, or by reflection in their kindred, their friends, their nation, their profession, or their name.

Out of civil states, there is always war of every one against every one. Hereby it is manifest, that during the time men live without a common power to keep them all in awe, they are in that condition which is called war; and such a war, as is of every man, against every man. For *war,* consisteth not in battle only, or the act of fighting; but in a tract of time, wherein the will to contend by battle is sufficiently known: and therefore the notion of *time,* is to be considered in the nature of war; as it is in the nature of weather. For as the nature of foul weather, lieth not in a shower or two of rain; but in an inclination thereto of many days together: so the nature of war, consisteth not in actual fighting; but in the known disposition thereto, during all the time there is no assurance to the contrary. All other time is *peace.*

The incommodities of such a war. Whatsoever therefore is consequent to a time of war, where every man is enemy to every man; the same is consequent to the time, wherein men live without other security, than what their own strength, and their own invention shall furnish them withal. In such condition, there is no place for industry; because the fruit thereof is uncertain: and consequently no culture of the earth; no navigation, nor use of the commodities that may be imported by sea; no commodious building; no instruments of moving, and removing, such things as require much force; no knowledge of the face of the earth; no account of time; no arts; no letters; no society; and which is worst of all, continual fear, and danger of violent death; and the life of man, solitary, poor, nasty, brutish, and short.

It may seem strange to some man, that has not well weighed these things; that nature should thus dissociate, and render men apt to invade, and destroy one another: and he may therefore, not trusting to this inference, made from the passions, desire perhaps to have the same confirmed by experience. Let him therefore consider with himself, when taking a journey, he arms himself, and seeks to go well accompanied; when going to sleep, he locks his doors; when even in his house he locks his chests; and this when he knows there be laws, and public officers, armed, to revenge all injuries shall be done him; what opinion he has of his fellow-subjects, when he rides armed; of his fellow citizens, when he locks his doors; and of his children, and servants, when he locks his chests. Does he not there as much accuse mankind by his actions, as I do by my words? But neither of us accuse man's nature in it. The desires, and other passions of man, are in themselves no sin. No more are the actions, that proceed from those passions, till they know a law that forbids them: which till laws be made they cannot know: nor can any law be made, till they have agreed upon the person that shall make it.

It may peradventure be thought, there was never such a time, nor condition of war as this; and I believe it was never generally so, over all the world: but there are many places, where they live so now. For the savage people in many places of America, except the government of small families, the concord whereof dependeth on natural lust, have no government at all; and live at this day in that brutish manner, as I said before. Howsoever, it may be perceived what manner of life there would be, where there were

no common power to fear, by the manner of life, which men that have formerly lived under a peaceful government, use to degenerate into, in a civil war.

But though there had never been any time, wherein particular men were in a condition of war one against another; yet in all times, kings, and persons of sovereign authority, because of their independency, are in continual jealousies, and in the state and posture of gladiators; having their weapons pointing, and their eyes fixed on one another; that is, their forts, garrisons, and guns upon the frontiers of their kingdoms; and continual spies upon their neighbours; which is a posture of war. But because they uphold thereby, the industry of their subjects; there does not follow from it, that misery, which accompanies the liberty of particular men.

In such a war nothing is unjust. To this war of every man, against every man, this also is consequent; that nothing can be unjust. The notions of right and wrong, justice and injustice have there no place. Where there is no common power, there is no law: where no law, no injustice. Force, and fraud, are in war the two cardinal virtues. Justice, and injustice are none of the faculties neither of the body, nor mind. If they were, they might be in a man that were alone in the world, as well as his senses, and passions. They are qualities, that relate to men in society, not in solitude. It is consequent also to the same condition, that there be no propriety, no dominion, no *mine* and *thine* distinct; but only that to be every man's, that he can get: and for so long, as he can keep it. And thus much for the ill condition, which man by mere nature is actually placed in; though with a possibility to come out of it, consisting partly in the passions, partly in his reason.

The passions that incline men to peace. The passions that incline men to peace, are fear of death; desire of such things as are necessary to commodious living; and a hope by their industry to obtain them. And reason suggesteth convenient articles of peace, upon which men may be drawn to agreement. These articles, are they, which otherwise are called the Laws of Nature.

• • •

The *right of nature,* which writers commonly call *jus naturale,* is the liberty each man hath, to use his own power, as he will himself, for the preservation of his own nature; that is to say, of his own life; and consequently, of doing any thing, which in his own judgment, and reason, he shall conceive to be the aptest means thereunto.

By *liberty,* is understood, according to the proper signification of the word, the absence of external impediments: which impediments, may oft take away part of a man's power to do what he would; but cannot hinder him from using the power left him, according as his judgment, and reason shall dictate to him.

A *law of nature, lex naturalis,* is a precept or general rule, found out by reason, by which a man is forbidden to do that, which is destructive of his life, or taketh away the means of preserving the same; and to omit that, by which he thinketh it may be best preserved.

• • •

And because the condition of man, as hath been declared in the precedent chapter, is a condition of war of every one against every one; in which case every one is governed by his own reason; and there is nothing he can make use of, that may not be a help unto him, in preserving his life against his enemies; it followeth, that in such a condition, every man has a right to every thing; even to one another's body. And therefore, as long as this natural right of every man to every thing endureth, there can be no security to any man, how strong or wise soever he be, of living out the time, which nature ordinarily alloweth men to live. And consequently it is a precept, or general rule of reason, *that every man, ought to endeavour peace, as far as he has hope of obtaining it; and when he cannot obtain it, that he may seek, and use, all helps, and advantages of war.* The first branch of which rule, containeth the first, and fundamental law of nature; which is, *to seek peace, and follow it.* The second, the sum of the right of nature; which is, *by all means we can, to defend ourselves.*

The second law of nature. From this fundamental law of nature, by which men are commanded to endeavour peace, is derived this second law; *that a man be willing, when others are so too, as far-forth, as for peace, and defence of himself he shall think it necessary, to lay down this right to all things; and be contented with so much liberty against other men, as he would allow other men against himself.* For as long as every man holdeth this right, of doing any thing he liketh; so long are all men in the condition of war. But if other men will not lay down their right, as well as he; then there is no reason for any one, to divest himself of his: for that were to expose himself to prey, which no man is bound to, rather than to dispose himself to peace. This is that law of the Gospel; *whatsoever you require that others should do to you, that do ye to them.* And that law of all men, *quod tibi fieri non vis, alteri ne feceris.*

• • •

It is true, that certain living creatures, as bees, and ants, live sociably one with another, which are therefore by Aristotle numbered amongst political creatures; and yet have no other direction, than their particular judgments and appetites; nor speech, whereby one of them can signify to another, what he thinks expedient for the common benefit: and therefore some man may perhaps desire to know, why mankind cannot do the same. To which I answer,

First, that men are continually in competition for honour and dignity, which these creatures are not; and consequently amongst men there ariseth on that ground, envy and hatred, and finally war; but amongst these not so.

Secondly, that amongst these creatures, the common good differeth not from the private; and being by nature inclined to their private, they procure thereby the common benefit. But man, whose joy consisteth in comparing himself with other men, can relish nothing but what is eminent.

Thirdly, that these creatures, having not, as man, the use of reason, do not see, nor think they see any fault, in the administration of their common business; whereas amongst men, there are very many, that think themselves wiser, and abler to govern the public, better than the rest; and these strive to reform and innovate, one this way, another that way; and thereby bring it into distraction and civil war.

Fourthly, that these creatures, though they have some use of voice, in making known to one another their desires, and other affections; yet they want that art of words, by which some men can represent to others, that which is good, in the likeness of evil; and evil, in the likeness of good; and augment, or diminish the apparent greatness of good and evil; discontenting men, and troubling their peace at their pleasure.

Fifthly, irrational creatures cannot distinguish between *injury,* and *damage;* and therefore as long as they be at ease, they are not offended with their fellows: whereas man is then most troublesome, when he is most at ease: for then it is that he loves to shew his wisdom, and control the actions of them that govern the commonwealth.

Lastly, the agreement of these creatures is natural; that of men, is by covenant only, which is artificial: and therefore it is no wonder if there be somewhat else required, besides covenant, to make their agreement constant and lasting; which is a common power, to keep them in awe, and to direct their actions to the common benefit.

The generation of a commonwealth. The definition of a commonwealth. The only way to erect such a common power, as may be able to defend them from the invasion of foreigners, and the injuries of one another, and thereby to secure them in such sort, as that by their own industry, and by the fruits of the earth, they may nourish themselves and live contentedly; is, to confer all their power and strength upon one man, or upon one assembly of men, that may reduce all their wills, by plurality of voices, unto one will: which is as much as to say, to appoint one man, or assembly of men, to bear their person; and every one to own, and acknowledge himself to be author of whatsoever he that so beareth their person, shall act, or cause to be acted, in those things which concern the common peace and safety; and

therein to submit their wills, every one to his will, and their judgments, to his judgment. This is more than consent, or concord; it is a real unity of them all, in one and the same person, made by covenant of every man with every man, in such manner, as if every man should say to every man, *I authorize and give up my right of governing myself, to this man, or to this assembly of men, on this condition, that thou give up thy right to him, and authorize all his actions in like manner.* This done, the multitude so united in one person, is called a *commonwealth,* in Latin *civitas.* This is the generation of that great *leviathan,* or rather, to speak more reverently, of that *mortal god,* to which we owe under the *immortal God,* our peace and defence. For by this authority, given him by every particular man in the commonwealth, he hath the use of so much power and strength conferred on him, that by terror thereof, he is enabled to form the wills of them all, to peace at home, and mutual aid against their enemies abroad. And in him consisteth the essence of the commonwealth; which, to define it, is *one person, of whose acts a great multitude, by mutual covenants one with another, have made themselves every one the author, to the end he may use the strength and means of them all, as he shall think expedient, for their peace and common defence.*

Sovereign, and subject, what. And he that carrieth this person is called *sovereign,* and said to have *sovereign power;* and every one besides, his *subject.*

The attaining to this sovereign power, is by two ways. One by natural force; as when a man maketh his children, to submit themselves, and their children to his government, as being able to destroy them if they refuse; or by war subdueth his enemies to his will, giving them their lives on that condition. The other, is when men agree amongst themselves, to submit to some man, or assembly of men, voluntarily, on confidence to be protected by him against all others. This latter, may be called a political commonwealth, or commonwealth by *institution;* and the former, a commonwealth by *acquisition.*

MUTUAL AID

Petr Kropotkin

The conception of struggle for existence as a factor of evolution, introduced into science by Darwin and Wallace, has permitted us to embrace an immensely wide range of phenomena in one single generalization, which soon became the very basis of our philosophical, biological, and sociological speculations. An immense variety of facts:—adaptations of function and structure of organic beings to their surroundings; physiological and anatomical evolution; intellectual progress, and moral development itself, which we formerly used to explain by so many different causes, were embodied by Darwin in one general conception. We understood them as continued endeavours—as a struggle against adverse circumstances—for such a development of individuals, races, species and societies, as would result in the greatest possible fullness, variety, and intensity of life. It may be that at the outset Darwin himself was not fully aware of the generality of the factor which he first invoked for explaining one series only of facts relative to the accumulation of individual variations in incipient species. But he foresaw that the term which he was introducing into science would lose its philosophical and its only true meaning if it were to be used in its narrow sense only—that of a struggle between separate individuals for the sheer means of existence. And at the very beginning of his memorable work he insisted upon the term being taken in its "large and metaphorical sense including dependence of one being on another, and including (which is more important) not only the life of the individual, but success in leaving progeny."[1]

While he himself was chiefly using the term in its narrow sense for his own special purpose, he warned his followers against committing the error (which he seems once to have committed himself)

of overrating its narrow meaning. In *The Descent of Man* he gave some powerful pages to illustrate its proper, wide sense. He pointed out how, in numberless animal societies, the struggle between separate individuals for the means of existence disappears, how *struggle* is replaced by *co-operation,* and how that substitution results in the development of intellectual and moral faculties which secure to the species the best conditions for survival. He intimated that in such cases the fittest are not the physically strongest, nor the cunningest, but those who learn to combine so as mutually to support each other, strong and weak alike, for the welfare of the community. "Those communities," he wrote, "which included the greatest number of the most sympathetic members would flourish best, and rear the greatest number of *offspring*" (2nd edit., p. 163). The term, which originated from the narrow Malthusian conception of competition between each and all, thus lost its narrowness in the mind of one who knew Nature.

• • •

As soon as we study animals—not in laboratories and museums only, but in the forest and the prairie, in the steppe and the mountains—we at once perceive that though there is an immense amount of warfare and extermination going on amidst various species, and especially amidst various classes of animals, there is, at the same time, as much, or perhaps even more, of mutual support, mutual aid, and mutual defence amidst animals belonging to the same species or, at least, to the same society. Sociability is as much a law of nature as mutual struggle. Of course it would be extremely difficult to estimate, however roughly, the relative numerical importance of both these series of facts. But if we resort to an indirect test, and ask Nature: "Who are the fittest: those who are continually at war with each other, or those who support one another?" we at once see that those animals which acquire habits of mutual aid are undoubtedly the fittest. They have more chances to survive, and they attain, in their respective classes, the highest development of intelligence and bodily organization. If

---

[1] *Origin of Species,* chap. iii.

the numberless facts which can be brought forward to support this view are taken into account, we may safely say that mutual aid is as much a law of animal life as mutual struggle, but that, as a factor of evolution, it most probably has a far greater importance, inasmuch as it favours the development of such habits and characters as insure the maintenance and further development of the species, together with the greatest amount of welfare and enjoyment of life for the individual, with the least waste of energy.

Of the scientific followers of Darwin, the first, as far as I know, who understood the full purport of Mutual Aid *as a law of Nature and the chief factor of evolution,* was a well-known Russian zoologist, the late Dean of the St. Petersburg University, Professor Kessler. He developed his ideas in an address which he delivered in January 1880, a few months before his death, at a Congress of Russian naturalists; but, like so many good things published in the Russian tongue only, that remarkable address remains almost entirely unknown.[2]

"As a zoologist of old standing," he felt bound to protest against the abuse of a term—the struggle for existence—borrowed from zoology, or, at least,

against overrating its importance. Zoology, he said, and those sciences which deal with man, continually insist upon what they call the pitiless law of struggle for existence. But they forget the existence of another law which may be described as the law of mutual aid, which law, at least for the animals, is far more essential than the former. He pointed out how the need of leaving progeny necessarily brings animals together, and, "the more the individuals keep together, the more they mutually support each other, and the more are the chances of the species for surviving, as well as for making further progress in its intellectual development." "All classes of animals," he continued, "and especially the higher ones, practise mutual aid," and he illustrated his idea by examples borrowed from the life of the burying beetles and the social life of birds and some mammalia. The examples were few, as might have been expected in a short opening address, but the chief points were clearly stated; and, after mentioning that in the evolution of mankind mutual aid played a still more prominent part, Professor Kessler concluded as follows:—

> I obviously do not deny the struggle for existence, but I maintain that the progressive development of the animal kingdom, and especially of mankind, is favoured much more by mutual support than by mutual struggle. . . . All organic beings have two essential needs: that of nutrition, and that of propagating the species. The former brings them to a struggle and to mutual extermination, while the needs of maintaining the species bring them to approach one another and to support one another. But I am inclined to think that in the evolution of the organic world—in the progressive modification of organic beings—mutual support among individuals plays a much more important part than their mutual struggle."[3]

• • •

Happily enough, competition is not the rule either in the animal world or in mankind. It is limited among animals to exceptional periods, and natural

---

[2]Leaving aside the pre-Darwinian writers, like Toussenel, Fée, and many others, several works containing many striking instances of mutual aid—chiefly, however, illustrating animal intelligence—were issued previously to that date. I may mention those of Houzeau, *Les facultés mentales des animaux,* 2 vols., Brussels, 1872; L. Büchner's *Aus dem Geistesleben der Thiere,* 2nd ed. in 1877; and Maximilian Perty's *Ueber das Seelenleben der Thiere,* Leipzig, 1876. Espinas published his most remarkable work, *Les Sociétés animales,* in 1877, and in that work he pointed out the importance of animal societies, and their bearing upon the preservation of species, and entered upon a most valuable discussion of the origin of societies. In fact, Espinas's book contains all that has been written since upon mutual aid, and many good things besides. If I nevertheless make a special mention of Kessler's address, it is because he raised mutual aid to the height of a law much more important in evolution than the law of mutual struggle. The same ideas were developed next year (in April 1881) by J. Lanessan in a lecture published in 1882 under this title: *La lutte pour l'existence et l'association pour la lutte.* G. Romanes's capital work, *Animal Intelligence,* was issued in 1882, and followed next year by the *Mental Evolution in Animals.* About the same time (1883), Büchner published another work, *Liebe und Liebes-Leben in der Thierwelt,* a second edition of which was issued in 1885. The idea, as seen, was in the air.

[3]*Memoirs (Trudy) of the St. Petersburg Society of Naturalists,* vol. xi. 1880.

selection finds better fields for its activity. Better conditions are created by the *elimination of competition* by means of mutual aid and mutual support.[4] In the great struggle for life—for the greatest possible fullness and intensity of life with the least waste of energy—natural selection continually seeks out the ways precisely for avoiding competition as much as possible. The ants combine in nests and nations; they pile up their stores, they rear their cattle—and thus avoid competition; and natural selection picks out of the ants' family the species which know best how to avoid competition, with its unavoidably deleterious consequences. Most of our birds slowly move southwards as the winter comes, or gather in numberless societies and undertake long journeys—and thus avoid competition. Many rodents fall asleep when the time comes that competition should set in; while other rodents store food for the winter, and gather in large villages for obtaining the necessary protection when at work. The reindeer, when the lichens are dry in the interior of the continent, migrate towards the sea. Buffaloes cross an immense continent in order to find plenty of food. And the beavers, when they grow numerous on a river, divide into two parties, and go, the old ones down the river, and the young ones up the river—and avoid competition. And when animals can neither fall asleep, nor migrate, nor lay in stores, nor themselves grow their food like the ants, they do what the titmouse does, and what Wallace (*Darwinism,* ch. v.) has so charmingly described: they resort to new kinds of food—and thus, again, avoid competition.

"Don't compete!—competition is always injurious to the species, and you have plenty of resources to avoid it!" That is the *tendency* of nature, not always realized in full, but always present. That is the watchword which comes to us from the bush, the forest, the river, the ocean. "Therefore combine—

practise mutual aid! That is the surest means for giving to each and to all the greatest safety, the best guarantee of existence and progress, bodily, intellectual, and moral." That is what Nature teaches us; and that is what all those animals which have attained the highest position in their respective classes have done. That is also what man—the most primitive man—has been doing; and that is why man has reached the position upon which we stand now, as we shall see in the subsequent chapters devoted to mutual aid in human societies.

The immense part played by mutual aid and mutual support in the evolution of the animal world has been briefly analyzed in the preceding chapters. We have now to cast a glance upon the part played by the same agencies in the evolution of mankind. We saw how few are the animal species which live an isolated life, and how numberless are those which live in societies, either for mutual defence, or for hunting and storing up food, or for rearing their offspring, or simply for enjoying life in common. We also saw that, though a good deal of warfare goes on between different classes of animals, or different species, or even different tribes of the same species, peace and mutual support are the rule within the tribe or the species; and that those species which best know how to combine, and to avoid competition, have the best chances of survival and of a further progressive development. They prosper, while the unsociable species decay.

It is evident that it would be quite contrary to all that we know of nature if men were an exception to so general a rule: if a creature so defenceless as man was at his beginnings should have found his protection and his way to progress, not in mutual support, like other animals, but in a reckless competition for personal advantages, with no regard to the interests of the species. To a mind accustomed to the idea of unity in nature, such a proposition appears utterly indefensible. And yet, improbable and unphilosophical as it is, it has never found a lack of supporters. There always were writers who took a pessimistic view of mankind. They knew it, more or less superficially, through their own limited experience; they knew of history what the annalists, al-

---

[4]"One of the most frequent modes in which Natural Selection acts is, by adapting some individuals of a species to a somewhat different mode of life, whereby they are able to seize unappropriated places in Nature" (*Origin of Species,* p. 145)—in other words, to avoid competition.

ways watchful of wars, cruelty, and oppression, told of it, and little more besides; and they concluded that mankind is nothing but a loose aggregation of beings, always ready to fight with each other, and only prevented from so doing by the intervention of some authority.

Hobbes took that position; and while some of his eighteenth-century followers endeavoured to prove that at no epoch of its existence—not even in its most primitive condition—mankind lived in a state of perpetual warfare; that men have been sociable even in "the state of nature," and that want of knowledge, rather than the natural bad inclinations of man, brought humanity to all the horrors of its early historical life,—his idea was, on the contrary, that the so-called "state of nature" was nothing but a permanent fight between individuals, accidentally huddled together by the mere caprice of their bestial existence. True, that science has made some progress since Hobbes's time, and that we have safer ground to stand upon than the speculations of Hobbes or Rousseau. But the Hobbesian philosophy has plenty of admirers still; and we have had of late quite a school of writers who, taking possession of Darwin's terminology rather than of his leading ideas, made of it an argument in favour of Hobbes's views upon primitive man, and even succeeded in giving them a scientific appearance. Huxley, as is known, took the lead of that school, and in a paper written in 1888 he represented primitive men as a sort of tigers or lions, deprived of all ethical conceptions, fighting out the struggle for existence to its bitter end, and living a life of "continual free fight"; to quote his own words—"beyond the limited and temporary relations of the family, the Hobbesian war of each against all was the normal state of existence."[5]

It has been remarked more than once that the chief error of Hobbes, and the eighteenth-century philosophers as well, was to imagine that mankind began its life in the shape of small straggling families, some-

thing like the "limited and temporary" families of the bigger carnivores, while in reality it is now positively known that such was *not* the case. Of course, we have no direct evidence as to the modes of life of the first man-like beings. We are not yet settled even as to the time of their first appearance, geologists being inclined at present to see their traces in the pliocene, or even the miocene, deposits of the Tertiary period. But we have the indirect method which permits us to throw some light even upon that remote antiquity. A most careful investigation into the social institutions of the lowest races has been carried on during the last forty years, and it has revealed among the present institutions of primitive folk some traces of still older institutions which have long disappeared, but nevertheless left unmistakable traces of their previous existence. A whole science devoted to the embryology of human institutions has thus developed in the hands of Bachofen, MacLennan, Morgan, Edwin Tylor, Maine, Post, Kovalevsky, Lubbock, and many others. And that science has established beyond any doubt that mankind did *not* begin its life in the shape of small isolated families.

Far from being a primitive form of organization, the family is a very late product of human evolution. As far as we can go back in the palæo-ethnology of mankind, we find men living in societies—in tribes similar to those of the highest mammals; and an extremely slow and long evolution was required to bring these societies to the gentile, or clan organization, which, in its turn, had to undergo another, also very long evolution, before the first germs of family, polygamous or monogamous, could appear. Societies, bands, or tribes—not families—were thus the primitive form of organization of mankind and its earliest ancestors. That is what ethnology has come to after its painstaking researches. And in so doing it simply came to what might have been foreseen by the zoologist. None of the higher mammals, save a few carnivores and a few undoubtedly-decaying species of apes (orang-outans and gorillas), live in small families, isolatedly straggling in the woods. All others live in societies. And Darwin so well understood that isolately-living apes never could have developed into man-like beings, that he was inclined to consider man

---

[5]*Nineteenth Century,* February 1888, p. 165.

as descended from some comparatively weak *but social species,* like the chimpanzee, rather than from some stronger but unsociable species, like the gorilla.[6] Zoology and palæo-ethnology are thus agreed in considering that the band, not the family, was the earliest form of social life. The first human societies simply were a further development of those societies which constitute the very essence of life of the higher animals.

WAR AND AGGRESSION

Ashley Montagu

TERRITORY AND WAR

"We must face the fact," writes Lorenz, "that militant enthusiasm has evolved from the hackle-raising and chin-protruding communal defense instinct of our prehuman ancestors and that the key stimulus situations which release it still bear the earmarks of this origin."

Robert Ardrey tells us that the "territorial drive, as one ancient, animal foundation for the form of human misconduct known as war, is so obvious as to demand small attention . . . But the drive to defend and maintain territory can be regarded not as a cause but only as a condition of war." "Human warfare comes about only when the defensive instinct of a determined territorial proprietor is challenged by the predatory compulsions of an equally determined territorial neighbor."

"The principal cause of modern warfare," Ardrey informs us, "arises from the failure of an intruding power correctly to estimate the defensive resources of a territorial defender." In other words, if Hitler had known he would lose the war, there would have been no second world war, a claim entirely dis-

proven by the historic facts. To oversimplify the matter greatly, Hitler made war because he was a psychopathic monster, suffering among other things from delusions of grandeur, and not on the basis of an erroneous estimate of the war's outcome. Commenting on this "nursery-floor view" of human affairs, Professor Edmund Leach remarks, "This is the Hobbesian notion that if there were no policemen each of us would immediately set about murdering everyone else in sight, and it is total rubbish."

Niko Tinbergen, in his inaugural address as professor of animal behavior at Oxford University, delivered in February 1968, stated that man has developed similarities to wolves, lions, and hyenas, and that as a social, hunting primate he must originally have been organized on the principle of group territories. Territorialism, Tinbergen believes, is one of our ancestral traits. "In order to understand what makes us go to war," he writes, "we have to recognize that man behaves like a group-territorial species." What causes war, according to Tinbergen, is the upsetting of the balance between aggression and fear, and this upsetting is due to a number of the consequences of cultural evolution. These are: the outpacing of man's limited behavior adjustability by the culturally determined changes in his social environment, the enormous increase in the pressures of population, the advent of long-distance communication, mobility, intergroup contacts, and the exposure to continuous external provocation of aggression. These alone would not explain man's increased tendency to kill his fellow man; such conditions would merely lead to continuous threat behavior. What upsets the balance between aggression and fear is the brainwashing into all-out fighting that our warriors are made to undergo, the use of long-range weapons, and hence, the removal of appeasement and distress signals of opponents which would stop our warriors short of killing. It is these last three factors alone that Tinbergen considers as sufficient to explain how we have become such unhinged killers. Tinbergen believes that Lorenz is right when he claims that the elimination, through education, of the internal urge to fight will turn out to be very difficult, if not impossible.

---

[6]*The Descent of Man,* end of ch. ii. pp. 63 and 64 of the 2nd edition.

Desmond Morris, a student of Tinbergen's, had earlier developed these views of his teacher in his widely read book *The Naked Ape,* and later in *The Human Zoo.* Under natural conditions, Morris points out, the goal of aggression is domination, not destruction, but this goal has become blurred in the case of man "because of the vicious combination of attack remoteness and group co-operativeness." Men fight now to support their comrades rather than to dominate the enemy, "and their inherent susceptibility to direct appeasement is given little chance to express itself. This unfortunate development may yet prove to be our undoing and lead to the rapid extinction of the species."

Lorenz, like Tinbergen and Morris, believes that human cultural evolution has been so rapid that we have not had time to develop those inhibitions which would have served to restrain our aggressive drives. It seems never to have occurred to these writers that possibly humans have never developed such inhibitions because they really have no biologically determined aggressive drives, that the aggression exhibited is largely culturally conditioned, that the only forms of inhibition humans have found it necessary to develop are also cultural, and that as an instinctless creature the human requires no inbuilt biological behavioral controls.

In his book *Human Aggression* Anthony Storr, an English psychiatrist, tells us: "It is obvious that man could never have attained his present dominance, nor even have survived as a species, unless he possessed a large endowment of aggressiveness." Since Dr. Storr uses the terms "aggression" and "aggressiveness" in so many different senses it is difficult to say whether or not he means that humans owe their present dominance, even their survival, to warfare. In any event, he agrees with Lorenz, Tinbergen, and Morris that humans lack strong inhibitions against killing their own species because they are ill-equipped with natural weapons. "If men had tusks or horns they would be less, rather than more, likely to kill one another. The artificial weapon is too cerebral a device for nature to have provided adequate safeguards against it." In passing it may be remarked that nature—to employ Dr. Storr's phrasing—would

most probably have done nothing of the sort, since with the equipment Dr. Storr describes it would have been easy to produce power imbalances completely altering the cost-benefit ratio in regard to aggression. Such aggression could have been very destructive of human groups.

ADAPTABILITY, INHIBITION, AND CONTROL

Lorenz and Ardrey, as we have seen, claim that man has aggressively employed weapons from the very beginning of his attainment of human status, that, in fact, he owes his emergence as a human being to his use of artificial weaponry. That would be a matter of some five million years or longer, a more than sufficient time for "nature" to have provided the necessary safeguards countering the continued use of weapons against his fellow man. When the innate aggressionists speak of man's cultural development having outpaced his limited behavioral adjustability to the environment they forget a most important fact—namely, that man has evolved as the most malleable, flexible, and educable of all creatures for the reason that he has constantly been making those adaptively successful behavioral responses to the challenges of the environment which, under the pressures of natural selection, have enabled him to make himself what he has become. Furthermore, were the function of that organ through which all these changes are principally expressed—the human brain—to be characterized by one word, that word would be "inhibition." The human brain is the organ of inhibition. It is the organ of deliberation and of choice. As Delgado has said, to behave is to choose one pattern among many. The human brain is the organ that permits voluntary rather than biologically predetermined inhibition. What, however, the innate aggressionists have in mind when they speak of inhibition is the biologically determined variety they attribute to other animals in response to appeasement behavior.

I am not convinced that either appeasement behavior or the response to it is innately determined. It seems to me much more likely that in mammals, at any rate, such appeasement behavior is to an appreciable extent learned. But however that may be, a considerable number of human societies have cultivated inhibition of aggressive response in their members. The gatherer-hunters discussed earlier . . . as examples of peoples who have the expression of aggression well under control were the Australian aborigines, the Bushmen of the Kalahari Desert, the Eskimos, the Pygmies of the Ituri forest, the Hadza of Tanzania, the Lepchas of Sikkim, the Birhor of southern India, the Semang of Malaya and the Punan of Borneo (both peoples who until recently were exclusively gatherer-hunters), and the Tasaday of Mindanao who, until their discovery, were exclusively foodgatherers. To these may be added the Comanche and western Shoshoni Indians, the Papago and the Pueblo Indians, the Ifaluk of the Pacific, and a good many other peoples. The Israeli and Arab nations have become formidable military powers not out of militant enthusiasm or a desire to react to the stimulus of threat or attack, but because their governments and citizens have been forced to protect themselves against the artificially created militant enthusiasm of their respective enemies. Arabs as a whole and Israelis in particular despise and deplore any form of violence. But in a world of tension, threat, and violence they have no choice other than to resort to arms. In the case of the Israelis it is their dearly purchased right to existence as a persecuted people rather than territory that they seek to defend. This in no way implies that it is some archaic territorial instinct that fuels their resistance to attack, or that they are unable to inhibit the driving power of such a putative instinct, when they respond to attacks upon them. The Israelis would like nothing better than to live at peace with their neighbors, and to be of help to them, and, indeed, to turn the sword into a plowshare. They would prefer nothing more than to practice total inhibition of all hostile responses to threatening behavior. But their hostile neighbors do not stop at threats, and the Israelis know this, and so they have no alternative other than to be prepared for whatever onslaught from whatever side it may come. Indeed, if one needed an example of inhibition of aggressive behavior in the

face of real threats to a people's continued existence, a more striking example could hardly be found than that presented by the Israelis.

The point I am endeavoring to make is that inbuilt, innate inhibitions against any form of behavior are quite unnecessary in malleable creatures such as humans, who can be trained or train themselves to the most rigorous and consistent forms of inhibition. That this has always been the case may be dependably inferred from the fact that, for example, so powerful a drive as the desire for sexual intercourse has been successfully inhibited by countless numbers of human beings in the face of the most powerful temptations. The Nambikwara, of Brazil, for example, after the birth of a child abstain from sexual intercourse until the child is weaned—that is, until about its third year. This deliberate spacing of children is made as a response to their nomadic existence and the meager resources of the environment. The vows that monks and nuns have taken for generations constitute impressive examples of the power of voluntary inhibition of which human beings are capable.

It is not for lack, then, of the capacity for inhibition that many societies show such a frightful record of killing, for most peoples have developed such inhibitions, but rather that in the matter of sanctioned killing of the enemy in time of war most societies of the civilized world have actively discouraged any inhibitory reservations the individual might have. Indeed, in such societies those are most highly rewarded who behave as if they have no inhibitions about killing the enemy. The hero is he who kills or makes it possible to kill the greatest number of the enemy. Virtually all our institutions, traditions, and public media conspire to elevate and sanctify the uninhibited killing of the enemy as the most noble of moral obligations in the service of one's country. Those who refuse to participate in such killing, either by conscientious objection, or by evading the draft, by desertion, or by any other means, are condemned, jailed, or otherwise penalized. The rewards and encouragements for sanctioned killing are everywhere so constantly emphasized that even were humans to possess innate inhibitions against killing the defeated "enemy," they would be so overlaid with positively reinforced rewards for killing that such inhibitions would hardly have a chance to express themselves. But since humans naturally lack any drive to kill their fellow humans—or to kill anything, for the matter of that—they need no innate inhibition to inhibit what they do not possess. Since, however, they are capable of learning to kill other animals as well as their own kind, such social inhibitions are required in order to limit and control their behavior. Hence, every society has instituted rules and regulations relating to such conduct, and these are gradually absorbed by the growing member of society.

So the answer to the innate aggressionists is that humans have no innate inhibitions against killing, nor do they possess any innate mechanism for responding to appeasement gestures, not because cultural has outrun biological development, but simply because humans have no innate tendencies directed toward killing. And although they are at least as capable of learning to develop such inhibitions as other animals, in many human societies they are encouraged to regard the killing of the enemy as a sacred and patriotic duty. It is absurd, therefore, to cite the lack of inhibition in such societies against sanctioned killing as a reason for that killing, or an explanation of it. Where, as in those human societies in which the prohibitions against intragroup killing become part of the socialization process, human beings do not kill each other. The small proportion who commit such killings are generally abnormal persons who have suffered significant failures of need satisfaction, especially of maternal love, during the socialization process.

THE UNWARLIKE NATURE OF MANY PEOPLES

The fact that modern societies with all their resources must devote so much time and energy to the cultivation and development of aggressive and "warlike virtues" in their citizens suggests that such allegedly instinctual drives toward war do not exist. If wars were due to the arousal of instinctive drives,

nations would not have to resort to conscription and the draft in order to raise armies. Dr. Richard G. van Gelder, chairman of the Department of Mammalogy at the American Museum of Natural History, has remarked in this connection, "There is no more reason to believe that man fights wars because fish or beavers are territorial than to think that man can fly because bats have wings."

Blithely made assumptions, such as Tinbergen's that since humans were originally small hunting primates they must therefore have been organized on the principle of group territories, are typical of the overgeneralizations of the innate aggressionists. We have seen in the preceding chapter that our closest relations, the gorilla and chimpanzee, are nonterritorial.

Dr. Storr tells us that anthropologists report "a few cases of people amongst whom aggressive behavior and war are relatively rare." Most of these people, he goes on to say, "seem to be living under the dominance of neighboring societies who are more aggressive than themselves, and have simply adopted a form of submissive adaptation in the face of perpetual threat."

Again, this is a typical innate aggressionist statement, and there is no truth in it. It has already been made clear that there are many unaggressive peoples, and with very few exceptions these do not live under the domination of anyone but themselves. Nor are the peoples "few" in number who do not engage in war. It may be taken as the general rule that peoples who are not politically organized are also not given to war, and gatherer-hunter societies lack political organization. Such political functions as are carried out in these societies are performed partially or wholly by institutions such as religious or kinship organizations, and these exist primarily for ritual purposes and the regulation of initiation, marriage, and inheritance. As Beals and Hoijer put it, "Bands, tribes, and confederacies appear to represent the most frequent types of political organization found among nonliterate peoples, and it is of interest to note that these political forms are perhaps universal among peoples who have never developed warfare for conquest. The warfare that does exist in such societies is generally a matter of petty raiding for small economic gain or for purposes of vengeance or prestige." The possession of others' territory, political or economic exploitation or subjugation, is never the end of petty raiding—raiding which is in no way comparable with the warfare waged by politically more sophisticated peoples. Warfare, in the sense of an armed attack by one group against another for the purposes of conquest and exploitation, does not occur among any of the gatherer-hunter peoples. Horse-raiding and vengeance parties have been known to occur among American Indians of the Plains. These groups were usually very small, a few men in the case of a vengeance party, eight or ten in the horse-raiding party. In the vengeance party the object was to kill a member of the offender's tribe. Raiding for horses was often sanctioned and encouraged in a vision, and as for the killing of the member of another tribe, the mission was considered completed when a killing occurred.

Most of the peoples of the Arctic, Subarctic, Great Basin, northeast Mexico, and probably Baja California, lacked anything resembling true warfare before European contact. They had no permanent military organization, special fighting regalia, or associated public ceremonies.

Freud, like Dr. Storr, also found it difficult to believe that there existed any unaggressive unwarlike people on this earth. In his famous answer to Einstein's question, "Is there any way of delivering mankind from the menace of war?" he wrote: "In some happy corners of the earth, they say, where nature brings forth abundantly whatever man desires, there flourish races whose lives go gently by, unknowing of aggression and constraint. This I can hardly credit."

Unfortunately, one of the hazards attendant on addiction to one's own theories is that it tends to make one insensible to the facts. The evidence for the existence of such unaggressive peoples was available in Freud's day, had he taken the trouble to seek it out. It is a pity that he did not do so. He preferred, instead, to disbelieve in the existence of such peoples, presumably because he would have found it difficult to reconcile them with his theories. Nev-

ertheless, such peoples exist to this present day, and they can be neither denied nor explained away.

The important fact for us to recognize is that at the level of the non-politically organized gatherer-hunter stage of human development the coefficient of aggressiveness is relatively low, and with the exception of the Andaman Islanders, the Ona and the Yaghan of Tierra del Fuego, and three or four other gatherer-hunting groups, the organized attack of one group against another in anything resembling warfare is a rarity.

The late Verrier Elwin, the distinguished Anglo-Indian anthropologist, in his book on the Baiga, a hunting-cultivating people of the Satpura Mountains in Central India, tells how during the Second World War an old Baiga woman grew concerned for the welfare of Elwin's English countrymen. "This," she said, "is how God equalizes things. Our sons and daughters die young, of hunger or disease or the attacks of wild beasts. The sons and daughters of the English could grow old in comfort and happiness. But God sends madness upon them, and they destroy each other, and so in the end their great knowledge and their religion are useless and we are all the same." Alas.

One day a party of Baigas, anxious to help their English friend's countrymen, came to Elwin with a bundle of bows and arrows which they wanted him to forward to the British government to aid in the war. When Elwin explained to them that modern battles were no longer fought with such weapons they were much perturbed. "But if they use guns," they said, "people will really get killed." The gentle, unaggressive Baiga could be roused to sympathy for the cause of their white friend's people, but they themselves could not imagine anyone seriously attempting to kill anyone. The only aggression they understood was sympathetic magic against some other person.

• • •

Another completely unaggressive, weaponless, unwarlike people are the reindeer-herding Lapps. Their gentleness has been a matter of history for several hundred years, yet, somehow, in the discussion of unaggressive unwarlike peoples they have, in common with a good many other peoples, been overlooked. But everyone who has lived among them has commented enthusiastically on their peaceableness and gentle character. We seem to have a selective capacity for overlooking the obvious. Even though the Lapps are a Christianized people and live in Europe, writers like Dr. Storr appear to be unaware of their existence, for had he known of them one can hardly imagine his writing of them as among those rare unwarlike peoples who live under the domination of neighboring societies who are more aggressive than themselves. The Lapps live under the domination of no one; even though the Finns, the Swedes, and the Norwegians are their neighbors, they maintain the integrity of their own way of life.

It has already been mentioned that the peoples of the Arctic and Subarctic before European contact were, with few exceptions, not given to warfare. From the Aleuts to the Zeshaks there are more than 500 populations in Siberia alone—most of them unstudied. But from what we do know of them aggressive behavior seems to have varied from frequent to rare. Keith Otterbein in his cross-cultural study of war found that of the sample of thirty uncentralized political societies he surveyed six engaged in warfare, i.e., 20 percent.

The existence of so many different peoples at all levels of cultural development, gatherer-hunters, pastoral, agricultural, urban, and industrial, who are or were unwarlike, certainly renders very dubious the claims of the innate aggressionists for the existence of a powerful drive toward war.

The simple fact appears to be that stateless societies do not as a rule indulge in war, and that it usually takes organization of a society into a political state before those conditions that lead to genuine warfare come into play. These conditions may be conflict of interest, material or ideal, actual or traditional, economic objectives, territorial expansion (or its prevention), nationalism, the prevention of ideological conquest imagined or real, and the like.

The existence of nonaggressive and unwarlike peoples does not, of course, disprove the possible existence of predispositions to aggression or warfare. What the existence of such peoples does prove is that aggressive behavior and warfare are not ineluctable accompaniments of the human condition, that do what we will they must and will find expression.

In the light of the facts we have thus far considered it seems hardly necessary to appeal to any innate drive which can be meaningfully attached to such artificial purposes. If some humans behave "very much like a group territorial species," as indeed they sometimes appear to do, it is not due, it may be suggested, to genetics, but to frenetics, to tribalism closely identified with an emotional attachment to a particular territory.

THE CAUSES OF WAR

Modern wars are not made by nations or peoples, nor are they made by men in a state of aggression welling over with an instinct of territory. Wars are usually made by a few individuals in positions of great power, "great leaders," "thoughtful" and "respected" statesmen generally advised by "the best and the brightest," almost always with calm and deliberation, and the pretense if not the conviction of complete moral rectitude. Generals, removed far from the battlefront, give orders for the annihilation of the "enemy" with no more aggressiveness or emotion than when they order the gardener at home to mow the lawn a little closer. The "fighting" man shoots at or drops his bombs on an "enemy" he hardly ever sees, and from whom his emotional disengagement could scarcely be more remote. He is engaged in "hostilities" in which there is no emotional enmity, and in "aggressive" behavior in which there is no feeling of aggression. His behavior is not instinctively but state-directed toward the enemy. Such aggression falls into the class that Professor Karl E. Scheibe of the Department of Psychology at Wesleyan University has called "legitimized aggression." Such "aggression" is justified and legitimized by a collectivity, whether state, political party, a cause, or a self-appointed prophet, and is acted out by individuals for reasons that are self-transcending rather than self-assertive.

Neither physiological processes, instincts, nor learning paradigms are involved in such "aggression," and it is virtually empty of cultural content. Enemies are indicated and the subjects are called upon to show their loyalty. The potentiation of legitimized aggression is like the arming of a weapon, while the assignment of the enemy, of evil, is like pointing it at a specific target. "An order is given and the harm is done."

Jean Rostand, the French biologist, has put it very well. "In war," he said, "man is much more a sheep than a wolf. He follows, he obeys. War is servility, rather—a certain fanaticism and credulity— but not aggressiveness."

Bernard Brodie, professor of political science at the University of California at Los Angeles, has pointed out that war is a rather poor outlet for human aggression or rage. It is too dangerous and too costly, and the enemy is too impersonal and remote. Aggression and rage are more suitably immediately expended on visible, tangible persons close at hand. Furthermore, the intervention of enormous, overorganizing policy-directed bureaucracies, is not very satisfactory for getting any kind of a job done. Aggression seeks immediate relief against a target. War machines succeed in rendering weak or wanting any aggressiveness that may have been present. The truth is—and this is perhaps the greatest of all paradoxes—motivationally, war represents one of the least aggressive forms of man's behavior. A state is not a natural creation but an artificial entity, and it is as such artificial entities that states wage war, with artificial weapons from artificial motives for artificial purposes, conducted for artificial ends.

• • •

The evidence discussed in this book, on the contrary, suggests that up to some twelve thousand years ago war played an insignificant role, if any, in human evolution. Since the Neolithic, when the first village communities came into being, war, if anything, has become increasingly dysgenic and humanly socially destructive. It now threatens the very survival of all life on earth. Plunged as we are into crises before we are aware that there are problems, we cast about for ready solutions. In order to save us

from the final Armageddon the innate aggressionists have offered a variety of dubious solutions.

THE REDIRECTION OF AGGRESSION

• • •

Lorenz tells us that "a simple and effective way of discharging aggression in an innocuous manner is to redirect it at a substitute object." Sport, which Lorenz believes contains elements of contest rendering it akin to serious fighting, has as its main function today the cathartic discharge of aggressive urge. More important, it educates man to conscious and responsible control of his own fighting behavior. Transgressions in sport are quickly punished. The demands for fairness and chivalry, according to Lorenz, must be respected even in the face of the strongest aggression-eliciting stimuli. The most important function of sport, however, is to serve as a safety valve for the dangerous pressures of collective military enthusiasm. So Lorenz recommends sporting contests of every kind between nations as outlets for their collective militant enthusiasm. The suggestion is that such contests would promote personal acquaintance between the people of different nations, and they would therefore unite in enthusiasm for a common cause people who would otherwise have little in common.

Dr. Storr agrees with Lorenz on the efficacy of sports in the redirection of aggression, and goes on to suggest that annual competitions between nations could take the form of competing to see which one could produce the most efficient mental hospital, the safest car, the best-designed house for a worker, and so on, through an endless range of possibilities.

The idea that competitive sports can serve to deflect aggression into more useful and less damaging channels than warfare is subject to testing. If there is any truth in the idea then societies that are peaceful should indulge, according to the Drive Discharge theory, in a good many competitive sports which serve to drain off the assumed otherwise dangerous aggression. Conversely, warlike societies should be lacking in such competitive sports. Societies tend to be internally consistent in their attitudes and behaviors manifested in different activities. This being so we would expect to find, according to the Culture Pattern Model (that aggressive behavior is primarily learned), that combative sports are more likely to occur in warlike societies than in peaceful ones. Rather than alternatives to war, such combative sports would represent the embodiments of the same theme or outlook on war. These possibilities have been investigated by Dr. Richard D. Sipes of the Department of Anthropology of the State University of New York at Buffalo. In his study entitled "War, Sports and Aggression: An Empirical Test of Two Rival Theories," Dr. Sipes used two test strategies: a cross-cultural correlation study and a developmental (diachronic) case study of the United States. A careful statistical analysis of 130 different societies revealed that, in the cross-cultural study, there were only four exceptions to the rule "that where we find warlike behavior we typically find combative sports and where war is relatively rare combative sports tend to be absent." The hypothesis is, therefore, refuted that combative sports constitute alternatives to war as discharge channels of accumulated aggressive tension. "It casts strong doubt on the idea that there is such a thing as accumulable aggressive tension . . . It clearly supports the validity of the Culture Pattern Model (that aggressive behavior is primarily learned), and as clearly tends to discredit the Drive Discharge Model," namely, that aggressive sports tend to reduce aggressive tension.

In the years since the turn of the century the United States has been engaged in 28 military actions, an average of 1 every 2.7 years. According to innate aggressionist theory, the combative sports are more likely and the noncombative sports less likely to discharge accumulated tension successfully. If this were, in fact, the case we should, according to the Drive Discharge theory, expect an inverse relationship to be found between combative sports (hunting and football) and military activity, and no, or a smaller, inverse relationship between noncombative (betting and baseball) sports and military activity. On the other hand, the Culture Pattern Model would lead one to expect either no or a direct relationship between combative sports and military activity, and no or a smaller direct relationship between noncombative and military activity. Dr. Sipes's findings tended strongly to support the Culture Pattern Model. "We

need not postulate," Dr. Sipes concludes, "an innate propensity in the individual toward violent aggression and killing nor speculate on the mechanics involved in natural selection for warlike or combative killing behavior in humans when it is not found in animals. The tendency for a group of men to engage in war can be more parsimoniously and satisfactorily explained as being carried in their society's culture than in the individual men's genes."

Dr. Sipes also draws attention to the fact that the prevalence of combative sports throughout a large part of the world does not require resort to individual hunting patterns, aggression, the need to excel, or the like. Such sports form components of a combative culture theme, integral parts of a combative culture pattern, and wherever one finds a warlike society there one will find combative sports. The internal consistencies shown in the behavioral patterns of such societies render cultural explanations of these behaviors rather more cogent than the appeal to "innate" propensities. There is much other evidence which shows that sporting contests, far from siphoning off or deflecting or sublimating aggression, tend, in fact, to reinforce it and even to exacerbate it.

Even though the borders between Canada and the United States remain open and undefended, Canadian and U.S. hockey teams when in competition seldom manage to avoid getting into a fight. "War on ice," as ice hockey has come to be called, is expected by the spectators to involve fighting. When, in Czechoslovakia, in March 1969 the Czechs defeated the Russians in hockey, the supporters of the opposing teams battled one another. Such conflicts have occurred with increasing frequency and violence in recent years in England, Mexico, Uruguay, Italy, Chile, and a number of other countries. In 1964, in Peru, a referee disallowed a goal during an Olympic soccer match, whereupon the supporters of the penalized team rioted, and before the melee was over a hundred people were dead and 500 injured, while numerous buildings were destroyed. During a soccer match between El Salvador and Honduras in 1969 each side claimed the other had used unfair tactics. This led not only to a riot but to a three-day war between the two nations, during which 1,000 people died. Fights at competitions between Blacks and Whites during high school sports in the United States do not speak highly for sports as a means of reducing or deflecting aggressive tensions. Nor, unfortunately, does the violence which has occurred at sporting events in many other countries tend to support the notion that sports offer any kind of a solution to the problem of individual, national, or international aggression. Even when a team wins its supporters are often so aroused they seem to be only too eager to exhibit their pleasure in responding to the aggressive behavior of the supporters of the other side. Crook has pointed out that the wanton destruction of train interiors by British football fans on their way to a game played away from "home" would suggest that the whole context of such games does not contribute to a lessening of tension. And certainly it is becoming increasingly evident that the organization of major sporting events can no longer take place without the institution of effective rules of management and crowd control.

Aggressive behavior at sporting events, if anything, often seems to elicit similar behavior from the spectators. This is especially frequently seen at boxing and wrestling matches, when many of the spectators appear to be not merely vicariously but actively engaged in worsting their man's opponent. There are a great many studies in this particular connection which show that it is not so much tension reduction that is achieved on these occasions as reinforcement of aggression. Those who find this kind of "sporting" aggression rewarding are not likely to undergo any long-lasting reduction in their aggression, but will continue to be at least as aggressive as they ever were, if their aggression is not, in fact, augmented.

• • •

There is, as we have seen, good reason to believe that competitive sports often evoke and worsen the aggressiveness of the competitors. This is as true of children as it is of adults. The evidence from many studies both on children and adults shows that far from producing a cathartic reduction of aggression, the expression of aggressive behavior tends either to maintain or increase it. Surely, if one wishes to train children in cooperation it is more sensible to do so in games that are cooperative rather than those that

are competitive. Indeed, the National Commission on the Causes and Prevention of Violence deplored the reigning competitive attitudes of winning at all costs, and emphasized the desirability of cultivating and producing a graceful loser. There are few among us who seem to understand that the true winner in a race is often the one who comes in last.

What seems evident is that if it is assumed that sports constitute proper occasions for the expenditure of aggression, then they will only serve to encourage and perpetuate aggression, rather than diminish it or result in its redirection.

Recently Lorenz has somewhat modified his views, and now expresses "strong doubts whether watching aggressive behavior even in the guise of sport has any cathartic effect at all." His doubts, however, do not appear to extend to active participation in sports.

It appears, then, that the recommendations of the innate aggressionists for the control of aggression are unsound and impracticable on several counts. First, aggressive behavior is not ineradicable; since its expression is learned, no matter how firmly based the "wiring" of that behavior may be in the brain, it can be prevented or controlled by not being taught, and untaught when learned. Second, whatever aggression is, it is not an energy or a fluid which tends to overflow after it has reached a certain level or pressure, and third, therefore, it cannot be siphoned off or sublimated in activities such as sports or some other display of energetics. If, then, we are to find a solution to the problem of human aggression, it must lie rather in careful and detailed research into the conditions of human experience that influence the development or nondevelopment of aggressive behavior.

THERE IS NO HUMAN NATURE

Jean-Paul Sartre

What is meant by the term *existentialism?*

Most people who use the word would be rather embarrassed if they had to explain it, since, now that the word is all the rage, even the work of a musician or painter is being called existentialist. A gossip columnist in *Clartés* signs himself *The Existentialist,* so that by this time the word has been so stretched and has taken on so broad a meaning, that it no longer means anything at all. It seems that for want of an advance-guard doctrine analogous to surrealism, the kind of people who are eager for scandal and flurry turn to this philosophy which in other respects does not at all serve their purposes in this sphere.

Actually, it is the least scandalous, the most austere of doctrines. It is intended strictly for specialists and philosophers. Yet it can be defined easily. What complicates matters is that there are two kinds of existentialist; first, those who are Christian, among whom I would include Jaspers and Gabriel Marcel, both Catholic; and on the other hand the atheistic existentialists, among whom I class Heidegger, and then the French existentialists and myself. What they have in common is that they think that existence precedes essence, or, if you prefer, that subjectivity must be the starting point.

Just what does that mean? Let us consider some object that is manufactured, for example, a book or a paper-cutter: here is an object which has been made by an artisan whose inspiration came from a concept. He referred to the concept of what a paper-cutter is and likewise to a known method of production, which is part of the concept, something which is, by and large, a routine. Thus, the paper-cutter is at once an object produced in a certain way and, on the other hand, one having a specific use; and one can not postulate a man who produces a paper-cutter but does not know what it is used for. Therefore, let us say that, for the paper-cutter, essence—that is, the ensemble of both the production routines and the properties which enable it to be both produced and defined—precedes existence. Thus, the presence of the paper-cutter or book in front of me is determined. Therefore, we have here a technical view of the world whereby it can be said that production precedes existence.

When we conceive God as the Creator, He is generally thought of as a superior sort of artisan. Whatever doctrine we may be considering, whether one like that of Descartes or that of Leibnitz, we al-

ways grant that will more or less follows understanding or, at the very least, accompanies it, and that when God creates He knows exactly what He is creating. Thus, the concept of man in the mind of God is comparable to the concept of paper-cutter in the mind of the manufacturer, and, following certain techniques and a conception, God produces man, just as the artisan, following a definition and a technique, makes a paper-cutter. Thus, the individual man is the realization of a certain concept in the divine intelligence.

In the eighteenth century, the atheism of the *philosophes*[1] discarded the idea of God, but not so much for the notion that essence precedes existence. To a certain extent, this idea is found everywhere; we find it in Diderot, in Voltaire, and even in Kant. Man has a human nature; this human nature, which is the concept of the human, is found in all men, which means that each man is a particular example of a universal concept, man. In Kant, the result of this universality is that the wild-man, the natural man, as well as the bourgeois, are circumscribed by the same definition and have the same basic qualities. Thus, here too the essence of man precedes the historical existence that we find in nature.

Atheistic existentialism, which I represent, is more coherent. It states that if God does not exist, there is at least one being in whom existence precedes essence, a being who exists before he can be defined by any concept, and that this being is man, or, as Heidegger[2] says, human reality. What is meant here by saying that existence precedes essence? It means that, first of all, man exists, turns up, appears on the scene, and, only afterwards, defines himself. If man, as the existentialist conceives him, is indefinable, it is because at first he is nothing. Only afterward will he be something, and he himself will

---

[1]The term refers to the French Enlightenment philosophers of the eighteenth century, including Voltaire (1694–1778), Jean Jacques Rousseau (1712–1778), and Denis Diderot (1713–1784). These philosophers extolled reason against religion and superstition and generally advocated social and political reform (Eds.).

[2]Martin Heidegger (1889–1976) was a German existentialist philosopher whose major work *Being and Time* greatly influenced Sartre's philosophical development (Eds.).

have made what he will be. Thus, there is no human nature, since there is no God to conceive it. Not only is man what he conceives himself to be, but he is also only what he wills himself to be after this thrust toward existence.

Man is nothing else but what he makes of himself. Such is the first principle of existentialism. It is also what is called subjectivity, the name we are labeled with when charges are brought against us. But what do we mean by this, if not that man has a greater dignity than a stone or table? For we mean that man first exists, that is, that man first of all is the being who hurls himself toward a future and who is conscious of imagining himself as being in the future. Man is at the start a plan which is aware of itself, rather than a patch of moss, a piece of garbage, or a cauliflower; nothing exists prior to this plan; there is nothing in heaven; man will be what he will have planned to be. Not what he will want to be. Because by the word "will" we generally mean a conscious decision, which is subsequent to what we have already made of ourselves. I may want to belong to a political party, write a book, get married; but all that is only a manifestation of an earlier, more spontaneous choice that is called "will." But if existence really does precede essence, man is responsible for what he is. Thus, existentialism's first move is to make every man aware of what he is and to make the full responsibility of his existence rest on him. And when we say that a man is responsible for himself, we do not only mean that he is responsible for his own individuality, but that he is responsible for all men.

The word subjectivism has two meanings, and our opponents play on the two. Subjectivism means, on the one hand, that an individual chooses and makes himself; and, on the other, that it is impossible for man to transcend human subjectivity. The second of these is the essential meaning of existentialism. When we say that man chooses his own self, we mean that every one of us does likewise; but we also mean by that that in making this choice he also chooses all men. In fact, in creating the man that we want to be, there is not a single one of our acts which does not at the same time create

an image of man as we think he ought to be. To choose to be this or that is to affirm at the same time the value of what we choose, because we can never choose evil. We always choose the good, and nothing can be good for us without being good for all.

If, on the other hand, existence precedes essence, and if we grant that we exist and fashion our image at one and the same time, the image is valid for everybody and for our whole age. Thus, our responsibility is much greater than we might have supposed, because it involves all mankind. If I am a workingman and choose to join a Christian trade-union rather than be a communist, and if by being a member I want to show that the best thing for man is resignation, that the kingdom of man is not of this world, I am not only involving my own case—I want to be resigned for everyone. As a result, my action has involved all humanity. To take a more individual matter, if I want to marry, to have children; even if this marriage depends solely on my own circumstances or passion or wish, I am involving all humanity in monogamy and not merely myself. Therefore, I am responsible for myself and for everyone else. I am creating a certain image of man of my own choosing. In choosing myself, I choose man.

This helps us understand what the actual content is of such rather grandiloquent words as anguish, forlornness, despair. As you will see, it's all quite simple.

First, what is meant by anguish? The existentialists say at once that man is anguish. What that means is this: the man who involves himself and who realizes that he is not only the person he chooses to be, but also a lawmaker who is, at the same time, choosing all mankind as well as himself, can not help escape the feeling of his total and deep responsibility. Of course, there are many people who are not anxious; but we claim that they are hiding their anxiety, that they are fleeing from it. Certainly, many people believe that when they do something, they themselves are the only ones involved, and when someone says to them, "What if everyone acted that way?" they shrug their shoulders and answer, "Everyone doesn't act that way." But really, one should always ask himself, "What would happen if everybody looked at things that way?" There is no escaping this disturbing thought except by a kind of double-dealing. A man who lies and makes excuses for himself by saying "not everybody does that," is someone with an uneasy conscience, because the act of lying implies that a universal value is conferred upon the lie.

Anguish is evident even when it conceals itself. This is the anguish that Kierkegaard[3] called the anguish of Abraham. You know the story: an angel has ordered Abraham to sacrifice his son; if it really were an angel who has come and said, "You are Abraham, you shall sacrifice your son," everything would be all right. But everyone might first wonder, "Is it really an angel, and am I really Abraham? What proof do I have?"

There was a madwoman who had hallucinations; someone used to speak to her on the telephone and give her orders. Her doctor asked her, "Who is it who talks to you?" She answered, "He says it's God." What proof did she really have that it was God? If an angel comes to me, what proof is there that it's an angel? And if I hear voices, what proof is there that they come from heaven and not from hell, or from the subconscious, or a pathological condition? What proves that they are addressed to me? What proof is there that I have been appointed to impose my choice and my conception of man on humanity? I'll never find any proof or sign to convince me of that. If a voice addresses me, it is always for me to decide that this is the angel's voice; if I consider that such an act is a good one, it is I who will choose to say that it is good rather than bad.

Now, I'm not being singled out as an Abraham, and yet at every moment I'm obliged to perform exemplary acts. For every man, everything happens as if all mankind had its eyes fixed on him and were guiding itself by what he does. And every man ought to say to himself, "Am I really the kind of man who has the right to act in such a way that humanity might guide itself by my actions?" And if he does not say that to himself, he is masking his anguish.

There is no question here of the kind of anguish which would lead to quietism, to inaction. It is a matter of a simple sort of anguish that anybody who has had responsibilities is familiar with. For example, when a military officer takes the responsibility for an attack and sends a certain number of men to death, he chooses to do so, and in the main he alone makes the choice. Doubtless, orders come from above, but they are too broad; he interprets them, and on this interpretation depend the lives of ten or fourteen or twenty men. In making a decision he can not help having a certain anguish. All leaders know this anguish. That doesn't keep them from acting; on the contrary, it is the very condition of their action. For it implies that they envisage a number of possibilities, and when they choose one, they realize that it has value only because it is chosen. We shall see that this kind of anguish, which is the kind that existentialism describes, is explained, in addition, by a direct responsibility to the other men whom it involves. It is not a curtain separating us from action, but is part of action itself.

When we speak of forlornness, a term Heidegger was fond of, we mean only that God did not exist and that we have to face all the consequences of this. The existentialist is strongly opposed to a certain kind of secular ethics which would like to abolish God with the least possible expense. About 1880, some French teachers tried to set up a secular ethics which went something like this: God is a useless and costly hypothesis; we are discarding it; but, meanwhile, in order for there to be an ethics, a society, a civilization, it is essential that certain values be taken seriously and that they be considered as having an *a priori*[4] existence. It must be obligatory, *a priori,* to be honest, not to lie, not to beat your wife, to have children, etc., etc. So we're going to try a little device which will make it possible to show that values exist all the same, inscribed in a heaven of

---

[3]Soren Kierkegaard (1813–1855) was a Danish existentialist philosopher and religious thinker (Eds.).

---

[4]*a priori* is a Latin phrase meaning, literally, "from what comes before." In philosophy, it refers to something which precedes or is independent of sensory experience. Thus, what is *a priori* is true, valid, or exists by necessity (Eds.).

ideas, though otherwise God does not exist. In other words—and this, I believe, is the tendency of everything called reformism in France—nothing will be changed if God does not exist. We shall find ourselves with the same norms of honesty, progress, and humanism, and we shall have made of God an outdated hypothesis which will peacefully die off by itself.

The existentialist, on the contrary, thinks it very distressing that God does not exist, because all possibility of finding values in a heaven of ideas disappears along with Him; there can no longer be an *a priori* Good, since there is no infinite and perfect consciousness to think it. Nowhere is it written that the Good exists, that we must be honest, that we must not lie; because the fact is we are on a plane where there are only men. Dostoievsky said, "If God didn't exist, everything would be possible." That is the very starting point of existentialism. Indeed, everything is permissible if God does not exist, and as a result man is forlorn, because neither within him nor without does he find anything to cling to. He can't start making excuses for himself.

If existence really does precede essence, there is no explaining things away by reference to a fixed and given human nature. In other words, there is no determinism, man is free, man is freedom. On the other hand, if God does not exist, we find no values or commands to turn to which legitimize our conduct. So, in the bright realm of values, we have no excuse behind us, nor justification before us. We are alone, with no excuses.

That is the idea I shall try to convey when I say that man is condemned to be free. Condemned, because he did not create himself, yet, in other respects is free; because, once thrown into the world, he is responsible for everything he does. The existentialist does not believe in the power of passion. He will never agree that a sweeping passion is a ravaging torrent which fatally leads a man to certain acts and is therefore an excuse. He thinks that man is responsible for his passion.

The existentialist does not think that man is going to help himself by finding in the world some omen by which to orient himself. Because he thinks that man will interpret the omen to suit himself. Therefore, he thinks that man, with no support and no aid, is condemned every moment to invent man. Ponge, in a very fine article, has said, "Man is the future of man." That's exactly it. But if it is taken to mean that this future is recorded in heaven, that God sees it, then it is false, because it would really no longer be a future. If it is taken to mean that, whatever a man may be, there is a future to be forged, a virgin future before him, then this remark is sound. But then we are forlorn.

To give you an example which will enable you to understand forlornness better, I shall cite the case of one of my students who came to see me under the following circumstances: his father was on bad terms with his mother, and, moreover, was inclined to be a collaborationist; his older brother had been killed in the German offensive of 1940, and the young man, with somewhat immature but generous feelings, wanted to avenge him. His mother lived alone with him, very much upset by the half-treason of her husband and the death of her older son; the boy was her only consolation.

The boy was faced with the choice of leaving for England and joining the Free French Forces—that is, leaving his mother behind—or remaining with his mother and helping her to carry on. He was fully aware that the woman lived only for him and that his going-off—and perhaps his death—would plunge her into despair. He was also aware that every act that he did for his mother's sake was a sure thing, in the sense that it was helping her to carry on, whereas every effort he made toward going off and fighting was an uncertain move which might run aground and prove completely useless; for example, on his way to England he might, while passing through Spain, be detained indefinitely in a Spanish camp; he might reach England or Algiers and be stuck in an office at a desk job. As a result, he was faced with two very different kinds of action: one, concrete, immediate, but concerning only one individual; the other concerned an incomparably vaster group, a national collectivity, but for that very reason was dubious, and might be interrupted en route. And, at the same time, he was wavering between two kinds of ethics. On the one hand, an ethics of sympathy, of personal devotion; on the other, a broader ethics, but one whose efficacy was more dubious. He had to choose between the two.

Who could help him choose? Christian doctrine? No. Christian doctrine says, "Be charitable, love your neighbor, take the more rugged path, etc., etc." But which is the more rugged path? Whom should he love as a brother? The fighting man or his mother? Which does the greater good, the vague act of fighting in a group, or the concrete one of helping a particular human being to go on living? Who can decide *a priori?* Nobody. No book of ethics can tell him. The Kantian ethics says, "Never treat any person as a means, but as an end." Very well, if I stay with my mother, I'll treat her as an end and not as a means; but by virtue of this very fact, I'm running the risk of treating the people around me who are fighting, as means; and, conversely, if I go to join those who are fighting, I'll be treating them as an end, and, by doing that, I run the risk of treating my mother as a means.

If values are vague, and if they are always too broad for the concrete and specific case that we are considering, the only thing left for us is to trust our instincts. That's what this young man tried to do; and when I saw him, he said, "In the end, feeling is what counts. I ought to choose whichever pushes me in one direction. If I feel that I love my mother enough to sacrifice everything else for her—my desire for vengeance, for action, for adventure—then I'll stay with her. If, on the contrary, I feel that my love for my mother isn't enough, I'll leave."

But how is the value of a feeling determined? What gives his feeling for his mother value? Precisely the fact that he remained with her. I may say that I like so-and-so well enough to sacrifice a certain amount of money for him, but I may say so only if I've done it. I may say "I love my mother well enough to remain with her" if I have remained with her. The only way to determine the value of this affection is, precisely, to perform an act which confirms and defines. But, since I require this affection to justify my act, I find myself caught in a vicious circle.

On the other hand, Gide has well said that a mock feeling and a true feeling are almost indistinguishable; to decide that I love my mother and will remain with her, or to remain with her by putting on an act, amount somewhat to the same thing. In other words, the feeling is formed by the acts one performs; so, I can not refer to it in order to act upon it. Which means that I can neither seek within myself the true condition that will impel me to act, nor apply to a system of ethics for concepts which will permit me to act. You will say, "At least, he did go to a teacher for advice." But if you seek advice from a priest, for example, you have chosen this priest; you already knew, more or less, just about what advice he was going to give you. In other words, choosing your adviser is involving yourself. The proof of this is that if you are a Christian, you will say, "Consult a priest." But some priests are collaborating, some are just marking time, some are resisting. Which to choose? If the young man chooses a priest who is resisting or collaborating, he has already decided on the kind of advice he's going to get. Therefore, in coming to see me he knew the answer I was going to give him, and I had only one answer to give: "You're free, choose, that is, invent." No general ethics can show you what is to be done; there are no omens in the world. The Catholics will reply, "But there are." Granted—but, in any case, I myself choose the meaning they have.

When I was a prisoner, I knew a rather remarkable young man who was a Jesuit. He had entered the Jesuit order in the following way: he had had a number of very bad breaks; in childhood, his father died, leaving him in poverty, and he was a scholarship student at a religious institution where he was constantly made to feel that he was being kept out of charity; then, he failed to get any of the honors and distinctions that children like; later on, at about eighteen, he bungled a love affair; finally, at twenty-two, he failed in military training, a childish enough matter, but it was the last straw.

This young fellow might well have felt that he had botched everything. It was a sign of something, but of what? He might have taken refuge in bitterness or despair. But he very wisely looked upon all this as a sign that he was not made for secular triumphs, and that only the triumphs of religion, holiness, and faith were open to him. He saw the hand of God in all this, and so he entered the order. Who can help seeing that he alone decided what the sign meant?

Some other interpretation might have been drawn from this series of setbacks; for example, that he might have done better to turn carpenter or revolutionist. Therefore, he is fully responsible for the interpretation. Forlornness implies that we ourselves choose our being. Forlornness and anguish go together.

As for despair, the term has a very simple meaning. It means that we shall confine ourselves to reckoning only with what depends upon our will, or on the ensemble of probabilities which make our action possible. When we want something, we always have to reckon with probabilities. I may be counting on the arrival of a friend. The friend is coming by rail or street-car; this supposes that the train will arrive on schedule, or that the street-car will not jump the track. I am left in the realm of possibility; but possibilities are to be reckoned with only to the point where my action comports with the ensemble of these possibilities, and no further. The moment the possibilities I am considering are not rigorously involved by my action, I ought to disengage myself from them, because no God, no scheme, can adapt the world and its possibilities to my will. When Descartes said, "Conquer your self rather than the world," he meant essentially the same thing.

The Marxists to whom I have spoken reply, "You can rely on the support of others in your action, which obviously has certain limits because you're not going to live forever. That means: rely on both what others are doing elsewhere to help you, in China, in Russia, and what they will do later on, after your death, to carry on the action and lead it to its fulfillment, which will be the revolution. You even *have* to rely upon that, otherwise you're immoral." I reply at once that I will always rely on fellow-fighters insofar as these comrades are involved with me in a common struggle, in the unity of a party or a group in which I can more or less make my weight felt; that is, one whose ranks I am

in as a fighter and whose movements I am aware of at every moment. In such a situation, relying on the unity and will of the party is exactly like counting on the fact that the train will arrive on time or that the car won't jump the track. But, given that man is free and that there is no human nature for me to depend on, I can not count on men whom I do not know by relying on human goodness or man's concern for the good of society. I don't know what will become of the Russian revolution; I may make an example of it to the extent that at the present time it is apparent that the proletariat plays a part in Russia that it plays in no other nation. But I can't swear that this will inevitably lead to a triumph of the proletariat. I've got to limit myself to what I see.

Given that men are free and that tomorrow they will freely decide what man will be, I can not be sure that, after my death, fellow-fighters will carry on my work to bring it to its maximum perfection. Tomorrow, after my death, some men may decide to set up Fascism, and the others may be cowardly and muddled enough to let them do it. Fascism will then be the human reality, so much the worse for us.

Actually, things will be as man will have decided they are to be. Does that mean that I should abandon myself to quietism? No. First, I should involve myself; then, act on the old saw, "Nothing ventured, nothing gained." Nor does it mean that I shouldn't belong to a party, but rather that I shall have no illusions and shall do what I can. For example, suppose I ask myself, "Will socialization, as such, ever come about?" I know nothing about it. All I know is that I'm going to do everything in my power to bring it about. Beyond that, I can't count on anything. Quietism is the attitude of people who say, "Let others do what I can't do." The doctrine I am presenting is the very opposite of quietism, since it declares, "There is no reality except in action." Moreover, it goes further, since it adds, "Man is nothing else than his plan; he exists only to the extent that he fulfills himself; he is therefore nothing else than the ensemble of his acts, nothing else than his life."

According to this, we can understand why our doctrine horrifies certain people. Because often the only way they can bear their wretchedness is to think, "Circumstances have been against me. What I've been and done doesn't show my true worth. To be sure, I've had no great love, no great friendship, but that's because I haven't met a man or woman who was worthy. The books I've written haven't been very good because I haven't had the proper leisure. I haven't had children to devote myself to because I didn't find a man with whom I could have spent my life. So there remains within me, unused and quite viable, a host of propensities, inclinations, possibilities, that one wouldn't guess from the mere series of things I've done."

Now, for the existentialist there is really no love other than one which manifests itself in a person's being in love. There is no genius other than one which is expressed in works of art; the genius of Proust[5] is the sum of Proust's works; the genius of Racine is his series of tragedies. Outside of that, there is nothing. Why say that Racine could have written another tragedy, when he didn't write it? A man is involved in life, leaves his impress on it, and outside of that there is nothing. To be sure, this may seem a harsh thought to someone whose life hasn't been a success. But, on the other hand, it prompts people to understand that reality alone is what counts, that dreams, expectations, and hopes warrant no more than to define a man as a disappointed dream, as miscarried hopes, as vain expectations. In other words, to define him negatively and not positively. However, when we say, "You are nothing else than your life," that does not imply that the artist will be judged solely on the basis of his works of art; a thousand other things will contribute toward summing him up. What we mean is that a man is nothing else than a series of undertakings, that he is the sum, the organization, the ensemble of the relationships which make up these undertakings.

• • •

From these few reflections it is evident that nothing is more unjust than the objections that have been raised against us. Existentialism is nothing else than an attempt to draw all the consequences of a coherent atheistic position. It isn't trying to plunge man into despair at all. But if one calls every attitude of unbelief despair, like the Christians, then the word is not being used in its original sense. Existentialism isn't so atheistic that it wears itself out showing that God doesn't exist. Rather, it declares that even if God did exist, that would change nothing. There you've got our point of view. Not that we believe that God exists, but we think that the problem of His existence is not the issue. In this sense existentialism is optimistic, a doctrine of action, and it is plain dishonesty for Christians to make no distinction between their own despair and ours and then to call us despairing.

MAN WITHOUT THEORY

Francisco Miró Quesada

Man cannot live without theory, for he is the theoretical animal par excellence. Ancient wisdom characterized him as "rational animal," because theories were formulated by reason. No longer does anyone hold that there are theoretical men and practical men, men dedicated to thought and others dedicated to action. All men are theoretical, only some know it and are distinguished by their determination to develop theoretical perspectives, whereas others are satisfied to live submerged in the theory and to use it to obtain pressing needs. Our life, however, is surrounded by theory. From our confidence in the firmness of the earth we walk on, all is the fruit of theory, of scientific thought, of our capacity to think about events and to interpret them. Thanks to theory we are able to confront the world, to have a world, to predict events, manage them, direct them, and take advantage of them. It is because there have been men dedicated to discovering how the world is that the "practical men" can dedicate themselves to

---

[5]Marcel Proust (1871–1922) was a French novelist most famous for his *Remembrance of Things Past* (Eds.).

modifying it through technology, a late and secondary product of theory.

Theory, the knowledge of things and events, emerges as a necessity in man's defense against the assault of the world. Theory is born as a function of man and for man to find a perspective within the endless labyrinth of events as he orders his world. He structures the world so he can reach his self-proposed goals. He must know himself to know what he pursues and what the true relationships to his world are. This is to say that every theory concerning the world, concerning the things that surround him, necessarily implies a theory concerning himself, for to think about the world is to think about one's self, since the world is only the terminus of action. Furthermore, it is to think that thought has particular possibilities, that it is capable of dominating specified situations. It is to think about what is going to be done with the knowledge acquired about the world, and to think about one's own destiny.

However, at this point by their very nature things begin to be quite different, because the reality of man is infinitely more complex than that of the world. To theorize about the world is much easier than to theorize about man. In the surrounding world, simple patterns are more or less common, like the successions of various cyclical states such as day and night, tides, and movements of the stars. Given this simplicity and regularity, all theory can be verified, elaborate as it may be. One need only deduce the various consequences implicit in the presuppositions. As long as the consequences coincide with the facts one can continue to accept the theory as true, but if the facts contradict it, then one will have to reject, modify, or adapt the theory; otherwise it becomes untenable. This process of verification is the foundation of all possible knowledge of realities and is what has permitted man to evolve from the most primitive and infantile theories to the present elaborate systems of physics, astronomy, and biology.

The more complicated a segment of reality, the more difficult it is to elaborate a theory that will account for it and allow man to know it. It is more probable , also, that one will find a theoretical consequence that does not coincide with the facts and

will make the theory fail. However, by means of corrections and reelaborations, it is always possible to improve it and to adapt it to the new demands of the facts, achieving thereby a knowledge of nature that is more or less uniform and progressive. When we are concerned with human beings, however, this procedure is practically impossible. Because man's complexity is such and the intertwining of the facts that characterize him is so great that to elaborate a reasonably acceptable theory concerning his nature, it becomes necessary to rely on a dense skein of concepts and hypotheses. From this theoretical mire an endless series of consequences unfold that must be correlated with the facts about man. And in the long run the facts ruin the theory because, unfortunately, some and often many of the consequences of the theory contradict the facts. In addition to this insuperable difficulty, there is another that is perhaps even greater, the phenomenon of freedom. Human freedom is not a theory, it is a fact—the fact of the unpredictability of our actions. Whereas in nature the smooth, simple recurrences of phenomena permit astounding predictions, the possibility of man making decisions that go counter to what is foreseen makes it impossible to achieve rigorous knowledge of what we are. In principle, every man can show any theory concerning man to be inadequate. All he has to do is act so as to contradict what the theory permits one to predict concerning his actions. In some cases, of course, the predictions are fulfilled, but it is on a superficial or pathological level. Ultimately, no one can predict anything concerning what a human being will do. Yet, the essence of theory consists in deriving consequences, that is, making predictions.

However, if formulating theories about man is such a difficult and demanding task, all our other theories concerning the world and life also incur a subtle, grave danger. For, as we have seen, to formulate a theory concerning nature one must presuppose something about man himself, about his capacity to formulate theories and about life's purpose that is his lot to pursue. Every radical change in the theory of man leads inevitably to change in our way of seeing the world, and this produces insecurity and distress. For, to change a theory concerning the world forces us to recognize that what we believed is not so certain, that the earth we walk on has suddenly become moving sand in which we may sink. Further, to have to change our perspective on ourselves forces us to recognize that we were in error, that what we believed was eternally true about our possibilities and destiny has been seriously questioned. Suddenly, as with the psychopath, we are strangers to ourselves, we no longer recognize ourselves. Nothing is more terrifying to man than to discover that he is not what he believed he was. For years, centuries, perhaps even millennia, he struggled for security only to have it dissolved in a gust of mysterious theoretical wind. Hence the furor, the resentment, and the hatred toward those who dare attack this security, for without it we are not able to live. . . .

The process in which theories concerning man dissolve is inflexible and its successive stages are easily describable. The first step is the general elaboration of the theory. In a majority of cultures this step has been simple and spontaneous. In the modern world it is conscious and has scientific and philosophical pretensions, as for example in Nazism, fascism, and Marxism. In all cases, however, the point of departure is the same: a tangled mass of extremely complicated hypotheses that are taken to be the sublime, incontrovertible, and definitive truth. For some people this truth is of a divine origin and in some cases these hypotheses seem quite simple when first proposed. . . .

In order to understand these issues, it is important to have a clear concept of what a theory is, especially of the relationship between a theory and its logical implications. As we have seen, a theory is a series of hypotheses about some aspect of reality, and it may be restricted or broad and encompassing. Once the hypotheses have been formulated a series of consequences can be derived logically. The fundamental aspect of this logical derivability is the immensity of its range, since, beginning with a small number of hypotheses one can derive innumerable consequences, so many, in fact, that they are practically infinite. This is the main characteristic of any

theory whatever, constituting its greatness as well as its limitation, its usefulness as well as its terrible danger. Through the power of derivation, atomic energy has been developed, so that it will be possible within a few years to improve the world in unforeseen ways or to destroy it by pressing a button. Through this strange and almost magical power we have made airplanes fly, we have burned witches, invented the telescope and the microscope, committed atrocious genocides, saved millions of lives, and made martyrs of millions of human beings.

A theory's power of derivation is so immense that it is difficult to understand without a concrete example. If we take arithmetic as an example, it will be sufficient to clarify what we want to say. Those who know what mathematical theories are and how they are organized know that all, absolutely all arithmetical knowledge can be derived from the seven postulates of Peano. These hypotheses are extraordinarily simple and can be understood by a child. However, in spite of being only seven, an immense number of conclusions is derived from them, a number so great that, although our knowledge of arithmetic has been increasing for 2500 years, it still continues to increase, and will continue to increase in the coming centuries. Aside from being numerous, the consequences are so complicated that no one can foresee where they will eventually lead. This example permits us to see clearly the incalculable power of a theory, for, once hypotheses are formulated, we can deduce an incalculable number of conclusions from them by means of logic.

This example demonstrates that from a few, simple hypotheses one can derive an infinite number of consequences that because they are so rich and numerous are unforeseeable, for once the hypotheses are formulated, no one can foresee what the future consequences will be. These consequences follow a rigorous, logical line and as the investigators continue to deduce them, their derivation follows necessarily from the hypotheses. However, no one can foresee what the consequences will be or where they will lead. If this is true in the case of a theory that has only seven, very simple hypotheses, what would happen with a theory concerning man that, as we have seen, consists of a great number of complicated hypotheses?

Let us turn now to a third dimension of all theories about man, their strange quality and inevitable failure. To obtain security in the world and to make headway through life's complexities, man elaborates a complicated theory concerning himself. The complication is inevitable because man, the subject of the theory, is the most complicated being in the universe. Due to the inextricable complications of being human, every theory concerning man, in spite of its inevitable complication, is incomplete. In spite of this incompleteness but because the theory is so complicated, the consequences derived from it are numerically overwhelming. The liability, however, is not found in the number of the consequences, but in their unpredictability. Thus, in the case of arithmetic or for that matter, all mathematical theories, the hypotheses are few and simple, the consequences are so numerous that they become unforeseeable and leave the most perceptive minds stupefied. In the case of a theory as complicated as theories concerned with man, however, this impressive array of consequences must be multiplied by infinity. And this has always been true. Due to the complexity of the theories he has elaborated concerning himself, man has drawn very odd, strange, and stupefying conclusions concerning his own being. Beginning with hypotheses that for him were more or less evident, man has come to conclusions that in the beginning were quite foreign to his thought. We only need to review history to support the claim that the doctrines man has elaborated concerning himself have carried him to unanticipated extremes. Calvinism, for example, begins with ascetic principles but comes to the inevitable conclusion that wealth is a sign of having been chosen by God for salvation. From this perspective to modern colonialism is only a small step, a step that naturally was taken in the most sincere conviction of its being just. Think for example of the strange character of funeral rituals, of human sacrifices, of the auto-da-fé, of the differences of sexual morality that exist in diverse cultures, of religious wars. One must recognize that all these actions that seem so foreign to the

points of departure are only their inevitable consequences. They lead to the failure of the theory, because given their great quantity, there comes a point at which the theory is obviously opposed to the facts. And then man ceases to believe in them or he tries to adapt them, if he can, to new demands. We must recognize that every theory concerning man is incomplete and thus has inherent limitations. However, because the theory is so complex it allows for the derivation of unexpected consequences, and in the long run one of the consequences will be evidence in support of the limitation or imperfection of the theory. Since man is such a complex reality, in the first theorizing efforts consequences usually coincide with the facts, but even if they do not one can pretend they do. The theory however, like Pandora's box, continues producing consequences that are added to the initial hypothesis, in turn leading to other more complex and wondrous consequences until it would seem the whole theoretical machinery had gone wild. A theory, however, is inflexible, the most inflexible thing in the world, much more so than machines or the will of man, and once placed in motion it has a terrifying force, like a monster that devours everything and can be detained by nothing. In a spontaneous manner as generally happens, or in a conscious manner, once the primitive hypotheses have been formulated, the consequences unfold and continue to do so without stopping, falling like grenades on a battlefield with increasing precision and explosive potential. It is as if man were a spider and the theory were his web, but a web that continued to expand unceasingly until it had imprisoned him in its own strands and slowly, inevitably asphyxiated him. When this happens, he realizes for the first time that the complicated theory that he created concerning himself is betraying him. Man does not create theories for his pleasure. He creates theories as a fundamental way of life, for it is his method of overcoming the chaos of existence. When consciously and often implicitly in secular pursuits, he elaborates a theory concerning himself, his nature, his relationship to the universe, or his ultimate destiny, it is in order to handle in a more adequate fashion the dangerous complexity of his existence, in order to feel more secure and well grounded. However, if the contrary occurs, it means that this theory is inadequate, that it must be amplified, restructured, or perhaps radically changed. . . .

The history of humanity is an impressive succession of complicated, yet false theories that man has woven around himself. Along the millennial pathway of history, theories lay semidestroyed and rusted like military equipment left behind by an army in retreat. Each great theoretical crisis, each great change, each new development marks the shift from one culture to another, from one age to another. In earlier days men were not sufficiently aware of what was happening, although they were aware that something was happening and expectantly waited the new. At times their desires were implemented in a conscious, more or less rapid manner. At other times, however, the restructuring process lasted centuries. Intuitively men grasped the significance of the situation, but the mechanism for restructuring was not grasped for two reasons: the lack of historical consciousness, that is, awareness of the relationship between their world view and historic era, and the lack of understanding of what a theory is. In the nineteenth century a great movement began that culminated in our day and overcame both limitations. For this reason, in the present, in this modern, troubled atomic era, the era of the machine and technology, we are aware nevertheless of what is really happening. We have a clear understanding that history is a succession of ways of conceiving the world and man, of ways considered absolute by men of different ages but that today are no more than vague shadows, difficult to understand. Our civilization, therefore, is the most philosophical of all, because none has had as clear an awareness of its limitation and relativity. In truth, our age is characteristically an age of search, of disorientation, and of acute consciousness of its negative traits. Contemporary man is one who experiences in his own flesh the failure of a great theory concerning himself: European rationalism, in all its facets, from the liberalism of "laissez faire" to Nazism and Marxism. Ortega has said of our age that it is an "age of disillusioned living," but to be

more precise we should say, "an age of disillusioned theorizing." Scheler begins one of his books, perhaps his best, with the celebrated phrase, "Never has man been such an enigma to himself."

Given this situation the inevitable question is "What shall we do?" The depth of the question does permit a dogmatic answer. Indeed, perhaps this essay should end here. However, to be human means to try unceasingly to overcome every "non plus ultra" and since we do not wish to deny our human condition, we have no alternative but to forge ahead. Yet, before continuing we wish to emphasize that what follows is no more than the point of view of a particular individual who, along with all other individuals in this age, is faced with an immense problem that by its very nature transcends any purely individual response.

The first thought that might come to mind, and perhaps a majority already favors it, is to commit our efforts to the reconstruction of the old theory, making it more comprehensive and adapting it to the demands of our modern circumstance. Or, should this not be possible, to elaborate a new theory that may or may not be related to the old or to earlier theories, but would constitute an organic system, capable of providing answers to the most pressing questions and have the scope and flexibility necessary to permit men of our day to work with the total range of their problems. In actual experience, the normal or spontaneous attitude always develops a theory. So we, although disillusioned by theories, in seeing ourselves in a bind, think of amplifying or creating theories, like men of other ages. In this day, however, there is a difference: men of previous ages were not aware of the relativity or limits of their theories, nor of the horrible dangers implicit in creating a complicated theory concerning man from which unforeseeable and mortal consequences were derived. Furthermore, they did not suspect that their theories ran the same risks as all preceding theories. Therefore they created under illusion, but in faith, and so their theories had "vital force" and served to resolve human problems since men believed in them and were convinced that all previous ages had been in error whereas they were in the truth. In this day, however, we are not convinced our position is unique, true, or definitive. Indeed, we know that whatever we do, our theory about man will suffer the same end as the others.

Yet, instead of searching for a new theory and instinctively following the destiny of Sisyphus, what if we assume a completely different attitude? Instead of inventing a new and dangerous theory, why not simply give up formulating theories about ourselves? Now this proposal may well produce a scandal and for two good reasons. First, because man is so accustomed to formulating theories about himself, to taking for granted that he knows what he is, to feeling himself at the helm of a world of structures and hierarchies, to renounce theory leaves him with the impression that he is giving up the possibility of finding solutions, that he is spineless and morally decadent, that he has given up the struggle for good and against evil. Second, because it is believed, more for theoretical than practical considerations, that no matter what man does he is condemned to theorize and that he can give up everything except formulating a complete concept of the world, of things, and of himself. It is believed that man needs theory to live, that without it he flounders and does not know what to hold on to, he is a lost soul on a ship without a rudder. For, although he may deny theory, implicitly he is always constructing a system of concepts for clarifying the meaning of his life.

To be sure, this second argument is much more powerful than the first. Its strength, however, lies in its inclusive breadth, for its detailed analysis of situations is slipshod. For example, if one analyzes all the elements constituting the world within which man includes himself, one sees there are various dimensions. One dimension is the surrounding world. This dimension, naturally, is undeniable. If man does not possess a well-formulated theory concerning the surrounding world he is not even able to walk down the street. The simple act of dodging an automobile indicates the possession of a rather clear concept of the principles of causality and the laws of dynamics. Further, our cultural crisis is not a crisis in knowledge of the natural world. The cosmic world, our surrounding environment is known with

increasingly greater certainty and vigor. It is perhaps the only part of our general vision of the world that at present follows a linear evolution. We have reached such a comprehension of what physical theory is, that the elaboration of that type theory is carried out in the awareness that in time it will be surpassed, and that it will be necessary to amplify it to include new facts. For this reason, it is possible that the nuclear emphasis of the old theory may be preserved intact and that it may be possible to consider it as a special case of a new theory. Some might believe that this procedure is applicable to the theory about the nature of man. However, given the complexity of all anthropological theory, this is not possible. Physical as well as mathematical theories are very simple, since they are based on broad abstractive processes. Therefore, this approach is not adequate for anthropological theory. But if we do not make use of it, we encounter the earlier objection, namely, that every theory concerning the surrounding world presupposes an integrated theory of the human being. And here we come to the crux of the issue. For, if this affirmation is true, then we will never be able to free ourselves from a theory concerning ourselves and we will always return to that monotonous, well-beaten path. This, however, we believe to be false, because even though it is undeniable that every theory concerning the cosmos presupposes a theory concerning man, it does not presuppose necessarily that the theory of the cosmos is complete. In order to grant validity to a theory about the cosmos, we must presuppose certain epistemological postulates, certain beliefs concerning the structure and organization of our consciousness, but in no way does such a theory necessarily include hypotheses about the moral life or destiny of man. The most to be said is that from these epistemological presuppositions, one can derive many consequences as to the possibilities of knowing the world in general and even ourselves and that these consequences may be positive or negative in some or in many aspects. However, this does not invalidate our point of view because what we are specifically trying to do is place brackets around our cognitive faculties insofar as these are applied to ourselves.

However, man is so accustomed to living on the theoretical level that he does not conceive the possibility of refraining from decisions about his own nature and fundamental relationships with the surrounding world. Thus he always finds arguments that justify his use of theories. In the present case, those who deny the possibility of avoiding theory about man adduce that this avoidance is impossible because determining one's orientation in the world without language is impossible. To establish inter-human communication, whatever it may be, is impossible without speech, but speech is in itself a theory. The philosophical analysis of language shows unequivocally that every expressive system acquires its ultimate meaning from theoretical presuppositions about the nature of the world and of man. Thus the very possibility of language implies the immersion of the human being in a complete theory concerning himself, a theory that refers not only to his objective relationship with the environing world, but also to his norms of action and destiny. Philological analysis of the most trivial words reveals, in a surprising way at times, the immense background of cosmological, metaphysical, and ethical theory upon which all possible language rests. The argument, then, would seem to be definitive: man cannot live without an orientation in the world and to seek an orientation in the world requires a specific theory concerning the physical structure of the cosmos. This theory, however, cannot be elaborated without language, but language is the great, universal theory, the expression of what in the ultimate, collective, anonymous, and therefore inevitable sense man believes about the world and himself. Thus, it is impossible to live as a human being without presupposing certain theoretical axioms concerning our nature and our destiny.

The inference from this last bulwark of the theory is sound. The error, however, is not found in the conclusion but in the point of departure. The error is found in the lack of theory as to what a theory is. For if one analyzes what a theory really is one sees immediately that it is always possible to do without it. Better said, there are two classes of theories, one that is implicit and spontaneous, formulated by the primitive collective mind that creates language, and the other is conscious, elaborated and created for specific purposes of knowledge. *The first cannot be avoided, but the second can* and this is our concern. The first cannot be avoided because it is implicit in language and it is impossible to do without language. Even if it is a theory that decisively influences our manner of seeing the world and of being ourselves, it is an implicit, practically unconscious theory, a theory so remote that we have forgotten its true meaning. Words that in a primitive beginning embodied terrifying revelations about nature, about the world, and about ourselves are now applied mechanically to specific, concrete objects. "To exist" signifies etymologically, "to place oneself outside himself." Enormous theoretical ranges are implicit in this meaning. Nevertheless, for the man who is not specialized, who does not meditate philosophically on the meanings of words, "to exist" means simply "to live" if he refers to a human being and "to be real" if he refers to things. "Devil" meant "slanderer" for the primitive man. Much feeling is wrapped up in this meaning. However, in modern Western languages when speaking of the devil, one does not think specifically of a slanderer in spite of the biblical passage in which the devil tempts Eve, slandering God. In pursuing the analysis of the primitive meaning of language, one comes to the following conclusion: as constituted, language is an original theory about the world and ourselves, a theory containing ethical and metaphysical principles. In an indirect and inevitable manner it influences our manner of being. This influence, however, is weakened by distance and by forgetting the primitive meanings. With the passage of time, with the progress of expressive flexibility, in the coming of the scientific spirit words acquire a new seal, a precise meaning of associative reference to things, persons, and actions over their primitive, vague, and metaphorical meaning. Therefore, in spite of the theoretical "pressure" of language, we are quite capable of overcoming the primitive world view. Thus, any of our Western languages of Indo-European origin presupposes in its beginning a theological vision of the world, a special conception of "being" and a specified taxonomy of moral values and disvalues centered in a paternalistically organized society. However, these meanings are so worn by time and so covered with semantic accumulations that it is perfectly possible for a Western man to see the world in a completely different manner. To be sure, the liberation can never be complete, although it is sufficiently radical that the Indo-European origin of our languages does not oblige us to consider a man a scoundrel who does not believe in God or who believes, with respect to sexual morality, that men and women have equal rights. This shift is the focus of our concern.

Let us now take a look at the other type of theory, *conscious theory* or if one prefers "scientific-philosophical" theory in a very broad sense. *Every theory formulated by man about the world, life, and its destiny, belongs to this type of theory.* Every human being, in addition to the theoretical background imposed by language, lives subsumed in some scientific-philosophical theory. However, an analysis of the human situation shows quite readily that it is also possible to avoid this type theory. To do this only a clear concept of the epistemological significance of the word "theory" is needed. Every theory presupposes the existence of "facts" and although facts cannot be interpreted without a theory, this does not prevent them from existing as such. A completely convincing example is that in spite of the change in theories, facts remain the same. Thus, the orbital path of Jupiter can be explained by Newton's theory as well as by Einstein's theory of generalized relativity. Nevertheless, in spite of the difference between these two theories, Jupiter's orbital path, as fact, remains the same. It can be explained also by primitive concepts, for example, as the movement of a lamp carried by a nocturnal god as he travels his circular path through the firmament. Still, all men will inevitably see Jupiter in the same manner. And seeing it they will consciously or unconsciously formulate some theory about it. The facts are nevertheless undeniably there; the blue of the sky, the white of the clouds, the brilliance of the light, the green of the fields are facts that are seen alike by all men in spite of the theories.

And just as in nature, in spite of the change of theories or perhaps precisely because of this change, one can clearly identify the facts, so in the human realm the facts remain stable over against the changes in the understanding of life. Between the theory whose consequences lead to the sacrifice of human lives and the theory that interprets such action as intolerable there is, to be sure, a significant distance. Nevertheless, all men who lived with these theories have undeniable characteristics in common. All were capable of suffering and rejoicing, all wept and laughed at least once in their life. All spoke, all felt emotions, all loved and hated at one time or another. One might object that in these affirmations we are formulating a theory, for to affirm that all were men is to universalize a concept of man. For among savages there are many groups that do not consider others to be human, but see them as animals, and some tribes even see themselves as dispossessed of the human condition. To this, however, we respond that what presupposes a theory is not the description of the facts, but dividing men into men and other things. For one must have a theory that is thoroughly elaborated and proclaimed with zealous fanaticism in order to come to believe that a person that speaks as we speak and communicates with us is not equal to us. In such interpretations of the facts, complicated ethico-metaphysical theories of the totem and the taboo are at play. However, if one insists that the universal application of the word "man" is the direct or indirect implication of some theory, we can dispense with the term. We only need observe the facts directly: there is something animated that laughs and cries, sings and shouts, hates and loves, suffers and rejoices, and above all speaks and communicates with others by means of symbols. And this type of animated something we decide to call "man." We presuppose nothing concerning its nature, origin, destiny, or obligations. There it is before us with curious demeanor, mysterious gestures, and different looks. Its history develops through the centuries, elaborating strange theories for which it has strong attraction, an attraction that is so strong that in support of their truth it is capable of anything, even of killing and torturing a fellow man. However, just as some men are capable of killing and torturing to support a theory, others are incapable of doing so in spite of all theories, in spite of all the demands and pressures of their environment. There are men who love other men and there are others that do not feel any special love but nevertheless rebel and draw back in the face of suffering and injustice. Within the range of these attitudes of cruelty and brotherhood man displays all his possibilities. All human life is tinted with these two attitudes that are like the two ultimate but opposing colors of an infinite spectrum. When man takes hold of a theory to justify his desire to make others suffer, he descends to the level of the demonic. When he rises to the level of self-sacrifice in order to prevent the suffering of others, he attains sainthood. Between these two extremes are all other men. This is the great fact, the formidable fact of the human condition down through history. Through all changes and ages, all cultural cycles and crises, all great achievements and catastrophes, we find the same fact: there are men who make others suffer and there are men capable of suffering so that others will not suffer. There are men who struggle against man and there are men who struggle for man. This fact follows two possibilities, *two ways from which to choose:* One can decide either to exploit man or to defend him. These are the fundamental attitudes. All others belong in some degree to these two, for even indifference is the zero point at which one attitude shifts into the other. The course of history is guided by the way men have organized to implement some gradation of these two activities.

QUESTIONS FOR DISCUSSION

1. Is there an innate human nature? If there is, what is it? If you believe that there is no human nature, then how do you explain why people act the way they do? Defend your position with respect to these questions and refer to at least two of the writers in this section.

2. Imagine Mencius, Hsün Tzu, Thomas Hobbes, and Petr Kropotkin sitting in a room together. They are discussing the question: Is human nature good or evil? What would they say to each other?

3. War has been with us through most of recorded history. Is war inevitable, and is there some feature of human nature that makes it so? If not, what are the basic causes of war? Is there an alternative to war? In your answer, refer to Montague and to at least one other thinker in this section.

4. Explain what Sartre means by "existence precedes essence" and why this claim entails that there is no human nature. Compare Sartre's position with the position of at least one other thinker in this section. With whom do you most agree (and why)?

5. Miró Quesada writes that "the history of humanity is an impressive succession of complicated, yet false theories that man has woven about himself." How does he argue for this claim? Why, according to him, is it impossible to formulate an adequate theory of human nature? Consider Miró Quesada's position in relation to the position of one of the other thinkers in this section.

GENDER NATURE

That the human species is divided into male and female is hardly problematic. The problem arises when we ask what it means to be male or female. The most immediate response is that males and females have different sexual anatomies. But this does not in itself explain the wide range of social phenomena encompassed by these terms. As Simone de Beauvoir observes: "to go for a walk with one's eyes open is enough to demonstrate that humanity is divided into two classes of individuals whose clothes, faces, bodies, smiles, gaits, interests, and occupations are manifestly different." The question, then, cannot be simply answered by referring to sex. Or rather the question needs to be reformulated more precisely: Why are there two social classes built upon the foundation of physical sexual difference? We might then distinguish between sex (in the physical sense) and *gender,* which is a social and psychological category; in other words, we can distinguish between male and female as physical beings and the socio-psychological characteristics of *masculinity* and *femininity.*

Gender differences refer to a difference in social roles and social identity. There are at least two fundamental kinds of explanations that can be given to account for gender difference. The first is that these differences are somehow *natural,* which is why the question of gender is placed in this chapter on human nature. The second is that these differences are socially constructed, which is to say that those with different sexual anatomies are, for reasons extraneous to sex as such, given positions within the social order and are socialized to identify themselves with those positions. The implication of the first position is that gender difference is innate and, therefore, unchangeable in its general forms. The implication of the second position is that such differences can be significantly altered or perhaps eliminated altogether.

We begin this section with two Islamic views concerning women's nature. The first is that of the eleventh-century Islamic philosopher Abu Hamid Muhammad Al-Ghazali (1058–1111). Al-Ghazali

was born in what is now northeastern Iran, was for a time a University professor in Baghdad, but eventually left the academic life to become a Sufi mystic. Many of his philosophical works are concerned with the possibility of metaphysical knowledge. In this selection he attempts to characterize the role of women within the Islamic social order. He develops several major claims through a set of anecdotes and aphorisms: that a woman should be pious, a good helpmate, and obedient to her husband, that men must be merciful to their wives since they "are prisoners in the hands of men"; and that many of the evils in the world are caused by women.

This last characterization is examined by Fatima Mernissi, who teaches sociology at the University of Mohammed V in Rabat, Morocco. She argues that there are, in fact, two theories concerning women within Islam—an explicit theory that sees man as aggressive and women as passive; and an implicit and unconscious theory that she derives from the writings of Al-Ghazali. In the implicit theory women are not inherently inferior but must be controlled precisely because of their potential equality and power. Their power, according to this implicit theory, lies in their sexual ability to attract men and weaken their will, thus distracting men from their higher spiritual and intellectual pursuits. Women are, therefore, always a destructive force, and so their sexuality must be veiled and regulated. Thus, argues Mernissi, "the entire Muslim social structure can be seen as an attack on, and a defense against, the disruptive power of female sexuality." One of the implications she draws from this analysis is that, for Islam, humanity is constituted only by males, women being perceived as an external threat.

The next selection in this section is by Simone de Beauvoir (1908–1986), a well-known feminist and French existentialist philosopher, novelist, and playwright. *The Second Sex,* from which the following selection is taken, was first published in France in 1949. As one of the first major works to document women's biological, social, political, and sexual oppression, it anticipated today's feminist movement and is generally considered one of its most important theoretical works. De Beauvoir's main claim in the selection in this section is that while man is defined in his own terms, woman is defined by her role in relation to man. The problem here is not only one of semantic asymmetry, but that this asymmetry also reflects a fundamental inequality between men and women. Hence, a woman is always the "other," always "the second sex."

De Beauvoir's feminist challenge to masculine status provoked a response by the Spanish existential philosopher José Ortega y Gasset (1883–1955). Ortega was for many years the chair of the department of metaphysics at the University of Madrid and the editor of several cultural and philosophical journals. He was one of the leading intellectuals of the Spanish Republic and became a member of Parliament. When the Spanish civil war broke out, he went into exile in Europe and Argentina and did not return to Spain until after World War II. He was a prolific writer on a wide range of cultural, artistic, and philosophical topics. Albert Camus once said that, other than Nietzsche, Ortega was perhaps the greatest European writer.

In contrast to de Beauvoir, Ortega argues that both "men and women are constituted by their reference to one another." While he admits that the situation is not exactly symmetrical, he denies that the asymmetry should pose a problem for women. Indeed, he asserts that a woman fulfills her destiny precisely through her reference to a man. As an existentialist, he argues that this destiny was not imposed upon her by biology but was the invention of history, "the result of a series of free creations . . . that have sprung as much from her as from man." Ortega further claims that the feminine ego is radically different from the masculine ego in that the body exists more for a woman than it does for a man; in effect, he claims that her soul is more corporeal. Thus, what defines a woman is not her physical features but her feminine "soul," which permeates these features. Ortega concludes that what attracts a man to a woman is not her body as such but rather that men "desire women because Her body is a soul."

Since de Beauvoir's *The Second Sex,* many contemporary feminists have explored the ways in which the two genders, masculine and feminine, are socially constructed to the advantage of the male. For some feminists, including de Beauvoir, part of the problem lies in the way in which women are taught to identify with their bodies. The conclusion that these feminists sometimes draw is that women need to disassociate themselves from their bodies. The next selection in this section, by Elizabeth V. Spelman, challenges this prescription, calling it a form of somatophobia (a fear and disdain for the body). Spelman, who currently teaches philosophy at Smith College, argues that the refusal of feminists to take the body seriously contributes to "white solipsism," or the inability to understand that sexism for black women is different than it is for white women. If women's liberation means abstracting the idea of women from their bodies, then black liberation means that blacks must ignore their blackness. But the oppression of women and of blacks works by assigning negative significance to certain bodily characteristics. Without our bodies, we would not be identified as men or women, as black and white. Therefore, the failure to recognize our embodiment results in a sex and color blindness that cannot see the different ways in which different groups of people (white women, black women, etc.) are oppressed in their unique cultural and historical contexts.

Claims about the innateness of certain masculine and feminine characteristics often appeal to some idea of an ancient past in which our "primitive" ancestors relegated certain roles to men and others to women. Such claims are sometimes buttressed by observations about the patriarchal practices of certain indigenous peoples—for example, American Indians. In the final selection of this section, Paula Gunn Allen argues that such patriarchal practices that currently exist are not the original tradition of the tribes that lived in what is now the Americas before Columbus but precisely the result of the European conquest and genocide of indigenous cultures.

Paula Gunn Allen is part Laguna Indian, part Sioux, part Lebanese, part Scottish, and part American. She is a highly respected poet, essayist, and novelist, generally writing about Native American and feminist themes. In her work *The Sacred Hoop: Recovering the Feminine in American Indian Tradition,* from which our selection is taken, Gunn Allen discusses the ways in which the conquest of the American Indians was a cultural genocide that destroyed the women-centered and egalitarian traditions and practices of many of the indigenous tribes, replacing them with European patriarchal attitudes. She emphasizes that before the conquest, women-centered traditions were central to spiritual life, that shamans were often trained across gender lines, that men's status in the clan system was dependent on women, and that certain women were designated as "men," and assigned the roles of men. These women were those that in our society would be labeled "lesbians." Indeed, in preconquest tribal societies, lesbianism and homosexuality were generally accepted, and Gunn Allen links the homophobia that resulted from colonization to the devaluation of women.

WOMEN'S NATURE: TWO ISLAMIC VIEWS

THE PROPER ROLE FOR WOMEN

Abu Hamid Muhammad Al-Ghazali

The Apostle, God bless him, stated that the best and most blessed of women are those who are most prolific in child-bearing, fairest in countenance, and least costly in dowry. He also stated, "In so far as you are able, seek a free woman in marriage; they are the purest."

The Prince of the Believers 'Umar (ibn al-Khaṭṭāb) said, "Take refuge in God from the evils caused by women, and beware (even) of the most pious of them." This means, let not (even) your own wife receive praise.

The author of this book declares that any man who desires to be sound in his religion and sound as master of his house ought not to care about nobility of birth and beauty of countenance; for a pious (wife) is the best and most beautiful.

• • •

ANECDOTE

Abū Saʿīd related that in the time of the Children of Israel there was a good man who had a pious, judicious and tactful wife. An inspiration came down to the Prophet of the Age saying, "Inform that good man that We have predestined him to spend one half of his life in poverty and one half in wealth. Let him choose now whether the poverty shall be during his youth or during his old age." The young man on hearing this went to his wife and said, "O wife, this is the command which has come down from God on High. How do you suggest that I choose?" "What is your choice?" she asked. "Come," he replied, "let us choose the poverty during our youth, so that when hardship comes we may have strength to endure it. (Moreover), when we grow old we shall need something to eat if we are to be free from cares and capable of properly obeying (God's commands)." Thereupon his wife said, "O husband, if we are poor during our youth, we shall be unable to obey God's (commands) properly then; and thereafter, when we shall have thrown to the winds the prime of our life and grown weak, how shall we perform the duties involved in obeying (God)? Let us therefore choose the wealth now, so that we may during our youth have strength both to obey God's commands and to practise charity." "Your opinion is the right one," said the husband; "let us act accordingly." Then (another) inspiration came down to the Prophet of the Age, (and the message for that man and his wife was this): "Now that you are striving to obey Us and that your intention is good, I who am the Sustainer of all life will cause you to pass (straight) to wealth. Continue striving to obey My commands, and of whatever I give you give part for alms so that both this world and the next may be yours."

The author of this book declares that he has related this story to help you understand that a good helpmate will do (you) good in this world's and the next world's affairs alike.

TRADITION

Ibn 'Abbās, God be pleased with him, has related that the Prophet went into the house of Umm Salamah, God be pleased with her, and saw that she had performed the morning prayer and was reciting God's epithets. "O Umm Salamah," he asked her, "why do not you join in the congregational prayer and go to the Friday service? Why do not you make the pilgrimage and go to fight for God against the infidels? Why do not you finish memorizing the Qur'ān?" "O Apostle of God," she replied, "all these are men's activities." Then the Prophet, peace be upon him, stated: "For women too there are activities of equal worth." "Which are they, God's Apostle?" she respectfully inquired. He answered: "Whenever a woman who fulfils God's requirements and is obedient to her husband takes hold of a spinning-wheel and turns it, this is as if she were reciting God's epithets, joining in congregational prayer, and fighting against infidels."

As long as (a woman) spins at the wheel, sins vanish from her. Spinning at the wheel is women's bridge and stronghold. Three things' sounds reach to the throne of God on High: (i) the sound of bows being drawn by warriors fighting infidels; (ii) the sound of the pens of scholars; (iii) the sound of spinning by virtuous women.

APHORISM

Aḥnaf ibn Qays has said: "If you want women to like you, satisfy them sexually and treat them tenderly."

'Umar (ibn al-Khaṭṭāb), peace be upon him, has said: "Do not speak to women of love, because their hearts will be corrupted. For women are like meat left in a desert; God's (help) is needed to preserve them."

• • •

TRADITION

Salmān al-Fārsī, God be pleased with him, has related that the Prophet, God bless him, was (once) asked, "Which women are best?" He answered, "Those who obey you, whatever be your commands." Then he was asked, "Which are the worst?" He answered, "Those who avoid pleasing their husbands."

APHORISM

A teacher was teaching girls how to write. A sage passed by and said, "This teacher is teaching wickedness to the wicked."

APHORISM

An intelligent woman was asked, "What are the virtues of women?" ("And what," she rejoined, "are the faults of men?") "Niggardliness and cowardice," (they answered). ("These," she said,) "are among the virtues of women."

APHORISM

A sage wished (that) his short wife (might have been) tall. People asked him, "Why did not you marry a wife of full stature?" "A woman is an evil thing," he answered, "and the less (there is) of an evil thing the better."

APHORISM

A sage has said, "Men who marry women get four sorts of wife: (i) the wife who belongs wholly to her husband; (ii) the wife who belongs half to her husband; (iii) the wife who belongs one-third to her husband; (iv) the wife who is her husband's enemy. The wife who belongs wholly to her husband will be a woman who is a virgin. The wife who belongs half to her husband will be [a woman whose former husband has died but has no children]. The wife who belongs one-third to her husband will be a woman whose former husband has died but who has children by the first husband. The wife who is her husband's enemy will be a (divorced) woman whose former husband is still living. Therefore the best wives are virgins.

• • •

EXCURSUS DESCRIBING THE TYPES OF WOMEN

The race of women consists of ten species, and the character of each (of these) corresponds and is related to the distinctive quality of one of the animals. One (species) resembles the pig, another the ape, another the dog, another the snake, another the mule, another the scorpion, another the mouse, another the pigeon, another the fox, and another the sheep. The woman who resembles the pig in character knows full well how to eat, break (crockery), and cram her stomach, and she does not mind where she comes and goes. She does not trouble herself with religion, prayer and fasting, and she never thinks about death, resurrection, reward and punishment, about (God's) promises, threats, commands and prohibitions, or about (His) pleasure and displeasure. She is heedless of her husband's rights and careless about nurturing and disciplining her children and teaching them knowledge of the Qur'ān. She always wears filthy clothes, and an unpleasant smell issues from her. The woman who has the character and peculiarities of the ape concerns herself with clothes of many colours—green, red, and yellow, with trinkets and jewels—pearls or rubies, and with gold and silver. She boasts of these to her relatives, but maybe her secret (self) is not the same as her (outward) appearance. The woman who has the character of the dog is one who, whenever her husband speaks, jumps at his face and shouts at him and snarls at him. If her husband's purse is full of silver and gold and the household is blessed with prosperity, she says to him, "You are the whole world to me. May God on High never let me see evil befall you, and may my own death come before yours!" But if her husband becomes insolvent, she

insults and chides him, saying "You are a poor wretch," and everything is the opposite of what it was before. The woman who has the character of the mule is like a restive mule which will not stay in one place. She is stubborn and goes her own way, and is conceited. The woman who has the peculiarities of the scorpion is always visiting the houses of the neighbours, gossiping and collecting gossip; she does her utmost to cause enmity and hatred among them and to stir up strife. Like the scorpion she stings wherever she goes. She is not afraid to be one of those concerning whom the Prophet, blessings upon him, stated: "No instigator of strife will enter Paradise," meaning (in Persian) "No tale-teller will go to heaven." The woman who has the character of the mouse is a thief who steals from her husband's purse (and hides what she has stolen) in the houses of the neighbours. She steals barley, wheat, rice and miscellaneous supplies and gives away yarn for spinning. The woman who has the peculiarities of the pigeon flits about all day long and is never still. She says to her husband, "Where are you going and whence have you come?" and she does not speak affectionately. The woman who has the peculiarities of the fox lets her husband out of the house and eats everything there is (in it), then does not stir and pretends to be sick, and when her husband comes in, starts a quarrel and says, "You left me (alone in the house) sick." The woman who has the peculiarities of the sheep is blessed like the sheep, in which everything is useful. The good woman is the same. She is useful to her husband and to (his) family and the neighbours, compassionate with her own kinsfolk, affectionate towards the (members of the) household and towards her children, and obedient to Almighty God. The pious, veiled woman is a blessing from God on High, and few men (are able to find) a pious, veiled woman (for a wife).

• • •

(ANECDOTE)

It is related that there once lived in Bukhārā a water-carrier, who for thirty years had been carrying water to the house of a certain goldsmith. Now the goldsmith had an exceedingly beautiful and virtuous wife. One day when the water-carrier had brought the water, he saw her standing in the courtyard. Suddenly he walked up, took her hand, and squeezed it. Then he departed. When the goldsmith returned home, his wife said to him, "Tell me truly. Did you do something (in the bazaar) today which has displeased God on High? What was it?" He replied, "I did nothing, except that at lunch-time I made a bracelet for a certain woman, and she put it on her arm. The woman was intensely beautiful, and I took her hand and squeezed it." "God is most great!" exclaimed his wife; "that is what you did, and this is the reason why the water-carrier who has been coming to this house for thirty years and has never played false with us today at lunch-time squeezed my hand (too)." "I have repented," her husband said. On the following day the water-carrier came. He grovelled on the ground before her and said, "Absolve me. It was the devil who led me astray yesterday." "It was not your fault," she replied, "because my husband the master of the house (who was at the shop) had committed the same offence; (God repaid him in kind, here in this lower world)."

A wife must be contented with her husband, whether he be capable of much or of little. She must follow the examples of the blessed Fāṭimah and of 'Ā'ishah, in order that she may become one of the Ladies of Paradise; as the following story shows.

ANECDOTE

It is related that Fāṭimah, God be pleased with her, (had been doing a lot of grinding on the hand-mill). She showed her hands to 'Alī, God ennoble his face, and they were blistered. "Tell your father," said 'Alī, "and perhaps he will buy a maidservant for you." Fāṭimah laid the matter before the Apostle, peace be upon him, and said, "O Apostle of God, buy me a maidservant. I am becoming desperate with all the work (I have to do)." The Prophet, God bless him, answered, "I will teach you something which is dearer than servants and higher than the seven heavens and earths." "What is it, God's Apostle?" she asked. He answered,

"When you are about to go to sleep, say three times: "Praise be to God," "Thanks be to God," "There is no God but God" and "God is Most Great." This will be better for you than any maidservant."

In the Traditions it is reported that the Prophet, blessings be upon him, owned a rug and that when the members of his household pulled it over their heads, their legs were left bare. On the night when Fāṭimah went to 'Alī as a bride, ('Alī) had a sheepskin on which they slept. Fāṭimah owned (none of the goods) of this world (except) a rug and a palm-fibre pillow. It will therefore assuredly be proclaimed on the Resurrection Day, "Lower your eyes that the Lady of Paradise may pass!"

A wife will become dear to her husband and gain his affection, firstly by honouring him; secondly by obeying him when they are alone together; and (further) by bearing in mind his advantage and disadvantage, adorning herself (for him), keeping herself concealed from (other) men and secluding herself in the house; by coming to him tidy and pleasantly perfumed, having meals ready (for him) at the (proper) times and cheerfully preparing whatever he desires, by not making impossible demands, not nagging, keeping her nakedness covered at bedtime, and keeping her husbands' secrets during his absence and in his presence.

The author of this book declares that it is the duty of gentlemen to respect the rights of their wives and veiled ones and to show mercy, kindness and forbearance to them. A man who wishes to become merciful and affectionate towards his wife must [remember] ten things (which will help him) to act fairly: (i) she cannot divorce you, while you can (divorce her whenever you wish); (ii) she can take nothing from you, while you can take everything from her; (iii) as long as she is in your net she can have no other husband, while you can have another wife; (iv) (without your permission she cannot go out of the house, while you can;) (vi) she is afraid of you, while you are not afraid of her; (vii) she is content with a cheerful look and a kind word from you, while you are not content with any action of hers; (viii) she is taken away from her mother, father and kinsfolk (for your sake), while you are not separated from any person unless you so wish; (ix) you may buy concubines and prefer them to her, while she has to endure this; (x) she kills herself (with worry) when you are sick, while you do not worry when she dies. For (all) these reasons, intelligent men will be merciful towards their wives and will not treat them unjustly; because women are prisoners in the hands of men. The intelligent man will (also) have forbearance for women; because they are deficient in intelligence. Referring to their scant intelligence, the Prophet, peace be upon him, stated: "They are deficient in (their) intellects and (their) religion. Moreover, no man ought to act upon (women's) plans; if he does, he will lose, as the following story shows.

ANECDOTE

King Parvīz was extremely fond of fish. One day when he was sitting on the terrace with Shīrīn, a fisherman brought a large fish and laid it before them. Parvīz ordered that he be given four thousand *dirhams.* Shīrīn said, "You were not right to give this fisherman four thousand *dirhams.*" "Why (not)?" he asked. Shīrīn answered, "Because henceforward whenever you give four thousand *dirhams* to one of your servants and retainers, he will say "(The king) gave me the same as he gave to a fisherman"; and whenever you give less, he will say, "(The king) gave me less than he gave to a fisherman." "You are right," said Parvīz; "but it is over now, and kings cannot decently go back on their word." "(I have) a plan for dealing with the matter," said Shīrīn; "call back the fisherman, and ask him whether the fish is male or female. If he says that it is male, tell him that you wanted a female one; and if he says that it is female, tell him that you wanted a male one." So Parvīz called back the fisherman. He was a clever and very knowing man, and when Parvīz asked him "Is this fish male or female?" he kissed the ground and said: 'This fish is neither male nor female. It is hermaphrodite." Parvīz laughed and ordered that he be given a further four thousand *dirhams.* The man then went to the treasurer, drew eight thousand *dirhams,* and put them into a knapsack which he slung over his shoulder. When he came out into the courtyard,

one *dirham* dropped from the knapsack. He put down the knapsack and picked the *dirham* up; and Parvīz and Shīrīn saw him do this. Shīrīn turned to Parvīz and said, "What a poor mean fellow this fisherman is! One *dirham* out of the eight thousand dropped and he objected to parting with it." Parvīz was annoyed and replied, "What you say is true." Then he ordered that the fisherman be called back, and said to him, "What a poor fellow you must be! When one *dirham* out of the eight thousand dropped from your knapsack, you put down the knapsack from your shoulder and picked the *dirham* up." The fisherman kissed the ground and said, "May the king's life be long! I picked up that one *dirham* because of its importance. It has the king's face stamped on one side and the king's name inscribed on the other. I feared that some person might unknowingly trample upon it and dishonour the king's name and face, and that I should be (responsible for) the offence." Parvīz was pleased (with this answer) and ordered that he be given a further four thousand *dirhams.* So the fisherman returned (home) with twelve thousand *dirhams.* Then Parvīz said, "A man who acts upon a woman's suggestion will lose two *dirhams* for every one."

The author of this book declares that the prosperity and peopling of the world depend on women. True prosperity, however, will not be achieved without (sound) planning. It is men's duty, especially after coming of age, to take precautions in matters of choosing wives and giving daughters in marriage, and so avoid falling into disgrace and embarrassment. It is a fact that all the trials, misfortunes and woes which befall men come from women, and that few men get in the end what they long and hope for from them; as the poet has said,

> When slaves rebel against the Merciful,
>   when men in fear and dread of Sulṭāns stand,
>   it's due to women.
> When robbers put their lives into the balance,
> when men incur disgrace, invariably
>   it's due to women.
> The disobedience and sad fate of Adam,
> Joseph's incarceration in the dungeon,
>   were due to women.

Hārūt's long stay in Babylon, where he writhes
suspended by a hair, making loud groans,
    was due to women.

Majnūn's flight to the nomads, sick with love,
the tale of Sindibād which makes you smile,
    were due to women.

Ruin in the two worlds, and last of all
unfaithfulness, you'll learn, are what men get
    from women.

BEYOND THE VEIL

Fatima Mernissi

Islam transformed a group of individuals into a
community of believers. This community is defined
by characteristics that determine the relations of the
individuals within the *umma* both with each other
and with non-believers:

"In its internal aspect the *umma* consists of the
totality of individuals bound to one another by
ties, not of kinship or race, but of religion, in that
all its members profess their belief in the one God,
Allah, and in the mission of his prophet, Muhammad. Before God and in relation to Him, all are
equal without distinction of race . . . In its external
aspect, the *umma* is sharply differentiated from all
other social organizations. Its duty is to bear witness to Allah in the relations of its members to one
another and with all mankind. They form a single
indivisible organization, charged to uphold the
true faith, to instruct men in the ways of God, to
persuade them to the good and to dissuade them
from evil by *word and deed.*[1]

One of the devices the Prophet used to implement the *umma* was the creation of the institutions
of the Muslim family, which was quite unlike any

existing sexual unions.[2] Its distinguishing feature
was its strictly defined monolithic structure.

Because of the novelty of the family structure in
Muhammad's revolutionary social order, he had to
codify its regulations in detail. Sex is one of the instincts whose satisfaction was regulated at length
by religious law during the first years of Islam. The
link in the Muslim mind between sexuality and the
shari'a has shaped the legal and ideological history
of the Muslim family structure[3] and consequently
of relations between the sexes. One of the most enduring characteristics of this history is that the family structure is assumed to be unchangeable, for it is
considered divine.

Controversy has raged throughout this century
between traditionalists who claim that Islam prohibits any change in sex roles, and modernists who
claim that Islam allows for the liberation of women,
the desegregation of society, and equality between
the sexes. But both factions agree on one thing: Islam
should remain the sacred basis of society. In this
book I want to demonstrate that there is a fundamental contradiction between Islam as interpreted in official policy and equality between the sexes. Sexual
equality violates Islam's premise, actualized in its
laws, that heterosexual love is dangerous to Allah's
order. Muslim marriage is based on male dominance.
The desegregation of the sexes violates Islam's ideology on women's position in the social order: that
women should be under the authority of fathers,
brothers, or husbands. Since women are considered
by Allah to be a destructive element, they are to be
spatially confined and excluded from matters other
than those of the family. Female access to non-domestic space is put under the control of males.

Paradoxically, and contrary to what is commonly
assumed, Islam does not advance the thesis of
women's inherent inferiority. Quite the contrary, it
affirms the potential equality between the sexes. The
existing inequality does not rest on an ideological or
biological theory of women's inferiority, but is the
outcome of specific social institutions designed to
restrain her power: namely, segregation and legal

---

[1]H. A. R. Gigg, "Constitutional Organization" in *Origin and Development of Islamic Law,* ed. M. Khâduri and H. J. Liebesny,
Vol. I (Washington, D.C.: Middle East Institute, 1955), p. 3.
[2]Gertrude Stern, *Marriage in Early Islam* (London: The Royal
Asiatic Society, 1931), p. 71.

[3]Joseph Schacht, *An Introduction to Islamic Law* (London: Oxford University Press, 1964), p. 161.

subordination in the family structure. Nor have these institutions generated a systematic and convincing ideology of women's inferiority. Indeed, it was not difficult for the male initiated and male-led feminist movement to affirm the need for women's emancipation, since traditional Islam recognizes equality of potential. The democratic glorification of the human individual, regardless of sex, race, or status, is the kernel of the Muslim message.

In Western culture, sexual inequality is based on belief in women's biological inferiority. This explains some aspects of Western women's liberation movements, such as that they are almost always led by women, that their effect is often very superficial, and that they have not yet succeeded in significantly changing the male-female dynamics in that culture. In Islam there is no such belief in female inferiority. On the contrary, the whole system is based on the assumption that women are powerful and dangerous beings. All sexual institutions (polygamy, repudiation, sexual segregation, etc.) can be perceived as a strategy for containing their power.

This belief in women's potence is likely to give the evolution of the relationship between men and women in Muslim settings a pattern entirely different from the Western one. For example, if there are any changes in the sex status and relations, they will tend to be more radical than in the West and will necessarily generate more tension, more conflict, more anxiety, and more aggression. While the women's liberation movement in the West focuses on women and their claim for equality with men, in Muslim countries it would tend to focus on the mode of relatedness between the sexes and thus would probably be led by men and women alike. Because men can see how the oppression of women works against men, women's liberation would assume the character of a generational rather than sexual conflict. This could already be seen in the opposition between young nationalists and old traditionalists at the beginning of the century, and currently it can be seen in the conflict between parents and children over the dying institution of arranged marriage.

At stake in Muslim society is not the emancipation of women (if that means only equality with men), but the fate of the heterosexual unit. Men and women were and still are socialized to perceive each other as enemies. The desegregation of social life makes them realize that besides sex, they can also give each other friendship and love. Muslim ideology, which views men and women as enemies, tries to separate the two, and empowers men with institutionalized means to oppress women. But whereas fifty years ago there was coherence between Muslim ideology and Muslim reality as embodied in the family system, now there is a wide discrepancy between that ideology and the reality that it pretends to explain. This book explores many aspects of that discrepancy and describes the *sui generis* character of male-female dynamics in Morocco, one of the most striking mixtures of modernity and Muslim tradition.

• • •

THE FUNCTION OF INSTINCTS

The Christian concept of the individual as tragically torn between two poles—good and evil, flesh and spirit, instinct and reason—is very different from the Muslim concept. Islam has a more sophisticated theory of the instincts, more akin to the Freudian concept of the libido. It views the raw instincts as energy. The energy of instincts is pure in the sense that it has no connotation of good or bad. The question of good and bad arises only when the social destiny of men is considered. The individual cannot survive except within a social order. Any social order has a set of laws. The set of laws decides which uses of the instincts are good or bad. It is the use made of the instincts, not the instincts themselves, that is beneficial or harmful to the social order. Therefore, in the Muslim order it is not necessary for the individual to eradicate his instincts or to control them for the sake of control itself, but he must use them according to the demands of religious law.

When Muhammad forbids or censures certain human activities, or urges their omission, he does not want them to be neglected altogether, nor does he want them to be completely eradicated, or the powers from which they result to remain altogether unused. He wants those powers to be employed as much as possible for the right aims. Every intention should thus eventually become the right one and the direction of all human activities one and the same.[4] Aggression and sexual desire, for example, if harnessed in the right direction, serve the purposes of the Muslim order; if suppressed or used wrongly, they can destroy that very order:

> Muhammad did not censure wrathfulness with the intention of eradicating it as a human quality. If the power of wrathfulness were no longer to exist in man, he would lose the ability to help the truth to become victorious. There would no longer be holy war or glorification of the word of God. Muhammad censured the wrathfulness that is in the service of Satan and reprehensible purposes, but the wrathfulness that is one in God and in the service of God deserves praise.[5]
>
> ... Likewise when he censures the desires, he does not want them to be abolished altogether, for a complete abolition of *concupiscence* in a person would make him defective and inferior. He wants the desire to be used for permissible purposes to serve the public interests, so that man becomes an active servant of God who willingly obeys the divine commands.[6]

Imam Ghazali (1050–1111) in his book *The Revivification of Religious Sciences*[7] gives a detailed description of how Islam integrated the sexual instinct in the social order and placed it at the service of God. He starts by stressing the antagonism between sexual desire and the social order: "If the desire of the flesh dominates the individual and is not controlled by the fear of God, it leads men to commit destructive acts.[8] But used according to God's

will, the desire of the flesh serves God's and the individual's interests in both worlds, enhances life on earth and in heaven. Part of God's design on earth is to ensure the perpetuity of the human race, and sexual desires serve this purpose:

> Sexual desire was created solely as a means to entice men to deliver the seed and to put the woman in a situation where she can cultivate it, bringing the two together softly in order to obtain progeny, as the hunter obtains his game, and this through copulation.[9]

He created two sexes, each equipped with a specific anatomic configuration which allows them to complement each other in the realization of God's design.

> God the Almighty created the spouses, he created the man with his penis, his testicles and his seed in his kidneys [kidneys were believed to be the semen-producing gland]. He created for it veins and channels in the testicles. He gave the woman a uterus, the receptacle and depository of the seed. He burdened men and women with the weight of sexual desire. All these facts and organs manifest in an eloquent language the will of their creator, and address to every individual endowed with intelligence an unequivocal message about the intention of His design. Moreover, Almighty God did clearly manifest His will through his messenger (benediction and salvation upon him) who made the divine intention known when he said "Marry and multiply." How then can man not understand that God showed explicitly His intention and revealed the secret of His creation? Therefore, the man who refuses to marry fails to plant the seed, destroys it and reduces to waste the instrument created by God for this purpose.[10]

Serving God's design on earth, sexual desire also serves his design in heaven.

> Sexual desire as a manifestation of God's wisdom has, independently of its manifest function, another function: when the individual yields to it and satisfies it, he experiences a delight which would be without match if it were lasting. It is a foretaste of the delights secured for men in Paradise, because to make a promise

---

[4]Ibn Khaldūn, *The Muqaddimah, An Introduction to History,* translated by Franz Rosenthal (Princeton, N.J.: Princeton University Press, Bollingen Series, 1969) pp. 160–161.
[5]*Ibid.*, p. 161.
[6]*Ibid.*
[7]Abu-Hamid al-Ghazali, *Ihya Ulum ad-Din, ("The Revivification of Religious Sciences")* (Cairo: al-Maktaba at Tijariya al-Kubra, n.d.).
[8]*Ibid.*, p. 28.

[9]*Ibid.*, p. 25.
[10]*Ibid.*, p. 25.

to men of delights they have not tasted before would be ineffective. . . . This earthly delight, imperfect because limited in time, is a powerful motivation to incite men to try and attain the perfect delight, the eternal delight and therefore urges men to adore God so as to reach heaven. Therefore the desire to reach the heavenly delight is so powerful that it helps men to persevere in pious activities in order to be admitted to heaven.[11]

Because of the dual nature of sexual desire (earthly and heavenly) and because of its tactical importance in God's strategy, its regulation had to be divine as well. In accordance with God's interests, the regulation of the sexual instinct was one of the key devices in Muhammad's implementation on earth of a new social order in then-pagan Arabia.

FEMALE SEXUALITY:
ACTIVE OR PASSIVE?

According to George Murdock, societies fall into two groups with respect to the manner in which they regulate the sexual instinct. One group enforces respect of sexual rules by a "strong internalization of sexual prohibitions during the socialization process," the other enforces that respect by "external precautionary safeguards such as avoidance rules," because these societies fail to internalize sexual prohibitions in their members.[12] According to Murdock, Western society belongs to the first group while societies where veiling exists belong to the second.

> Our own society clearly belongs to the former category, so thoroughly do we instil our sex mores in the consciences of individuals that we feel quite safe in trusting our internalized sanctions. . . . We accord women a maximum of personal freedom, knowing that the internalized ethics of premarital chastity and post-marital fidelity will ordinarily suffice to prevent abuse of their liberty through fornication or adultery whenever a favourable opportunity presents itself. Societies of the other type . . . attempt to preserve pre-

marital chastity by secluding their unmarried girls or providing them with duennas or other such external devices as veiling, seclusion in harems or constant surveillance.[13]

However, I think that the difference between these two kinds of societies resides not so much in their mechanisms of internalization as in their concept of female sexuality. In societies in which seclusion and surveillance of women prevail, the implicit concept of female sexuality is active; in societies in which there are no such methods of surveillance and coercion of women's behaviour, the concept of female sexuality is passive.

In his attempt to grasp the logic of the seclusion and veiling of women and the basis of sexual segregation, the Muslim feminist Qasim Amin came to the conclusion that women are better able to control their sexual impulses than men and that consequently sexual segregation is a device to protect men, not women.[14]

He started by asking who fears what in such societies. Observing that women do not appreciate seclusion very much and conform to it only because they are compelled to, he concluded that what is feared is *fitna:* disorder or chaos. (*Fitna* also means a beautiful woman—the connotation of a *femme fatale* who makes men lose their self-control. In the way Qasim Amin used it *fitna* could be translated as chaos provoked by sexual disorder and initiated by women.) He then asked who is protected by seclusion.

> If what men fear is that women might succumb to their masculine attraction, why did they not institute veils for themselves? Did men think that their ability to fight temptation was weaker than women's? Are men considered less able than women to control themselves and resist their sexual impulse? . . . Preventing women from showing themselves unveiled expresses men's fear of losing control over their minds, falling prey to *fitna* whenever they are confronted with a non-veiled woman. The implications of such an institution lead us to think that women are believed to be better equipped in this respect than men.[15]

---

[11]*Ibid.,* p. 27.
[12]George Peter Murdock, *Social Structure* (New York: MacMillan & Co. Free Press), 1965, p. 273.

[13]*Ibid.*
[14]Kacem Amin, *The Liberation of the Woman,* (Cairo: 'Umum al-Makatib Bimisr Wa-Iharij, 1928), p. 64.
[15]*Ibid.,* p. 65.

Amin stopped his inquiry here and, probably thinking that his findings were absurd, concluded jokingly that if men are the weaker sex, they are the ones who need protection and therefore the ones who should veil themselves.

Why does Islam fear *fitna?* Why does Islam fear the power of female sexual attraction over men? Does Islam assume that the male cannot cope sexually with an uncontrolled female? Does Islam assume that women's sexual capacity is greater than men's?

Muslim society is characterized by a contradiction between what can be called "an explicit theory" and "an implicit theory" of female sexuality, and therefore a double theory of sexual dynamics. The explicit theory is the prevailing contemporary belief that men are aggressive in their interaction with women, and women are passive. The implicit theory, driven far further into the Muslim unconscious, is epitomized in Imam Ghazali's classical work.[16] He sees civilization as struggling to contain women's destructive, all-absorbing power. Women must be controlled to prevent men from being distracted from their social and religious duties. Society can survive only by creating institutions that foster male dominance through sexual segregation and polygamy for believers.

The explicit theory, with its antagonistic, machismo vision of relations between the sexes is epitomized by Abbas Mahmud al-Aqqad.[17] In *Women in the Koran* Aqqad attempted to describe male-female dynamics as they appear through the Holy Book. Aqqad opened his book with the quotation from the Koran establishing the fact of male supremacy ("the men are superior to them by a degree") and hastily concludes that "the message of the Koran, which makes men superior to women is the manifest message of human history,

the history of Adam's descendants before and after civilization."[18]

What Aqqad finds in the Koran and in human civilization is a complementarity between the sexes based on their antagonistic natures. The characteristic of the male is the will to power, the will to conquer. The characteristic of the female is a negative will to power. All her energies are vested in seeking to be conquered, in wanting to be overpowered and subjugated. Therefore, "She can only expose herself and wait while the man wants and seeks."[19]

Although Aqqad has neither the depth nor the brilliant systematic deductive approach of Freud, his ideas on the male-female dynamic are very similar to Freud's emphasis on the "law of the jungle" aspect of sexuality. The complementarity of the sexes, according to Aqqad, resides in their antagonistic wills and desires and aspirations.

> Males in all kinds of animals are given the power—embodied in their biological structure—to compel females to yield to the demands of the instinct (that is, sex). . . . There is no situation where that power to compel is given to women over men.[20]

Like Freud, Aqqad endows women with a hearty appetite for suffering. Women enjoy surrender.[21] More than that, for Aqqad women experience pleasure and happiness only in their subjugation, their defeat by males. The ability to experience pleasure in suffering and subjugation is the kernel of femininity, which is masochistic by its very nature. "The woman's submission to the man's conquest is one of the strongest sources of women's pleasure."[22] The machismo theory casts the man as the hunter and the woman as his prey. This vision is widely

---

[16]al-Ghazali, *The Revivification of Religious Sciences,* Vol. II, chapter on marriage; and Mizan al-'Amal ("Criteria for Action") (Cairo: Dar al-Ma'arif, 1964).

[17]'Abbas Mahmud al-Aqquad, *The Women in the Koran* (Cairo: Dar al-Hilal, n.d.).

[18]*Ibid.,* p. 7; the verse he refers to is verse 228 of Surah II which is striking by its inconsistency. The whole verse reads as follows: And they [women] have rights similar to those [of men] over them in kindness, and men are a degree above them.

[19]*Ibid.,* p. 24.

[20]*Ibid.,* p. 25. The biological assumptions behind Aqquad's sweeping generalizations are obviously fallacious.

[21]*Ibid.,* p. 18.

[22]*Ibid.,* p. 26.

shared and deeply ingrained in both men's and women's vision of themselves.

The implicit theory of female sexuality, as seen in Imam Ghazali's interpretation of the Koran, casts the woman as the hunter and the man as the passive victim. The two theories have one component in common, the woman's *qaid* power ("the power to deceive and defeat men, not by force, but by cunning and intrigue"). But while Aqqad tries to link the female's *qaid* power to her weak constitution, the symbol of her divinely decreed inferiority, Imam Ghazali sees her power as the most destructive element in the Muslim social order, in which the feminine is regarded as synonymous with the satanic.

The whole Muslim organization of social interaction and spacial configuration can be understood in terms of women's *qaid* power. The social order then appears as an attempt to subjugate her power and neutralize its disruptive effects.

• • •

In the actively sexual Muslim female aggressiveness is seen as turned outward. The nature of her aggression is precisely sexual. The Muslim woman is endowed with a fatal attraction which erodes the male's will to resist her and reduces him to a passive acquiescent role. He has no choice; he can only give in to her attraction, whence her identification with *fitna,* chaos, and with the anti-divine and anti-social forces of the universe.

> The Prophet saw a woman. He hurried to his house and had intercourse with his wife Zaynab, then left the house and said, "When the woman comes towards you, it is Satan who is approaching you. When one of you sees a woman and he feels attracted to her, he should hurry to his wife. With her, it would be the same as with the other one."[23]

Commenting on this quotation, Imam Muslim, an established voice of Muslim tradition, reports that the Prophet was referring to the

. . . fascination, to the irresistible attraction to women God instilled in man's soul, and he was referring to the pleasure man experiences when he looks at the woman, and the pleasure he experiences with anything related to her. She resembles Satan in his irresistible power over the individual.[24]

This attraction is a natural link between the sexes. Whenever a man is faced with a woman, *fitna* might occur: "When a man and a woman are isolated in the presence of each other, Satan is bound to be their third companion."[25]

The most potentially dangerous woman is one who has experienced sexual intercourse. It is the married woman who will have more difficulties in bearing sexual frustration. The married woman whose husband is absent is a particular threat to men: "Do not go to the women whose husbands are absent. Because Satan will get in your bodies as blood rushes through your flesh."[26]

In Moroccan folk culture this threat is epitomized by the belief in Aisha Kandisha, a repugnant female demon. She is repugnant precisely because she is libidinous. She has pendulous breasts and lips and her favourite pastime is to assault men in the streets and in dark places, to induce them to have sexual intercourse with her, and ultimately to penetrate their bodies and stay with them for ever.[27] They are then said to be inhabited. The fear of Aisha Kandisha is more than ever present in Morocco's daily life. Fear of the castrating female is a legacy of tradition and is seen in many forms in popular beliefs and practices and in both religious and mundane literature, particularly novels.

Moroccan folk culture is permeated with a negative attitude towards femininity. Loving a woman is popularly described as a form of mental illness,

---

[23] Abbi 'Issa at-Tarmidi, *Sunan at-Tarmidi* (Medina: al-Maktaba as Salafiya, n.d.) Vol. II, p. 413. Bab: 9, Hadith: 1167. (Hereinafter Bab will be indicated by the letter B, and Hadith by the letter H.)

[24] Abu al-Hassan Muslim, *al-Jami' as-Sahih* (Beirut: al-Maktaba at-Tijariya, n.d.) Vol. III, Book of Marriage, p. 130.

[25] at-Tarmidi, *Sunan at-Tramidi,* p. 419, B: 16, H: 1181. See also al-Bukhari, *Kitab al-Jami' as-Sahih* (Leyden, Holland: Ludolph Krehl, 1868) Vol. III, Kitab 67, B: 11. (Hereinafter Kitab will be indicated by the letter K.)

[26] at-Tarmidi, *Sunan at-Tramidi,* p. 419, B: 17, H: 1172.

[27] Edward Westermarck, *The Belief in Spirits in Morocco* (Abo, Finland: Abo-Akademi, 1920).

a self-destructive state of mind. A Moroccan proverb says

Love is a complicated matter
If it does not drive you crazy, it kills you.[28]

• • •

The Muslim order faces two threats: the infidel without and the woman within.

> The Prophet said, "After my disappearance there will be no greater source of chaos and disorder for my nation than women."[29]

• • •

Different social orders have integrated the tensions between religion and sexuality in different ways. In the Western Christian experience sexuality itself was attacked, degraded as animality and condemned as anti-civilization. The individual was split into two antithetical selves: the spirit and the flesh, the ego and the id. The triumph of civilization implied the triumph of soul over flesh, of ego over id, of the controlled over the uncontrolled, of spirit over sex.

Islam took a substantially different path. What is attacked and debased is not sexuality but women, as the embodiment of destruction, the symbol of disorder. The woman is *fitna,* the epitome of the uncontrollable, a living representative of the dangers of sexuality and its rampant disruptive potential. We have seen that Muslim theory considers raw instinct as energy which is likely to be used constructively for the benefit of Allah and His society if people live according to His laws. Sexuality *per se* is not a danger. On the contrary, it has three positive, vital functions. It allows the believers to perpetuate themselves on earth, an indispensable condition if the social order is to exist at all. It serves as a "foretaste of the delights secured for men in Paradise,[30]

thus encouraging men to strive for paradise and to obey Allah's rule on earth. Finally, sexual satisfaction is necessary to intellectual effort.

The Muslim theory of sublimation is entirely different from the Western Christian tradition as represented by Freudian psychoanalytic theory. Freud viewed civilization as a war against sexuality.[31] Civilization is sexual energy "turned aside from its sexual goal and diverted towards other ends, no longer sexual and socially more valuable."[32] The Muslim theory views civilization as the outcome of satisfied sexual energy. Work is the result not of sexual frustration but of a contented and harmoniously lived sexuality.

> The soul is usually reluctant to carry out its duty because duty [work] is against its nature. If one puts pressures on the soul in order to make it do what it loathes, the soul rebels. But if the soul is allowed to relax for some moments by the means of some pleasures, it fortifies itself and becomes after that alert and ready for work again. And in the woman's company, this relaxation drives out sadness and pacifies the heart. It is advisable for pious souls to divert themselves by means which are religiously lawful.[33]

According to Ghazali, the most precious gift God gave humans is reason. Its best use is the search for knowledge. To know the human environment, to know the earth and galaxies, is to know God. Knowledge (science) is the best form of prayer for a Muslim believer. But to be able to devote his energies to knowledge, man has to reduce the tensions within and without his body, avoid being distracted by external elements, and avoid indulging in earthly pleasures. Women are a dangerous distraction that must be used for the specific purpose of providing the Muslim nation with offspring and quenching the tensions of the sexual instinct. But in no way should women be an object of emotional investment or the focus of attention,

---

[28]Edward Westermarck, *Wit and Wisdom in Morocco: A Study of Native Proverbs* (London: MacMillan and Co., 1926), p. 330.
[29]Abu Abd Allah Muhammad Ibn Ismail al-Bukhari, *Kitab al-Jami' as-Sahih* (Leyden, Holland: Ludolph Krehl, 1868), p. 419, K: 67, B:18.
[30]al-Ghazali, *Revivification,* p. 28.

[31]Sigmund Freud, *Civilization and Its Discontents* (New York: Norton and Co., Inc., 1962).
[32]Sigmund Freud, *A General Introduction to Psychoanalysis* (New York: Pocket Books, 1952) p. 27.
[33]al-Ghazali, *Revivification,* p. 32.

which should be devoted to Allah alone in the form of knowledge-seeking, meditation, and prayer.

Ghazali's conception of the individual's task on earth is illuminating in that it reveals that the Muslim message, in spite of its beauty, considers humanity to be constituted by males only. Women are considered not only outside of humanity but a threat to it as well. Muslim wariness of heterosexual involvement is embodied in sexual segregation and its corollaries: arranged marriage, the important role of the mother in the son's life, and the fragility of the marital bond (as revealed by the institutions of repudiation and polygamy). The entire Muslim social structure can be seen as an attack on, and a defence against, the disruptive power of female sexuality.

THE SECOND SEX

Simone de Beauvoir

For a long time I have hesitated to write a book on woman. The subject is irritating, especially to women; and it is not new. Enough ink has been spilled in the quarreling over feminism, now practically over, and perhaps we should say no more about it. It is still talked about, however, for the voluminous nonsense uttered during the last century seems to have done little to illuminate the problem. After all, is there a problem? And if so, what is it? Are there women, really? Most assuredly the theory of the eternal feminine still has its adherents who will whisper in your ear: "Even in Russia women still are *women*"; and other erudite persons—sometimes the very same—say with a sigh: "Woman is losing her way, woman is lost." One wonders if women still exist, if they will always exist, whether or not it is desirable that they should, what place they occupy in this world, what their place should be. "What has become of women?" was asked recently in an ephemeral magazine.

But first we must ask: what is a woman? *"Tota mulier in utero,"* says one, "woman is a womb." But in speaking of certain women, connoisseurs declare that they are not women, although they are equipped with a uterus like the rest. All agree in recognizing the fact that females exist in the human species; today as always they make up about one half of humanity. And yet we are told that femininity is in danger; we are exhorted to be women, remain women, become women. It would appear, then, that every female human being is not necessarily a woman; to be so considered she must share in that mysterious and threatened reality known as femininity. Is this attribute something secreted by the ovaries? Or is it a Platonic essence, a product of the philosophic imagination? Is a rustling petticoat enough to bring it down to earth? Although some women try zealously to incarnate this essence, it is hardly patentable. It is frequently described in vague and dazzling terms that seem to have been borrowed from the vocabulary of the seers, and indeed in the times of St. Thomas it was considered an essence as certainly defined as the somniferous virtue of the poppy.

But conceptualism[1] has lost ground. The biological and social sciences no longer admit the existence of unchangeably fixed entities that determine given characteristics, such as those ascribed to woman, the Jew, or the Negro. Science regards any characteristic as a reaction dependent in part upon a *situation.* If today femininity no longer exists, then it never existed. But does the word *woman,* then, have no specific content? This is stoutly affirmed by those who hold to the philosophy of the enlightenment, of rationalism, of nominalism;[2] women, to them, are merely the human beings arbitrarily designated by the word *woman.* Many American

[1] *Conceptualism* is a philosophical position holding that universal concepts exist in the mind and that, therefore, general terms—such as *"man"* and *"woman"*—refer to some universal essence (Eds.).
[2] *Nominalism* is a philosophical position holding that general terms are simply words designating a collection of individuals and that there is no abstract universal essence to which they refer (Eds.).

women particularly are prepared to think that there is no longer any place for woman as such; if a backward individual still takes herself for a woman, her friends advise her to be psychoanalyzed and thus get rid of this obsession. In regard to a work, *Modern Woman: The Lost Sex,* which in other respects has its irritating features, Dorothy Parker has written: "I cannot be just to books which treat of woman as woman. . . . My idea is that all of us, men as well as women, should be regarded as human beings." But nominalism is a rather inadequate doctrine, and the antifeminists have had no trouble in showing that women simply *are not* men. Surely woman is, like man, a human being; but such a declaration is abstract. The fact is that every concrete human being is always a singular, separate individual. To decline to accept such notions as the eternal feminine, the black soul, the Jewish character, is not to deny that Jews, Negroes, women exist today—this denial does not represent a liberation for those concerned, but rather a flight from reality. Some years ago a well-known woman writer refused to permit her portrait to appear in a series of photographs especially devoted to women writers; she wished to be counted among the men. But in order to gain this privilege she made use of her husband's influence! Women who assert that they are men lay claim none the less to masculine consideration and respect. I recall also a young Trotskyite standing on a platform at a boisterous meeting and getting ready to use her fists, in spite of her evident fragility. She was denying her feminine weakness; but it was for love of a militant male whose equal she wished to be. The attitude of defiance of many American women proves that they are haunted by a sense of their femininity. In truth, to go for a walk with one's eyes open is enough to demonstrate that humanity is divided into two classes of individuals whose clothes, faces, bodies, smiles, gaits, interests, and occupations are manifestly different. Perhaps these differences are superficial, perhaps they are destined to disappear. What is certain is that right now they do most obviously exist.

If her functioning as a female is not enough to define woman, if we decline also to explain her through "the eternal feminine," and if nevertheless we admit, provisionally, that women do exist, then we must face the question: what is a woman?

To state the question is, to me, to suggest, at once, a preliminary answer. The fact that I ask it is in itself significant. A man would never get the notion of writing a book on the peculiar situation of the human male.[3] But if I wish to define myself, I must first of all say: "I am a woman"; on this truth must be based all further discussion. A man never begins by presenting himself as an individual of a certain sex; it goes without saying that he is a man. The terms *masculine* and *feminine* are used symmetrically only as a matter of form, as on legal papers. In actuality the relation of the two sexes is not quite like that of two electrical poles, for man represents both the positive and the neutral, as is indicated by the common use of *man* to designate human beings in general; whereas woman represents only the negative, defined by limiting criteria, without reciprocity. In the midst of an abstract discussion it is vexing to hear a man say: "You think thus and so because you are a woman"; but I know that my only defense is to reply: "I think thus and so because it is true," thereby removing my subjective self from the argument. It would be out of the question to reply: "And you think the contrary because you are a man," for it is understood that the fact of being a man is no peculiarity. A man is in the right in being a man; it is the woman who is in the wrong. It amounts to this: just as for the ancients there was an absolute vertical with reference to which the oblique was defined, so there is an absolute human type, the masculine. Woman has ovaries, a uterus; these peculiarities imprison her in her subjectivity, circumscribe her within the limits of her own nature. It is often said that she thinks with her glands. Man superbly ignores the fact that his anatomy also includes glands, such as the testicles, and that they secrete hormones. He thinks of his body as a direct and normal

---

[3]The Kinsey Report [Alfred C. Kinsey and others: *Sexual Behavior in the Human Male* (W. B. Saunders Co., 1948)] is no exception, for it is limited to describing the sexual characteristics of American men, which is quite a different matter.

connection with the world, which he believes he apprehends objectively, whereas he regards the body of woman as a hindrance, a prison, weighed down by everything peculiar to it. "The female is a female by virtue of a certain *lack* of qualities," said Aristotle; "we should regard the female nature as afflicted with a natural defectiveness." And St. Thomas for his part pronounced woman to be an "imperfect man," an "incidental" being. This is symbolized in Genesis where Eve is depicted as made from what Bossuet called "a supernumerary bone" of Adam.

Thus humanity is male and man defines woman not in herself but as relative to him; she is not regarded as an autonomous being. Michelet writes: "Woman, the relative being. . . ." And Benda is most positive in his *Rapport d'Uriel:* "The body of man makes sense in itself quite apart from that of woman, whereas the latter seems wanting in significance by itself. . . . Man can think of himself without woman. She cannot think of herself without man." And she is simply what man decrees; thus she is called "the sex," by which is meant that she appears essentially to the male as a sexual being. For him she is sex—absolute sex, no less. She is defined and differentiated with reference to man and not he with reference to her; she is the incidental, the inessential as opposed to the essential. He is the Subject, he is the Absolute—she is the Other.

•   •   •

A free individual blames only himself for his failures, he assumes responsibility for them; but everything happens to women through the agency of others, and therefore these others are responsible for her woes. Her mad despair spurns all remedies; it does not help matters to propose solutions to a woman bent on complaining: she finds none acceptable. She insists on living in her situation precisely as she does—that is, in a state of impotent rage. If some change is proposed she throws up her hands: "That's the last straw!" She knows that her trouble goes deeper than is indicated by the pretexts she advances for it, and she is aware that it will take more than some expedient to deliver her from it. She holds the entire world responsible because it

has been made without her, and against her; she has been protesting against her condition since her adolescence, ever since her childhood. She has been promised compensations, she has been assured that if she would place her fortune in man's hands, it would be returned a hundredfold—and she feels she has been swindled. She puts the whole masculine universe under indictment. Resentment is the reverse side of dependence: when one gives all, one never receives enough in return.

•   •   •

There are many aspects of feminine behavior that should be interpreted as forms of protest. We have seen that a woman often deceives her husband through defiance and not for pleasure; and she may be purposely careless and extravagant because he is methodical and economical. Misogynists who accuse woman of always being late think she lacks a sense of punctuality; but as we have seen, the fact is that she can adjust herself very well to the demands of time. When she is late, she has deliberately planned to be. Some coquettish women think they stimulate the man's desire in this way and make their presence the more highly appreciated; but in making the man wait a few minutes, the woman is above all protesting against that long wait: her life.

In a sense her whole existence is waiting, since she is confined in the limbo of immanence and contingence, and since her justification is always in the hands of others. She awaits the homage, the approval of men, she awaits love, she awaits the gratitude and praise of her husband or her lover. She awaits her support, which comes from man; whether she keeps the checkbook or merely gets a weekly or monthly allowance from her husband, it is necessary for him to have drawn his pay or obtained that raise if she is to be able to pay the grocer or buy a new dress. She waits for man to put in an appearance, since her economic dependence places her at his disposal; she is only one element in masculine life while man is her whole existence. The husband has his occupations outside the home, and the wife has to put up with his absence all day long; the lover—passionate as he may be—is the one who decides on their meetings and separations in accordance with his obligations. In bed, she awaits the male's desire, she awaits—sometimes anxiously—her own pleasure.

All she can do is arrive later at the rendezvous her lover has set, not be ready at the time designated by her husband; in that way she asserts the importance of her own occupations, she insists on her independence; and for the moment she becomes the essential subject to whose will the other passively submits. But these are timid attempts at revenge; however persistent she may be in keeping men waiting, she will never compensate for the interminable hours she has spent in watching and hoping, in awaiting the good pleasure of the male.

Woman is bound in a general way to contest foot by foot the rule of man, though recognizing his over-all supremacy and worshipping his idols. Hence that famous "contrariness" for which she has often been reproached. Having no independent domain, she cannot oppose positive truths and values of her own to those asserted and upheld by males; she can only deny them. Her negation is more or less thoroughgoing, according to the way respect and resentment are proportioned in her nature. But in fact she knows all the faults in the masculine system, and she has no hesitation in exposing them.

Women have no grasp on the world of men because their experience does not teach them to use logic and technique; inversely, masculine apparatus loses its power at the frontiers of the feminine realm. There is a whole region of human experience which the male deliberately chooses to ignore because he fails to *think* it: this experience woman *lives*. The engineer, so precise when he is laying out his diagrams, behaves at home like a minor god: a word, and behold, his meal is served, his shirts starched, his children quieted; procreation is an act as swift as the wave of Moses' wand; he sees nothing astounding in these miracles. The concept of the miracle is different from the idea of magic: it presents, in the midst of a world of rational causation, the radical discontinuity of an event without cause, against which the weapons of thought are shattered; whereas magical phenomena are unified by hidden forces the continu-

ity of which can be accepted—without being understood—by a docile mind. The newborn child is miraculous to the paternal minor god, magical for the mother who has experienced its coming to term within her womb. The experience of the man is intelligible but interrupted by blanks; that of the woman is, within its own limits, mysterious and obscure but complete. This obscurity makes her weighty; in his relations with her, the male seems light: he has the lightness of dictators, generals, judges, bureaucrats, codes of law, and abstract principles. This is doubtless what a housekeeper meant when she said, shrugging her shoulders: "Men, they don't think!" Women say, also: "Men, they don't know, they don't know life." To the myth of the praying mantis, women contrast the symbol of the frivolous and obtrusive drone bee.

It is understandable, in this perspective, that woman takes exception to masculine logic. Not only is it inapplicable to her experience, but in his hands, as she knows, masculine reasoning becomes an underhand form of force; men's undebatable pronouncements are intended to confuse her. The intention is to put her in a dilemma: either you agree or you do not. Out of respect for the whole system of accepted principles she should agree; if she refuses, she rejects the entire system. But she cannot venture to go so far; she lacks the means to reconstruct society in different form. Still, she does not accept it as it is. Halfway between revolt and slavery, she resigns herself reluctantly to masculine authority. On each occasion he has to force her to accept the consequences of her halfhearted yielding. Man pursues that chimera, a companion half slave, half free: in yielding to him, he would have her yield to the convincingness of an argument, but she knows that he has himself chosen the premises on which his rigorous deductions depend. As long as she avoids questioning them, he will easily reduce her to silence; nevertheless he will not convince her, for she senses his arbitrariness. And so, annoyed, he will accuse her of being obstinate and illogical; but she refuses to play the game because she knows the dice are loaded.

WOMAN AS BODY

José Ortega y Gasset

As a young man, I once traveled back to Spain from Buenos Aires on a great liner. Among my fellow passengers there was a small group of American ladies, young and extremely beautiful. Although my acquaintance with them never even reached a footing of intimacy, it was obvious that I spoke to each of them as a man speaks to a woman who is in the full flower of her feminine attributes. One of these ladies felt rather offended in her American dignity. Evidently Lincoln had not struggled to win the War of Secession in order that I, a young Spaniard, could permit myself to treat her like a woman. In the United States of that time women were so modest that they thought there was something better than "being a woman." At any rate, she said to me, "I insist that you talk to me as if I were a human being." I could not help answering: "Madam, I am not acquainted with this person whom you call a 'human being.' I know only men and women. As it is my good fortune that you are not a man but a woman—and certainly a magnificent one—I behave accordingly." The poor creature had gone through some college where she had suffered the rationalistic education of the time, and rationalism is a form of intellectual bigotry which, in thinking about reality, tries to take it into account as little as possible. In this case it had produced the hypothesis of the abstraction "human being." It should always be remembered that the species—and the species is the concrete and real—reacts on the genus and specifies it.

• • •

In the presence of Woman we men immediately divine a creature who on the level of "humanness" has a vital station somewhat lower than ours. No other being has this twofold condition—being human, and being less so than a man is. This duality is the source of the unparalleled delight that woman is for the masculine man. The aforesaid equalitarian

mania has recently resulted in an attempt to minimize what is one of the fundamental facts in human destiny—the fact of sexual duality. Simone de Beauvoir—a distinguished writer in that capital of graphomania, Paris—has written a very long book on "The Second Sex." This estimable lady finds it intolerable that woman should be considered—and consider herself—constitutively referable to man and hence not centered in herself, as man would seem to be. Mademoiselle de Beauvoir thinks that to consist in "reference to another" is incompatible with the idea of person, which is rooted in "freedom toward oneself." But it is not clear why there must be such incompatibility between being free and consisting in reference to another human being. After all, the amount of reference to woman which constitutes the human male is by no means small. But the human male consists pre-eminently in reference to his profession. Professionality—even in the most primitive of primitive men—is probably the most masculine trait of all, to the point where "doing nothing," having no profession, is felt to be something effeminating in a man. Mademoiselle de Beauvoir's book, so prodigal of pages, leaves us with the impression that the writer, very fortunately, confuses things and thus displays in her work the characteristic confusion that assures us of the genuineness of her feminine being. On the other hand, to believe, as follows from her argument, that a woman is more a person when she does not "exist" preoccupied by man but occupied in writing a book on "the second sex," seems to us something decidedly more than simple confusion.

The duality of the sexes has as its consequence that men and women are constituted by their reference to one another—and to such a degree that any insufficiency in either men's or women's living in reference to the other sex is something that in every case requires explanation and justification. It is another matter that this reference to the other sex, though constitutive in both, has a preeminent place in woman, while in man its autonomy is reduced by other references. With all the qualifications and reservations that "case histories" would suggest, we may affirm that woman's destiny is "*to be* in view of man." But this formula in no way diminishes her freedom. The human being, as free, is free before and in the face of his destiny. He can accept it or resist it, or, what is the same thing, he can be it or not be it. Our destiny is not only what we have been and now are; it is not only the past, but, coming from the past, it projects itself, in openness, toward the future. This retrospective fatality—what we now are—does not enslave our future, does not inexorably predetermine what we are not yet. Our future being emerges from our freedom, a continuous spring forever flowing out of itself. But freedom presupposes plans of action among which to choose, and these plans can only be created by using the past—our own and others'—as a material that inspires us to new combinations. The past then—our destiny—does not influence us in imperative and mechanical form, but as the guiding thread of our inspirations. We are not inexorably circumscribed in it; rather, at every moment it launches us upon free creation of our future being. Hence the antique formula could not be improved: *Fata ducunt, non trahunt,* "Destiny directs, it does not drag." For, great as is the radius of our freedom, there is a limit to it—we cannot escape maintaining continuity with the past. Nothing more clearly shows us in what this ineluctable continuity with the past consists than those occasions when the plan we make and adopt consists in the radical negation of a past. Then we see that one of the methods the past employs to inspire us is to urge us to do the opposite of what it had done.

• • •

All this brief "philosophical" embroidery on past and future, destiny and freedom, comes down to opposing the tendency of certain present-day "philosophers" who invite woman to plan her "future being" by ceasing to be what she has been until now, namely, woman—all in the name of freedom and the idea of the person. Now, what woman has been in the past, her femininity, does not derive from her freedom and person having been negated, either by men or by a biological fatality; on the contrary, it is the result of a series of

free creations, of fertile inspirations that have sprung as much from her as from man. For the human being, the zoological duality of the sexes is not—just as the other subhuman conditions are not—something inexorably imposed, but the very opposite—a theme for inspiration. What we call "woman" is not a product of nature but an invention of history, just as art is. This is why the copious pages that Mademoiselle de Beauvoir devotes to the biology of the sexes are so little fertile, so completely beside the point. Only when we are engaged in imagining the origin of man need we keep constantly in mind the facts which the biology of evolution presents to us today—even though we can be certain that tomorrow it will present us others. But once man is man, we enter a world of freedom and creation. Instead of studying woman zoologically, it would be infinitely more fertile to contemplate her as a literary genre or an artistic tradition.

So let us, without a blush that would be pure snobbery, go back to calling woman the "weaker sex" with perfectly quiet consciences. Indeed, let us proclaim it in a more radical sense. I said that, besides the characteristic of confusion, the other characteristic with which woman appears to us is her lower vital rank on the human plane. This last qualification serves only to introduce us to the phenomenon to be considered, but it is insufficient because it implies a comparison with man, and nothing, in its true reality, is a comparison. We are not, then, considering the fact that, in comparison with man, woman seems to us to be less strong vitally than he is. There is no occasion, at least for the present, to talk of more or less; what we must consider is the fact that, when we see a woman, what we see consists in *weakness.* This is so obvious that, for that very reason, we completely pass over it when we discuss what woman is. When Aristotle says that woman is a sick man, it is not likely that he was referring to her periodical sufferings but precisely to this constitutive characteristic of weakness. But to call it "sickness" is to go out of one's way to use a secondary expression that supposes comparing her with the healthy man.

This patent characteristic of weakness is the basis of woman's inferior vital rank. But, as it could not but be, this inferiority is the source and origin of the peculiar value that woman possesses in reference to man. For by virtue of it, woman makes us happy and *is happy herself, is happy in feeling that she is weak.* Indeed, only a being inferior to man can radically affirm his basic being—not his talents or his triumphs or his achievements, but the elemental condition of his person. The greatest admirer of the gifts that we may have does not corroborate and confirm us as does the woman who falls in love with us. And this is because, in sober truth, only woman knows how to love and is able to love—that is, to disappear in the other.

•   •   •

The feminine ego is so radically different from our male ego that it displays the difference from the very first in something that could not be more elementary —in the fact that its relation to its body is different from the relation in which the masculine ego stands to its body.

•   •   •

For it is too much overlooked that the feminine body is endowed with a more lively internal sensibility than man's; that is, our organic intracorporeal sensations are vague and as it were muffled in comparison with woman's. In this fact I see one of the roots from which—ever suggestive, charming, and admirable—the resplendent spectacle of femininity comes to flower.

The comparative hyperesthesia of woman's organic sensations brings it about that her body exists for her more than man's does for him. Normally, we men forget our brother the body; we are not aware of possessing it except at the chill or burning hour of extreme pain or extreme pleasure. Between our purely psychic I and the outer world, nothing seems to be interposed. Woman, on the contrary, is constantly having her attention claimed by the liveliness of her intracorporeal sensations; she is always aware of her body as interposed between the world and her I, she always carries it before her, at once as

a shield of defense and a vulnerable hostage. The consequences are clear: woman's whole psychic life is more involved with her body than man's; in other words, her soul is more corporeal—but, vice versa, her body lives more constantly and closely with her spirit; that is, her body is more permeated with soul. In fact, the feminine person displays a far higher degree of interpenetration between body and spirit than man. In man, comparatively speaking, each normally takes its own course; body and soul know little of each other and are not allied, rather, they act like irreconcilable enemies.

In this observation I believe we can find the cause for an eternal and enigmatic fact which runs through human history from one end to the other, and of which all the explanations so far given have been stupid or superficial—I refer to woman's age-old propensity to adorn and ornament her body. In the light of the idea that I am expounding, nothing could be more natural and at the same time inevitable. Her native physiological structure imposes on woman the habit of noticing, paying attention to her body, which ends by being the closest object in the perspective of her world. And since culture is only sustained reflection on that to which our attention prefers to turn, woman has created the remarkable culture of the body, which, historically, began in adornment, continued in cleanliness, and has ended in courtesy, that inspired feminine invention, which, finally, is the subtle culture of the gesture.[1]

The result of this constant attention that woman devotes to her body is that her body appears to us from the first as impregnated, as wholly filled with soul. This is the foundation for the impression of weakness that her presence creates in us. Because in contrast to the firm and solid appearance of the body, the soul is a little tremulous, the soul is a little weak. In short, the erotic attraction that woman produces in man is not—as the ascetics have always told us in their blindness on these matters—aroused

---

[1]In these last three paragraphs, I have made use of my essay "La percepción del prójimo" ["The Perception of One's Fellowman"; *Obras completas,* Vol. VI, pp. 161 ff.].

by the feminine body as body; rather, we desire woman because Her body *is* a soul.

GENDER AND RACE

Elizabeth V. Spelman

Feminist theorists as politically diverse as Simone de Beauvoir, Betty Friedan, and Shulamith Firestone have described the conditions of women's liberation in terms that suggest that the identification of woman with her body has been the source of our oppression, and hence that the source of our liberation lies in sundering that connection.[1] For example, de Beauvoir introduces *The Second Sex* with the comment that woman has been regarded as "womb"; and she later observes that woman is thought of as planted firmly in the world of "immanence," that is, the physical world of nature, her life defined by the dictates of her "biologic fate."[2] In contrast, men live in the world of "transcendence," actively using their minds to create "values, mores, religions."[3] Theirs is the world of culture as opposed to the world of nature. Among Friedan's central messages is that women should be allowed and encouraged to be "culturally" as well as "biologically" creative, because the former activities, in contrast to childbearing and rearing, are "mental" and are of "highest value to society"—"mastering the secrets of atoms, or the stars, composing symphonies, pioneering a new concept in government or society."[4]

This view comes out especially clearly in Firestone's work. According to her, the biological difference between women and men is at the root of women's oppression. It is woman's body—in particular, our body's capacity to bear children—that

makes, or makes possible, the oppression of women by men. Hence we must disassociate ourselves from our bodies—most radically—by making it possible, or even necessary, to conceive and bear children outside the womb, and by otherwise generally disassociating our lives from the thankless tasks associated with the body.[5]

In predicating women's liberation on a disassociation from our bodies, Firestone oddly enough joins the chorus of male voices that has told us over the centuries about the disappointments entailed in being embodied creatures. What might be called "somatophobia" (fear of and disdain for the body) is part of a centuries-long tradition in Western culture. As de Beauvoir so thoroughly described in *The Second Sex,* the responsibility for being embodied creatures has been assigned to women: we have been associated, indeed virtually identified, with the body; men (or some men) have been associated and virtually identified with the mind. Women have been portrayed as possessing bodies in a way men have not. It is as if women essentially, men only accidentally, have bodies. It seems to me that Firestone's (as well as Friedan's and de Beauvoir's) prescription for women's liberation does not challenge the negative attitude toward the body; it only hopes to end the association between the body, so negatively characterized, and women.

I think the somatophobia we see in the work of Firestone and others is a force that contributes to white solipsism in feminist thought, in at least three related ways. First, insofar as feminists ignore, or indeed accept, negative views of the body in prescriptions for women's liberation, we will also ignore an important element in racist thinking. For the superiority of men to women (or, as we have seen, of some men to some women) is not the only hierarchical relationship that has been linked to the superiority of the mind to the body. Certain kinds, or "races," of people have been held to be more body-like than others, and this has meant that they are perceived as more animal-like and less god-like. For example, in

---

[1]Spelman, "Woman as Body."
[2]De Beauvoir, *The Second Sex,* xii, 57.
[3]Ibid., 119.
[4]Friedan, *The Feminine Mystique,* 247–77.

[5]Firestone, *The Dialectic of Sex,* chap. 10.

The White Man's Burden, Winthrop Jordan describes ways in which white Englishmen portrayed
black Africans as beastly, dirty, highly sexual beings.[6] Lillian Smith tells us in *Killers of the Dream*
how closely run together were her lessons about the
evil of the body and the evil of Blacks.[7]

We need to examine and understand somatophobia and look for it in our own thinking, for the idea
that the work of the body and for the body has no part
in real human dignity has been part of racist as well
as sexist ideology. That is, oppressive stereotypes of
"inferior races" and of women (notice that even in order to make the point in this way, we leave up in the
air the question of how we shall refer to those who
belong to both categories) have typically involved
images of their lives as determined by basic bodily
functions (sex, reproduction, appetite, secretions,
and excretions) and as given over to attending to the
bodily functions of others (feeding, washing, cleaning, doing the "dirty work"). Superior groups, we
have been told from Plato on down, have better
things to do with their lives. It certainly does not follow from the presence of somatophobia in a person's
writings that she or he is a racist or a sexist. But disdain for the body historically has been symptomatic
of sexist and racist (as well as classist) attitudes.

Human groups know that the work of the body and
for the body is necessary for human existence, and
they make provisions for that necessity. Thus even
when a group views its liberation in terms of being
free of association with, or responsibility for, bodily
tasks, its own liberation is likely to be predicated on
the oppression of other groups—those assigned to do
the body's work. For example, if feminists decide that
women are not going to be relegated to doing such
work, who do we think is going to do it? Have we attended to the role that racism and classism historically
have played in settling that question? We may recall
why Plato and Aristotle thought philosophers and citizens needed leisure from this kind of work and who
they thought ought to do it.

Finally, if one thinks—as de Beauvoir, Friedan,
and Firestone do—that the liberation of women requires abstracting the notion of woman from the notion of woman's body, then one might logically
think that the liberation of Blacks requires abstracting the notion of a Black person from the notion of
a black body. Since the body, or at least certain of its
aspects, may be thought to be the culprit, the solution may seem to be: Keep the person and leave the
occasion for oppression behind. Keep the woman,
somehow, but leave behind her woman's body; keep
the Black person but leave the Blackness behind.

• • •

Once the concept of woman is divorced from the
concept of woman's body, conceptual room is made
for the idea of a woman who is no particular historical woman—she has no color, no accent, no particular characteristics that require having a body. She
is somehow all and only woman; that is her only
identifying feature. And so it will seem inappropriate or beside the point to think of women in terms
of any physical characteristics, especially if their
oppression has been rationalized by reference to
those characteristics.

None of this is to say that the historical and cultural identity of being Black or white is the same
thing as, or is reducible to, the physical feature of
having black or white skin. Historical and cultural
identity is not constituted by having a body with
particular identifying features, but it cannot be
comprehended without such features and the significance attached to them.

Adrienne Rich was perhaps the first well-known
contemporary white feminist to have noted "white
solipsism" in feminist theorizing and activity. I think
it is no coincidence that she also noticed and attended to the strong strain of somatophobia in feminist theory. *Of Woman Born* updates the connection
between somatophobia and misogyny/gynephobia
that Simone de Beauvoir described at length in *The
Second Sex*.[8] But unlike de Beauvoir or Firestone,

---

[6]Winthrop P. Jordan, *The White Man's Burden* (New York: Oxford University Press, 1974), chap. 1.
[7]Smith, *Killers of the Dream,* 83–98.

[8]Adrienne Rich, *Of Woman Born* (New York: Norton, 1976).

Rich refuses to throw out the baby with the bathwater: she sees that the historical negative connection between woman and body (in particular, between woman and womb) can be broken in more than one way. Both de Beauvoir and Firestone wanted to break it by insisting that women need be no more connected—in thought or deed—with the body than men have been. In their view of embodiment as a liability, de Beauvoir and Firestone are in virtual agreement with the patriarchal cultural history they otherwise question. Rich, however, insists that the negative connection between woman and body be broken along other lines. She asks us to think about whether what she calls "flesh-loathing" is the only attitude it is possible to have toward our bodies. Just as she explicitly distinguishes between motherhood as experience and motherhood as institution, so she implicitly asks us to distinguish between embodiment as experience and embodiment as institution. Flesh-loathing is part of the well-entrenched beliefs, habits, and practices epitomized in the treatment of pregnancy as a disease. But we need not experience our flesh, our body, as loathsome.

I think it is not a psychological or historical accident that having examined the way women view their bodies, Rich also focused on the failure of white women to see Black women's experiences as different from their own. For looking at embodiment is one way (though not the only one) of coming to recognize and understand the particularity of experience. Without bodies we could not have personal histories. Nor could we be identified as woman or man, Black or white. This is not to say that reference to publicly observable bodily characteristics settles the question of whether someone is woman or man, Black or white; nor is it to say that being woman or man, Black or white, just means having certain bodily characteristics (that is one reason some Blacks want to capitalize the term; "Black" refers to a cultural identity, not simply a skin color). But different meanings are attached to having certain characteristics, in different places and at different times and by different people, and those differences affect enormously the kinds of lives we lead or experiences we have. Women's op-

pression has been linked to the meanings assigned to having a woman's body by male oppressors. Blacks' oppression has been linked to the meanings assigned to having a black body by white oppressors. (Note how insidiously this way of speaking once again leaves unmentioned the situation for Black women.) We cannot hope to understand the meaning of a person's experiences, including her experiences of oppression, without first thinking of her as embodied, and second thinking about the particular meanings assigned to that embodiment. If, because of somatophobia, we think and write as if we are not embodied, or as if we would be better off if we were not embodied, we are likely to ignore the ways in which different forms of embodiment are correlated with different kinds of experience.

Rich—unlike de Beauvoir—asks us to reflect on the culturally assigned differences between having a Black or a white body, as well as on the differences between having the body of a woman or of a man. Other feminists have reflected on the meaning of embodiment and recognized the connection between flesh-loathing and woman-hatred, but they have only considered it far enough to try to divorce the concept of woman from the concept of the flesh. In effect, they have insisted that having different bodies does not or need not mean men and women are any different as humans; and having said that, they imply that having different colored bodies does not mean that Black women and white women are any different. Such statements are fine if interpreted to mean that the differences between woman and man, Black and white, should not be used against Black women and white women and Black men. But not paying attention to embodiment and to the cultural meanings assigned to different forms of it is to encourage sexblindness and colorblindness. These blindnesses are vicious when they are used to support the idea that all experience is male experience or that all experience is white experience. Rich does not run away from the fact that women have bodies, nor does she wish that women's bodies were not so different from men's. That healthy regard for the ground of our differences from men is logically connected to—though of course does not ensure—a healthy regard for the ground of the differences between Black women and white women.

> "Colorblindness" . . . implies that I would look at a Black woman and see her as white, thus engaging in white solipsism to the utter erasure of her particular reality.[9]

Colorblindness denies the particularity of the Black woman and rules out the possibility both that her history has been different and that her future might be different in any significant way from the white woman's.

• • •

On the one hand, what unifies women and justifies us in talking about the oppression of women is the overwhelming evidence of the worldwide and historical subordination of women to men. On the other, while it may be possible for us to speak about women in a general way, it also is inevitable that any statement we make about women in some particular place at some particular time is bound to suffer from ethnocentrism if we try to claim for it more generality than it has. So, for example, to say that the image of woman as frail and dependent is oppressive is certainly true. But it is oppressive to white women in the United States in quite a different way than it is oppressive to Black women, for the sexism Black women experience is in the context of their experience of racism. In Toni Morrison's *The Bluest Eye,* the causes and consequences of Pecola's longing to have blue eyes are surely quite different from the causes and consequences of a white girl with brown eyes having a similar desire.[10] More to the point, the consequences of *not* having blue eyes are quite different for the two. Similarly, the family may be the locus of oppression for white middle-class women, but to claim that it is the locus of oppression for all women is to ignore the fact that for Blacks in America the family has been a source of resistance against white oppression.[11]

In short, the claim that all women are oppressed is fully compatible with, and needs to be explicated in terms of, the many varieties of oppression that different populations of women have been subject to. After all, why should oppressors settle for uniform kinds of oppression, when to oppress their victims in many different ways—consciously or unconsciously—makes it more likely that the oppressed groups will not perceive it to be in their interest to work together?

Finally, it is crucial not to see Blackness only as the occasion for oppression—any more than one sees being a woman only as the occasion for oppression. No one ought to expect the forms of our liberation to be any less various than the forms of our oppression. We need to be at least as generous in imagining what women's liberation will be like as our oppressors have been in devising what women's oppression has been.

THE SACRED HOOP

Paula Gunn Allen

In the beginning were the people, the spirits, the gods; the four-leggeds, the two-leggeds, the wingeds, the crawlers, the burrowers, the plants, the trees, the rocks. There were the moon, the sun, the earth, the waters of earth and sky. There were the stars, the thunders, the mountains, the plains, the mesas and the hills. There was the Mystery. There were the Grandmothers, the Mothers, the clans, the people. At the end of the fifteenth century, Anglo-European time, the old world that the tribes, Nations, and Confederacies lived in began to be torn apart. At first the tear seemed small enough, and for various reasons we did not grasp the enormity of the threat; indeed, many tribes did not know there was a threat for another two to three hundred years.

The wars of conquest that began with the landing of Christopher Columbus on an isolated little is-

---

[9]Rich, "Disloyal to Civilization," 300.
[10]Toni Morrison, *The Bluest Eye* (New York: Pocketbooks, 1972).
[11]See, for example, Carol Stack, *All Our Kin* (New York: Harper and Row, 1974).

land on the edge of the southeastern sea gained momentum until every tribe and every aspect of traditional life was swept up in it; during the centuries of those wars everything in our lives was affected and much was changed, even the earth, the waters, and the sky. We went down under wave after wave of settlement, each preceded, accompanied by, and followed by military engagements that were more often massacres of our people than declared wars. These wars, taken together, constitute the longest undeclared war neo-Americans have fought, and no end is in sight.

It is still being fought on reservations, in urban communities, along Indian-white frontiers (which occur wherever Indian and non-Indian interface); in Mexico and in Central America—Guatemala, El Salvador, Nicaragua, Honduras, and Costa Rica; in South America—Brazil, Argentina, Chile, Venezuela, Peru. In some areas we have been all but extinguished, as in the islands of the Caribbean, Canada, and the United States; in others we continue to survive in large numbers, though usually characterized as peasants and disguised as Hispanics by the Anglo-European/Hispanic media, scholars, officials, and political activists. Still we endure, and many of our old values, lifeways, and philosophies endure with us, for they, like us, are inextricably linked to the land, the sky, the waters, and the spirits of this Turtle Island, this Earth-Surface place, that the whites call "the New World."

FROM GYNECENTRIC TO PATRIARCHAL

During the five hundred years of Anglo-European colonization, the tribes have seen a progressive shift from gynecentric, egalitarian, ritual-based social systems to secularized structures closely imitative of the European patriarchal system. During this time women (including lesbians) and gay men— along with traditional medicine people, holy people, shamans, and ritual leaders—have suffered severe loss of status, power, and leadership. That these groups have suffered concurrent degradation is not coincidental; the woman-based, woman-centered traditions of many precontact tribes were tightly bound to ritual, and ritual was based on spiritual understandings rather than on economic or political ones.

The genocide practiced against the tribes is aimed systematically at the dissolution of ritual tradition. In the past this has included prohibition of ceremonial practices throughout North and Meso-America, Christianization, enforced loss of languages, reeducation of tribal peoples through government-supported and Christian mission schools that Indian children have been forced to attend, renaming of the traditional ritual days as Christian feast days, missionization (incarceration) of tribal people, deprivation of language, severe disruption of cultures and economic and resource bases of those cultures, and the degradation of the status of women as central to the spiritual and ritual life of the tribes.

Along with the devaluation of women comes the devaluation of traditional spiritual leaders, female and male, and, largely because of their ritual power and status, the devaluation of lesbian and gay tribal members as leaders, shamans, healers, or ritual participants. Virtually all customary sexual customs among the tribes were changed—including marital, premarital, homosexual, and ritual sexual practices, along with childhood and adult indulgence in open sexuality, common in many tribes.

Colonization means the loss not only of language and the power of self-government but also of ritual status of all women and those males labeled "deviant" by the white Christian colonizers. The usual divisions of labor—generally gender-based (if you count homosexual men as women and dikes as men)—were altered, prohibited, or forced underground, from whence they have only recently begun to reemerge as the tribes find themselves engaged in a return to more traditional ways of life.

In considering gender-based roles, we must remember that while the roles themselves were fixed in most archaic American cultures, with divisions of "women's work" and "men's work," the individuals fit into these roles on the basis of proclivity, inclination, and temperament. Thus men who in contemporary

European and American societies are designated gay or homosexual were gender-designated among many tribes as "women" in terms of their roles; women who in contemporary societies are designated as lesbians (actually, "dikes" is more accurate) were designated as men in tribal cultures. As an example, the Kaska of Canada would designate a daughter in a family that had only daughters as a boy. When she was small, around five, her parents would tie a pouch of dried bear ovaries to her belt. She would dress in male clothing and would function in the Kaska male role for the rest of her life. Interestingly, if a male attempted to make sexual advances to this male-designated person, he was liable to punishment, because the Kaska felt this violation would ruin the "dike's" luck in hunting.[1]

The Yuma had a tradition of gender designation based on dreams; a female who dreamed of weapons became a male for all practical purposes. In this the Yumas were similar to the neighboring Mohaves and Cocopah, except the gender-role designation was based on the choice of companions and play objects of a young person. In such systems a girl who chose to play with boys or with boys' objects such as a bow and arrow became a male functionary. Among the Mohave, another dream-culture people related to the Yuma, the hwame, a term roughly corresponding to "dike" in English, took a male name and was in all respects subject to ritual male taboos vis à vis females, such as avoidance of contact with a menstruating wife. The hwame's wife was not considered hwame but simply a woman.[2]

In addition to these tribes, others that display a positive acceptance of lesbianism include the Navajo (who considered lesbians an asset), the Mohave (who thought that from the inception of the world homosexuals were a natural and necessary part of society), the Quinault, the Apache, the Ojibwa, and the Eskimo.[3]

In her brilliant, comprehensive gay cultural history *Another Mother Tongue: Gay Words, Gay Worlds,* poet and writer Judy Grahn devotes a large chapter to the existence of lesbians and homosexuals as ritually and socially valued tribal members. Citing numerous sources including Jonathan Katz, Sue Ellen Jacobs, myself, Carolyn Neithammer, Arthur Evans, Edward Carpenter, Michael Wilken, John (Fire) Lame Deer, Hamilton Tyler, John Gunn, and various contemporary gay and lesbian American Indian poets and writers, Grahn writes a lengthy chronicle about the place gays held among many American Indian peoples. Grahn cites anthropologist Sue Ellen Jacobs as listing eighty-eight tribes whose recorded cultural attributes include references to gayness, with twenty of these including specific references to lesbianism. According to Jacobs, eleven tribes denied any homosexuality to anthropologists or other writers (which doesn't necessarily mean it wasn't openly sanctioned and practiced, acknowledged, or valued), and those denials came from tribes located in areas of heaviest, lengthiest, and most severely puritanical white encroachment. Among the eighty-eight tribes who admitted homosexuality among them and referred to it in positive ways are the Apache, Navajo, Winnebago, Cheyenne, Pima, Crow, Shoshoni, Paiute, Osage, Acoma, Zuñi, Sioux, Pawnee, Choctaw, Creek, Seminole, Illinois, Mohave, Shasta, Aleut, Sac and Fox, Iowa, Kansas, Yuma, Aztec, Tlingit,

---

[1]Carolyn Neithammer, *Daughters of the Earth* (New York: Collier, 1977), p. 231. It must be said that Neithammer is as homophobic in her reporting on lesbianism as she is racist in her accounts of tribal views of womanhood. In her three-page treatment, she begins with accounts of positive valuing of lesbians, then moves to tolerance of lesbianism, and ends the section with a rousing tale of how the good villagers of a heterosexist Eskimo village routed the evil lesbian and her lover and forced them to give up their unconventional lifestyle and return to the ways of their village. Sadly, her book is often the main title featured on the Native American Women shelf at women's bookstores across the country.

[2]Neithammer, *Daughters,* pp. 231–234.

---

[3]In an unpublished paper, Evelyn Blackwood cites Kaj Birket-Smith's *The Chugach Eskimo* (Copenhagen: National Museum, 1953) on the interesting point that evidently only the Chugash Eskimo and the Navajo literally perceive the berdache as "half-man/half-woman," which, Blackwood says, is not a common perception. "Sexuality, Gender and Mode of Production: The Case of Native American Female Homosexuality (Berdache)," unpublished manuscript, 1983.

Maya, Naskapi, Ponca, Menomini, Maricopa, Klamath, Quinault, Yuki, Chilula, and Kamia— indicating the presence of lesbianism and homosexuality in every area of North America.[4]

• • •

Recent scholarly work reveals the universal or nearly universal presence of homosexuality and lesbianism among tribal peoples, the special respect and honor often accorded gay men and women, and the alteration in that status as a result of colonization of the continent by Anglo-Europeans. These studies demonstrate the process by which external conquest and colonization become internalized among the colonized with vivid clarity. Homophobia, which was rare (perhaps even absent entirely) among tribal peoples in the Americas, has steadily grown among them as they have traded traditional tribal values for Christian industrial ones.

Gay historian Walter Williams records particularly poignant stories about contemporary homosexuals in which colonization is clearly linked to homophobia and racist colonial attempts to eradicate tribal cultures. Citing numerous scholarly sources, Williams refers to homosexuality among the Maya, Ojibwa, various branches of the Sioux, the Sac and Fox, the Osage, unspecified California and Alaskan Indians, the Papago, Crow, Hopi, Navajo, Klamath, Winnebago, Yokuts, Zuñi, Iroquois, Cheyenne, Omaha, and Aleut.[5]

Among the many accounts Williams cites, the stark homophobia of the white recorders contrasts sharply with the easy acceptance the Indians accord the presence of gays among themselves. This is particularly notable in the earliest white reports; as colonization deepens its hold on tribal lifeways, the reported attitudes of Indians split: some, usually the most traditional, continue to accord high respect to homosexuals, even to the present day. Of these,

many, perhaps most, will not discuss the subject with non-Indians because they are unwilling to have institutions or practices that they value subjected to ridicule or contempt. They also may feel a strong need to protect the homosexuals and lesbians among them and the tribe as a whole from further life-threatening assaults which for too long have been directed against them.

Other Indians, more acculturated and highly Christianized, treat the presence of lesbianism or homosexuality among them with fear and loathing. They do not confine that loathing to homosexuality but direct it to other aspects of tribal ceremonial life, particularly when it has to do with sexuality. Thus a Hopi man despairs of his people, saying that there is nothing good in the old Hopi ways. This man, Kuanwikvaya, testified to U.S. officials: "There is nothing good in the Hopi religion. It is all full of adultery and immorality. I cannot tell all the dirt and filth that is in these ceremonies." Another Hopi man, Tuwaletstiwa, testified that before he accepted Christianity his life "was unspeakably evil . . . When a Hopi becomes a Christian he quits attending these dances. He knows the evil in them is so great."[6] These testimonies were taken in 1920, when U.S. officials suppressed the Hopi dances. The men's statements were used as "local witness" proof that the traditional ceremonies were properly banned.

But the pattern of colonized psychology and social valuation among Indian people may be being reversed. Recently, Russell Means of the American Indian Movement—a man not always noted for his liberal attitudes toward women and other devalued individuals—said, in defense of homosexuals and their anciently valued place among the people: "The Indian looked upon these unique individuals as something special the Great Mystery created to teach us. These people had something special to tell us."[7] And the Oglala Sioux holy man John (Fire) Lame Deer

[4]Judy Grahn, *Another Mother Tongue: Gay Words, Gay Worlds* (Boston: Beacon Press, 1984), pp. 55–56.
[5]Walter Williams, "American Indian Responses to the Suppression of the Homosexual Berdache Tradition," presented at the Organization of American Historians convention, Spring 1983.

[6]Martin Duberman, ed., "Documents in Hopi Indian Sexuality," *Radical History Review* 20 (Spring 1979), pp. 109, 112, 113.
[7]Russell Means, Interview, *Penthouse Magazine* (April 1981), p. 138.

said, "To us a man is what nature, or his dreams, make him. We accept him for what he wants to be. That's up to him . . . There are good men among the *winktes* and they have been given certain powers."[8]

It is significant, I think, that those who are homophobic are also very likely to be misogynist. Indeed, the latter often masquerade as the former. The colonizers' treatment of gays is analogous to their treatment of healers, holy people, dreamers, and other traditional leaders, foremost among whom have traditionally been the women—the matrons, clan mothers, dreamers, and makers of ritual and tribal life in the western hemisphere.

Before the coming of the white man, or long ago, so far, as the people say, the Grandmother(s) created the firmament, the earth, and all the spirit beings in it. She (or they) created, by thinking into being, the Women, or the Woman, from whom the people sprang. The Women thus thought into being also gave thought, and the people and all the orders of being in this world came into being, including the laws, the sciences, agriculture, householding, social institutions— everything. Long ago the peoples of this hemisphere knew that their power to live came to them from the Grandmother or Grandmothers (depending on the tribe) not only originally but continuously, even to the present. Many old mythologies and most ceremonial cycles (if taken within their entire cultural framework) reiterate and celebrate this central fact of tribal Native American existence. Many of the tribes retain this old knowledge—a knowledge that they have kept hidden from the whites and often from their own tribespeople but that they have preserved. Only recently have the women begun to raise our voices again, at the behest of the Grandmother(s), to tell the story as it is told and to lay claim to the ancient power that is vested in Woman since before time.

In a recent interview published in the West German feminist monthly *Emma,* three Native American representatives of a movement called Concerned Aboriginal Women discussed the pres-

ent crisis among American Indians in Canada and the part the women are taking in their struggle to retain title to their lands. One of the women, identified as Vera, said: "You know, for such a long long time our men struggled and struggled, and things got worse. Then the grandmothers and mothers decided that now we must intervene! Among our people we have a tradition that the women make the decisions. Later we can go back to taking care of our children." Another woman, Judalon, continued: "The government corrupted our leaders and it took the women to realize it." The third woman, Dinah, added, "They've turned our men around the way they want them, so that they have lost their direction and no longer know where they should be going."

The interviewer asked the women why they sound like they want to "step back" to taking care of the children when German women are struggling to do more than housework and childrearing. German women "want to be able to participate in public decisions," the interviewer said. Judalon explained that Native American women have always participated in public decisions.

> For example, in my mother's tribe, the Mohawks, the women made all the decisions. In the Longhouse the clan mothers would gather and sit on one side. The chiefs would sit on the other side. On the other two sides, the rest of the people would sit and the current problem would be discussed. The clan mothers would decide what should happen, but the men would speak for them. The men never made decisions. It was that way in the tribe and also in a clan's household. The women were responsible and made the decisions.
>
> Everything has changed since we've had contact with the Europeans. First, our leaders were brainwashed. They became vain and thought that they alone could decide things . . . Today many Indian men behave like European men.

The other two women agree, noting that traditionally respect for women by Indian men was high and that all work was valued because it was all important. At this the interviewer asked about division of labor into gender roles, and the Iroquois women responded that work was generally divided along gender lines,

[8]John (Fire) Lame Deer and Richard Erdoes, *Lame Deer: Seeker of Visions* (New York: Simon and Schuster, 1972), p. 149.

but I think with us there were never such sharp divisions between these areas as with you. The men had to be able to cook since, for example, they were often away hunting or fighting. And there were also girl warriors. In some tribes there were also women leaders. Of course, there are great differences between the Indian nations, but most of them did not have this sharp division of roles. There were also girls who were raised as boys, if, for example, a family only had daughters. And these women would then marry other women. We even have special initiation rites for transvestites . . . In those families which lead a traditional lifestyle, it is still the case that the men have great respect for the women. And with the help of the spiritual movement, things have been changing over the last ten years. More and more Indians are returning to the traditional ways. The old people are teaching us.[9]

The way it is now is generally very different from the way it was; the devaluation of women that has accompanied Christianization and westernization is not a simple matter of loss of status. It also involves increases in violence against women by men, a phenomenon not experienced until recently and largely attributable to colonization and westernization.

Many people believe that Indian men have suffered more damage to their traditional status than have Indian women, but I think that belief is more a reflection of colonial attitudes toward the primacy of male experience than of historical fact. While women still play the traditional role of housekeeper, childbearer, and nurturer, they no longer enjoy the unquestioned positions of power, respect, and decision making on local and international levels that were not so long ago their accustomed functions. Only in some tribes do they still enjoy the medicine or shamanistic power they earlier possessed. No longer, except in backwoods pockets of resistance, do they speak with the power and authority of inviolable law.

It is true that colonization destroyed roles that had given men their sense of self-esteem and identity, but the significant roles lost were not those of hunter and warrior. Rather, colonization took away

[9] Interview in *Emma* (June 1982). Reprinted in *Connexions: An International Women's Quarterly,* no. 8 (Spring 1983) pp. 6–8.

the security of office men once derived from their ritual and political relationship to women. Men's status in all tribes that use clan systems, and perhaps in others, came to them through the agency of women, who got their own status from the spirit people, particularly the Grandmother powers that uphold and energize the universe. But with the coming of the white man and his patriarchal system, the powers of the women were systematically undermined in countless ways, and this undermining was and is reinforced willingly by many of the men.

The history of the subjugation of women under the dominant patriarchal control of males is a long and largely ugly one, and it affects every tribe and Nation now as much as ever. It is synchronistic rather than coincidental that most of the Indian women known to the general non-Indian public have been convicted of playing into the white man's game and betraying the Indian; all have been accused of doing so because of sexual or romantic connections with white men, and all have been blamed by many Indians for white conquest. Patriarchy requires that powerful women be discredited so that its own system will seem to be the only one that reasonable or intelligent people can subscribe to.

The nature of the change in the images of women and gays among American Indians caused by patriarchal propaganda is historical, cultural, and political. In that change can be seen the history of patriarchy on this continent and, by extension, all over the world. As American Indian women emerge from the patriarchally imposed ignominy of the past centuries, the falsity of all the colonizers' stories about Native Americans, about spirituality, gayness, and femaleness, becomes increasingly apparent. And as we articulate a feminine analysis of the effects of colonization, we are more and more able to demonstrate that the colonizers' image of Indian women has, more than any other factor, led to the high incidence of rape and abuse of Indian women by Indian men. This violent behavior is tacitly approved of by the tribes through the refusal of tribal governments across the country and in urban Indian enclaves to address the issue and provide care, shelter, and relief for the women victims and competent, useful treatment for the offenders. The white and recently Indian image of powerful Indian women as traitors is another chapter in the patriarchal folktale that begins with Eve causing Adam's fall from grace into divine disgrace.

WOMEN AS HEALERS, DREAMERS, AND SHAMANS

• • •

Traditional American Indian systems depended on basic concepts that are at present being reformulated and to some extent practiced by western feminists, including cooperation (but by that traditional Indians generally meant something other than non-competitiveness or passivity), harmony (again, this did not necessarily mean absence of conflict), balance, kinship, and respect. Their material, social, and ritual systems were predicated on these essential values, which might be seen as objectives, parameters, norms, or principles depending on how they were being applied in a given situation. They did not rely on external social institutions such as schools, court, and prisons, kings, or other political rulers, but rather on internal institutions such as spirit-messengers, guides, teachers, or mentors; on tradition, ritual, dream and vision; on personal inclination (understood more in a geological sense than in a hedonistic one) and the leadership of those who had demonstrated competence with the foregoing characteristics.

Thus to traditional American Indians, social and personal life is governed by internal rather than external factors, and systems based on spiritual orders rather than on material ones are necessarily heavily oriented toward internal governing mechanisms.

Among traditionals the psychospiritual characteristics of the individual are channeled to blend harmoniously with those of the rest of the group. This channeling is done by applying custom, by sharing appropriate items from the oral tradition, and by helping and encouraging children in tribally approved endeavors that are matched to individual inclinations but that will provide useful skills, understandings, and abilities for the good of the entire group. The young person is trained in a number of ways, formal and informal, and by a number of individuals in the tribe. Traditionally, female children (or female surrogates) are trained by women, while male children (or male surrogates) are trained by men in learning their ritual roles within their social system. In some groups such as the Cherokee, however, shamans are typically trained along cross-gender rather than same gender lines. Thus male shamans train female apprentices, and female shamans train male apprentices. Traditionally, proper behavior falls along gender lines, as did expectations, but gender is understood in a psychological or psychospiritual sense much more than in a physiological one.

Thus the high position held by women as a group and by certain women as individuals results from certain inclinations that the women are born with and that they demonstrate through temperament, interest, competence, spirit-direction, and guidance. Women are by the nature of feminine "vibration" graced with certain inclinations that make them powerful and capable in certain ways (all who have this temperament, ambience, or "vibration" are designated women and all who do not are not so designated). Their power includes bearing and rearing children (but in tribal life everyone is in some sense "raising" the children); cooking and similar forms of "woman's work"; decision making; dreaming and visioning; prophesying; divining, healing, locating people or things; harvesting, preserving, preparing, storing, or transporting food and healing stuffs; producing finished articles of clothing; making houses and laying them out in the proper village arrangement; making and using all sorts of technological equipment such as needles, scrapers, grinders, blenders, harvesters, diggers, fire makers, lathes, spindles, looms, knives, spoons, and ladles; locating and/or allocating virtually every resource used by the people. Guiding young women through the complex duties of womanhood must have taxed the creative, physical, psychic, and spiritual powers of all the women. In addition, they bore responsibility for preserving and using the oral tradition; making important tribal decisions about the life or death of captives and other outsiders; and overseeing ritual occasions, including making spiritual and physical provisions for ceremonies in cultures that devoted as much as two-thirds of their time to ritual/ceremonial pursuits. In short, the women did—and wherever possible still do—everything that maintains the life and stability of their tribal people. It is no wonder that Indian people in general insist that among them women are considered sacred. Nor, as perhaps you can see, is this an empty compliment in a society that depends for its life upon the sacred.

As shamans, the women in many tribes function in all ways that male shamans are known to. They perform healings, hunting ceremonies, vision quests and the guidance for them, acts of psychokinesis, teleportation, weather direction, and more. In the various tribes according to each one's customs, the shaman also creates certain artifacts—clothing, baskets, ornaments, objects to be worn in pouches or under skirts or sewed into belts. She officiates at burials, births, child naming and welcoming into this world, menstrual and pregnancy rituals and rites, psychic manipulation of animals, metamorphoses or transformations. She does much of this through dancing and chanting, and a large part of the method, symbols, significances, and effects of her shamanic efforts are recorded in the stories she tells, the songs she sings, and the knowledge she possesses. Much of this knowledge she transmits to others in ways that will be of use to them, and much of it she keeps to herself, teaches in formal settings to her apprentices, or shares with other shamans.

One of the primary functions of the shaman is her effect on tribal understandings of "women's roles," which in large part are traditional in Mrs. McCabe's sense of the word. It is the shaman's connection to the spirit world that Indian women writers reflect most strongly in our poetry and fiction. If there is any Indian woman's tradition that informs our work, it is the spiritual understanding of womanhood as an expression of spirit. That understanding is formed on the recognition that everything is alive, that the spirit people are part of our daily world, that all life lives in harmony and kinship with and to all other life, and that sickness of all kinds and of all orders comes about because of our resistance to surrendering to the complexity and multidimensionality of existence.

So we acknowledge that the violation of the Mothers' and Grandmothers' laws of kinship, respect, balance, and harmony brings about social, planetary, and personal illness and that healing is a matter of restoring the balance within ourselves and our communities. To this restoration of balance, of health, and wellness (wealth) we contribute our energies. For we are engaged in the work of reclaiming our minds, our gods, and our traditions. The sacred hoop cannot be restored unless and until its sacred center is recognized.

QUESTIONS FOR DISCUSSION

1. Do "male" and "female" signify two different natures? How do you account for the observable behavior and characterological differences between men and women? Would you want there to be a society in which there were no specific sex-identified social roles? Is an androgynous human being a possible and/or desirable ideal?
2. Discuss the significance of the role of women within Islam with reference to Fatima Mernissi's analysis and Simone de Beauvoir's claim that women are the second sex.
3. Simone de Beauvoir writes: "A free individual blames only himself for his failures, he assumes responsibility for them; but everything happens to women through the agency of others, and therefore these others are responsible for her woes." Evaluate this position in the light of Sartre's claim that we are absolutely free and responsible for our actions.
4. Why, according to Simone de Beauvoir, are women "the Other"? Evaluate her position with respect to Ortega y Gasset's response. What do you think?
5. Does Spelman's insistence on the importance of the body in understanding women's oppression imply that there is an innate female nature? Why, for her, does the recognition of the importance of the body imply that sexism is different for white and black women? Do you agree with her analysis?
6. What are the implications of Allen's analysis of the effects of the European conquest on Native Americans for the issue of gender nature?

SEXUAL NATURE

In the last selection in the previous section, general acceptance of homosexuality and lesbianism by Native Americans before the advent of colonization was discussed. Homosexuality was also very much accepted in ancient Greece, at least among the aristocracy. A typical scenario for the young aristocratic male was to have an older male mentor who was also a lover. When the young man reached maturity, he would marry and have a family. Eventually, he would become the older lover and mentor of a younger male, and the pattern would repeat itself. The general European and American attitude toward homosexuality and lesbianism is, however, quite different. Often drawing on biblical references, this tradition has been decidedly homophobic, claiming that homosexuality is unnatural and immoral. The underlying premise is that a heterosexual orientation is the only natural form of sexuality. The central question that the articles in this section will raise is whether there is any reason to assume that some forms of sexuality are natural, while others are not. Specifically, is there any reason to assume that homosexuality is unnatural? This question is closely related to another: Is there any reason to claim, as is often done in this culture, that homosexuality is immoral? It is precisely these two questions that are addressed by Richard Mohr, who has written extensively about gay issues and who is a philosopher at the University of Illinois. Mohr notes that those who claim that homosexuality is immoral often claim that it violates the natural function of the genitals. But do those or any other organ need have only one function? Is there anything unnatural, for example, in using the mouth to lick stamps or, for that matter, to have sex?

Mohr also suggests that homosexuality is more a discovery than it is a choice, in which case it would make no sense to hold the homosexual morally responsible for his or her homosexuality. This implies that while there is no sexual orientation that is inherently unnatural, sexual orientation is determined by one's nature, which is to say, by one's biology. It is precisely this claim that is challenged by Ruth Hubbard, who is professor emerita of biology at Harvard University.

Hubbard has written several major works and numerous articles concerned with the political implications of biology and especially its implications for women's issues. In this selection, taken from *The Politics of Women's Biology,* Hubbard argues that people are not born homosexual or heterosexual. Is sexual orientation, then, something which is socially constructed? She doesn't precisely answer this question, but as a long-term critic of biological determinism, she seems to be arguing against any form of determinism. Instead, she argues for a non-deterministic model of sexual development, placing emphasis on our diversity, flexibility, and ability to change. Society may channel and limit our sexual imagination, but, in the last analysis, "people fall in love with individuals, not with a sex."

IS HOMOSEXUALITY UNNATURAL?

Richard D. Mohr

WHO ARE GAYS ANYWAY?

A recent Gallup poll found that only one in five Americans reports having a gay or lesbian acquaintance.[1] This finding is extraordinary given the number of practicing homosexuals in America. Alfred Kinsey's 1948 study of the sex lives of 12,000 white males shocked the nation: 37 percent had at least one homosexual experience to orgasm

---

[1]"Public Fears—And Sympathies," *Newsweek,* August 12, 1985, p. 23.

in their adult lives; an additional 13 percent had homosexual fantasies to orgasm; 4 percent were exclusively homosexual in their practices; another 5 percent had virtually no heterosexual experience; and nearly 20 percent had at least as many homosexual as heterosexual experiences.[2]

Two out of five men one passes on the street have had orgasmic sex with men. Every second family in the country has a member who is essentially homosexual and many more people regularly have homosexual experiences. Who are homosexuals? They are your friends, your minister, your teacher, your bank teller, your doctor, your mail carrier, your officemate, your roommate, your congressional representative, your sibling, parent, and spouse. They are everywhere, virtually all ordinary, virtually all unknown.

Several important consequences follow. First, the country is profoundly ignorant of the actual experience of gay people. Second, social attitudes and practices that are harmful to gays have a much greater overall harmful impact on society than is usually realized. Third, most gay people live in hiding—in the closet—making the "coming out" experience the central fixture of gay consciousness and invisibility the chief characteristic of the gay community.

• • •

BUT AREN'T THEY UNNATURAL?

The most noteworthy feature of the accusation of something being unnatural (where a moral rather than an advertising point is being made) is that the plaint is so infrequently made. One used to hear the charge leveled against abortion, but that has pretty much faded as anti-abortionists have come to lay all their chips on the hope that people will come to view abortion as murder. Incest used to be considered unnatural but discourse now usually assimilates it to

the moral machinery of rape and violated trust. The charge comes up now in ordinary discourse only against homosexuality. This suggests that the charge is highly idiosyncratic and has little, if any, explanatory force. It fails to put homosexuality in a class with anything else so that one can learn by comparison with clear cases of the class just exactly what it is that is allegedly wrong with it.

Though the accusation of unnaturalness looks whimsical, in actual ordinary discourse when applied to homosexuality, it is usually delivered with venom aforethought. It carries a high emotional charge, usually expressing disgust and evincing queasiness. Probably it is nothing but an emotional charge. For people get equally disgusted and queasy at all sorts of things that are perfectly natural—to be expected in nature apart from artifice—and that could hardly be fit subjects for moral condemnation. Two typical examples in current American culture are some people's responses to mothers' suckling in public and to women who do not shave body hair. When people have strong emotional reactions, as they do in these cases, without being able to give good reasons for them, we think of them not as operating morally, but rather as being obsessed and manic. So the feelings of disgust that some people have to gays will hardly ground a charge of immorality. People fling the term "unnatural" against gays in the same breath and with the same force as when they call gays "sick" and "gross." When they do this, they give every appearance of being neurotically fearful and incapable of reasoned discourse.

When "nature" is taken in *technical* rather than ordinary usages, it looks like the notion also will not ground a charge of homosexual immorality. When unnatural means "by artifice" or "made by humans," it need only be pointed out that virtually everything that is good about life is unnatural in this sense, that the chief feature that distinguishes people from other animals is their very ability to make over the world to meet their needs and desires, and that their well-being depends upon these departures from nature. On this understanding of human nature and the natural, homosexuality is perfectly unobjectionable.

---

[2]Alfred C. Kinsey, *Sexual Behavior in the Human Male* (Philadelphia: Saunders, 1948), pp. 650–651. On the somewhat lower incidences of lesbianism, see Alfred C. Kinsey, *Sexual Behavior in the Human Female* (Philadelphia: Saunders, 1953), pp. 472–475.

Another technical sense of natural is that something is natural and so, good, if it fulfills some function in nature. Homosexuality on this view is unnatural because it allegedly violates the function of genitals, which is to produce babies. One problem with this view is that lots of bodily parts have lots of functions and just because some one activity can be fulfilled by only one organ (say, the mouth for eating) this activity does not condemn other functions of the organ to immorality (say, the mouth for talking, licking stamps, blowing bubbles, or having sex). So the possible use of the genitals to produce children does not, without more, condemn the use of the genitals for other purposes, say, achieving ecstasy and intimacy.

The functional view of nature will only provide a morally condemnatory sense to the unnatural if a thing which might have many uses has but one proper function to the exclusion of other possible functions. But whether this is so cannot be established simply by looking at the thing. For what is seen is all its possible functions. The notion of function seemed like it might ground moral authority, but instead it turns out that moral authority is needed to define proper function. Some people try to fill in this moral authority by appeal to the "design" or "order" of an organ, saying, for instance, that the genitals are designed for the purpose of procreation. But these people cheat intellectually if they do not make explicit *who* the designer and orderer is. If it is God, we are back to square one—holding others accountable for religious beliefs.

Further, ordinary moral attitudes about childbearing will not provide the needed supplement which in conjunction with the natural function view of bodily parts would produce a positive obligation to use the genitals for procreation. Society's attitude toward a childless couple is that of pity not censure—even if the couple could have children. The pity may be an unsympathetic one, that is, not registering a course one would choose *for oneself,* but this does not make it a course one would *require* of others. The couple who discovers they cannot have children are viewed not as having thereby had a debt canceled, but rather as having to forgo some

of the richness of life, just as a quadriplegic is viewed not as absolved from some moral obligation to hop, skip, and jump, but as missing some of the richness of life. Consistency requires then that, at most, gays who do not or cannot have children are to be pitied rather than condemned. What *is* immoral is the willful preventing of people from achieving the richness of life. Immorality in this regard lies with those social customs, regulations, and statutes that prevent lesbians and gay men from establishing blood or adoptive families, not with gays themselves.

Sometimes people attempt to establish authority for a moral obligation to use bodily parts in a certain fashion simply by claiming that moral laws are natural laws and vice versa. On this account, inanimate objects and plants are good in that they follow natural laws by necessity, animals by instinct, and persons by a rational will. People are special in that they must first discover the laws that govern them. Now, even if one believes the view—dubious in the post-Newtonian, post-Darwinian world—that natural laws in the usual sense ($E = mc^2$, for instance) have some moral content, it is not at all clear how one is to discover the laws in nature that apply to people.

On the one hand, if one looks to people themselves for a model—and looks hard enough—one finds amazing variety, including homosexuality as a social ideal (upper-class fifth-century Athens) and even as socially mandatory (Melanesia today). When one looks to people, one is simply unable to strip away the layers of social custom, history, and taboo in order to see what's really there to any degree more specific than that people are the creatures that make over their world and are capable of abstract thought. That this is so should raise doubts that neutral principles are to be found in human nature that will condemn homosexuality.

On the other hand, if one looks to nature apart from people for models, the possibilities are staggering. There are fish that change gender over their lifetimes: should we "follow nature" and be operative transsexuals? Orangutans, genetically our next of kin, live completely solitary lives without social organization of any kind: ought we to "follow nature" and be hermits? There are many species where only two members per generation reproduce: should we be bees? The search in nature for people's purpose, far from finding sure models for action, is likely to leave one morally rudderless.

BUT AREN'T GAYS WILLFULLY THE WAY THEY ARE?

It is generally conceded that if sexual orientation is something over which an individual—for whatever reason—has virtually no control, then discrimination against gays is especially deplorable, as it is against racial and ethnic classes, because it holds people accountable without regard for anything they themselves have done. And to hold a person accountable for that over which the person has no control is a central form of prejudice.

Attempts to answer the question whether or not sexual orientation is something that is reasonably thought to be within one's own control usually appeal simply to various claims of the biological or "mental" sciences. But the ensuing debate over genes, hormones, twins, early childhood development, and the like, is as unnecessary as it is currently inconclusive.[3] All that is needed to answer the question is to look at the actual experience of gays in current society and it becomes fairly clear that sexual orientation is not likely a matter of choice. For coming to have a homosexual identity simply does not have the same sort of structure that decision making has.

On the one hand, the "choice" of the gender of a sexual partner does not seem to express a trivial desire that might be as easily well fulfilled by a simple substitution of the desired object. Picking the

gender of a sex partner is decidedly dissimilar, that is, to such activities as picking a flavor of ice cream. If an ice-cream parlor is out of one's flavor, one simply picks another. And if people were persecuted, threatened with jail terms, shattered careers, loss of family and housing, and the like, for eating, say, rocky road ice cream, no one would ever eat it; everyone would pick another easily available flavor. That gay people abide in being gay even in the face of persecution shows that being gay is not a matter of easy choice.

On the other hand, even if establishing a sexual orientation is not like making a relatively trivial choice, perhaps it is nevertheless relevantly like making the central and serious life choices by which individuals try to establish themselves as being of some type. Again, if one examines gay experience, this seems not to be the case. For one never sees anyone setting out to become a homosexual, in the way one does see people setting out to become doctors, lawyers, and bricklayers. One does not find "gays-to-be" picking some end—"At some point in the future, I want to become a homosexual"—and then setting about planning and acquiring the ways and means to that end, in the way one does see people deciding that they want to become lawyers, and then sees them plan what courses to take and what sort of temperaments, habits, and skills to develop in order to become lawyers. Typically gays-to-be simply find themselves having homosexual encounters and yet at least initially resisting quite strongly the identification of being homosexual. Such a person even very likely resists having such encounters, but ends up having them anyway. Only with time, luck, and great personal effort, but sometimes never, does the person gradually come to accept her or his orientation, to view it as a given material condition of life, coming as materials do with certain capacities and limitations. The person begins to act in accordance with his or her orientation and its capacities, seeing its actualization as a requisite for an integrated personality and as a central component of personal well-being. As a result, the experience of coming out to oneself has for gays the basic structure of a discovery, not the structure of a choice. And

---

[3]The preponderance of the scientific evidence supports the view that homosexuality is either genetically determined or a permanent result of early childhood development. See the Kinsey Institute's study by Alan Bell, Martin Weinberg, and Sue Hammersmith, *Sexual Preference: Its Development in Men and Women* (Bloomington: Indiana University Press, 1981); Frederick Whitam and Robin Mathy, *Male Homosexuality in Four Societies* (New York: Praeger, 1986), ch. 7.

far from signaling immorality, coming out to others affords one of the few remaining opportunities in ever more bureaucratic, mechanistic, and socialistic societies to manifest courage.

THE SOCIAL CONSTRUCTION OF SEXUALITY

Ruth Hubbard

There is no "natural" human sexuality. This is not to say that our sexual feelings are "unnatural" but that whatever feelings and activities our society interprets as sexual are channeled from birth into socially acceptable forms of expression.

Western thinking about sexuality is based on the Christian equation of sexuality with sin, which must be redeemed through making babies. To fulfill the Christian mandate, sexuality must be intended for procreation, and thus all forms of sexual expression and enjoyment other than heterosexuality are invalidated. Actually, for most Christians nowadays just plain heterosexuality will do, irrespective of whether it is intended to generate offspring.

These ideas about sexuality set up a major contradiction in what we tell children about sex and procreation. We teach them that sex and sexuality are about becoming mommies and daddies and warn them not to explore sex by themselves or with playmates of either sex until they are old enough to have babies. Then, when they reach adolescence and the entire culture pressures them into heterosexual activity, whether they themselves feel ready for it or not, the more "enlightened" among us tell them how to be sexually (meaning heterosexually) active without having babies. Surprise: It doesn't work very well. Teenagers do not act "responsibly"—teenage pregnancies and abortions are on the rise and teenage fathers do not acknowledge and support their partners and babies. Somewhere we forget that we have been telling lies. Sexuality and procreation

are not linked in societies like ours. On the contrary, we expect youngsters to be heterosexually active from their teens on but to put off having children until they are economically independent and married, and even then to have only two or, at most, three children.

Other contradictions: This society, on the whole, accepts Freud's assumption that children are sexual beings from birth and that society channels their polymorphously perverse childhood sexuality into the accepted forms. Yet we expect our children to be asexual. We raise girls and boys together more than is done in many societies while insisting that they must not explore their own or each other's sexual parts or feelings.

What if we acknowledged the separation of sexuality from procreation and encouraged our children to express themselves sexually if they were so inclined? What if we, further, encouraged them to explore their own bodies as well as those of friends of the same and the other sex when they felt like it? They might then be able to feel at home with their sexuality, have some sense of their own and other people's sexual needs, and know how to talk about sexuality and procreation with their friends and sexual partners before their ability to procreate becomes an issue for them. In this age of AIDS and other serious sexually transmitted infections, such a course of action seems like essential preventive hygiene. Without the embarrassment of unexplored and unacknowledged sexual needs, contraceptive needs would be much easier to confront when they arise. So, of course, would same-sex love relationships.

Such a more open and accepting approach to sexuality would make life easier for children and adolescents of either sex, but it would be especially advantageous for girls. When a boy discovers his penis as an organ of pleasure, it is the same organ he is taught about as his organ of procreation. A girl exploring her pleasurable sensations finds her clitoris, but when she is taught about making babies, she hears about the functions of the vagina in sex and birthing. Usually, the clitoris goes unmentioned, and she doesn't even learn its name until much later.

Therefore for boys there is an obvious link between procreation and their own pleasurable, erotic explorations; for most girls, there isn't.

INDIVIDUAL SEXUAL SCRIPTS

Each of us writes our own sexual script out of the range of our experiences. None of this script is inborn or biologically given. We construct it out of our diverse life situations, limited by what we are taught or what we can imagine to be permissible and correct. There is no unique female sexual experience, no male sexual experience, no unique heterosexual, lesbian, or gay male experience. We take the experiences of different people and sort and lump them according to socially significant categories. When I hear generalizations about *the* sexual experience of some particular group, exceptions immediately come to mind. Except that I refuse to call them exceptions: They are part of the range of our sexual experiences. Of course, the similar circumstances in which members of a particular group find themselves will give rise to group similarities. But we tend to exaggerate them when we go looking for similarities within groups or differences between them.

This exaggeration is easy to see when we look at the dichotomy between "the heterosexual" and "the homosexual." The concept of "the homosexual", along with many other human typologies, originated toward the end of the nineteenth century. Certain kinds of behavior stopped being attributed to particular persons and came to define them. A person who had sexual relations with someone of the same sex became a certain kind of person, a "homosexual"; a person who had sexual relations with people of the other sex, a different kind, a "heterosexual."

This way of categorizing people obscured the hitherto accepted fact that many people do not have sexual relations exclusively with persons of one or the other sex. (None of us has sex with a kind of person; we have sex with a person.) This categorization created the stereotypes that were popularized by the sex reformers, such as Havelock Ellis and Edward Carpenter, who biologized the "difference." "The homosexual" became a person who is different by nature and therefore should not be made responsible for his or her so-called deviance. This definition served the purpose of the reformers (although the laws have been slow to change), but it turned same-sex love into a medical problem to be treated by doctors rather than punished by judges—an improvement, perhaps, but not acceptance or liberation.

THEORIES OF SEXUAL DEVELOPMENT

Freud was unusual for his time (and still is, to some extent, for ours) by insisting that sexual development is not innate and automatic. He considered it scientifically as valid to ask how people come to love individuals of the other sex as of their own. Nonetheless, he then plotted a course of "normal" development which involved his newly invented Oedipus complex, castration anxiety, and penis envy, to explain how men come to form affective attachments to women and women to men. Thus, loving people of one's own sex continued to be seen as pathological.

Feminist revisions of Freud by Nancy Chodorow and Dorothy Dinnerstein delineate affective development by putting the main emphasis on the maturing child's relationship to the mother rather than to the father, as Freud had done. Because a child's first loving relationship usually is with the mother or some other woman, for girls this relationship is with a person of the same sex, whereas for boys, with a person of the other sex. Therefore their analysis, like Freud's, posits a crucial difference between the ways girls and boys develop sexual identities and erotic relationships with members of the other sex.

Freud delineated a course that was clearer and more direct for boys and fuzzier and more problematical for girls. Chodorow and Dinnerstein suggest that male psychosexual development is the more problematical. They argue that because all children initially identify with their primary caretaker, who is usually a woman, girls can maintain their initial gender identification. Because boys must grow up to be men, they have to become ostentatiously unlike the person who cares for them and who was their first love. Yet boys, like girls, usually are not nearly so familiar with a man as they are with their female caretaker. This necessity to differentiate themselves in kind from the person they know and love best engenders a fragility in the male ego that women need not cope with. It is surprising that neither Chodorow nor Dinnerstein addressed the question of why, in that case, so many women later form affective ties with men rather than transferring their primary bond from the mother, or other female caretaker, to other women. Their model readily lends itself to suggesting that, from a developmental point of view, for both men and women love for women is less problematical than love for men. But they did not explore these implications.

TOWARD A NONDETERMINISTIC MODEL OF SEXUALITY

I do not want to imply that they are worth pursuing in that form. I am no more comfortable with models that posit a psychological determinism, in which what happens in early childhood is all-important, than I am with biodeterminism. I find Chodorow's and Dinnerstein's analyses more interesting than Freud's but no more convincing. With sexuality, as with other aspects of our lives, I prefer to stress human diversity, flexibility, and our ability to change. Alfred Kinsey and his collaborators showed a long time ago that most people can love people of either sex and that our choices often change over time and with social circumstances.

Some gay men and lesbians feel that they were born "different" and have always been homosexual. They recall feeling strongly attracted to members of their own sex when they were children and adolescents. But many women who live with men and think of themselves as heterosexual also had strong affective and erotic ties to girls and women while they were growing up. If they were now in loving relationships with women, they might look back on their earlier loves as proof that they were always lesbians. But if they are now involved with men, they may be tempted to devalue their former feelings as "puppy love" or "crushes."

Even within the preferred sex, most of us feel a greater affinity for certain "types" than for others. Not any man or woman will do. No one has seriously suggested that something in our innate makeup makes us light up in the presence of only certain women or men. We would think it absurd to look to hormone levels or any other simplistic biological cause for our preference for a specific "type" within a sex. In fact, scientists rarely bother to ask what in our psychosocial experience shapes these kinds of tastes and preferences. We assume it must have something to do with our relationship to our parents or with other experiences, but we do not probe deeply unless people prefer the "wrong" sex. Then, suddenly, scientists begin to look for specific causes.

Because of our recent history and political experiences, feminists tend to reject simplistic, causal models of how our sexuality develops. Many women who have thought of themselves as heterosexual for much of their life and who have been married and have had children have fallen in love with a woman (or women) when they have had the opportunity to rethink, refeel, and restructure their lives.

The society in which we live channels, guides, and limits our imagination in sexual as well as other matters. Why some of us give ourselves permission to love people of our own sex whereas others cannot even imagine doing so is an interesting question. But I do not think it will be answered by measuring our hormone levels or by trying to unearth our earliest affectional ties. As women begin to speak freely about our sexual experiences, we are getting a varied range of information with which we can reexamine, reevaluate, and change ourselves. Lately, increasing numbers of women have begun to acknowledge their "bisexuality"—the fact that they can love women and men in succession or simultaneously. People fall in love with individuals, not with a sex. Gender need not be a significant factor in our choice, although for some of us it may be.

QUESTIONS FOR DISCUSSION

1. Is homosexuality unnatural? Is it immoral? Defend your position with reference to Richard Mohr's analysis and to Hubbard's claim that there is no natural sexuality.

2. Does one choose to be homosexual or heterosexual? Consider Mohr's and Hubbard's answers to this question. Consider Sartre's answer. What is your own answer to this question (and why)?

René Magritte, *The False Mirror,* 1928, oil on canvas, 21 1/4″ × 31 7/8″. Collection, The Museum of Modern Art, New York. Purchase.

CHAPTER 5

SELF, MIND AND BODY

The early Christian philosopher Saint Augustine in his *Confessions* says, "What then is time? If no one asks me I know; if I try to explain it to someone who asks me, I know not." He might have said the same of *self*. For most of us, the concept of self when used unexamined is—like Augustine's concept of time—among the most basic and obvious that we use. But once we enter into a philosophical reflection on this concept—asking "Who am I?" or "What am I?", "Am I identical with my mind? My body? A soul that is different than either?"—the clarity of our notion is quickly seen to vanish.

Thinkers in nearly every culture have asked such questions and come up with a variety of answers—answers that affect not only our psychological view of ourselves but also our approach to matters of the spirit. The answer we give to the question of what and who we are will determine to a great extent the way we view our relation to this life and this body we call "my body." It will affect our views on the question of whether or not we will survive death and—if we do—what form an afterlife or -lives will take. Finally, it will affect our relations with others—with other "selves"—and, through this, our ethics and our view of the community of selves we term "society."

The selections in this chapter begin with a controversy that has appeared both in Western thought and the thought of ancient India: Is the "self" that we talk about so confidently in our everyday life a permanent underlying substance or a mere "bundle" of thoughts and whims and feelings, a "stream of consciousness" without any underlying "river bed" to give it stability in the world? Or should we, as the Argentine philosopher Risieri Frondizi suggests, look for this stability in the stream of consciousness itself? The first four sections of the chapter wind through several centuries and cultures as we pursue these questions. Starting with the controversy between substance and bundle theorists in the Western tradition, as exemplified in the philosophies of the two best-known advocates of each view, René Descartes in the seventeenth century and David Hume writing almost exactly 100 years later, we move on next to the same debate as it plays itself out in Asian thought. Here we begin with two versions of the substance view of self as it appears in two seminal works of orthodox Hinduism, the *Bhagavad Gita* and the *Upanishads*. We then turn to the rival bundle view of early Buddhism and see it develop into the "middle way" and "mind-only" philosophies of the later Mahayana Buddhist schools. Finally, we come back to the contemporary Western world with a defense of the bundle theory by a modern analytic philosopher, Derek Parfit, and the suggested compromise that was alluded to above by the twentieth-century Latin American, Frondizi.

In the fifth and final section of the chapter, the reader is invited to take a brief tour of some philosophical reflections on the question of an afterlife in several cultures, both ancient and modern.

THE SELF: A CONTROVERSY IN
THE MODERN WESTERN TRADITION

The term *modern,* as it is used in philosophy, refers to the development in thought that has taken place since the time of the very beginnings of modern science. Modern philosophy thus extends from the seventeenth century to the present day. Its founder is usually declared to be René Descartes (1596–1650), from whose *Meditations on First Philosophy* our first selection is taken.

The seventeenth century in Descartes' Europe was a time of dramatic change. Not only was Christendom immersed in a brutal civil war in which Catholicism was pitted against the new Protestant churches, it also was experiencing the challenge of a new kind of science. This new science was growing out of Copernius' revolution in astronomy in the previous century; it appeared to be in conflict with the traditional, religious world view that had earlier grown out of the medieval synthesis of Aristotle and the Bible. The new view held that the earth was not the center of the universe and stationary; it moved. Furthermore, its motion—in fact, all motion—could be explained by the principles of mechanics. The human body, like any other object, was also subject to these principles. God and "soul" seemed no longer needed for an explanation of nature.

It was at this point in history that philosophy became truly crucial. Throughout the Middle Ages, philosophy had been dominated by religious assumptions. Now those assumptions seemed to be competing with a new way of understanding the world. It was a time of great questioning and great doubt. "Better to not take anything for granted," said many, "neither the assumptions of religion nor the assumptions of science. For how is anyone to know which view of reality is correct?" Each of the world views claimed its own unique path to knowledge; the foundations of knowledge were themselves at issue.

René Descartes took up this skeptical challenge. As someone who was both a devout Catholic Christian and one of the new scientists who was question-

ing the traditional view, the matter was of vital importance to him. In our selection, Descartes begins by declaring that he will not accept anything as true unless it is demonstrated to be beyond doubt. He thus starts his reflections with a method that has come to be called "the method of doubt"—a method that begins with a philosophical doubt of everything that can be doubted, regardless of whether or not these things are really doubted in ordinary daily life. Thus, even our basic commonsense beliefs are called into question. Even the most basic "truths" of arithmetic and geometry are initially dismissed by Descartes.

However, he continues, there is one thing that is absolutely certain. I cannot doubt that there is a doubter. I cannot doubt the existence of the self that has these doubts. There is an "I" that thinks, a thinking thing, a mind as distinct from and independent of the body. One cannot, under any circumstances, deny this.

A century later, however, the Scottish philosopher David Hume (1711–1776) does just that. Not only does he question the *certainty* of Descartes' assertion, he also argues that it is in fact false. There is no single entity of which we are conscious that we can call a self. In effect, Hume is arguing that Descartes' doubting was not radical enough; what Descartes took to be certain is entirely unfounded.

It is important to understand that Hume's analysis begins from the premise that every true idea must be derived from experience—from some concrete sense impression. This view is known as "empiricism" in philosophy. From the empiricist standpoint, if we had an accurate idea of the self, it would have to be derived from some sense impression. However, as Hume declares, we cannot upon reflection find any distinct impression that corresponds to a "self." What we call a "self" is merely "a bundle or collection of different perceptions, which succeed each other with an inconceivable rapidity, and are in a perpetual flux and movement."

MEDITATIONS

René Descartes

MEDITATION I

Concerning the Things of which we may doubt

It is now several years since I first became aware how many false opinions I had from my childhood been admitting as true, and how doubtful was everything I have subsequently based on them. Accordingly I have ever since been convinced that if I am to establish anything firm and lasting in the sciences, I must once for all, and by a deliberate effort, rid myself of all those opinions to which I have hitherto given credence, starting entirely anew, and building from the foundations up. But as this enterprise was evidently one of great magnitude, I waited until I had attained an age so mature that I could no longer expect that I should at any later date be better able to execute my design. This is what has made me delay so long; and I should now be failing in my duty, were I to continue consuming in deliberation such time for action as still remains to me.

Today, then, as I have suitably freed my mind from all cares, and have secured for myself an assured leisure in peaceful solitude, I shall at last apply myself earnestly and freely to the general overthrow of all my former opinions. In doing so, it will not be necessary for me to show that they are one and all false; that is perhaps more than can be done. But since reason has already persuaded me that I ought to withhold belief no less carefully from things not entirely certain and indubitable than from those which appear to me manifestly false, I shall be justified in setting all of them aside, if in each case I can find any ground whatsoever for regarding them as dubitable. Nor in so doing shall I be investigating each belief separately—that, like inquiry into their falsity, would be an endless labor. The withdrawal of foundations involves the downfall of whatever rests on these foundations, and what I shall therefore begin by examining are the principles on which my former beliefs rested.

Whatever, up to the present, I have accepted as possessed of the highest truth and certainty I have learned either from the senses or through the senses. Now these senses I have sometimes found to be deceptive; and it is only prudent never to place complete confidence in that by which we have even once been deceived.

But, it may be said, although the senses sometimes deceive us regarding minute objects, or such as are at a great distance from us, there are yet many other things which, though known by way of sense, are too evident to be doubted; as, for instance, that I am in this place, seated by the fire, attired in a dressing-gown, having this paper in my hands, and other similar seeming certainties. Can I deny that these hands and this body are mine, save perhaps by comparing myself to those who are insane, and whose brains are so disturbed and clouded by dark bilious vapors that they persist in assuring us that they are kings, when in fact they are in extreme poverty; or that they are clothed in gold and purple when they are in fact destitute of any covering; or that their head is made of clay and their body of glass, or that they are pumpkins. They are mad; and I should be no less insane were I to follow examples so extravagant.

None the less I must bear in mind that I am a man, and am therefore in the habit of sleeping, and that what the insane represent to themselves in their waking moments I represent to myself, with other things even less probable, in my dreams. How often, indeed, have I dreamt of myself being in this place, dressed and seated by the fire, whilst all the time I was lying undressed in bed! At the present moment it certainly seems that in looking at this paper I do so with open eyes, that the head which I move is not asleep, that it is deliberately and of set purpose that I extend this hand, and that I am sensing the hand. The things which happen to the sleeper are not so clear nor so distinct as all of these are. I cannot, however, but remind myself that on many occasions I have in sleep been deceived by similar illusions; and on more careful study of them

I see that there are no certain marks distinguishing waking from sleep; and I see this so manifestly that, lost in amazement, I am almost persuaded that I am now dreaming.

Let us, then, suppose ourselves to be asleep, and that all these particulars—namely, that we open our eyes, move the head, extend the hands—are false and illusory; and let us reflect that our hands perhaps, and the whole body, are not what we see them as being. Nevertheless we must at least agree that the things seen by us in sleep are as it were like painted images, and cannot have been formed save in the likeness of what is real and true. The types of things depicted, eyes, head, hands, etc.—these at least are not imaginary, but true and existent. For in truth when painters endeavor with all possible artifice to represent sirens and satyrs by forms the most fantastic and unusual, they cannot assign them natures which are entirely new, but only make a certain selection of limbs from different animals. Even should they excogitate something so novel that nothing similar has ever before been seen, and that their work represents to us a thing entirely fictitious and false, the colors used in depicting them cannot be similarly fictitious; they at least must truly exist. And by this same reasoning, even should those general things, viz., a body, eyes, a head, hands and such like, be imaginary, we are yet bound to admit that there are things simpler and more universal which are real existents and by the intermixture of which, as in the case of the colors, all the images of things of which we have any awareness be they true and real or false and fantastic, are formed. To this class of things belong corporeal nature in general and its extension, the shape of extended things, their quantity or magnitude, and their number, as also the location in which they are, the time through which they endure, and other similar things.

This, perhaps, is why we not unreasonably conclude that physics, astronomy, medicine, and all other disciplines treating of composite things are of doubtful character, and that arithmetic, geometry, etc., treating only of the simplest and most general things and but little concerned as to whether or not they are actual existents, have a content that is certain and indubitable. For whether I am awake or dreaming, 2 and 3 are 5, a square has no more than four sides; and it does not seem possible that truths so evident can ever be suspected of falsity.

Yet even these truths can be questioned. That God exists, that He is all-powerful and has created me such as I am, has long been my settled opinion. How, then, do I know that He has not arranged that there be no Earth, no heavens, no extended thing, no shape, no magnitude, no location, while at the same time securing that all these things appear to me to exist precisely as they now do? Others, as I sometimes think, deceive themselves in the things which they believe they know best. How do I know that I am not myself deceived every time I add 2 and 3, or count the sides of a square, or judge of things yet simpler, if anything simpler can be suggested? But perhaps God has not been willing that I should be thus deceived, for He is said to be supremely good. If, however, it be repugnant to the goodness of God to have created me such that I am constantly subject to deception, it would also appear to be contrary to His goodness to permit me to be sometimes deceived, and that He does permit this is not in doubt.

There may be those who might prefer to deny the existence of a God so powerful, rather than to believe that all other things are uncertain. Let us, for the present, not oppose them; let us allow, in the manner of their view, that all which has been said regarding God is a fable. Even so we shall not have met and answered the doubts suggested above regarding the reliability of our mental faculties; instead we shall have given added force to them. For in whatever way it be supposed that I have come to be what I am, whether by fate or by chance, or by a continual succession and connection of things, or by some other means, since to be deceived and to err is an imperfection, the likelihood of my being so imperfect as to be the constant victim of deception will be increased in proportion as the power to which they assign my origin is lessened. To such argument I have assuredly nothing to reply; and thus at last I am constrained to confess that there is no one of all my former opinions which is not open to doubt, and this not merely owing to want of thought on my part, or through levity, but from cogent and maturely considered reasons. Henceforth, therefore, should I desire to discover something certain, I ought to refrain from assenting to these opinions no less scrupulously than in respect of what is manifestly false.

But it is not sufficient to have taken note of these conclusions; we must also be careful to keep them in mind. For long-established customary opinions perpetually recur in thought, long and familiar usage having given them the right to occupy my mind, even almost against my will, and to be masters of my belief. Nor shall I ever lose this habit of assenting to and of confiding in them, not at least so long as I consider them as in truth they are, namely, as opinions which, though in some fashion doubtful (as I have just shown), are still, none the less, highly probable and such as it is much more reasonable to believe than to deny. This is why I shall, as I think, be acting prudently if, taking a directly contrary line, I of set purpose employ every available device for the deceiving of myself, feigning that all these opinions are entirely false and imaginary. Then, in due course, having so balanced my old-time prejudices by this new prejudice that I cease to incline to one side more than to another, my judgment, no longer dominated by misleading usages, will not be hindered by them in the apprehension of things. In this course there can, I am convinced, be neither danger nor error. What I have under consideration is a question solely of knowledge, not of action, so that I cannot for the present be at fault as being over-ready to adopt a questioning attitude.

Accordingly I shall now suppose, not that a true God, who as such must be supremely good and the fountain of truth, but that some malignant genius exceedingly powerful and cunning has devoted all his powers in the deceiving of me; I shall suppose that the sky, the earth, colors, shapes, sounds, and all external things are illusions and impostures of which this evil genius has availed himself for the abuse of my credulity; I shall consider myself as having no hands, no eyes, no flesh, no blood, nor any senses, but as falsely opining myself to possess all these things. Further, I shall obstinately persist in this way of thinking; and even if, while so doing, it may not

be within my power to arrive at the knowledge of any truth, there is one thing I have it in me to do, viz., to suspend judgment, refusing assent to what is false. Thereby, thanks to this resolved firmness of mind, I shall be effectively guarding myself against being imposed upon by this deceiver, no matter how powerful or how craftily deceptive he may be.

This undertaking is, however, irksome and laborious, and a certain indolence drags me back into the course of my customary life. Just as a captive who has been enjoying in sleep an imaginary liberty, should he begin to suspect that his liberty is a dream, dreads awakening, and conspires with the agreeable illusions for the prolonging of the deception, so in similar fashion I gladly lapse back into my accustomed opinions. I dread to be wakened, in fear lest the wakefulness may have to be laboriously spent, not in the tranquilizing light of truth, but in the extreme darkness of the above-suggested questionings.

MEDITATION II

Concerning the Nature of the Human Mind, and how it is more easily known than the Body

So disquieting are the doubts in which yesterday's meditation has involved me that it is no longer in my power to forget them. Nor do I yet see how they are to be resolved. It is as if I had all of a sudden fallen into very deep water, and am so disconcerted that I can neither plant my feet securely on the bottom nor maintain myself by swimming on the surface. I shall, however, brace myself for a great effort, entering anew on the path which I was yesterday exploring; that is, I shall proceed by setting aside all that admits even of the very slightest doubt, just as if I had convicted it of being absolutely false; and I shall persist in following this path, until I have come upon something certain, or, failing in that, until at least I know, and know with certainty, that in the world there is nothing certain.

Archimedes, that he might displace the whole earth, required only that there might be some one point, fixed and immovable, to serve in leverage; so likewise I shall be entitled to entertain high hopes if

I am fortunate enough to find some one thing that is certain and indubitable.

I am supposing, then, that all the things I see are false; that of all the happenings my memory has ever suggested to me, none has ever so existed; that I have no senses; that body, shape, extension, movement and location are but mental fictions. What is there, then, which can be esteemed true? Perhaps this only, that nothing whatsoever is certain.

But how do I know that there is not something different from all the things I have thus far enumerated and in regard to which there is not the least occasion for doubt? Is there not some God, or other being by whatever name we call Him, who puts these thoughts into my mind? Yet why suppose such a being? May it not be that I am myself capable of being their author? Am I not myself at least a something? But already I have denied that I have a body and senses. This indeed raises awkward questions. But what is it that thereupon follows? Am I so dependent on the body and senses that without them I cannot exist? Having persuaded myself that outside me there is nothing, that there is no heaven, no Earth, that there are no minds, no bodies, am I thereby committed to the view that I also do not exist? By no means. If I am persuading myself of something, in so doing I assuredly do exist. But what if, unknown to me, there be some deceiver, very powerful and very cunning, who is constantly employing his ingenuity in deceiving me? Again, as before, without doubt, if he is deceiving me, I exist. Let him deceive me as much as he will, he can never cause me to be nothing so long as I shall be thinking that I am something. And thus, having reflected well, and carefully examined all things, we have finally to conclude that this declaration, *Ego sum, ego existo,* is necessarily true every time I propound it or mentally apprehend it.

But I do not yet know in any adequate manner what I am, I who am certain that I am; and I must be careful not to substitute some other thing in place of myself, and so go astray in this knowledge which I am holding to be the most certain and evident of all that is knowable by me. This is why I shall now meditate anew on what, prior to my venturing on

these questionings, I believed myself to be. I shall withdraw those beliefs which can, even in the least degree, be invalidated by the reasons cited, in order that at length, of all my previous beliefs, there may remain only what is certain and indubitable.

What then did I formerly believe myself to be? Undoubtedly I thought myself to be a man. But what is a man? Shall I say a rational animal? No, for then I should have to inquire what is "animal," what "rational"; and thus from the one question I should be drawn on into several others yet more difficult. I have not, at present, the leisure for any such subtle inquiries. Instead, I prefer to meditate on the thoughts which of themselves sprang up in my mind on my applying myself to the consideration of what I am, considerations suggested by my own proper nature. I thought that I possessed a face, hands, arms, and that whole structure to which I was giving the title "body," composed as it is of the limbs discernible in a corpse. In addition, I took notice that I was nourished, that I walked, that I sensed, that I thought, all of which actions I ascribed to the soul. But what the soul might be I did not stop to consider; or if I did, I imaged it as being something extremely rare and subtle, like a wind, a flame or an ether, and as diffused throughout my grosser parts. As to the nature of "body," no doubts whatsoever disturbed me. I had, as I thought, quite distinct knowledge of it; and had I been called upon to explain the manner in which I then conceived it, I should have explained myself somewhat thus: by body I understand whatever can be determined by a certain shape, and comprised in a certain location, whatever so fills a certain space as to exclude from it every other body, whatever can be apprehended by touch, sight, hearing, taste or smell, and whatever can be moved in various ways, not indeed of itself but something foreign to it by which it is touched and impressed. For I nowise conceived the power of self-movement, of sensing or knowing, as pertaining to the nature of body: on the contrary I was somewhat astonished on finding in certain bodies faculties such as these.

But what am I now to say that I am, now that I am supposing that there exists a very powerful, and if I may so speak, malignant being, who employs all his powers and skill in deceiving me? Can I affirm that I possess any one of those things which I have been speaking of as pertaining to the nature of body? On stopping to consider them with closer attention, and on reviewing all of them, I find none of which I can say that it belongs to me; to enumerate them again would be idle and tedious. What then, of those things which I have been attributing not to body, but to the soul? What of nutrition or of walking? If it be that I have no body, it cannot be that I take nourishment or that I walk. Sensing? There can be no sensing in the absence of body; and besides I have seemed during sleep to apprehend things which, as I afterwards noted, had not been sensed. Thinking? Here I find what does belong to me: it alone cannot be separated from me. *I am, I exist.* This is certain. How often? As often as I think. For it might indeed be that if I entirely ceased to think, I should thereupon altogether cease to exist. I am not at present admitting anything which is not necessarily true; and, accurately speaking, I am therefore [taking myself to be] only a thinking thing, that is to say, a mind, an understanding or reason— terms the significance of which has hitherto been unknown to me. I am, then, a real thing, and really existent. What thing? I have said it, a thinking thing.

And what more am I? I look for aid to the imagination. [But how mistakenly!] I am not that assemblage of limbs we call the human body; I am not a subtle penetrating air distributed throughout all these members; I am not a wind, a fire, a vapor, a breath or anything at all that I can image. I am supposing all these things to be nothing. Yet I find, while so doing, that I am still assured that I am a something.

But may it not be that those very things which, not being known to me, I have been supposing nonexistent, are not really different from the self that I know? As to that I cannot say, and am not now discussing it. I can judge only of things that are known to me. Having come to know that I exist, I am inquiring as to what I am, this I that I thus know to exist. Now quite certainly this knowledge, taken in the precise manner as above, is not dependent on things

the existence of which is not yet known to me; consequently and still more evidently it does not depend on any of the things which are feigned by the imagination. Indeed this word *feigning* warns me of my error; for I should in truth be feigning were I to *image* myself to be a something; since imaging is in no respect distinguishable from the contemplating of the shape or image of a *corporeal*[1] thing. Already I know with certainty that I exist, and that all these imaged things, and in general whatever relates to the nature of body, may possibly be dreams merely or deceptions. Accordingly, I see clearly that it is no more reasonable to say, "I will resort to my imagination in order to learn more distinctly what I am," than if I were to say, "I am awake and apprehend something that is real, true; but as I do not yet apprehend it sufficiently well, I will of express purpose go to sleep, that my dreams may represent it to me with greater truth and evidence." I know therefore that nothing of all I can comprehend by way of the imagination pertains to this knowledge I [already] have of myself, and that if the mind is to determine the nature of the self with perfect distinctness, I must be careful to restrain it, diverting it from all such imaginative modes of apprehension.

What then is it that I am? A thinking thing.[2] What is a thinking thing? It is a thing that doubts, understands, affirms, denies, wills, abstains from willing, that also can be aware of images and sensations.

Assuredly if all these things pertain to me, I am indeed a something. And how could it be they should not pertain to me? Am I not that very being who doubts of almost everything, who none the less also apprehends certain things, who affirms that one thing only is true, while denying all the rest, who yet desires to know more, who is averse to being deceived, who images many things, sometimes even despite his will, and who likewise apprehends many things which seem to come by way of the senses? Even though I should be always dreaming, and though he who has created me employs all his ingenuity in deceiving me,

---

[1]Italics not in original text.
[2]*Res cogitans;* Fr. *une chose qui pense.*

is there any one of the above assertions which is not as true as that I am and that I exist? Any one of them which can be distinguished from my thinking? Any one of them which can be said to be separate from the self? So manifest is it that it is I who doubt, I who apprehend, I who desire, that there is here no need to add anything by way of rendering it more evident. It is no less certain that I can apprehend images. For although it may happen (as I have been supposing) that none of the things imaged are true, the imaging, *quâ* active power, is none the less really in me, as forming part of my thinking. Again, I am the being who senses, that is to say, who apprehends corporeal things, as if by the organs of sense, since I do in truth see light, hear noise, feel heat. These things, it will be said, are false, and I am only dreaming. Even so, it is none the less certain that it seems to me that I see, that I hear, and that I am warmed. This is what in me is rightly called sensing, and as used in this precise manner is nowise other than thinking.

PERSONAL IDENTITY

David Hume

There are some philosophers who imagine we are every moment intimately conscious of what we call our *self;* that we feel its existence and its continuance in existence; and are certain, beyond the evidence of a demonstration, both of its perfect identity and simplicity. The strongest sensation, the most violent passion, say they, instead of distracting us from this view, only fix it the more intensely and make us consider their influence on *self* either by their pain or pleasure. To attempt a further proof of this were to weaken its evidence; since no proof can be derived from any fact of which we are so intimately conscious; nor is there anything of which we can be certain if we doubt of this.

Unluckily all these positive assertions are contrary to that very experience which is pleaded for

them; nor have we any idea of *self,* after the manner it is here explained. For from what impression[1] could this idea be derived? This question it is impossible to answer without a manifest contradiction and absurdity; and yet it is a question which must necessarily be answered, if we would have the idea of self pass for clear and intelligible. It must be some one impression that gives rise to every real idea. But self or person is not any one impression, but that to which our several impressions and ideas are supposed to have a reference. If any impression gives rise to the idea of self, that impression must continue invariably the same, through the whole course of our lives; since self is supposed to exist after that manner. But there is no impression constant and invariable. Pain and pleasure, grief and joy, passions and sensations succeed each other, and never all exist at the same time. It cannot therefore be from any of these impressions, or from any other, that the idea of self is derived; and consequently there is no such idea.

But further, what must become of all our particular perceptions upon this hypothesis? All these are different, and distinguishable, and separable from each other, and may be separately considered, and may exist separately, and have no need of anything to support their existence. After what manner therefore do they belong to self, and how are they connected with it? For my part, when I enter most intimately into what I call *myself,* I always stumble on some particular perception or other, of heat or cold, light or shade, love or hatred, pain or pleasure. I never can catch *myself* at any time without a perception, and never can observe anything but the perception. When my perceptions are removed for any time, as by sound sleep, so long am I insensible of *myself,* and may truly be said not to exist. And were all my perceptions removed by death, and could I neither think, nor feel, nor see, nor love, nor hate, after the dissolution of my body, I should be entirely annihilated, nor do I conceive what is fur-

---

[1]Hume uses the term *impression* to refer to those sense experiences that are neither memories nor the result of acts of imagination; as such, impressions are, for him, either sensations, passions, or emotions (Eds.).

ther requisite to make me a perfect nonentity. If any one, upon serious and unprejudiced reflection, thinks he has a different notion of *himself,* I must confess I can reason no longer with him. All I can allow him is, that he may be in the right as well as I, and that we are essentially different in this particular. He may, perhaps, perceive something simple and continued, which he calls *himself;* though I am certain there is no such principle in me.

But setting aside some metaphysicians of this kind, I may venture to affirm of the rest of mankind, that they are nothing but a bundle or collection of different perceptions, which succeed each other with an inconceivable rapidity, and are in a perpetual flux and movement. Our eyes cannot turn in their sockets without varying our perceptions. Our thought is still more variable than our sight; and all our other senses and faculties contribute to this change; nor is there any single power of the soul, which remains unalterably the same, perhaps for one moment. The mind is a kind of theatre, where several perceptions successively make their appearance; pass, repass, glide away, and mingle in an infinite variety of postures and situations. There is properly no *simplicity* in it at one time, nor *identity* in different, whatever natural propension we may have to imagine that simplicity and identity. The comparison of the theatre must not mislead us. They are the successive perceptions only, that constitute the mind; nor have we the most distant notion of the place where these scenes are represented, or of the materials of which it is composed.

What then gives us so great a propension to ascribe an identity to these successive perceptions, and to suppose ourselves possessed of an invariable and uninterrupted existence through the whole course of our lives? In order to answer this question we must distinguish betwixt personal identity, as it regards our thought or imagination, and as it regards our passions or the concern we take in ourselves. The first is our present subject; and to explain it perfectly we must take the matter pretty deep, and account for that identity, which we attribute to plants and animals; there being a great analogy betwixt it and the identity of a self or person.

We have a distinct idea of an object that remains invariable and uninterrupted through a supposed variation of time; and this idea we call that of *identity* or *sameness.* We have also a distinct idea of several different objects existing in succession, and connected together by a close relation; and this to an accurate view affords as perfect a notion of *diversity* as if there was no manner of relation among the objects. But though these two ideas of identity, and a succession of related objects, be in themselves perfectly distinct, and even contrary, yet it is certain that, in our common way of thinking, they are generally confounded with each other. That action of the imagination, by which we consider the uninterrupted and invariable object, and that by which we reflect on the succession of related objects, are almost the same to the feeling; nor is there much more effort of thought required in the latter case than in the former. The relation facilitates the transition of the mind from one object to another, and renders its passage as smooth as if it contemplated one continued object. This resemblance is the cause of the confusion and mistake, and makes us substitute the notion of identity, instead of that of related objects. However at one instant we may consider the related succession as variable or interrupted, we are sure the next to ascribe to it a perfect identity, and regard it as invariable and uninterrupted. Our propensity to this mistake is so great from the resemblance above mentioned, that we fall into it before we are aware; and though we incessantly correct ourselves by reflection, and return to a more accurate method of thinking, yet we cannot long sustain our philosophy, or take off this bias from the imagination. Our last resource is to yield to it, and boldly assert that these different related objects are in effect the same, however interrupted and variable. In order to justify to ourselves this absurdity, we often feign some new and unintelligible principle, that connects the objects together, and prevents their interruption or variation. Thus we feign the continued existence of the perceptions of our senses, to remove the interruption; and run into the notion of a *soul,* and *self,* and *substance,* to disguise the variation. But, we may further observe, that where we do not give rise to such a fiction, our propension to confound identity with relation is so great, that we are apt to imagine something unknown and mysterious, connecting the parts, beside their relation; and this I take to be the case with regard to the identity we ascribe to plants and vegetables. And even when this does not take place, we still feel a propensity to confound these ideas, though we are not able fully to satisfy ourselves in that particular, nor find anything invariable and uninterrupted to justify our notion of identity.

Thus the controversy concerning identity is not merely a dispute of words. For when we attribute identity, in an improper sense, to variable or interrupted objects, our mistake is not confined to the expression, but is commonly attended with a fiction, either of something invariable and uninterrupted, or of something mysterious and inexplicable, or at least with a propensity to such fictions. What will suffice to prove this hypothesis to the satisfaction of every fair inquirer, is to show,

from daily experience and observation, that the objects which are variable or interrupted, and yet are supposed to continue the same, are such only as consist of a succession of parts, connected together by resemblance, contiguity, or causation. For as such a succession answers evidently to our notion of diversity, it can only be by mistake we ascribe to it an identity; and as the relation of parts, which leads us into this mistake, is really nothing but a quality, which produces an association of ideas, and an easy transition of the imagination from one to another, it can only be from the resemblance, which this act of the mind bears to that by which we contemplate one continued object, that the error arises.

QUESTION FOR DISCUSSION

1. Compare Descartes' view of the self with that of Hume. With which of the two philosophers do you most agree? Why?

HINDUISM AND BUDDHISM: A SIMILAR CONTROVERSY

In the West, Hindu philosophy is often thought to be a monolithic structure—a view of the world as a mere appearance of God or the Brahman-Atman, the Ultimate Transcendent Self, a nondual "Absolute Spirit" that is, in the last analysis, open only to mystical vision. In reality, this is just one of many philosophical interpretations of Hinduism, though it *is* strongly supported by those *Upanishads* which we have looked at previously in the first chapter of this book. Our second selection in this chapter, which is also from the *Upanishads,* is often cited in support of this nondualist view as well. Since the *Upanishads* is a sacred text—being a record of the teachings of the earliest philosopher-gurus of Hinduism—the passages we have included in this volume are given a special place in the Hindu religion. Still, their interpretations have been many and they form only a portion of the large body of literature included in Hindu thought. In reality, the only position that the many philosophies of Hinduism share is a belief in some form of unified subject or soul. The view that this soul is the nondual Absolute Spirit is one of many and not, in fact, the most popular. It is probably also not the oldest. That honor goes to the Samkhya philosophy described in another sacred Indian text, the *Bhagavad Gita* or Song of God. Samkhya is a dualism, though not precisely the mind-body dualism described in Descartes. It is rather a dualism of nature and spirit. Reality consists of the natural world or *Prakriti* on the one hand and the Spirit or pure transcendental ego, *Purusha,* which lies beyond the world, on the other—the "field," as the *Gita* puts it, and the "knower of the field." The psychological self, which we know by ordinary means, is a part of *Prakriti,* not the pure ego *Purusha.* The *Purusha,* or pure ego, to use a metaphor taken from the Western philosopher Ludwig Wittgenstein, is to the world as the eye is to the field of vision. As you do not see the eye that does the looking, so also the pure ego stands beyond the "field" of the world of nature. It is not to be identified with the personality that acts in this world. The search for this pure ego, if carried to completion, would result in enlightenment, as would also, however, the realization of the self interpreted as Absolute Spirit or its realization under any of the other varieties of philosophical description known to Hinduism. Just as in Western philosophy, where St. Thomas and Descartes share the same basic Christian outlook though their views of soul differ greatly, so also in Hinduism a basic religious agreement can override philosophical disputes.

The passion for this quest for pure ego or "true self" reached a zenith in the sixth century B.C., when countless young men began to flock to the forest to find enlightenment and an end to suffering by discovering what and who they truly were. Among them was a young prince from the Himalayan foothills, Gotama Siddhartha. Having exhausted the Hindu teachings and still finding himself unsatisfied and seemingly far from the knowledge of his true nature, he began to develop his own path to wisdom. The path is the eightfold path of Buddhism, and its creator is known to history as Buddha, the one who has awakened from the sleep of everyday awareness. At the end of the path, the Buddha discovered not a true self but the nonexistence of self or *anatman* in much the same manner that 2,300 years later David Hume in distant Scotland was to reach the same conclusion but, apparently, not the attendant bliss. In the selection included in this section, the doctrine is defended by the philosopher-monk Nagasena in a dialogue with the Greek-born Indian King Milinda, which has become a classic of Buddhist philosophy and a bridge to Western thought.

At a still later time in Indian history, Buddhism itself underwent a transformation, the development of the Mahayana or Great Vehicle school of Buddhism, which came to dominate Buddhist thought in China and Japan. Out of this school there developed two new philosophies, both of which attempted a synthesis between the early Buddhist and the Hindu view of self. The first, Madhyamika or Middle Way between self and no-self, is represented in a selection from the contemporary scholar T. R. V. Murti's work, *The Central*

Philosophy of Buddhism. The second and later Yogacara philosophy, used extensively by the famous Zen meditational school of Buddhism, is expounded in an essay by another twentieth-century thinker, the Japanese Buddhist teacher Toshihiko Izutsu.

The reader of this section is strongly advised to read these selections in conjunction with related selections in other portions of the anthology. In particular, those interested in the *Upanishads* are advised to consult also the selections from it in the first chapter, as well as the commentary on the *Upanishads* by Sri Ramana Maharshi found there. To understand more fully the implications of the selections on Buddhism, the reader should turn to the general account of its philosophy found in Chapter 8, H. Saddhatissa's account of the Four Noble Truths of Buddhism.

SAMKHYA DUALISM

Bhagavad-Gita[*]

THE BODY CALLED THE FIELD, THE SOUL CALLED THE KNOWER OF THE FIELD, AND DISCRIMINATION BETWEEN THEM

THE FIELD AND
THE KNOWER OF THE FIELD

Arjuna said:

Prakṛti and *puruṣa,* the field and the knower of the field,[1] knowledge and the object of knowledge—these I should like to know, O Késava (Kṛṣṇa).[2]

The Blessed Lord said:

1. This body, O Son of Kunti (Arjuna), is called the field, and him who knows this those who know thereof call the knower of the field.

• • •

3. Hear briefly from Me what the field is, of what nature, what its modifications are, whence it is, what he [the knower of the field] is, and what his powers are.
4. This has been sung by sages in many ways and distinctly, in various hymns and also in well-reasoned and conclusive expressions of the aphorisms of the Absolute [*Brahma Sūtra*].[3]
5. The great [five gross] elements, self-sense, understanding, as also the unmanifested, the ten senses and mind, and the five objects of the senses,
6. Desire and hatred, pleasure and pain, the aggregate [the organism], intelligence, and steadfastness described—this in brief is the field along with its modifications.

KNOWLEDGE

7. Humility [absence of pride], integrity [absence of deceit], nonviolence, patience, uprightness, service of the teacher, purity of body and mind, steadfastness, and self-control,
8. Indifference to the objects of sense, self-effacement, and the perception of the evil of birth, death, old age, sickness, and pain,
9. Non-attachment, absence of clinging to son, wife, home, and the like, and a constant equal-mindedness to all desirable and undesirable happenings,

---

*The "Gita" consists of a conversation that takes place on a battlefield between the famous warrior, Arjuna, and his chariot driver, the God-man Krsna (Krishna). The beginning of that conversation can be found in Chapter 7 of this volume (Eds.).

[1]*Prakṛti* (Nature) is unconscious activity, and *puruṣa* (the self) is inactive consciousness. The body is called the field in which events happen; all growth, decline, and death take place in it. The conscious principle, inactive and detached, which lies behind all active states as witness, is the knower of the field.

---

[2]This verse is not found in some editions. If it is included, the total number of verses in the *Bhagavad-gītā* will be 701 and not 700, which is the number traditionally accepted. So we do not include it in the numbering of the verses.

[3]The *Gītā* suggests that it is expounding the truths already contained in the Vedas, the Upaniṣads, and the *Brahma Sūtra* or the aphorisms of *Brahman* later systematized by Bādarāyaṇa.

10. Unswerving devotion to Me with wholehearted discipline, resort to solitary places, dislike for a crowd of people,

11. Constancy in the knowledge of the Spirit, insight into the end of the knowledge of Truth—this is declared to be true knowledge, and all that is different from it is non-knowledge.

12. I will describe that which is to be known and by knowing which life eternal is gained. It is the Supreme *Brahman* who is beginningless and who is said to be neither existent nor non-existent.

THE KNOWER OF THE FIELD

13. With his hands and feet everywhere, with eyes, heads, and faces on all sides, with ears on all sides, He dwells in the world, enveloping all.

14. He appears to have the qualities of all the senses and yet is without any of the senses, unattached and yet supporting all, free from the *guṇas* [dispositions of *prakṛti*] and yet enjoying them.

15. He is without and within all beings. He is unmoving as also moving. He is too subtle to be known. He is far away and yet is He near.

16. He is undivided [indivisible] and yet He seems to be divided among beings. He is to be known as supporting creatures, destroying them and creating them afresh.

17. He is the Light of lights, said to be beyond darkness. Knowledge, the object of knowledge, and the goal of knowledge—He is seated in the hearts of all.

THE FRUIT OF KNOWLEDGE

18. Thus the field, also knowledge and the object of knowledge have been briefly described. My devotee who understands thus becomes worthy of My state.

NATURE AND SPIRIT

19. Know thou that *prakṛti* [Nature] and *puruṣa* [soul] are both beginningless; and know also that the forms and modes are born of *prakṛti*.

20. Nature is said to be the cause of effect, instrument, and agent(ness) and the soul is said to be the cause, in regard to the experience of pleasure and pain.

21. The soul in nature enjoys the modes born of nature. Attachment to the modes is the cause of its births in good and evil wombs.

22. The Supreme Spirit in the body is said to be the Witness, the Permitter, the Supporter, the Experiencer, the Great Lord and the Supreme Self.

23. He who thus knows soul (*puruṣa*) and Nature (*prakṛti*) together with the modes (*guṇas*)—though he act in every way, he is not born again.

THE TRUE SELF

The Upanishads

Hari*h*, Om.[1] There is this city of Brahman (the body), and in it the palace, the small lotus (of the heart), and in it that small ether. Now what exists within that small ether, that is to be sought for, that is to be understood.

And if they should say to him: "Now with regard to that city of Brahman,[2] and the palace in it, i.e. the small lotus of the heart, and the small ether within the heart, what is there within it that deserves to be sought for, or that is to be understood?"

Then he should say: "As large as this ether (all space) is, so large is that ether within the heart. Both heaven and earth are contained within it, both fire and air, both sun and moon, both lightning and stars; and whatever there is of him (the Self) here in the world, and whatever is not (i.e. whatever has been or will be), all that is contained within it."

---

[1] An invocation to God (Eds.).

[2] "Brahman" refers to God in God's deepest Being, as one finds God within oneself. Thus, Brahman in the *Upanishads* is also identified with the true "Self" (Eds.).

And if they should say to him: "If everything that exists is contained in that city of Brahman, all beings and all desires (whatever can be imagined or desired), then what is left of it, when old age reaches it and scatters it, or when it falls to pieces?"

Then he should say: "By the old age of the body, that (the ether, or Brahman within it) does not age; by the death of the body, that (the ether, or Brahman within it) is not killed. That (the Brahman) is the true Brahma-city (not the body). In it all desires are contained. It is the Self, free from sin, free from old age, from death and grief, from hunger and thirst, which desires nothing but what it ought to desire, and imagines nothing but what it ought to imagine. Now as here on earth people follow as they are commanded, and depend on the object which they are attached to, be it a country or a piece of land.

"And as here on earth, whatever has been acquired by exertion, perishes, so perishes whatever is acquired for the next world by sacrifices and other good actions performed on earth. Those who depart from hence without having discovered the Self and those true desires, for them there is no freedom in all the worlds. But those who depart from hence, after having discovered the Self and those true desires, for them there is freedom in all the worlds.

NO SELF

Questions of King Milinda

Now Milinda the king went up to where the venerable Nâgasena was, and addressed him with the greetings and compliments of friendship and courtesy, and took his seat respectfully apart. And Nâgasena reciprocated his courtesy, so that the heart of the king was propitiated.

And Milinda began by asking, "How is your Reverence known, and what, Sir, is your name?"

"I am known as Nâgasena, O king, and it is by that name that my brethren in the faith address me.

But although parents, O king, give such a name as Nâgasena, or Sûrasena, or Vîrasena, or Sihasena, yet this, Sire,—Nâgasena and so on—is only a generally understood term, a designation in common use. For there is no permanent individuality (no soul) involved in the matter."

Then Milinda called upon the Yonakas and the brethren to witness: "This Nâgasena says there is no permanent individuality (no soul) implied in his name. Is it now even possible to approve him in that?" And turning to Nâgasena, he said: "If, most reverend Nâgasena, there be no permanent individuality (no soul) involved in the matter, who is it, pray, who gives to you members of the Order your robes and food and lodging and necessaries for the sick? Who is it who enjoys such things when given? Who is it who lives a life of righteousness? Who is it who devotes himself to meditation? Who is it who attains to the goal of the Excellent Way, to the Nirvâna of Arahatship? And who is it who destroys living creatures? who is it who takes what is not his own? who is it who lives an evil life of worldly lusts, who speaks lies, who drinks strong drink, who (in a word) commits any one of the five sins which work out their bitter fruit even in this life? If that be so there is neither merit nor demerit; there is neither doer nor causer of good or evil deeds; there is neither fruit nor result of good or evil Karma.—If, most reverend Nâgasena, we are to think that were a man to kill you there would be no murder, then it follows that there are no real masters or teachers in your Order, and that your ordinations are void.—You tell me that your brethren in the Order are in the habit of addressing you as Nâgasena. Now what is that Nâgasena? Do you mean to say that the hair is Nâgasena?"

"I don't say that, great king."

"Or the hairs on the body, perhaps?"

"Certainly not."

"Or is it the nails, the teeth, the skin, the flesh, the nerves, the bones, the marrow, the kidneys, the heart, the liver, the abdomen, the spleen, the lungs, the larger intestines, the lower intestines, the stomach, the fæces, the bile, the phlegm, the pus, the blood, the sweat, the fat, the tears, the serum, the saliva, the mucus, the oil that lubricates the joints, the urine, or the brain, or any or all of these, that is Nâgasena?"[1]

And to each of these he answered no.

"Is it the outward form then (Rûpa) that is Nâgasena, or the sensations (Vedanâ), or the ideas (Saññâ), or the confections (the constituent elements of character, Samkhârâ), or the consciousness (Viññâna), that is Nâgasena?"[2]

And to each of these also he answered no.

"Then is it all these Skandhas combined that are Nâgasena?"

"No! great king."

"But is there anything outside the five Skandhas that is Nâgasena?"

And still he answered no.

"Then thus, ask as I may, I can discover no Nâgasena. Nâgasena is a mere empty sound. Who then is the Nâgasena that we see before us? It is a falsehood that your reverence has spoken, an untruth!"

And the venerable Nâgasena said to Milinda the king: "You, Sire, have been brought up in great luxury, as beseems your noble birth. If you were to walk this dry weather on the hot and sandy ground, trampling under foot the gritty, gravelly grains of the hard sand, your feet would hurt you. And as your body would be in pain, your mind would be disturbed, and you would experience a sense of bodily suffering. How then did you come, on foot, or in a chariot?"

"I did not come, Sir, on foot. I came in a carriage."

"Then if you came, Sire, in a carriage, explain to me what that is. Is it the pole that is the chariot?"

"I did not say that."

"Is it the axle that is the chariot?"

"Certainly not."

"Is it the wheels, or the framework, or the ropes, or the yoke, or the spokes of the wheels, or the goad, that are the chariot?"

And to all these he still answered no.

"Then is it all these parts of it that are the chariot?"

"No, Sir."

"But is there anything outside them that is the chariot?"

And still he answered no.

"Then thus, ask as I may, I can discover no chariot. Chariot is a mere empty sound. What then is the chariot you say you came in? It is a falsehood that your Majesty has spoken, an untruth! There is no such thing as a chariot! You are king over all India, a mighty monarch. Of whom then are you afraid that you speak untruth?" And he called upon the Yonakas and the brethren to witness, saying: "Milinda the king here has said that he came by carriage. But when asked in that case to explain what the carriage was, he is unable to establish what he averred. Is it, forsooth, possible to approve him in that?"

When he had thus spoken the five hundred Yonakas shouted their applause, and said to the king: "Now let your Majesty get out of that if you can?"

And Milinda the king replied to Nâgasena, and said: "I have spoken no untruth, reverend Sir. It is on account of its having all these things—the pole, and the axle, the wheels, and the framework, the ropes, the yoke, the spokes, and the goad—that it comes under the generally understood term, the designation in common use, of 'chariot.'"

"Very good! Your Majesty has rightly grasped the meaning of 'chariot.' And just even so it is on account of all those things you questioned me about—the thirty-two kinds of organic matter in a human body, and the five constituent elements of being—that I come under the generally understood term, the designation in common use, of 'Nâgasena.' For it was said, Sire, by our Sister Vagirâ in the presence of the Blessed One:

"Just as it is by the condition precedent of the co-existence of its various parts that the word 'chariot' is used, just so is it that when the Skandhas are there we talk of a 'being.'"

"Most wonderful, Nâgasena, and most strange. Well has the puzzle put to you, most difficult though it was, been solved. Were the Buddha himself here he would approve your answer. Well done, well done, Nâgasena!"

---

[1]This list of the thirty-two forms (âkâras) of organic matter in the human body occurs already in the Khuddaka Pâtha, §3. It is the standard list always used in similar connections; and is, no doubt, supposed to be exhaustive. There are sixteen (half as many) âkâras of the mind according to Dîpavamsa I, 42.

[2]These are the five Skandhas, which include in them the whole bodily and mental constituents of any being.

• • •

"How many years seniority have you, Nâgasena?"

"Seven, your Majesty."

"But how can you say it is your 'seven?' Is it you who are 'seven,' or the number that is 'seven?' "

Now that moment the figure of the king, decked in all the finery of his royal ornaments, cast its shadow on the ground, and was reflected in a vessel of water. And Nâgasena asked him: "Your figure, O king, is now shadowed upon the ground, and reflected in the water, how now, are you the king, or is the reflection the king?"

"I am the king, Nâgasena, but the shadow comes into existence because of me."

"Just even so, O king, the number of the years is seven, I am not seven. But it is because of me, O king, that the number seven has come into existence; and it is mine in the same sense as the shadow is yours."

• • •

The king said: "Is there, Nâgasena, such a thing as the soul?"

"What is this, O king, the soul (Vedagu)?"

"The living principle within which sees forms through the eye, hears sounds through the ear, experiences tastes through the tongue, smells odours through the nose, feels touch through the body, and discerns things (conditions, 'dhammâ') through the mind—just as we, sitting here in the palace, can look out of any window out of which we wish to look, the east window or the west, or the north or the south."

The Elder replied: "I will tell you about the five doors,[3] great king. Listen, and give heed attentively. If the living principle within sees forms through the eye in the manner that you mention, choosing its window as it likes, can it not then see forms not only through the eye, but also through each of the other five organs of sense? And in like manner can it not then as well hear sounds, and experience taste, and

smell odours, and feel touch, and discern conditions through each of the other five organs of sense, besides the one you have in each case specified?"

"No, Sir."

"Then these powers are not united one to another indiscriminately, the latter sense to the former organ, and so on. Now we, as we are seated here in the palace, with these windows all thrown open, and in full daylight, if we only stretch forth our heads, see all kinds of objects plainly. Can the living principle do the same when the doors of the eyes are thrown open? When the doors of the ear are thrown open, can it do so? Can it then not only hear sounds, but see sights, experience tastes, smell odours, feel touch, and discern conditions? And so with each of its windows?"

"No, Sir."

"Then these powers are not united one to another indiscriminately. Now again, great king, if Dinna here were to go outside and stand in the gateway, would you be aware that he had done so?"

"Yes, I should know it."

"And if the same Dinna were to come back again, and stand before you, would you be aware of his having done so?"

"Yes, I should know it."

"Well, great king, would the living principle within discern, in like manner, if anything possessing flavour were laid upon the tongue, its sourness, or its saltness, or its acidity, or its pungency, or its astringency, or its sweetness?"

"Yes, it would know it."

"But when the flavour had passed into the stomach would it still discern these things?"

"Certainly not."

"Then these powers are not united one to the other indiscriminately. Now suppose, O king, a man were to have a hundred vessels of honey brought and poured into one trough, and then, having had another man's mouth closed over and tied up, were to have him cast into the trough full of honey. Would he know whether that into which he had been thrown was sweet or whether it was not?"

"No, Sir."

"But why not?"

---

[3]It is odd he does not say six.

"Because the honey could not get into his mouth."

"Then, great king, these powers are not united one to another indiscriminately."[4]

"I am not capable of discussing with such a reasoner. Be pleased, Sir, to explain to me how the matter stands."

Then the Elder convinced Milinda the king with discourse drawn from the Abhidhamma, saying: "It is by reason, O king, of the eye and of forms that sight arises, and those other conditions—contact, sensation, idea, thought, abstraction, sense of vitality, and attention—arise each simultaneously with its predecessor. And a similar succession of cause and effect arises when each of the other five organs of sense is brought into play. And so herein there is no such thing as soul (Vedagu)."

THE MIDDLE WAY

T. R. V. Murti

There are two main currents of Indian philosophy—one having its source in the ātma-doctrine of the Upaniṣads and the other in the anātma-doctrine of Buddha. They conceive reality on two distinct and exclusive patterns. The Upaniṣads and the systems following the Brāhmanical tradition conceive reality on the pattern of an inner core or soul (ātman), immutable and identical amidst an outer region of impermanence and change, to which it is unrelated or but loosely related. This may be termed the Substance-view of reality (ātma-vāda). In its radical form, as in the Advaita Vedānta, it denied the reality of the apparent, the impermanent and the many; and equated that with the false. The Sāṃkhya did not go so far; still it inclined more towards the substantial,

the permanent and the universal. The Nyāya-Vaiśeṣika, with its empirical and pluralist bias, accords equal status to both substance and modes. Not only did these systems accept the ātman, but what is more, they conceived all other things also on the substance-pattern.[1] The ātman is the very pivot of their metaphysics, epistemology and ethics. In epistemology, substance makes for unity and integration of experience; it explains perception, memory and personal identity better than other theories. Bondage is ignorance of the self or the wrong identification of the non-self with the self. Freedom is the discrimination between the two.

The other tradition[2] is represented by the Buddhist denial of substance (ātman) and all that it implies. There is no inner and immutable core in things; everything is in flux. Existence for the Buddhist is momentary (kṣaṇika), unique (svalakṣaṇa) and unitary (dharmamātra). It is discontinuous, discrete and devoid of complexity. The substance (the universal and the identical) was rejected as illusory; it was but a thought-construction made under the influence of wrong belief (avidyā). This may be taken as the *Modal view of reality.* The Buddhists brought their epistemology and ethics in full accord with their metaphysics. Their peculiar conception of perception and inference and the complementary doctrine of mental construction (vikalpa) are necessary consequences of their denial of substance. Heroic attempts were made to fit this theory with the doctrine of Karma and rebirth. Avidyā (ignorance), which is the root-cause of suffering, is the wrong belief in the ātman; and prajñā (wisdom) consists in the eradication of this belief and its attendant evils.

• • •

Ātman is the chief category of the permanent. In a restricted but more prevalent usage, it means the

[4]That is: "Your 'living principle within' cannot make use of whichever of its windows it pleases. And the simile of a man inside a house does not hold good of the soul."

[1]The Nyāya-Vaiśeṣika is a philosophical system of Hinduism like Sāṃkhya and Vedānta. A selection on this system is not included in this reader (Eds.).
[2]The term 'Tradition' is used here not in the sense of dogmatic authoritarianism, but to mean a fountain-source from which stems a continuous stream of thought and culture.

soul or spirit, the subject of experience; in a wider and more logical sense it is substance in general. There are two principal views of the Self (ātman): one is the conception, in vogue with the Brāhmanical systems, of a permanent and immutable entity identical amidst changing states and therefore different from them; the other is the Buddhistic conception of ātman as a conventional name for a series of discrete momentary states (skandharūpa), sensation and feeling, intellection and conation. There is nothing unitary or identical amidst the changing states, and nothing hidden beneath them as the ātman. Like all existence, the mental states too are in a state of continual flux. The Buddhists coined a very unattractive word—"pudgala"—for the ātman. Besides these two principal views, there is the intermediary standpoint not only of the Jainas,[3] but of the Vātsīputrīyas (Sāmmitīyas) within the Buddhist fold itself. They held that the ātman or pudgala was a sort of quasi-permanent entity neither different from nor identical with the states like fire and fuel. The Pudgalātmavāda has been universally condemned as a heresy by the Buddhist schools, including the Mādhyamika.

If the ātman were identical with the states, it would be subject to birth, decay and death. There would be as many selves (ātman) as there are states. Of each self it could be urged that it was non-existent before it was born and would cease to exist later. Further, it would have been produced without causes, each self being a discrete independent entity, having no relation with the previous. The full weight of this criticism is realised when we consider moral responsibility. As the former self has ceased to exist and a new one has emerged into existence, the deeds done by the previous also cease to exist; for, there is no longer that entity which performed them. If the later self were to experience the result of the acts of the previous self, it would be a clear case of gratuitous burdening of responsibility. All this is repugnant to the implications of the moral act and its consequences, as done and enjoyed by the *same* agent.

This view of the states being the self really identifies the act with the agent, the feeling with the person who experiences the feeling. Such identification is unwarranted and cannot account for experience. The feeling itself is not the feeler, a content is not the *knowing* of the content. The subject of experience has to be accepted as indispensable for the occurrence of any mental state. The Buddhists, as rigorous exponents of the modal view, eschew the ātman and replace it completely by the states of feeling, sensation, conception and volition. Memory, recognition, moral responsibility and transmigration are all attempted to be explained on this hypothesis of substanceless momentary states. It speaks not a little for the dialectical insight of Nāgārjuna and his followers that they are acutely alive to the halting nature of the modal view.[4]

"The self is not the states that originate and cease; how can the experiencing subject be identical with the experienced states?" His main criticism of the modal view is that it wrongly identifies the agent with the act, the subject and the object. A multitude of qualities is not substance; a bundle of states is not the self. Bereft of unity, they fall asunder and make for disorder. The substance or self is the unifying factor which integrates several acts, making mental life continuous and coherent.

The rejection of the Buddhist modal view of the ātman by the Mādhyamika does not of itself mean that he is committed to the opposite view of an identical and changeless self (substance) different from the states. As a keen dialectician, the Mādhyamika is equally aware of the pitfalls of the substance-view of the ātman. He rejects that too as a false view of the real.

The conception of the ātman is variously formulated by the different non-Buddhistic systems; but they all agree in considering it as eternal, and as existing apart from the states and as identical amidst change. The main criticism of the Mādhyamika is that if the ātman were totally different from the

---

[3]The Jainas are a small sect in India, separate from both the Hindus and Buddhists; they are known chiefly for their extreme commitment to nonviolence (Eds.).

[4]Nagarjuna is the founder and leading philosopher of the Mādhyamika or Middle Way school of Mahayana Buddhism, which rejects both earlier Buddhist claims and those of the Hindus (Eds.).

states, it would be apprehended apart from them, as the table is perceived apart from the chair. It is not so perceived, and hence it is merely thought to exist owing to transcendental thought-construction. The ātman is the egoity reflected in the states, enjoying a semblance of independence, identity and permanence. It is thus a construct read into the manifold of states.

If the ātman were a real entity, there should be agreement about it. On the contrary one's (self) ātman is anātma (non-self) for another, and vice versa; and this should not be the case if it were an objective reality.

The relation of the ātman with the states cannot be formulated in any conceivable manner: whether the states are the self or different from them; whether the states are in it, or it is in them; whether the states belong to it, or vice versa, etc. There are obvious difficulties in every formulation, and most of them have been considered already.

It might be asked: if the ātman were not a real spiritual entity, then who is the mover and controller of the bodily movements? But how can an immaterial principle actuate a material thing like the body or the sense-organs and mind etc. Changeless and all-pervasive, ātman is not active; and without action, the ātman cannot be an agent. He cannot even co-ordinate and synthesise the different states into a unity.

As in the modal view, here too moral and spiritual life becomes impossible, though for an opposite reason; an unchanging ātman cannot be benefited by any spiritual discipline, nor can it deteriorate if that effort were not made. In spiritual progress the ātman cannot be identical at any two stages of development. To say that the ātman is not really bound or free, but owing to avidyā he wrongly identifies himself with the body, sense-organs and mind, is to say that phenomenal life is the work of false belief and imagination. The saving knowledge then is not that the real is ātman or anātma, but that none of our conceptual patterns applies to it.

On the modal view, there are the different momentary states only; there is no principle of unity.

Mental life is inexplicable without the unity of the self. On the substance-view, there is the unitary and identical self rigid and standing aloof from the states which the ātman is presumed to shape into order. The self of the Brāhmanical systems is a bare colourless unity bereft of difference and change, which alone impart significance to it. The self has no meaning apart from the states and mental activity. The two are mutually dependent, and hence unreal.

• • •

After an examination of the several views (dṛṣṭis) with regard to the ātman, Nāgārjuna concludes: "The self is not different from the states, nor identical with them; (there) is no self without the states; nor is it to be considered non-existent."

The Mādhyamika position may appear to be at variance with the teaching of the Buddha; on several occasions he seems to have asserted the existence of the self. But there are texts which declare quite unequivocally that he denied the self. The contradiction, however, is but apparent. "The self does exist, the Buddhas have declared; they have taught the 'no-self' doctrine too; they have (finally) taught that there is neither self nor non-self." Buddha's teaching is adjusted to the need of the taught as the medicine of the skilled physician is to the malady of the patient. He does not blindly, mechanically, prescribe one remedy to all and sundry, He corrects those with a nihilistic tendency by affirming the self, as there is continuity of karma and its result; to those addicted to the dogmatic belief in a changeless substantial ātman and who cling to it, he teaches the 'no-self doctrine' as an antidote; his ultimate teaching is that there is neither self nor not-self as these are subjective devices. The Real as the Indeterminate (sūnya) is free from conceptual construction. The indeterminacy of the Absolute allows freedom of approach; numberless are the ways by which it could be reached. The sole condition is that the method chosen should suit the disciple's disposition; this is the doctrine of upāya-kauśalya (excellence in the choice of means), and it applies to every doctrine.

EGO-LESS CONSCIOUSNESS: A ZEN VIEW

Toshihiko Izutsu

THE FIRST PERSON PRONOUN "I"

In dealing with the topic of the two dimensions of ego-consciousness in Zen, it might be thought more in line with Jungian psychology to use the word "Self" instead of the word "Ego" to designate what I am going to explain as ego-consciousness in the second or deeper dimension. But there is a reason why I prefer in this particular case to use one and the same word, "ego," in reference to the two dimensions of consciousness which I shall deal with in this Essay. For it is precisely one of the most important points which Zen makes that the empirical I which is the very center of human existence in our ordinary, daily life and the other I which is supposed to be actualized through the experience of enlightenment are ultimately identical with one another. The two "egos" are radically different from each other and look almost mutually exclusive in the eyes of those who are in the pre-enlightenment stage of Zen discipline. From the viewpoint of the post-enlightenment stage, however, they are just one and the same. In the eyes of the truly enlightened Zen master, there is nothing special, nothing extraordinary about what is often called by such grandiose names as Cosmic Ego, Cosmic Unconscious, Transcendental Consciousness and the like. It is no other than the existential ground of the ordinary, commonplace man who eats when he is hungry, drinks when he is thirsty, and falls asleep when he is sleepy, that is, in short, the ordinary self which we are accustomed to regard as the subject of the day-to-day existence of the plain man.

But let us start from the beginning. The starting-point is provided by our ego-consciousness as we find it in the pre-enlightenment stage. Historically as well as structurally, Zen has always been seriously concerned with our consciousness of ourselves. Indeed, it is not going too far to say that the problem of how to deal with ego-consciousness is *the* sole and exclusive problem for Zen Buddhism. Says Dōgen,[1] one of the greatest Zen masters of Japan in the thirteenth century A.D.: "To get disciplined in the way of the Buddha means nothing other than getting disciplined in properly dealing with your own I." That is to say, an intense, unremitting self-inquiry exhausts the whole of Buddhism. It constitutes the first step into the Way of the Buddha and it constitutes the ultimate end of the same Way. There is no other problem in Zen.

Another Japanese Zen master of the 15th century, Ikkyū,[2] admonishes his disciples in a similar way saying: "Who or what am I? Search for your I from the top of your head down to your bottom." And he adds: "No matter how hard you may search after it, you will never be able to grasp it. *That* precisely is your I." In this last sentence there is a clear suggestion made as to how the problem of ego-consciousness is to be posed and settled in Zen Buddhism.

Our ordinary view of the world may be symbolically represented as a circle with the ego as its autonomous center. With individual differences that are clearly to be recognized, each circle delimits a certain spatial and temporal expanse within the boundaries of which alone everything knowable is knowable. Its circumference sets up a horizon beyond which things disappear in an unfathomable darkness. The center of the circle is occupied by what Karl Jaspers called *Ich als Dasein,* i.e. the empirical ego, the I as we ordinarily understand it.

The circle thus constituted is of a centrifugal nature in the sense that everything, every action, whether mental or bodily, is considered to originate from its center and move toward its periphery. It is also centripetal in the sense that whatever happens within the circle is referred back and reduced to the center as its ultimate ground.

The center of the circle comes in this way to be vaguely represented as a permanent and enduring

---

[1]Dōgen (1200–1253).
[2]Master Ikkyū (1394–1481). The quotation is from his *Mizukagami.*

entity carrying and synthesizing all the disparate and divergent elements to be attributed to the various aspects and functions of the mind-body complex. Thus is born an image of the personal identity underlying all mental operations and bodily movements, remaining always the same through all the intra-organic and extra-organic processes that are observable in the mind-body complex. Linguistic usage expresses this inner vision of personal identity by the first person pronoun "I."

In our actual life we constantly use the first person pronoun as the grammatical subject for an infinite number of predicates. Long before the rise of Zen, Buddhism in India had subjected this usage of the first person pronoun to a thoroughgoing scrutiny in connection with the problem of the unreality of the ego, which, as is well known, was from the beginning the fundamental tenet of Buddhist philosophy and which, insofar as it was an idea distinguishing Buddhism from all other schools of Indian philosophy, was for the Buddhists of decisive importance.

We often say for instance "I am fat" or "I am lean" in reference to our bodily constitution. We say "I am healthy" or "I am ill" in accordance with whether our bodily organs are functioning normally or not. "I walk," "I run," etc., in reference to our bodily movements. "I am hungry," "I am thirsty," etc., in reference to the intra-organic physiological processes. "I see," "I hear," "I smell," etc., in reference to the activity of our sense organs. The first person pronoun behaves in fact as the grammatical subject of many other types of sentences, descriptive or otherwise.

Under all those propositions with the first person pronoun as the subject there is clearly observable the most primitive, primal certainty of "I am." This primal certainty we have of our "I am," that is, the consciousness of ego, derives its supreme importance from the fact that it constitutes the very center of the existential circle of each one of us. As the center sets itself into motion, a whole world of things and events spreads itself out around it in all directions, and as it quiets down the same variegated world is reduced to the original single point. The spreading-out of the empirical world in all its possible forms

around the center is linguistically reflected in the sentences whose grammatical subject is "I."

The most serious question here for Zen is: Does the grammatical subject of all these sentences represent the real personal subject in its absolute suchness? Otherwise expressed: Does the first person pronoun appearing in each of the sentences of this sort indicate pure subjectivity, the true Subject as understood by Zen Buddhism? The answer will definitely be in the negative.

The nature of the problem before us may be clarified in the following way. Suppose someone asks me "Who are you?" or "What are you?" To this question I can give an almost infinite number of answers. I can say, for example, "I am a Japanese," "I am a student," etc. Or I can say "I am so-and-so," giving my name. None of these answers, however, presents the *whole* of myself in its absolute "suchness." And no matter how many times I may repeat the formula "I am *X*," changing each time the semantic referent of the *X,* I shall never be able to present directly and immediately the "whole man" that I am. All that is presented by this formula is nothing but a partial and relative aspect of my existence, an objectified qualification of the "whole man." Instead of presenting the pure subjectivity that I am as the "whole man," the formula presents myself only as a relative object. But what Zen is exclusively concerned with is precisely the "whole man." And herewith begins the real Zen problem concerning the ego consciousness. Zen may be said to take its start by putting a huge question mark to the word "I" as it appears as the subject-term of all sentences of the type: "I am *X*" or "I do *X*." One enters into the world of Zen only when one realizes that his own I has itself turned into an existential question mark.

In the authentic tradition of Zen Buddhism in China it was customary for a master to ask a newcomer to his monastery questions in order to probe the spiritual depth of the man. The standard question, the most commonly used for this purpose, was: "Who are you?" This simple, innocent-looking question was in reality one which the Zen disciples were most afraid of. We shall have later occasion to see how vitally important this question is in Zen. But it will already be clear enough that the question is of such grave importance because it demands of us that we reveal immediately and on the spot the reality of the I underlying the common usage of the first person pronoun, that is, the "whole man" in its absolute subjectivity. Without going into theoretical details, I shall give here a classical example.[3] Nan Yüeh Huai Jang (J.: Nangaku Ejō, 677–744) who was later to become the successor to the Sixth Patriarch of Zen Buddhism in China, the famous Hui Nêng (J.: Enō, 637–713), came to visit the latter. Quite abruptly Hui Nêng asked him: "What is *this thing* that has come to me in this way?" This put the young Nan Yüeh completely at a loss for a reply. He left the master. And it took him eight years to solve the problem. In other words, the question "What are you?" functioned for the young Nan Yüeh as a *kōan*. And, let me add, it can be or is in fact a *kōan* for anyone who wants to have an insight into the spirit of Zen. The answer, by the way, which Nan Yüeh presented to the master after eight years' struggle was a very simple one: "Whatever I say in the form of *I am X* will miss the point. That exactly is the real I."

Making reference to this famous anecdote, Master Musō, an outstanding Zen master of fourteenth century Japan,[4] makes the following remark. "To me, too," he says, "many men of inferior capacity come and ask various questions about the spirit of Buddhism. To these people I usually put the question: 'Who is the one who is actually asking me such a question about the spirit of Buddhism?' To this there are some who answer: 'I am so-and-so,' or 'I am such-and-such.' There are some who answer: 'Why is it necessary at all to ask such a question? It is too obvious.' There are some who answer not by words but by gestures meant to symbolize the famous dictum: 'My own Mind, that is the Buddha.' There are still others who answer (by repeating or imitating like a parrot the sayings of ancient masters, like) 'Looking above, there is nothing to be sought after. Looking below, there is nothing to be

thrown away.' All these people will never be able to attain enlightenment."

This naturally reminds us of what is known in the history of Zen as the "concluding words of Master Pai Chang." Pai Chang Huai Hai (J.: Hyakujō Ekai, 720–814) was one of the greatest Zen masters of the T'ang dynasty. It is recorded that whenever he gave a public sermon to the monks of his temple, he brought it to an end by directly addressing the audience: "You people!" And as all turned towards the master in a state of unusual spiritual tension, at that very moment he flung down upon them like a thunderbolt the shout: "WHAT IS THAT?" Those among the audience who were mature enough to get enlightened were supposed to attain enlightenment on the spot.

"What is that?" "Who are you?" "What are you?" "Where do you come from?" These and other similar questions addressed by an enlightened master to a newcomer all directly point to the real I of the latter which ordinarily lies hidden behind the veil of his empirical I. These questions are extremely difficult to answer in a Zen context. Let us recall that Nan Yüeh had to grapple with his *kōan* for eight years before he found his own solution for it—not, of course, a verbal solution, but an existential one. The difficulty consists in that a question of this sort in the Zen context of a dialogue between master and disciple demands of the latter an immediate realization of the I as pure and unconditioned subjectivity. This is difficult almost to the extent of being utterly impossible because at the very moment that the disciple turns his attention to his own self which under ordinary conditions he is wont to express quite naïvely and unreflectingly by the first person pronoun, the self becomes objectified, or we should say, petrified, and the sought-for pure subjectivity is lost. The pure Ego can be realized only through a total transformation of the empirical ego into something entirely different, functioning in an entirely different dimension of human existence.

ZEN THEORY OF CONSCIOUSNESS

In order to elucidate the nature of the problem, let me go back once again to the image of the circle with which I proposed to represent symbolically the world as experienced by man at the pre-enlightenment

---

[3]*Wu Têng Hui Yüan*, III.

[4]The National Teacher, Musō (1275–1351), particularly famous for initiating the tradition of landscape gardening in Japanese culture. The following passage is found in his work *Muchū Mondō Shū*, II.

stage. The world in the view of the plain man, I said, may conveniently be represented as a vaguely illumined circle with the empirical ego at its center as the source of illumination. Around the empirical ego there spreads out a more or less narrowly limited circle of existence within which things are perceived and events take place. Such is the world-view of the plain man.

The circle of existence seen in this way would seem to have a peculiar structure. The center of the circle, the empirical ego, establishes itself as the "subject" and, as such, cognitively opposes itself to the "object" which is constituted by the world extending from and around it. Each of the things existing in the world and the world itself, indeed everything other than the "subject," is regarded as an "object." Zen does not necessarily criticize this structure as something entirely false or baseless. Zen takes a definitely negative attitude toward such a view as a falsification of the reality only when the "subject" becomes conscious of itself as the "subject," that is to say, when the "subjective" position of the center of the circle comes to produce the consciousness of the ego as an enduring individual entity. For in such a context, the "subject" turns into an "object." The "subject" may even then conceptually still remain "subjective," but insofar as it is conscious of itself as a self-subsistent entity, it belongs to the sphere of the "objective." It is but another "object" among myriads of other "objects." Viewed in such a light, the entire circle of the world of Being together with its center, the ego, proves to be an "objective" order of things. That is to say, what is seemingly the center of the circle is not the real center; the "subject" is not the real Subject.

In fact, it is characteristic of the psychological mechanism of man that no matter how far he may go in search of his real self in its pure and absolute subjectivity, it goes on escaping his grip. For the very act of turning attention to the "subject" immediately turns it into an "object."

What Zen primarily aims at may be said to be the reinstatement of the "subject" in its proper, original position, at the very center of the circle, not as an "object" but in its absolute subjectivity, as the real Subject or pure Ego. But the essential nature of the "subject"

being such as has just been indicated, the task of reinstating it in this sense cannot possibly be accomplished unless the illuminated circle of existence surrounding the "subject" be also completely transformed. We may perhaps describe the situation by saying that the primary aim of Zen consists in trying to broaden the "circle" to infinity to the extent that we might actualize an infinitely large circle with its circumference nowhere to be found, so that its center be found everywhere, always mobile and ubiquitous, fixed at no definite point. Only as the center of such a circle could the "subject" be the pure Ego.

In ancient Indian Buddhism, the pure Ego thus actualized used to be designated by the word *prajñā* or Transcendental Wisdom. Zen, using the traditional, common terminology of Buddhism that has developed in China, often calls it the "Buddha Nature," or simply "Mind." But Zen possesses also its specific vocabulary which is more colorful and more characteristically Chinese, for designating the same thing, like "No-Mind," the "Master," the "True-Man-without-any-rank," "your-original-Face-which-you-possessed-prior-to-the-birth-of-your-own-father-and-mother," or more simply, "This Thing," "That" or still more simply "It." All these and other names are designed to point to the transfigured ego functioning as the center of the transfigured "circle."

For a better understanding of the transfiguration of the ego here spoken of, we would do well to consider the Zen idea of the structure of consciousness. Buddhism, in conformity with the general trend of Indian philosophy and spirituality, was concerned from the earliest periods of its historical development in India, and later on in China, with a meticulous analysis of the psychological processes ranging from sensation, perception and imagination to logical thinking, translogical thinking and transcendental intuition. As a result, many different psychological and epistemological theories have been proposed. And this has been done in terms of the structure of consciousness. Characteristic of these theories of consciousness is that consciousness is represented as something of a multilayer structure. Consciousness, in this view, consists of a number of layers or different dimensions organically related to each other but each functioning in its own way.

The most typical of all theories of consciousness that have developed in Mahayana Buddhism is that of the Yogācāra School (otherwise called the Vijñaptimātratā School, i.e., Consciousness-Only School). The philosophers of this school recognize in human consciousness three distinctively different levels. The first or "surface" level is the ordinary psychological dimension in which the sense-organs play the preponderant role producing sensory and perceptual images of the external things. Under this uppermost layer comes the *mano-vijñāna* or Manas-Consciousness. This is the dimension of the ego-consciousness.

According to the Yogācāra School, the consciousness of ego which we ordinarily have is but an infinitesimal part of the Manas-Consciousness. It is only the tip of a huge iceberg that shows above the surface. The greater part of the iceberg is submerged beneath the water. The submerged part of the iceberg consists of the so-called "egotistic attachments" which have been accumulated there since time immemorial and which are intensely alive and active in the invisible depths of the psyche, sustaining, as it were, from below what we are ordinarily conscious of as our "I."

The Manas-Consciousness itself is sustained from below by the *ālaya-vijñāna,* the Storehouse-Consciousness which constitutes the deepest layer of human consciousness. Unlike the Manas-Consciousness of which at least the smallest part is illumined in the form of the empirical ego-consciousness, the Storehouse-Consciousness lies entirely in darkness. It is a "storehouse" or repository of all the karmic effects of our past actions, mental and bodily. They are "stored" there under the form of primordial Images which constantly come up to the above-mentioned surface level of consciousness arousing there the sensory and perceptual images of the phenomenal things and producing at the second level of consciousness i.e., the level of *mano-vijñāna,* the consciousness of the ego. What is remarkable about the nature of the Storehouse-Consciousness is that, in the view of the Yogācāra School, it is not confined to the individual person. It exceeds the boundaries of an individual mind extending even beyond the personal uncon-

scious that belongs to the individual, for it is the "storehouse" of all the karmic vestiges that have been left by the experiences of mankind since the beginning of time. As such the concept of the Storehouse-Consciousness may be said to be the closest equivalent in Buddhism to the Collective Unconscious.

However, the philosophers of the Yogācāra School speak of transcending the Storehouse-Consciousness by the force of a spiritual illumination that issues forth from the World of Purest Reality as they call it, which they say could be opened up by man's going through the arduous process of the spiritual discipline of meditation.

As a branch of Mahayana Buddhism closely connected with the Yogācāra School, Zen bases itself philosophically on a similar conception of the structure of consciousness. However, being by nature averse to all theorizing, let alone philosophizing, Zen has elaborated no special doctrine concerning this problem, at least in an explicit form. But under the innumerable anecdotes, *kōans,* poems, and popular sermons which constitute the main body of Zen literature, a group of major ideas about the structure of consciousness is clearly discernible. And it is not so hard for us to bring them out in a theoretic form and develop them into a Zen doctrine of consciousness.

It immediately becomes clear that Zen also holds a multilayer theory of consciousness. Here, however, as in all other cases, Zen greatly simplifies the matter. It regards consciousness as consisting of two entirely different, though intimately related, layers which we may distinguish as (1) the intentional and (2) the non-intentional dimension of consciousness, the word "intentional" being used in the original sense as exemplified by the use of the Latin word *intentio* in Medieval philosophy.

In the intentional dimension, the I as the "subject" is empirically given as a correlate of the "object." There is an essential correlation between the "subject" and "object." All noetic experience in this dimension is necessarily of dualistic structure. I regard myself as "I" only insofar as I am aware of external things and events as "objects" of cognition.

There would be no ego-consciousness if there were absolutely no "object" to be cognized. More generally, it is characteristic of this dimension that our consciousness is always and necessarily a "consciousness-of." It is an awareness *intending* something, i.e., directed toward something; it is an awareness with an objective reference.

It is, in other words, of the very nature of consciousness in this dimension that it cannot but objectify whatever appears before it. And paradoxically or ironically enough, this holds true even of the "subject." The very moment I become aware of myself, my I turns into an objectified I, an "object" among all other "objects." This is the main reason, as I said earlier, why it is so difficult to realize the "subject" in its pure subjectivity. One can never hope to actualize the pure Ego as long as one remains in the intentional dimension of consciousness.

Zen, however, recognizes—and knows through experience—another dimension of consciousness which is what I have called above the "non-intentional" dimension, and in which consciousness functions without being divided into the subjective and objective. It is a noetic dimension which is to be cultivated through the yogic, introspective techniques of *zazen*, a special dimension in which consciousness is activated not as "consciousness-of" but as Consciousness pure and simple. This would exactly correspond to what Vasubandhu, a representative philosopher of the Yogācāra School, once said:[5] "As the mind perceives no object, it remains as pure Awareness."

The non-intentional awareness is found to be at work, albeit usually in vague and indistinct form, even in our day-to-day experience. Already the Sautrāntika School of Hinayana Buddhism[6] noticed the existence of the non-intentional aspect in the mind of the plain man. The proposition, for example, "I feel happy" in contradistinction to a proposi-

tion like "I see a mountain," expresses a kind of non-intentional awareness. For being-happy is an awareness of a pleasurable mode of being, an elation which is vaguely diffused in the whole of my mind-body complex, with no definite, particular "object" of which I can say I am conscious, unless I become by *intentio secunda* conscious of my being-happy. The proposition "I see a mountain," on the contrary, is clearly a description of a perceptual event taking place between the "subject" and the "object."

What Zen is interested in, however, is not a non-intentional awareness such as is expressed by propositions of the type: "I am happy." Rather Zen is interested in opening up a special dimension of consciousness which is, we might say, systematically non-intentional. It is a dimension in which even a proposition like "I see the mountain" for example will be found to signify a peculiar state of awareness of such a nature that exactly the same propositional content may be expressed interchangeably by four linguistically different sentences: (1) "I see the mountain," (2) "The mountain sees me," (3) "The mountain sees the mountain," (4) "I see myself." The non-intentional dimension of consciousness in which Zen is interested is such that these four sentences are exactly synonymous with each other. Until these four sentences are realized to be exactly synonymous with each other, you are still in the intentional dimension of consciousness. Furthermore, in the non-intentional dimension of consciousness these four synonymous sentences can very well be reduced to a one word sentence: "Mountain!" and this word again can freely be reduced to one single word "I."

Here we observe how the original sentence: "I see the mountain" from which we started has ultimately been condensed into one single point of "I." The "I" thus actualized conceals within itself all the sentential variants that have been passed through, so that it can at any moment reveal itself as the "Mountain!" or expand into any of the four full sentences. In whichever form it may appear, it is a pure non-intentional awareness, a pure consciousness instead of "consciousness-of." Nothing is here

---

[5]In his *Trimshika-Vijñaptimātratā-Siddhi.*
[6]See an excellent exposition of the matter by H. Guenther: *Buddhist Philosophy,* Harmondsworth-Baltimore, 1972, pp. 68–70.

objectified. What Zen considers to be the true Self or absolute Ego is precisely the I actualized in such a dimension of consciousness as an immediate self-expression of this very dimension.

QUESTIONS FOR DISCUSSION

1. The Samkhya dualism of the *Bhagavad Gita* is somewhat different from Descartes' dualism. Compare and contrast Samkhya and Cartesian dualism. (*Note: Cartesianism* is the term usually used by philosophers to describe the work of Descartes and his followers.)

2. Compare the early Buddhist view of self with that of the Hindu *Upanishads.*

3. Compare the early Buddhist view of self with those of the Western philosophers presented in the previous section of this chapter.

4. Both the Madhyamika philosophy explained by Murti and the later Yogacara philosophy expounded by Izutsu claim to be philosophies of Mahayana Buddhism. On the basis of what you have read, do they appear to you to be different or essentially similar interpretations of this viewpoint?

A DEFENSE OF HUME AND BUDDHA
BASED ON WESTERN PSYCHOLOGY

During the 1960s, it was discovered that surgical separation of the two hemispheres of the brain was beneficial in cases of severe epilepsy. Unfortunately, the procedure had unanticipated side effects of a disturbing and unusual nature. When separated, the two hemispheres and the body parts they separately controlled assumed an independence of amazing proportions. In one frightening and dramatic instance, the patient reported an argument with his wife that resulted in his one hand attempting to strike her while his other hand tried to protect her from the blow. In the following article, the contemporary British analytic philosopher Derek Parfit draws upon this incredible psychological discovery in an attempt to defend the "bundle" theory of the self developed by both David Hume and the Buddha against the "ego theory" of philosophers such as Descartes and the orthodox Hindu sages.

DIVIDED MINDS AND THE
"BUNDLE" THEORY OF SELF

Derek Parfit

It was the split-brain cases which drew me into philosophy. Our knowledge of these cases depends on the results of various psychological tests, as described by Donald MacKay. These tests made use of two facts. We control each of our arms, and see what is in each half of our visual fields, with only one of our hemispheres. When someone's hemispheres have been disconnected, psychologists can thus present to this person two different written questions in the two halves of his visual field, and can receive two different answers written by this person's two hands.

Here is a simplified imaginary version of the kind of evidence that such tests provide. One of these people looks fixedly at the centre of a wide screen, whose left half is red and right half is blue. On each half in a darker shade are the words, "How many colours can you see?" With both hands the person writes, "Only one." The words are now changed to read, "Which is the only colour that you can see?" With one of his hands the person writes "Red," with the other he writes "Blue."

If this is how such a person responds, I would conclude that he is having two visual sensations—that he does, as he claims, see both red and blue. But in seeing each colour he is not aware of seeing the other. He has two streams of consciousness, in each of which he can see only one colour. In one stream he sees red, and at the same time, in his other stream, he sees blue. More generally, he could be having at the same time two series of thoughts and sensations, in having each of which he is unaware of having the other.

This conclusion has been questioned. It has been claimed by some that there are not *two* streams of consciousness, on the ground that the sub-dominant hemisphere is a part of the brain whose functioning involves no consciousness. If this were true, these cases would lose most of their interest. I believe that it is not true, chiefly because, if a person's dominant hemisphere is destroyed, this person is able to react in the way in which, in the split-brain cases, the sub-dominant hemisphere reacts, and we do not believe that such a person is just an automaton, without consciousness. The sub-dominant hemisphere is, of course, much less developed in certain ways, typically having the linguistic abilities of a three-year-old. But three-year-olds are conscious. This supports the view that, in split-brain cases, there *are* two streams of consciousness.

Another view is that, in these cases, there are two persons involved, sharing the same body. Like

Professor MacKay, I believe that we should reject this view. My reason for believing this is, however, different. Professor MacKay denies that there are two persons involved because he believes that there is only one person involved. I believe that, in a sense, the number of persons involved is none.

THE EGO THEORY AND
THE BUNDLE THEORY

To explain this sense I must, for a while, turn away from the split-brain cases. There are two theories about what persons are, and what is involved in a person's continued existence over time. On the *Ego Theory,* a person's continued existence cannot be explained except as the continued existence of a particular *Ego,* or *subject of experiences.* An Ego Theorist claims that, if we ask what unifies someone's consciousness at any time—what makes it true, for example, that I can now both see what I am typing and hear the wind outside my window—the answer is that these are both experiences which are being had by me, this person, at this time. Similarly, what explains the unity of a person's whole life is the fact that all of the experiences in this life are had by the same person, or subject of experiences. In its best-known form, the *Cartesian view,* each person is a persisting purely mental thing—a soul, or spiritual substance.

The rival view is the *Bundle Theory.* Like most styles in art—Gothic, baroque, rococo, etc.—this theory owes its name to its critics. But the name is good enough. According to the Bundle Theory, we can't explain either the unity of consciousness at any time, or the unity of a whole life, by referring to a person. Instead we must claim that there are long series of different mental states and events—thoughts, sensations, and the like—each series being what we call one life. Each series is unified by various kinds of causal relation, such as the relations that hold between experiences and later memories of them. Each series is thus like a bundle tied up with string.

In a sense, a Bundle Theorist denies the existence of persons. An outright denial is of course absurd. As Reid protested in the eighteenth century, "I am not thought, I am not action, I am not feeling; I am something which thinks and acts and feels." I am not a series of events, but a person. A Bundle Theorist admits this fact, but claims it to be only a fact about our grammar, or our language. There are persons or subjects in this language-dependent way. If, however, persons are believed to be more than this—to be separately existing things, distinct from our brains and bodies, and the various kinds of mental states and events—the Bundle Theorist denies that there are such things.

The first Bundle Theorist was Buddha, who taught 'anatta', or the *No Self view.* Buddhists concede that selves or persons have "nominal existence," by which they mean that persons are merely combinations of other elements. Only what exists by itself, as a separate element, has instead what Buddhists call "actual existence." Here are some quotations from Buddhist texts:

> At the beginning of their conversation the king politely asks the monk his name, and receives the following reply: "Sir, I am known as 'Nagasena'; my fellows in the religious life address me as 'Nagasena.' Although my parents gave me the name . . . it is just an appellation, a form of speech, a description, a conventional usage. 'Nagasena' is only a name, for no person is found here."

> A sentient being does exist, you think, O Mara? You are misled by a false conception. This bundle of elements is void of Self. In it there is no sentient being. Just as a set of wooden parts Receives the name of carriage, So do we give to elements The name of fancied being.

> Buddha has spoken thus: "O Brethren, actions do exist, and also their consequences, but the person that acts does not. There is no one to cast away this set of elements, and no one to assume a new set of them. There exists no Individual, it is only a conventional name given to a set of elements."[1]

---

[1] For the sources of these and similar quotations, see my *Reasons and Persons* (1984), pp. 502–3, 532. Oxford: Oxford Univ. Press.

Buddha's claims are strikingly similar to the claims advanced by several Western writers. Since these writers knew nothing of Buddha, the similarity of these claims suggests that they are not merely part of one cultural tradition, in one period. They may be, as I believe they are, true.

WHAT WE BELIEVE OURSELVES TO BE

Given the advances in psychology and neurophysiology, the Bundle Theory may now seem to be obviously true. It may seem uninteresting to deny that there are separately existing Egos, which are distinct from brains and bodies and the various kinds of mental states and events. But this is not the only issue. We may be convinced that the Ego Theory is false, or even senseless. Most of us, however, even if we are not aware of this, also have certain beliefs about what is involved in our continued existence over time. And these beliefs would only be justified if something like the Ego Theory was true. Most of us therefore have false beliefs about what persons are, and about ourselves.

These beliefs are best revealed when we consider certain imaginary cases, often drawn from science fiction. One such case is *teletransportation*. Suppose that you enter a cubicle in which, when you press a button, a scanner records the states of all of the cells in your brain and body, destroying both while doing so. This information is then transmitted at the speed of light to some other planet, where a replicator produces a perfect organic copy of you. Since the brain of your Replica is exactly like yours, it will seem to remember living your life up to the moment when you pressed the button, its character will be just like yours, and it will be in every other way psychologically continuous with you. This psychological continuity will not have its normal cause, the continued existence of your brain, since the causal chain will run through the transmission by radio of your "blueprint."

Several writers claim that, if you chose to be teletransported, believing this to be the fastest way of travelling, you would be making a terrible mistake. This would not be a way of travelling, but a way of dying. It may not, they concede, be quite as bad as ordinary death. It might be some consolation to you that, after your death, you will have this Replica, which can finish the book that you are writing, act as parent to your children, and so on. But, they insist, this Replica won't be you. It will merely be someone else, who is exactly like you. This is why this prospect is nearly as bad as ordinary death.

Imagine next a whole range of cases, in each of which, in a single operation, a different proportion of the cells in your brain and body would be replaced with exact duplicates. At the near end of this range, only 1 or 2 per cent would be replaced; in the middle, 40 or 60 per cent; near the far end, 98 or 99 per cent. At the far end of this range is pure teletransportation, the case in which all of your cells would be "replaced."

When you imagine that some proportion of your cells will be replaced with exact duplicates, it is natural to have the following beliefs. First, if you ask, "Will I survive? Will the resulting person be me?," there must be an answer to this question. Either you will survive, or you are about to die. Second, the answer to this question must be either a simple "Yes" or a simple "No." The person who wakes up either will or will not be you. There cannot be a third answer, such as that the person waking up will be half you. You can imagine yourself later being half-conscious. But if the resulting person will be fully conscious, he cannot be half you. To state these beliefs together: to the question, "Will the resulting person be me?" there must always *be* an answer, which must be all-or-nothing.

There seem good grounds for believing that, in the case of teletransportation, your Replica would not be you. In a slight variant of this case, your Replica might be created while you were still alive, so that you could talk to one another. This seems to show that, if 100 per cent of your cells were replaced, the result would merely be a Replica of you. At the other end of my range of cases, where only 1 per cent would be replaced, the resulting person clearly *would* be you. It therefore seems that, in the cases in between, the resulting person must be either you, or merely a Replica. It seems that one of these must be true, and that it makes a great difference which is true.

HOW WE ARE NOT WHAT WE BELIEVE

If these beliefs were correct, there must be some critical percentage, somewhere in this range of cases, up to which the resulting person would be you, and beyond which he would merely be your Replica. Perhaps, for example, it would be you who would wake up if the proportion of cells replaced were 49 per cent, but if just a few more cells were also replaced, this would make all the difference, causing it to be someone else who would wake up.

That there must be some such critical percentage follows from our natural beliefs. But this conclusion is most implausible. How could a few cells make such a difference? Moreover, if there is such a critical percentage, no one could ever discover where it came. Since in all these cases the resulting person would believe that he was you, there could never be any evidence about where, in this range of cases, he would suddenly cease to be you.

On the Bundle Theory, we should reject these natural beliefs. Since you, the person, are not a separately existing entity, we can know exactly what would happen without answering the question of what will happen to you. Moreover, in the cases in the middle of my range, it is an empty question whether the resulting person would be you, or would merely be someone else who is exactly like you. These are not here two different possibilities, one of which must be true. These are merely two different descriptions of the very same course of events. If 50 per cent of your cells were replaced with exact duplicates, we could call the resulting person you, or we could call him merely your Replica. But since these are not here different possibilities, this is a mere choice of words.

As Buddha claimed, the Bundle Theory is hard to believe. It is hard to accept that it could be an empty question whether one is about to die, or will instead live for many years.

What we are being asked to accept may be made clearer with this analogy. Suppose that a certain club exists for some time, holding regular meetings. The meetings then cease. Some years later, several people form a club with the same name, and the same rules. We can ask, "Did these people revive the very same club? Or did they merely start up another club which is exactly similar?" Given certain further details, this would be another empty question. We could know just what happened without answering this question. Suppose that someone said: "But there must be an answer. The club meeting later must either be, or not be, the very same club." This would show that this person didn't understand the nature of clubs.

In the same way, if we have any worries about my imagined cases, we don't understand the nature of persons. In each of my cases, you would know that the resulting person would be both psychologically and physically exactly like you, and that he would have some particular proportion of the cells in your brain and body—90 per cent, or 10 per cent, or, in the case of teletransportation, 0 per cent. Knowing this, you know everything. How could it be a real question what would happen to you, unless you are a separately existing Ego, distinct from a brain and body, and the various kinds of mental state and event? If there are no such Egos, there is nothing else to ask a real question about.

Accepting the Bundle Theory is not only hard; it may also affect our emotions. As Buddha claimed, it may undermine our concern about our own futures. This effect can be suggested by redescribing this change of view. Suppose that you are about to be destroyed, but will later have a Replica on Mars. You would naturally believe that this prospect is about as bad as ordinary death, since your Replica won't be you. On the Bundle Theory, the fact that your Replica won't be you just consists in the fact that, though it will be fully psychologically continuous with you, this continuity won't have its normal cause. But when you object to teletransportation you are not objecting merely to the abnormality of this cause. You are objecting that this cause won't get *you* to Mars. You fear that the abnormal cause will fail to produce a further and all-important fact, which is different from the fact that your Replica will be psychologically continuous with you. You do not merely want there to be psychological continuity between you and some future person. You want to *be* this future person. On the Bundle Theory, there is no such special further fact. What you fear will not happen, in this imagined case, *never* happens. You want the person on Mars to be you in a specially intimate way in which no future person will ever be you. This means that, judged from the standpoint of your natural beliefs, even ordinary survival is about as bad as teletransportation. *Ordinary survival is about as bad as being destroyed and having a Replica.*

HOW THE SPLIT-BRAIN CASES SUPPORT THE BUNDLE THEORY

The truth of the Bundle Theory seems to me, in the widest sense, as much a scientific as a philosophical conclusion. I can imagine kinds of evidence which would have justified believing in the existence of separately existing Egos, and believing that the continued existence of these Egos is what explains the continuity of each mental life. But there is in fact very little evidence in favour of this Ego Theory, and much for the alternative Bundle Theory.

Some of this evidence is provided by the split-brain cases. On the Ego Theory, to explain what unifies our experiences at any one time, we should simply claim that these are all experiences which are being had by the same person. Bundle Theorists reject this explanation. This disagreement is hard to resolve in ordinary cases. But consider the simplified split-brain case that I described. We show to my imagined patient a placard whose left half is blue and right half is red. In one of this person's two streams of consciousness, he is aware of seeing only blue, while at the same time, in his other stream, he is aware of seeing only red. Each of these two visual experiences is combined with other experiences, like that of being aware of moving one of his hands. What unifies the experiences, at any time, in each of this person's two streams of con-

sciousness? What unifies his awareness of seeing only red with his awareness of moving one hand? The answer cannot be that these experiences are being had by the same person. This answer cannot explain the unity of each of this person's two streams of consciousness, since it ignores the disunity between these streams. This person is now having all of the experiences in both of his two streams. If this fact was what unified these experiences, this would make the two streams one.

These cases do not, I have claimed, involve two people sharing a single body. Since there is only one person involved, who has two streams of consciousness, the Ego Theorist's explanation would have to take the following form. He would have to distinguish between persons and subjects of experiences, and claim that, in split-brain cases, there are *two* of the latter. What unifies the experiences in one of the person's two streams would have to be the fact that these experiences are all being had by the same subject of experiences. What unifies the experiences in this person's other stream would have to be the fact that they are being had by another subject of experiences. When this explanation takes this form, it becomes much less plausible. While we could assume that "subject of experiences," or "Ego," simply meant "person," it was easy to believe that there are subjects of experiences. But if there can be subjects of experiences that are not persons, and if in the life of a split-brain patient there are at any time two different subjects of experiences—two different Egos—why should we believe that there really are such things? This does not amount to a refutation. But it seems to me a strong argument against the Ego Theory.

As a Bundle Theorist, I believe that these two Egos are idle cogs. There is another explanation of the unity of consciousness, both in ordinary cases and in split-brain cases. It is simply a fact that ordinary people are, at any time, aware of having several different experiences. This awareness of several different experiences can be helpfully compared with one's awareness, in short-term memory, of several different experiences. Just as there can be a single memory of just having had several experiences, such as hearing a bell strike three times, there can be a single state of awareness both of hearing the fourth striking of this bell, and of seeing, at the same time, ravens flying past the bell-tower.

Unlike the Ego Theorist's explanation, this explanation can easily be extended to cover split-brain cases. In such cases there is, at any time, not one state of awareness of several different experiences, but two such states. In the case I described, there is one state of awareness of both seeing only red and of moving one hand, and there is another state of awareness of both seeing only blue and moving the other hand. In claiming that there are two such states of awareness, we are not postulating the existence of unfamiliar entities, two separately existing Egos which are not the same as the single person whom the case involves. This explanation appeals to a pair of mental states which would have to be described anyway in a full description of this case.

I have suggested how the split-brain cases provide one argument for one view about the nature of persons. I should mention another such argument, provided by an imagined extension of these cases, first discussed at length by David Wiggins.[2]

In this imagined case a person's brain is divided, and the two halves are transplanted into a pair of different bodies. The two resulting people live quite separate lives. This imagined case shows that personal identity is not what matters. If I was about to divide, I should conclude that neither of the resulting people will be me. I will have ceased to exist. But this way of ceasing to exist is about as good— or as bad—as ordinary survival.

Some of the features of Wiggins's imagined case are likely to remain technically impossible. But the case cannot be dismissed, since its most striking feature, the division of one stream of consciousness into separate streams, has already happened. This is a second way in which the actual split-brain cases have great theoretical importance. They challenge some of our deepest assumptions about ourselves.[3]

QUESTION FOR DISCUSSION

1. Does the evidence that Derek Parfit presents really warrant, in your opinion, the conclusion about the nature of the self that he draws from it? Are there other possible interpretations of the data? If so, what are they?

---

[2]At the end of his *Identity and Spatio-temporal Continuity* (1967), Oxford: Blackwell.

[3]I discuss these assumptions further in part 3 of my *Reasons and Persons.*

THE SELF AS ACTIVITY

We see here yet another view of self. The twentieth-century Argentine philosopher Risieri Frondizi (1910–1983) puts it succinctly: The self is constituted, not by a static, unchanging substance, but by its actions. It is our behavior that constitutes the self. In developing this view, he relies heavily upon psychology, invoking the psychological concept of Gestalt rather than "substance" to explain the unity of the self. Interestingly, Frondizi's essay is not, as one might expect, a translation from the Spanish. He spent much time lecturing in the United States as well as Argentina during his career and at times wrote in English as well as Spanish. Consequently, he was and is a presence in North American as well as Latin American philosophy in this century.

THE DYNAMIC UNITY OF THE SELF

Risieri Frondizi

THE BEING AND THE DOING OF THE SELF

Experience shows us that the self does not depend upon any obscure or hidden substantial core but depends upon what it does, has done, proposes to do, or is able to do. The self is revealed in its action; it reveals itself and constitutes itself by acting. It is nothing before acting, and nothing remains of it if experiences cease completely. Its *esse* is equivalent to its *facere*. We are not given a ready-made self; we create our own self daily by what we do, what we experience. Our behavior—in which both our actual doing and our intentions should properly be included—is not an expression of our self but the very stuff which constitutes it.

What holds experiences together, what gives us personality, is not, therefore, a substantial bond but a functional one, a coordinated structure of activities.

The self is not something already made but something that is always in the making. It is formed throughout the course of its life, just as any institution is formed—a family, a university, a nation. There is no aboriginal nucleus of the self that exists prior to its actions; the self arises and takes on existence as it acts, as it undergoes experiences. The category of substance must be supplanted by that of function if we wish to interpret adequately the nature of the self. The concept of function connotes, in this case, the concepts of activity, process, and relation.

The functional link by no means includes only our past experiences. The self is memory, but it is not memory alone. Our personality depends upon what has happened to us, but it cannot be reduced to our personal history; the self is not the blind aggregate of our experiences. We get the push of the past, but we also get the pull of the future. There is, in the self, a note of novelty and creativity, a free will, an ability to control the eventual course of our experiences. Activity, therefore, contains an element of novelty; it cannot be grasped or comprehended by referring exclusively to its past. The self is not inert matter, deposited on the shore by the tide of experience, but creative will, plotting its own course for itself. It depends upon its past history but is able to mold its own history-to-be, to orient its life according to new courses. It is memory but memory projected toward the future, memory hurled ahead. The future conditions the nature of our self not only as it merges with the present but also while it is still more distantly future. What we plan to do, even if we never get to do it, gives sense to our activities. The future, however, is not a part of our self merely as a system of ideas and intentions; it also enters into the formation of the self through our emotions. In times of confusion and disaster the thought of the future of our country, our child, our own lives grieves us. Though it is true that this suffering is a present and not a future experience, its object is the future. It is like the pain caused by a splinter; the pain is not the splinter, but it could not exist without the presence of the splinter. Hope, despair, and many other experiences would be impossible if the future were not an element in our lives.

The self is a function already performed but also a function to be fulfilled, a capacity, a potentiality. Our being consists of what we have done but also of what we intend and are able to do. The past creates ability; the ability gives a sense of direction to the past. Even the capacity that was never realized, the potentiality that never had the chance of becoming actual, forms an integral part of our self.

The past and the future of the self are not, strictly speaking, separable parts; they form an indissoluble whole. The past acquires meaning in the light of the future; the future, in turn, depends upon the past. We cannot do whatever we want; our abilities depend upon our past experiences.

Some people have denied the dynamic character of the self or have relegated it to a position of secondary importance, thinking it to be incompatible with its unity. Unable to conceive of the unity of a changing being, they have considered that the process of alteration of the self only scratches its surface and that the self keeps an immutable central core. It is true that there is only one Ego for each experiential stream, but it is also true that the self is not immutable. We have seen that the self is constantly changing, that everything that happens to us enriches and modifies our self. But change does not mean substitution; rather, it means an alteration of the inner pattern. Thus, former experiences never quite disappear completely, though they can change their nature and meaning with the development of the self.

• • •

ANALYSIS AND ANALYTICISM[*]

A study of the validity of the procedure utilized by the atomists reveals its weaknesses even more clearly than does an analysis of the results of the procedure itself.

The analysis of psychic complexes and their reduction to supposed primary elements has no empirical justification; it makes its appearance in atomism as a presupposition which, on the face of it, has the same philosophic value as the rationalist presupposition. We are aware of the difficulties which one has to face in an attempt to eliminate all presuppositions. It is nevertheless evident that atomism has made no serious effort to justify or examine critically the procedure which it employs. It has accepted and used the procedure with no thought for its philosophic basis or for the consequences which would result from its application.

As is well known, the method that is used conditions the nature of the object under observation. If, blinded by the prestige acquired by the scientific method, we commit the stupid blunder of the modern tourist who tries to examine under the microscope a city which he is visiting for the first time, we shall not succeed in seeing the houses, the people, the plants, and the flowers. It would imply an even greater blindness to maintain that in the city there are neither houses nor people nor flowers, without realizing that they have disappeared as a consequence of the instrument chosen. The naked eye, in such a case, is a better instrument than the microscope, which, though it shows us the detail, keeps us from seeing the whole.

The analytic method has often worked like a microscope. It has revealed details which no one had ever seen before, but it has impeded our view of the whole. Again, the naked eye and the free-ranging glances of the spirit are superior to the intellect provided with the perfected technique and instruments of analysis. We need only to glance within, if we hold no prejudicial theories, to see what is hidden from the philosophers using analytic methods and blinded by the postulates of their theory and by their technique of observation.

Why should we be surprised that the wholes are not perceived if it has already been accepted in advance that analysis is the only form of apprehension? That which has been previously eliminated cannot be discovered, and it is impossible to reconstruct what should never have been destroyed.

[*]Although there are references to its failures in the following section, Frondizi's full critique of Descartes' approach—the "substantialist" or, as Frondizi calls it below, the "rationalist" viewpoint—has not been included in the selection. We have emphasized rather his critique of the Humean "analytic" approach (Eds.).

The analytic philosophy which sprang from Hume's atomism is subject to an almost demoniac desire for destruction—destruction by reductions. When confronted by a whole, these philosophers make no effort to comprehend its nature and find the sense of the whole. They proceed immediately to chop the whole into as many parts as possible and to submit each part to the thoroughgoing test of analysis. It is like the little boy who wants to find out what makes his toy work and ends up defiantly facing a heap of loose nuts and bolts.

This destructive drive is based upon a metaphysical postulate from which another postulate, an epistemological one, is derived; these two postulates support what we might call "the fallacy of reduction." The metaphysical postulate may be stated thus: elements have a more actual reality than wholes. The epistemological consequence is obvious: the goal of philosophic knowledge is to come to grips with the basic elements which constitute reality.

From these two postulates a series of principles is derived and conditions the whole attitude of the analytic philosophers. There are two principles which particularly concern us in the study which we are making: *a*) that the "parts" or elements can be separated from the "whole" without undergoing any change; *b*) that these elements can be discovered by analysis and defined in such a way that leaves no room for doubt.

• • •

I am not proposing, of course, the abandonment of analysis as a philosophic method. It is not clear how analysis could be abandoned without falling into an attitude of contemplative mysticism, which would bring as its immediate consequence greater confusion and obscurity to the field of philosophy. What I am criticizing is *analyticism,* if we may so call it, which attempts to reduce to analysis every philosophic task and actually analyzes away what is really important.

Analysis involves the disarticulation of a complex reality whose unity is destroyed when its component members are separated. It can be used in the realm of psychic life with a great deal of profit and very little

danger, provided that one is constantly aware of its limitations and consequences and never loses sight of the fact that the elements which have been separated by analysis are members of a totality which must, of necessity, remain united. Analysis should therefore be used—always, of course, keeping the totality in mind—only in order to make clear the meaning of the whole and to comprehend its inner mechanism, not in order to eliminate the whole or reduce it to a heap of disjointed pieces. Hence analysis should be applied to a structure only after the structure has been taken in and recognized as a whole; reality should not be sacrificed to the method used.

• • •

The analytic attitude is moreover complemented by a mechanical conception of the psychic life which tries to "explain" everything by means of simple elements and the forces that move them. When the psychic life has been put together again in this way, it has lost its organic unity, its spontaneity, its very life—all that characterizes the human being. Hence the final result seems more like a robot than a man: the parts that make it up remain unalterable, and the forces that move it are completely mechanical. The process of reconstruction cannot give us what analysis has previously destroyed—the organic coherence of the inner life. Reconstruction is neither necessary nor possible, for this organic unity is a primary reality and not the conclusion of a system.

THE CONCEPT OF GESTALT

What is the self before its unity has been broken down by analysis? In what does its organic or structural unity consist?

Let us first make clear that this unity is not one that transcends the empirical world, the world of experiences. It is a unity derived from the very experiences themselves. There is nothing under or above the totality of experiences. If one overlooks the word "totality" or interprets it in an atomistic sense, this statement would be equivalent of subscribing to Hume's theory. But we should never interpret the totality or structure of experiences as a mere sum or aggregate of the same. The experiential totality has qualities which are not possessed by the members which constitute it. Consequently the characteristics of the total structure of the self cannot be deduced, necessarily, from the characteristics of each of the experiences taken separately.

• • •

What is it that characterizes a Gestalt? Like any other fundamental concept, that of Gestalt presents a degree of complexity which does not allow one to enunciate in a few words all the richness of its content. Nevertheless, there are certain characteristics which seem to be fundamental. First, there is the one that has already been emphasized: a structural whole—a Gestalt—has qualities not possessed by any of the elements which form it. In this sense, a Gestalt or structure is set in contrast with a mere sum of elements. The physical and chemical qualities of a cubic yard of water are the same as those of each gallon that makes it up. The whole, in this case, is no more than the mere sum of its parts. In the case of a structure, on the other hand, this is not so, as we have seen in considering the character of a melody; it possesses qualities which cannot be found in any of the notes, for it can be transposed without being changed into another melody.

The above-mentioned characteristic does not mean, of course, that a Gestalt is completely independent of the members which constitute it. In the first place, there can be no structure without members. But the dependence of structure upon members does not stop here—the removal, addition, or fundamental alteration of a member modifies the whole structure, as can be seen in the case of an organism.[1] Any important alteration or suppression of a member alters the totality of an organism and may even cause its disappearance. This does not happen in the case of a sum. We can remove one, two, thirty, or forty gallons of water without causing the rest to undergo any important change in quality.

But not only does the structural whole suffer alteration when one of its members is taken away, the member that is taken away is also basically altered. A hand separated from the body is unable to feel or to seize an object—it ceases to be a hand—whereas the gallon of water separated from the rest retains practically all of its properties. This characteristic, taken along with the foregoing one, will suffice for the definition of a member of a structure. A member of a structure is that which cannot be removed without affecting the whole structure and losing its own nature when separated from the "whole." Conversely, we can characterize the "mere sum" as something made up of "parts" or "elements" that undergo no change when joined to other "parts" and which can be removed without producing any change either in itself or in what remains. The relationship between the parts is that of mere juxtaposition.

The difference between structure and mere sum does not stem solely from the fact that the parts of the latter are independent of the whole and that the members of the former are conditioned by the structure. There is also the fact that the parts may be homogeneous, whereas the members must offer diversity and even opposition of characteristics. One gallon of water is just as much water as any other gallon or measure. The same is true of one brick in a pile of bricks or of each grain of sand in the desert. On the contrary, in an organism each member has its own specific nature—the heart is the heart and cannot perform the functions of the liver or kidneys. There is not only diversity among the members but also opposition; and this opposition is subsumed into the unity which organizes them. The unification and organization of the members which make up a structure do not come about at the expense of the peculiar and distinctive qualities of each member. Organization is not the equivalent of homogenization, and unity does not contradict the multiplicity and diversity of the elements. This multiplicity and diversity must always be maintained as absolutely essential. Thus we find structure to be the result of a dialectic play of oppo-

---

[1]Lewin defines a Gestalt in his *Principles of Topological Psychology* (p. 208) as a "system whose parts are dynamically connected in such a way that a change of one part results in a change of all the other parts."

sites, of a struggle between the members; it seems to hang by the thread which establishes a dynamic balance. But this unity is not of an abstract sort. A concept which organizes different members into a unity by grouping them in agreement with a common note does not constitute a structure. One essential aspect of the structure is lacking: its unity must be concrete. For that reason I use the term "structure" rather than "form" or "configuration" to translate the German word Gestalt, which, besides carrying the connotation of these two latter concepts, designates a unity that is *concrete*.

THE STRUCTURAL UNITY OF THE SELF

When we considered the applicability of the category of substance to the self, we noticed that none of the three classic characteristics of this concept—immutability, simplicity, and independence—belonged to the self. We obtained a similarly negative result from the consideration of the atomistic conception. In the first place, the supposed psychic atom is a poorly defined unit which, when one attempts to fix it with any precision, vanishes into thin air, becoming a mere arbitrary instant in an uninterrupted process. In the second place, the aggregation of atoms, which can have only a relationship of juxtaposition one to another, looks like a grotesque caricature of the real organic unity of the self. Let us now see if the category which we have called Gestalt or structure is any more successful.

It seems unquestionable that the psychic life is not chaotic, that each state or experience is connected to all the rest. This connection, however, is not of experience to experience, like the links of a chain, for if this were so there would be a fixed order of connections and in order to get to one link we should necessarily have to go by way of the preceding ones. But in the same way that Köhler showed that there is no constant relation between stimulus and response, it would be easy to show that in like manner there is no constant relation between one experience and another. No laboratory experiment is needed to prove this, for our daily experiences supply all the material we require—

the sound and sight of the sea is exhilarating one day and depressing the next; the same piece of music arouses in us different reactions according to the situation in which we hear it; our arrival at the same port and in the same ship can start altogether different trains of reflection in us, depending on whether we have arrived to stay for the rest of our life or only for a short vacation; the memory of a disagreement with a friend, which irritated us so much when it happened, may now provoke only an indifferent smile. The relations of experiences to each other resemble the relations between stimuli and responses in the fact that they arise within a given context.

These undeniable data of the psychic life are founded on the fact that the self is not a sum of experiences or an aggregate of parts in juxtaposition but a structure—in the sense defined above; whatever happens to one of its elements affects the whole, and the whole in turn exerts an influence upon each element. It is because the whole reacts as a structural unity and not as a mechanism that a stimulus can provoke consequences in an altogether different field from the one in which it has arisen. Thus, a strictly intellectual problem can give rise to emotional torment, and a fact of an emotional sort can have far-reaching volitional consequences. The self is not departmentalized—like modern bureaucracy—but constitutes an organic unity with intimate, complex, and varied interrelations.

The self presents itself, then, as an organized whole, an integrated structure, and experiences are related to one another not through but within the whole. For that reason, when the structure is modified the nature of the experiences and of the relationships between them are also modified. The interdependence of the different experiential groups shows that the self is a structure which is organized and "makes sense" and that each member occupies its proper place within the structure.

This does not mean, of course, that the structure which constitutes the self cannot be analyzed and broken down, theoretically, into less complex structures. It does mean, however, that we are in fact dealing with a unity that is formed upon substructures and the intimate and complex interrelation of these substructures.[2]

And here we notice another characteristic of the concept of structure which is directly applicable to the self: the members of a structure are heterogeneous in contrast with the homogeneity of the parts of a nonstructural unity. Let us state, first of all, that the structure which constitutes the self, being a very complex structure, is made up not of "simple members" but of substructures; it is consequently to the heterogeneity of these substructures that we are referring. It must also be kept in mind that the substructures are not of an abstract nature, like concepts, and that we are not trying to reconstruct a reality by juxtaposing abstractions such as the so-called "faculties of the soul."

The complexity and heterogeneity of the structure are twofold: on the one hand there is the complexity which we may call transversal; on the other there is the horizontal or, better, the temporal complexity. In actuality the self embraces the combination of both complexes, which do not and cannot exist in separation.

If we make a cross section at a given moment in our life, we find that we have a slice of a process that is made up of bundles of three different kinds of experience: the intellectual, the emotive, and the volitive. This shows that not even in the briefest moment of our life is it possible to catch ourselves concentrated upon a single type of experience.

• • •

The atomists should not be blamed too much for their failure to perceive the structure that goes through time, its development and evolution. Their error in this case is due to their conception of time as an empty and indifferent form which may be filled by either one content or another, without making any difference. Psychological time, however, is not empty, and it is impossible to separate its content from its form. It cannot be disintegrated into the sup-

posed instants which constitute it, for each psychological "moment" is a structure with unity of meaning. And, what is more, the "present" conceived of by the atomists is arbitrary. It aspires to be a fragment without extension. But for the present to make real sense it must contain the past and the future.

The gradual change of structure through time can be seen both by observing the development of the process itself and by comparing cross sections made at different points in the process. If one makes such a comparison, one will notice not only that the experiences vary but also that the type of structure does. At one moment the emotive is predominant and the intellectual and volitional are secondary; at another the intellectual is predominant, etc. The only thing that remains is the presence of a structure made up of three types of experiences.

This diversity and opposition among the elements which constitute the self should not lead us to forget the unity which characterizes every structure. The self is no exception. Its multiplicity does not exclude its unity or vice versa. And this is not the abstract unity of a concept which points to what is common; it is a concrete unity, of "flesh and blood" as Unamuno would say, for there is nothing more real and concrete than our self. Diversity underlies the structure but is in turn lost within it, for the elements uphold each other mutually in an intimate sort of interweaving in which it is impossible to distinguish warp from woof. This is not because the three types of substructure have equivalent strength and no one of them dominates the other two—as in the theory of the so-called balance of power—but because they vary constantly. At a given moment one element stands forth as the figure and the others form the ground; after a while there is a change of roles. These changes are explained by the fact that the self is a dynamic structure and thus resembles a symphony rather than a painting.

We should perhaps stress the point that the changes undergone by the self are not due exclusively to a different distribution of the members, for the members themselves are of a dynamic nature. Moreover, the self is constituted not only of members but also of the *tensions* produced by the recip-

---

[2]By substructure I mean any of the structural parts that constitute the total Gestalt that makes up the self. (Frondizi)

rocal play of influences. The breakdown of the equilibrium of tensions is what generally produces the most important changes.

It now appears obvious that the relations between the experiences are not fixed, for each experience as it is incorporated into the structure modifies its former state. This member in turn undergoes the influence of the whole, which is another characteristic of a Gestalt easy to find in the self. Thus, the perceptions which we have at this moment depend upon our former state. The new experience immediately acquires the coloration given it both by the basic structure of the self and by the particular situation in which it finds itself at that moment. If we are happy and in pleasant company, for example, the color of the spectacles we happen to be wearing has very little effect upon the emotive state of our spirit. This is not because visual perception ceases to have emotional tonality but because a greater affective tone—the happiness which results from a different cause—completely overshadows it. What is more, the stable nature of the self colors the transitory state. There are people who give the impression of seeing the world in the rosiest colors, whatever the tint of the spectacles they wear, and there are others who see clouds in the clearest sky.

This is the influence of the whole upon the member which is incorporated, but there is also an influence of the member upon the whole. We must not forget that a structure is not suspended in thin air but rests solely upon the members which constitute it. A symphonic orchestra is something more than the sum of the musicians that go to form it, but it cannot exist without the musicians. A self without the experiential structures that go to make it up would be the same as an orchestra without musicians, that is, a pure fantasy, the fantasy of a spiritual entity that would be unable to love, hate, decide, want, perceive, etc., and would pretend to be immutable substance. Such a concept would be immutable without doubt, but it would have the immutability of nothingness.

In the same way that the total suppression of the experiential structures would mean the suppression of the self, any change or alteration of a member has repercussions on the whole structure. By this I do not mean a man lacking in emotional life, for example, for it is obvious that he would not be a man but a mere caricature, or projection on a plane of two dimensions, of a three-dimensional reality. I am referring to the alteration of a structural subcomplex. Abulia, for example, is a disease of the will, but the changes which it provokes are not limited to the volitional—it has immediate repercussions in the emotive and intellectual spheres and consequently in the total structure. Its intellectual repercussions are easily seen, for the person suffering from abulia is unable to concentrate his attention, and thus his intellectual processes break down completely. And the emotional sphere is impaired too, for the sufferer is unable, by an act of the will, to get rid of the emotion which has taken control of him, so he lets himself be so possessed by this emotion that it changes his whole personality.

Of the characteristics of the structure that are applicable to the self we have only to consider now the first and most important, that is, the fact that the structure possesses qualities not possessed by the members that make it up. At this stage in our inquiry it seems a waste of time to insist that this is one of the characteristics of the self. Let us consider only the most obvious reasons. The self has a permanence—in the sense of constant presence—and a stability that the experiences and experiential groups do not have. Experiences are totally unstable; transiency is their characteristic. The self, on the other hand, remains stable in the face of the coming and going of experiences. If experiences do not have stability, even less can they have permanence, which is the fundamental characteristic of the self. And this is not all. The structure of the self is such that the members that make it up cannot exist in separation from it. There is no experience that does not belong to a particular self. The self depends, then, upon the experiences, but it is not equivalent to their sum. It is a structural quality.

• • •

PROBLEMS SOLVED BY THE STRUCTURAL CONCEPTION

A. Permanence and Mutability of the Self

At the beginning of this chapter we saw that both substantialism and atomism were unable to give an adequate picture of the self because they could not comprehend how its permanence and continuity could be compatible with the changes that it undergoes. Substantialism emphasized the permanence and atomism the mutability.

The structural conception that we are here proposing allows us to see that the two characteristics are not only compatible but also complementary. The historical survey of past thought on the subject . . . showed us that substantialism could not understand the changing nature of the self because it held fast to an irreducible and immutable nucleus and that Hume's atomism, in its effort to destroy the doctrine of a substantial nucleus, confused it with the very real permanence and continuity of the self.

If we free ourselves of the limitations of both historical positions and observe reality just as it presents itself, we shall see that the permanence and continuity of the self are based upon its structural character, for it is a dynamic structure made up not only of the elements which we can isolate in a cross section of our life but also of the substructures that form the complex longitudinal bundles that constitute the self. And change occurs each time a new element is taken in, which alters but does not destroy the structure.

In this way the constant alteration of the self insures its stability. It is undeniable that a new experience modifies, or can modify, the structure of the self. The loss of a child or a friend, a war, a religious experience, etc. can produce such an inner commotion that they may alter the total structure. From that time on we are not the same person as before. We act in a different way, we see life in a different perspective, and it may be that not only the future but also the past is colored by the new attitude. But it is

just this experience causing us to change which gives endurance to the self. From now on we shall be the man who has lost his son or his friend or who had this or that religious experience. Other children that we may have or the new friends which we may take into our hearts may cover up but can never completely obliterate the existence of an experience that at one time shook us deeply and persists in the structure of our spirit despite all that may happen to us in the future.

What happens on a large scale in the case of experiences that are profoundly moving happens on a smaller scale in all the other experiences of our life. Each new experience alters the structure or substructure to which it is connected, and thus it is incorporated "definitively," so to speak. Whatever happens afterward may alter the meaning of the experience within the whole—increasing it or diminishing it—but it can never erase the experience completely.

An analogy of a physical sort, even though inadequate to characterize our psychic life, may perhaps make clear the meaning of what I am trying to put across. The self resembles, in this respect, a mixture of colors. If we add to the mixture a new color—for example, blue—the mixture will be altered to a degree that will depend upon the quantity and shade of blue added and upon the combination of colors that were there before. This quantity of blue which produces a change in the former mixture is incorporated definitively into the whole, and however many more colors we add we shall never be able completely to counteract its presence.

The nature of the whole and the influence of the element incorporated into it are controlled, in the case of the analogy, by certain stable physical laws in which quantity plays an important role. This is not the case with psychic structures, in which quantity gives way to equality. Psychic structures obey certain principles, carefully studied by the Gestalt psychologists in the case of visual perception, which also exist in all the other orders of life and in the constitution of the total structure of the self. These general principles governing the organization of our total personality are what the most psychologically acute educators use as the basis for their choice of one type of experience rather than another in their endeavor to devise a system of corrective education for an aberrant personality.

Every self has a center or axis around which its structure is organized. When the personality has already developed, this axis is what gives direction and organization to our life, not only in that new experiences do not succeed in dislodging it from its route but also in that it chooses the type of experience that it finds to be in tune with it. But it is not a nucleus immutable in itself or fixed in relation to the rest of the structure. In the first place it undergoes an evolution which we can consider normal. The axis that predominates changes at the different stages of our life. In our earliest childhood the predominant experiential substructure is that related to alimentation, later it is play, and so on through life.

What is more, the center undergoes sudden displacements caused by new experiences that shake and modify the total structure. This is the case with the soldier who, according to war records, after devoting his life to the acquisition or intensification of his capacity for destruction and after exercising this capacity for years at the cost of many lives, suddenly discovers "the truth," "finds himself," decides that "we are all brothers." The center of his personality is completely displaced. His technical capacity as a killer, in which he formerly took pride—and centered his whole personality—is now a source of humiliation and shame. His personality must retrace its steps and choose another route.

These changes are due to many varied and complex reasons. Usually they have a long period of germination, as it were, in the world of the subconscious and burst forth full blown at a propitious moment. I recall the case of an American pilot who fought for several years in the Pacific; all of a sudden "the truth was revealed to him" while he was reading, more or less by chance, certain passages in the Bible. At other times the change comes about because of the intensification of the means of destruction; the explosion of the atomic bomb produced a psychological shock in many of those who had launched 200-pound bombs under the same

flag. Most commonly it comes about because of the shock of contrast; the soldier, in the midst of hatred, destruction, and death, comes across people who are devoting their lives to healing, in a spirit of disinterested love, the physical and moral wounds that other men cause. These external situations usually act as the immediate cause for the eruption of subterranean currents; at other times they stir up for the first time currents that burst forth later on, if a propitious situation presents itself.

We should not be surprised that an apparently insignificant fact may be able to change the total structure of our personality after it has been stable for many years; in the psychological realm quantities are of no great importance. The principle, *causa aequat effectum,* is not valid in the interrelations of the different elements. Gestalt psychology has shown us how the constitution of the structure and its alteration are governed by principles that have nothing to do with the principle of causality in its simplistic interpretation as the equal of cause and effect.

• • •

B. Immanence and Transcendence of the Self

Another apparent paradox—similar to that of permanence and mutability—which is resolved by the structural conception is that of the immanence and transcendence of the self. For both atomism and substantialism, immanence and transcendence are incompatible. Either the self is equivalent to the totality of experiences—and in this sense is immanent to them—or it is something that transcends the experiences. Atomism holds the first position and substantialism the second.

According to the theory that I am proposing, the self is immanent and transcends experiences at the same time, though admittedly the terms have different meanings from those attributed to them both by atomism and by substantialism. The self is immanent because it is, indeed, equivalent to the totality of experiences; but this totality, in turn, should be interpreted not as the sum or aggregate of the experiences but as a structure that has properties that cannot be found in its parts. According to this interpretation of the concept of totality, the self transcends the experiences and becomes a structural quality, in the sense in which Ehrenfels used this expression. Nevertheless, this is not the transcendence defended by the substantialists when they affirm the existence of a being that supports states or experiences. Mine is a transcendence that not only does not exclude immanence but actually takes it for granted.

Let us look at the problem from another point of view. The relation between the self and its experiences is so intimate that every experience reveals some aspect of the self; what is more, every experience forms part of the self. In this sense, the self seems to be represented in each one of the experiences, to be nothing but them. No experience, however, is able to reveal to us the self in its entirety. Not even the sum of all the experiences can do that. The self is able to transcend its autobiography; hence the possibility of a true repentance, a conversion, a new life. In the first instance the self seems to be immanent; in the second it is seen to be something that transcends its experiences.

The problem is clarified considerably if one turns his attention to those two propositions which Hume, and many others after him, considered to be incompatible: *a*) that the self is nothing apart from its experiences; *b*) that the self cannot be reduced to its experiences. I, of course, affirm that both propositions are true. When Hume maintained that the self should be reduced to a bundle of perceptions because it could not exist without them, he let himself be misled by the substantialist prejudice in favor of the so-called independence of the self. But the self, though not independent of the perceptions, is not reducible to the mere sum of them.

The paradox of the immanence and transcendence of the self, just like the paradox which we examined before, has arisen as a consequence of the way in which substantialists stated the problem of the self, a statement that the atomists accepted without realizing its consequences. The problem, as stated, presupposes a metaphysics and a logic which our conception rejects. First, it conceives of real existence as substance, independent and immutable; and second, it interprets the principles of identity and of noncontradiction in a very rigid way. My concept, on the other hand, gives a very dynamic interpretation to both principles, to the point of seeing in contradiction much of the essence of the real. What is more, I believe that there is nothing independent and immutable. I can hardly believe, therefore, in the independence and immutability of the self, the stuff of which is relationship and the essence of which is creative process.

C. Unity and Multiplicity

A variant of the preceding paradoxes is that of unity and multiplicity. When atomism took over the analysis of the self, its unity was destroyed forever and the self was turned into a great mosaic of loose pieces. Each perception became a reality in itself, independent, separable, sharply delimited. With this conception of the elements it proved impossible to rewin the lost unity. Atomists maintained, therefore, the plurality of the self, even though they sighed from time to time for the unity that they themselves had destroyed. When atomists—and men like William James who criticized atomism without being able to free themselves from the source of its confusion—ask what unites the different parts constituting the self, one must simply answer that the self never ceased to constitute a unity. Atomism's difficulties in reaching the unity of the self are merely a consequence of the arbitrary way in which it was dismembered. First they build a wall; then they complain they cannot see beyond the wall.

Substantialism, on the other hand, takes as its point of departure the postulate of unity and relegates multiplicity to accidents. The self is only one, although many different things happen to it.

With the importance that these "happenings" have for us—the self is made up of what it does—the whole statement of the problem collapses; the self is one or multiple according to how one looks at it. It is one if one focuses on the whole; it is multiple if one focuses on the members that constitute it. The self is the unity of the multiplicity of its experiences.

The unity of the self is not like the pseudo unity of a concept that is arrived at by abstraction. Its unity is quite concrete and is arrived at by a process of integration. It is a unity that does not abolish but preserves the differences in the members that make it up. That the self has members does not mean that it can be divided, as one divides a generic concept into the different species that it contains. The self is indivisible, though this does not keep us from dis-

tinguishing the different members that constitute it. The self has no existence apart from its members, nor do the members, if separated from the totality of the self, have existence.

QUESTION FOR DISCUSSION

1. Is the self, as Frondizi argues, best viewed as an activity rather than a substance? Can its unity be constituted in the manner in which he thinks it can?

THE SELF BEYOND DEATH

The doctrine of reincarnation has been officially frowned upon in the Christian world since the earliest days of Christianity. Although there are— even today—Hassidic Jewish sects that find evidence for it in the Bible, it has generally had a marginal and shadow history in the Western world. A shadow history is still, however, a history, and following the advent of religious freedom in the modern democracies, a fairly sizable number of people entertain some form of the belief in the West today. In recent years especially, the reports of out-of-body experiences recorded by Raymond Moody in his best-selling *Life After Life* seem to have kindled a great interest in the idea of reincarnation.

Previously, the view had remained largely dormant in the West, emerging only in sporadic reports of heresy trials from medieval Italy and Germany. Only in southern France did the idea have a real social impact. There, in the thirteenth century, the Church waged a war against the forces of a great heretical movement, the Cathar faith, which had won the allegiance of a majority in the countryside. The Cathars taught a strange version of Christianity indeed. The Devil, not God, they said, created this world; and we, the embodied souls that inhabit it, are fallen angels, doomed to perpetual reincarnation until, following the teachings of Christ, we perfect ourselves and again ascend to the Heaven from which we fell.

In setting forth this unique interpretation of Christian scripture, the heretics seem to have relied heavily on the thought of Plato. For the belief in reincarnation, though not the norm, was fairly widespread—in part due to his influence—in the pre-Christian ancient world. There are, however, also traces of Buddhism in Cathar Christianity. An order of monks and nuns, following rules that would be familiar in many Buddhist monasteries, constituted the clergy of the faith, its "perfected ones"; they were vegetarian, did not drink alcohol, refrained from all violence, and lived celibate lives.

They saw themselves as living among the people as an example for the people in much the way that the traditional Buddhist orders, even today, see their role in society. Jesus, for them, was only a master teacher on the model of the Buddha. The drama of the crucifixion, moreover, seems to have interested the Cathars not at all.

And Buddha, of course, taught a doctrine of rebirth, which accompanied his teachings wherever they traveled in Asia. In Tibet, this doctrine of rebirth reached a level of detail unparalleled anywhere in the world. Strictly speaking, as readers of the second section of this chapter will realize, there is no self or soul in Buddhist philosophy to *re*-incarnate—that is, to go back into another body; so the Buddhists generally prefer the term *rebirth,* which we have used above. In early Buddhist teachings, the gap between death and rebirth was usually thought to be momentary, the last moment of consciousness in this life leading to the first in the next. The *karma* that glued the two together was a connection in the nature of the consciousness itself. Thus, a person who died angry might, for example, be reborn as a choleric infant, to use a clear, if perhaps oversimplified, case. In the Tibetan Buddhist tradition, the period between death and rebirth is, however, extended to forty-nine days. In our first selection, an abridgement of the famous *Tibetan Book of the Dead,* this journey of the consciousness is sketched out for the dying person in order to help her or him to negotiate the journey, and perhaps, with luck, even to win enlightenment on the way.

It is often thought that reincarnation holds a prominent place in African thought as well as Asian. It seems to have been present in some form in ancient Egyptian thought. Indeed there are those who see Egypt as a possible origin for the doctrine in Plato and the other Greek philosophers who advanced the view. And Egypt is, both geographically and culturally, very much a part of Africa, whatever the racial composition of its probably heterogeneous population turns out to be. But the doctrine of reincarnation is not, in fact, the standard African belief, according to Professor Innocent Onyewuenyi of the University of Nsukka in Nigeria, a contemporary African philosopher. The African view that is often mistaken for reincarnation is in fact a somewhat subtler doctrine in which the vital force of an ancestor, but not his or her soul or personality, is embodied in a particular descendent.

Plato, whose dialogue, *Phaedo,* we turn to next, is, on the other hand, a clear advocate of the doctrine. The dialogue is set on the day of the execution of Plato's great teacher, Socrates, who has been condemned to death, as an old man, for corruption of the youth of Athens and disbelief in the traditional Greek gods. In the selection from the dialogue presented here, Socrates calmly explains to his friends why he is convinced that the soul does not die with the body but is born again and again into this and the other world.

Unlike Plato—who commits himself to both an afterlife and reincarnation—Aristotle, his former student and philosophical rival, is not convinced that the soul does survive the death of the body. Being the "form" of the body, in his view, it seems to be inseparable from it. The impossibility of an afterlife is even more forcefully argued by the ancient Indian materialists, who defy our Western stereotypes in almost all respects.

India is viewed in the popular Western imagination as a land in which spirituality predominates over the practical side of life. Like most cliches, this is, perhaps, partially true. And yet modern India is one of the largest industrial nations in the world, while traditional India enjoyed a material culture far greater than that of Europe for most of its history. Moreover, though it is true that India's philosophies have, in the main, reflected a profound sense of spirituality, it is also true that India has always had its religious skeptics and materialist debunkers of the spiritual. The selection below is taken from the oldest of these iconoclasts—the Carvaka philosophers of the time of the Buddha; or rather, it is taken from their opponents' accounts of them, very few of their original works having survived the censorship of the orthodox over the centuries. "There is no heaven, no final liberation, nor any soul in another world," say the Carvaka, according to these sources. "There is no evidence for any self distinct from the body." The ego dies with the body's death.

The same doctrine is expounded in England in the 1930s by the world-famous logician-philosopher Bertrand Russell, who debates these questions with Anglican bishops rather than Brahmin priests and saddhus. The ultimate argument, though bolstered with new forms of scientific evidence, remains the same in both cases: The data, the materialists claim, show that the relation of mind and body is such that we cannot expect mind and spirit to exist except where a living body sustains them.

DEATH AND REBIRTH

The Tibetan Book of the Dead

This is what the Lama reads to the dying person:

Preamble

I now transmit to you the profound teachings which I have myself received from my Teacher, and, through him, from the long line of initiated Gurus. Pay attention to it now, and do not allow yourself to be distracted by other thoughts! Remain lucid and calm, and bear in mind what you hear! If you suffer, do not give in to the pain! If restful numbness overtakes you, if you swoon away into a peaceful forgetting—do not surrender yourself to that! Remain watchful and alert!

The factors which made up the person known as E.C. are about to disperse. Your mental activities are separating themselves from your body, and they are about to enter the intermediary state. Rouse your energy, so that you may enter this state self-possessed and in full consciousness!

I. THE MOMENT OF DEATH, AND THE CLEAR LIGHT OF PURE REALITY

First of all there will appear to you, swifter than lightning, the luminous splendour of the colourless light of Emptiness, and that will surround you on all sides. Terrified, you will want to flee from the radiance, and you may well lose consciousness. Try to submerge yourself in that light, giving up all belief in a separate self, all attachment to your illusory ego. Recognize that the boundless Light of this true Reality is your own true self, and you shall be saved!

Few, however, are those who, having missed salvation during their life on earth, can attain it during this brief instant which passes so quickly. The overwhelming majority are shocked into unconsciousness by the terror they feel.

The Emergence of a Subtle Body

If you miss salvation at that moment, you will be forced to have a number of further dreams, both pleasant and unpleasant. Even they offer you a chance to gain understanding, as long as you remain vigilant and alert. A few days after death there suddenly emerges a subtle illusory dream-body, also known as the "mental body." It is impregnated with the after-effects of your past desires, endowed with all sense-faculties, and has the power of unimpeded motion. It can go right through rocks, hills, boulders, and walls, and in an instant it can traverse any distance. Even after the physical sense-organs are dissolved, sights, sounds, smells, tastes, and touches will be perceived, and ideas will be formed. These are the result of the energy still residing in the six kinds of consciousness, the after-effects of what you did with your body and mind in the past. But you must know that all you perceive is a mere vision, a mere illusion, and does not reflect any really existing objects. Have no fear, and form no attachment! View it all even-mindedly, without like or dislike!

II. THE EXPERIENCE OF THE SPIRITUAL REALITIES

Three and a half days after your death, Buddhas and Bodhisattvas will for seven days appear to you in their benign and peaceful aspect. Their light will shine upon you, but it will be so radiant that you will scarcely be able to look at it. Wonderful and delightful though they are, the Buddhas may nevertheless frighten you. Do not give in to your fright! Do not run away! Serenely contemplate the spectacle before you! Overcome your fear, and feel no desire! Realize that these are the rays of the grace of the Buddhas, who come to receive you into their Buddha-realms. Pray to them with intense faith and humility, and, in a halo of rainbow light, you will merge into the heart of the divine Father-Mother, and take up your abode in one of the realms of the Buddhas. Thereby you may still at this moment win your salvation.

But if you miss it, you will next, for another seven days, be confronted with the angry deities, and the Guardians of the Faith, surrounded by their followers in tumultuous array, many of them in the form of animals which you have never seen in the life you left. Bathed in multicoloured light they stand before you, threatening you and barring your passage. Loud are their voices, with which they shout, 'Hit him! Hit him! Kill him! Kill him!' This is what you have to hear, because you turned a deaf ear to the saving truths of religion! All these forms are strange to you, you do not recognize them for what they are. They terrify you beyond words, and yet it is you who have created them. Do not give in to your fright, resist your mental confusion! All this is unreal, and what you see are the contents of your own mind in conflict with itself. All these terrifying deities, witches, and demons around you—fear them not, flee them not! They are but the benevolent Buddhas and Bodhisattvas, changed in their outward aspect. In you alone are the five wisdoms, the source of the benign spirits! In you alone are the five poisons, the source of the angry spirits! It is from your own mind therefore that all this has sprung. What you see here is but the reflection of the contents of your own mind in the mirror of the Void. If at this point you should manage to understand that, the shock of this insight will stun you, your subtle body will disperse into a rainbow, and you will find yourself in paradise among the angels.

III. SEEKING REBIRTH

But if you fail to grasp the meaning of what you were taught, if you still continue to feel a desire to exist as an individual, then you are now doomed to again re-enter the wheel of becoming.

The Judgement

You are now before Yama, King of the Dead. In vain will you try to lie, and to deny or conceal the evil deeds you have done. The Judge holds up before you the shining mirror of Karma, wherein all your deeds are reflected. But again you have to deal with dream images, which you yourself have made, and which you project outside, without recognizing them as your own work. The mirror in which Yama seems to read your past is your own memory, and also his judgement is your own. It is you yourself who pronounce your own judgement, which in its turn determines your next rebirth. No terrible God pushes you into it; you go there quite on your own. The shapes of the frightening monsters who take hold of you, place a rope round your neck and drag you along, are just an illusion which you create from the forces within you. Know that apart from these karmic forces there is no Judge of the Dead, no gods, and no demons. Knowing that, you will be free!

The Desire for Rebirth

At this juncture you will realize that you are dead. You will think, "I am dead! What shall I do?" and you will feel as miserable as a fish out of water on red-hot embers. Your consciousness, having no object on which to rest, will be like a feather tossed about by the wind, riding on the horse of breath. At about that time the fierce wind of karma, terrific and hard to bear, will drive you onwards, from behind, in dreadful gusts. And after a while the thought will occur to you, "O what would I not give to possess a body!" But because you can at first find no place for you to enter into, you will be dissatisfied and have the sensation of being squeezed into cracks and crevices amidst rocks and boulders.

The Dawning of the Lights of the Six Places of Rebirth

Then there will shine upon you the lights of the six places of rebirth. The light of the place in which you will be reborn will shine most prominently, but it is your own karmic disposition which decides about your choice. The rays of lights which will guide you to the various worlds will seem to you restful and friendly compared with the blinding flash of light which met you at first.

If you have deserved it by your good deeds, a white light will guide you into one of the heavens, and for a while you will have some happiness among the gods. Habits of envy and ambition will attract you to the red light, which leads to rebirth among the warlike Asuras, forever agitated by anger and envy. If you feel drawn to a blue light, you will find yourself again a human being, and well you remember how little happiness that brought you! If you had a heavy and dull mind, you will choose the green light, which leads you to the world of animals, unhappy because insecure and excluded from the knowledge which brings salvation. A ray of dull yellow will lead you to the world of the ghosts, and, finally, a ray of the colour of darkish smoke into the hells. Try to desist, if you can! Think of the Buddhas and Bodhisattvas! Recall that all these visions are unreal, control your mind, feel amity towards all that lives! And do not be afraid! You alone are the source of all these different rays. In you alone they exist, and so do the worlds to which they lead. Feel not attracted or repelled, but remain evenminded and calm!

Reincarnation

If so far you have been deaf to the teaching, listen to it now! An overpowering craving will come over you for the sense-experiences which you remember having had in the past, and which through your lack of sense-organs you cannot now have. Your desire for rebirth becomes more and more urgent; it becomes a real torment to you. This desire now racks you; you do not, however, experience it for what it is, but feel it as a deep thirst which parches you as you wander along, harassed, among deserts of burning sands. Whenever you try to take some rest, monstrous forms rise up before you. Some have animal heads on human bodies, others are gigantic birds with huge wings and claws. Their howlings and their whips drive you on, and then a hurricane carries you along, with those demonic beings in hot pursuit. Greatly anxious, you will look for a safe place of refuge.

Everywhere around you, you will see animals and humans in the act of sexual intercourse. You envy them, and the sight attracts you. If your karmic coefficients destine you to become a male, you feel attracted to the females and you hate the males you see. If you are destined to become a female, you will feel love for the males and hatred for the females you see. Do not go near the couples you see, do not try to interpose yourself between them, do not try to take the place of one of them! The feeling which you would then experience would make you faint away, just at the moment when egg and sperm are about to unite. And afterwards you will find that you have been conceived as a human being or as an animal.

AFRICA AND REINCARNATION: A REAPPRAISAL

Innocent Onyewuenyi

INTRODUCTION

"The task of philosophy is not to throw the common man's view into the dustbin mainly because it is unreflective. Philosophical investigation and reflection is supposed to discover and find out the inherent difficulties in the common sense view, redefine, refine and remodel them."[1] This paper is an attempt to apply philosophical investigation and reflection on African belief in reincarnation which I regard as an unreflective common man's view; it is an attempt to discover the inherent inconsistencies in such a belief; it also essays to redefine the African concept of reincarnation in line with African ontology or theory of being, so that the term "reincarnation," which, according to African philosophy of language, is just a "raw material," may be given appropriate meaning or be dropped entirely. For in African language words cannot become stereotyped *a priori* in their meaning but are constantly being reinterpreted and charged with new meaning. "The phoneme is therefore only a raw material, the 'flesh' of the meaning. And it is the Muntu [man] who designates the vocable as a word, and gives it 'meaning-force' or nommo-force, then this makes it into a symbol, a picture."[2]

For the European a word like "God" conveys a stable concept; it is not so for the African. Dr. Idowu in a lecture given at the University College, Ibadan in 1957, gave five interpretations of the Yoruba word for "God" (Olodumare): (1) Olodu-Omo-Ere: The supreme one, offspring of the boa; (2) Olodu Ma Re: The supreme one who remains constant; (3) Olodu Mo Are: The supreme one, wearing the crown; (4) Olodu Kari: The perfect one; (5) Olodumare: The one to whom I must return.[3] This shows the many different meanings that can be attached to the African Yoruba word for "God."

Similarly "reincarnation" is a European word which conveys a definite constant concept. It would be erroneous, therefore, to limit African interpretations of concepts which explain the vital influences of the dead forebears on the living, and for which there are no proper translations in European languages, to the stable concept of reincarnation. It is as incorrect to say that Africans believe in reincarnation as it is to say that African religion is animism—a term invented by the English anthropologist E. B. Tylor in an article in 1866 and later in his book *Primitive Mentality* in 1871. The

---

[1]Olaosebikan Adeyinka, "A Critique of the Empiricists' and Rationalists' Theories of Knowledge," unpublished M.A. thesis, University of Lagos, 1981, p. 58.

[2]Janheinz Jahn, *Muntu: An Outline of the New African Culture* (New York: Grove Press, 1961), p. 150.
[3]*Ibid.,* p. 152.

same is true of the phrase "ancestor worship" used by Herbert Spencer in his book, *Principles of Sociology,* to describe his speculation that "savage" peoples associated the spirits of the dead with certain objects, and in order to keep in good terms with the spirits of their ancestors people made sacrifices to them.

These and similar inaccurate and derogatory terms are descriptions of speculations of foreign scholars and/or evolués, who in many cases have little access to the proper sources of African beliefs and practices or had little more than a chance opportunity of a fleeting glimpse of the vast continent. John S. Mbiti speaks for Africa when he states that

> Worship is the wrong word to apply in this situation. . . . The departed whether parents, brothers, sisters or children, form part of the family, and must therefore be kept in touch with their surviving relatives. Libation and the giving of food to the departed are tokens of fellowship, hospitality and respect; the drink and food so given are symbols of family continuity and contact.[4]

WHAT IS REINCARNATION?

The word is derived from two Latin words: *re* = again; and *incarnare* = to enter into the body. Reincarnation is simply the theory that when the soul separates from the body at death, it informs another body for another span of earthly life. It has different variations like metempsychosis or transmigration of souls where the soul of a person informs an animal or tree. "The soul may enter its human tenement from the ghost realm, the tree world or the animal kingdom."

INSTANCES OF BELIEF IN REINCARNATION

Belief in reincarnation is attested to by all known world cultures. Pythagoras of Samos, who lived in the fourth century B.C. and founded a philosophico-

religious society, believed in the transmigration of souls or in "being born again." He taught his followers to abstain from animal flesh on the grounds that there was a kinship between men and animals, and "for fear that the soul of one's friend might be inhabiting the body of some animal killed for the table."[5] For the Greeks and the Western world, body/soul dualism is a datum. Every living human being is made up of body and soul, the material and the spiritual. When death strikes, the soul leaves the body and either incarnates another body or goes to the house of Hades to receive reward or punishment for its actions on earth.

Socrates was of the group who believed in the latter. His life of justice and obedience to the Law which resulted in his death, despite its didactic purpose, was aimed at happiness in the next life:

> . . . to be in company with Orpheus and Musaios and Hesiod and Homer, how much would one of you give for that? For myself, I am willing to die many times, if this is true; since I myself should find staying there a wonderful thing. . . . To converse with them there, and to be with them, and cross-examine them would be an infinity of happiness.[6]

The Christian New Testament records instances of Jewish belief in reincarnation. The story of the man born blind and the rumours that Christ was Jeremias or Elias come back to life, come readily to mind: "And Jesus came into the quarters of Caesarea Philippi and he asked his disciples saying: who do men say that the Son of man is? But they said: some John the Baptist, and some others Elias or one of the prophets."[7] Even Herod seems to think that Jesus was John the Baptist risen from the dead: "And king Herod heard and he said: John the Baptist is risen again from the dead: and therefore mighty works show forth themselves in him."[8]

---

[4] John S. Mbiti, *African Religions and Philosophy* (New York: Doubleday, 1970), p. 11.

---

[5] Rex Warner, *The Greek Philosophers* (New York: New American Library, 1958), p. 21.
[6] Edith Hamilton and Huntington Cairns, eds., *The Collected Dialogues of Plato* (New York: Random House, 1966), p. 25.
[7] Matthew 16: 13–16.
[8] Mark 6: 14–16.

The Hindu position is beautifully summarized by Sir Edwin Arnold in his verse translation of the *Bhagavad-Gita* thus:

> Nay, but as when one layeth
>   His worn-out robes away,
> And taking new ones, sayeth,
>   "These will I wear today!"
> So putteth by the spirit
>   Lightly its garb of flesh
> And passeth to inherit
>   A residence afresh.[9]

Evidently this is belief in reincarnation or transmigration of souls. Death is of the body which is temporary garment of an individual's karma, which passes from form to form with intervals of rest between. There is no hell or heaven (eternal life) because "a man's hereafter is the aggregate effects of the causes generated by him in the past. The cause was limited, equally so will be the effects. The limited and finite cannot cause eternity."[10] Rather it is the complex aggregate of all experiences of past lives clothed with diverse attributes and qualities which undergoes purification through the principle of circles and periodicity until every weakness is overcome. Finally ultimate success for men is assured and infinite time provided for by the enfolding or eventual merging of the spiritual self of every man.

AFRICAN BELIEF IN REINCARNATION

Belief in reincarnation is reported among many African societies. The Igbos convince themselves that a child is a reincarnate of a dead ancestor if that child exhibits human features or characteristics of the living-dead. The Igbo word for reincarnation is *Ilo Uwa* = a return to the world. The occurrence of child prodigies (*ebibiuwa*) with their preincarnation intellectual and physical acquisitions is cited by Africans as proof for their belief in reincarnation. Godfrey Hudson refers to this as "the strange genius

. . . brought from former lives in which mastery of their subjects had been attained."[11] The Igbos explain that such geniuses in their lives suffered in any number of ways owing to a lack of those qualities which they now exhibit. Hence in their new life, having obtained parentage and body through which the acquired genius can be expressed, they display these quite early in life. Such children are referred to as "being older than their ages." Another attempt at explaining child prodigies is that the child is a reincarnate of a deceased intelligent, crafty and successful person from his lineage.

Reappearance of bodily marks of a deceased person on the body of a newborn child is another basis for the Africans' belief in reincarnation. I will explain by narrating my own family experience in 1946. My father's aunt, who loved him very dearly, was sick, suffering from a cough. Naturally my father took very good care of her, calling in one native doctor after another to treat the ailment. The woman's own children and our other relatives were not as involved as my father in looking after her. When it became clear that she was going to die, she made her will. She willed many stocks of yams and domestic animals, cash crops, and farmlands to her children and other relatives. She gave nothing to my father. Since she loved my father so much and did not include him in her will, the talk began to spread that she would reincarnate into my family.

When the woman died, a surgery was performed to remove the "bag of cough" so that she would be free of this deadly malady in her next life. The chest was stitched back. The curious thing happened!! When my mother had a baby-girl months after this woman's death, the marks of the stitches appeared on the child's chest and can be seen to this day. For the villagers no further proof was needed to prove that my sister is a reincarnate of my father's aunt. To this day, the children of that deceased woman call my sister *Nne* = mother. It will be pertinent, for the purpose of this paper, to note that my mother was al-

---

[9]Christmas Humphreys, *Buddhism* (London: Wyman, 1954), p. 105.
[10]*Ibid.,* p. 106.

[11]Godfrey Hudson, *Lecture Notes: The School of the Wisdom* (Adyar, India: Theosophical Publishing House, 1962), p. 172.

ready pregnant before my father's auntie died; and that my father's uncle also regards one of his own daughters as a reincarnate of the same woman.

First names also betray African belief in reincarnation. At birth, babies are scrutinized to identify any resemblances they bear to past parents. Sometimes an oracle is consulted to know who has "come back." The principal name of the child indicates this: "father has returned," "mother has returned." The Yoruba call the child who is born immediately after the death of his grandfather *Babatunde* (= father has returned) and the girl born immediately after the death of her grandmother *Yetunde* (mother has returned). The Igbos give names such as *Nne-Nna* = the mother of her father; *Nna-Nna* = the father of his father; *Nne-ji* = my brother/sister; *Nna-ji* = my half brother/half sister. None of these names is repeated in the same family because they specify the return of specific ancestors. Invariably people pay to the child the same reverence they were accustomed to pay to the deceased grandparent.

I have gone to some length in giving instances of the common man's unreflective views on reincarnation and the "reasons" for such views, as a setting for the aims of this paper, namely, a philosophical investigation and reappraisal of African belief in reincarnation and its attendant inconsistencies. These noted instances are what one might call non-philosophical data of African culture which require philosophical reflection and analysis in order "to find out their inherent difficulties, redefine, refine and remodel them."

AFTER-LIFE: INCONSISTENCIES OF BELIEF IN REINCARNATION

The African is a firm believer in life after death, i.e. the existence of the individual in an incorporeal, yet real form, in a life beyond. The Igbos call it *Ala-Muo;* the Yorubas call it *Ehin-Iwa.* The whole fuss about decent burial ceremonies, and the so-called "ancestor-worship" betray Africans' invincible conviction that the dead exist as individuals in the spirit world. From the spirit world, the ancestors who are now released from the restraints imposed by this earth, and who are possessors of limitless

potentialities can exploit these for the benefit or to the detriment of those who still live on earth. Hence survivors pay respect and acts of recognition to these ancestors in order to be favoured. States Prof. Idowu, "The deceased . . . still remain the father and mother which they were before their death, capable of exercising their parental functions, though now in a more powerful and unhampered way, over the survivors. The Yoruba say still *Baba mi* ('my father') or *Iya mi* ('my mother'), when they speak of their deceased parents. Although they speak of bringing the spirit of the deceased into the house, they rarely say that 'I am going to speak to the "spirit" of my father'; what they say is, 'I am going to speak to my father.' "[12] The individuality of the deceased father or mother is recognized as existing in the spirit world from where it maintains unbroken family relationship with the living offspring.

Just as the Athenians had an altar to the "unknown god," Africans recognize as individuals even ancestors whose names cannot be remembered any longer. The recently deceased ancestors are requested to transmit the family prayers and acts of respectful recognition to the unknown ancestors.

The behaviour of the children of my father's aunt is another example of African recognition of the individual permanent existence of the dead. Despite the fact that they call my sister *Nne* ("Mother") whenever they see her, they still render traditional ancestral filial duties to their deceased mother who still retains her role as their mother. They know too well that if they do not render these filial duties, it would amount to a repudiation of natural dependence which may bring about untold hardship to themselves. Placide Tempels testifies, "It would be tantamount to uttering his own death sentence. It would be in the nature of a revolt. It would constitute exclusion from the source of vital force which flows among Bantu by strict rules of primogeniture from fathers and ancestors."[13]

---

[12]E. Bolaji Idowu, *Olodumare: God in Yoruba Belief* (London: Longmans, Green, 1962), p. 192.

[13] Placide Tempels, *Bantu Philosophy* (Paris: Présence Africaine, 1969), p. 153.

A further support for the individual existence of ancestors in the spirit world, from where they perform their roles as guardians and protectors of families and ethics of the community, is given by John S. Mbiti:

> The living-dead know and have interest in what is going on in the family. When they appear, which is generally to the oldest members of the household, they are recognized by name as "so and so"; they inquire about family affairs and may even warn of impending danger or rebuke those who failed to follow their special instructions. They are the guardians of family affairs, traditions, ethics and activities.[14]

The question then arises: how can Africans sincerely and truly believe in reincarnation while at the same time recognizing the personal individual existence in the spirit world of the ancestors who are believed to have reincarnated? What do they really mean by reincarnation? Could they mean reincarnation in the classical sense, namely "the passage of the soul from one body to another . . . the lot of the soul in each being determined by its behaviour in a former life?"[15]

One can see the logic in the Pythagorean theory of reincarnation in that when the soul of a deceased person informs another body or animal or tree, it does not exist any longer in the spirit world. This is also true of Jewish and Hindu positions. They uphold the principle of contradiction which states that a thing cannot be and not be at the same time in the same manner. They maintain that at death the soul separates from the body and has a bodiless immaterial existence until such a time as it puts on a new garb of flesh. At one particular time the soul or spirit is either in the spirit world or in a corporeal residence.

The dilemma posed by the so-called belief in reincarnation was outlined by Prof. Idowu thus:

> Nevertheless we find ourselves confronted with the paradox involved in the belief of the Yoruba that the deceased persons do "reincarnate" in their grandchildren. In the first place it is believed that in spite of this reincarnation, the deceased continue to live in After-Life. Those who are still in the world can have communion with them, and they are there with all their ancestral qualities unimpaired. Secondly, it is believed that they do reincarnate, not only in one grand child or great grand child, but also in several contemporary grand children or great grand children, who are brothers and sisters and cousins, aunts and nephews, uncles and nieces, ad infinitum."[16]

How then can this paradox be resolved? The same author attempts a solution by stating that "in African belief, there is no reincarnation in the classical sense. One can only speak of partial or, more precisely, apparent reincarnation, if the word must be used at all."[17] He further explains that the specific belief of the Yoruba about those who depart from this world is that once they have entered After-Life, there they remain, and there the survivors and their children after them can keep unbroken intercourse with them, especially if they have been good persons while on earth and were ripe for death when they died. This is also true of most African traditional cultures.

In another attempt at the resolution of the dilemma, the Nupe tribe of Nigeria come up with the conception that each person has two souls; after death one of the souls goes and resides permanently with the Maker, while the other one reincarnates. This solution is too simplistic to warrant much discussion. Suffice it to say that it contradicts the concept of personality and personal identity.

Coming back to Prof. Idowu's answer to the paradox, the present writer ventures to submit that, following the meaning of reincarnation in the classical sense, it is no solution at all to say that there is "partial" or "apparent" reincarnation. I rather share his view that "the word must (not) be used at all."

• • •

The essence or nature of anything is conceived by the African as "force." It is not even correct to say that "being" in the African thought has the nec-

---

[14]J. S. Mbiti, *op. cit.,* p. 108.
[15]*Encyclopaedia of Religion and Ethics,* XII, 245.

[16]E. Bolaji Idowu, *op. cit.,* p. 194.
[17]E. Bolaji Idowu, *African Traditional Religion* (London: S.C.M. Press, 1973), p. 187.

essary element or quality of force. The precision of their concept of being will not be attained if their notion of being is expressed as "being is that which *possesses* force." Rather "the concept of force is inseparable from the definition of 'being.' There is no idea among Bantu of 'being' divorced from the idea of 'force.' Without the element 'force,' 'being' cannot be conceived. . . . Force is the nature of being, force is being; being is force."[18] Care must be taken here not to confuse this dynamic notion of reality with some kind of universal force animating all existence.

For Africans there is a clear distinction and essential difference between different forces or inner realities of beings, just as there are differences between categories of material visible things.

> When you say in terms of western philosophy, that beings are differentiated by their essences or nature; Africans say that forces differ in their essences or nature. There is the divine force, terrestrial or celestial forces, human forces, and vegetable and even mineral forces.[19]

In addition to different categories of forces, Africans maintain that these forces follow a hierarchical order such that God precedes the spirits; then come the founding fathers and the living-dead, according to the order of primogeniture; then the living according to their rank in terms of seniority.

• • •

REINCARNATION IMPOSSIBLE IN THE FRAMEWORK OF AFRICAN ONTOLOGY

Bearing in mind our earliest treatment of the African concept of being as "force" and its dynamic nature, we further add that in the category of visible beings the Africans distinguish that which is perceived by the senses and the "thing in itself" namely, the inner nature or "force" of the thing

whether man, animal, or tree. When a person dies, the traditional African does not say that the "soul" of the dead has gone to the spirit-world. It is not the "soul" or "part of man" that has gone to the world of the spirits but the whole man though not in a visible but invisible state. Tempels explains

> What lives on after death is not called by the Bantu by a term indicating part of man. I have always heard their elders speak of "the man himself," "himself"; or it is "the little man" who was formerly hidden behind the perceptible manifestation of the man; or *muntu* which at death has left the living, . . . *Muntu* signifies vital force endowed with intelligence and will.[20]

The dichotomy of soul and body is not applicable such that at death, the soul separates and inhabits another body. Rather "the man" still exists as this person in a spiritual invisible form. His bodily energy goes but his vital force persists and waxes stronger and stronger ontologically.

In line with the hierarchy of "forces" the dead ancestors assume an enhanced vital superiority of intelligence and will over the living; "the departed must therefore have gained in deeper knowledge of the forces and nature"[21] and because of the ontological relationship existing among members of the clan, they interact with the living. What interacts with the living is "the man himself" who is now essentially "force." Vital force grows and/or weakens through the interaction of forces. A person is "really dead" when his vital force is totally diminished. Due to their preoccupation with immortality and deathlessness, the ancestors are concerned with the increase of their and their descendants' vital force for the well-being and continuity of the clan.

One of the ways of increasing the ancestor's vital force is by sacrifices and prayers from the living descendants. Hence the wish of Africans to have many children who will offer sacrifices to them after death. By an inverse movement the "force" of the ancestor flows into the sacrifices and into the community which he embodies and the living

---

[18]Placide Tempels, *op. cit.,* p. 51.
[19]*Ibid.,* p. 37.

[20]*Ibid.,* p. 53.
[21]Janheinz Jahn, *op. cit.,* p. 106.

receive the "strengthening influence" of the ancestor. "The whole weight of an extinct race lies on the dead . . . for they have for the whole time of their infinite deathlessness, missed the goal of their existence, that is, to perpetuate themselves through reproduction in the living person."[22]

This "perpetuation of themselves through reproduction" is what has been mistakenly called reincarnation. It is rather the "life-giving will" or "vital influence" or "secretion of vital power" of the ancestor on his living descendants. This is understandable because the ancestor who is now pure dynamic force can influence and effect many births in his clan without emptying his personality. This explains Prof. Idowu's "partial or more precisely apparent reincarnation." Reincarnation cannot be partial or apparent. Either it is or is not. "The dead are esteemed," says Tempels, "only to the extent to which they increase and perpetuate their vital force in their progeny."[23]

The vital force of an ancestor is comparable to the sun, which is not diminished by the number and extent of its rays. The sun is present in its rays and heats and brightens through its rays; yet the rays of the sun singly or together are not the sun. In the same way the "vital force" which is the being of the ancestor can be presented in one or several of the living members of his clan, through his life-giving will or vital influence, without its being diminished or truncated. Just as the sun is the causal agent of heat, so is an ancestor a causal agent of his descendants who are below him in the ontological hierarchy. This vital influence is subordinate and distinct from the creative influence which is the domain of God. Tempels clarifies the point:

> Man is not the first or creative cause of life, but he sustains and adds to the life of the forces which he finds below him within his ontological hierarchy. And man, in Bantu thought, although in a more circumscribed sense than God, is also a causal force of life.[24]

This is the philosophical basis for the African claim that a certain ancestor has been "reborn" in one or several living members of the same clan. What the Africans mean by "return" or "reborn" cannot be translated by "reincarnation" because for them the child or children are not *identified* with the dead, since the birth of the little one(s) in no wise puts an end to the existence of the deceased ancestor in the spirit-world. This becomes clearer still when one realises that Africans do not hold that conception is caused by the spirit of the ancestor. The biological conception of the child results from the concurrent act of God and the parents. The influence of the ancestor, which has been called "reincarnation," comes later on. "It is the human being, who already possesses life in the womb of his mother (by divine influence), who finds himself under the vital, the ontological influence of a predestined ancestor or of a spirit."[25] This explains the "Paradox" which Prof. Idowu identified in the belief of the Yorubas that deceased persons do "reincarnate" in their grandchildren and still continue to live in After-Life. The dynamic nature of the "being" of the deceased, the theory of ontological hierarchy and interaction of forces in African metaphysics explain how the deceased ancestor can be in the spirit-world and yet his presence is felt in the land of the living.

• • •

The imposition of the "belief in reincarnation" on Africans has undermined African cultural identity in that their cultural respects to their ancestors, which are tokens of fellowship, hospitality, and family continuity, are misconstrued as beliefs in reincarnation. The situation becomes more disturbing when "educated" Africans are in the forefront in "imposing" the concepts of reincarnation on Africans. Other terminologies such as "vital influence," "life-strengthening," "personal ray," "vital participation," should be used in place of "reincarnation." Instead of saying that a newborn child is a "reincarnate" of an ancestor, we should rather say that he is the "vital influence" or the "life-

[22]*Ibid.,* p. 109.
[23]Placide Tempels, *op. cit.,* p. 46.
[24]*Ibid.,* p. 99.
[25]*Ibid.,* p. 111.

share" or "personal ray," or "living-perpetuation" of the ancestor. If these suggested terminologies seem inadequate to the reader, I invite him to suggest an alternative, so that with the benefit of his collaboration, we can approach more nearly to perfection and exactitude.

THE PHAEDO

Plato

"Then from all this," said Socrates, "genuine philosophers must come to some such opinion as follows, so as to make to one another statements such as these: 'A sort of direct path, so to speak, seems to take us to the conclusion that so long as we have the body with us in our enquiry, and our soul is mixed up with so great an evil, we shall never attain sufficiently what we desire, and that, we say, is the truth. For the body provides thousands of busy distractions because of its necessary food; besides, if diseases fall upon us, they hinder us from the pursuit of the real. With loves and desires and fears and all kinds of fancies and much rubbish, it infects us, and really and truly makes us, as they say, unable to think one little bit about anything at any time. Indeed, wars and factions and battles all come from the body and its desires, and from nothing else. For the desire of getting wealth causes all wars, and we are compelled to desire wealth by the body, being slaves to its culture; therefore we have no leisure for philosophy, from all these reasons. Chief of all is that if we do have some leisure, and turn away from the body to speculate on something, in our searches it is everywhere interfering, it causes confusion and disturbance, and dazzles us so that it will not let us see the truth; so in fact we see that if we are ever to know anything purely we must get rid of it, and examine the real things by the soul alone; and then, it seems, after we are dead, as the reasoning shows, not while we live, we shall possess that which we

desire, lovers of which we say we are, namely wisdom. For if it is impossible in company with the body to know anything purely, one thing of two follows: either knowledge is possible nowhere, or only after death; for then alone the soul will be quite by itself apart from the body, but not before. And while we are alive, we shall be nearest to knowing, as it seems, if as far as possible we have no commerce or communion with the body which is not absolutely necessary, and if we are not infected with its nature, but keep ourselves pure from it, until God himself shall set us free. And so, pure and rid of the body's foolishness, we shall probably be in the company of those like ourselves, and shall know through our own selves complete incontamination, and that is perhaps the truth. But for the impure to grasp the pure is not, it seems, allowed.' So we must think, Simmias, and so we must say to one another, all who are rightly lovers of learning; don't you agree?"

"Assuredly, Socrates."

"Then," said Socrates, "if this is true, my comrade, there is great hope that when I arrive where I am travelling, there if anywhere I shall sufficiently possess that for which all our study has been pursued in this past life. So the journey which has been commanded for me is made with good hope, and the same for any other man who believes he has got his mind purified, as I may call it."

"Certainly," replied Simmias.

"And is not purification really that which has been mentioned so often in our discussion, to separate as far as possible the soul from the body, and to accustom it to collect itself together out of the body in every part, and to dwell alone by itself as far as it can, both at this present and in the future, being freed from the body as if from a prison?"

"By all means," said he.

"Then is not this called death—a freeing and separation of soul from body?"

"Not a doubt of that," said he.

"But to set it free, as we say, is the chief endeavour of those who rightly love wisdom, nay of those alone, and the very care and practice of the philosophers is nothing but the freeing and separation of soul from body, don't you think so?"

"It appears to be so."

"Then, as I said at first, it would be absurd for a man preparing himself in his life to be as near as possible to death, so to live, and then when death came, to object?"

"Of course."

"Then in fact, Simmias," he said, "those who rightly love wisdom are practising dying, and death to them is the least terrible thing in the world. Look at it in this way: If they are everywhere at enmity with the body, and desire the soul to be alone by itself, and if, when this very thing happens, they shall fear and object—would not that be wholly unreasonable? Should they not willingly go to a place where there is good hope of finding what they were in love with all through life (and they loved wisdom), and of ridding themselves of the companion which they hated? When human favourites and wives and sons have died, many have been willing to go down to the grave, drawn by the hope of seeing there those they used to desire, and of being with them; but one who is really in love with wisdom and holds firm to this same hope, that he will find it in the grave, and nowhere else worth speaking of—will he then fret at dying and not go thither rejoicing? We must surely think, my comrade, that he will go rejoicing, if he is really a philosopher; he will surely believe that he will find wisdom in its purity there and there alone. If this is true, would it not be most unreasonable, as I said just now, if such a one feared death?"

• • •

When Socrates had thus finished, Cebes took up the word: "Socrates," he said, "on the whole I think you speak well; but that about the soul is a thing which people find very hard to believe. They fear that when it parts from the body it is nowhere any more; but on the day when a man dies, as it parts from the body, and goes out like a breath or a whiff of smoke, it is dispersed and flies away and is gone and is nowhere any more. If it existed anywhere, gathered together by itself, and rid of these evils which you have just described, there would be great and good hope, Socrates, that what you say is true; but this very thing needs no small reassurance and

faith, that the soul exists when the man dies, and that it has some power and sense."

"Quite true," said Socrates, "quite true, Cebes; well, what are we to do? Shall we discuss this very question, whether such a thing is likely or not?"

"For my part," said Cebes, "I should very much like to know what your opinion is about it."

Then Socrates answered, "I think no one who heard us now could say, not even a composer of comedies,[1] that I am babbling nonsense and talking about things I have nothing to do with! So if you like, we must make a full enquiry.

"Let us enquire whether the souls of dead men really exist in the house of Hades or not. Well, there is the very ancient legend which we remember, that they are continually arriving there from this world, and further that they come back here and are born again from the dead. If that is true, and the living are born again from the dead, must not our souls exist there? For they could not be born again if they did not exist; and this would be sufficient proof that it is true, if it should be really shown that the living are born from the dead and from nowhere else. But if this be not true, we must take some other line."

"Certainly," said Cebes.

"Then don't consider it as regards men only," he said; "if you wish to understand more easily, think of all animals and vegetables, and, in a word, everything that was birth, let us see if everything comes into being like that, always opposite from opposite and from nowhere else; whenever there happens to be a pair of opposites, such as beautiful and ugly, just and unjust, and thousands of others like these. So let us enquire whether everything that has an opposite must come from its opposite and from nowhere else. For example, when anything becomes bigger, it must, I suppose, become bigger from being smaller before."

"Yes."

"And if it becomes smaller, it was bigger before and became smaller after that?"

"True," he said.

_____

[1]As Aristophanes had done in his play *The Clouds.*

"And again, weaker from stronger, and slower from quicker?"

"Certainly."

"Very well, if a thing becomes worse, is it from being better, and more just from more unjust?"

"Of course."

"Have we established that sufficiently, then, that everything comes into being in this way, opposite from opposite?"

"Certainly."

"Again, is there not the same sort of thing in them all, between the two opposites two becomings, from the first to the second, and back from the second to the first; between greater and lesser increase and diminution, and we call one increasing and the other diminishing?"

"Yes," he said.

"And being separated and being mingled, growing cold and growing hot, and so with all; even if we have sometimes no names for them, yet in fact at least it must be the same everywhere, that they come into being from each other, and that there is a becoming from one to the other?"

"Certainly," said he.

"Well then," he said, "is there something opposite to being alive, as sleeping is opposite to being awake?"

"There is," he said.

"What?"

"Being dead," he said.

"Well, all these things come into being from each other, if they are opposites, and there are two becomings between each two?"

"Of course."

"Then," said Socrates, "I will speak of one of the two pairs that I mentioned just now, and its becomings; you tell me about the other. My pair is sleeping and being awake, and I say that being awake comes into being from sleeping and sleeping from being awake, and that their becomings are falling asleep and waking up. Is that satisfactory?"

"Quite so."

"Then you tell me in the same way about life and death. Do you not say that to be alive is the opposite of to be dead?"

"I do."

"And that they come into being from each other?"

"Yes."

"From the living, then, what comes into being?"

"The dead," he said.

"And what from the dead?"

"The living, I must admit."

"Then from the dead, Cebes, come living things and living men?"

"So it appears," he said.

"Then," said he, "our souls exist in the house of Hades."

"It seems so."

"Well, of the two becomings between them, one is quite clear. For dying is clear, I suppose, don't you think so?"

"Oh yes," said he.

"Then what shall we do?" he said. "Shall we refuse to grant in return the opposite becoming; and shall nature be lame in this point? Is it not a necessity to grant some becoming opposite to dying?"

"Surely it is," he said.

"What is that?"

"Coming to life again."

"Then," said he, "if there is coming to life again, this coming to life would be a being born from the dead into the living."

"Certainly."

"It is agreed between us, then, in this way also that the living are born from the dead, no less than the dead from the living: and since this is true, there would seem to be sufficient proof that the souls of the dead must of necessity exist somewhere, whence we assume they are born again."

• • •

"Another thing," said Cebes, putting in, "you know that favourite argument of yours, Socrates, which we so often heard from you, that our learning is simply recollection: that also makes it necessary, I suppose, if it is true, that we learnt at some former time what we now remember; but this is impossible unless our soul existed somewhere before it was born in this human shape. In this way also the soul seems to be something immortal."

Then Simmias put in, "But, Cebes, what are the proofs of this? Remind me, for I don't quite remember now."

"There is one very beautiful proof," said Cebes, "that people, when asked questions, if they are properly asked, say of themselves everything correctly; yet if there were not knowledge in them, and right reason, they would not be able to do this. You see, if you show someone a diagram or anything like that, he proves most clearly that this is true."[2]

Socrates said, "If you don't believe this, Simmias, look at it in another way and see whether you agree. You disbelieve, I take it, how what is called learning can be recollection?"

"Disbelieve you," said Simmias, "not I! I just want to have an experience of what we are now discussing—recollection. I almost remember and believe already from what Cebes tried to say; yet none the less I should like to hear how *you* were going to put it."

"This is how," he answered. "We agree, I suppose, that if anyone remembers something he must have known it before at some time."

"Certainly," he said.

"Then do we agree on this also, that when knowledge comes to him in such a way, it is recollection? What I mean is something like this: If a man has seen or heard something or perceived it by some other sense, and he not only knows that, but thinks of something else of which the knowledge is not the same but different, is it not right for us to say he remembered that which he thought of?"

"How do you mean?"

"Here is an example: Knowledge of a man and knowledge of a lyre are different."

"Of course."

"Well, you know about lovers, that when they see a lyre or a dress or anything else which their beloved uses, this is what happens to them: they know the lyre, and they conceive in the mind the figure of the boy whose lyre it is? Now this is recollection; just as when one sees Simmias, one often remembers Cebes, and there would be thousands of things like that."

"Thousands, indeed!" said Simmias.

"Then is that sort of thing," said he, "a kind of recollection? Especially when one feels this about things which one had forgotten because of time and neglect?"

"Certainly," he said.

"Very well then," said Socrates. "When you see a horse in a picture, or a lyre in a picture, is it possible to remember a man? And when you see Simmias in a picture, to remember Cebes?"

"Yes indeed."

"Or when you see Simmias in a picture, to remember Simmias himself?"

"Oh yes," said he.

["These being either like or unlike?"

"Yes."

"It makes no difference," he said. "Whenever, seeing one thing, from sight of this you think of another thing whether like or unlike, it is necessary," he said, "that that was recollection."

"Certainly."][3]

"Does it not follow from all this that recollection is both from like and from unlike things?"

"It does."

"But when a man remembers something from like things, must this not necessarily occur to him also—to reflect whether anything is lacking or not from the likeness of what he remembers?"

"He must."

---

[2]The version of the argument to which Cebes here refers is found in another of Plato's dialogues, the *Meno.* There Socrates shows that an uneducated slave boy can be led to solve a simple problem in geometry by means of asking him questions alone. When the boy has solved the problem and is confident of his answer, Socrates argues that he is so because he has brought into memory knowledge from a past life. Previous to this, Socrates had been questioning the boy's master, Meno, in a similar way about the nature of virtue. The implication is thus that all knowledge of the general concepts that we use comes from a prior birth in the higher world of the perfect forms (Eds.).

---

[3]The bracketed passage has been transposed from 74 C-D of the Greek text, p. 478, where it would appear to be meaningless.

"Consider then," he said, "if this is true. We say, I suppose, there is such a thing as the equal, not a stick equal to a stick, or a stone to a stone, or anything like that, but something independent which is alongside all of them, the equal itself, equality; yes or no?"

"Yes, indeed," said Simmias, "upon my word, no doubt about it."

"And do we understand what that is?"

"Certainly," he said. "Where did we get the knowledge of it? Was it not from such examples as we gave just now, by seeing equal sticks or stones and so forth, from these we conceived that which was something distinct from them? Don't you think it is distinct? Look at it this way also: Do not the same stones or sticks appear equal to one person and unequal to another?"

"Certainly."

"Well, did the really-equals ever seem unequal to you, I mean did equality ever seem to be inequality?"

"Never, Socrates."

"Then those equal things," said he, "are not the same as the equal itself."

"Not at all, I think, Socrates."

"Yet from these equals," he said, "being distinct from that equal, you nevertheless conceived and received knowledge of that equal?"

"Very true," he said.

"Well," said he, "how do we feel about the sticks as compared with the real equals we spoke of just now; do the equal sticks seem to us to be as equal as equality itself, or do they fall somewhat short of the essential nature of equality; or nothing short?"

"They fall short," he said, "a great deal."

"Then we agree on this: When one sees a thing, and thinks, 'This which I now see wants to be like something else—like one of the things that are, but falls short and is unable to be such as that is, it is inferior,' it is necessary, I suppose, that he who thinks thus has previous knowledge of that which he thinks it resembles but falls short of?"

"That is necessary."

"Very well, do we feel like that or not about equal things and the equal?"

"Assuredly, we do."

"It is necessary then that we knew the equal before that time when, first seeing the equal things, we thought that all these aim at being such as the equal, but fall short."

"That is true."

"Well, we go on to agree here also: we did not and we could not get a notion of the equal by any other means than by seeing or grasping, or perceiving by some other sense. I say the same of equal and all the rest."

"And they are the same, Socrates, for what the argument wants to prove."

"Look here, then; it is from the senses we must get the notion that all these things of sense aim at that which is the equal, and fall short of it; or how do we say?"

"Yes."

"Then before we began to see and hear and use our other senses, we must have got somewhere knowledge of what the equal is, if we were going to compare with it the things judged equal by the senses and see that all things are eager to be such as that equal is, but are inferior to it."

"This is necessary from what we agreed, Socrates."

"Well, as soon as we were born we saw and heard and had our other senses?"

"Certainly."

"Then, we say, we must have got knowledge of the equal before that?"

"Yes."

"Before we were born, then, it is necessary that we must have got it."

"So it seems."

"Then if we got it before we were born and we were born having it, we knew before we were born and as soon as we were born, not only the equal and the greater and the less but all the rest of such things? For our argument now is no more about the equal than about the beautiful itself, and the good itself, and the just and the pious, and I mean everything which we seal with the name of 'that which is,' the essence, when we ask our questions and respond with our answers in discussion. So we must have got the proper knowledge of each of these before we were born."

• • •

"When did our souls get the knowledge of these things? For surely it is not since we became human beings."

"Certainly not."

"Then before."

"Yes."

"So, Simmias, our souls existed long ago, before they were in human shape, apart from bodies, and then had wisdom."

• • •

It appears to me that bigness itself never consents to be big and small at the same time, and not only that, even the bigness in us never accepts smallness and will not be surpassed; but one of two things, it must either depart and retreat whenever its opposite, smallness, comes near, or else must perish at its approach; it does not consent to submit and receive the smallness, and so to become other than what it was. Just so I, receiving and submitting to smallness, am still the man I am, I'm still this same small person; but the bigness in me, being big, has not dared to become small! In the same way, the smallness in us does not want to become or be big, nor does any other of the opposites, being still what it was, want to become and be the opposite; but either it goes away or it is destroyed in this change."

"Certainly," said Cebes, "that is what I think."

One of those present, hearing this, said—I do not clearly remember who it was—"Good heavens, didn't we admit in our former discussion the very opposite of what we are saying now—that the greater came from the less and the less from the greater, and in fact this is how opposites are generated, from opposites? Now it seems to be said that this could never be."

Socrates bent down his head to listen, and said, "Spoken like a man! I thank you for reminding me, but you don't understand the difference between what we are saying now and what we said then. For then we said that the practical opposite thing is generated from its practical opposite, but now we are saying that the opposite quality itself could never become the quality opposite to itself, either in us or in nature. Then, my

friend, we were speaking of things which have opposites, these being named by the name of their (opposite) qualities, but now we are speaking of the opposite qualities themselves, from which being in the things, the things are named: those qualities themselves, we say, could never accept generation from each other." Then, with a glance at Cebes, he added, "Is it possible that you too, Cebes, were disturbed by what our friend spoke of?"

"No, not by this," replied Cebes, "but I don't deny that I get disturbed a good deal."

"Well, then, are we agreed," said Socrates, "simply on this, that nothing will ever be opposite to itself?"

"Quite agreed," he said.

"Here is something else," he said,"see if you will agree to this. You speak of hot and cold?"

"Yes."

"Is it the same as fire and snow?"

"Not at all."

"But the hot is something other than fire, and the cold other than snow?"

"Yes."

"Well, I suppose you agree that snow receiving fire (to use our former way of putting it) will never be what it was, snow, and also be hot, but when the hot approaches it will either retreat from it or be destroyed."

"Certainly."

"Fire, also, when the cold approaches, will either go away from it or be destroyed, but it will never endure to receive the coldness and still be what it was, fire, and cold too."

"True," said he.

"Then it is possible," he said, "with some such things, that not only the essence is thought worthy of the same name forever, but something else also is worthy, which is not that essence but which, when it exists, always has the form of that essence. Perhaps it will be a little clearer as follows. Odd numbers must always be called odd, I suppose, mustn't they?"

"Yes."

"Of all things do we use this name only for oddness, for that is what I ask, or is there something else, not oddness, but what must be called always by that name because its nature is never to be deserted by oddness? For example, triplet and so forth. Now consider the triplet: Don't you think it should be called always both by its own name and also by the name of odd, although oddness is not the same as triplet? Still it is the nature of triplet and quintet and half of all the numbers, that each of them is odd although it is not the same thing as oddness; so also two and four and all the other row of numbers are each of them always even, although none is the same thing as evenness; do you agree?"

"Of course," he said.

"Now attend, this is what I want to make clear. It seems that not only those real opposites do not receive each other, but also things which not being opposites of each other yet always have those real opposites in them, these also do not look like things which receive that reality which is opposite to the reality in them, but when it approaches they either are destroyed or retire. We shall say, for example, that a triplet will be destroyed before any such thing happens to it, before it remains and becomes even, while it is still three?"

"Certainly," said Cebes.

"Nor, again," he said, "is twin the opposite of triplet."

"Not at all."

"Then not only the opposite essences do not remain at the approach of each other, but some other things do not await the approach of the opposites."

"Very true," he said.

"Then shall we distinguish what sorts of things these are," he said, "if we can?"

"Certainly."

"Then, Cebes, would they be those which compel whatever they occupy not only to get their own essence but also the essence of some opposite?"

"How so?"

"As we said just now. You know, I suppose, that whatever the essence of three occupies must necessarily be not only three but odd."

"Certainly."

"And the essence opposite to that which does this we say could never come near such a thing."

"It could not."

"And what has done this? Was not it oddness?"

"Yes."

"And opposite to this is the essence of even?"

"Yes."

"Then the essence of even will never approach three."

"No."

"So three has no part in the even."

"None."

"Then the triplet is uneven."

"Yes."

"Now for my distinction. What things, not being opposite to something, yet do not receive the opposite itself which is in that something? For instance now, the triplet is not the opposite to the even, yet still does not receive it because it always brings the opposite against it; and a pair brings the opposite against the odd, and fire against cold, and so with very many others. Just look then, if you distinguish thus, not only the opposite does not receive the opposite, but that also which brings anything opposite to whatever it approaches never receives the opposite to that which it brings. Recollect once more; there's no harm to hear the same thing often. Five will not receive the essence of even, or its double ten the essence of odd; yet this same double will not receive the essence of odd, although it is not opposite to anything. Again, one and a half and other such things with a half in them will not receive the essence of whole, nor will one-third and all such fractions, if you follow and agree with me in this."

"I do agree certainly, and I follow."

"Once more, then," he said, "go back to the beginning. And don't answer the questions I ask, till I show you how. I want something more than the first answer I mentioned, the safe one; I see a new safety from what we have been saying now. If you ask me what must be in any body if that body is to be hot, I will not give you that safe answer, the stupid answer, 'Heat,' but a more subtle answer from our present reasoning, 'Fire'; or if you ask what must be in a body if it is to be diseased, I will not answer 'Disease,' but 'Fever'; or if you ask what must be in a number if it is to be odd, I will not say 'Oddness,' but 'Onehood,' and so forth. Now then, do you know clearly enough what I want?"

"Oh yes," he said.

"Answer then," said he, "what must be in a body if it is to be living?"

"Soul," said he.

"Is this always true?"

"Of course," he said.

"Well now, whatever the soul occupies, she always comes to it bringing life?"

"She does, indeed," he said.

"Is there an opposite to life, or not?"

"There is."

"What?"

"Death."

"Then soul will never receive the opposite to that which she brings, as we have agreed already."

"Most assuredly," said Cebes.

"Well, what name did we give just now to that which did not receive the essence of the even?"

"Uneven," he said.

"And what name to that which does not receive what is just, or to that which does not receive music?"

"Unmusical," he said, "and unjust the other."

"Very well. What do we call that which does not receive death?"

"Immortal," he said.

"And the soul does not receive death?"

"No."

"Then the soul is a thing immortal?"

"It is," he said.

ON THE SOUL

Aristotle

Now let us start afresh, as it were, and try to determine what the soul is, and what definition of it will be most comprehensive. We describe one class of existing things as substance; and this we subdivide into three: (1) matter, which in itself is not an individual thing; (2) shape or form, in virtue of which individuality is directly attributed, and (3) the compound of the two. Matter is potentiality, while form is realization or actuality, and the word actuality is used in two senses, illustrated by the possession of knowledge and the exercise of it. Bodies seem to be pre-eminently substances, and most particularly those which are of natural origin; for these are the sources from which the rest are derived. But of natural bodies some have life and some have not; by life we mean the capacity for self-sustenance, growth, and decay. Every natural body, then, which possesses life must be substance, and substance of the compound type. But since it is a body of a definite kind, *viz.*, having life, the body cannot be soul, for the body is not something predicated of a subject, but rather is itself to be regarded as a subject, *i.e.*, as matter. So the soul must be substance in the sense of being the form of a natural body, which potentially has life. And substance in this sense is actuality. The soul, then, is the actuality of the kind of body we have described. But actuality has two senses, analogous to the possession of knowledge and the exercise of it. Clearly actuality in our present sense is analogous to the possession of knowledge; for both sleep and waking depend upon the presence of soul, and waking is analogous to the exercise of knowledge, sleep to its possession but not its exercise. Now in one and the same person the possession of knowledge comes first. The soul may therefore be defined as the first actuality of a natural body potentially possessing life; and such will be any body which possesses organs. (The parts of plants are organs too, though very simple ones: *e.g.*, the leaf protects the pericarp, and the pericarp protects the seed; the roots are analogous to the mouth, for both these absorb food.) If then one is to find a definition which will apply to every soul, it will be "the first actuality of a natural body possessed of organs." So one need no more ask whether body and soul are one than whether the wax and the impression it receives are one, or in general whether the matter of each thing is the same as that of which it is the matter; for admitting that the terms unity and being are used in many senses, the paramount sense is that of actuality.

We have, then, given a general definition of what the soul is: it is substance in the sense of formula; *i.e.,* the essence of such-and-such a body. Suppose that an implement, *e.g.* an axe, were a natural body; the substance of the axe would be that which makes it an axe, and this would be its soul; suppose this removed, and it would no longer be an axe, except equivocally. As it is, it remains an axe, because it is not of this kind of body that the soul is the essence or formula, but only of a certain kind of natural body which has in itself a principle of movement and rest. We must, however, investigate our definition in relation to the parts of the body. If the eye were a living creature, its soul would be its vision; for this is the substance in the sense of formula of the eye. But the eye is the matter of vision, and if vision fails there is no eye, except in an equivocal sense, as for instance a stone or painted eye. Now we must apply what we have found true of the part to the whole living body. For the same relation must hold good of the whole of sensation to the whole sentient body *qua* sentient as obtains between their respective parts. That which has the capacity to live is not the body which has lost its soul, but that which possesses its soul; so seed and fruit are potentially bodies of this kind. The waking state is actuality in the same sense as the cutting of the axe or the seeing of the eye, while the soul is actuality in the same sense as the faculty of the eye for seeing, or of the implement for doing its work. The body is that which exists potentially; but just as the pupil and the faculty of seeing make an eye, so in the other case the soul and body make a living creature. It is quite clear, then, that neither the soul nor certain parts of it, if it has parts, can be separated from the body; for in some cases the actuality belongs to the parts themselves. Not but what there is nothing to prevent some parts being separated, because they are not actualities of any body. It is also uncertain whether the soul as an actuality bears the same relation to the body as the sailor to the ship. This must suffice as an attempt to determine in rough outline the nature of the soul.

ANCIENT INDIAN MATERIALISM

The Cārvāka School

The efforts of Cārvāka are indeed hard to be eradicated, for the majority of living beings hold by the current refrain—

> While life is yours, live joyously;
> None can escape Death's searching eye:
> When once this frame of ours they burn,
> How shall it e'er again return?

The mass of men, in accordance with the Śāstras of policy and enjoyment, considering wealth and desire the only ends of man and denying the existence of any object belonging to a future world, are found to follow only the doctrine of Cārvāka. Hence another name for that school is Lokāyata,—a name well accordant with the thing signified.[1]

In this school the four elements, earth, &c., are the original principles; from these alone, when transformed into the body, intelligence is produced, just as the inebriating power is developed from the mixing of certain ingredients; and when these are destroyed, intelligence at once perishes also. They quote the *śruti* [Vedic text] for this [*Brhadāraṇyaka Upaniṣad* II.iv 12]; "Springing forth from these elements, itself solid knowledge, it is destroyed when they are destroyed,—after death no intelligence remains." Therefore the soul is only the body distinguished by the attribute of intelligence, since there is no evidence for any self distinct from the body, as such cannot be proved, since this school holds that perception is the only source of knowledge and does not allow inference, &c.

The only end of man is enjoyment produced by sensual pleasures. Nor may you say that such cannot be called the end of man as they are always

---

[1] "Loka" is Sanskrit for the material world. The Śāstras referred to above are essays of a purely secular nature (Eds.).

mixed with some kind of pain, because it is our wisdom to enjoy the pure pleasure as far as we can, and to avoid the pain which inevitably accompanies it; just as the man who desires fish takes the fish with their scales and bones, and having taken as many as he wants, desists; or just as the man who desires rice, takes the rice, straw and all, and having taken as much as he wants, desists. It is not therefore for us, through a fear of pain, to reject the pleasure which our nature instinctively recognises as congenial. Men do not refrain from sowing rice, because forsooth there are wild animals to devour it; nor do they refuse to set the cooking-pots on the fire, because forsooth there are beggars to pester us for a share of the contents. If any one were so timid as to forsake a visible pleasure, he would indeed be foolish like a beast, as has been said by the poet—

The pleasure which arises to men from contact
　　with sensible objects,
Is to be relinquished as accompanied by pain,—
　　such is the reasoning of fools;
The berries of paddy, rich with the finest white
　　grains,
What man, seeking his true interest, would fling
　　away because covered with husk and dust?

If you object that, if there be no such thing as happiness in a future world, then how should men of experienced wisdom engage in the *Agnihotra*[2] and other sacrifices, which can only be performed with great expenditure of money and bodily fatigue, your objection cannot be accepted as any proof to the contrary, since the *Agnihotra*, &c., are only useful as means of livelihood, for the Veda is tainted by the three faults of untruth, self-contradiction, and tautology; then again the impostors who call themselves Vaidic [or Vedic] pandits are mutually destructive, as the authority of the *jñāna-kāṇḍa* (section on knowledge) is overthrown by those who maintain that of the *karma-kāṇḍa* (section on ac-

tion), while those who maintain the authority of the *jñāna-kāṇḍa* reject that of the *karma-kāṇḍa;* and lastly, the three Vedas themselves are only the incoherent rhapsodies of knaves, and to this effect runs the popular saying—

The *Agnihotra,* the three Vedas, the ascetic's three
　　staves, and smearing oneself with ashes,—
Bṛhaspati says these are but means of livelihood
　　for those who have no manliness nor sense.

Hence it follows that there is no other hell than mundane pain produced by purely mundane causes, as thorns, &c.; the only Supreme is the earthly monarch whose existence is proved by all the world's eyesight; and the only liberation is the dissolution of the body. By holding the doctrine that the soul is identical with the body, such phrases as "I am thin," "I am black," &c., are at once intelligible, as the attributes of thinness, &c., and self-consciousness will reside in the same subject (the body); and the use of the phrase "my body" is metaphorical like "the head of Rāhu" [Rāhu being really *all head*].

All this has been thus summed up—
In this school there are four elements, earth, water,
　　fire, and air;
And from these four elements alone is intelligence
　　produced,—
Just like the intoxicating power from *kiṇva*, &c.,
　　mixed together;
Since in "I am fat," "I am lean," these attributes
　　abide in the same subject,
And since fatness, &c., reside only in the body, it
　　alone is the soul and no other,
And such phrases as "my body" are only
　　significant metaphorically.

• • •

An opponent will say, if you thus do not allow *adṛṣṭa,*[3] the various phenomena of the world become destitute of any cause. But we cannot accept

---

[2]Sacrificial offering to fire.

[3]The unseen force.

this objection as valid, since these phenomena can all be produced spontaneously from the inherent nature of things. Thus it has been said—

The fire is hot, the water cold, refreshing cool the
    breeze of morn;
By whom came this variety? from their own
    nature was it born

• • •

If beings in heaven are gratified by our offering
    the Śrāddha here,
Then why not give the food down below to those
    who are standing on the housetop?
While life remains let a man live happily, let him
    feed on ghee[4] even though he runs in debt;
When once the body becomes ashes, how can it
    ever return again?
If he who departs from the body goes to another
    world,
How is it that he comes not back again, restless for
    love of his kindred?
Hence it is only as a means of livelihood that
    brāhmins have established here
All these ceremonies for the dead—there is no
    other fruit anywhere.
The three authors of the Vedas were buffoons,
    knaves, and demons.
All the well-known formulas of the pandits,
    jarpharī, turpharī, &c.
And all the obscene rites for the queen
    commanded in the Aśvamedha.[5]
These were invented by buffoons, and so all the
    various kinds of presents to the priests,
While the eating of flesh was similarly
    commanded by night-prowling demons.

    Hence in kindness to the mass of living beings must we fly for refuge to the doctrine of Cārvāka. Such is the pleasant consummation.

---

[4]Clarified butter.
[5]A Vedic sacrificial ritual: the "horse sacrifice."

PRABODHA-CANDRODAYA OR THE RISE OF THE MOON OF INTELLECT

A Drama of Ancient India[6]

(A MATERIALIST and one of his pupils enter.)

Materialist: My son, you know that Legislation [the law of punishment by fear of which alone are men influenced in their conduct] is the only Science, and that it comprises everything else. The three Vedas are a cheat. Behold if Heaven be obtained through the officiating priest, sacrificial rites, and the destruction of the substances employed, why is not abundance of excellent fruit obtained from the ashes of a tree which has been burnt up by the fire of the forest. If the victims slain in sacrifices ascend to heaven, why are not parents offered up in sacrifice by their children? If funeral oblations nourish the deceased, why is not the flame of an extinguished taper renovated by pouring on oil?

Pupil: Venerable tutor, if to gratify the appetites be the principal end of life, why do these men renounce sensual pleasures, and submit to pain arising from the severest mortifications?

Materialist: These fools are deceived by the lying Śāstras, and are fed with the allurements of hope. But can begging, fasting, penance, exposure to the burning heat of the sun, which emaciate the body, be compared with the ravishing embraces of women with large eyes, whose prominent breasts are compressed with one's arms?

Pupil: Do these pilgrims indeed torture themselves in order to remove the happiness which is mingled with this miserable existence?

Materialist: (Smiling.) You ignorant boy, such are the fooleries of these unenlightened men. They conceive that you ought to throw away the pleasures of life, because they are mixed with pain; but what prudent man will throw away unpeeled rice

---

[6]This second selection on the Cārvāka school is taken from a popular drama of ancient India. The school's doctrines are thus seen to be a source of controversy that is not limited to the debates of scholars alone (Eds.).

which incloses excellent grain because it is covered with the husk?

PERSONS, DEATH, AND THE BODY

Bertrand Russell

Before we can profitably discuss whether we shall continue to exist after death, it is well to be clear as to the sense in which a man is the same person as he was yesterday. Philosophers used to think that there were definite substances, the soul and the body, that each lasted on from day to day, that a soul, once created, continued to exist throughout all future time, whereas a body ceased temporarily from death till the resurrection of the body.

The part of this doctrine which concerns the present life is pretty certainly false. The matter of the body is continually changing by processes of nutriment and wastage. Even if it were not, atoms in physics are no longer supposed to have continuous existence; there is no sense in saying: this is the same atom as the one that existed a few minutes ago. The continuity of a human body is a matter of appearance and behavior, not of substance.

The same thing applies to the mind. We think and feel and act, but there is not, in addition to thoughts and feelings and actions, a bare entity, the mind or the soul, which does or suffers these occurrences. The mental continuity of a person is a continuity of habit and memory: there was yesterday one person whose feelings I can remember, and that person I regard as myself of yesterday; but, in fact, myself of yesterday was only certain mental occurrences which are now remembered and are regarded as part of the person who now recollects them. All that constitutes a person is a series of experiences connected by memory and by certain similarities of the sort we call habit.

If, therefore, we are to believe that a person survives death, we must believe that the memories and habits which constitute the person will continue to be exhibited in a new set of occurrences.

No one can prove that this will not happen. But it is easy to see that it is very unlikely. Our memories and habits are bound up with the structure of the brain, in much the same way in which a river is connected with the riverbed. The water in the river is always changing, but it keeps to the same course because previous rains have worn a channel. In like manner, previous events have worn a channel in the brain, and our thoughts flow along this channel. This is the cause of memory and mental habits. But the brain, as a structure, is dissolved at death, and memory therefore may be expected to be also dissolved. There is no more reason to think otherwise than to expect a river to persist in its old course after an earthquake has raised a mountain where a valley used to be.

All memory, and therefore (one may say) all minds, depend upon a property which is very noticeable in certain kinds of material structures but exists little if at all in other kinds. This is the property of forming habits as a result of frequent similar occurrences. For example: a bright light makes the pupils of the eyes contract; and if you repeatedly flash a light in a man's eyes and beat a gong at the same time, the gong alone will, in the end, cause his pupils to contract. This is a fact about the brain and nervous system—that is to say, about a certain material structure. It will be found that exactly similar facts explain our response to language and our use of it, our memories and the emotions they arouse, our moral or immoral habits of behavior, and indeed everything that constitutes our mental personality, except the part determined by heredity. The part determined by heredity is handed on to our posterity but cannot, in the individual, survive the disintegration of the body. Thus both the hereditary and the acquired parts of a personality are, so far as our experience goes, bound up with the characteristics of certain bodily structures. We all know that memory may be obliterated by an injury to the brain, that a virtuous person may be rendered vicious by encephalitis lethargica, and that a clever child can be turned into an idiot by lack of iodine. In view of such familiar facts, it seems scarcely probable that the mind survives the total destruction of brain structure which occurs at death.

It is not rational arguments but emotions that cause belief in a future life.

The most important of these emotions is fear of death, which is instinctive and biologically useful. If we genuinely and wholeheartedly believed in the future life, we should cease completely to fear death. The effects would be curious, and probably such as most of us would deplore. But our human and subhuman ancestors have fought and exterminated their enemies throughout many geological ages and have profited by courage; it is therefore an advantage to the victors in the struggle for life to be able, on occasion, to overcome the natural fear of death. Among animals and savages, instinctive pugnacity suffices for this purpose; but at a certain stage of development, as the Mohammedans first proved, belief in Paradise has considerable military value as reinforcing natural pugnacity. We should therefore admit that militarists are wise in encouraging the belief in immortality, always supposing that this belief does not become so profound as to produce indifference to the affairs of the world.

Another emotion which encourages the belief in survival is admiration of the excellence of man. As the Bishop of Birmingham says, "His mind is a far finer instrument than anything that had appeared earlier—he knows right and wrong. He can build Westminster Abbey. He can make an airplane. He can calculate the distance of the sun. . . . Shall, then, man at death perish utterly? Does that incomparable instrument, his mind, vanish when life ceases?"

The Bishop proceeds to argue that "the universe has been shaped and is governed by an intelligent purpose," and that it would have been unintelligent, having made man, to let him perish.

To this argument there are many answers. In the first place, it has been found, in the scientific investigation of nature, that the intrusion of moral or aesthetic values has always been an obstacle to discovery. It used to be thought that the heavenly bodies must move in circles because the circle is the most perfect curve, that species must be immutable because God would only create what was perfect and what therefore stood in no need of improvement, that it was useless to combat epidemics except by repentance because they were sent as a punishment for sin, and so on. It has been found, however, that, so far as we can discover, nature is indifferent to our values and can only be understood by ignoring our notions of good and bad. The Universe may have a purpose, but nothing that we know suggests that, if so, this purpose has any similarity to ours.

Nor is there in this anything surprising. Dr. Barnes tells us that man "knows right and wrong." But, in fact, as anthropology shows, men's views of right and wrong have varied to such an extent that no single item has been permanent. We cannot say, therefore, that man knows right and wrong, but only that some men do. Which men? Nietzsche argued in favor of an ethic profoundly different from Christ's, and some powerful governments have accepted his teaching. If knowledge of right and wrong is to be an argument for immortality, we must first settle whether to believe Christ or Nietzsche, and then argue that Christians are immortal, but Hitler and Mussolini are not, or vice versa. The decision will obviously be made on the battlefield, not in the study. Those who have the best poison gas will have the ethic of the future and will therefore be the immortal ones.

Our feelings and beliefs on the subject of good and evil are, like everything else about us, natural facts, developed in the struggle for existence and not having any divine or supernatural origin. In one of Aesop's fables, a lion is shown pictures of huntsmen catching lions and remarks that, if he had painted them, they would have shown lions catching huntsmen. Man, says Dr. Barnes, is a fine fellow because he can make airplanes. A little while ago there was a popular song about the cleverness of flies in walking upside down on the ceiling, with the chorus: "Could Lloyd George do it? Could Mr. Baldwin do it? Could Ramsay Mac do it? Why, NO." On this basis a very telling argument could be constructed by a theologically-minded fly, which no doubt the other flies would find most convincing.

Moreover, it is only when we think abstractly that we have such a high opinion of man. Of men in the concrete, most of us think the vast majority very bad. Civilized states spend more than half their revenue on killing each other's citizens. Consider the long history of the activities inspired by moral fervor: human sacrifices, persecutions of heretics, witch-hunts, pogroms leading up to wholesale extermination by poison gases, which one at least of Dr. Barnes's episcopal colleagues must be supposed to favor, since he holds pacifism to be un-Christian. Are these abominations, and the ethical doctrines by which they are prompted, really evidence of an intelligent Creator? And can we really wish that the men who practiced them should live forever? The world in which we live can be understood as a result of muddle and accident; but if it is the outcome of deliberate purpose, the purpose must have been that of a fiend. For my part, I find accident a less painful and more plausible hypothesis.

QUESTIONS FOR DISCUSSION

1. Western psychology often claims to find new meaning in ancient literature. The psychologist Carl Jung read the *Tibetan Book of the Dead* backwards and said that he found a record of the unconscious mind in it, beginning with the Freudian sexually oriented unconscious and progressing ever deeper and deeper. Do you think that this is a plausible reading of the *Book of the Dead?* Why or why not?

2. In what ways does the African belief system concerning an afterlife differ, in Onyewuenyi's interpretation, from the belief in reincarnation? In what ways, if any, are the two beliefs similar?

3. Socrates feels that he has rational grounds for believing in immortality. Do you think that he really does—that is, that he really has demonstrated that it is highly probable, and not just a matter of faith, that the soul lives forever?

4. Compare Plato's view of the soul with that of Aristotle. With which do you most agree? Why? Compare Plato's view also with that of Russell and the ancient Indian materialists.

5. Russell believes that "all that constitutes a person is a series of experiences connected by memory and by certain similarities of the sort we call habit." Does this seem to you a correct analysis of what a person is? Why or why not?

Patrick J. Sullivan, *The Fourth Dimension,* 1938, oil on canvas, 24 1/4″ × 30 1/4″. The Museum of Modern Art, New York. The Sidney and Harriet Janis Collection. Photograph © 1994 The Museum of Modern Art, New York.

CHAPTER 6

DESTINY, DETERMINISM, AND FREEDOM

What does it mean to be free? There is an obvious sociopolitical answer to this question. We are free insofar as we are permitted to do certain things; or conversely, insofar as there is nothing interfering with our acting as we wish. If we are enslaved or in prison, we are clearly not free. When governmental authorities tell us what we can read or say, what sexual acts we can and cannot perform, with whom we can associate, where we can travel—in short, when we are prevented from doing what we believe it is our right to do—we lack political freedom. On a smaller social scale, when someone physically threatens us, we experience ourselves as unfree. Some would extend this social and political concept to include nonphysical threats—for example, when the boss threatens to fire us—and to situations where we lack the social and/or material resources to achieve our goals. In this last sense, we are not free if we cannot find employment (freedom to work) or lack access to certain educational institutions (freedom to learn) or cannot obtain sufficient food or shelter (freedom from want). Where we draw the boundary lines has been a major source of political debate between liberals, conservatives, and radicals.

However, there is another issue of freedom, perhaps more subtle but, at least to those with a philosophical turn of mind, of equal importance. This is the issue of freedom versus determinism, which is the focus of our present chapter. Consider the following hypothetical example. A woman lives in a society that grants what we believe are the appropriate political and human rights. She is gainfully employed in an agreeable situation. She has had a reasonable education and does not lack for material security. During her free time she goes to certain restaurants, supermarkets, and stores and consumes whatever she pleases. Is she free? If asked this question directly, she answers in the affirmative. Now, before the reader also does the same, let us add one additional piece of information to our hypothetical scenario. She has been acting under the influence of a series of posthypnotic suggestions, but she has no memory of having been hypnotized. Is she still free?

The reader may protest at this point: "but I haven't been hypnotized. No one tells me what to buy, what career to pursue, whom I may decide to marry, whether to join a political movement, and so on." Let us think about our choices once again. Does modern advertising have anything to do with our choice of products? Does our socialization as males or females have anything to do with our choice of career, or whom we marry, or our political orientation? How do we come to choose the things we do? Even if our choices cannot be traced to a straightforward suggestion by one or more persons, were there not some indirect suggestions? Were there not, at least, some factors in our personal history that motivated the choice?

Now, consider one of the key assumptions of modern science—the assumption of a universal cause and effect. If something occurs, we assume it was caused by something else. If psychology and the social sciences are to be truly scientific, must they not also assume that human action, emotions, and ideas are caused by certain factors in our past experience and perhaps partly by our genetic structure? This is the thesis of determinism. Then, if our actions and choices are themselves determined, how can we be free?

The selections in this chapter consider the philosophical problem of freedom from a number of points of view. In the first section, we consider a problem that precedes the scientific age but that still has many adherents—the problem of destiny. The idea of destiny is often equated with a fatalism that holds not merely that we are determined but that we are *predetermined* by certain universal cosmic forces—for example, by the laws of Karma or the positions of the planets and stars as understood by astrology. This postulate seems to rule out the possibility of free will. The first reading in this section, by the twentieth-century Indian philosopher Sarvepalli Radhakrishnan, challenges the idea that Karma implies a predetermined destiny and argues that we can, in fact, change our destiny. The second reading, by the contemporary African philosopher Kwame Gyekye, explicates the Akan concept of destiny and argues that it is not incompatible with the idea of free will.

The readings in the second section of this chapter argue for a radical concept of freedom, sometimes called metaphysical freedom, or free will. Both the nineteenth-century Russian novelist Fyodor Dostoevsky and the contemporary French existentialist philosopher Jean-Paul Sartre insist that choice cannot be explained by reference to scientific, or causal, laws and that we have complete free will.

Finally, in the third section of this chapter, we ask whether freedom is compatible with determinism. The first reading, by Moritz Schlick, argues yes unequivocally; the second reading, by John Hospers, uses Schlick's analysis against him and argues no just as unequivocally. The third reading, by Nancy Holmstrom, argues yes but only under certain conditions; and the final reading, by Kitaro Nishida, also argues yes but for reasons that are significantly different from those advanced by Schlick and Holmstrom.

Readers of Section One might also want to look at the selection by Sarvepalli Radhakrishnan in Section Two of Chapter 3. Readers of Section Two of this chapter might want to consider also reading the selection by Sartre in Section One of Chapter 4. For those who want to learn more about the logical positivist method that Schlick employs, see the selection by Antony Flew in Section One of Chapter 3.

DESTINY AND FREEDOM

In the general introduction to this chapter we mentioned that destiny is often taken to mean that we are not only determined but predetermined by some universal cosmic force. In ancient China, for example, it was often said that "Heaven decreed" whether we were rich or poor, industrious or lazy, happy or unhappy, or whether our life would be long or short. In India the idea of Karma, of a universal moral law, was often interpreted to mean that our present destiny was predetermined by our good or bad actions in former lives. In this section, Sarvepalli Radhakrishnan takes issue with this interpretation.

Sarvepalli Radhakrishnan (1888–1975) was a major contemporary Indian philosopher and statesman—he was both vice president and president of India—who attempted to reinterpret Hinduism in a way that reconciles some of its internal divisions and makes it more accessible to Western philosophical thought. In the selection in this chapter, he denies that the idea of Karma implies predestination.

Karma is understood as a moral counterpart to physical law. Just as there is cause and effect in the physical universe, so it exists in the moral universe. We reap morally as we have sown. If we do evil, we can expect evil to befall us, and similarly if we do good; and given the Hindu belief in reincarnation, it is often assumed that our destiny in this life is predestined by what we have done in our former lives.

While Radhakrishnan would agree that the laws of Karma rule our free will in the sense of an undetermined action and that we always carry our whole past with us, he does not believe that our destiny is predetermined. He insists that the laws of Karma should be understood not as mechanical but as a spiritual principle and that while our past is determined, our future is only conditioned. He compares the situation to a card game: "Cards in the game of life are given to us," but we can still choose how to play our hand. In short, we must confront the moral effects of our past actions, but we decide how to confront them, thus making it possible for us to change our destiny.

Kwame Gyekye is a professor of philosophy at the University of Ghana and is one of the foremost interpreters and architects of contemporary African philosophy. Gyekye's work, *An Essay on African Philosophical Thought: The Akan Conceptual Scheme,* from which the second selection in this section is taken, is an attempt to reconstruct the ideas of members of this major ethnic group in Ghana as a philosophical system and to develop a plausible philosophical interpretation and defense of its key concepts. In this selection, he attempts to reconstruct and evaluate the Akan's concept of destiny. In contrast to Radhakrishnan's analysis of Karma, Gyekye argues that the Akan understanding of destiny does imply predestination and rules out the idea that we can change our destiny. The Akan concept of destiny insists that every human being has a destiny that was fixed beforehand and that it is precisely this destiny that makes each individual unique. It also assumes a completely deterministic conception of the world. Nonetheless, Gyekye insists that the Akan concept of destiny does not lead to an attitude of resignation, nor does it rule out free will. It does not lead to an attitude of resignation because, first, it assumes that destiny is at work only after repeated attempts by a person have failed to achieve the desired goals; second, because it allows for the idea of accidents and contingencies; and, third, having a destiny means that each of us has a sphere of action for which he or she is naturally suited, thus implying that we should strive to discover what that is. The Akan concept of destiny is compatible with free will because while determinism implies that all events are caused, an action is not an event; and because what are predetermined and fixed are only certain key events within which a large range of choice is possible.

KARMA AND FREEDOM

Sarvepalli Radhakrishnan

The doctrine of Karma is sometimes interpreted as implying a denial of human freedom, which is generally regarded as the basis of all ethical values. But when rightly viewed the law does not conflict with the reality of freedom. It is the principle of science which displaces belief in magic or the theory that we can manipulate the forces of the world at our pleasure. The course of nature is determined not by the passions and prejudices of personal spirits lurking behind it but by the operation of immutable laws. If the sun pursues his daily and the moon her nightly journey across the sky, if the silent procession of the seasons moves in light and shadow across the earth, it is because they are all guided in their courses by a power superior to them all. "Verily O Gārgī, at the command of that Imperishable, the sun and the moon stand apart, the earth and the sky stand apart . . . The moments, the hours, the days, the nights, the fortnights, the months, the seasons and the years stand apart. Verily O Gārgī, at the command of that Imperishable, some rivers flow from the snowy mountains to the east, others to the west in whatever direction each flows."[1] There is the march of necessity everywhere. The universe is lawful to the core.

The theory of Karma recognizes the rule of law not only in outward nature, but also in the world of mind and morals. *Ṛta* manifests itself equally in nature and in human society. We are every moment making our characters and shaping our destinies. "There is no loss of any activity which we commence nor is there any obstacle to its fulfilment. Even a little good that we may do will protect us against great odds."[2] What we have set our hearts on will not perish with this body. This fact inspires life with the present sense of eternity.

At a time when people were doing devil's work under divine sanction and consoling themselves by attributing everything to God's will, the principle of Karma insisted on the primacy of the ethical and identified God with the rule of law. All's law, yet all's God. Karma is not a mechanical principle but a spiritual necessity. It is the embodiment of the mind and will of God. God is its supervisor, karmādhyakṣaḥ.[3] Justice is an attribute of God. Character of God is represented by St. James as one "with whom can be no variation neither shadow that is cast by turning." Every act, every thought is weighed in the invisible but universal balance-scales of justice. The day of judgment is not in some remote future, but here and now, and none can escape it. Divine laws cannot be evaded. They are not so much imposed from without as wrought into our natures. Sin is not so much a defiance of God as a denial of soul, not so much a violation of law as a betrayal of self. We carry with us the whole of our past. It is an ineffaceable record which time cannot blur nor death erase.

There is room for repentance and consequent forgiveness on this scheme. The critic who urges that belief in Karma makes religious life, prayer and worship impossible has not a right understanding of it. In his opinion God has abdicated in favour of his law. To pray to God is as futile a superstition as to bid the storm give us strength, or the earthquake to forgive us our sins. Of course the Hindu does not look upon prayer as a sort of Aladdin's lamp to produce anything we want. God is not a magician stopping the sun in its course and staying the bullet in its march. But his truth and constancy, his mercy and justice find their embodiment in the implacable working of the moral law. Forgiveness is not a mitigation of God's justice but only an expression of it. We can insist with unflinching rigour on the inexorability of the moral law and yet believe in the forgiveness of sins. Spiritual growth and experience are governed by laws similar to those which rule the rest of the universe. If we sow to the flesh we shall of the flesh reap corruption. The punishment for a

[1] *Bṛh. Up.*, iii. 8. 9.
[2] *Bhagavadgītā*, iii. 40.
[3] *Śvet. Up.*, vi. II.

desecrated body is an enfeebled understanding and a darkened soul. If we deliberately fall into sin, shutting our eyes to moral and spiritual light, we may be sure that in God's world sin will find us out and our willful blindness will land us in the ditch. A just God cannot refuse to any man that which he has earned. The past guilt cannot be wiped away by the atoning suffering of an outward substitute.[4] Guilt cannot be transferred. It must be atoned for through the sorrow entailed by self-conquest. God cannot be bought over and sin cannot be glossed over.

The principle of Karma reckons with the material or the context in which each individual is born. While it regards the past as determined, it allows that the future is only conditioned. The spiritual element in man allows him freedom within the limits of his nature. Man is not a mere mechanism of instincts. The spirit in him can triumph over the automatic forces that try to enslave him. The *Bhagavadgītā* asks us to raise the self by the self. We can use the material with which we are endowed to promote our ideals. The cards in the game of life are given to us. We do not select them. They are traced to our past Karma, but we can call as we please, lead what suit we will, and as we play, we gain or lose. And there is freedom.

What the individual will be cannot be predicted beforehand, though there is no caprice. We can predict an individual's acts so far as they are governed by habit, that is, to the extent his actions are mechanical and not affected by choice. But choice is not caprice. Free will in the sense of an undetermined, unrelated, uncaused factor in human action is not admitted, but such a will defies all analysis. It has nothing to do with the general stream of cause and effect. It operates in an irregular and chaotic way. If human actions are determined by such a will, there is no meaning in punishment or training of character. The theory of Karma allows man the freedom to use the material in the light of his knowledge. Man controls the uniformities in na-

ture, his own mind and society. There is thus scope for genuine rational freedom, while indeterminism and chance lead to a false fatalism.

The universe is not one in which every detail is decreed. We do not have a mere unfolding of a pre-arranged plan. There is no such thing as absolute prescience on the part of God, for we are all his fellow-workers. God is not somewhere above us and beyond us, he is also in us. The divine in us can, if utilized, bring about even sudden conversions. Evolution in the sense of epigenesis is not impossible. For the real is an active developing life and not a mechanical routine.

The law of Karma encourages the sinner that it is never too late to mend. It does not shut the gates of hope against despair and suffering, guilt and peril. It persuades us to adopt a charitable view towards the sinner, for men are more often weak than vicious. It is not true that the heart of man is desperately wicked and that he prefers evil to good, the easy descent to hell to the steep ascent to heaven.

Unfortunately, the theory of Karma became confused with fatality in India when man himself grew feeble and was disinclined to do his best. It was made into an excuse for inertia and timidity and was turned into a message of despair and not of hope. It said to the sinner, "Not only are you a wreck, but that is all you ever could have been. That was your preordained being from the beginning of time." But such a philosophy of despair is by no means the necessary outcome of the doctrine of Karma.

DESTINY AND FREE WILL: AN AFRICAN VIEW

Kwame Gyekye

Although much has been written about it, the Akan concept of destiny (*nkrabea:* also fate) has not been thoroughly analyzed. Many of the attempts to define it have been thin and pedestrian. There have

---

[4]Cp. munir manute mūrkho mucyate. The monk meditates and the fool is freed.

been a number of different interpretations of the concept, resulting either from the ambiguity of the concept among the Akan thinkers themselves, or from the lack of profound and satisfactory analysis by scholars. My intention in this chapter is to clarify fully the nature of the concept and to explore its implications for human freedom and responsibility.

BASIS OF BELIEF IN DESTINY

Akan thinkers hold that every human being has a destiny that was fixed beforehand . . . the soul (*ōkra*) is thought to be the bearer of the destiny of man. It is held that before the soul sets out to enter this world, it takes leave of or bids farewell (*kra*) to the Supreme Being, Onyame. At this juncture it receives from Onyame the message (*nkra*) that will determine the course of the individual's life on earth. From the outset, that is, in Akan conceptions there is a close link between destiny and the soul. Here are some proverbs that underline this belief:

There is no bypass to God's destiny.
No living man can subvert the order of God.
Unless you die of God, let living man attempt to
   kill you and you will not perish.
The yam that will burn when fried, will also burn
   when boiled.
The tree that will shed its leaves, knows no rainy
   season.
If you are destined to die by the gun, you will not
   die by the arrow.
What is destined to prosper or succeed cannot be
   otherwise.
If a piece of wood remains in a river for thousands
   of years, it cannot become a crocodile.
If you are destined to gain fortunes, the vulture
   will not be abominable to your soul.[1]

What is the basis of Akan belief in destiny? In his critical examination Wiredu stated: "There is however a very much more intractable difficulty which emerges when we ask the question why it comes to be supposed in the first place that man has unalterable pre-appointed destiny. A question of this sort is of the last consequence in the assessment of a philosophy, for the real meaning of a philosophical thesis remains more or less hidden until the *reasoning* behind it is known."[2] Wiredu's point is of course fundamental and applies to a great number of beliefs and assumptions. However, before I take up the reasoning of the Akan thinkers concerning the basis of their belief in human destiny, I should like to make one general remark.

The belief in destiny is of course not peculiar to the Akan people; it is probably found in all cultures. The question of destiny is of great import for human beings, and hence has been raised and explored by thinkers and theologians in all philosophies and religions. It is enmeshed with such genuine philosophical themes as determinism, freedom of the will, punishment, moral responsibility, etc. Regarding the reasons for this universal belief in destiny two observations may be made.

The first relates to the link that a number of thinkers find between language and thought, or more precisely in the present context, between language and metaphysics. They claim that there is some kind of reality antecedent to language that language is developed to express or depict. Language or linguistic structure, they hold, reflects a deep-lying structure of reality (or being). On this showing, the Akan expression *nkrabea* was developed to depict a reality. Thus, a well-known discussant stated that "if there were no accident (*asiane*), the word *asiane* would not exist in the Akan language."[3] He stated that "the situation or matter that is not real has no name" (*asēm a enni hō no enni*

[1]*Wōabō wo dē ibenya adze a, wo 'kra nnkyir pētē.* J. A. Annobil (interview, 31 August 1976, Cape Coast) explained the proverb thus: the vulture is believed to be a sign of misfortune, and yet it cannot be an impediment to the person who is destined to be fortunate.

[2]K. Wiredu, "Philosophy and Our Culture," *Proceedings of the Ghana Academy of Arts and Sciences,* Vol. XV, 1977, p. 48; my italics.
[3]Interview with Nana Osei-Bonsu of Kumasi, 8–11 January, 1974.

din). In other words, anything that is named must be presumed to be real.

Second, the universal belief in destiny derives from another belief, namely, that humans are the product of a Creator. It is possible to assume that if humans were fashioned, they were fashioned in a way which would determine their inclinations, dispositions, talents, etc. Thus, an Akan fragment says: "All men have one head but heads[4] differ" (*nnipa nyinaa wō ti baako nanso wōn ti nsē*). That is, all people are basically alike as people—they are all created in the same way—but they differ in their fortunes, luck, capacities, etc. Just as the maker of a car can determine its speed, size, and shape, so the Creator can determine a number of things about human beings. The notion of a preappointed destiny, therefore, may also have arisen in this way. It might not have arisen if man were supposed to have evolved and not been created by a Creator. Thus, Western humanism that maintains "that man is an evolutionary product of the Nature of which he is part" goes on appropriately to deny "that there is any overarching fate, either in the form of a Divine Providence or a malignant Satanism, that is either helping or hindering man's progress and well-being."[5]

How did the Akan thinkers come by their concept of destiny? What is the basis or reasoning behind their concept of destiny? The basis of the Akan concept of destiny, like the bases of most of their concepts and thoughts, is essentially experiential. Human life (*abrabō*) itself, therefore, provides the setting for their thought on destiny. A well-known researcher on Akan language and culture said in a discussion: "It is in *life* itself that we see that there is destiny."[6] Another discussant stated: "Destiny reveals itself clearly in life"[7] (that is, in human experiences). Patterns of individual lives, habitual or persistent traits of persons, fortunes

and misfortunes, successes and failures, the traumas and enigmas of life; the ways in which propensities, inclinations, capacities, and talents show themselves in individuals; the observed uniqueness of the individual—all these suggest to the Akan that there is and must be some basis or reason for this individuality. That basis is destiny.

For the Akan, the striking features of these phenomena do much to clinch the idea about destiny. These features include the repetition and persistence of particular actions of the individual, the apparent unalterability and inexplicability of elements in one's character, the inexplicability of events in the life of an individual, the apparent irremediability of particular failures in the life of an individual, the constancy of one's good fortunes, and so on. It is the existence of such features of their experiences that, in the view of Akan thinkers, suggests the reality of a concept of destiny. With regard to the unalterability of a trait in one's character, for instance, it is held that if a person commits an accidental act (*asiane*), which for them means not influenced by destiny, he or she will not commit it again; that action is thus easily corrigible. A discussant[8] explained that if one day the cocoa bags of a farmer who has become wealthy through buying and selling cocoa catch fire, the occurrence would be considered an accident. On the other hand, if every time he buys cocoa it catches fire, then this repeated event will be ascribed to his destiny: Selling and buying cocoa is just not his destined occupation; he ought to give it up and look elsewhere for his "real" occupation. In other words, it is the persistence of an action or a behavior pattern or the inexplicability of an event that induces a belief in destiny.

The Akan concept of destiny is thus not mysterious; it is reached through a profound analysis of the realities of human life. The reasoning behind the concept, like all reasoning based on experience, is inductive. This does not, however, detract from its plausibility or validity, and supports the view that the philosophical enterprise proceeds from experience.

---

[4]The first use of "head" (*ti*) refers to the physical head, the second to the *soul,* the bearer of destiny.

[5]Corliss Lamont, *The Philosophy of Humanism,* pp. 13, 109.

[6]Interview with J. A. Annobil (*abrabō no mu na yehu sē nkrabea bi wō hō*).

[7]Interview with Oheneba Kwabena Bekoe of Akropong-Akuapem, 30 July 1976: (*nkrabea no yi ne ho adi pefee wō abrabō mu*).

[8]Interview with J. A. Annobil, 1 September 1976.

The concept of destiny is thus reached by reflecting upon the experiences of individuals. This implies that destiny is that which determines the uniqueness and individuality of a person. It is your destiny (*nkrabea*) that makes you you, and my destiny that makes me me. The *nkrabea* of a person is unique and idiosyncratic, as we see in the following proverbs:

Each destiny is different from the other.
All men have one head but heads differ.
Antelope's soul (destiny) is one, duiker's another.[9]
Oh cock, do not compare your destiny with that of the hen.

In Akan conceptions each person is unique, for, as they often say, "each and his destiny," that is, each person has his own destiny (*obiara ne ne nkrabea*). A person's destiny is the crucial determinant or basis of individuality and uniqueness. The characteristics of individuals reflect the differences in their destiny.

• • •

THE GENERAL NATURE OF DESTINY

The conception of destiny held by most of the traditional wise persons with whom I had discussions makes the destiny of man a *general* destiny. That is, the message (*nkra*) borne by the soul is said to be comprehensive; it determines only the broad outlines of an individual's mundane life, not the specific details. It follows that not every action a person performs or every event that occurs in one's life comes within the ambit of his destiny. Two problems, perhaps the most difficult problems in the Akan conception of destiny, immediately come up. The first is: How can we determine the exact level of generality of one's destiny? The second is: What are the elements of destiny, that is, what attributes are contained in the message of destiny? The second question appears to be more fundamen-

tal, for if we can determine the nature of the content of the message, we have some idea of the level of generality of destiny. I shall therefore attempt the second question first.

My discussants were generally unsure about the elements that are included in one's destiny. They were, however, unanimous in claiming that the time of a person's death and possibly also the manner and place of death are stipulated in his destiny. Rank and occupation are included, according to two discussants.[10] Thus the level of the generality of destiny remains vague. All the discussants, however, agreed that the inexplicable events in one's life, the unalterable and persistently habitual traits of character, the persistent actions and behavior patterns of an individual are all traceable to destiny. It is important to note that only when all human or physical explanations for events or actions are exhausted that recourse is had to a person's destiny. This being so, one might say that only certain "key" events and actions are embodied in destiny. Perhaps better, the destiny of an individual comprises certain basic attributes. The proverbs on destiny . . . refer to such key events or basic attributes. What these basic attributes are is of course difficult to say with certainty. Nevertheless, it is clear that the Akan notion of destiny is a general one, which implies that not everything that a person does or that happens to him or her represents a page from the "book of destiny."

Construing the message (*nkra*) of destiny in terms of basic attributes provides a solution for another knotty problem in the Akan conception of destiny. The problem is that of the alterability or unalterability of one's destiny. This problem is of great consequence, for it has been supposed that its solution determines the place of human effort in human activities and the development of society. It will be shown, however, that the place of human effort depends on something other than the alterable or unalterable nature of one's destiny. On the ques-

---

[9]Akan proverbs are ultimately about mankind, its life, its conception of the universe, etc., although nonhumans such as animals, trees, rivers, also figure in the language of the proverb.

[10]Interviews with Opanin Apenkwa, Keeper of the Shrine, Ghana National Cultural Centre, Kumasi, 6 September 1974, and Krontihene Boafo-Ansah of Akropong-Akuapem, 17 July 1976.

tion of whether or not one can alter one's destiny, my discussants were about equally divided. Bishop Sarpong[11] claims that destiny can be changed by magic or religious means. Opoku,[12] however, denies that it can be changed. The Akan proverbs on destiny I have examined seem to imply the unalterability and unavoidability of destiny. Perhaps there are some proverbs that imply otherwise. But if the message of destiny is conceived in terms of basic attributes, as I am construing it, it is clear why destiny cannot be changed: Basic attributes do not change. Moreover, if as I have argued destiny is determined by the *omnipotent* Supreme Being, it obviously cannot be changed. Hence, the insistence of the proverbs I have seen that God's destiny cannot be avoided or changed is logical.

Changing one's destiny is not only an impossible idea, but it is also one that should, strictly speaking, not arise in a system in which destiny is divinely determined. The reason is, since the Supreme Being is regarded in Akan thought as good—a view that is expressed in these proverbs:

Goodness is the prime characteristic of God.
The hawk says: "Whatever God does is good."

—the destiny fixed by God must be good. My discussants were unanimous in asserting that "everyone's leave-taking was good" (*obiara kraa yie*); "nobody's leave-taking was evil" (*obiara ankra bōne*); "God created everyone well" (*Nyame bōō abiara yie*). Thus, bad things are not included in the message of destiny. Wherein, then, lies the necessity for changing one's destiny, for changing what is good? There is really no such necessity, for the talk of changing destiny really refers to the attempt to better one's condition. For instance, a person's path may be strewn with failures, either because of his or her own actions, desires, decisions, and intentions, or because of the activities of some supposed evil forces. A person in such a situation may try to do something about the situation by, say, consulting priests and diviners. But in so doing he or she would certainly not be changing destiny as such; rather, he or she would in fact be trying to better the conditions of life (*abrabō*) by some means. Therefore one should speak of improving one's circumstances in life rather than of "changing" one's destiny.

Destiny in Akan thought, interpreted as the basic attributes of an individual, may be contrasted with the German philosopher Leibniz's (1646–1716) concept of the individual. Leibniz wrote:

> We have said that the concept of an individual substance includes once for all everything which can ever happen to it, and that in considering this concept one will be able to see everything which can truly be said concerning the individual, just as we are able to see in the nature of a circle all the properties which can be derived from it.[13]

The view that the concept of the individual "includes once for all everything which can ever happen to it" is in fact antithetical to the message of destiny, the basis of individuality in Akan thought. For the Akan notion does not include everything that can ever happen to the individual.

Akan thinkers maintain that the message of destiny of an individual is not known by any living man, a view that is expressed, for instance, in the proverb:

When someone was taking leave of the Supreme Being, no one else was standing by.
(*obi kra ne Nyame no na obi nnyina hō bi*)

Since no one else observed the act of leave-taking of another person, no one knows the destiny of any other person. The individual does not know his or her own destiny either; the message of destiny cannot be remembered since a large portion of the soul (*ōkra*) is said to remain unconscious. Only the Supreme Being (Onyame) knows an individual's destiny. But divine knowledge of an individual's destiny does not appear to be fatal to the latter's exercise of free will, since the individual does not presume to have access

[11]Sarpong, "Aspects," p. 42.
[12]Kofi A. Opoku, "The Destiny of Man in Akan Traditional Religious Thought," in *Conch,* Vol. VII, Nos. 1 and 2, 1975, pp. 21ff.

[13]G. W. Leibniz, *Discourse on Metaphysics: Correspondence with Arnauld and Monadology,* trans. G. R. Montgomery (Open Court, La Salle, IL, 1968), pp. 19–20.

to this knowledge of God. More on free will in Akan thought anon.

Finally, we turn to the resignation that is alleged to be involved in, or induced by, the Akan concept of human destiny. Wiredu wrote:

> . . . adversity may lead a man to resignation. This happens every where and in all cultures. *But in our culture the notions about destiny just mentioned are apt to facilitate the resignation of a despairing soul.*[14]

Again:

> But our traditional philosophy is probably highly remarkable in the personal directness and individual immediacy of the doctrine of fate and, further, in the sincerity and practical seriousness with which it is entertained in the day to day life of our people.[15]

Kwesi Dickson has argued successfully against the view that the Akan concept of *nkrabea* induces resignation. Referring specifically to the Akan notion of destiny, *nkrabea,* he wrote: "Resignation, with its consequent passivity, does not appear to be encouraged in African thought."[16] Some of the arguments I advance against the view that the Akan concept of destiny induces an immediate feeling of doom have been made by Dickson.

First, only after *repeated* attempts in the pursuit of some aim have failed do the Akans normally blame a person's failure on destiny, *nkrabea.* This means that striving is highly esteemed by the Akans and that it is never considered normal to give up easily or immediately unless one is brought to a situation from which there is no escape. Resignation should not be the immediate response to failure; it is appropriate only after all possible recourse has been exhausted. Resignation is thus a response or attitude to a humanly impossible situation. In such a situation the Akans would say:

Man came to play only a part of the drama of life,
   not the whole.
   (*onipa bēyēē bi, na wōammēyē ne nyinaa*)

On this saying Antubam comments: "*When after a sincere strenuous effort* the Ghanaian fails to reach the highest height in a competition, he cheers himself up in resignation by saying to himself" the above proverb.[17] It is implicit in the proverb that something must have been achieved, some effort expended. The feeling of resignation wells up only when one recognizes that one's efforts have been misplaced, or are otherwise unavailing. Such resignation, however, does not imply a feeling of doom or a belief that future success is impossible, nor does it induce in that individual the feeling that trying other pursuits would be useless. After repeated failure, resignation is a rational, realistic, and necessary attitude for an individual who believes that luck, success, and fortune are to be looked for elsewhere.

Second, everyone wishes to avoid evil and escape disaster; hence the strong belief in the beneficial activities of the traditional diviners and priests. In all libation prayers, the spiritual beings, from Onyame down to the ancestors, are implored to avert disaster (*musuo*) and to bring peace, happiness, prosperity, good harvest, etc.

Third, as observed earlier, Akans believe in the existence of accidents (*asiane, akwanhyia*)—events or actions that are not "in one's destiny." As one discussant put it, "Accident is not in the *nkrabea*" (*asiane, enni nkrabea no mu*).[18] The word *asiane* is generally used to refer to an unintended effect, although this does not mean that it is uncaused, or occurring by chance. An Akan proverb has it that,

The death of *funtum* affects *mmatatwene.*
(*funtum wuo saa mmatatwene*)

Funtum is a tree. *Mmatatwene* is a creeping plant that grows along and around the main stem of the *funtum* tree. Now, if one fells the *funtum* tree, at the same time, though unintentionally as far as one is concerned, one destroys the *mmatatwene* plant around it.

---

[14]K. Wiredu, "Philosophy and Our Culture," p. 46; my italics.
[15]Ibid., p. 47.
[16]K. A. Dickson, *Aspects of Religion and Life in Africa,* p. 9.

[17]Kofi Antubam, *Ghana's Heritage of Culture,* p. 44; my italics.
[18]Interview with J. A. Annobil of Cape Coast, 1 September 1976.

Thus, the destruction or death of the *mmatatwene* plant is an accident, that is, an effect not intended by the person who felled the *funtum* tree. The proverb makes it clear that there are, according to the Akan thinkers, accidents or contingencies in human life, a fact also recognized or implicit in the general character of *nkrabea*.

Finally, by stressing the uniqueness and individuality of people, the Akan concept of destiny implies that each individual is naturally fitted for a particular sphere of action, and that he or she has capacities and aptitudes for the activities of that sphere. This means that while one does not have a capacity or talent for every conceivable or desirable pursuit, one certainly has capacities for particular pursuits or endeavors. This position emerges in such proverbs as:

If God did not give the swallow anything, He gave it agility.[19]
If the cat does not have anything, it has swiftness.

Since each individual has some talents, a series of failures would suggest that he or she might be in the wrong sphere of action and that those talents are therefore misplaced and are consequently being denied the opportunity for their full exercise. Thus, if the Akan concept of destiny is fully and properly understood, it would have far-reaching beneficial consequences for individuals in society.

CAUSALITY, FATE, FREE WILL, AND RESPONSIBILITY

I now turn to the external and internal influences on human life and the implications of these for free will and moral responsibility . . . Akan thinkers hold a strongly deterministic conception of the world: For them every event has a cause; nothing is attributable to chance. We learned in our analysis of the Akan concept of a person . . . that some characteristics, due to the *ntoro* and *mogya* elements, are in-

herited from parents or relatives and that moral attributes are generally ascribed to the *sunsum* (spirit) . . . We saw that fate or destiny is unalterable. Even an individual's day of birth, called *krada,* is thought to influence one's personal characteristics. Thus, people born on Monday are said to be calm (*odwo*), those born on Thursday are said to be courageous (*prēko:* warlike), and so on. One's *krada,* and hence time, is believed to be a factor in determining one's individuality and uniqueness. In the light of such a deterministic conception of the world and of life, can humans be said to be free in their actions and behavior? Can they be moral agents? Akan thinkers answer these questions in the affirmative.

The argument in Western philosophy pertaining to human free will and responsibility is this: If every event is caused, as determinism holds, then human action and behavior too are caused, and hence we cannot be held to be free and therefore cannot be held morally responsible for those actions. There is a suppressed premise in the argument, which is that human actions are (a species of) events. This premise is, in my view, not wholly correct. There is a sense in which human actions cannot be considered as events. Events are mere happenings or occurrences, which do not have their origin in human design and motivation. Thus, we speak of the flooding of a river, the erosion of the sea, a tremor of the earth, the capsizing of a boat during a storm, the disruption of electrical supply following lightning, and the crash of an aircraft during a thunderstorm, as events. Human "events," insofar as they originate in human thought, deliberation, desire, etc., cannot strictly be regarded as events. Although the word "event" may be used to refer to humanly motivated action, as in "The French Revolution was a momentous *event* in the history of France," "The Bond of 1844 was a significant *event* in the history of Ghana," "Intertribal wars in Africa were tragic *events,*" "Egyptian President Sadat's visit to Jerusalem in December 1977 was a historic *event,*" the sense of "event" in these statements is plainly different from the sense it has in the occurrences mentioned earlier. The flooding of a river and the warring among ethnic groups in

---

[19]Akrofi comments: this proverb is "used in showing that every human being has a special talent." C. A. Akrofi, *Twi Proverbs,* proverb no. 791.

Africa are different kinds of "events." The former is an event simply: It just occurred, without any human intervention. The latter is, strictly speaking, not an event, for it did not simply occur; it was an *action* brought about as a result of human deliberation, intention, decision, and desire; it was planned and executed by people. The French Revolution did not erupt by itself, like a volcano; it was planned and executed by humans. Sadat's historic visit to Jerusalem resulted from his desire for peace in that area of the world. Such human actions may later be described as "events," but they are not events, properly speaking.

. . . Akan thinking about causation is confined to events, natural and nonhuman, that are beyond the control or power of people, to the exclusion of human actions (*nneyēe*). I think it is correct to maintain that in Akan thought the doctrine of causality or determinism is irrelevant as far as human actions are concerned. This means that the doctrine of determinism is not fatal to the freedom a person has in actions and behavior. For the fact that every event is caused does not, in the Akan system, eliminate or subvert the role of the individual in human actions. Now Akan thinkers conceive of cause in terms of spirit or power (*sunsum*), and humans also have a spirit, even if of a lower potency, that is the basis of thought, deliberation, will and so on. It follows that man also is a causal agent. Determinism therefore does not negate the effectiveness of human beings as causal and therefore moral agents. The *sunsum* of a person is held to be developable; a weak power or capacity can be improved or strengthened. Moral failures, then, which are in fact spiritual defects, can be rectified. Therefore, neither the Akan deterministic conception of the world nor Akan moral psychology is fatal to human free will and responsibility.

The concept of destiny (*nkrabea*) might be held to be subversive of the reality of humans as causal free agents. For if actions are predetermined, then thoughts, deliberations, decisions are of no consequence; there is nothing that a person might think of or do that will affect the result. Therefore, the effects of the concept of destiny on volitional causality are relevant to the questions of free will and moral responsibility. Is the Akan concept of destiny destructive of human free will?

Because *nkrabea* (destiny) expresses only the basic attributes of the individual, and because *nkrabea* is *general* and not specific, human actions are not fated or necessitated; this fact gives viability and meaningfulness to the concept of choice. Even if one considered free will not to be absolute in the light of human creatureliness, it must nevertheless be granted that the individual can make his or her own existence meaningful through the exercise of free will within the scope of destiny.

That actions and behavior originate from thought, desire, choice, etc., is implicit in the concept of *asiane*, accident, which is invariably tied to the concept of *nkrabea*. In Akan thought, "accident" refers to an action or event that is unintended but that has a cause. As far as human actions are concerned, the cause is, of course, the person himor herself. Consequently, if a hunter, for instance, accidentally mistakes a man for an animal and shoots him, he is held responsible, even though as far as he is concerned it was an unintended action. It was his action in that he was the cause of it; he should or could have been more careful. Also relevant here is that of "doing something premeditatedly or purposely" (*se wo hyēda*). However, for it to be applicable here, it appears in the negative: *wōanhyēda*, that is, "He did not do it premeditatedly (or deliberately)." But it is implicit that this does not mean that action is automatic or predetermined. Our hypothetical hunter cannot absolve himself of the responsibility by claiming that his action was unpremeditated; he accepts the responsibility for the action because he willed and executed it, even though the consequences of his action turned out to be different from what he intended. Thus, the general nature of *nkrabea* allows room for the exercise by the person of free will and, consequently, "accidental" and "unpremeditated" actions are considered as deriving from the exercise of free will and hence are the person's responsibility.

Humanity is endowed with capacity (or power) for thought and action. This capacity is implied in the concept of *sunsum*. Humans then should employ this capacity to improve themselves. The Akans highly esteem effort, for as the proverb has it,

> Trying hard breaks the back of misfortune.
> (*mmōdenbō bu musuo abasa so*)

Thus, if a person fails to do the right thing either in a moral situation or otherwise he or she should be held responsible, for it was within human capacity to do it correctly.

Akan thinkers maintain that character, which is given an important place in the ethical life of a person, is reformable; it can be trained and developed. Moral habits are acquired through habituation and obedience to good advice. Thus, they say:

> We offer advice (in order to reform one's
>   character),
> but we do not change destiny.
> (*yetufo, yentu hyēbrē*)
> One is not born with "bad head" but one takes it
>   on the earth.
> (*ti bōne wofa no fam, wōmfa nnwo*)

The latter proverb means that bad habits are acquired by people; misfortunes and failures are their own making. Accordingly, an unhappy or miserable life is attributed to a person's behavior or conduct:

> If a man is unhappy, his conduct is the cause.
> (*onipa ho antō no a, na efi n'asēm*)

Because character can be reformed, such an attribution, it seems to me, is appropriate. A person is responsible for the state of his or her character, for he or she is endowed with the capacity to reform and to improve. In sum, then, Akan philosophy maintains that human beings are free and must therefore be held morally responsible for their actions and behavior.

QUESTIONS FOR DISCUSSION

1. Consider one example of belief in destiny in our society—for example, belief in astrology, belief that you will die when it is your time, belief that there is one "soulmate" whom you are destined to be with—in relation to one of the analyses in this section. What do you think is the psychological and/or social function of this belief? Does this belief imply resignation? Does it rule out free will? Do you believe in predestination in any form? Why or why not?

2. Evaluate Radhakrishnan's claim that according to the laws of Karma the past is determined but the future is only conditioned. Do you believe that our actions for good or evil can determine our destiny? Do you think that you can change your destiny?

3. Gyekye claims that the Akan concept of destiny assumes that each of us has a destiny that was fixed beforehand and that we cannot change. Nonetheless, he argues that this concept of destiny is not destructive of free will. Explain how this is possible according to Gyekye, and evaluate his position.

RADICAL FREEDOM

It is not easy to categorize the Russian writer Fyodor Dostoevsky (1821–1881). Generally considered one of the greatest novelist of all times—his novels include *Crime and Punishment* and *The Brothers Karamazov*—his fiction has profound psychological, social, and philosophical merit. The main character in *Notes from the Underground,* from which this selection is taken, is an isolated, alienated, and self-avowedly spiteful and perverse individual who spends the first part of this work alternatively engaging in philosophical reflections and taunting a reader who, as far as he is concerned, does not exist. It is his philosophical musings that concern us in this section, but they cannot be entirely divorced from the character he creates.

The key claim made by this "underground" man is that what is most important to human beings is the assumption of a radical freedom—a freedom that challenges natural laws, reason, and even enlightened self-interest. Throughout history, he asserts, "men, *consciously,* that is, fully understanding their real interests, have left them in the background and have rushed headlong on another path." This is because human beings will not (and must not) allow themselves to become the object of scientific laws or mathematical predictions, for then they would be, in his words, mere "piano-keys" and "organ-stops." If human desires can be determined by the precision of a mathematical formula, they lose their quality as desires, as life can be predicted and plotted in advance. Human beings will do anything, he insists, to assert their freedom of will, even what is injurious and stupid "in order to have the right to desire for himself even what is stupid." This is why, in the last analysis, Dostoevsky believes that social reform is at best useless and more often pernicious. He decries the "Palace of Crystal," a phrase that refers to Russian proponents of utopian socialist ideas. Dostoevsky's specific target was the literary critic and novelist N. G. Chernyshevsky, whose novel *What Is to Be Done?* inspired Vladimir I. Lenin to write a revolutionary treatise of the same name.

Dostoevsky's ideas can be appreciated as an overture to the more systematic view of human freedom proposed by the French existentialist philosopher and novelist Jean-Paul Sartre (1905–1980). For Sartre, as for Dostoevsky, freedom is absolute and entails an absolute responsibility. This aspect of Sartre's position is expressed forcefully in the selection in Chapter 4. The selection that we are now going to consider comes from his major work *Being and Nothingness* and is an attempt to analyze the nature of choice and to demonstrate how it is possible for our choices to be absolutely free.

Sartre's position rests on his claim about how motives are formed. Our actions, he acknowledges, are always determined in the sense that they have motives. But it is human consciousness that freely creates these motives. Our choices are free, not in the sense that they are unconnected to our motives, but insofar as consciousness, which always operates "for-itself," has the power to withdraw from what *is,* the "in-itself," at any moment, to recognize that something is lacking in the present state of affairs, and, thus, to present this "negation" as a motive for action. Since, according to this view, it is the absence of something rather than its presence that motivates us, no existing state of affairs can be said to cause my actions. However, in contrast to Dostoevsky's analysis of freedom as pure capriciousness, this does not mean that my choices are arbitrary and that they have no relation to my character or to my past experience; for each individual choice is part of an ensemble of choices, of the sum of my projects which form an organic totality. This ensemble, this totality, must, in turn, be referred to my original project of being who I am; and this original project is itself a choice that relates my consciousness to my body and both my consciousness and my body to the world and to other persons. It is the fundamental choice of my "being-in-the-world." As I am always free to make a new fundamental choice, I am ultimately free to reconstruct myself.

NOTES FROM THE UNDERGROUND[1]

Fyodor Dostoevsky

I am a sick man . . . I am a spiteful man. I am an unattractive man. I believe my liver is diseased. However, I know nothing at all about my disease, and do not know for certain what ails me. I don't consult a doctor for it, and never have, though I have a respect for medicine and doctors. Besides, I am extremely superstitious, sufficiently so to respect medicine, anyway (I am well-educated enough not to be superstitious, but I am superstitious). No, I refuse to consult a doctor from spite. That you probably will not understand. Well, I understand it, though. Of course, I can't explain who it is precisely that I am mortifying in this case by my spite: I am perfectly well aware that I cannot "pay out" the doctors by not consulting them; I know better than any one that by all this I am only injuring myself and no one else. But still, if I don't consult a doctor it is from spite. My liver is bad, well—let it get worse!

I have been going on like that for a long time—twenty years. Now I am forty. I used to be in the government service, but am no longer. I was a spiteful official. I was rude and took pleasure in being so. I did not take bribes, you see, so I was bound to find a recompense in that, at least. (A poor jest, but I will not scratch it out. I wrote it thinking it would sound very witty; but now that I have seen myself

that I only wanted to show off in a despicable way, I will not scratch it out on purpose!)

• • •

I was lying when I said just now that I was a spiteful official. I was lying from spite. I was simply amusing myself with the petitioners and with the officer, and in reality I never could become spiteful. I was conscious every moment in myself of many, very many elements absolutely opposite to that. I felt them positively swarming in me, these opposite elements. I knew that they had been swarming in me all my life and craving some outlet from me, but I would not let them, would not let them, purposely would not let them come out. They tormented me till I was ashamed: they drove me to convulsions and—sickened me, at last, how they sickened me! Now, are not you fancying, gentlemen, that I am expressing remorse for something now, that I am asking your forgiveness for something? I am sure you are fancying that . . . However, I assure you I do not care if you are . . .

It was not only that I could not become spiteful, I did not know how to become anything: neither spiteful nor kind, neither a rascal nor an honest man, neither a hero nor an insect. Now, I am living out my life in my corner, taunting myself with the spiteful and useless consolation that an intelligent man cannot become anything seriously, and it is only the fool who becomes anything. Yes, a man in the nineteenth century must and morally ought to be pre-eminently a characterless creature; a man of character, an active man, is pre-eminently a limited creature. That is my conviction of forty years. I am forty years old now, and you know forty years is a whole lifetime; you know it is extreme old age. To live longer than forty years is bad manners, is vulgar, immoral. Who does live beyond forty? Answer that, sincerely and honestly. I will tell you who do: fools and worthless fellows. I tell all old men that to their face, all these venerable old men, all these silver-haired and reverend seniors! I tell the whole world that to its face. I have a right to say so, for I shall go on living to sixty myself. To seventy! To eighty! . . . Stay, let me take breath . . .

---

[1]The author of the diary and the diary itself are, of course, imaginary. Nevertheless it is clear that such persons as the writer of these notes not only may, but positively must, exist in our society, when we consider the circumstances in the midst of which our society is formed. I have tried to expose to the view of the public more distinctly than is commonly done one of the characters of the recent past. He is one of the representatives of a generation still living. In this fragment, entitled "Underground," this person introduces himself and his views, and, as it were, tries to explain the causes owing to which he has made his appearance and was bound to make his appearance in our midst. In the second fragment there are added the actual notes of this person concerning certain events in his life. —AUTHOR'S NOTE.

You imagine no doubt, gentlemen, that I want to amuse you. You are mistaken in that, too, I am by no means such a mirthful person as you imagine, or as you may imagine; however, irritated by all this babble (and I feel that you are irritated) you think fit to ask me who am I—then my answer is, I am a collegiate assessor. I was in the service that I might have something to eat (and solely for that reason), and when last year a distant relation left me six thousand roubles in his will I immediately retired from the service and settled down in my corner. I used to live in this corner before, but now I have settled down in it. My room is a wretched, horrid one in the outskirts of the town. My servant is an old country-woman, ill-natured from stupidity, and, moreover, there is always a nasty smell about her. I am told that the Petersburg climate is bad for me, and that with my small means it is very expensive to live in Petersburg. I know all that better than all these sage and experienced counsellors and monitors . . . But I am remaining in Petersburg; I am not going away from Petersburg! I am not going away because . . . ech! Why, it is absolutely no matter whether I am going away or not going away.

But what can a decent man speak of with most
    pleasure?

Answer: Of himself.

Well, so I will talk about myself.

I want now to tell you, gentlemen, whether you care to hear it or not, why I could not even become an insect. I tell you solemnly, that I have many times tried to become an insect. But I was not equal even to that. I swear, gentlemen, that to be too conscious is an illness—a real thorough-going illness. For man's everyday needs, it would have been quite enough to have the ordinary human consciousness, that is, half or a quarter of the amount which falls to the lot of a cultivated man of our unhappy nineteenth century, especially one who has the fatal ill-luck to inhabit Petersburg, the most theoretical and intentional town on the whole terrestrial globe. (There are intentional and unintentional towns.) It would have been quite enough, for instance, to have the consciousness by which all so-called direct persons and men of action live. I bet you think I am

writing all this from affectation, to be witty at the expense of men of action; and what is more, that from ill-bred affectation, I am clanking a sword like my officer. But, gentlemen, whoever can pride himself on his diseases and even swagger over them?

Though, after all, every one does do that; people do pride themselves on their diseases, and I do, may be, more than any one. We will not dispute it; my contention was absurd. But yet I am firmly persuaded that a great deal of consciousness, every sort of consciousness, in fact, is a disease. I stick to that. Let us leave that, too, for a minute. Tell me this: why does it happen that at the very, yes, at the very moments when I am most capable of feeling every refinement of all that is "good and beautiful," as they used to say at one time, it would, as though of design, happen to me not only to feel but to do such ugly things, such that . . . Well, in short, actions that all, perhaps, commit; but which, as though purposely, occurred to me at the very time when I was most conscious that they ought not to be committed. The more conscious I was of goodness and of all that was "good and beautiful," the more deeply I sank into my mire and the more ready I was to sink in it altogether. But the chief point was that all this was, as it were, not accidental in me, but as though it were bound to be so. It was as though it were my most normal condition, and not in the least disease or depravity, so that at last all desire in me to struggle against this depravity passed. It ended by my almost believing (perhaps actually believing) that this was perhaps my normal condition. But at first, in the beginning, what agonies I endured in that struggle! I did not believe it was the same with other people, and all my life I hid this fact about myself as a secret. I was ashamed (even now, perhaps, I am ashamed): I got to the point of feeling a sort of secret abnormal, despicable enjoyment in returning home to my corner on some disgusting Petersburg night, acutely conscious that that day I had committed a loathsome action again, that what was done could never be undone, and secretly, inwardly gnawing, gnawing at myself for it, tearing and consuming myself till at last the bitterness turned into a sort of shameful accursed sweetness, and at last—

into positive real enjoyment! Yes, into enjoyment, into enjoyment! I insist upon that. I have spoken of this because I keep wanting to know for a fact whether other people feel such enjoyment. I will explain: the enjoyment was just from the too intense consciousness of one's own degradation; it was from feeling oneself that one had reached the last barrier, that it was horrible, but that it could not be otherwise; that there was no escape for you; that you never could become a different man; that even if time and faith were still left you to change into something different you would most likely not wish to change; or if you did wish to, even then you would do nothing; because perhaps in reality there was nothing for you to change into.

And the worst of it was, and the root of it all, that it was all in accord with the normal fundamental laws of overacute consciousness, and with the inertia that was the direct result of those laws, and that consequently one was not only unable to change but could do absolutely nothing. Thus it would follow, as the result of acute consciousness, that one is not to blame in being a scoundrel; as though that were any consolation to the scoundrel once he has come to realize that he actually is a scoundrel. But enough . . . Ech, I have talked a lot of nonsense, but what have I explained? How is enjoyment in this to be explained? But I will explain it. I will get to the bottom of it! That is why I have taken up my pen. . .

· · ·

But these are all golden dreams. Oh, tell me, who was it first announced, who was it first proclaimed, that man only does nasty things because he does not know his own interests; and that if he were enlightened, if his eyes were opened to his real normal interests, man would at once cease to do nasty things, would at once become good and noble because, being enlightened and understanding his real advantage, he would see his own advantage in the good and nothing else, and we all know that not one man can, consciously, act against his own interests, consequently, so to say, through necessity, he would begin doing good? Oh, the babe! Oh, the pure, innocent child! Why, in the first place, when in all

these thousands of years has there been a time when man has acted only from his own interest? What is to be done with the millions of facts that bear witness that men, *consciously,* that is, fully understanding their real interests, have left them in the background and have rushed headlong on another path, to meet peril and danger, compelled to this course by nobody and by nothing, but, as it were, simply disliking the beaten track, and have obstinately, willfully, struck out another difficult, absurd way, seeking it almost in the darkness. So, I suppose, this obstinacy and perversity were pleasanter to them than any advantage . . . Advantage! What is advantage?

And will you take it upon yourself to define with perfect accuracy in what the advantage of man consists? And what if it so happens that a man's advantage, *sometimes,* not only may, but even must, consist in his desiring in certain cases what is harmful to himself and not advantageous. And if so, there can be such a case, the whole principle falls into dust. What do you think—are there such cases? You laugh; laugh away, gentlemen, but only answer me: have man's advantages been reckoned up with perfect certainty? Are there not some which not only have not been included but cannot possibly be included under any classification? You see, you gentlemen have, to the best of my knowledge, taken your whole register of human advantages from the averages of statistical figures and politico-economical formulas. Your advantages are prosperity, wealth, freedom, peace—and so on, and so on. So that the man who should, for instance, go openly and knowingly in opposition to all that list would, to your thinking, and indeed mine too, of course, be an obscurantist or an absolute madman: would not he? But, you know, this is what is surprising: why does it so happen that all these statisticians, sages and lovers of humanity, when they reckon up human advantages invariably leave out one? They don't even take it into their reckoning in the form in which it should be taken and the whole reckoning depends upon that. It would be no great matter, they would simply have to take it, this advantage, and add it to the list. But the trouble is, that this strange advantage does not fall under any classification and is not in place in any list. I have a friend for instance . . . Ech! gentlemen, but of course he is your friend, too; and indeed there is no one, no one, to whom he is not a friend!

When he prepares for any undertaking this gentleman immediately explains to you, elegantly and clearly, exactly how he must act in accordance with the laws of reason and truth. What is more, he will talk to you with excitement and passion of the true normal interests of man; with irony he will upbraid the short-sighted fools who do not understand their own interests, nor the true significance of virtue; and, within a quarter of an hour, without any sudden outside provocation, but simply through something inside him which is stronger than all his interests, he will go off on quite a different tack—that is, act in direct opposition to what he has just been saying about himself, in opposition to the laws of reason, in opposition to his own advantage—in fact, in opposition to everything . . . I warn you that my friend is a compound personality, and therefore it is difficult to blame him as an individual. The fact is, gentlemen, it seems there must really exist something that is dearer to almost every man than his greatest advantages, or (not to be illogical) there is a most advantageous advantage (the very one omitted of which we spoke just now) which is more important and more advantageous than all other advantages, for the sake of which a man if necessary is ready to act in opposition to all laws; that is, in opposition to reason, honour, peace, prosperity—in fact, in opposition to all those excellent and useful things if only he can attain that fundamental, most advantageous advantage which is dearer to him than all. "Yes, but it's advantage all the same" you will retort. But excuse me, I'll make the point clear, and it is not a case of playing upon words. What matters is, that this advantage is remarkable from the very fact that it breaks down all our classifications, and continually shatters every system constructed by lovers of mankind for the benefit of mankind. In fact, it upsets everything. But before I mention this advantage to you, I want to compromise myself personally, and therefore I boldly declare that all these fine systems—all these theories for explaining to mankind their real normal interests, in order that inevitably striving to pursue these interests they may at once become good and noble—are, in my opinion, so far, mere logical exercises! Yes, logical exercises. Why, to maintain this theory of the regeneration of mankind by means of the pursuit of his own advantage is to my mind almost the same thing as . . . as to affirm, for instance, following Buckle, that through civilization mankind becomes softer, and consequently less bloodthirsty, and less fitted for warfare.

Logically it does seem to follow from his arguments. But man has such a predilection for systems and abstract deductions that he is ready to distort the truth intentionally, he is ready to deny the evidence of his senses only to justify his logic. I take this example because it is the most glaring instance of it. Only look about you: blood is being spilt in streams, and in the merriest way, as though it were champagne. Take the whole of the nineteenth century in which Buckle lived. Take Napoleon—the Great and also the present one. Take North America—the eternal union. Take the farce of Schleswig-Holstein[2] . . . And what is it that civilization softens in us? The only gain of civilization for mankind is the greater capacity for variety of sensations—and absolutely nothing more. And through the development of this many-sidedness man may come to finding enjoyment in bloodshed. In fact, this has already happened to him. Have you noticed that it is the most civilized gentlemen who have been the subtlest slaughterers, to whom the Attilas and Stenka Razins could not hold a candle, and if they are not so conspicuous as the Attilas and Stenka Razins it is simply because they are so often met with, are so ordinary and have become so familiar to us. In any case civilization has made mankind if not more bloodthirsty, at least more vilely, more loathsomely blood-thirsty. In old days he saw justice in bloodshed and with his conscience at peace

---

[2]The nineteenth-century controversy about the status of the territories of Schleswig and Holstein led to two German-Danish wars (Eds.).

exterminated those he thought proper. Now we do think bloodshed abominable and yet we engage in this abomination, and with more energy than ever. Which is worse? Decide that for yourselves.

They say that Cleopatra (excuse an instance from Roman history) was fond of sticking gold pins into her slave-girls' breasts and derived gratification from their screams and writhings. You will say that that was in the comparatively barbarous times; that these are barbarous times too, because also, comparatively speaking, pins are stuck in even now; that though man has now learned to see more clearly than in barbarous ages, he is still far from having learnt to act as reason and science would dictate. But yet you are fully convinced that he will be sure to learn when he gets rid of certain old bad habits, and when common sense and science have completely re-educated human nature and turned it in a normal direction. You are confident that then man will cease from *intentional* error and will, so to say, be compelled not to want to set his will against his normal interests. That is not all; then, you say, science itself will teach man (though to my mind it's a superfluous luxury) that he never has really had any caprice or will of his own, and that he himself is something of the nature of a piano-key or the stop of an organ, and that there are, besides, things called the laws of nature; so that everything he does is not done by his willing it, but is done of itself, by the laws of nature. Consequently we have only to discover these laws of nature, and man will no longer have to answer for his actions and life will become exceedingly easy for him. All human actions will then, of course, be tabulated according to these laws, mathematically, like tables of logarithms up to 108,000, and entered in an index; or, better still, there would be published certain edifying works of the nature of encyclopaedic lexicons, in which everything will be so clearly calculated and explained that there will be no more incidents or adventures in the world.

Then—this is all what you say—new economic relations will be established, all ready-made and worked out with mathematical exactitude, so that every possible question will vanish in the twinkling of an eye, simply because every possible answer to it will be provided. Then the "Palace of Crystal" will be built. Then . . . In fact, those will be halcyon days. Of course there is no guaranteeing (this is my comment) that it will not be, for instance, frightfully dull then (for what will one have to do when everything will be calculated and tabulated?), but on the other hand everything will be extraordinarily rational. Of course boredom may lead you to anything. It is boredom sets one sticking golden pins into people, but all that would not matter. What is bad (this is my comment again) is that I dare say people will be thankful for the gold pins then. Man is stupid, you know, phenomenally stupid; or rather he is not at all stupid, but he is so ungrateful that you could not find another like him in all creation. I, for instance, would not be in the least surprised if all of a sudden, apropos of nothing, in the midst of general prosperity a gentleman with an ignoble, or rather with a reactionary and ironical, countenance were to arise and putting his arms akimbo, say to us all: "I say, gentlemen, hadn't we better kick over the whole show and scatter rationalism to the winds, simply to send these logarithms to the devil, and to enable us to live once more at our own sweet foolish will!" That again would not matter; but what is annoying is that he would be sure to find followers—such is the nature of man. And all that for the most foolish reason, which, one would think, was hardly worth mentioning: that is, that man everywhere and at all times, whoever he may be, has preferred to act as he chose and not in the least as his reason and advantage dictated. And one may choose what is contrary to one's own interests, and sometimes one *positively ought* (that is my idea). One's own free unfettered choice, one's own caprice—however wild it may be, one's own fancy worked up at times to frenzy—is that very "most advantageous advantage" which we have overlooked, which comes under no classification and against which all systems and theories are continually being shattered to atoms. And how do these wiseacres know that man wants a normal, a virtuous choice? What has made them conceive that man must want a rationally advantageous choice? What man wants is simply *independent* choice, whatever that independence may cost and wherever it may lead. And choice, of course, the devil only knows what choice . . .

"Ha! ha! ha! But you know there is no such thing as choice in reality, say what you like," you will interpose with a chuckle. "Science has succeeded in so far analyzing man that we know already that choice and what is called freedom of will is nothing else than—"

Stay, gentlemen, I meant to begin with that myself. I confess, I was rather frightened. I was just going to say that the devil only knows what choice depends on, and that perhaps that was a very good thing, but I remembered the teaching of science . . . and pulled myself up. And here you have begun upon it. Indeed, if there really is some day discovered a formula for all our desires and caprices—that is, an explanation of what they depend upon, by what laws they arise, how they develop, what they are aiming at in one case and in another and so on, that is, a real mathematical formula—then, most likely, man will at once cease to feel desire, indeed, he will be certain to. For who would want to choose by rule? Besides, he will at once be transformed from a human being into an organ-stop or something of the sort; for what is a man without desires, without free will and without choice, if not a stop in an organ? What do you think? Let us reckon the chances—can such a thing happen or not?

"H'm!" you decide. "Our choice is usually mistaken from a false view of our advantage. We sometimes choose absolute nonsense because in our foolishness we see in that nonsense the easiest means for attaining a supposed advantage. But when all that is explained and worked out on paper (which is perfectly possible, for it is contemptible and senseless to suppose that some laws of nature man will never understand), then certainly so-called desires will no longer exist. For if a desire should come into conflict with reason we shall then reason and not desire, because it will be impossible retaining our reason to be *senseless* in our desires, and in that way knowingly act against reason and desire to injure ourselves. And as all choice and reasoning can be really calculated—because there will some day be discovered the laws of our so-called free will—so, joking apart, there may one day be something like a table constructed of them, so that we really shall choose in accordance with it. If, for instance, some day they calculate and prove to me that I made a long nose at some one because I could not help making a long nose at him and that I had to do it in that particular way, what *freedom* is left me, especially if I am a learned man and have taken my degree somewhere? Then I should be able to calculate my whole life for thirty years beforehand. In short, if this could be arranged there would be nothing left for us to do; anyway, we should have to understand that. And, in fact, we ought unwearyingly to repeat to ourselves that at such and such a time and in such and such circumstances Nature does not ask our leave; that we have got to take her as she is and not fashion her to suit our fancy, and if we really aspire to formulas and tables of rules, and well, even . . . to the chemical retort, there's no help for it, we must accept the retort too, or else it will be accepted without our consent . . ."

Yes, but here I come to a stop! Gentlemen, you must excuse me for being over-philosophical; it's the result of forty years underground! Allow me to indulge my fancy. You see, gentlemen, reason is an excellent thing, there's no disputing that, but reason is nothing but reason and satisfies only the rational side of man's nature, while will is a manifestation of the whole life, that is, of the whole human life including reason and all the impulses. And although our life, in this manifestation of it, is often worthless, yet it is life and not simply extracting square roots. Here I, for instance, quite naturally want to live, in order to satisfy all my capacities for life, and not simply my capacity for reasoning, that is, not simply one-twentieth of my capacity for life. What does reason know? Reason only knows what it has succeeded in learning (some things, perhaps, it will never learn; this is a poor comfort, but why not say so frankly?) and human nature acts as a whole, with everything that is in it, consciously or unconsciously, and, even if it goes wrong, it lives. I suspect, gentlemen, that you are looking at me with compassion; you tell me again that an enlightened and developed man, such, in short, as the future man will be, cannot consciously desire anything disadvantageous to himself, that that can be proved mathematically. I thoroughly agree, it can—by mathematics.

But I repeat for the hundredth time, there is one case, one only, when man may consciously, purposely, desire what is injurious to himself, what is stupid, very stupid—simply in order to have the right to desire for himself even what is very stupid and not to be bound by an obligation to desire only what is sensible. Of course, this very stupid thing, this caprice of ours, may be in reality, gentlemen, more advantageous for us than anything else on earth, especially in certain cases. And in particular it may be more advantageous than any advantage even when it does us obvious harm, and contradicts the soundest conclusions of our reason concerning our advantage—for in any circumstances it preserves for us what is most precious and most important—that is, our personality, our individuality. Some, you see, maintain that this really is the most precious thing for mankind; choice can, of course, if it chooses, be in agreement with reason; and especially if this be not abused but kept within bounds. It is profitable and sometimes even praiseworthy. But very often, and even most often, choice is utterly and stubbornly opposed to reason . . . and . . . and . . . Do you know that that, too, is profitable, sometimes even praiseworthy? Gentlemen, let us suppose that man is not stupid. (Indeed one cannot refuse to suppose that, if only from the one consideration, that, if man is stupid, then who is wise?) But if he is not stupid, he is monstrously ungrateful! Phenomenally ungrateful. In fact, I believe that the best definition of man is the ungrateful biped. But that is not all, that is not his worst defect; his worst defect is his perpetual moral obliquity, perpetual—from the days of the Flood to the Schleswig-Holstein period.

Moral obliquity and consequently lack of good sense; for it has long been accepted that lack of good sense is due to no other cause than moral obliquity. Put it to the test and cast your eyes upon the history of mankind. What will you see? Is it a grand spectacle? Grand, if you like. Take the Colossus of Rhodes,[3] for instance, that's worth something. With good reason Mr. Anaevsky testifies of it that some say that it is the work of man's hands, while others maintain that it has been created by Nature herself. Is it many-coloured? It may be it is many-coloured, too: if one takes the dress uniforms, military and civilian, of all peoples in all ages—that alone is worth something, and if you take the undress uniforms you will never get to the end of it; no historian would be equal to the job. Is it monotonous? It may be it's monotonous too: it's fighting and fighting; they are fighting now, they fought first and they fought last—you will admit that it is almost too monotonous. In short, one may say anything about the history of the world—anything that might enter the most disordered imagination.

The only thing one can't say is that it's rational. The very word sticks in one's throat. And, indeed, this is the odd thing that is continually happening; there are continually turning up in life moral and rational persons, sages and lovers of humanity, who make it their object to live all their lives as morally and rationally as possible, to be, so to speak, a light to their neighbours simply in order to show them that it is possible to live morally and rationally in this world. And yet we all know that those very people sooner or later have been false to themselves, playing some queer trick, often a most unseemly one. Now I ask you: what can be expected of man since he is a being endowed with such strange qualities? Shower upon him every earthly blessing, drown him in a sea of happiness, so that nothing but bubbles of bliss can be seen on the surface; give him economic prosperity, such that he should have nothing else to do but sleep, eat cakes and busy himself with the continuation of his species, and even then out of sheer ingratitude, sheer spite, man would play you some nasty trick. He would even risk his cakes and would

---

[3]The *Colossus of Rhodes* was a bronze statue over 100 feet high representing the ancient sun god Helios. It took twelve years to build (292–280 B.C.E.) and commemorated the raising of the siege in Rhodes twelve years earlier (Eds.).

deliberately desire the most fatal rubbish, the most uneconomical absurdity, simply to introduce into all this positive good sense his fatal fantastic element. It is just his fantastic dreams, his vulgar folly, that he will desire to retain, simply in order to prove to himself—as though that were so necessary—that men still are men and not the keys of a piano, which the laws of nature threaten to control so completely that soon one will be able to desire nothing but by the calendar. And that is not all: even if man really were nothing but a piano-key, even if this were proved to him by natural science and mathematics, even then he would not become reasonable, but would purposely do something perverse out of simple ingratitude, simply to gain his point. And if he does not find means he will contrive destruction and chaos, will contrive sufferings of all sorts, only to gain his point! He will launch a curse upon the world, and as only man can curse (it is his privilege, the primary distinction between him and other animals) it may be by his curse alone he will attain his object—that is, convince himself that he is a man and not a piano-key! If you say that all this, too, can be calculated and tabulated—chaos and darkness and curses, so that the mere possibility of calculating it all beforehand would stop it all, and reason would reassert itself—then man would purposely go mad in order to be rid of reason and gain his point! I believe in it, I answer for it, for the whole work of man really seems to consist in nothing but proving to himself every minute that he is a man and not a piano-key! It may be at the cost of his skin, it may be by cannibalism! And this being so, can one help being tempted to rejoice that it has not yet come off, and that desire still depends on something we don't know?

You will scream at me (that is, if you condescend to do so) that no one is touching my free will, that all they are concerned with is that my will should of itself, of its own free will, coincide with my own normal interests, with the laws of nature and arithmetic.

Good heavens, gentlemen, what sort of free will is left when we come to tabulation and arithmetic, when it will all be a case of twice two makes four? Twice two makes four without my will. As if free will meant that!

FREEDOM AND ACTION

Jean-Paul Sartre

It is strange that philosophers have been able to argue endlessly about determinism and free-will, to cite examples in favor of one or the other thesis without ever attempting first to make explicit the structures contained in the very idea of *action*. The concept of an act contains, in fact, numerous subordinate notions which we shall have to organize and arrange in a hierarchy: to act is to modify the *shape* of the world; it is to arrange means in view of an end; it is to produce an organized instrumental complex such that by a series of concatenations and connections the modification effected on one of the links causes modifications throughout the whole series and finally produces an anticipated result. But this is not what is important for us here. We should observe first that an action is on principle *intentional*. The careless smoker who has through negligence caused the explosion of a powder magazine has not *acted*. On the other hand the worker who is charged with dynamiting a quarry and who obeys the given orders has acted when he has produced the expected explosion; he knew what he was doing or, if you prefer, he intentionally realized a conscious project.

This does not mean, of course, that one must foresee all the consequences of his act. The emperor Constantine when he established himself at Byzantium, did not foresee that he would create a center of Greek culture and language, the appearance of which would ultimately provoke a schism in the Christian Church and which would contribute to weakening the Roman Empire. Yet he performed an act just in so far as he realized his project of creating a new residence for emperors in the Orient. Equating the result with the intention is here sufficient for us to be able to speak of action. But if this is the case, we establish that the action necessarily implies as its condition the recognition of a "desideratum"; that is, of an objective lack or again of a *négatité*.[1] The *intention* of providing a rival for Rome can come to Constantine only through the apprehension of an objective lack: Rome lacks a counterweight; to this still profoundly pagan city ought to be opposed a Christian city which at the moment is *missing*. Creating Constantinople is understood as an *act* only if first the conception of a new city has preceded the action itself or at least if this conception serves as an organizing theme for all later steps. But this conception can not be the pure representation of the city as *possible*. It apprehends the city in its essential characteristic, which is to be a *desirable* and not yet realized possible.

• • •

In so far as man is immersed in the historical situation, he does not even succeed in conceiving of the failures and lacks in a political organization or determined economy; this is not, as is stupidly said, because he "is accustomed to it," but because he apprehends it in its plenitude of being and because he can not even imagine that he can exist in it otherwise. For it is necessary here to reverse common opinion and on the basis of what it is not, to acknowledge the harshness of a situation or the sufferings which it imposes, both of which are motives for conceiving of another state of affairs in which things would be better for everybody. It is on the day that we can conceive of a different state of affairs that a new light falls on our troubles and our suffering and that we *decide* that these are unbearable. A worker in 1830 is capable of revolting if his salary is lowered, for he easily conceives of a situation in which his wretched standard of living would be not as low as the one which is about to be imposed on him. But he does not represent his sufferings to himself as unbearable; he adapts himself to them not through resignation but because he lacks the education and reflection necessary for him to conceive of a social state in which these sufferings would not exist. Consequently *he does not act*. Masters of

Lyon following a riot, the workers at Croix-Rousse do not know what to do with their victory; they return home bewildered, and the regular army has no trouble in overcoming them. Their misfortunes do not appear to them "habitual" but rather *natural;* they *are,* that is all, and they constitute the worker's condition. They are not detached; they are not seen in the clear light of day, and consequently they are integrated by the worker with his being. He suffers without considering his suffering and without conferring value upon it. To suffer and to *be* are one and the same for him. His suffering is the pure affective tenor of his nonpositional consciousness, but he does not *contemplate* it. Therefore this suffering can not be in itself a *motive* for his acts. Quite the contrary, it is after he has formed the project of changing the situation that it will appear intolerable to him. This means that he will have to give himself room, to withdraw in relation to it, and will have to have effected a double nihilation: on the one hand, he must posit an ideal state of affairs as a pure *present* nothingness; on the other hand, he must posit the actual situation as nothingness in relation to this state of affairs. He will have to conceive of a happiness attached to his class as a pure possible—that is, presently as a certain nothingness—and on the other hand, he will return to the present situation in order to illuminate it in the light of this nothingness and in order to nihilate it in turn by declaring: "I *am not* happy."

Two important consequences result. (1) No factual state whatever it may be (the political and economic structure of society, the psychological "state," *etc.*) is capable by itself of motivating any act whatsoever. For an act is a projection of the for-itself toward what is not, and what is can in no way determine by itself what is not. (2) No factual state can determine consciousness to apprehend it as a *négatité* or as a lack.

• • •

This means evidently that it is by a pure wrenching away from himself and the world that the worker can posit his suffering as unbearable suffering and consequently can *make of it the motive* for his revolutionary action. This implies for consciousness the permanent possibility of effecting a

---

[1]*Négatité* is Sartre's word for what is experienced as lacking or absent in the situation, e.g., that which is desired but does not exist (Eds.).

rupture with its own past, of wrenching itself away from its past so as to be able to consider it in the light of a non-being and so as to be able to confer on it the meaning which *it has* in terms of the project of a meaning which it *does not have.*

• • •

Does this mean that one must view freedom as a series of carpricious jerks comparable to the Epicurean clinamen? Am I free to wish anything whatsoever at any moment whatsoever? And must I at each instant when I wish to explain this or that project encounter the irrationality of a free and contingent choice? Inasmuch as it has seemed that the recognition of freedom had as its consequence these dangerous conceptions which are completely contradictory to experience, worthy thinkers have turned away from a belief in freedom. One could even state that determinism—if one were careful not to confuse it with fatalism—is "more human" than the theory of free will. In fact while determinism throws into relief the strict conditioning of our acts, it does at least give the *reason* for each of them. And if it is strictly limited to the psychic, if it gives up looking for a conditioning in the ensemble of the universe, it shows that the reason for our acts is in ourselves: we act as we are, and our acts contribute to making us.

• • •

Thus we do not intend here to speak of anything arbitrary or capricious. An existent which as consciousness is necessarily separated from all others because they are in connection with it only to the extent that they are *for it,* an existent which decides its past in the form of a tradition in the light of its future instead of allowing it purely and simply to determine its present, an existent which makes known to itself what it is by means of *something other than it* (that is, by an end which it is not and which it projects from the other side of the world)—that is what we call a free existent. This does not mean that I am free to get up or to sit down, to enter or to go out, to flee or to face danger—if one means by freedom here a pure capricious, unlawful, gratuitous, and in-

comprehensible contingency. To be sure, each one of my acts, even the most trivial, is entirely free in the sense which we have just defined; but this does not mean that my act can be anything *whatsoever* or even that it is *unforeseeable.* Someone, nevertheless may object and ask how if my act can be understood *neither* in terms of the state of the world *nor* in terms of the ensemble of my past taken as an irremediable thing, it could possibly be anything but gratuitous. Let us look more closely.

Common opinion does not hold that to be free means only to choose oneself. A choice is said to be free if it is such that it could have been other than what it is. I start out on a hike with friends. At the end of several hours of walking my fatigue increases and finally becomes very painful. At first I resist and then suddenly I let myself go, I give up, I throw my knapsack down on the side of the road and let myself fall down beside it. Someone will reproach me for my act and will mean thereby that I was free— that is, not only was my act not determined by any thing or person, but also I could have succeeded in resisting my fatigue longer, I could have done as my companions did and reached the resting place before relaxing. I shall defend myself by saying that I was *too tired.* Who is right? Or rather is the debate not based on incorrect premises? There is no doubt that I could have done otherwise, but that is not the problem. It ought to be formulated rather like this: could I have done otherwise without perceptibly modifying the organic totality of the projects which I am; or is the fact of resisting my fatigue such that instead of remaining a purely local and accidental modification of my behavior, it could be effected only by means of a radical transformation of my being-in-the-world—a transformation, moreover, which is *possible?* In other words: I could have done otherwise. Agreed, But *at what price?*

We are going to reply to this question by first presenting a *theoretical* description which will enable us to grasp the principle of our thesis. We shall see subsequently whether the concrete reality is not shown to be more complex and whether without contradicting the results of our theoretical inquiry, it will not lead us to enrich them and make them more flexible.

Let us note first that the fatigue by itself could not provoke my decision. As we saw with respect to physical pain, fatigue is only the way in which I exist my body.[2] It is not at first the object of a positional consciousness,[3] but it is the very facticity of my consciousness. If then I hike across the country, what is revealed to me is the surrounding world; this is the object of my consciousness, and this is what I transcend toward possibilities which are my own—those, for example, of arriving this evening at the place which I have set for myself in advance. Yet to the extent that I apprehend this countryside with my eyes which unfold distances, my legs which climb the hills and consequently cause new sights and new obstacles to appear and disappear, with my back which carries the knapsack—to this extent I have a non-positional consciousness (of) this body which rules my relations with the world and which signifies my engagement in the world, in the form of fatigue. Objectively and in correlation with this non-thetic consciousness the roads are revealed as interminable, the slopes as *steeper,* the sun as more burning, *etc.* But I do not yet *think* of my fatigue; I apprehend it as the quasi-object of my reflection. Nevertheless there comes a moment when I do seek to consider my fatigue and to recover it. We really ought to provide an interpretation for this same intention; however, let us take it for what it is. It is not at all a contemplative apprehension of my fatigue; rather, as we saw with respect to pain, I *suffer* my fatigue. That is, a reflective consciousness is directed upon my fatigue in order to live it and to confer on it a value and a practical relation to myself. It is only on this plane that the fatigue will appear to me as bearable or intolerable. It will never be anything in itself, but it is the reflective For-itself which rising up suffers the fatigue as intolerable.

Here is posited the essential question: my companions are in good health—like me; they have had

practically the same training as I so that although it is not possible to *compare* psychic events which occur in different subjectivities, I usually conclude—and witnesses after an objective consideration of our bodies-for-others conclude—that they are for all practical purposes "as fatigued as I am." How does it happen therefore that they suffer their fatigue differently? Someone will say that the difference stems from the fact that I am a "sissy" and that the others are not. But although this evaluation undeniably has a practical bearing on the case and although one could take this into account when there arose a question of deciding whether or not it would be a good idea to take me on another expedition, such an evaluation can not satisfy us here. We have seen that to be ambitious is to project conquering a throne or honors; it is not a *given* which would incite one to conquest; it is this conquest itself. Similarly to be a "sissy" can not be a factual given and is only a name given to the way in which I suffer my fatigue. If therefore I wish to understand under what conditions I can suffer a fatigue as unbearable, it will not help to address oneself to so-called factual givens, which are revealed as being only a choice; it is necessary to attempt to examine this choice itself and to see whether it is not explained within the perspective of a larger choice in which it would be integrated as a secondary structure. If I question one of my companions, he will explain to me that he is fatigued, of course, but that he *loves* his fatigue; he gives himself up to it as to a bath; it appears to him in some way as the privileged instrument for discovering the world which surrounds him, for adapting himself to the rocky roughness of the paths, for discovering the "mountainous" quality of the slopes. In the same way it is this light sunburn on the back of his neck and this slight ringing in his ears which will enable him to realize a direct contact with the sun. Finally the feeling of effort is for him that of fatigue overcome. But as his fatigue is nothing but the passion which he endures so that the dust of the highways, the burning of the sun, the roughness of the roads may exist to the fullest, his effort (*i.e.,* this sweet familiarity with a fatigue which he loves, to which he abandons himself and

---

[2]Sartre is intentionally using the phrase "*exist my body*" to indicate that I do not exist in my body, for that would mean that I am separate from my body (Eds.).

[3]*Positional consciousness* is consciousness which is aware of itself, according to Sartre. If it is only conscious of any object (and not reflecting upon itself), it is nonpositional consciousness (Eds.).

which nevertheless he himself directs) is given as a way of appropriating the mountain, of suffering it to the end and being victor over it. We shall see in the next chapter what is the meaning of the word *having* and to what extent *doing* is a method of *appropriating*. Thus my companion's fatigue is lived in a vaster project of a trusting abandon to nature, of a passion consented to in order that it may exist at full strength, and at the same time the project of sweet mastery and appropriation. It is only in and through this project that the fatigue will be able to be understood and that it will have meaning for him.

But this meaning and this vaster, more profound project are still by themselves *unselbständig*. They are not sufficient. For they precisely presuppose a particular relation of my companion to his body, on the one hand, and to things, on the other.

• • •

. . . It is evident following our analysis that the way in which my companion *suffers* his fatigue necessarily demands—if we are to understand it—that we undertake a regressive analysis which will lead us back to an initial project. Is this project we have outlined finally *selbständig?* Certainly—and it can be easily proved to be so. In fact by going further and further back we have reached the original relation which the for-itself chooses with its facticity and with the world. But this original relation is nothing other than the for-itself's being-in-the-world inasmuch as this being-in-the-world is a choice—that is, we have reached the original type of nihilation by which the for-itself has to be its own nothingness. No interpretation of this can be attempted, for it would implicitly suppose the being-in-the-world of the for-itself just as all the demonstrations attempted by Euclid's Postulate implicitly suppose the adoption of this postulate.

Therefore if I apply this same method to interpret the way in which I suffer my fatigue, I shall first apprehend in myself a distrust of my body—for example, a way of wishing not "to have anything to do with it," wanting not to take it into account, which is simply one of numerous possible modes in which I can *exist my body*. I shall easily discover an analogous distrust with respect to the in-itself and, for example, an original project for recovering the in-itself which I nihilate *through the intermediacy of others,* which project in turn refers me to one of the initial projects which we enumerated in our preceding discussion. Hence my fatigue instead of being suffered "flexibly" will be grasped "sternly" as an importunate phenomenon which I want to get rid of—and this simply because it incarnates my body and my brute contingency in the midst of the world at a time when my project is to preserve my body and my presence in the world by means of the looks of others. I am referred to myself as well as to my original project; that is, to my being-in-the-world in so far as this being is a choice.

QUESTIONS FOR DISCUSSION

1. Is Dostoevsky's underground man expressing any truths about the human condition (if so, what are they), or is he merely expressing his own very peculiar personality?

2. Analyze Sartre's example of the hiker who says that he is too tired to continue. How does Sartre interpret this situation as an example of freedom? What is your evaluation of Sartre's position?

3. Sartre believes that we are absolutely free in the sense that nothing but our free choices determine what we do and who we are. Do you agree or disagree? In arguing for your own position, use examples from your own life.

CAN WE RECONCILE FREEDOM AND DETERMINISM?

There are two kinds of determinism—often labeled, respectively, "hard" and "soft" determinism. The difference between these two revolves around the problem of moral responsibility. We might recall that for Sartre—in Section Two of this chapter and in Chapter 4—since human beings are free, they must be responsible for their actions. Hard determinism would accept this implication but, insofar as it denies the antecedent, would draw a very different conclusion: since human beings are *not* free, they cannot be held morally responsible for their actions. This implication of determinism might be "hard" to accept, but the hard determinism insists that this is the way things are.

The soft determinist, in contrast, is a determinist who is uncomfortable with the above conclusion. While equally deterministic, soft determinists want to hold human beings morally responsible for their actions. They would also agree that unless human beings are free in a significant sense, they cannot be held responsible. The only possible solution to this dilemma is to claim that while human beings are determined, they are nonetheless free in a sense that is necessary for moral responsibility to exist. Thus, the soft determinist position is often called *compatibilism* or *reconciliationism,* because it takes freedom and moral responsibility to be compatible with determinism, and it claims to reconcile determinism with freedom.

The article by Moritz Schlick is one of the classic attempts to accomplish this task. Moritz Schlick was born in Berlin in 1882 and was shot to death in 1936 by a graduate student to whom he had denied the doctoral degree. Schlick was a founding member of the Vienna Circle, a small group of philosophers that came together in the early 1920s and who formulated a philosophical position that has come to be known as "logical positivism." Logical positivism maintains that philosophy's chief task is to determine the conditions under which statements can be meaningful—in effect, to clarify the meaning or to expose the lack of meaning of a variety of concepts. They claimed that many problems posed by traditional metaphysics turn out, on careful analysis, to be meaningless, hence, pseudoproblems.

In the selection that follows, Schlick analyzes the problem of free will as a pseudoproblem. The opposite of freedom is not determinism, he declares, but rather compulsion. As long as I can act upon my desires, as long as I am free from external compulsion, I have all the freedom I need to be considered morally responsible for my actions. Thus, the opposition "freedom versus determinism" is a pseudo-opposition.

Schlick maintains that psychological laws should not be understood as compelling our actions but simply as describing the desires on the basis of which we act. One possible problem with his analysis is that he does not inquire into the causes of these desires. Specifically, if human actions are motivated by desires, which are themselves determined by forces over which we have no control, then, even in the absence of external constraints, it is difficult to construe them as free actions. In other words, the problem of freedom, then, is not only, as Schlick would have it, the problem of external compulsion, but it is also the problem of internal psychological constraints and their causes. On this analysis, the program of soft determinism—to reconcile determinism and freedom—becomes problematic.

In the second selection of this section, the American philosopher John Hospers challenges Schlick's position in its own terms and argues for a hard determinism grounded in psychoanalytic theory. By appealing to Freud's theory of unconscious motivation, Hospers argues that most, if not all, of our conscious desires, deliberations, and choices are facades for unconscious forces and, therefore, may be properly regarded as *compelled* (from the outside) by those forces. In other words, actions that appear to be free because they are performed in the absence of external physical compulsion are, in fact, psychologically compelled and, therefore, in a deeper sense, not free at all. Insofar as most of our actions are of this sort, it follows that (unconscious) psychological determinism is incompatible with moral freedom; in short, that human beings are neither free nor morally responsible for their actions.

Hospers does, however, make one qualification. Near the end of his article, he briefly suggests another possible criteria for distinguishing between free and unfree acts—freedom is in inverse proportion to one's neuroticism. In this sense of freedom, one may be considered free or unfree by degrees.

Hospers presents a strong case for hard determinism. The next article, by Nancy Holmstrom, who teaches philosophy at Rutgers University, attempts to "firm up" soft determinism by considering different ways in which our beliefs and desires are determined. She recognizes that at the heart of the question of freedom is not only being able to act upon our beliefs and desires but also having control over those beliefs and desires. In other words, soft determinism, in order to make good its compatibilist claim, must show how people can have control over the sources of the beliefs and desires that ultimately motivate them.

In the course of her analysis, Holmstrom indicates how a free action can be distinguished from an action performed as a result of brainwashing, subliminal advertising, and other forms of conditioning in which one's desires are acquired through coercion. The conclusion of her analysis ties the question of human freedom in the philosophical sense to social and political freedom, for only if people have control over the social conditions that shape their desires and beliefs can they be said to have control over their actions.

The last selection offers a very different attempt to reconcile freedom and determinism. Kitaro Nishida, a twentieth-century Japanese philosopher and Zen Buddhist, has attempted to give the Eastern mode of thinking a Western philosophical foundation, in effect, to synthesize the insights of East and West. His *Inquiry into the Good,* from which this selection is taken, is heavily influenced by the phenomenological method.

Nishida criticizes both the notion of an absolute freedom and a mechanical determinism. He criticizes the former because a will without a cause would be unintelligible and would, in any case, not

be felt as free. He criticizes mechanical determinism because consciousness is self-determined; it is not determined from without but is, nonetheless, determined by laws governing its own activity. Consciousness is free not because it acts without reason, not because it determines which ideas will initially arise, but because it can, through synthesizing and analyzing the ideas that do arise, come to know its own reason. Therefore, the more knowledge we have, the freer we become.

FREEDOM AND RESPONSIBILITY

Moritz Schlick

WHEN IS A MAN RESPONSIBLE?

1. The Pseudo-Problem of Freedom of the Will

With hesitation and reluctance I prepare to add this chapter to the discussion of ethical problems. For in it I must speak of a matter which, even at present, is thought to be a fundamental ethical question, but which got into ethics and has become a much discussed problem only because of a misunderstanding. This is the so-called problem of the freedom of the will. Moreover, this pseudo-problem has long since been settled by the efforts of certain sensible persons; and, above all, the state of affairs just described has been often disclosed—with exceptional clarity by Hume. Hence it is really one of the greatest scandals of philosophy that again and again so much paper and printer's ink is devoted to this matter, to say nothing of the expenditure of thought, which could have been applied to more important problems (assuming that it would have sufficed for these). Thus I should truly be ashamed to write a chapter on "freedom." In the chapter heading, the word "responsible" indicates what concerns ethics, and designates the point at which misunderstanding arises. Therefore the concept of responsibility constitutes our theme, and if in the process of its clarification I also must speak of the concept of freedom I shall, of course, say only what others have already said better; consoling myself with the thought that in this way alone can anything be done to put an end at last to that scandal.

• • •

The main task of ethics is to explain moral behavior. To explain means to refer back to laws: every science, including psychology, is possible only in so far as there are such laws to which the events can be referred. Since the assumption that *all* events are subject to universal laws is called the principle of causality, one can also say, "Every science presupposes the principle of causality." Therefore every explanation of human behavior must also assume the validity of causal laws; in this case the existence of psychological laws.

• • •

All of our experience strengthens us in the belief that this presupposition is realized, at least to the extent required for all purposes of practical life in intercourse with nature and human beings, and also for the most precise demands of technique. Whether, indeed, the principle of causality holds universally, whether, that is, *determinism* is true, we do not know; no one knows. But we do know that it is impossible to settle the dispute between determinism and indeterminism by mere reflection and speculation, by the consideration of so many reasons for and so many reasons against (which collectively and individually are but pseudo-reasons). Such an attempt becomes especially ridiculous when one considers with what enormous expenditure of experimental and logical skill contemporary physics carefully approaches the question of whether causality can be maintained for the most minute intra-atomic events.

But the dispute concerning "freedom of the will" generally proceeds in such fashion that its advocates attempt to refute, and its opponents to prove, the validity of the causal principle, both using

hackneyed arguments, and neither in the least abashed by the magnitude of the undertaking.

• • •

Fortunately, it is not necessary to lay claim to a final solution of the causal problem in order to say what is necessary in ethics concerning responsibility; there is required only an analysis of the concept, the careful determination of the meaning which is in fact joined to the words "responsibility" and "freedom" as these are actually used. If men had made clear to themselves the sense of those propositions, which we use in everyday life, that pseudo-argument which lies at the root of the pseudo-problem, and which recurs thousands of times within and outside of philosophical books, would never have arisen.

The argument runs as follows: "If determinism is true, if, that is, all events obey immutable laws, then my will too is always determined, by my innate character and my motives. Hence my decisions are necessary, not free. But if so, then I am not responsible for my acts, for I would be accountable for them only if I could do something about the way my decisions went; but I can do nothing about it, since they proceed with necessity from my character and the motives. And I have made neither, and have no power over them: the motives come from without, and my character is the necessary product of the innate tendencies and the external influences which have been effective during my lifetime. Thus determinism and moral responsibility are incompatible. Moral responsibility presupposes freedom, that is, exemption from causality."

This process of reasoning rests upon a whole series of confusions, just as the links of a chain hang together. We must show these confusions to be such, and thus destroy them.

2. Two Meanings of the Word "Law"

It all begins with an erroneous interpretation of the meaning of "law." In practice this is understood as a rule by which the state prescribes certain behavior to its citizens. These rules often contradict the natural desires of the citizens (for if they did not do so, there would be no reason for making them), and are in fact not followed by many of them; while others obey, but under *compulsion*. The state does in fact compel its citizens by imposing certain sanctions (punishments) which serve to bring their desires into harmony with the prescribed laws.

In natural science, on the other hand, the word "law" means something quite different. The natural law is not a *pre*scription as to how something should behave, but a formula, a *des*cription of how something does in fact behave. The two forms of "laws" have only this in common: both tend to be expressed in *formulae*. Otherwise they have absolutely nothing to do with one another, and it is very blameworthy that the same word has been used for two such different things; but even more so that philosophers have allowed themselves to be led into serious errors by this usage. Since natural laws are only descriptions of what happens, there can be in regard to them no talk of "compulsion." The laws of celestial mechanics do not prescribe to the planets how they have to move, as though the planets would actually like to move quite otherwise, and are only forced by these burdensome laws of Kepler to move in orderly paths; no, these laws do not in any way "compel" the planets, but express only what in fact planets actually do.

If we apply this to volition, we are enlightened at once, even before the other confusions are discovered. When we say that a man's will "obeys psychological laws," these are not civic laws, which compel him to make certain decisions, or dictate desires to him, which he would in fact prefer not to have. They are laws of nature, merely expressing which desires he *actually has* under given conditions; they describe the nature of the will in the same manner as the astronomical laws describe the nature of planets. "Compulsion" occurs where man is prevented from realizing his natural desires. How could the rule according to which these natural desires arise itself be considered as "compulsion"?

3. Compulsion and Necessity

But this is the second confusion to which the first leads almost inevitably: after conceiving the laws of nature, anthropomorphically, as order imposed *nolens*

volens upon the events, one adds to them the concept of "necessity." This word, derived from "need," also comes to us from practice, and is used there in the sense of inescapable compulsion. To apply the word with this meaning to natural laws is of course senseless, for the presupposition of an opposing desire is lacking; and it is then confused with something altogether different, which is actually an attribute of natural laws. That is, universality. It is of the essence of natural laws to be universally valid, for only when we have found a rule which holds of events without exception do we *call* the rule a law of nature. Thus when we say "a natural law holds necessarily" this has but one legitimate meaning: "It holds in *all* cases where it is applicable." It is again very deplorable that the word "necessary" has been applied to natural laws (or, what amounts to the same thing, with reference to causality), for it is quite superfluous, since the expression "universally valid" is available. Universal validity is something altogether different from "compulsion"; these concepts belong to spheres so remote from each other that once insight into the error has been gained one can no longer conceive the possibility of a confusion.

The confusion of two concepts always carries with it the confusion of their contradictory opposites. The opposite of the universal validity of a formula, of the existence of a law, is the nonexistence of a law, indeterminism, acausality; while the opposite of compulsion is what in practice everyone calls "freedom." Here emerges the nonsense, trailing through centuries, that freedom means "exemption from the causal principle," or " not subject to the laws of nature." Hence it is believed necessary to vindicate indeterminism in order to save human freedom.

4. Freedom and Indeterminism

This is quite mistaken. Ethics has, so to speak, no moral interest in the purely theoretical question of "determinism or indeterminism?" but only a theoretical interest, namely: in so far as it seeks the laws of conduct, and can find them only to the extent that causality holds. But the question of whether man is morally free (that is, has that freedom which, as we shall show, is the presupposition of moral responsibility) is altogether different from the problem of determinism. Hume was especially clear on this point. He indicated the inadmissible confusion of the concepts of "indeterminism" and "freedom"; but he retained, inappropriately, the word "freedom" for both, calling the one freedom of "the will," the other, genuine kind, "freedom of conduct." He showed that morality is interested only in the latter, and that such freedom, in general, is unquestionably to be attributed to mankind. And this is quite correct. Freedom means the opposite of compulsion; a man is *free* if he does not act under *compulsion,* and he is compelled or unfree when he is hindered from without in the realization of his natural desires. Hence he is unfree when he is locked up, or chained, or when someone forces him at the point of a gun to do what otherwise he would not do. This is quite clear, and everyone will admit that the everyday or legal notion of the lack of freedom is thus correctly interpreted, and that a man will be considered quite free and responsible if no such external compulsion is exerted upon him. There are certain cases which lie between these clearly described ones, as, say, when someone acts under the influence of alcohol or a narcotic. In such cases we consider the man to be more or less unfree, and hold him less accountable, because we rightly view the influence of the drug as "external," even though it is found within the body; it prevents him from making decisions in the manner peculiar to his nature. If he takes the narcotic of his own will, we make him completely responsible for *this* act and transfer a part of the responsibility to the consequences, making, as it were, an average or mean condemnation of the whole. In the case also of a person who is mentally ill we do not consider him free with respect to those acts in which the disease expresses itself, because we view the illness as a disturbing factor which hinders the normal functioning of his natural tendencies. We make not him but his disease responsible.

5. The Nature of Responsibility

But what does this really signify? What do we mean by this concept of responsibility which goes along with that of "freedom," and which plays such an important role in morality? It is easy to attain complete clarity in this matter; we need only carefully determine the manner in which the concept is used. What is the case in practice when we impute "responsibility" to a person? What is our aim in doing this? The judge has to discover who is responsible for a given act in order that he may *punish* him. We are inclined to be less concerned with the inquiry as to who deserves *reward* for an act, and we have no special officials for this; but of course the principle would be the same. But let us stick to punishment in order to make the idea clear. What is punishment, actually? The view still often expressed, that it is a natural *retaliation* for past wrong, ought no longer to be defended in cultivated society; for the opinion that an increase in sorrow can be "made good again" by further sorrow is altogether barbarous. Certainly the origin of punishment may lie in an impulse of retaliation or vengeance; but what is such an impulse except the instinctive desire to destroy the *cause* of the deed to be avenged, by the destruction of or injury to the malefactor? Punishment is concerned only with the institution of causes, of *motives* of conduct, and this alone is its meaning. Punishment is an educative measure, and as such is a means to the formation of motives, which are in part to prevent the wrongdoer from repeating the act (reformation) and in part to prevent others from committing a similar act (intimidation). Analogously, in the case of reward we are concerned with an incentive.

Hence the question regarding responsibility is the question: Who, in a given case, is to be punished? Who is to be considered the true wrongdoer? This problem is not identical with that regarding the original instigator of the act; for the great-grandparents of the man, from whom he inherited his character, might in the end be the cause, or the statesmen who are responsible for his social milieu, and so forth. But the "doer" is the one *upon whom the motive must have acted* in order, with certainty, to have prevented the act (or called it forth, as the case may be). Consideration of remote causes is of no help here, for in the first place their actual contribution cannot be determined, and in the second place they are generally out of reach. Rather, we must find the person in whom the decisive junction of causes lies. The question of who is responsible is the question concerning the *correct point of application of the motive.* And the important thing is that in this its meaning is completely exhausted; behind it there lurks no mysterious connection between transgression and requital, which is merely *indicated* by the described state of affairs. It is a matter only of knowing who is to be punished or rewarded, in order that punishment and reward function as such—be able to achieve their goal.

Thus, all the facts connected with the concepts of responsibility and imputation are at once made intelligible. We do not charge an insane person with responsibility, for the very reason that he offers no unified point for the application of a motive. It would be pointless to try to affect him by means of promises or threats, when his confused soul fails to respond to such influence because its normal mechanism is out of order. We do not try to give him motives, but try to heal him (metaphorically, we make his sickness responsible, and try to remove its causes). When a man is forced by threats to commit certain acts we do not blame him, but the one who held the pistol at his breast. The reason is clear: the act would have been prevented had we been able to restrain the person who threatened him; and this person is the one whom we must influence in order to prevent similar acts in the future.

6. The Consciousness of Responsibility

But much more important than the question of when a man is said to be responsible is that of when he *himself* feels responsible. Our whole treatment would be untenable if it gave no explanation of this. It is, then, a welcome confirmation of the view here developed that the subjective feeling of responsibility coincides with the objective judgment. It is a fact of experience that, in general, the person blamed or condemned is conscious of the fact that he was "rightly" taken to account—of course, under the supposition that no error has been made, that the assumed state of affairs actually occurred. What is this consciousness of having been the true doer of the act, the actual instigator? Evidently not merely that it was he who took the steps required for its performance; but there must be added the awareness that he did it "independently,"

"of his own initiative," or however it be expressed. This feeling is simply the consciousness of *freedom,* which is merely the knowledge of having acted of one's *own* desires. And "one's own desires" are those which have their origin in the regularity of one's character in the given situation, and are not imposed by an external power, as explained above. The absence of the external power expresses itself in the well-known feeling (usually considered characteristic of the consciousness of freedom) *that one could also have acted otherwise.* How this indubitable experience ever came to be an argument in favor of indeterminism is incomprehensible to me. It is of course obvious that I should have acted differently had I *willed* something else; but the feeling never says that I could also have willed something else, even though this is true, if, that is, other motives had been present. And it says even less that under *exactly the same* inner and outer conditions I could also have willed something else. How could such a feeling inform me of anything regarding the purely theoretical question of whether the principle of causality holds or not? Of course, after what has been said on the subject, I do not undertake to demonstrate the principle, but I do deny that from any such fact of consciousness the least follows regarding the principle's validity. This feeling is not the consciousness of the absence of a cause, but of something altogether different, namely, of *freedom,* which consists in the fact that I can act as I desire.

Thus the feeling of responsibility assumes that I acted freely, that my own desires impelled me; and if because of this feeling I willingly suffer blame for my behavior or reproach myself, and thereby admit that I might have acted otherwise, this means that other behavior was compatible with the laws of volition—of course, granted other motives. And I myself desire the existence of such motives and bear the pain (regret and sorrow) caused me by my behavior so that its repetition will be prevented. To blame oneself means just to apply motives of improvement to oneself, which is usually the task of the educator. But if, for example, one does something under the influence of torture, feelings of guilt and regret are absent, for one knows that according to the laws of volition no other behavior was possible—no matter what ideas, because of their feeling tones, might have functioned as motives. The important thing, always, is that the feeling of responsibility means the realization that one's self, one's own psychic processes constitute the point at which motives must be applied in order to govern the acts of one's body.

7. Causality as the Presupposition of Responsibility

We can speak of motives only in a causal context; thus it becomes clear how very much the concept of responsibility rests upon that of causation, that is, upon the regularity of volitional decisions. In fact if we should conceive of a decision as utterly without any cause (this would in all strictness be the indeterministic presupposition) then the act would be entirely a matter of *chance,* for chance is identical with the absence of a cause; there is no other opposite of causality. Could we under such conditions make the agent responsible? Certainly not. Imagine a man, always calm, peaceful and blameless, who suddenly falls upon and begins to beat a stranger. He is held and questioned regarding the motive of his action, to which he answers, in his opinion truthfully, as we assume: "There was no motive for my behavior. Try as I may I can discover no reason. My volition was without any cause—I desired to do so, and there is simply nothing else to be said about it." We should shake our heads and call him insane, because we have to believe that there was a cause, and lacking any other we must assume some mental disturbance as the only cause remaining; but certainly no one would hold him to be responsible. If decisions were causeless there would be no sense in trying to influence men; and we see at once that this is the reason why we could not bring such a man to account, but would always have only a shrug of the shoulders in answer to his behavior. One can easily determine that in practice we make an agent the more responsible the more motives we can find for his conduct. If a man guilty of an atrocity was an enemy of his victim, if previously he had shown violent tendencies, if some special circumstance angered him, then

we impose severe punishment upon him; while the fewer the reasons to be found for an offense the less do we condemn the agent, but make "unlucky chance," a momentary aberration, or something of the sort, responsible. We do not find the causes of misconduct in his character, and therefore we do not try to influence it for the better: this and only this is the significance of the fact that we do not put the responsibility upon him. And he too feels this to be so, and says, "I cannot understand how such a thing could have happened to me."

In general we know very well how to discover the causes of conduct in the characters of our fellow men; and how to use this knowledge in the prediction of their future behavior, often with as much certainty as that with which we know that a lion and a rabbit will behave quite differently in the same situation. From all this it is evident that in practice no one thinks of questioning the principle of causality, that, thus, the attitude of the practical man offers no excuse to the metaphysician for confusing freedom from compulsion with the absence of a cause. If one makes clear to himself that a causeless happening is identical with a chance happening, and that, consequently, an indetermined will would destroy all responsibility, then every desire will cease which might be father to an indeterministic thought. No one can prove determinism, but it is certain that we assume its validity in all of our practical life, and that in particular we can apply the concept of responsibility to human conduct only in so far as the causal principle holds of volitional processes.

For a final clarification I bring together again a list of those concepts which tend, in the traditional treatment of the "problem of freedom," to be confused. In the place of the concepts on the left are put, mistakenly, those of the right, and those in the vertical order form a chain, so that sometimes the previous confusion is the cause of that which follows:

Natural Law.	Law of State.
Determinism (Causality).	Compulsion.
(Universal Validity).	(Necessity).
Indeterminism (Chance).	Freedom.
(No Cause).	(No Compulsion).

FREE WILL AND PSYCHOANALYSIS

John Hospers

The free act is the uncompelled act, says Schlick, and controversies about causality and determinism have nothing to do with the case. When one asks whether an act done of necessity is free, the question is ambiguous: if "of necessity" means "by compulsion," then the answer is no; if, on the other hand, "of necessity" is a way of referring to "causal uniformity" in nature—the sense in which we may misleadingly speak of the laws of nature as "necessary" simply because there are no exceptions to them—then the answer is clearly yes; every act is an instance of some causal law (uniformity) or other, but this has nothing to do with its being free in the sense of uncompelled.

For Schlick, this is the end of the matter. Any attempt to discuss the matter further simply betrays a failure to perceive the clarifying distinctions that Schlick has made.

> Freedom means the opposite of compulsion; a man is *free* if he does not act under *compulsion,* and he is compelled or unfree when he is hindered from without in the realization of his natural desires. Hence, he is unfree when he is locked up, or chained, or when someone forces him at the point of a gun to do what otherwise he would not do. This is quite clear, and everyone will admit that the everyday or legal notion of the lack of freedom is thus correctly interpreted, and that a man will be considered quite free . . . if no such external compulsion is exerted upon him.[1]

This all seems clear enough. And yet if we ask whether it ends the matter, whether it states what we "really mean" by "free," many of us will feel qualms. We remember statements about human beings being pawns of their environment, victims of conditions beyond their control, the result of causal influences stemming from parents, etc., and we think, "Still, are we really free?" We do not want to say that the uniformity of nature itself binds us or renders us unfree; yet is there not something in what generations of wise men have said about man being fettered? Is there not something too facile, too sleight-of-hand, in Schlick's cutting of the Gordian knot?

It will be noticed that we have slipped from talking about acts as being free into talking about human beings as free. Both locutions are employed, I would say about 50–50. Sometimes an attempt is made to legislate definitely between the two: Stebbing, for instance, says that one must never call acts free, but only the doers of the acts.[2]

Let us pause over this for a moment. If it is we and not our acts that are to be called free, the most obvious reflection to make is that we are free to do some things and not free to do other things; we are free to lift our hands but not free to lift the moon. We cannot simply call ourselves free or unfree *in toto;* we must say at best that we are free in respect of certain actions only. G. E. Moore states the criterion as follows: we are free to do an act if we can do it *if* we want to; that which we can do if we want to is what we are free to do.[3] Some things certain people are free to do while others are not: most of us are free to move our legs, but paralytics are not; some of us are free to concentrate on philosophical reading matter for three hours at a stretch while others are not. In general, we could relate the two approaches by saying that a *person* is free *in respect of* a given action if he can do it if he wants to, and in this case his *act* is free.

Moore himself, however, has reservations that Schlick has not. He adds that there *is* a sense of "free" which fulfills the criterion he has just set forth; but that there may be *another* sense in which man cannot be said to be free in all the situations in which he could rightly be said to be so in the first sense.

And surely it is not necessary for me to multiply examples of the sort of thing we mean. In practice

---

[1]Moritz Schlick, *The Problems of Ethics,* Chapter VII, p. 150.

[2]L. Susan Stebbing, *Philosophy and the Physicists,* p. 242.

[3]G. E. Moore, *Ethics,* p. 205.

most of us would not call free many persons who behave voluntarily and even with calculation aforethought, and under no compulsion either of any obvious sort. A metropolitan newspaper headlines an article with the words "Boy Killer Is Doomed Long before He Is Born,"[4] and then goes on to describe how a twelve-year-old boy has just been sentenced to thirty years in Sing Sing for the murder of a girl; his family background includes records of drunkenness, divorce, social maladjustment, epilepsy, and paresis. He early displays a tendency to sadistic activity to hide an underlying masochism and "prove that he's a man"; being coddled by his mother only worsens this tendency, until, spurned by a girl in his attempt on her, he kills her—not simply in a fit of anger, but calculatingly, deliberately. Is he free in respect of his criminal act, or for that matter in most of the acts of his life? Surely to ask this question is to answer it in the negative. Perhaps I have taken an extreme case; but it is only to show the superficiality of the Schlick analysis the more clearly. Though not everyone has criminotic tendencies, everyone has been molded by influences which in large measure at least determine his present behavior; he is literally the product of these influences, stemming from periods prior to his "years of discretion," giving him a host of character traits that he cannot change now even if he would. So obviously does what a man is depend upon how a man comes to be, that it is small wonder that philosophers and sages have considered man far indeed from being the master of his fate. It is not as if man's will were standing high and serene above the flux of events that have moulded him; it is itself caught up in this flux, itself carried along on the current. An act is free when it is determined by the man's character, say moralists; but when there was nothing the man could do to shape his character, and even the degree of will power available to him in shaping his habits and disciplining himself to overcome the influence of his early environment is a factor over which he has no control, what are we to say of this kind of

"freedom?" Is it not rather like the freedom of the machine to stamp labels on cans when it has been devised for just that purpose? Some machines can do so more efficiently than others, but only because they have been better constructed.

It is not my purpose here to establish this thesis in general, but only in one specific respect which has received comparatively little attention, namely, the field referred to by psychiatrists as that of unconscious motivation. In what follows I shall restrict my attention to it because it illustrates as clearly as anything the points I wish to make.

Let me try to summarize very briefly the psychoanalytic doctrine on this point.[5] The conscious life of the human being, including the conscious decisions and volitions, is merely a mouthpiece for the unconscious—not directly for the enactment of unconscious drives, but of the compromise between unconscious drives and unconscious reproaches. There is a Big Three behind the scenes which the automaton called the conscious personality carries out: the id, an "eternal gimme," presents its wish and demands its immediate satisfaction; the super-ego says no to the wish immediately upon presentation, and the unconscious ego, the mediator between the two, tries to keep peace by means of compromise.[6]

To go into examples of the functioning of these three "bosses" would be endless; psychoanalytic case books supply hundreds of them. The important point for us to see in the present context is that it is the unconscious that determines what the conscious impulse and the conscious action shall be. Hamlet, for example, had a strong Oedipus wish, which was

---

[4]*New York Post,* Tuesday, May 18, 1948, p. 4.

[5]I am aware that the theory presented below is not accepted by all practicing psychoanalysts. Many non-Freudians would disagree with the conclusions presented below. But I do not believe that this fact affects my argument, as long as the concept of unconscious motivation is accepted. I am aware, too, that much of the language employed in the following descriptions is animistic and metaphorical; but as long as I am presenting a view I would prefer to "go the whole hog" and present it in its strongest possible light. The theory can in any ease be made clearest by the use of such language, just as atomic theory can often be made clearest to students with the use of models.

[6]This view is very clearly developed in Edmund Bergler, *Divorce Won't Help,* especially Chapter I.

violently counteracted by super-ego reproaches; these early wishes were vividly revived in an unusual adult situation in which his uncle usurped the coveted position from Hamlet's father and won his mother besides. This situation evoked strong strictures on the part of Hamlet's super-ego, and it was this that was responsible for his notorious delay in killing his uncle. A dozen times Hamlet could have killed Claudius easily; but every time Hamlet "decided" not to: a free choice, moralists would say— but no, listen to the super-ego: "What you feel such hatred toward your uncle for, what you are plotting to kill him for, is precisely the crime which you yourself desire to commit: to kill your father and replace him in the affections of your mother. Your fate and your uncle's are bound up together." This paralyzes Hamlet into inaction. Consciously all he knows is that he is unable to act; this conscious inability he rationalizes, giving a different excuse each time.[7]

We have always been conscious of the fact that we are not masters of our fate in every respect—that there are many things which we cannot do, that nature is more powerful than we are, that we cannot disobey laws without danger of reprisals, etc. Lately we have become more conscious, too, though novelists and dramatists have always been fairly conscious of it, that we are not free with respect to the emotions that we feel—whom we love or hate, what types we admire, and the like. More lately still we have been reminded that there are unconscious motivations for our basic attractions and repulsions, our compulsive actions or inabilities to act. But what is not welcome news is that our very acts of volition, and the entire train of deliberations leading up to them, are but facades for the expression of unconscious wishes, or rather, unconscious compromises and defenses.

A man is faced by a choice: shall he kill another person or not? Moralists would say, here is a free choice—the result of deliberation, an action con-

sciously entered into. And yet, though the agent himself does not know it, and has no awareness of the forces that are at work within him, his choice is already determined for him: his conscious will is only an instrument, a slave, in the hands of a deep unconscious motivation which determines his action. If he has a great deal of what the analyst calls "free-floating guilt," he will not; but if the guilt is such as to demand immediate absorption in the form of self-damaging behavior, this accumulated guilt will have to be discharged in some criminal action. The man himself does not know what the inner clockwork is; he is like the hands on the clock, thinking they move freely over the face of the clock.

A woman has married and divorced several husbands. Now she is faced with a choice for the next marriage: shall she marry Mr. A, or Mr. B, or nobody at all? She may take considerable time to "decide" this question, and her decision may appear as a final triumph of her free will. Let us assume that A is a normal, well-adjusted, kind, and generous man, while B is a leech, an impostor, one who will become entangled constantly in quarrels with her. If she belongs to a certain classifiable psychological type, she will inevitably choose B, and she will do so even if her previous husbands have resembled B, so that one would think that she "had learned from experience." Consciously, she will of course "give the matter due consideration," etc., etc. To the psychoanalyst all this is irrelevant chaff in the wind— only a camouflage for the inner workings about which she knows nothing consciously. If she is of a certain kind of masochistic strain, as exhibited in her previous set of symptoms, she *must* choose B: her superego, always out to maximize the torment in the situation, seeing what dazzling possibilities for self-damaging behavior are promised by the choice of B, compels her to make the choice she does, and even to conceal the real basis of the choice behind an elaborate facade of rationalizations.

A man is addicted to gambling. In the service of his addiction he loses all his money, spends what belongs to his wife, even sells his property and neglects his children. For a time perhaps he stops; then, inevitably, he takes it up again, although he himself

---

[7]See *The Basic Writings of Sigmund Freud,* Modern Library Edition, p. 310. (In *The Interpretation of Dreams.*) Cf. also the essay by Ernest Jones, "A Psycho-analytical Study of Hamlet."

may think he chose to. The man does not know that he is a victim rather than an agent; or, if he sometimes senses that he is in the throes of something-he-knows-not-what, he will have no inkling of its character and will soon relapse into the illusion that he (his conscious self) is freely deciding the course of his own actions. What he does not know, of course, is that he is still taking out on his mother the original lesion to his infantile narcissism, getting back at her for her fancied refusal of his infantile wishes—and this by rejecting everything identified with her, namely education, discipline, logic, common sense, training. At the roulette wheel, almost alone among adult activities, chance—the opposite of all these things—rules supreme; and his addiction represents his continued and emphatic reiteration of his rejection of Mother and all she represents to his unconscious.

This pseudo-aggression of his is of course masochistic in its effects. In the long run he always loses; he can never quit while he is winning. And far from playing in order to win, rather one can say that his losing is a *sine qua non* of his psychic equilibrium (as it was for example with Dostoyevsky): guilt demands punishment, and in the ego's "deal" with the super-ego the super-ego has granted satisfaction of infantile wishes in return for the self-damaging conditions obtaining. Winning would upset the neurotic equilibrium.[8]

A man has wash-compulsion. He must be constantly washing his hands—he uses up perhaps 400 towels a day. Asked why he does this, he says, "I need to, my hands are dirty"; and if it is pointed out to him that they are not really dirty, he says "They feel dirty anyway, I feel better when I wash them." So once again he washes them. He "freely decides" every time; he feels that he must wash them, he deliberates for a moment perhaps, but always ends by washing them. What he does not see, of course, is the invisible wires inside him pulling him inevitably to do the thing he does: the infantile id-wish concerns preoccupation with dirt, the super-ego charges him with this, and the terrified ego must respond, "No, I don't like dirt, see how clean I like to be, look how I wash my hands!"

Let us see what further "free acts" the same patient engages in (this is an actual case history): he is taken to a concentration camp, and given the worst of treatment by the Nazi guards. In the camp he no longer chooses to be clean, does not even try to be—on the contrary, his choice is now to wallow in filth as much as he can. All he is aware of now is a disinclination to be clean, and every time he must choose he chooses not to be. Behind the scenes, however, another drama is being enacted: the super-ego, perceiving that enough torment is being administered from the outside, can afford to cease pressing its charges in this quarter—the outside world is doing the torturing now, so the super-ego is relieved of the responsibility. Thus the ego is relieved of the agony of constantly making terrified replies in the form of washing to prove that the super-ego is wrong. The defense no longer being needed, the person slides back into what is his natural predilection anyway, for filth. This becomes too much even for the Nazi guards: they take hold of him one day, saying "We'll teach you how to be clean!" drag him into the snow, and pour bucket after bucket of icy water over him until he freezes to death. Such is the end-result of an original id-wish, caught in the machinations of a destroying super-ego.

Let us take, finally, a less colorful, more everyday example. A student at a university, possessing wealth, charm, and all that is usually considered essential to popularity, begins to develop the following personality-pattern: although well taught in the graces of social conversation, he always makes a *faux pas* somewhere, and always in the worst possible situation; to his friends he makes cutting remarks which hurt deeply—and always apparently aimed in such a way as to hurt the most: a remark that would not hurt A but would hurt B he invariably makes to B rather than to A, and so on. None of this

---

[8]See Edmund Bergler's article on the pathological gambler in *Diseases of the Nervous System* (1943). Also "Suppositions about the Mechanism of Criminosis," *Journal of Criminal Psychopathology* (1944) and "Clinical Contributions to the Psychogenesis of Alcohol Addiction," *Quarterly Journal of Studies on Alcohol,* 5:434 (1944).

is conscious. Ordinarily he is considerate of people, but he contrives always (unconsciously) to impose on just those friends who would resent it most, and at just the times when he should know that he should not impose: at 3 o'clock in the morning, without forewarning, he phones a friend in a nearby city demanding to stay at his apartment for the weekend; naturally the friend is offended, but the person himself is not aware that he has provoked the grievance ("common sense" suffers a temporary eclipse when the neurotic pattern sets in, and one's intelligence, far from being of help in such a situation, is used in the interest of the neurosis), and when the friend is cool to him the next time they meet, he wonders why and feels unjustly treated. Aggressive behavior on his part invites resentment and aggression in turn, but all that he consciously sees is other's behavior toward him—and he considers himself the innocent victim of an unjustified "persecution."

Each of these choices is, from the moralist's point of view, free: he chose to phone his friend at 3 a.m.; he chose to make the cutting remark that he did, etc. What he does not know is that an ineradicable masochistic pattern has set in. His unconscious is far more shrewd and clever than is his conscious intellect; it sees with uncanny accuracy just what kind of behavior will damage him most, and unerringly forces him into that behavior. Consciously, the student "doesn't know why he did it"—he gives different "reasons" at different times, but they are all, once again, rationalizations cloaking the unconscious mechanism which propels him willy-nilly into actions that his "common sense" eschews.

The more of this sort of thing you see, the more you can see what the psychoanalyst means when he talks about "the illusion of free-will." And the more of a psychiatrist you become, the more you are overcome with a sense of what an illusion this precious free-will really is. In some kinds of cases most of us can see it already: it takes no psychiatrist to look at the epileptic and sigh with sadness at the thought that soon this person before you will be as one possessed, not the same thoughtful intelligent person you knew. But people are not aware of this

in other contexts, for example when they express surprise at how a person whom they have been so good to could treat them so badly. Let us suppose that you help a person financially or morally or in some other way, so that he is in your debt; suppose further that he is one of the many neurotics who unconsciously identify kindness with weakness and aggression with strength, then he will unconsciously take your kindness to him as weakness and use it as the occasion for enacting some aggression against you. He can't help it, he may regret it himself later; still, he will be driven to do it. If we gain a little knowledge of psychiatry, we can look at him with pity, that a person otherwise so worthy should be so unreliable—but we will exercise realism too and be aware that there are some types of people that you cannot be good to in "free" acts of their conscious volition, they will use your own goodness against you.

Sometimes the persons themselves will become dimly aware that "something behind the scenes" is determining their behavior. The divorcee will sometimes view herself with detachment, as if she were some machine (and indeed the psychoanalyst does call her a "repeating-machine"): "I know I'm caught in a net, that I'll fall in love with this guy and marry him and the whole ridiculous merry-go-round will start all over again."

We talk about free will, and we say, yes, the person is free to do so-and-so if he can do so *if* he wants to—and we forget that his wanting to is itself caught up in the stream of determinism, that unconscious forces drive him into the wanting or not wanting to do the thing in question. The idea of the puppet whose motions are manipulated from behind by invisible wires, or better still, by springs inside, is no mere figure of speech. The analogy is a telling one at almost every point.

And the pity of it is that it all started so early, before we knew what was happening. The personality-structure is inelastic after the age of five, and comparatively so in most cases after the age of three. Whether one acquires a neurosis or not is determined by that age—and just as involuntarily as if it had been a curse of God. If, for example, a masochistic pattern was set up, under pressure of hyper-narcissism combined with real or fancied infantile deprivation, then the masochistic snowball was on its course downhill long before we or anybody else knew what was happening, and long before anyone could do anything about it. To speak of human beings as "puppets" in such a context is no mere metaphor, but a stark rendering of a literal fact: only the psychiatrist knows what puppets people really are; and it is no wonder that the protestations of philosophers that "the act which is the result of a volition, a deliberation, a conscious decision, is free" leave these persons, to speak mildly, somewhat cold.

• • •

Now, what of the notion of responsibility? What happens to it on our analysis?

Let us begin with an example, not a fictitious one. A woman and her two-year-old baby are riding on a train to Montreal in mid-winter. The child is ill. The woman wants badly to get to her destination. She is, unknown to herself, the victim of a neurotic conflict whose nature is irrelevant here except for the fact that it forces her to behave aggressively toward the child, partly to spite her husband whom she despises and who loves the child, but chiefly to ward off super-ego charges of masochistic attachment. Consciously she loves the child, and when she says this she says it sincerely, but she must behave aggressively toward it nevertheless, just as many children love their mothers but are nasty to them most of the time in neurotic pseudo-aggression. The child becomes more ill as the train approaches Montreal; the heating system of the train is not working, and the conductor advises the woman to get off the train at the next town and get the child to a hospital at once. The woman says no, she must get to Montreal. Shortly afterward, the child's condition worsens, and the mother does all she can to keep it alive, without, however, leaving the train, for she declares that it is absolutely necessary that she reach her destination. But before she gets there the child is dead. After that, of course, the mother grieves, blames herself, weeps hysterically, and joins the church to gain surcease from the guilt

that constantly overwhelms her when she thinks of how her aggressive behavior has killed her child.

Was she responsible for her deed? In ordinary life, after making a mistake, we say, "Chalk it up to experience." Here we say, "Chalk it up to the neurosis." No, she is not responsible. She could not help it if her neurosis forced her to act this way—she didn't even know what was going on behind the scenes, she merely acted out the part assigned to her. This is far more true than is generally realized: criminal actions in general are not actions for which their agents are responsible; the agents are passive, not active—they are victims of a neurotic conflict. Their very hyper-activity is unconsciously determined.

To say this is, of course, not to say that we should not punish criminals. Clearly, for our own protection, we must remove them from our midst so that they can no longer molest and endanger organized society. And, of course, if we use the word "responsible" in such a way that justly to hold someone responsible for a deed is by definition identical with being justified in punishing him, then we can and do hold people responsible. But this is like the sense of "free" in which free acts are voluntary ones. It does not go deep enough. In a deeper sense we cannot hold the person responsible: we may hold his neurosis responsible, but he is not responsible for his neurosis, particularly since the age at which its onset was inevitable was an age before he could even speak.

The neurosis is responsible—but isn't the neurosis a part of *him?* We have been speaking all the time as if the person and his unconscious were two separate beings; but isn't he one personality, including conscious and unconscious departments together?

I do not wish to deny this. But, it hardly helps us here; for what people want when they talk about freedom, and what they hold to when they champion it, is the idea that the *conscious* will is the master of their destiny. "I am the master of my fate, I am the captain of my soul"—and they surely mean their conscious selves, the self that they can recognize and search and introspect. Between an unconscious that willy-nilly determines your actions, and an external force which pushes you, there is little if anything to choose. The unconscious is just *as if* it were an outside force; and indeed, psychiatrists will assert that the inner Hitler can torment you far more than any external Hitler can. Thus the kind of freedom that people want, the only kind they will settle for, is precisely the kind that psychiatry says that they cannot have.

Heretofore it was pretty generally thought that, while we could not rightly blame a person for the color of his eyes or the morality of his parents, or even for what he did at the age of three, or to a large extent what impulses he had and whom he fell in love with, one *could* do so for other of his adult activities, particularly the acts he performed voluntarily and with premeditation. Later this attitude was shaken. Many voluntary acts came to be recognized, at least in some circles, as compelled by the unconscious. Some philosophers recognized this too—Ayer[9] talks about the kleptomaniac being unfree, and about a person being unfree when another person exerts a habitual ascendancy over his personality. But this is as far as he goes. The usual examples, such as the kleptomaniac and the schizophrenic, apparently satisfy most philosophers, and with these exceptions removed, the rest of mankind is permitted to wander in the vast and alluring fields of freedom and responsibility. So far, the inroads upon freedom left the vast majority of humanity untouched; they began to hit home when psychiatrists began to realize, though philosophers did not, that the domination of the conscious by the unconscious extended, not merely to a few exceptional individuals, but to all human beings, that the "big three behind the scenes" are not respecters of persons, and dominate us all, even including that *sanctum sanctorum* of freedom, our conscious will. To be sure, the domination in the case of "normal" individuals is somewhat more benevolent than the tyranny and despotism exercised in neurotic cases, and therefore the former have evoked less comment; but the principle remains in all cases the same: the unconscious is the master of every fate and the captain of every soul.

We speak of a machine turning out good products most of the time but every once in a while it turns out a "lemon." We do not, of course, hold the product responsible for this, but the machine, and via the machine, its maker. Is it silly to extend to inanimate objects the idea of responsibility? Of course. But is it any less silly to employ the notion in speaking of human creatures? Are not the two kinds of cases analogous in countless important ways? Occasionally a child turns out badly too, even when his environment and training are the same as that of his brothers and sisters who turn out "all right." He is the "bad penny." His acts of rebellion against parental discipline in adult life (such as the case of the gambler, already cited) are traceable to early experiences of real or fancied denial of infantile wishes. Sometimes the denial has been real, though many denials are absolutely necessary if the child is to grow up to observe the common decencies of civilized life; sometimes, if the child has an unusual quantity of narcissism, every event that occurs is interpreted by him as a denial of his wishes, and nothing a parent could do, even granting every humanly possible wish, would help. In any event, the later neurosis can be attributed to this. Can the person himself be held responsible? Hardly. If he engages in activities which are a menace to society, he must be put into prison, of course, but responsibility is another matter. The time when the events occurred which rendered his neurotic behavior inevitable was a time long before he was capable of thought and decision. As an adult, he is a victim of a world he never made—only this world is inside him.

What about the children who turn out "all right"? All we can say is that "it's just lucky for them" that what happened to their unfortunate brother didn't happen to them; *through no virtue of their own* they are not doomed to the life of unconscious guilt, expiation, conscious depression, terrified ego-gestures for the appeasement of a tyrannical super-ego that he is. The machine turned them out with a minimum of damage. But if the brother cannot be blamed for his evils, neither can they be praised for their good. It will take society a long time to come round to this attitude. We do not blame people for the color of their eyes, but we have not attained the same attitude toward their socially significant activities.

---

[9] A. J. Ayer, "Freedom and Necessity," *Polemic* (September-October 1946), pp. 40–43.

We all agree that machines turn out "lemons," we all agree that nature turns out misfits in the realm of biology—the blind, the crippled, the diseased; but we hesitate to include the realm of the personality, for here, it seems, is the last retreat of our dignity as human beings. Our ego can endure anything but this; this island at least must remain above the encroaching flood. But may not precisely the same analysis be made here also? Nature turns out psychological "lemons" too, in far greater quantities than any other kind; and indeed all of us are "lemons" in some respect or other, the difference being one of degree. Some of us are lucky enough not to have a gambling-neurosis or criminotic tendencies or masochistic mother-attachment or overdimensional repetition-compulsion to make our lives miserable, but most of our actions, those usually considered the most important, are unconsciously dominated just the same. And, if a neurosis may be likened to a curse of God, let those of us, the elect, who are enabled to enjoy a measure of life's happiness without the hell-fire of neurotic guilt, take this, not as our own achievement, but simply for what it is—a gift of God.

Let us, however, quit metaphysics and put the situation schematically in the form of a deductive argument.

1. An occurrence over which we had no control is something we cannot be held responsible for.
2. Events E, occurring during our babyhood, were events over which we had no control.
3. Therefore events E were events which we cannot be held responsible for.
4. But if there is something we cannot be held responsible for, neither can we be held responsible for something that inevitably results from it.
5. Events E have as inevitable consequence Neurosis N, which in turn has as inevitable consequence Behavior B.
6. Since N is the inevitable consequence of E and B is the inevitable consequence of N, B is the inevitable consequence of E.
7. Hence, not being responsible for E, we cannot be responsible for B.

In Samuel Butler's Utopian satire *Erewhon* there occurs the following passage, in which a judge is passing sentence on a prisoner:

> It is all very well for you to say that you came of unhealthy parents, and had a severe accident in your childhood which permanently undermined your constitution; excuses such as these are the ordinary refuge of the criminal; but they cannot for one moment be listened to by the ear of justice. I am not here to enter upon curious metaphysical questions as to the origin of this or that—questions to which there would be no end were their introduction once tolerated, and which would result in throwing the only guilt on the tissues of the primordial cell, or on the elementary gases. There is no question of how you came to be wicked, but only this—namely, are you wicked or not? This has been decided in the affirmative, neither can I hesitate for a single moment to say that it has been decided justly. You are a bad and dangerous person, and stand branded in the eyes of your fellow countrymen with one of the most heinous known offenses.[10]

As moralists read this passage, they may perhaps nod with approval. But the joke is on them. The sting comes when we realize what the crime is for which the prisoner is being sentenced: namely, consumption. The defendant is reminded that during the previous year he was sentenced for aggravated bronchitis, and is warned that he should profit from experience in the future. Butler is employing here his familiar method of presenting some human tendency (in this case, holding people responsible for what isn't their fault) to a ridiculous extreme and thereby reducing it to absurdity. How soon will mankind appreciate the keen edge of Butler's bitter irony? How long will they continue to read such a passage, but fail to smile, or yet to wince?

• • •

Can human beings, in the light of psychiatric knowledge, be called "free" in any respect at all?

We must remember that every term that can be significantly used must have a significant opposite. If the opposite cannot significantly be asserted, neither

---

[10]Samuel Butler, *Erewhon* (Modern Library edition), p. 107.

can its original. If the term "unfree" can be significantly used, so can the term "free." Even though there may be no actual denotation of a term naming an opposite, one must know what it would be like—what it would mean to speak of it; even though there are no white crows, it must be significant, as indeed it is, to speak of them. Now is the case of freedom like that of the white crows that don't exist but can be significantly spoken of, or like the black crows that do exist and can be significantly spoken of as well?

Unless "freedom" is taken to mean the same as "lack of cause" and a principle of universal causality is taken for granted, I think the latter must be the case.

If we asked the psychoanalysts for their opinion on this, they would doubtless reply somewhat as follows. They would say that they were not accustomed to using the term "free" at all, but that if they had to suggest a criterion for distinguishing the free from the unfree, they would say that a person's freedom occurs in inverse proportion to his neuroticism; the more he is compelled in his behavior by a *malevolent* unconscious, the less free he is. We speak of degrees of freedom—and the psychologically normal and well-adjusted individual is comparatively the freest, even though most of his behavior is determined by his unconscious.

But suppose it is the determination of his behavior by his unconscious, no matter what kind, that we balk at? We may then say that a man is free only to the extent that his behavior is *not* unconsciously motivated at all. If this be our criterion, most of our behavior could not be called free: everything, including both impulses and volitions, having to do with our basic attitudes toward life, the general tenor of our tastes, whether we become philosophers or artists or business men, our whole affective life including our preferences for blondes or brunettes, active or passive, older or younger, has its inevitable basis in the unconscious. Only those comparatively vanilla-flavored aspects of life—such as our behavior toward people who don't really matter to us—are exempted from this rule.

These, I think, are the two principal criteria for distinguishing freedom from the lack of it which we might set up on the basis of psychoanalytic knowl-

edge. Conceivably we might set up others. In every case, of course, it remains trivially true that "it all depends on how we choose to use the word." The facts are what they are, regardless of how we choose to label them. But if we choose to label facts in a way which is out of accordance with people's deep-seated and traditional methods of labeling them, as we would be doing if we labeled "free" human actions which we know as much about as we now do through modern psychiatry, then we shall only be manipulating words to mislead our fellow creatures.

FIRMING UP SOFT DETERMINISM

Nancy Holmstrom

I

An important position on the question of freedom and determinism holds that determinism and predictability *per se* constitute no threat to the freedom and responsibility of an agent. What matters, according to this view, called soft determinism, is the basis on which the prediction is made or the nature of the conditions such that given those conditions, the agent will do what he/she does.[1] When the agent does what he does because of his beliefs and de-

---

My thanks are due to all those whose comments on a closely related paper were of invaluable help to me in writing this one and especially to Berent Enc, Haskell Fain, Bernard Gendron and Gary Young.
[1]Representative of contemporary approaches but somewhat different and less adequate in my opinion than the version I present are Moritz Schlick's "When Is a Man Responsible?" and R. E. Hobart's "Free Will as Involving Determinism and Inconceivable Without It" in *Free Will and Determinism* ed. by Bernard Berofsky (N.Y.: Harper and Row, 1966). Earlier versions are found in J. S. Mill, *An Examination of Sir William Hamilton's Philosophy* (London: Longmans Green and Co., Ltd., 1872) and David Hume's "Of Liberty and Necessity" in *An Inquiry Concerning Human Understanding* (Los Angeles: Henry Regnery Co., 1956).

sires[2] to do it, then what the agent does is "up to him"; the causal chain goes through the person or the self, as it were. In such cases the agent can be said to be the cause of the action. Such actions are free. On the other hand, when the causes of an action, or, more generally, of what a person does, are not his/her beliefs and desires to do that action, then what happens is not "up to him" and the action is not free. However, it may not be compelled either. It is where the action is in contradiction to what the agent wants that the act can be said to be compelled. The agent is not responsible for the action because the action occurs in spite of him.

Among the objections that have been raised to this account of the distinction between free and unfree acts is that it provides an insufficient account of what it is for an agent to do an act freely. The problem is the source of the sources of one's allegedly free actions, i.e., the sources of one's beliefs and desires. Many philosophers have felt that if an agent's beliefs and desires are themselves determined, then actions proceeding from them must be as unfree as actions that are not caused by the agent's beliefs and desires. For example, Richard Taylor bids us to suppose that:

> while my behavior is entirely in accordance with my own volitions, and thus "free" in terms of the conception of freedom we are examining, my volitions themselves are caused. To make this graphic, we can suppose that an ingenious physiologist can induce in me any volition he pleases, simply by pushing various buttons on an instrument to which, let us suppose, I am attached by numerous wires. All the volitions I have in that situation, are, accordingly, precisely the ones he gives me . . . This is the description of a man who is acting in accordance with his inner volitions, a man

whose body is unimpeded and unconstrained in its motions, these motions being the effects of those inner states. It is hardly the description of a free and responsible agent. It is the perfect description of a puppet.[3]

The same point can be made by examples of beliefs and desires acquired by brainwashing, hypnosis, subliminal advertising, etc. If a person acts because of beliefs and desires acquired in such ways, the action is clearly not free even though the action was done because of the agent's beliefs and desires. This shows that it is not the case that an act is free just because it is caused by the beliefs and desires of the agent to do the act. The standard soft determinist position is inadequate as it stands.

One way of dealing with the objection might be to distinguish freedom of action and freedom of will and to maintain that the act was free but the will was not.[4] However, I think such examples show that these concepts cannot be so easily separated. Because the "will" is unfree in such cases, we would not call the act free. Taylor thinks his point applies much more generally than just to these sorts of examples and concludes that the standard conception of determinism cannot apply to a free act. He introduces, instead, a special notion of "agent causality."[5] I prefer to explore a response to the above objection that remains within the standard compatibilist framework.

I think that the objection I raised to soft determinism shows that soft determinists have too limited a notion of what is required for an agent to be the source of his/her actions. All that they require is that the agent do what he or she pleases. They ignore the question of whether the agent has control over the sources of the actions, his/her desires and beliefs. Taylor inferred that if the desires causing an action

[2]I intend "beliefs" and "desires" to cover all mental sources of action whatever exactly these are. I will not consider the question of the differences between these ostensible causes, (intentions, motives, wants, etc.), and their mutual relations, as this is a very involved issue and not crucial to my arguments. I use the word "desire" rather than "want" because there is one very weak sense of "want" in which I want to do everything I do intentionally. When I do use "want" it should be understood in the stronger sense in which it is equivalent to "desire."

[3]Richard Taylor. Metaphysics (Englewood Cliffs, N.J.: Prentice Hall, Inc., 1963), p. 45.
[4]Harry Frankfurt seems to do this although it is not entirely clear what he would say about this sort of example, in "Freedom of Will and the Concept of a Person." *Journal of Philosophy,* Vol. LXVIII, No. 1, January 14, 1971.
[5]Richard Taylor. *Action and Purpose* (Englewood Cliffs, N.J.: Prentice Hall, Inc., 1966).

are themselves caused then the action is not free. This does not follow. Just because some causes of desires and beliefs, such as brainwashing, make actions resulting from them unfree, it does not follow that any cause of desires and beliefs has the same implications for the freedom of actions resulting from them.

Since the notion of having control is the heart of the notion of freedom for me,[6] let me stop to clarify the concept briefly. If I have control over x then x depends on what I do or do not do. I am an important part of the causal process producing x, such that if I did something different x would be different. Moreover, I must be conscious of x's dependence on me in order for x to be under my control. Whether some insect lives or not depends on whether or not I step on him as I walk down the street. But if I do not know he is there his life is not under my control. So for x to be under my control what I do or do not do must be an important part of the cause of x and I must know this. X therefore must depend on what I want or on my "will" in order for x to be under my control. Now since one can make more or less of a difference, be more or less important a part of the causal process, it therefore follows that one can have more or less control over something. The more control a person has the freer that person is. Clearly, then, a person is not simply free or unfree. Nor is every action simply free or unfree. Rather, there is a continuum between free and unfree with many or most acts lying somewhere in between. When I say that an act is free what I mean is that the act falls on the free side of the continuum. Or, since there is no line in the middle of a continuum, it might be clearer to say that a free act falls in the direction of the free end of the continuum. Acts are more or less free according to how close they are to the free end of the continuum.[7]

What I want to argue in this paper is that people can have differing amounts of control over what they desire and what they believe. People can be more or less important a part of the causal process leading to their having the desires and beliefs that they do. Our discussion thus far shows that only if they have control over their beliefs and desires do they really have control over their actions. The key question, then is whether this idea of having control over one's beliefs and desires makes any sense and whether in fact we do have such control. Many people would probably say that while what we do is often up to us, what we believe and desire depends on factors completely beyond our control. Speaking generally, it depends on the way the world is; more specifically, it depends on our biological and psychological natures, the society in which we live, and our particular portion of it (i.e., our class, race, ethnic group, etc.). Others would object that it makes no sense to separate the person or self from his/her desires and beliefs, and hence makes no sense to talk of the person having control over his/her desires and beliefs. My major purpose in this paper will be to give substance to the idea that people can have control over the sources of their actions, that is, have control over their desires and beliefs.

If an agent can be said to be the source of his/her beliefs and desires, then it makes sense to say that the agent is a self-determining being. This is a concept that many have taken to be at the heart of freedom, whether they be determinists, indeterminists or hold to the idea of "agent causality."[8] If we can give substance to this notion of a person having control over his desires and beliefs, we will have given substance to the notion of a self-determining being.

II

Before turning directly to the central task, I wish to raise another sort of counterexample to soft determinism. Some acts that are done because of the

[6]If there are other conceptions of freedom in which control is not central then I am simply not interested in them and what I say may not apply to these other senses.

[7]It should be clear that I am using "free" and "unfree" (or "compelled") as contraries and not contradictories. Many acts we do every day, such as putting on our shoes, cannot sensibly be said to be either free or unfree. They belong in the middle of the continuum or—better perhaps—not on the continuum at all. Of other acts, it makes good sense to ask whether they are free or unfree; it is the answer that is complicated and which would place them somewhere in the middle of the continuum.

[8]"The principle of free will says 'I produce my volitions. Determinism says: My volitions are produced by me.' Determinism is free will expressed in the passive voice." R. E. Hobart, *op. cit.,* p. 71.

agent's desires and beliefs to do them are neverthe-less unfree, but for reasons other than the source of those desires and beliefs. However, we will see that these counterexamples do not challenge the funda-mental thrust of soft determinism because the exam-ples are all such that we have reason to say that the actions in the examples are not truly self-determined.

A heroin addict steals some money and uses it to buy heroin which he then takes. It might be said that all three acts (stealing, buying the drug and taking it) are done because of the addict's desire to achieve a certain state and the belief that these are ways of achieving it. If we imagine that this addict does not want to be an addict,[9] as is the case with most ad-dicts, then these acts of his are crucially different from most acts done because of the agent's beliefs and desires. While the addict wants the heroin he also wants to not take the drug. Moreover, he wants a great number of things which he believes to be in-compatible with taking the drug, e.g., health, self-respect, an ordinary life, etc. These contrary desires, values and beliefs are greater in number and also are part of an integrated whole. The desire to take the drug is not part of such an integrated whole, but nev-ertheless it outweighs all these contrary desires and beliefs. A kleptomaniac's desire to steal would prob-ably be similar. Most actions done because of the agent's desires are not in conflict with a greater number of his/her integrated desires and beliefs. I think it is this factor which leads compatibilists to reject such cases as not really counterexamples to their analysis of a free act as one resulting from the wants of the agent. An act resulting from such a con-flict does not seem to proceed from the self as a free act must; it occurs in spite of the person. Moritz Schlick says "We rightly consider the man to be more or less unfree, and hold him less responsible, because we rightly view the influence of the drug as "external" even though it is found within the body; it prevents him from making decisions in the man-ner peculiar to his nature."[10] This integrated set of

desires, beliefs and values might be said to consti-tute the person's nature or self as it is at that time.[11] Acts proceeding from desires that are external to this and yet dominant would seem to be unfree. There are certain exceptions to this, however, which we will discover as we progress.

III

I wish at this point to introduce the notion of a sec-ond order volition as discussed by Harry Frankfurt in "Free Will and the Concept of a Person."[12] Some-one has a volition of the second order when he wants to have a certain desire and, moreover, wants that desire to be his effective desire, i.e., his will, in Frankfurt's terminology. The addict in our example may simply suffer from a conflict between the desire to take the drug and a number of contradictory or in-compatible desires. However, he may, further, want that the latter desires be his effective desires. If so, then the addict's desire to take the drug is in conflict not only with a greater number of integrated desires and beliefs, but with a second order volition as well. Yet it still determines the addict's actions. By being in conflict with the will he wants to have, it is in con-flict with the want with which he has thereby identi-fied himself. Hence, when this desire determines action, the action is in sharp contrast to most acts done because of the agent's beliefs and desires. In-stead of being an act that depends on the agent, that is "up to him," it happens against his will. This pro-vides further grounds for saying that the act does not proceed from the self. Quite aside from the nature of

---

[9]If, on the other hand, we suppose that the addict does not mind being an addict, then none of the following holds.
[10][Schlick,] *op. cit.*, p. 59.

[11]It might be questioned whether the addict really does have such an integrated set at the time he/she is intent on procuring the heroin. (Alastair Hannay raised this question.) I think that when we ascribe wants or beliefs to a person we are talking of dispo-sitions that a person has over some longish time period (the pre-cise duration of which I could not say). So their having certain beliefs and desires is not contradicted by their behaving incon-sistently with them on some occasion. If one prefers to say that they do not have these beliefs and desires when their behavior is inconsistent with them, then we could talk about the self as con-sisting of the integrated set of beliefs and desires that exist over some longish period of time, the precise duration of which it would be impossible to set.
[12][Frankfurt,] *op. cit.*

the desire that is in conflict with the second order volition in our example, (i.e., the desire to take heroin), it would seem plausible to take as a sufficient condition for making an act unfree that it proceed from beliefs and desires that are in conflict with a second order volition. A necessary condition, then, of a free act is that it proceed from desires and beliefs that are consistent with second order volitions. This should be seen as a development of the compatibilist account of a free act as one caused by the self, specifically the agent's beliefs and desires.

IV

Consistency with an integrated set of beliefs and desires and with second order volitions is not sufficient for an act to be free. We saw at the outset that the source of the beliefs and desires causing an act is relevant to the freedom of that act. The sorts of examples which first showed us that the soft determinist position was unsatisfactory as thus far presented were examples of acts done because of beliefs and desires that seemed in some way to have been forced upon the agent. Whether the person acquired beliefs and desires (volitions or the reasons for doing what he/she does) by being hooked up to a machine someone else controls, or by being brainwashed or exposed to subliminal advertising, the following is true. The beliefs and desires were acquired by measures taken by others in order to induce them, which measures were taken either explicitly against the person's will (brainwashing), and/or without his/her knowledge (subliminal advertising). (Taylor's case could be either.) Being ignorant of the measures taken to induce the beliefs and desires, the person is as much lacking in control over them as if they were taken explicitly against his/her will. In both cases the person, as an active determining being, is irrelevant to what happens. He/she has no control, and—more importantly—no possibility of control over the beliefs and desires he/she acquires. Actions done because of beliefs and desires acquired under such conditions are not free.

Now is it really necessary that a person's beliefs and desires be caused by other people in order for it

to be the case that they were forced upon him/her? Although it was true of our original examples, I do not think it is a necessary condition. While it may sound odd to say they were the result of force or coercion where no persons were the cause, it can certainly be said that the desires were not acquired freely, or even that they were acquired under coercive conditions. The issue about causation of beliefs and desires that is crucial to the freedom of acts resulting from them is whether the person enters into the causal process as an active determinant. If the person does not, then the beliefs and desires were not acquired freely, and acts resulting from them are not free because not self-determined. If, on the contrary, the beliefs and desires are opposed to the person's desires, first or second order, then acts resulting from them are unfree or compelled. All this can be true even though the causes of the beliefs and desires were not measures taken by others to induce them. Suppose that a person lives under conditions of economic scarcity, which entails that not everyone will get what he/she needs and wants. A consequence of a person getting enough for himself and his family is that others will not have enough. A person in these conditions might, partly as a survival mechanism, come to desire that others not have enough—and might act on this desire. If this occurred, it seems to me that such an act would be an unfree one, (although perhaps not at the very end of the continuum). If the person did not want to want that others not have enough, if in fact he/she wanted not to want this, then the desire would conflict with a second order volition. Acts resulting from such desires are unfree. However, in the absence of a conflicting or reinforcing second order volition, I would still wish to put the act on the unfree end of the continuum because the desires causing the act were produced under coercive conditions. The conditions were coercive because the person had no control over them, their existence was contrary to his/her desires, and his/her personality and character had little or no effect on their influence. Remove economic scarcity and the desire would be removed, (although perhaps not immediately). Similar examples could be given of beliefs and desires caused by particular social systems and particular institutions within a social system.

V

Let us examine in some greater detail the conditions I have given under which desires could be said to have been acquired unfreely or coercively. It might be thought that my conditions apply too widely and would make too many desires turn out to have been unfreely acquired. For example, suppose a person has a strong desire to hear Bach because her parents regularly played Bach records in order to induce that desire. Her desire was acquired because of her parents' efforts to induce the desire. Their efforts consisted of intensively exposing her to the object they wished her to desire. If my conditions apply to such cases then her going to a concert as an adult because she wants to hear Bach played would be unfree—and this is an unattractive conclusion. However, my conditions do not lead to this conclusion, because the conditions I set are not met in the example. The child was not unaware of the causes of her later desire, which is what my condition requires; in fact it was by being aware of the music that was regularly played that she came to desire to hear it. Conceivably, but improbably, she was unaware that hearing the music was the cause of her later desire or that her parents regularly played it in order to produce that desire in her. However, these are different conditions than the one I gave. In general, where the measures taken to induce a desire simply amount to exposing a person to the object of the hoped-for desire, this does not meet my conditions, because the person cannot be unaware of the causes of the desire, (although he/she may be unaware that they are the causes).[13]

I am inclined to think that my conditions as they stand thus far are in need of revision in the other direction, that is, to make them apply more widely. Suppose that what was done to induce the desire was not mere exposure to the object, but rather conditioning. If they had conditioned her, the parents would have accompanied the playing of the music with pleasurable stimuli and they would have negatively reinforced any expressions of negative feeling toward the music. If this had been done, the desire would be the result of more than the interrelation of the person and the object of the desire, as is the case when the desire for something comes into being because of exposure to it. A desire that is the result of conditioning is the result of pleasures and pains that accompany the object, but are external to the person, the object and the relation between them. When a person acquires desires and aversions for things because of pleasures and pains that are intrinsic to those things, such as the pleasures of eating good food, the pains of overeating, then those desires and aversions are freely acquired. Where the pleasures and pains are external, the *person* (i.e., his/her personality, reasoning capacities, etc.), is bypassed in the process. This should make the process coercive. However, as my conditions stand they do not give this result. The person could be aware of the elements of the conditioning process, (the music, the accompanying pleasures and pains), though unaware of the connections between them, the purposes behind them and their effect. She was aware of the measures taken and, therefore, if it were not explicitly against her will, the conditioning would not be coercive according to what I have said about coercion thus far. I take this to indicate that something more must be said.

In the hopes of working out how conditioning differs from mere exposure, let us go back to the example of the person who acquired a desire to hear the music of Bach because of repeated exposure to his music as a child. Whether the exposure was the deliberate work of others, as in our example, or not, acquisition of a desire through exposure differs from clearly coercive ways of acquiring desires. When people acquire a desire through being acquainted with the object or experience, they have the possibility of coming to have that desire or not.

---

[13]A desire acquired merely by exposure to the object or experience will not be a free desire if it meets other criteria for *unfree* desires. An example of such a desire might be the desire for heroin. The need for this qualification was pointed out to me by Gary Young.

Whether they do or not will depend on facts about them: their aptitudes, beliefs, personality, other desires, etc. Where this is the case they can be said to have control, or at least the possibility of control, over the desires they acquire. Where, on the other hand, the causes of their beliefs and desires would exist and would effectively operate regardless of the fact that their personality, character, other beliefs and desires are opposed to these causes, then they obviously have no chance of controlling what beliefs and desires they come to have.

We can distinguish, then, between cases where people can have control over their beliefs and desires and those where they cannot. Knowledge is necessary in order that a person have this possibility of control. In the account I gave of when a person could be said to have freely acquired his/her desires I only required that the person have knowledge of the causes, (and also that they not be against the person's will), in order that the causes not be coercive. Oftentimes, however, one needs to have more than simple knowledge of the causes. Conditioning is a case where the person being conditioned might know the causes, that is, might know the elements of the causal process, but might not know their interconnections or the purposes behind them. The person is acquainted with the causes but unaware that they are the causes or how and why they operate. If conditioning would operate regardless of whether a person knew the latter, then it is a causal process that the person cannot have any control over. Hence it is coercive.

Sometimes the efficacy of causal conditions depends on people's ignorance of them, that they are or may be causes, and how and why they operate. In such cases, people's ignorance of these facts would deprive them of whatever control knowledge might give them. People are less free to the extent that they operate on unconscious motives. Successful psychoanalysis can increase the patient's control and therefore freedom, by making conscious things that had hithertofore been unconscious. Sometimes just knowing the purposes behind potential causes, (e.g., that it is designed to convince you, scare you, buy you off, or get you to buy something), can make a difference to whether those purposes are realized. Without the knowledge, one's attitudes towards these purposes cannot come into play and one cannot exercise any control over them. If the efficacy of the causes depends on one's ignorance of such facts about the causes, then the causes are coercive. It is where knowledge about the causes would have made a difference that ignorance makes the causes coercive. Causes of beliefs and desires are coercive where they operate contrary to the person's other beliefs, desires, character and personality. This is so when the causes are explicitly against the person's will, or unknown to the person, or when they depend for their efficacy on the person's ignorance of certain facts about them. According to these conditions, conditioning would usually be coercive, which, I think, is as it should be.

Suppose one came to know that one was being conditioned and the knowledge made no difference to the efficacy of the causes. Is this a coercive way of acquiring desires? The answer depends on whether the conditioning process was against the person's will. If the causes operate against his/her will then they are coercive. On the other hand, suppose they are not operating against the person's will; in other words, suppose a person voluntarily chooses to be conditioned. A person might deliberately expose himself to conditions which will cause him to have (or not have) certain desires, e.g., not to smoke. Once he puts himself into the situation, the causes operate independent of his other beliefs and desires, personality, etc. His new effective desire not to smoke will be the result of conditioning, and we have said that conditioning is a form of coercion. However, I think that the circumstances of this kind of case make a significant difference. The person's self does enter into the causal process as an active determinant, whereas in most cases of conditioning this is not so. The person in our example who voluntarily has himself conditioned has a second order volition not to smoke, which is in conflict with his or her volition to smoke. If the second order volition were sufficiently strong to outweigh the first order volition by itself, then the new effective desire would be acquired in a completely free manner. However, it is not sufficiently strong to do this by itself. Causes that are independent of the person are necessary to change his desire. However, these other causes come into play only because of his second order volition. He had himself conditioned because he has a desire not to desire to smoke. So I think we can say that the cause of his new effective desire not to smoke is his second order volition. The new desire is not the result of coercion; it does spring from the self. However, it does not only spring from the self. It was not acquired in as free a manner as if the second order volition was sufficient by itself to cause it, but I would still put it towards the free end of the continuum.

What we have come up with is what we started with and that is, that to the extent that the causes of one's actions are themselves caused by things over which people have no control, (even with knowledge of them), to that extent one's actions are unfree. What I have tried to do is to make sense of the idea of having control over one's desires. In order to say that one has control over one's desires it is necessary that what we identify as the self determines what one desires and what desires one acts on. To put together the criteria elaborated thus far: in order for actions caused by desires to be free, these desires must first of all not have been coercively acquired. What this means has been explained. Knowledge was seen to be a key factor. Secondly, they must not be contrary to the person's second order volitions. This second condition implies that the person has second order volitions. We will not be able to say that these desires are the desires the person wants to have unless a) he/she has second order volitions and unless b) these volitions outweigh first order volitions in the case of a conflict. Thirdly, the desire must be in harmony with an integrated set of desires and beliefs—hence one's self at that given time. This third requirement must be qualified. A desire causing a free action may be inconsistent with this integrated set if the set does not meet one of the necessary conditions and the desire fulfills both the conditions. If the set was coercively acquired and the conflicting desire was not, or if the conflicting desire is supported by a second order volition and the set is not, then an action caused by the conflicting desire would

be free. Any person missing second order volitions is missing an important kind of control over his/her actions, and hence an important dimension of freedom.[14] That is why an action that proceeds from a conflicting desire which is supported by a second order volition is freer than one that proceeded from the integrated set, where there are no effective second order volitions. This sort of situation could lead to a revision of the set—a restructuring of the self. However, lacking an integrated set which is responsible for his/her actions, the person is divided, and it is less possible for that person to be a self-determining being. Therefore, the person is most free when there is an integrated set which is in accordance with his/her second order volitions. Then we can say that this is a self-determining person.[15]

• • •

VII

As a prelude to concluding, I wish to consider the implications of my general and abstract analysis to the concrete question of just how free most people are today. We shall see that although my view implies that people can be free, though determined, it is also an implication of my view that most people are quite unfree today. The answer to this question

---

[14]What Frankfurt says is somewhat different. According to him, such a being would not be a person because having second order volitions is essential to being a person in this sense: a being without them is a wanton. We also differ in that I connect freedom of will and freedom of action whereas he separates them, and thirdly, in that I give a sense to the idea of controlling one's desires (freedom of will) independent of the idea of second order volitions.

[15]It may be worth pointing out that all of my criteria allow for the possibility that two people could perform the same act for the same reasons but one does it freely, the other unfreely. I do not see this as an objection of my account (Paul Teller raised it as an objection.) All accounts of freedom allow the possibility of the same act (type) performed by one person being free and by another person being unfree. The act's (un)freedom depends on facts about its cause. Incompatibilists would say it depends on whether it's caused; compatibilists would say it depends on what the cause is. Since my account goes beyond the act, and its causes or lack thereof, to the causes of the causes of the act, it makes sense that the (un)freedom of the act would depend on facts about the causes of the causes.

of how free people are is not one that applies to all people just in virtue of their being human, but rather depends on who the people are and where and when they are living. It turns out, then, on my view, that human freedom is closely tied to social and political freedom and is not a distinct metaphysical question. (In considering this part of the philosophical question we are inevitably drawn into empirical issues, including political ones, so my own opinion on these matters will certainly intrude.)

Desires arise in us because of a whole complex set of conditions which affect one another. (Neither they nor their influence can actually be separated so the following remarks are unavoidably artificial.) These determining conditions include physical and psychological conditions, which to some extent we share with others, but which also differ from person to person. People today are capable of some but not much control over these conditions. Greater knowledge, aided by money, gives a person greater possibilities of control, but there are still very definite limits which no one today is capable of transcending. Greater knowledge will give greater possibilities of human control, but it is probable that there will always be limits that one cannot transcend. What is possible is for a person to exercise some control over the form of the desires these conditions tend to produce, and also over whether and how these desires are acted upon.

How much control a person can exercise over the social and political conditions causing his/her desires depends on the particular social system in which the person lives, and also the place that the person occupies in the system. Some changes are possible in the latter in most societies but usually quite little. In any case, it is only within the framework allowed by that system and it is not possible within the framework of *any* present society for *most* people to change their positions within that framework. As for the framework itself, one cannot change the time in which one lives, and since what social systems are possible depends on the time and place, there is a certain inevitable limitation. However, there are many fewer inevitable limitations on the degree of control one can exercise over social causes than over physical causes—in the future, but

also in the present. Given the limitations of time and place, there is great potential today for people to collectively control the social conditions under which they live, and hence the beliefs and desires these conditions tend to produce, even if there are some conditions they still would not be able to control. However, with some notable exceptions, the ability to control the social conditions in which one lives is only potential today, not actual. This is partially because people do not realize they have this ability.[16] This lack of realization is strongly supported, of course, by the social system in which they live and by those who do control it. There is, again, the possibility of exercising some control over the form of the desires likely to be produced by these conditions, and also over whether and how these desires are acted upon. However, so long as one does not control the social causes of one's beliefs and desires, one does not have much chance of controlling the actual beliefs and desires one comes to have.

Leaving aside the nature of the influence, what is necessary in order to be able to exercise control over the influences acting upon one, is to be a certain kind of person, as well as to have knowledge and the cooperation of others. A person who is critical and discriminating and sees him/herself as actively shaping the world, history and also him/herself, is capable of doing just that—not alone, but in cooperation with others. There are, of course, varying conditions where people may be more or less aware and/or more or less able not to be passive products. However, it seems that most people today are quite uncritical and undiscriminating and lack this self-conception. Many feel themselves to be more like passive products of history and their own particular environment—and their environment makes them feel that way. However, in the course of struggle against the oppressive aspects of their environment, they can come to realize their potential to bring the

---

[16]This is the phenomenon of fetishism that Marx discusses. "Such conditions are . . . independent of individuals and appear, although they are created by society, to be the same as natural conditions, i.e., uncontrollable by the individual." *The Grundrisse—Karl Marx,* edited by David McLellan (New York, Harper and Row, 1971), p. 72.

world under their conscious collective control. The realization of this is a first step towards changing the framework that keeps them without control. This capacity to change the world and consequently their own nature is unique to human beings. It gives them the potential of being free in the fullest sense that is possible in a deterministic world.[17]

FREEDOM OF THE WILL

Kitaro Nishida

I argued . . . that in psychological terms the will is simply one phenomenon of consciousness but that in terms of its fundamental nature it is the base of reality. We now must consider whether the will is a free or determined activity, a question that has perplexed scholars since ancient times and that holds important implications for morality. Through this discussion we can clarify the philosophical character of the will.

Judging from what people usually believe, we all consider the will to be free. Given our experience of our consciousness, within a certain sphere of action we are able to do something while also being able not to do it—that is, we believe we are free within that sphere. For this reason ideas of responsibility, irresponsibility, self-confidence, regret, praise, and blame arise in us. But let us now give careful thought to what is meant by "within a certain sphere."

We cannot freely control all things in the external world. Even our own bodies cannot be freely manipulated in any absolute sense. The voluntary movement of muscles seems to be free, but if we become ill we are no longer able to move our muscles freely. The only things we can freely manage are our own phenomena of consciousness. Even so, we have neither the freedom to create ideas anew nor the freedom to recall at any time something we once experienced. That which we regard as truly free is simply the activity of a union of ideas—that is, how we analyze ideas and how we synthesize them derive from the freedom of the self. And yet, an indisputable, a priori law functions in the analysis and synthesis of ideas, so we are not here able to do as we please either. Moreover, when a union of ideas stands alone or when a certain union is especially strong, we must fully obey it. We possess total freedom of choice only in the context of the a priori law of the establishment of ideas, and only when of two or more ways to unite ideas none has the strength to dominate.

Many of those who expound theories about the freedom of the will base their arguments on the facts of experience in the internal world. According to them, within that scope the selection of motives is in all respects a matter of our freedom and has no other reason than ourselves. They argue that decision is based on a type of mystical power—called the will—that is independent of both the various conditions in the external world and disposition, habit, and character in the internal world. In short, they posit a power that exists apart from the union of ideas while controlling it.

In contrast, those who expound deterministic theories of the will generally do so on the basis of observations of facts in the external world. According to them, the phenomena of the universe do not occur fortuitously; even extremely minute matters, when investigated in detail, necessarily possess a sufficient cause. This is the idea behind scholarly inquiry, and with the development of science it becomes increasingly certain. The causes and effects of natural phenomena formerly considered mysterious have since become clear, and we have advanced to the point where we can calculate them mathematically. At present, only our will is still regarded as having

---

[17]This perspective is similar to that expressed by Marx in *Capital* where he says, "The freedom in this field [i.e., the realm of necessity] cannot consist of anything else but the fact that socialized man, the associated producers regulate their interchange with nature rationally, bring it under their human control, instead of being ruled by it as by some blind power; then they accomplish their task with the least expenditure of energy and under conditions most adequate to their human nature and most worthy of it. But it always remains a realm of necessity. Beyond it begins that development of human power, which is its own end, the true realm of freedom, which, however, can flourish only upon that realm of necessity as its basis." *Capital,* Vol. III, English translation, p. 820.

no cause. Even the will, however, cannot escape from the great, unchanging laws of nature. We continue to think that the will is free because the development of science is still in its infancy and because we cannot explain each of the causes of the will. It is true that in individual instances the action of the will appears to be irregular and devoid of any fixed cause, but if we look statistically at the actions of a large number of people, we discern that the actions are surprisingly orderly and that they have certain causes and effects. These observations strengthen our conviction that there are causes related to our will and bring us to the conclusion that our will, just like all other phenomena of nature, is ruled by a necessary, mechanical law of cause and effect and therefore is not some sort of mysterious power.

Which of these opposing theories is correct? As I stated before, those who uphold theories of free will in an extreme form tell us that we have a mysterious ability to choose motives freely without any cause or reason. But this assertion is totally mistaken, for there must be a sufficient reason for our choice of motives. Even if the reason does not appear clearly in consciousness, it must exist beneath consciousness. Moreover, if—as the proponents of free will contend—something decides things fortuitously without any reason, then at the time of decision we would not feel that the will is free; rather we would feel the decision to be a fortuitous event that has functioned from without, and our feeling of responsibility for the decision would be weak. Those who advance theories of free will set forth their arguments on the basis of experience in the internal world, but such internal experience actually proves the opposite—determinism.

Let us now offer a criticism of the determinist argument. These proponents claim that because natural phenomena are controlled by the law of mechanical necessity, phenomena of consciousness must be controlled by it as well. This stance is based on the assumption that phenomena of consciousness and natural phenomena (that is, material phenomena) are identical and controlled by the same law. But is this assumption correct? Whether phenomena of consciousness and material phenomena are controlled by the same law is an unsettled issue,

and arguments marshalled on this assumption are extremely weak. Even if modern physiological psychology advances to the point where we can physically or chemically explain each of the functions of the brain at the base of consciousness, will we thereby be able to assert that phenomena of consciousness are controlled by a mechanical law of necessity? For example, the bronze that serves as the raw material of a statue perhaps cannot escape the domination of the laws of mechanical necessity, but can we not say that the meaning expressed by the statue exists apart from those laws? So-called spiritual meaning cannot be seen, heard, or counted; it transcends the laws of mechanical necessity.

In summary, the kind of will described by those who argue for the freedom of the will—a will that is totally without cause or reason—does not exist. Such a contingent will would not be felt to be free; rather, it would be felt to be oppressive. When we function for a certain reason, that is, from the internal character of the self, we feel ourselves to be free. And we feel most free when the cause of a motive emerges from the most profound internal character of the self. The reason behind the will, however, is not a mechanical cause as described by determinists. Our spirit contains a law governing its activity, and when spirit functions in accordance with its own law, it is truly free.

Freedom thus has two possible meanings: (1) being totally without cause, that is, fortuitous or contingent, and (2) having no external restrictions and therefore functioning of and by oneself. The latter indicates autonomous freedom, and this is the freedom of the will. At this point, the following problem arises. Assuming that freedom means to function according to one's character, we see that amongst the countless things around us nothing fails to function so. The flowing of water and the burning of fire are examples of this. Why then is only the will considered to be free and other things to be determined?

The occurrence of a phenomenon in the natural world is determined strictly by its circumstances. Only one, certain phenomenon—and no others—arises from a particular set of circumstances. All natural phenomena arise according to this sort of blind necessity. Phenomena of consciousness, however, do not simply arise, for they are phenomena of which we are conscious—that is, they arise and we know that they have arisen. Knowing something or being conscious of it includes other possibilities. To be conscious of taking something includes the possibility of not taking it. To put it more exactly, consciousness always possesses a universal character—consciousness always includes an idealistic element, otherwise it is not consciousness. That consciousness has such a character means that it harbors possibilities other than actual events. Being actual yet including ideals, being idealistic and yet not separating from actuality—this is the distinctive character of consciousness. Consciousness is in fact never controlled by other things, for it is always controlling them. Knowing this, even if our conduct occurs according to necessary laws we are not confined by the conduct. Moreover, actuality is simply one particular instance of the ideals that constitute the base of consciousness; that is, it is simply one process in which the ideals actualize themselves. Conduct therefore is not generated from without, but from within. And because we see actuality as simply one instance of the ideals, consciousness comes to include numerous other possibilities.

Consciousness is free not because it functions fortuitously beyond the laws of nature, but rather because it follows its own nature. It is free not because it functions for no reason, but because it knows well the reasons behind its functioning. As our knowledge advances, we become freer people. Even if we are controlled or oppressed by others, when we know this we extricate ourselves from the oppression. If we go even farther and realize the unavoidable reason for the situation, then the oppression turns into freedom—Socrates was freer than the Athenians who poisoned him. Pascal said that a person is as weak as a reed, but because he or she is a thinking reed, even if the whole world tries to destroy him, he is greater than that which kills him, for he himself knows that he will die.

As discussed earlier . . . the idealistic element—that is, the unifying activity—that constitutes the base of consciousness is not a product of nature; rather, it is because of this unity that nature comes to exist. This unity is the infinite power at the base of reality, and it cannot be limited quantitatively. It exists independently of the necessary laws of nature. Because our will is an expression of that power, it is free and goes beyond the control of such natural laws.

QUESTIONS FOR DISCUSSION

1. Discuss: Freedom is a problem of both external physical constraints—consider Schlick's analysis of freedom as the absence of compulsion—and internal psychological constraints. What can we do to become more free in both senses?

2. Is freedom compatible with determinism? In your answer consider: (a) Schlick's analysis of freedom; and (b) the problem of conditioning and our ability to have control over the sources of our beliefs and desires.

3. Hospers claims that "our very acts of volition and the entire train of deliberations leading up to them are but facades for the expression of unconscious wishes, or rather, unconscious compromises and defenses." In light of this claim, analyze an important choice that you have made. Was it really a free choice?

4. Does Nancy Holmstrom's analysis of freedom really succeed in "firming up" soft determinism—in particular, does it succeed in drawing a clear distinction between conditioned acts that are unfree and those that are free? Does it provide an adequate response to Hospers' analysis of the implications of unconscious motivation?

5. If human beings are not free, they cannot be held morally responsible for their actions. Does soft determinism provide enough "freedom" for human beings to be considered morally responsible? In answering this question, refer to Schlick and at least one other thinker in this section.

6. Discuss Nishida's claim that consciousness is determined by laws governing its own activity. To what extent do you believe that consciousness is free from external determination? What is the role of knowledge and reason in human freedom?

Two Ragamuffins, "Didn't Live Nowhere," The Jacob A. Riis Collection, Museum of the City of New York.

CHAPTER 7

ETHICS

Of what does *ethics* consist? Is it the response to a moral law? Is it obedience to God? Or obedience to the rational? Or is it to be understood entirely in terms of its human function, its role in the promotion of human happiness? Both the *Bhagavad-Gita* and philosopher Immanuel Kant consider ethics to be based on duty, which is respect for a moral law. The *Bhagavad-Gita* sees that moral law ordained by God and written into human social roles. Kant discerns the universal moral law through use of reason. Both assert that if all humanity followed this moral law, there would be harmony in society. Both Kant and the *Bhagavad-Gita* put forward deontological ethical positions (emphasizing duty), but while their views are similar, they are also distinct, insofar as the *Bhagavad-Gita*'s ethics of duty has a liberatory aspect to it. While the goal of Kant's ethics of duty would be a world in which rationality and morality guided all individuals and governments, the goal set by the *Bhagavad-Gita* entails spiritual freedom.

There are, however, critics of an ethics of duty. Mill's utilitarian theory insists that the right action is the one that would increase human happiness. Although we could try to reconcile the two and say that it is one's "duty" to increase happiness for oneself

and others, Kant's notion of duty specifically rules out concerns for happiness, so that "right" alone will prevail. In similar fashion, in the *Bhagavad-Gita,* the hero, Arjuna, on the promise that it will lead to liberation from suffering, is counseled to put aside all feelings of sadness and compassion so that he can do his duty.

It is the above abstract and "unfeeling" aspect of the ethics of duty that Virginia Held criticizes in her analysis. The idea of a detached, rational analysis providing a guide for action belittles the positive role of emotion and care for others. It puts asunder all relationships of care between persons and replaces them with respect for an abstract law. Such ethical systems are skewed, according to Held, because they come wholly from a male point of view and have neglected women's ethical experience.

Another theme, explored in the second section of this chapter, examines the issue of altruism or other-centered moral theories, in contrast to egoistic or self-centered theories. Throughout the centuries, moral theories and religious world views have described the moral life as opposed to the usual, amoral, and self-centered "survival instinct" acted upon naturally by so many humans. In our chapter, Motse argues that an adequate ethics would advocate universal love for all humans. But not everyone agrees that one must give up one's egoistic concerns of survival and thriving, merely to fulfill the whims of others. Twentieth-century thinker Ayn Rand delivers a searing critique of altruistic moral theories and propounds what she considers a superior, egoistic basis for ethics. In contrast, our third author, Gunapala Dharmasiri, argues that an accurate understanding of the self would lead us to question the distinction between self and others; a real egoism would have to be altruistic. Finally, Carlo Filice also walks a middle ground between egoism and altruism while exploring the question: Do I have an obligation to help others in need? Our duty to help others in emergencies entails a daily readiness to help.

It is obvious to even the casual student of history or anthropology that different people have held different moral views at different times and places. Is this because, as absolutists would claim, only some people were right and others were wrong? Or can the same action be right in one context, wrong in another? Nowadays, with the emphasis put by many people on sensitivity toward cultures other than one's own, several questions concerning tolerance and pluralism arise: Should I apologize for my own views? Should I refrain from trying to convert others to my philosophy, for fear that I may damage their own valuable belief system? Can I ever say that anyone else is wrong? Can we ever use force to stop someone from acting on his or her beliefs?

Wherever two cultures meet and the one tries to supplant the other, issues of how moral systems get their legitimacy and authority arise. Such cultural clashes bring to life the perennial moral dilemmas posed in the third section by our three authors, Alejandro Korn, Alain Locke, and David Wong. Korn and Locke were active primarily in the first half of the twentieth century, while Wong is a contemporary philosopher.

Alejandro Korn, the Argentinian philosopher well-known in Latin America, argues that indeed all moral judgments are subjective. There is no universal standard, and no criteria by which to tell if a moral stance is the correct one. But Korn thinks this subjectivity presents no substantive problem. Others, of course,

would disagree. African-American philosopher Alain Locke, influenced by a pragmatist approach to truth and value, also charges that universalists who think values are objective and unchanging are wrong. But values are not arbitrary either; rather, values change and progress over time as circumstances change and as people have greater experience. Old values are not simply rejected but found to be inadequate and so are superseded by better views. In addition, he believes it is important through self-education to become more cosmopolitan in one's tastes so that a wider variation of value can be experienced and appreciated.

Contemporary Asian-American philosopher David Wong explains that relativism is often dismissed by its critics, who put relativist arguments in their most extreme form so that they can easily be defeated. For example, the relativist says judging others is wrong; but since the relativist is criticizing others, he or she is engaging in judging others as well. Wong argues that a more moderate version of relativism is defensible, since such a view would still allow one to speak out against societies that practice grave evil. He adds that relativism can more adequately account for the nature of dilemmas that arise because different societies hold values that are different yet reasonable ethical ideals.

To explore further the issues of the Buddhist view of reality and the Buddhist conception of the self, as background to Dharmasiri's article, see "Questions of King Milinda" in Chapter 5, Sivaraska's article in Chapter 3, and the Saddhatissa selection in Chapter 8. Those interested in relativism may also be interested in Section One of Chapter 9, where our ability to understand others' point of view is discussed by several authors. Motse's argument for universal love is paralleled in the works of Gandhi and King, included in Section Three of Chapter 9. Those interested in moral theories might like to study Aristotle's ethics, which concentrate on the cultivation of virtuous character, included in Section One of Chapter 8. Finally, those who would like to explore feminist critiques of philosophy along the lines of Held's approach might want to look at Beauvoir, Spelman, and Hubbard in Sections Two and Three of Chapter 4, and Carol Christ in Section Three of Chapter 3.

THE ETHICS OF DUTY AND ITS CRITICS

Our first account of an ethics of duty is taken from India. The *Bhagavad-Gita* was a poem passed down through time by oral tradition. It found its way into the Hindu epic poem the *Mahabharata,* which is the longest poem in the world. It is regarded as a sacred text in the Hindu religious and philosophical tradition. The story line of the *Mahabharata* is a struggle between the forces of good and evil, and it culminates with a war on a large battlefield. The "good" is represented by the Pandavas family, and Arjuna is one of the sons of Pandu. The "evil" is represented by the Kurava family. The specific conflict that tears these related families apart has to do with rivalry caused by choosing an heir-apparent to the throne. Although many scholars argue that the story line of the *Mahabharata* points to an actual historical event, the dialogue between Krishna and Arjuna is considered to be a spiritual masterpiece, set in the context of the larger story line of the epic poem but possessing a spiritual insight that does not depend on its historical connection to any actual battle. Estimates of its dates run as early as 800 BCE.

In this selection, from Chapters 1 through 3 of the *Bhagavad-Gita,* we witness a dialogue between Arjuna, a young warrior, and Krishna, an avatar or incarnation of God, who advises him on the battleground. The story is used in the Hindu tradition to illustrate the proper attitude toward life and responsibility. In this particular battle, Arjuna does not want to fight, because he is moved by the sight of his friends, relatives, and teachers who are assembled to fight him on the battlefield. Yet, as a member of the warrior caste, it is his job to serve his community through selflessly fighting, and so it is not proper that he be moved to tears and put down his arms. This is explained to Arjuna by Krishna, who suggests that Arjuna should not be attached to the repercussions of his actions but should do his duty in a detached manner. Wars should not be fought for personal gain and power but for a just cause. If one resists desire and the pleasures of sense, the mind will not be clouded and the soul will find peace.

Since Arjuna seems to be trying to enact a life of renunciation, as he has explained that he would rather be killed on the battlefield than fight, Krishna counsels against a life of renunciation, and in favor of a life of duty, where one fulfills the tasks assigned and works happily with detachment: a spiritual practice called karma yoga. It is aptly described as an ethics of duty, in which not only must one do one's duty because God has ordained it, but also because it is the way to true, spiritual happiness, in contrast to other pleasures that are passing and end in despair.

It should be noted that throughout the centuries there have been alternative interpretations of this passage that draw from it different conclusions about action. Although many might conclude that this passage attempts to reconcile young men to their position in military service, seeing it as a duty, Mohandas Gandhi, for example, held a somewhat unorthodox interpretation of the story. He insisted that the story did not describe a literal battlefield, and was not really about war. Rather, it was metaphorical, and represented the struggle between good and evil in the mind of each individual. In this way, one could regard the passage as not necessarily advocating violence, a position that was more consistent with Gandhi's devotion to the principle of *ahimsa* or nonviolence.

Although the practice of caste cannot be found in eighteenth-century Konigsberg, it is hard not to notice some similarities in disposition between the doctrines in the *Bhagavad-Gita* and Kant's concept of duty. Kant, like the *Bhagavad-Gita,* voices a fear of emotions that might sway one from the right course. However, the discernment of just what is one's duty he sees differently. The *Bhagavad-Gita* emphasizes God's ordination, presumably known through tradition; Kant emphasizes reason's ability to discern right action.

Immanuel Kant (1724–1804) was born in Konigsberg, Prussia (now Kaliningrad, Russia), to pietist parents. Kant decided he did not want to be like his parents, whose emotionally religious fervor did not suit him. Instead, he wrote a book entitled

Religion Within the Limits of Reason Alone, which summed up his stance that whatever is rational in religion should be accepted, while the rest discarded. Kant spent his whole life in Konigsberg, where he was a popular philosophy professor. He begins the essay included here by emphasizing the central importance of the good will, meaning the intention to do good. Regardless of its ability to enact what it desires, it is valuable and praiseworthy for its own sake. Kant discerns that the goal of life is to do the good—in other words, to do one's moral duty—which means to act in respect to the moral law. Kant asserts that an action has moral worth only if it is done from duty; to do what is right out of sympathy and compassion can no more give an action moral worth than a right action done for the motive of self-interest. Each of us can discern the proper course of action by making sure that the maxim of our action could become a universal law. This formula is known as Kant's "categorical imperative." As universality is the basic property of reason, it is pure reason itself—that is, reason free of emotions—from which our sense of duty is derived.

Kant's position is often contrasted to that of J. S. Mill (1806–1873). Mill was a British philosopher who was greatly influenced by Jeremy Bentham, who had been the founder of an ethical view known as "utilitarianism."

Mill argues that the goal of human life is happiness, and his "utilitarian" formulation of ethics argues that an action is the correct one if it results in the greatest happiness for the greatest number of people. Mill's position offers a challenge to Kant in several ways. Firstly, Mill's position is hedonistic; he believes pleasure is the goal of human life. Of course, he makes distinctions, asserting that humans are capable of a pleasure more sophisticated than animal gratification. But that all humans seek pleasure as the highest end is a fact that Mill considers obvious. Secondly, Mill contends that intentions aren't important, as long as the consequences of an action increase happiness for the greatest number of people. This is what is referred to as the "consequentialist" aspect of his view, with its emphasis on consequences as justification for action,

as opposed to Kant's emphasis on intentions. As one would expect, a view entitled "utilitarianism" emphasizes the practical consequences that result from an action or policy. Although certainly in opposition to Kant's view, Mill himself thought there was an implicit consequentialism in Kant's intentional theory, in that the latter was implicitly appealing to the consequences of adopting the maxim of your action as a universal law.

Needless to say, many philosophers have joined in this ethical debate between Kant and Mill, taking one side or the other or even criticizing both. For example, it could be argued that accepting Kant's "categorical imperative" is accepting too subjective a criterion, for it allows the callous to accept the possibility of harsh treatment, while the overly sensitive will rule out even minor inconveniences towards others. ("It is acceptable to hurt others' feelings" may be a maxim accepted by some and not by others, as well as "It is acceptable to abandon people in need of help"). Criticisms of Mill's utilitarianism involve the unpredictability of the future, an aspect that especially wreaks havoc on an ethical view based wholly on the weighing of future consequences.

Our fourth author in this section, Virginia Held, a contemporary American philosophy professor who teaches at Hunter College and the Graduate School of the City University of New York, has her own unique angle on the shortcomings of both Kant's and Mill's ethical theories. Her article puts forward not only her own view but attempts to represent some common threads of thought in the contemporary ethical theorizing of many women philosophers. Traditional ethical theories, she asserts, have been written from the male standpoint. Praise of reason and denigration of emotion, rather than being the obviously preferable moral position, is biased in favor of men's experience and relegates to women an inferior status. Male ethicists tend to abstract individuals from their families and their general social context, which obscures the true human situation, framing ethical obligations by means of a contextless, abstract, fictitious individual. Both Kant's and Mill's approach to any moral dilemma is too abstracted from the concrete situation; such a cool, calculated approach to moral dilemmas denigrates the positive role of emotion, involvement, and the nuances of concrete situations. An alternative women's moral theory would entail appreciating the context of the dilemma. A fruitful resolution of a moral dilemma would show itself in the restoration of human relationships, not the upholding of a rule such as the principle of utility or the categorical imperative. An "ethic of care" may be more important than the more abstract and legalistic "ethic of justice."

RIGHT ACTION

Bhagavad-Gita

CHAPTER 1. THE HESITATION AND DESPONDENCY OF ARJUNA

The question

Dhṛtarāṣṭra said:

1. In the field of righteousness, the field of the Kurus,[1] when my people and the sons of Pāṇḍu had gathered together, eager for battle, what did they do, O Saṁjaya?[2]

Saṁjaya said:

2. Then, Duryodhana the prince, having seen the army of the Pāṇḍavas drawn up in battle order, approached his teacher and spoke this word:

3. Behold, O Teacher, this mighty army of the sons of Pāṇḍu organized by thy wise pupil, the son of Drupada.

4. Here are heroes, great bowmen equal in battle to Bhīma[3] and Arjuna[4]—Yuyudhāna, Virāṭa, and Drupada, a mighty warrior;

5. Dhṛṣṭaketu, Cekitāna and the valiant King of Kāśi, also Purujit, Kuntibhoja and Śaibya, the foremost of men;

6. Yudhāmanyu, the strong and Uttamauja, the brave; and also the son of Subhadrā and sons of Draupadī, all of them great warriors.

7. Know also, O best of the twiceborn,[5] the leaders of my army, those who are most distinguished among us. I will name them now for thine information:

8. Thyself and Bhīṣma and Karṇa and Kṛpa, ever victorious in battle; Asvatthāman, Vikarṇa, and also the son of Somadatta;

9. And many other heroes who have risked their lives for my sake. They are armed with many kinds of weapons and are all well skilled in war.

10. Unlimited is this army of ours which is guarded by Bhīṣma, while that army of theirs, which is guarded by Bhīma, is limited.

11. Therefore do ye all support Bhīṣma, standing firm in all the fronts, in your respective ranks.

12. In order to cheer him up, the aged Kuru, his valiant grandsire, roared aloud like a lion and blew his conch.

---

[1]Kurukṣetra is the land of the Kurus, a leading clan of the period. It is a vast field near Hastināpura in the neighborhood of modern Delhi. When Dhṛtarāṣṭra, the blind king of the Kurus, decided to give his throne to Yudhiṣṭhira, who is also known as Dharmarāja, the embodiment of virtue, in preference to his own eldest son, Duryodhana, the latter, by tricks and treachery, secured the throne for himself and attempted to destroy Yudhiṣṭhira and his four brothers. Kṛṣṇa, the head of the Yādava clan, sought to bring about a reconciliation between the cousins. When all attempts failed, a fratricidal war between the Kauravas and the Pāṇḍavas became inevitable. Kṛṣṇa proposed that he and his vassals would join the two sides and left the choice to the parties. The vassals were selected by Duryodhana, and Kṛṣṇa himself joined the Pāṇḍavas as the charioteer of Arjuna.
[2]Saṁjaya is the charioteer of the blind king, Dhṛtarāṣṭra, who reports to him the events of the war. (Many of the other names used in the text are without philosophical significance and no attempt will be made to explain them.)

---

[3]Bhīma is Yudhiṣṭhira's Commander-in-Chief, though nominally Dhṛṣṭadyumna holds that office.
[4]Arjuna is the friend of Kṛṣṇa and the great hero of the Pāṇḍavas. Other names used for Arjuna are Bhārata (descended of Bhārata), Dhanaṁjaya (winner of wealth), Gudākeśa (having the hair in a ball), Pārtha (son of Pṛthā), Paraṁtapa (oppressor of the enemy).
[5]One who is twice-born is one who is invested with the sacred thread, the symbol of initiation into the life of spirit, which is the aim of education.

13. Then conches and kettledrums, tabors and drums and horns suddenly blared forth and the noise was tumultuous.

14. When stationed in their great chariot yoked to white horses, Kṛṣṇa and Arjuna blew their celestial conches.

15. Kṛṣṇa blew his Pāñcajanya and Arjuna his Devadatta and Bhīma of terrific deeds blew his mighty conch, Pauṇḍra.

16. Prince Yudhiṣṭhira, the son of Kuntī, blew his Anantavijaya and Nakula and Sahadeva blew their Sughoṣa and Maṇipuṣpaka.

17. And the king of Kāśi, the Chief of archers, Śikhaṇḍin, the great warrior, Dhṛṣṭadyumna and Virāṭa and the invincible Sātyaki;

18. Drupada and the sons of Draupadī, O Lord of earth, and the strong-armed son of Subhadrā, on all sides blew their respective conches.

19. The tumultuous uproar resounding through earth and sky rent the hearts of Dhṛtarāṣṭra's sons.

20. Then Arjuna, whose banner bore the crest of Hanumān, looked at the sons of Dhṛtarāṣṭra drawn up in battle order; and as the flight of missiles [almost] started, he took up his bow.

21. And, O Lord of earth, he spoke this word to Hṛṣīkeśa (Kṛṣṇa): Draw up my chariot, O Acyuta (Kṛṣṇa),[6] between the two armies.

22. So that I may observe these men standing, eager for battle, with whom I have to contend in this strife of war.

23. I wish to look at those who are assembled here, ready to fight and eager to achieve in battle what is dear to the evil-minded son of Dhṛtarāṣṭra.

24. Thus addressed by Guḍākeśa (Arjuna), Hṛṣīkeśa (Kṛṣṇa) drew up that best of chariots, O Bhārata (Dhṛtarāṣṭra), between the two armies.

25. In front of Bhīṣma, Droṇa, and all the chiefs he said: "Behold, O Pārtha (Arjuna), these Kurus assembled here."

26. There saw Arjuna standing fathers and grandfathers, teachers, uncles, brothers, sons and grandsons, as also companions;

27. And also fathers-in-law and friends in both the armies. When the son of Kuntī (Arjuna) saw all these kinsmen thus standing arrayed,

28. He was overcome with great compassion and uttered this in sadness:

The Distress of Arjuna

When I see my own people arrayed and eager for fight, O Kṛṣṇa,

29. My limbs quail, my mouth goes dry, my body shakes and my hair stands on end.

30. The bow Gāṇḍiva slips from my hand, and my skin too is burning all over. I am not able to stand steady. My mind is reeling.

31. And I see evil omens, O Keśava (Kṛṣṇa), nor do I foresee any good by slaying my own people in the fight.

32. I do not long for victory, O Kṛṣṇa, nor kingdom nor pleasures. Of what use is kingdom to us, O Kṛṣṇa, or enjoyment or even life?

33. Those for whose sake we desire kingdom, enjoyments and pleasures—they stand here in battle, renouncing their lives and riches:

34. Teachers, fathers, sons, and also grandfathers; uncles and fathers-in-law, grandsons and brothers-in-law, and other kinsmen.

35. These I would not consent to kill, though killed myself, O Madhusūdana (Kṛṣṇa), even for the kingdom of the three worlds; how much less for the sake of the earth?

36. What pleasure can be ours, O Kṛṣṇa, after we have slain the sons of Dhṛtarāṣṭra? Only sin will accrue to us if we kill these criminals.

37. So it is not right that we slay our kinsmen, the sons of Dhṛtarāṣṭra. Indeed, how can we be happy, O Mādhava (Kṛṣṇa), if we kill our own people?

---

[6]Acyuta (immovable) is another name for Kṛṣṇa. Other names used for Kṛṣṇa are Madhusūdana (slayer of the demon Madhu), Ariśūdana (slayer of enemies), Govinda (herdsman or giver of enlightenment), Vāsudeva (son of Vasudeva), Yādava (descendent of Yadu), Keśava (having fine hair), Mādhava (the husband of Lakṣmī), Hṛṣīkeśa (lord of the senses, *hṛṣika, īśa*), Janārdana (the liberator of men).

38. Even if these whose minds are overpowered by greed see no wrong in the destruction of the family and no crime in treachery to friends;

39. Why should we not have the wisdom to turn away from this sin, O Janārdana (Kṛṣṇa), we who see the wrong in the destruction of the family?

40. In the ruin of a family, its ancient laws are destroyed: and when the laws perish, the whole family yields to lawlessness.

41. And when lawlessness prevails, O Vārṣṇeya (Kṛṣṇa), the women of the family become corrupted, and when women are corrupted, confusion of castes arises.

42. And to hell does this confusion bring the family itself as well as those who have destroyed it. For the spirits of their ancestors fall, deprived of their offerings of rice and water.

43. By the misdeeds of those who destroy a family and create confusion of *varṇas* [castes], the immemorial laws of the race and the family are destroyed.

44. And we have heard it said, O Janārdana (Kṛṣṇa), that the men of the families whose laws are destroyed needs must live in hell.

45. Alas, what a great sin have we resolved to commit in striving to slay our own people through our greed for the pleasures of the kingdom!

46. Far better would it be for me if the sons of Dhṛtarāṣṭra, with weapons in hand, should slay me in the battle, while I remain unresisting and unarmed.

47. Having spoken thus on the field of battle, Arjuna sank down on the seat of his chariot, casting away his bow and arrow, his spirit overwhelmed by sorrow.

In the Upaniṣad of the *Bhagavad-gītā,* the science of the Absolute, the scripture of *yoga,* and the dialogue between Śrīkṛṣṇa and Arjuna, this is the first chapter, entitled "The Depression of Arjuna."[7]

---

[7]This is the usual colophon, which is not a part of the text. There are slight variations in the titles of the chapters in the different versions, but they are not worth recording.

CHAPTER 2: SĀṂKHYA THEORY[8] AND YOGA PRACTICE

Kṛṣṇa's rebuke and exhortation to be brave

Saṃjaya said:

1. To him who was thus overcome by pity, whose eyes were filled with tears and troubled and who was much depressed in mind, Madhusūdana (Kṛṣṇa) spoke this word.

The Blessed Lord said:

2. Whence has come to thee this stain (this dejection) of spirit in this hour of crisis? It is unknown to men of noble mind [not cherished by the Āryans]; it does not lead to heaven; on earth it causes disgrace, O Arjuna.

3. Yield not to this unmanliness, O Pārtha (Arjuna), for it does not become thee. Cast off this petty faintheartedness and arise, O Oppressor of the foes (Arjuna).

Arjuna said:

4. How shall I strike Bhīṣma and Droṇa, who are worthy of worship, O Madhusūdana (Kṛṣṇa), with arrows in battle, O Slayer of foes (Kṛṣṇa)?

5. It is better to live in this world by begging than to slay these honoured teachers. Though they are mindful of their gains, they are my teachers, and by slaying them, I would enjoy in this world delights which are smeared with blood.

6. Nor do we know which for us is better, whether we conquer them or they conquer us. The sons of Dhṛtarāṣṭra, whom if we slew we should not care to live, are standing before us in battle array.

7. My very being is stricken with the weakness of sentimental pity. With my mind bewildered about my duty, I ask Thee. Tell me, for certain, which is better. I am Thy pupil; teach me, who am seeking refuge in Thee.

---

[8]The teacher explains in brief in verses 11–38 the wisdom of the Sāṃkhya philosophy. The Sāṃkhya does not refer to Kapila's system but to the teaching of the Upaniṣads. Sāṃkhya and Yoga are not in the *Gītā* discordant systems. They have the same aim but differ in their methods.

8. I do not see what will drive away this sorrow which dries up my senses even if I should attain rich and unrivalled kingdom on earth or even the sovereignty of the gods.

Saṁjaya said:

9. Having thus addressed Hṛṣīkeśa (Kṛṣṇa), the mighty Guḍākeśa (Arjuna) said to Govinda (Kṛṣṇa), "I will not fight," and became silent.
10. To him thus depressed in the midst of the two armies, O Bhārata (Dhṛtarāṣṭra), Hṛṣīkeśa (Kṛṣṇa), smiling as it were, spoke this word.

The distinction between self and body: we should not grieve for what is imperishable

The Blessed Lord said:

11. Thou grievest for those whom thou shouldst not grieve for, and yet thou speakest words about wisdom. Wise men do not grieve for the dead or for the living.
12. Never was there a time when I was not, nor thou, nor these lords of men, nor will there ever be a time hereafter when we shall cease to be.[9]
13. As the soul passes in this body through childhood, youth and age, even so is its taking on of another body. The sage is not perplexed by this.
14. Contacts with their objects, O son of Kuntī (Arjuna), give rise to cold and heat, pleasure and pain. They come and go and do not last forever; these learn to endure, O Bhārata (Arjuna).
15. The man who is not troubled by these, O Chief of men (Arjuna), who remains the same in pain and pleasure, who is wise, makes himself fit for eternal life.
16. Of the non-existent there is no coming to be; of the existent there is no ceasing to be. The conclusion about these two has been perceived by the seers of truth.

17. Know thou that that by which all this is pervaded is indestructible. Of this immutable being, no one can bring about the destruction.
18. It is said that these bodies of the eternal embodied soul, which is indestructible and incomprehensible, come to an end. Therefore fight, O Bhārata (Arjuna).
19. He who thinks that this slays and he who thinks that this is slain; both of them fail to perceive the truth; this one neither slays nor is slain.
20. He is never born, nor does he die at any time, nor having once come to be does he again cease to be. He is unborn, eternal, permanent, and primeval. He is not slain when the body is slain.
21. He who knows that it is indestructible and eternal, uncreated and unchanging—how can such a person slay any one, O Pārtha (Arjuna), or cause any one to slay?
22. Just as a person casts off worn-out garments and puts on others that are new, even so does the embodied soul cast off worn-out bodies and take on others that are new.
23. Weapons do not cleave this self; fire does not burn him; waters do not make him wet; nor does the wind make him dry.
24. He is uncleavable. He cannot be burnt. He can be neither wetted nor dried. He is eternal, all-pervading, unchanging, and immovable. He is the same forever.
25. He is said to be unmanifest, unthinkable, and unchanging. Therefore, knowing him as such, thou shouldst not grieve.

We should not grieve over what is perishable

26. Even if thou thinkest that the self is perpetually born and perpetually dies, even then, O Mighty-armed (Arjuna), thou shouldst not grieve,
27. For to the one that is born death is certain, and certain is birth for the one that has died. Therefore, for what is unavoidable thou shouldst not grieve.

---

[9]While the Sāṁkhya system postulates a plurality of souls, the *Gītā* reconciles this with unity.

28. Beings are unmanifest in their beginnings, manifest in the middles, and unmanifest again in their ends, O Bhārata (Arjuna). What is there in this for lamentation?

29. One looks upon Him as a marvel; another likewise speaks of Him as a marvel; another hears of Him as a marvel; and even after hearing, no one whatsoever has known Him.

30. The dweller in the body of every one, O Bhārata (Arjuna), is eternal and can never be slain. Therefore, thou shouldst not grieve for any creature.

Appeal to a sense of duty

31. Further, having regard for thine own duty, thou shouldst not falter; there exists no greater good for a kṣatriya [warrior] than a war enjoined by duty.

32. Happy are the kṣatriyas, O Pārtha (Arjuna), for whom such a war comes of its own accord as an open door to heaven.

33. But if thou doest not this lawful battle, then thou wilt fail thy duty and glory and will incur sin.

34. Besides, men will ever recount thy ill-fame, and for one who has been honoured ill-fame is worse than death.

35. The great warriors will think that thou hast abstained from battle through fear, and they by whom thou wast highly esteemed will make light of thee.

36. Many unseemly words will be uttered by thine enemies, slandering thy strength. Could anything be sadder than that?

37. Either slain thou shalt go to heaven; or victorious thou shalt enjoy the earth; therefore arise, O Son of Kuntī (Arjuna), resolve on battle.

38. Treating alike pleasure and pain, gain and loss, victory and defeat, then get ready for battle. Thus thou shalt not incur sin.

The insight of Yoga

39. This is the wisdom of the Sāṁkhya given to thee, O Pārtha (Arjuna). Listen now to the Yoga. If your intelligence accepts it, thou shalt cast away the bondage of works.

40. In this path, no effort is ever lost and no obstacle prevails; even a little of this righteousness (dharma) saves from great fear.

41. In this, O joy of the Kurus (Arjuna), the resolute understanding is single; but the thoughts of the irresolute are many-branched and endless.

No wisdom for the worldly-minded

42–43. The undiscerning, who rejoice in the letter of the Veda, who contend that there is nothing else, whose nature is desire, and who are intent on heaven, proclaim these flowery words that result in rebirth as the fruit of actions and lay down various specialized rites for the attainment of enjoyment and power.

44. The intelligence which is to be trained, of those who are devoted to enjoyment and power and whose minds are carried away by these words [of the Veda], is not well-established in the Self [or concentration].

45. The action of the threefold modes [10] is the subject matter of the Veda; but do thou become free, O Arjuna, from this threefold nature; be free from the dualities [the pairs of opposites]; be firmly fixed in purity, not caring for acquisition and preservation; and be possessed of the Self.

46. As is the use of a pond in a place flooded with water everywhere, so is that of all the Vedas for the brāhmin who understands.[11]

Work without concern for the results

47. To action alone hast thou a right and never at all to its fruit; let not the fruits of action be thy motive; neither let there be in thee any attachment to inaction.

---

[10]The three modes (guṇas) are goodness (sattva), passion (rajas), and dullness or inertia (tamas). These are the primary constituents of nature and are the bases of all substances.
[11]That is, for those of illumined consciousness or spiritual insight ritual observances are of little value.

48. Fixed in *yoga,* do thy work, O winner of wealth (Arjuna), abandoning attachment, with an even mind in success and failure, for evenness of mind is called *yoga.*

49. Far inferior indeed is mere action to the discipline of intelligence, O winner of wealth (Arjuna); seek refuge in intelligence. Pitiful are those who seek for the fruits of their action.

50. One who has yoked his intelligence [with the Divine] (or is established in his intelligence) casts away even here both good and evil. Therefore strive for *yoga; yoga* is skill in action.

51. The wise who have united their intelligence [with the Divine], renouncing the fruits which their action yields and freed from the bonds of birth, reach the sorrowless state.

52. When thine intelligence shall cross the whirl of delusion, then shalt thou become indifferent to what has been heard and what is yet to be heard.[12]

53. When thine intelligence, which is bewildered by the Vedic texts, shall stand unshaken and stable in spirit (*samādhi*), then shalt thou attain to insight (*yoga*).

The characteristics of the perfect sage

Arjuna said:

54. What is the description of the man who has this firmly founded wisdom, whose being is steadfast in spirit; O Keśava (Kṛṣṇa)? How does the man of settled intelligence speak; how does he sit; how does he walk?

The Blessed Lord said:

55. When a man puts away all the desires of his mind, O Pārtha (Arjuna), and when his spirit is content in itself, then is he called stable in intelligence.

56. He whose mind is untroubled in the midst of sorrows and is free from eager desire amid pleasures, he from whom passion, fear, and rage have passed away—he is called a sage of settled intelligence.

57. He who is without affection on any side, who does not rejoice or loathe as he obtains good or evil—his intelligence is firmly set [in wisdom].

58. He who draws away the senses from the objects of sense on every side as a tortoise draws in his limbs into the shell—his intelligence is firmly set [in wisdom].

59. The objects of sense turn away from the embodied soul who abstains from feeding on them, but the taste for them remains. Even the taste turns away when the Supreme is seen.

60. Even though a man may ever strive [for perfection] and be ever so discerning, O Son of Kuntī (Arjuna), his impetuous senses will carry off his mind by force.

61. Having brought all the senses under control, he should remain firm in *yoga,* intent on Me; for he, whose senses are under control, his intelligence is firmly set.

62. When a man dwells in his mind on the objects of sense, attachment to them is produced. From attachment springs desire, and from desire comes anger.

63. From anger arises bewilderment, from bewilderment loss of memory, and from loss of memory the destruction of intelligence; and from the destruction of intelligence he perishes.

64. But a man of disciplined mind, who moves among the objects of sense, with the senses under control and free from attachment and aversion—he attains purity of spirit.

65. And in that purity of spirit, there is produced for him an end of all sorrow; the intelligence of such a man of pure spirit is soon established [in the peace of the self].

66. For the uncontrolled, there is no intelligence; nor for the uncontrolled is there the power of concentration; and for him without concentration, there is no peace; and for the unpeaceful, how can there be happiness?

67. When the mind runs after the roving senses, it carries away the understanding, even as a wind carries away a ship on the waters.

68. Therefore, O Mighty-armed (Arjuna), he whose senses are all withdrawn from their objects—his intelligence is firmly set.

---

[12]Scriptures are unnecessary for the man who has attained insight.

69. What is night for all beings is the time of waking for the disciplined soul; and what is the time of waking for all beings is night for the sage who sees (or the sage of vision).[13]

70. He unto whom all desires enter as waters into the sea, which, though ever being filled, is ever motionless, attains to peace, and not he who hugs his desires.

71. He who abandons all desires and acts free from longing, without any sense of mineness or egotism—he attains to peace.

72. This is the divine state, O Pārtha (Arjuna); having attained thereto, one is not again bewildered; fixed in that state at the end [at the hour of death] one can attain to the bliss of God.

This is the second chapter, entitled "The *Yoga* of Knowledge."

CHAPTER 3: KARMA-YOGA OR THE METHOD OF WORK

Why then work at all?

Arjuna said:

1. If thou deemest that the path of understanding is more excellent than the path of action, O Janārdana (Kṛṣṇa), why then dost thou urge me to do this savage deed, O Keśava (Kṛṣṇa)?

2. With an apparently confused utterance thou seemest to bewilder my intelligence. Tell me, then, decisively the one thing by which I can attain to the highest good.

Life is work; unconcern for results is needful

The Blessed Lord said:

3. O blameless One, in this world a twofold way of life has been taught of yore by Me, the path of knowledge for men of contemplation and that of works for men of action.

4. Not by abstention from work does a man attain freedom from action; nor by mere renunciation does he attain to his perfection.

5. For no one can remain even for a moment without doing work; every one is made to act helplessly by the impulses born of nature.

6. He who restrains his organs of action but continues in his mind to brood over the objects of sense, whose nature is deluded, is said to be a hypocrite [a man of false conduct].

7. But he who controls the senses by the mind, O Arjuna, and without attachment engages the organs of action in the path of work, he is superior.

The importance of sacrifice

8. Do thou thine allotted work, for action is better than inaction; even the maintenance of thy physical life cannot be effected without action.

9. Save work done as and for a sacrifice,[14] this world is in bondage to work. Therefore, O son of Kuntī (Arjuna), do thy work as a sacrifice, becoming free from all attachment.

10. In ancient days the Lord of creatures created men along with sacrifice, and said, "By this shall ye bring forth and this shall be unto you that which will yield the milk of your desires."

11. By this foster ye the gods and let the gods foster you; thus fostering each other you shall attain to the supreme good.

12. Fostered by sacrifice, the gods will give the enjoyments you desire. He who enjoys these gifts without giving to them in return is verily a thief.

13. The good people who eat what is left from the sacrifice are released from all sins, but those wicked people who prepare food for their own sake—verily they eat their sin.

14. From food creatures come into being; from rain is the birth of food; from sacrifice rain comes into being, and sacrifice is born of work.

15. Know the origin of *karma* [of the nature of sacrifices] to be in *Brahman* [the Veda], and the

---

[13]When all beings are attracted by the glitter of sense-objects, the sage is intent on understanding reality. He is wakeful to the nature of reality to which the unwise is asleep or indifferent.

---

[14]All work is to be done in a spirit of sacrifice, for the sake of the Divine.

Brahman springs from the Imperishable. Therefore the *Brahman,* which comprehends all, ever centres round the sacrifice.

16. He who does not, in this world, turn the wheel thus set in motion, is evil in his nature, sensual in his delight, and he, O Pārtha (Arjuna), lives in vain.

Be satisfied In the Self

17. But the man whose delight is in the Self alone, who is content with the Self, who is satisfied with the Self—for him there exists no work that needs to be done.
18. Similarly, in this world he has no interest whatever to gain by the actions that he has done and none to be gained by the actions that he has not done. He does not depend on all these beings for any interest of his.
19. Therefore, without attachment, perform always the work that has to be done, for man attains to the highest by doing work without attachment.

Set an example to others

20. It was even by works that Janaka [15] and others attained to perfection. Thou shouldst do works also with a view to the maintenance of the world.[16]
21. Whatsoever a great man does, the same is done by others as well. Whatever standard he sets, the world follows.
22. There is not for me, O Pārtha (Arjuna), any work in the three worlds which has to be done or anything to be obtained which has not been obtained; yet I am engaged in work.

---

[15]Janaka was the king of Mithilā and the father of Sītā, the wife of Rāma. Janaka ruled, giving up his personal sense of being the worker.

[16]"The maintenance of the world" (*lokasaṁgraha*) stands for the unity of the world, the interconnectedness of society. If the world is not to sink into a condition of physical misery and moral degradation, if the common life is to be decent and dignified, religious ethics must control social action.

23. For, if ever I did not engage in work unwearied, O Pārtha (Arjuna), men would in every way follow my path.
24. If I should cease to work, these worlds would fall in ruin, and I should be the creator of disordered life and destroy these people.
25. As the unlearned act from attachment to their work, so should the learned also act, O Bhārata (Arjuna), but without any attachment, with the desire to maintain the world-order.
26. Let him not unsettle the minds of the ignorant who are attached to action. The enlightened man doing all works in a spirit of *yoga* should set others to act (as well).

The Self is no doer

27. While all kinds of work are done by the modes of nature (*guṇas*), he whose soul is bewildered by the self-sense thinks, "I am the doer."
28. But he who knows the true character of the distinction of the soul from the modes of nature and their works, O Mighty-armed (Arjuna), understanding that it is the modes which are acting on the modes themselves, does not get attached.
29. Those who are misled by the modes of nature get attached to the works produced by them. But let no one who knows the whole unsettle the minds of the ignorant who know only a part.
30. Resigning all thy works to Me, with thy consciousness fixed in the Self, being free from desire and egoism, fight, delivered from thy fever.
31. Those men, too, who, full of faith and free from cavil, constantly follow this teaching of Mine are released from the bondage of works.
32. But those who slight My teaching and do not follow it, know them to be blind to all wisdom, lost and senseless.

Nature and duty

33. Even the man of knowledge acts in accordance with his own nature. Beings follow their nature. What can repression accomplish?

34. For every sense-attachment and [every] aversion are fixed in regard to the objects of that sense. Let no one come under their sway, for they are his two enemies.

35. Better is one's own law though imperfectly carried out than the law of another carried out perfectly. Better is death in the fulfilment of one's own law, for to follow another's law is perilous.

The enemy is desire and anger

Arjuna said:

36. But by what is a man impelled to commit sin, as if by force, even against his will, O Vārṣṇeya (Kṛṣṇa)?

The Blessed Lord said:

37. This is craving, this is wrath, born of the mode of passion, all devouring and most sinful. Know this to be the enemy here.

38. As fire is covered by smoke, as a mirror by dust, as an embryo is enveloped by the womb, so is this covered by that [passion].

39. Enveloped is wisdom, O Son of Kuntī (Arjuna), by this insatiable fire of desire, which is the constant foe of the wise.

40. The senses, the mind, and the intelligence are said to be its seat. Veiling wisdom by these, it deludes the embodied soul.

41. Therefore, O Best of Bhāratas (Arjuna), control thy senses from the beginning and slay this sinful destroyer of wisdom and discrimination.

42. The senses, they say, are great; greater than the senses is the mind; greater than the mind is the intelligence; but greater than the intelligence is he [the self].

43. Thus knowing him who is beyond the intelligence, steadying the [lower] self by the Self, smite, O Mighty-armed (Arjuna), the enemy in the form of desire, so hard to get at.

This is the third chapter, entitled "The *Yoga* of Works."

MORAL DUTY

Immanuel Kant

It is impossible to conceive of anything anywhere in the world or even anywhere out of it that can without qualification be called good, except a Good Will. Reasoning, wit, judgment, or whatever the *talents* of the intellect may be called, or such qualities of *temperament* as courage, determination and constancy of purpose, are doubtless good and desirable in many respects. But they may also be extremely evil and harmful unless the will be good which is to make use of these natural gifts and whose particular quality we therefore designate as *character*. The same is true of the *gifts of fortune*. Power, riches, honor, even health, all comfort and contentment with one's condition which is called *happiness* frequently engender together with courage also an insolence, unless a good will is present which properly directs and thus fits to a general purpose their influence upon the mind and with it the entire principle of activity. Even an impartial sane witness can never take pleasure in the uninterrupted well-being of a person who shows no trace of a pure and good will. Consequently the good will seems to be the indispensable condition even of being worthy of happiness.

Certain qualities are even conducive to this good will itself and yet they have no intrinsic unquestioned value. Rather they still presuppose a good will which detracts from the esteem which we properly have for them and which makes it impossible to consider them absolutely good. Moderation in emotion and passion, self-control and sober consideration are not only in many respects good but they seem even to constitute a part of the *inner* worth of a person. And yet one can hardly call them unreservedly good (however much the ancients may have praised them). For without the principles of a good will they may become very evil indeed. The cold-bloodedness of a villain not only makes him far more dangerous, but also directly makes him seem more despicable to us than he would have seemed without it.

The good will is good not because of what it causes or accomplishes, not because of its usefulness in the attainment of some set purpose, but alone because of the willing, that is to say, of itself. Considered by itself, without any comparison, it is to be valued far more highly than all that might be accomplished through it in favor of some inclination or of the sum of all inclinations. Even though by some special disfavor of fortune or because of the meager provision of a stepmotherly nature this will were entirely lacking in ability to carry out its intentions; if with the greatest of efforts nothing were to be accomplished by it, and nothing were to remain except only the good will (not, to be sure, as a pious wish but as an exertion of every means in our power), it would still sparkle like a jewel by itself, like something that has its full value in itself. Its usefulness or fruitfulness can neither add nor detract from its worth. This would be, as it were, merely the setting to enable an easier handling of it in ordinary intercourse or to draw to it the attention of those who are not yet sufficiently expert in the knowledge of it, but not to recommend it to experts or to determine its worth.

There seems to be something so surprising in the idea of the absolute value of the mere will with no regard for its utility that, though even ordinary reason thoroughly agrees with it, we still must suspect that perhaps merely an extravagant fancy is at the basis of this assertion, and that we are interpreting wrongly the purpose of nature in making reason the ruler of our will. Therefore we will examine this idea from this point of view.

In the natural endowment of an organized being, that is, a being suitably adapted to life, we assume the principle that every organ to be found in it is best fitted and suited to it. If, therefore, in a being which possesses reason and a will the real purpose of nature were its *preservation* and its welfare, in a word, its *happiness,* then nature would have made a bad choice in selecting the reason of this being to carry out its intention. For all actions which such a being must perform to carry out this intention and the entire code of behavior could have been dictated far better and the purpose have been far better main-

tained by instinct than by reason. If the being was to be endowed also with reason, then the latter should have served only to make observations on the fortunate disposition of the nature of the being, to rejoice in it and be grateful for the beneficent cause of it; but it would not have wanted to entrust its desires to the weak and deceptive direction of reason and thus awkwardly to interfere with the intentions of nature. In a word, it would have prevented reason from breaking forth into *practical use* and assuming the impertinence to plan with its poor insight the structure of its happiness and the means of its attainment. Nature itself would have undertaken the selection not only of its purposes but also of the means of their attainment and with wise foresight would have entrusted both to instinct.

We do indeed find that the more a cultivated reason concerns itself with the meaning of happiness and the enjoyment of life, the farther away man gets from true satisfaction. Because of this there arises in many and even in those most tried in the use of reason, if only they are honest enough to admit it, a certain degree of *misology,* that is to say, a hatred of reason; because after viewing all the advantages which they derive, perhaps not merely from the discovery of the various arts of ordinary life but even from the sciences (which after all seem to them also a luxury of reason), they still find that they have burdened themselves with more trouble than they have won of happiness. Finally they envy rather than despise the common run of men who are more nearly directed by the mere natural instincts and allow their reason to have little influence upon their conduct. In so far one must admit that the judgment of those, who belittle and even rate below zero the boastful glorification of the advantages which reason is supposed to give us in regard to the happiness and satisfaction of life, is in no sense peevish or lacking in gratitude to the kindness of providence. On the contrary, secretly there lies at the basis of this judgment the idea of another and much worthier purpose of the existence of reason, for which, rather than for the sake of happiness, it is really intended, and to which as a supreme condition the private intentions of man must for the most part yield.

However, reason is not sufficiently adapted to guide the will with certainty in respect to its objects and the satisfaction of all our needs which it in part even multiplies and for which purpose the inborn natural instincts would have served far better. Nevertheless reason has been allotted to us as a practical faculty, that is to say, a faculty which is meant to influence the *will.* Therefore, if we are to assume that nature in the distribution of its capacities has everywhere proceeded with expediency, the real destination of reason cannot be to serve as a means to other ends but to produce *a will good in itself,* for which reason is absolutely indispensable. Thus this will, though not the sole and entire good, must nevertheless be the highest good and a condition of every other, even of all desire for happiness. Therefore it is quite in accordance with the wisdom of nature when we realize that the cultivation of reason, demanded by the foremost and unconditional purpose, in various ways restricts, in this life at least, the attainment of the second and generally conditioned purpose, namely our happiness. Yes, it may even reduce its value to below nothing without injury to nature's purpose. For reason, which recognizes its highest office to be the establishing of a good will, in the attainment of this purpose is capable only of its own peculiar satisfaction which arises from the fulfilment of its purpose, even though it meets with many an obstruction raised by the inclinations.

Now, in order to develop the idea of a good will to be esteemed for no other reason than for itself, just as sound common sense already contains it and it therefore needs less to be taught than clarified, and which is foremost in the evaluation of all our actions and the condition of everything else, we will take the concept of duty. Duty includes the notion of a good will with certain subjective restrictions and hindrances. However, far from hiding and obscuring it, these rather serve to bring it out by contrast and make it shine forth all the brighter.

I shall pass over all those actions which are at once recognized as being contrary to duty however useful they may be in one or another respect. There can be no question whether or not they have arisen from duty since they plainly contradict the latter. I shall also omit those actions which really conform to duty but to which men have *no* immediate *inclination* because they are impelled to them by some other inclination. For in such actions it is easy to distinguish whether the dutiful action has been performed *out of duty* or for some selfish reason. It is much more difficult to observe the distinction where an action conforms to duty and the subject besides has an immediate inclination for it. For example, it is indeed a matter of duty that a merchant should not take advantage of an inexperienced customer and where business is flourishing no merchant will do so, but he will rather maintain a fixed common price for all. One is therefore served *honestly.* But that is not nearly reason enough to believe that the merchant has been acting out of duty or principles of honesty. It was his advantage to act so. It cannot be assumed in this case that he has besides a direct inclination for his customers which impels him out of love, as it were, to give none of them the advantage in price over the other. Consequently his action arose neither from duty nor from an immediate inclination, but merely out of some selfish purpose.

On the other hand, it is a duty to preserve one's life and besides everyone has an immediate inclination to do so. But the frequently anxious care which most men take of it has no intrinsic value and their maxim no moral content. They indeed preserve their life *dutifully,* but not *out of duty.* However, when adversities and hopeless grief have wholly destroyed the desire for living; when the unfortunate person, stout of soul and angered by his fate rather than dejected or despondent, nevertheless loves his life not because of inclination or fear, but as a matter of duty, then his maxim has a moral content.

It is a duty to help others wherever possible, and there is many a sympathetic soul that, without a trace of vanity or self-interest, takes delight in making others happy and is able to rejoice in the contentment of others, in so far as he has helped produce it. But I maintain that, however dutiful and amiable such an action may be, in this case it still has no moral value, but goes hand in hand with other inclinations as, for example, the inclination toward honor which, when it by chance coincides with what is in fact for the common good and in accordance with duty, and therefore honorable, deserves praise but not a high esteem. For the maxim lacks the moral content, namely, that such actions be done *from duty* and not from inclination. Let us assume, however, that the mind of such a philanthropist is beclouded by a private grief which destroys all his interest in the fate of others; that he still has the ability to alleviate the suffering of others, but that the strange need does not move him because he is sufficiently occupied with his own. If now, when there is no inclination to urge him to it, he nevertheless rouses himself from this deadly indifference and performs the act without any inclination, solely out of duty, then the action for the very first time has genuine moral value. Let us assume further still that nature has allotted very little power of sympathy to a certain person, he is cold by temperament and indifferent to the suffering of others, perhaps because he himself possesses the special gift of patience and the power of endurance in respect to his own suffering and presupposes or even demands the same in others. While such a person, who certainly is not its poorest product, has not been fashioned by nature into a philanthropist, will he not still find within himself a source which will afford him a far higher value than that of a friendly temperament can be? Assuredly! This is the very point at which that value of character begins to show which is moral and incomparably highest, namely, to do good, not from inclination, but from duty.

To safeguard one's happiness is a duty, at least indirectly; for discontent with one's condition amidst the press of worries and unsatisfied wants may easily become a great *temptation to the transgression of duties.* But, even without having regard for duty, all men already possess of themselves the strongest and deepest inclination to happiness, because in this very idea all inclinations unite. On the other hand, the prescription for happiness is often such that it greatly detracts from certain inclinations and thus makes it impossible for man to make a definite and certain concept of the satisfaction of all inclinations under the name of happiness. Therefore it is not hard to understand how a single inclination,

because of what it promises and the time in which its gratification may be attained, is able to prove more powerful than such a fluctuating idea. For example, a gouty person may choose to enjoy what pleases his palate and suffer greatly because he calculates that, in this instance at least, he has not deprived himself of the enjoyment of the moment for the sake of the, perhaps groundless, expectation of the benefits that are said to lie in health. But also in this case, even though a general inclination to happiness did not determine his will and he did not consider health so necessary, at least for himself, there is still the law, here as in all other cases, namely the law to further his happiness not from inclination, but from duty. And that law alone will give his conduct its real moral worth.

That undoubtedly is the true interpretation of the Scriptures, where we are commanded to love our neighbor, even our enemy. For love from inclination cannot be commanded; but to do good out of duty, even though no inclination at all impels toward it, yes, even when a very natural and uncontrollable disinclination opposes it, is a *practical* and not a *pathological* love. Such a love lies in the will and not in some propensity of affection, in the principles of action and not in tender sympathy. And such love alone can be commanded.

The second proposition is this: An action from duty does *not* have its moral worth *in the purpose* which is to be attained by it, but in the maxim according to which it has been formed. It therefore does not depend upon the actuality of the object of the action, but only on the *principle of volition* according to which the action has taken place, irrespective of all objects of desire. From what has been said above it is clear that, whatever the purpose of our actions, and whatever their effects as ends and drives of the will, these can afford the actions no absolute and moral value. In what then can this value be if it does not lie in the will or in relation to the expected effect? It can be nowhere except *in the principle of the will,* irrespective of the purposes that the action is to realize. For the will stands at the crossroads, as it were, between its *a priori* principle, which is formal, and its *a posteriori* drive, which is material. Since it must be determined by something, it follows that it must be determined by the formal principle of general volition, whenever an action is done from duty and consequently every material principle has been withdrawn from it.

The third proposition, a consequence of the two preceding, I would formulate thus: *Duty is the necessity of an action out of respect for the law.* For the object as the effect of my intended action I may indeed have an inclination, *but never respect,* for the very reason that it is merely an effect and not the activity of a will. Just so, I can have no respect for any inclination whatever, whether it be my own or another's. At most I may approve of my own and on occasion even have a fondness for another's, that is, consider it favorable to my interests. Only that can be an object of my respect, and hence a command, which has the relation of a basic principle to my will, but never that of an effect; which, instead of serving, rather outweighs my inclination or at least excludes it entirely from consideration in the making of a choice. Since then an action from duty must eliminate entirely the influence of the inclinations and thus every object of the will, there is nothing left to determine the will, except objectively the *law* and subjectively *pure respect* for this practical law, that is to say, the maxim to obey such a law, even at the expense of all my inclinations.

The moral worth of an action then does not lie in the effect which is expected of it, and consequently in no principle of an action which must borrow its motive from the expected effect. For all these effects (the comfort of one's condition or even the promotion of the happiness of others) could have been brought about by other causes and did not need the will of a rational being, in which alone, however, the highest and unconditioned good can be found. Therefore the supreme good which we call moral can consist only in *the conception of the law* in itself, *which indeed is possible only in a rational being,* in so far as this conception, and not the hoped-for effect, determines his will. This good, however, is already present in the person himself who acts in accordance with it, and it does not need to wait upon the effect to put in its appearance.

But of what sort can this law possibly be, the conception of which, even without regard for the effect expected from it, must determine the will, in order that the latter may without qualification be called purely and simply good? Since I have deprived the will of every stimulus which it might receive from the results of a law, so there is nothing left to serve as principle for the will except the universal lawfulness of actions in general. That is to say, I am never to act otherwise than *so that I could at the same time will that my maxim should become a universal law.* Here the pure lawfulness in general, without the basis of any law whatever which is directed upon definite actions, is that which serves and must serve as principle for the will, unless duty everywhere is to be an empty delusion and a chimerical notion. Ordinary human reason in its practical judgment fully agrees with this and always has this suggested principle in view.

Take this question, for example. If I am sorely pressed, may I make a promise with the intention not to keep it? I readily distinguish between the two principal meanings of this question, whether it is clever or else a matter of duty to make a false promise. The first undoubtedly may quite often be the case. To be sure, I realize that it is not enough to want to extricate myself from a momentary embarrassment by means of this subterfuge, but that I ought to consider whether from this lie there might not arise later much greater difficulties than those from which I am at present freeing myself. Since the results of my assumed *cleverness* cannot easily be foreseen, I ought to consider whether the loss of confidence in me might not constitute a far greater harm than all the evil I am trying to avoid at present; whether I would not be acting *more prudently* if I proceeded according to a universal law and developed the habit of never making a promise except with the intention to keep it. However I soon realize that the basis of such a maxim is after all fear of the consequences of my action. Certainly it is a very different thing to be truthful from duty than because of fear of disadvantageous results. In the first case the very conception of the action in itself contains a law for me to follow, in the other case I must first look about to see what consequences might be connected with it for me. For if I deviate from the principle of duty then it is most certainly evil; if, however, I act against my maxim of cleverness I may at some time greatly profit by this faithlessness, even though it be safer for the present to adhere to it. However, in order to take the shortest and yet surest way toward an answer to this problem, whether or not a deceitful promise is in accordance with duty, I ask myself: Would I indeed be satisfied to have my maxim (to extricate myself from an embarrassing situation by a false promise) considered a universal law? Would I be able to say to myself: Everybody has the right to make a false promise if he finds himself in a difficulty from which he can escape in no other way? In that manner I soon realize that I may will the lie, but never a universal law to lie. For according to such a law there really would be no promise at all, because it would be vain to make a pretense of my will in respect to my future actions to those who have no faith in my pretensions or who, if they were rash enough to do so, would repay me in my own coin. Therefore my maxim would destroy itself as soon as it got to be a universal law.

Therefore I have need of no far-reaching perspicacity to know what to do in order that my volition may be morally good. Inexperienced in understanding the course of the world, incapable of being prepared for all that happens in it, I merely ask myself: Can you will that your maxim becomes a universal law? If not, then it is unsound; and indeed not because of a disadvantage arising from it for you or for others, but because it is not suited as a principle for a possible universal code of law. But reason forces upon me an immediate respect for this code, even though I do not yet *comprehend* upon what it is based (that is a matter for investigation by philosophers). But I at least understand this much: that it is an appreciation of that value which far outweighs all the worth of that which is esteemed by inclination; that the necessity of my action out of *pure* respect for the practical law is what constitutes duty and that, to duty, every other motive must yield

because it is the condition of a will good *in itself,* than which there is no greater value.

UTILITARIANISM

John Stuart Mill

There are few circumstances among those which make up the present condition of human knowledge more unlike what might have been expected, or more significant of the backward state in which speculation on the most important subjects still lingers, than the little progress which has been made in the decision of the controversy respecting the criterion of right and wrong. From the dawn of philosophy, the question concerning the *summum bonum,* or, what is the same thing, concerning the foundation of morality, has been accounted the main problem in speculative thought, has occupied the most gifted intellects and divided them into sects and schools carrying on a vigorous warfare against one another. And after more than two thousand years the same discussions continue, philosophers are still ranged under the same contending banners, and neither thinkers nor mankind at large seem nearer to being unanimous on the subject than when the youth Socrates listened to the old Protagoras and asserted (if Plato's dialogue be grounded on a real conversation) the theory of utilitarianism against the popular morality of the so-called sophist. . . .

To inquire how far the bad effects of this deficiency have been mitigated in practice, or to what extent the moral beliefs of mankind have been vitiated or made uncertain by the absence of any distinct recognition of an ultimate standard, would imply a complete survey and criticism of past and present ethical doctrine. It would, however, be easy to show that whatever steadiness or consistency these moral beliefs have attained has been mainly due to the tacit influence of a standard not recognized. Although the nonexistence of an acknowledged first principle has made ethics not so much a guide as a consecration of men's actual sentiments, still, as men's sentiments, both of favor and of aversion, are greatly influenced by what they suppose to be the effects of things upon their happiness, the principle of utility, or, as Bentham latterly called it, the greatest happiness principle, has had a large share in forming the moral doctrines even of those who most scornfully reject its authority. Nor is there any school of thought which refuses to admit that the influence of actions on happiness is a most material and even predominant consideration in many of the details of morals, however unwilling to acknowledge it as the fundamental principle of morality and the source of moral obligation. I might go much further and say that to all those *a priori* moralists who deem it necessary to argue at all, utilitarian arguments are indispensable. It is not my present purpose to criticize these thinkers; but I cannot help referring, for illustration, to a systematic treatise by one of the most illustrious of them, the *Metaphysics of Ethics* by Kant. This remarkable man, whose system of thought will long remain one of the landmarks in the history of philosophical speculation, does, in the treatise in question, lay down a universal first principle as the origin and ground of moral obligation; it is this: "So act that the rule on which thou actest would admit of being adopted as a law by all rational beings." But when he begins to deduce from this precept any of the actual duties of morality, he fails, almost grotesquely, to show that there would be any contradiction, any logical (not to say physical) impossibility, in the adoption by all rational beings of the most outrageously immoral rules of conduct. All he shows is that the *consequences* of their universal adoption would be such as no one would choose to incur.

On the present occasion, I shall, without further discussion of the other theories, attempt to contribute something toward the understanding and appreciation of the "utilitarian" or "happiness" theory, and toward such proof as it is susceptible of. It is evident that this cannot be proof in the ordinary and popular meaning of the term. Questions of ultimate ends are not amenable to direct proof. Whatever can be proved to be good must be so by being shown to be a means to something admitted to be good without proof. The medical art is proved to be good by its conducing to health; but how is it possible to prove that health is good? The art of music is good, for the reason, among others, that it produces pleasure; but what proof is it possible to give that pleasure is good? If, then, it is asserted that there is a comprehensive formula, including all things which are in themselves good, and that whatever else is good is not so as an end but as a means, the formula may be accepted or rejected, but is not a subject of what is commonly understood by proof. We are not, however, to infer that its acceptance or rejection must depend on blind impulse or arbitrary choice. There is a larger meaning of the word "proof," in which this question is as amenable to it as any other of the disputed questions of philosophy. The subject is within the cognizance of the rational faculty; and neither does that faculty deal with it solely in the way of intuition. Considerations may be presented capable of determining the intellect either to give or withhold its assent to the doctrine; and this is equivalent to proof.

We shall examine presently of what nature are these considerations; in what manner they apply to the case, and what rational grounds, therefore, can be given for accepting or rejecting the utilitarian formula. But it is a preliminary condition of rational acceptance or rejection that the formula should be correctly understood. I believe that the very imperfect notion ordinarily formed of its meaning is the chief obstacle which impedes its reception, and that, could it be cleared even from only the grosser misconceptions, the question would be greatly simplified and a large proportion of its difficulties removed. Before, therefore, I attempt to enter into the philosophical grounds which can be given for assenting to the utilitarian standard, I shall offer some illustrations of the doctrine itself, with the view of showing more clearly what it is, distinguishing it from what it is not, and disposing of such of the practical objections to it as either originate in, or are closely connected with, mistaken interpretations of its meaning. Having thus prepared the ground, I shall afterwards endeavor to throw such light as I can call upon the question considered as one of philosophical theory.

· · ·

A passing remark is all that needs be given to the ignorant blunder of supposing that those who stand up for utility as the test of right and wrong use the term in that restricted and merely colloquial sense in which utility is opposed to pleasure. An apology is due to the philosophical opponents of utilitarianism for even the momentary appearance of confounding them with anyone capable of so absurd a misconception; which is the more extraordinary, inasmuch as the contrary accusation, of referring everything to pleasure, and that, too, in its grossest form, is another of the common charges against utilitarianism: and, as has been pointedly remarked by an able writer, the same sort of persons, and often the very same persons, denounce the theory "as impracticably dry when the word 'utility' precedes the word 'pleasure,' and as too practicably voluptuous when the word 'pleasure' precedes the word 'utility.'" Those who know anything about the matter are aware that every writer, from Epicurus to Bentham, who maintained the theory of utility meant by it, not something to be contradistinguished from pleasure, but pleasure itself, together with exemption from pain; and instead of opposing the useful to the agreeable or the ornamental, have always declared that the useful means these, among other things. Yet the common herd, including the herd of writers, not only in newspapers and periodicals, but in books of weight and pretension, are perpetually falling into this shallow mistake. Having caught up the word "utilitarian," while knowing nothing whatever about it but its sound, they habitually express by it the rejection or the neglect of pleasure in some of its forms: of beauty, of ornament, or of amusement. Nor is the term thus ignorantly misapplied solely in disparagement, but occasionally in compliment, as though it implied superiority to frivolity and the mere pleasures of the moment. And this perverted use is the only one in which the word is popularly known, and the one from which the new generation are acquiring their sole notion of its meaning. Those who introduced the word, but who had for many years discontinued it as a distinctive appellation, may well feel themselves called upon to resume it if by doing so they can hope to contribute anything toward rescuing it from this utter degradation.

The creed which accepts as the foundation of morals "utility" or the "greatest happiness principle" holds that actions are right in proportion as they tend to promote happiness; wrong as they tend to produce the reverse of happiness. By happiness is intended pleasure and the absence of pain; by unhappiness, pain and the privation of pleasure. To give a clear view of the moral standard set up by the theory, much more requires to be said; in particular, what things it includes in the ideas of pain and pleasure, and to what extent this is left an open question. But these supplementary explanations do not affect the theory of life on which this theory of morality is grounded—namely, that pleasure and freedom from pain are the only things desirable as ends; and that all desirable things (which are as numerous in the utilitarian as in any other scheme) are desirable either for pleasure inherent in themselves or as means to the promotion of pleasure and the prevention of pain.

Now such a theory of life excites in many minds, and among them in some of the most estimable in feeling and purpose, inveterate dislike. To suppose that life has (as they express it) no higher end than pleasure—no better and nobler object of desire and pursuit—they designate as utterly mean and groveling, as a doctrine worthy only of swine, to whom the followers of Epicurus were, at a very early period, contemptuously likened; and modern holders of the doctrine are occasionally made the subject of equally polite comparisons by its German, French, and English assailants.

When thus attacked, the Epicureans have always answered that it is not they, but their accusers, who represent human nature in a degrading light, since the accusation supposes human beings to be capable of no pleasures except those of which swine are capable. If this supposition were true, the charge could not be gainsaid, but would then be no longer an imputation; for if the sources of pleasure were precisely the same to human beings and to swine, the rule of life which is good enough for the one would be good enough for the other. The comparison of the Epicurean life to that of beasts is felt as degrading, precisely because a beast's pleasures do not satisfy a human being's conceptions of happiness. Human beings have faculties more elevated than the animal appetites and, when once made conscious of them, do not regard anything as happiness which does not include their gratification. I do not, indeed, consider the Epicureans to have been by any means faultless in drawing out their scheme of consequences from the utilitarian principle. To do this in any sufficient manner, many Stoic, as well as Christian, elements require to be included. But there is no known Epicurean theory of life which does not assign to the pleasures of the intellect, of the feelings and imagination, and of the moral sentiments a much higher value as pleasures than to those of mere sensation. It must be admitted, however, that utilitarian writers in general have placed the superiority of mental over bodily pleasures chiefly in the greater permanency, safety, uncostliness, etc., of the former—that is, in their circumstantial advantages rather than in their intrinsic nature. And on all these points utilitarians have fully proved their case; but they might have taken the other and, as it may be called, higher ground with entire consistency. It is quite compatible with the principle of utility to recognize the fact that some kinds of pleasure are more desirable and more valuable than others. It would be absurd that, while in estimating all other things quality is considered as well as quantity, the estimation of pleasure should be supposed to depend on quantity alone.

If I am asked what I mean by difference of quality in pleasures, or what makes one pleasure more valuable than another, merely as a pleasure, except its being greater in amount, there is but one possible answer. Of two pleasures, if there be one to which all or almost all who have experience of both give a decided preference, irrespective of any feeling of moral obligation to prefer it, that is the more desirable pleasure. If one of the two is, by those who are competently acquainted with both, placed so far above the other that they prefer it, even though knowing it to be attended with a greater amount of discontent, and would not resign it for any quantity of the other pleasure which their nature is capable of, we are justified in ascribing to the preferred enjoyment a superiority in quality so far outweighing quantity as to render it, in comparison, of small account.

Now it is an unquestionable fact that those who are equally acquainted with and equally capable of appreciating and enjoying both do give a most marked preference to the manner of existence which employs their higher faculties. Few human creatures would consent to be changed into any of the lower animals for a promise of the fullest allowance of a beast's pleasures; no intelligent human being would consent to be a fool, no instructed person would be an ignoramus, no person of feeling and conscience would be selfish and base, even though they should be persuaded that the fool, the dunce, or the rascal is better satisfied with his lot than they are with theirs. They would not resign what they possess more than he for the most complete satisfaction of all the desires which they have in common with him. If they ever fancy they would, it is only in cases of unhappiness so extreme that to escape from it they would exchange their lot for almost any other, however undesirable in their own eyes. A being of higher faculties requires more to make him happy, is capable probably of more acute suffering, and certainly accessible to it at more points, than one of an inferior type; but in spite of these liabilities, he can never really wish to sink into what he feels to be a lower grade of existence. We may give what explanation we please of this unwillingness; we may attribute it to pride, a name which is given indiscriminately to some of the most and to some of the least estimable feelings of which mankind are capable; we may refer it to the love of liberty and personal independence, an appeal to which was with the Stoics one of the most effective means for the inculcation of it; to the love of power or to the love of excitement, both of which do really enter into and contribute to it; but its most appropriate appellation is a sense of dignity, which all human beings possess in one form or other, and in some, though by no means in exact, proportion to their higher faculties, and which is so essential a part of the happiness of those in whom it is strong that nothing which conflicts with it could be otherwise than momentarily an object of desire to them. Whoever supposes that this preference takes place at a sacrifice of happiness—that the superior being, in anything like equal circumstances, is not happier than the inferior—confounds the two very different ideas of happiness and content. It is indisputable that the being whose capacities of enjoyment are low has the greatest chance of having them fully satisfied; and a highly endowed being will always feel that any happiness which he can look for, as the world is constituted, is imperfect. But he can learn to bear its imperfections, if they are at all bearable; and they will not make him envy the being who is indeed unconscious of the imperfections, but only because he feels not at all the good which those imperfections qualify. It is better to be a human being dissatisfied than a pig satisfied; better to be Socrates dissatisfied than a fool satisfied. And if the fool, or the pig, are of a different opinion, it is because they only know their own side of the question. The other party to the comparison knows both sides.

It may be objected that many who are capable of the higher pleasures occasionally, under the influence of temptation, postpone them to the lower. But this is quite compatible with a full appreciation of the intrinsic superiority of the higher. Men often, from infirmity of character, make their election for the nearer good, though they know it to be the less valuable; and this no less when the choice is between two bodily pleasures than when it is between bodily and mental. They pursue sensual indulgences to the injury of health, though perfectly aware that health is the greater good. It may be further objected that many who begin with youthful enthusiasm for everything noble, as they advance in years, sink into indolence and selfishness. But I do not believe that those who undergo this very common change voluntarily choose the lower description of pleasures in preference to the higher. I believe that, before they devote themselves exclusively to the one, they have already become incapable of the other. Capacity for the nobler feelings is in most natures a very tender plant, easily killed, not only by hostile influences, but by mere want of

sustenance; and in the majority of young persons it speedily dies away if the occupations to which their position in life has devoted them, and the society into which it has thrown them, are not favorable to keeping that higher capacity in exercise. Men lose their high aspirations as they lose their intellectual tastes, because they have not time or opportunity for indulging them; and they addict themselves to inferior pleasures, not because they deliberately prefer them, but because they are either the only ones to which they have access or the only ones which they are any longer capable of enjoying. It may be questioned whether anyone who has remained equally susceptible to both classes of pleasures ever knowingly and calmly preferred the lower, though many, in all ages, have broken down in an ineffectual attempt to combine both.

From this verdict of the only competent judges, I apprehend there can be no appeal. On a question which is the best worth having of two pleasures, or which of two modes of existence is the most grateful to the feelings, apart from its moral attributes and from its consequences, the judgment of those who are qualified by knowledge of both, or, if they differ, that of the majority among them, must be admitted as final. And there needs be the less hesitation to accept this judgment respecting the quality of pleasures, since there is no other tribunal to be referred to even on the question of quantity. What means are there of determining which is the acutest of two pains, or the intensest of two pleasurable sensations, except the general suffrage of those who are familiar with both? Neither pains nor pleasures are homogeneous, and pain is always heterogeneous with pleasure. What is there to decide whether a particular pleasure is worth purchasing at the cost of a particular pain, except the feelings and judgment of the experienced? When, therefore, those feelings and judgment declare the pleasures derived from the higher faculties to be preferable *in kind,* apart from the question of intensity, to those of which the animal nature, disjoined from the higher faculties, is susceptible, they are entitled on this subject to the same regard.

I have dwelt on this point as being a necessary part of a perfectly just conception of utility or happiness considered as the directive rule of human conduct. But it is by no means an indispensable condition to the acceptance of the utilitarian standard; for that standard is not the agent's own greatest happiness, but the greatest amount of happiness altogether; and if it may possibly be doubted whether a noble character is always the happier for its nobleness, there can be no doubt that it makes other people happier, and that the world in general is immensely a gainer by it. Utilitarianism, therefore, could only attain its end by the general cultivation of nobleness of character, even if each individual were only benefited by the nobleness of others, and his own, so far as happiness is concerned, were a sheer deduction from the benefit. But the bare enunciation of such an absurdity as this last renders refutation superfluous.

According to the greatest happiness principle, as above explained, the ultimate end, with reference to and for the sake of which all other things are desirable—whether we are considering our own good or that of other people—is an existence exempt as far as possible from pain, and as rich as possible in enjoyments, both in point of quantity and quality; the test of quality and the rule for measuring it against quantity being the preference felt by those who, in their opportunities of experience, to which must be added their habits of self-consciousness and self-observation, are best furnished with the means of comparison. This, being according to the utilitarian opinion the end of human action, is necessarily also the standard of morality, which may accordingly be defined "the rules and precepts for human conduct," by the observance of which an existence such as has been described might be, to the greatest extent possible, secured to all mankind; and not to them only, but, so far as the nature of things admits, to the whole sentient creation.

• • •

It has already been remarked that questions of ultimate ends do not admit of proof, in the ordinary acceptation of the term. To be incapable of proof by reasoning is common to all first principles, to the first premises of our knowledge, as well as to those of our conduct. But the former, being matters of fact, may be the subject of a direct appeal to the faculties which judge of fact—namely, our senses and our internal consciousness. Can an appeal be made to the same faculties on questions of practical ends? Or by what other faculty is cognizance taken of them?

Questions about ends are, in other words, questions [about] what things are desirable. The utilitarian doctrine is that happiness is desirable, and the only thing desirable, as an end; all other things being only desirable as means to that end. What ought to be required of this doctrine, what conditions is it requisite that the doctrine should fulfill—to make good its claim to be believed?

The only proof capable of being given that an object is visible is that people actually see it. The only proof that a sound is audible is that people hear it; and so of the other sources of our experience. In like manner, I apprehend, the sole evidence it is possible to produce that anything is desirable is that people do actually desire it. If the end which the utilitarian doctrine proposes to itself were not, in theory and in practice, acknowledged to be an end, nothing could ever convince any person that it was so. No reason can be given why the general happiness is desirable, except that each person, so far as he believes it to be attainable, desires his own happiness. This, however, being a fact, we have not only all the proof which the case admits of, but all which it is possible to require, that happiness is a good, that each person's happiness is a good to that person, and the general happiness, therefore, a good to the aggregate of all persons. Happiness has made out its title as *one* of the ends of conduct and, consequently, one of the criteria of morality.

FEMINIST TRANSFORMATION OF MORAL THEORY

Virginia Held

The history of philosophy, including the history of ethics, has been constructed from male points of view, and has been built on assumptions and concepts that are by no means gender-neutral.[1] Feminists characteristically begin with different concerns and give different emphases to the issues we consider than do non-feminist approaches. And, as Lorraine Code expresses it, "starting points and focal points shape the impact of theoretical discussion."[2] Within philosophy, feminists often start with, and focus on, quite different issues than those found in standard philosophy and ethics, however "standard" is understood. Far from providing mere additional insights which can be incorporated into traditional theory, feminist explorations often require radical transformations of existing fields of inquiry and theory. From a feminist point of view, moral theory along with almost all theory will have to be transformed to take adequate account of the experience of women.

• • •

Women have been seen as emotional rather than as rational beings, and thus as incapable of full moral personhood. Women's behavior has been interpreted as either "natural" and driven by instinct, and thus as irrelevant to morality and to the construction of moral principles, or it has been interpreted as, at best, in need of instruction and supervision by males better able to know what morality requires and better able to live up to its demands.

The Hobbesian conception of reason is very different from the Platonic or Aristotelian conceptions before it, and from the conceptions of Rousseau or Kant or Hegel later; all have in common that they ignore and disparage the experience and reality of women. Consider Hobbes' account of man in the state of nature contracting with other men to establish society. These men hypothetically come into existence fully formed and independent of one another, and decide on entering or staying outside of civil society. As Christine Di Stefano writes, "What we find in Hobbes's account of human nature and political

order is a vital concern with the survival of a self conceived in masculine terms . . . This masculine dimension of Hobbes's atomistic egoism is powerfully underscored in his state of nature, which is effectively built on the foundation of denied maternity."[3] In *The Citizen,* where Hobbes gave his first systematic exposition of the state of nature, he asks us to "consider men as if but even now sprung out of the earth, and suddenly, like mushrooms, come to full maturity, without all kind of engagement with each other."[4] As Di Stefano says, it is a most incredible and problematic feature of Hobbes's state of nature that the men in it "are not born of, much less nurtured by, women, or anyone else."[5] To abstract from the complex web of human reality an abstract man for rational perusal, Hobbes has, Di Stefano continues, "expunged human reproduction and early nurturance, two of the most basic and typically female-identified features of distinctively human life, from his account of basic human nature. Such a strategy ensures that he can present a thoroughly atomistic subject . . ."[6] From the point of view of women's experience, such a subject or self is unbelievable and misleading, even as a theoretical construct. The Leviathan, Di Stefano writes, "is effectively comprised of a body politic of orphans who have reared themselves, whose desires are situated within and reflect nothing but independently generated movement . . ."[7]

Rousseau, and Kant, and Hegel, paid homage to the emotional power, the aesthetic sensibility, and the familial concerns, respectively, of women. But since in their views morality must be based on rational principle, and women were incapable of full rationality, or a degree or kind of rationality comparable to

[1]See e.g. Cheshire Calhoun, "Justice, Care, Gender Bias," *The Journal of Philosophy* 85 (September, 1988): 451–63.
[2]Lorraine Code, "Second Persons," in *Science, Morality and Feminist Theory,* ed. Marsha Hanen and Kai Nielsen (Calgary: University of Calgary Press, 1987), p. 360.

[3]Christine Di Stefano, "Masculinity as Ideology in Political Theory: Hobbesian Man Considered," *Women's Studies International Forum* (Special Issue: *Hypatia*), Vol. 6, No. 6 (1983): 633–44, p. 637.
[4]Thomas Hobbes, *The Citizen: Philosophical Rudiments Concerning Government and Society,* ed. B. Gert (Garden City, New York: Doubleday, 1972 (1651)), p. 205.
[5]Di Stefano, op. cit., p. 638.
[6]Ibid.
[7]Ibid., p. 639.

that of men, women were deemed, in the view of these moralists, to be inherently wanting in morality. For Rousseau, women must be trained from childhood to submit to the will of men lest their sexual power lead both men and women to disaster. For Kant, women were thought incapable of achieving full moral personhood, and women lose all charm if they try to behave like men by engaging in rational pursuits. For Hegel, women's moral concern for their families could be admirable in its proper place, but is a threat to the more universal aims to which men, as members of the state, should aspire.[8]

These images, of the feminine as what must be overcome if knowledge and morality are to be achieved, of female experience as naturally irrelevant to morality, and of women as inherently deficient moral creatures, are built into the history of ethics.

Annette Baier recently speculated about why it is that moral philosophy has so seriously overlooked the trust between human beings that in her view is an utterly central aspect of moral life. She noted that "the great moral theorists in our tradition not only are all men, they are mostly men who had minimal adult dealings with (and so were then minimally influenced by) women."[9] They were for the most part "clerics, misogynists, and puritan bachelors," and thus it is not surprising that they focus their philosophical attention "so single-mindedly on cool, distanced relations between more or less free and equal adult strangers . . ."[10]

• • •

And so we are groping to shape new moral theory. Understandably, we do not yet have fully worked out feminist moral theories to offer. But we can suggest some directions our project of developing such theories is taking. As Kathryn Morgan points out, there is not likely to be a "star" feminist moral theorist on the order of a Rawls or Nozick: "There will be no individual singled out for two reasons. One reason is that vital moral and theoretical conversations are taking place on a large dialectical scale as the feminist community struggles to develop a feminist ethic. The second reason is that this community of feminist theoreticians is calling into question the very model of the individualized autonomous self presupposed by a star-centered male-dominated tradition . . . We experience it as a common labour, a common task."[11]

• • •

In the area of moral theory in the modern era, the priority accorded to reason has taken two major forms. A) On the one hand has been the Kantian, or Kantian-inspired search for very general, abstract, deontological, universal moral principles by which rational beings should be guided. Kant's Categorical Imperative is a foremost example: it suggests that all moral problems can be handled by applying an impartial, pure, rational principle to particular cases. It requires that we try to see what the general features of the problem before us are, and that we apply an abstract principle, or rules derivable from it, to this problem. On this view, this procedure should be adequate for all moral decisions. We should thus be able to act as reason recommends, and resist yielding to emotional inclinations and desires in conflict with our rational wills.

B) On the other hand, the priority accorded to reason in the modern era has taken a Utilitarian form. The Utilitarian approach, reflected in rational choice theory, recognizes that persons have desires and interests, and suggests rules of rational choice for maximizing the satisfaction of these. While some philosophers in this tradition espouse egoism, especially of an

[8]For examples of relevant passages, see *Philosophy of Woman: Classical to Current Concepts,* ed. Mary Mahowald (Indianapolis: Hackett, 1978); and *Visions of Women,* ed. Linda Bell (Clifton, New Jersey: Humana, 1985). For discussion, see Susan Moller Okin, *Women in Western Political Thought* (Princeton, New Jersey: Princeton University Press, 1979); and Lorenne Clark and Lynda Lange, eds., *The Sexism of Social and Political Theory* (Toronto: University of Toronto Press, 1979).
[9]Annette Baier, "Trust and Anti-Trust," *Ethics* 96 (1986): 231–60, pp. 247–48.
[10]Ibid.

[11]Kathryn Morgan, "Women and Moral Madness," in *Science, Morality and Feminist Theory,* ed. Hanen and Nielsen, p. 223.

intelligent and long-term kind, many do not. They begin, however, with assumptions that what are morally
relevant are gains and losses of utility to theoretically
isolatable individuals, and that the outcome at which
morality should aim is the maximization of the utility
of individuals. Rational calculation about such an outcome will, in this view, provide moral recommendations to guide all our choices. As with the Kantian
approach, the Utilitarian approach relies on abstract
general principles or rules to be applied to particular
cases. And it holds that although emotion is, in fact,
the source of our desires for certain objectives, the
task of morality should be to instruct us on how to pursue those objectives most rationally. Emotional attitudes toward moral issues themselves interfere with
rationality and should be disregarded. Among the
questions Utilitarians can ask can be questions about
which emotions to cultivate, and which desires to try
to change, but these questions are to be handled in the
terms of rational calculation, not of what our feelings
suggest.

Although the conceptions of what the judgments
of morality should be based on, and of how reason
should guide moral decision, are different in Kantian
and in Utilitarian approaches, both share a reliance
on a highly abstract, universal principle as the appropriate source of moral guidance, and both share the
view that moral problems are to be solved by the application of such an abstract principle to particular
cases. Both share an admiration for the rules of reason to be appealed to in moral contexts, and both
denigrate emotional responses to moral issues.

Many feminist philosophers have questioned
whether the reliance on abstract rules, rather than the
adoption of more context-respectful approaches, can
possibly be adequate for dealing with moral problems,
especially as women experience them.[12] Though Kan-
tians may hold that complex rules can be elaborated
for specific contexts, there is nevertheless an assumption in this approach that the more abstract the reason-

ing applied to a moral problem, the more satisfactory.
And Utilitarians suppose that one highly abstract principle, The Principle of Utility, can be applied to every
moral problem no matter what the context.

A genuinely universal or gender-neutral moral
theory would be one which would take account of the
experience and concerns of women as fully as it
would take account of the experience and concerns
of men. When we focus on the experience of women,
however, we seem to be able to see a set of moral
concerns becoming salient that differs from those of
traditional or standard moral theory. Women's experience of moral problems seems to lead us to be especially concerned with actual relationships between
embodied persons, and with what these relationships
seem to require. Women are often inclined to attend
to rather than to dismiss the particularities of the context in which a moral problem arises. And we often
pay attention to feelings of empathy and caring to
suggest what we ought to do rather than relying as
fully as possible on abstract rules of reason.

Margaret Walker, for instance, contrasts feminist
moral "understanding" with traditional moral
"knowledge." She sees the components of the former as involving "attention, contextual and narrative appreciation, and communication in the event
of moral deliberation."[13] This alternative moral
epistemology holds that "the adequacy of moral understanding decreases as its form approaches generality through abstraction."[14]

The work of psychologists such as Carol Gilligan
and others has led to a clarification of what may be
thought of as tendencies among women to approach
moral issues differently. Rather than interpreting
moral problems in terms of what could be handled
by applying abstract rules of justice to particular
cases, many of the women studied by Gilligan

---

[12]For an approach to social and political as well as moral issues
that attempts to be context-respectful, see Virginia Held, *Rights
and Goods, Justifying Social Action* (Chicago: University of
Chicago Press, 1989).

[13]Margaret Urban Walker, "Moral Understandings: Alternative
'Epistemology' for a Feminist Ethics," *Hypatia* 4 (Summer,
1989): 15–28, p. 19.

[14]Ibid., p. 20. See also Iris Marion Young, "Impartiality and the
Civic Public: Some Implications of Feminist Critiques of Moral
and Political Theory," in Seyla Benhabib and Drucilla Cornell,
Feminism as Critique (Minneapolis: University of Minnesota
Press, 1987).

tended to be more concerned with preserving actual human relationships, and with expressing care for those for whom they felt responsible. Their moral reasoning was typically more embedded in a context of particular others than was the reasoning of a comparable group of men.[15] One should not equate tendencies women in fact display with feminist views, since the former may well be the result of the sexist, oppressive conditions in which women's lives have been lived. But many feminists see our own consciously considered experience as lending confirmation to the view that what has come to be called "an ethic of care" needs to be developed. Some think it should supersede "the ethic of justice" of traditional or standard moral theory. Others think it should be integrated with the ethic of justice and rules.

In any case, feminist philosophers are in the process of reevaluating the place of emotion in morality in at least two respects. First, many think morality requires the development of the moral emotions, in contrast to moral theories emphasizing the primacy of reason. . . .

Secondly, emotion will be respected rather than dismissed by many feminist moral philosophers in the process of gaining moral understanding. The experience and practice out of which feminist moral theory can be expected to be developed will include embodied feeling as well as thought. In a recent overview of a vast amount of writing, Kathryn Morgan states that "feminist theorists begin ethical theorizing with embodied, gendered subjects who have particular histories, particular communities, particular allegiances, and particular visions of human flourishing. The starting point involves valorizing what has frequently been most mistrusted and despised in the western philosophical tradition . . ."[16] Among the elements being reevaluated are feminine emotions. The "care" of the alternative feminist approach to morality appreciates rather than rejects emotion. The caring relationships important to feminist morality cannot be understood in terms of abstract rules or moral reasoning. And the "weighing" so often needed between the conflicting claims of some relationships and others cannot be settled by deduction or rational calculation. A feminist ethic will not just acknowledge emotion, as do Utilitarians, as giving us the objectives toward which moral rationality can direct us. It will embrace emotion as providing at least a partial basis for morality itself, and for moral understanding.

Annette Baier stresses the centrality of trust for an adequate morality.[17] Achieving and maintaining trusting, caring relationships is quite different from acting in accord with rational principles, or satisfying the individual desires of either self or other. Caring, empathy, feeling with others, being sensitive to each other's feelings, all may be better guides to what morality requires in actual contexts than may abstract rules of reason, or rational calculation, or at least they may be necessary components of an adequate morality.

The fear that a feminist ethic will be a relativistic "situation ethic" is misplaced. Some feelings can be as widely shared as are rational beliefs, and feminists do not see their views as reducible to "just another attitude."[18] In her discussion of the differences between feminist medical ethics and non-feminist medical ethics, Susan Sherwin gives an example of how feminists reject the mere case by case approach that has come to predominate in nonfeminist medical ethics. The latter also rejects the excessive reliance on abstract rules characteristic of standard ethics, and in this way resembles feminist ethics. But the very focus on cases in isolation from one another deprives this approach from attending to general features in the institutions and practices of medicine that, among other faults, systematically contribute to the oppression of women.[19] The difference of approach can be seen in

---

[15]See especially Carol Gilligan, *In a Different Voice: Psychological Theory and Women's Development* (Cambridge, Massachusetts: Harvard University Press, 1988); and Eva Feder Kittay and Diana T. Meyers eds., *Women and Moral Theory* (Totowa, New Jersey: Rowman and Allanheld, 1987).

[16]Kathryn Pauly Morgan, "Strangers in a Strange Land...," p. 2.

[17]Annette Baier, "Trust and Anti-Trust."

[18]See especially Kathryn Pauly Morgan, "Strangers in a Strange Land . . ."

[19]Susan Sherwin, "Feminist and Medical Ethics: Two Different Approaches to Contextual Ethics," *Hypatia* 4 (Summer, 1989): 57–72.

the treatment of issues in the new reproductive technologies, where feminists consider how the new technologies may further decrease the control of women over reproduction.

This difference might be thought to be one of substance rather than of method, but Sherwin shows the implications for method also. With respect to reproductive technologies one can see especially clearly the deficiencies of the case by case approach: what needs to be considered is not only choice in the purely individualistic interpretation of the case by case approach, but control at a more general level and how it affects the structure of gender in society. Thus, a feminist perspective does not always counsel attention to specific case versus appeal to general considerations, as some sort of methodological rule. But the general considerations are often not the purely abstract ones of traditional and standard moral theory, they are the general features and judgments to be made about cases in actual (which means, so far, patriarchal) societies. A feminist evaluation of a moral problem should never omit the political elements involved; and it is likely to recognize that political issues cannot be dealt with adequately in purely abstract terms any more than can moral issues.

The liberal tradition in social and moral philosophy argues that in pluralistic society and even more clearly in a pluralistic world, we cannot agree on our visions of the good life, on what is the best kind of life for humans, but we can hope to agree on the minimal conditions for justice, for coexistence within a framework allowing us to pursue our visions of the good life.[20] Many feminists contend that the commitment to justice needed for agreement *in actual conditions* on even minimal requirements of justice is as likely to demand relational feelings as a rational recognition of abstract principles. Human beings can and do care, and are capa-

ble of caring far more than at present, about the sufferings of children quite distant from them, about the prospects for future generations, and about the well-being of the globe. The liberal tradition's mutually disinterested rational individualists would seem unlikely to care enough to take the actions needed to achieve moral decency at a global level, or environmental sanity for decades hence, as they would seem unable to represent caring relationships within the family and among friends. . . .

The possibilities as well as the problems (and we are well aware of some of them) in a feminist reenvisioning of emotion and reason need to be further developed, but we can already see that the views of nonfeminist moral theory are unsatisfactory.

QUESTIONS FOR DISCUSSION

1. In what ways might it be fulfilling to, as the Bhagavad-Gita suggests, accept one's position in society, and do what one must do, in an attitude of detachment from results? What popular ideas in our society counsel against such an attitude? What is your own position on this debate, and why? Illustrate with an example or two from your own life.

2. Do you agree with Kant that practical love, which acts in response to duty, is more in line with morality than "pathological" love, based on feelings of affection that come and go? Or do you think that there is some moral value to a "feeling" like love? Would the contemporary crisis of marriage and divorce be abated if more people married due to practical love, rather than pathological love? (Many contemporary societies still practice the tradition of arranged marriages, based on practical considerations.)

3. Can you think of moral dilemmas in which the "ethics of care" that Held describes would differently solve moral dilemmas compared to a utilitarian or Kantian approach? Which way of solving the moral dilemma would be more satisfactory to you? Why?

---

[20]See especially the work of John Rawls and Ronald Dworkin; see also Charles Larmore, *Patterns of Moral Complexity* (Cambridge: Cambridge University Press, 1987).

UNIVERSAL CARE FOR OTHERS: ALTRUISM VERSUS EGOISM

Does behaving ethically involve caring for others? If so, to what extent should I care? Should I care for all equally, or only for persons in certain situations or relationships, such as those related to me, or those I love? Is my duty to aid others unlimited, or can I limit it to those who need emergency assistance?

Motse (or Mo Tzu) is an ancient Chinese philosopher (470–391 BCE) who was at first a Confucianist but later chose to reject Confucianism (because of its overemphasis on ritual and social elegance) and start his own school of Moism. Like Confucius, Motse wanted to reduce the military conflicts that were rampant in China. The problem became acute during the Warring States period of China's history (403–222 BCE). Noticing that the people's suffering at the time was great, Motse attributed the suffering to a particular source. The problem was that people loved others only partially; while they loved some people, they hated or neglected to love others. The key to ending the conflicts was to advocate universal love of others. Only by regarding others' suffering as one's own could fighting cease.

Motse argues that one would prefer as one's friend or one's ruler someone who cared for the needs of others. One who feeds the hungry, clothes the naked, and buries the dead is to be preferred over someone who cares not for the troubles of others. When it is objected that no person or ruler has the resources or will to minister to the needs of all in the way that Motse describes, he replies that it has been done in the past, and so is possible in the future. In contrast to the Confucian tradition, Motse upholds the need to administer justice impartially, without regard for family members and relatives. One should treat one's own parents as one would anyone's parents, and not save special treatment for them. Could people actually be transformed so as to act upon a motivation of universal love? Motse assures us that if only rulers encourage this attribute in their subjects, the people will be able to develop it.

While Motse spent many years traveling to visit feudal lords and princes to offer his services as a counselor and to attempt to prevent the outbreak of wars, he finally settled down to run a school to train youths in the skills needed for public office.

Is it wrong to care more for the self than for others? Arguing in defense of egoism is Ayn Rand, who was born in 1905 in St. Petersburg, Russia, but lived in the United States from 1926 onward. Rand is famous for her ethics of egoism, and she defends it against the ethics of altruism of the sort found in Motse's work, Buddhism, Christianity, Utilitarianism, or even certain versions of Marxism. In her own life, Rand fled a Soviet government that often advocated the benefit of the society as a whole over individual rights, condemning the capitalist ethic of getting ahead by exploiting others. To counter those notions, Rand developed her ethics of selfishness, which is unembarrassed by its egoistic claims. She first protects egoism from stereotypes. Since egoism has to do with achieving one's own interests, the "brute's" grab at pleasure is not in the true self-interest of the individual, and so can be ruled out. The evil of a robber's actions, for example, does not lie in the robber pursuing his or her interests, but rather in what the robber chooses as a goal and the way in which the goal is attained. In this way, she distinguishes her position from the justification of any action that the strong may choose in pursuit of his or her own interests. In fact, she has a theory of rights that must be upheld even by the egoist.

Rand considers altruism to be psychologically harmful because it implies that the desire to live is selfish and evil and it suggests that any special love one might have for a family member, friend, or spouse is unwarranted or morally dangerous. She combats a view that she calls "moral cannibalism," which consists of the notion that any time one does something for oneself, someone else must be being hurt. In fact, the opposite may be the case.

Gunapala Dharmasiri is a contemporary scholar who was born in Sri Lanka and studied at the University of Sri Lanka as well as the University of Lancaster in England. He is now teaching at the

University of Sri Lanka. Dharmasiri argues that for a Buddhist, there is no such thing as egoism apart from altruism, because ultimately we are all interrelated, since there is no such thing as a self apart from others. He explains that Buddhist ethics' first challenge is to constitute an ethics without the concept of a substantial person who possesses a soul. For Buddhism, the person is a temporary arrangements of parts. However, there is still the notion that preceding events have a relationship to later events. And so one still has a notion of causal responsibility, even without the permanent subject. Another metaphysical distinction influences Buddhist morality in that Buddhism considers there to be two orders of "reality"—the conventional reality of our daily lives, and the higher, absolute reality in which there are no such things as persons and morality. However, the absolutely "realized" person will naturally act in such a way as to seem moral in the conventional sphere.

But why should one devote oneself to the well-being of others if there "are" no others, in a substantive sense? Our actions must be informed by an acknowledgement of dependency. Since all of reality is interrelated, the extreme notions of altruism and egoism don't make sense; after all, one is part of a larger whole. A person who believes he or she is separate is in a state of illusion. Even the personality is a social construction, being shaped in interaction with others. One who mistreats nature or others sets off a causal chain of events that is bound to bounce back. One consequence of this view is the lifestyle of *ahimsa* or nonviolence, where one ideally refrains from killing even the smallest of animals.

Our fourth author, Carlo Filice, is a contemporary philosopher who teaches at the State University of New York at Geneseo. He asks the question whether we have any obligation to help those who are experiencing serious suffering such as genocide and human rights violations. Our obligation may be limited by what can be reasonably expected of us, considering that we have many obligations that may compete with the obligation to help others in need. But the question still remains: Just how far does our obligation extend? To say that one has any obligation at all

to others departs from the strict egoist view, but even Rand agrees that we should help others in emergencies. Filice argues, step by step, that we have a moral obligation, not only to inconvenience ourselves to help others in dire need, but also to remained poised (by being informed) so as to be able to act quickly in case an atrocity happens. Our obligation increases if our own country is a contributor to the disaster. Our obligation, however, falls short, he argues, of an altruistic view that would consider any suffering of others as no less important than our own.

UNIVERSAL LOVE

Motse

Motse said: The purpose of the magnanimous lies in procuring benefits for the world and eliminating its calamities. Now among all the current calamities, which are the most important? The attack on the small states by the large ones, disturbances of the small houses by the large ones, oppression of the weak by the strong, misuse of the few by the many, deception of the simple by the cunning, disdain towards the humble by the honoured—these are the misfortunes in the empire. Again, the lack of grace on the part of the ruler, the lack of loyalty on the part of the ruled, the lack of affection on the part of the father, the lack of filial piety on the part of the son—these are further calamities in the empire. Also, the mutual injury and harm which the unscrupulous do to one another with weapons, poison, water, and fire is still another calamity in the empire.

When we come to think about the cause of all these calamities, how have they arisen? Have they arisen out of love of others and benefiting others? Of course we should say no. We should say they have arisen out of hate of others and injuring others. If we should classify one by one all those who hate others and injure others, should we find them to be universal in love or partial? Of course we should say they are partial. Now, since partiality against one another is the cause of the major calamities in the empire, then partiality is wrong.

Motse continued: Whoever criticizes others must have something to replace them. Criticism without suggestion is like trying to stop flood with flood and put out fire with fire. It will surely be without worth.

Motse said: Partiality is to be replaced by universality. But how is it that partiality can be replaced by universality? Now, when every one regards the states of others as he regards his own, who would attack the others' states? Others are regarded like self. When every one regards the capitals of others as he regards his own, who would seize the others' capitals? Others are regarded like self. When every one regards the houses of others as he regards his own, who would disturb the others' houses? Others are regarded like self. Now, when the states and cities do not attack and seize each other and when the clans and individuals do not disturb and harm one another—is this a calamity or a benefit to the world? Of course it is a benefit. When we come to think about the several benefits in regard to their cause, how have they arisen? Have they arisen out of hate of others and injuring others? Of course we should say no. We should say they have arisen out of love of others and benefiting others. If we should classify one by one all those who love others and benefit others, should we find them to be partial or universal? Of course we should say they are universal. Now, since universal love is the cause of the major benefits in the world, therefore Motse proclaims universal love is right.

And, as has already been said, the interest of the magnanimous lies in procuring benefits for the world and eliminating its calamities. Now that we have found out the consequences of universal love to be the major benefits of the world and the consequences of partiality to be the major calamities in the world; this is the reason why Motse said partiality is wrong and universality is right. When we try to develop and procure benefits for the world with universal love as our standard, then attentive ears and keen eyes will respond in service to one another,

then limbs will be strengthened to work for one another, and those who know the Tao will untiringly instruct others. Thus the old and those who have neither wife nor children will have the support and supply to spend their old age with, and the young and weak and orphans will have the care and admonition to grow up in. When universal love is adopted as the standard, then such are the consequent benefits. It is incomprehensible, then, why people should object to universal love when they hear it.

Yet the objection is not all exhausted. It is asked: "It may be a good thing, but can it be of any use?"

Motse replied: If it were not useful then even I would disapprove of it. But how can there be anything that is good but not useful? Let us consider the matter from both sides. Suppose there are two men. Let one of them hold to partiality and the other to universality. Then the advocate of partiality would say to himself, how can I take care of my friend as I do of myself, how can I take care of his parents as my own? Therefore when he finds his friend hungry he would not feed him, and when he finds him cold he would not clothe him. In his illness he would not minister to him, and when he is dead he would not bury him. Such is the word and such is the deed of the advocate of partiality. The advocate of universality is quite unlike this both in word and in deed. He would say to himself, I have heard that to be a superior man one should take care of his friend as he does of himself, and take care of his friend's parents as his own. Therefore when he finds his friend hungry he would feed him, and when he finds him cold he would clothe him. In his sickness he would serve him, and when he is dead he would bury him. Such is the word and such is the deed of the advocate of universality.

These two persons then are opposed to each other in word and also in deed. Suppose they are sincere in word and decisive in deed so that their word and deed are made to agree like the two parts of a tally, and that there is no word but what is realized in deed, then let us consider further: Suppose a war is on, and one is in armour and helmet ready to join the force, life and death are not predictable. Or suppose one is commissioned a deputy by the ruler to such far countries like Pa, Yüeh, Ch'i, and Ching, and the arrival and return are quite uncertain. Now (under such circumstances) let us inquire upon whom would one lay the trust of one's family and parents. Would it be upon the universal friend or upon the partial friend? It seems to me, on occasions like these, there are no fools in the world. Even if he is a person who objects to universal love, he will lay the trust upon the universal friend all the same. This is verbal objection to the principle but actual selection by it—this is self-contradiction between one's word and deed. It is incomprehensible, then, why people should object to universal love when they hear it.

Yet the objection is not all exhausted. It is objected: Maybe it is a good criterion to choose among ordinary men, but it may not apply to the rulers.

Let us again consider the matter from both sides. Suppose there are two rulers. Let one of them hold partiality and the other universality. Then the partial ruler would say to himself, how can I take care of the people as I do of myself? This would be quite contrary to common sense. A man's life on earth is of short duration, it is like a galloping horse passing by. Therefore when he finds his people hungry he would not feed them, and when he finds them cold he would not clothe them. When they are sick he would not minister to them, and upon their death he would not bury them. Such is the word and such is the deed of the partial ruler. The universal ruler is quite unlike this both in word and in deed. He would say to himself, I have heard that to be an upright ruler of the world one should first attend to his people and then to himself. Therefore when he finds his people hungry he would feed them, and when he finds them cold he would clothe them. In their sickness he would minister to them, and upon their death he would bury them. Such is the word and such is the deed of the universal ruler.

These two rulers, then, are opposed to each other in word and also in deed. Suppose they are sincere in word and decisive in deed so that their word and deed are made to agree like the two parts of a tally, and that there is no word but what is realized in deed, then let us consider further: Suppose, now, that there is a disastrous pestilence, that most peo-

ple are in misery and privation, and that many lie dead in ditches. (Under such circumstances) let us inquire, if a person could choose one of the two rulers, which would he prefer? It seems to me on such occasions there are no fools in the world. Even if he is a person who objects to universal love, he will choose the universal ruler. This is verbal objection to the principle but actual selection by it—this is self-contradiction between one's word and deed. It is incomprehensible, then, why people should object to universal love when they hear it.

Yet the objection is still not exhausted. It points out that universal love may be magnanimous and righteous, but how can it be realized? Universal love is impracticable just as carrying Mt. T'ai and leaping over rivers. So, then, universal love is but a pious wish, how can it be actualized?

Motse replied: To carry Mt. T'ai and leap over rivers is something that has never been accomplished since the existence of man. But universal love and mutual aid has been personally practised by six ancient sage-kings.

How do we know they have done it?

Motse said: I am no contemporary of theirs, neither have I heard their voice or seen their faces. The sources of our knowledge lie in what is written on the bamboos and silk, what is engraved in metal and stones, and what is cut in the vessels to be handed down to posterity.

The "Great Declaration" proclaims: "King Wen was like the sun and the moon, shedding glorious and resplendent light in the four quarters as well as over the Western land." This is to say that the love of King Wen is so wide and universal that it is like the sun and the moon shining upon the world without partiality. Here is universal love on the part of King Wen; what Motse has been talking about is really derived from the example of King Wen.

Moreover it is true not only in the "Great Declaration," but also with the "Oath of Yü." Yü said (therein): "Come all you hosts of people, take heed and hearken to my words. It is not that I, a single person, would willingly stir up this confusion. The Prince of Miao is more and more unreasonable, he deserves punishment from Heaven. Therefore I lead you to appoint the lords of the states and go to punish the Prince of Miao." It was not for the sake of increasing his wealth and multiplying his felicitations and indulging his ears and eyes but for that of procuring benefits for the world and eliminating its annoyances that Yü went to war against the Prince of Miao. This is universal love on the part of Yü, and what Motse has been talking about is really derived from the example of Yü.

Again it is true not only in the "Oath of Yü" but also with the "Oath of T'ang." T'ang said: "Unworthy Lü presumed to do sacrifice with a first-born male animal to Heaven on high and mother Earth, saying, 'Now there is a great drought from heaven. It happens right in my, Lü's, time. I do not know whether I have wronged Heaven or men. Good, I dare not cover up; guilt, I dare not let go—this is clearly seen in the mind of God. If there is sin anywhere hold me responsible for it; if I myself am guilty may the rest be spared.' "[1] This is to say that though having the honour of being an emperor and the wealth of possessing the whole world, T'ang did not shrink from offering himself as sacrifice to implore God and the spirits. This is universal love on the part of T'ang, and what Motse has been talking about is really derived from the example of T'ang.

Still again, it is true not only in the "Oath of Yü" and the "Oath of T'ang" but also with the "Poems of Chou." To quote: "the way of the (good) emperor is wide and straight, without partiality and without favouritism. The way of the (good) emperor is even and smooth, without favouritism and without partiality. It is straight like an arrow and just like a balance. The superior man follows it, (even) the unprincipled looks on (without resentment)." Thus the principle that I have been expounding is not to be regarded as a mere doctrinaire notion. In the past, when Wen and Wu administered the government both of them rewarded the virtuous and punished the wicked without partiality to their relatives and brothers. This is just the universal love of Wen

and Wu. And what Motse has been talking about is really derived from the examples of Wen and Wu. It is incomprehensible then why people should object to universal love when they hear it.

Yet the objection is still not exhausted. It raises the question, when one does not think in terms of benefits and harm to one's parents would it be filial piety?

Motse replied: Now let us inquire about the plans of the filial sons for their parents. I may ask, when they plan for their parents, whether they desire to have others love or hate them? Judging from the whole doctrine (of filial piety), it is certain that they desire to have others love their parents. Now, what should I do first in order to attain this? Should I first love others' parents in order that they would love my parents in return, or should I first hate others' parents in order that they would love my parents in return? Of course I should first love others' parents in order that they would love my parents in return. Hence those who desire to be filial to one another's parents, if they have to choose (between whether they should love or hate others' parents), had best first love and benefit others' parents. Would any one suspect that all the filial sons are stupid and incorrigible (in loving their own parents)? We may again inquire about it. It is said in the "Ta Ya"[2] among the books of the ancient kings: "No idea is not given its due value; no virtue is not rewarded. When a peach is thrown to us, we would return with a prune." This is to say whoever loves others will be loved and whoever hates others will be hated. It is then quite incomprehensible why people should object to universal love when they hear it.

Is it because it is hard and impracticable? There are instances of even much harder tasks done. Formerly, Lord Ling of the state of Ching liked slender waists. In his time people in the state of Ching ate not more than once a day. They could not stand up without support, and could not walk without leaning against the wall. Now, limited diet is quite hard to endure, and yet

---

[1] The passage is not found in the "Oath of T'ang." The several sentences are scattered through the "Announcement of T'ang" in *Shu Ching.* Cf. Legge, vol. iii, pp. 184–90.

[2] "Ta Ya" is the name of a group of odes in *Shih Ching*. Only the first two lines of the following quotation appear in the ode "Yi." Legge, vol. iv, p. 514, renders it:

Every word finds its answer;
Every good deed has its recompense.

it was endured. While Lord Ling encouraged it, his people could be changed within a generation to conform to their superior. Lord Kou Chien of the state of Yüeh admired courage and taught it his ministers and soldiers three years. Fearing that their knowledge had not yet made them efficient he let a fire be set on the boat, and beat the drum to signal advance. The soldiers at the head of the rank were even pushed down. Those who perished in the flames and in water were numberless. Even then they would not retreat without signal. The soldiers of Yüeh would be quite terrified (ordinarily). To be burnt alive is a hard task, and yet it was accomplished. When the Lord of Yüeh encouraged it, his people could be changed within a generation to conform to their superior. Lord Wen of the state of Chin liked coarse clothing. And so in his time the people of Chin wore suits of plain cloth, jackets of sheep skin, hats of spun silk, and big rough shoes. Thus attired, they would go in and see the Lord and come out and walk in the court. To dress up in coarse clothing is hard to do, yet it has been done. When Lord Wen encouraged it his people could be changed within a generation to conform to their superior.

Now to endure limited diet, to be burnt alive, and to wear coarse clothing are the hardest things in the world, yet when the superiors encouraged them the people could be changed within a generation. Why was this so? It was due to the desire to conform to the superior. Now, as to universal love and mutual aid, they are beneficial and easy beyond a doubt. It seems to me that the only trouble is that there is no superior who encourages it. If there is a superior who encourages it, promoting it with rewards and commendations, threatening its reverse with punishments, I feel people will tend toward universal love and mutual aid like fire tending upward and water downwards—it will be unpreventable in the world.

Therefore, universal love is really the way of the sage-kings. It is what gives peace to the rulers and sustenance to the people. The gentleman would do well to understand and practise universal love; then he would be gracious as a ruler, loyal as a minister, affectionate as a father, filial as a son, courteous as an elder brother, and respectful as a younger brother. So, if the gentleman desires to be a gracious ruler, a loyal

minister, an affectionate father, a filial son, a courteous elder brother, and a respectful younger brother, universal love must be practised. It is the way of the sage-kings and the great blessing of the people.

THE VIRTUE OF SELFISHNESS

Ayn Rand*

In popular usage, the word "selfishness" is a synonym of evil; the image it conjures is of a murderous brute who tramples over piles of corpses to achieve his own ends, who cares for no living being and pursues nothing but the gratification of the mindless whims of any immediate moment.

Yet the exact meaning and dictionary definition of the word "selfishness" is: *concern with one's own interests.*

This concept does *not* include a moral evaluation; it does not tell us whether concern with one's own interests is good or evil; nor does it tell us what constitutes man's actual interests. It is the task of ethics to answer such questions.

The ethics of altruism has created the image of the brute, as its answer, in order to make men accept two inhuman tenets: (a) that any concern with one's own interests is evil, regardless of what these interests might be, and (b) that the brute's activities are *in fact* to one's own interest (which altruism enjoins man to renounce for the sake of his neighbors).

Altruism declares that any action taken for the benefit of others is good, and any action taken for one's own benefit is evil. Thus the *beneficiary* of an action is the only criterion of moral value—and so long as that beneficiary is anybody other than oneself, anything goes.

*The Estate of Ayn Rand has requested the following: "The following are brief and potentially misleading excerpts from three different articles by Ayn Rand. An ellipsis sign indicates each omission of material from the original text."

Hence the appalling immorality, the chronic injustice, the grotesque double standards, the insoluble conflicts and contradictions that have characterized human relationships and human societies throughout history, under all the variants of the altruist ethics.

Observe the indecency of what passes for moral judgments today. An industrialist who produces a fortune, and a gangster who robs a bank are regarded as equally immoral, since they both sought wealth for their own "selfish" benefit. A young man who gives up his career in order to support his parents and never rises beyond the rank of grocery clerk is regarded as morally superior to the young man who endures an excruciating struggle and achieves his personal ambition. A dictator is regarded as moral, since the unspeakable atrocities he committed were intended to benefit "the people," not himself.

Observe what this beneficiary-criterion of morality does to a man's life. The first thing he learns is that morality is his enemy; he has nothing to gain from it, he can only lose; self-inflicted loss, self-inflicted pain and the gray, debilitating pall of an incomprehensible duty is all that he can expect. He may hope that others might occasionally sacrifice themselves for his benefit, as he grudgingly sacrifices himself for theirs, but he knows that the relationship will bring mutual resentment, not pleasure—and that, morally, their pursuit of values will be like an exchange of unwanted, unchosen Christmas presents, which neither is morally permitted to buy for himself. Apart from such times as he manages to perform some act of self-sacrifice, he possesses no moral significance: morality takes no cognizance of him and has nothing to say to him for guidance in the crucial issues of his life; it is only his own personal, private, "selfish" life and, as such, it is regarded either as evil or, at best, *amoral.*

Since nature does not provide man with an automatic form of survival, since he has to support his life by his own effort, the doctrine that concern with one's own interests is evil means that man's desire to live is evil—that man's life, as such, is evil. No doctrine could be more evil than that.

Yet that is the meaning of altruism, implicit in such examples as the equation of an industrialist with a robber. There is a fundamental moral difference between a man who sees his self-interest in production and a man who sees it in robbery. The evil of a robber does *not* lie in the fact that he pursues his own interests, but in *what* he regards as to his own interest; *not* in the fact that he pursues his values, but in *what* he chose to value; *not* in the fact that he wants to live, but in the fact that he wants to live on a subhuman level.[1]

If it is true that what I mean by "selfishness" is not what is meant conventionally, then *this* is one of the worst indictments of altruism: it means that altruism *permits no concept* of a self-respecting, self-supporting man—a man who supports his life by his own effort and neither sacrifices himself nor others. It means that altruism permits no view of men except as sacrificial animals and profiteers-on-sacrifice, as victims and parasites—that it permits no concept of a benevolent co-existence among men—that it permits no concept of *justice.*

If you wonder about the reasons behind the ugly mixture of cynicism and guilt in which most men spend their lives, these are the reasons: cynicism, because they neither practice nor accept the altruist morality—guilt, because they dare not reject it.

To rebel against so devastating an evil, one has to rebel against its basic premise. To redeem both man and morality, it is the concept of *"selfishness"* that one has to redeem.

The first step is to assert *man's right to a moral existence*—that is: to recognize his need of a moral code to guide the course and the fulfillment of his own life.

---

[1]Ayn Rand accepts Aristotle's definition of the human essence as that of a "rational animal" but feels that, by itself, this does not give a full account of human nature. Man is also an animal that must create and produce in order to survive—unlike, for example, a cow, which merely grazes on the grass while it is there and then moves on. It is, in fact, chiefly this productive need that human reason serves. The thief thus chooses to deny his human nature in trying to take another's fruits of production and lives a "subhuman" life (Eds.).

The Objectivist ethics holds that the actor must always be the beneficiary of his action and that man must act for his own *rational* self-interest. But his right to do so is derived from his nature as man and from the function of moral values in human life—and, therefore, is applicable *only* in the context of a rational, objectively demonstrated and validated code of moral principles which define and determine his actual self-interest. It is not a license "to do as he pleases" and it is not applicable to the altruists' image of a "selfish" brute nor to any man motivated by irrational emotions, feelings, urges, wishes or whims.

This is said as a warning against the kind of "Nietzschean egoists" who, in fact, are a product of the altruist morality and represent the other side of the altruist coin: the men who believe that any action, regardless of its nature, is good if it is intended for one's own benefit. Just as the satisfaction of the irrational desires of others is *not* a criterion of moral value, neither is the satisfaction of one's own irrational desires. Morality is not a contest of whims.

• • •

The *moral cannibalism* of all hedonist and altruist doctrines lies in the premise that the happiness of one man necessitates the injury of another.

Today, most people hold this premise as an absolute not to be questioned. And when one speaks of man's right to exist for his own sake, for his own rational self-interest, most people assume automatically that this means his right to sacrifice others. Such an assumption is a confession of their own belief that to injure, enslave, rob or murder others is in man's self-interest—which he must selflessly renounce. The idea that man's self-interest can be served only by a non-sacrificial relationship with others has never occurred to those humanitarian apostles of unselfishness, who proclaim their desire to achieve the brotherhood of men. And it will not occur to them, or to anyone, so long as the concept "rational" is omitted from the context of "values," "desires," "self-interest" and *ethics.*

The Objectivist ethics proudly advocates and upholds *rational selfishness*—which means: the val-

ues required for man's survival *qua* man—which means: the values required for *human* survival—not the values produced by the desires, the emotions, the "aspirations," the feelings, the whims or the needs of irrational brutes, who have never outgrown the primordial practice of human sacrifices, have never discovered an industrial society and can conceive of no self-interest but that of grabbing the loot of the moment.

The Objectivist ethics holds that *human* good does not require human sacrifices and cannot be achieved by the sacrifice of anyone to anyone. It holds that the *rational* interests of men do not clash—that there is no conflict of interests among men who do not desire the unearned, who do not make sacrifices nor accept them, who deal with one another as *traders,* giving value for value.

The principle of *trade* is the only rational ethical principle for all human relationships, personal and social, private and public, spiritual and material. It is the principle of *justice.*

A trader is a man who earns what he gets and does not give or take the undeserved. He does not treat men as masters or slaves, but as independent equals. He deals with men by means of a free, voluntary, unforced, uncoerced exchange—an exchange which benefits both parties by their own independent judgment. A trader does not expect to be paid for his defaults, only for his achievements. He does not switch to others the burden of his failures, and he does not mortgage his life into bondage to the failures of others.

In spiritual issues—(by "spiritual" I mean: "pertaining to man's consciousness")—the currency or medium of exchange is different, but the principle is the same. Love, friendship, respect, admiration are the emotional response of one man to the virtues of another, the spiritual *payment* given in exchange for the personal, selfish pleasure which one man derives from the virtues of another man's character. Only a brute or an altruist would claim that the appreciation of another person's virtues is an act of selflessness, that as far as one's own selfish interest and pleasure are concerned, it makes no difference whether one deals with a genius or a fool, whether one meets a hero or a thug, whether one marries an ideal woman or a slut. In spiritual issues, a trader is a man who does not seek to be loved for his weaknesses or flaws, only for his virtues, and who does not grant his love to the weaknesses or the flaws of others, only to their virtues.

To love is to value. Only a rationally selfish man, a man of *self-esteem,* is capable of love—because he is the only man capable of holding firm, consistent, uncompromising, unbetrayed values. The man who does not value himself, cannot value anything or anyone.

• • •

Love and friendship are profoundly personal, selfish values: love is an expression and assertion of self-esteem, a response to one's own values in the person of another. One gains a profoundly personal, selfish joy from the mere existence of the person one loves. It is one's own personal, selfish happiness that one seeks, earns and derives from love.

A "selfless," "disinterested" love is a contradiction in terms: it means that one is indifferent to that which one values.

Concern for the welfare of those one loves is a rational part of one's selfish interests. If a man who is passionately in love with his wife spends a fortune to cure her of a dangerous illness, it would be absurd to claim that he does it as a "sacrifice" for *her* sake, not his own, and that it makes no difference to *him,* personally and selfishly, whether she lives or dies.

Any action that a man undertakes for the benefit of those he loves is *not a sacrifice* if, in the hierarchy of his values, in the total context of the choices open to him, it achieves that which is of greatest *personal* (and rational) importance to *him.* In the above example, his wife's survival is of greater value to the husband than anything else that his money could buy, it is of greatest importance to his own happiness and, therefore, his action is *not* a sacrifice.

But suppose he let her die in order to spend his money on saving the lives of ten other women, none of whom meant anything to him—as the ethics of altruism would require. *That* would be a sacrifice.

Here the difference between Objectivism and altruism can be seen most clearly: if sacrifice is the moral principle of action, then that husband *should* sacrifice his wife for the sake of ten other women. What distinguishes the wife from the ten others? Nothing but her value to the husband who has to make the choice—nothing but the fact that *his* happiness requires her survival.

The Objectivist ethics would tell him: your highest moral purpose is the achievement of your own happiness, your money is yours, use it to save your wife, *that* is your moral right and your rational, moral choice.

Consider the soul of the altruistic moralist who would be prepared to tell that husband the opposite. (And then ask yourself whether altruism is motivated by benevolence.)

The proper method of judging when or whether one should help another person is by reference to one's own rational self-interest and one's own hierarchy of values: the time, money or effort one gives or the risk one takes should be proportionate to the value of the person in relation to one's own happiness.

• • •

The virtue involved in helping those one loves is not "selflessness" or "sacrifice," but *integrity.* Integrity is loyalty to one's convictions and values; it is the policy of acting in accordance with one's values, of expressing, upholding and translating them into practical reality. If a man professes to love a woman, yet his actions are indifferent, inimical or damaging to her, it is his lack of integrity that makes him immoral.

The same principle applies to relationships among friends. If one's friend is in trouble, one should act to help him by whatever nonsacrificial means are appropriate. For instance, if one's friend is starving, it is not a sacrifice, but an act of integrity to give him money for food rather than buy some insignificant gadget for oneself, because his welfare is important in the scale of one's personal values. If the gadget means more than the friend's suffering, one had no business pretending to be his friend.

The practical implementation of friendship, affection and love consists of incorporating the welfare (the *rational* welfare) of the person involved into one's own hierarchy of values, then acting accordingly.

But this is a reward which men have to earn by means of their virtues and which one cannot grant to mere acquaintances or strangers.

What, then, should one properly grant to strangers? The generalized respect and good will which one should grant to a human being in the name of the potential value he represents—until and unless he forfeits it.

A rational man does not forget that *life* is the source of all values and, as such, a common bond among living beings (as against inanimate matter), that other men are potentially able to achieve the same virtues as his own and thus be of enormous value to him. This does not mean that he regards human lives as interchangeable with his own. He recognizes the fact that his own life is the *source,* not only of all his values, but of *his capacity to value.* Therefore, the value he grants to others is only a consequence, an extension, a secondary projection of the primary value which is himself.

"The respect and good will that men of self-esteem feel toward other human beings is profoundly egoistic; they feel, in effect: 'Other men are of value because they are of the same species as myself.' In revering living entities, they are revering their *own* life. This is the psychological base of any emotion of sympathy and any feeling of 'species solidarity.'"[2]

•　•　•

It is only in emergency situations that one should volunteer to help strangers, if it is in one's power. For instance, a man who values human life and is caught in a shipwreck, should help to save his fellow passengers (though not at the expense of his own life). But this does not mean that after they all reach shore, he should devote his efforts to saving his fellow passengers from poverty, ignorance, neurosis or whatever other troubles they might have. Nor does it mean that he should spend his life sailing the seven seas in search of shipwreck victims to save.

Or to take an example that can occur in everyday life: suppose one hears that the man next door is ill and penniless. Illness and poverty are not metaphysical emergencies, they are part of the normal risks of existence; but since the man is temporarily helpless, one may bring him food and medicine, *if* one can afford it (as an act of good will, not of duty) or one may raise a fund among the neighbors to help him out. But this does not mean that one must support him from then on, nor that one must spend one's life looking for starving men to help.

In the normal conditions of existence, man has to choose his goals, project them in time, pursue them and achieve them by his own effort. He cannot do it if his goals are at the mercy of and must be sacrificed to any misfortune happening to others. He cannot live his life by the guidance of rules applicable only to conditions under which human survival is impossible.

The principle that one should help men in an emergency cannot be extended to regard all human suffering as an emergency and to turn the misfortune of some into a first mortgage on the lives of others.

•　•　•

The moral purpose of a man's life is the achievement of his own happiness. This does not mean that he is indifferent to all men, that human life is of no value to him and that he has no reason to help others in an emergency. But it *does* mean that he does not subordinate his life to the welfare of others, that he does not sacrifice himself to their needs, that the relief of their suffering is not his primary concern, that any help he gives is an *exception,* not a rule, an act of generosity, not of moral duty, that it is *marginal* and *incidental*—as disasters are marginal and incidental in the course of human existence—and that *values,* not disasters, are the goal, the first concern and the motive power of his life.

---

[2]Nathaniel Branden, "Benevolence versus Altruism," *The Objectivist Newsletter,* July 1962.

BUDDHIST ETHICS

Gunapala Dharmasiri

There are some interesting issues that are specific to the Buddhist theory of ethics. These issues originate from the nature of the Buddhist theory of reality. A person does not have a self or a soul and is said to be made up of five factors. When these five factors come together, they constitute the person, just as a chariot is made up of the parts that constitute it. And, it is further said that these five factors are incessantly changing or are always in a state of flux. In this state of affairs, can one meaningfully speak of "a person"? If there is no person, there are problems for moral discourse, because ethical discourse presupposes the notions of "personal responsibility," "personal identity," "personal initiative" and "moral commitment."

One could imagine these problems easily solved if we were to accept the theory of a self. But for the Buddha, the idea of a self could not be made meaningful in any way. The only way to make the idea of self meaningful is to verify it, and if we look at ourselves objectively in order to verify it, all we see is the above five factors. And if we introspect and subjectively look for a self, all we see is an ever changing series of thoughts and sensations. Therefore, if the idea of self or soul is not meaningful, we will have to explain things with the help of existing facts.

Although Buddhism does not accept the idea of a person as an enduring entity, it accepts the existence of a person as a composite of factors. Two criteria are used in determining the identity of a person. A person is made up of two types of groups of events, physical and mental. As all these groups are ever changing, the preceding events disappear, giving birth to succeeding events. Thus the succeeding events inherit the characteristics of the preceding events. This results in a causal sequence of events. In Buddhism, it is through this "unbroken continuity or coherence of the series of events" (*avicchinna santati sāmaggi*—Buddhaghosa), that personal identity is traced. The person who lives at 9 a.m. this morning is a result of the person who lived at 7 a.m. this morning.

DOCTRINE OF KARMA

It is in this sense that the Buddhist doctrine of karma has to be interpreted. Though some assume that the doctrine of karma is a metaphysical doctrine, it is actually a psychological principle or a law based on the law of causation as applied to a series of mental events. If a person has a "bad" thought now, this will generate further "bad" thoughts, thus gradually leading to the formation of a karmic mental complex. This complex can generate various types of mental illnesses like anxiety and guilt, which gradually lead to further complications such as physical illnesses. The Buddha said that karma is a principle that can be verified in this life itself by looking into the causal relationships between mental phenomena and between mental and physical phenomena. A "bad" thought leads to tension and anxiety, while a "good" thought leads to calmness and relaxation. Thus, the problem of personal identity and moral responsibility is solved in terms of causal connectedness.

Another problem that arises within Buddhist ethics is how to justify altruistic or "other-regarding" action. If real "persons" do not exist, how can we make the idea of moral commitment to others meaningful? A difficult problem that comes up in the Buddhist teaching of egolessness is "why should I do anything at all"?

Before we discuss acting or working for others, we must first be clear about what is meant by "work." Ordinarily, work is supposed to be physical. But Buddhism accepts two kinds of work: physical and spiritual. For example, a Brahmin farmer called Kasībhāradvāja accused the Buddha of leading an idle life, not doing any physical work or labor. The Buddha replied that he was also engaged in labor and that he was perhaps engaged in a task more important and arduous than what physical labor involves. Further, he said that if necessary, his work could also be easily described in the jargon of the physical labor of a farmer. The Buddha answers, "I also, O Brahmana, both plough and sow, and having ploughed and sown, I eat." Then the Brahmin retorts: "Thou professest to be a ploughman, and yet we do not see thy ploughing; asked about thy ploughing, tell us of it, that we may know thy ploughing." The Buddha answers, "Faith is the seed, penance the rain, understanding my yoke and plough, modesty the pole of the plough, mind the tie, thoughtfulness my ploughshare and goad . . . Exertion is my beast of burden; carrying me to *Nibbāna*,[1] he goes without turning back to the place where, having gone, one does not grieve. So this ploughing is ploughed, it bears the fruit of immortality; having ploughed this ploughing, one is freed from all pain."[2] Therefore, the Buddhist approach to asceticism should be properly understood. The Buddha recommended forests and lonely places only as ideal sites for training in meditation, but never for living, and he always advised monks that they "should travel around for the benefit and happiness of the multitude of human beings" (*Caratha bhikkhave cārikaṃ bahu jana hitāya bahujana sukhāya*).

CONVENTIONAL REALITY AND ABSOLUTE REALITY

Buddhism also formulates another distinction we should be aware of, that between two levels of reality: conventional reality and absolute reality. Persons and morality exist in the conventional realm, while in the realm of absolute reality both these ideas do not make much sense. Ordinary moral theory presupposes the sense of "a person." Ordinary moral theory is valid and meaningful for one who believes that he is "a person." Once one realizes that there is no person, then he goes beyond this type of morality. However, it should be clearly noted that by going beyond morality one does not get permission to contravene ordinary moral values. In other words, the absolute dimension has no power or privilege to abrogate ordinary moral values. The Buddha shows this distinction by saying that an ordinary person,

when he is moral, is conditioned by morality (*sīla-mayo*), but an enlightened person is moral by "nature" (*sīlavā*), because the nature of Nirvana is moral perfection, *i.e.*, when viewed from the conventional standpoint. Therefore, when we discuss morality we must be aware of the conventional level of reality which is presupposed in our analysis.

"OTHER REGARDING" ACTIONS

How does Buddhism recommend and justify "other-regarding" actions? It has several grounds for doing so. One reason stems from the theory of dependent origination (*paṭicca-samuppāda*), which emphasizes that everything originates dependent on everything else. Therefore, everything owes its existence to everything else. Actually, it is the *Anatta* doctrine that involves one in altruistic actions. The doctrine of interdependence rules out the possibility of a separate soul, because nothing can be independent in a world where everything is interrelated. I cannot think of myself as separate from the rest of the universe because, for example, if I take my body, it is dependent on food (which means that my body is dependent on plants, animals, water, oxygen, *etc.*). My mind also exists dependently because the existence of thoughts is dependent on sense data derived from the external world of objects and persons.

A Buddha's altruistic commitment to others and other objects originates from this dependency. Because my existence is dependent on the rest of the universe, I naturally owe a debt and an obligation to the rest of the universe. Therefore, my attitude to others and other objects should be one of respect and gratitude. Thus, Buddhism advocates a sense of awe and respect towards living beings and nature. Here, it is important to note that in Buddhism, the distinction between altruism and egoism breaks down as a meaningless distinction. The ideal moral attitude to other beings advocated by the Buddha is the "love a mother shows towards her one and only child" and the love relationship between mother and child cannot be characterized as egoistic or altruistic because it is a fluid mixture

---

[1]Sometimes spelled "nirvana," this is the desireless state that is the goal of Buddhism [Eds.].

[2]*Samyutta Nikāya* (Polytechnic Society, London).

of both. Likewise, helping others is a way of helping oneself.

One has to understand that one is a part of a larger whole, and is not a separate person. That is why the ordinary unenlightened man is, in Buddhist terminology, called a 'Puthujjana' (puthu = separate; jana = people), or a person who believes that he is separate. The relationship between the part and whole is organic. In the way the whole creates the part, the part also creates the whole. Therefore one should realize that one can play a creative (in a cosmic sense) part in the cosmic order of events. In a way, the whole determines the part. But, the Buddhist point is that the part can also play a role in determining the whole. This is, of course, an inevitable implication of the principle of interrelatedness. . . .

What the doctrine of interdependence emphasizes is, from the fact that the rest of the universe is responsible for me, it follows that I too am responsible for the rest of the universe. In the *Sigālovāda Sutta,* the Buddha emphasizes that rights and duties imply each other. If the rights are not well reciprocated by the duties, a moral imbalance is bound to result. From the fact that nature treats us rightly, it follows that we should treat nature rightly. Buddhism strongly believes that morality is the best way to communicate with nature because morality is the nature of nature. If we mishandle or mistreat nature we are bound to get back our due.

LOVE THAT EMBRACES ALL BEINGS

It is from the above considerations that an attitude of deepest love towards other beings and nature, which the Buddha advocates is derived. It is important to note that Buddhism is much more than merely humanistic, because the Buddhist love embraces all types of beings. Whenever the Buddha talks about loving others, he always speaks of "all beings" (*sabbe satta*). The same love that prompts a mother to care for her one and only son should prompt persons to do their best to help the rest of the community. This attitude fosters virtues like sharing and sympathy.

Another reason why we should do anything at all is grounded on sympathy. A central theme in Buddhist ethics is that "one should treat others in exactly the same way as one treats oneself" (*attānam upamam katvā*). In the *Anumāna Sutta,* the Buddha states that the basis of the "other-regarding" principle is an inference from oneself to another. The inference works in two ways. The first is thinking of oneself in terms of others. According to the Buddha, the sense of the value of oneself or of one's own personality is derived from others. Therefore, "personality" itself being a value concept, if one is to become a "person" in the proper sense, it must necessarily be done in a social medium. For that reason, one should always be considerate of the value of others. Man's personality is largely a product and an item of the society around him. One becomes good or derives any value to one's personality only through the society, which is why one must consider and respect others. One does not become oneself without the help of others. Here, the so-called distinction between altruism and egoism breaks down. The Buddha states his inferential principle: "Therein, your reverences, self ought to be measured against self thus by a monk: 'That person who is of evil desires and who is in the thrall of evil desires, that person is displeasing and disagreeable to me; and similarly, if I were of evil desires and in the thrall of evil desires, I would be displeasing and disagreeable to other.' "[3] The dichotomy between egoism and altruism breaks down when he repeatedly emphasizes the necessity of "other-regarding" virtues for one's development as a person, not only on a social level, but even on the spiritual level where progress is impossible without cultivating "other-regarding" virtues.

• • •

In the *Karanīya Metta Sutta* he says that, in spreading love, one must think of all possible types

---

[3]*Majjhima Nikāya* (Polytechnic Society, London), I. 97.

of beings: "Whatever living beings there may be: feeble or strong, long (or tall), stout, or medium, short, small, or large, seen or unseen, those dwelling far or near, those who are born and those who are yet to be born: may all beings, without exception, be happy-minded."[4] We must respect all forms of life. What the Buddha believes is that whatever form it takes, life is life. As the Mahayanists say, all life forms are sacred because they all contain the seeds of Buddhahood or perfection. If one does not have this reverence towards life, one alienates oneself from life. Whether it is one's own or another's, life is treated as a commonly shared property. If one disrespects life that is manifested in any form, one deteriorates morally and spiritually because one becomes alienated from the most basic and intrinsic value of the world. Here, it is important to note the significant fact that the Buddha prohibited monks from harming trees and plants because "they are creatures with one sense-faculty (*ekindriya*), (*i.e.* touch)" and therefore, "people are of the opinion that there is life in trees."[5] He also forbade monks to dig the earth because that would harm "tiny creatures living in earth"[6] (But he did not enjoin these rules for laymen because of the practical difficulties).

Although a complete practice of *Ahiṃsā* (non-injury) is even theoretically impossible because the process of living itself automatically involves a process of killing or injuring many beings, perfect *Ahiṃsā* is always regarded as the ideal that one should always try to live up to as far as possible. What truly matters is this genuine desire or motive to respect life. The Buddha says that the ultimate and intrinsic value of life will be self evident to any one who will care to look at one's own life. The Buddha's appeal to us is to realize that all other beings also think of themselves exactly in the same way one thinks about oneself. Therefore, in Buddhism, the sacredness of life is an ultimate ethical

fact which is proved and made meaningful self-evidently, *i.e.,* through empathy.

ON THE OBLIGATION TO KEEP INFORMED ABOUT DISTANT ATROCITIES

Carlo Filice

One must know about far away moral atrocities if one is to attempt to remedy them. Ignorance of these atrocities is at times a legitimate excuse for failure to make such attempts but not generally. It certainly is not a legitimate excuse when one deliberately keeps oneself uninformed of major atrocities; an example of such a person would be the well-educated, refined hedonist whose world revolves, by conscious choice, around private pleasure. On the other hand, it is a legitimate excuse in many cases when one simply lacks the means for being informed; an example of such would be the seriously underprivileged, culturally deprived, illiterate person.

But what about the cases of those people who fall somewhere between these two extremes? What about the single mother, working full-time as a nurse, who takes care of her children's needs most of the remainder of her hours? What about the young businessman almost wholly preoccupied with his struggle to make it in the business world? What about the medical student whose workload saps her of all desire to look at additional printed pages? What about the secretary whose after-work life is dedicated to cultivating her interest in French literature? What about the real estate agent in constant pursuit of new listings and loan agreements, who finds barely enough time to spend with her family? What about the small farmer in whose circle of friends and relatives questions about what might be happening in China, Brazil, or Mozambique do not come up? Is their relative ignorance of

---

[4]*Sutta Nipāta* (Polytechnic Society, London), 146–147.
[5]*Vinaya*, IV, 34.
[6]*Vinaya*, IV, 32–3.

major moral atrocities excusable? Is their consequent inaction excusable?

This is the issue I would like to explore in this essay. My claim will be that this type of ignorance is not excusable in most cases of "average" Westerners and of "average" US citizens in particular. Consequently this ignorance does not excuse their doing nothing about large-scale abuses.

Consider the events in East Timor during the last fifteen years. They constitute a typical major moral atrocity. The choice of this example is recommended by a number of factors: (1) the relative magnitude of the evil; (2) the supportive (military, economic, diplomatic) role played by the US government and others in this bloody episode; (3) the fact that most of us are unaware of this atrocity; (4) the fact that some sources of information concerning it can be found in the public arena, though they generally must be sought out.

The following are the basic facts of the East Timor situation as reported by Noam Chomsky and Edward S. Herman who gathered them from various uncontestable sources:

> On December 7, 1975 Indonesian armed forces invaded the former Portuguese colony of East Timor, only a few hours after the departure of President Gerald Ford and Henry Kissinger from a visit to Jakarta. Although Indonesia has effectively sealed off East Timor from the outside world, reports have filtered through indicating that there have been massive atrocities, with estimates running to 100,000 killed, about one-sixth of the population. An assessment by the Legislative Research Service of the Australian Parliament concluded that there is "mounting evidence that the Indonesians have been carrying out a brutal operation in East Timor," involving "indiscriminate killing on a scale unprecedented in post-World War II history."[1]

The above account reflects the number of dead as of 1979. A 1987 estimate as reported by the *New York Times* is 150,000. The entire population of East Timor was estimated by the *New York Times* in 1975 to be 620,000. That means that by now nearly one fourth of the population of this tiny, backward area has been killed. The main reason for the Indonesian invasion was the 1975 popular victory in East Timor (one year after East Timor was granted independence from Portugal) of a party named FRETILIN and the defeat of more conservative parties. FRETILIN's character is summarized by Chomsky and Herman on the basis of independent reports:

> FRETILIN was a moderate reformist national front, headed by a Catholic seminarian and initially involving largely urban intellectuals, among them young Lisbon-educated radical Timorese who "were most eager to search for their cultural origins" and who were "to lead the FRETILIN drive into the villages, initiating consumer and agricultural co-operatives, and a literary campaign conducted in [the native language] along the lines used by Paulo Freire in Brazil." . . . It was "more reformist than revolutionary," calling for gradual steps towards complete independence, agrarian reform, transformation of uncultivated land and large farms to people's cooperatives, educational programs, steps towards producer-consumer cooperatives supplementing existing Chinese economic enterprises "for the purposes of supplying basic goods to the poor at low prices," controlled foreign aid and investment, and a foreign policy of non-alignment.[2]

This victorious party's platform did not please the Indonesian leadership which ten years earlier had carried out an internal purge of half a million suspected "communists." Thus, under a pretext to end a civil war in East Timor (there had in fact been some fighting between followers of FRETILIN and of UDT that had, however, quickly come to an end due to the former's preponderance of public support), Indonesia invaded and sealed the area from international observers and organizations, including the International Red Cross, and finding widespread indigenous resistance, proceeded to carry out the slaughter.

---

[1] Noam Chomsky and Edward S. Herman, *The Washington Connection and Third World Fascism,* vol. 1 of *The Political Economy of Human Rights* (Boston: South End Press, 1979), 130.

[2] Ibid., 134. The internal quotation quotes Jill Joliffe, *East Timor: Nationalism and Colonialism* (Australia: University of Queensland Press, 1978), 79.

It is important to note that between 1973 and 1977 Indonesia received $254 million of military aid (in arms, military aid grants, and military sales credit), and $634 million in economic aid from the US.[3] Moreover, during this time 1,272 Indonesian military officers received US military training.[4] These facts, together with the timing of the invasion (just after high-level consultations with Ford and Kissinger), the traditionally close ties between the Indonesian and the US governments, and the lack of serious protests by the United States in the years since the invasion, show complicity on the part of the US government and establishment, which included the media and the intellectual community.

The attempt by Indonesia to "pacify" East Timor has continued during the last thirteen years. While this was happening, the few books and reports on the massacre have generally escaped wide public attention in both the United States and in Europe. When mainstream publications such as the *New York Times* and *Newsweek* have reported on the invasion, they have generally distorted what actually occurred, by relying upon official Indonesian accounts, by ignoring reports offered by refugees in Portugal, and at least on one occasion, by deliberately altering the published version of events given by an Australian reporter who was in East Timor during the early weeks of the invasion.[5]

One could go on with such depressing details. One could also tell similar stories about other states within the US sphere of influence such as Guatemala, Thailand, El Salvador, and Brazil. The point is that the case of East Timor is not an anomaly. The factors which make it an example of a slaughter relevant for the present essay apply to many other cases. In nearby El Salvador, for example, we find a regime which has permitted, or perhaps sponsored, the death-squad killing of tens of thousands during the last twelve years.[6] That same regime has received consistent US economic, military, and diplomatic aid. Again, despite the magnitude of the evil, its proximity to the United States, and its greater news coverage, most of us are unable to locate El Salvador on a world map.

Because the "average" US citizen does not know these massacres occur, nor of the government's relatively close ties to the regimes perpetrating them, the average citizen does nothing to help end the slaughters. Is this ignorance and resulting inaction morally excusable? The following is one line of argument in favor of a "no" answer. It tries to establish that most of us are under a *prima facie* obligation to keep informed about cases such as East Timor. What it maintains about US citizens would also apply to citizens of other major powers whose governments play supportive roles in the atrocities of other governments.

1. One has a *prima facie* obligation to help prevent harm, especially major, avoidable suffering and death, whenever helping to do so requires only trivial sacrifices, such as buying fewer or no luxury items, spending less time

---

[3]Ibid., 45. The original sources of these data are the following: United States Department of Defense, *Foreign Military Sales and Military Assistance Facts* (Washington, 1976); U.S. Department of Defense, *Security Assistance Program, Presentation to Congress, F.Y. 1978* (Washington, 1977); U.S. Agency for International Development, *U.S. Overseas Loans and Grants,* 1 July 1945–30 June 1975 (Washington, 1976).
[4]Chomsky and Herman, 45.
[5]Ibid., 136–38.

[6]According to a 1985 Americas Watch Report these were the relevant statistics: "more than 40,000 civilian noncombatants killed—murdered by government forces and "death squads" allied to them; another 3,000 disappeared; 750,000 or so (15 percent of the population) . . . homeless or 'displaced' within its borders." "With Friends Like These," in Cynthia Brown, ed., *Americas Watch Report on Human Rights and U.S. Policy in Latin America* (New York: Pantheon Books, 1985), 115.

According to *New York Times* reporter James LeMoyne, "The Civil War has killed more than 70,000 people, most of them civilians shot by the army during the early 1980's." The victims have included nuns, priests, and an archbishop. No one has been successfully prosecuted and arrested for any of these thousands of killings. James LeMoyne, "The Guns of Salvador," *New York Times Magazine,* 5 Feb. 1989, 20.

watching television, etc., and whenever there is some chance that one's efforts will produce at least some success.[7]

2. One will not be in a position to help prevent harm if one is unaware of the occurrence of this harm.

3. One who has a *prima facie* obligation to help prevent X also has a *prima facie* obligation to attempt to position oneself so as to be able to help prevent X, particularly if these positional attempts are likely to be successful (e.g., if A has a *prima facie* duty to prevent his own violent behavior, A also has a *prima facie* duty to attempt to remain sober if drunkenness tends to make A violent, and if A's attempts to remain sober are not absolutely hopeless).

4. Therefore, each of us has a *prima facie* obligation to make serious attempts to become and remain informed about the occurrence of major, avoidable harm whenever these attempts at gaining the necessary information are likely to succeed and require small sacrifices, and whenever there is some chance for the prevention of at least some harm.

5. Major moral atrocities, such as the systematic and large-scale torture and killing by a government for political reasons, constitute one class of major avoidable harm.

6. Therefore, each of us has a *prima facie* obligation to make serious attempts to be informed about the occurrence of major moral atrocities (whenever the conditions in 4 above obtain).

7. Most people in developed countries who attempt to gain the necessary information are likely to succeed.

8. Most people in developed countries can make serious attempts to gain the necessary information about current moral atrocities without such attempts resulting in major sacrifices.

9. The preventive actions based on such information have some likelihood of leading to the prevention of at least some harm resulting from major moral atrocities.

10. Therefore, most people in developed countries have a *prima facie* obligation to make serious attempts to become informed about the current major moral atrocities, especially those occurring within their country's sphere of influence.

I will enlarge on this argument by considering a number of likely objections.

• • •

OBJECTION I: CITIZENS ARE TOO POWERLESS TO FIND OUT

Should the average US citizen decide to seek the relevant information, are there not a number of factors which show that he or she most likely will not succeed in finding out about affairs such as the East Timor or the El Salvador bloodshed? Consider the following: large numbers of people are only semi-literate and would not walk into a library or bookstore or even read a newspaper. Others more literate lack knowledge of geography, history, international affairs, economics, and political and religious ideologies. They lack the general intellectual sophistication to know where to start looking and how to interpret what they find. Should this large majority of people not be exempt from the obligation to seek knowledge of matters beyond their intellectual reach? ...

This ... objection shows how difficult it is for most people to become informed about atrocities. Most people would first, or in the process, have to broaden themselves on many different fronts

---

[7]The notion of "*prima facie* obligation" employed in this argument is most naturally derivable from consequentialist moral theories. However, I believe that it can also be grounded on deontological theories of rights and obligations. I would think that victims of torture and killing are entitled, by virtue of having basic "negative" rights, to receiving our help in avoiding being tortured and killed. However, this topic is too vast for it to be properly addressed here. I choose not to rely on the notion of rights generally, because I find rights to be metaphysically suspect unless they are taken as derived from more basic values such as harm and benefit.

before they would be armed to do the requisite research. This intellectual broadening most people will choose not to do. However, I find it excessive to say that most people cannot do it.[8] Help can always be found, whether from the parish priest, the local librarian, or the college educated daughter-in-law. Naturally, sacrifices would have to be made.

But, our opponent might continue, most parish priests, librarians, and college educated daughters-in-law have never even heard of places like East Timor, and they may barely recognize names such as El Salvador, Indonesia, Guatemala, and Paraguay. How can they be counted on to inform the rest of us about what is going on there? If such information is available mainly in relatively obscure publications such as *The Nation* or Amnesty International reports which are not found in most libraries and bookstores, and they are not mentioned in most university courses, how can the average citizen be held morally accountable for being unaware of it? Should the blame not go to the mainstream press and to mainstream educators instead?

Undoubtedly, the press and the intellectual corps are preeminent bearers of moral responsibility for not taking sufficient measures to inform themselves and the public of various moral atrocities. But given that there are publications, albeit off the main media routes, which do report on these matters, is this responsibility not shared also by average middle-class literate citizens? Perhaps their responsibility is diminished due to their greater difficulty in attaining access to this information. But clearly one would not want to accept the principle that major wrongdoing can be ignored whenever information about it is hard to obtain, since such ignorance would have justi-

fied ignoring Nazi atrocities during the 1930s and 1940s.

• • •

OBJECTION II: HELP ONLY THOSE YOU CAN, I.E., YOUR NEIGHBORS

The average individual's attempt to influence matters like the Indonesian policy *vis-à-vis* East Timor, runs this objection, is not likely to lead to the prevention of any harm. . . .

Would one not be more effectively beneficent by helping instead local charities, an alcoholic relative, or the neighborhood stray cats? And if so, why waste time and effort in trying to become informed about distant atrocities?

Naturally, there is some validity to this line of thinking. One's replies might include the following observations. . . .

[T]he ideal conditions for "local morality" cannot be obtained in the actual world. Perhaps in an ideal world where power and resources are somewhat equitably distributed, if each tends only to her own locality where a noticeable difference can be affected, the global result would probably be morally acceptable (though protection of common resources, such as the ozone layer, would require global and collective attention). But in a world like ours, where resources and power are disproportionately distributed, often through past and present injustice, the policy of each tending to her own property and community will not lead to morally acceptable global results. In this askew world, pursuing one's personal interests and community interests may mean keeping those in Timor or Brazil dispossessed; and one's power to do so is likely to more than offset another's power to improve his or her position. Any view that justifies the pursuit of ends benefiting only oneself and one's own, and that neglects to consider seriously the implications of such pursuits for "others," does not deserve the appellation "moral." Impartiality must be one of the essential features of the moral viewpoint. One aim of this viewpoint is the transcendence of the "one's

---

[8]Whether one has the right not to change and improve oneself is a complex issue. At the very least, however, such a right may conflict with the rights of others (to be given help in preventing their being tortured and killed) which may generate a duty that one keep informed on the condition of these others. I discuss this issue more fully in non-rights terms below. See note 9.

own/others" dichotomy, hard as this may be.[9] Impartiality in an interconnected world implies a cosmopolitan outlook. . . .

Needless to say, having an obligation to find out about, and speak out on, distant matters does not exempt one from obligations to help the local indigent, alcoholic, or cat. Many of us can do both. In fact, since parochial and distant matters often causally interact, one may need to do both. But, one might ask, where does one draw the line? And where does one find the time? One does have to earn a living so as to be in a position to help both the local and the distant needy. One does have to fulfill one's family obligations. And one needs to take care of oneself, to do things for sheer pleasure, or to develop artistic and other skills, and not out of moral considerations.

Obviously these questions lead to immense complexities. One suggestion may be that in the interest of time and effectiveness what each individual should devote herself to, in addition to providing for self, family, and friends, depends on the individual's circumstances and expertise. For instance, the lawyer might most effectively use some of her time to defend the interests of the local disenfranchised and speak out about the misuses of the legal system in South Africa or about the US government's selective and self-serving compliance with World Court decisions; the local radio announcer might best use her position to insert unusual and personally researched news items into ordinary broadcasts; the corporate employee might best explore the policies of the firm's international division, and if necessary blow the whistle on ethically dubious practices. Despite countless idiosyncrasies and complications, it remains a fact that most (or at least many) individuals can afford to sacrifice some of the time and resources ordinarily allotted for personal pleasure for the sake of those less fortunate.

These sacrifices need not result in significant "losses." One might, in fact, find that these "moral" pursuits will turn into creative and satisfying projects. These projects may even become replacements for some of one's more mindless leisure activities.

• • •

OBJECTION III: THE INDIVIDUAL IS IMPOTENT IN THE FACE OF HISTORICAL FORCES

The individual, according to this objection, is impotent to prevent or arrest events such as the East Timor massacre because such periodical massacres are after all necessary products of the present world order. To prevent these occurrences, one would have to change this world order. But the individual is as ineffectual in producing this change as a single cell is ineffectual in altering the psychological temperament of the person. . . .

---

[9]This claim has been contested by a number of contemporary philosophers: Philippa Foot, *Virtues and Vices and Other Essays in Moral Philosophy* (Berkeley: University of California Press, 1978); Bernard Williams, *Moral Luck* (Cambridge: Cambridge University Press, 1981); Susan Wolf, "Moral Saints," *Journal of Philosophy* 79 (1982): 419–31; Michael Slote, *Goods and Virtues* (Oxford: Clarendon Press, 1983); and Thomas Nagel, *The View From Nowhere.* In different ways each argues that it is not necessarily immoral to pursue personal, familial, or local goals at the expense of "common good" goals. The personal vs. impersonal dilemma is at the center of Nagel's moral and general philosophy. His opinion is that "the impartial standpoint of morality . . . will give to everyone a dispensation for a certain degree of partiality—in recognition of the fact that it is one aspect of the human perspective." In other words, an objective moral theory, in acknowledging all the facts in our universe, must take into account the fact that humans encounter the world from the subjective perspective of self, family, race, and nationality. The theory's moral demands cannot ignore this human fact. Consequently, an objective moral theory, such as utilitarianism, cannot be strictly impartial. I admit that the issue is profound and fascinating. But I would lean toward the hard line considered, but finally rejected, by Nagel: "One might take the severe line that moral requirements result from a correct assessment of the weight of good and evil, impersonally revealed, that it is our job to bring our motives into line with this, and that if we cannot do it because of personal weakness, this shows not that the requirements are excessive but that we are bad—though one might refrain from being too censorious about it." This view strikes me as rationally unavoidable once one grants the equal moral value of virtually every human. The partiality toward self that the above-mentioned philosophers defend goes directly against this moral axiom, particularly in a world of limited resources where my having x often deprives another or others. Were each of us insulated from others, the case might be different. Thomas Nagel, *The View From Nowhere,* 202–05.

This objection to the presumed power of individuals to affect world events does have some plausibility. This plausibility derives in part from the alleged biology-psychology parallel. Individual biological cells are hard put to affect the condition of the local bodily organ, much less that of the entire organism. Does this also hold true for persons *vis-à-vis* the corporation, the nation, and the international system? There are obvious differences between the positions of cells and of persons relative to their respective environments. Unlike cells, persons can come to understand the behavior of the larger system and the forces which help shape it. Unlike cells, persons are not cognitively confined to their narrow surroundings; they can establish chains of communication which cover distant parts of the larger system and which may lead to the formation of international organizations such as human rights groups, labor federations, and scientific world bodies. These organizations will then collectively form a moral subsystem inserted among other large-scale systemic forces. In short, cells are generally passive victims of the behavior of larger scale biological-psychological units.

Persons appear to be much more capable of understanding and of actively influencing large scale units, such as unions, churches, corporations, and nations. While it is tempting to overestimate an individual's potency within systemic units, one must also take care not to reduce the individual's position to complete insignificance.

If, in fact, individuals can create or offer support to competitive systemic moral forces like Amnesty International or Greenpeace, which in turn can produce some moral impact on the otherwise amoral world order, then individuals can affect this world order albeit indirectly. Perhaps the impact of these "moral" organizations is negligible. However, that is not so obvious, and in fact their influence appears to be growing. Certainly, their impact would be strengthened by the support of additional individuals. Hence, we come full circle to the moral necessity for individual action aimed at large-scale matters.

OBJECTION IV: IT WOULD BE GREAT TO HELP, BUT IS IT WRONG NOT TO HELP?

Philosophers of ethics distinguish between acts that are morally required and acts that, while commendable if done, are not obligatory, called "supererogatory" acts. Sharing one's salary with some group of destitute strangers constitutes a commendable but not an obligatory act. What about taking steps to broaden oneself culturally and intellectually in order to be able to keep abreast of foreign developments so as to help fight against major moral abuses? Wouldn't this also be a commendable but not required course of action? If so, the average citizen is not under any compelling obligation to engage in this course of action.

Let us assume that the commendable/obligatory distinction is valid. Even so, by appealing to certain considerations of compensatory justice it can be shown that the information-seeking course of action is obligatory. Consider the salary sharing example. While generally your sharing your salary with some poor strangers is not morally required (though some historical figures, like Jesus, have thought otherwise), what if you have contributed— even if only to a tiny degree—to their systematic impoverishment and have done so in some unfair way? One would think then that by way of compensation you owe them at least some help or some fraction of your possessions.

Has the average citizen contributed to a tiny degree, and in an unfair way, to the moral atrocities committed by foreign governments and the US government in Vietnam? Those who would answer "yes" can advance the following argument:

1. In a democratic country, the government speaks for citizens and invests some of their tax money in foreign affairs. It performs this general function with their knowledge and approval. It is, thus, their agent or broker.
2. The US government has helped, and continues to help, many brutal foreign regimes, often with some of its citizens' tax money.
3. Therefore, US citizens' agent has clearly supported brutal foreign regimes.

4. A person shares responsibility with the agent for what the latter does while carrying out the duties with which it is charged; and the responsibility is shared even when the agent's actions are taken without the person's knowledge, so long as the agent is granted broad powers of action.

5. The US government is given broad powers of action, especially in foreign affairs, and often does not fully inform the citizens about its foreign policies.

6. Therefore, the average US citizen shares responsibility with the government for its foreign affairs policies which often support brutal foreign regimes.

Having thus contributed to moral atrocities, US citizens are morally obligated to help the victims of such atrocities by way of compensation, if nothing else.[10]

But what about the case of those citizens who oppose the government's policies and vote for or otherwise support candidates and parties who call for an end to support to brutal regimes? Are these citizens not exempt from any complicity in these atrocities? Must they take further and more drastic actions, such as not paying a proportional share of their income taxes, in order to satisfy their moral obligations? Considered in its own right, this is a very difficult issue. For our purposes it suffices to say that this group constitutes a very small minority (most people, again, do not cast their votes and support on the basis of a candidate's position on foreign policy issues). Moreover, the type of person who is aware of and opposes these immoral foreign policies has thereby shown currency with the relevant world events and has already taken steps to help al-

leviate the atrocities. For most of the rest of us, the argument still stands.

But what if the government, as our agent, conceals from us or at least fails to explicitly inform us about its activities in other parts of the world? Would this not relieve us of the responsibility for the related atrocities despite our contribution to these atrocities through, for example, unwitting financial support? To answer this, we would have to know how actively we tend to seek the relevant information from our agent; how willing we are to close our eyes to its practices; and whether there are sources which can, if necessary, provide us with the relevant information. What has already been said on these issues shows that we can uncover our government's role in foreign atrocities.[11] In that case we, the citizens, remain partially responsible for its foreign deeds, and our compensatory obligation stands. In fact, once the moral obligation is seen as deriving from the principle of compensatory justice, our duty to help alleviate systematic human rights abuses becomes much stronger than would be the case if it derived merely from a general obligation to prevent harm to people we have in no way affected. Our actions and omissions have affected and do affect distant people, however unwitting we may be in this.

Because of this contribution to the harm, we have a particularly compelling duty to inform ourselves about these distant atrocities. Indeed, there are many other major sources of harm in our world, such as famines, diseases, environmental destruction, and the nuclear arms threat. My earlier argument, based on a general obligation to prevent harm, can also be used to spur us into keeping informed about these other evils. But if the demands upon our personal time and energy become too burdensome, and we must choose among subjects about which to keep informed, then we ought to inform ourselves first about those major evils to which we contribute—directly, through our actions, and indirectly, through

---

[10]A similar point is made by Slote in discussing whether wealthy individuals and nations who omit to share some of their wealth with the poor are justified in this omission. He observes that "[o]missions may not be permissible . . . if they in some sense preserve or perpetuate commissive wrongdoings." And since he thinks that in fact most wealthy individuals and nations become and remain wealthy by immoral means, they are obligated to share their wealth with those at whose expense this wealth becomes accumulated. M. Slote, "The Morality of Wealth," 141–45.

[11]Note that here I am not relying on the conclusion of my earlier argument based on the general obligation to prevent harm. I am merely borrowing one premise from that argument.

the actions of our representative government. And while such major evils will not be confined to distant atrocities, some of these atrocities will surely fall under this most stringent category.

One must add that this argument has made no mention of the economic benefits that accrue to us through big business's exploitation of favorable foreign conditions (e.g., cheap labor, cheap resources, lenient safety regulations, low taxes, etc.). These favorable investment conditions are often systematically maintained by repressive regimes at steep human rights costs. Most of us benefit considerably from the success of these multinational firms. We benefit as consumers through cheaper products. We benefit as investors in stocks, banks, pension funds, and through greater dividends. And we benefit in many other ways, given the support by multinationals for media organizations, hospitals, universities, and the arts. Accordingly, are we not obligated to compensate those who are violently repressed so that such benefits will continue to flow our way?

OBJECTION V: BUT EVEN MORE PEOPLE WILL DROWN IF WE ROCK THE INTERNATIONAL BOAT

This argument runs as follows: Yes, our government and multinational business institutions often cooperate with violent oligarchic regimes, and these regimes do engage in large-scale abuses, but one must consider the alternatives. The serious alternatives have often been left-wing regimes that tend to produce even greater evils and abuses by radically suspending "the market system" in favor of some centralized command system; by creating a one-party political system; and by carrying out massive purges of suspected opponents. . . .

Thus, is our foreign policy not morally justified, caught as it is between two inevitable evils? . . .

A systematic reply to this objection would take us far indeed from our present limited scope. The following remarks will have to suffice. First, this argument relies, I believe, on a false dichotomy. The choice of "third world" regimes is not necessarily between violent oligarchies and violent Stalinist-

type left-wing systems. There have been humane, neutral, and semi-left-wing systems based on democracy and on a mixed economy, such as those of the Scandinavian countries. Others were not given much of a chance, e.g., Chile under Allende, and recently, Nicaragua. . . .

When left-wing parties gain power electorally, as in Greece, Chile, and Spain, the result is far from violent and repressive; quite the opposite tends to happen. The movement in the countries listed is toward more open and tolerant systems. Moreover, the presumed dichotomy also ignores options such as religiously inspired regimes, perhaps not all of which will be violent and repressive like Iran's.

Second, even if the above dichotomy were valid, and morally we had to support anti-left-wing regimes, our government, and other governments, could surely exert enough real pressure on them so as to avert the massive and systematic abuses that characterize their rule. The record, as with the slaughter of Timorese and of Salvadorans, shows a repeated failure to exert such pressure. Surely the present world order could be maintained in a less brutal way. Our present relations with criminal regimes is surely not the best we can do, particularly since the Soviet threat has significantly diminished.

OBJECTION VI: ONE CANNOT CHANGE THE PAST

Is it not the case that by the time the average citizen finds out about a major moral atrocity it has already occurred, and hence it cannot be helped?

This is so in a few cases. In other cases, the tragedy goes on for years as in East Timor, El Salvador, Guatemala, and Paraguay, to name a few. During this time, governments and corporations continue to conduct business as usual with the regime, often supplying the very weapons used to carry out the massacres. Moreover, future atrocities can be averted by helping to create an international climate hostile to regimes which tend to engage in atrocities.

One final note: none of what I've said precludes other grounds for the obligation to keep informed about current and historical events. One may be morally obligated as a Christian or as a democratic citizen to keep informed. There may also be prudential grounds for keeping informed. However, these matters fall outside the scope of this paper.

To sum up, I have argued that harm prevention and compensatory justice factors oblige most of us to help prevent and remedy distant, systematic atrocities. To do this, we need to keep informed about such atrocities. Keeping informed becomes, thus, a moral obligation. If one's neighbors systematically abuse their children, and there is clear evidence of this ongoing abuse available, who can and who will listen to the children's cries? One would be seriously remiss if he or she were not to pay attention and call the authorities. One would be particularly remiss if he or she had benefitted from the abuse and had, perhaps unwittingly, helped to provide the means for carrying out the abuse.

The victims in El Salvador, East Timor, and elsewhere are not simply children, and perhaps they are not our "neighbors," but in our current global village, their cries can be heard by most of us, if we are willing to listen. And many of us unwittingly benefit from and contribute to their suffering. In such circumstances, one would think that the distance of the victims would not lessen our obligation to pay attention and take action.

QUESTIONS FOR DISCUSSION

1. Is it possible to love all persons equally, as Motse argues? Would it really end all war? You may want to compare Motse's ideas to the similar and more recent ideas of Gandhi and Martin Luther King, Jr. (in Chapter 9).

2. Certainly Rand's view is at odds with other views in this section. What would be some of our other authors' criticisms of Rand's ethics of "selfishness"? What would be Rand's criticisms of the others? Might there be some points of agreement between her view and that of the others in the section?

3. If Dharmasiri is right and there is no "person," and personality is largely a product of social context, then whom can we blame for evil deeds? Can there be an ethics without a potentially guilty subject? Why wouldn't Buddhist egoless ethics end in the attitude, "why should I do anything at all?" How would a Buddhist defend him- or herself from the above challenges?

4. How would Filice's argument about moral obligation apply to today's college students? Are you aware of any present atrocities? If so, what do you think would be Filice's argument in that particular case about what you should do? Do you agree with him? Why or why not?

SUBJECTIVISM AND THE PROBLEM OF RELATIVISM

Can there be universal moral claims? Many of our ethicists in other sections of this chapter argue that they have a formula for deducing which actions are best. Kant argues that there are imperatives that are categorical—applicable to all circumstances. Mill's utilitarian approach, while weighing the pros and cons of individual situations, still insists that the utilitarian method should apply to all times and cultures. And what shall we do about the clash of cultural values, when some cultures uphold egoistic values while others uphold altruistic values? Can both be right, in their own spheres? Or is one more correct than the other?

We will look first at the views of Argentinean philosopher Alejandro Korn. Korn (1860–1936) was born in San Vincente, a district of Buenos Aires. He had, over the years, a great personal influence on many thinkers in Argentina, and his inspiration helped overcome the positivism that had predominated in Argentinean philosophy before him. Korn argues that insofar as there is no God who can provide the standard for absolute, intrinsic claims of value for certain objects or concepts, valuation is always subjective. Valuation is always influenced by social context, and values change throughout time. Values proposed to be universal are never really upheld in practice. Korn insists instead that something is valuable only if humans value it. Each individual tends to keep his or her right of judging flexible at all times. And, of course, there is no consensus among all people in all times as to what is valuable or not.

Korn insists that although values have always been subjective, that has not reduced human history to anarchy. During certain time frames, certain arguments, authorities, or interests hold sway over most people and introduce some temporary uniformity in values. Logical argumentation in itself is not sufficient to throw off the subjective aspect, for even logic is influenced by the times and the context. Those who claim that ideal values exist, especially philosophers, deal only with word play. This is because ideal values are just abstract ideas for unrealized ultimate aspirations. They can only become effective and efficacious

when through action they are objectivized in concrete form, destined to be a historical episode in the evolution of human culture. The historical process is the searchlight for those values that are to triumph and prevail, although it need not necessarily be our own society's values that will triumph.

Alain Locke's ideas complement those of Korn. Locke is an African-American philosopher whose philosophical works are slowly commanding more and more attention from the academic philosophical community. Locke was born in Philadelphia and lived from 1885 to 1954. He began his career with his first philosophy degree from Harvard. Even though he won the prestigious Rhodes scholarship to study at the graduate level at Oxford University, five Oxford colleges refused to admit him. When the American Club held a Thanksgiving dinner for the scholarship winners, they refused to admit Locke because of his race. Locke had to battle against prejudice in one way or another during his entire career. He joined the Baha'i religion, heartened by its insistence on the unity of humanity and its practice of holding interracial religious meetings (a rarity, since Christianity in America at the time was highly segregated).

While a member and sometimes chair of the philosophy department for many years at Howard University, Locke continued to expand his interests beyond philosophy to religion, history, and art. Locke considered the study of African culture and race relations of central importance. He visited Egypt and Sudan in 1924 and promoted and collected African art. Locke is perhaps best known for his contributions to the Harlem Renaissance, such as his collection of articles and artwork called *The New Negro.* Locke's message was the cultural continuity between Africa and African-Americans. He encouraged artists to take up the theme of struggling against racism in their artistic and literary works.[1]

---

[1]Leonard Harris, "Rendering the Text," *The Philosophy of Alain Locke: Harlem Renaissance and Beyond,* ed. Leonard Harris (Philadelphia: Temple University Press, 1989), pp. 3–27.

In this essay, we witness Locke's interest in European value theory, to which he was exposed at Oxford, as well as the influence of pragmatism from his time at Harvard. He notes that there has been a major problem in theorizing value (a pursuit called *axiology*). Value formalism argues that values are objective and permanent, in some sense fixed by nature or essence (harking back to Plato's idea of the forms), tending toward authoritarianism, fundamentalism, and dogmatism. He argues that value realists are guilty of making entities out of modes of behavior. In contrast, Locke insists that values have to be understood in their relational and changing context. That values can change does not mean that they are not normative. As he explains, his position is not just that what's good today is bad tomorrow, but rather that what is revealed by experience as better becomes the new good. Rather than discarding old values, what happens is a retrospective revaluation of the old value, which makes corrective revision possible. He goes on to illustrate a functionalist approach to value by drawing on examples from logic and art in addition to moral clashes. Locke is concerned that people develop a cosmopolitan taste in both art and morality; only by widening appreciation for values that are new or complex can current value conflicts be resolved.

David Wong is a professor of philosophy at Brandeis University. He has written many articles and books exploring the relevance of ancient Chinese philosophy to present-day society. In the article in this section, he explores two aspects of relativism that are important: meta-ethical moral relativism, which asserts that moral truth and justifiability are culturally and historically contingent; and normative relativism, which claims that it is wrong to pass judgment on those who hold values different from oneself and wrong to try to make them conform to one's own values.

Wong argues that extreme versions of relativism are easily proven wrong, self-contradictory, or dangerous. But it would be wrong to conclude that absolutism and/or universalism would be more satisfactory. Relativists can successfully show that particular differences in moral belief between cultures are best explained by a theory that denies that there is a single true morality. You may have two societies that each focus on a good that is reasonable. This is possible because the range of human goods is too rich and diverse to be summed up in a single moral ideal. Functionalism alone could not resolve which morality is the best since two different moralities may be able to perform practical functions equally well. Without asserting that the one true morality could be found, it could nevertheless be argued that moralities could be evaluated by whether they succeed in reducing interpersonal conflict and promote persons who consider the interest of others.

Regarding normative relativism, Wong offers his analysis of the twin dangers of, on the one hand, judging one's own values to be the best while condemning the values of others; and on the other hand, neglecting to condemn values and behaviors that lead to universally recognized and grave harm.

VALUES ARE SUBJECTIVE

Alejandro Korn

Valuation is a complex process in which all psychical activities participate in various proportions, as part of a whole, until they are synthesized in a volition. Psychological analysis can identify the confluence of the most elemental biological impulses, the most instinctive appetites, the most refined sensibility, the most prudent reflection, the most remote memories, the most headstrong faith, the most idealistic or mystical vision—all of which come together in the act of valuation, in the movement of will that approves or repudiates. The genesis of valuation is influenced by the historical moment in which we live, the collective atmosphere—cultural, ethnic, and associational—that envelops us, and the more or less social features of our character. In short, there is a slippery, personal dimension to valuation, which eludes all logical coercion. Although psychological analysis, armed with the intuition of a Dostoyevski, may penetrate to the murkiest depths of the human soul, there will always remain something, an undecipherable *x*. And this is to say nothing of those professional psychologists who are condemned to skim the surface.

If we judge another person's valuation to be naive or stupid, wise or brilliant, this is a valuation in its own right. Even valuations that are personally repugnant to us—that strike us as paradoxical, cynical, or extravagant—originate in a conscience that can declare them whenever it assumes the responsibility. They do not bind us, to be sure; they cannot even command our respect since we accept or reject them according to our own judgment. A universal conscience can deny the most pampered valuation, however attired in dogmatic authority. So many valuations, originally scorned and vilified, come to win general assent. Many others become silent, without echo, because they were isolated occurrences. We should realize not only that the valuations of our contemporaries disagree among themselves to infinity, but also that there is a continuing transformation of values throughout successive generations. How strange, indeed, if even in the course of our own brief existence we change our minds as we do!

We should not be led into error by the apparent existence of valuations that seem to be supported by indisputable evidence, as well as by our own assent. They would vanish as soon as one barely squeezed them. There is no need to choose a trivial example. Let us take the fifth of the Ten Commandments, but with its tacit qualifications: you shall not kill, if you are not a warrior, judge, or priest; you shall not kill, except for members of another tribe; you shall not kill but those who profess a different creed; you shall not kill, except in defense of your life, your honor, or your property; you shall not openly kill, although you may exploit the life of your neighbor; you shall not kill, as long as you have no motive for it. The author of this commandment was never concerned with living up to it; he must have been a very word-minded person. History is the history of human slaughter. Thinkers have justified it; poets have glorified it.

There is no need to multiply examples; they all lead to the same conclusion. Normative valuations may assume airs of universality, but that claim can be, and is, converted into a lie by historical reality. Effective valuation dwells in our inner authority; there is no judge outside the conscious will. We insist: it is impossible to point out a universal, permanent, or constant valuation that is esteemed by all people in all times. Conscience always reserves the right to choose or refuse the presumed obligation. I like it when someone else agrees with my evaluation; but I am not disposed to submit mine to an extraneous authority, whether that of the overwhelming majority of men or that of the highest magistrate. The decision is in the last resort that of the autonomous person. This is the common root of the infinite number of concrete valuations, and also the reason for their divergence.

Well, someone may say, these conclusions reflect historical and empirical reality, and in this sense they are beyond attack. And yet, valuations are not arbitrary: the will does not adopt them capriciously, nor can it ignore the existence of values independent of human whim—indeed, of human valuation. In other words, we do not create value, we are limited to discovering it, and the concept of it is independent of the psychological or historical process. Let us now examine this new problem.

Value, we have said, is the object of an affirmative valuation. It has to do with real or ideal objects. No one should attribute intrinsic value to real objects. Neither natural nor made objects have value if no one appreciates them, if they are unrelated to human interest. There are no values for science; there are only equally interesting or equally indifferent facts. When we attribute value to a thing, it is a shaky title; it is not the same for me as for another, nor the same today as yesterday. The Arab who was lost in the desert found what he took to be a sack of dates in the track of a caravan. He looked inside, and threw it away in disgust. They're only pearls, he said. The conditional value of real objects depends on our estimation of them. But let us leave the case of real objects: it is too simple.

We have examined the historical creations that pertain to the different order of valuations. The value of these creations depends on our evaluation. We can withhold it. The religious dogma, the work of art, the judicial formula, the practical advice, the philosophical truth—what other value should they have than what they receive from our assent? Has not the protest of the martyr or of the reforming genius always come under the scrutiny of the dominant valuation, armed perhaps with material power? When a secular value ceases to rule, first in one conscience and then in many, it ends by disappearing or by being replaced. Each person can bring this about, individually, within the jurisdiction of his own conscience, and he will do it if the dominant value strikes him as coercive. Historical, like material values, remain subject to our personal valuation.

Let us, then, get down to a discussion of the most important concepts: the great ideal values. Positivism manages to convert them into subjective postulates derived from the cosmic mechanism. The current metaphysical reaction classifies them as absolutes. In either case they are regarded as constant and immutable values, set apart from any act of will. They would continue to exist, whether or not any human mind conceived or esteemed them. Their own authority is enough to establish them; they cannot be denied: who would dare deny justice, beauty, truth?

It is commonsensical that such values do not exist. One does not find them in spatiotemporal reality. In what superreality or in what unreal limbo can one place them? They are the abstract name for still unrealized ultimate aspirations, and they put us in contact with the transcendent as we think about their fulfillment. They are pure ideas; they come to be but are not. Word on our lips, ideal concept in consciousness, they only become effective and efficacious when, through action, they are objectivized in concrete, relative, and deficient form, destined to be a historical episode in the evolution of human culture. These creations of will symbolize its ultimate aims. We cannot conceive of purposes as part of the mechanical process of nature as it is interpreted by science; only will proclaims them. Causal and teleological conceptions cannot be reconciled; they constitute a basic antinomy that is deepened, rather than avoided, by rational analysis. Let this be said for the naturalists.

Those axiological theories that make use of objective, unreal, and atemporal values represent a shamefaced metaphysics scarcely disguised by its mask of logic. We are by no means denying metaphysical need. Man keeps trying new roads to escape the greatest of his anxieties. Unfortunately, reason is no help. We deny the possibility of a logical and rational metaphysics and we require philosophies to set a neat boundary between empirical reality and metaphysical poetry. The "Great Demolisher" did his work to give the neo-rationalists a chance to hide amid the ruins of their miserable shacks. Any rational metaphysics is a sin against logic. We have no words—hardly even metaphors—to express the eternal—that is, the ineffable. There is no scholastic technique for finding the *coincidentia oppositorum* of irreducible antinomies. That can come only from the great creations of art and mystical vision, aesthetic and religious emotion.

The authors who are committed to discovering absolute values, valid *a priori,* have already invented an *ad hoc* gnoseology. They will not discuss the historical and psychological consequences of valuations; they will maintain, however, that this process arises from values and does not create them. This assumes that our axiological knowledge transcends empirical reality and arrives at the notion of timeless values. In effect, they rely on a theory according to which spatiotemporal objects are only one kind of object within a multiplicity of objective orders. The unreal as well as the real can be an object. This is another effort to open the royal road to metaphysical truth.

It affirms, first, the autonomy of logical values, and then the autonomy of ethical values. They are objective and not subjective. They are born following a psychological gestation but, once the umbilical cord is cut, they have their own destiny. We know the offspring: the "substantial forms" of scholasticism, the old "rational entities," which prudent criticism, not daring to hypostasize, deprives of "being" and reduces to vague nonsense in a kingdom where they neither are, exist, nor act. If this paradox does not captivate us, it is, according to Rickert, because our mental habits are deficient.

We are dealing with wordplay, in which talented men waste their great erudition in byzantine discourse, a marvelous mixture of logical subtlety and essential intuitions *(Wesenschau)*. They claim to have captured the unreal object, but they have only lost contact with reality. . . .

But now some terrified soul will break in: "In this case we are without fixed and binding values!" And indeed, we never had them; they do not exist. Is not the historical change of values an obvious fact, along with the incompatibility of contemporary values? One finds different values at each geographical latitude, in each ethnic group, in each political alliance, and with each social interest. Within each group, however homogeneous it may seem, we find persons who resist the current valuation. There is always some dissent on the way to triumph or failure. Is it not amusing how the satisfied bourgeoisie try to turn their profit into a timeless value, or how the true believer hawks the promptings of his fanaticism like dogmas?

Philosophers are no better; indeed, they provide the most disconcerting spectacle. It is the very nature of philosophy, they say, to aspire to universality. Philosophical truth must be one. It is impossible to conceive it as circumscribed by geographical limits, or determined by the historical moment, or by the interests of a social level. Nevertheless, this is what happens. As in so many cases, the paradox is the real. We know of a Western philosophy and of another that is Eastern; of a Greek philosophy and of another that is modern, of an empirical position opposed to rationalism, skepticism to dogmatism, realism to idealism. All systems are logical, but their pied multiplicity simply shows how ineffective logical argumentation is. Each different philosophy is the expression of a different valuation. Thus it has to run the same risks as all valuations. Each philosophy is systematized as a legal brief for the will that inspires it. Sometimes, though, in periods of decadence, the professor's poor and empty pedantry reveals a lack of will, a lack of vital conviction.

People should not be so afraid of subjective valuation. Humanity has not fallen into anarchy just because valuations have always been subjective.

Aristotle alerts us, with his usual sagacity, by his observation that man is a gregarious animal. An isolated individual is a rare event; as a member of a group, his personal impulses are toned down by the rule of the gregarious instinct. Without feeling himself restrained, he will recite the liturgical formula that he has been taught, he will revere the established legal norms, he will respect the hallowed commonplaces, and will dress according to the current fad. No one rebels against an oppression he does not feel. Satisfied souls do not change collective values.

If rebellious evaluation appears, it will take its chances. Only a closed mind would object to it; while if many experience the same coercion, the rebellious judgment will be generalized. But a subjective valuation will be extinguished without consequences if, after a short or long conflict, it comes to have no historical dignity. Expressions of the general will, to be effective, should at least express the will of a more or less large group.

How, then, are we to choose from among the available valuations those that ought to prevail? The historical process does this; those that triumph prevail. It is not always the most just valuation—namely, ours—that triumphs. So, to conciliate them, we have recourse to argumentation, to persuasion, to the coincidence of interests, or to authority—if we have it. And yet, let us not forget that valuations represent our reaction to a physical or historical reality that is given to us, that common setting within which the individual and the collectivity act. . . .

A FUNCTIONAL VIEW OF VALUE ULTIMATES

Alain Locke

Quite patently, the core problem in theory of value is the satisfactory explanation of the formal value ultimates, such as beauty, truth and goodness. . . . I confess at the outset to a preference for a functionalist theory of value, but my brief for a functional analysis of value norms is . . . made . . . because a functional approach, even should it lead to a non-functionalist theory of value, of necessity treats the value varieties in terms of their interrelationships, guaranteeing a comparative approach and a more realistic type of value analysis. . . .

This wide field of comparative and differential analysis of values should all along have been a major emphasis in value theory, as seems to have been intended by the pioneer axiologists in their demand for a *general* psychology of value. But value formalism has, it seems, [been] deprived of this. Formalism in value theory, moreover, leads so easily to value fundamentalism and its dogmatisms. Many current value theories are in substance extensions of preformulated epistemologies and already adopted metaphysical positions, with a projection of these into a theory of value as a new set of weapons to be used in the traditional warfare of ideologies. On such grounds, it seems wise, therefore, to canvas the possibilities of the functional approach to the problem of value ultimates.

• • •

One question, however, must be settled favorably before a functional analysis of the normative element in so-called value "ultimates" can assure itself of safe clearance. That is an adequate answer to the contention of the value realists that functional value analysis can only yield a descriptive account of value assertions and cannot, therefore, account for their normative character or their role in evaluative judgment. The most outspoken form of this argument regards all varieties of value functionalism as merely attenuated forms of the extremist position in value relativism, logical positivism, and reducible to it in final analysis on the presumption that they deny by implication what positivism denies explicitly, *viz.,* the basic normative property of values. An example of such criticism is Urban's quite categorical statement, "It is coming to be seen that there is no middle ground between this positivism and some form of objective axiology," going on to add: "Many, it is true, have sought such a middle ground in pragma-

tism, with its quasi-objectivity and its instrumental notion of verification. But it is becoming increasingly clear that such a position is untenable."[1]

Such a reduction of the position of all value functionalism to the ultra-relativism of the positivists is arbitrary and unwarranted. Granted that some relativist interpretations of value are so subjective as to be completely atomistic and anarchistic, that is not the case with all. Particularly is this so with a type of analysis whose main objective is to give a consistent account of the relative permanencies of value-modes and their normative criteria *and* the readily observable phenomena of value change and value transposition in a way that they will not contradict one another.

Value content is observably variable and transposable with regard to its value norms. There is no warrant of fact for considering values as fixed permanently to certain normative categories or pegged in position under them or attached intrinsically by nature or "essence" to that mode of valuation to which they may be relevantly referred. Only in our traditional stereotyping of values is this so: in actuality, something in the way they are felt or apprehended establishes their normative relevancy. On this point, it may well turn out that some psychological coerciveness in value feeling or some dispositional role or cue in behavior is an adequate and more verifiable explanation of the relation between the particular value and its referential "ultimate" or norm.

It is, moreover, an oversimplification of the form of relativism under discussion, functional relativism, to say that it merely calls to our attention that what is good today is bad tomorrow [or vice versa]. This interpretation of value is more properly represented by a statement that what is revealed or developed in experience as *better* becomes *the new good,* shifting to the position of normative acceptance or urgency formerly occupied by the older value content. The process continuity of the normative character of values is demonstrated not merely

---

[1]Wilbur Urban, "Axiology," in D. Runes (ed.), *Twentieth Century Philosophy,* p. 62.

by the substitution of new value content for the old, but even more clearly by the displacement and retroactive devaluing of the old, a procedure which transforms yesterday's good into a relatively bad. That which is felt or judged as relatively better (or truer to the systematic value quality in the case of other types of value than the ethical) is normally preferred and so becomes normatively imperative. When explicit judgment ensues, it is revamped in evaluative thought accordingly.

To my way of construing the situation, it is the retrospective revaluation of the value which, by guaranteeing the stability of the norm and the value system it supports exhibits most clearly the really functional force and character of the normative principle. Paradoxically, in actual practise, it seems to be the progressively corrective character of the value norm more than stability of specific value content which endows our abstract values with normative ultimacy. It is by such a criterion, for example, that we can best explain why a lesser evil becomes a comparative good.

There are, of course, value situations where this functionally normative reaction is lacking, but on close scrutiny they turn out to be situations which even as exceptions prove the rule. For they are situations where the inhibitions and dogmatisms of habit block the corrective revision of the value content. In such cases either the intelligence or feeling or both, entrenched in irrational fixation on the orthodox content, refuses to follow through, and invariably does so by the technique of asserting an inseparable connection between the value form and its value content. I have elsewhere in greater detail[2] attempted to characterize value norms as system values rather than fixed intrinsic values, as process imperatives rather than intrinsic absolutes.

The most effective reply, however, to value realism's rejection of this functionalist interpretation is to challenge the value realist under his presuppositions to explain, in addition to such value change as

has just been cited, the numerous observable cases of value transposition. For instance, a demonstration or proof, normally logical in value reverence and criterion, is appraised, because of its virtuosity or style of proof as "neat," "pretty," "elegant" or even "beautiful." Unless this type of value occurrence is illusory or mere metaphorical confusion in the language of value description, it presents an almost unexplainable character to the value realist. If he is consistent with his doctrine of the value type as intrinsic, he must dismiss such situations as mere analogies. But inside acquaintance with the experience shows it to be a genuinely aesthetic value reference both in its valuational and evaluational phases, vested with the characteristic attitudes, feelings and judgment of the aesthetic norm rather than just a metaphorical transfer of aesthetic predicates. It actually becomes an aesthetic value *qua* something admired for its perfection of form and the contemplative satisfaction which this admiration of it yields. Formalizations of values, traditional in attitude association or orthodox in logical evaluation, do stereotype certain content with value references that become typical and characteristic; but there are not only many exceptions in actual valuation but in all specific cases, where the value attitude as experienced or felt is that appropriate to another value-genre, the value reference and judgment as indicated qualitatively by the descriptive predicates, however unorthodox the reference, follow, it seems, the actualities of the value attitude.

On the other hand, the value realist's reasoning, in addition to being an inadequate explanation of the real situation, in its form of thinking would seem to involve another instance of what Reiser aptly calls the "inveterate tendency to make entities out of modes of behavior."[3] Certainly this value objectification upon an intrinsic basis exhibits *usteron proteron* reasoning by reversing the natural order of the value and its content reference, as though the discrimination of the value led to the discovery of

[2]Alain Locke, "Values and Imperatives," in Sidney Hook and Horace M. Kallen (eds.), *American Philosophy Today and Tomorrow* (New York: Lee Furman, 1935), p. 313.

[3]Oliver L. Reiser, *The Promise of Scientific Humanism: Toward a Unification of Scientific, Religious, Social, and Economic Thought* (New York: D. Piest, 1940), p. 123.

the "true" nature of the object, rather than realizing that the valuing of the object in a certain way leads to its apprehension in a certain value context. Ehrenfels has a pithy analysis of such fallaciousness: "Philosophy itself," he says, "at the beginning followed this urge for objectification which transfers the content of the inner experience to the thing itself as absolutely determinant, endeavoring thus to discover that which had *value in itself,* with about as much justification [he shrewdly adds] as one might claim in contending whether the direction toward the north pole or that toward the south pole pointed upwards in itself, or whether the earth by itself was a large or small body."[4] This, I take it, is both an apt description and refutation of the classic fallacy involved in the value absolutist's position. From the functionalist's point of view the basic error lies in regarding the formal value as the cause of the valuation or as an essence of the value object rather than the system value of the mode of valuing, which is sometimes the symbol, sometimes its rationale, but in practise an implementation of the value as apprehended. Of course, to the degree that values are regarded abstractly, they take on a quality of universality and seeming independence, but this is merely a common characteristic of all generalizations. But If we can sufficiently explain the character of value-generals as system norms, functional in value discrimination and comparison, they need not then be unrealistically raised to the status of hypostasized absolutes or perennial essences.

At this point it becomes quite proper to leave behind formal counterargument of opposing views, and turn to the more concrete and congenial consideration of concrete cases, functionally interpreted. Time will permit only a single example from each of the major value-genres, the moral, the logical and the aesthetic, each instance selected to illustrate what we may call the contextual basis of the normative character involved. Each case, involving

as it does value change and the displacement of older traditional material by new value content, ought to exhibit the type of relative normativity of the kind we have been delineating, that is, flexible as to material content permitting value change and reconstruction but nonetheless systematic and normatively coercive in its function of value control.

As a case illustrating several important facets of functional relativism in moral values, I choose a profoundly analytic value problem propounded in a play by the Soviet dramatist, Korneichuk, I believe, which deeply impressed me when I saw it some years ago. I think he made out a clear case for the contextual but systematic character of normative value control. He was enabled to do so because he chose a situation involving a complete reversal of value for the same act, but showed how though diametrically opposed one to the other, as between the two systems of values, each was imperatively right in the context of its own appropriate system. By taking an act that most of us find impossible to imagine out of our orthodox context of the greatest of all evils and crimes, Korneichuk dramatically and illuminatingly sets the action and conflict in a setting where the greatest of crimes is not only a virtue but a sacrosanct duty. The act is parricide, and the setting is the changing life of a nomadic Eskimo tribe making their first sustained contact with Western civilization and its moral codes.

Age-old custom, on the very reasonable basis of the peculiar uselessness of the old and feeble in the hazardous life of a nomadic Arctic people, has decreed the custom of ritualistic parricide, with the eldest son obligated by custom to push the aged parent off into the sea from an icefloe after a feast in which both the shaman and the aged victim give ritualistic consent. The hero of the play, however, has been away at a Soviet training center and has been exposed to another code in terms of which pardonable parricide has become unpardonable murder, and in addition functionally unnecessary. Returning, he is in general conflict with the tribal values, but has been taught to minimize the impact of the conflict with understanding tolerance and piecemeal reform. But peace cannot be made on that basis with the shaman

---

[4]C. F. von Ehrenfels, "Werttheorie und Ethik," *Vierteljahrsschrift für wissenschaftliche Philosophie* 17 (1893), p. 87. [In the original Locke noted Volume I; however, the reference seems to be to Volume 17.]

who represents the unyielding authority of the old system as a whole. The shaman's moment inevitably comes when the time arrives for the father's custom sanctioned death, for at that point the two systems meet in irreconcilable contradiction.

The dramatist has carefully and sympathetically conveyed the imperative logic of the older value system which makes parricide acceptable to the aged parent and a filial duty expected of his son. Though an obsolescent way of life, with its justifying function gone, the old value is presented, correctly, I think, as "right" on its own level, that is, in the mind of the father and the relatives. As he vacillates between the two loyalties, the son's hesitancy and grief over the tragic dilemma emotionally concedes this; at several moments he is pictured as about to perform what to him is a crime but to the others a dutiful favor. But the reappearance of the shaman reinstates the duel between the systems, and it is clear that from that point on the son will never concede in action. The old man, still convinced of the rightness of his going, shocked by his son's hesitancy and yet dimly aware of the new set of values which hinder him, walks off into the sea without benefit of ceremony. The effective dramatization at one and the same time of the respective truths in conflict and of the value system principle as the root of the coercive normativeness of each affords deep insight into the nature of the functional normativity we are discussing. It is an exemplary instance of functional normativity, and one calculated to disprove the value formalist's charge of the non-normative character of the functionalist value interpretation.

The case example for logical values is taken deliberately from scientific theory rather than abstract logic, because although the same principle of systematic consistency is the functioning norm, the scientific example, in addition, will point up the fact that modern scientific theory has fully accepted the relativistic criterion of truth as its normative methodological criterion. It is now a commonplace that science at any given time acknowledges a final truth only in the sense of the most recently accepted consensus of competent experience, and contrary to traditional logic, knows no absolute or irreplaceable truth. Almost any of the larger general theories in

science could equally well be taken as illustration of this. But I take the electron theory as most convenient to show in addition to the superiority of the electronic view of the atom as an explanatory concept for the observed behavior of matter, its greater normative range and force as a concept of greater systematic consistency and coverage than the older theory which it has displaced. As von Mach pointed out long ago, we realize that the extension of the system coverage of a theoretical truth is an important factor in its preferability as a theoretical satisfactory and acceptable explanation. As such, the proper interpretation would seem to be to regard this criterion as an evaluative form principle with a normative validity which is functionally based and attested.

But to turn more directly to the problem at hand, no physicist accepting the electronic view would style the older classical theory of the atom as false in its entirety but only in certain of its aspects. Indeed for a long period it was quite satisfactory as a consistent explanation of the nature of matter. However, until radically revised, it was not satisfactory or consistent as an interpretation of matter as energy. The electron theory is, therefore, a *truer* theory of the atom, and I stress truer, because, occupying the same relative position in the systematic analytical explanation of matter, it consistently includes and interprets more observable phenomena than the older atomic theory. For in addition to what it explained before—qualitative description and identification, serial position and relative weight and valence—it now also explains energy structure and energy potential. But the main point is that the new truth incorporates, on the basis of consistency, a good part of the previous theory, although perforce, also in the interest of consistency it has to discard certain other theoretically postulated properties now inconsistent with the enlarged range of known facts. Instrumental logic regards it as important to point out that, though now false, these elements were acceptable and useful in their context and time, and led up to the interpretations we now have substituted for general acceptance.

We should notice that important aspects of the present theory are hypothetical, and are regarded as true because of their systematic value in the explanation of the facts. Some of these items are just as hypothetical as the displaced and discredited elements in the older theory, but their present acceptability is based on the restored consistency, the wider coverage and the greater inclusiveness of the theoretical system as now conceived. The functionally normative character, in contradistinction to a permanent and intrinsic view of the nature of the truth value seems obvious, and this example is typical. A functionally based or relative ultimacy is all that is required, and more than that, at least in scientific procedures is definitely preferable.

Our value judgments in art, though none the less critical today and certainly more technical than ever, are also far from the traditionalism of the older aesthetics. Modern art theory and practise have broken almost completely with the former authoritarian conception of beauty. Indeed, on both the consumer and the productive or creative level, we have actually witnessed in less than a generation the basic criteria of a major value mode going completely relativistic with regard to styles, idioms, art rationales and judgmental evaluation. Creative expression in modern art has particularly operated on radically extended canons of beauty and its appreciation. There are those, I am aware, who will say that art expression today has become so utterly relativistic that there is no longer a standard of beauty left or a valid set of stylistic criteria. But impartial examination of modern art will show rather contrary results. The widening of the variety of styles and aesthetic has actually been accompanied by a deepening of aesthetic taste and a sharpening of critical discrimination.

Certainly normative control has not been lost or sacrificed, as is proved by a double line of evidence. In the first place the appreciation of new forms and varieties has not caused us to lose grasp on our appreciation of the older varieties, the classical heritage of past artistic expression. Indeed, on the contrary, modernist art has never in its best expressions undermined the appreciation of traditional art. In the second place, critical discrimination as tested by genuine knowledge appreciation of the technical aspects of art styles has increased manyfold. Vari-

ety, on the whole, has not led to greater confusion, but by actual comparisons, critical taste and judgment have improved. Our current art pluralism is attested by the contemporary tolerance of many mutually incompatible styles, whose growth has been accompanied by a growing liberation of taste from formalism and superficially imposed standards, as concrete examples will show.

The musical formalist or aesthetic authoritarian has to confess his inability to judge the contemporary musical situation and usage. But the modernist, who is a sub-conscious or semi-conscious relativist, finds little or no difficulty in interpreting what has actually happened in modern art. In music, for example, what has the modern composer done? He has changed musical content substantially, but instead of destroying the musical norm has really enlarged its scope. He has not changed, in fact is not able to change the basic attitudinal qualities of musical apprehension nor has he broken down its discriminatory effectiveness. His new forms have developed critical criteria appropriate to their idiom and at the same time not inconsistent with the older criteria after habituation. What the modernist styles have done is really, by conditioning, to enlarge both by bringing them into the orbit of the same favorable aesthetic reaction. The new style and idiom—certainly it is not our hearing but our appreciative apprehension which has improved—has succeeded in bringing into the realm of immediately felt concordance what was previously felt as irregular and cacophonic, and could not, therefore, be apprehended pleasurably and integrated into an aesthetically toned reaction.

A person who cannot, however, synthesize his auditory and emotional experiences on hearing Stravinsky or Hindemith cannot appreciate the musical language of modernist music. He can realize the technical musicianship and also concede its potential musicality for those who can genuinely appreciate it. But that same person can by repeated exposure to such music bring it not only within the range of appreciation but within now enlarged criteria of evaluative judgment, as good, bad or mediocre of its kind. The cacophony by repeated experience has become concordant, meaningful and therefore "beautiful." Now the illuminating aspect of this is that Stravinsky and Hindemith have not to such a matured taste upset the approach to and the appreciation of Mozart and Beethoven; nor for that matter has jazz upset the apprehension of classical musical forms and idioms, except temporarily. One hastens to add good jazz, which has developed for jazz idioms and forms more and more professionalized devotees and rigidly normative criteria of taste and critical musical analysis.

We may cite, quite briefly, the same sequence of results in another phase of art, painting and sculpture. In these forms, too, modernist art at first acquaintance seems a welter of uncoordinated styles and their rival aesthetics. But the anarchy is in large part illusory. Modern art has about solved the problem of art tolerance, by making each style a systematic criterion for itself and whatever is relevant to it. More than that both creative activity and appreciation have broadened base perceptably. Modern art creativity may not be as Alpine as it was in certain periods of the past, but there is undeniably a higher plateau of appreciation and performance.

Incidentally this widening of the range of appreciation and participation is as good an example as we can find of what democratization can mean in a value field. First our exposure to Oriental art with its markedly different idioms and form criteria inaugurated the artistic value revolution we call modernism. The appreciative understanding and creative use of the formerly strange and to us unaesthetic idioms of African and other primitive art followed, and a revolutionary revision of taste and creative outlook was fully on.

Since then, with ever-increasing experimentalism, art forms have been multiplied and taste extended. But here again in this field, as in music, modernistic relativism has not served to invalidate but rather to enhance the appreciation of the classical and traditional expressions of the beautiful.

Certainly this is a good augury for the resolution of certain hitherto irresolvable types of value conflict. I merely throw out the suggestion that through modernism and its enforced but not normatively chaotic relativism we have forged a psychological key for the

active and simultaneous appreciation of diverse styles within our own culture, in fact within our own culture period. It seems to serve for the wider but none the less vivid appreciative understanding of alien art forms and idioms, and to give us some insight into their correlated aesthetics. Already through such enlargement we are able to appreciate a good measure of primitive art of all varieties, children's art and the art forms of many cultures that were dead letters to our eyes previously. In an approaching world interchange of culture it is just such widening of taste to a cosmopolitan range and level which seems most desirable, if indeed not imperative. That accents what has previously been mentioned, the functional superiority in explicit terms of improved comprehension of values and their more effective correlation as a direct consequence of relativistic as over against authoritarian approaches to the sets of values involved. If this is extendable to other value fields, and I think it is, we have in this principle of analysis and rearrangement an effective base for resolving large segments of our current value conflicts.

Instrumentalism or functionalism as I prefer to stress it has already pointed out that scientific knowledge operates on the methodological postulates of relativism and the constant revision of a progressively organized body of systematized experience. Art, we have just seen, in its contemporary theory and practise of values has moved in a similar direction, without losing hold on normative criteria that are effective and functional, though not arbitrarily static and absolute. We would do well to remember that both science and art once had doctrines of the finality of beauty and truth, but have been able to abandon them. Absolutism, however, with its corollary of fundamentalism is still fairly generally entrenched in moral theory, in goodly measure still in speculative philosophy and in the orthodox varieties of religious faith and belief. The continuation of the older tradition of absolutism is, of course, closely bound in with the question of the nature of value ultimates and the type of normativeness they are supposed to exercise. This was our starting point. We come back to it to suggest that the more tenable interpretations of value theory as to the actual functioning of value norms aligns value theory on the side of the relativist position. Should that be true, value theory in the next steps of its development may exert the deciding influence among the value disciplines in turning away from absolutism and dogmatism on the one hand and relativism of the revisionist and progressive stripe on the other. Having become accommodated to a progressive truth and an ever-expanding and creatively exploratory quest for beauty, it may be that we shall tend toward a relativistic but not anarchic ethics, world view and religion which will be more functionally correlated with the actualities of life and conduct and more effectively normative without rigidly imposed and dictatorial authority. Our value ultimates from that point of definition and enforcement will no longer be unrealistic as principles and from the cultural point of view provincial tyrants.

RELATIVISM

David Wong

I. INTRODUCTION

Moral relativism is a common response to the deepest conflicts we face in our ethical lives. Some of these conflicts are quite public and political, such as the apparently intractable disagreement in the United States over the moral and legal permissibility of abortion. Other conflicts inviting the relativistic response are of a less dramatic but more recurrent nature. This author's experience as a first-generation Chinese American exemplifies a kind of conflict that others have faced: that between inherited values and the values of the adopted country. As a child I had to grapple with the differences between what was expected of me as a good Chinese son and what was expected of my non-Chinese friends. Not only did they seem bound by duties that were much less rigorous in the matter of honouring parents and upholding the

family name, but I was supposed to feel superior to them because of that. It added to my confusion that I sometimes felt envy at their freedom.

Moral relativism, as a common response to such conflicts, often takes the form of a denial that any single moral code has universal validity, and an assertion that moral truth and justifiability, if there are any such things, are in some way relative to factors that are culturally and historically contingent. This doctrine is *meta-ethical* relativism, because it is about the relativity of moral truth and justifiability. Another kind of moral relativism, also a common response to deep moral conflict, is a doctrine about how one ought to act toward those who accept values very different from one's own. This *normative* moral relativism holds that it is wrong to pass judgement on others who have substantially different values, or to try to make them conform to one's values, for the reason that their values are as valid as one's own. Another common response to deep moral conflict, however, contradicts moral relativism in its two major forms. It is the universalist or absolutist position that both sides of a moral conflict cannot be equally right, that there can be only one truth about the matter at issue. This position is so common, in fact, that William James was led to call us "absolutists by instinct."[1] The term "universalism" will be used hereafter, because "absolutism" is used not only to refer to the denial of moral relativism, but also to the view that some moral rules or duties are absolutely without exception.

II. META-ETHICAL RELATIVISM

The debate between moral relativism and universalism accounts for a significant proportion of philosophical reflection in ethics. In ancient Greece at least some of the "Sophists" defended a version of moral relativism, which Plato attempted to refute. Plato attributes to the first great Sophist, Protagoras, the argument that human custom determines what is fine

___

[1] W. James, "The will to believe," *Essays in Pragmatism,* ed. Aubrey Castell (New York: Harner, 1948).

and ugly, just and unjust. Whatever is communally judged to be the case, the argument goes, actually comes to be the case.[2] Now the Greeks, through trade, travel, and war, were fully aware of wide variation in customs, and so the argument concludes with the relativity of morality. The question with this argument, however, is whether we can accept that custom determines in a strong sense what is fine and ugly, just and unjust. It may influence what people *think* is fine and just. But it is quite another thing for custom to determine what *is* fine and just. Customs sometimes change under the pressure of moral criticism, and the argument seems to rely on a premise that contradicts this phenomenon.

Another kind of argument given for relativism is premised on the view that the customary ethical beliefs in any given society are functionally necessary for that society. Therefore, the argument concludes, the beliefs are true for that society, but not necessarily in another. The sixteenth-century essayist, Michel de Montaigne, sometimes makes this argument ("Of custom, and not easily changing an accepted law")[3], but it has had its greatest acceptance among anthropologists of the twentieth century who emphasize the importance of studying societies as organic wholes of which the parts are functionally interdependent. The problem with the functional argument, however, is that moral beliefs are not justified merely on the grounds that they are necessary for a society's existence in anything like its present form. Even if a society's institutions and practices crucially depend on the acceptance of certain beliefs, the justifiability of those beliefs depends on the moral acceptability of the institutions and practices. To show that certain beliefs are necessary for maintaining a fascist society, for instance, is not to justify those beliefs.

Despite the weaknesses of these arguments for moral relativism, the doctrine has always had its ad-

herents. Its continuing strength has always been rooted in the impressiveness of the variation in ethical belief to be found across human history and culture. In an ancient text (*Dissoi Logoi* or the *Contrasting Arguments*)[4] associated with the Sophists, it is pointed out that for the Lacedaemonians, it was fine for girls to exercise without tunics, and for children not to learn music and letters, while for the Ionians, these things were foul. Montaigne assembled a catalogue of exotic customs, such as male prostitution, cannibalism, women warriors, killing one's father at a certain age as an act of piety, and recites from the Greek historian Herodotus the experiment of Darius. Darius asked Greeks how much they would have to be paid before they would eat the bodies of their deceased fathers. They replied that no sum of money could get them to do such a thing. He then asked certain Indians who customarily ate the bodies of their deceased fathers what they would have to be paid to burn the bodies of their fathers. Amidst loud exclamations, they bade him not to speak of such a thing.[5]

But while many have been moved by such examples to adopt moral relativism, the argument from diversity does not support relativism in any simple or direct way. As the Socrates of Plato's dialogues observed, we have reason to listen only to the wise among us.[6] The simple fact of diversity in belief is no disproof of the possibility that there are some beliefs better to have than the others because they are truer or more justified than the rest. If half the world still believed that the sun, the moon, and the planets revolved around the earth, that would be no disproof of the possibility of a unique truth about the structure of the universe. Diversity in belief, after all, may result from varying degrees of wisdom. Or it may be that different people have their own limited perspectives of the truth, each perspective being distorted in its own way.

---

[2]Plato, *Theaetetus,* 172 AB; trans. E. Hamilton and H. Cairns, *Collected Dialogues of Plato* (Princeton: Princeton University Press, 1961). It is unclear, however, whether the real Protagoras actually argued in this manner.
[3]M. de Montaigne, *Complete Essays* (1595): trans. Donald M. Frame (Stanford: Stanford University Press, 1973).

[4]T. M. Robinson, trans.: *Contrasting Arguments: an edition of the Dissoi Logoi* (New York: Arno Press, 1979).
[5]Montaigne, op. cit., "Of custom." Book III, 38. Herodotus: *The Persian Wars,* trans. George Rawlinson (New York: Modern Library, 1942).
[6]Plato, *Crito* (44 C D) in E. Hamilton and H. Cairns, trans., *Collected Dialogues.*

It is sometimes thought that the extent and depth of disagreement in ethics indicates that moral judgements are simply not judgements about facts, that they assert nothing true or false about the world but straightforwardly express our own subjective reactions to certain facts and happenings, whether these be collective or individual reactions.[7]

A more complicated view is that moral judgements purport to report objective matters of fact, but that there are no such matters of fact.[8] The success of modern science in producing a remarkable degree of convergence of belief about the basic structure of the physical world probably reinforces these varieties of scepticism about the objectivity of moral judgements. It is hard to deny that there is a significant difference in the degree of convergence of belief in ethics and in science. Yet there are possible explanations for that difference that are compatible with claiming that moral judgements are ultimately about facts in the world. These explanations might stress, for instance, the special difficulties of acquiring knowledge of subjects that pertain to moral knowledge.

An understanding of human nature and human affairs is necessary for formulating an adequate moral code. The enormously difficult and complex task of reaching such an understanding could be a major reason for differences in moral belief. Furthermore, the subject matter of ethics is such that people have the most intense practical interest in what is established as truth about it, and surely this interest engenders the passions that becloud judgement.[9] Universalists could point out that many apparently exotic moral beliefs presuppose certain religious and metaphysical beliefs, and that these beliefs, rather than any difference in fundamental values, explain the apparent strangeness. Consider, for example, the way our view of Darius' Indians would change if we were to attribute to them the belief that eating the body of one's deceased father is a way of preserving his spiritual substance. Finally, some of the striking differences in moral belief across societies may not be rooted in differences in fundamental values but in the fact that these values may have to be implemented in different ways given the varying conditions that obtain across societies. If one society contains many more women than men (say, because men are killing each other off in warfare), it would not be surprising if polygamy were acceptable there, while in another society, where the proportion of women to men is equal, monogamy is required. The difference in accepted marriage practice may come down to that difference in the proportion of women to men, and not to any difference in basic moral ideals of marriage or of the proper relationships between women and men.

The mere existence of deep and wide disagreements in ethics, therefore, does not disprove the possibility that moral judgements can be objectively correct or incorrect judgements about certain facts. Moral relativists must chart some other more complicated path from the existence of diversity to the conclusion that there is no single true or most justified morality. I believe (and have argued)[10] that the relativist argument is best conducted by pointing to particular kinds of differences in moral belief, and then by claiming that these particular differences are best explained under a theory that denies the existence of a single true morality. This would involve denying that the various ways that universalists have for explaining ethical disagreement are sufficient for explaining the particular differences in question.[11]

One apparent and striking ethical difference that would be a good candidate for this sort of argument concerns the emphasis on individual rights that is embodied in the ethical culture of the modern West and that seems absent in traditional cultures found in Africa, China, Japan and India. The content of

[7]For example, see C. L. Stevenson, *Ethics and Language* (New Haven: Yale University Press, 1944).

[8]J. L. Mackie, *Ethics: Inventing Right and Wrong* (Harmondsworth: Penguin, 1977).

[9]For a reply in this spirit, see T. Nagel, *The View from Nowhere* (New York: Oxford University Press, 1986), 172 AB; pp. 185–88.

[10]D. B. Wong, *Moral Relativity* (Berkeley: University of California Press, 1984).

[11]For another strategy of argument that relies more on an analysis of the meaning of moral judgements, see G. Harman: "Moral relativism defended". *Philosophical Review* 84 (1975), 3–22.

duties in such traditional cultures instead seems organized around the central value of a common good that consists in a certain sort of ideal community life, a network of relationships, partially defined by social roles, again, ideal, but imperfectly embodied in ongoing existing practice. The ideal for members is composed of various virtues that enable them, given their place in the network of relationships, to promote and sustain the common good.

Confucianism, for instance, makes the family and kinship groups the models for the common good, with larger social and political units taking on certain of their features, such as benevolent leaders who rule with the aim of cultivating virtue and harmony among their subjects. Moralities centered on such values would seem to differ significantly from ones centered on individual rights to liberty and to other goods, if the basis for attributing such rights to persons does not seem to lie in their conduciveness to the common good of a shared life, but in a moral worth independently attributed to each individual. By contrast a theme frequently found in ethics of the common good is that individuals find their realization as human beings in promoting and sustaining the common good. Given this assumption of the fundamental harmony between the highest good of individuals and the common good, one might expect the constraints on freedom to have greater scope and to be more pervasive when compared to a tradition in which no such fundamental harmony between individual and common goods is assumed.

If the contrast between the two types of morality is real, it raises the question of whether one or the other type is truer or more justified than the other. The argument for a relativistic answer may start with the claim that each type focuses on a good that may reasonably occupy the centre of an ethical ideal for human life. On the one hand, there is the good of belonging to and contributing to a community; on the other, there is the good of respect for the individual apart from any potential contribution to community. It would be surprising, the argument goes, if there were just one justifiable way of setting a priority with respect to the two goods. It should not be surprising, after all, if the range of human

goods is simply too rich and diverse to be reconciled in just a single moral ideal.

Such an argument could be supplemented by an explanation of why human beings have such a thing as a morality. Morality serves two universal human needs. It regulates conflicts of interest between people, and it regulates conflicts of interest within the individual born of different desires and drives that cannot all be satisfied at the same time. Ways of dealing with those two kinds of conflict develop in anything recognizable as human society. To the extent that these ways crystallize in the form of rules for conduct and ideals for persons, we have the core of a morality. Now in order to perform its practical functions adequately, it may be that a morality will have to possess certain general features. A relatively enduring and stable system for the resolution of conflict between people, for instance, will not permit the torture of persons at whim.

But given this picture of the origin and functions of morality, it would not be surprising if significantly different moralities were to perform the practical functions equally well, at least according to standards of performance that were common to these moralities. Moralities, on this picture, are social creations that evolve to meet certain needs. The needs place conditions on what could be an adequate morality, and if human nature has a definite structure, one would expect further constraining conditions on an adequate morality to derive from our nature. But the complexity of our nature makes it possible for us to prize a variety of goods and to order them in different ways, and this opens the way for a substantial relativism to be true.

The picture sketched above has the advantage of leaving it open as to how strong a version of relativism is true. That is, it holds that there is no single true morality, yet does not deny that some moralities might be false and inadequate for the functions they all must perform. Almost all polemics against moral relativism are directed at its most extreme versions: those holding that all moralities are equally true (or equally false, or equally lacking in cognitive content). Yet a substantial relativism need not be so radically egalitarian. Besides ruling out moralities that would aggravate interpersonal conflict, such as the one described above, relativists could also recognize that adequate moralities must promote the production of persons capable of considering the interests of others. Such persons would need to have received a certain kind of nurturing and care from others. An adequate morality, then, whatever else its content, would have to prescribe and promote the sorts of upbringing and continuing interpersonal relationships that produce such persons.

A moral relativism that would allow for this kind of constraint on what could be a true or most justified morality might not fit the stereotype of relativism, but would be a reasonable position to hold. One reason, in fact, that not much progress has been made in the debate between relativists and universalists is that each side has tended to define the opponent as holding the most extreme position possible. While this makes the debating easier, it does nothing to shed light on the vast middle ground where the truth indeed may lie. Many of the same conclusions could be drawn about the debate over normative moral relativism: much heat, and frequent identification of the opponent with the most extreme position possible.

III. NORMATIVE RELATIVISM

The most extreme possible position for the normative relativist is that no one should ever pass judgement on others with substantially different values, or try to make them conform to one's own values. Such a definition of normative relativism is usually given by its opponents, because it is an indefensible position. It requires self-condemnation by those who act according to it. If I pass judgement on those who pass judgement, I must condemn myself. I am trying to impose a value of tolerance on everyone, when not everyone has that value, but this is not what I am supposed to be doing under the most extreme version of normative relativism. Philosophers are usually content with such easy dismissals of the most extreme version of normative relativism, but there is reason to consider whether more moderate versions might be more tenable. The reason is that normative

relativism is not just a philosophical doctrine but a stance adopted toward morally troubling situations.

Anthropologists are sometimes identified with this stance, and it is instructive to understand how this identification emerged from a historical and sociological context. The birth of cultural anthropology in the late nineteenth century was in part subsidized by colonizing governments needing to know more about the nature and status of "primitive" peoples. Influenced by Darwinian theory, early anthropological theory tended to arrange the peoples and social institutions of the world in an evolutionary series, from primordial man to the civilized human being of nineteenth-century Europe. Many anthropologists eventually reacted against the imperialism of their governments and to its rationalization supplied by their predecessors. More importantly, they came to see the peoples they studied as intelligent men and women whose lives had meaning and integrity. And this led to questioning the basis for implicit judgements of the inferiority of their ways of life, especially after the spectacle of the civilized nations in brutal struggle with one another in the First World War.[12]

The normative relativism of some of the anthropologists of that period, then, was a response to real moral problems concerning the justifiability of colonization and more generally concerning intervention in another society so as to cause major changes in previously accepted values or in people's ability to act on those values. No simple version of normative relativism is the answer to these problems, as was illustrated by the fact that an ethic of non-judgemental tolerance would self-destruct when used to condemn the intolerant. The inadequacy of the simple versions also is illustrated by the swing in anthropology on the question of normative relativism after the Second World War. That war, many realized, was a battle against enormous evil. Such a realization brought

---

[12]See, for example Ruth Benedict, *Patterns of Culture* (New York: Penguin, 1934); and more recently, Melville Herskovits, *Cultural Relativism: Perspectives in Cultural Pluralism* (New York: Vintage, 1972).

vividly to the forefront the necessity of passing judgement at least sometimes and of acting on one's judgement. And accordingly there was a new trend within cultural anthropology toward finding a basis for making judgements that would depend on criteria to be applied to all moral codes.

A more reasonable version of normative relativism would have to permit us to pass judgement on others with substantially different values. Even if these different values are as justified as our own from some neutral perspective, we still are entitled to call bad or evil or monstrous what contradicts our most important values. What we are entitled to do in the light of such judgements, however, is another matter. Many of us who are likely to read this book would be reluctant to intervene in the affairs of others who have values substantially different from ours, when the reason for intervention is the enforcement of our own values, and when we think that we have no more of an objective case for our moral outlook than the others have for theirs. The source of this reluctance is a feature of our morality. A liberal, contractualist outlook is very much part of our ethical life in the postmodern West, whether we acknowledge it or not. We want to act toward others in such a way that our actions could be seen as justified by them if they were fully reasonable and informed of all relevant facts. If we hold a meta-ethical moral relativism, however, then we must recognize that there will be occasions when some otherwise desirable course of action toward others with different values will violate this feature of our morality.

At that point, there is no general rule that will tell us what to do. It would seem to depend on what other values of ours are at stake. If a practice performed by others were to involve human sacrifice, for example, then the value of tolerance might indeed be outweighed, and we may decide to intervene to prevent it. The disagreement over the legal permissibility of abortion demonstrates how difficult the weighing can be, however. Consider the position of those who believe that abortion is morally wrong because it is the taking of life that has moral status. Within this group some seem undisturbed by the fact that there is deep disagreement over the moral status of the fetus. They

wish to prohibit abortion. But others in this group, while holding that abortion is wrong, admit that reasonable persons could disagree with them and that human reason seems unable to resolve the question. For this reason they oppose legal prohibitions of abortion. The former believe that the latter do not take the value of human life seriously, while the latter believe that the former fail to recognize the depth and seriousness of the disagreement between reasonable persons.

Each position has some force, and clearly normative relativism offers no simple solution to the dilemma. What the doctrine provides, however, is a set of reasons for tolerance and non-intervention that must be weighed against other reasons. The doctrine applies not only to proposed interventions by one society in another, but also, as in the case of abortion, to deep moral disagreements within pluralistic societies containing diverse moral traditions. If meta-ethical relativism is true, even if only with respect to a limited set of moral conflicts such as abortion, then our moral condition is immeasurably complicated. We must strive to find what will be for us the right or the best thing to do, and also deal with the feelings of unease caused by the recognition that there is no single right or best thing to do. This task, no matter how difficult, is not the end of moral reflection. It instead may be the beginning of a different sort of reflection that involves on the one hand an effort to reach an understanding with those who have substantially different values, and on the other the effort to stay true to one's own values. Some of those who believe that abortion is the taking of a life with moral status, for instance, have chosen to oppose it by placing their efforts into organizations that aim to lessen the perceived need for abortion, organizations that aid unwed mothers, for example.

One final issue regarding relativism needs addressing. Relativism has a bad name in some quarters because it is associated with a lack of moral conviction, with a tendency toward nihilism. Part of the reason for the bad name may be the identification of relativism with its most extreme forms. If these forms are true, then everything is permitted, on someone's morality. But another reason for the bad name is the assumption that one's moral confidence, one's commitment to act on one's values, is somehow dependent on maintaining the belief that one's morality is the only true or the most justified one. But surely some reflection will reveal that such a belief alone would not guarantee a commitment to act. The commitment to act involves a conception of what one's morality means to the self, whether it be the only true one or not. It involves making a connection between what one desires, what one aspires to, and the substantive content of one's moral values. It is being able to see morality as important to us in these ways that allows us to avoid nihilism. The belief that our morality is the only true or most justified one does not automatically create this kind of importance, nor is it a necessary condition for this kind of importance, because the values I may see as important and part of what makes life most meaningful to me may not have to be values that all reasonable persons would accept or recognize to be true.

Here, as in other matters concerning relativism, the emotion provoked by the mere name tends to muddle the issues and to polarize unnecessarily. When we get through defending and attacking what most people conceive as relativism or what they associate with it, then most of the real work remains to be done. What is left is a moral reality that is quite messy and immune to neat solutions. But why should we have expected anything else?

QUESTIONS FOR DISCUSSION

1. Given Korn's position, in what way could ethics be seen as a social enterprise? In what way is it a personal affair? What are the strengths or dangers of each (the social and the individual) approach?

2. If values are subjective, how will it be possible to arbitrate between diverse or opposing groups holding different values? Perhaps even the person chosen to arbitrate with a view to harmonizing the grieving parties may instead impose his or her own values. Refer to any of our authors in this section to answer this question.

3. How can we be assured, if values are subjective as Korn suggests, that the best view will prevail throughout history? Perhaps might makes right in too many cases of values. Can you think of some examples, or counterexamples? Include Locke's argument about the progressive nature of reevaluation.

4. What are common arguments in criticism of relativism, recounted by Locke and Wong? How could a relativist answer these objections? Which side do you think has the better argument, and why?

Happiness and the Good Life
  Aristotle, *The Rational Life*
  Tabataba'i, *Islam Is the Road to Happiness*
  Joan Chittister, *Living the Rule of St. Benedict Today*
  H. Saddhatissa, *The Four Noble Truths*
  Herbert John Benally, *Navajo Ways of Knowing*
  Albert Camus, *The Myth of Sisyphus*

Taoist and Confucian Views
  Lao Tzu, *Living in the Tao*
  Chuang Tzu, *Lost in the Tao*

  Raymond M. Smullyan, *Whichever the Way*
  Fung Yu-Lan, *The Spheres of Living*

Facing Death
  Native Mesoamerican, *Thought of the Sages*
  Gregory Baum, *Social Conceptions of Death*
  Etty Hillesum, *Facing Death*

Avery Architectural and Fine Arts Library, Columbia University in the City of New York.

CHAPTER 8

THE MEANING OF LIFE AND DEATH

Does life have a meaning? What kind of a thing might the meaning of life be? If it is seen as an ultimate reason for our existence, must that reason lie outside life? Or could it be found within life itself? Suppose life is found to have no meaning. Would that make it worthless? Would animal instinct and the force of habit then constitute our only reason to live? Or perhaps are we, in asking this, approaching the problem in the wrong way? Might it not be that life's meaning is found within human satisfaction? In that case, the achievement of something like happiness would seem to be the meaning of life. But can it be any kind of happiness? And what is happiness anyway? These are among the questions debated in the following chapter by thinkers from a great variety of cultures.

In the chapter's opening section, we are presented with several authors who see human happiness as life's goal. However, their ideas of what happiness is, and how it is attained, differ greatly. Therefore, readers should proceed with caution—we should be careful to understand in what precise sense this happiness is meant, for if we take for granted our everyday conception of happiness as "having a good time," we will come to conclusions that differ greatly from those of our authors. In fact, striving after happiness

in the "fun" sense may be, by some of our author's accounts, the surest way to be miserable!

Aristotle, the ancient Greek philosopher, asserts that we humans find the best kind of happiness in achieving excellence. Our next author, Tabataba'i, a modern Shi'ite Muslim theologian, suggests that happiness is to be found through adherence to the precepts of the Qur'an, the chief scripture of Islam. In fact, a long historical dialogue, in which Aristotle's works were preserved and popularized through medieval times by Arabic scholars, accounts for the parallels between Aristotle's and Tabataba'i's emphasis on happiness; they are not accidental.

Just as Tabataba'i insists that his religion, Islam, is the key to happiness, members of other religions suggest that their own spiritual path puts forward the best guide for life. Joan Chittister, a contemporary Catholic nun, explains how the *Rule of St. Benedict,* a spiritual guide written in the fifth century, helps her to find meaning in her life in the United States today. H. Saddhatissa, a contemporary Buddhist scholar from Sri Lanka, argues that Buddhism has the most helpful guidelines for life. However, he maintains that Buddhism is not a religion, and the precepts he proposes are not to be accepted on faith but based only on one's own experience. He also says that it is important that we do not strive after anything, not even ordinary happiness; the goal of life, he explains, is to attain a state of nibbana (nirvana), which constitutes contentment far beyond our usual idea of happiness.

Herbert John Benally, who lives on the Navajo reservation in Sweetwater, Arizona, explains the Navajo ideas of how to achieve *hózhó,* or harmony, also referred to as walking the "beauty way" of life. The Four Directions symbolize the different values that should influence our life in order to attain harmony with the earth and each other.

Finally, Albert Camus, a French Algerian philosopher of this century, puts forward an atheist's response to spiritual approaches to happiness and meaning in life. Ironically, he finds "happiness" in the suffering but persevering character of Sisyphus, from Greek mythology. Camus uses Sisyphus as a metaphor for understanding and accepting our struggles in life today, without the "comfort" of a loving God's help or rewards in an afterlife.

Our second section's topics are closely related to the topics of Section One. Taoist and Confucian philosophers from ancient and contemporary times speak of what attitude one should take toward life in order to reach contentment and/or wisdom. The Taoists suggest that an openness to whatever life has to offer is the surest way to happiness, whereas struggling to control or force the outcomes of life to goals we have chosen will lead to self-defeating frustration. Fung Yu-Lan, a contemporary Confucianist and well-known Chinese philosopher, suggests that the highest goal in life is to become a "sage," one who is fully aware of his or her thoughts and actions, who does the ordinary things of daily life with enlightened awareness.

No discussion of the meaning of life would be complete without taking serious note of the fact that our life in our human bodies comes to an end. What attitude should we take to our impending death, our finitude? How will our mortality affect our ability to be happy, and/or to find meaning in life? As readers of Chapter 5 have seen, Plato quotes Socrates as saying, as he waited in prison for his execution, that a philosopher's whole life's goal is to prepare for death.

It is not, however, only the anticipation of an afterlife that has led philosophers to ponder death. Martin Heidegger, a German existentialist philosopher of this century, suggested that it wasn't possible to lead an authentic life until one took stock of one's human finitude, for only the sense of dread that this produces can lift us out of scurrying self-forgetfulness.

This section concerns the issue of how to face that dread—one's attitude toward death. Should it be feared? Challenged? Accepted? The question of death has been pondered by humanity for at least as far back in time as we have records. Our first selection is from Native Mesoamerica, in what is today central Mexico, and was originally written in a language called Nahuatl, the language of the Aztec people. Various Mesoamerican sages argued about whether we should enjoy our moments of life while we can or set our sights on a future life after death.

Next, Gregory Baum, a Canadian sociologist of religion, suggests that the contemporary individual longing for immortality is a product of our individualistic culture. In earlier Christian accounts, individual survival of death was not central, and the focus was rather on the coming kingdom of God and the survival and well-being of the community. Baum suggests we could revive the communal sense and face death from a different perspective. Our last author, Etty Hillesum, a Dutch Jew, shares her experience of confronting death at Auschwitz at the hands of the Nazis, and seeing her people's worldly existence destroyed. By clinging to spiritual values, she learns to accept her death without feeling destroyed as a person.

Often one's attitude toward death is shaped by one's beliefs concerning an afterlife. It is therefore suggested that those interested look at the philosophical debates of Chapter 5, which consider whether there is an immaterial and spiritual aspect to human existence. Section Five of Chapter 5 is of particular interest, as it asks: What might life after death be like? As with so many other philosophical topics, this one goes beyond factual evidence, and our authors must speculate, using reason and persuasion in putting forth their views.

HAPPINESS AND THE GOOD LIFE

Our section begins with Aristotle (384–322 B.C.E.). Born in Macedonia, Aristotle traveled to Athens where he studied Plato's philosophy in the Academy for twenty years. Aristotle is known for criticizing Plato's views, but in some ways he continues the Platonic tradition. Aristotle's interests were broad, encompassing biology and politics in addition to philosophy. Aristotle was tutor to Alexander the Great, who conquered a vast empire, and on Alexander's death, he had to flee Athens and return to Macedonia to save his own life.

In this passage from *Nichomachean Ethics,* a book named after his son, Aristotle asserts that all things that exist have a goal embedded in their nature, and that goal is to embody perfection as their nature would allow. We are all attracted and drawn toward perfection because we are attracted to God, who is perfection Itself. Aristotle's god is not an "agent cause" like the Judaeo-Christian God, who chose to act in history; or like the Greek gods who lived on Mt. Olympus—Olympic gods were considered to be interested in human affairs, occasionally deciding to sink a ship here, help a battle there, or cause people to fall in love or hate each other. In contrast, Aristotle's god was a "final cause," causing activity in the world only indirectly by drawing all things forth to attain their limited perfection, motivating them as happens with a tired runner who, on catching sight of the finish line, may suddenly be moved to accelerate. Aristotle's god is not meant to be worshipped in any religious sense; the god's role is, by self-absorbed contemplation of his own perfection, to encourage each of us toward our own perfection.

Aristotle argues that happiness is what all humans seek; but our ideas of what makes us happy might be flawed. Some find happiness in enjoyment, some find it in devoting their lives to politics and trying to change the world for the good, while others find happiness in exercising their soul, meaning both their intellectual and moral capacities, in attaining the perfection of virtue and a life devoted to contemplation. These various happinesses are not all of the

same quality; a concert pianist who plays a concerto excellently experiences a different kind of joy than the person who buys a CD of the pianist playing the concerto and sits on the sofa listening to it. Aristotle is also concerned that our natural desire for happiness, without being shaped by moral training, could lead us to vices like gluttony and sloth; our goal should be to shape our moral characters so that we become the kind of person who finds pleasure by doing what is good and feels pain when engaging in wrongdoing. Aristotle himself does not posit an afterlife at which time we can experience joy. He is more interested in the happiness that comes at life's end, when we look back over our accomplishments and take stock of whom we've become.

In this context, it is interesting to look at the parallels and divergences between Aristotle and our next author, Allamah Sayyid Muhammad Husayn Tabataba'i. Tabataba'i was born in 1903 in Tabriz, Iran. He studied Arabic, math, science, religion, and philosophy in Najaf, Iran. After 1945, he went to Qum, Iran, where he lived until his death in 1982. He often traveled to Tehran to meet with other Shi'ite scholars, such as Mutahhari, included in our text in Chapter 2.

Tabataba'i, like Aristotle—indeed, influenced by him—argues that happiness is the aim of life. This happiness is found for humans, plants, and animals of all sorts through the pursuit of a natural goal, given by God. However, his insistence on the centrality of religion, particularly Islam, for reaching happiness is not found in Aristotle. Tabataba'i suggests we search for the *din/* (deen) which is God's code, to which we humans must submit. He argues that the Qur'an provides a comprehensive program of activity for life, covering the areas of religious belief, moral virtues, and the legal system. On Judgment Day, humans will be judged and then rewarded or punished for their behavior during their lives. There is a social aspect to evil, in that persons can discourage others from pursuing the path of God. It is therefore important to have a society that is ruled by truth and justice, and not by a tyrant or by "the majority," as in a democracy.

Tabataba'i refers to the twin "dangers" posed to Islam: the "tyrant" most probably refers to the former Shah of Iran, while the democratic "majority" is a criticism of secular Western democracy. Iran, because of the influence of its Shi'ite Muslim population, has chosen to have the Qur'an as its constitution, making it an Islamic state; perhaps this is the country ruled by truth and justice to which Tabataba'i alludes. Here it may be interesting to pause and note that Aristotle as well cautioned against tyrannies and democracies, since in both cases those who govern do so for self-gain; the only good government would be one that governs for the common good. Aristotle's notion of the "common good," however, is decidedly more secular than Tabataba'i's notion.

Our next author searches for the meaning of life from a Christian perspective. Joan Chittister, O.S.B., is a contemporary Catholic Benedictine Sister. She was formerly prioress of her community in Erie, Pennsylvania, and has been the executive director of the Alliance for International Monasticism (AIM). She has been an active leader in Pax Christi, an international Catholic movement for peace and justice, and was awarded the Pope Paul VI Teacher of Peace award by Pax Christi in 1990.

In this passage, Chittister reflects on living the "Rule of Benedict" in our contemporary times. The "Rule of Benedict" was written by St. Benedict of Nursia, an Italian monk who lived from 480 to about 543 A.C.E. Benedict lived in the time of the collapse of Rome. Scandalized by the behaviors he witnessed and the crumbling of a civilization, he fled Rome where he had been studying and went to Subiaco, where he lived for many years as a hermit. He began to get a reputation as a wise man. Finally, several monks asked him if he would lead their community. He wrote the Rule of Benedict, which was promoted by Pope Gregory; Charlemagne, the Frankish King (750–820), later declared it the official rule for all religious monks and nuns of the time. It can be argued that Benedict and his sister Scholastica had a profound influence on the stability of Europe by the emphasis of the Rule on nor-

malcy and moderate behavior, while the monastic tradition kept preserved many ancient texts through diligent copying, as well as the literacy skills needed to read them.

As Chittister explains, the Rule was meant to be understood not in the legalistic sense but as a guide or a way of life. Chittister explains that the Rule is not just about the purposes of life understood in the terms of worldly goals and productivity. The question of meaning asks us to think of our actions: Who will care? Who will profit? Who will be forgotten or hurt? We must look for the global results of our actions. Contemplation, she explains, is the pursuit of meaning. That meaning is found through a balance of work (understood as our gift to the world, our co-creativity with God) and holy leisure, which gives us time to evaluate our work. In this way we avoid the twin dangers of our times: workaholism and pseudocontemplation.

H. Saddhatissa is a contemporary Buddhist scholar who reflects upon the insights of the Buddha, who lived in the sixth century B.C.E. As Saddhatissa explains it, Buddhism is not a "revealed religion" that depends, like Judaism, Christianity, or Islam, on some special messenger imparting revealed truths that most persons would otherwise not know; rather, Buddhism is based wholly on human experience. He therefore challenges us to "try out" the truths of Buddhism to see if they can explain our lives.

The Buddha had formulated "Four Noble Truths," which contained the insight for freedom from suffering. His insight did not involve "running away" from suffering, for ills like poverty, old age, disease, and death are inevitable. Rather, it was his profound psychological insight that it is our clinging to and craving for happiness that ultimately make us miserable. If we could let go of our desire, even for life itself, then we would no longer be made miserable.

But how can we ever get into the frame of mind in which we can let go of desires? Here, Saddhatissa suggests following the "Middle Way" outlined by the Buddha. A self-disciplined life can lead to the sustained ability to let go of destructive and tumultuous desires. We easily see a connection between the Buddhist "Middle Way" and Aristotle's later understanding of virtue as the means between two extremes. For both thinkers, moderation is the way to avoid suffering and vice.

Herbert John Benally is a contemporary thinker who has lived for many years on the Navajo reservation in Sweetwater, Arizona. He thinks the Navajo community has valuable spiritual insights for today's secular society. He explains that the goal of life is to achieve harmony or *hózhó,* called the "beauty way" of life. He insists that the world is full of intelligence, and that humans have the ability to learn from and imitate nature. He explains that the four directions each have a message that helps to give direction to our lives, resulting ultimately in balance.

Finally, we have the ideas of Albert Camus (1913–1960), who is a French Algerian (meaning that he was born in Algeria of French settler parents who lived in Algeria during the time when it was still a French colony). Camus is well known for both his philosophical novels and essays. Camus is convinced that life has no pregiven meaning; nonetheless he is concerned whether life can be worth living. Using the image of the torment of Sisyphus from ancient Greek mythology, he argues that it can be. Sisyphus was condemned by the gods to push a rock up a hill each day, only to have it roll down again; and so his work would begin again. Despite the eternally futile task the gods have given him, Camus insists, "one must imagine Sisyphus happy." Stuck in a routine that cannot be escaped, it seems Sisyphus finds happiness in his way of relating to his situation, in his way of finding satisfaction in the repetition and struggle.

Camus' works are considered part of existential philosophy, an intellectual movement made popular by Camus' contemporary, Jean-Paul Sartre. While Camus' existentialism (as well as Sartre's) is atheistic, one can nevertheless ponder whether there might be some rough parallel between Camus' notion of happiness in the midst of unending struggle and the Buddhist stance. One is also reminded of the emphasis on detachment from the fruits of one's

actions found in both the Bhagavad-Gita and Kant's philosophy, covered earlier in Chapter 7.

THE RATIONAL LIFE

Aristotle

Every art and every inquiry, and similarly every action and pursuit, is thought to aim at some good; and for this reason the good has rightly been declared to be that at which all things aim. But a certain difference is found among ends; some are activities, others are products apart from the activities that produce them. Where there are ends apart from the actions, it is the nature of the products to be better than the activities. Now, as there are many actions, arts, and sciences, their ends also are many; the end of the medical art is health, that of ship-building a vessel, that of strategy victory, that of economics wealth. But where such arts fall under a single capacity—as bridle-making and the other arts concerned with the equipment of horses fall under the art of riding, and this and every military action under strategy, in the same way other arts fall under yet others—in all of these the ends of the master arts are to be preferred to all the subordinate ends; for it is for the sake of the former that the latter are pursued. It makes no difference whether the activities themselves are the ends of the actions, or something else apart from the activities, as in the case of the sciences just mentioned.

Let us resume our inquiry and state, in view of the fact that all knowledge and every pursuit aims at some good, what it is that we say political science aims at and what is the highest of all goods achievable by action. Verbally there is very general agreement; for both the general run of men and people of superior refinement say that it is happiness, and identify living well and doing well with being happy; but with regard to what happiness is they differ, and the many do not give the same account as the wise. For the former think it is some plain and obvious thing, like pleasure, wealth, or honour; they differ, however, from one another—and often even the same man identifies it with different things, with health when he is ill, with wealth when he is poor; but, conscious of their ignorance, they admire those who proclaim some great ideal that is above their comprehension. Now some thought that apart from these many goods there is another which is self-subsistent and causes the goodness of all these as well. To examine all the opinions that have been held were perhaps somewhat fruitless; enough to examine those that are most prevalent or that seem to be arguable.

Let us not fail to notice, however, that there is a difference between arguments from and those to the first principles. For Plato, too, was right in raising this question and asking, as he used to do, "are we on the way from or to the first principles?"[1] There is a difference, as there is in a race-course between the course from the judges to the turning-point and the way back. For, while we must begin with what is known, things are objects of knowledge in two senses—some to us, some without qualification. Presumably, then, *we* must begin with things known to *us*. Hence any one who is to listen intelligently to lectures about what is noble and just and, generally, about the subjects of political science must have been brought up in good habits. For the fact is the starting-point, and if this is sufficiently plain to him, he will not at the start need the reason as well; and the man who has been well brought up has or can easily get starting-points. And as for him who neither has nor can get them, let him hear the words of Hesiod:

Far best is he who knows all things himself;
Good, he that hearkens when men counsel right;
But he who neither knows, nor lays to heart
Another's wisdom, is a useless wight.

Let us, however, resume our discussion from the point at which we digressed. To judge from the lives that men lead, most men, and men of the most vulgar type, seem (not without some ground) to identify

the good, or happiness, with pleasure; which is the reason why they love the life of enjoyment. For there are, we may say, three prominent types of life—that just mentioned, the political, and thirdly the contemplative life. Now the mass of mankind are evidently quite slavish in their tastes, preferring a life suitable to beasts, but they get some ground for their view from the fact that many of those in high places share the tastes of Sardanapallus. A consideration of the prominent types of life shows that people of superior refinement and of active disposition identify happiness with honour; for this is, roughly speaking, the end of the political life. But it seems too superficial to be what we are looking for, since it is thought to depend on those who bestow honour rather than on him who receives it, but the good we divine to be something proper to a man and not easily taken from him. Further, men seem to pursue honour in order that they may be assured of their goodness; at least it is by men of practical wisdom that they seek to be honoured, and among those who know them, and on the ground of their virtue; clearly, then, according to them, at any rate, virtue is better. And perhaps one might even suppose this to be, rather than honour, the end of the political life. But even this appears somewhat incomplete; for possession of virtue seems actually compatible with being asleep, or with lifelong inactivity, and, further, with the greatest sufferings and misfortunes; but a man who was living so no one would call happy, unless he were maintaining a thesis at all costs. But enough of this; for the subject has been sufficiently treated even in the current discussions. Third comes the contemplative life, which we shall consider later.

• • •

Let us again return to the good we are seeking, and ask what it can be. It seems different in different actions and arts; it is different in medicine, in strategy, and in the other arts likewise. What then is the good of each? Surely that for whose sake everything else is done. In medicine this is health, in strategy victory, in architecture a house, in any other sphere something else, and in every action and pursuit the end; for it is for the sake of this that

---

[1]Plato, *Republic* 511B.

all men do whatever else they do. Therefore, if there is an end for all that we do, this will be the good achievable by action, and if there are more than one, these will be the goods achievable by action.

So the argument has by a different course reached the same point; but we must try to state this even more clearly. Since there are evidently more than one end, and we choose some of these (e.g. wealth, flutes, and in general instruments) for the sake of something else, clearly not all ends are final ends; but the chief good is evidently something final. Therefore, if there is only one final end, this will be what we are seeking, and if there are more than one, the most final of these will be what we are seeking. Now we call that which is in itself worthy of pursuit for the sake of something else, and that which is never desirable for the sake of something else more final than the things that are desirable both in themselves and for the sake of that other thing, and therefore we call final without qualification that which is always desirable in itself and never for the sake of something else.

Now such a thing happiness, above all else, is held to be; for this we choose always for itself and never for the sake of something else, but honour, pleasure, reason, and every virtue we choose indeed for themselves (for if nothing resulted from them we should still choose each of them), but we choose them also for the sake of happiness, judging that by means of them we shall be happy. Happiness, on the other hand, no one chooses for the sake of these, nor, in general, for anything other than itself.

From the point of view of self-sufficiency the same result seems to follow; for the final good is thought to be self-sufficient. Now by self-sufficient we do not mean that which is sufficient for a man by himself, for one who lives a solitary life, but also for parents, children, wife, and in general for his friends and fellow citizens, since man is born for citizenship. But some limit must be set to this; for if we extend our requirement to ancestors and descendants and friends' friends we are in for an infinite series. Let us examine this question, however, on another occasion; the self-sufficient we now define as that which when isolated makes life desirable and lack-

ing in nothing; and such we think happiness to be; and further we think it most desirable of all things, without being counted as one good thing among others—if it were so counted it would clearly be made more desirable by the addition of even the least of goods; for that which is added becomes an excess of goods, and of goods the greater is always more desirable. Happiness, then, is something final and self-sufficient, and is the end of action.

Presumably, however, to say that happiness is the chief good seems a platitude, and a clearer account of what it is is still desired. This might perhaps be given, if we could first ascertain the function of man. For just as for a flute-player, a sculptor, or any artist, and, in general, for all things that have a function or activity, the good and the "well" is thought to reside in the function, so would it seem to be for man, if he has a function. Have the carpenter, then, and the tanner certain functions or activities, and has man none? Is he born without a function? Or as eye, hand, foot, and in general each of the parts evidently has a function, may one lay it down that man similarly has a function apart from all these? What then can this be? Life seems to be common even to plants, but we are seeking what is peculiar to man. Let us exclude, therefore, the life of nutrition and growth. Next there would be a life of perception, but *it* also seems to be common even to the horse, the ox, and every animal. There remains, then, an active life of the element that has a rational principle; of this, one part has such a principle in the sense of being obedient to one, the other in the sense of possessing one and exercising thought. And, as "life of the rational element" also has two meanings, we must state that life in the sense of activity is what we mean; for this seems to be the more proper sense of the term. Now if the function of man is an activity of soul which follows or implies a rational principle, and if we say "a so-and-so" and "a good so-and-so" have a function which is the same in kind, e.g. a lyre-player and a good lyre-player, and so without qualification in all cases, eminence in respect of goodness being added to the name of the function (for the function of a lyre-player is to play the lyre, and that of a good lyre-player is to do so well): if this is the case, [and we state the function of man to be a certain kind of life, and this to be an activity or actions of the soul implying a rational principle, and the function of a good man to be the good and noble performance of these, and if any action is well performed when it is performed in accordance with the appropriate excellence: if this is the case,] human good turns out to be activity of soul in accordance with virtue, and if there are more than one virtue, in accordance with the best and most complete.

But we must add "in a complete life." For one swallow does not make a summer, nor does one day; and so too one day, or a short time, does not make a man blessed and happy.

· · ·

Virtue, then, being of two kinds, intellectual and moral, intellectual virtue in the main owes both its birth and its growth to teaching (for which reason it requires experience and time), while moral virtue comes about as a result of habit, whence also its name (ἠθική) is one that is formed by a slight variation from the word ἔθος (habit). From this it is also plain that none of the moral virtues arises in us by nature; for nothing that exists by nature can form a habit contrary to its nature. For instance the stone which by nature moves downwards cannot be habituated to move upwards, not even if one tries to train it by throwing it up ten thousand times; nor can fire be habituated to move downwards, nor can anything else that by nature behaves in one way be trained to behave in another. Neither by nature, then, nor contrary to nature do the virtues arise in us; rather we are adapted by nature to receive them, and are made perfect by habit.

Again, of all the things that come to us by nature we first acquire the potentiality and later exhibit the activity (this is plain in the case of the senses; for it was not by often seeing or often hearing that we got these senses, but on the contrary we had them before we used them, and did not come to have them by using them); but the virtues we get by first exercising them, as also happens in the case of the arts as well. For the things we have to learn before we

can do them, we learn by doing them, e.g. men become builders by building and lyre-players by playing the lyre; so too we become just by doing just acts, temperate by doing temperate acts, brave by doing brave acts.

This is confirmed by what happens in states; for legislators make the citizens good by forming habits in them, and this is the wish of every legislator, and those who do not effect it miss their mark, and it is in this that a good constitution differs from a bad one.

Again, it is from the same causes and by the same means that every virtue is both produced and destroyed, and similarly every art; for it is from playing the lyre that both good and bad lyre-players are produced. And the corresponding statement is true of builders and of all the rest; men will be good or bad builders as a result of building well or badly. For if this were not so, there would have been no need of a teacher, but all men would have been born good or bad at their craft. This, then, is the case with the virtues also; by doing the acts that we do in our transactions with other men we become just or unjust, and by doing the acts that we do in the presence of danger, and being habituated to feel fear or confidence, we become brave or cowardly. The same is true of appetites and feelings of anger; some men become temperate and good-tempered, others self-indulgent and irascible, by behaving in one way or the other in the appropriate circumstances. Thus, in one word, states of character arise out of like activities. This is why the activities we exhibit must be of a certain kind; it is because the states of character correspond to the differences between these. It makes no small difference, then, whether we form habits of one kind or of another from our very youth; it makes a very great difference, or rather *all* the difference.

Since, then, the present inquiry does not aim at theoretical knowledge like the others (for we are inquiring not in order to know what virtue is, but in order to become good, since otherwise our inquiry would have been of no use), we must examine the nature of actions, namely how we ought to do them; for these determine also the nature of the states of character that are produced, as we have said. Now, that we must act according to the right rule is a common principle and must be assumed—it will be discussed later, i.e. both what the right rule is, and how it is related to the other virtues. But this must be agreed upon beforehand, that the whole account of matters of conduct must be given in outline and not precisely, as we said at the very beginning that the accounts we demand must be in accordance with the subject-matter; matters concerned with conduct and questions of what is good for us have no fixity, any more than matters of health. The general account being of this nature, the account of particular cases is yet more lacking in exactness; for they do not fall under any art or precept but the agents themselves must in each case consider what is appropriate to the occasion, as happens also in the art of medicine or of navigation.

But though our present account is of this nature we must give what help we can. First, then, let us consider this, that it is the nature of such things to be destroyed by defect and excess, as we see in the case of strength and of health (for to gain light on things imperceptible we must use the evidence of sensible things); both excessive and defective exercise destroys the strength, and similarly drink or food which is above or below a certain amount destroys the health, while that which is proportionate both produces and increases and preserves it. So too is it, then, in the case of temperance and courage and the other virtues. For the man who flies from and fears everything and does not stand his ground against anything becomes a coward, and the man who fears nothing at all but goes to meet every danger becomes rash; and similarly the man who indulges in every pleasure and abstains from none becomes self-indulgent, while the man who shuns every pleasure, as boors do, becomes in a way insensible; temperance and courage, then, are destroyed by excess and defect, and preserved by the mean.

But not only are the sources and causes of their origination and growth the same as those of their destruction, but also the sphere of their actualization will be the same; for this is also true of the things which are more evident to sense, e.g. of

strength; it is produced by taking much food and undergoing much exertion, and it is the strong man that will be most able to do these things. So too is it with the virtues; by abstaining from pleasures we become temperate, and it is when we have become so that we are most able to abstain from them; and similarly too in the case of courage; for by being habituated to despise things that are terrible and to stand our ground against them we become brave, and it is when we have become so that we shall be most able to stand our ground against them.

We must take as a sign of states of character the pleasure or pain that ensues on acts; for the man who abstains from bodily pleasures and delights in this very fact is temperate, while the man who is annoyed at it is self-indulgent, and he who stands his ground against things that are terrible and delights in this or at least is not pained is brave, while the man who is pained is a coward. For moral excellence is concerned with pleasures and pains; it is on account of the pleasure that we do bad things, and on account of the pain that we abstain from noble ones. Hence we ought to have been brought up in a particular way from our very youth, as Plato says, so as both to delight in and to be pained by the things that we ought; for this is the right education.

Again, if the virtues are concerned with actions and passions, and every passion and every action is accompanied by pleasure and pain, for this reason also virtue will be concerned with pleasures and pains. This is indicated also by the fact that punishment is inflicted by these means; for it is a kind of cure, and it is the nature of cures to be effected by contraries.

Again, as we said but lately, every state of soul has a nature relative to and concerned with the kind of things by which it tends to be made worse or better; but it is by reason of pleasures and pains that men become bad, by pursuing and avoiding these—either the pleasures and pains they ought not or when they ought not or as they ought not, or by going wrong in one of the other similar ways that may be distinguished. Hence men even define the virtues as certain states of impassivity and rest; not well, however, because they speak absolutely, and do not say "as one ought" and "as one ought not" and "when one ought or ought not," and the other things that may be added. We assume, then, that this kind of excellence tends to do what is best with regard to pleasures and pains, and vice does the contrary.

The following facts also may show us that virtue and vice are concerned with these same things. There being three objects of choice and three of avoidance, the noble, the advantageous, the pleasant, and their contraries, the base, the injurious, the painful, about all of these the good man tends to go right and the bad man to go wrong, and especially about pleasure; for this is common to the animals, and also it accompanies all objects of choice; for even the noble and the advantageous appear pleasant.

Again, it has grown up with us all from our infancy; this is why it is difficult to rub off this passion, engrained as it is in our life. And we measure even our actions, some of us more and others less, by the rule of pleasure and pain. For this reason, then, our whole inquiry must be about these; for to feel delight and pain rightly or wrongly has no small effect on our actions.

Again, it is harder to fight with pleasure than with anger, to use Heraclitus'[2] phrase, but both art and virtue are always concerned with what is harder; for even the good is better when it is harder. Therefore for this reason also the whole concern both of virtue and of political science is with pleasures and pains; for the man who uses these well will be good, he who uses them badly bad.

That virtue, then, is concerned with pleasures and pains, and that by the acts from which it arises it is both increased and, if they are done differently, destroyed, and that the acts from which it arose are those in which it actualizes itself—let this be taken as said.

The question might be asked, what we mean by saying that we must become just by doing just acts, and temperate by doing temperate acts; for if men do just and temperate acts, they are already just and temperate, exactly as, if they do what is in accordance with the laws of grammar and of music, they are grammarians and musicians.

Or is this not true even of the arts? It is possible to do something that is in accordance with the laws of grammar, either by chance or at the suggestion of another. A man will be a grammarian, then, only when he has both done something grammatical and done it grammatically; and this means doing it in accordance with the grammatical knowledge in himself.

Again, the case of the arts and that of the virtues are not similar; for the products of the arts have their goodness in themselves, so that it is enough that they should have a certain character, but if the acts that are in accordance with the virtues have themselves a certain character it does not follow that they are done justly or temperately. The agent also must be in a certain condition when he does them; in the first place he must have knowledge, secondly he must choose the acts, and choose them for their own sakes, and thirdly his action must proceed from a firm and unchangeable character. These are not reckoned in as conditions of the possession of the arts, except the bare knowledge; but as a condition of the possession of the virtues knowledge has little or no weight, while the other conditions count not for a little but for everything, i.e. the very conditions which result from often doing just and temperate acts.

Actions, then, are called just and temperate when they are such as the just or the temperate man would do; but it is not the man who does these that is just and temperate, but the man who also does them *as* just and temperate men do them. It is well said, then, that it is by doing just acts that the just man is produced, and by doing temperate acts the temperate man; without doing these no one would have even a prospect of becoming good.

But most people do not do these, but take refuge in theory and think they are being philosophers and will become good in this way, behaving somewhat like patients who listen attentively to their doctors, but do none of the things they are ordered to do. As the latter will not be made well in body by such a

---

[2]Heraclitus (540–480 B.C.E.) was an ancient Greek philosopher who believed that reality was constantly in motion and changing (Eds.).

course of treatment, the former will not be made well in soul by such a course of philosophy.

• • •

Now that we have spoken of the virtues, the forms of friendship, and the varieties of pleasure, what remains is to discuss in outline the nature of happiness, since this is what we state the end of human nature to be. Our discussion will be the more concise if we first sum up what we have said already. We said, then, that it is not a disposition; for if it were it might belong to some one who was asleep throughout his life, living the life of a plant, or, again, to some one who was suffering the greatest misfortunes. If these implications are unacceptable, and we must rather class happiness as an activity, as we have said before, and if some activities are necessary, and desirable for the sake of something else, while others are so in themselves, evidently happiness must be placed among those desirable in themselves, not among those desirable for the sake of something else; for happiness does not lack anything, but is self-sufficient. Now those activities are desirable in themselves from which nothing is sought beyond the activity. And of this nature virtuous actions are thought to be; for to do noble and good deeds is a thing desirable for its own sake.

Pleasant amusements also are thought to be of this nature; we choose them not for the sake of other things; for we are injured rather than benefited by them, since we are led to neglect our bodies and our property. But most of the people who are deemed happy take refuge in such pastimes, which is the reason why those who are ready-witted at them are highly esteemed at the courts of tyrants; they make themselves pleasant companions in the tyrants' favourite pursuits, and that is the sort of man they want. Now these things are thought to be of the nature of happiness because people in despotic positions spend their leisure in them, but perhaps such people prove nothing; for virtue and reason, from which good activities flow, do not depend on despotic position; nor, if these people, who have never tasted pure and generous pleasure, take refuge in the bodily pleasures, should these for that reason

be thought more desirable; for boys, too, think the things that are valued among themselves are the best. It is to be expected, then, that, as different things seem valuable to boys and to men, so they should to bad men and to good. Now, as we have often maintained those things are both valuable and pleasant which are such to the good man; and to each man the activity in accordance with his own disposition is most desirable, and, therefore, to the good man that which is in accordance with virtue. Happiness, therefore, does not lie in amusement; it would, indeed, be strange if the end were amusement, and one were to take trouble and suffer hardship all one's life in order to amuse oneself. For, in a word, everything that we choose we choose for the sake of something else—except happiness, which is an end. Now to exert oneself and work for the sake of amusement seems silly and utterly childish. But to amuse oneself in order that one may exert oneself, as Anacharsis puts it, seems right; for amusement is a sort of relaxation, and we need relaxation because we cannot work continuously. Relaxation, then, is not an end; for it is taken for the sake of activity.

The happy life is thought to be virtuous; now a virtuous life requires exertion, and does not consist in amusement. And we say that serious things are better than laughable things and those connected with amusement, and that the activity of the better of any two things—whether it be two elements of our being or two men—is the more serious; but the activity of the better is *ipso facto* superior and more of the nature of happiness. And any chance person—even a slave—can enjoy the bodily pleasures no less than the best man; but no one assigns to a slave a share in happiness—unless he assigns to him also a share in human life. For happiness does not lie in such occupations, but, as we have said before, in virtuous activities.

If happiness is activity in accordance with virtue, it is reasonable that it should be in accordance with the highest virtue; and this will be that of the best thing in us. Whether it be reason or something else that is this element which is thought to be our natural ruler and guide and to take thought of things noble and divine, whether it be itself also divine or only the most divine element in us, the activity of this in accordance with its proper virtue will be perfect happiness. That this activity is contemplative we have already said.

Now this would seem to be in agreement both with what we said before and with the truth. For, firstly, this activity is the best (since not only is reason the best thing in us, but the objects of reason are the best of knowable objects); and, secondly, it is the most continuous, since we can contemplate truth more continuously than we can *do* anything. And we think happiness has pleasure mingled with it, but the activity of philosophic wisdom is admittedly the pleasantest of virtuous activities; at all events the pursuit of it is thought to offer pleasures marvellous for their purity and their enduringness, and it is to be expected that those who know will pass their time more pleasantly than those who inquire. And the self-sufficiency that is spoken of must belong most to the contemplative activity. For while a philosopher, as well as a just man or one possessing any other virtue, needs the necessaries of life, when they are sufficiently equipped with things of that sort the just man needs people towards whom and with whom he shall act justly, and the temperate man, the brave man, and each of the others is in the same case, but the philosopher, even when by himself, can contemplate truth, and the better the wiser he is; he can perhaps do so better if he has fellow-workers, but still he is the most self-sufficient. And this activity alone would seem to be loved for its own sake; for nothing arises from it apart from the contemplating, while from practical activities we gain more or less apart from the action. And happiness is thought to depend on leisure; for we are busy that we may have leisure, and make war that we may live in peace. Now the activity of the practical virtues is exhibited in political or military affairs, but the actions concerned with these seem to be unleisurely. Warlike actions are completely so (for no one chooses to be at war, or provokes war, for the sake of being at war; any one would seem absolutely murderous if he were to make enemies of his friends in order to bring about battle and slaughter); but the action of the statesman is also un-

leisurely, and—apart from the political action itself—aims at despotic power and honours, or at all events happiness, for him and his fellow citizens—a happiness different from political action, and evidently sought as being different. So if among virtuous actions political and military actions are distinguished by nobility and greatness, and these are unleisurely and aim at an end and are not desirable for their own sake, but the activity of reason, which is contemplative, seems both to be superior in serious worth and to aim at no end beyond itself, and to have its pleasure proper to itself (and this augments the activity), and the self-sufficiency, leisureliness, unweariedness (so far as this is possible for man), and all the other attributes ascribed to the supremely happy man are evidently those connected with this activity, it follows that this will be the complete happiness of man, if it be allowed a complete term of life (for none of the attributes of happiness is *in*complete).

But such a life would be too high for man; for it is not in so far as he is man that he will live so, but in so far as something divine is present in him; and by so much as this is superior to our composite nature is its activity superior to that which is the exercise of the other kind of virtue. If reason is divine, then, in comparison with man, the life according to it is divine in comparison with human life. But we must not follow those who advise us, being men, to think of human things, and, being mortal, of mortal things, but must, so far as we can, make ourselves immortal, and strain every nerve to live in accordance with the best thing in us; for even if it be small in bulk, much more does it in power and worth surpass everything. This would seem, too, to be each man himself, since it is the authoritative and better part of him. It would be strange, then, if he were to choose not the life of his self but that of something else. And what we said before will apply now; that which is proper to each thing is by nature best and most pleasant for each thing; for man, therefore, the life according to reason is best and pleasantest, since reason more than anything else *is* man. This life therefore is also the happiest.

But in a secondary degree the life in accordance with the other kind of virtue is happy; for the activities in accordance with this befit our human estate. Just and brave acts, and other virtuous acts, we do in relation to each other, observing our respective duties with regard to contracts and services and all manner of actions and with regard to passions; and all of these seem to be typically human. Some of them seem even to arise from the body, and virtue of character to be in many ways bound up with the passions. Practical wisdom, too, is linked to virtue of character, and this to practical wisdom, since the principles of practical wisdom are in accordance with the moral virtues and rightness in morals is in accordance with practical wisdom. Being connected with the passions also, the moral virtues must belong to our composite nature; and the virtues of our composite nature are human; so, therefore, are the life and the happiness which correspond to these. The excellence of the reason is a thing apart; we must be content to say this much about it, for to describe it precisely is a task greater than our purpose requires. It would seem, however, also to need external equipment but little, or less than moral virtue does. Grant that both need the necessaries, and do so equally, even if the statesman's work is the more concerned with the body and things of that sort; for there will be little difference there; but in what they need for the exercise of their activities there will be much difference. The liberal man will need money for the doing of his liberal deeds, and the just man too will need it for the returning of services (for wishes are hard to discern, and even people who are not just pretend to wish to act justly); and the brave man will need power if he is to accomplish any of the acts that correspond to his virtue, and the temperate man will need opportunity; for how else is either he or any of the others to be recognized? It is debated, too, whether the will or the deed is more essential to virtue, which is assumed to involve both; it is surely clear that its perfection involves both; but for deeds many things are needed, and more, the greater and nobler the deeds are. But the man who is contemplating the truth needs no such

thing, at least with a view to the exercise of his activity; indeed they are, one may say, even hindrances, at all events to his contemplation; but in so far as he is a man and lives with a number of people, he chooses to do virtuous acts; he will therefore need such aids to living a human life.

But that perfect happiness is a contemplative activity will appear from the following consideration as well. We assume the gods to be above all other beings blessed and happy; but what sort of actions must we assign to them? Acts of justice? Will not the gods seem absurd if they make contracts and return deposits, and so on? Acts of a brave man, then, confronting dangers and running risks because it is noble to do so? Or liberal acts? To whom will they give? It will be strange if they are really to have money or anything of the kind. And what would their temperate acts be? Is not such praise tasteless, since they have no bad appetites? If we were to run through them all, the circumstances of action would be found trivial and unworthy of gods. Still, every one supposes that they *live* and therefore that they are active; we cannot suppose them to sleep like Endymion. Now if you take away from a living being action, and still more production, what is left but contemplation? Therefore the activity of God, which surpasses all others in blessedness, must be contemplative; and of human activities, therefore, that which is most akin to this must be most of the nature of happiness.

This is indicated, too, by the fact that the other animals have no share in happiness, being completely deprived of such activity. For while the whole life of the gods is blessed, and that of men too in so far as some likeness of such activity belongs to them, none of the other animals is happy, since they in no way share in contemplation. Happiness extends, then, just so far as contemplation does, and those to whom contemplation more fully belongs are more truly happy, not as a mere concomitant but in virtue of the contemplation; for this is in itself precious. Happiness, therefore, must be some form of contemplation.

But, being a man, one will also need external prosperity; for our nature is not self-sufficient for the purpose of contemplation, but our body also must be healthy and must have food and other attention. Still, we must not think that the man who is to be happy will need many things or great things, merely because he cannot be supremely happy without external goods; for self-sufficiency and action do not involve excess, and we can do noble acts without ruling earth and sea; for even with moderate advantages one can act virtuously (this is manifest enough; for private persons are thought to do worthy acts no less than despots—indeed even more); and it is enough that we should have so much as that; for the life of the man who is active in accordance with virtue will be happy. Solon, too, was perhaps sketching well the happy man when he described him as moderately furnished with externals but as having done (as Solon thought) the noblest acts, and lived temperately; for one can with but moderate possessions do what one ought. Anaxagoras also seems to have supposed the happy man not to be rich nor a despot, when he said that he would not be surprised if the happy man were to seem to most people a strange person; for they judge by externals, since these are all they perceive. The opinions of the wise seem, then, to harmonize with our arguments. But while even such things carry some conviction, the truth in practical matters is discerned from the facts of life; for these are the decisive factor. We must therefore survey what we have already said, bringing it to the test of the facts of life, and if it harmonizes with the facts we must accept it, but if it clashes with them we must suppose it to be mere theory. Now he who exercises his reason and cultivates it seems to be both in the best state of mind and most dear to the gods. For if the gods have any care for human affairs, as they are thought to have, it would be reasonable both that they should delight in that which was best and most akin to them (i.e. reason) and that they should reward those who love and honour this most, as caring for the things that are dear to them and acting both rightly and nobly. And that all these attributes belong most of all to the philosopher is manifest. He, therefore, is the dearest to the gods. And he who is that will presum-

ably be also the happiest; so that in this way too the philosopher will more than any other be happy.

ISLAM IS THE ROAD TO HAPPINESS

Tabataba'i

The religion of Islam is superior to any other in that it guarantees happiness in man's life. For Muslims, Islam is a belief system with moral and practical laws that have their source in the Qur'an.

God, may He be exalted, says, *"Indeed this Qur'an guides to the path which is clearer and straighter than any other"* [XVII:9]. He also says, *"We have revealed to you the book which clarifies every matter"* [XVI:89].

These references exemplify the numerous Qur'anic verses (*āyāt*) which mention the principles of religious belief, moral virtues and a general legal system governing all aspects of human behaviour.

A consideration of the following topics will enable one to understand that the Qur'an provides a comprehensive programme of activity for man's life.

Man has no other aim in life but the pursuit of happiness and pleasure, which manifests itself in much the same way as love of ease or wealth. Although some individuals seem to reject this happiness, for example, by ending their lives in suicide, or by turning away from a life of leisure, they too, in their own way, confirm this principle of happiness; for, in seeking an end to their life or of material pleasure, they are still asserting their own personal choice of what happiness means to them. Human actions, therefore, are directed largely by the prospects of happiness and prosperity offered by a certain idea, whether that idea be true or false.

Man's activity in life is guided by a specific plan or programme. This fact is self-evident, even though it is sometimes concealed by its very apparentness.

Man acts according to his will and desires; he also weighs the necessity of a task before undertaking it.

In this he is promoted by an inherent scientific law, which is to say that he performs a task for "himself" in fulfilling needs which he perceives are necessary. There is, therefore, a direct link between the objective of a task and its execution.

Any action undertaken by man, whether it be eating, sleeping or walking, occupies its own specific place and demands its own particular efforts. Yet an action is implemented according to an inherent law, the general concept of which is stored in man's perception and is recalled by motions associated with that action. This notion holds true whether or not one is obliged to undertake the action or whether or not the circumstances are favourable.

Every man, in respect of his own actions, is as the state in relation to its individual citizens, whose activity is controlled by specific laws, customs and behaviour. Just as the active forces in a state are obliged to adapt their actions according to certain laws, so is the social activity of a community composed of the actions of each individual. If this were not the case, the different components of society would fall apart and be destroyed in anarchy in the shortest time imaginable.

If a society is religious, its government will reflect that religion; if it is secular, it will be regulated by a corresponding code of law. If a society is uncivilized and barbaric, a code of behaviour imposed by a tyrant will appear; otherwise, the conflict of various belief-systems within such a society will produce lawlessness.

Thus man, as an individual element of society, has no option but to possess and pursue a goal. He is guided in the pursuit of his goal by the path which corresponds to it and by the rules which must necessarily accompany his programme of activity. The Qur'an affirms this idea when it says that *"every man has a goal to which he is turning, so compete with each other in good action"* [II:148]. In the usage of the Qur'an, the word *dīn* is basically applied to a way, a pattern of living, and neither the believer nor the non-believer is without a path, be it prophetic or man-made.

God, may He be exalted, describes the enemies of the divine *dīn* (religion) as those *"who prevent others from the path of God and would have it crooked"* [VII:45].

This verse shows that the term *Sabīl Allāh*—the path of God—used in the verse refers to the *dīn* of *fiṭrah*—the inherent pattern of life intended by God for man). It also indicates that even those who do not believe in God implement His *dīn,* albeit in a deviated form; this deviation, which becomes their *dīn,* is also encompassed in God's programme.

The best and firmest path in life for man is the one which is dictated by his innate being and not by the sentiments of any individual or society. A close examination of any part of creation reveals that, from its very inception, it is guided by an innate purpose towards fulfilling its nature along the most appropriate and shortest path; every aspect of each part of creation is equipped to do so, acting as a blueprint for defining the nature of its existence. Indeed all of creation, be it animate or inanimate, is made up in this manner.

As an example, we may say that a green-tipped shoot, emerging from a single grain in the earth, is "aware" of its future existence as a plant which will yield an ear of wheat. By means of its inherent characteristics, the shoot acquires various mineral elements for its growth from the soil and changes, day by day, in form and strength until it becomes a fully-matured grain-bearing plant—and so comes to the end of its natural cycle.

Similarly, if we investigate the life-cycle of the walnut tree, we observe that it too is "aware," from the very beginning, of its own specific purpose in life, namely, to grow into a big walnut tree. It reaches this goal by developing according to its own distinct inherent characteristics; it does not, for example, follow the path of the wheat-plant in fulfilling its goal just as the wheat-plant does not follow the life pattern of the walnut tree.

Since every created object which makes up the visible world is subject to this same general law, there is no reason to doubt that man, as a species of creation, is not. Indeed his physical capabilities are the best proof of this rule; like the rest of creation, they allow him to realize his purpose, and ultimate happiness, in life.

Thus, we observe that man, in fact, guides himself to happiness and well-being merely by applying the fundamental laws inherent in his own nature.

This law is confirmed by God in the Qur'an, through His Prophet Moses, when he says, *"Our Lord is He who gave everything its nature, then guided it"*[XX:50]. It is further explained in LXXXVII:2–3 as *"He who created and fashioned in balanced proportion and He who measures and guides."*

As to the creation and the nature of man, the Qur'an says,

> *By the soul and Him who fashioned it and then*
> *inspired it with wrong action and fear of God;*
> *he is truly successful who causes it to grow and*
> *purifies it and he is a failure who corrupts and*
> *destroys it* [XCI:7–10].

God enjoins upon man the duty to *"strive towards a sincere application of the dīn,"* (that is, the *fiṭrah* of God, or the natural code of behaviour upon which He has created mankind), since *"there is no changing (the laws of) the creation of God"*[XXX:30].

He also says that *"In truth, the only deen recognized by God is Islam"* [III:19]. Here, Islam means submission, the method of submission to these very laws. The Qur'an further warns that *"the actions of the man who chooses a dīn other than Islam will not be accepted"* [III:85].

The gist of the above verses, and other references on the same subject, is that God has guided every creature—be it man, beast or vegetable—to a state of well-being and self-fulfillment appropriate to its individual make-up.

Thus the appropriate path for man lies in the adoption of personal and social laws particular to his own *fiṭrah* (or innate nature), and in avoiding people who have become "denaturalized" by following their own notions or passions. It is clearly underlined that *fiṭrah,* far from denying man's feelings and passions, accords each its proper due and allows man's conflicting spiritual and material needs to be fulfilled in a harmonious fashion.

Thus, we may conclude that the intellect *'aql* should rule man in matters pertaining to individual or personal decisions, rather than his feelings. Similarly, truth and justice should govern society and not the whim of a tyrant or even the will of a majority, if that be contrary to a society's true benefit.

From this we may conclude that only God is empowered to make laws, since the only laws useful to man are those which are made according to his inherent nature.

It also follows that man's needs, arising from his outward circumstance and his inner reality, are fulfilled only by obeying God's instructions (or laws). These needs may arise through events beyond man's control or as a result of the natural demands of his body.

Both are encompassed in the plan of life that God has designated for man. For, as the Qur'an says, the *"decision rests with God only,"* [XII:40,67] which is to say that there is no governance (of man or society, of the inner or the outer) except that of God.

Without a specific creational plan, based on the innate disposition of man, life would be fruitless and without meaning. We may understand this only through belief in God and a knowledge of his Unity, as explained in the Qur'an.

From here we may proceed to an understanding of the Day of Judgement, when man is rewarded or punished according to his deeds. Thereafter, we may arrive at a knowledge of the prophets and of prophetic teachings, since man cannot be judged without being first instructed in the matter of obedience and disobedience. These three fundamental teachings are considered to be the roots of the Islamic way of life.

To these we may add the fundamentals of good character and morals which a true believer must possess, and which are a necessary extension of the three basic beliefs mentioned above. The laws governing daily activity not only guarantee man's happiness and moral character but, more importantly, increase his understanding of these beliefs and of the fundamentals of Islam.

THE RULE:
A BOOK OF WISDOM

Joan D. Chittister, O.S.B.

Are you hastening toward your heavenly home? Then with Christ's help, keep this little rule that we have written for beginners. After that, you can set out for the loftier summits of the teaching and virtues we mentioned above, and under God's protection you will reach them. Amen.
—RB 73:8–9

The ancients tell a story of the spiritual life that may best explain this book:

A young monastic came upon an elder one day sitting among a group of praying, working, meditating people.

"I have the capacity to walk on water," the young disciple said. "So, let's you and I go onto that small lake over there and sit down and carry on a spiritual discussion."

But the Teacher answered, "If what you are trying to do is to get away from all of these people, why do you not come with me and fly into the air and drift along in the quiet, open sky and talk there."

And the young seeker replied, "I can't do that because the power you mention is not one that I possess."

And the Teacher explained, "Just so. Your power of remaining still on top of the water is one that is possessed by fish. And my capacity of floating through the air can be done by any fly. These abilities have nothing to do with real truth and, in fact, may simply become the basis of arrogance and competition, not spirituality. If we're going to talk about spiritual things, we should really be talking here."

Just about every person I have ever met who was serious about spiritual things thinks the point of the story is true: daily life is the stuff of which high sanctity can be made. But just about nobody I have ever met, however, really thinks it is easily possible. Spirituality, we have all learned somehow, is something I have to leave where I am in order to find it. I get it in small doses, in special places and under rarefied conditions. I hope I get enough at one time

in life to carry me through all the other times. The idea that sanctity is as much a part of the married life or the single life as it is of the religious life or the clerical life is an idea dearly loved but seldom deeply believed.

In our own times, too, just as at the time of the story, fads crowd into the spiritual life. We are told that novenas are the answer one year and retreats another and meditation centers a third. True believers tell us that the cult of their choice is the only answer to the struggles of life. The occultists promise salvation in the stars or from ancient oriental lore. The therapeutic community offers marathon encounters or anger-release workshops to cleanse the soul. Over and over again, cures and cults and psychological exercises are regularly tried and regularly discarded while people look for something that will make them feel good, steady their perspective, and bring meaning and direction to their lives. But, as the ancient story demonstrates, if we are not spiritual where we are and as we are, we are not spiritual at all. We are simply consumers of the latest in spiritual gadgetry that numbs our confusions but never fills our spirits or frees our hearts.

After years of monastic life I have discovered that unlike spiritual fads, which come and go with the teachers or cultures that spawned them, the Rule of Benedict looks at the world through interior eyes and lasts. Here, regardless of who we are or what we are, life and purpose meet.

The Rule of Benedict has been a guide to the spiritual life for common people since the sixth century. Anything that has lasted that long and had that kind of impact in a throwaway society is certainly worthy of consideration. This book looks at these questions. "How do we account for a way of life that has lasted for over fifteen hundred years, and what, if anything, does it have to say to the spiritual life in our world today?"

Benedictine spirituality offers exactly what our times are lacking. Benedictine spirituality seeks to fill up the emptiness and heal the brokenness in which most of us live in ways that are sensible, humane, whole, and accessible to an overworked, overstimulated, overscheduled human race.

The Rule of Benedict called the class-centered Roman world to community and calls us to the same on a globe that is fragmented. The Rule called for hospitality in times of barbarian invasions and calls us to care in a world of neighborhood strangers. It called for equality in a society full of classes and castes and calls us to equality in a world that proclaims everyone equal but judges everyone differently. Benedict, who challenged the patriarchal society of Rome to humility, challenges our own world, too, whose heroes are Rambo and James Bond, military powers and sports stars, the macho and the violent.

Benedictine spirituality calls for depth in a world given over almost entirely to the superficial and the tinny. It offers a set of attitudes to a world that has been seduced by gimmicks and quick fixes. Benedictine spirituality offers insight and wisdom where pieties have lost meaning and asceticisms have lost favor.

Most of all, Benedictine spirituality is good news for hard times. It teaches people to see the world as good, their needs as legitimate, and human support as necessary. Benedictine spirituality doesn't call for either great works or great denial. It simply calls for connectedness. It shows us how to connect with God, with others, and with our inmost selves.

All in all, the Rule of Benedict is designed for ordinary people who live ordinary lives. It was not written for priests or mystics or hermits or ascetics; it was written by a layman for laymen. It was written to provide a model of spiritual development for the average person who intends to live life beyond the superficial or the uncaring. It is written for people with deeply spiritual sensibilities and deeply serious concerns who have no intention of setting out to escape their worlds but only to infuse their moral lights with the vision of the Divine.

The Rule of Benedict is wisdom distilled from the daily. This book is simply an account of how I, having lived this Rule in a monastic community for over thirty years, have come to understand the implications of a Benedictine spirituality for our own times. . . .

The question is, What are the spiritual values enshrined now for nearly fifteen hundred years in the Rule of Benedict and what do they have to say, if anything, to our own age and our own attempts to live calmly in the middle of chaos, productively in an arena of waste, lovingly in a maelstrom of individualism, and gently in a world full of violence? What do they have to say to us who seek answers to the great questions of life while our work overwhelms us and our debts expand, while our families vie for our attention and our friends minimize our concerns, while our politicians tell us that life is getting better when we know that, for many at least, much in life is actually getting worse. . . .

The Rule of Benedict is not a set of spiritual exercises and not a set of proscriptions and not a set of devotions and not a set of disciplines. The Rule of Benedict, in fact, is not a rule at all, in the modern sense of that word.

Where "rule" is interpreted to mean controls or laws or demands, the Rule of Benedict does not qualify for that category. On the contrary, The Rule of Benedict is simply a plan of life, a set of principles that is clearly meant to be nearer to the original meaning of the Latin word *regula,* or guide, than to the concept *lex,* or law. Law is what we have come to expect from religion; direction is what we need.

Regula, the word now translated to mean "rule," in the ancient sense meant "guidepost" or "railing," something to hang on to in the dark, something that leads in a given direction, something that points out the road, something that gives us support as we climb. The Rule of Benedict, in other words, is more wisdom than law. The Rule of Benedict is not a list of directives. The Rule of Benedict is a way of life.

And that's the key to understanding the Rule. It isn't one.

That's why it can be just as important to lay people as it is to monastics. "Listen . . . whoever you are," Benedict says in the Prologue to the Rule. *Whoever* you are.

The Rule of Benedict is simply a piece of Wisdom Literature designed to deal with the great questions of life in ways that make them understandable and present and clear and achievable.

But coming to realize that in both a church and a world that want either all law or no law at all is not easy. Formula and license are so much simpler than steady, steady attention to the quality of life we are creating as well as seeking. It is very difficult when we're young, in other words, to realize that to get where we want to go in life we must often do things we would not choose to do. To rise early in the morning to pray and read is very foreign thinking to the corporate climber who is sure that what really needs to be done is to store up sleep and conserve strength for the difficult day ahead. To the monastic mentality, though, nothing more sensible can possibly occur. Without the praying and the reading, the monastic believes, who will ever understand what the climbing is meant to reach or the achieving is all about? To halt work for prayer in the middle of a chaotic day seems, to many a young monastic whose work or study is magnetizing and good, to be sheer unreality. But years later it becomes clear that the daily process of stopping to remember what life is really all about at its *giddiest* peaks may have been the only unvarnished reality of that whole period of life.

• • •

In the monastic mind, work is not for profit. In the monastic mentality, work is for giving, not just for gaining. In monastic spirituality, other people have a claim on what we do. Work is not a private enterprise. Work is not to enable me to get ahead; the purpose of work is to enable me to get more human and to make my world more just. The questions for contemporary society and the technological age are clear: Is non-work really an ideal? What should we be doing when we are not working? And, how is work in the monastic spirit different from work done out of other perspectives?

There are two poles pulling at the modern concept of work. One pole is workaholism; the other pole is pseudocontemplation.

The workaholic does not work to live. The workaholic lives to work. The motives are often confusing and sometimes even misleading. Some workaholics give their entire lives to work because they have learned in a pragmatic culture that what they do is the only value they have. Many workaholics don't work for work's sake at all; they work

for money and more money and more money. Other workaholics work simply to avoid having to do anything else in life. Work is the shield that protects them from having to make conversation or spend time at home or broaden their social skills. Sometimes, ironically enough, work becomes the shield that enables people to get out of other work. As a result, although the workaholic often makes a very good contribution to society, it is often only at the expense of their fuller, wiser selves.

Pseudocontemplatives, on the other hand, see work as an obstacle to human development. They want to spend their hours lounging or drifting or gazing, or "processing." They work only to sustain themselves and even then as little as possible. Pseudocontemplatives say they are seeking God in mystery, but as a matter of fact they are actually missing the presence of God in the things that give meaning to life. The biggest shock of my early life in the community was to find out that novices were not permitted to go to chapel between the regular times for prayer. Were not permitted. Now what kind of a place was this? Here I was, set to get instant holiness and impress the novice mistress at the same time, but someone apparently had figured out both motives and moved to block the whole idea. In fact, they had something much better in mind for all of us. They wanted us to work. Why?

Genesis is very clear on the subject. "Then God took Adam," Scripture says, "and put him in the garden to cultivate and to care for it" (Gen 2:15). Adam was put in the garden to till it and to keep it, not to contemplate it; not to live off of it; not to lounge. Even in an ideal world, it seems, God expected us to participate in the co-creation of the world.

The early Christians, including Paul, worked to sustain themselves. "You know that these hands of mine have served both my needs and those of my companions. I have always pointed out to you that it is by such hard work that you must help the weak" (Acts 20:34–35). And the Rule is equally clear: "When they live by the works of their hands, as our fathers and the apostles did before us, then are they really monks" (RB 48:8). The Desert Monastics, too, always worked. They braided baskets for sale to support themselves and to provide something of use to others, of course, but also to avoid what the ancients called *acedia,* a kind of lethargy that made the continued efforts of the spiritual life too much for the soul that was undisciplined and unexercised.

None of the great religious figures withdrew from reality intent on rapture alone. The rapture came from making reality better. And work was the key to it all.

Work is a Christian duty. Paul's rule was "Those who would not work should not eat" (2 Thess. 3:6–12). And Benedict's rule was "Idleness is the enemy of the soul. Therefore, the monastic should have specified periods for manual labor as well as for prayerful reading . . . Even the weak and delicate should be given some work or craft" (RB 48:24).

Now those are crucial concepts. In one swift phrase, work and meditation are put on the same level in Benedict's rule. Work is not a nuisance to be avoided. Work is a gift to be given. Clearly, holiness and work are not mutually exclusive ideas. Work, on the contrary, is a necessary part of holiness in Benedictine life.

Surprisingly enough, in a document on the spiritual life, Benedict treats work first after prayer and at more length than *lectio,* the meditative reading of Scripture. There is to be no doubt about it: the monastic life is not an escape from responsibility nor is it membership in the local country club. The Benedictine is to be about tilling and keeping the garden of life in the most serious of ways. Western culture has not treated work kindly. We have a history of serfs who worked like slaves and sweatshops that robbed people of their human dignity and basic rights. We have lived in a capitalism that bred brutal competition and unequal distribution of goods as well as inventiveness and profit. We are watching the poor get poorer even while they are working. We see the rich get richer even when they don't. And we realize that the middle class must work harder every year just to stay where they were last year. What can possibly be good about all of that? That depends on the work we do and why we're doing it.

In Benedictine spirituality, work is what we do to continue what God wanted done. Work is co-creative.

Keeping a home that is beautiful and ordered and nourishing and artistic is co-creative. Working in a machine shop that makes gears for tractors is co-creative. Working in an office that processes loan applications for people who are themselves trying to make life more humane is co-creative. Working on a science project, on the other hand, whose sole intent is to destroy life makes a mockery of creation. To say that science is blind, that science is objective, that science is neutral when what you make is napalm and the components of germ warfare and plutonium trigger-fingers is to raise ethical questions of overwhelming proportions. Here Benedictine spirituality confronts the casuistry and clever moral gyrations of this time with the sign of the accusing presence of Christ. Benedictine work is intent on building the Kingdom, not on destroying it.

In Benedictine spirituality, work is purposeful and perfecting and valuable. It is not a time-filler or a money-maker or a necessary evil. We work because the world is unfinished and it is ours to develop. We work with a vision in mind. After the person with a Benedictine soul has been there, the world ought to be a little closer to the way the Kingdom will look. . . .

Time, we learned through regularity and responsibility, is the treasure that cannot be recovered and must not be taken for granted. Time is all we have to make our lives bright-colored, warm, and rich. Time spent on an artificial high is time doomed to failure. Time spent amassing what I cannot possibly use and which will not change my measure of myself even if I do use it, is time wasted. Time spent in gray, dry aimlessness is a prison of the thickest walls. But good work that leaves the world softer and fuller and better than ever before is the stuff of which human satisfaction and spiritual value are made. There will come a moment in life when we will have to ask ourselves what we spent our lives on and how life in general was better as a result of it. On that day we will know the sanctifying value of work.

Work has been one thing that our culture has done best. Every American child is encouraged to get a paying job from the age of six. We have been trained to be responsible and productive. As a result, the Western world fast became the industrial center of the world where a few people could out-farm, out-produce, and out-organize every other area of the world. But we have some serious by-products of the Puritan notion that hard work is a claim on God's blessings and a sign of God's favor as well. Success and efficiency and opportunity and elitism and alienation have marked us too. The drive for success at work, instead of success in life, continues to make people ill and to destroy marriages and to increase the level of personal dissatisfaction.

Efficiency has become a god that will accept the sacrifice of people for the sake of the production line. The days of hand-carved chairs from an artist's hands have given way to plastic molds for the sake of profit though it's clear that we need beauty and community in this world today more than we need one more product of anything. We need to learn that there are some things worth doing in life that are worth doing poorly, if doing them perfectly means we will have destroyed people for the sake of producing the product. Do we need paper clips in this world? Absolutely. Do we need to make them faster and distribute them more broadly than anyone else in the world in order to make more money than anyone else in the paper clip business? Not if it means that we must drive the workers who make them beyond their endurance and ourselves beyond the humane to do it.

Opportunity has made dilettantes of us all. We run through the candy store of life always looking for the better job and the better pay and the better office. Nothing is ever good enough in the quest for success. Instead of settling down, we work constantly with one eye on the next office, the next opening, the next promotion. Instead of being who we are where we are, we are always on our way to somewhere else in this culture. So making friends with the neighbors is not a high priority. After all, we won't be here long. Keeping the word that sold the product is of little consequence. We won't be here when the customer complains. Developing a conscience about what we do and how we do it is hardly important. By the time it fails or is uncovered we will have been long gone. And our family lives and human development will have been long gone with it.

The disassociation that comes from being only one small point on the assembly line of modern life has dulled our consciences and blinded our eyes to our own part in a world where death is our greatest export. The days are gone when the family that tilled the field also planted and harvested it together. Now owners own and planters plant and sprayers spray and pickers pick and sellers sell and none of them takes responsibility for the pesticides that reach our tables. Scientists calculate and designers design and welders weld and punchers punch and assemblers assemble and none of them takes responsibility for a nuclear world.

The implications of a Benedictine spirituality of work in a world such as this are clear, it seems:

- Work is my gift to the world. It is my social fruitfulness. It ties me to my neighbor and binds me to the future. It lights up that spark in me that is most like the God of Genesis. I tidy the garden and plant the garden and distribute the goods of the garden and know that it is good.
- Work is the way I am saved from total self-centeredness. It gives me a reason to exist that is larger than myself. It makes me part of possibility. It gives me hope. . . .

Work, it is clear from the Rule of Benedict, must not exist in a vacuum. Monastics do not exist to work. Work is to be integrated into monastic life without doing violence to either. In the Benedictine vision of life, no one dimension of life is to be exclusive. Prayer, community, and personal development are all as essential to the good life as work. And that takes a sense of holy leisure.

Scholars of the Talmud say that the Sabbath is emphasized in Genesis not to show that God needed rest, because that would be heresy, but to show that God created rest and that God demanded rest. Rest, Sabbath, the rabbis insisted, were essential to creation for three reasons.

First, they argued, the Sabbath equalized the rich and the poor. For one day a week, at least, everyone was the same. On the Sabbath, the rich could not oppress the poor or control the poor or consume the poor. On the Sabbath, rich and poor were equally free. Second, the rabbis taught, the purpose of the Sabbath was to give us time to evaluate our work as God had evaluated the work of creation to see if our work, too, was "good." Finally, the rabbis declared, the purpose of the Sabbath was to give us time to contemplate the meaning of life.

In fact, the rabbis pointed out, if one-seventh of every week is rest, then one-seventh of life is rest: 52 days a year, 3,640 days in seventy years—or ten years of sabbath, rest, and reflection in a lifetime, which are all designed to be used for reflection on meaning. Sabbath, in other words, is that period for holy leisure when I take time to look at life in fresh, new ways.

In his plan of life, Benedict set aside four hours a day for prayer, six to nine hours a day for work, seven to nine hours for sleep, about three hours for eating and rest, and three hours a day for reading and reflection time. I remember the kind of surprise that came over me when, after years in the community, I suddenly realized one morning in chapel at the daily oral reading of the Rule that Benedict wasn't saying that someone should be sent around the monastery to see if people were doing their work. He was saying that they should be sent around the monastery to see if the monastics were doing their reading and reflecting (RB 48). The community should be mindful, in other words, to see that people were taking time to live a thoughtful as well as a productive life.

Benedict's schedule, of course, is an agrarian and monastic one. It does not work for families with small children. It does not work for people who commute across large cities. It does not work for those whose workday runs from early office hours to evening appointments. But if Benedict's hours don't compute for us, his ideas are more important than ever. We may not be able to keep that particular schedule, you and I, but we must find a life rhythm that somehow satisfies each of those elements.

The question for a time of rapid transit and conference calls and triple-shift work days is balance. And the answer is balance too.

But what is balance in a society whose skewing of time has it totally off balance? What is balance in a culture that has destroyed the night with perpetual light and keeps equipment going twenty-four hours

a day because it is more costly to turn machines on and off than it is to pay people to run them at strange and difficult hours? In the first place, balance for us is obviously not a mathematical division of the day. For most of us, our days simply do not divide that easily. In the second place, balance for us is clearly not equivalence. Because I have done forty hours of work this week does not mean that I will get forty hours of prayer and leisure. What it does mean, however, is that somehow I must make time for both. I must make time, or die inside.

Leisure has two dimensions, play and rest. The Benedictine Rule does not talk about play because play was built right into sixth century life by the church calendar. One of the functions of holy days and festivals, most of which started in churches and religious communities, was to provide both the privileged and the peasants of the society with space and time for common enjoyment. On Church feasts commoners could not be required to work. Play was the Church's gift to the working class in a day before labor unions and industrialization.

Now, in this century, we even have to learn how to play. Indeed we have more opportunities for play than generations before us, but we have managed to make most of our play simply a special kind of work. We organize our ball teams into leagues and our running into races and our swimming into exercise programs and our tennis into tournaments. The movies are violent and the plays are expensive. It costs money to take children to the zoo to see animals that once could be seen in the backyard for nothing. Toys must be educational and of infinite variety. Play has become big business in the United States, and so most of America has taken to television watching instead to avoid their anxieties and their exhaustion, with the Fourth of July and the Memorial Day weekend the only recognized deviations from the anesthetizing social norm.

The notion of celebrating life as communities and families together, the underlying value of the old church feasts, is long gone. The balance of family and social recreation is becoming harder and harder to come by. The balance of work and real play, activities done for no purpose at all except the release and recapture of energy, is becoming foreign. As a consequence our souls are drying up in work and our minds are being numbed by TV nothingness. We need to learn to play again if our spiritual lives are going to be healthy at all.

But play is not the only indicator of non-work or personal growth, and it is not at all the dimension that Benedict treated. The leisure that Benedictine spirituality deals with is holy leisure, leisure that is for holy things, leisure that makes the human more human by engaging the heart and broadening the vision and deepening the insight and stretching the soul. Benedictine spirituality is more intent on developing thinking people than it is on developing pious people. It is one thing to pray prayers; it is another thing to be prayerful.

To understand leisure is to avoid being one of the lemmings of life who follow the crowd and follow the boss and follow the party line. Holy leisure asks, What is it to follow the gospel in this situation, now, here? Holy leisure means I take time to step back and ask what's going on in this, in them, in me. I take time to try to understand what the Jesus-life demands in this situation. . . .

Holy leisure, in other words, is the foundation of contemplation. There is an idea abroad in the land that contemplation is the province of those who live in cloistered communities and that it is out of reach to the rest of us who bear the noonday heat in the midst of the maddening crowd. But if that's the case, then Jesus who was followed by people and surrounded by people and immersed in people was not a contemplative. And Francis of Assisi was not a contemplative. And Teresa of Avila was not a contemplative. And Catherine of Siena was not a contemplative. And Thomas Merton was not a contemplative. And Mahatma Gandhi was not a contemplative. Obviously, some of our greatest contemplatives have been our most active and most effective people. No, contemplation is not withdrawal from the human race.

The problem is that we must learn to distinguish between purpose and meaning in life. Purpose is part of what it means to be white, Western, American. Purpose has something to do with being pro-

ductive and setting goals and knowing what needs to be done and doing it. It is easy to have purpose. To write seven letters today, to wax that floor, to finish this legal brief, to make out those reports, to complete this degree, that's purpose. Meaning, on the other hand, depends on my asking myself who will care and who will profit and who will be touched and who will be forgotten or hurt or affected by my doing those things. Purpose determines what I will do with this part of my life. Meaning demands to know why I'm doing it and with what global results.

Contemplation, therefore, is not a vacation from life. Contemplation is the pursuit of meaning. The contemplative is intent on determining the relative value of things in life. The contemplative believes that everything we do either advances or obstructs our search for meaning in life. Those who find the will of God everywhere and feel the presence of God anywhere are the real contemplatives.

Real contemplatives don't separate political morality and private morality. They know that all of life is one. Real contemplatives don't think in terms of this world and the next. They know that life is simply an ongoing process, only part of which is clear to us at any one time. Real contemplatives don't substitute daydreaming for doing the will of God. In the midst of the greatest spiritual moments in the record of humankind, Moses was sent away from the burning bush, Joseph was sent to take care of Mary, Mary Magdalene was sent to tell the apostles of the resurrection. The moment of enlightenment, it seems, comes not for itself but for the sake of the mission. Immersion in the God-life demands a response, not a rest. Real contemplatives don't spend life staring into space. That kind of contemplation can simply become a disguise for pure escape, or worse, for selfishness. Idleness is not a synonym for contemplation.

Real contemplation, in other words, is not for its own sake. It doesn't take us out of reality. On the contrary, it puts us in touch with the world around us by giving us the distance we need to see where we are more clearly. To contemplate the gospel and not respond to the wounded in our own world cannot be contemplation at all. That is prayer used as an excuse for not being Christian. That is spiritual dissipation.

Contemplation is the ability to see the world around us as God sees it. Contemplation is a sacred mindfulness of my holy obligation to care for the world I live in. Contemplation is awareness of God within me and in the people around me. Contemplation is consciousness of the real fullness of life. Contemplatives don't let one issue in life consume all their nervous energy or their hope. God is bigger than this problem at work or this irritating neighbor at home or this dependent relative in the family. God is calling me on and on and on, beyond all these partial things, to the goodness of the whole of life and my responsibility to it.

That's enlightenment. When I myself am the total square footage of my own small world, that's darkness. When my pains and my successes and my agendas are my only concern, that's darkness. When I see no larger meaning in my life than my own interests, that's darkness. But when I begin to look at life through the eyes of God, then enlightenment has finally come.

But enlightenment and contemplation, the relationship between the goals of my life and the meaning of my life, take more than wishing. Inner vision and direction can only come from keeping my heart centered on God and my mind open. That's where Benedictine spirituality is balm and blessing in a world gone wild with activity for its own sake. . . .

And so Benedict calls all of us to mindfulness. No life is to be so busy that there is no time to take stock of it. No day is to be so full of business that the gospel dare not intrude. No schedule is to be so tight that there is no room for reflection on whether what is being done is worth doing at all. No work should be so all-consuming that nothing else can ever get in: not my husband, not my wife, not my hobbies, not my friends, not nature, not reading, not prayer. How shall we ever put on the mind of Christ if we never take time to determine what the mind of Christ was then and is now, for me.

So, contemplation does not take non-work; contemplation takes holy leisure. Contemplation takes discipline. . . .

At the end of a long day, it is so much easier to curl up with the newspaper or slump in front of the TV than it is to wrestle with the Scriptures. At the beginning of a busy day, it is so much more tempting to get an early start on what won't get finished anyway than it is to stay in chapel and let the Word of God seep slowly in as a guide to the day's reality. We all tell ourselves that things are just too hectic, that what we really need is play, not holy leisure. We all say we'll do better tomorrow and then do not. We all say the schedule is too crowded and the children are too noisy and the exhaustion is too deep. But, if we do nothing to change it, the schedule just gets worse and the noise gets more unrelenting and the fatigue goes deeper into the bone. The fact is that it is our souls, not our bodies, that are tired. That fact is that we are so overstimulated and so underenergized that the same old things stay simply the same old things, always. The sense of excitement that comes with newness and freshness is gone. Only contemplation, the recognition of meaning in life, can possibly bring that kind of energy back. But that means we have to make time for ourselves for holy reading and gentle awareness and deep reflection. How else can we come to understand what relationship really means in life? How else can we hope to make sense out of the senseless? How else can we come to control what has control of us, if not by putting things in perspective and putting self in perspective and putting the God-life in perspective.

THE FOUR NOBLE TRUTHS

H. Saddhatissa

THE FIRST NOBLE TRUTH

Including a Discussion of Impermanence *(Anicca)*

Buddhism not being a revealed religion, at least not in the usual sense of the word, is based wholly on human experience. The follower of the Buddha is exhorted to believe nothing until he has experienced it and found it to be true.

We shall consider now . . . the main tenets of Buddhist philosophy. It must at all times be remembered, however, that these "truths" are not presented to the would-be Buddhist as articles of faith in which he must believe in order to be saved. They are the result of one man's search for truth and freedom, and they have been found valid by many millions who followed after him; but each individual, in so far as he is a true follower of the Buddha, must reason out each step for himself, and must in time come to experience the truth, not by hearsay but by direct knowledge during his own lifetime. Until that day of his own enlightenment, he will not be able to appreciate fully the profundity and sublimity of the Buddha's teaching.

The first truth to which the Buddha awakened on the night of the full moon of May was the truth of suffering (*dukkha*).

The most placid and happy-natured among us would admit that many things in this life are *dukkha*. There is physical and mental sickness, there is pain. There is the grief and sorrow occasioned by the loss of, or separation from, that which one loves. There is death:

> Not in the sky, nor in mid-ocean, nor in entering a mountain cave, is found that place on earth where abiding one will not be overcome by death.[1]

Those of a less contented nature might add to this list the frustration that results from not getting what one wants, or from being tied to what one hates. Who of us have not experienced the suffering attendant upon anger, who has never known fear, loneliness and despair?

Long before chemistry and physics discovered the transience and instability of matter/energy, the Buddha had "realized" the fundamental impermanence of all phenomena—including everything that a man can call his "self"; body and mind, sensations, perceptions and feelings are impermanent and subject to change. And since they are impermanent, they are un-

satisfactory, they are *dukkha*. Two thousand five hundred years before the Existential *angst* shattered the complacency of industrial Europe, Buddhist monks sat in meditation and were silently shattered by the same anguish as the knowledge arose within them that all things are in a state of flux, and that suffering is built into the very structure of existence.

The realization that existence itself is suffering, that pleasure is but "gilded pain," and that death is the only certainty—this realization has led many men into many different paths. For some the experience has been so catastrophic that only suicide or madness could release them from the memory of it. For others there has been a less dramatic but equally tragic flight into the realms of the *acte gratuit* or of *l'humeur noir*. Others have turned to drugs, to drink, to perversions or diversions of one kind and another. Some have become power maniacs, some tramps. Some have taken to gambling, others have "seen the light and been saved." The Buddha went on into the centre of the knowledge of the truth of suffering, and penetrated its cause. And this is what Buddhists call the "second noble truth": the truth of the cause of suffering.

THE SECOND NOBLE TRUTH

(Including a Discussion of *Paṭiccasamuppāda* and Rebirth)

If we are to understand, even in a rudimentary fashion, the truth of the cause of suffering, we must touch upon and attempt to unravel some of the most complex and subtle aspects of the Buddha's teaching. We shall have to consider, for example, the "chain of dependent origination" and the doctrine of rebirth.

Starting with the experiential fact of the transient and unsatisfactory nature of human existence, the Buddha set out to discover the implications of that impermanence and the cause of that unease. He found that the two threads were intertwined and interdependent. It is through failure to realize the truth of impermanence, through grasping at the "constant flux" as though it were something stable, that man is caught up in the whirlpool of suffering.

[1] Dh., v. 128.

The chain of interdependent links that binds men to the wheel of suffering is called *Paṭiccasamuppāda*. This is a cycle of causation; Buddhism posits no first cause but a series of interconnected links in a (vicious) circle from which there is no apparent escape.

The doctrine of *paṭiccasamuppāda* (dependent origination) is one of the most subtle teachings in the scriptures of the world; the Buddha himself claimed:

> Profound indeed is this teaching of *paṭiccasamup-pāda*. . . . It is through not understanding and penetrating this doctrine that beings have become entangled like a matted ball of thread.[2]

To penetrate the doctrine of *paṭiccasamuppāda* is to penetrate to the very core of existence. All we shall attempt to do here is to present an outline of the teaching in as simple terms as possible. As we grow older, more experienced and, we hope, wiser, new depths of the teaching and new possibilities of interpretation will become apparent.

• • •

The first-named link in the chain is ignorance—the failure to realize the truth, the lack of insight into the reality of things. In this soil of delusion subconscious impulses or drives arise. Because of our basic ignorance, these drives are not recognized for what they are—impermanent and illusory—but are allowed to flourish and bear fruit. Finally, though still unrecognized, they erupt into the conscious mind. Consciousness, as unenlightened as the subconscious drives from which it arose, immediately begins to classify and arrange. Instead of the "constant flux," consciousness posits a stable world of identifiable things. This world of "ten thousand things" impinges on our senses, and forthwith an emotional reaction is produced. We find the experience pleasant or unpleasant or we "couldn't care less" and sink back into sleep. This emotional reaction creates a craving; if the experience is pleasant we seek it out, if unpleasant we recoil from it. Out of this craving arises clinging as we lapse into the habit

of grabbing or of rejecting. Our response is no longer attuned to the stimulus, which may in fact have ceased to please or displease us, but we continue to cling to it because it is familiar. In this way we are led on towards a new situation but still encumbered with the attitudes of the past. The new situation arises, comes to maturity, decays and passes away. We are back where we started. The experience has taught us nothing. All it has done for us is to add another thread to the rope that binds us to the wheel of suffering.

This terrifying prospect—worthy of the imaginative art of the middle ages—of man, blind and naked, spinning on a wheel of torment, might well prompt us to jump off the wheel by means of suicide. But here we are checked abruptly by the doctrine of rebirth. Suicide will not enable us to jump off the wheel; we are tied to it beyond death.

During the night of his enlightenment the Buddha experienced two aspects of rebirth. He reviewed his own previous lives and he witnessed the arising and passing away of others. The doctrine of dependent origination itself is usually taught, at least in the East, as a description of the process whereby one life is linked to the next. We must be careful here to distinguish between transmigration and rebirth. Transmigration posits a soul that migrates from one life to another. Rebirth does not speak of a soul nor of any "thing" passing over.

During one lifetime we fondly imagine that we and our world are stable. Despite the obvious examples of change and decay, of erratic feelings and unpredictable moods, despite the process of growth and decline, despite the microscopic experiments of scientists, we continue to behave as though we were something permanent, something identifiable and "real." The Buddha's answer to this attitude was to ask: Where is the "I"? Is it the body? Is it the feelings? Is it the will? or the mind? Nowhere can be found a permanent identity. What then "passes over" after death?

The reply is simple yet unexpected. Life is a constant flux. What we recognize as one lifetime is merely a specific manifestation of this flux. At death the pattern is disturbed but the flux continues. If we try to jump off the wheel by committing suicide we

---

[2]D., II, p. 55; S., II, p. 92, iv, p. 158.

merely interrupt one manifestation of flux. In so far as "we" existed before, we continue to exist.

The various schools of Buddhism have elaborated different explanations of the way in which the patterns, established during one lifetime, are interrupted at death, reform and re-establish themselves. It may be that the moment of death is followed immediately by the rebirth moment. It may be that there is an intervening period during which the patterns have time to recluster themselves and form new combinations. But just as we cannot destroy the energy mass that we call our body—though we crush it, burn it or blow it to pieces—so we cannot destroy the other aspects of "our" life: mind with its feelings, sensations, etc. The flux continues, the chain of dependent origination remains unbroken, the cause of suffering persists—whether we will or not.

The second noble truth is the truth of the cause of suffering. Briefly that cause is craving: craving for sensual satisfaction, craving for existence, craving for non-existence. Freud was remarkably close to Buddhist classifications when he defined the basic human drives as libido and morbido. Conjoined with craving is delusion. These two root-causes breed the illusion of possession: this is my house, my reputation, my life. We grasp at an illusion and run chasing after it "down the days and down the nights," dreaming and waking, from one life to the next.

THE THIRD NOBLE TRUTH

(Including a Discussion of *Anattā*)

The Buddha said: I teach but two things—*dukkha* and the release from *dukkha*.[3] The third noble truth is the truth of the cessation of *dukkha*. It has been said that if you hurl a stick and hit a dog, a dog will snarl at the stick and attack it; if you hurl a stick at a lion, the lion will ignore the stick and attack you. A similar comparison was drawn by the Buddha between the teachings of others and his own teaching; other religions have attacked the symptoms, spread-

ing a salve of one kind or another on the raw wound of human suffering; the teaching of the Buddha, on the other hand, maintains that only by the eradication of the cause of *dukkha* can a state be reached in which *dukkha,* no longer arises.

This state, the state of the non-arising of *dukkha,* is called *Nibbāna.*[4]

Nibbāna defies description in the same way as does "the kingdom of heaven" of the *Gospel according to St. Thomas.* It has been called the deathless, the other shore. Being uncompounded, it is not subject to the three characteristics of all compounded things: impermanence, *dukkha* and substancelessness. It is compared to the wind. "*Nibbāna* is uncompounded; it is made of nothing at all. One cannot say of *Nibbāna* that it arises or that it does not arise, or that it is to be produced, or that it is past or future or present, or that it is cognizable by the eye, ear, nose, tongue or body." It is, however, cognizable by the mind.

There are two extremes which one must avoid in trying to *understand* the concept of *Nibbāna.* Firstly, one must avoid comparing *Nibbāna* with any kind of personal god. The doctrine of no-self, which we mentioned in . . . in connection with an individual human life, applies too in connection with *Nibbāna.* Even the uncompounded, the deathless *Nibbāna* is *anattā*—without a self. *Nibbāna,* though not bound by the phenomenal world of suffering, is not separate from it. The other pitfall to be avoided is to identify the attainment of *Nibbāna* with annihilation. Here we should refer the reader to the discussion on suicide; just as there is no "self" that can jump off the wheel, so there is no self that can be annihilated by the attainment of *Nibbāna. Nibbāna* is the non-arising of all conditioned states; there will no longer be any "being" swept away on the round of suffering.

The fourth noble truth outlines the practical means by which *Nibbāna* is to be realized; but be-

---

[3]M., I, p. 140.

[4]*Nibbāna* is a Pali term (*Nirvana* in Sanscrit); literally, it means "blowing out" or "extinction." For Buddhism, it is the extinction of suffering, the freedom from desire and illusion, the Ultimate Reality, the Absolute Truth, total liberation, and, in any case, a state beyond words (Eds.).

fore announcing it the Buddha cleared away certain misconceptions which were current at the time and which had proved a serious hindrance in the quest for truth. In the first discourse after his Enlightenment, delivered to the five disciples who had deserted him when he abandoned the path of self-mortification, he explained that there are two extreme courses to be avoided; on the one hand that of excessive sensual indulgence, which is unprofitable and ignoble, and on the other the practice of extreme physical asceticism, which is painful, impure, vain and unprofitable.

In contrast to these stands "The Middle Path" which the Buddha discovered; the Path which enables one to see and to know, which leads to peace, to discernment, to full knowledge, to *Nibbāna.*

THE FOURTH NOBLE TRUTH

(Including a Discussion of *Kamma/Vipāka*)

The fourth noble truth is the truth of the way leading to the cessation of suffering; it is a map of the path to *Nibbāna.* It has been said of *Nibbāna* that it is causeless, that it is not born of *kamma,*[5] but the way leading to the realization of Nibbana is subject to the law of cause and effect.

Here we must digress a little to discuss some of the salient points of the Buddhist doctrine of *kamma/vipāka*—the interdependence of cause and effect.

The Buddhist path to liberation is built on the universal law—which to the Buddha and to many who came after him, was an experienced fact—of the interdependence of cause and effect. Nothing, according to the Buddhist view, arises without a cause. The doctrine of *kamma/vipāka* cuts firmly across the controversy between fatalism and free will. We are con-

ditioned by all that we have been, by all that has been said, thought or done in countless previous lives; yet in this present moment we are, consciously or unconsciously, determining the future. Our life now, at this very moment, is both the *vipāka* of the past and the *kamma* of the future. The *kamma/vipāka* law explains why Buddhism is often referred to as the teaching of the here and now. For here and now is the only sphere in which man can influence—and may eventually interrupt—the chain of *kamma/vipāka.*

The intricate interplay of the myriad strands of *kamma/vipāka,* some reinforcing each other, some counterbalancing, some fading, some waxing strong, is said to have been one of the meditational experiences which arose in the mind of the Buddha during the night of his Enlightenment.

In Buddhist terminology all thought, action and speech is said to be rooted in one of two types of consciousness—*kusala* or *akusala,* wholesome or unwholesome. If the root is generosity, compassion or insight, the resultant act constitutes wholesome *kamma* and will produce correspondingly beneficial effects. If the root is greed, hatred or delusion, unwholesome *kammic* acts result, leading to undesirable effects. The initial function of the "way leading to the cessation of suffering" is to help one to eliminate unwholesomely rooted *kamma* and begin to cultivate those states of mind which will bring only beneficial results. It has been frequently pointed out, however, that one cannot in this teaching expect quick returns; although our present actions may be reasonably, even uncomfortably, "wholesome," we may find ourselves overwhelmed by misfortunes and distress; this does not disprove the law of *kamma/vipāka,* however, nor is it an excuse for returning to our old comfortable rut. Our present distress is but the effect (*vipāka*) of the past, and in order to forestall its recurrence in the future we need to consider what crop we are now sowing.

The path leading to the release from suffering is said to be eight-fold. These are not consecutive steps. The eight factors are interdependent and must be perfected simultaneously, the fulfilment of one factor being unlikely without at least the partial development of the others. These eight factors are:

---

[5] *Kamma,* in Pali, and *karma,* in Sanskrit, in its most general sense means all good and bad actions. *Kamma* is neither fatalism nor a doctrine of predetermination. The past influences the present, for *kamma* is past as well as present. The past and present influence the future—in this life or in the life to come. The Buddha has said: "It is mental volition, O monks, that I call *kamma.* Having willed, one acts through body, speech or mind." (A., III, p. 415.)

1. sammā diṭṭhi	right understanding or views
2. sammā saṅkappa	right thought or motives
3. sammā vācā	right speech
4. sammā kammanta	right action
5. sammā ājīva	right means of livelihood
6. sammā vāyāma	right effort
7. sammā sati	right mindfulness
8. sammā samādhi	right concentration

It is important to realize that the word *sammā* prefixing each of the eight factors has a wide range of meaning. In this context it can mean right as opposed to wrong, or it can, in the developed follower of the path, come to mean completed or perfected.

The initial task of one wishing to follow the eight-fold path is to observe oneself carefully and see which factors have already been developed to a certain extent and which are still in a very rudimentary condition. (Some people, for example, have developed their thinking faculty but their ability to communicate with other people is almost non-existent. Others, on the contrary, find it easy to form relationships but have an undeveloped reflective faculty.) The weak aspects of character or of life will then have to be brought into balance and harmony with the strong.

We shall proceed now to consider each factor of the path in turn. Our method will be similar to that employed in connection with the doctrine of *paticcasamuppāda,* and a similar warning must be given. The interpretations here are suggestions only. As with every other philosophical "truth," the truth of the way to the cessation of suffering will have little meaning or relevance if it is studied coldly and objectively; but as each factor is quietly reviewed and gradually assimilated into daily life, some of its value and depth will begin to be appreciated.

1. Sammā diṭṭhi (right understanding or views) in the initial stages of one's practice of the path need mean little more than a vague recognition that "all is not what it seems." Right understanding implies in the first instance having seen through the delusion that material security automatically brings peace of mind, or that ceremonies and ritual can wipe out the effects of a past act. Gradually, as the

path is perfected, right views, based on knowledge, replace the previous delusions or superstitions that were based on ignorance and lack of insight.

The first factor of the path is then concerned with the contents of the mind. In order to develop this factor one must cease to think mechanically, and begin to question one's previous assumptions, until all erroneous views have been replaced by views based on an understanding of things as they really are.

One must see life as it is, in accordance with its three characteristics of impermanence (*anicca*), dissatisfactoriness (*dukkha*) and egolessness (*anattā*); one must possess a clear understanding of the nature of existence, of the moral law, of the factors and component elements that go to make up *samsārd.*[6] In short, one must have a clear understanding of *paticcasamuppāda* and the Four Noble Truths. On the basis of understanding these facts one can perceive the causes of the vicissitudes of life.

2. Sammā saṅkappa, usually translated as right thought or right motives, seems to apply to the emotional basis of thought rather than to thinking itself. As the first factor of the path is concerned with the content and direction of thought, the second factor is concerned with the quality of the drive behind the thinking.

It is quite possible, and even at present quite fashionable, to hold opinions that would be called by a Buddhist "right views," and yet the emotional drive behind those views may not be "right" at all. It is possible, for example, to be driven by an unrecognized fear of involvement to adopt the view that "all is impermanent." Similarly a pathological inability to relax or to enjoy oneself can lead one to grasp at the view that "all is suffering"—the fault being thereby shifted from within to without. The doctrine that there is no permanent, abiding soul or personal identity can easily find favour with one who has never succeeded in forming a satisfactory relationship with another—or with himself. The development of "right thought" implies gradually uncovering and resolving

---

[6]*Samsara* is the cycle of existence, in contrast to Nirvana. It is the illusory struggle to find happiness through control of the external world (Eds.).

these unrecognized drives. It implies weeding out the "unwholesome" roots and encouraging the "wholesome" roots of generosity and unselfishness, kindness and compassion, wisdom and insight.

Sammā saṅkappa (right thought or motives) is that quality of consciousness wherein there is no obstruction to the thought processes. Sometimes, although to an observer one may seem to be reasoning logically and clearly, one is dimly aware of an emotional block that is in fact controlling the direction of one's reasoning and preventing it from penetrating beyond a certain point. *Sammā saṅkappa* is the absence of all such emotional obstructions. It denotes a state of consciousness that is limpid, clear, cool, free from the limiting considerations of self-interest, without tension or veiled uneasiness.

This means that one's mind should be pure, free from carnal "thirst" (*rāga*), malevolence (*vyāpāda*), cruelty (*vihiṃsā*) and the like. At the same time, one should be willing to relinquish anything that obstructs one's onward march.

3. Sammā vācā (right speech). By not indulging in, or listening to, lying, back-biting, harsh talk and idle gossip, we can establish a connecting link between "right thought" and "right action." *Sammā vācā* is free from dogmatic assertions and from hypnotic suggestions; it is an instrument whereby one can learn and teach, comfort and be comforted. We are practising right speech when we use conversation as a means of coming to know people, to understand them and ourselves. This last sentence may seem a little ridiculous if looked at superficially: What else, one might ask, could conversation be used for? Yet one has only to sit in a bus or train and listen to the "conversations" going on around to realize that they are very rarely examples of right speech. Most so-called conversations are a series of interrupted monologues: each member of the group speaks more or less in order, but no one listens or makes any attempt to respond.

The practice of this third factor of the path implies a gradual but radical change in our use of language. At the time the eight-fold path was expounded the spoken word was the main medium of communication; but what is here set down as "right speech" could now be interpreted as "right communication"—whether that take the form of radio or TV programmes, advertising material, newspapers, magazines or books. The development of *sammā vācā* should lead to a gradual refining of our use of all forms of communication. We shall come to realize the destructive nature of hypnotic TV advertisements, sensational newspaper articles and escapist literature of all kinds. We shall come to realize the dangers as well as the immense potential value of conversation.

Right speech, then, means using the various modes of communication to further our search for understanding and insight.

It would not only be characterized by wisdom but also by kindness. Right speech should not be unduly excitable, not prompted by infatuation or selfish interests. It should not be such as to inflame the passions.

The person of right speech has been explained by the Buddha as follows:

> He avoids lying. He speaks the truth. Wherever he may be he never knowingly speaks a lie, either for the sake of his own advantage, or for the sake of another person's advantage, or for the sake of any advantage whatsoever. He avoids tale bearing. What he has heard here, he does not repeat there, so as to cause dissension there; and what he has heard there, he does not repeat here, so as to cause dissension here. Thus he unites those that are divided; and those that are united, he encourages. Concord gladdens him, he delights and rejoices in concord; and it is concord that he spreads by his words. He avoids harsh language. He speaks such words as are gentle, soothing to the ear, loving, such words as go to the heart, and are courteous and friendly, and agreeable to many. He avoids vain talk. He speaks at the right time, in accordance with facts, speaks what is useful, speaks of the law and the discipline; his speech is like a treasure, uttered at the right moment, accompanied by arguments, moderate and full of sense.[7]

> He uses such speech which is harmless, pleasant to the ear, agreeable, touching the heart, courteous, delightful to many and pleasant to many. This one is called "the honey-tongued."[8]

---

[7]A., v, p. 264 f.
[8]*Ibid.,* I, p. 128.

4. Sammā kammanta (right action). This involves much more than just keeping the precepts. In the early stages of the practice of the path, keeping the precepts will probably require such an effort that there will be little energy left for any more advanced development of right action. Gradually, however, as the unwholesome patterns are weakened and we begin to build up some positive virtues, the further implications of *sammā kammanta* can be considered.

Right action is any action that proceeds from an unobstructed mind. Whereas morality, in the usual sense of the word, can be practised by one who is blind to the motives behind this behaviour right action is impossible without a clear and deep understanding.

The *path* of right action involves abstaining from unwholesome *kamma* and performing only those actions which will lead to beneficial results. The *goal* of right action, however, is to transcend even *kusala* (wholesome) *kamma,* for once the enlightenment experience has arisen in life, actions will cease to produce any *kammic* results, harmful or beneficial. The *Upanishads* put it slightly differently: "Only actions done in God bind not the soul of man,"[9] but the meaning is similar. Although for many years and perhaps for many lifetimes we shall have to strive to develop the fourth factor in the sense of "wholesome practices," when once the path has been fully perfected, actions will no longer have any binding effect, will no longer form part of the *kamma/vipāka* chain.

5. Sammā ājīva (right means of livelihood). The simplest interpretation of this factor of the path is based on the five precepts. Conscientious observance of the five precepts automatically vetos certain trades and professions. The first precept—not to harm living things—requires that we do not earn our living by means of butchering cattle, dealing in flesh, fishing, hunting and so forth. Neither may one make or use weapons, nor engage in any form of warfare. Similarly the fifth precept—not to in-

dulge in drinks or drugs that tend to cloud the mind—prevents us not only from trafficking in drugs, but also from engaging in the manufacture or distribution of alcohol. This straightforward interpretation of *sammā ājīva* makes a very useful beginning, but it is only a beginning. As soon as we delve a little deeper into the concept of right livelihood, a host of problems and further shades of meaning becomes apparent.

We shall list a few of the problems, without attempting to give any answers. The reader, if he tries to practise this factor of the path, will evolve his own answers—and, of course, an infinite number of further questions. Among the problems raised by an attempt to practice *sammā ājīva* are:

1. whether one can support, by working, paying taxes and accepting benefits, a government which is engaged in warfare, or actively preparing for it;
2. whether, in the name of the relief of human suffering, one can engage in medical research that involves sacrificing the lives of countless animals; and, more subtly, whether one can prescribe, sell—or even use—those drugs which have been discovered and tested by means of such experiments;
3. whether one has the right to destroy disease-bearing insects, or work in the preparation of materials for that purpose;
4. whether the third and fourth precepts would prohibit one from working in advertising or mass production work.

The list is endless. The questions are all ones that can only be answered by careful analysis of the circumstances, the motives and the attitudes of the people involved.

Even if one manages more or less to avoid the wrong means of livelihood, the problems are not yet over. *Sammā ājīva* implies much more than the mere avoiding of wrong means of livelihood. It implies a careful weighing up of our attributes and potentialities, and the selecting of a job that will use the talents we have and at the same time help to develop our weak points.

---

[9]Isopaniṣad, v. 2.

Briefly, then, we might say that the fifth factor of the path requires us to stop and consider how and why we are spending our working hours. It requires us to take time to think out and find some means of occupation which will be conducive to our own growth and development and which will, if possible, be beneficial to others. If a job helps us in our search for an understanding both of ourselves and of the world around us then it is, for us, *sammā ājīva*—no matter how futile and crazy it may seem to our friends and neighbours.

6. Sammā vāyāma (right effort). Although the canonical division of right effort into four categories seems at first sight to be rather pedantic and meaningless it has, if one studies it more closely, a sound practical and psychological validity. The four-fold division of right effort consists of:

1. the effort to cut off unwholesome states that have already arisen;
2. the effort to prevent the arising of unwholesome states that have not yet arisen;
3. the effort to preserve wholesome states that have already arisen;
4. the effort to encourage wholesome states that have not yet arisen.

Right effort requires the development of insight, intuition and will power. We need to develop insight in order to perceive which of the states of mind habitually present are to be preserved and which are to be weeded out. We need to develop intuition so that we can gauge when we are sailing close to a hitherto unknown state of mind and whether we should go ahead or withdraw from it.

This sixth factor, though dependent on insight and intuition, is primarily concerned with the development of the will. Buddhism insists on the development of wisdom rather than of will power; nevertheless it recognizes the need for the latter and provides scope for the perfecting of it in this factor of the path. Without the constant and deliberate practice of right effort, no sure progress can be made.

7. Sammā sati (right mindfulness) is the pivotal factor of the path. Without it none of the other factors can be brought to completion. Right mindful-

ness serves too as a control over the other factors, preventing the excessive development of one at the expense of the others. In Christian terminology *sammā sati* might be translated as "the practice of the presence of God"; it implies gradually extending one's awareness until every action, thought and word is performed in the full light of consciousness.

The practice of mindfulness has been described under four headings known as the four foundations of mindfulness, *satipaṭṭhāna*. Firstly, mindfulness of the body: this consists in becoming gradually more aware of the body. We can begin this practice by trying to watch the various changes in the postures of the body—lying, sitting, standing, walking. Care must be taken to be neither too objective nor too subjective; we are not being asked to look at our bodies as "things" moving puppet-like before the watching mind; nor are we asked to "feel" very acutely every movement and gesture. What is required rather is that we try to live here and now "in our bodies." This may seem a bizarre request, but once we try to experience this state we realize how rarely in fact we are "living in our bodies," how rarely we are aware of the movements of our limbs and the interplay of muscles. Mindfulness of the body can be practised too by watching the breath flowing in and out of the nostrils, by listening to sound impinging on the ear, not pausing to name and pass judgement on them, but just noting their arising and passing away. We can learn to become aware of the taste and texture of food, not after the manner of the gourmet or the connoisseur, not for the sake of becoming an expert in the detection of spices or in the selection of wines, but simply in order to intensify our awareness, noting the order and intensity of sensations, the variety of flavours, temperatures, colours, etc.

For some, and particularly for the intellectual types, mindfulness of the body is at first difficult. It is difficult to know what it is all about, what in fact one is supposed to be doing. But once we begin to get the feel of it, it becomes very simple. We forget about it of course, maybe for hours on end, then suddenly the memory returns, and we begin again. "Happy is he who dwells mindful of the body," it has been said. Whenever we become tense, nervous, exhausted, if we can remember the "feel" of mindfulness of the body and re-establish it, the tension and weariness dissolve.

When we find ourselves becoming too relaxed and complacent, then is the time to move on to the second foundation of mindfulness. (Not that the four are to be practised in strictly water-tight compartments, but it is probably wisest to become fairly conversant with one before setting out on the next.) Mindfulness of the feelings requires us to take up a similarly quiet and detached attitude towards our feelings as towards our bodies. By feelings is meant here the emotional reaction that follows any stimulus: pleasure, pain or indifference. We can watch this reaction occurring in response to both physical and mental stimuli. A warm wind blows, the reaction is pleasant; our pride is trampled on, the reaction is painful; we succeed in accomplishing a difficult task, the reaction is pleasant; we get angry about something, the reaction is painful; etc., etc. Again we must be careful not to adopt an objective, mechanistic attitude towards feelings; that would be as erroneous as our old method of clinging passionately to them. What is required is that we watch the arising and the passing away of each feeling—without trying to hold on to it, if it is pleasant, or trying to hurry it away, if it is unpleasant. Gradually we find that our sense of perspective is developing; we no longer identify ourselves with each fleeting feeling or let it carry us away to say or do things that we later regret. It is not at all a question of suppressing any feelings that arise—that would be completely at variance with the practice of mindfulness. But we watch each feeling arise, and, without tampering with it, let it pass away.

Mindfulness of the mind seems to be something of a tautology, yet it is perfectly feasible. In this third foundation of mindfulness we watch the constantly changing quality of the state of mind. Now the mind is joyful, limpid, enthusiastic; now it has become clouded over, sullen, lethargic; now it is sentimental, now reflective, now angry, now compassionate. Always the same advice: watch, do not tamper, allow each state to come and go unimpeded. . . .

8. *Sammā samādhi.* Right concentration or meditation is the last factor of the path leading to the cessation of suffering. Meditation and its counterpart in daily life—mindfulness (*sati*)—form together the essence of the Buddha's teaching. . . .

It has been said of the mind that it is like a pool. Too often that pool is agitated and muddy, reflecting nothing but its own turbidity. Buddhist meditation is designed to quieten the mind until it becomes perfectly still. Then the deep recesses of the pool can be seen clearly, and it will reflect a true picture of whatever is presented to it. There are many hindrances in the way of one who seeks to quieten the mind in this way: violent emotions of desire or of hatred, restlessness and discontent, hesitation and doubt, laziness, weariness and sloth. Meditation manuals list the different obstacles that are likely to arise and explain how each one can be dealt with.

Sammā samādhi (right concentration) should not be equated with what the Christian Church calls meditation. Certain elements are, of course, similar, but *sammā samādhi* includes also those states which the Christian would call contemplation rather than meditation. Whether Buddhist *samādhi* goes even beyond contemplation as it is known to the Christian Church—though not, of course, to some of its mystics—or whether it falls short of that goal, is for each one of us to decide, in the light of our own experience.

NAVAJO WAYS OF KNOWING

Herbert John Benally

Traditional Navajo wisdom recognizes spirituality as the foundation of all knowledge necessary for achieving harmony, or *hózhǫ́,* the Beauty Way of Life. This foundation is as relevant today as it ever was, and could serve as the basis of an approach to teaching which avoids the separation of secular and spiritual knowledge that characterizes Western society. The connection between that separation and the problems of contemporary life is apparent, and calls for a close re-examination of this traditional wisdom. The Navajo organized their knowledge, as well as their life activities, around the parts of the day and the four cardinal directions. This system of organization was placed by the Holy People in the primordial era. At that time the gods laid the foundation of this world with grandfathers and grandmothers fire, water, air, and soil. Around that foundation they placed the four different lights and four forms of sacred knowledge which would regulate man and all life's activities. With the dawn they placed "that which gives direction to life" (*bik'ehgo da'iináanii*) and with the blue twilight they placed "sustenance" (*nihigááł*). "The gathering of family" (*aha'áná'oo'nííł*) was placed with the yellow evening twilight and "rest, contentment and respect for creation" (*háá'ayííh, sihasin dóó hodílzin*) was placed with the darkness. "All of these things placed will direct all lives from here on," it was said.

I. BIK'EHGO DA'IINÁANII

The first area of knowledge, "that which gives direction to life," emphasizes character development, particularly excellence of heart and mind. This encompasses all knowledge which enables the individual to make intelligent decisions whenever a choice involving values is to be made. Just as dawn brings light, this area of knowledge brings clarity and perspective to the mind, permeating all aspects of one's life. This area of learning includes beliefs, self-discipline, and values that provide standards of behavior and give meaning to life.

The Navajo believe that the gods pass over the country at dawn. If an individual is up and about he will be blessed by them with health and prosperity. Corn pollen is usually offered to these gods and a petition extended to them at this time. It was believed that the things which they petitioned for became part of one's thoughts, planning, teaching and life. In time the petitioner becomes one with his prayer. It was important to pray. It helped one to organize the priorities in his life and to clarify his

thinking. His spirituality was recognized as the source of both his strength and his enlightenment.

It was also believed that one should get up at dawn and run. To the elders this was not just a physical exercise but an activity that brought about physical, mental and spiritual well-being. By running at dawn one disciplines and strengthens his mind in order to be in control in all situations. With a well-developed constitution he can overcome any adversity that may arise.

Another way of establishing a strong foundation is by listening to the wisdom of the elders and keeping their words close to one's heart. "If things are to be it's up to you," "remember the young and the old and those yet to be born," and "stability comes from a clear purpose for being" are some of the teachings that have survived. This wisdom has been passed from generation to generation and finds roots in one's being, becoming the source of strength throughout one's life.

The dawn provides the blueprint for building a good life. It is the source of fortitude, sound teaching, standards of conduct and appreciation for life. Without the guiding principles provided by the dawn there would be no standards by which people could evaluate the effectiveness of their thoughts and actions. They would be unable to fully experience life or to develop a genuine appreciation for themselves, others and nature. They would run the risk of falling into great disharmony, hunger, illness, poverty and other social ills which are so prevalent today.

II. NIHIGÁÁL

The second area of knowledge, associated with the blue twilight, is sustenance. This area focuses on obtaining self-reliance, providing for the family and being a contributing member of the community. To achieve these goals one must recognize work in all its dimensions including the ethical, vocational, social and environmental. All of these areas are connected and interdependent. For instance, traditional Navajo wisdom views objects of material wealth as having spirit and personality. There is a Navajo saying, "*Yódí dóó nitl'iz soosáadoo,*" "May the spirit of all good things show favor upon me." Attracting these good spirits requires a certain attitude and personality. They come to the person who exercises prudence, order, industry, patience and kindness, and most importantly, to one who is prayerful. These qualities are all founded on the principle of receiving and giving. Sharing promotes happiness, while excessiveness inclines one toward evil. Conversely, when one sleeps late he attracts the being of poverty and his cousins—hunger, shame, apathy, disorder and ignorance. The good spirits will avoid a house that is disorganized, where vulgar and abusive language is used and where there is idleness.

Another aspect of sustenance involves learning how to work and becoming responsible. Children learn specific skills "on the job" well before they are able to understand the nature of the work or the responsibility involved. It was said that the livestock teach the child dependability, resourcefulness and responsibility. For example, when a sheep is lost the child is sent back to find it. The job was not considered complete until every sheep was accounted for. This might sometimes be a hard lesson but was absolutely necessary for adult life. Elders would advise parents to "Teach the children while they are yet tender and when their minds can still be bent and shaped like a young willow" and remind them that "It is harder when their minds have formed. Instill in them appropriate habits and they will discover reasons for their behavior when they come of age."

Cooperation was the basis of Navajo communal existence. On the other hand, competition was never foreign to the Navajo—in fact, it was the basis of their traditional games. However, making competition a part of one's life was frowned upon because it led to pride, which was considered an evil. Everyone was expected to come to the aid of their neighbors in time of need. "My people are my insurance" was how one woman put it when describing the events surrounding the loss of a loved one. Her people had come from miles around to console her and to help her with the substantial expenses with which she was faced. Helping in Navajo society was an opportunity to show the person being helped respect and regard.

The elders watch the stars, particularly Pleiades, the . . . "seeds of all kinds." They were instructed to watch this constellation in order to know when to start planting. The community performs a blessing on the seeds when . . . the "seeds of all kinds" set in the west. During the seed blessing ceremony, offerings are made at sacred places to the gods for moisture and for a good harvest. The seeds which had been blessed are then planted. Everyone worked together as a single unit to plant and harvest. When the harvest and winter storage were completed a special ceremony of thanksgiving was made to the gods.

Work, which is central to the blue twilight, is a life-sustaining principle. It is essential for obtaining and preserving one's dignity. Dignity and respectability are not possible unless a person is able to provide for his family and help those that need assistance. The worker understands that material possessions are based upon the principles of giving and receiving, and of industry and integrity. He is a skilled provider who understands the forces of nature and is able to use them to his benefit. He understands that cooperation within the community is the key to assuring the general welfare of the community. In order to maintain prosperity he continues to offer prayers for blessings and thanksgiving to the creators, who are the source of sustenance. A person who is ignorant or neglectful of these principles invites poverty, apathy, health problems and discord in the family and community.

III. AHA'ÁNAÁ'OO'NÍÍT

The third category of knowledge is associated with the yellow evening twilight. It focuses on *k'é,* a term which encompasses emotional ties and relationships associated with the family, extended family, community, nation as a whole, and the natural environment. The term *k'é* in Navajo conveys love, cherishing, caring, esteem, as well as the simple acknowledgment of the inherent value of others.

This learning begins at home. One of the teachings within our tribe centers on the relationship between husband and wife. A primary source for this teaching comes from the relationship between Father Sky and

Mother Earth. When the plants, animals, seasons and constellations were completed and ready to be put into motion, Mother Earth is said to have asked, "Who will be responsible for all of these creations and their movements?" The Holy People replied that this responsibility will be placed in the hands of Sky Father. He will awake and put all things in motion. In the spring he will awaken you with thunder from your rest and with his help you will make all things grow and mature. In the fall he will once again sound the thunder, his scepter of leadership, at which time your work will be completed and you will rest. Father Sky then covers Mother Earth with a white blanket for the winter months. His primary work begins and woe to those who have been lazy and unprepared. Cold and hunger will find them and teach them the value of industry and preparation.

Mother Earth, the prototypical mother, is gentle and kind—no one who truly understands the nature of things must suffer from cold or hunger during the summer months. She nurtures and strengthens all living things and prepares them for the future. She follows the lead of her husband Father Sky. Father Sky exemplifies fatherhood, which includes unwavering leadership, tenderness toward Mother Earth, sternness in teaching, and gentleness to those of his children who are industrious and prepared.

Our elders taught that a man carries his shield on his left arm, protecting his family, his beliefs, his land and his freedom. The mother carries her cooking utensils in her right hand to represent her shield against hunger, illness and other adversities. Between the two parents a great deal of security is provided to the children from which they can achieve maturity. It is the weak, undisciplined and immature parent who does not understand what is required in the role of a parent who leaves the children in darkness, hunger, cold, to be ravaged by all manner of afflictions.

Appreciation for all that is included in the concept of *k'é* originates within the home where kinship terms, rather than names, are generally used to address family members. It is very difficult to translate the expression of endearment that these terms convey into another tongue. Kinship relationship terms communicate and reinforce an acceptance and a sense of belonging and caring to the person to whom they are

directed. For example, the word that the mother uses with her children is *shee'awee shiyazhi,* my dear little one. Notice in these kinship expressions the word "my": my child, my sister, my mother, my grandfather, etc. The kinship terms are not just empty expressions, but living words that lie at the foundation of self-esteem. When terms of endearment are absent a gray area of doubt emerges in the mind of the young person regarding acceptance and belonging. The loneliness, alienation and rejection felt by the young person may become contributing factors in the young person trying to seek acceptance in negative ways.

The use of appropriate kinship terms between siblings and other family members defines their respective roles and encourages positive family ties. I have personally observed that children in a family that uses kinship terms to address each other tend to get along much better than children in families where personal names are used.

The Navajo family system employs a hierarchical structure in which people are recognized according to their age. With maturity comes the responsibility to care, to teach and to set an example for those that are younger. The younger were obligated to respect and obey those that were older. It reflected very poorly on both the older and younger sibling when they argued. This system of relating remained with the individual throughout his life. One is not necessarily respected simply on the basis of how much he may have or what he can do. Respect is primarily based on age. When we use personal names we become equals, and being at the same level seems to encourage competition and bickering. The two systems can be compared by observing that one encourages respect and cooperation and the other conflict and competition.

A child's identity is based on his immediate family and clan membership. He represents his family wherever he goes, and in whatever he does. A person is never alone; he carries with him his family's reputation and their expectations. Any behavior contrary to that expected behavior reflects negatively both on that individual and his family. An individual can never divorce himself from his family. As long as parents and grandparents are living, it is expected that their positions in the family hierarchy will be honored.

Another major element involved in establishing relations among Navajos is the clan system. One is born *into* the mother's clan and is born *for* the father's clan. The maternal and paternal grandfathers usually are of different clans. One addresses a member of his clan as brother and sister. Members of the father's clan are addressed as paternal aunts and uncles and are thought of as the father's relatives. Individuals who are members of one's maternal or paternal grandfather's clans are thought of as that grandfather's relative and treated accordingly. The Navajo people function like one large extended family according to the clan system. The knowledge and use of the clan system in our tribe is therefore very important. It is the basis for holding each other in high regard and for dealing with each other as family. The interpersonal relationships learned in the home are thus lived out in the community. Family relationships are the foundation of all social interaction on the reservation.

Our elders are constantly reminding us to question the aims of schools and churches operating on the reservation. What is the point of having schools and churches if they do not teach compassion for the elders and for those who are less fortunate? We see on the reservation senior citizens alone during the winter without anyone to take care of them, to take them to the hospital or to the store to buy food. Frequently, their children had been educated or baptized and moved away, leaving their families behind. "Where is the compassion, concern, and kindness that we thought were being taught in the classroom and in the churches?" they often inquire. The old way was to care for the elders who occupied positions of honor in the community. We are losing respect for this great source of moral support as well as a vital link with our heritage. Learning must be sought which will increase our level of concern for the welfare of our children, youth and elders.

IV. HÁÁ'ÁYÍÍH, SIHASIN DÓÓ HÓDÍLZIN

The fourth area of knowledge is associated with darkness. The focus in this area is on reverence and respect for nature. The Navajo sees the world full of life and intelligence. He learns to interact with the intelligence around him with appropriate respect and dignity. There is a great natural order to the universe of which man is an integral part. Man is endowed with the ability to observe and imitate this order. For example, the Navajo have found that certain birds mate for life and have become symbols of fidelity in marriage. Proper interaction with this order requires knowledge of one's position and moving from there with reverence or, as a Navajo would put it, with *k'é*.

There is tremendous power in the natural order. We move with this power interdependently. We follow a course that is followed by all intelligence, or creation—a world of order and prosperity. As one recognizes his being as a part of a great circle manifested in the seasons, including birth and old age and the movement of the celestial bodies, he finds renewing power and strength. To the Navajo people all creation is endowed with great powers and the ability to bestow blessings in each of their respective seasons.

To understand this power we must return to the time of the placement of all things. The mountains, for example, were endowed with thinking, planning, prayer, teaching and material things. They were placed and dressed in that way for our benefit. As the clouds rest upon the mountains and the rains fall, the water begins to flow, taking with it the blessings of the mountains. When we utilize this water it unfolds the gifts of prayer, thinking, planning, teaching, and prosperity that it carries from the mountains. We may either use this blessing that was provided by the Holy People for our benefit, or destroy it through improper or disrespectful use.

All creation is connected and interdependent. If any part of the system is upset, the whole system is affected, creating an imbalance. The contemporary threats of pollution, toxicity and destruction of our ozone attest to this connection and interdependence. I believe we are only now finally beginning to understand this circle of connection.

Gratitude is at the very heart of respect and reverence for nature. Gratitude is directed to the water, the trees, plants and animals that nourish and shelter, and especially to the creators, that their blessings would never diminish. In this way the great law of receiving and giving is recognized.

In the Navajo world spiritual understanding is that which gives vitality and meaning to all life. The Western educational system requires us to separate the religious from the secular. Native Americans prefer to maintain their spiritually holistic perspective. When they are forced to put holism aside they find their lives and the values that give them meaning disintegrating or diminishing, and replaced with a fragmented and incoherent philosophy that leads into the mire of social disintegration.

FINDING A BALANCE

The essence of the Navajo philosophy is holism and the goal it sets for life is peace and harmony. By balancing the four cardinal areas of Navajo knowledge the individual will develop sound beliefs and values and be prepared to make responsible decisions. He will develop knowledge and skills so that he will be able to provide for his family, demonstrate good leadership within the family and community, and retain a sense of reverence for all things, both those on the earth and in the heavens. There is a great central focus where all forms of knowledge converge. In Navajo, this point of convergence is the synthesis of knowledge obtained from the cardinal points that find expression in appreciation, reverence, and love for harmony.

The Navajo organized their lives according to these four areas of knowledge. It seems that if we were all educated in this way we would find balance. This "balance" is similar to the way a nutritionist would speak about a balanced diet. If a person does not eat properly he will not have vitality and general good health. When we are not taught in this way, drawing on all four areas of knowledge, we become spiritually, emotionally, socially, physically and environmentally impoverished. We become narrow in our views and cannot see the connection between all knowledge. We wind up perpetuating the imbalance within and between ourselves, other people and the natural world.

This traditional wisdom is not only relevant today, but is even necessary to restore the balance which many of us have lost along with our most cherished traditions. Understanding and practicing

the essence of the principles placed in each of the four directions will give us a strong foundation to make wise decisions for ourselves, our families and our communities. The internalization of these principles immunizes us from many of the adversities of life. When we recognize and become one with the divine power of the circle of creation we experience the Beauty Way of Life, or *hózhǫ́*.

THE MYTH OF SISYPHUS

Albert Camus

The gods had condemned Sisyphus to ceaselessly rolling a rock to the top of a mountain, whence the stone would fall back of its own weight. They had thought with some reason that there is no more dreadful punishment than futile and hopeless labor.

If one believes Homer, Sisyphus was the wisest and most prudent of mortals. According to another tradition, however, he was disposed to practice the profession of highwayman. I see no contradiction in this. Opinions differ as to the reasons why he became the futile laborer of the underworld. To begin with, he is accused of a certain levity in regard to the gods. He stole their secrets. Ægina, the daughter of Æsopus, was carried off by Jupiter. The father was shocked by that disappearance and complained to Sisyphus. He, who knew of the abduction, offered to tell about it on condition that Æsopus would give water to the citadel of Corinth. To the celestial thunderbolts he preferred the benediction of water. He was punished for this in the underworld. Homer tells us also that Sisyphus had put Death in chains. Pluto could not endure the sight of his deserted, silent empire. He dispatched the god of war, who liberated Death from the hands of her conqueror.

It is said also that Sisyphus, being near to death, rashly wanted to test his wife's love. He ordered her to cast his unburied body into the middle of the public square. Sisyphus woke up in the underworld. And there, annoyed by an obedience so contrary to human love, he obtained from Pluto permission to return to earth in order to chastise his wife. But when he had seen again the face of this world, enjoyed water and sun, warm stones and the sea, he no longer wanted to go back to the infernal darkness. Recalls, signs of anger, warnings were of no avail. Many years more he lived facing the curve of the gulf, the sparkling sea, and the smiles of earth. A decree of the gods was necessary. Mercury came and seized the impudent man by the collar and, snatching him from his joys, led him forcibly back to the underworld, where his rock was ready for him.

You have already grasped that Sisyphus is the absurd hero. He *is,* as much through his passions as through his torture. His scorn of the gods, his hatred of death, and his passion for life won him that unspeakable penalty in which the whole being is exerted toward accomplishing nothing. This is the price that must be paid for the passions of this earth. Nothing is told us about Sisyphus in the underworld. Myths are made for the imagination to breathe life into them. As for this myth, one sees merely the whole effort of a body straining to raise the huge stone, to roll it and push it up a slope a hundred times over; one sees the face screwed up, the cheek tight against the stone, the shoulder bracing the clay-covered mass, the foot wedging it, the fresh start with arms outstretched, the wholly human security of two earth-clotted hands. At the very end of his long effort measured by skyless space and time without depth, the purpose is achieved. Then Sisyphus watches the stone rush down in a few moments toward that lower world whence he will have to push it up again toward the summit. He goes back down to the plain.

It is during that return, that pause, that Sisyphus interests me. A face that toils so close to stones is already stone itself! I see that man going back down with a heavy yet measured step toward the torment of which he will never know the end. That hour like a breathing-space which returns as surely as his suffering, that is the hour of consciousness. At each of those moments when he leaves the heights and gradually sinks toward the lairs of the gods, he is superior to his fate. He is stronger than his rock.

If this myth is tragic, that is because its hero is conscious. Where would his torture be, indeed, if at every step the hope of succeeding upheld him? The workman of today works every day in his life at the same tasks, and this fate is no less absurd. But it is tragic only at the rare moments when it becomes conscious. Sisyphus, proletarian of the gods, powerless and rebellious, knows the whole extent of his wretched condition: it is what he thinks of during his descent. The lucidity that was to constitute his torture at the same time crowns his victory. There is no fate that cannot be surmounted by scorn.

• • •

If the descent is thus sometimes performed in sorrow, it can also take place in joy. This word is not too much. Again I fancy Sisyphus returning toward his rock, and the sorrow was in the beginning. When the images of earth cling too tightly to memory, when the call of happiness becomes too insistent, it happens that melancholy rises in man's heart: this is the rock's victory, this is the rock itself. The boundless grief is too heavy to bear. These are our nights of Gethsemane.[1] But crushing truths perish from being acknowledged. Thus, Œdipus at the outset obeys fate without knowing it. But from the moment he knows, his tragedy begins. Yet at the same moment, blind and desperate, he realizes that the only bond linking him to the world is the cool hand of a girl. Then a tremendous remark rings out: "Despite so many ordeals, my advanced age and the nobility of my soul make me conclude that all is well." Sophocles' Œdipus, like Dostoevsky's Kirilov,[2] thus gives the recipe for the absurd victory. Ancient wisdom confirms modern heroism.

One does not discover the absurd without being tempted to write a manual of happiness. "What! by such narrow ways—?" There is but one world, however. Happiness and the absurd are two sons of

---

[1]Gethsemane is the garden where Jesus prayed the night of his arrest and before he was crucified.

[2]Œdipus is the protagonist of the ancient Greek playwright Sophocles' play, *Œdipus Rex.* Kirilov is a character in Dostoevsky's writings.

the same earth. They are inseparable. It would be a mistake to say that happiness necessarily springs from the absurd discovery. It happens as well that the feeling of the absurd springs from happiness. "I conclude that all is well," says Œdipus, and that remark is sacred. It echoes in the wild and limited universe of man. It teaches that all is not, has not been, exhausted. It drives out of this world a god who had come into it with dissatisfaction and a preference for futile sufferings. It makes of fate a human matter, which must be settled among men.

All Sisyphus' silent joy is contained therein. His fate belongs to him. His rock is his thing. Likewise, the absurd man, when he contemplates his torment, silences all the idols. In the universe suddenly restored to its silence, the myriad wondering little voices of the earth rise up. Unconscious, secret calls, invitations from all the faces, they are the necessary reverse and price of victory. There is no sun without shadow, and it is essential to know the night. The absurd man says yes and his effort will henceforth be unceasing. If there is a personal fate, there is no higher destiny, or at least there is but one which he concludes is inevitable and despicable. For the rest, he knows himself to be the master of his days. At that subtle moment when man glances backward over his life, Sisyphus returning toward his rock, in that slight pivoting he contemplates that series of unrelated actions which becomes his fate, created by him, combined under his memory's eye and soon sealed by his death. Thus, convinced of the wholly human origin of all that is human, a blind man eager to see who knows that the night has no end, he is still on the go. The rock is still rolling.

I leave Sisyphus at the foot of the mountain! One always finds one's burden again. But Sisyphus teaches the higher fidelity that negates the gods and raises rocks. He too concludes that all is well. This universe henceforth without a master seems to him neither sterile nor futile. Each atom of that stone, each mineral flake of that night-filled mountain, in itself forms a world. The struggle itself toward the heights is enough to fill a man's heart. One must imagine Sisyphus happy.

QUESTIONS FOR DISCUSSION

1. For which of our authors does God play an important role in discerning whether life has meaning? Does your own belief or disbelief in a certain kind of God influence your idea of life's meaning?

2. Several of our authors posit happiness as the goal of life. Do they all mean the same thing by happiness? Do you agree or disagree that happiness is or should be our goal in life, and if so, what do you mean by "happiness"?

3. Several of our authors counsel moderation of appetites and emotions, sometimes positing a "mean" between two extremes. Do you agree that moderation is virtuous? Might there be difficulties in discerning moderation in certain situations? Might detachment from desires sometimes seem inappropriate? Think of some concrete examples.

4. Do any of our authors suggest connections between how an individual might find his or her goal in life, and how a society should be structured to promote such goal-oriented activity? Are some of our philosophers calling for change on a personal level, and/or a social and political level as well? If so, what kind of changes are needed, and why?

TAOIST AND CONFUCIAN VIEWS

Taoism is a mysticism. It does not believe that life's meaning can be expressed in words. The *Tao Te Ching,* the Chinese classic written in the sixth century B.C.E. and attributed to the ancient sage referred to as Lao Tzu, appears to state this when it says:

> The ancient Masters were profound and subtle
> Their wisdom was unfathomable
> There is no way to describe it;
>   all we can describe is their appearance

So we are to understand wisdom through observing the actions and styles of the wise. Will this show us what life's meaning is? Do those who have wisdom necessarily know what life means? How will we ever know the answer to this, if wisdom cannot be described? But then, how can there be a question about life's meaning, if the meaning of life is also beyond words?

The author of the *Tao Te Ching* is traditionally said to be Lao Tzu, who, legend tells us, was a contemporary of Confucius, which would date the book from the fifth or sixth century B.C.E. However, "Lao Tzu" is probably not a name but a phrase meaning "the old sage"; so the author is, in a sense, anonymous. And the "history" of his life and of his meeting with Confucius is, as likely as not, a fiction, the latter story merely serving to dramatize the tension between the aloof mysticism of the Tao and Confucian moralism in classical Chinese thought.

The basic message of the *Tao Te Ching* is that each person should follow his or her *te,* or natural power, which expresses itself in spontaneity and natural harmony. Being ruled by either the intellect or desires interferes with *te.* Taoism advocates *wu-wei,* often translated as inaction, but better understood as allowing action to occur spontaneously without effort, as a letting be rather than an aggressive approach to life.

The fourth-century B.C.E. Chinese sage Chaung Tzu, our second author, expresses this idea by describing the actions of Prince Wen Hui's cook, who used Tao to cut up oxen; Ch'ui, the draftsman, who draws perfect circles freehand; Chi Hsing Tzu, the patient trainer of fighting cocks; and himself, Chaung Tzu, when he turned down the offer to be prime minister.

The same spirit as that exemplified in these tales is also found in the dialogue and essays of the contemporary American logician-philosopher Raymond Smullyan, who plays in his works with the Taoist paradoxes of action and inaction. As a variation of the same theme in our earlier section in this chapter, we see again the idea that one must effortlessly "act" in the world in such a way that one will not be disappointed with the results. In sum, within the Taoist context, "inaction" does not literally mean being immobile; rather, it means going with the flow, not forcing or attempting to control what happens.

Contemporary Confucian philosopher Fung Yu-Lan discusses the contribution of philosophy to our understanding of life. Philosophy is not about increasing our knowledge of matters of fact; rather, it's about elevating the mind. Philosophy is about how to become a sage. A sage is not merely a "moral" person, searching for perfection, perhaps as Aristotle imagines it, or struggling against self-interest to engage instead in moral duty, as portrayed by Kant. A sage reaches a transcendent sphere, where the sage realizes his or her identification with the universe, so that from then on all one's actions are performed to benefit that universe. As Yu-Lan explains, the sage doesn't do anything extraordinary, but does what he or she does in a state of enlightenment.

LIVING IN THE TAO

Lao Tzu

1

Tao can be talked about, but not the Eternal Tao.
Names can be named, but not the Eternal Name.

As the origin of heaven-and-earth, it is nameless:
As "the Mother" of all things, it is nameable.

So, as ever hidden, we should look at its inner
  essence:
As always manifest, we should look at its outer
  aspects.

These two flow from the same source, though
  differently named;
And both are called mysteries.

The Mystery of mysteries is the Door of all
  essence.

• • •

4

The Tao is like an empty bowl,
Which in being used can never be filled up.
Fathomless, it seems to be the origin of all things.
It blunts all sharp edges,
It unties all tangles,
It harmonizes all lights,
It unites the world into one whole.
Hidden in the deeps,
Yet it seems to exist for ever.
I do not know whose child it is;
It seems to be the common ancestor of all, the
  father of things.

8

The highest form of goodness is like water.
Water knows how to benefit all things without
  striving with them.

It stays in places loathed by all men.
Therefore, it comes near the Tao.

In choosing your dwelling, know how to keep to
  the ground.
In cultivating your mind, know how to dive in the
  hidden deeps.
In dealing with others, know how to be gentle
  and kind.
In speaking, know how to keep your words.
In governing, know how to maintain order.
In transacting business, know how to be
  efficient.
In making a move, know how to choose the right
  moment.

If you do not strive with others,
You will be free from blame.

9

As for holding to fullness,
Far better were it to stop in time!

Keep on beating and sharpening a sword,
And the edge cannot be preserved for long.

Fill your house with gold and jade,
And it can no longer be guarded.

Set store by your riches and honour,
And you will only reap a crop of calamities.

Here is the Way of Heaven:
When you have done your work, retire!

• • •

12

The five colours blind the eye.
The five tones deafen the ear.
The five flavours cloy the palate.
Racing and hunting madden the mind.
Rare goods tempt men to do wrong.

Therefore, the Sage takes care of the belly, not
  the eye.
He prefers what is within to what is without.

13

"Welcome disgrace as a pleasant surprise.
Prize calamities as your own body."

Why should we "welcome disgrace as a pleasant
 surprise"?
Because a lowly state is a boon:
Getting it is a pleasant surprise,
And so is losing it!
That is why we should "welcome disgrace as a
 pleasant surprise."

Why should we "prize calamities as our own
 body"?
Because our body is the very source of our
 calamities.
If we have no body, what calamities can we have?

Hence, only he who is willing to give his body for
 the sake of the world is fit to be entrusted with
 the world.
Only he who can do it with love is worthy of
 being the steward of the world.

• • •

15

The ancient adepts of the Tao were subtle and
flexible, profound and comprehensive.
Their minds were too deep to be fathomed.

Because they are unfathomable,
One can only describe them vaguely by their
 appearance.

Hesitant like one wading a stream in winter;
Timid like one afraid of his neighbours on all
 sides;
Cautious and courteous like a guest;
Yielding like ice on the point of melting;
Simple like an uncarved block;
Hollow like a cave;
Confused like a muddy pool;
And yet who else could quietly and gradually
 evolve from the muddy to the clear?
Who else could slowly but steadily move from the
 inert to the living?

He who keeps the Tao does not want to be full.
But precisely because he is never full,
He can always remain like a hidden sprout,
And does not rush to early ripening.

16

Attain to utmost Emptiness.
Cling single-heartedly to interior peace.
While all things are stirring together,
I only contemplate the Return.
For flourishing as they do,
Each of them will return to its root.
To return to the root is to find peace.
To find peace is to fulfill one's destiny.
To fulfill one's destiny is to be constant.
To know the Constant is called Insight.

If one does not know the Constant,
One runs blindly into disasters.
If one knows the Constant,
One can understand and embrace all.
If one understands and embraces all,
One is capable of doing justice.
To be just is to be kingly;
To be kingly is to be heavenly;
To be heavenly is to be one with the Tao;
To be one with the Tao is to abide forever.
Such a one will be safe and whole
Even after the dissolution of his body.

• • •

22

Bend and you will be whole.
Curl and you will be straight.
Keep empty and you will be filled.
Grow old and you will be renewed.

Have little and you will gain.
Have much and you will be confused.

Therefore, the Sage embraces the One,
And becomes a Pattern to all under Heaven.
He does not make a show of himself,

Hence he shines;
Does not justify himself,
Hence he becomes known;
Does not boast of his ability,
Hence he gets his credit;
Does not brandish his success,
Hence he endures;
Does not compete with anyone,
Hence no one can compete with him.
Indeed, the ancient saying: "Bend and you
    will remain whole" is no idle word.
Nay, if you have really attained wholeness,
    everything will flock to you.

• • •

24

One on tip-toe cannot stand.
One astride cannot walk.
One who displays himself does not shine.
One who justifies himself has no glory.
One who boasts of his own ability has no merit.
One who parades his own success will not endure.
In Tao these things are called "unwanted food and
    extraneous growths,"
Which are loathed by all things.
Hence, a man of Tao does not set his heart
    upon them.

• • •

34

The Great Tao is universal like a flood.
How can it be turned to the right or
    to the left?

All creatures depend on it,
And it denies nothing to anyone.

It does its work,
But it makes no claims for itself.

It clothes and feeds all,
But it does not lord it over them:
Thus, it may be called "the Little."
All things return to it as to their home,

But it does not lord it over them:
Thus, it may be called "the Great."

It is just because it does not wish to
    be great
That its greatness is fully realized.

• • •

38

High Virtue is non-virtuous;
Therefore it has Virtue.
Low Virtue never frees itself from
    virtuousness;
Therefore it has no Virtue.

High Virtue makes no fuss and has no private ends
    to serve;
Low Virtue not only fusses but has private ends
    to serve.

High humanity fusses but has no private ends
    to serve;
High morality not only fusses but has private ends
    to serve.

High ceremony fusses but finds no response;
Then it tries to enforce itself with rolled-up
    sleeves.

Failing Tao, man resorts to Virtue.
Failing Virtue, man resorts to humanity.
Failing humanity, man resorts to morality.
Failing morality, man resorts to
    ceremony.

Now, ceremony is the merest husk of faith
    and loyalty;
It is the beginning of all confusion
    and disorder.

As to foreknowledge, it is only the flower
    of Tao,
And the beginning of folly.

Therefore, the full-grown man sets his
    heart upon the substance rather than
    the husk;
Upon the fruit rather than the flower.
Truly, he prefers what is within to what is
    without.

• • •

43

The softest of all things
Overrides the hardest of all things.
Only Nothing can enter into no-space.
Hence I know the advantages of Non-Ado.

Few things under heaven are as instructive as the
  lessons of Silence,
Or as beneficial as the fruits of Non-Ado.

44

As for your name and your body, which is the
  dearer?
As for your body and your wealth, which is the
  more to be prized?
As for gain and loss, which is the more painful?

Thus, an excessive love for anything will cost you
  dear in the end.
The storing up of too much goods will entail a
  heavy loss.

To know when you have enough is to be immune
  from disgrace.
To know when to stop is to be preserved from
  perils.
Only thus can you endure long.

45

The greatest perfection seems imperfect,
And yet its use is inexhaustible.
The greatest fullness seems empty,
And yet its use is endless.

The greatest straightness looks like crookedness.
The greatest skill appears clumsy.
The greatest eloquence sounds like stammering.

Restlessness overcomes cold,
But calm overcomes heat.

The peaceful and serene
Is the Norm of the World.

• • •

63

Do the Non-Ado.
Strive for the effortless.
Savour the savourless.
Exalt the low.
Multiply the few.
Requite injury with kindness.

Nip troubles in the bud.
Sow the great in the small.

Difficult things of the world
Can only be tackled when they are easy.
Big things of the world
Can only be achieved by attending to their small
  beginnings.
Thus, the Sage never has to grapple with big
  things,
Yet he alone is capable of achieving them!

He who promises lightly must be lacking in faith.
He who thinks everything easy will end by finding
  everything difficult.
Therefore, the Sage, who regards everything as
  difficult,
Meets with no difficulties in the end.

• • •

68

A good soldier is never aggressive;
A good fighter is never angry.
The best way of conquering an enemy
Is to win him over by not antagonizing him.
The best way of employing a man
Is to serve under him.
This is called the virtue of non-striving!
This is called using the abilities of men!
This is called being wedded to Heaven as of old!

• • •

74

When the people are no longer afraid of death,
Why scare them with the spectre of death?

If you could make the people always afraid of death,
And they still persisted in breaking the law,
Then you might with reason arrest and execute them,
And who would dare to break the law?

Is not the Great Executor always there to kill?
To do the killing for the Great Executor
Is to chop wood for a master carpenter,
And you would be lucky indeed if you did not hurt
    your own hand!

• • •

76

When a man is living, he is soft and supple.
When he is dead, he becomes hard and rigid.
When a plant is living, it is soft and tender.
When it is dead, it becomes withered and dry.

Hence, the hard and rigid belongs to the company
    of the dead:
The soft and supple belongs to the company of the
    living.

Therefore, a mighty army tends to fall by its own
    weight,
Just as dry wood is ready for the axe.

The mighty and great will be laid low;
The humble and weak will be exalted.

• • •

81

Sincere words are not sweet,
Sweet words are not sincere.
Good men are not argumentative,
The argumentative are not good.
The wise are not erudite,
The erudite are not wise.

The Sage does not take to hoarding.
The more he lives for others, the fuller is his life.
The more he gives, the more he abounds.

The Way of Heaven is to benefit, not to harm.
The Way of the Sage is to do his duty, not to strive
    with anyone.

LOST IN THE TAO

Chuang Tzu

CUTTING UP AN OX

Prince Wen Hui's cook
Was cutting up an ox.
Out went a hand,
Down went a shoulder,
He planted a foot,
He pressed with a knee,
The ox fell apart
With a whisper,
The bright cleaver murmured
Like a gentle wind.
Rhythm! Timing!
Like a sacred dance,
Like "The Mulberry Grove,"
Like ancient harmonies!

"Good work!" the Prince exclaimed,
"Your method is faultless!"
"Method?" said the cook
Laying aside his cleaver,
"What I follow is Tao
Beyond all methods!

"When I first began
To cut up oxen
I would see before me
The whole ox
All in one mass.

"After three years
I no longer saw this mass.
I saw the distinctions.

"But now, I see nothing
With the eye. My whole being
Apprehends.
My senses are idle. The spirit
Free to work without plan
Follows its own instinct
Guided by natural line,
By the secret opening, the hidden
    space,

My cleaver finds its own way.
I cut through no joint, chop no bone.

"A good cook needs a new chopper
Once a year—he cuts.
A poor cook needs a new one
Every month—he hacks!

"I have used this same cleaver
Nineteen years.
It has cut up
A thousand oxen.
Its edge is as keen
As if newly sharpened.

"There are spaces in the joints;
The blade is thin and keen:
When this thinness
Finds that space
There is all the room you need!
It goes like a breeze!
Hence I have this cleaver nineteen
    years
As if newly sharpened!

"True, there are sometimes
Tough joints. I feel them coming,
I slow down, I watch closely,
Hold back, barely move the blade,
And whump! the part falls away
Landing like a clod of earth.

"Then I withdraw the blade,
I stand still
And let the joy of the work
Sink in.
I clean the blade
And put it away."

Prince Wan Hui said,
"This is it! My cook has shown me
How I ought to live
My own life!"

• • •

MAN IS BORN IN TAO

Fishes are born in water
Man is born in Tao.
If fishes, born in water,

Seek the deep shadow
Of pond and pool,
All their needs
Are satisfied.
If man, born in Tao,
Sinks into the deep shadow
Of non-action
To forget aggression and concern,
He lacks nothing
His life is secure.

Moral: "All the fish needs
Is to get lost in water.
All man needs is to get lost
In Tao."

• • •

CRACKING THE SAFE

For security against robbers who snatch purses,
    rifle luggage, and crack safes,
One must fasten all property with ropes, lock it up
    with locks, bolt it with bolts.
This (for property owners) is elementary good
    sense.
But when a strong thief comes along he picks up
    the whole lot,
Puts it on his back, and goes on his way with only
    one fear:
That ropes, locks, and bolts may give way.
Thus what the world calls good business is only a
    way
To gather up the loot, pack it, make it secure
In one convenient load for the more enterprising
    thieves.
Who is there, among those called smart,
Who does not spend his time amassing loot
For a bigger robber than himself? . . .
In the land of Khi, from village to village,
You could hear cocks crowing, dogs barking.
Fishermen cast their nets,
Ploughmen ploughed the wide fields,
Everything was neatly marked out
By boundary lines. For five hundred square miles
There were temples for ancestors, altars
For field-gods and corn-spirits.

Every canton, county, and district
Was run according to the laws and statutes—
Until one morning the Attorney General, Tien
    Khang Tzu,
Did away with the King and took over the whole
    state.
Was he content to steal the land? No,
He also took over the laws and statutes at the same
    time,
And all the lawyers with them, not to mention the
    police.
They all formed part of the same package.

Of course, people called Khang Tzu a robber,
But they left him alone
To live as happy as the Patriarchs.
No small state would say a word against him,
No large state would make a move in his direction,
So for twelve generations the state of Khi
Belonged to his family. No one interferred
With his inalienable rights. . . .

The invention
Of weights and measures
Makes robbery easier.
Signing contracts, settings seals,
Makes robbery more sure.
Teaching love and duty
Provides a fitting language
With which to prove that robbery
Is really for the general good.
A poor man must swing
For stealing a belt buckle
But if a rich man steals a whole state
He is acclaimed
As statesman of the year.

Hence if you want to hear the very best speeches
On love, duty, justice, etc.,
Listen to statesmen.

But when the creek dries up
Nothing grows in the valley.
When the mound is levelled
The hollow next to it is filled.
And when the statesmen and lawyers
And preachers of duty disappear
There are no more robberies either

And the world is at peace.

Moral: the more you pile up ethical principles
And duties and obligations
To bring everyone in line
The more you gather loot
For a thief like Khang.
By ethical argument
And moral principle
The greatest crimes are eventually shown
To have been necessary, and, in fact,
A signal benefit
To mankind.

· · ·

ACTION AND NON-ACTION

The non-action of the wise man is not inaction.
It is not studied. It is not shaken by anything.
The sage is quiet because he is not moved,
Not because he *wills* to be quiet.
Still water is like glass.
You can look in it and see the bristles on your
    chin.
It is a perfect level;
A carpenter could use it.
If water is so clear, so level,
How much more the spirit of man?
The heart of the wise man is tranquil.
It is the mirror of heaven and earth
The glass of everything.
Emptiness, stillness, tranquillity, tastelessness,
Silence, non-action: this is the level of heaven and
    earth.
This is perfect Tao. Wise men find here
Their resting place.
Resting, they are empty.

From emptiness comes the unconditioned.
From this, the conditioned, the individual things.
So from the sage's emptiness, stillness arises:
From stillness, action. From action, attainment.
From their stillness comes their non-action, which
    is also action
And is, therefore, their attainment.
For stillness is joy. Joy is free from care

Fruitful in long years.

Joy does all things without concern:
For emptiness, stillness, tranquillity, tastelessness,
Silence, and non-action
Are the root of all things.

• • •

THE MAN OF TAO

The man in whom Tao
Acts without impediment
Harms no other being
By his actions
Yet he does not know himself
To be "kind," to be "gentle."

The man in whom Tao
Acts without impediment
Does not bother with his own interests
And does not despise
Others who do.
He does not struggle to make money
And does not make a virtue of poverty.
He goes his way
Without relying on others
And does not pride himself
On walking alone.
While he does not follow the crowd
He won't complain of those who do.
Rank and reward
Make no appeal to him;
Disgrace and shame
Do not deter him.
He is not always looking
For right and wrong
Always deciding "Yes" or "No."
The ancients said, therefore:

> *"The man of Tao*
> *Remains unknown*
> *Perfect virtue*
> *Produces nothing*
> *'No-Self'*
> *Is 'True-Self.'*
> *And the greatest man*
> *Is Nobody."*

THE TURTLE

Chuang Tzu with his bamboo pole
Was fishing in Pu river.

The Prince of Chu
Sent two vice-chancellors
With a formal document:
"We hereby appoint you
Prime Minister."

Chuang Tzu held his bamboo pole.
Still watching Pu river,
He said:
"I am told there is a sacred tortoise,
Offered and canonized
Three thousand years ago,
Venerated by the prince,
Wrapped in silk,
In a precious shrine
On an altar
In the Temple.

"What do you think:
Is it better to give up one's life
And leave a sacred shell
As an object of cult
In a cloud of incense
Three thousand years,

Or better to live
As a plain turtle
Dragging its tail in the mud?"

"For the turtle," said the Vice-Chancellor,
"Better to live
And drag its tail in the mud!"

"Go home!" said Chuang Tzu.
"Leave me here
To drag my tail in the mud!"

• • •

PERFECT JOY

Is there to be found on earth a fullness of joy, or is
there no such thing? Is there some way to make life
fully worth living, or is this impossible? If there is
such a way, how do you go about finding it? What

should you try to do? What should you seek to avoid? What should be the goal in which your activity comes to rest? What should you accept? What should you refuse to accept? What should you love? What should you hate?

What the world values is money, reputation, long life, achievement. What it counts as joy is health and comfort of body, good food, fine clothes, beautiful things to look at, pleasant music to listen to.

What it condemns is lack of money, a low social rank, a reputation for being no good, and an early death.

What it considers misfortune is bodily discomfort and labor, no chance to get your fill of good food, not having good clothes to wear, having no way to amuse or delight the eye, no pleasant music to listen to. If people find that they are deprived of these things, they go into a panic or fall into despair. They are so concerned for their life that their anxiety makes life unbearable, even when they have the things they think they want. Their very concern for enjoyment makes them unhappy.

The rich make life intolerable, driving themselves in order to get more and more money which they cannot really use. In so doing they are alienated from themselves, and exhaust themselves in their own service as though they were slaves of others.

The ambitious run day and night in pursuit of honors, constantly in anguish about the success of their plans, dreading the miscalculation that may wreck everything. Thus they are alienated from themselves, exhausting their real life in service of the shadow created by their insatiable hope.

The birth of a man is the birth of his sorrow.

The longer he lives, the more stupid he becomes, because his anxiety to avoid unavoidable death becomes more and more acute. What bitterness! He lives for what is always out of reach! His thirst for survival in the future makes him incapable of living in the present. . . .

I cannot tell if what the world considers "happiness" is happiness or not. All I know is that when I consider the way they go about attaining it, I see them carried away headlong, grim and obsessed, in the general onrush of the human herd, unable to stop themselves or to change their direction. All the while they claim to be just on the point of attaining happiness.

For my part, I cannot accept their standards, whether of happiness or unhappiness. I ask myself if after all their concept of happiness has any meaning whatever.

My opinion is that you never find happiness until you stop looking for it. My greatest happiness consists precisely in doing nothing whatever that is calculated to obtain happiness: and this, in the minds of most people, is the worst possible course.

I will hold to the saying that: "Perfect joy is to be without joy. Perfect praise is to be without praise."

If you ask "what ought to be done" and "what ought not to be done" on earth in order to produce happiness, I answer that these questions do not have an answer. There is no way of determining such things.

Yet at the same time, if I cease striving for happiness, the "right" and the "wrong" at once become apparent all by themselves.

Contentment and well-being at once become possible the moment you cease to act with them in view, and if you practice non-doing (*wu wei*), you will have both happiness and well-being.

Here is how I sum it up:

> Heaven does nothing: its non-doing is
>   its serenity.
> Earth does nothing: it non-doing is its rest.
>
> From the union of these two non-doings
> All actions proceed,
> All things are made.
> How vast, how invisible
> This coming-to-be!
> All things come from nowhere!
> How vast, how invisible—
> No way to explain it!
> All beings in their perfection
> Are born of non-doing.
> Hence it is said:
> "Heaven and earth do nothing

Yet there is nothing they do not do."

Where is the man who can attain
To this non-doing?

• • •

THE FIGHTING COCK

Chi Hsing Tzu was a trainer of fighting cocks
For King Hsuan.
He was training a fine bird.
The King kept asking if the bird were
Ready for combat.
"Not yet," said the trainer.
"He is full of fire.
He is ready to pick a fight
With every other bird. He is vain and confident
Of his own strength."
After ten days, he answered again:
"Not yet. He flares up
When he hears another bird crow."
After ten more days:
"Not yet. He still gets
That angry look
And ruffles his feathers."
Again ten days:
The trainer said, "Now he is nearly ready.
When another bird crows, his eye
Does not even flicker.
He stands immobile
Like a cock of wood.
He is a mature fighter.
Other birds
Will take one look at him
And run."

• • •

WHEN THE SHOE FITS

Ch'ui the draftsman
Could draw more perfect circles freehand
Than with a compass.

His fingers brought forth
Spontaneous forms from nowhere. His mind

Was meanwhile free and without concern
With what he was doing.

No application was needed
His mind was perfectly simple
And knew no obstacle.

So, when the shoe fits
The foot is forgotten,
When the belt fits
The belly is forgotten,
When the heart is right
"For" and "against" are forgotten.

No drives, no compulsions,
No needs, no attractions:
Then your affairs
Are under control.
You are a free man.

Easy is right. Begin right
And you are easy.
Continue easy and you are right.
The right way to go easy
Is to forget the right way
And forget that the going is easy.

• • •

MEANS AND ENDS

The gatekeeper in the capital city of Sung became such an expert mourner after his father's death, and so emaciated himself with fasts and austerities, that he was promoted to high rank in order that he might serve as a model of ritual observance.

As a result of this, his imitators so deprived themselves that half of them died. The others were not promoted.

The purpose of a fish trap is to catch fish, and when the fish are caught, the trap is forgotten.

The purpose of a rabbit snare is to catch rabbits. When the rabbits are caught, the snare is forgotten.

The purpose of words is to convey ideas. When the ideas are grasped, the words are forgotten.

Where can I find a man who has forgotten words?
He is the one I would like to talk to.

FLIGHT FROM THE SHADOW

There was a man who was so disturbed by the sight of his own shadow and so displeased with his own footsteps that he determined to get rid of both. The method he hit upon was to run away from them.

So he got up and ran. But every time he put his foot down there was another step, while his shadow kept up with him without the slightest difficulty.

He attributed his failure to the fact that he was not running fast enough. So he ran faster and faster, without stopping, until he finally dropped dead.

He failed to realize that if he merely stepped into the shade, his shadow would vanish, and if he sat down and stayed still, there would be no more footsteps.

WHICHEVER THE WAY

Raymond M. Smullyan

1. MY SYSTEM OF ETHICS

Whichever the way the wind blows,
Whichever the way the world goes,
Is perfectly all right with me!
　　　　　　　　　—*Anonymous Taoist*

2. WHICHEVER THE WAY

Moralist: I have just read your poem:

Whichever the way the wind blows,
Whichever the way the world goes,
Is good enough for me!

Taoist: You misquoted it. The last line is "Is perfectly all right with me." But I like your version at least as well as mine—in a way, even better.

Moralist: At any rate, I regard the poem as childish, irresponsible, illogical and morally reprehensible.

Taoist: That's perfectly all right with me!

Moralist: No, seriously, I cannot go along with the quietistic philosophy in your poem.

Taoist: I don't think of it as quietistic.

Moralist: Of course it is! Superficially your poem bears a resemblance to the Zen poem:

Sitting quietly doing nothing,
Spring comes, and the grass grows by itself.[1]

Taoist: I love that poem; I think it is my favorite.

Moralist: You would love it! Actually, I myself have nothing against that poem. There is nothing wrong with sitting quietly while the grass is growing because growing grass is something of value. But it is a very different thing to sit quietly while the world is going up in flames!

Taoist: I never advocated sitting quietly while the world goes up in flames. I never advocated sitting quietly at all. In fact, my poem does not advocate anything.

Moralist: You say the way things are going is good enough for you. Well, it may be good enough for you, but it sure is not good enough for me! With all the misery and injustice in the world, you might be content to sit quietly doing nothing, letting the wind blow where it listeth, but *I* intend to go out in the world and do something about it, whether you like it or not!

Taoist: Whether *I* like it or not! Whether *I* like it? I just told you:

Whichever the way the wind blows,
Whichever the way the world goes,
Is good enough for me!

So if you wish to go out and make changes in the world, your doing so is good enough for me.

Moralist: Sure it's good enough for you if *I* go to the trouble of making changes in the world, but it evidently is not good enough for you if you have to go to the trouble of making the changes.

---

[1]See Alan Watts, *The Way of Zen* (Vintage Books, 1957), p. 134.

Taoist: Why not? If I go out in the world and make changes, that is also good enough for me.

Moralist: But if things are already good enough for you, why would you want to make any changes?

Taoist: Why not?

Moralist: Oh come now, don't be silly! Either things are good enough for you or they are not. You can't have it both ways. If things are good enough for you, then there is no need for you to make changes; if not, then there is. I judge whether things really are good enough for you on the basis of how you act.

Taoist: I don't see it that way. I lead a very active life, as a matter of fact; I am always busy with some project or other. But I still say that whatever happens is good enough for me. Suppose some of my projects fail. Then I keep trying further until I succeed. Some of my projects I may not succeed in accomplishing in my lifetime. And this very fact is good enough for me.

Moralist: Suppose you were a doctor and were working hard to save a patient's life. Would you honestly say to yourself, "I am trying my best to save the patient's life, but if he dies, it is perfectly all right with me"?

Taoist: Of course not! I would think it highly inappropriate to express this sentiment at such a time.

Moralist: Ah, I've caught you! You are being inconsistent! On the one hand you say that *all* the things which happen are good enough for you, and yet you admit of a particular happening that it is not good enough for you. So plainly you are inconsistent!

Taoist: Oh, for God's sake, come off it! You the great logician have caught *me* in an inconsistency! I affirm a universal statement and yet I deny an instance! Tut, tut, isn't that just terrible!

Moralist: Well, what do you have to say for yourself?

Taoist: What do I have to say for myself? Mainly that you are a first-class dope! That is the main thing I have to say.

Now look, will it make you any happier if I change the poem as follows? Suppose some very unpleasant event occurs—call it event E—then I can change the poem thus:

Whichever the way the wind blows,
Whichever the way the world goes,
Is perfectly all right with me
Except for event E.

Moralist: That is still no good. This means that you have to change the poem every time you come across a different unpleasant event.

Taoist: Not at all! I can simply use the symbol "E" once and for all as a variable ranging over all unpleasant events.

Moralist: I think you are being facetious!

Taoist: Of course I am! My facetiousness is obviously only an annoyance reaction to your pedantry.

Moralist: But honestly now, why should you regard it as pedantic that I object to a simple inconsistency? How can you seriously maintain that everything that happens is all right with you and yet admit that certain things which happen are not all right with you.

Taoist: I never maintained that everything that happens is all right with me. I never said that taking each thing that happens, that very thing is all right with me. I said "whichever the way the world goes" is all right with me. I was thinking of the direction of the world as a whole as one *unit*. The fact that I like the world as a whole does not mean that I like each part in isolation from the rest.

Moralist: It has suddenly occurred to me that maybe I have misjudged you. Perhaps all you are trying to say is that you accept the will of God. Maybe you are trying to say, "Let thy will, not mine, be done."

Taoist: If it makes you happy to think of it in these theological terms, by all means do so. I would not put it in those words, but perhaps they are not too far from what I have in mind. Your first suggestion, that I accept the will of God, comes closer than "Let thy will, not mine, be done."

Moralist: What is the difference between the two?

Taoist: To me they are, at least psychologically, very different. I recall in my bachelor days I spent one summer in Chicago in which I resided in a theological seminary. I had many conversations with the resident minister. One day he asked me whether I would not attend the evening services for the house. Although I did not feel quite right about it, I accepted as a matter of courtesy. And so I went, and at one point we were to fold our hands and pray to God, "Let thy will, not mine, be done." I vividly recall at this point that I felt hypocritical—indeed as if I actually were lying. Could I in all sincerity really wish that God would do his will rather than mine? Suppose, for example, that Christianity were true, and that God would will that I be damned and suffer eternal punishment. Could I really *sanction* God doing this to me? Or to anyone else, for that matter? Even Satan himself? Besides, if the Christian God really exists, it would seem rather ludicrous for a weak defenceless creature like myself to have to give his approval of God carrying out his own will. Obviously God will do what he wills, whether I like it or not. I'm sure this sentiment has often been expressed before, but I cannot help expressing it again. Anyhow, for these reasons, the phrase "Let thy will, not mine, be done" has never sounded right in my ears. Your first idea of "accepting the will of God" is different. Accepting something is not the same as desiring it. And that is why I say that your first suggestion comes closer to my meaning than your second although it still is not quite what I mean.

Moralist: Well, if this is not what your poem means, then I am still puzzled as to what it really means.

Taoist: Why do you work so hard trying to find its *meaning?* Can't you just accept it for what it is, and simply say "It's a good poem" or "It's a rotten poem"?

Moralist: No, no, there must be a meaning in it. You say you are not advocating quietism, surely you are not advocating activism. I guess you are just advocating accepting the world as it is.

Taoist: No, I am not *advocating* anything.

Moralist: Surely your idea must somehow affect your attitude towards the world, and have some effect on your behavior.

Taoist: Attitude, yes; behavior, no.

Moralist: Have you always had this attitude?

Taoist: Definitely not.

Moralist: Well, since you had it, would you say that you have become more or less active than formerly?

Taoist: Neither. My external actions have undergone no appreciable change.

Moralist: But you must have *some* ethical message in your poem. Why did you choose such a pompous title as "My System of Ethics"? According to the last few things you have said, you seem to have no system at all.

Taoist (laughing): I deliberately chose such a pompous title as a jest at moralists, who tend to take themselves so seriously! I was delighted at the very pomposity of the title "My System of Ethics" leading the reader to expect that I was going to come out with some ponderous analysis of what is the ultimate nature of the "Good," and how people should conduct their lives. And then all that comes out is this silly little poem. And yet, in a way, I honestly believe that this poem does contain—mainly, perhaps, on an unconscious level—a very serious message.

Moralist: But you cannot tell me what the message is?

Taoist: I have the same difficulty I would have in trying to explain why a joke is funny.

Moralist: Well, now, you say that the message does not so much concern people's actions.

Taoist: That's right.

Moralist: It just concerns change in attitudes.

Taoist: Right.

Moralist: Can you give me any inkling as to what attitude you have in mind? Do you have any idea of what attitudes you hope your message might engender?

Taoist: I think so. I think it would tend to make one's actions no less directed or efficient than before—indeed, hopefully even more so—but it would tend to make the actions performed with less fear and anxiety.

Moralist: Oh, then you *do* have a significant message. In which case I think you owe it to yourself and others to express it more precisely and clearly.

Taoist: The clearest way *I* can express it is by saying:

Whichever the way the wind blows,
Whichever the way the world goes,
It's all the same to me!

EPILOGUE

Several days after I completed this chapter, there was a storm during the night and the wind blew out many of the screens from the porch. Next morning I was standing there looking at the desolation, and my wife came down and said: "Well Raymond, are you still satisfied with whichever the way the wind blows?"

THE SPHERES OF LIVING

Fung Yu-Lan

What is the function of philosophy? . . . I suggested that, according to Chinese philosophical tradition, its function is not the increase of positive knowledge of matters of fact, but the elevation of the mind. Here it would seem well to explain more clearly what I mean by this statement.

In my book, *The New Treatise on the Nature of Man,* I have observed that man differs from other animals in that when he does something, he understands what he is doing, and is conscious that he is doing it. It is this understanding and self-consciousness that give significance for him to what he is doing. The various significances that thus attach to his various acts, in their totality, constitute what I call his sphere of living. Different men may do the same things, but according to their different degrees of understanding and self-consciousness, these things may have varying significance to them. Every individual has his own sphere of living, which is not quite the same as that of any other individual. Yet in spite of these individual differences, we can classify the various spheres of living into four general grades. Beginning with the lowest, they are: the innocent sphere, the utilitarian sphere, the moral sphere, and the transcendent sphere.

A man may simply do what his instinct or the custom of his society leads him to do. Like children and primitive people, he does what he does without being self-conscious or greatly understanding what he is doing. Thus what he does has little significance, if any, for him. His sphere of living is what I call the innocent sphere.

Or man may be aware of himself, and be doing everything for himself. That does not mean that he is necessarily an immoral man. He may do something, the consequences of which are beneficial to others, but his motivation for so doing is self-benefit. Thus everything he does has the significance of utility for himself. His sphere of living is what I call the utilitarian sphere.

Yet again a man may come to understand that a society exists, of which he is a member. This society constitutes a whole and he is a part of that whole. Having this understanding, he does everything for the benefit of the society, or as the Confucianists say, he does everything "for the sake of righteousness, and not for the sake of personal profit." He is the truly moral man and what he does is moral action in the strict sense of the word. Everything he does has a moral significance. Hence his sphere of living is what I call the moral sphere.

And finally, a man may come to understand that over and above society as a whole, there is the great whole which is the universe. He is not only a member of society, but at the same time a member of the universe. He is a citizen of the social organization, but at the same time a citizen of Heaven, as Mencius says. Having this understanding, he does everything for the benefit of the universe. He understands the significance of what he does and is self-conscious of the fact that he is doing what he does. This understanding and self-consciousness constitute for him a higher sphere of living which I call the transcendent sphere.

Of the four spheres of living, the innocent and the utilitarian are the products of man as he is, while the moral and the transcendent are those of man as he ought to be. The former two are the gifts of nature, while the latter two are the creations of the spirit. The innocent sphere is the lowest, the utilitarian comes next, then the moral, and finally the transcendent. They are so because the innocent sphere requires almost no understanding and self-consciousness, whereas the utilitarian and the moral require more, and the transcendent requires most. The moral sphere is that of moral values, and the transcendent is that of supermoral values.

According to the tradition of Chinese philosophy, the function of philosophy is to help man to achieve the two higher spheres of living, and especially the highest. The transcendent sphere may also be called the sphere of philosophy, because it cannot be achieved unless through philosophy one gains some understanding of the universe. But the moral sphere, too, is a product of philosophy. Moral actions are not simply actions that accord with the moral rule, nor is moral man one who simply cultivates certain moral habits. He must act and live with an understanding of the moral principles involved, and it is the business of philosophy to give him this understanding.

To live in the moral sphere of living is to be a *hsien* or morally perfect man, and to live in the transcendent sphere is to be a *sheng* or sage. Philosophy teaches the way of how to be a sage. . . . to be a sage is to reach the highest perfection of man as man. This is the noble function of philosophy.

In the *Republic*, Plato said that the philosopher must be elevated from the "cave" of the sensory world to the world of intellect. If the philosopher is in the world of intellect, he is also in the transcendent sphere of living. Yet the highest achievement of the man living in this sphere is the identification of himself with the universe, and in this identification, he also transcends the intellect.

. . . Chinese philosophy has always tended to stress that the sage need do nothing extraordinary in order to be a sage. He cannot perform miracles, nor need he try to do so. He does nothing more than most people do, but, having high understanding, what he does has a different significance to him. In other words, he does what he does in a state of enlightenment, while other people do what they do in a state of ignorance. As the Ch'an monks say: "Understanding—this one word is the source of all mysteries." It is the significance which results from this understanding that constitutes his highest sphere of living.

Thus the Chinese sage is both of this world and the other world, and Chinese philosophy is both this-worldly and other-worldly. With the scientific advancement of the future, I believe that religion with its dogmas and superstitions will give way to science; man's craving for the world beyond, however, will be met by the philosophy of the future— a philosophy which is therefore likely to be both this-worldly and other-worldly. In this respect Chinese philosophy may have something to contribute.

QUESTIONS FOR DISCUSSION

1. Discuss the *Tao Te Ching's* claim that true wisdom seems foolish. In addition, look for the various metaphors used to illustrate that softness and flexibility are "stronger" than rigidity. Do you agree? Can you illustrate your point with concrete examples from life situations?

2. Evaluate Smullyan's dialogue between the Taoist and the Moralist. With whom do you agree more and why? Or do you disagree with both? What is your opinion on "whichever way the wind blows"? Can you point to times in your life that can be understood by appealing to either the Taoist or the moralist philosophy?

3. Keeping Smullyan's comments on the Moralist in the back of your mind, what do you think of Fung Yu-Lan's claim that there is a higher kind of living than moralism? Can you imagine a state of mind in which you would realize your interconnection with the universe? How would this state of mind be different from the moralist stance?

FACING DEATH

Our experience of life most certainly influences our attitude toward death. We probably can't figure out the meaning of death apart from our reflections on the meaning of life. One very interesting collection of passages reflecting on life and death comes from Native Mesoamerica, located for thousands of years in an area which is presently called Mexico. The texts were gathered in the sixteenth century and were originally written in Nahuatl, an Aztec language. The texts point to the misfortunes of this world. The author or authors (they are anonymous) note that we must all perish, and that our pleasures in this world are all temporary. As for what should be our attitude toward life given this fact of death, a dialogue ensues that could be between various thinkers, or perhaps is a dialogue within the mind of one thinker. Two attitudes are possible: either enjoy life's passing pleasures while you can, or bear the pains of this life while waiting for the life after this one, which will hopefully be better.

Our next author, Gregory Baum of McGill University, argues that the desire of the individual to live forever is a product of our times, with its emphasis on the individual ego. In earlier times, the community was more important; the early Christian church had a much different understanding of life after death than the contemporary Christian church.

Gregory Baum's course of studies is a fascinating one. Born a Jew in Berlin, Baum fled Germany in 1939 at age 16, taking refuge first in England and then in Canada, which became his permanent home. He converted to Christianity in 1946 and became well known as a theologian. Later pursuing studies in sociology at the New School for Social Research, he combined the two fields and began to produce works such as *Religion and Alienation,* from which our selection is an excerpt.

Baum argues that death, like any other aspect of life, must be understood in its social context, for society gives the act meaning and to a large extent shapes the individual's reaction to death. In contrast to views of heaven meant to placate the suffering,

toiling masses, the Bible accounts speak of a coming kingdom of God to happen in this world in the near future. Baum suggests that attitudes toward death are socially grounded, and depending on the society's imagination of the future, death will be either feared or accepted. Death is a dreaded enemy only for those who love the self, an attitude encouraged by our contemporary individualistic society. However, if Christians are able to have as their longing a just society for others, focus can be taken off the self and death loses its fearfulness.

Etty Hillesum, our final author in this last section, perhaps exemplifies what Baum describes as fearlessness in the face of death born of caring for others. Hillesum was a Dutch Jew, born in 1914 in Middleburg, Netherlands. The selections here are excerpts from her diary and letters, entitled *An Interrupted Life,* that was published after her death at the Auschwitz concentration camp in 1943. Her diary, which begins in 1941, gives a detailed description of the slowly dawning realization, experienced by so many Jews in Nazi-occupied countries, that they were methodically being exterminated as a people. What is first experienced as restriction and discrimination finally results in annihilation. Hillesum's diaries and letters give a close account, not only of her own states of mind, but also of those of the people around her. Not a philosopher by profession, Hillesum's reflections yet show evidence of a philosophy formed and lived in the crucible of trying times.

Holland had capitulated to the Nazis in May 1940, and the Germans were working at isolating the Jews, throwing them out of jobs, forcing them to wear the star of David, and finally deporting them to work camps.

Because Hillesum saw physical death as inevitable, she sought not to flee it but to accept it. Since she was convinced of the spirituality of the self, she interpreted death as no loss, so long as one could face it with calm happiness and in selfless service. Hillesum preferred this attitude of quiet bravery to attempts at saving oneself, which she saw as selling one's integrity, snatching at a few brief moments of worldly life, while losing the spiritual significance of the moment and lack of solidarity with the suffering of others.

Though some have criticized such attitudes toward the Holocaust, Hillesum's account remains insightful and moving as an account of one young woman's coming to terms with the finitude of her own life and the moral collapse of the society around her.

The selections contained here begin with entries during March 1942. By that summer, she had a job with the Jewish Council. Working in these offices briefly, Hillesum decided by August that what she really wanted to do was to accompany Jews sent to Westerbork work camp and minister to their needs within the camp. Westerbork was a temporary community, uprooted weekly by transport trains that were packed with prisoners bound for Auschwitz. Hillesum traveled back to Amsterdam frequently, and one of our excerpts is from a time when she returned there because of poor health. Eventually her whole family, and even Hillesum herself, were packed onto the Poland-bound trains. The last piece of writing collectors have found is a postcard thrown off from the moving train on which Hillesum was sent to her death in Auschwitz in autumn 1943. In the postcard, she asserts that she and others left the camp singing; these brave last words attest to her consistency in her attitude even to her end.

THE THOUGHT OF THE SAGES*

Native Mesoamerican

SORROWFUL CERTAINTY OF DEATH

Meditate upon it, O princes of Huexotzinco;
although it be jade, although it be gold,
it too must go to the place of the fleshless.

It too must go to the region of mystery;
we all perish, no one will remain!

We came only to be born.
Our home is beyond:
In the realm of the defleshed ones.
I suffer:
Happiness, good fortune never comes my way.
Have I come here to struggle in vain?
This is not the place to accomplish things.
Certainly nothing grows green here:
Misfortune opens its blossoms.[1]

It is true that we leave, truly we part.
We leave the flowers, the songs, and the earth.
It is true that we go; it is true that we part![2]

May your heart open!
May your heart draw near!
You bring me torment,
you bring me death.
I will have to go there
where I must perish.
Will you weep for me one last time?
Will you feel sad for me?

Really we are only friends,
I will have to go,
I will have to go.[3]

Let us consider things as lent to us, O friends;
only in passing are we here on earth;
tomorrow or the day after,
as Your heart desires, Giver of Life,
we shall go, my friends, to His home.

Meditate, remember the region of mystery;
beyond is His house; truly we all go
to where the fleshless are, all of us men;
our hearts shall go to know His face.
What are you meditating?
What are you remembering, O my friends?
Meditate no longer!
At our side the beautiful flowers bloom;
so does the Giver of Life concede pleasure to man.

---

*The compositions included in this selection convey personal feelings in relation to death and the possibility of an afterlife. All of them are poems and songs in Nahuatl. Their translation has been prepared by Miguel Leon-Portilla.

[1]*Collection of Mexican Songs,* manuscript preserved in the National Library of Mexico, fol. 14 v. and 4 v.
[2]*Ibid.,* fol. 61 v.
[3]*Ibid.,* fol. 26 r.

All of us, if we meditate, if we remember,
become sad here.[4]

I shall have to leave the precious flowers;
I shall have to descend to the place where those,
in one way or another, live.[5]

TO THE REGION OF MYSTERY

This song accompanies the march
To the region of mystery!
You are fêted,
You have spoken divine words,
But you have died. . . ![6]

So when I remember Itzcoatl,[7]
Sadness invades my heart.
Is it that you were tired?
Or did laziness defeat the Lord of the house?
The Giver of Life resists no one. . . .
So the cortege continues:
It is the universal march![8]

ANGUISHED DOUBTS[9]

Where do we go, oh! where do we go?
Are we dead beyond, or do we yet live?
Will there be existence again?
Will the joy of the Giver of Life be there again?[10]

Do flowers go to the region of the dead?
In the Beyond, are we dead or do we still live?

Where is the source of light, since that which
    gives life hides itself?[11]

Perchance, are we really true beyond?
Will we live where there is only sadness?
Is it true, perchance is it not true . . . ?
How many can truthfully say
that truth is or is not there?
Let our hearts not be troubled.[12]

Given over to sadness
we remain here on earth.

Where is the road
that leads to the Region of the Dead,
the place of our downfall,
the country of the fleshless?

Is it true perhaps that one lives
there, where we all go?
Does your heart believe this?
He hides us
in a chest, in a coffer,
the Giver of Life,
He who shrouds people forever.

Will I be able to look upon,
able to see perhaps, the face
of my mother, of my father?
Will they loan me
a few songs, a few words?
I will have to go down there;
nothing do I expect.
They leave us,
given over to sadness.[13]

Where shall I go?
Where shall I go?
Which is the path to the God of Duality?

Perchance, is Your Home
in the place of the fleshless?
In the innermost of heaven?
Or is the place of the fleshless
only here on earth?[14]

---

[4]*Ibid.,* fol. 14 v.

[5]*Ibid.,* fol. 62 r.

[6]The deeds of a great warrior are here recalled. He had spoken divine words and accomplished extraordinary things but one has to accept that now he is dead.

[7]*Itzcoatl,* the well-known Aztec ruler, reigned from 1428 to 1440.

[8]This poem is included in the already quoted *Collection of Mexican songs,* fol. 30 r.

[9]In the already transcribed poems, the sages' expression is directly concerned with the sorrowful certainty of death. Now the examples I will present are testimonies of their anguished doubts about what we can expect to experience beyond our earthly reality.

[10]*Collection of Mexican Songs,* National Library of Mexico, fol. 61 v.

---

[11]*Ibid.,* fol. 61 r.

[12]*Ibid.,* fol. 62 r.

[13]*Ibid.,* fol. 14 r.

[14]*Ibid.,* fol. 14 v.

Are we to live a second time?
Your heart knows it:
Only once have we come to live.[15]

Am I going to disappear,
Like the withered flowers?
How will my heart do it?
Nothing will remain of me?
At least poetry: flower and song![16]

LET US ENJOY OURSELVES HERE AND NOW[17]

For only here on earth
shall the fragrant flowers last
and the songs that are our bliss.
Enjoy them now![18]

One day we must go,
one night we will descend into the region of
    mystery.
Here, we only come to know ourselves;
only in passing are we here on earth.
In peace and pleasure let us spend our lives; come,
    let us enjoy ourselves.[19]

Let us have friends here!
It is the time to know our faces.
Only with flowers
can our song enrapture.
We will have gone to His house,
but our word
shall live here on earth.
We will go, leaving behind
our grief, our song.
For this will be known,
the song shall remain real.
We will have gone to His house,

but our word
shall live here on earth.[20]

I weep, I feel forlorn;
I remember that we must leave flowers and songs.
Let us enjoy ourselves now, let us sing now!
For we go, we disappear.[21]

Remove trouble from your hearts, O my friends.
As I know, so do others:
Only once do we live.
Let us in peace and pleasure spend our lives;
come, let us enjoy ourselves!
Let not those who live in anger join us,
the earth is so vast.
Oh! that one could live forever!
Oh! that one never had to die![22]

BEYOND IS THE PLACE WHERE ONE LIVES[23]

Truly earth is not the place of reality.
Indeed one must go elsewhere;
beyond, happiness exists.
Or is it that we come to earth in vain?
Certainly some other place is the abode of life.[24]

Beyond is the place where one lives.
I would be lying to myself were I to say,
"Perhaps everything ends on this earth;
here do our lives end."

No, O Lord of the Close Vicinity,
it is beyond, with those who dwell in Your house,
that I will sing songs to You, in the innermost of
    heaven.
My heart rises;
I fix my eyes upon You,

---

[15]*Ibid.,* fol. 12 r.

[16]*Ibid.,* fol. 10 r.

[17]The following compositions convey the feelings and ideas of some of the sages, those in particular who had adopted a sort of "Epicurean attitude" in their lives. If we have to disappear from the earth, and if we are ignorant about our destiny, "let us enjoy ourselves now, for as long we can. . . ."

[18]*Collection of Mexican Songs,* fol. 61 v.

[19]*Ibid.,* fol. 25 v.

---

[20]*Romances de los Señores de Nueva España,* Library of the University of Texas, Austin, fol. 27 v.

[21]*Collection of Mexican Songs,* fol. 35 r.

[22]*Ibid.,* fol. 25 v. and 26 r.

[23]Followers of a different trend of thought were the sages who, while being persuaded that "earth is not the place of reality," accepted the idea that "one must go elsewhere," to that place, in the beyond, where happiness really exists. Otherwise, they said, we would have to admit that man had come to live in vain.

[24]*Collection of Mexican Songs,* fol. 1 v.

next to You, beside You,
O Giver of Life![25]

Thus the dead were addressed,
when they died.
If it was a man, they spoke to him,
invoked him as a divine being,
in the name of pheasant;
if it was a woman, in the name of owl;
and they said to them:

"Awaken, already the sky is tinged with red,
already the dawn has come,
already the flame-colored pheasants are singing,
the fire-colored swallows,
already butterflies are on the wing."

For this reason the ancient ones said,
he who has died, he becomes a god.
They said: "He became a god there,"
which means that he died.[26]

SOCIAL CONCEPTIONS OF DEATH

Gregory Baum

The great critics of religion have looked upon the Christian teaching on the kingdom of God and the expectation of eternal life as principal causes of human alienation. Otherworldliness, according to these critics, leads to the contempt of this world. The hope for an eternal life of happiness makes people shrug their shoulders in regard to their earthly existence and prevents them from becoming concerned enough about their situation to change the conditions of social life. The doctrine of eternal life trivializes history. A religion that promises heaven consoles people in their misery, makes them

patient and meek, and protects the existing social and political orders. Otherworldly religion, according to this analysis, is inevitably ideological.

Since critical theology intends to make the church assume theological responsibility for the unintended, social consequences of its religion and free the proclamation of the gospel from the alienating trends associated with it, contemporary theologians regard the Christian teaching on the last things as a topic of special challenge. Is it possible to understand Christ's preaching of the kingdom as utopian rather than ideological religion? The great critics of religion have measured Christian teaching in the light of the common understanding held by the church over the last centuries, with its almost exclusive concentration on individual destiny. The message of the kingdom has been reduced, in the church's preaching and in the minds of the faithful, to an assurance of personal survival after death and entry into the happiness of heaven. Hell was preached as a possibility for the unrepentant sinner, and in the Catholic Church purgatory was presented as the realm where the faithful departed of good will undergo the painful transformation that enables them to enter into eternal bliss. What we find in this common understanding is an almost complete privatization of the gospel promises. The first task of critical theology then, here as in connection with other doctrines, is the deprivatization of the church's teaching.

According to the New Testament the center of Christ's preaching was the kingdom of God. Jesus was the servant and instrument of God's reign in the lives of men, promised to Israel in the ancient days, inaugurated in his person, and about to be made manifest in all its power. This kingdom was no "otherworldly reality"; it was God's reign, promised from the beginning, anticipated in the covenanted people and the sacramental church, and finally coming upon history as judgment and new creation. This kingdom was not conceived as a realm parallel to history; it was not a heavenly dominion above the realms of the earth; the kingdom was, rather, the divine reign that emerged in history as the longing of the cosmos and the fulfillment of the people's hopes. The kingdom was preached as

---

[25]*Ibid.,* fol. 2 r.
[26]*Codex Matritensis,* fol. 195 r.

the new age. It will destroy the sin in the hearts of men and the injustices present in their institutions, it will rectify the inequalities in the world and give people access to the sources of life. It was this kingdom that was to have no end. The promises made in the New Testament, then, affect individual people as well as society, the heart as well as the world, the body as well as the soul, present history as well as the world to come. The Christian promises are offered globally; they are not sorted out in detail. We admit, of course, that the New Testament language regarding the kingdom is dualistic, but this refers not to a dualism between mind and body, or between person and society, but to the contrast between the old age and the new. Christ ushered in a new age. The New Testament records the different ways in which the early Christians understood God's promises, from the eager expectation of the final judgment and the end of the world, to the patient confidence that the kingdom present in Christ and his church would be a source of a gradual humanization in history.

In the patristic age the message of eternal life remained focused on the community. It is true that the eschatological tension of the early church was lost very soon, but if we are to believe Henri de Lubac's famous study, *Catholicism,*[1] in the age of the fathers the thrust of the church's teaching, including the doctrine of eternal life, focused on the redemption and destiny of the whole community. Lubac developed the thesis of his book in the thirties, after prolonged conversation with Marxist thought; he tried to demonstrate that the individualism implicit in modern Christianity was due to the privatization of religion which had distorted, against the genius of Catholicism, the collectivist understanding of sin, grace and glory proclaimed and celebrated by the church of the fathers. The church as God's people was the bearer of the divine promises, and it was this people that was to live eternally. The church was the sign and symbol of the whole human race, the one human family, whose

destiny was disclosed and made visible in the fellowship of the faithful. The doctrine of eternal life revealed first and foremost the divine end and purpose of history. It directed people's imagination toward the last days of God's ultimate victory of evil and the creation of a new heaven and a new earth. The question of personal survival after death was not in the foreground. The liturgy of Christian burial confined itself to the simple words of *requies, lux* and *pax.* Dominant in the Christian imagination and the church's liturgy was the hope for the final accomplishment, the completion of history, and the resurrection of the entire people.

For the first thousand years the Christian people looked forward to the resurrection of the last day as the complete fulfillment of the divine promises and showed comparatively little interest in the state of the soul after the death of the body. This changed gradually. When the theologians in the 14th century, responding to the religion of the faithful, taught that after death the soul encounters the living God, undergoes the particular judgment, and if approved is admitted to eternal bliss in the *visio beatifica,*[2] Pope John XXII, relying on the more ancient tradition, condemned this new trend. "The soul separated from the body," he taught, "does not enjoy the vision of God which is its total reward and will not enjoy it prior to the resurrection."[3] Pope John XXII was the last witness of the ancient church's collectivist imagination, which saw salvation primarily as the entry of the entire people into grace and glory. However individualistic culture had superseded the Pope. He himself changed his mind; and the next pontiff, Pope Benedict XII, revoked the position of his predecessor, solemnly proposed the new teaching, and confirmed the shift of the church's religious longing from the crowning of history in the new creation to the soul's eternal happiness after death. Until recently, this has been the common stance of modern Christianity.

---

[1]Henri de Lubac, *Catholicism,* trans. L. C. Sheppard, Burns & Oates, London, 1962, especially pp. 49-62.

[2]Literally, "beatific vision": a state of bliss in which the human soul beholds God's presence [Eds.].
[3]*Enchiridion Symbolorum,* edit. Denzinger-Schönmetzer, Herder, Freiburg, 1963, p. 295.

In the modern period the church's teaching of eternal life was understood almost exclusively in terms of the fate that awaited the individual after his or her death. The eschatological framework of the gospel was largely abandoned. Christians no longer experienced themselves as a people on pilgrimage, as a people with an historical destiny; instead they regarded the society to which they belonged, and the church within it, as abiding elements of the divine plan and reduced the great Christian adventure to the personal journey from birth to death. Church and society were the unchanging stage on which people worked out their personal salvation. The Church's liturgy, on the whole, retained the historical vision and recalled that God had acted in Christ on behalf of all mankind and brought history to the new and final age, but the individualistic culture did not allow this ancient teaching to affect the people's piety. Death became the end of the journey and salvation the pledge of one's own personal happiness beyond the grave.

This privatizing trend in religion corresponds to the growing individualism in secular culture, which has reached its high point in modern, *Gesellschaft*-type society. Here the individual is wholly severed from the social matrix. At the same time, acting as impersonal agents in a rationalized society, people feel that they have lost the sense of self. The triumph and agony of individualism have made people focus on personal death as the great enemy which threatens the meaning of their lives in the present. Modern secularity imitates the church's concentration on death. For Heidegger, the fear of death marks a person's entire life and produces a metaphysical anguish that reveals man's authentic nature. This concentration on personal death has even found entry into sociological reflection. Alfred Schutz integrates Heidegger's view of death into his phenomenology of the social world, and Peter Berger assigns personal death a primary role in his sociology of religion and the construction of reality.[4] The fear of death

overshadows the whole of a person's life; it convicts her efforts of building the world and her quest for happiness of finitude and imbues them with a peculiar anxiety. This anguish, this fear of death, the horror of chaos is, according to Berger's sociology, the generating force that makes people seek a safe and stable world, and create sacred symbols that legitimate the present order and promise future security. Religion is created as the answer to personal death and its anxiety-producing power. What we have here, it seems to me, is a psychology rather than a sociology of religion.

While it may not be surprising that such a privatizing perspective takes hold of philosophers in the modern age, it is curious to see this perspective applied in sociology. For why should a social thinker hold that death is the universal fact that has meaning apart from the social context in which it occurs? Is the reaction of people to their mortality a transcendent phenomenon, independent of their cultural world, and hence a solid ground, beyond the changing social circumstances, on which to construct a sociology of religion? The old-fashioned literature glorifying the self-sacrifice of soldiers on the battlefield is a good illustration that the attitude toward one's own death depends on social environment. Max Weber may have been only half-serious when he suggested that death has become such an absurd event only in modern, competitive, achievement-oriented society because there people daily sacrifice happiness for the sake of work, and when they finally encounter death, they feel that after having postponed happiness all their lives, they are now cheated of their reward and their entire life is being mocked and invalidated. Weber may have thought that in other cultures people were willing to live more wholeheartedly in the present with its joys and pains, and when death awaited them as the long sleep at the end of their lives, they may not have been that frightened by it. Even the attitude toward death is socially grounded. To regard the anxiety over one's mortality as a primary principle of human behavior. I conclude, corresponds not to the nature of reality but to the privatizing trend of the social world.

---

[4] Peter Berger, *The Sacred Canopy,* pp. 23-28: *The Social Construction of Reality,* pp. 27, 101-102.

The attitude toward death depends on the imagination of the future, mediated throughout society by cultural or religious movements. In tribal society, the imagination of people projected the ongoing existence of the tribe and hence they found it easy to speak of life beyond the grave. They felt themselves embedded in a living reality that would perdure in the future. In the ages of nationalism and its accompanying conflicts and wars, to give another example, people's imagination of the future circled around the emergence and flowering of the nation, and when confronted with death in this struggle, they did not fear for themselves but dreamt of their nation's future. Nationalist poetry is full of accounts of such sacrificial deaths. In modern society, people's imagination of the future tends to be caught in their own personal lives. They dream of what life will be like for them in ten years, in twenty years, in thirty years. In the consumers' society of today our imagination is taught to concentrate on the rising standard of living and the ever greater personal well-being. Death, in such a context, seems utterly frightful. But already if a person is profoundly attached to her children and their families, then her imagination will circle around their future and her own personal death will not appear as the great enemy. Herbert Marcuse, the great atheistic social philosopher, has made one of the most profound remarks about death, one that one might expect to find in the great literatures of religion. "Men can die without anxiety," Marcuse wrote, "if they know that what they love is protected from misery and oblivion."[5] If the object of a person's love is protected from harm and assured of well-being, then the nothingness of her own tomorrow, threatened in death, is not a great source of anguish. But if we love ourselves, and our future imagination circles around our own well-being—this is almost inevitable in *Gesellschaft*-type society—then what we love is wholly unprotected, and death becomes the dreaded enemy. How does Marcuse's important

remark apply to the Christian faith? If we yearn for the kingdom of God, if we long for God's victory over evil and all the enemies of life and believe that in Christ this victory is assured, then what we love is protected and it should not be so difficult to die.

The Christian teaching of eternal life, we conclude, rather than making the believers focus on their own death and worry about what happens to them after they die, liberates them for a greater love and makes them yearn for the reconciliation and deliverance of all peoples. The Christian message of resurrection, understood in this deprivatizing perspective, far from making Christians concentrate on their own heaven, frees them from anxiety about their own existence and directs their hope to the new creation. The doctrine of God's approaching kingdom, the central Christian symbol, summons people to forget themselves, to serve the kingdom of God coming into the lives of men and women, and to rejoice with the Christian community, gathered at worship, that in Christ God's final victory has been assured. God will have the last word. Evil will not be allowed to stand. The entry into personal salvation and future life is not prepared by concentrating on one's own life but by trusting and loving God's coming reign. The dialect of personal-and-social, which we observed when speaking of sin and grace, must also be observed when interpreting the Christian doctrine of eternal life.

This deprivatizing trend is operative in contemporary spirituality. Perhaps one of the first signs of this reorientation was given by a remarkable woman who in many ways was a conventional saint, Thérèse of Lisieux.[6] In her oft-quoted statement, "I want to spend my heaven doing good on earth," she subtly criticized the individualism of traditional Catholic spirituality. She thought that she would not be able to rest with God as long as people were still suffering and the promised king-

---

[5]Herbert Marcuse, *Eros and Civilization,* Vintage Books, New York, 1962, p. 216.

[6]Author of the religious classic *Story of a Soul,* Thérèse of Lisieux was born in 1873 in Alencon, France. She joined the Carmelite Monastery at age 15, and died an early death in 1897. Devotion to Thérèse, and claims of her ongoing help and influence, continue to this day [Eds.].

dom had not been established. This was then a startling innovation. In contemporary spiritual writers, such as Thomas Merton, Daniel Berrigan, Ernesto Cardinale, and James Douglas, the passage to a more collective understanding of divine salvation has been completed. While these authors attach much importance to personal life and one's personal union with God as the ground for a life that will never die, they understand this personal life as participation in the human community and a share in the salvation which is meant for all. Here each person is damaged by the misery inflicted on others. In this new spirituality there is no communion with God unless mediated by Jesus, that is, by a total solidarity with humanity, especially the underprivileged and dispossessed. Here entry into eternal life is again understood, following the New Testament, as repentance and identification with God's coming reign. Anguish about one's death and concern about one's personal heaven are not the entry into the Christian life. Nor is the question of personal survival after death the best way to approach the Christian teaching on eternal life.

The common theological approach to death and dying has also been privatized from another point of view. Usually, in sermons and books on pastoral theology, we speak of death as if people normally die peacefully in their beds. Death is here looked upon as the startling end of a person's life in a settled context of friendly faces. Yet by thinking of death in this way, we forget that vast numbers of people die very differently as victims of society. A glance at statistics of people killed by wars, acts of genocide, unrelieved famines, and other forms of collective violence reminds us that a peaceful death in bed is by no means the normal way for people to die in the 20th century. A certain, highly private theology of dying, it seems to me, disguises from consciousness the cruel world to which we belong. We tend to think that the terms which make sense to us in our protected context apply to people everywhere. But death in bed, after a life well spent, is for many people the object of great hope. To focus on this kind of death as if it were the great enemy overlooks the political realities of the 20th century. Asking the reader's permission for a very personal remark, I recall that my own mother, hiding in Berlin from Nazi persecution of the Jews and deportation to the death camps, became overwhelmed with exhaustion, fell gravely ill, and still died in a bed surrounded by friendly faces, not by enemies. This was a grace. A Christian theology of death ought to take the political dimension seriously. To die in bed, after a long, affirmative life, is not so bad, and we can't really wish anything better for ourselves. At the same time, we do not want an imagination of the future that circles around our own personal fate. The Christian message of the coming kingdom promises deliverance from evil on a universal scale including all the peoples of the earth, and thanks to this message we want to think of our personal lives as situated in this holy, dread and universal drama.

FACING DEATH

Etty Hillesum

The branches of the tree outside my window have been lopped off.

The night before the stars had still hung like glistening fruit in the heavy branches, and now they climbed, unsure of themselves, up the bare, ravaged trunk. Oh, yes, the stars: for a few nights, some of them, lost, deserted, grazed over the wide, forsaken, heavenly plain.

For a moment, when the branches were being cut, I became sentimental. And for that moment I was deeply sad. Then I suddenly knew: I should love the new landscape, too, love it in my own way. Now the two trees rise up outside my window like imposing, emaciated ascetes, thrusting into the bright sky like two daggers.

And on Thursday evening the war raged once again outside my window and I lay there watching it all from my bed. Bernard was playing a Bach record next door. It had sounded so powerful and glowing, but then, suddenly, there were planes, ack-ack fire, shooting, bombs—much noisier than they have been for a long time. It seemed to go on right beside the house. And it suddenly came to me again: there must be so many houses all over the world which are collapsing each day under just such bombs as these.

And Bach went gallantly on, now faint and small. And I lay there in my bed in a very strange mood. Filaments of light along the menacing bare trunk outside my window. A constant pounding. And I thought to myself: any minute now a piece of shrapnel could come through that window. It's quite possible. And it's equally possible that there would be a lot of pain. And yet I felt so deeply peaceful and grateful, there in my bed, and meekly resigned to all the disasters and pains that might be in store for me.

• • •

SATURDAY MORNING, 7:30 . . . The bare trunks which climb past my window now shelter under a cover of young green leaves. A springy fleece along their naked, tough, ascetic limbs.

I went to bed early last night and from my bed I stared out through the large open window. And it was once more as if life with all its mysteries was close to me, as if I could touch it. I had the feeling that I was resting against the naked breast of life, and could feel her gentle and regular heartbeat. I felt safe and protected. And I thought: how strange. It is wartime. There are concentration camps. I can say of so many of the houses I pass: here the son has been thrown into prison, there the father has been taken hostage, and an 18-year-old boy in that house over there has been sentenced to death. And these streets and houses are all so close to my own. I know how very nervous people are, I know about the mounting human suffering. I know the persecution and oppression and despotism and the impotent fury and the terrible sadism. I know it all.

And yet—at unguarded moments, when left to myself, I suddenly lie against the naked breast of life and her arms round me are so gentle and so protective and my own heartbeat is difficult to describe: so slow and so regular and so soft, almost muffled, but so constant, as if it would never stop.

That is also my attitude to life and I believe that neither war nor any other senseless human atrocity will ever be able to change it.

• • •

Many accuse me of indifference and passivity when I refuse to go into hiding; they say that I have given up. They say everyone who can must try to stay out of their clutches, it's our bounden duty to try. But that argument is specious. For while everyone tries to save himself, vast numbers are nevertheless disappearing. And the funny thing is I don't feel I'm in their clutches anyway, whether I stay or am sent away. I find all that talk so cliché-ridden and naive and can't go along with it any more. I don't feel in anybody's clutches; I feel safe in God's arms, to put it rhetorically, and no matter whether I am sitting at this beloved old desk now, or in a bare room in the Jewish district or perhaps in a labour camp under SS guards in a month's time—I shall always feel safe in God's arms. They may well succeed in breaking me physically, but no more than that. I may face cruelty and deprivation the likes of which I cannot imagine in even my wildest fantasies. Yet all this is as nothing to the immeasurable expanse of my faith in God and my inner receptiveness.

I shall always be able to stand on my own two feet even when they are planted on the hardest soil of the harshest reality. And my acceptance is not indifference or helplessness. I feel deep moral indignation at a regime that treats human beings in such a way. But events have become too overwhelming and too demonic to be stemmed with personal resentment and bitterness. These responses strike me as being utterly childish and unequal to the fateful course of events.

People often get worked up when I say it doesn't really matter whether I go or somebody else does, the main thing is that so many thousands *have* to go. It is not as if I want to fall into the arms of destruction with a resigned smile—far from it. I am only bowing to the inevitable and even as I do so I am sustained by the certain knowledge that ultimately they cannot rob us of anything that matters. But I don't think I would feel happy if I were exempted from what so many others have to suffer. They keep telling me that someone like me has a duty to go into hiding, because I have so many things to do in life, so much to give. But I know that whatever I may have to give to others, I can give it no matter where I am, here in the circle of my friends or over there, in a concentration camp. And it is sheer arrogance to think oneself too good to share the fate of the masses.

And if God Himself should feel that I still have a great deal to do, well then, I shall do it after I have suffered what all the others have to suffer. And whether or not I am a valuable human being will only become clear from my behaviour in more arduous circumstances. And if I should not survive, how I die will show me who I really am. Of course that doesn't mean I will turn down a medical exemption if they give me one on account of my inflamed kidneys and bladder. And I have been recommended for some sort of soft job with the Jewish Council. They had permission to hire 180 people last week, and the desperate are thronging there in droves, as shipwrecked people might cling for dear life to a piece of driftwood. But that is as far as I am prepared to go and, beyond that, I am not willing to pull any strings. In any case, the Jewish Council seems to have become a hotbed of intrigue, and resentment against this strange agency is growing by the hour. And sooner or later it will be their turn to go, anyway.

But, of course, by then the English may have landed. At least that's what those people say who have not yet abandoned all political hope. I believe that we must rid ourselves of all expectations of help from the outside world, that we must stop guessing about the duration of the war and so on. And now I am going to set the table.

• • •

14 JULY, TUESDAY EVENING. Everyone must follow the way of life that suits him best. I simply cannot make active preparations to save myself, it seems so pointless to me and would make me nervous and unhappy. My letter of application to the Jewish Council on Jaap's urgent advice has upset my cheerful yet deadly serious equilibrium. As if I had done something underhand. Like crowding on

to a small piece of wood adrift on an endless ocean after a shipwreck and then saving oneself by pushing others into the water and watching them drown. It is all so ugly. And I don't think much of this particular crowd, either. I would much rather join those who prefer to float on their backs for a while, drifting on the ocean with their eyes turned towards heaven and who then go down with a prayer. I cannot help myself. My battles are fought out inside, with my own demons; it is not in my nature to tilt against the savage, cold-blooded fanatics who clamour for our destruction. I am not afraid of them either, I don't know why; I am so calm it is sometimes as if I were standing on the parapets of the palace of history looking down over far-distant lands. This bit of history we are experiencing right now is something I know I can stand up to. I know what is happening and yet my head is clear. But sometimes I feel as if a layer of ashes were being sprinkled over my heart, as if my face were withering and decaying before my very eyes, and as if everything were falling apart in front of me and my heart were letting everything go. But these are brief moments; then everything falls back into place, my head is clear again and I can once more bear and stand up to this piece of history which is ours. For once you have begun to walk with God, you need only keep on walking with Him and all of life becomes one long stroll—such a marvellous feeling.

We go too far in fearing for our unhappy bodies, while our forgotten spirit shrivels up in some corner.

• • •

Maria, hallo,

Ten thousand have passed through this place, the clothed and the naked, the old and the young, the sick and the healthy—and I am left to live and work and stay cheerful. It will be my parents' turn to leave soon, if by some miracle not this week then certainly one of the next. And I must learn to accept this as well. Mischa insists on going along with them and it seems to me that he probably should; if he has to watch his parents leave this place it will totally unhinge him. I shan't go, I just can't. It is easier to pray for someone from a distance than to see him suffer by your side. It is not fear of Poland that keeps me from going along with my parents, but fear of seeing them suffer. And that, too, is cowardice.

This is something people refuse to admit to themselves: at a given point you can no longer *do,* but can only *be* and accept. And although that is something I learned a long time ago, I also know that one can only accept for oneself and not for others. And that is what is so desperately difficult for me here. Mother and Mischa still want to "do," to turn the whole world upside down, but I know we can't do anything about it. I have never been able to "do" anything; I can only let things take their course and if need be suffer. This is where my strength lies and it is great strength indeed.

QUESTIONS FOR DISCUSSION

1. Many of our authors in this section find the courage to face death because of a belief in an afterlife. But not all of them describe the afterlife, or the self who survives death, in the same way. What are some of the differences? And similarities?

2. Do you agree, or disagree, that whether there is life after death plays a big role in whether our lives are meaningful or not? Draw upon the ideas of several of our authors.

3. Baum suggests a theological interpretation of the Christian position on life after death that is quite different from the average layman's understanding. Is his view convincing? Or is it difficult to give up the standard view of individual survival after death?

4. What do you think of the idea, proposed by Hillesum, and suggested by Baum through his example of Thérèse of Lisieux, that we can't really experience life's full meaning unless we engage in compassionate action to help others?

Birmingham, Alabama, May 1963. (Charles Moore/Black Star)

554

CHAPTER 9

SOCIAL JUSTICE

Philosophy is essentially a theoretical discipline, but theories are related to practice. In social and political philosophy, philosophers turn their thoughts to the question of human social formations and forms of government: What is the ideal government? What is the individual's relationship to government? What is required in our social relationship to one another? What constitutes exploitation, or discrimination? What do demands for equality mean, politically and economically?

In matters of politics, philosophers throughout history have been more than armchair speculators. Some have helped to legitimate the governments under which they lived; other philosophers have questioned that legitimation and helped to topple governments. We now live in a world where a "global economy" unites people from different countries. But this global economy includes vast differences in wealth, power, and health. Typically in many countries, including the United States, a relatively small number of rich people own the majority of property and have the most wealth. At the same time, nearly one-fourth of the world's people live in absolute poverty, with incomes of less than one dollar a day. While some people hook up on the Internet to communicate with all corners of the globe, over 90 percent of the world's people do not have telephones.[1]

How shall we understand each other when we have such vastly different cultural, political, and economic experiences of life? Books and technological means such as the Internet are helpful, but they can't accomplish the task alone. A great deal of our ability to understand others depends upon our own minds and the narrow or broad perspective from which we look out onto our world. How each of us sees the world is, however, influenced by our social upbringing and how we were taught to perceive and evaluate the actions of others. In other words, some philosophers argue, we don't just see the world "as it is." The schema of ideas that we receive through our upbringing encourages us to notice certain things and not notice others, to give certain aspects of experience moral importance and

---

[1]See Richard A. Hoehn, "Introduction," and Marc C. Cohen, "World Hunger in a Global Economy," in *Hunger in a Global Economy: Hunger 1998, Eighth Annual Report on the State of World Hunger* (Silver Spring, MD: Bread for the World Institute, 1998), pp. 2–21.

to think of other aspects with indifference. Our perspectives may also be narrowed, quite innocently at times, by our lack of firsthand experience of how our society may seem to others who do not occupy the same position that we do. Our ability to evaluate what is the best course of action and to incarnate certain values such as justice and equality may be contingent upon our ability to take into consideration the points of view of others with whom we share the public realm. Such is the theme of our first section, "Perspectives, Difference, and Moral Respect." We hear first from Peggy McIntosh, who tells us about her becoming aware of how being white in contemporary America gave her an unearned privilege, making life easier for her than if she were black, Hispanic, Native American, or Asian. Laurence Thomas argues that people who aren't members of a socially oppressed group should listen to the testimonies of those who experience racism firsthand, rather than project their own ideas and belittle the firsthand accounts that they hear; he calls such careful and respectful listening "moral deference." Paula Moya explains how she came to her awareness of herself as a Chicana woman who is politically committed to overcoming racism and sexism in society. And Karen Fiser exposes many people's mistaken notions about what it's like to live with a disability, tracing these conceptual problems back to their philosophical counterparts: a philosophy of person that presumes ablebodiedness.

Our second section, "Social Equality," examines just distribution of wealth and position in society. Are inequalities sometimes justified? For what reasons? Does a commitment to political equality necessarily entail economic equality? It may be the case that humans are equal in some ways and unequal in others. What would be the implications of this?

Contemporary Indian author Satyavrata Siddhantalankar argues for social stratification based on what he considers sound spiritual principles found in the Vedas, contending that a strict equality would go against the natural differences in human temperaments. John Rawls, a well-known American philosopher, tries to reconstruct mentally the ideal social situation in which issues of fairness can be decided. He argues that economic inequalities would be good if they resulted in benefits for the common good. H. Odera Oruka, a Kenyan philosopher, argues that Rawls' licence for economic inequality would inevitably result in political inqualities, and so Rawls' position must be rejected or modified.

In the third section, we look at the results when people are oppressed by unjust political or economic systems. Many political theorists echo the sentiments of the U.S. Declaration of Independence and assert that the dominated have a right to fight for their dignity and freedom. But just how that fight will be waged—through violence and threat of violence, nonviolent activism, or education— differs from author to author. Marx and Engels offer a revolutionary challenge to the political and economic systems of capitalism. Mohandas Gandhi thinks that nonviolent action in the spirit of love can overcome the system of foreign oppression in colonial India; he uses the same rationale as well to combat the caste discrimination that exists in his society. Martin Luther King, Jr., explains why Gandhi's philosophy is needed in our present world, which is increasingly globally interconnected on the political and economic level. Malcolm X sees the need to challenge and eradicate racist practices in the United States; violent threats may be needed to startle a complacent and entrenched system. Finally, Enrique Dussel explains, from his perspective of liberation philosophy, why it is just for the poor to engage in violent struggle within the Latin American context.

PERSPECTIVES, DIFFERENCE, AND MORAL RESPECT

In this section, our authors discuss the need for an expanded awareness of the experience, insights, and needs of others, who may have unique perspectives that we can learn about only by listening to their accounts. Learning about the struggles of others may then cause us to question things we take for granted regarding our own experience. Such an ability to understand others could be considered a prerequisite for being able to solve any other social and political issue of the day.

Peggy McIntosh is the associate director of the Wellesley College Center for Research on Women. She realized through her work with feminist issues that many men are unwilling to grant that they are over-privileged compared to women. Her idea of *overprivilege* means that someone has an unearned advantage. Men have a tendency to experience their own situation as neutral; while they might admit that women are disadvantaged in comparison, they are reluctant to admit that their own successes may be due to overreward. McIntosh shares her insight about her own realization of the ways in which she was overprivileged by being white in a racist society. As she explains, "The appearance of being a good citizen rather than a troublemaker comes in large part from having all sorts of doors open automatically because of my color."

Although privilege sounds like something we'd like to have, McIntosh explains that it's actually harmful, not only to others but to the privileged person him- or herself. Privilege gives one the "permission" not to take other cultures seriously. This could have wide-ranging repercussions for us if we want to learn how to live with each other in a just society.

Laurence Thomas, a contemporary African-American professor of philosophy at Syracuse University, explains why it is important to listen to members of racial and cultural minorities when they describe what it is like to live in a racist society. It is not enough just to imagine oneself in the other person's shoes—such flights of imagination might lead to serious misconceptions. Thomas argues that members of dominated social categories are owed moral

deference; this means that persons of goodwill from the dominated social group, who can speak intelligently about experiences that they alone can have, should be listened to and believed. Otherwise, this puts members of the dominated social category at a constant disadvantage, in that every time they try to speak, people will insist that they are giving a biased account.

Paula Moya echoes Thomas's point on moral deference in her description of epistemic privilege: She argues that someone who has had key experiences will be able to provide the information we all need for understanding the effects of the power structure in a society. She argues that granting epistemic privilege is not just a nice gesture; rather, it is necessary for social objectivity. She explains that her identity as "Chicana" is truer, and more objective, than if she were to identify herself as Hispanic, American, or Mexican-American. She argues that in order for any of us to really understand our world, we must understand our own social location.

An interesting example of the problem of projecting one's own experience onto others occurred recently in the state of Oregon. A group of people with disabilities brought charges against the state, saying that the allocation of state health resources discriminated against those with disabilities. In response, the state of Oregon argued that its allocations were based on popular and democratic criteria. They had conducted a telephone poll in which Oregon residents were asked to rank the relative importance of various forms of health care. When it came to the category of disabilities such as blindness, those polled often claimed that they'd rather be dead than disabled; therefore, they ranked services for those with disabilities as the lowest priority. This is a result of people trying to imagine how they themselves would feel if they were disabled, rather than asking a disabled person what life is really like for someone who is disabled.[1]

---

[1]Cited in Iris Marion Young, "Asymmetrical Reciprocity: On Moral Respect, Wonder, and Enlarged Mentality," *Constellations* 3 no. 3 (1997), pp. 340–63, especially pp. 343–44.

Karen Fiser, a contemporary philosopher and poet who teaches at Stanford University, addresses this issue of disability from the disabled person's perspective. She argues that disabled people can enrich our understanding of what it means to be human. She expresses her frustration with the philosophical literature on the topic: it seems philosophers only want to talk about disabilities in the context of whether it's allowable to kill a disabled person. They never talk about life with a disability. Our own society's overvaluing of personal autonomy makes it difficult for the disabled person to ask for help, in Fiser's view. Too many able persons see people with disabilities as a special expense and trouble, rather than accepting their legal right to equal access. Fiser concludes by exploring the complex situation of the intersection of race and gender with disability.

WHITE PRIVILEGE AND MALE PRIVILEGE

Peggy McIntosh

Through work to bring materials and perspectives from Women's Studies into the rest of the curriculum, I have often noticed men's unwillingness to grant that they are overprivileged in the curriculum, even though they may grant that women are disadvantaged. Denials that amount to taboos surround the subject of advantages that men gain from women's disadvantages. These denials protect male privilege from being fully recognized, acknowledged, lessened, or ended.

Thinking through unacknowledged male privilege as a phenomenon with a life of its own, I realized that since hierarchies in our society are interlocking, there was most likely a phenomenon of white privilege that was similarly denied and protected, but alive and real in its effects. As a white person, I realized I had been taught about racism as something that puts others at a disadvantage, but had

been taught not to see one of its corollary aspects, white privilege, which puts me at an advantage.

I think whites are carefully taught not to recognize white privilege, as males are taught not to recognize male privilege. So I have begun in an untutored way to ask what it is like to have white privilege. This paper is a partial record of my personal observations and not a scholarly analysis. It is based on my daily experiences within my particular circumstances.

I have come to see white privilege as an invisible package of unearned assets that I can count on cashing in each day, but about which I was "meant" to remain oblivious. White privilege is like an invisible weightless knapsack of special provisions, assurances, tools, maps, guides, codebooks, passports, visas, clothes, compass, emergency gear, and blank checks.

Since I have had trouble facing white privilege, and describing its results in my life, I saw parallels here with men's reluctance to acknowledge male privilege. Only rarely will a man go beyond acknowledging that women are disadvantaged to acknowledging that men have unearned advantage, or that unearned privilege has not been good for men's development as human beings, or for society's development, or that privilege systems might ever be challenged and *changed*.

I will review here several types or layers of denial that I see at work protecting, and preventing awareness about, entrenched male privilege. Then I will draw parallels, from my own experience, with the denials that veil the facts of white privilege. Finally, I will list forty-six ordinary and daily ways in which I experience having white privilege, by contrast with my African American colleagues in the same building. This list is not intended to be generalizable. Others can make their own lists from within their own life circumstances.

Writing this paper has been difficult, despite warm receptions for the talks on which it is based.[1]

---

[1]This paper was presented at the Virginia Women's Studies Association conference in Richmond in April, 1986, and the American Education Research Association conference in Boston in October, 1986, and discussed with two groups of participants in the Dodge seminars for Secondary School Teachers in New York and Boston in the spring of 1987.

For describing white privilege makes one newly accountable. As we in Women's Studies work to reveal male privilege and ask men to give up some of their power, so one who writes about having white privilege must ask, "Having described it, what will I do to lessen or end it?"

Counter-Arguements

The denial of men's overprivileged state takes many forms in discussions of curriculum change work. Some claim that men must be central in the curriculum because they have done most of what is important or distinctive in life or in civilization. Some recognize sexism in the curriculum but deny that it makes male students seem unduly important in life. Others agree that certain *individual* thinkers are male oriented but deny that there is any *systemic* tendency in disciplinary frameworks or epistemology to overempower men as a group. Those men who do grant that male privilege takes institutionalized and embedded forms are still likely to deny that male hegemony has opened doors for them personally. Virtually all men deny that male overreward alone can explain men's centrality in all the inner sanctums of our most powerful institutions. Moreover, those few who will acknowledge that male privilege systems have overempowered them usually end up doubting that we could dismantle these privilege systems. They may say they will work to improve women's status, in the society or in the university, but they can't or won't support the idea of lessening men's. In curricular terms, this is the point at which they say that they regret they cannot use any of the interesting new scholarship on women because the syllabus is full. When the talk turns to giving men less cultural room, even the most thoughtful and fair-minded of the men I know will tend to reflect, or fall back on, conservative assumptions about the inevitability of present gender relations and distributions of power, calling on precedent or sociobiology and psychobiology to demonstrate that male domination is natural and follows inevitably from evolutionary pressures. Others resort to arguments from "experience" or religion or social responsibility or wishing and dreaming.

After I realized, through faculty development work in Women's Studies, the extent to which men work from a base of unacknowledged privilege, I understood that much of their oppressiveness was unconscious. Then I remembered the frequent charges from women of color that white women whom they encounter are oppressive. I began to understand why we are justly seen as oppressive, even when we don't see ourselves that way. At the very least, obliviousness of one's privileged state can make a person or group irritating to be with. I began to count the ways in which I enjoy unearned skin privilege and have been conditioned into oblivion about its existence, unable to see that it put me "ahead" in any way, or put my people ahead, over-rewarding us and yet also paradoxically damaging us, or that it could or should be changed.

My schooling gave me no training in seeing myself as an oppressor, as an unfairly advantaged person, or as a participant in a damaged culture. I was taught to see myself as an individual whose moral state depended on her individual moral will. At school, we were not taught about slavery in any depth; we were not taught to see slaveholders as damaged people. Slaves were seen as the only group at risk of being dehumanized. My schooling followed the pattern which Elizabeth Minnich has pointed out: whites are taught to think of their lives as morally neutral, normative, and average; and also ideal, so that when we work to benefit others, this is seen as work that will allow "them" to be more like "us." I think many of us know how obnoxious this attitude can be in men.

After frustration with men who would not recognize male privilege, I decided to try to work on myself at least by identifying some of the daily effects of white privilege in my life. It is crude work, at this stage, but I will give here a list of special circumstances and conditions I experience that I did not earn but that I have been made to feel are mine by birth, by citizenship, and by virtue of being a conscientious law-abiding "normal" person of goodwill. I have chosen those conditions that I think in my case *attach somewhat more to skin-color privilege* than to class, religion, ethnic status, or geographical location, though these other privileging factors are intricately intertwined. As far as I can see, my Afro-American co-workers, friends, and acquaintances with whom I come into daily or frequent contact in this particular time, place, and line of work cannot count on most of these conditions.

1. I can, if I wish, arrange to be in the company of people of my race most of the time.

2. I can avoid spending time with people whom I was trained to mistrust and who have learned to mistrust my kind or me.

3. If I should need to move, I can be pretty sure of renting or purchasing housing in an area which I can afford and in which I would want to live.

4. I can be reasonably sure that my neighbors in such a location will be neutral or pleasant to me.

5. I can go shopping alone most of the time, fairly well assured that I will not be followed or harassed by store detectives.

6. I can turn on the television or open to the front page of the paper and see people of my race widely and positively represented.

7. When I am told about our national heritage or about "civilization," I am shown that people of my color made it what it is.

8. I can be sure that my children will be given curricular materials that testify to the existence of their race.

9. If I want to, I can be pretty sure of finding a publisher for this piece on white privilege.

10. I can be fairly sure of having my voice heard in a group in which I am the only member of my race.

11. I can be casual about whether or not to listen to another woman's voice in a group in which she is the only member of her race.

12. I can go into a book shop and count on finding the writing of my race represented, into a supermarket and find the staple foods that fit with my cultural traditions, into a hairdresser's shop and find someone who can deal with my hair.

13. Whether I use checks, credit cards, or cash, I can count on my skin color not to work against the appearance that I am financially reliable.

14. I could arrange to protect our young children most of the time from people who might not like them.

15. I did not have to educate our children to be aware of systemic racism for their own daily physical protection.

16. I can be pretty sure that my children's teachers and employers will tolerate them if they fit school and workplace norms; my chief worries about them do not concern others' attitudes toward their race.

17. I can talk with my mouth full and not have people put this down to my color.

18. I can swear, or dress in secondhand clothes, or not answer letters, without having people attribute these choices to the bad morals, the poverty, or the illiteracy of my race.

19. I can speak in public to a powerful male group without putting my race on trial.

20. I can do well in a challenging situation without being called a credit to my race.

21. I am never asked to speak for all the people of my racial group.

22. I can remain oblivious to the language and customs of persons of color who constitute the world's majority without feeling in my culture any penalty for such oblivion.

23. I can criticize our government and talk about how much I fear its policies and behavior without being seen as a cultural outsider.

24. I can be reasonably sure that if I ask to talk to "the person in charge," I will be facing a person of my race.

25. If a traffic cop pulls me over or if the IRS audits my tax return, I can be sure I haven't been singled out because of my race.

26. I can easily buy posters, postcards, picture books, greeting cards, dolls, toys, and children's magazines featuring people of my race.

27. I can go home from most meetings of organizations I belong to feeling somewhat tied in, rather than isolated, out of place, outnumbered, unheard, held at a distance, or feared.

28. I can be pretty sure that an argument with a colleague of another race is more likely to jeopardize her chances for advancement than to jeopardize mine.

29. I can be fairly sure that if I argue for the promotion of a person of another race, or a program centering on race, this is not likely to cost me heavily within my present setting, even if my colleagues disagree with me.

30. If I declare there is a racial issue at hand, or there isn't a racial issue at hand, my race will

lend me more credibility for either position than a person of color will have.

31. I can choose to ignore developments in minority writing and minority activist programs, or disparage them, or learn from them, but in any case, I can find ways to be more or less protected from negative consequences of any of these choices.

32. My culture gives me little fear about ignoring the perspectives and powers of people of other races.

33. I am not made acutely aware that my shape, bearing, or body odor will be taken as a reflection on my race.

34. I can worry about racism without being seen as self-interested or self-seeking.

35. I can take a job with an affirmative action employer without having my co-workers on the job suspect that I got it because of my race.

36. If my day, week, or year is going badly, I need not ask of each negative episode or situation whether it has racial overtones.

37. I can be pretty sure of finding people who would be willing to talk with me and advise me about my next steps, professionally.

38. I can think over many options, social, political, imaginative, or professional, without asking whether a person of my race would be accepted or allowed to do what I want to do.

39. I can be late to a meeting without having the lateness reflect on my race.

40. I can choose public accommodation without fearing that people of my race cannot get in or will be mistreated in the places I have chosen.

41. I can be sure that if I need legal or medical help, my race will not work against me.

42. I can arrange my activities so that I will never have to experience feelings of rejection owing to my race.

43. If I have low credibility as a leader, I can be sure that my race is not the problem.

44. I can easily find academic courses and institutions that give attention only to people of my race.

45. I can expect figurative language and imagery in all of the arts to testify to experiences of my race.

46. I can choose blemish cover or bandages in "flesh" color and have them more or less match my skin.

I repeatedly forgot each of the realizations on this list until I wrote it down. For me, white privilege has turned out to be an elusive and fugitive subject. The pressure to avoid it is great, for in facing it I must give up the myth of meritocracy. If these things are true, this is not such a free country; one's life is not what one makes of it; many doors open for certain people through no virtues of their own. These perceptions mean also that my moral condition is not what I had been led to believe. The appearance of being a good citizen rather than a troublemaker comes in large part from having all sorts of doors open automatically because of my color.

A further paralysis of nerve comes from literary silence protecting privilege. My clearest memories of finding such analysis are in Lillian Smith's unparalleled *Killers of the Dream* and Margaret Andersen's review of Karen and Mamie Fields' *Lemon Swamp*. Smith, for example, wrote about walking toward black children on the street and knowing they would step into the gutter; Andersen contrasted the pleasure that she, as a white child, took on summer driving trips to the south with Karen Fields' memories of driving in a closed car stocked with all necessities lest, in stopping, her black family should suffer "insult, or worse." Adrienne Rich also recognizes and writes about daily experiences of privilege, but in my observation, white women's writing in this area is far more often on systemic racism than on our daily lives as light-skinned women.[2]

In unpacking this invisible knapsack of white privilege, I have listed conditions of daily experience that I once took for granted, as neutral, normal, and

---

[2]Andersen, Margaret. "Race and the Social Science Curriculum: A Teaching and Learning Discussion." *Radical Teacher,* November, 1984, pp. 17–20. Smith, Lillian, *Killers of the Dream,* New York: W. W. Norton, 1949.

universally available to everybody, just as I once thought of a male-focused curriculum as the neutral or accurate account that can speak for all. Nor did I think of any of these perquisites as bad for the holder. I now think that we need a more finely differentiated taxonomy of privilege, for some of these varieties are only what one would want for everyone in a just society, and others give license to be ignorant, oblivious, arrogant, and destructive. Before proposing some more finely tuned categorization, I will make some observations about the general effects of these conditions on my life and expectations.

In this potpourri of examples, some privileges make me feel at home in the world. Others allow me to escape penalties or dangers that others suffer. Through some, I escape fear, anxiety, insult, injury, or a sense of not being welcome, not being real. Some keep me from having to hide, to be in disguise, to feel sick or crazy, to negotiate each transaction from the position of being an outsider or, within my group, a person who is suspected of having too close links with a dominant culture. Most keep me from having to be angry.

I see a pattern running through the matrix of white privilege, a pattern of assumptions that were passed on to me as a white person. There was one main piece of cultural turf; it was my own turf, and I was among those who could control the turf. I could measure up to the cultural standards and take advantage of the many options I saw around me to make what the culture would call a success of my life. *My skin color was an asset for any move I was educated to want to make.* I could think of myself as "belonging" in major ways and of making social systems work for me. I could freely disparage, fear, neglect, or be oblivious to anything outside of the dominant cultural forms. Being of the main culture, I could also criticize it fairly freely. My life was reflected back to me frequently enough so that I felt, with regard to my race, if not to my sex, like one of the real people.

Whether through the curriculum or in the newspaper, the television, the economic system, or the general look of people in the streets, I received daily signals and indications that my people counted and that others *either didn't exist or must be trying, not*

very successfully, to be like people of my race. I was given cultural permission not to hear voices of people of other races or a tepid cultural tolerance for hearing or acting on such voices. I was also raised not to suffer seriously from anything that darker-skinned people might say about my group, "protected," though perhaps I should more accurately say *prohibited,* through the habits of my economic class and social group, from living in racially mixed groups or being reflective about interactions between people of differing races.

In proportion as my racial group was being made confident, comfortable, and oblivious, other groups were likely being made unconfident, uncomfortable, and alienated. Whiteness protected me from many kinds of hostility, distress, and violence, which I was being subtly trained to visit in turn upon people of color.

For this reason, the word "privilege" now seems to me misleading. Its connotations are too positive to fit the conditions and behaviors which "privilege systems" produce. We usually think of privilege as being a favored state, whether earned, or conferred by birth or luck. School graduates are reminded they are privileged and urged to use their (enviable) assets well. The word "privilege" carries the connotation of being something everyone must want. Yet some of the conditions I have described here work to systemically overempower certain groups. Such privilege simply *confers dominance,* gives permission to control, because of one's race or sex. The kind of privilege that gives license to some people to be, at best, thoughtless and, at worst, murderous should not continue to be referred to as a desirable attribute. Such "privilege" may be widely desired without being in any way beneficial to the whole society.

Moreover, though "privilege" may confer power, it does not confer moral strength. Those who do not depend on conferred dominance have traits and qualities that may never develop in those who do. Just as Women's Studies courses indicate that women survive their political circumstances to lead lives that hold the human race together, so "underprivileged" people of color who are the world's majority have survived their oppression and lived survivors' lives from which the white global minority can and must learn. In some groups, those dominated have actually become strong through *not* having all of these unearned advantages, and this gives them a great deal to teach the others. Members of so-called privileged groups can seem foolish, ridiculous, infantile, or dangerous by contrast.

I want, then, to distinguish between earned strength and unearned power conferred systemically. Power from unearned privilege can look like strength when it is, in fact, permission to escape or to dominate. But not all of the privileges on my list are inevitably damaging. Some, like the expectation that neighbors will be decent to you, or that your race will not count against you in court, should be the norm in a just society and should be considered as the entitlement of everyone. Others, like the privilege not to listen to less powerful people, distort the humanity of the holders as well as the ignored groups. Still others, like finding one's staple foods everywhere, may be a function of being a member of a numerical majority in the population. Others have to do with not having to labor under pervasive negative stereotyping and mythology.

We might at least start by distinguishing between positive advantages that we can work to spread, to the point where they are not advantages at all but simply part of the normal civic and social fabric, and negative types of advantage that unless rejected will always reinforce our present hierarchies. For example, the positive "privilege" of belonging, the feeling that one belongs within the human circle, as Native Americans say, fosters development and should not be seen as privilege for a few. It is, let us say, an entitlement that none of us should have to earn; ideally it is an *unearned entitlement*. At present, since only a few have it, it is an *unearned advantage* for them. The negative "privilege" that gave me cultural permission not to take darker-skinned Others seriously can be seen as arbitrarily conferred dominance and should not be desirable for anyone. This paper results from a process of coming to see that some of the power that I originally saw as attendant on being a human being in the United States consisted in *unearned advantage* and *conferred dominance,* as well

as other kinds of special circumstance not universally taken for granted.

In writing this paper I have also realized that white identity and status (as well as class identity and status) give me considerable power to choose whether to broach this subject and its trouble. I can pretty well decide whether to disappear and avoid and not listen and escape the dislike I may engender in other people through this essay, or interrupt, answer, interpret, preach, correct, criticize, and control to some extent what goes on in reaction to it. Being white, I am given considerable power to escape many kinds of danger or penalty as well as to choose which risks I want to take.

There is an analogy here, once again, with Women's Studies. Our male colleagues do not have a great deal to lose in supporting Women's Studies, but they do not have a great deal to lose if they oppose it either. They simply have the power to decide whether to commit themselves to more equitable distributions of power. They will probably feel few penalties whatever choice they make; they do not seem, in any obvious short-term sense, the ones at risk, though they and we are all at risk because of the behaviors that have been rewarded in them.

Through Women's Studies work I have met very few men who are truly distressed about systemic, unearned male advantage and conferred dominance. And so one question for me and others like me is whether we will be like them, or whether we will get truly distressed, even outraged, about unearned race advantage and conferred dominance and if so, what we will do to lessen them. In any case, we need to do more work in identifying how they actually affect our daily lives. We need more down-to-earth writing by people about these taboo subjects. We need more understanding of the ways in which white "privilege" damages white people, for these are not the same ways in which it damages the victimized. Skewed white psyches are an inseparable part of the picture, though I do not want to confuse the kinds of damage done to the holders of special assets and to those who suffer the deficits. Many, perhaps most, of our white students in the United States think that racism doesn't affect them because they are not people of color; they do not see "whiteness" as a racial identity. Many men likewise think that Women's Studies does not bear on their own existences because they are not female; they do not see themselves as having gendered identities. Insisting on the universal "effects" or "privilege" systems, then, becomes one of our chief tasks, and being more explicit about the *particular* effects in particular contexts is another. Men need to join us in this work.

In addition, since race and sex are not the only advantaging systems at work, we need to similarly examine the daily experience of having age advantage, or ethnic advantage, or physical ability, or advantage related to nationality, religion, or sexual orientation. Professor Marnie Evans suggested to me that in many ways the list I made also applies directly to heterosexual privilege. This is a still more taboo subject than race privilege: the daily ways in which heterosexual privilege makes some persons comfortable or powerful, providing supports, assets, approvals, and rewards to those who live or expect to live in heterosexual pairs. Unpacking that content is still more difficult, owing to the deeper imbeddedness of heterosexual advantage and dominance and stricter taboos surrounding these.

But to start such an analysis I would put this observation from my own experience: The fact that I live under the same roof with a man triggers all kinds of societal assumptions about my worth, politics, life, and values and triggers a host of unearned advantages and powers. After recasting many elements from the original list I would add further observations like these:

1. My children do not have to answer questions about why I live with my partner (my husband).
2. I have no difficulty finding neighborhoods where people approve of our household.
3. Our children are given texts and classes that implicitly support our kind of family unit and do not turn them against my choice of domestic partnership.

4. I can travel alone or with my husband without expecting embarrassment or hostility in those who deal with us.
5. Most people I meet will see my marital arrangements as an asset to my life or as a favorable comment on my likability, my competence, or my mental health.
6. I can talk about the social events of a weekend without fearing most listeners' reactions.
7. I will feel welcomed and "normal" in the usual walks of public life, institutional and social.
8. In many contexts, I am seen as "all right" in daily work on women because I do not live chiefly with women.

Difficulties and dangers surrounding the task of finding parallels are many. Since racism, sexism, and heterosexism are not the same, the advantages associated with them should not be seen as the same. In addition, it is hard to isolate aspects of unearned advantage that derive chiefly from social class, economic class, race, religion, region, sex, or ethnic identity. The oppressions are both distinct and interlocking, as the Combahee River Collective statement of 1977 continues to remind us eloquently.[3]

One factor seems clear about all of the interlocking oppressions. They take both active forms that we can see and embedded forms that members of the dominant group are taught not to see. In my class and place, I did not see myself as racist because I was taught to recognize racism only in individual acts of meanness by members of my group, never in invisible systems conferring racial dominance on my group from birth. Likewise, we are taught to think that sexism or heterosexism is carried on only through intentional, individual acts of discrimination, meanness, or cruelty, rather than in invisible systems conferring unsought dominance on certain groups. Disapproving of the systems

[3]"A Black Feminist Statement," The Combahee River Collective, pp. 13–22 in G. Hull, P. Scott, B. Smith, Eds., *All the Women Are White, All the Blacks are Men, But Some of Us Are Brave: Black Women's Studies,* Old Westbury, NY: The Feminist Press, 1982.

won't be enough to change them. I was taught to think that racism could end if white individuals changed their attitudes; many men think sexism can be ended by individual changes in daily behavior toward women. But a man's sex provides advantage for him whether or not he approves of the way in which dominance has been conferred on his group. A "white" skin in the United States opens many doors for whites whether or not we approve of the way dominance has been conferred on us. Individual acts can palliate, but cannot end, these problems. To redesign social systems, we need first to acknowledge their colossal unseen dimensions. The silences and denials surrounding privilege are the key political tool here. They keep the thinking about equality or equity incomplete, protecting unearned advantage and conferred dominance by making these taboo subjects. Most talk by whites about equal opportunity seems to me now to be about equal opportunity to try to get into a position of dominance while denying that *systems* of dominance exist.

Obliviousness about white advantage, like obliviousness about male advantage, is kept strongly inculturated in the United States so as to maintain the myth of meritocracy, the myth that democratic choice is equally available to all. Keeping most people unaware that freedom of confident action is there for just a small number of people props up those in power and serves to keep power in the hands of the same groups that have most of it already. Though systemic change takes many decades, there are pressing questions for me and I imagine for some others like me if we raise our daily consciousness on the perquisites of being light-skinned. What will we do with such knowledge? As we know from watching men, it is an open question whether we will choose to use unearned advantage to weaken invisible privilege systems and whether we will use any of our arbitrarily awarded power to try to reconstruct power systems on a broader base.

MORAL DEFERENCE*

Laurence Thomas

Why is this peach-tree said to be better than that other; but because it produces more or better fruit? . . . In morals, too, is not the tree known by the fruit?
—DAVID HUME, *ENQUIRY CONCERNING THE PRINCIPLES OF MORALS* (V, IINL)

In "What Is It Like to Be a Bat?," Thomas Nagel tells us that we hardly come to know what it is like to be a bat by hanging upside down with our eyes closed.[1] That experience simply tells us what it is like to be a human behaving or attempting to behave like a bat. If bats were intelligent creatures possessing a natural language, which we could translate, surely we would have to take their word

*This paper owes its inspiration to my 1991 Winter Quarter class on the Gilligan-Kohlberg debate (which I taught while visiting at the University of Chicago); Alison M. Jaggar's, "Love and Knowledge: Emotion in Feminist Epistemology," in eds. Alison M. Jaggar and Susan R. Bordo, *Gender/Body/Knowledge: Feminist Reconstructions of Being and Knowing* (New Brunswick: Rutgers University Press, 1989); and Seyla Benhabib's "The Generalized and the Concrete Other: The Kohlberg-Gilligan Controversy and Moral Theory," in eds. Eva Feder Kittay and Diana T. Meyers, *Women and Moral Theory* (Rowman and Littlefield, 1978). I see moral deference as a way of responding to the moral significance of the concreteness of others. I received instructive comments from Norma Field, John Pittman, and Julian Wuerth. At various times, conversations with Linda Alcoff, Alan J. Richard, Michael Stocker (always a present help), and Thomas Nagel (over the penultimate draft) were very helpful. A special debt of gratitude is owed to writer Jamie Kalven whose life reveals the richness that moral deference can yield.

Some recent works on the subject of racism have been most illuminating: David Theo Goldberg, "Racism and Rationality: The Need for a New Critique," *Philosophy of the Social Sciences,* Vol. 20 (1990); Adrian M. S. Piper's paper "Higher-Order Discrimination," in Owen Flanagan and Amelie Oksenberg Rorty, *Identity, Character, and Morality: Essays in Moral Psychology* (Cambridge: Massachusetts Institute of Technology Press, 1990); Elizabeth V. Spelman, *Inessential Women: Problems of Exclusion in Feminist Thought* (Beacon Press, 1988). My essay has very nearly turned out to be something of a companion piece to Michael Stocker's wonderful essay "How Emotions Reveal Value" (unpublished).
[1]In *Mortal Questions* (Cambridge University Press, 1979).

for what it is like to be a bat. If, in batese, bats—including the most intelligent and articulate ones—generally maintained that "Hanging upside down is extraordinarily like experiencing death through colors," we human beings would probably not know how to get a handle on what was being claimed, since the notion of experiencing death already strains the imagination. Just so, we would be in no position to dismiss their claim as so much nonsense because we cannot get a handle on it—because, after all, we humans experience no such thing when we engage in bat-like behavior. On this matter, bats would be owed deference.

Some people are owed deference—moral deference, that is. Moral deference is meant to stand in opposition to the idea that there is a vantage point from which any and every person can rationally grasp whatever morally significant experiences a person might have. A fundamentally important part of living morally is being able to respond in the morally appropriate way to those who have been wronged. And this ability we cannot have in the absence of a measure of moral deference. David Hume's position on the human sentiments gives us insight regarding the matter. Or so I claim in Section III. The full account of moral deference is offered in Section IV, the final section. I maintain that the attitude of moral deference is, as it were, a prelude to bearing witness to another's pain, with that person's authorization—the person's blessings, if you will.

On my view, moral deference is the bridge between individuals with different emotional category configurations owing to the injustices of society. I do not claim that moral deference will serve as a bridge between intelligent creatures who differ radically in their biological constitution from one another, though moral deference may nonetheless be owed. Moral deference, as I conceive of it, is not about whether individuals are innocent with respect to those who have been treated unjustly; rather, it is simply about the appropriate moral attitude to take when it comes to understanding the ways in which another has been a victim of social injustice. A person's innocence or lack thereof is irrelevant.

SOCIAL CATEGORIES

If one encounters a Holocaust survivor, it would be moral hubris of the worst sort—unless one is also such a survivor—to assume that by way of rational imaginative role-taking, à la Kohlberg,[2] one could even begin to grasp the depth of that person's experiences—the hurts, pains, and anxieties of that individual's life. There is not enough good will in the world to make it possible for persons (who are not Holocaust survivors) to put themselves imaginatively in the mind of a Holocaust survivor, to do so simply as an act of ratiocination.

The slaveowners who lived among slaves and, in fact, ruled the very lives of slaves knew a great deal about slaves. In many cases, slaveowners knew more about the intimate lives of slaves than a person has the right to know about another's intimate life (unless such information is freely and voluntarily offered in a noncoercive context). Yet, for all that white slaveowners knew about black slaves, the owners did not know what it was like to be a slave. Naturally, there were slave uprisings; but no slaveowner knew what it was like to be a slave on account of being a victim of such uprisings.

If a woman has been raped, it is clear that the last thing in the world that a heterosexual man should say is, "I can imagine how you feel." A great many men can barely imagine or grasp the fear of rape that, to varying degrees, permeates the lives of women, let alone the profoundly violent act of rape itself. Few actions could be more insensitive to victims of rape than a man's supposition that via a feat of imagination he can get a grip on the pain that a victim of rape has experienced.

I am, of course, aware that heterosexual men can be raped. But given the assumption of heterosexuality, male victims of rape, unlike female victims of rape, do not in general have the awkwardness of seeking to be personally fulfilled romantically by forming a relationship with a person who belongs to

---

[2]*The Philosophy of Moral Development* (New York: Harper & Row, 1981). See especially the essay entitled "From Is to Ought: How to Commit the Naturalistic Fallacy and Get Away with It."

the very same social category as does the person who has harmed them. Nor, in any case, do males have to contend with social attitudes—some subtle, some ever so explicit—that make them the target of sexual violence or that minimize the significance of their consent as an appropriate condition of sexual intercourse. Lesbians do not escape this latter injustice; gay men who have been raped do. Given the assumption of heterosexuality, while both a woman and a man have to recover from the mental anguish of having been violated, complete recovery for a man does not involve being able to have sex with a man again. Thus, a fortiori, complete recovery is not a matter of his being able to do so without that act conjuring up the pain of rape. By contrast, complete recovery for a woman is generally seen along precisely these lines. Hence, recovery for a heterosexual man involves nothing like the phenomenal ambivalence that it involves for a woman.

Why is it that we cannot simply imaginatively put ourselves in the shoes of a Holocaust survivor or, in the case of a man, in the shoes of a rape victim? The answer is painfully obvious: even if we had a complete description of the person's experiences, we would nonetheless not be the subject of those experiences. Nor would we have the painful memory of being the subject of those experiences. So a description, no matter how full and complete, would fail on two counts to capture the subjective element of an experience. The latter count—namely, the memories—is far from trivial, because part of the way in which experiences shape our lives is through the memories of them impressing themselves upon our lives. In fact, there are times when the impact of a bad experience upon our lives would be virtually nugatory but for the way in which our lives are affected by the memories of it.

Suppose that one has been robbed at gunpoint. The actual loss may not amount to much at all, say $20 or $30. Suppose one has not suffered any physical or mental abuse, since two police officers came on the scene just in time. Yet, the event may alter the way in which one lives for years to come. Of course, one will realize how lucky one was. It is just that one cannot help thinking about what might

have happened but for a fluke of luck—a mode of thought that very nearly cripples one emotionally. Rehearsing an experience in one's mind can frighteningly reveal just how lucky one was. A woman who has been raped can be having sex with her male partner, which has been ever so explicitly consensual, only to find that she can no longer continue the act because she has suddenly been assailed by the painful memories of being raped.

No amount of imagination in the world can make it the case that one has the subjective imprimatur of the experiences and memories of another. And an individual's subjective imprimatur makes a very real difference. Let me tie some things together.

There can be appropriate and inappropriate responses to the moral pain of another. When a person has suffered a grave misfortune the type of moral response that will serve to help that person to recover must be sensitive to the adverse ways in which the misfortune is likely to affect her or his life. This includes not just the physical damage that has been wrought to the person's body, but the ways in which the person will be haunted by painful memories, the person's feelings of emotional and social vulnerability, and so on. For as I have noted, the bodily damage can, itself, be negligible. It is not in the damage done to the body that the horror of armed robbery necessarily lies—since there might be none—but in the damage done to the victim's sense of self. Again, while rape can certainly be physically violent, it need not be, as the idea gaining acceptance of acquaintance rape reveals.[3]

Now, to be sure, there are many misfortunes, at the hands of other, which any human being can experience, and so which are independent of social categories. We may think of these as generalized misfortunes. Anyone can be robbed, or be the victim of a car accident caused by an intoxicated driver, or be hit by a stray bullet. Anyone can lose a loved one owing to a flagrant disregard for human rights. These misfortunes do not know the

---

[3]See, for instance, "Tougher Laws Mean More Cases are Called Rape," *The New York Times,* 27 May 1991: p. 9.

boundaries of social categories. And though there can be difficulties, perhaps insuperable ones in some instances, with how to individuate (events that are) misfortunes, when people have experienced generalized misfortunes of the same type, then they have considerable insight into one another's suffering. The experience of losing a leg as a teenager is perhaps qualitatively different from that of losing a leg as an adult of 50, but no doubt the two experiences are far closer qualitatively than is either to the experience of losing a parent as a teenager or as an adult of 50. And between two teenagers both of whom lose a leg, it perhaps matters if one is an athlete and one is not.[4]

To be contrasted with generalized misfortunes are misfortunes that are quite tied to diminished social categories—misfortunes owing to oppressive, if not prevailing, negative attitudes about the members of well-defined diminished social categories. As it happens, the diminished social category may be coextensive with a natural category, as may be the case with gender.[5] I shall use the euphemism "hostile misfortunes" to refer to these misfortunes, where "hostile" is intended to capture both that the misfortune is owing to agency and that the agency, with respect to the relevant set of acts, is owing to morally objectionable attitudes regarding the diminished social category. I shall often refer to a person in such a category as a category person.

Not everyone in a diminished social category experiences all, and to the same extent, the hostile misfortunes specific to that category, but being in a diminished social category makes it exceedingly likely that one's life will be tinged with some of the hostile misfortunes specific to that diminished social category. Moreover, if one is not in that diminished social category, the likelihood of one's experiencing

any of the hostile misfortunes will be virtually nil. I regard gender, ethnicity, and race as obviously involving diminished social categories of this kind, though there need not be hostile misfortunes specific to every ethnic and racial group. Although people of the same diminished social category do not all endure the same hostile experiences, the relevant experiential psychological distances between their lives will be less than such distances between their lives and the lives of those who do not belong to any diminished social category or to a very different one. Interestingly, there can be subgroups within a diminished social category, and hostile misfortunes tied to those subgroups. For instance, there are very light-complexioned blacks (some of whom are phenotypically indistinguishable from whites) and there are darker-complexioned blacks; and each subgroup has its own hostile misfortunes, in addition to those associated simply with being black. Finally, it is possible for the hostile misfortunes of two different diminished social categories to parallel one another to a considerable degree. Such may be the case with the hostile misfortunes of African-American and Hispanic-American peoples. Individuals from these groups do not experience exactly the same hostile misfortunes. But there appears to be considerable overlap. The hostile misfortunes of a diminished social category group need not be fixed. Hence, there could be less overlap between two groups at one time than at another time.

As with generalized misfortunes, though, I shall assume that when two people of the same diminished social category experience the same type of hostile misfortune, then they have considerable insight into one another's experiencing of that misfortune. Of course, the problem of individuating types of events does not disappear here. Numerous refinements are possible. However, I shall leave such matters aside. Furthermore, there is the very thorny issue of when the hostile misfortunes of two diminished social category groups are similar enough to one another that each group has some insight into the moral pains of the other. There is certainly no reason to rule this out of court on conceptual grounds; on the other hand, one of the worst mis-

---

[4]For a very important discussion of events, and their individuation, see Judith Jarvis Thomson, *Acts and Other Events* (Cornell University Press, 1977).

[5]That gender is both a biological and a social category is developed at length in my essay "Sexism and Racism: Some Conceptual Differences," *Ethics* (1980).

takes that can be made is for one diminished social category group to assume, without having attended to the matter, that its suffering gives it insight into the suffering of another diminished social category group. But this issue, too, I shall leave aside.

Now, the knowledge that someone belongs to a diminished social category group does not, in and of itself, give one insight into the subjective imprimatur of that individual's experiences of and memories stemming from the hostile misfortunes tied to the category to which the person belongs. If so, then a very pressing question is: how is it possible to be morally responsive in the appropriate way to those belonging to a diminished social category if one does not belong to that category? Here is where moral deference enters into the picture, though first more needs to be said about being a member of a diminished social category.

BEING SOCIALLY CONSTITUTED

David Hume observed that "Human nature cannot by any means subsist, without the association of individuals . . ."[6] His point can be rendered in a contemporary vein as follows: we are constituted through others, by which I mean that the way in which we conceive of ourselves is, at least in part, owing to how others conceive of us, and necessarily so. The way in which we think of ourselves is inextricably tied to the way in which others think of us. In a fully just world, all would be constituted through others so as to be full and equal members of society. That is, each member would be constituted so as to see her or himself in this way. By contrast, in an oppressive society, the victims of oppression—diminished social category persons, I mean—are constituted, in both masterfully subtle ways and in ever so explicit ways, so as not to see themselves as full and equal members of society. I shall refer to this as downward social constitution. Each group of diminished social category persons in

society experiences different forms of downward social constitution, although I have allowed that there may be overlap. Painfully, social groups that are themselves victims of downward social constitution may engage in downward social constitution of one another. Victims of sexism can be antisemitic; victims of racism can be sexist. And so on for each diminished social category group. Even worse, perhaps, there can be downward social constitution by members within a group. In an oppressive society, downward social constitution is an ongoing and pervasive phenomenon, which is not to deny that there can be pockets of relief to varying degrees. Needless to say, a society with diminished social categories will have one or more privileged social categories, the members of which are favored and have full access to the goods of society.

One of the most important ways in which downward social constitution occurs pertains to expectations. It is just assumed, often without awareness of what is being done, that this or that category person cannot measure up in an important way. The reality that we do not expect much of a person on account of her category can be communicated in a thousand and one ways. One may listen inattentively, or interrupt ever so frequently, or not directly respond to what the person actually says, or not respond with the seriousness that is appropriate to the persons concerned. Most significantly, owing to meager expectations, one may fail to give the benefit of the doubt to the diminished social category person. We often do not realize that we are participating in the downward constitution of others because communicating favorable and negative expectations with regard to others is a natural part of life. Further, behavior that contributes to the downward constitution of another may manifest itself in other contexts that have nothing to do with downward constitution. After all, one can listen inattentively simply because one is preoccupied. Or, one can fail to respond directly because one misunderstood what the person said. Accordingly, negative expectations toward a member of a diminished social category need not feel any different from negative expectations toward any other member of society, nor need

[6]*Enquiries Concerning the Principles of Morals* (Section IV, para. 165).

the behavior bear a special mark. Except for the blatant bigot or sexist, participating in the downward social constitution of another rarely has any special phenomenological feel to it.

Thus, it is interesting that for most people the evidence that they do not engage in downwardly constituting behavior is that they do not have the appropriate feelings. It is true that if one has and sustains the appropriate feelings, then one is an X-ist (racist, sexist, and so forth), or one has acted in an X-ist way if such feelings fuel one's behavior; on the other hand, it is manifestly false that if one lacks such feelings, then X-ism is not a part of one's life.

I have said that in an oppressive society downward social constitution is an ongoing and pervasive phenomenon despite pockets of relief. Such constitution may show up in advertisement, in the casting of characters for a film (play or television program), in the assumptions about the interests (as well as professional aims and hobbies) that a person has or what such a person should be satisfied with. The list goes on. Further, an expression of downward constitution may manifest itself at almost any time in almost any context. An expression of downward constitution may come from those who are so eager to put up an appearance of caring that they deceive themselves in believing that they actually care. Such an expression may even come from those who in fact care.[7]

To be a member of a diminished social category group is invariably to have to contend with what I shall call the problem of social category ambiguity. Often enough the question will be: was that remark or piece of behavior a manifestation of downward social constitution or something else or both? It may not have been, but the very nature of the context and one's social reality as a diminished social category person does not allow one to rule out that possibility with the desired confidence. On the one hand, one does not want to accuse someone falsely; on the other, one may not want to put up with an af-

front owing to being a member of a diminished social category. Yet, there may be no way to inquire about the matter without giving the appearance of doing the former. Finally, there is the painful reality that one may not be able to share one's feelings about one's social category status with those who do not belong to that category, without giving the impression of being overly concerned with such matters—even with those who regard themselves as friends. It is a reality that sometimes requires a kind of profound disassociation from one's own experiences, at least momentarily.

Together, these things all speak to a profound sense of vulnerability that comes with being a member of a diminished social category. Part of that vulnerability is owing not just to being a subject of downward social constitution, but to the memories of such experiences. Invariably, the diminished social category person will be haunted by some of these memories to varying degrees. Then there is the fact that a memory (sometimes painful, sometimes not) of an experience of downward social constitution can be triggered by any number of things, including the witnessing of another's experience of downward social constitution, or another such experience of one's own. There is a sense in which one can be assailed by the memories of past undesirable experiences. A diminished social category person is vulnerable in this way. People who are downwardly constituted socially are victims of a social claim about them—not just any old claim but the claim that they lack the wherewithal to measure up in an important social dimension. In this regard, diminished social category persons are vulnerable on several counts. First, there is the vulnerability owing to being weary of always feeling the need to prove that this social claim is a lie—if not to themselves then to others. Second, there is the vulnerability owing to the reality that there is almost nothing that diminished social category persons can do which will decisively establish the falsity of the social claim. Third, there is the vulnerability owing to the weariness of it all that stems from the feeling that one must speak up because no one else will, although one is concerned that con-

---

[7]For an absolutely masterful discussion of these matters, see Adrian Piper, "Higher-Order Discrimination."

tinually speaking up will diminish one's effectiveness. Obviously, diminished social category persons cope with these vulnerabilities in a variety of different ways and with varying degrees of success. But successfully coping with a vulnerability is hardly tantamount to not being vulnerable, any more than not showing anger is tantamount to not being angry.

The remarks in the preceding two paragraphs are meant to bring out the sense of *otherness* that inescapably comes with being a person belonging to a diminished social category, the sense of what it means to be socially constituted as such a person. This sense of otherness is not something that a person who does not belong to one's particular diminished social category can grasp simply by an act of ratiocination. In particular, it is not something to which people belonging to privileged social categories can grasp. People who belong to a privileged social category can, of course, experience insults and affronts to their person, even at the hands of those belonging to a diminished social category. Indeed, privileged social category persons can experience these things precisely because they belong to a privileged social category. But, clearly, just as a person does not know what it is like to be a bat by hanging upside down with closed eyes, a person does not know what it is like to be a member of a diminished social category merely on account of having been affronted and insulted by diminished social category persons for being a privileged social category person. For the hallmark of a diminished social category person is that of being a person whose life has been downwardly constituted socially, with all that this implies in terms of vulnerability as noted above. A privileged social category person who has experienced affronts at the hands of diminished social category persons has no more had a downwardly constituted life on that account, with all that this implies in terms of vulnerability, than has a seventy-year-old person led a life marred by sickness for having had to spend three weeks at twenty in the hospital for exposure to meningitis and again at fifty for exposure to hepatitis.

EMOTIONAL CONFIGURATION

Hume seems to have held that if our natural capacity for sympathy and benevolence were sufficiently cultivated, we would have adequate insight into the weal and woe of others.[8] I disagree, although I think that his heart was in the right place. In a world without hostile misfortunes and diminished social category groups, and so without privileged social category groups, I think that Hume's position would, indeed, be correct or very nearly that. I hesitate only because it might be that even in a perfectly just world some differences might be impassable despite unqualified good will on all accounts. Hume's point holds given two assumptions: (a) the emotional capacities of people are essentially the same; (b) the configuration of these emotional capacities through society is essentially the same, the primary difference with respect to the latter being in their development. Thus, for Hume, Nero is simply one whose capacity for benevolence and sympathy virtually went uncultivated. By contrast, Hume thought it obvious that anyone who had benefited from some cultivation of these sentiments could not help but see that Nero's actions were criminal.[9]

Such social phenomena as downward social constitution and diminished social categories would not have occurred to Hume. Specifically, and more pointedly, it would not have occurred to him that a person's emotions could be configured along a dimension other than the extent of their cultivation, the case of gender aside.[10] So, given Hume's moral psychology, anyone whose capacity for sympathy and benevolence was properly cultivated was in a position to understand sufficiently the moral experiences of all

---

[8]*Enquiries Concerning the Principles of Morals:* V, pt. II, pars. 183, 189; IX, pt. I, par. 220.

[9]*Principles of Morals,* Appen. 1, 241.

[10]For an important discussion of Hume regarding gender, see Annette Baier. *A Progress of Sentiments* (Cambridge: Harvard University Press, 1991), pp. 273–75. Hume thought that women who desired to become wives and to bear children should be held to stricter standards of chastity than men. Cf. David Hume, *Enquiries Concerning the Principles of Morals.* Section V, Section VIII, par. 215 and, especially, Section VI, part I, par. 195.

others. I am suggesting that Hume's moral psychology must be adjusted to take into account the reality that the emotional makeup of persons can be configured along dimensions other than cultivation. There is what I shall call emotional category configuration.

In a sexist society, a politically correct male who abhors violence against females, and understands ever so well why a victim of rape would rather be comforted by a female than a male nonetheless does not have the emotional configuration of a female. This is because the kind of fears that he experiences when he walks alone at night do not have as their source a concern about sexual violence; whereas they do for a woman whether or not she has been raped.[11] In a sexist society, at any rate, the emotional category configurations of women and men are different. This follows from women and men being socially constituted differently.

Likewise, a white can be attacked by blacks, and that attack can be brutal and absolutely inexcusable. As a result, the person may be emotionally crippled in terms of his fear of interacting with blacks. This is painfully sad. All the same, this suffering experience does not parallel the suffering of blacks. His fear of blacks may very well be a reminder of the random brutality of some blacks and of the moral squalor in which some wallow. The experience may seal his conviction that blacks lack the wherewithal to live morally decent lives.

But for all of that, the experience will not be a reminder that he is a second-class citizen. It will not make him vulnerable to that pain. He will not have the pain of being scarred by those who in fact have power over so very much of his life. By and large, the white will not really have to concern himself with having to trust blacks who have power over him, as with a little effort and creativity the white

can avoid situations of this kind; whereas for the black, having to trust whites who have power over him is a real possibility. So, whereas some physical distance from blacks, coupled with time, might serve to heal the wounds of the white, this healing route is not a genuine possibility for a black. This is yet another dimension along which the black will live with his pain in a quite different manner than the white. Certainly no innocent white should be a victim of black anger and hostility; certainly no innocent black should be either. The moral wrong may be equal in either case. My point is that because the black and the white have different emotional category configurations, each will experience their respective pain in a radically different manner. While economic differences could be factored in here, I did not develop the point with such differences in mind. The force of the point is not diminished in the least if both the white and the black are quite upper middle-class people enjoying equal salaries.

A fortiori, we have a difference in emotional category configuration here rather than a difference in the cultivation of the emotions if we suppose that the black and the white went to the very same kind of schools, read many of the same books, and have overlapping interests and musical tastes. We can imagine that they have similar personalities, and have had similar maturation experiences and wrestled with many of the same issues. Nonetheless, it is most likely they will be socially constituted in different ways. In the case of the black, strangers might be surprised that he was not born poor, or wonder where he learned to speak so well. The police at the university where he has just joined the faculty might regard him with suspicion. Or, at the checkout desk at the university library, the staff person might ask him for a piece of photo-identification to confirm that he is actually the owner of the university library card (which does not have a photograph on it) that he presented. These experiences will not be a part of the white person's life.

The cumulative effect of these experiences contributes to the significant difference in the emotional category configuration of which I have been speaking. Time and time again, a well-off black must steel

---

[11]Perhaps male child victims of male rape can approximate such fears in their own lives. Still the adult life of such males will be qualitatively different from the adult life of females, owing to great differences in the way in which society portrays women and men as sex objects. See the discussion in Section I above. This, of course, hardly diminishes the pain of having been a male victim of child rape.

himself against such experiences in settings of equality, while a white need not. Ironically, some of the experiences of downward social constitution— some of the insults—that a black will encounter, the person could only encounter if she were well-off, since a black in the throes of poverty would be too far removed from such social situations in the first place.[12] A black American in the throes of poverty is not apt to experience racism in a Middle Eastern or European hotel by a white American.

Nothing that I have experienced in my entire life had prepared me for the shock of being taken as a would-be purse snatcher in a Middle Eastern hotel by a white American who saw me enter the hotel lobby from the guest rooms. The person leapt for her pocketbook on the counter as if she had springs on her feet, although people had been sitting in the lobby all along. Worse still, she and I had been sitting in the lobby opposite one another only two days earlier. As I play back the experience in my mind, it seems so incredibly surrealistic to me that I continually find myself stunned. Even granting racism, and that she had been robbed by a black man while she was in Harlem, just how reasonable under the circumstances could it have been for her to suppose that *I* was a poor black out to steal her purse? After all, it takes more than cab fare to get from New York, New York, to any place in the Middle East.[13] I have been called a "nigger" to my face three times in my life. One of them was in Harvard Yard between Widner and Emerson. If I were to walk around with a fear that whites might call me "nigger," I would surely be taken as mad by most of my friends and acquaintances. Or, I would be seen as having enormous and unjustified hostility against whites.

Hume's moral psychology cannot account for the emotional vulnerability that comes with the above experience. This is because it would not have occurred to him that a person would be treated as anything other than a full citizen of the world on a par with all others—at least among other equally cultivated individuals—*if* the individual displayed the refinements of education and culture. It would not have occurred to him that persons displaying such refinements could be the object of hostile misfortunes. For on his view, the display of these things should suffice to elicit admiration.[14]

THE IDEA OF MORAL DEFERENCE

Moral deference is owed to persons of good will when they speak in an informed way regarding experiences specific to their diminished social category from the standpoint of an emotional category configuration to which others do not have access. The idea behind moral deference is not that a diminished social category person can never be wrong about the character of his own experiences. Surely he can, since anyone can. Nor is it that silence is the only appropriate response to what another says when one lacks that individual's emotional category configuration. Rather, the idea is that there should be a presumption in favor of the person's account of her experiences. This presumption is warranted because the individual is speaking from a vantage point to which someone not belonging to her diminished social category group does not have access. It is possible to play a major role in helping a person to get clearer about the character of an experience delivered from the vantage point of an emotional category configuration. But helping someone get clearer is qualitatively different from

---

[12]Bernard Boxill, in a very powerful essay, "Dignity, Slavery, and the 13th Amendment," has demonstrated the deep and profound way in which slavery was insulting. His essay appears in Michael J. Meyer and William A. Parent (eds.), *Human Dignity, the Bill of Rights and Constitutional Values* (Cornell University Press, 1992).

[13]I was so enraged by the experience that it was clear to me that I had better channel my rage lest I do something that I would regret. Fortunately, I had a micro-cassette recorder with me. I walked the streets of Tel Aviv and taped the essay "Next Life, I'll Be White," *The New York Times*/Op-Ed page (13 August 1990), an expanded version of which appeared in *Ebony Magazine* (December, 1990). It is, among other things, profoundly insulting when the obvious is discounted at one's own expense.

---

[14]*Enquiries Concerning the Principles of Morals:* V, pt. II–180; VIII.

being dismissive. Indeed, how a person feels about a matter can be of the utmost importance even if the individual's feelings are inappropriate, since inappropriate feelings can shed considerable light on the very appearances of things in themselves.

While I do not think that moral deference is owed only to persons of good will who are members of diminished social categories, my account begins with such persons. The assumption here is that in characterizing their feelings and experiences as diminished social category persons, those of good will do not tell an account that is mired and fueled by feelings of rancor and bitterness. This is not to suggest that persons of good will never experience tremendous anger and rage on account of experiences of downward social constitution. They sometimes do, and rightly so. Occasionally experiencing anger and rage, though, is by no means the same thing as becoming consumed by these feelings. A complete account of moral deference would have to be extended to include those who, understandably or not, have come to be full of bitterness and rancor owing to the ways in which they have been downwardly constituted socially. It becomes especially important to extend the account in this direction if one considers that oppression, itself, can render its victims so full of rancor and bitterness that the manifestation of these sentiments can blind us to their underlying cause, namely oppression itself.

Moral deference is meant to reflect the insight that it is wrong to discount the feelings and experiences of persons in diminished social category groups simply because their articulation of matters does not resonate with one's imaginative take on their experiences. Moral deference acknowledges a vast difference between the ideal moral world and the present one. In the ideal moral world there would be only one category of emotional configuration, namely the human one—or at most two, allowing for differences in the sexes. So, given adequate cultivation of emotions and feelings, everyone would be able to get an imaginative take on the experiences of others. Interestingly, this way of understanding the role of emotions in the ideal world might point to a reason for making them irrelevant entirely; for

if rightly cultivated emotions would result in everyone's making the same moral judgments on the basis of them, then the emotions do not make for a morally relevant difference between people, at least not among those with rightly cultivated emotions. On this view, the emotions can only make a morally relevant difference if they are seen as a constitutive feature of what it means to be a person, and so of moral personhood. But, alas, philosophers often seem anxious to deny that the emotions have any moral relevance, in and of themselves, at the foundational conception of moral personhood.[15]

In a far from ideal moral world, such as the one we live in, which privileges some social categories and diminishes others, it stands to reason that there will be emotional boundaries between people, owing to what I have called emotional category configuration. This is one of the bitter fruits of immorality. Recall Hume's question: "In morals, too, is not the tree known by its fruits?" The idea of moral deference is true to the moral reality that the mark of an immoral society is the erection of emotional walls between persons. It is true to the reality that social immorality cannot be eliminated in the absence of a firm grasp of how it has affected its victims. It is not enough to be confident that social immorality harms. One must also be sensitive to the way in which it harms. Thus, the idea of moral deference speaks to an attitude that a morally decent person should have in an immoral society.

We can best get at what moral deference involves, and its importance, by thinking of what it means to bear witness to another's moral pain with that person's authorization. To bear witness to the moral pain of another, say, Leslie, with Leslie's authorization, is to have won her confidence that one can speak informedly and with conviction on her behalf to another about the moral pain she has endured. It is to have won her confidence that one will tell her story with her voice, and not with one's own voice. Hence, it is to have won her trust that one will render salient

---

[15]Cf. my "Rationality and Affectivity: The Metaphysics of the Moral Self," *Social Philosophy and Policy* 5 (1988): 154–72.

what was salient for her in the way that it was salient for her; that one will represent her struggle to cope in the ways that she has been in getting on with her life; that one will convey desperation where desperation was felt, and hurt where hurt was felt. And so on.

To bear witness to Leslie's pain is not to tell Leslie's story of pain as a means to explicating how her pain has affected one's own life. Accordingly, to be authorized by Leslie to bear witness to her pain is to have won her confidence that telling her story of pain will not take a back seat to telling one's own story of pain as caused by her story. Not that it will always be impossible for people to make reasonable inferences about how one has been affected. It stands to reason that how one has been affected will surely be obvious in some cases. Rather, whatever inferences reasonable people might be able to draw, the point of bearing witness to the moral pain of another will not be so that others can see how one has been affected by the other person's pain. Thus, to be authorized to bear witness for another is to have won her confidence that one will tell her story with a certain motivational structure.

Now, it may be tempting to think that bearing witness to the moral pain of others requires something amounting to a complete diminution of the self, to becoming a mere mouthpiece for another. But this is to think of bearing witness to the moral pain of others as something that happens to one—a state that one falls into or whatever. Perhaps there are such cases of bearing witness. I do not write with them in mind, however. Instead, as I conceive of the idea, bearing witness to the moral pain of another is very much an act of agency and, as such, it can be an extremely courageous thing to do. During the time of slavery, whites who endeavored to bear witness to the moral pain of blacks were sometimes called "nigger lovers." In Nazi Germany, some who endeavored to bear witness to the moral pain of the Jews were killed. Nowadays, those who endeavor to bear witness to the moral pain of lesbians and homosexuals are often branded as such themselves. Far from being an activity only for the faint of heart, bearing witness to the moral pain of others can require extraordinary courage and resoluteness of will.

Well, needless to say, there can be no bearing witness, as I have explicated it, to the moral pain of another without having heard his story and heard it well. One will have had to have heard the glosses on the story and the nuances to the story. One will have had to have been sensitive to the emotions that manifested themselves as the story was told, and to the vast array of nonverbal behavior with which the story was told. One will have to have heard his story well enough to have insight into how his life has been emotionally configured by his experiences. One rightly authorizes a person to bear witness to his moral pain only if these things are true.

In an important essay entitled "The Need for More than Justice," Annette Baier explains the significance of departing from John Rawls's claim that justice is the first virtue of social justice.[16] One thing that is needed is the appropriate moral posture toward those who have been oppressed. Without it, we often blithely trample upon those whom we mean to help. The notion of moral deference is meant to give expression to one aspect of what that posture calls for. It is impossible to responsively help those who have been hurt if one does not understand the nature of their pain. And while it may be true that we can know what is right and wrong behavior for others without consulting them, it is simply false that, in the absence of similar experiences, we can know how others are affected by wrongdoing without consulting them.

Let me repeat a point made at the outset: the idea of moral deference helps us to understand the inadequacy of the response that one has not contributed to

---

[16]*Morality and Feminist Theory, Canadian Journal of Philosophy,* Supp. Vol. 13 (1987). Rawls's first sentence is "Justice is the first virtue of social institutions as truth is of systems of thought," *A Theory of Justice* (Cambridge: Harvard University Press, 1971), p. 3.

As I was typing the final draft of this essay, Martha Minow's book, *Making All the Difference: Inclusion, Exclusion, and American Law* (Ithica: Cornell University Press), was brought to my attention. But I did read the Afterword in which she writes: "Claiming that we are impartial is insufficient if we do not consider changing how we think. Impartiality is the guise that partiality takes to seal bias against exposure" (p. 376). This essay points to a way in which that change must go.

another's oppression. To the extent that it is true, the response does not entail that one understands another's downward social constitution. Moral innocence does not entail understanding. Neither, for that matter, does good will. Nor does either entail that one has earned the trust of one who has been downwardly constituted by society. It goes without saying that the innocence of others should never be discounted; neither should it be trumpeted for what it is not, namely understanding and the earned trust of others.

A final comment: the account of moral deference offered suggests why both those who have been downwardly constituted by society and those who have not been should think differently of one another. If, as I have argued, those who have not been should be willing to earn the trust of the downwardly constituted, then the downwardly constituted must not insist that, as a matter of principle, this is impossible. Understandably, it may be difficult to earn the trust of those who have been downwardly constituted by society. And it may, in fact, not be possible for some outside of the social category in question actually to do so. But what has to be false is that, as a matter of principle, it is impossible for anyone outside of that social category to do so.

Apart from the context of the loves of friendship and romance, there is no greater affirmation that we can want from another than that which comes in earning her or his trust. If we should be willing to accept moral affirmation from others, then surely we are more likely to treat them justly. Moral deference embodies this idea.

CHICANA IDENTITY

Paula M. L. Moya

In the following section I will draw upon Satya Mohanty's essay "The Epistemic Status of Cultural Identity: On *Beloved* and the Postcolonial Condition,"[1] to articulate a realist account of Chicana

identity that theorizes the linkages between social location, experience, epistemic privilege, and cultural identity. I must emphasize that this project is not an attempt to rehabilitate an essentialist view of identity. The critiques of essentialism are numerous; the aporias of an essentialist notion of identity have been well documented.[2] The mistake lies in assuming that our options for theorizing identities are inscribed within the postmodernism/essentialism binary—that we are either completely fixed and unitary or unstable and fragmented selves. The advantage of a realist theory of identity is that it allows for an acknowledgment of how the social facts of race, class, gender, and sexuality function in individual lives without *reducing* individuals to those social determinants.

I will begin by clarifying my claims and defining some terms. "Epistemic privilege," as I will use it in this essay, refers to a special advantage with respect to possessing or acquiring knowledge about how fundamental aspects of our society (such as race, class, gender, and sexuality) operate to sustain matrices of power. Although I will claim that oppressed groups may have epistemic privilege, I am not implying that social locations have epistemic or political meanings in a self-evident way. The simple fact of having been born a person of color in the United States or of having suffered the effects of heterosexism or of economic deprivation does not, in and of itself, give someone a better understanding or knowledge of the structure of our society.

[1]Satya P. Mohanty, "The Epistemic Status of Cultural Identity: On *Beloved* and the Postcolonial Condition." *Cultural Critique* 24 (Spring 1993), 41–80; and Mohanty, "Colonial Legacies, Multicultural Futures: Relativism, Objectivity, and the Challenge of Otherness," *PMLA* 110, no. 1 (1995), 108–18.
[2]When I refer to essentialism, I am referring to the notion that individuals or groups have an immutable and discoverable "essence"—a basic, unvariable, and presocial nature. As a theoretical concept, essentialism expresses itself through the tendency to see *one* social fact (class, gender, race, sexuality, etc.) as determinate in the last instance for the cultural identity of the individual or group in question. As a political strategy, essentialism has had both liberatory and reactionary effects. For one poststructuralist critique of essentialism that does not quite escape the postmodernist tendency I am critiquing in this essay, see Diana Fuss's book *Essentially Speaking*.

The key to claiming epistemic privilege for people who have been oppressed in a particular way stems from an acknowledgment that they have experiences—experiences that people who are not oppressed in that same way usually lack—that *can* provide them with information we all need to understand how hierarchies of race, class, gender, and sexuality operate to uphold existing regimes of power in our society. Thus, what is being claimed is not any *a priori* link between social location or identity and knowledge, but a link that is historically variable and mediated through the interpretation of experience.

"Experience," in this essay, refers to the fact of personally observing, encountering, or undergoing a particular event or situation. By this definition, experience is admittedly subjective. Experiences are not wholly external events; they do not just happen. Experiences happen to us, and it is our theoretically mediated interpretation of an event that makes it an "experience." The meanings we give our experiences are inescapably conditioned by the ideologies and "theories" through which we view the world. But what is at stake in my argument is not that experience is theoretically mediated, but rather that experience *in its mediated form* contains a "cognitive component" through which we can gain access to knowledge of the world.[3] It is this contention, that it is "precisely in this *mediated* way that [personal experience] yields knowledge," that signals a theoretical departure from the opposed camps of essentialism and postmodernism.[4]

The first claim of a realist theory of identity is that the different social facts (such as gender, race, class, and sexuality) that mutually constitute an individual's social location are causally relevant for the experiences she will have. Thus, a person who is racially coded as "white" in our society will usually face situations and have experiences that are significantly different from those of a person who is racially coded as "black."[5] Similarly, a person who is racially coded as "black" and who has ample financial resources at her disposal will usually face situations and have experiences that are significantly different from those of a person who is racially coded as "black" and lacks those resources. The examples can proliferate and become increasingly complex, but the basic point is this: the experiences a person is likely to have will be largely determined by her social location in a given society.[6] In order to appreciate the structural causality of the experiences of any given individual, we must take into account the mutual interaction of *all* the different social facts which constitute her social location, and situate them within the particular social, cultural, and historical matrix in which she exists.

The second basic claim of a realist theory of identity is that an individual's experiences will influence, but not entirely determine, the formation of her cultural identity. Thus, while I am suggesting that members of a group may share experiences as a result of their (voluntary or involuntary) membership in that group, I am not suggesting that they all come to the same conclusions about those experiences.[7] Because the theories through which humans interpret their experiences vary from individual to individual, from time to time, and from situation to situation, it follows that different

---

[3]Mohanty, "Epistemic Status," 45
[4]Ibid.

[5]This can happen even if both individuals in the example are born into an African-American community and consider themselves "black." It should be clear that I am not talking about race as a biological category. I am talking about people who, for one reason or another, appear to others as "white" or "black." As I will demonstrate in my discussion of Moraga's work, this is an important distinction for theorizing the link between experience and cultural identity for people with real, but not visible, biological or cultural connections to minority communities.
[6]For an illuminating discussion of the way in which the social fact of gender has structured the experiences of at least one woman, and has profoundly informed the formation of her cultural identity, see Mohanty's "Epistemic Status," esp. pp. 46–51.
[7]It is not even necessary that they recognize themselves as members of that group. For example, a dark-skinned immigrant from Puerto Rico who refuses identification with African-Americans may nevertheless suffer racist experiences arising from the history of black/white race relations within the U.S. due to mainland U.S. citizens' inability to distinguish between the two distinct cultural groups.

people's interpretations of the same kind of experience will differ. For example, one woman may interpret her jealous husband's monitoring of her interactions with other men as a sign that "he really loves her," while another may interpret it in terms of the social relations of gender domination, in which a man may be socialized to see himself as both responsible for and in control of his wife's behavior. The kinds of identities these women construct for themselves will both condition and be conditioned by the kinds of interpretations they give to the experiences they have. (The first woman may see herself as a treasured wife, while the second sees herself as the victim in a hierarchically organized society in which, by virtue of her gender, she exists in a subordinate position.)

The third claim of a realist theory of identity is that there is a cognitive component to identity which allows for the possibility of error and of accuracy in interpreting experience. It is a feature of theoretically mediated experience that one person's understanding of the same situation may undergo revision over the course of time, thus rendering her subsequent interpretations of that situation more or less accurate. I have as an example my own experience of the fact that the other women in my freshman dorm at Yale treated me differently than they treated each other. My initial interpretation of the situation led me to conclude that they just did not like me—the individual, the particular package of hopes, dreams, habits, and mannerisms that I was. Never having had much trouble making friends, this experience was both troubling and humbling to me. As a "Spanish" girl from New Mexico, neither race nor racism were social realities that I considered as being relevant to me. I might have wondered (but I did not) why I ended up spending my first semester at Yale with the other brown-skinned, Spanish-surnamed woman in my residential college. It was only after I moved to Texas, where prejudice against Mexicans is much more overt, that I realized that regardless of how I saw myself, other people saw me as "Mexican." Reflecting back, I came to understand that while I had not seen the other women in my dorm as being particularly different from me, the reverse was not the case. Simultaneous with that understanding came the suspicion that my claim to a

Spanish identity might be both factually and ideologically suspect. A little digging proved my suspicion correct.[8] In Texas, then, I became belatedly and unceremoniously Mexican-American. All this to illustrate the point that identities both condition and are conditioned by the kinds of interpretations people give to the experiences they have. As Mohanty says, "identities are ways of making sense of our experiences." They are "theoretical constructions that enable us to read the world in specific ways."[9]

The fourth claim of a realist theory of identity is that some identities, because they can more adequately account for the social facts constituting an individual's social location, have greater epistemic value than some others that same individual might claim. If, as in the case of my Spanish identity, I am forced to ignore certain salient facts of my social location in order to maintain my self-conception, we can fairly conclude that my identity is epistemically distorted. While my Spanish identity may have a measure of epistemic validity (mine is a Spanish surname; I undoubtedly have some "Spanish blood"), we can consider it less valid than an alternative identity which takes into consideration the ignored social facts (my "Indian blood," my Mexican cultural heritage) together with all the other social facts that are causally relevant for the experiences I might have. Identities have more or less epistemic validity to the extent that they "refer" outward to the world, that they accurately describe and explain the complex interactions between the multiple determinants of an individual's social location.[10] According to the realist the-

---

[8]For an explanation of the historical origins of the myth that Spanish-surnamed residents of New Mexico are direct descendants of Spanish *conquistadores,* see Rodolfo Acuña, *Occupied America,* 55–60; Nancie González, *The Spanish-Americans of New Mexico,* 78–83; and John Chavez, *The Lost Land,* 85–106.

[9]Mohanty, "Epistemic Status," 55.

[10]Identities can be evaluated, according to Mohanty, "using the same complex epistemological criteria we use to evaluate 'theories.'" He explains: "Since different experiences and identities refer to different aspects of *one* world, one complex causal structure that we call 'social reality,' the realist theory of identity implies that we can evaluate them comparatively by considering how adequately they explain this structure" ("Epistemic Status," 70–71).

ory of identity, identities are neither self-evident, unchanging, and uncontestable, nor are they absolutely fragmented, contradictory, and unstable. Rather, identities are subject to multiple determinations and to a continual process of verification which takes place over the course of an individual's life through her interaction with the society she lives in. It is in this process of verification that identities can be (and often are) contested, and that they can (and often do) change.

I want to consider now the possibility that my identity as a "Chicana" can grant me a knowledge about the world that is "truer," and more "objective," than an alternative identity I might claim as either a "Mexican-American," a "Hispanic," or an "American" (who happens to be of Mexican descent). When I refer to a Mexican-American, I am referring to a person of Mexican heritage born and/or raised in the United States whose nationality is U.S. American. The term for me is descriptive, rather than political. The term "Hispanic" is generally used to refer to a person of Spanish, Mexican, Puerto Rican, Dominican, Cuban, Chilean, Peruvian, etc. heritage who may or may not have a Spanish-surname, who may or may not speak Spanish, who can be of any racial extraction, and who resides in the U.S. As it is currently deployed, the term is so general as to be virtually useless as a descriptive or analytical tool. Moreover, the term has been shunned by progressive intellectuals for its overt privileging of the "Spanish" part of what, for many of the people it claims to describe, is a racially and culturally mixed heritage. A Chicana, according to the usage of women who identify that way, is a politically aware woman of Mexican heritage who is at least partially descended from the indigenous people of Mesoamerica and who was born and/or raised in the United States. What distinguishes a Chicana from a Mexican-American, a Hispanic, or an American of Mexican descent is her political awareness; her recognition of her disadvantaged position in a hierarchically organized society arranged according to categories of class, race, gender, and sexuality; and her propensity to en-

gage in political struggle aimed at subverting and changing those structures.[11]

The fifth claim of a realist theory of identity is that our ability to understand fundamental aspects of our world will depend on our ability to acknowledge and understand the social, political, economic, and epistemic consequences of our own social location. If we can agree that our *one* social world is, as Mohanty asserts, "constitutively defined by relations of domination,"[12] then we can begin to see how my cultural identity as a Chicana, which takes into account an acknowledgment and understanding of those relations, may be more epistemically valid than an alternative identity I might claim as a Mexican-American, a Hispanic, or an American. While a description of myself as a Mexican-American is not technically incorrect, the description implies a structural equivalence with other hyphenated Americans (Italian-Americans, German-Americans, African-Americans, etc.) that erases the differential social, political, and economic relations that obtain for different groups. This erasure is even more marked in the cultural identity of the Hispanic or American (of Mexican descent), whose self-conception often depends upon the idea that she is a member of one more assimilable ethnic group in what is simply a nation of immigrants.[13] Factors of race, gender, and class get obscured in these identities, while

---

[11] Historically, the term "Chicano" was a pejorative name applied to lower-class Mexican-Americans. Like the term "Black," it was consciously appropriated and revalued by (primarily) students during the Chicano Movement of the 1960s. According to the *Plan de Santa Barbara,* the term specifically implies a politics of resistance to Anglo-American domination.

[12] Mohanty, "Epistemic Status," 72.

[13] An example of the assimilationist "Hispanic" is Linda Chavez whose book, *Out of the Barrio: Toward a New Politics of Hispanic Assimilation* suggests that Hispanics, like "previous" white ethnic groups, are rapidly assimilating into the mainstream of U.S. culture and society (2). Not only does Chavez play fast and loose with sociological and historical evidence, but her thesis cannot account for the social fact of race. She does not mention race as being causally relevant for the experiences of Hispanics, and she repeatedly refers to "non-Hispanic whites," a grammatical formulation which assumes that all Hispanics are white. She accounts for Puerto Ricans and Dominicans by considering them as "dysfunctional" "exceptions" to the white-Hispanic rule (139–59).

a normative heterosexuality is simply presumed. We find that in order to maintain her identity, the Hispanic or American (of Mexican descent) may have to repress or misinterpret her own or others' experiences of oppression. Moreover, she will most likely view her material situation (her "success" or "failure") as entirely a result of her individual merit, and dismiss structural relations of domination as irrelevant to her personal situation. Thus, my claim that social locations have epistemic consequences is not the same as claiming that a particular kind of knowledge inheres in a particular social location. An individual's understanding of herself and the world will be mediated, more or less accurately, through her cultural identity.

The sixth and final claim of a realist theory of identity is that oppositional struggle is fundamental to our ability to understand the world more accurately. Mohanty, drawing upon the work of Sandra Harding and Richard Boyd, explains this Marxian idea in this way:

> In the case of social phenomena like sexism and racism, whose distorted representation benefits the powerful and the established groups and institutions, an attempt at an objective explanation is necessarily continuous with oppositional political struggles. Objective knowledge of such social phenomena is in fact often dependent on the theoretical knowledge that activism creates. For without these alternative constructions and accounts, our capacity to interpret and understand the dominant ideologies and institutions is limited to those created or sanctioned by these very ideologies and institutions.[14]

The "alternative constructions and accounts" generated through oppositional struggle provide new ways of looking at our world that always complicate and often challenge dominant conceptions of what is "right," "true," and "beautiful." They call to account the distorted representations of peoples, ideas, and practices whose subjugation is fundamental to the colonial, neo-colonial, imperialist, or capitalist project. Furthermore, because the well-being (and sometimes even survival) of the groups

or individuals who engage in oppositional struggle depends on their ability to refute or dismantle dominant ideologies and institutions, their vision is usually more critical, their efforts more diligent, and their arguments more comprehensive than those of individuals or groups whose well-being is predicated on the maintenance of the status quo. Oppressed groups and individuals have a stake in knowing "*what it would take* to change [our world], on . . . identifying the central relations of power and privilege that sustain it and make the world what it is."[15] This is why "granting the possibility of epistemological privilege to the oppressed might be more than a sentimental gesture; in many cases in fact it is the only way to push us toward greater social objectivity."[16] Thus, a realist theory of identity demands oppositional struggle as a necessary (although not sufficient) step toward the achievement of an epistemically privileged position.

PHILOSOPHY AND DISABILITY

Karen Fiser

A few years after I became disabled, I began to notice how seldom philosophers acknowledge the existence of disability and chronic pain. It is probably important that, because I had been trained as a philosopher, it took me years to notice, though I myself had a disability. As human beings, we inevitably undergo physical limitation and loss, disease, disability, and chronic pain. If we do not suffer now, we will later. If we do not suffer ourselves, we love someone who does. By one recent estimate, there are close to 44 million disabled people in the United States.[1] In 1983 it was estimated that 60 mil-

[14]Mohanty, "Epistemic Status," 51–52.

[15]Ibid., 53.
[16]Ibid., 72.
[1]Congressional Research Service, *Digest of Data on Persons with Disabilities,* Library of Congress, Report #84-115 EPW, 1984, principal investigator John L. Czajka.

lion Americans were either partially or totally disabled by chronic pain.[2] Yet there is an absence in philosophy of meaningful discussion of these familiar facts of our human condition, even in contexts where one might expect to find it.

Philosophical discussions of personal identity, for example, commonly feature brains in vats, rational Martians, and person stages. I have never seen a deep or careful discussion by a philosopher of the terrifying crises of personal identity familiar to people who become disabled as adults. Similarly, philosophical discussions of pain, though they abound, seem oddly trivial and jejune next to any real experience of pain, especially chronic pain. One could simply never tell from reading philosophy that disabled people contribute to society or that their experience might enrich our understanding of what it is to live a human life.[3]

Disabled people do sometimes appear in the philosophical literature. But, as Susan Wendell has noted, almost always the same two questions are being discussed: (1) How severely disabled does a person have to be before we are justified in withholding medical treatment and letting that person die? and (2) How disabled does a fetus need to be before it is permissible to prevent its being born?[4] Imagine yourself disabled, and see how this linkage of disability and death might strike you. It is as if there is no question of a *life* with disability, at all. It is simply assumed that disability in itself can be an appropriate basis for ending a human life, and the only morally troubling question is, *When?*

Involved in such a point of view is a cluster of attitudes and assumptions philosophers ought to

question but apparently don't: *we,* the subjects here, can decide when persons whose disability places *them* at the margins (relative to *us*) may be allowed to live. There is a presumption that *we* have the right to ask this question, and that *we* have the capacity to answer it for ourselves on moral or conceptual or medical grounds, in the absence of any detailed knowledge of the lives of persons with disabilities or any real conversation with them on these issues. Related to this assumption is the fact that the philosophers prescribing life or death for persons with disabilities are themselves able-bodied; if they weren't, they would not write as they do. There is no sense that disabled people are fully human subjects who can speak for themselves. Why does this seem plausible? We can see what is wrong with it by substituting any other minority group for persons with disabilities; what we have then is obviously, shockingly wrong. What does it mean that we don't notice this?

Even when philosophers do (rarely) attempt to discuss examples from the point of view of a person with a disability, their discussions are often marred by the same ignorant and contemptuous attitudes. Consider this passage from *Real People* by Kathleen V. Wilkes, in which she is comparing mental with physical disabilities:

> It is of course true that physical deficiency too may prevent him from engaging in such activities; but physical problems would at least leave open the possibility that he could pursue his interests indirectly—the physically handicapped can, for example, tell his friends and children, or write books, about how to care for begonias, what are the best routes up mountains, which philosophy books he would reread if only he were not blind, what he would say or do to support unilateralism or multilateralism if only he had the physical capacity.[5]

I suspect that most readers would read right past the offensive attitudes expressed in this passage without

[2]David B. Morris, *The Culture of Pain* (Berkeley and Los Angeles: University of California Press, 1991), p. 19.

[3]Interestingly, two important books on the nature of pain have been written recently by nonphilosophers: Elaine Scarry's *The Body in Pain: The Making and Unmaking of the World* (New York: Oxford University Press, 1987); and Morris, *The Culture of Pain*). For further detailed descriptions of the experience of pain, especially chronic pain, see Karen Fiser, "Privacy and Pain," *Philosophical Investigations* 9, no. I (January 1986), pp. 1–17.

[4]Susan Wendell, "Toward a Feminist Theory of Disability," *Hypatia* 4, no. 2 (Summer 1989), pp. 104–24 (see especially p. 104).

[5]Kathleen Wilkes, *Real People* (Oxford: Clarendon, 1988), pp. 94–95.

noticing them.[6] A "physically handicapped" person could tell people how to care for begonias or write a book about it—*as opposed to* gardening? But, of course, disabled people do garden, and they also write books about topics more important than begonias. Stephen Hawking, a physicist with profound disabilities who wrote *A Brief History of Time,* did his important scientific work only *after* he became disabled.[7] Mark Wellman, a paraplegic, climbs mountains, he doesn't just write about it. Blind people do read philosophy, and they write it as well. What "physical capacity" is required to support a political position or even to be active in politics? Franklin Roosevelt had an orthopedic disability, as we know, as have present Senators Kerrey and Dole. The clear implication of this paragraph is that disabled people usually don't do these things or can do them only "indirectly" or vicariously, simply because of their physical disabilities. But this is just not true.

Why would a philosopher make claims so at odds with facts we know very well when reminded of them? What accounts for the absence from our theories of real persons with real disabilities? Why can't we hear ourselves when we say offensive things about disabled people? I would like to suggest that we cannot end discrimination against persons with disabilities until we fundamentally change the way we think about and describe disability. We must reject the assumption (made by Wilkes in the paragraph quoted) that it even makes sense to say that if we know a person has a disability (belongs to a class of persons, for instance, persons with Down's syndrome or wheelchair users) we know what that person can do. We must stop making assumptions about what groups of people can do, and let them tell us.

DISABLING ASSUMPTIONS

I once gave my introductory ethics class an article to read, one of these Sunday supplement "super-crip" stories about people who triumph over their so-called handicaps. The story involved a man who refused to be beaten by his muscular dystrophy. It recounted how he insisted on driving and forcing himself to walk using crutches; the whole point of the article was to praise him for pushing himself always to do more. He and his wife went to a movie. He drove around until he finally found a parking place, and then they walked several blocks to the theater. But this had made them late, so he got angry at himself and insisted that they go home.

I asked my (all able-bodied) class to list the assumptions made by the author of the story. They didn't see any. Here are several: (1) It is better to use crutches than to use a wheelchair, even when using crutches is slower and makes you late for the movie; (2) using crutches to walk rather than a chair is courageous; (3) it is better for a disabled man to drive, even if it means he has to walk farther, than for his wife to drive and let him off in front of the theater; and (4) anger at himself for taking longer to get to the movie is an appropriate, healthy response (which *also* means he's courageous).

The members of my class did not notice these as assumptions because they shared them all. But most people with orthopedic disabilities do not hold these views; or, rather, if they do at first, they must (sometimes painfully) learn to discard them as disabling assumptions. The fact is, the dominant society is wheelchairphobic. People seem to feel a lot of emotion about wheelchairs, and they sometimes react oddly and unpredictably.[8] I have had perfect strangers shout at me to *get out of that chair.* Once

---

[6]The terminology Wilkes uses—the "senile and the retarded"—to describe those with mental disabilities is itself objectionable. She assumes, without evidence or argument, that a person with a mental disability could not do the activities described in this passage. But of many persons with such disabilities this is plainly false; it depends on the kind and severity of the disability, as well as the person's circumstances, including the enabling or disabling attitudes of people around them.

[7]Michael White and John Gribben, *Stephen Hawking: A Life in Science* (New York: Dutton, 1992).

---

[8]"The occupant of a wheelchair is a living *memento mori*—a visible, unwelcome reminder of the chaos that can at any moment shatter our illusion of a fair and orderly universe . . . [O]ne is the object of stares, avoidance, fawning, condescension, and the combined ignorance, insensitivity and outright cruelty that prompts total strangers to volunteer details of the worst possible cases of whatever one's illness happens to be." Carol Easton, *Jacqueline du Pre* (New York: Summit, 1990), p. 187.

a woman congratulated the person standing next to me for having the courage it takes to walk! Sometimes people seem to feel called upon to *do* something, so they start pushing your chair vigorously without asking or speaking to you first.

Most people seem to assume you must be worse off if you're using a chair than you would be if you were standing. Many assume that if you use a chair, you're "confined" to it and can't walk. This is social prejudice born of ignorance. As one rehabilitation professional put it, "There are even times when the person who is walking is more disabled—because it takes twice as much energy to walk as it does if he would just sit down and wheel his chair."[9]

Many wheelchair users are in their chairs only half the day, or only when they are walking long distances. When I am walking, I am in pain with every step; when I am in my chair, I am in less pain, so I can do more. The chair empowers me. Pity is therefore not an appropriate response to someone using a wheelchair to walk. But if pity is inappropriate, so is the view that it takes more courage to walk with crutches. If you spent one day in a chair, you would know better. (By the way, doctors are not immune to these prejudices. Knowledge of the disease process does not equate to understanding the lives of people with disabilities.)

I myself went through a learning process. Like many others with my disability, I fought as hard as I could against using a wheelchair. I was especially afraid to teach in one. I endured many months of standing in front of my classes with excruciating, burning pain in my back and knees. Finally someone pointed out to me that it was actually *disabling* me to stand up, first because my obvious pain was distracting my class, and second because on days after I had stood I could not get out of bed. The price I was paying to keep standing on my own two feet was much too high.

As to assumption 3, that it's better for the man to drive than for his wife to drop him off, we over-

value personal autonomy in this culture, especially in men. But insisting on doing everything for oneself can be unrealistic and wrong, damaging to oneself and to others, when the circumstances have changed. Many disabled people go through a humbling transformation, learning to depend on others and to ask for help while not becoming overly dependent. The man in this story is going to have trouble if he keeps making his wife miss the movie because he insists on driving.

Finally, about assumption 4: people with any serious disability know that part of having a disability is constantly thinking out new ways to get something done and calculating how long it will take. Simple tasks become complex, requiring imagination and negotiation with others. Even one's relation to time has to change. In his memoir on becoming blind, John Hull tells of the profound changes in the sense of time and space occasioned by the onset of disability, describing a friend with multiple sclerosis who takes forty-five minutes to get his shoes tied.[10] Everything takes longer.[11] You have to become more patient, not only with yourself, but with those for whom you must wait to receive help. Getting angry at oneself is the worst thing one could do. In this man's case, it seems a symptom of serious denial.

I have gone into such detail to make a point. People with disabilities are full, not diminished, human beings: they have real nonvicarious human lives to lead. You would not know that from reading philosophy.[12] There are many things to know about living a good life with a disability; most people begin to

---

[9]Ed Hooper, "More than a Long Walk," *Disability Rag,* January–February 1986, p. 21.

[10]John M. Hull, *Touching the Rock: An Experience of Blindness* (New York: Pantheon, 1990), p. 79.

[11]In his moving book of essays *Broken Vessels,* Andre Dubus quotes a friend's rule: "There comes a time in the life of an amputee when he realizes that everything takes three times as long." Andre Dubus, *Broken Vessels* (Boston: Godine, 1991), p. 167. For a discussion of the effect of chronic illness on time, see Kathy Charmaz, *Good Days, Bad Days* (New Brunswick, N.J.: Rutgers University Press, 1991).

[12]On the ethical significance of "having a human life to lead," see Cora Diamond, "The Importance of Being Human," in *Human Beings,* ed. David Cockburn (Cambridge: Cambridge University Press, 1991).

learn them only after they become disabled or someone close to them does. The accumulated wisdom and experience of disabled people is disregarded, as if it concerned only themselves. Its human importance is overlooked and discounted. For a long time in this country we have lived with what amounts to social and cultural segregation of people with disabilities. We seem content to remain ignorant about their lives and circumstances, and this ignorance often results in mistreatment and misunderstanding. But why should this be? Why do we think that ignorance and prejudice about people with disabilities is acceptable? Why do we think there is nothing important to learn from them about life?

If Kathleen Wilkes knew any disabled people well, I do not believe she would write philosophy as she does. Ethical theorists who knew about the lives of persons with Down's syndrome would not presume to generalize about their "diminished quality of life" or to give this as a reason for withholding medical treatment a "normal" child would receive.[13] When people refuse to look at the circumstances of a disabled person's life, they make abusive assumptions that disable the person. For example, in the case of Phillip Becker, a child with Down's syndrome who was institutionalized by his parents at birth, it was the refusal of the parents to see what he actually was like and was capable of that disabled him.[14] Because they saw him as someone who could not live a worthwhile life, they withheld their consent for Phillip to have his heart defect surgically repaired. The Heaths, a volunteer couple who had grown to love Phillip and saw him as a lively, likeable child who could learn and could enjoy his life, fought for him to have the same quality

medical care he would have received without question if he had not been disabled.

There are many less dramatic examples of how the ignorant assumptions of the able-bodied actually create a handicap where the physical limitation involved need not do so. John Hull describes how sighted people do not understand that when a blind person is lost, he needs to be told precisely where he is; giving directions as one would to a sighted person (turn left at the corner, and then right) does not help. Similarly, when a blind person walks along with a friend, he must put a finger under the friend's elbow to stay with him. He therefore can't use his stick or attend in the same way to the route. This creates a dependency that the sighted person may assume is normal, when it is only a consequence of being with someone sighted.[15]

Many persons previously thought to be "retarded" all their lives are now able to speak as a result of new techniques of facilitated communication on a computer keyboard. Men and women had been described and treated as if they were completely unable to learn, when in fact we were unable to communicate with them to find out what they knew. Many have lived whole lives waiting for us to find the key to unlock the prison of silence. Clearly, part of what was disabling them was other people's assumptions in the absence of real knowledge about what they could do.

Here is another, more everyday, kind of case. When I became disabled, I was constantly shamed by the fact that I would make plans and then have to change them. I would plan to attend a meeting and not be able to go. I would bend all my efforts to meet a certain professional goal and fail miserably because of unforeseen circumstances. When your pain level and energy are unpredictable, you feel as if you are at the mercy of factors you cannot control. That's because you are. You have to learn to take what a day bestows, even if it's not what you planned, and so do your friends, colleagues, and family. Before I understood this, I

---

[13]On this topic, see Adrienne Asch and Michelle Fine, *Women with Disabilities* (Philadelphia: Temple University Press, 1988), p. 299: "People who decide that Down's Syndrome or spina bifida automatically renders children or adults 'vegetables' or 'better off dead' simply know nothing about the lives of such people today—much less what those lives could be in a more inclusive, person-oriented society."

[14]Martha Minow, *Making All the Difference: Inclusion, Exclusion, and American Law* (Ithaca, N.Y.: Cornell University Press, 1990), pp. 341–49.

[15]Hull, *Touching the Rock*, pp. 145, 100–101.

blamed myself and let others blame me. This shame was disabling.[16]

Finally a wise friend whose husband had MS told me that this inability to predict even one's own future goes with the territory. You buy an adapted van so you can drive, only to find that your worsening condition makes further driving impossible. You fight for six months to have your employer accept the idea that a changed work schedule would enable you to function in your workplace, only to find that the new schedule is too much for you, and you have to start all over again.

Sometimes relationships cannot withstand the strain. Friends get hurt and angry that you don't do what you said you would do. Employers take it as your personal failing that you can't control your own life. All disabled persons can tell stories about problems at work, even jobs lost, because employers could not understand their behavior, and about friends and lovers who could not accept the realities of their situation and chose to disappear.

The important point here is that a person with a disability cannot be understood as the same person, with one added property—a disability. Or, to put this point differently: one cannot understand a person with a disability without coming to understand the nature of that particular disability and the demands it places on the person involved. For instance, if you don't understand that a person with multiple sclerosis suffering exacerbations of her condition can't predict what she will be able to do, you might wrongly conclude, from her failure to do, that she's unreliable or irresponsible.

THE INVISIBLE MINORITY

Often disabled people seem to be the invisible minority. Able-bodied people, even those who mean well, sometimes seem to overlook them or to view their problems as merely personal ones. Many peo-ple do not understand that discrimination against persons with disabilities is a serious problem that will not be solved easily. I heard a woman speak whose daughter had recently been a high school student who used a wheelchair. Her senior prom had been scheduled by the school in an inaccessible place. When the daughter protested that she wanted to attend and could not, many people got angry at her for causing so much trouble—after all, she was the only one affected.

When I heard this story, my thought was that if one student were excluded from a prom because the dance was held in a racially segregated country club, people would see that exclusion as clearly wrong and speak up for her. But when I tried that analogy out on able-bodied friends, they didn't think it was a good one. First of all, why would a wheelchair user need to go to a dance? If the school changed the dance to an accessible place, they thought, it would be a good thing to do, but they could not see that the student had a legal right to an accessible prom. This reaction troubled me. I began to fear that my able-bodied friends unconsciously saw people with disabilities as "less than," as if the disability *in itself* diminished their humanity, removing their right to choose for themselves. First of all, they tended to identify (somewhat defensively, it seemed to me) with the school authorities, seeing the problem in terms of expense and trouble to the school to benefit one person, and not of the student's civil rights.[17] But, even more damaging, they seemed to take for granted that it was permissible for others to define the interests and abilities of a disabled person: she was disabled, so she could not dance and could have no interest in dancing. They did not perceive the obvious lack of respect inherent in this point of view.

Sometimes this lack of respect comes out in sadistic and abusive behavior. In *The Illness Narratives,*

---

[16]For a good account of these feelings of shame, see Nancy Mairs, "On Being a Cripple" (1987), p. 120, Marsha Saxton and Florence Howe, eds. *With Wings* (New York: Feminist Press, 1987).

[17]Perhaps Pl, 101–336, the Americans with Disabilities Act of 1990, will help to change people's thinking. It forbids discrimination against persons with disabilities in employment, public accommodations, transportation, telecommunications, and activities of state and local government.

Arthur Kleinman tells the story of Paul Sensabaugh, a man who suffered brain injury and coma with severe injuries to the frontal and temporal lobes.[18] As a result, he underwent personality changes. His behavior became childish and impulsive. He was left with limited cognition. For him it became a struggle to do the simplest things. The biggest event of his day was going out to buy a paper. His daily routine became crucial to his sense of self-respect; it was important to be independent, to look "just the same as the others." Though his life had become severely circumscribed after his accident, he remained extremely conscious of other people's reactions and anxious to avoid shame. Dr. Kleinman remarks:

> I came to realize just how often he was shamed: by children in the hospital who gawked at him and mimicked his behavior; by patients or families who avoided sitting near him; by the hospital security personnel, who had a habit of making faces when he walked by; by the woman at the cash register who would say, "Come on, get goin', we can't wait all day while you count your change"; and worst of all, by the janitorial staff who called him "dummy."

One day the doctor was in a hurry and was brusque with Paul, impatiently cutting off his slow, painstaking attempts to talk. Paul responded:

> That's OK, Dr. Kleinman. I'm accustomed to it. I'm just a small person. I'm hardly a grownup anymore. I know the truth [beginning to cry]. I'm not altogether up here. I'm a half-wit like they said, aren't I? The world is too fast for me, isn't it? The people are too big. And when they get angry they can hurt you, can't they? It really is too dangerous a place for me. Maybe I should live in a home, you know what I mean, a home for people like me.

To me, the humanity and dignity of Paul's response provide the best answer to those who think that his disability, severe as it is, makes him less human or in any way renders his life less than a wholly human life. The point is, how do we as a society provide what he needs to live the best life possible *for him?* Yet many

people, meeting Paul on the street, would react to him with distaste, fear, condescension, or impatience, utterly failing to see that their own behavior is now creating the pain in his life and needs to change.

In fact, people with disabilities are often easy targets for verbal and physical abuse. Shocking as it is, many are victimized in their own homes. On the street, it is not unusual for wheelchair users to be taunted, beaten, and robbed.[19] Even when disabled people are not overtly abused, their dignity and personhood are continually assaulted. They are ignored, infantilized, treated as if they weren't there, spoken about in the third person: "Will you look after him? Will his chair fit in the elevator?" Taxi drivers pass wheelchair users by, because they think it's not worth their time to deal with the chair.[20]

Able-bodied people often have great difficulty seeing how they contribute to the problems disabled people face. I once had a politically progressive colleague who loved Vietnamese peasants and every single member of the working class. Yet he kept scheduling meetings of a group to which we both belonged up a steep flight of stairs, which made it impossible for me to attend. He never could grasp that this was a political issue, much less a moral one. I could not get him to see the point. I wanted to call him a racist, because that's what it felt like: he refused to see what his privilege allowed him not to see, and I never had any power to make him act differently. (And that experience taught me a valuable lesson: never assume that someone who understands one form of oppression will necessarily notice or understand the oppression of disabled people. On the contrary, sometimes progressives are the worst, because they assume they're on your side, that they aren't among those who need to change, and that their behavior is beyond criticism. In other words, they do not think they need to learn anything from a disabled person because they already have the correct position.)

---

[18]Arthur Kleinman, *The Illness Narratives: Suffering, Healing, and the Human Condition* (New York: Basic Books, 1988), pp. 165–69.

[19]Personal communication from Bob Alexander, then chair of the Cambridge Commission on Handicapped Persons, in 1986.
[20]Sucheng Chan, "You're Short, Besides!" In *Making Face, Making Soul,* ed. Gloria Anzaldua (San Francisco: Aunt Lute Foundation, 1990), p. 164; Hull, *Touching the Rock,* p. 60; Saxton and Howe, *With Wings,* p. 80.

• • •

DISABILITY AND THE ESSENTIALISM DEBATE

Categories are quick to congeal, and the experiences of women whose lives do not fit the categories will appear as anomalous, when in fact the theory should have grown out of them as much as others from the beginning.
—María C. Lugones and Elizabeth V. Spelman, *"Have We Got a Theory for You!"*

María Lugones and Vicky Spelman have written passionately and convincingly about the cultural imperialism of white feminists whose theorizing omits and distorts the reality lived by women of color.[21] They argue that feminist claims about what women experience *as women* can themselves be acts of domination, in that they erase the realities of some women's lives in favor of a false universality.

In her wonderful book *Inessential Woman,* Spelman argues: "If feminism is essentially about gender, and gender is taken to be neatly separable from race and class, then race and class don't need to be talked about except in some peripheral way. And if race and class are peripheral to women's identities as women, then racism and classism can't be of central concern to feminism."[22] She is arguing against what she calls the "additive" analysis of the oppression of women.[23] What is wrong with this view, she says, is that if we think that what it is to be a woman (as opposed to a man) is a unitary thing that can be understood in isolation from what it is to be black, for example, we end up falsifying the experience of black women. That is because we are treating the "oppression of a black woman in a society that is racist as well as sexist as if it were a further burden when, in fact, it is a different burden." For example,

the way a black woman is distinguished from white men may be different from the ways she is distinguished from black men.[24] Generalizations about the treatment of women (for example, that they are "put on a pedestal" by men) overlook the experience of black women, who certainly have not been put on a pedestal by white men.[25] Similarly, characterizing the family as a locus of oppression (without qualification) may falsify the experience of black women, for whom the family also has been "a source of resistance against white oppression."[26]

I think these arguments have great value; they demonstrate the inadequacy of any account of how women are oppressed that does not try to characterize the interplay of the various aspects of a woman's identity. And I think Spelman is right to say that a person from a dominant point of view who attempts to generalize or to characterize another person's or group's experience runs the risk of overlooking, erasing, or falsifying that experience. I also agree that we must be careful when we exercise the power to characterize, not only to be as faithful as we can to that person's or group's experience but to question our right to speak for and about others.

Yet if we apply Spelman's arguments to disability, some problems emerge. The first is that Spelman herself has omitted any mention of the experience of women with disabilities.[27] Yet, if her argument is correct, if a theorist thinks that a woman's gender is neatly separable from disability, that theorist must think that disability is peripheral

---

[21]María C. Lugones and Elizabeth V. Spelman, "Have We Got a Theory for You! Feminist Theory, Cultural Imperialism, and the Demand for 'The Woman's Voice,'" in *Hypatia Reborn: Essays in Feminist Philosophy,* ed. Azizah Y. Al-Hibri and Margaret A. Simons (Bloomington: Indiana University Press, 1990).
[22]Elizabeth V. Spelman, *Inessential Woman: Problems of Exclusion in Feminist Thought* (Boston: Beacon, 1988), p. 112.
[23]Ibid. p. 123.
[24]Ibid., p. 135.
[25]Ibid, p. 120.
[26]Ibid. p. 132.
[27]Women with disabilities are never mentioned in the article by Lugones and Spelman, "Have We Got." They are also omitted in María C. Lugones, "On the Logic of Pluralist Feminism," in *Feminist Ethics,* ed. Claudia Card (Lawrence: University Press of Kansas, 1991). In Spelman's book, I found one reference to "handicap," and given its context it is unfortunate that this is the only one: "Or I might think it important to resist a term altogether—for example, 'handicapped.' I might think it important to embrace joyfully a term such as 'lesbian' or 'Black' and to try with others to invest it with new meaning" (Spelman, *Inessential Woman* p. 152). Even when Spelman gives a list of aspects of identity she believes theorists must always consider—including race, class, ethnicity, sexual orientation, language, religion, and nationality—she leaves out disability.

and can't be of central concern to feminism. What are we to make of the fact that Spelman never discusses women with disabilities? The difficulty here goes deeper than leaving disability off the list of significant aspects of identity. If disability were considered, the analysis itself would have to change. In the course of making her argument, Spelman relies, at least implicitly, on generalizations about, for instance, black women's experience and white women's experience that may not apply without qualification to women with disabilities. To the extent that her arguments are successful and we understand the contrasts she intends between black women's and white women's historical experience, the generalizations must be in some sense useful and true. Yet they do not take account of, for example, the experience of white women with disabilities, who also have hardly been placed on a pedestal by men. Over and over again in the descriptions many disabled women (from different races and cultural backgrounds) give of their own lives, we find them saying that their oppression consists not in being forced to fill traditional female roles, but in not being seen by many others as women or as sexual beings at all.[28] (But of course for other women, this generalization would *not* be true; it is difficult to give a nuanced account of the role of disability in relation to other factors. And nothing guarantees the truth of one's own account, anyway: in the end, we are left with the person's own *interpretation and beliefs,* which themselves may be influenced by factors like age, race, class, cultural origin, ideology, political consciousness, etc.)

This means that, for many disabled women, being a woman—being an embodied, gendered, sexual being—is not experienced as separate from one's disability and cannot be understood that way. At one point, Spelman contrasts white women's experiences of their bodies with black women's experiences of their bodies, arguing against the culturally entrenched "somatophobia" of Western theory.[29] Why does she fail to notice or think worthy of mention the profoundly different experiences disabled people, both men and women, have of their bodies? After all, if there is a group who can be said more than any other to bear the burden of our fear and hatred of the mortal body, it is disabled people. Why does Spelman find it plausible to generalize about the experience of white women and black women, without noticing how the exclusion of disability limits her own theorizing?

I think we can answer this question by turning to the essay Spelman wrote with María Lugones. In that essay, the authors characterize the dominant voice in the United States as white, middle class, heterosexual, and Christian (or at any rate not self-identified non-Christian).[30] My question is, Is the hidden assumption here that this voice belongs to an able-bodied woman? Because women with disabilities historically have *not* been included or heard, any more than women of color. (Of course, the *exceptional* disabled woman may be heard, like the *exceptional* woman of color. This is no objection to the general claim.) In a strange way, Lugones and Spelman seem to privilege race, and, because they do, they fail to notice that the "oppressor class" they describe also excludes many disabled white women, as well as women of color.

To me it is clear that Lugones and Spelman are imagining the white oppressor class as able-bodied. But notice what happens if you reimagine this class as including women with Down's syndrome; blind women; women deaf since birth; women with mental disabilities; women with multiple sclerosis, cerebral palsy, and spina bifida; as well as women living their lives inside institutions and women living on the street who have been deinstitutionalized. Are they part of the oppressor class, or not? Are they a different class altogether?

---

[28]Marian Blackwell-Stratton et al., "Smashing Icons: Disabled Women and the Disability and Women's Movements," in Asch and Fine, *Women with Disabilities,* pp. 13, 29; Debra Kent, "In Search of Liberation," in Saxton and Howe, *With Wings,* p. 82.

[29]Spelman, *Inessential Woman,* pp. 129–30.
[30]Lugones and Spelman, "Have We Got," p. 20.

When Spelman and Lugones identify an "asymmetry" between white women and women of color, it is hard to avoid feeling that a complexity has been reduced to a duality.[31] Neither women of color nor white women, if they have no experience of disability, can rightly be said to speak for women with disabilities, much less for the full range of these women—not until these theorists have learned something, educated themselves about disability, and this they cannot do without involvement, activity, and self-change. . . .

What does seem certain is that the only way we have to transcend these limits and to learn about the other, as Martha Minow has noted, is to talk with that person.[32] As a disabled person, I would like to see philosophers, including feminist theorists, stop merely consulting their intuitions about disability and start listening to disabled people talk about their own experiences. I would like to see them stop repeating biased and offensive language and assumptions about disability. And, finally, I would hope to see them working to correct not only the appalling silence about the lives of real human beings with real disabilities, but also the conditions underneath the silence.

QUESTIONS FOR DISCUSSION

1. Can you relate the experiences our authors share to your own experiences? Did the authors point to something you never noticed before, or shed light on an issue about which you were unsure? Explain, using concrete examples.

2. Explain in your own words the concepts of epistemic privilege and moral deference. Do you agree with these concepts? Why or why not? Can you give an example of when such a practice may be important in discerning the truth of a situation?

---

[31]Ibid., p. 31.
[32]Minow, *Making All the Difference*, p. 263.

SOCIAL EQUALITY

This second section explores the inner dynamics of coexistence within a society. Most societies are not ethnically homogeneous, and most have economic and social classes. When are various economic and social rewards for our differences legitimate and justified, and when are they unfair? How should societies be reshaped, or why should they remain as they are?

Our first author, Satyavrata Siddhantalankar, was for many years vice chancellor of Gurukula University, in Hardwar, India. He has written extensively on Vedic culture. In this selection, he argues that although the caste system as practiced in India today brings with it social tyranny, nevertheless its beginnings were noble and in accord with human nature. According to this system, there are four possible natures or temperaments for human beings; these distinguish propensities, not professions. So, properly understood, Brahmana, Kshatriya, Vaishya, and Shudra are four ways in which to approach spiritual self-fulfillment. If "division of labor" is based on material circumstances, then economic classes will spring up with their concomitant class struggles; but if profession follows spiritual nature, this predicament will be avoided.

John Rawls is one of the foremost political philosophers in the analytic tradition. His work is known in the fields of sociology and economics as well as in philosophy. In this selection, Rawls is concerned with a fair, and therefore just, distribution of economic wealth in any society. To find his paradigm, he asks us to engage in a thought experiment, necessarily abstract, but whose conclusions will be helpful in the concrete by serving as an ideal model. He wants to articulate and make explicit the rules by which people would regulate their social cooperation in the ideal, just society, where rational, equal, and unconstrained people would come together and freely agree to abide by certain tenets. A social system based on fairness would have the advantage that members of the society would accept the rules voluntarily, closely approximating the idea

of the "social contract" as described by Locke and other traditional political philosophers. Rawls suggests that this thought experiment be conducted under a "veil of ignorance," in which none of the judges would be able to foretell their own position in society; only then could we trust that their judgments were disinterested and based on fairness. Under these circumstances, Rawls is confident that people would accept inequalities in wealth and status in their society only if such inequalities could be shown to be to everyone's advantage. Also, positions of authority and command must be equally open to all. As he explains, there must be equal liberty of citizens: for example, political liberty, liberty of conscience, the freedom or right to hold personal property, and freedom from arbitrary arrest and seizure.

H. Odera Oruka offers us a critique of Rawls's position. Odera Oruka (1944–1995) was a philosophy professor and founder of the philosophy department at the University of Nairobi in Kenya. He was born in Nyanza Province, Western Kenya, and got his advanced degrees in the United States and Sweden. He was well known for his contributions to the field of African philosophy. Odera Oruka was very active in the World Futures Studies Federation, and he was especially concerned about the future of development and the environment. According to Odera Oruka, Rawls is mistaken in his belief that a society can sustain economic inequalities while preserving political equality. To make his point, he takes us on an imaginative journey to a future society in which the rich are able to afford to extend their lives. (This society, of course, is not so much unlike our present world, where those in rich nations have a longer life expectancy than those from poor nations.) Wouldn't such life extension mean that one had more time in which to exercise one's political rights? If so, how can it be that unequal distribution could be to everyone's advantage?

Odera Oruka challenges Rawls's claim that his paradigm for justice, based on the veil of ignorance, is really neutral regarding economic schemes. Instead, Odera Oruka argues, Rawls presumes a capitalist framework, and such a presumption may be unjustified.

A DEFENSE OF VARNA (CASTE)

Satyavrata Siddhantalankar

Spiritualism builds and binds, whereas materialism destroys and disintegrates. Spiritualism razes to the ground the barriers which separate man from man, materialism only leaves behind its vistas and edifices of separation. Is not, then, one fully justified in inquiring as to how it could ever be that Vedic culture, whose fundamental postulate is spiritualism, devise a system of social stratification known as the caste system or *Jati Vyavastha* which set man against man in the form of *Brahmanas, Kshatriyas, Vaishyas,* and *Shudras,* and relegated an appreciable section of its own humanity to the heinous lot of untouchability? Is such a system consistent with the spiritual claims of India's culture? Does it not make the inquiring and intelligent mind say to itself: "Yes, in India, theory and practice must really be poles apart"?

There can be no two opinions about the devastating effects of the caste system on Indian society. It has been an outrageous social tyranny. It has created an artificial hierarchy of superior and inferior human beings which can be said to have violated every spiritual postulate advocated by this culture. Even the constitutions of materialistically advanced countries guarantee "equality before the law" to each and every citizen. But is it not clearly apparent that the spiritualistic law of Vedic culture, as reflected by its workings through the caste system, has guaranteed through the centuries naught else but inequality to the members of its own fold? All this is no doubt true, but the fact to be borne in mind is that this was not the perspective with which the

Vedic masters viewed the system; or to put it differently and more affirmatively, this was not the system evolved by Vedic culture. Is not history replete with instances of various social, religious, political, and economic institutions which after passing through the heyday of their glory have so degenerated as to be completely irreconcilable with every original concept of them? How else would Tennyson say, "God fulfils Himself in many ways, Lest one good custom should corrupt the world"?

The caste system, if viewed through the eyes of the present century, can and must only be regarded as that social system which evolved as a result of certain social, religious, economic, and political compulsions of the post-Vedic and medieval periods, and which prevented the Hindu society from disintegration against the onslaughts of the invaders. It was through these rigid disciplinary measures that both Indian society and culture were able to maintain their compactness as well as hold their own against the foreigners. It was a boon so long as it served its purpose but has turned into a bane after having outlived its utility. The original conception of Vedic sociologists based upon spiritual philosophy was called the *Varna* system and not *Jati* or caste system.

DIFFERENCE BETWEEN VARNA AND JATI OR CASTE

The two words in Sanskrit literature which are often confused with each other, giving rise to misconception regarding the Indian social system, are *Varna* and *Jati.* Both *Varna* and *Jati* are translated as caste by English writers but actually they are poles asunder. Both denote differences in human nature; but whereas *Varna* is spiritual, *Jati* is social; *Varna* is the old Vedic conception, *Jati* is purely a medieval and a post-Vedic idea. When we speak of the *Varna* system of Vedic culture, we do not mean the *Jati* or caste system of the medieval period, based upon birth, which as we have already stated is the bane of Indian society. Thus we see that the term caste refers to *Jati* and not to *Varna;* and it is *Varna* about the spiritual significance of which we are concerned here. . . . The entire scope of life was covered by the Vedic concept of *Varna.*

What is *Varna?* The word *Varna* is derived from the root *Vri* which means to choose or to select. But wherein lies the selection? Or, what is that which we have to select? According to Vedic philosophy, each human being is capable of falling into one of the four categories of propensities, or temperaments, or innate natures; and *Varna* is the selection of one of these four propensities for the development of one's soul. Thus, there are four *Varnas* or four *Pravrittees* (propensities) of life; and these must be distinguished, at the very outset, from the many *Vrittees* (professions) of life. The *Varna* system, thus, reduces itself not to a fourfold classification of professions or to an application of the socio-economic principle of the division of labour, but rather to a spirituo-psychological classification of human beings with regard to their natures on the basis of their temperament.

The *Varna* system did not regard man as merely an economic automaton, it viewed man as a whole. None can say that to eat, to drink, and to be merry is the be-all and the end-all of human existence; all must endorse Longfellow's statement: "Dust thou art, to dust returnest, Was not spoken of the soul." The body must perish, but there is some entity of eternal value beyond the body; for whom the body is and who is not for the body; who uses the body as its instrument and is master of the body. Labour and capital are no doubt for the preservation and upkeep of the body, but is the body only for the body? How can such a proposition be tenable? The body must be for something apart from and beyond the body, and this something is what we call the spirit.

According to the teachings of Vedic philosophy, the ultimate goal or target which each and every human being should place before himself is realization of the divine and self-fulfilment, and it is towards this end that our entire life's pursuits should be directed. It was essentially to help men to move collectively towards this end that the *Varna* system was evolved. Thus the *Brahmana, Kshatriya, Vaishya,* and *Shudra* are not, as is generally believed, the four professions; they are the four propensities of human beings which point out the four different directions accessible to the soul in its journey through life. It is only one of these four propensities that are available at the option of the individual which leads one to acquire material possessions and permits him to involve himself in the physical world. This propensity was known as *Vaishya* temperament, but even this was so channellized that it was not made the be-all and the end-all of one's existence. In the *Varna* system, as we shall see in the course of this chapter, even this material nature of man was spiritualized. Thereby a scheme was evolved whose fundamental objective was that both individually and collectively the entire nation should move towards the attainment of self-realization after setting before itself the ideal of *Atmic* development. This was the quintessence of *Varna* philosophy.

DETAILS OF THE FOUR SPIRITUAL PROPENSITIES

We have said that there are four human propensities. What are they, and how do they arise, are but the logical questions that must present themselves at this point. The explanations are forthcoming from the Sankhya philosophy. According to this philosophy the evolution of the world of matter and life is from *Prakriti* (matter). What is *Prakriti? Prakriti* is the homogeneous state of matter in which *Sattva* (unactivity), *Rajas* (activity), and *Tamas* (inactivity) are in equilibrium. When this state of equilibrium was disturbed, the world in its heterogeneous visible form appeared which is called *Vikriti.* It is this very substance or *Vikriti,* which comes into existence from the disturbed state of *Prakriti* with the three qualities of *Sattva, Rajas,* and *Tamas,* that goes into the formation of the *Manas* (mind).

Thus the mind has three qualities or attributes, i.e., *Sattvika* (unactive), *Rajasika* (active), and *Tamasika* (inactive). These three attributes of the mind, which work their way out in society, were treated by Vedic sociologists as being equivalent to four different types of human beings. Those in whom the *Sattvika* quality dominates are called *Brahmanas,* those in whom the *Sattvika*-cum-*Rajasika* quality is all powerful are called *Kshatriyas,* those in whom the *Rajasika*-cum-*Tamasika* quality holds its sway are called *Vaishyas,* and those in whom the *Tamasika* quality is all embracing are called *Shudras.* These are not the four professions but, psychologically speaking, are the four main propensities of the human mind. Every profession and all forms of trade, commerce, and industry are included only in the *Vaishya* propensity. Thus it is absolutely clear that Vedic metaphysics underlies Vedic psychology, and it is Vedic psychology which is at the root of Vedic sociology wherein this fourfold division of human society has been visualized. *Varna* only indicates a particular spiritual or psychological frame, bent, or direction of the human mind.

And so it is that now, with the mists of misconception having been cleared from before our eyes, does not our heart leap up when we behold as it were a rainbow shining across from our erstwhile darkened horizons and stormy skies, as we pensively recall Shri Krishna's immortal line from the Gita: "The four orders of society (*Brahmana, Kshatriya, Vaishya,* and *Shudra*) were created by me corresponding to the different types of *Gunas* and *Karmas.* Though the author of this creation, I am also its nondoer. It is in this light and perspective that one should dwell upon Shri Krishna's advice to Arjuna: "One's own duty, though devoid of merit, is preferable to the duty of another well performed." What else is this if not a home truth as well as a piece of friendly advice given out by Shri Krishna to all of us? Can we ever hope to contradict our innate natures and attempt any work for which we are most unsuited? Yes, it is a far better thing for each of us to confine ourselves to that piece of work for which the *Guna* is lying latent within us, rather than be caught up in a whirlpool of other activities whose fountainhead is not within ourselves. Even today, in a world of stark materialism, with every banner bearing the emblem: "All men are equal," did not Bernard Shaw rise up to contradict the prevailing consensus of opinion when he poured out that all men are basically unequal? Of course Shaw was only referring to the differences in nature, temperament, capabilities, etc., as manifested by the different human beings; he was not concerned with the reasons or the causes of these disparities. It was Vedic culture alone that concerned itself with these problems and shouldered the cross of finding their solutions. Hence the modern world, if it wants to bridge the gap left in this knowledge by one of the greatest thinkers of the day, should turn to the teachings of the Vedic seers.

A person of a *Sattvika* bent of mind with a thorough spiritual outlook on life is a *Brahmana.* One with an admixture of *Sattvika* and *Rajasika* qualities but in whom the *Rajas* predominates comes into the fold of the *Kshatriya.* They both confine their activities to social welfare not because it is their livelihood or profession, but on account of the fact that the *Brahmana* and the *Kshatriya* can fulfil their spiritual urges only by serving society with the power of the brain and the might of the arm respectively. Their self is consistently progressing from manifoldness to oneness, from disunity to unity, from selfishness to selflessness, and instead of entangling itself in the meshes of *Prakriti,* it has well set itself on the onward march to self-realization. Their disinterested service is rewarded by society which caters to their physical needs.

It has been ordained that a *Brahmana* should never beg for his needs, even though he may be at the point of death, neither should he accumulate nor hoard. His lot is only to serve unfettered and unbidden. He should lead a life of voluntary poverty. Every richness for him lies in self-abnegation. The *Kshatriya* is also forbidden from hankering after wealth. He is a combination of *Sattva* and *Rajas* but his *Rajas* must be *Sattva*-oriented. Despite all his war and other activities, the ideal which he is required to set before himself is the progress towards the *Sattvika* life of the spirit. The *Vaishya* is an admixture of *Rajas* and *Tamas* in his mental attitude or make-up, but the predominance is of the *Rajas* over *Tamas.* Whereas the *Brahmanas* and the *Kshatriyas* lead a life of disinterestedness and selflessness, the *Vaishya* keeps the torch of his self-interest burning before him. The *Shudra* is the one in whom *Tamas* dominates and this makes him inactive, dull, and inert.

We have explained that the Sankhya philosophy visualizes the entire hierarchy of human creation standing as it were on four steps, each step being constructed out of a different *Varna* building material. Modern psychology has also arrived at the same conclusion but only uses different terminology. In modern parlance we can say that the mind has three functions to perform, namely, knowing, willing, and feeling. The men of knowledge who disinterestedly serve society with the dominance of the *Sattvika* quality may be designated as *Brahmanas.* The men of action who are willing to lay down their lives for the cause of the nation and in whom the *Rajasika* quality predominates may be styled as *Kshatriyas.* The men of desire who are attracted and attached to the world of matter, who view life with a feeling of self-interest, and in whom the *Rajasika*-cum-*Tamasika* quality holds its own against everything else may be called *Vaishyas.* And the men whose doings are neither channelled towards knowledge, nor action, nor self-interest, but who are overpowered by the *Tamasika* qualities may be looked upon as the *Shudras.*

It is thus clearly apparent, from the above, that the *Varna* system of social stratification was based upon metaphysical and psychological foundations. It was a positive effort made by the Vedic sociologists to guide, with a conscious effort, social evolution towards a predetermined goal or end, instead of letting the blind, unconscious law of nature mould the social structure. And this could only be brought about by the introduction of a well devised scheme into which each and every individual was required to fit and which, in its turn, was also suited to as well as catered for the needs of all. Thus the *Varna* system of Vedic culture is naught else but the application of the four fundamental propensities or natures of the different individuals collectively to society in general.

DIVISION OF LABOUR IS A PART OF VAISHYA PROPENSITY ONLY

The four *Varnas,* as we have explained, are not the four professions or means of livelihood, they are rather the four basic natures of human beings. If these *Varnas* were to be regarded as professions as they are by certain people, the question that would present itself would undoubtedly be as to whether the Vedic Aryans were only aware of four means of

livelihood. How is this possible? Professions have always been innumerable. These four *Varnas* are essentially propensities, natures, or temperaments, and the *Vaishya Varna* or the acquisitive propensity which finds its outlet into various economic professions, is only one of them.

Division of labour is associated only with the *Vaishya* temperament and with none other. We can say that a person of this nature constitutes the economic man who looks at everything from a purely monetary angle. But as this *Vaishya* propensity constitutes only one-fourth of the total human propensity as visualized by the *Varna* system, the other three-fourths being embraced by the remaining three *Varnas,* the principle of the division of labour touches only the fringes of the *Varna* system.

The *Varna* system and the principle of the division of labour are neither correlated nor interchangeable. The *Varnas* are the four *Pravrittees* or the four natures of human beings, whereas the division of labour includes the numberless *Vrittis* or professions. These numberless *Vrittis* or professions are merely the ramifications of the same basic human nature known as the *Vaishya* temperament.

A CO-ORDINATED AND WELL BALANCED SOCIAL EVOLUTION WAS THE AIM AND OBJECTIVE OF THE VARNA SYSTEM

The word *Varna* means to choose. But the question is: what is there to be chosen? *Varna* system upholds that it is not a profession that has to be chosen, but rather a path of life which will be in conformity with the innate nature of the individual and will enable him to attain the goal for which the soul has taken birth in human form. Hence, *Varna* was a spiritual conception and not an economic interpretation of life. The economic nature, propensity, or potential of man is only one-fourth of the total human propensity. Hence if a person who was supposed to be a *Brahmana* or *Kshatriya* by nature used his talents for the earning of money, he would no longer be considered as a *Brahmana* or a *Kshatriya* but would come into the fold of the *Vaishya.* In Vedic terminology, anything that was done for the sake of money was immediately designated as the function of a *Vaishya,* regardless of the fact as to how very noble was the act. The fundamental thing was the propensity, the nature, the temperament. For it is this which was considered to be real because it sprang out of the inner self; whereas the various professions were only considered to be the outer expressions of merely one of the four basic propensities of man.

Social evolution left to the unconscious, blind forces of nature brings in its wake the economic principle of the division of labour, for it is in this direction that we are driven by the materialistic world. This process can only terminate in the creation of economic inequalities which, in turn, give rise to class conflicts, wars, and social revolutions. The same social evolution, if properly guided and controlled along the psychological principles enunciated in the *Varna* system of Vedic culture, can usher in an era of peace, co-operation, and mutual goodwill.

A THEORY OF JUSTICE

John Rawls

My aim is to present a conception of justice which generalizes and carries to a higher level of abstraction the familiar theory of the social contract as found, say, in Locke, Rousseau, and Kant.[1] In order to do this we are not to think of the original contract as one to enter a particular society or to set up a particular form of government. Rather, the guiding idea is that the principles of justice for the basic structure of society are the object of the original agreement. They are the principles that free and rational persons concerned to further their own interests would accept in an initial position of equality as defining the fundamental terms of their association. These principles are to regulate all further agreements; they specify the kinds of social cooperation that can be entered into and the forms of government that can be established. This way of regarding the principles of justice I shall call justice as fairness.

Thus we are to imagine that those who engage in social cooperation choose together, in one joint act, the principles which are to assign basic rights and duties and to determine the division of social benefits. Men are to decide in advance how they are to regulate their claims against one another and what is to be the foundation charter of their society. Just as each person must decide by rational reflection what constitutes his good, that is, the system of ends which it is rational for him to pursue, so a group of persons must decide once and for all what is to count among them as just and unjust. The choice which rational men would make in this hypothetical situation of equal liberty, assuming for the present that this choice problem has a solution, determines the principles of justice.

In justice as fairness the original position of equality corresponds to the state of nature in the traditional theory of the social contract. This original position is not, of course, thought of as an actual historical state of affairs, much less as a primitive condition of culture. It is understood as a purely hypothetical situation characterized so as to lead to a certain conception of justice.[2] Among the essential features of this situation is that no one knows his

[1]As the text suggests, I shall regard Locke's *Second Treatise of Government,* Rousseau's *The Social Contract,* and Kant's ethical works beginning with *The Foundations of the Metaphysics of Morals* as definitive of the contract tradition. For all of its greatness, Hobbes's *Leviathan* raises special problems. A general historical survey is provided by J. W. Gough, *The Social Contract,* 2nd ed. (Oxford, The Clarendon Press, 1957), and Otto Gierke, *Natural Law and the Theory of Society,* trans. with an introduction by Ernest Barker (Cambridge, The University Press, 1934). A presentation of the contract view as primarily an ethical theory is to be found in G. R. Grice, *The Grounds of Moral Judgment* (Cambridge, The University Press, 1967).

[2]Kant is clear that the original agreement is hypothetical. See *The Metaphysics of Morals,* pt. I (*Rechtslehre*), especially §§ 47, 52; and pt. II of the essay "Concerning the Common Saying: This May Be True in Theory but It Does Not Apply in Practice," in *Kant's Political Writings,* ed. Hans Reiss and trans. by H. B. Nisbet (Cambridge, The University Press, 1970), pp. 73–87. See Georges Vlachos, *La Pensée politique de Kant* (Paris, Presses Universitaires de France, 1962), pp. 326–335; and J. G. Murphy, *Kant: The Philosophy of Right* (London, Macmillan, 1970), pp. 109–112, 133–136, for a further discussion.

place in society, his class position or social status, nor does any one know his fortune in the distribution of natural assets and abilities, his intelligence, strength, and the like. I shall even assume that the parties do not know their conceptions of the good or their special psychological propensities. The principles of justice are chosen behind a veil of ignorance. This ensures that no one is advantaged or disadvantaged in the choice of principles by the outcome of natural chance or the contingency of social circumstances. Since all are similarly situated and no one is able to design principles to favor his particular condition, the principles of justice are the result of a fair agreement or bargain. For given the circumstances of the original position, the symmetry of everyone's relations to each other, this initial situation is fair between individuals as moral persons, that is, as rational beings with their own ends and capable, I shall assume, of a sense of justice. The original position is, one might say, the appropriate initial status quo, and thus the fundamental agreements reached in it are fair. This explains the propriety of the name "justice as fairness": it conveys the idea that the principles of justice are agreed to in an initial situation that is fair. The name does not mean that the concepts of justice and fairness are the same, any more than the phrase "poetry as metaphor" means that the concepts of poetry and metaphor are the same.

Justice as fairness begins, as I have said, with one of the most general of all choices which persons might make together, namely, with the choice of the first principles of a conception of justice which is to regulate all subsequent criticism and reform of institutions. Then, having chosen a conception of justice, we can suppose that they are to choose a constitution and a legislature to enact laws, and so on, all in accordance with the principles of justice initially agreed upon. Our social situation is just if it is such that by this sequence of hypothetical agreements we would have contracted into the general system of rules which defines it. Moreover, assuming that the original position does determine a set of principles (that is, that a particular conception of justice would be chosen), it will then be true that whenever social institu-

tions satisfy these principles those engaged in them can say to one another that they are cooperating on terms to which they would agree if they were free and equal persons whose relations with respect to one another were fair. They could all view their arrangements as meeting the stipulations which they would acknowledge in an initial situation that embodies widely accepted and reasonable constraints on the choice of principles. The general recognition of this fact would provide the basis for a public acceptance of the corresponding principles of justice. No society can, of course, be a scheme of cooperation which men enter voluntarily in a literal sense; each person finds himself placed at birth in some particular position in some particular society, and the nature of this position materially affects his life prospects. Yet a society satisfying the principles of justice as fairness comes as close as a society can to being a voluntary scheme, for it meets the principles which free and equal persons would assent to under circumstances that are fair. In this sense its members are autonomous and the obligations they recognize self-imposed.

One feature of justice as fairness is to think of the parties in the initial situation as rational and mutually disinterested. This does not mean that the parties are egoists, that is, individuals with only certain kinds of interests, say in wealth, prestige, and domination. But they are conceived as not taking an interest in one another's interests. They are to presume that even their spiritual aims may be opposed, in the way that the aims of those of different religions may be opposed. Moreover, the concept of rationality must be interpreted as far as possible in the narrow sense, standard in economic theory, of taking the most effective means to given ends. I shall modify this concept to some extent, as explained later, but one must try to avoid introducing into it any controversial ethical elements. The initial situation must be characterized by stipulations that are widely accepted.

In working out the conception of justice as fairness one main task clearly is to determine which principles of justice would be chosen in the original position. To do this we must describe this situation in some detail and formulate with care the problem of choice which it presents. These matters I shall take up in the immediately succeeding chapters. It may be observed, however, that once the principles of justice are thought of as arising from an original agreement in a situation of equality, it is an open question whether the principle of utility would be acknowledged. Offhand it hardly seems likely that persons who view themselves as equals, entitled to press their claims upon one another, would agree to a principle which may require lesser life prospects for some simply for the sake of a greater sum of advantages enjoyed by others. Since each desires to protect his interests, his capacity to advance his conception of the good, no one has a reason to acquiesce in an enduring loss for himself in order to bring about a greater net balance of satisfaction. In the absence of strong and lasting benevolent impulses, a rational man would not accept a basic structure merely because it maximized the algebraic sum of advantages irrespective of its permanent effects on his own basic rights and interests. Thus it seems that the principle of utility is incompatible with the conception of social cooperation among equals for mutual advantage. It appears to be inconsistent with the idea of reciprocity implicit in the notion of a well-ordered society. Or, at any rate, so I shall argue.

I shall maintain instead that the persons in the initial situation would choose two rather different principles: the first requires equality in the assignment of basic rights and duties, while the second holds that social and economic inequalities, for example inequalities of wealth and authority, are just only if they result in compensating benefits for everyone, and in particular for the least advantaged members of society. These principles rule out justifying institutions on the grounds that the hardships of some are offset by a greater good in the aggregate. It may be expedient but it is not just that some should have less in order that others may prosper. But there is no injustice in the greater benefits earned by a few provided that the situation of persons not so fortunate is thereby improved. The intuitive idea is that since everyone's well-being depends upon a scheme of cooperation without which no one could have a satisfactory life, the division of advantages should be such as to draw forth the willing cooperation of everyone taking part in it, including those less well situated. Yet this can be expected only if reasonable terms are proposed. The two principles mentioned seem to be a fair agreement on the basis of which those better endowed, or more fortunate in their social position, neither of which we can be said to deserve, could expect the willing cooperation of others when some workable scheme is a necessary condition of the welfare of all.[3] Once we decide to look for a conception of justice that nullifies the accidents of natural endowment and the contingencies of social circumstance as counters in quest for political and economic advantage, we are led to these principles. They express the result of leaving aside those aspects of the social world that seem arbitrary from a moral point of view.

The problem of the choice of principles, however, is extremely difficult. I do not expect the answer I shall suggest to be convincing to everyone. It is, therefore, worth noting from the outset that justice as fairness, like other contract views, consists of two parts: (1) an interpretation of the initial situation and of the problem of choice posed there, and (2) a set of principles which, it is argued, would be agreed to. One may accept the first part of the theory (or some variant thereof), but not the other, and conversely. The concept of the initial contractual situation may seem reasonable although the particular principles proposed are rejected. To be sure, I want to maintain that the most appropriate conception of this situation does lead to principles of justice contrary to utilitarianism and perfectionism, and therefore that the contract doctrine provides an alternative to these views. Still, one may dispute this contention even though one grants that the contractarian method is a useful way of studying ethical theories and of setting forth their underlying assumptions.

Justice as fairness is an example of what I have called a contract theory. Now there may be an

---

[3]For the formulation of this intuitive idea I am indebted to Allan Gibbard.

objection to the term "contract" and related expressions, but I think it will serve reasonably well. Many words have misleading connotations which at first are likely to confuse. The terms "utility" and "utilitarianism" are surely no exception. They too have unfortunate suggestions which hostile critics have been willing to exploit; yet they are clear enough for those prepared to study utilitarian doctrine. The same should be true of the term "contract" applied to moral theories. As I have mentioned, to understand it one has to keep in mind that it implies a certain level of abstraction. In particular, the content of the relevant agreement is not to enter a given society or to adopt a given form of government, but to accept certain moral principles. Moreover, the undertakings referred to are purely hypothetical: a contract view holds that certain principles would be accepted in a well-defined initial situation.

The merit of the contract terminology is that it conveys the idea that principles of justice may be conceived as principles that would be chosen by rational persons, and that in this way conceptions of justice may be explained and justified. The theory of justice is a part, perhaps the most significant part, of the theory of rational choice. Furthermore, principles of justice deal with conflicting claims upon the advantages won by social cooperation; they apply to the relations among several persons or groups. The word "contract" suggests this plurality as well as the condition that the appropriate division of advantages must be in accordance with principles acceptable to all parties. The condition of publicity for principles of justice is also connoted by the contract phraseology. Thus, if these principles are the outcome of an agreement, citizens have a knowledge of the principles that others follow. It is characteristic of contract theories to stress the public nature of political principles. Finally there is the long tradition of the contract doctrine. Expressing the tie with this line of thought helps to define ideas and accords with natural piety. There are then several advantages in the use of the term "contract." With due precautions taken, it should not be misleading.

· · ·

THE ORIGINAL POSITION AND JUSTIFICATION

I have said that the original position is the appropriate initial status quo which insures that the fundamental agreements reached in it are fair. This fact yields the name "justice as fairness." It is clear, then, that I want to say that one conception of justice is more reasonable than another, or justifiable with respect to it, if rational persons in the initial situation would choose its principles over those of the other for the role of justice. Conceptions of justice are to be ranked by their acceptability to persons so circumstanced. Understood in this way the question of justification is settled by working out a problem of deliberation: we have to ascertain which principles it would be rational to adopt given the contractual situation. This connects the theory of justice with the theory of rational choice.

If this view of the problem of justification is to succeed, we must, of course, describe in some detail the nature of this choice problem. A problem of rational decision has a definite answer only if we know the beliefs and interests of the parties, their relations with respect to one another, the alternatives between which they are to choose, the procedure whereby they make up their minds, and so on. As the circumstances are presented in different ways, correspondingly different principles are accepted. The concept of the original position, as I shall refer to it, is that of the most philosophically favored interpretation of this initial choice situation for the purposes of a theory of justice.

But how are we to decide what is the most favored interpretation? I assume, for one thing, that there is a broad measure of agreement that principles of justice should be chosen under certain conditions. To justify a particular description of the initial situation one shows that it incorporates these commonly shared presumptions. One argues from widely accepted but weak premises to more specific conclusions. Each of the presumptions should by itself be natural and plausible; some of them may seem innocuous or even trivial. The aim of the contract approach is to establish that taken together they impose significant bounds on acceptable principles of justice. The ideal outcome would be that these conditions determine a unique set of principles; but I shall be satisfied if they suffice to rank the main traditional conceptions of social justice.

One should not be misled, then, by the somewhat unusual conditions which characterize the original position. The idea here is simply to make vivid to ourselves the restrictions that it seems reasonable to impose on arguments for principles of justice, and therefore on these principles themselves. Thus it seems reasonable and generally acceptable that no one should be advantaged or disadvantaged by natural fortune or social circumstances in the choice of principles. It also seems widely agreed that it should be impossible to tailor principles to the circumstances of one's own case. We should insure further that particular inclinations and aspirations, and persons' conceptions of their good do not affect the principles adopted. The aim is to rule out those principles that it would be rational to propose for acceptance, however little the chance of success, only if one knew certain things that are irrelevant from the standpoint of justice. For example, if a man knew that he was wealthy, he might find it rational to advance the principle that various taxes for welfare measures be counted unjust; if he knew that he was poor, he would most likely propose the contrary principle. To represent the desired restrictions one imagines a situation in which everyone is deprived of this sort of information. One excludes the knowledge of those contingencies which sets men at odds and allows them to be guided by their prejudices. In this manner the veil of ignorance is arrived at in a natural way. This concept should cause no difficulty if we keep in mind the constraints on arguments that it is meant to express. At any time we can enter the original position, so to speak, simply by following a certain procedure, namely, by arguing for principles of justice in accordance with these restrictions.

It seems reasonable to suppose that the parties in the original position are equal. That is, all have the same rights in the procedure for choosing principles; each can make proposals, submit reasons for their acceptance, and so on. Obviously the purpose of these conditions is to represent equality between human beings as moral persons, as creatures having a conception of their good and capable of a sense of justice. The basis of equality is taken to be similarity in these two respects. Systems of ends are not ranked in value; and each man is presumed to have the requisite ability to understand and to act upon whatever principles are adopted. Together with the veil of ignorance, these conditions define the principles of justice as those which rational persons concerned to advance their interests would consent to as equals when none are known to be advantaged or disadvantaged by social and natural contingencies.

There is, however, another side to justifying a particular description of the original position. This is to see if the principles which would be chosen match our considered convictions of justice or extend them in an acceptable way. We can note whether applying these principles would lead us to make the same judgments about the basic structure of society which we now make intuitively and in which we have the greatest confidence; or whether, in cases where our present judgments are in doubt and given with hesitation, these principles offer a resolution which we can affirm on reflection. There are questions which we feel sure must be answered in a certain way. For example, we are confident that religious intolerance and racial discrimination are unjust. We think that we have examined these things with care and have reached what we believe is an impartial judgment not likely to be distorted by an excessive attention to our own interests. These convictions are provisional fixed points which we presume any conception of justice must fit. But we have much less assurance as to what is the correct distribution of wealth and authority. Here we may be looking for a way to remove our doubts. We can check an interpretation of the initial situation, then, by the capacity of its principles to accommodate our firmest convictions and to provide guidance where guidance is needed.

In searching for the most favored description of this situation we work from both ends. We begin by describing it so that it represents generally shared and preferably weak conditions. We then see if these conditions are strong enough to yield a significant set of principles. If not, we look for further premises equally reasonable. But if so, and these principles match our considered convictions of justice, then so far well and good. But presumably there will be discrepancies. In this case we have a choice. We can either modify the account of the initial situation or we can revise our existing judgments, for even the judgments we take provisionally as fixed points are liable to revision. By going back and forth, sometimes altering the conditions of the contractual circumstances, at others withdrawing our judgments and conforming them to principle, I assume that eventually we shall find a description of the initial situation that both expresses reasonable conditions and yields principles which match our considered judgments duly pruned and adjusted. This state of affairs I refer to as reflective equilibrium.[4] It is an equilibrium because at last our principles and judgments coincide; and it is reflective since we know to what principles our judgments conform and the premises of their derivation. At the moment everything is in order. But this equilibrium is not necessarily stable. It is liable to be upset by further examination of the conditions which should be imposed on the contractual situation and by particular cases which may lead us to revise our judgments. Yet for the time being we have done what we can to render coherent and to justify our convictions of social justice. We have reached a conception of the original position.

I shall not, of course, actually work through this process. Still, we may think of the interpretation of the original position that I shall present as the result of such a hypothetical course of reflection. It represents the attempt to accommodate within one scheme both reasonable philosophical conditions on principles as well as our considered judgments of justice. In arriving at the favored interpretation of the initial situation there is no point at which an appeal is made to self-evidence in the traditional sense either of general conceptions or particular convictions. I do not claim for the principles of justice proposed that they are necessary truths or derivable from such truths. A conception of justice cannot be deduced from self-evident premises or conditions on principles; instead, its justification is a matter of the mutual support of many considerations, of everything fitting together into one coherent view.

A final comment. We shall want to say that certain principles of justice are justified because they would be agreed to in an initial situation of equality. I have emphasized that this original position is purely hypothetical. It is natural to ask why, if this agreement is never actually entered into, we should take any interest in these principles, moral or otherwise. The answer is that the conditions embodied in the description of the original position are ones that we do in fact accept. Or if we do not, then perhaps we can be persuaded to do so by philosophical reflection. Each aspect of the contractual situation can be given supporting grounds. Thus what we shall do is to collect together into one conception a number of conditions on principles that we are ready upon due consideration to recognize as reasonable. These constraints express what we are prepared to regard as limits on fair terms of social cooperation. One way to look at the idea of the original position, therefore, is to see it as an expository device which sums up the meaning of these conditions and helps us to extract their consequences.

•   •   •

TWO PRINCIPLES OF JUSTICE

I shall now state in a provisional form the two principles of justice that I believe would be chosen in the original position. In this section I wish to make only the most general comments, and therefore the first formulation of these principles is tentative. As we go on I shall run through several formulations

---

[4]The process of mutual adjustment of principles and considered judgments is not peculiar to moral philosophy. See Nelson Goodman, *Fact, Fiction, and Forecast* (Cambridge, Mass., Harvard University Press, 1955), pp. 65–68, for parallel remarks concerning the justification of the principles of deductive and inductive inference.

and approximate step by step the final statement to be given much later. I believe that doing this allows the exposition to proceed in a natural way.

The first statement of the two principles reads as follows.

> First: each person is to have an equal right to the most extensive basic liberty compatible with a similar liberty for others.
>
> Second: social and economic inequalities are to be arranged so that they are both (a) reasonably expected to be to everyone's advantage, and (b) attached to positions and offices open to all. . . .

By way of general comment, these principles primarily apply, as I have said, to the basic structure of society. They are to govern the assignment of rights and duties and to regulate the distribution of social and economic advantages. As their formulation suggests, these principles presuppose that the social structure can be divided into two more or less distinct parts, the first principle applying to the one, the second to the other. They distinguish between those aspects of the social system that define and secure the equal liberties of citizenship and those that specify and establish social and economic inequalities. The basic liberties of citizens are, roughly speaking, political liberty (the right to vote and to be eligible for public office) together with freedom of speech and assembly; liberty of conscience and freedom of thought; freedom of the person along with the right to hold (personal) property; and freedom from arbitrary arrest and seizure as defined by the concept of the rule of law. These liberties are all required to be equal by the first principle, since citizens of a just society are to have the same basic rights.

The second principle applies, in the first approximation, to the distribution of income and wealth and to the design of organizations that make use of differences in authority and responsibility, or chains of command. While the distribution of wealth and income need not be equal, it must be to everyone's advantage, and at the same time, positions of authority and offices of command must be accessible to all. One applies the second principle by holding positions open, and then, subject to this constraint, arranges social and economic inequalities so that everyone benefits.

These principles are to be arranged in a serial order with the first principle prior to the second. This ordering means that a departure from the institutions of equal liberty required by the first principle cannot be justified by, or compensated for, by greater social and economic advantages. The distribution of wealth and income, and the hierarchies of authority, must be consistent with both the liberties of equal citizenship and equality of opportunity.

It is clear that these principles are rather specific in their content, and their acceptance rests on certain assumptions that I must eventually try to explain and justify. A theory of justice depends upon a theory of society in ways that will become evident as we proceed. For the present, it should be observed that the two principles (and this holds for all formulations) are a special case of a more general conception of justice that can be expressed as follows.

> All social values—liberty and opportunity, income and wealth, and the bases of self-respect—are to be distributed equally unless an unequal distribution of any, or all, of these values is to everyone's advantage.

Injustice, then, is simply inequalities that are not to the benefit of all. Of course, this conception is extremely vague and requires interpretation.

As a first step, suppose that the basic structure of society distributes certain primary goods, that is, things that every rational man is presumed to want. These goods normally have a use whatever a person's rational plan of life. For simplicity, assume that the chief primary goods at the disposition of society are rights and liberties, powers and opportunities, income and wealth. (Later on in Part Three the primary good of self-respect has a central place.) These are the social primary goods. Other primary goods such as health and vigor, intelligence and imagination, are natural goods; although their possession is influenced by the basic structure, they are not so directly under its control. Imagine, then, a hypothetical initial arrangement in which all the social primary goods are equally distributed: everyone has similar rights and duties, and income and wealth are evenly shared. This state of affairs provides a benchmark for judging improvements. If certain inequalities of wealth and organizational powers would make everyone better off than in this hypothetical starting situation, then they accord with the general conception.

Now it is possible, at least theoretically, that by giving up some of their fundamental liberties men are sufficiently compensated by the resulting social and economic gains. The general conception of justice imposes no restrictions on what sort of inequalities are permissible; it only requires that everyone's position be improved. We need not suppose anything so drastic as consenting to a condition of slavery. Imagine instead that men forgo certain political rights when the economic returns are significant and their capacity to influence the course of policy by the exercise of these rights would be marginal in any case. It is this kind of exchange which the two principles as stated rule out; being arranged in serial order they do not permit exchanges between basic liberties and economic and social gains. The serial ordering of principles expresses an underlying preference among primary social goods. When this preference is rational so likewise is the choice of these principles in this order.

In developing justice as fairness I shall, for the most part, leave aside the general conception of justice and examine instead the special case of the two principles in serial order. The advantage of this procedure is that from the first the matter of priorities is recognized and an effort made to find principles to deal with it. One is led to attend throughout to the conditions under which the acknowledgment of the absolute weight of liberty with respect to social and economic advantages, as defined by the lexical order of the two principles, would be reasonable. Offhand, this ranking appears extreme and too special a case to be of much interest; but there is more justification for it than would appear at first sight. Or at any rate, so I shall maintain. Furthermore, the distinction between fundamental rights and liberties and economic and social benefits marks a difference

among primary social goods that one should try to exploit. It suggests an important division in the social system. Of course, the distinctions drawn and the ordering proposed are bound to be at best only approximations. There are surely circumstances in which they fail. But it is essential to depict clearly the main lines of a reasonable conception of justice; and under many conditions anyway, the two principles in serial order may serve well enough. When necessary we can fall back on the more general conception.

The fact that the two principles apply to institutions has certain consequences. Several points illustrate this. First of all, the rights and liberties referred to by these principles are those which are defined by the public rules of the basic structure. Whether men are free is determined by the rights and duties established by the major institutions of society. Liberty is a certain pattern of social forms. The first principle simply requires that certain sorts of rules, those defining basic liberties, apply to everyone equally and that they allow the most extensive liberty compatible with a like liberty for all. The only reason for circumscribing the rights defining liberty and making men's freedom less extensive than it might otherwise be is that these equal rights as institutionally defined would interfere with one another.

Another thing to bear in mind is that when principles mention persons, or require that everyone gain from an inequality, the reference is to representative persons holding the various social positions, or offices, or whatever, established by the basic structure. Thus in applying the second principle I assume that it is possible to assign an expectation of well-being to representative individuals holding these positions. This expectation indicates their life prospects as viewed from their social station. In general, the expectations of representative persons depend upon the distribution of rights and duties throughout the basic structure. When this changes, expectations change. I assume, then, that expectations are connected: by raising the prospects of the representative man in one position we presumably increase or decrease the prospects of representative men in other positions. Since it applies to institutional forms, the second principle (or rather the first part of it) refers to the expectations of representative individuals. As I shall discuss below, neither principle applies to distributions of particular goods to particular individuals who may be identified by their proper names. The situation where someone is considering how to allocate certain commodities to needy persons who are known to him is not within the scope of the principles. They are meant to regulate basic institutional arrangements. We must not assume that there is much similarity from the standpoint of justice between an administrative allotment of goods to specific persons and the appropriate design of society. Our common sense intuitions for the former may be a poor guide to the latter.

Now the second principle insists that each person benefit from permissible inequalities in the basic structure. This means that it must be reasonable for each relevant representative man defined by this structure, when he views it as a going concern, to prefer his prospects with the inequality to his prospects without it. One is not allowed to justify differences in income or organizational powers on the ground that the disadvantages of those in one position are outweighed by the greater advantages of those in another. Much less can infringements of liberty be counterbalanced in this way. Applied to the basic structure, the principle of utility would have us maximize the sum of expectations of representative men (weighted by the number of persons they represent, on the classical view); and this would permit us to compensate for the losses of some by the gains of others. Instead, the two principles require that everyone benefit from economic and social inequalities. It is obvious, however, that there are indefinitely many ways in which all may be advantaged when the initial arrangement of equality is taken as a benchmark. How then are we to choose among these possibilities? The principles must be specified so that they yield a determinate conclusion.

CRITIQUE OF RAWLS

H. Odera Oruka

In *A Theory of Justice*[1] John Rawls introduces an egalitarian formula in the concept of justice.[2] But he does so on the plane of a liberal-capitalist conception of justice that corrodes the formula, and the theory turns out as a subtle defence of welfare-capitalism. Rawls' claim that his theory could be accommodated within both the private economic system and the socialist-oriented one is therefore incorrect.[3] One of the aims of this chapter is to substantiate this fact and explicate the true ideological position of the theory. I shall also attempt to salvage and purify the egalitarian element in Rawls. But this can only be done by making a fundamental reversal and reorganisation of his lexical order in the special conception of justice. Although this is damaging to Rawls' ideological affinity and still falls short of a full conception of justice as egalitarian fairness, it nevertheless makes his theory more suitable and attractive for the realisation of justice in a modern underdeveloped country.

I am beginning to think that it is difficult to formulate a universal theory of social justice, which, to be relevant, needs to take into account the level of economic advancement, historical traditions and experience and ideological realities of the societies for which it is meant. It is precisely these factors that would dictate what the people regard or ought to treat as primary goods and fundamental rights in any society which they must want to have whatever else they may want. Rawls, for example, stipulates that wealth and income are primary goods. But this would be true inasmuch as we define wealth and in-

---

[1] J. Rawls, *A Theory of Justice* (Oxford: Oxford University Press, 1973).
[2] Ibid., p. 538. Rawls writes, "While there are many forms of equality, and egalitarianism admits of degrees, there are conceptions of justice that are recognizably egalitarian, even though significant disparities are permitted. The two principles of justice fall, I assume, under this heading."
[3] Ibid., pp. 270–274.

come in the context of a capitalist economy such as that of the United States;[4] it cannot, without qualification, be true in a society in which the cardinal principle of social existence is the self-denial of the religious type as the worker-controlled socialism[5] or the communal free-for-all economy, claimed in some parts of traditional Africa. In such kinds of society, wealth and income would be to the individual either unnecessary possessions or a welcome fortune that he has no legitimate right to treat as personal. Therefore, when they happen to come his way he has to hand them out for collective use.

JUSTICE AND DISTRIBUTION OF GOODS

According to his general conception of justice, Rawls treats justice as fairness. This fairness is to be applied in the distribution of goods in a society in which "rights and liberties, opportunities and powers, income and wealth" are regarded as the basic social goods which everyone must want, whatever else he may want.

Moreover, the distribution is to be conducted according to the special conception of justice based on two basic principles: (i) the liberty principle and (ii) the socio-economic principle (the difference principle). These are treated as the two basic principles of justice. Their formulation is as follows:

1. Each person is to have an equal right to the most extensive total system of equal basic liberties compatible with a similar system of liberty for all.

2. Social and economic inequalities are to be arranged so that they are both (a) to the greatest benefit of the least advantaged, consistent with the just savings principle, and (b) attached to offices and positions open to all under conditions of fair equality of opportunity.[6]

The two principles are lexically ordered such that the liberty principle is prior to the socio-economic one, and the former cannot be infringed for the sake of the latter. Rawls states that "justice denies that the loss of freedom for some is made right by a greater good shared by others."[7] This is "the priority of liberty." Liberty can be restricted only for the sake of liberty, but not for the sake of economic or social gain.[8] But even when restriction is acceptable, it is necessary that it does enhance the quality of civilisation and freedom of all.[9]

The first principle, Rawls explains, caters for fundamental liberties such as the right to vote and stand for public office, freedom of speech and assembly, freedom of thought and conscience, and the right to hold *personal property* (emphasis mine). These constitute, according to Rawls, the fundamental rights and liberties that are inviolable. We should, however, note that with the exception of the right to personal property, all the other liberties fall under what can generally be referred to as political and intellectual liberty.

The second principle then takes care of the social goods such as wealth and income and all the rights that derive from these goods. This principle is supposed to guarantee that the inequalities are to the highest advantage of the poor or less fortunate members of the society! In other words, the poor must have in the system the best of all alternatives. Although their liberty may in practice be worth far less than that enjoyed by the rich, Rawls argues that this loss is nevertheless compensated for by the very nature of the system:

---

[4]Sensitive to this type of criticism, Rawls, in "Fairness to Goodness," *Philosophical Review* 84 (October) 1975, defines wealth and income so broadly that the desire for them becomes, in his view, "characteristic of societies generally," no matter whether the society is built on individualistic or communitarian values. Wealth in his view refers to food, land, buildings, machines, etc., as well as legal right to service and benefits from such items.

[5]For our purpose, a very relevant and lucid account of a "worker-controlled socialism" is given in David Schweickart's "Should Rawls Be a Socialist?", *Social Theory and Practice* vol. 5, no. 1 (Fall 1978). See also Mihailo Markovic's concept of "self-governing bodies" in "The Distribution of Power in a Just Society," Schweickart, op. cit., pp. 64–76.

[6]J. Rawls, op. cit., p. 302.
[7]Ibid., pp. 3–4.
[8]Ibid., p. 303.
[9]Ibid., p. 152.

The lesser worth of liberty is, however, compensated for since the capacity of the less fortunate members of the society to achieve their aims would be even less were they not to accept the existing inequalities.[10]

Rawls' egalitarianism and its limitation need to be clearly spelled out in order to locate the true ideological position of his theory. He has in mind an equalitarian formula which I wish to sketch out as follows:

The distribution of social goods is to be equal to the extent that the less fortunate receive no less than what they can obtain given and using their own capacity in a free-market competition.

Although the more fortunate may not be as well-off as they can be, assuming their capability, the less fortunate have to be. However, if on the basis of this arrangement a further improvement in the position of the well-off would improve or have no diminishing effect on the position of the less fortunate, then this should be permitted as being in line with justice.

The above sketch, I judge, is supported by the following formulations by Rawls:

Everyone is assured an equal liberty to pursue whatever plan of life he pleases as long as it does not violate what justice demands. Men share in primary goods on the principle that some can have more if they are acquired in ways which improve the situation of those who have less.

If there are inequalities in the basic structure that work to make everyone better off in comparison with the benchmark of initial equality, why not permit them?

Inequalities are permissible when they maximize, or at least all contribute to, the long-term expectations of the least fortunate group in society.[11]

Given Rawls' theory, what should one understand by the phrase, "what justice demands"?

This implies that given the lexical order and priority of liberty, any development of inequality which is not detrimental to "the benchmark of equality" (whatever this mark may be) would be in line with justice. Thus as long as the two principles are lexically ordered and the distribution is or is believed to be to the greatest advantage of the poor subject to the principle of saving and fair equality of opportunity, any widening of the socio-economic gap would not violate the demand of justice.[12]

That this can be so implies that something must be seriously wrong with the egalitarian nature of Rawls' theory. The effect of this is that the theory still falls far short of offering a formula that would be acceptable in proper egalitarian or socialist camps.

One of the characteristics of capitalism (a characteristic that egalitarian theory has no room for) is its capacity to promote or allow an *infinite* socio-economic gap between the rich and the poor. This gap is part of the meaning of the "unjust distribution of wealth" often levelled against capitalism, but we should make a distinction between laissez-faire capitalism and modern or welfare capitalism. Both allow a large socio-economic gap, but the latter strives to mitigate the charge of "unjust distribution" by preaching economic improvement of the conditions of the poor as a cardinal principle. Welfare capitalism thus appears to extend human rights from the civil sphere to the economic sphere. But this, however, is significant only in theory since in practice it leaves the reign of private property and individualism intact.

Great inequality is not compatible with the ethics of egalitarianism. Egalitarianism requires equality even as an end in itself and excludes the possibility that a gain for others could be a sufficient justification for allowing a large gap in inequality. And it does not matter even if the gain is a sufficient measure of what the beneficiaries deserve. Egalitarianism in any society strives to eradicate social and economic inequality as an intrinsic evil. On the world scene, the inequality that currently exists—for example,

---

[10]Ibid.,p. 204.
[11]Ibid., pp. 94 and 151.

[12]He writes, "in theory the difference principle permits indefinite large inequalities in return for small gains to less favored" (p. 536).

between the affluent North (Europe and America) and the destitute South (Africa, Asia and Latin America)—is grossly antithetical to egalitarianism, no matter what aid the North gives to the South.

Thus in global terms, egalitarianism would be more in line with global justice rather than international justice.[13] The former requires equal distribution of the world's wealth among its population, regardless of the national, racial, technological or geographical differences. It requires total eradication of inequality in the world. But the latter, on the other hand, requires an internationally recognised law that would ensure that everyone has a right to a minimum standard of living. It is at best for the elimination of abject poverty. International justice thus is open to large inequality as long as everyone has a right to a minimum standard of living.

EGALITARIAN SOCIETY

As an example of the wide gap in inequality in wealth and income and even in basic liberties that Rawls' theory would allow, imagine a society called *SUWJ* (Society of Unbalanced or Wild Justice). *SUWJ* has an advanced technology and a well-developed culture. In *SUWJ* the well-off form a tiny minority compared to the rest of the populace, who, though well above the abject poverty line, are still relatively poor in their own society. Now, due to its highly developed technology, skills and education, *SUWJ* discovers a means of extending the human lifespan threefold and keeping a human being immune from all diseases during his lifespan.[14] The cost of doing this for any individual is so much that it is impossible for the society to afford it for the majority of the citizens or even for all its elite and

intelligentsia. Yet a tiny minority, the well-off members of the society, can individually save from their income and afford the lifespan extension and complete immunity. When this is done to the well-off, they find in practice that the worth of their liberty and all conditions of their life are highly enriched compared to the rest of the society. Although the rest of the society has reasonable healthcare, it is not immune from many diseases and life expectancy is not beyond one lifespan.

Now the situation in *SUWJ* would not, I judge, violate the demands of justice as stipulated by Rawls. The capital for life extension and complete immunity comes from the savings (hence personal property) of those who go in for them. Indeed, that everybody is above the abject poverty line and has reasonable healthcare in *SUWJ* can be used to give the impression that everybody has attained the benchmark of equality. The extension of life and complete immunity for the few can thus be defended as a contribution to the long-term expectations of the less fortunate group in the society.

Life extension and complete immunity for the minority in *SUWJ* would cause an infinite gap of inequality between the lives of the rich and those of the poor. And this inequality would be felt both in terms of wealth and income and in terms of the Rawlsian basic liberties such as freedom to vote and stand for public office and the right or opportunity to acquire and hold personal property. Since Rawls does, in a recent work, define wealth not only as ownership of goods such as land, buildings, capital and machines but also as a right to personal services and benefits that derive from such goods, it follows that life extension and complete immunity would be considered as forms of wealth.

It may be argued that given Rawls' theory, *SUWJ* would be impossible. First, that the taxation of the rich to further improve the conditions of the poor would not allow savings enabling anyone to afford the extension of life threefold. Second, it can be argued that the citizens in a Rawlsian society are rationalists who would not allow excessive differences in wealth given the requisite background institutions stipulated in Chapter 26 of his work.

---

[13]See for example, Lars O. Ericsson's "Two Principles of International Justice," *Justice: Social or Global* (Stockholm: 1981), pp. 20–22 in which he compares these two forms of justice.
[14]That the human lifespan can be extended is really not a wild dream. Medical research has established that aging can be slowed down by slowing down the rate at which the cells age using medical means. See the report on "Secrets of the Human Cell" in *Newsweek,* 20 August 1979.

This objection will not do. Any taxation or reduction of the wealth of the rich is subject to the requirement that justice has not been violated if the poor do already receive no less than what the benchmark of initial equality stipulates. After this benchmark is satisfied, there is "fair equality of opportunity" in free-market competition. And whatever the poor end up with, no matter how small, compared to the gain of the rich, must be a just measure of what they deserve given their capability. Second, with Rawls, the demand of justice is not contravened when the differences between the rich and the poor arise from the worth of liberty—i.e., from substantive liberty (which depends on one's resources), not from formal liberty (which in law is guaranteed for everyone no matter what one's means are).

So there would be no reason to limit or hinder individual savings for the extension of life and complete immunity argument given Rawls in *SUWJ*. First, everyone has a right to hold personal property and can use it to pursue whatever plan of life he pleases. And this right is enshrined in the first principle, which cannot be violated for the sake of the second principle, even if this involves extending the benchmark of equality and socio-economic benefit to the less fortunate. Therefore, personal saving for whatever plan of life would be in line with Rawls' theory. But even if the first principle is not at stake and the matter is one only of the second principle, it can be argued that the minimum standard of living in *SUWJ* is more than what the less fortunate can afford on their own.

The argument that Rawls' citizens are rationalists who would not wish excessive differences in wealth is counterbalanced by the fact that they are also egoists who would not shun the chance to improve themselves when the opportunity arises.

The example of *SUWJ* is not so far damaging to Rawls' theory. So far we have only tried to show that *SUWJ* would manifest a great gap in inequality between the rich and the poor, and that this inequality would be both in wealth and income and in fundamental rights and liberties, and that there is no restriction in Rawls' theory against this development.

But inequality, however great, is not negative for Rawls' theory, for, logically, the theory has the capacity to accommodate and justify inequality so long as it is to the advantage of the less fortunate. Therefore, to be damaging to Rawls' theory *SUWJ* must be shown to be unjust.

Rawls claims that his theory is egalitarian oriented. Assuming the ethics of egalitarian fairness, *SUWJ* can be shown to be unjust for two main reasons: First, great inequality in wealth and income, even in services and benefits derived from these items, is in conflict with the nature of equality required by egalitarian social existence. Part of the aim of egalitarian fairness is to suppress and eradicate, as a matter of cardinal ethical principle, any development toward inequality in wealth and liberty. Equality in egalitarian terms is an end in itself and inequality an evil to be eliminated, even at a high price. Second, the possibility for some people (a minority) in one society to acquire the means for such a good life while others (the majority) cannot afford such means, would ensure serious disharmony, envy and distrust in the society. Yet a just society, in communitarian terms, must be free of such problems; social harmony and mutual trust and understanding between the fortunate and the unfortunate must be a condition of justice treated as fairness. If in Rawls' theory a society analogous to *SUWJ* is possible, then the theory cannot actually be suitable in a communitarian-oriented social order. And so, the egalitarian principles or expressions found in it are only formal, not substantive, requirements.

Some may object that *SUWJ* is merely a figment of the imagination that has no parallel in reality. But it is, in my judgement, fairly easy to find analogous situations in world history. Feudalism, colonialism and the South African racial regime (apartheid) are historical examples. In feudalism, the inequality in terms of wealth and liberty between a lord and his serf or vassal is enormous, but the mutual conviction is that this relationship is to the greatest advantage of the latter rather than the former. The field or land that the serf utilises is merely a loan from the lord. The chance of the serf to possess or utilise his holding would be almost nil, were he not to accept this relationship.

In the feudal Ethiopia of Emperor Haile Selassie, an appalling inequality existed between the Emperor and his associates, who owned almost all the land, and the peasants, who had to till the land for their subsistence and make payment to the landlords.

A typical colonial situation in Africa was one in which the very small minority (the settlers and colonial administrators) owned great wealth, had very good healthcare and a life expectancy of 70 to 80 years. Yet the majority (the colonised) owned nothing of significance, had perpetual ill-health and a life expectancy of only about 30 years. Yet there were arguments justifying colonialism as a blessing for the colonised population. It was argued, for example, that the settler had come to civilise and help develop the native, and that the latter would be much worse off were it not for colonialism. The colonial situation was thus seen to be to the greatest benefit of the colonised. A similar argument was sometimes used by the supporters of the South African regime. They argued that the blacks in South Africa are economically better off than their fellows elsewhere in Africa, the implication being that the South African situation is to the advantage of the blacks, considering what they would have elsewhere in Africa. Therefore, if the blacks in South Africa have less liberty compared to the whites, this, it is believed, is compensated for in socio-economic benefits. I do not mean to argue that Rawls' theory justifies feudalism, colonialism or apartheid. I mean to explain only that the position of the less fortunate in these situations can be justified by arguments similar to the ones Rawls uses for allowing inequalities in wealth and the worth of liberty.

LIBERTY TO PROPERTY

The main characteristics of capitalism as supported by the liberal political philosophy are private property, individual formal (not substantive) liberty and political (not economic) democracy. Capitalism emerges as welfare-capitalism when a fourth element is added to it, namely formal economic equality. This element aims to mitigate the problem of great inequality in socio-economic well-being and

opportunity in laissez-faire capitalism. It therefore stipulates that the less fortunate be accorded equal opportunity in the economic sphere and that the worst-off or the most helpless of them be considered for state subsidy. I have referred to this element as "formal economic equality" because substantive or meaningful economic equality is impossible in capitalism. And this is because capitalism cannot exist without private property, and the latter is incompatible with substantive socio-economic equality. This incompatibility, I sense, has made Rawls appear to play down the issue of private property in order to give the impression that the theory is actually for substantive social equality.[15] But the truth in the final analysis is that private property is indirectly very subtly defended. Rawls does not directly talk of the right to private property as one of the liberties embodied in the first principle. He talks of the right to personal property. This may lead others to take it that the property referred to here excludes productive property and individual possession of "the means of production." There is a distinction found in the English law between the "real property" and "personal property." The former is considered immovable and inheritable, while the latter is movable and easily distributable at death. The impression given thus is that personal property is insignificant as far as productive property and the generation of huge private wealth are concerned.

It is not clear if Rawls treats personal property in the same way. But whether he does so or not, the safe place he reserves for the right to personal property does logically entail the right to productive or private property. To see this, we should distinguish between socially significant and socially insignificant

---

[15] In "Rawlsian Justice and Economic Systems," Barry Clark and Herbert Gentis write, "Modern liberal political economy sensitive to the potential inconsistency between private property and social equity has undergone one of the most abrupt transformations ever witnessed in the history of social thought. Without great fanfare the commitment to private property has been dropped." See *Philosophy and Public Affairs* vol. 7, no. 4 (Summer 1978).

It is not true that the commitment to private property has been dropped. What has happened is that the use of the expression has been avoided. But its substance is expressed in terms such as "fair equality of opportunity" and the "right to personal property."

personal property. The former gives the owner social and economic power over others. It involves the sole ownership by an individual or family of such things as land, factories, mines or capital. The possession of any of these economic means gives one an important status in productive property. Socially insignificant personal property does not give one any social power over others. It involves the possession of such things as clothes, furniture and books.

The distinction between what is purely personal property that gives one no social power in production and that which does give this power is difficult to find in Rawls' theory. Wealth is treated, in the individual plan of life, as a primary social good which he must want. In such a situation, the right to socially insignificant personal property becomes inseparable from the right to private or productive property. The accumulation of capital may start originally simply as the use of small personal savings to generate more money and again to continue for more and more money. Thus personal property in Rawls' theory can emerge as private property without involving any interference with the demands of justice. And it can, according to the principles of justice, be defended as a fundamental right embodied in the first principle. When secured, private property would be inheritable and be defended as personal property. Rawls writes,

> The unequal inheritance of wealth is no more inherently unjust than the unequal inheritance of intelligence.[16]

In an authentic socialist or egalitarian society, it would be absurd to treat differences in wealth as differences in intelligence. Now Rawls cannot (seriously speaking) just mean the socially trivial personal property when he talks of "the right to hold personal property." Personal property in the trivial sense might be a problem in the state of nature, but it is taken for granted in all modern states. It would therefore be amazing for Rawls to treat it as a problematic issue in a theory of justice. I submit that all

private property whose ownership is limited to an individual or a family is still personal property and the right to it must, on Rawls' account, be treated as a basic liberty. So Rawls includes economic liberty in the first principle.[17]

The theoretical possibility for unlimited socio-economic inequality in Rawls' theory and the high place he assigns to personal property make the theory unsuitable for a socialist-oriented social system.

POLITICAL AND INTELLECTUAL LIBERTY

Generally, Rawls considers political liberty (the right to vote and stand for public office, freedom of speech and assembly) and intellectual liberty (freedom of thought and conscience) to be more fundamental than economic equality and social welfare. But in a society where the majority are illiterate and there is widespread poverty, political and intellectual liberties are luxuries. The people either do not understand them, or they have no motivation to exercise them. Poverty-stricken people want bread, not freedom of thought and speech. Neither do they care about the right to vote and stand for public office, unless this is clearly explained to them in terms of their social frustration. Otherwise, a potential voter would easily sell his voting card for a loaf of bread or a small sum of money. What the majority of semi-literate and poverty-stricken people want is not liberty as "equal freedom." What they want is "the worth of liberty." They may want freedom of religion, but this only as an opiate to help them forget their earthly conditions. Such people long for economic equality, not for the materially valueless political democracy.

Rawls may object to this by the argument that ignorance of a person's right is no excuse for denying him that right. The poor and illiterate people, he can

---

[16]J. Rawls, op. cit., p. 278.

[17]That Rawls avoids mention of productive property in the first principle has led some to infer that "economic liberty" (a cardinal principle of capitalism) is not treated as basic in his theory of justice. See for example Jan Narveson's "A Puzzle About Economic Justice in Rawls' Theory," *Social Theory and Practice* vol. 4, no. 1 (Fall 1976), p. 7.

explain, do not bother about the named fundamental rights and liberties because they are ignorant of the fact that it is their right to exercise them. But fairly and justly speaking, they ought to exercise those rights. Our argument actually is not that these liberties are not what the majority of people in an underdeveloped world ought to have. Our argument is that as things stand, such rights would not be their priorities.

Hence they are less fundamental to them than the rights to economic and social equality. To them, the right to act and the means to improve their social and economic conditions are more fundamental than freedom of thought and conscience; "Freedom of thought without freedom of action is illusory."[18]

That economic needs are always more primary than political needs is generally true for all people. However, when the fulfilment of one's economic needs is beyond reproach, one may perhaps mistake political needs as being more basic than the economic ones.

CONCLUSION

In my judgment, in order for Rawls' theory to be suitable for a typical Third World country, it ought to be revised as follows: The first principle should be the second and vice-versa, and the lexical order is to be retained. In the first principle clause, (b) should be reformed and replaced with the clause attached to offices and positions open to those whose ideological inclination is to advance the requirement in (a). In sketch,

1. Social and economic differences are to be arranged so that they are both (a) to the greatest benefit of the least advantaged, consistent with the just savings principle, and (b) attached to offices and positions open to those whose ethical inclination is to advance the requirement in (a).
2. Each person is to have an equal right to the most extensive total system of equal basic liberties compatible with a similar system of liberty for all.

[18]M. Markovic, "The Distribution of Power in a Just Society," *Social Theory and Practice* vol. 5, no. 1 (Fall 1978).

The purpose of the above reorganisation is to salvage the egalitarian element in Rawls' theory and to make it serve the aims of ensuring a communitarian social order. As it stands originally, it has the egalitarianism suppressed or at best serves only to hide the excesses of capitalism. But in essence it is a capitalist-democracy-tending social theory.

Putting Rawls' first principle second and vice-versa would help to ensure that liberty as "equal freedom," which in itself is hollow without "the worth of liberty," is relegated to the backstage. The first principle in Rawls says only that everyone's formal or constitutional liberty be maximised, provided every other person has the same liberty. In other words, this liberty is no more than the "equality of everybody before the law." All men are *ipso facto* equal before the law, but some are more equal than others anyway. The latter derive their position from wealth and power—from their social and economic position in the society. It is they who have the worth of liberty; the rest only have the liberty to be free. But they may not yet really be free. Therefore, it is in Rawls' second principle where the worth of liberty lies. This is why it is the first principle in our formulation.

The less fortunate are usually the majority. In Africa they form over 90 per cent of the population. It is therefore fitting that they are given priority. There will also be a need for planning and saving for the future generation as Rawls had foreseen. It is therefore proper that the saving principle is placed where it is.

Our society is to be an egalitarian or authentically socialist-oriented social order. It would therefore be absurd to grant those whose tendency is for a different social order equal opportunity as those for the egalitarian system. This might give the great capitalist sharks and tycoons a chance to dominate the market and tread on the less fortunate. This allowance would jeopardise the requirement in (a). So if the ethics of (a) are to be fulfilled, it is only logical and moral that fair equality of opportunity be confined to egalitarianism.

QUESTIONS FOR DISCUSSION

1. What are Siddhantalankar's criticisms of the caste system of India today, and how has it, in his view, fallen from its proper ideal? Do you think that a society can uphold differences without discrimination? Why or why not?

2. Are you able to imagine yourself behind the veil of ignorance, as Rawls suggests? If so, what kind of world do you think would be fair? Are you fairly sure that your perspective from the "original position" is an accurate one, or are you experiencing difficulties reenacting Rawls' decision-making method?

3. There are great disparities in our world regarding the wealth and income of people and countries. Following the criteria put forward by our various authors, should such large differences be morally tolerated or not? What arguments would be advanced both for and against such disparities?

4. Recent 1998 statistics show that the average life expectancy for males and females in fifteen African countries is under fifty years old.[1] Given that fact, do you think there may be any present truth in the thought experiment in which Odera Oruka asks us to engage? If so, what should be done about it?

---

[1] See Richard A. Hoehn, "Introduction," and Marc C. Cohen, "World Hunger in a Global Economy," in *Hunger in a Global Economy: Hunger 1998, Eighth Annual Report on the State of World Hunger* (Silver Spring, MD: Bread for the World Institute, 1998), pp. 2–21.

SOCIAL CHANGE: VIOLENCE OR NONVIOLENCE?

This section focuses on the ever-recurrent political problem that stems from abuses of government. What constitutes unjust governing or domination? Dictionary accounts define *domination* as an "exercise of power in ruling," but add that the term also refers to "arbitrary or insolent sway." Not all thinkers agree on where to draw the line, in specific instances as well as in theory, between legitimate authority and use of power, and brutal or disrespectful abuse of power. However, there comes a time when people are ready to join together to change an abusive social order. But how should they do so? Should their means be nonviolent or violent? Would violence be wrong? Would nonviolence be ineffective?

According to Marx and Engels, what counts as virtue and what counts as criminal activity are always decided by the ruling class of any given era and framed in such a way as to legitimate its own actions while appealing to universal impartiality. Karl Marx (1818–1883) was born in Trier in the Rhineland of Germany of a Jewish family. He received a doctorate in philosophy from the University of Jena. He was involved in journalism that criticized the government's policies and soon found himself exiled, first to France and then to England. His partnership with German-born Friedrich Engels (1820–1895) solidified in England, where Engels managed his father's textile industry, and both collaborated with and helped to support Marx in his studies.

In *The Communist Manifesto,* Marx and Engels describe first how societies through the ages, from ancient to feudal to modern times, have always been set up in order to legitimate exploitation. Although capitalism has served its purpose in society by furthering the means of production, its usefulness has passed. In the future, they predict, the time will be ripe for the workers to become self-aware and gather their forces together, to oust the capitalists from their position of privilege.

Our next author, Mohandas K. Gandhi, argues that colonial India should only attempt to win its freedom from British rule by nonviolent means. Gandhi was born in 1869 in Porbandar, India, an area highly influenced by Jainism, with its emphasis on the practice of "ahimsa" or nonviolence. Gandhi would change the emphasis of this traditional spiritual virtue from "refraining to act," to acting in a context of resistance while using nonviolent means. He termed his actions "satyagraha," meaning "soul-force" or "truth-force," and was determined to reinforce through his actions this new method of seeking social change and justice.

As the selection in our chapter mentions, there was much concern in India in the years preceding independence as to whether Gandhi's nonviolent methods would work. There had been a massacre at Jalianwala Bagh, located in Amritsar, in April 1919. General Dyer of the British forces decided to order his troops to open fire on a peaceful assembly of protestors because they disobeyed the order against holding public meetings. Over 300 people were killed and over 1,000 were wounded. Although Gandhi mourned for those who were killed, he said that he felt worse when he heard reports of Indians who had used violence in retaliation against the British, so determined was he to show that India could use the method of nonviolence to win freedom.

Gandhi was a Hindu, and there were many more Hindus than Muslims in the India of his day; yet his movement was vigorously in favor of Hindu–Muslim Unity. The Khalifat Committee mentioned in the following passages was created to show united support in India for the Caliph, or religious leader of Islam, who was in a troubled position after the defeat of Turkey in World War I. Both Hindus and Muslims braved arrests and beatings in many satyagraha campaigns. The Great Salt Satyagraha was one of the most famous and widespread of the nonviolent campaigns, and its success resulted in the Round Table talks in London between British government officials, Gandhi, and other members of the Indian National Congress in 1931, as a prelude to independence.

Martin Luther King, Jr., is by now well known in the United States and around the world. He was an African-American preacher and activist leader involved in the Civil Rights movement in the 1960s, and he was killed by an assassin in 1968. King was deeply impressed by Gandhi's experiments with nonviolent action in India and decided that the same approach was needed in America to end the continuing racial discrimination against African-Americans.

In this essay King explains how means and ends must cohere in one's struggle for freedom and equality. He enjoins us to transcend loyalties of race, ethnicity, class, and nation, and to develop a world perspective. Since we are mutually interdependent, he argues, we have a single destiny. He talks about the three different concepts of love, and the importance of practicing *agape,* a creative, redemptive goodwill toward all, while seeking nothing in return. It is clear that while King found inspiration in Gandhi, he was also able to find this message of nonviolent love in his reading of the Christian scriptures. Our excerpt comes from a sermon delivered on Christmas day.

Malcolm X, who later took the name El Hajj Malik El Shabazz, describes his struggle for respect and self-recognition for all African-Americans in their attempt to combat American racism. Malcolm X was born Malcolm Little in Michigan. His father was killed by Ku Klux Klan members when he was still a child, and his mother struggled with poverty in the years that followed. Years later, in prison, he studied Islam, prompted by correspondence with the founder of the black-based Nation of Islam, Elijah Muhammad. An eloquent and fiery spokesman on his release from prison, he became a preacher for the Nation of Islam and was well known to Americans for not mincing words about the situation of race relations in the United States. He was heralded by some as a truth-teller and derided by others as a hate-monger; it is important to scrutinize his works to accurately understand his message.

The speech included in this section was delivered on December 3, 1964, during a debate at Britain's Oxford University, in which he and others on his debate team defended the proposition, "Extremism in defense of liberty is no vice, moderation in the pursuit of justice is no virtue." Many in the audience were loudly enthusiastic in their applause of Malcolm; however, in the vote recorded after the debate, Malcolm's position received 137 votes, compared to 228 votes against. In this excerpt from the speech, Malcolm explains what he means by his now famous saying, "By Any Means Necessary."

Malcolm argues that since racism is such a terrible blight upon society, extreme measures are justified in eradicating unjust racist structures. Certainly he argues, as he summed up elsewhere, the ballot would be better than the bullet; but if we look more closely at the so-called democratic system of government in the United States, we see that racist structures make reform impossible. In this context Malcolm insists that fear born from threats of violence may be the only thing that will be able to shake the system.

It is important to note, however, that "any means necessary" did not necessarily mean violence. One important project for Malcolm X near the end of his life was to get the United Nations to pay attention to human rights violations happening in the United States. Also, he had addressed a summit meeting of the Organization of African Unity in Cairo, Egypt, in 1964, to ask African leaders to use their influence in the United Nations to this end.[1] So among the "means" to which Malcolm X resorted were the means of international politics.

Our final excerpt is from Enrique Dussel, an Argentinean philosopher who has been living and teaching at the University of Central Mexico for many years now. Dussel's works can be seen within the larger movement of liberation theology and philosophy, of which we have seen an earlier exposition in Chapter 3, by Leonardo and Clodovis Boff. Dussel argues against "reformism"—the position that only reform is ever desirable or possible. Rather, a revolution may be needed to challenge the two sins confronting what he calls peripheral nations

---

[1]Malcolm X, "Speech to African Summit Conference—Cairo, Egypt," in *Malcolm X: The Man and His Times,* ed. John Henrik Clarke (New York: MacMillan, 1969), pp. 288–93.

(insofar as they are on the margins of the power centers of Europe and the United States). One sin is the relationship between capital and the workers; the other is the relationship between the Northern and Southern nations. He argues that Northern nations extract wealth in the form of profit from Southern or developing nations while depriving workers of integrity and basic needs. He encourages us to notice the "violence of everyday," the institutional violence that presents domination as natural and acceptable.

While Dussel admires Gandhi and Martin Luther King, Jr., as suffering servants and martyrs, he suggests instead the need for a political hero. According to Dussel, the use of force, guided ethically and within limits, must be used to end domination and the everyday violence of the system.

THE COMMUNIST MANIFESTO

Karl Marx and Friedrich Engels

The history of all hitherto existing society[1] is the history of class struggles.

Freeman and slave, patrician and plebeian, lord and serf, guild-master[2] and journeyman, in a word, oppressor and oppressed, stood in constant opposition to one another, carried on an uninterrupted, now hidden, now open fight, a fight that each time ended, either in a revolutionary reconstitution of society at large, or in the common ruin of the contending classes.

In the earlier epochs of history, we find almost everywhere a complicated arrangement of society into various orders, a manifold gradation of social rank. In ancient Rome we have patricians, knights, plebeians, slaves; in the Middle Ages, feudal lords, vassals, guild-masters, journeymen, apprentices, serfs; in almost all of these classes, again, subordinate gradations.

The modern bourgeois society that has sprouted from the ruins of feudal society, has not done away with class antagonisms. It has but established new classes, new conditions of oppression, new forms of struggle in place of the old ones.

Our epoch, the epoch of the bourgeoisie, possesses, however, this distinctive feature: It has simplified the class antagonisms. Society as a whole is more and more splitting up into two great hostile camps, into two great classes directly facing each other—bourgeoisie and proletariat.[3]

From the serfs of the Middle Ages sprang the chartered burghers[4] of the earliest towns. From these burgesses the first elements of the bourgeoisie were developed.

The discovery of America, the rounding of the Cape, opened up fresh ground for the rising bourgeoisie. The East Indian and Chinese markets, the colonization of America, trade with the colonies, the increase in the means of exchange and in commodities generally, gave to commerce, to navigation, to industry, an impulse never before known,

---

[1]That is, all *written* history. In 1837, the pre-history of society, the social organization existing previous to recorded history, was all but unknown. Since then Haxthausen [August von, 1792–1866] discovered common ownership of land in Russia, Maurer [Georg Ludwig von] proved it to be the social foundation from which all Teutonic races started in history, and, by and by, village communities were found to be, or to have been, the primitive form of society everywhere from India to Ireland. The inner organization of this primitive communistic society was laid bare, in its typical form, by Morgan's [Lewis H., 1818–1881] crowning discovery of the true nature of the *gens* and its relation to the *tribe*. With the dissolution of these primeval communities, society begins to be differentiated into separate and finally antagonistic classes. I have attempted to retrace this process of dissolution in *The Origin of the Family, Private Property and the State.*

[2]Guild-master, that is, a full member of a guild, a master within, not a head of a guild.

[3]By bourgeoisie is meant the class of modern capitalists, owners of the means of social production and employers of wage-labor; by proletariat, the class of modern wage-laborers who, having no means of production of their own, are reduced to selling their labor power in order to live.

[4]Chartered burghers were freemen who had been admitted to the privileges of a chartered borough thus possessing full political rights.—*Ed.*

and thereby, to the revolutionary element in the tottering feudal society, a rapid development.

The feudal system of industry, in which industrial production was monopolized by closed guilds,[5] now no longer sufficed for the growing wants of the new markets. The manufacturing system took its place. The guild-masters were pushed aside by the manufacturing middle class; division of labor between the different corporate guilds vanished in the face of division of labor in each single workshop.

Meantime the markets kept ever growing, the demand ever rising. Even manufacture no longer sufficed. Thereupon, steam and machinery revolutionized industrial production. The place of manufacture was taken by the giant, modern industry, the place of the industrial middle class, by industrial millionaires—the leaders of whole industrial armies, the modern bourgeois.

Modern industry has established the world market, for which the discovery of America paved the way. This market has given an immense development to commerce, to navigation, to communication by land. This development has, in its turn, reacted on the extension of industry; and in proportion as industry, commerce, navigation, railways extended, in the same proportion the bourgeoisie developed, increased its capital, and pushed into the background every class handed down from the Middle Ages.

We see, therefore, how the modern bourgeoisie is itself the product of a long course of development, of a series of revolutions in the modes of production and of exchange.

Each step in the development of the bourgeoisie was accompanied by a corresponding political advance of that class. An oppressed class under the sway of the feudal nobility, it became an armed and self-governing association in the medieval commune,[6] here independent urban republic (as in Italy and Germany), there taxable "third estate" of the monarchy (as in France); afterwards, in the period of manufacture proper, serving either the semi-feudal or the absolute monarchy as a counterpoise against the nobility, and, in fact, cornerstone of the great monarchies in general—the bourgeoisie has at last, since the establishment of modern industry and of the world market, conquered for itself, in the modern representative state, exclusive political sway. The executive of the modern state is but a committee for managing the common affairs of the whole bourgeoisie.

The bourgeoisie has played a most revolutionary role in history. The bourgeoisie, wherever it has got the upper hand, has put an end to all feudal, patriarchal, idyllic relations. It has pitilessly torn asunder the motley feudal ties that bound man to his "natural superiors," and has left no other bond between man and man than naked self-interest, than callous "cash payment." It has drowned the most heavenly ecstasies of religious fervor, of chivalrous enthusiasm, of philistine sentimentalism, in the icy water of egotistical calculation. It has resolved personal worth into exchange value, and in place of the numberless indefeasible chartered freedoms, has set up that single, unconscionable freedom—Free Trade. In one word, for exploitation, veiled by religious and political illusions, it has substituted naked, shameless, direct, brutal exploitation.

The bourgeoisie has stripped of its halo every occupation hitherto honored and looked up to with reverent awe. It has converted the physician, the lawyer, the priest, the poet, the man of science, into its paid wage-laborers.

The bourgeoisie has torn away from the family its sentimental veil, and has reduced the family relation to a mere money relation.

---

[5]Craft guilds, made up of exclusive and privileged groups of artisans were, during the feudal period, granted monopoly rights to markets by municipal authorities. The guilds imposed minute regulations on their members controlling such matters as working hours, wages, prices, tools, and the hiring of workers.—*Ed.*

[6]"Commune" was the name taken in France by the nascent towns even before they had conquered from their feudal lords and masters local self-government and political rights as the "Third Estate." Generally speaking, for the economic development of the bourgeoisie, England is here taken as the typical country, for its political development, France.

The bourgeoisie has disclosed how it came to pass that the brutal display of vigor in the Middle Ages, which reactionaries so much admire, found its fitting complement in the most slothful indolence. It has been the first to show what man's activity can bring about. It has accomplished wonders far surpassing Egyptian pyramids, Roman aqueducts, and Gothic cathedrals; it has conducted expeditions that put in the shade all former migrations of nations and crusades.

The bourgeoisie cannot exist without constantly revolutionizing the instruments of production, and thereby the relations of production, and with them the whole relations of society. Conservation of the old modes of production in unaltered form, was, on the contrary, the first condition of existence for all earlier industrial classes. Constant revolutionizing of production, uninterrupted disturbance of all social conditions, everlasting uncertainty and agitation distinguish the bourgeois epoch from all earlier ones. All fixed, fast-frozen relations, with their train of ancient and venerable prejudices and opinions, are swept away, all new-formed ones become antiquated before they can ossify. All that is solid melts into air, all that is holy is profaned, and man is at last compelled to face with sober senses his real conditions of life and his relations with his kind.

The need of a constantly expanding market for its products chases the bourgeoisie over the whole surface of the globe. It must nestle everywhere, settle everywhere, establish connections everywhere.

The bourgeoisie has through its exploitation of the world market given a cosmopolitan character to production and consumption in every country. To the great chagrin of reactionaries, it has drawn from under the feet of industry the national ground on which it stood. All old-established national industries have been destroyed or are daily being destroyed. They are dislodged by new industries, whose introduction becomes a life and death question for all civilized nations, by industries that no longer work up indigenous raw material, but raw material drawn from the remotest zones; industries whose products are consumed, not only at home, but in every quarter of the globe. In place of the old

wants, satisfied by the production of the country, we find new wants, requiring for their satisfaction the products of distant lands and climes. In place of the old local and national seclusion and self-sufficiency, we have intercourse in every direction, universal inter-dependence of nations. And as in material, so also in intellectual production. The intellectual creations of individual nations become common property. National one-sidedness and narrow-mindedness become more and more impossible, and from the numerous national and local literatures there arises a world literature.

The bourgeoisie, by the rapid improvement of all instruments of production, by the immensely facilitated means of communication, draws all nations, even the most barbarian, into civilization. The cheap prices of its commodities are the heavy artillery with which it batters down all Chinese walls, with which it forces the barbarians' intensely obstinate hatred of foreigners to capitulate. It compels all nations, on pain of extinction, to adopt the bourgeois mode of production; it compels them to introduce what it calls civilization into their midst, i.e., to become bourgeois themselves. In a word, it creates a world after its own image.

The bourgeoisie has subjected the country to the rule of the towns. It has created enormous cities, has greatly increased the urban population as compared with the rural, and has thus rescued a considerable part of the population from the idiocy of rural life. Just as it has made the country dependent on the towns, so it has made barbarian and semi-barbarian countries dependent on the civilized ones, nations of peasants on nations of bourgeois, the East on the West.

More and more the bourgeoisie keeps doing away with the scattered state of the population, of the means of production, and of property. It has agglomerated population, centralized means of production, and has concentrated property in a few hands. The necessary consequence of this was political centralization. Independent, or but loosely connected provinces, with separate interests, laws, governments, and systems of taxation, became lumped together into one nation, with one government, one code of laws, one national class interest, one frontier, and one customs tariff.

The bourgeoisie, during its rule of scarce one hundred years, has created more massive and more colossal productive forces than have all preceding generations together. Subjection of nature's forces to man, machinery, application of chemistry to industry and agriculture, steam-navigation, railways, electric telegraphs, clearing of whole continents for cultivation, canalisation of rivers, whole populations conjured out of the ground—what earlier century had even a presentiment that such productive forces slumbered in the lap of social labour?

We see then, that the means of production and of exchange, which served as the foundation for the growth of the bourgeoisie, were generated in feudal society. At a certain stage in the development of these means of production and of exchange, the conditions under which feudal society produced and exchanged, the feudal organisation of agriculture and manufacturing industry, in a word, the feudal relations of property became no longer compatible with the already developed productive forces; they became so many fetters. They had to be burst asunder; they were burst asunder.

Into their place stepped free competition, accompanied by a social and political constitution adapted to it, and by the economic and political sway of the bourgeois class.

A similar movement is going on before our own eyes. Modern bourgeois society with its relations of production, of exchange and of property, a society that has conjured up such gigantic means of production and of exchange, is like the sorcerer who is no longer able to control the powers of the nether world whom he has called up by his spells. For many a decade past the history of industry and commerce is but the history of the revolt of modern productive forces against modern conditions of production, against the property relations that are the conditions for the existence of the bourgeoisie and of its rule. It is enough to mention the commercial crises that by their periodical return put the existence of the entire bourgeois society on trial, each time more threateningly. In these crises a great part

not only of the existing products, but also of the previously created productive forces, are periodically destroyed. In these crises there breaks out an epidemic that, in all earlier epochs, would have seemed an absurdity—the epidemic of over-production. Society suddenly finds itself put back into a state of momentary barbarism; it appears as if a famine, a universal war of devastation had cut off the supply of every means of subsistence; industry and commerce seem to be destroyed. And why? Because there is too much civilization, too much means of subsistence, too much industry, too much commerce. The productive forces at the disposal of society no longer tend to further the development of the conditions of bourgeois property; on the contrary, they have become too powerful for these conditions, by which they are fettered, and no sooner do they overcome these fetters than they bring disorder into the whole of bourgeois society, endanger the existence of bourgeois property. The conditions of bourgeois society are too narrow to comprise the wealth created by them. And how does the bourgeoisie get over these crises? On the one hand, by enforced destruction of a mass of productive forces; on the other, by the conquest of new markets, and by the more thorough exploitation of the old ones. That is to say, by paving the way for more extensive and more destructive crises, and by diminishing the means whereby crises are prevented.

The weapons with which the bourgeoisie felled feudalism to the ground are now turned against the bourgeoisie itself.

But not only has the bourgeoisie forged the weapons that bring death to itself; it has also called into existence the men who are to wield those weapons—the modern working class—the proletarians.

In proportion as the bourgeoisie, i.e., capital, is developed, in the same proportion is the proletariat, the modern working class, developed—a class of laborers, who live only so long as they find work, and who find work only so long as their labor increases capital. These laborers, who must sell themselves piecemeal, are a commodity, like every other article of commerce, and are consequently exposed to all the vicissitudes of competition, to all the fluctuations of the market.

Owing to the extensive use of machinery and to division of labor, the work of the proletarians has lost all individual character, and, consequently, all charm for the workman. He becomes an appendage of the machine, and it is only the most simple, most monotonous, and most easily acquired knack, that is required of him. Hence, the cost of production of a workman is restricted, almost entirely, to the means of subsistence that he requires for his maintenance, and for the propagation of his race. But the price of a commodity, and therefore also of labor, is equal to its cost of production. In proportion, therefore, as the repulsiveness of the work increases, the wage decreases. Nay more, in proportion as the use of machinery and division of labor increases, in the same proportion the burden of toil also increases, whether by prolongation of the working hours, by increase of the work exacted in a given time, or by increased speed of the machinery, etc.

Modern industry has converted the little workshop of the patriarchal master into the great factory of the industrial capitalist. Masses of laborers, crowded into the factory, are organized like soldiers. As privates of the industrial army they are placed under the command of a perfect hierarchy of officers and sergeants. Not only are they slaves of the bourgeois class, and of the bourgeois state; they are daily and hourly enslaved by the machine, by the overlooker, and, above all, by the individual bourgeois manufacturer himself. The more openly this despotism proclaims gain to be its end and aim, the more petty, the more hateful and the more embittering it is.

The less the skill and exertion of strength implied in manual labor, in other words, the more modern industry develops, the more is the labor of men superseded by that of women. Differences of age and sex have no longer any distinctive social validity for the working class. All are instruments of labor, more or less expensive to use, according to their age and sex.

No sooner has the laborer received his wages in cash, for the moment escaping exploitation by the manufacturer, than he is set upon by the other portions of the bourgeoisie, the landlord, the shopkeeper, the pawnbroker, etc.

The lower strata of the middle class—the small tradespeople, shopkeepers, and retired tradesmen generally, the handicraftsmen and peasants—all these sink gradually into the proletariat, partly because their diminutive capital does not suffice for the scale on which modern industry is carried on, and is swamped in the competition with the large capitalists, partly because their specialized skill is rendered worthless by new methods of production. Thus the proletariat is recruited from all classes of the population.

The proletariat goes through various stages of development. With its birth begins its struggle with the bourgeoisie. At first the contest is carried on by individual laborers, then by the work people of a factory, then by the operatives of one trade, in one locality, against the individual bourgeois who directly exploits them. They direct their attacks not against the bourgeois conditions of production, but against the instruments of production themselves; they destroy imported wares that compete with their labor, they smash machinery to pieces, they set factories ablaze, they seek to restore by force the vanished status of the workman of the Middle Ages.

At this stage the laborers still form an incoherent mass scattered over the whole country, and broken up by their mutual competition. If anywhere they unite to form more compact bodies, this is not yet the consequence of their own active union, but of the union of the bourgeoisie, which class, in order to attain its own political ends, is compelled to set the whole proletariat in motion, and is moreover still able to do so for a time. At this stage, therefore, the proletarians do not fight their enemies, but the enemies of their enemies, the remnants of absolute monarchy, the landowners, the nonindustrial bourgeois, the petty bourgeoisie. Thus the whole historical movement is concentrated in the hands of the bourgeoisie; every victory so obtained is a victory for the bourgeoisie.

But with the development of industry the proletariat not only increases in number; it becomes concentrated in greater masses, its strength grows, and it feels that strength more. The various interests and conditions of life within the ranks of the proletariat are more and more equalized, in proportion as machinery obliterates all distinctions of labor and nearly everywhere reduces wages to the same low level. The growing competition among the bourgeois, and the resulting commercial crises, make the wages of the workers ever more fluctuating. The unceasing improvement of machinery, ever more rapidly developing, makes their livelihood more and more precarious; the collisions between individual workmen and individual bourgeois take more and more the character of collisions between two classes. Thereupon the workers begin to form combinations (trade unions) against the bourgeoisie; they club together in order to keep up the rate of wages; they found permanent associations in order to make provision beforehand for these occasional revolts. Here and there the contest breaks out into riots.

Now and then the workers are victorious, but only for a time. The real fruit of their battles lies, not in the immediate result, but in the ever expanding union of the workers. This union is furthered by the improved means of communication which are created by modern industry, and which place the workers of different localities in contact with one another. It was just this contact that was needed to centralize the numerous local struggles, all of the same character, into one national struggle between classes. But every class struggle is a political struggle. And that union, to attain which the burghers of the Middle Ages, with their miserable highways, required centuries, the modern proletarians, thanks to railways, achieve in a few years.

This organization of the proletarians into a class, and consequently into a political party, is continually being upset again by the competition between the workers themselves. But it ever rises up again, stronger, firmer, mightier. It compels legislative recognition of particular interests of the workers, by taking advantage of the divisions among the bourgeoisie itself. Thus the ten-hour bill[7] in England was carried.

---

[7] The 10-Hour Bill, for which the English workers had been fighting for 30 years, was made a law in 1847.—*Ed.*

Altogether, collisions between the classes of the old society further the course of development of the proletariat in many ways. The bourgeoisie finds itself involved in a constant battle. At first with the aristocracy; later on, with those portions of the bourgeoisie itself whose interests have become antagonistic to the progress of industry, at all times with the bourgeoisie of foreign countries. In all these battles it sees itself compelled to appeal to the proletariat, to ask for its help, and thus, to drag it into the political arena. The bourgeoisie itself, therefore, supplies the proletariat with its own elements of political and general education, in other words, it furnishes the proletariat with weapons for fighting the bourgeoisie.

Further, as we have already seen, entire sections of the ruling classes are, by the advance of industry, precipitated into the proletariat, or are at least threatened in their conditions of existence. These also supply the proletariat with fresh elements of enlightenment and progress.

Finally, in times when the class struggle nears the decisive hour, the process of dissolution going on within the ruling class, in fact within the whole range of old society, assumes such a violent, glaring character, that a small section of the ruling class cuts itself adrift, and joins the revolutionary class, the class that holds the future in its hands. Just as, therefore, at an earlier period, a section of the nobility went over to the bourgeoisie, so now a portion of the bourgeoisie goes over to the proletariat, and in particular, a portion of the bourgeois ideologists, who have raised themselves to the level of comprehending theoretically the historical movement as a whole.

Of all the classes that stand face to face with the bourgeoisie today, the proletariat alone is a really revolutionary class. The other classes decay and finally disappear in the face of modern industry; the proletariat is its special and essential product.

The lower middle class, the small manufacturer, the shopkeeper, the artisan, the peasant, all these fight against the bourgeoisie, to save from extinction their existence as fractions of the middle class. They are therefore not revolutionary, but conservative. Nay more, they are reactionary, for they try to roll

back the wheel of history. If by chance they are revolutionary, they are so only in view of their impending transfer into the proletariat; they thus defend not
their present, but their future interests; they desert
their own standpoint to adopt that of the proletariat.

The "dangerous class," the social scum (*Lumpen-
proletariat*), that passively rotting mass thrown off by
the lowest layers of old society, may, here and there,
be swept into the movement by a proletarian revolution; its conditions of life, however, prepare it far more
for the part of a bribed tool of reactionary intrigue.

The social conditions of the old society no
longer exist for the proletariat. The proletarian is
without property; his relation to his wife and children has no longer anything in common with bourgeois family relations; modern industrial labor,
modern subjection to capital, the same in England
as in France, in America as in Germany, has
stripped him of every trace of national character.
Law, morality, religion, are to him so many bourgeois prejudices, behind which lurk in ambush just
as many bourgeois interests.

All the preceding classes that got the upper hand,
sought to fortify their already acquired status by sub-
jecting society at large to their conditions of appropriation. The proletarians cannot become masters of
the productive forces of society, except by abolishing
their own previous mode of appropriation, and
thereby also every other previous mode of appropriation. They have nothing of their own to secure and
to fortify; their mission is to destroy all previous se-
curities for, and insurances of, individual property.

All previous historical movements were movements of minorities, or in the interest of minorities.
The proletarian movement is the self-conscious, independent movement of the immense majority, in the
interest of the immense majority. The proletariat, the
lowest stratum of our present society, cannot stir, cannot raise itself up, without the whole superincumbent
strata of official society being sprung into the air.

Though not in substance, yet in form, the struggle of the proletariat with the bourgeoisie is at first
a national struggle. The proletariat of each country
must, of course, first of all settle matters with its
own bourgeoisie.

In depicting the most general phases of the development of the proletariat, we traced the more or
less veiled civil war, raging within existing society,
up to the point where that war breaks out into open
revolution, and where the violent overthrow of the
bourgeoisie lays the foundation for the sway of the
proletariat.

Hitherto, every form of society has been based, as
we have already seen, on the antagonism of oppress-
ing and oppressed classes. But in order to oppress a
class, certain conditions must be assured to it under
which it can, at least, continue its slavish existence.
The serf, in the period of serfdom, raised himself to
membership in the commune, just as the petty bourgeois, under the yoke of feudal absolutism, managed
to develop into a bourgeois. The modern laborer, on
the contrary, instead of rising with the progress of industry, sinks deeper and deeper below the conditions
of existence of his own class. He becomes a pauper,
and pauperism develops more rapidly than population and wealth. And here it becomes evident, that the
bourgeoisie is unfit any longer to be the ruling class
in society, and to impose its conditions of existence
upon society as an overriding law. It is unfit to rule
because it is incompetent to assure an existence to its
slave within his slavery, because it cannot help letting him sink into such a state, that it has to feed him,
instead of being fed by him. Society can no longer
live under this bourgeoisie, in other words, its existence is no longer compatible with society.

The essential condition for the existence and
sway of the bourgeois class, is the formation and
augmentation of capital; the condition for capital is
wage-labor. Wage-labor rests exclusively on competition between the laborers. The advance of industry, whose involuntary promoter is the
bourgeoisie, replaces the isolation of the laborers,
due to competition, by their revolutionary combination, due to association. The development of
modern industry, therefore, cuts from under its feet
the very foundation on which the bourgeoisie produces and appropriates products. What the bourgeoisie therefore produces, above all, are its own
grave-diggers. Its fall and the victory of the proletariat are equally inevitable.

NON-VIOLENT RESISTANCE

Mohandas K. Gandhi

MEANS AND ENDS

Reader: Why should we not obtain our goal, which is good, by any means whatsoever, even by using violence? Shall I think of the means when I have to deal with a thief in the house? My duty is to drive him out anyhow. You seem to admit that we have received nothing, and that we shall receive nothing by petitioning. Why, then, may we not do so by using brute force? And, to retain what we may receive we shall keep up the fear by using the same force to the extent that it may be necessary. You will not find fault with a continuance of force to prevent a child from thrusting its foot into fire? Somehow or other we have to gain our end.

Gandhi: Your reasoning is plausible. It has deluded many. I have used similar arguments before now. But I think I know better now, and I shall endeavour to undeceive you. Let us first take the argument that we are justified in gaining our end by using brute force because the English gained theirs by using similar means. It is perfectly true that they used brute force and that it is possible for us to do likewise, but by using similar means we can get only the same thing that they got. You will admit that we do not want that. Your belief that there is no connection between the means and the end is a great mistake. Through that mistake even men who have been considered religious have committed grievous crimes. Your reasoning is the same as saying that we can get a rose through planting a noxious weed. If I want to cross the ocean, I can do so only by means of a vessel; if I were to use a cart for that purpose, both the cart and I would soon find the bottom. "As is the God, so is the votary," is a maxim worth considering. Its meaning has been distorted and men have gone astray. The means may be likened to a seed, the end to a tree; and there is just the same inviolable connection between the means and the end as there is between the seed and the tree. I am not likely to obtain the result flowing from the worship of God by laying myself prostrate before Satan. If, therefore, any one were to say: "I want to worship God; it does not matter that I do so by means of Satan," it would be set down as ignorant folly. We reap exactly as we sow. The English in 1833 obtained greater voting power by violence. Did they by using brute force better appreciate their duty? They wanted the right of voting, which they obtained by using physical force. But real rights are a result of performance of duty; these rights they have not obtained. We, therefore, have before us in England the force of everybody wanting and insisting on his rights, nobody thinking of his duty. And, where everybody wants rights, who shall give them to whom? I do not wish to imply that they do no duties. They don't perform the duties corresponding to those rights; and as they do not perform that particular duty, namely, acquire fitness, their rights have proved a burden to them. In other words, what they have obtained is an exact result of the means they adopted. They used the means corresponding to the end. If I want to deprive you of your watch, I shall certainly have to fight for it; if I want to buy your watch, I shall have to pay for it; and if I want a gift, I shall have to plead for it; and, according to the means I employ, the watch is stolen property, my own property, or a donation. Thus we see three different results from three different means. Will you still say that means do not matter?

Now we shall take the example given by you of the thief to be driven out. I do not agree with you that the thief may be driven out by any means. If it is my father who has come to steal I shall use one kind of means. If it is an acquaintance I shall use another; and in the case of a perfect stranger I shall use a third. If it is a white man, you will perhaps say you will use means different from those you will adopt with an Indian thief. If it is a weakling, the means will be different from those to be adopted for dealing with an equal in physical strength; and if the thief is armed from top to toe, I shall simply remain quiet. Thus we have a variety of means between the father and the armed man. Again, I fancy that I should pretend to be sleeping whether the thief was my father or that strong armed man. The reason for this is that my father would also be armed and I should succumb to the strength possessed by either and allow my things to be stolen. The strength of my father would make me weep with pity; the strength of the armed man would rouse in me anger and we should become enemies. Such is the curious situation. From these examples we may not be able to agree as to the means to be adopted in each case. I myself seem clearly to see what should be done in all these cases, but the remedy may frighten you. I therefore hesitate to place it before you. For the time being I will leave you to guess it, and if you cannot, it is clear you will have to adopt different means in each case. You will also have seen that any means will not avail to drive away the thief. You will have to adopt means to fit each case. Hence it follows that your duty is not to drive away the thief by any means you like.

Let us proceed a little further. That well-armed man has stolen your property; you have harboured the thought of his act; you are filled with anger; you argue that you want to punish that rogue, not for your own sake, but for the good of your neighbours; you have collected a number of armed men, you want to take his house by assault; he is duly informed of it, he runs away; he too is incensed. He collects his brother robbers, and sends you a defiant message that he will commit robbery in broad daylight. You are strong, you do not fear him, you are prepared to receive him. Meanwhile, the robber pesters your neighbours. They complain before you. You reply that you are doing all for their sake, you do not mind that your own goods have been stolen. Your neighbours reply that the robber never pestered them before, and that he commenced his depredations only after you declared hostilities against him. You are between Scylla and Charybdis. You are full of pity for the poor men. What they say is true. What are you to do? You will be disgraced if you now leave the robber alone. You, therefore, tell the poor men: "Never mind. Come, my wealth is yours, I will give you arms, I will teach you how to use them; you should belabour the rogue; don't you leave him alone." And so the battle grows; the robbers increase in numbers; your neighbours have deliberately put themselves to inconvenience. Thus the result of wanting to take revenge upon the

robber is that you have disturbed your own peace; you are in perpetual fear of being robbed and assaulted; your courage has given place to cowardice. If you will patiently examine the argument, you will see that I have not overdrawn the picture. This is one of the means. Now let us examine the other. You set this armed robber down as an ignorant brother; you intend to reason with him at a suitable opportunity; you argue that he is, after all, a fellow man; you do not know what prompted him to steal. You, therefore, decide that, when you can, you will destroy the man's motive for stealing. Whilst you are thus reasoning with yourself, the man comes again to steal. Instead of being angry with him you take pity on him. You think that this stealing habit must be a disease with him. Henceforth, you, therefore, keep your doors and windows open, you change your sleeping-place, and you keep your things in a manner most accessible to him. The robber comes again and is confused as all this is new to him; nevertheless, he takes away your things. But his mind is agitated. He inquires about you in the village, he comes to learn about your broad and loving heart, he repents, he begs your pardon, returns you your things, and leaves off the stealing habit. He becomes your servant, and you will find for him honourable employment. This is the second method. Thus, you see, different means have brought about totally different results. I do not wish to deduce from this that robbers will act in the above manner or that all will have the same pity and love like you, but I only wish to show that fair means alone can produce fair results, and that, at least in the majority of cases, if not indeed in all, the force of love and pity is infinitely greater than the force of arms. There is harm in the exercise of brute force, never in that of pity.

Now we will take the question of petitioning. It is a fact beyond dispute that a petition, without the backing of force, is useless. However, the late Justice Ranade used to say that petitions served a useful purpose because they were a means of educating people. They give the latter an idea of their condition and warn the rulers. From this point of view, they are not altogether useless. A petition of an equal is a sign of courtesy; a petition from a slave is a symbol of his slavery. A petition backed by force is a petition from an equal and, when he transmits his demand in the form of a petition, it testifies to his nobility. Two kinds of force can back petitions. "We shall hurt you if you do not give this," is one kind of force; it is the force of arms, whose evil results we have already examined. The second kind of force can thus be stated: "If you do not concede our demand, we shall be no longer your petitioners. You can govern us only so long as we remain the governed; we shall no longer have any dealings with you." The force implied in this may be described as love-force, soul-force, or, more popularly but less accurately, passive resistance.[1] This force is indestructible. He who uses it perfectly understands his position. We have an ancient proverb which literally means: "One negative cures thirty-six diseases." The force of arms is powerless when matched against the force of love or the soul.

Now we shall take your last illustration, that of the child thrusting its foot into fire. It will not avail you. What do you really do to the child? Supposing that it can exert so much physical force that it renders you powerless and rushes into fire, then you cannot prevent it. There are only two remedies open to you—either you must kill it in order to prevent it from perishing in the flames, or you must give your own life because you do not wish to see it perish before your very eyes. You will not kill it. If your heart is not quite full of pity, it is possible that you will not surrender yourself by preceding the child and going into the fire yourself. You, therefore, helplessly allow it to go to the flames. Thus, at any rate, you are not using physical force. I hope you will not consider that it is still physical force, though of a low order, when you would forcibly prevent the child from rushing toward the fire if you could. That force is of a different order and we have to understand what it is.

Remember that, in thus preventing the child, you are minding entirely its own interest, you are exercising authority for its sole benefit. Your example does not apply to the English. In using brute force against the English you consult entirely your own,

that is the national, interest. There is no question here either of pity or of love. If you say that the actions of the English, being evil, represent fire, and that they proceed to their actions through ignorance, and that therefore they occupy the position of a child and that you want to protect such a child, then you will have to overtake every evil action of that kind by whomsoever committed and, as in the case of the evil child, you will have to sacrifice yourself. If you are capable of such immeasurable pity, I wish you well in its exercise.

(*Hind Swaraj or Indian Home Rule,* chap. xvi)

• • •

THE LAW OF SUFFERING

No country has ever risen without being purified through the fire of suffering. Mother suffers so that her child may live. The condition of wheat growing is that the seed grain should perish. Life comes out of Death. Will India rise out of her slavery without fulfilling this eternal law of purification through suffering?

If my advisers are right, evidently India will realize her destiny without travail. For their chief concern is that the events of April, 1919, should not be repeated. They fear non-co-operation because it would involve the sufferings of many. If Hampdon had argued thus he would not have withheld payment of ship-money, nor would Wat Tayler have raised the standard of revolt. English and French histories are replete with instances of men continuing their pursuit of the right irrespective of the amount of suffering involved. The actors did not stop to think whether ignorant people would not have involuntarily to suffer. Why should we expect to write our history differently? It is possible for us, if we would, to learn from the mistakes of our predecessors to do better, but it is impossible to do away with the law of suffering which is the one indispensable condition of our being. The way to do better is to avoid, if we can, violence from our side and thus quicken the rate of progress and to introduce greater purity in the methods of suffering. We can,

---

[1]Finding the word misleading Gandhiji later called the same force Satyagraha or non-violent resistance.—Ed.

if we will, refrain, in our impatience, from bending the wrong-doer to our will by physical force as Sinn Feiners are doing today, or from coercing our neighbours to follow our methods as was done last year by some of us in bringing about *hartal*. Progress is to be measured by the amount of suffering undergone by the sufferer. The purer the suffering, the greater is the progress. Hence did the sacrifice of Jesus suffice to free a sorrowing world. In his onward march he did not count the cost of suffering entailed upon his neighbours whether it was undergone by them voluntarily or otherwise. Thus did the sufferings of a Harishchandra suffice to re-establish the kingdom of truth. He must have known that his subjects would suffer involuntarily by his abdication. He did not mind because he could not do otherwise than follow truth.

I have already stated that I do not deplore the massacre of Jalianwala Bagh so much as I deplore the murders of Englishmen and destruction of property by ourselves. The frightfulness at Amritsar drew away public attention from the greater though slower frightfulness at Lahore where attempt was made to emasculate the inhabitants by slow processes. But before we rise higher we shall have to undergo such processes many more times till they teach us to take up suffering voluntarily and to find joy in it. I am convinced that the Lahorians never deserved the cruel insults that they were subjected to; they never hurt a single Englishman; they never destroyed any property. But a wilful ruler was determined to crush the spirit of a people just trying to throw off his chafing yoke. And if I am told that all this was due to my preaching Satyagraha, my answer is that I would preach Satyagraha all the more forcibly for that so long as I have breath left in me, and tell the people that next time they would answer O'Dwyer's insolence not by opening shops by reason of threats of forcible sales but by allowing the tyrant to do his worst and let him sell their all but their unconquerable souls. Sages of old mortified the flesh so that the spirit within might be set free, so that their trained bodies might be proof against any injury that might be inflicted on them by tyrants seeking to impose their will on them. And if India wishes to revive her ancient wisdom and

to avoid the errors of Europe, if India wishes to see the Kingdom of God established on earth instead of that of Satan which has enveloped Europe, then I would urge her sons and daughters not to be deceived by fine phrases, the terrible subtleties that hedge us in, the fears of suffering that India may have to undergo, but to see what is happening today in Europe and from it understand that we must go through suffering even as Europe has gone through, but not the process of making others suffer. Germany wanted to dominate Europe and the Allies wanted to do likewise by crushing Germany. Europe is no better for Germany's fall. The Allies have proved themselves to be just as deceitful, cruel, greedy and selfish as Germany was or would have been. Germany would have avoided the sanctimonious humbug that one sees associated with the many dealings of the Allies.

The miscalculation that I deplored last year was not in connection with the sufferings imposed upon the people, but about the mistakes made by them and violence done by them owing to their not having sufficiently understood the message of Satyagraha. What then is the meaning of non-co-operation in terms of the law of suffering? We must voluntarily put up with the losses and inconveniences that arise from having to withdraw our support from a Government that is ruling against our will. Possession of power and riches is a crime under an unjust Government, poverty in that case is a virtue, says Thoreau. It may be that in the transition state we may make mistakes; there may be avoidable suffering. These things are preferable to national emasculation.

We must refuse to wait for the wrong to be righted till the wrong-doer has been roused to a sense of his iniquity. We must not, for fear of ourselves or others having to suffer, remain participators in it. But we must combat the wrong by ceasing to assist the wrong-doer directly or indirectly.

If a father does an injustice it is the duty of his children to leave the parental roof. If the headmaster of a school conducts his institution on an immoral basis, the pupils must leave the school. If the chairman of a corporation is corrupt the members thereof must wash their hands clean of his corruption by withdrawing from it; even so if a Government does a grave injustice the subjects must withdraw co-operation wholly or partially, sufficiently to wean the ruler from his wickedness. In each case conceived by me there is an element of suffering whether mental or physical. Without such suffering it is not possible to attain freedom.

(*Young India,* 16-6-'20)

HOW TO WORK NON-CO-OPERATION

Perhaps the best way of answering the fears and criticism as to non-co-operation is to elaborate more fully the scheme of non-co-operation. The critics seem to imagine that the organizers propose to give effect to the whole scheme at once. The fact however is that the organizer have fixed definite, progressive four stages. The first is the giving up of titles and resignation of honorary posts. If there is no response or if the response received is not effective, recourse will be had to the second stage. The second stage involves much previous arrangement. Certainly not a single servant will be called out unless he is either capable of supporting himself and his dependents or the Khilafat Committee is able to bear the burden. All the classes of servants will not be called out at once and never will any pressure be put upon a single servant to withdraw himself from Government service. Nor will a single private employee be touched, for the simple reason that the movement is not anti-English. It is not even antiGovernment. Co-operation is to be withdrawn because the people must not be party to a wrong—a broken pledge—a violation of deep religious sentiment. Naturally, the movement will receive a check, is there is any undue influence brought to bear upon any Government servant, or if any violence is used or countenanced by any member of the Khilafat Committee. The second stage must be entirely successful, if the response is at all on an adequate scale. For no Government—much less the Indian Government—can subsist if the people cease to serve it. The withdrawal therefore of the police and the military—the third stage—is a distant goal. The organizers however wanted to be fair, open and above suspicion. They did not want to keep back from Government or the public a single step they had in contemplation even as a remote contingency. The fourth, i.e., suspension of taxes, is still more remote. The organizers recognize that suspension of general taxation is fraught with the greatest danger. It is likely to bring a sensitive class in conflict with the police. They are therefore not likely to embark upon it, unless they can do so with the assurance that there will be no violence offered by the people.

I admit, as I have already done, that non-co-operation is not unattended with risk, but the risk of supineness in the face of a grave issue is infinitely greater than the danger of violence ensuing from organizing non-co-operation. To do nothing is to invite violence for a certainty.

It is easy enough to pass resolutions or write articles condemning non-co-operation. But it is no easy task to restrain the fury of a people incensed by a deep sense of wrong. I urge those who talk or work against non-co-operation to descend from their chairs and go down to the people, learn their feelings and write, if they have the heart, against non-co-operation. They will find, as I have found, that the only way to avoid violence is to enable them to give such expression to their feelings as to compel redress. I have found nothing save non-co-operation. It is logical and harmless. It is the inherent right of a subject to refuse to assist a government that will not listen to him.

Non-co-operation as a voluntary movement can only succeed, if the feeling is genuine and strong enough to make people suffer to the utmost. If the religious sentiment of the Mohammedans is deeply hurt and if the Hindus entertain neighbourly regard towards their Muslim brethren, they both will count no cost too great for achieving the end. Non-co-operation will not only be an effective remedy but will also be an effective test of the sincerity of the Muslim claim and the Hindu profession of friendship.

(*Young India,* 5-5-'20)

• • •

MY FAITH IN NON-VIOLENCE

[From a talk after the evening prayer on board the ship at Suez on the way to London for the Round Table Conference.]

I have found that life persists in the midst of destruction and, therefore, there must be a higher law than that of destruction. Only under that law would a well-ordered society be intelligible and life worth living. And if that is the law of life, we have to work it out in daily life. Wherever there are jars, wherever you are confronted with an opponent, conquer him with love. In a crude manner I have worked it out in my life. That does not mean that all my difficulties are solved. I have found, however, that this law of love has answered as the law of destruction has never done. In India we have had an ocular demonstration of the operation of this law on the widest scale possible. I do not claim therefore that non-violence has necessarily penetrated the three hundred millions, but I do claim that it has penetrated deeper than any other message, and in an incredibly short time. We have not been all uniformly non-violent; and with the vast majority, non-violence has been a matter of policy. Even so, I want you to find out if the country has not made phenomenal progress under the protecting power of non-violence.

It takes a fairly strenuous course of training to attain to a mental state of non-violence. In daily life it has to be a course of discipline though one may not like it, like for instance, the life of a soldier. But I agree that, unless there is a hearty co-operation of the mind, the mere outward observance will be simply a mask, harmful both to the man himself and to others. The perfect state is reached only when mind and body and speech are in proper co-ordination. But it is always a case of intense mental struggle. It is not that I am incapable of anger, for instance, but I succeed on almost all occasions to keep my feelings under control. Whatever may be the result, there is always in me a conscious struggle for following the law of non-violence deliberately and ceaselessly. Such a struggle leaves one stronger for it. Non-violence is a weapon of the strong. With the weak it might easily be hypocrisy. Fear and love are contradictory terms. Love is reckless in giving away, oblivious as to what it gets in return. Love wrestles with the world as with the self and

ultimately gains a mastery over all other feelings. My daily experience, as of those who are working with me, is that every problem lends itself to solution if we are determined to make the law of truth and non-violence the law of life. For truth and non-violence are, to me, faces of the same coin.

The law of love will work, just as the law of gravitation will work, whether we accept it or not. Just as a scientist will work wonders out of various applications of the law of nature, even so a man who applies the law of love with scientific precision can work greater wonders. For the force of non-violence is infinitely more wonderful and subtle than the material forces of nature, like, for instance, electricity. The men who discovered for us the law of love were greater scientists than any of our modern scientists. Only our explorations have not gone far enough and so it is not possible for every one to see all its working. Such, at any rate, is the hallucination, if it is one, under which I am labouring. The more I work at this law the more I feel the delight in life, the delight in the scheme of this universe. It gives me a peace and a meaning of the mysteries of nature that I have no power to describe.

(*The Nation's Voice,* part II, pp. 109–10)

THE FUTURE

A friend writing from America propounds the following two questions:

1. Granted that Saytagraha is capable of winning India's independence, what are the chances of its being accepted as a principle of State policy in a free India? In other words, would a strong and independent India rely on Satyagraha as a method of self-preservation, or would it lapse back to seeking refuge in the age-old institution of war, however defensive its character? To restate the question on the basis of a purely theoretic problem: Is Satyagraha likely to be accepted only in an up-hill battle, when the phenomenon of martyrdom is fully effective, or is it also to be the instrument of a sovereign authority which has neither the need nor the scope of behaving on the principle of martyrdom?

2. Suppose a free India adopts Saytagraha as an instrument of State policy how would she defend herself against probable aggression by another sovereign State? To restate the question on the basis of a purely theoretic problem: What would be the Satyagrahic action-patterns to meet the invading army at the frontier? What kind of resistance can be offered the opponent before a common area of action, such as the one now existing in India between the Indian nationalists and the British Government, is established? Or should the Satyagrahis withhold their action until after the opponent has taken over the country?

The questions are admittedly theoretical. They are also premature for the reason that I have not mastered the whole technique of non-violence. The experiment is still in the making. It is not even in its advanced stage. The nature of the experiment requires one to be satisfied with one step at a time. The distant scene is not for him to see. Therefore, my answers can only be speculative.

In truth, as I have said before, now we are not having unadulterated non-violence even in our struggle to win independence.

As to the first question, I fear that the chances of non-violence being accepted as a principle of State policy are very slight, so far as I can see at present. If India does not accept non-violence as her policy after winning independence, the second question becomes superfluous.

But I may state my own individual view of the potency of non-violence. I believe that a State can be administered on a non-violent basis if the vast majority of the people are non-violent. So far as I know, India is the only country which has a possibility of being such a State. I am conducting my experiment in that faith. Supposing, therefore, that India attained independence through pure non-violence, India could retain it too by the same means. A non-violent man or society does not anticipate or provide for attacks from without. On the contrary, such a person or society firmly believes that nobody is going to disturb them. If the worst happens, there are two ways open to non-violence. To yield possession but non-co-operate with the aggressor. Thus, supposing that a modern edition of Nero descended upon India, the representatives of the State will let him in but tell him that he will get no assistance from the people. They will prefer death to submission. The second way would be non-violent resistance by the people who have been trained in the non-violent way. They would offer themselves unarmed as fodder for the aggressor's cannon. The underlying belief in either case is that even a Nero is not devoid of a heart. The unexpected spectacle of endless rows upon rows of men and women simply dying rather than surrender to the will of an aggressor must ultimately melt him and his soldiery. Practically speaking there will be probably no greater loss in men than if forcible resistance was offered; there will be no expenditure in armaments and fortifications. The non-violent training received by the people will add inconceivably to their moral height. Such men and women will have shown personal bravery of a type far superior to that shown in armed warfare. In each case the bravery consists in dying, not in killing. Lastly, there is no such thing as defeat in non-violent resistance. That such a thing has not happened before is no answer to my speculation. I have drawn no impossible picture. History is replete with instances of individual non-violence of the type I have mentioned. There is no warrant for saying or thinking that a group of men and women cannot by sufficient training act non-violently as a group or nation. Indeed the sum total of the experience of mankind is that men somehow or other live on. From which fact I infer that it is the law of love that rules mankind. Had violence, i.e. hate, ruled us, we should have become extinct long ago. And yet the tragedy of it is that the so-called civilized men and nations conduct themselves as if the basis of society was violence. It gives me ineffable joy to make experiments proving that love is the supreme and only law of life. Much evidence to the contrary cannot shake my faith. Even the mixed non-violence of India has supported it. But if it is not enough to convince an unbeliever, it is enough to incline a friendly critic to view it with favour.

(*Harijan*, 13-4-'40)

NON-VIOLENCE AND SOCIAL CHANGE

Martin Luther King, Jr.

We have experimented with the meaning of nonviolence in our struggle for racial justice in the United States, but now the time has come for man to experiment with nonviolence in all areas of human conflict, and that means nonviolence on an international scale.

Now let me suggest first that if we are to have peace on earth, our loyalties must become ecumenical rather than sectional. Our loyalties must transcend our race, our tribe, our class, and our nation; and this means we must develop a world perspective. No individual can live alone; no nation can live alone, and as long as we try, the more we are going to have war in this world. Now the judgment of God is upon us, and we must either learn to live together as brothers or we are all going to perish together as fools.

Yes, as nations and individuals, we are interdependent. I have spoken to you before of our visit to India some years ago. It was a marvelous experience; but I say to you this morning that there were those depressing moments. How can one avoid being depressed when one sees with one's own eyes evidences of millions of people going to bed hungry at night? How can one avoid being depressed when one sees with one's own eyes thousands of people sleeping on the sidewalks at night? More than a million people sleep on the sidewalks of Bombay every night; more than half a million sleep on the sidewalks of Calcutta every night. They have no houses to go into. They have no beds to sleep in. As I be-

held these conditions, something within me cried out: "Can we in America stand idly by and not be concerned?" And an answer came: "Oh, no!" And I started thinking about the fact that right here in our country we spend millions of dollars every day to store surplus food; and I said to myself: "I know where we can store that food free of charge—in the wrinkled stomachs of the millions of God's children in Asia, Africa, Latin America, and even in our own nation, who go to bed hungry at night."

It really boils down to this: that all life is interrelated. We are all caught in an inescapable network of mutuality, tied into a single garment of destiny. Whatever affects one directly, affects all indirectly. We are made to live together because of the interrelated structure of reality. Did you ever stop to think that you can't leave for your job in the morning without being dependent on most of the world? You get up in the morning and go to the bathroom and reach over for the sponge, and that's handed to you by a Pacific islander. You reach for a bar of soap, and that's given to you at the hands of a Frenchman. And then you go into the kitchen to drink your coffee for the morning, and that's poured into your cup by a South American. And maybe you want tea: that's poured into your cup by a Chinese. Or maybe you're desirous of having cocoa for breakfast, and that's poured into your cup by a West African. And then you reach over for your toast, and that's given to you at the hands of an English-speaking farmer, not to mention the baker. And before you finish eating breakfast in the morning, you've depended on more than half of the world. This is the way our universe is structured, this is its interrelated quality. We aren't going to have peace on earth until we recognize this basic fact of the interrelated structure of all reality.

Now let me say, secondly, that if we are to have peace in the world, men and nations must embrace the nonviolent affirmation that ends and means must cohere. One of the great philosophical debates of history has been over the whole question of means and ends. And there have always been those who argued that the end justifies the means, that the means really aren't important. The important thing is to get to the end, you see.

So, if you're seeking to develop a just society, they say, the important thing is to get there, and the means are really unimportant; any means will do so long as they get you there—they may be violent, they may be untruthful means; they may even be unjust means to a just end. There have been those who have argued this throughout history. But we will never have peace in the world until men everywhere recognize that ends are not cut off from means, because the means represent the ideal in the making, and the end in process, and ultimately you can't reach good ends through evil means, because the means represent the seed and the end represents the tree.

It's one of the strangest things that all the great military geniuses of the world have talked about peace. The conquerors of old who came killing in pursuit of peace, Alexander, Julius Caesar, Charlemagne, and Napoleon, were akin in seeking a peaceful world order. If you will read *Mein Kampf* closely enough, you will discover that Hitler contended that everything he did in Germany was for peace. And the leaders of the world today talk eloquently about peace. Every time we drop our bombs in North Vietnam, President Johnson talks eloquently about peace. What is the problem? They are talking about peace as a distant goal, as an end we seek, but one day we must come to see that peace is not merely a distant goal we seek, but that it is a means by which we arrive at that goal. We must pursue peaceful ends through peaceful means. All of this is saying that, in the final analysis, means and ends must cohere because the end is pre-existent in the means, and ultimately destructive means cannot bring about constructive ends.

Now let me say that the next thing we must be concerned about if we are to have peace on earth and goodwill toward men is the nonviolent affirmation of the sacredness of all human life. Every man is somebody because he is a child of God. And so when we say "Thou shalt not kill," we're really saying that human life is too sacred to be taken on the battlefields of the world. Man is more than a tiny vagary of whirling electrons or a wisp of smoke from a limitless smoldering. Man is a child of God, made in His image, and therefore must be respected as such. Until men see this everywhere, until nations see this everywhere, we will be fighting wars. One day somebody should remind us that, even though there may be political and ideological differences between us, the Vietnamese are our brothers, the Russians are our brothers, the Chinese are our brothers; and one day we've got to sit down together at the table of brotherhood. But in Christ there is neither Jew nor Gentile. In Christ there is neither male nor female. In Christ there is neither Communist nor capitalist. In Christ, somehow, there is neither bound nor free. We are all one in Christ Jesus. And when we truly believe in the sacredness of human personality, we won't exploit people, we won't trample over people with the iron feet of oppression, we won't kill anybody.

There are three words for "love" in the Greek New Testament; one is the word "*eros.*" *Eros* is a sort of aesthetic, romantic love. Plato used to talk about it a great deal in his dialogues, the yearning of the soul for the realm of the divine. And there is and can always be something beautiful about *eros,* even in its expressions of romance. Some of the most beautiful love in all of the world has been expressed this way.

Then the Greek language talks about "*philos,*" which is another word for love, and *philos* is a kind of intimate love between personal friends. This is the kind of love you have for those people that you get along with well, and those whom you like on this level you love because you are loved.

Then the Greek language has another word for love, and that is the word "*agapē .*" *Agapē* is more than romantic love, it is more than friendship. *Agapē* is understanding, creative, redemptive goodwill toward all men. *Agapē* is an overflowing love which seeks nothing in return. Theologians would say that it is the love of God operating in the human heart. When you rise to love on this level, you love all men not because you like them, not because their ways appeal to you, but you love them because God loves them. This is what Jesus meant when He said, "Love your enemies." And I'm happy that He didn't say, "Like your enemies," because there are some people that I find it pretty difficult to like. Liking is an affectionate emotion, and I can't like anybody who would bomb my home. I can't like anybody who would exploit me. I can't like anybody who would trample over me with injustices. I can't like them. I can't like anybody who threatens to kill me day in and day out. But Jesus reminds us that love is greater than liking. Love is understanding, creative, redemptive goodwill toward all men. And I think this is where we are, as a people, in our struggle for racial justice. We can't ever give up. We must work passionately and unrelentingly for first-class citizenship. We must never let up in our determination to remove every vestige of segregation and discrimination from our nation, but we shall not in the process relinquish our privilege to love.

I've seen too much hate to want to hate, myself, and I've seen hate on the faces of too many sheriffs, too many white citizens' councilors, and too many Klansmen of the South to want to hate, myself; and every time I see it, I say to myself, hate is too great a burden to bear. Somehow we must be able to stand up before our most bitter opponents and say: "We shall match your capacity to inflict suffering by our capacity to endure suffering. We will meet your physical force with soul force. Do to us what you will and we will still love you. We cannot in all good conscience obey your unjust laws and abide by the unjust system, because noncooperation with evil is as much a moral obligation as is cooperation with good, and so throw us in jail and we will still love you. Bomb our homes and threaten our children, and, as difficult as it is, we will still love you. Send your hooded perpetrators of violence into our communities at the midnight hour and drag us out on some wayside road and leave us half-dead as you beat us, and we will still love you. Send your propaganda agents around the country, and make it appear that we are not fit, culturally and otherwise, for integration, and we'll still love you. But be assured that we'll wear you down by our capacity to suffer, and one day we will win our freedom. We will not only win freedom for ourselves; we will so appeal to your heart and conscience that we will win you in the process, and our victory will be a double victory."

If there is to be peace on earth and goodwill toward men, we must finally believe in the ultimate morality of the universe, and believe that all reality hinges on moral foundations. Something must remind us of this as we once again stand in the Christmas season and think of the Easter season simultaneously, for the two somehow go together. Christ came to show us the way. Men love darkness rather than the light, and they crucified Him, and there on Good Friday on the Cross it was still dark, but then Easter came, and Easter is an eternal reminder of the fact that the truth-crushed earth will rise again. Easter justifies Carlyle in saying, "No lie can live for ever." And so this is our faith, as we continue to hope for peace on earth and goodwill toward men: let us know that in the process we have cosmic companionship.

BY ANY MEANS NECESSARY

Malcolm X

You make my point, that as long as a white man does it, it's all right. A Black man is supposed to have no feelings. So when a Black man strikes back, he's an extremist. He's supposed to sit passively and have no feelings, be nonviolent, and love his enemy. No matter what kind of attack, be it verbal or otherwise, he's supposed to take it. But if he stands up and in any way tries to defend himself, then he's an extremist.

No. I think that the speaker who preceded me is getting exactly what he asked for. My reason for believing in extremism—intelligently directed extremism, extremism in defense of liberty, extremism in quest of justice—is because I firmly believe in my heart that the day that the Black man takes an uncompromising step and realizes that he's within his rights, when his own freedom is being jeopardized, to use any means necessary to bring about his freedom or put a halt to that injustice, I don't think he'll be by himself.

I live in America, where there are only 22 million Blacks against probably 160 million whites. One of the reasons that I'm in no way reluctant or hesitant to do whatever is necessary to see that Black people do something to protect themselves [is that] I honestly believe that the day that they do, many whites will have more respect for them. And there will be more whites on their side than are now on their side with this little wishy-washy "love-thy-enemy" approach that they've been using up to now.

And if I'm wrong, then you are racialists.

As I said earlier, in my conclusion, I'm a Muslim. I believe in the religion of Islam. I believe in Allah, I believe in Muhammad, I believe in all of the prophets. I believe in fasting, prayer, charity, and that which is incumbent upon a Muslim to fulfill in order to be a Muslim. In April I was fortunate to make the *hajj* to Mecca, and went back again in September to try and carry out my religious functions and requirements.

But at the same time that I believe in that religion, I have to point out I'm also an American Negro, and I live in a society whose social system is based upon the castration of the Black man, whose political system is based on castration of the Black man, and whose economy is based upon the castration of the Black man. A society which, in 1964, has more subtle, deceptive, deceitful methods to make the rest of the world think that it's cleaning up its house, while at the same time the same things are happening to us in 1964 that happened in 1954, 1924, and in 1984.

They came up with what they call a civil rights bill in 1964, supposedly to solve our problem, and after the bill was signed, three civil rights workers were murdered in cold blood. And the FBI head, [J. Edgar] Hoover, admits that they know who did it. They've known ever since it happened, and they've done nothing about it. Civil rights bill down the drain. No matter how many bills pass, Black people in that country where I'm from—still, our lives are not worth two cents. And the government has shown its inability, or it unwillingness, to do whatever is necessary to protect life and property where the Black American is concerned.

So my contention is that whenever a people come to the conclusion that the government which they have supported proves itself unwilling or proves itself unable to protect our lives and protect our property because we have the wrong color skin, we are not human beings unless we ourselves band together and do whatever, however, whenever is necessary to see that our lives and our property is protected. And I doubt that any person in here would refuse to do the same thing, were he in the same position. Or I should say, were he in the same condition.

Just one step farther to see, am I justified in this stand? And I say, I'm speaking as a Black man from America, which is a racist society. No matter how much you hear it talk about democracy, it's as racist as South Africa or as racist as Portugal, or as racist as any other racialist society on this earth. The only difference between it and South Africa: South Africa preaches separation and practices separation; America preaches integration and practices segregation. This is the only difference. They don't practice what they preach, whereas South Africa preaches and practices the same thing. I have more respect for a man who lets me know where he stands, even if he's wrong, than one who comes up like an angel and is nothing but a devil.

The system of government that America has consists of committees. There are sixteen senatorial committees that govern the country and twenty congressional committees. Ten of the sixteen senatorial committees are in the hands of southern racialists, senators who are racialists. Thirteen of the twenty—well this was before the last election, I think it's even more so now. Ten of the sixteen committees, senatorial committees, are in the hands of senators who are southern racialists. Thirteen of the twenty congressional committees were in the hands of southern congressmen who are racialists. Which means out of the thirty-six committees that govern the foreign and domestic direction of that government, twenty-three are in the hands of southern racialists—men who in no way believe in the equality of man, and men who would do anything within their power to see that the Black man never gets to the same seat or to the same level that they are on.

The reason that these men from that area have that type of power is because America has a seniority system. And these who have that seniority have been there longer than anyone else because the Black people in the areas where they live can't vote. And it is only because the Black man is deprived of his vote that puts these men in positions of power, that gives them such influence in the government beyond their actual intellectual or political ability, or even beyond the number of people from the areas that they represent.

So we can see in that country that no matter what the federal government professes to be doing, the power of the federal government lies in these committees. And any time any kind of legislation is proposed to benefit the Black man or give the Black man his just due, we find it is locked up in these committees right here. And when they let something through the committee, usually it is so chopped up and fixed up that by the time it becomes law, it's a law that can't be enforced.

Another example is the Supreme Court desegregation decision that was handed down in 1954. This is a law, and they have not been able to implement this law in New York City, or in Boston, or in Cleveland, or Chicago, or the northern cities. And my contention is that any time you have a country, supposedly a democracy, supposedly the land of the free and the home of the brave, and it can't enforce laws—even in the northernmost, cosmopolitan, and progressive part of it—that will benefit a Black man, if those laws can't be enforced or that law can't be enforced, how much heart do you think we will get when they pass some civil rights legislation which only involves more laws? If they can't enforce this law, they will never enforce those laws.

So my contention is that we are faced with a racialistic society, a society in which they are deceitful, deceptive, and the only way we can bring about a change is to talk the kind of language—speak the language that they understand. The racialists never understand a peaceful language. The racialist never understands the nonviolent language. The racialist we have, he's spoken his language to us for four hundred years.

We have been the victim of his brutality. We are the ones who face his dogs that tear the flesh from our limbs, only because we want to enforce the Supreme Court decision. We are the ones who have our skulls crushed, not by the Ku Klux Klan but by policemen, only because we want to enforce what they call the Supreme Court decision. We are the ones upon whom water hoses are turned, with pressure so hard that it rips the clothes from our backs—not men, but the clothes from the backs of women and children. You've seen it yourselves. Only because we want to enforce what they call the law.

Well, any time you live in a society supposedly based upon law, and it doesn't enforce its own law because the color of a man's skin happens to be wrong, then I say those people are justified to resort to any means necessary to bring about justice where the government can't give them justice.

I don't believe in any form of unjustified extremism. But I believe that when a man is exercising extremism, a human being is exercising extremism in defense of liberty for human beings, it's no vice. And when one is moderate in the pursuit of justice for human beings, I say he's a sinner.

And I might add, in my conclusion—In fact, America is one of the best examples, when you read its history, about extremism. Old Patrick Henry said, "Liberty or death!" That's extreme, very extreme.

I read once, passingly, about a man named Shakespeare. I only read about him passingly, but I remember one thing he wrote that kind of moved me. He put it in the mouth of Hamlet, I think it was, who said, "To be or not to be"—he was in doubt about something. "Whether it was nobler in the mind of man to suffer the slings and arrows of outrageous fortune"—moderation—"or to take up arms against a sea of troubles and by opposing end them."

And I go for that. If you take up arms, you'll end it. But if you sit around and wait for the one who's in power to make up his mind that he should end it, you'll be waiting a long time.

And in my opinion the young generation of whites, Blacks, browns, whatever else there is— you're living at a time of extremism, a time of revolution, a time when there's got to be a change. People in power have misused it, and now there has to be a change and a better world has to be built, and the only way it's going to be built is with extreme methods. And I for one will join in with anyone, I don't care what color you are, as long as you want to change this miserable condition that exists on this earth.

Thank you.

ETHICS AND COMMUNITY

Enrique Dussel

16.6 REFORMISM AND DEVELOPMENTALISM

Let us face facts. First, the concrete, simple daily "changes" that we make very rarely touch the essence of our structures. In the second place, it is almost impossible that it should be otherwise. The fact is that it is very difficult to go beyond mere "reforms." Even the social teaching of the church, in its central aspect, merely proposes the reform of already existing systems. But this is not reform*ism.* By "reformism" we must understand the extreme position of those who regard reform as the only thing *ever* possible. Franz Hinkelammert has shown that Karl Popper's thinking is "reformist" in this negative, pejorative sense. But the frank, realistic admission that one must live in a situation that is merely "reformable" because reforms are the only thing actually possible here and now, is simply the daily practice of the prudent, realistic, even revolutionary militant who knows full well that revolutions are not a daily occurrence.

In this same spirit of realism, the development of productive forces, the development of a society's wealth, should be the ongoing intention of those who opt for the poor and the oppressed. "Development" enables the needy to have more goods so as to fulfill their needs—provided, of course, that the develop-ment in question is a *human* development, not merely the development of capital, as it is in most cases in Latin America, Africa, or Asia. "Developmentalism," on the other hand, is the pretense that the *only possible development is capitalist,* and that therefore money must be borrowed, and technology—the technology of the transnationals—employed.

With the collapse of populism, Latin American nationalistic capitalisms decided in the second half of the 1950s that the only hope for Latin American development lay in borrowing North American capital and technology. Ten years later the error of this notion became clear: instead of development, we had a still greater dependence, and the still wilder flight of our own capital—a greater loss of "surplus life" than ever before.

"Reformism" is a mistake, a sin against the reign of God. Its only ambition is the everlasting reproduction of the *same system.* "Developmentalism" is a transgression against the Spirit, for it believes only in *current means,* which are those of the system. It lacks the patience to seek new paths when necessary. It places its only hope in the "means" offered by the Prince of "this world."

16.7 DEPENDENCE, BREACH, AND REVOLUTION

Let no one think that an ethics of liberation is revolutionar*istic.* Revolutionar*ism* would be that anarchism that, here and now, before all else and always, come hell or high water, in season or out of season, would launch a revolution. Quite the contrary—only the patient, the humble, only those who hope, like our oppressed peoples over the years, the decades, the centuries are called in the *kairos*—the "fullness of time," the "Day of Yahweh"—to work the mighty deeds of the heroes, the prophets, the martyrs.

Our situation of dependence in the underdeveloped, peripheral nations points to a double sin: the social relationship of capital with workers, and the relationship of the developed North with the underdeveloped South. When the *kairos* is reached, the struggle with sin will no longer consist in the implementation of reforms. It will launch an attack upon the very *essence* of the structure of sin.

It is this breach with *essential structures,* which is possible only at rare moments in history—having ripened and matured over the course of centuries, suddenly to materialize in a matter of mere weeks or months—that is called "revolution." Cromwell's revolution in England in the seventeenth century, or the French Revolution in the eighteenth, or the Russian or Cuban revolutions in the twentieth, are *essential* social changes. In our own case, in the Latin America of the close of the twentieth century, the "*social* relationships" of domination that we have found to be constitutive of capital and dependence are being breached and dissolved, whether by way of the struggle with sin waged by the workers (as a class) against capital (the capitalists), or by way of the struggle of the poor countries with the rich nations—in other words, in a "class struggle" against the sin constituted by the vertical capital-labor relationship, or in a "struggle for national liberation" against the sin constituted by the horizontal relationship of a developed country with an underdeveloped country.

Revolution is essential breach with the structures of sin—sin as injustice, sin as anti-community, alienative, social relationship. Such a breach or rupture is necessary and possible only at certain moments in the multicentennial history of a people. It is a "once and for all" happening, perceived and exploited by the heroes and prophets of a people only once every so many centuries.

16.8 VIOLENCE

As Paul VI declared in Bogotá, Colombia, on August 23, 1968, "violence is neither evangelical nor Christian." Of course, the pope was referring to the violence of force, in Latin *vis,* the coercion of the will of others against their rights, against their justice. He spoke of the violence of sin. "It is clear," said Medellín, "that in many parts of Latin America we find a situation of injustice that can be called *institutionalized violence*" (*Medellín Document on Peace,* no. 16). This is the more visible violence, the

violence of every day, the violence of sin (2.2), institutional violence, the violence that produces weapons (15.10) or obliges the poor to sell their work.

This violence, that of the Prince of "this world," is frequently practiced with the consent of the oppressed. There is an ideological hegemony and domination in which the poor *accept* the system of domination, as something natural, as an obvious, eternal phenomenon. But the moment the oppressed (oppressed classes, oppressed nations, the poor) get on their feet, the moment they rebel, and oppose the domination under which they sweat and strain—this is the moment when *hegemonic* violence becomes *coercive.* Oppression becomes repression. All repression is perverse. There can never be a "legitimate" repression, as a certain conservative, right-wing group of bishops and others in the Latin American church say there can be.

Confronted with the active repression or violence of sin, many adopt the *tactics* or stance of "non-violence," as Mahatma Gandhi in India, Martin Luther King, Jr., in the United States, or Miguel D'Escoto in Nicaragua. This courageous position cannot, however, be elevated to the status of an absolute theoretical principle, an exclusive strategy for any and all situations. To the violence of sin the martyr opposes the valor of the suffering servant, who builds the church with his blood. But this martyr, this prophet, is not the political hero.

16.9 JUST DEFENSE AND A PEOPLE'S RIGHT TO LIFE

The exact contrary of the repulsive, unjust violence of the oppressor is the active *defense of the "innocent,"* of the oppressed poor, the repressed people. Saint Augustine teaches us that it is a requirement of charity or Christian love to *re-act* to unjust violence: "matters would be still worse, after all, were malefactors to lord it over the just" (*The City of God,* IV, 15). Saint Thomas likewise teaches that struggle is not sin (*Summa Theologiae,* II-II, q. 40, a. 1) if its cause is just. Further, he adds, "force is repelled with force" in the case of defending *life* (ibid., q. 64, a. 7).

The church has always held the "just war theory" where the authority of governments is involved, even in the Second Vatican Council (*Gaudium et Spes,* 79). But it happens that an innocent person or a people can be oppressed, repressed, colonized by a government. In that case the war is not a war of one state with another, but a liberation struggle between oppression and the defense of the innocent. Joan of Arc against the English, Washington against the established order, the *Résistance française* against Nazism, Bolívar or San Martín against Spain, Sandino against the North American occupation— none of these heroes represented the established *governments* of a state. They have their legitimacy in virtue of their *just cause* and their *right intention,* in virtue of their right to employ *adequate* means (even arms, as a "last resort") for the defense of the people—keeping in mind the principle of due proportion, of course, and not using more force than necessary to attain the realistic ends at stake. These are precisely the requisites that church tradition, including Saint Thomas, has always demanded for the use of force in defense of the innocent, the poor, the oppressed, in order that the use of force be just and legitimate. The Sandinista National Liberation Front, for example, complied with these requirements in its struggle with Somoza. And yet its members were labeled "subversives," "violent," and so on. In his Peace Day Message of 1982, Pope John Paul II asserted: "In the name of an elementary requisite of justice, peoples have the right and even *the duty* to protect their existence with *adequate means*" (no. 12). Peoples, then, and not merely governments, have this right and duty, and the means they are allowed to employ are "adequate means," in other words, even force of arms when necessary as a last resort to "repel force," as Saint Thomas put it—the force of sin and oppression.

But although the hero has need of "adequate means" to build the *future* state, the prophet and the martyr never need these means to build the present church, the Christian community. But political heroes cannot be forced to use the same means as do prophets and martyrs. A Camilo Torres will be a hero and an Oscar Romero a martyr. Their histori-

cal options were different. But both options can be legitimate. The political *legitimacy* of the actions of citizen Camilo will be judged by the future liberated state, not by theology or the church. In two encyclicals the popes condemned Latin American emancipation from Spain in the early nineteenth century. They committed the error of venturing into politics, and thus overstepping the bounds of their specific authority. Heroes are judged by heroes. Nor must we forget that there is such a thing as the charism of heroism, bestowed by the Holy Spirit.

16.10 REVOLUTION, MORALITY, ETHICS

I have already observed that daily life is a tissue of innumerable little repetitive acts, including, at best, "reforms," that may or may not enjoy transcendence (become institutional). Thus we have Christian moralities—prevailing moral systems that have taken their inspiration in Christianity, like the moralities of medieval European or colonial Latin American Christendom. Today, however, Latin America is caught up in a special stage of its history: that of its second emancipation. The first Latin American emancipation was its deliverance from dependence on Spain and Portugal, in the early years of the nineteenth century, or, in the Caribbean, from England, France, or Holland. In the first emancipation the agent and beneficiary of the revolution was the Creole oligarchy. Today, in the second emancipation, the subject or agent is the people of the poor as the "social bloc" of the oppressed.

As already indicated, revolution is not part of a people's normal experience. A revolution takes centuries to mature and materialize. But when a revolutionary process does break out, as in Nicaragua beginning in 1979, certain Christian ethical principles can function as norms to regulate and guide that exceptional praxis. The poor are the subject (agent) both of the reign of God, and of the revolution of liberation being conducted in Latin America here at the close of the twentieth century. Thus there will be an *essential* change in structures here. Prevailing "*social* relationships" (see chap. 13–15) will give place to other, more just structures and relationships (although they will *never* be perfect in human history before the Parousia, the Lord's return—Rev. 22:20).

As Moses abandoned the *morality* of Egypt only to find *ethical* norms to guide his praxis, so the heroes of the future homeland, along with the prophets, who frequently become martyrs (and this is why there have been so many martyrs in Latin America since 1969—because there are prophets), must have at their disposal a Christian ethics of revolution, a community ethics of liberation, an ethics capable of justifying "the *struggle* for social justice. This struggle must be seen as a normal dedication of the genuine good," says Pope John Paul II (*Laborem Exercens,* 20).

CONCLUSIONS

It might appear that the Christian may not theologize upon such current questions as class struggle, violence, or revolution. Those who do theorize upon these themes only too obviously do so in terms of their own ideologies, quickly taking sides in order to justify their daily praxis, be the latter one of domination, indifference, liberation, or what have you. But all these questions must be examined dispassionately, in the light of the principles sketched in part 1 of this treatise on community ethics.

Sin produces ethical discrepancies between persons—between dominator and dominated, hence between the dominating class or the "rich," and the dominated class or the "poor" (the oppressed as a social bloc). To deny the existence of classes is to deny the existence of sin. To deny that dominators struggle to institutionalize and eternalize their domination is the earmark of a naive mentality—if not of the bad faith of connivance. To deny the dominated their just right to defend their lives, defend the innocent, and rescue the people, and to call this defense sin, stigmatizing the "class struggle" as "hatred and nihilism" (for it is, after all, a movement to an*nihil*ate sin), is the praxis of a theology of domination. Just so, to regard the revolution of the poor as "sin," and the institutional violence of coercion and repression practiced by the dominators as the "nature of things," is to establish a diabolical morality and call it gospel. Values today are reversed, and the worst of principles and movements are presented as the Christian ethics of Jesus, the ethics of the gospel.

QUESTIONS FOR DISCUSSION

1. Familiarize yourself with some of the struggles of contemporary workers around the world. What would Marx and Engels have to say to them? How is the situation of workers in the United States different from, or similar to, the portrayal of proletarians that Marx and Engels give?
2. Several of our authors (Marx, Malcolm X, and Dussel) advocate violence to combat a situation of injustice. Gandhi and King, however, advocate nonviolence. Who do you think has the more effective method? Who do you think has the best moral position (or are both positions moral)?

PERMISSIONS
ACKNOWLEDGMENTS

Chapter 1

Plato, "The Symposium." From *The Great Dialogues of Plato* by Plato, pp. 90–106. Translated by W. H. D. Rouse. Translation copyright © 1956, renewed 1984 by J. C. G. Rouse. Used by permission of Dutton Signet, a division of Penguin Putnam Inc.

Plato, "The Parable of the Cave." "The Republic" from *The Great Dialogues of Plato* by Plato, pp. 312–317. Translated by W. H. D. Rouse. Translation copyright © 1956, renewed 1984 by J. C. G. Rouse. Used by permission of Dutton Signet, a division of Penguin Putnam Inc.

Black Elk, "Crazy Horse's Vision." Reprinted from *Black Elk Speaks,* pp. 85–87, by John G. Neihardt, by permission of the University of Nebraska of Press. Copyright 1932, 1959, 1972, by John G. Neihardt. Copyright © 1961 by the John G. Neihardt Trust.

Hannah Arendt, "The Value of the Surface." Excerpted from *Thinking,* vol. 1 of *The Life of the Mind* by Hannah Arendt, pp. 19–30. Copyright © 1978 by Harcourt Brace & Company; reprinted by permission of the publisher.

George Berkeley, "Subjective Idealism." From George Berkeley, "Three Dialogues between Hylas and Philonous . . . ," in *The Empiricists* (Garden City, NY: Doubleday, Dolphin Books, 1970), pp. 217–237, 252–256.

The Upanishads, "Thou Art That." From F. Frederick Max Müller, trans., *The Upanishads,* vol. 1 of *The Sacred Books of the East* (New York: Dover, 1962), pp. 101–105. Facsimile reprint of 1879 edition published by Clarendon Press, Oxford, England.

Sri Ramana Maharshi, "A Commentary on the Upanishads." Excerpted from Sri Ramana Maharshi, *Be as You Are: The Teachings of Sri Ramana Maharshi,* edited by David Godman (London and New York: Arkana, 1985), pp. 11–13, 201–204. Approximately 345 words on pp. 13 and 201 copyright © Sri Ramanasramam, 1985. Reproduced by permission of Penguin Books Ltd.

Arthur Schopenhauer, "The World as Will and Idea." From Arthur Schopenhauer, *The World as Will and Idea,* 4th ed., translated by R. B. Haldane and J. Kemp (London: Kegan Paul, Trench and Trubner, 1896), vol. 1, pp. 3–6, 133–134, 452–461.

Hui Neng, "The Sutra of Hui Neng." From *The Diamond Sutra and the Sutra of Hui Neng,* translated by A. F. Price and Wong Mou-lam, pp. 11–24. Reprinted by arrangement with Shambhala Publications, Inc., 300 Massachusetts Avenue, Boston, MA 02115.

Wang Fu-Chih, "Neo-Confucian Materialism." From Wang Fu-Chih, in *A Source Book in Chinese Philosophy,* translated and compiled by Wing-Tsit Chan, pp. 694–698. Copyright © 1963 and renewed 1991 by Princeton

Chapter 2

Vine Deloria, "Tribal Religious Realities." Excerpted by permission of the author from Vine Deloria, Jr., *The Metaphysics of Modern Existence* (San Francisco: Harper & Row, 1979), pp. 19–20, 151–159, 223 (notes), 230–231 (notes).

Chapter 3

Karl Marx and Friedrich Engels, "Critique of Religion." Reprinted from Karl Marx and Friedrich Engels, *On Religion* (New York: Schocken Books, 1964), pp. 41–42, 135–136, 147–149, 316–317, 82–84.

Leonardo Boff and Clodovis Boff, "Liberation Theology." Reprinted by permission from Leonardo Boff and Clodovis Boff, *Introducing Liberation Theology* (Maryknoll, NY: Orbis, 1987), pp. 1–10, 28–35, 49–58.

Sulak Sivaraksa, "Engaged Buddhism." Excerpted by permission from Sulak Sivaraksa, "Engaged Buddhism: Liberation from a Buddhist Perspective," in *World Religions and Human Liberation,* edited by Dan Cohn-Sherbok, pp. 78–92. Copyright © 1992 by Orbis Books, Maryknoll, New York.

Hassan Hanafi, "Islam and Revolution." Excerpted by permission from Hassan Hanafi, "The Revolution of the Transcendence," in *Islam in the Modern World, vol 2: Tradition, Revolution, and Culture* (Cairo, Egypt: Anglo-Egyptian Bookshop, n.d.), pp. 148–151, 159–181.

Carol P. Christ, "Why Women Need the Goddess." Reprinted by permission of the author from Carol P. Christ, "Why Women Need the Goddess," in Carol P. Christ and Judith Plaskow, eds., *Womanspirit Rising: A Feminist Reader in Religion* (New York: HarperCollins, 1992), pp. 273–287. Carol P. Christ is an internationally known feminist theologian. Her book *Laughter of Aphrodite: Reflections on a Journey to the Goddess* (Harper & Row) discusses issues raised in this essay in greater detail.

Chapter 4

Mencius, "Human Nature Is Good." Excerpted from Wang Fu-Chih, in *A Source Book in Chinese Philosophy,* translated and compiled by Wing-Tsit Chan, pp. 51–57, 59, 62–66, 75. Copyright © 1963 and renewed 1991 by Princeton University Press. Reprinted by permission of Princeton University Press.

Hsün Tzu, "Human Nature Is Evil." From Hsün Tzu, "Man's Nature Is Evil," in *Basic Writings of Mo Tzu, Hsün Tzu, and Han Fei Tzu,* translated by Burton Watson, pp. 157–165. © 1967, Columbia University Press. Reprinted with the permission of the publisher.

Thomas Hobbes, "Human Nature as Competitive." Excerpted from Thomas Hobbes, *Leviathan,* edited by Michael Oakeshott (New York: Collier Books, Macmillan Publishing, 1962), pp. 98–104, 131–133.

Petr Kropotkin, "Mutual Aid." From Petr Kropotkin, *Mutual Aid,* pp. 1–8, 74–80, Extending Horizons Books, 1976, Porter Sargent Publishers, Inc., 11 Beacon Street, Boston, MA 02108. Reprinted by permission.

Ashley Montagu, "War and Aggression." Excerpted from "War and Violence," in *The Nature of Human Aggression* by Ashley Montagu, pp. 258–284. Copyright © 1976 by Ashley Montagu. Used by permission of Oxford University Press, Inc.

Jean-Paul Sartre, "There Is No Human Nature." From *Existentialism and Human Emotions* by Jean-Paul Sartre, pp. 12–33, 51. Copyright © 1957, 1985 by Philosophical Library, Inc. Published by arrangement with Carol Publishing Group. A Citadel Press book.

Francisco Miró Quesada, "Man without Theory." From Francisco Miró Quesada, "Man without Theory," in *Latin American Philosophy in the Twentieth Century: Man, Values, and the Search for Philosophical Identity,* edited by Jorge J. E. Gracia, pp. 137–148 (Amherst, NY: Prometheus Books). Copyright 1986. Reprinted by permission of the publisher. Originally from Francisco Miró Quesada, *El hombre sin teoria* (Lima: Universidad Mayor de San Marcos, 1959), pp. 14–31.

Abuhamid Muhammad Al-Ghazali, "The Proper Role for Women." Reprinted from Abuhamid Muhammad Al-Ghazali, "Describing Women and Their Good and Bad Points," in *Ghazali's Book of Counsel for Kings,* translated by F. R. C. Bagley (University of Durham Publications, 1964), pp. 158–173, by permission of Oxford University Press.

Fatima Mernissi, "Beyond the Veil." Reprinted by permission from Fatima Mernissi, *Beyond the Veil: Male-Female Dynamics in Modern Muslim Society,* rev. ed. (Bloomington: Indiana University Press, 1987), pp. 18–20, 27–33, 41–45.

Simone de Beauvoir, "The Second Sex." From *The Second Sex* by Simone De Beauvoir, translated by H. M. Parshley, pp. xv–xix, 663–681. Copyright © 1952 and renewed 1980 by Alfred A. Knopf, Inc. Reprinted by permission of the publisher.

José Ortega y Gasset, "Women as Body." Excerpted from "More about Others and 'I,' " in *Man and People,* by José Ortega y Gasset, translated by Willard R. Trask, pp. 128–138. Translation copyright © 1957 by W. W. Norton & Company, Inc. Reprinted by permission of W. W. Norton & Company, Inc.

Elizabeth V. Spelman, "Gender and Race." Excerpted from "Gender and Race: The Ampersand Problem in Feminist Thought," in *Inessential Woman: Problems of Exclusion in Feminist Thought,* by Elizabeth V. Spelman, pp. 126–132, 209. © 1988 by Elizabeth V. Spelman. Reprinted by permission of Beacon Press, Boston.

Paula Gunn Allen, "The Sacred Hoop." Excerpted from "How the West Was Really Won," in *The Sacred Hoop: Recovering the Feminine in American Indian Traditions,* by Paula Gunn Allen, pp. 194–203, 206–208. © 1986, 1992 by Paula Gunn Allen. Reprinted by permission of Beacon Press, Boston.

Richard D. Mohr, "Is Homosexuality Unnatural?" Reprinted by permission of the author from Richard D. Mohr, "Gay Basics: Some Questions, Facts, and Values," in *The Right Thing to Do: Basic Readings in Moral Philosophy,* edited by James Rachels (New York: Random House, 1989), pp. 147–148, 155–160, 162–163.

Ruth Hubbard, "The Social Construction of Sexuality." From Ruth Hubbard, "The Social Construction of Sexuality," in *The Politics of Women's Biology,* pp. 130–135. Copyright © 1990 by Rutgers, The State University. Reprinted by permission of Rutgers University Press.

Chapter 5

René Descartes, "Meditations." Copyright © 1952 by St. Martin's Press, Inc. From *New Studies in the Philosophy of Descartes* by Norman Kemp Smith, pp. 176–187. Reprinted with permission of St. Martin's Press, Inc.

David Hume, "Personal Identity." Reprinted from David Hume, *A Treatise on Human Nature* (Cleveland: World Publishing, 1962), pp. 300–305.

Bhagavad-Gita, "Samkhya Dualism." From Sarvepalli Radhakrishnan and Charles Moore, eds., *A Sourcebook in Indian Philosophy,* pp. 145–147. Copyright © 1957, renewed 1988, by Princeton University Press. Reprinted by permission of Princeton University Press.

The Upanishads, "The True Self." From F. Frederick Max Müller, trans., *The Upanishads,* vol. 1 of *The Sacred Books of the East* (New York: Dover, 1962), pp. 125–127, 48. Facsimile reprint of 1879 edition published by Clarendon Press, Oxford, England.

Questions of King Milinda, "No Self." From *The Questions of King Milinda,* in vol. 35 of *The Sacred Books of the East,* translated by T. W. Rhys Davids (New York: Dover, 1963), pp. 40–45, 86–89. Facsimile reprint of 1874 edition published by Clarendon Press, Oxford, England.

T. R. V. Murti, "The Middle Way." From T. R. V. Murti, *The Central Philosophy of Buddhism* (London: George Allen & Unwin, 1955, 1960), pp. 10–11, 201–207. Reprinted by permission of HarperCollins Publishers Ltd.

Toshihiko Izutsu, "Ego-less Consciousness: A Zen View." From *Toward a Philosophy of Zen Buddhism,* by Toshihiko Izutsu, pp. 65–77, 82–83. © 1977 by the Imperial Iranian Academy of Philosophy. Reprinted by arrangement with Shambhala Publications, Inc., 300 Massachusetts Avenue, Boston, MA 02115.

Derek Parfit, "Divided Minds and the 'Bundle' Theory of Self." Reprinted by permission of Blackwell Publishers from Derek Parfit, "Divided Minds and the Nature of Persons," in *Mindwaves: Thoughts on Intelligence, Identity, and Consciousness,* edited by Colin Blakemore and Susan Greenfield (Oxford, England: Basil Blackwell, 1987), pp. 19–26.

Risieri Frondizi, "Dynamic Unity of the Self." Reprinted by permission of Josefina Frondizi from Risieri Frondizi, *The Nature of the Self: A Functional Interpretation* (Carbondale and Edwardsville: Southern Illinois University Press, 1971), pp. 145–147, 158–163, 170–177, 180–184, 188–193, 197–201.

The Tibetan Book of the Dead, "Death and Rebirth." From Edward Conze, trans., "Life after Death, and 'The Book of the Dead,'" in *Buddhist Scriptures* (Harmondsworth, Middlesex, England: Penguin Classics, 1959), pp. 227–232. Copyright © Edward Conze, 1959. Reproduced by permission of Penguin Books Ltd.

Innocent C. Onyewuenyi, "Africa and Reincarnation: A Reappraisal." Excerpted from Innocent C. Onyewuenyi,

"A Philosophical Reappraisal of African Belief in Reincarnation," *International Philosophical Quarterly* 22 (September 1982): 157–168.

Plato, "The Phaedo." From *The Great Dialogues of Plato* by Plato, pp. 469–480, 506–510. Translated by W. H. D. Rouse. Translation copyright © 1956, renewed 1984 by J. C. G. Rouse. Used by permission of Dutton Signet, a division of Penguin Putnam Inc.

Aristotle, "On the Soul." Reprinted by permission of the publishers and the Loeb Classical Library from Aristotle, *Aristotle on the Soul, Parva Naturalia, On Breath,* translated by W. S. Hett, Cambridge, MA: Harvard University Press, 1957, pp. 67–73.

The Cārvāka School, "Ancient Indian Materialism." First part from Madhava Acarya, *Sarvadarsanas-Samgraha,* translated by E. B. Cowell and A. E. Gough (London: Kegan Paul, Trench & Trubner, 1904), pp. 228–230, 233–234. Second part from Krsna Misra, *Prabodhacandrodaya,* translated by J. Taylor (Bombay, 1811), pp. 247–249.

Bertrand Russell, "Persons, Death, and the Body." From Bertrand Russell, "Do We Survive Death?" reprinted with the permission of Simon & Schuster, The Bertrand Russell Peace Foundation, and Routledge Ltd. from *Why I Am Not a Christian and Other Essays on Religion and Related Subjects* by Bertrand Russell, edited by Paul Edwards, pp. 88–93. Copyright © 1957 by George Allen & Unwin Ltd. Originally from Bertrand Russell, *The Mysteries of Life and Death* (London: Hutchinson and Company, 1936).

Chapter 6

Sarvepalli Radhakrishnan, "Karma and Freedom." From Sarvepalli Radhakrishnan, *The Hindu View of Life* (New York: Macmillan, 1969), pp. 52–55. Reprinted by permission of HarperCollins Publishers Ltd.

Kwame Gyekye, "Destiny and Free Will: An African View." Excerpted from Kwame Gyekye, "Destiny, Free Will, and Responsibility," in *An Essay on African Philosophical Thought: The Akan Conceptual Scheme,* rev. ed., pp. 104–107, 114–123, 227–229 (notes). © 1995 by Temple University. Reprinted by permission of Temple University Press.

Fyodor Dostoyevsky, "Notes from the Underground." From *Notes from Underground* by Fyodor Dostoyevsky, translated by Andrew MacAndrew, pp. 90–95, 105–115.

Translation copyright © 1961, renewed © 1989 by Andrew MacAndrew. Used by permission of Dutton Signet, a division of Penguin Putnam Inc.

Jean-Paul Sartre, "Freedom and Action." From *Being and Nothingness,* pp. 433–436, 452–455, 457, by Jean-Paul Sartre, translated by Hazel E. Barnes. Copyright 1956 by Philosophical Library. Published by arrangement with Carol Publishing Group. A Citadel Press Book.

Moritz Schlick, "Freedom and Responsibility." Reprinted by permission from Moritz Schlick, "When Is a Man Responsible?" in his *Problems of Ethics,* translated by David Rynin (Dover, 1939), pp. 143–158.

John Hospers, "Free Will and Psychoanalysis." Excerpted with permission from John Hospers, "Meaning and Free Will," *Philosophy and Phenomenological Research* 10, no. 3 (March 1950): 314–322, 324–330.

Nancy Holmstrom, "Firming Up Soft Determinism." Reprinted by permission of Blackwell Publishers from Nancy Holmstrom, "Firming Up Soft Determinism," *The Personalist,* vol. 58, no. 1 (January 1977).

Kitarō Nishida, "Freedom of the Will." Reprinted by permission from Kitarō Nishida, *An Inquiry into the Good,* translated by Masao Abe and Christopher Ives, pp. 95–99. Copyright © 1990 by Yale University Press.

Chapter 7

Bhagavad-Gita, "Right Action." From Sarvepalli Radhakrishnan and Charles Moore, eds., *A Sourcebook in Indian Philosophy,* pp. 102–116. Copyright © 1957, renewed 1988, by Princeton University Press. Reprinted by permission of Princeton University Press.

Immanuel Kant, "Moral Duty." From Immanuel Kant, *The Fundamental Principles of the Metaphysics of Ethics,* translated by Otto Manthey-Zorn (New York: Appleton-Century-Crofts, 1938), pp. 8–19.

John Stuart Mill, "Utilitarianism." From John Stuart Mill, *Utilitarianism,* edited by Oscar Priest (Library of Liberal Arts, Bobbs-Merrill, 1957), pp. 3–16, 44–45.

Virginia Held, "Feminist Transformations of Moral Theory." Reprinted by permission from Virginia Held, "Feminist Transformations of Moral Theory," *Philosophy and Phenomenological Research* 50, Supplement (Fall 1990): 321–334.

Motse, "Universal Love." From Motse, "Universal Love (III)," in *The Ethical and Political Works of Motse,* translated by Yi-Pao Mei (Westport, CT: Hyperion Press, 1973), pp. 87–97.

Ayn Rand, "The Virtue of Selfishness." Excerpts from *The Virtue of Selfishness* by Ayn Rand, pp. vii–xi, 34–35, 51–56. Copyright © 1961, 1964 by Ayn Rand. Used by permission of Dutton Signet, a division of Penguin Putnam Inc.

Gunapala Dharmasiri, "Buddhist Ethics." Reprinted by permission from Gunapala Dharmasiri, "Motivation in Buddhist Ethics," in *Fundamentals of Buddhist Ethics* (Antioch, CA: Golden Leaves, 1989), pp. 12–21.

Carlo Filice, "On the Obligation to Stay Informed about Distant Atrocities." Excerpted by permission from Carlo Filice, "On the Obligation to Keep Informed about Distant Atrocities," *Human Rights Quarterly* 12 (August 1990): 397–414. © 1990 The Johns Hopkins University Press.

Alejandro Korn, "Values Are Subjective." From Alejandro Korn, "Axiología," excerpted in *Latin American Philosophy in the Twentieth Century: Man, Values, and the Search for Philosophical Identity,* edited by Jorge J. E. Gracia, pp. 167–171 (Amherst, NY: Prometheus Books). Copyright 1986. Reprinted by permission of the publisher. Originally from *Obras* (La Plata: Universidad Nacional de La Plata, 1938), 1: 129–144.

Alain Locke, "A Functional View of Value Ultimates." From Alain Locke, "A Functional View of Value Ultimates," read at Columbia University, December 23, 1945, unpublished; reprinted with permission from the Alain Locke Papers, The Moorland-Spingarn Research Center, Howard University. In *The Philosophy of Alain Locke: Harlem Renaissance and Beyond,* edited by Leonard Harris (Philadelphia: Temple University Press, 1989), pp. 81–93.

David Wong, "Relativism." Reprinted by permission of Blackwell Publishers from David Wong, "Relativism," in *A Companion to Ethics,* edited by Peter Singer (Oxford, England: Basil Blackwell, 1991), pp. 442–450.

Chapter 8

Aristotle, "The Rational Life." Reprinted by permission of the publishers and the Loeb Classical Library from *Aristo-* *tle in Twenty-Three Volumes, xix: The Nichomachean Ethics,* translated by H. Rackham (Cambridge, MA: Harvard University Press, 1968), pp. 3–5, 11–17, 25–33, 71–87, 607–629.

Tabātabā'ī, "Islam Is the Road to Happiness." From Allāmah Sayyid M. H. Tabātabā'ī, *The Qur'an in Islam: Its Impact and Influence on the Life of Muslims* (London: Zahra Publications, Routledge & Kegan Paul, 1987), pp. 17–21.

Joan D. Chittister, "Living the Rule of St. Benedict Today." Excerpts from *Wisdom Distilled from the Daily: Living the Rule of St. Benedict Today* by Joan D. Chittister, pp. 1–4, 6–8, 83–86, 90–93, 98–106. Copyright © 1990 by Joan D. Chittister. Reprinted by permission of HarperCollins Publishers, Inc.

H. Saddhatissa, "The Four Noble Truths." Reprinted by permission of George Braziller Inc. and HarperCollins Ltd. from H. Saddhatissa, *The Buddha's Way* (New York: Braziller, 1971), pp. 37–57.

Herbert John Benally, "Navajo Ways of Knowing." Reprinted by permission of the author from Herbert John Benally, "Navajo Ways of Knowing," in *Expanding Philosophical Horizons: An Anthology of Nontraditional Writings,* edited by Max O. Hallman (Belmont, CA: Wadsworth, 1995), pp. 102–107.

Albert Camus, "The Myth of Sisyphus." From *The Myth of Sisyphus and Other Essays* by Albert Camus, translated by Justin O'Brien, pp. 3–4, 6, 13–21, 51–55, 119–123. Copyright © 1955 by Alfred A. Knopf, Inc. Reprinted by permission of the publisher.

Lao Tzu, "Living in the Tao." From Lao Tzu, *Tao Te Ching,* translated by John C. H. Wu: 8, 9, 12, 13, 15, 16, 22, 24, 38, 43–45, 63, 68, 74, 76, 81. © 1961 by St. John's University Press. Reprinted by arrangement with Shambhala Publications, Inc., 300 Massachusetts Avenue, Boston, MA 02115.

Chuang Tzu, "Lost in the Tao." From Thomas Merton, *The Way of Chuang-Tzu,* pp. 45–47, 65, 67–69, 80–81, 91–94, 99–102, 109, 112–113, 154, 155. Copyright © 1965 by The Abbey of Gethsemani. Reprinted by permission of New Directions Publishing Corp.

Raymond M. Smullyan, "Whichever the Way." Chapter 19 from *The Tao Is Silent* by Raymond Smullyan, pp. 61–67, 215. Copyright © 1977 by Raymond M.

Smullyan. Reprinted by permission of HarperCollins Publishers, Inc.

Fung Yu-Lan, "The Spheres of Living." Reprinted with the permission of The Free Press, a Division of Simon & Schuster, from *A Short History of Chinese Philosophy* by Fung Yu-Lan, edited by Derk Bodde, pp. 338–340. Copyright © 1948 by The Macmillan Company; copyright renewed 1976 by Chung Liao Fung and Derk Bodde.

Native Mesoamerican, "Thought of the Sages." From "The Thought of the Sages," translated by Miguel Léon-Portilla, in *Native Mesoamerican Spirituality,* edited by Miguel Léon-Portilla, pp. 181–187. © 1980 by The Missionary Society of St. Paul the Apostle in the State of New York. Used by permission of Paulist Press.

Gregory Baum, "Social Conceptions of Death." Reprinted from *Religion and Alienation: A Theological Reading of Sociology* by Gregory Baum, pp. 266–274, 292–293 (notes). © 1975 by the Missionary Society of St. Paul the Apostle in the State of New York. Used by permission of Paulist Press.

Etty Hillesum, "Facing Death." From *An Interrupted Life* by Etty Hillesum, pp. 98, 141–142, 184–186, 188–189, 249. English translation copyright © 1983 by Jonathan Cape Ltd. Reprinted by permission of Pantheon Books, a division of Random House, Inc., and Uitgeverij Balans BV.

Chapter 9

Peggy McIntosh, "White Privilege and Male Privilege." From Peggy McIntosh, "White Privilege and Male Privilege: A Personal Account of Coming to See Correspondences through Work in Women's Studies," in *Contemporary Moral Issues in a Diverse Society,* edited by Julie McDonald (Belmont, CA: Wadsworth, 1998), pp. 52–60. Copyright © 1988 by Peggy McIntosh. May not be reprinted without permission of author, at Wellesley College Center for Research on Women, Wellesley, MA 02181 (781/283-2520).

Laurence Thomas, "Moral Deference." Excerpted by permission from Laurence Thomas, "Moral Deference," *Philosophical Forum* 24 (Fall–Spring 1992–1993): 233–250 (including notes).

Paula M. L. Moya, "Chicana Identity." Copyright © 1996. From Paula M. L. Moya, "Postmodernism, 'Realism,' and the Politics of Identity," in *Feminist Genealogies, Colonial Legacies, Democratic Futures,* edited by M. Jacqui Alexander and Chandra Talpade Mohanty, pp. 136–141. Reproduced by permission of Routledge, Inc.

Karen Fiser, "Philosophy and Disability." Excerpted by permission from Karen Fiser, "Philosophy, Disability, and Essentialism," in *Defending Diversity: Contemporary Philosophical Perspectives on Pluralism and Multiculturalism,* edited by Lawrence Foster and Patricia Herzog (Amherst: The University of Massachusetts Press, 1994), pp. 83–101. Copyright © 1994 by The University of Massachusetts Press.

Satyavrata Siddhantalankar, "A Defense of Varna (Caste)." Excerpted by permission from Satyavrata Siddhantalankar, "The Theory of Varna Vyavashtha," in *Heritage of Vedic Culture: A Pragmatic Presentation* (Bombay, India: D. B. Taraporevala Sons & Co. Pvt. Ltd., 1969), pp. 169–170, 173–179.

John Rawls, "A Theory of Justice." Excerpted by permission of the publishers from *A Theory of Justice* by John Rawls, pp. 11–21, 60–65. Cambridge, MA: The Belknap Press of Harvard University Press. Copyright © 1971 by the President and Fellows of Harvard College.

H. Odera Oruka, "Critique of Rawls." Reprinted by permission from H. Odera Oruka, "John Rawls' Ideology: Justice as Egalitarian Fairness," in *Practical Philosophy: In Search of an Ethical Minimum* (Nairobi, Kenya: East African Educational Publishers Ltd., 1997), pp. 115–125.

Karl Marx and Friedrich Engels, "The Communist Manifesto." Reprinted by permission of International Publishers from Karl Marx and Friedrich Engels, *The Communist Manifesto,* translated by Gail Samuel Moore (New York: Washington Square Press, 1964), pp. 9–21.

Mohandas K. Gandhi, "Non-Violent Resistance." Reprinted by permission from M. K. Gandhi, *Non-Violent Resistance (Satyagraha)* (New York: Schocken Books, 1961), pp. 9–15, 112–117, 383–387. Copyright © 1951 by the Navajivan Trust.

Martin Luther King, Jr., "Non-Violence and Social Change." From Martin Luther King, Jr., "A Testament of Hope," which appeared in "A Christmas Sermon on Peace," *The Trumpet of Conscience* (New York: Harper &

Row, 1968), pp. 68–75. Reprinted by arrangement with The Heirs to the Estate of Martin Luther King, Jr., c/o Writers House, Inc., as agent for the proprietor. Copyright 1958 by Martin Luther King, Jr.; copyright renewed 1986 by Coretta Scott King.

Malcolm X, "By Any Means Necessary." From Malcolm X, "Any Means Necessary to Bring about Freedom," in *Malcolm X Talks to Young People,* edited by Steve Clark, pp. 184–188. Copyright © 1965, 1970, 1991 by Betty Shabazz and Pathfinder Press. Reprinted by permission.

Enrique Dussel, "Ethics and Community." Reprinted by permission from Enrique Dussel, *Ethics and Community,* Translated by Robert R. Barr, pp. 175–180. Copyright © 1988 by Orbis Books, Maryknoll, New York.

INDEX